HALSBURY'S

Laws of England

FOURTH EDITION
REISSUE

Volume 42

HALSBURY'S

Laws of England

FOURTH EDITION
REISSUE

LORD MACKAY OF CLASHFERN

Lord High Chancellor of Great Britain
1987-97

Volume 42

BUTTERWORTHS

LONDON   1999

United Kingdom	Butterworths, a Division of Reed Elsevier (UK) Ltd, Halsbury House, 35 Chancery Lane, LONDON WC2A 1EL and 4 Hill Street, EDINBURGH EH2 3JZ
Australia	Butterworths, a Division of Reed International Books, Australia Pty Ltd, CHATSWOOD, New South Wales
Canada	Butterworths Canada Ltd, MARKHAM, Ontario
Hong Kong	Butterworths Asia (Hong Kong), HONG KONG
India	Butterworths India, NEW DELHI
Ireland	Butterworth (Ireland) Ltd, DUBLIN
Malaysia	Malayan Law Journal Sdn Bhd, KUALA LUMPUR
New Zealand	Butterworths of New Zealand Ltd, WELLINGTON
Singapore	Butterworths Asia, SINGAPORE
South Africa	Butterworth Publishers (Pty) Ltd, DURBAN
USA	Lexis Law Publishing, CHARLOTTESVILLE, Virginia

FIRST EDITION

Published in 31 volumes between 1907 and 1917 under the Editorship of the Rt Hon the Earl of Halsbury, Lord High Chancellor of Great Britain, 1885–86, 1886–92 and 1895–1905

SECOND EDITION

Published in 37 volumes between 1931 and 1942 under the Editorship of the Rt Hon the Viscount Hailsham, Lord High Chancellor of Great Britain, 1928–29 and 1935–38

THIRD EDITION

Published in 43 volumes between 1952 and 1964 under the Editorship of the Rt Hon the Viscount Simonds, Lord High Chancellor of Great Britain, 1951–54

FOURTH EDITION

Published in 56 volumes between 1973 and 1987, with selective reissues between 1988 and 1998, under the Editorship of the Rt Hon Lord Hailsham of St Marylebone, Lord High Chancellor of Great Britain, 1970–74 and 1979–87. Reissue volumes since August 1998 published under the Editorship of the Rt Hon Lord Mackay of Clashfern, Lord High Chancellor of Great Britain, 1987–97

ISBN (complete set, standard binding) 0 406 03400 1

ISBN 0-406-89741-7

9 780406 897411

Printed and bound in Great Britain by The Bath Press, Bath.

website address: http://www.butterworths.co.uk

Editor in Chief

LORD MACKAY OF CLASHFERN

LORD HIGH CHANCELLOR OF GREAT BRITAIN

1987-97

The titles in Volume 42 have been contributed by:

SALE OF LAND

GRAHAM BATTERSBY, BA, JP, of Lincoln's Inn, Barrister;
Edward Bramley Professor of Law, University of Sheffield

SET-OFF AND COUNTERCLAIM

The Hon Sir ANTHONY MASON, AC, KBE, Former Chief Justice of Australia;
National Fellow, Australian National University; formerly Goodhart Professor
in Legal Science, Cambridge University

SETTLEMENTS

ROBERT WALLACE HAM, BCL, BA, one of Her Majesty's counsel,
of the Middle Temple and Lincoln's Inn

EMILY C CAMPBELL, BCL, MA, of Lincoln's Inn, Barrister

SHERIFFS

ALASTAIR BLACK, CBE, DL, a Solicitor of the Supreme Court;
former Under Sheriff of Greater London

CLAIRE SANDBROOK, LLB, a Solicitor of the Supreme Court;
Under Sheriff of Surrey

The permission of the Law Society and Solicitor's Law Stationery Society plc to reproduce extracts
from the Standard Conditions of Sale (3rd edition) is gratefully acknowledged.

The law stated in this volume is in general that in force on 28 February 1999.

Any future updating material will be found in the Current Service and annual Cumulative
Supplement to Halsbury's Laws of England.

TABLE OF CONTENTS

REFERENCES AND ABBREVIATIONS

ACT	Australian Capital Territory
AJIL	American Journal of International Law (1907 to date)
A-G	Attorney General
Adv-Gen	Advocate General
affd	affirmed
Alta	Alberta
affg	affirming
App	Appendix
art	article
Aust	Australia
B	Baron
BC	British Columbia
BYIL	British Yearbook of International Law
C	Command Paper (of a series published before 1900)
c	chapter number of an Act
CA	Court of Appeal
CAC	Central Arbitration Committee
CA in Ch	Court of Appeal in Chancery
CB	Chief Baron
CCA	Court of Criminal Appeal
CC Fees Order 1982	County Court Fees Order 1982 (SI 1982/1706) as subsequently amended (see the current County Court Practice)
CCR	County Court Rules 1981 (SI 1981/1687) as subsequently amended (see the current County Court Practice)
CCR	Court for Crown Cases Reserved
C-MAC	Courts-Martial Appeal Court
CO	Crown Office
COD	Crown Office Digest
CPR	Civil Procedure Rules 1998 (SI 1998/3132) (see the Civil Court Practice)
Can	Canada
Cd	Command Paper (of the series published 1900–18)
Cf	compare
ch	chapter
cl	clause
Cm	Command Paper (of the series published 1986 to date)
Cmd	Command Paper (of the series published 1919–56)

Cmnd	Command Paper (of the series published 1956–86)
Comr	Commissioner
Court Forms (2nd Edn)	Atkin's Encyclopaedia of Court Forms in Civil Proceedings, 2nd Edn. See note 2, p *16* post
Court Funds Rules 1987	Court Funds Rules 1987 (SI 1987/821) as subsequently amended (see the current Supreme Court Practice and County Court Practice)
DC	Divisional Court
DPP	Director of Public Prosecutions
EAT	Employment Appeal Tribunal
EC	European Community
ECJ	Court of Justice of the European Community
EComHR	European Commission of Human Rights
ECSC	European Coal and Steel Community
EEC	European Economic Community
EFTA	European Free Trade Association
Edn	Edition
Euratom	European Atomic Energy Community
Ex Ch	Court of Exchequer Chamber
ex p	ex parte
Fed	Federal
Forms & Precedents (5th Edn)	Encyclopaedia of Forms and Precedents other than Court Forms, 5th Edn. See note 2, p *16* post
GLC	Greater London Council
HC	High Court
HC	House of Commons
HL	House of Lords
ILPr	International Litigation Procedure
IRC	Inland Revenue Commissioners
Ind	India
Int Rels	International Relations
Ir	Ireland
J	Justice
JA	Judge of Appeal
JC	Justiciary Cases
Kan	Kansas
LA	Lord Advocate
LC	Lord Chancellor
LCC	London County Council
LCJ	Lord Chief Justice
LJ	Lord Justice of Appeal
LoN	League of Nations
LRC	Law Reports of the Commonwealth (1985–date)
MR	Master of the Rolls
Man	Manitoba
n	note
NB	New Brunswick
NI	Northern Ireland
NIJB	Northern Ireland Judgment Bulletin

NS	Nova Scotia
NSW	New South Wales
NZ	New Zealand
OJ	The Official Journal of the European Community published by the Office for Official Publications of the European Community
Ont	Ontario
P	President
PC	Judicial Committee of the Privy Council
PEI	Prince Edward Island
q	question
QBD	Queen's Bench Division of the High Court
Qld	Queensland
Que	Quebec
r	rule
RDC	Rural District Council
RPC	Restrictive Practices Court
RSC	Rules of the Supreme Court 1965 (SI 1965/1776) as subsequently amended (see the current Supreme Court Practice)
reg	regulation
Res	Resolution
revsd	reversed
Rly	Railway
s	section
SA	South Africa
S Aust	South Australia
SC	Supreme Court
SC Fees Order 1980	Supreme Court Fees Order 1980 (SI 1980/821) as subsequently amended (see the current Supreme Court Practice)
SI	Statutory Instruments published by authority
SR & O	Statutory Rules and Orders published by authority
SR & O Rev 1904	Revised Edition comprising all Public and General Statutory Rules and Orders in force on 31 December 1903
SR & O Rev 1948	Revised Edition comprising all Public and General Statutory Rules and Orders and Statutory Instruments in force on 31 December 1948
SRNI	Statutory Rules of Northern Ireland
Sask	Saskatchewan
Sch	Schedule
Sess	Session
Sing	Singapore
TS	Treaty Series
Tanz	Tanzania
Tas	Tasmania
UDC	Urban District Council
UN	United Nations
V-C	Vice-Chancellor

Vict	Victoria
W Aust	Western Australia
Zimb	Zimbabwe

NOTE 1. A general list of the abbreviations of law reports and other sources used in this work can be found in vol 54 (Reissue) Consolidated Table of Cases at p *v* et seq.

NOTE 2. Where references are made to other publications, the volume number precedes and the page number follows the name of the publication; eg the reference '12 Forms & Precedents (5th Edn) 44' refers to volume 12 of the Encyclopaedia of Forms and Precedents, page 44.

NOTE 3. An English statute is cited by short title or, where there is no short title, by regnal year and chapter number together with the name by which it is commonly known or a description of its subject matter and date. In the case of a foreign statute, the mode of citation generally follows the style of citation in use in the country concerned with the addition, where necessary, of the name of the country in parentheses.

NOTE 4. A statutory instrument is cited by short title, if any, followed by the year and number, or, if unnumbered, the date.

TABLE OF STATUTES

TABLE OF STATUTORY INSTRUMENTS

TABLE OF CASES

PARA

PARA

B

PARA

PARA

PARA

PARA

PARA

PARA

PARA

PARA

PARA

PARA

PARA

PARA

L

PARA

PARA

O

PARA

PARA

PARA

Q

R

S

PARA

PARA

PARA

U

SALE OF LAND

For		
auction sales	see	AUCTION
bankruptcy		BANKRUPTCY AND INSOLVENCY
boundaries		BOUNDARIES
building contracts		BUILDING CONTRACTS, ARCHITECTS, ENGINEERS AND SURVEYORS
building societies		BUILDING SOCIETIES
common rights		COMMONS
compulsory acquisition		COMPULSORY ACQUISITION OF LAND
contracts generally		CONTRACT
damages generally		DAMAGES
deeds		DEEDS AND OTHER INSTRUMENTS
development, control of		TOWN AND COUNTRY PLANNING
easements		EASEMENTS AND PROFITS À PRENDRE
estate agents		AGENCY
exchange of land		REAL PROPERTY
execution		EXECUTION
fraudulent conveyances		BANKRUPTCY AND INSOLVENCY; MISREPRESENTATION AND FRAUD; SETTLEMENTS
gifts		GIFTS
insurance		INSURANCE
interests in land		EASEMENTS AND PROFITS À PRENDRE; LANDLORD AND TENANT; MORTGAGE; REAL PROPERTY
land charges		LAND CHARGES
land registration		LAND REGISTRATION
leases		LANDLORD AND TENANT
limitation of actions		LIMITATION OF ACTIONS
local authorities, sales by		HOUSING; LANDLORD AND TENANT
mines and minerals		MINES, MINERALS AND QUARRIES
mistake		MISTAKE
misrepresentation		MISREPRESENTATION AND FRAUD
mortgagee's power of sale		MORTGAGE
open spaces		OPEN SPACES AND ANCIENT MONUMENTS
overreaching powers, conveyances under		EXECUTORS AND ADMINISTRATORS; MORTGAGE; REAL PROPERTY; SETTLEMENTS
partition		REAL PROPERTY
perpetuities		PERPETUITIES AND ACCUMULATIONS
personal representative power of		EXECUTORS AND ADMINISTRATORS
planning permission		TOWN AND COUNTRY PLANNING
powers		POWERS
real property generally		REAL PROPERTY
rectification generally		MISTAKE
registration of land		LAND REGISTRATION
rentcharges		RENTCHARGES
rescission generally		MISREPRESENTATION AND FRAUD
restrictive covenants		EQUITY
settled land		SETTLEMENTS

1. THE CONTRACT AND PRELIMINARY MATTERS

(1) INTRODUCTION

1. Procedure on the sale of land. A sale of land often falls into four distinct stages:
(1) the pre-contractual stage[1]; (2) the contractual stage[2]; (3) the completion stage[3]; and
(4) the post-completion stage[4]. At each stage it will be necessary to consider particular
aspects of the transaction.

Where the contract is by private treaty[5], the first stage is mainly concerned with the
fixing of the price, but certain other matters are of importance[6]. The purchaser frequently
enters into a preliminary agreement by which he agrees to buy the land from the vendor
at a price stated in the agreement. The preliminary agreement is usually expressed to be
subject to contract, in which event, until formal contracts are exchanged, either party may
retire from his bargain, even without giving a reason for so doing[7]. Such a preliminary
contract is often accompanied by the payment of a nominal deposit, the balance of the
full deposit being paid when the formal contract is signed[8].

After the preliminary agreement has been signed, the draft contract is prepared by the
vendor[9] and an inspection of the property (if it has not been inspected before the signing
of the preliminary agreement) and preliminary inquiries and searches[10] are made by the
purchaser before signing the contract[11], so as to ensure that he can safely enter into the
contract[12]. It is normally advisable for the purchaser to have a survey of the property
made[13].

The description of the property in a contract for sale of land, and of any exceptions
and reservations, or rights to be enjoyed, such as rights of drainage or light or other
easements, and the terms of any covenants to be inserted in the transfer, should be most
carefully prepared as, in general, these must be included subsequently in the transfer in
the precise terms in which they appear in the contract[14].

The time when the deposit is payable is a matter of arrangement; it will normally be
payable not later than the time of the signing of the contract and, if a nominal sum has
been paid on a preliminary agreement, a deduction is made in respect of the sum so paid[15].

1   See paras 4–22 post.
2   See paras 23–261 post.
3   See paras 262–325 post.
4   See paras 326–359 post.
5   On a sale by auction, the sale is subject to conditions of sale which have been prepared before the auction,
    and the purchaser must satisfy himself and preferably take legal advice that the conditions are such as he
    can in the circumstances accept and be bound by. As to conditions on sales by auction see paras 84–85
    post; and see generally AUCTION vol 2 (Reissue) para 935 et seq.
6   It may be desirable at this first stage to consider the applicability to the proposed transaction of capital
    gains tax (see CAPITAL GAINS TAXATION vol 5(1) (Reissue) para 3 et seq), inheritance tax (see
    INHERITANCE TAXATION vol 24 (Reissue) para 402 et seq), income tax (see INCOME TAXATION vol 23
    (Reissue) para 1 et seq), and value added tax (see VALUE ADDED TAX vol 49(1) (Reissue) para 1 et seq).
7   See CONTRACT vol 9(1) (Reissue) para 671; *Cohen v Nessdale Ltd* [1982] 2 All ER 97, [1982] 1 EGLR
    160, CA. As to the position where the agreement is subject to a condition, for example the obtaining of
    finance or a satisfactory survey see para 26 post.
8   As to giving credit for such a deposit see the text to note 15 infra.
9   The draft contract of sale now commonly incorporates the Standard Conditions of Sale (3rd Edn). Prior
    to 21 March 1990, two forms of standard contract were in general use in England and Wales: the Law
    Society's Conditions of Sale, and the National Conditions of Sale. In practice the choice of using one set
    of conditions in preference to the other tended to be governed by habit or tradition rather than being
    based on a reasoned decision that one set of conditions suited a particular transaction better than the other.
    Since 21 March 1990, a third standard form contract called the Standard Conditions of Sale has been in
    use and is now in its third edition. The Standard Conditions of Sale (3rd Edn) were published in 1995.

The new conditions emerged as a result of a merger between the Law Society's Conditions of Sale (1984 Revision) and the National Conditions of Sale (20th Edn) and are intended to replace both of these former sets of conditions, neither of which will again be published or revised. New editions of the Standard Conditions have indicated this by means of a sub-heading. So, the third edition is sub-titled 'National Conditions of Sale 23rd Edition, Law Society's Conditions of Sale 1995'. The Standard Conditions of Sale are designed to be used in both domestic and commercial transactions. However, a version of the Standard Conditions of Sale designed specifically for the sale of commercial land is due to be published in the summer of 1999.

10   These searches do not at this stage normally include a search for land charges as distinct from local land charges: see paras 19–22 post.

11   See para 4 et seq post. The practice is to deliver preliminary inquiries, requisitions and the draft transfer in duplicate, so that the vendor has a copy for his own use.

12   In approving the draft contract the purchaser should hesitate in accepting a title of less than the full statutory length of 15 years because he is deemed to have notice of everything he would have discovered if he had investigated the title for the statutory period (see para 90 post), and because, if he requires to finance the purchase by a mortgage, the mortgagee may insist on a full 15 year title. As to the statutory length of title see para 139 post.

13   As to the survey see para 7 post.

14   As to covenants in the transfer see para 81 post; and DEEDS AND OTHER INSTRUMENTS. As to the disposition of registered and unregistered land by transfer see para 262 note 2 post.

15   See para 86 post.

2. Procedure after signing contract. Upon the signing of the contract, the vendor prepares the abstract of title[1] and delivers it to the purchaser in accordance with the terms of the contract[2]. The purchaser then makes his requisitions on title and in some cases the draft transfer is delivered with the requisitions but, if its form depends upon the answers to the requisitions, its delivery must be deferred to a later stage[3]. Formerly, there were special requisitions on title and also what were termed general requisitions. The matters to which general requisitions related are now the subject of the preliminary inquiries and at the later stage when requisitions are delivered it may be sufficient merely to ask whether the answers to the inquiries are still true and complete in all respects[4].

It is necessary to search the registers again before completion, and these searches, which include searches in the land charges register as well as other necessary searches, must be made immediately before completion in order to secure priority over subsequent registrations[5]. It may be advisable in the case of land apparently unregistered to search at the Land Registry to ensure that the land has never in fact been registered[6].

The transfer when finally agreed is engrossed by the purchaser, the vendor delivers to the purchaser a completion statement[7], showing the balance actually due from the purchaser to the vendor[8], and this balance is then paid over and the transfer executed[9].

After transfer the remedies of the parties are very restricted[10].

1   As to the need for an abstract of title with respect to both unregistered and registered land see paras 138, 141–149 post.

2   As to the delivery of the abstract of title see paras 100–101, 138 post.

3   As to requisitions on title see paras 163–166 post. As to the disposition of registered and unregistered land by transfer see para 262 note 2 post.

4   As to the nature of requisitions see para 164 post. Apart from this request for confirmation, requisitions on title now relate almost entirely to matters of title and conveyance.

5   As to searches see paras 167–169 post.

6   As to index maps searches see LAND REGISTRATION vol 26 (Reissue) paras 797, 895. See also Greene 'Searches Before Contract' (1960) 110 LJo 147; and Garner 'The Control of Development Bill' (1960) 110 LJo 280. As to searches to be made when the land is known to be registered see para 169 post.

7   This is done as a matter of custom and practice; there is no legal obligation to provide a completion statement: *Carne v Debono* [1988] 3 All ER 485, [1988] 1 WLR 1107, CA. Where the only money payable on completion is the balance of the purchase price, a formal completion statement is often dispensed with: see *Carne v Debono* supra.

8   This debits the purchaser with the total purchase price and any outgoings, such as council tax or rates, which may have been paid by the vendor, so far as they relate to the period after the date at which

outgoings are apportionable. It credits the purchaser with any deposit which he may have paid, any sums (eg rent in advance where the property is let) which may have been received by the vendor so far as received in respect of the period after the date of apportionment, and any sums (eg rates) which the purchaser may have subsequently to pay, so far as they will relate to the period before that date. As to the date at which rents and profits and outgoings are apportionable see generally paras 124–125 post.

9   As to the stamping of transfers see paras 318–319 post; and STAMP DUTIES AND STAMP DUTY RESERVE TAX vol 44(1) (Reissue) para 1027 et seq. As to registration of dispositions of registered land and the effect of registration see LAND REGISTRATION vol 26 (Reissue) paras 718, 900 et seq.

10   As to these remedies see paras 352–359 post; and as to remedies under the implied covenants for title see para 343 et seq post.

3. Conveyancing services. Traditionally, conveyancing services have been provided by solicitors[1], but such services may now also be provided by licensed conveyancers[2].

It is an offence, subject to certain exceptions[3], for unqualified persons to draw or prepare any instrument of transfer or charge for the purposes of the Land Registration Act 1925, or to make any application or lodge any document for registration under that Act at the registry, or to draw or prepare any other instrument relating to real or personal estate, or any legal proceeding[4]. In addition an individual must not describe himself or hold himself out as a licensed conveyancer unless he holds a licence[5] which is in force under Part II[6] of the Administration of Justice Act 1985[7]. Provision is made in Part II of the Administration of Justice Act 1985[8] for the purpose of regulating the provision of conveyancing services[9] by persons who hold licences in force under that Act[10]. The statutory restriction[11] on a person preparing certain instruments when not qualified to act as a solicitor does not apply to any act done by a licensed conveyancer in the course of the provision of any conveyancing services if he is not precluded[12] from providing those services as a licensed conveyancer[13].

1   As to solicitors generally see SOLICITORS.
2   For the meaning of 'licensed conveyancer' see SOLICITORS vol 44(1) (Reissue) para 550.
3   See the Solicitors Act 1974 s 22(2) (as amended), s 22(2A) (as added): see SOLICITORS vol 44(1) (Reissue) para 528.
4   See ibid s 22(1) (as amended); and SOLICITORS vol 44(1) (Reissue) para 528. As to offences under the Solicitors Act 1974 see SOLICITORS vol 44(1) (Reissue) paras 526–531. As to the disposition of registered and unregistered land by transfer see para 262 note 2 post.
5   For the meaning of 'licence' see SOLICITORS vol 44(1) (Reissue) para 550.
6   Ie the Administration of Justice Act 1985 Pt II (ss 11–39) (as amended): see SOLICITORS vol 44(1) (Reissue) para 550 et seq.
7   Ibid s 35(1). As to the penalty for contravention of s 35(1) see SOLICITORS vol 44(1) (Reissue) para 535.
8   See note 6 supra.
9   For the meaning of 'conveyancing services' see SOLICITORS vol 44(1) (Reissue) para 550.
10   Administration of Justice Act 1985 s 11(1).
11   Ie under the Solicitors Act 1974 s 22(1) (as amended): see the text to note 4 supra; and SOLICITORS vol 44(1) (Reissue) para 528.
12   Ie precluded by any conditions imposed as mentioned in the Administration of Justice Act 1985 s 16(3)(a) (see SOLICITORS vol 44(1) (Reissue) para 560): s 11(4).
13   Ibid s 11(4).

(2) INQUIRIES AND SEARCHES BEFORE CONTRACT

(i) Inquiries and Inspection

A. IN GENERAL

4. Conditions designed to render inquiries unnecessary. Although the usual practice is now for the purchaser to make inquiries and searches before entering into a formal or binding contract[1], it is possible to draft conditions of sale designed to enable a binding contract to be entered into without certain kinds of preliminary inquiry. These would entitle the purchaser to rescind if the property proves to be subject to specified matters which, under the usual procedure, might have been discovered by preliminary inquiries and searches[2]. It is only in cases of exceptional urgency that acceptance of such conditions is to be recommended.

1   As to inquiries see para 5–18 post; and as to searches see paras 19–22 post.
2   There is no such condition in the Standard Conditions of Sale (3rd Edn). Cf the previously used National Conditions of Sale (20th Edn), conditions 3, 15(3); and The Law Society's Contract of Sale (1984 Revision), condition 4; and see also *Aquis Estates Ltd v Minton* [1975] 3 All ER 1043, [1975] 1 WLR 1452, CA. As to the Standard Conditions of Sale see para 1 note 9 ante.

5. Inquiries of vendor and local authorities. Preliminary inquiries are usually made in the first place of the vendor and in the second place of the local authorities[1]. Sets of inquiries relating to matters with which local authorities are concerned have been agreed between the associations representing those authorities and The Law Society and local authorities are prepared to answer those inquiries on payment of a small fee[2].

It seems that the answers to preliminary inquiries do not, in any case, amount to a warranty that the matters stated in them are true, so as to give rise to an action for breach of warranty after completion[3]. The answers, however, constitute representations, and, if they are material and incorrect and made by the vendor or his agent, they may entitle the purchaser to rescind the contract[4]. Alternatively, the purchaser will be entitled to damages unless the maker of the misrepresentation proves that, on reasonable grounds, he believed in the truth of the facts represented up to the time when the contract was made[5].

1   As to inquiries of tenants see para 6 post; and as to particular subjects of inquiry see paras 8–18 post.
2   The inquiries are addressed to the appropriate district or London borough council, which then obtains information as necessary from the appropriate county council. In practice these inquiries are usually sent with the application for an official search of the local land charges register: see para 20 post. As to fees see the Local Authorities (Charges for Land Searches) Regulations 1994, SI 1994/1885 (amended by SI 1996/525).
3   *Gilchester Properties Ltd v Gomm* [1948] 1 All ER 493; *Mahon v Ainscough* [1952] 1 All ER 337, CA.
4   See para 42 post. As to the court's discretionary power to order damages in lieu of rescission where the misrepresentation is proved by its maker to be purely innocent see para 42 post.
5   See the Misrepresentation Act 1967 s 2(1); para 42 post; and MISREPRESENTATION AND FRAUD vol 31 (Reissue) para 801. As to statutory regulation of attempts to exclude or restrict liability for misrepresentation see para 116 post; and *Walker v Boyle* [1982] 1 All ER 634, [1982] 1 WLR 495. The vendor is not protected by a statement that the replies to preliminary inquiries are believed to be correct but that their accuracy is not guaranteed, and that they do not obviate the need to make appropriate searches, inquiries and inspections (see the Standard Conditions of Sale (3rd Edn), conditions 3, 4; and para 116 post): *Walker v Boyle* supra. As to the Standard Conditions of Sale see para 1 note 9 ante.

6. Inspection of property and inquiries of tenants. Before entering into a formal contract, the purchaser must make an inspection of the property, since he is deemed to buy with notice of patent defects of title[1]. However, the constructive notice which arises from the occupation of land by someone other than the vendor[2] is not in itself sufficient to make the defect patent[3]. Where it appears that the property is subject to a lease or tenancy[4], inquiry should be made of the tenants, as well as the landlord, seeking to ascertain whether the tenants have statutory security of tenure and whether the rents are subject to statutory control[5].

1   As to patent defects see para 45 post; and as to the advisability of a survey see para 7 post.
2   See *Hunt v Luck* [1902] 1 Ch 428 at 433, CA; *Caunce v Caunce* [1969] 1 All ER 722, [1969] 1 WLR 286; *Williams and Glyn's Bank Ltd v Boland* [1981] AC 487, [1980] 2 All ER 408, HL; and *Kingsnorth Trust Ltd v Tizard* [1986] 2 All ER 54, sub nom *Kingsnorth Finance Co Ltd v Tizard* [1986] 1 WLR 783. A purchaser of unregistered land need not inquire whether a tenant has a right to rectification of the lease: *Smith v*

Jones [1954] 2 All ER 823, [1954] 1 WLR 1089. As to registered land see *Blacklocks v JB Developments (Godalming) Ltd* [1982] Ch 183, [1981] 3 All ER 392. See further para 329 post.

3   See *Yandle & Sons v Sutton* [1922] 2 Ch 199; and para 45 post. As to constructive notice in relation to dealings with land and statutory restrictions on constructive notice see EQUITY vol 16 (Reissue) paras 771–774; as to inquiries with regard to tenancies see paras 8–9 post; and as to the vendor's duty to disclose existing tenancies see para 58 post. The court will not grant an immediate decree of specific performance against a purchaser while there remain outstanding differences between the vendor and his tenant: *George v Thomas* (1904) 90 LT 505.

4   As to the general law of leases and tenancies see LANDLORD AND TENANT. Consider also the Leasehold Reform Act 1967 (see LANDLORD AND TENANT vol 27(2) (Reissue) para 1253 et seq). Where a tenant has statutory security of tenure, an agreement by the tenant to surrender possession on completion will not terminate the statutory right to security: *Appleton v Aspin* [1988] 1 All ER 904, [1988] 1 WLR 410, CA; and see *Woolwich Building Society v Dickman* [1996] 3 All ER 204, 72 P & CR 470, CA.

5   See *Goody v Baring* [1956] 2 All ER 11, [1956] 1 WLR 448 (action by a purchaser against a solicitor for failure to make proper inquiries). The intending purchaser should ask the tenant to produce the rent book: see LANDLORD AND TENANT vol 27(1) (Reissue) paras 222–225. He should also inspect the register of rents kept by the rent officer under the Rent Act 1977 s 66, or the register kept by the president of every rent assessment panel under s 79 (as amended): see LANDLORD AND TENANT vol 27(1) (Reissue) paras 766, 858. As to inquiries of the vendor as regards the application of the Rent Act 1977 and analogous legislation see para 8 post; and LANDLORD AND TENANT vol 27(1) (Reissue) para 655 et seq. As to inquiries of vendor and local authorities see para 5 ante.

7.   Survey. Since a purchaser cannot, in general, escape from being affected with notice of any patent defect in the property merely by pleading his own lack of the knowledge necessary to enable him to make a proper inspection[1], it is in general advisable for him to have the property surveyed by a qualified surveyor[2]. Where a valuation report is prepared by a valuer for a mortgagee, the valuer also owes a duty of care to the purchaser[3].

1   *Haywood v Cope* (1858) 25 Beav 140 at 148. See also para 45 note 5 post.
2   As to contracts subject to survey see para 26 post.
3   *Yianni v Edwin Evans & Sons* [1982] QB 438, [1981] 3 All ER 592; *Smith v Eric S Bush (a firm)* [1990] 1 AC 831, [1989] 2 All ER 514, HL; and see VALUERS AND SURVEYORS vol 49(1) (Reissue) para 416.

B.   PARTICULAR SUBJECTS OF INQUIRY

8.   Leaseholds and tenanted property. Where the property to be purchased is leasehold it is important that the purchaser should inspect the lease for the purpose of ascertaining the exact nature of the covenants and conditions contained in it, since those covenants, in so far as they run with the term, will be binding on him on the assignment of the lease[1]. If he has had a reasonable opportunity of inspecting the lease before contract, he will be bound to complete after signing the contract even though the lease contains onerous covenants[2]. Inquiry should also be made of the vendor whether any necessary licence of the landlord or any superior lessor has been or will be obtained[3], whether all rent accrued due has been duly paid[4], whether any breaches of covenant are known to the assignor and whether any notices[5] have been served in respect of such breaches[6].

Where the land sold is subject to a subsisting tenancy, the vendor should be asked to supply particulars of the tenancy and a copy of any lease or written tenancy agreement under which the tenant holds[7]. Such inquiries should be made as to the nature of the property, and the tenancy, so far as its nature can be ascertained, with a view to determining the applicability of various forms of statutory control, for example the legislation relating to protected tenancies of dwelling houses[8], to restricted contracts[9], to assured tenancies[10], to the protection of tenants holding under long tenancies[11] and to compensation for improvements and security of tenure in the case of business premises[12]. Inquiries should also be made as to the application or the possible future application of the statutory right of certain tenants, where the tenancy is a long tenancy at a low rent, to acquire the freehold or an extended lease[13]. It will be necessary also to inspect, as appropriate, the register of rents kept by the rent officer in respect of protected tenancies[14] or to the register of rents kept by the president of every rent assessment panel in respect of restricted contracts[15].

The necessity for making inquiries of tenants, as well as of landlords, as to their rights, including their rights under protective legislation, has already been mentioned[16].

1   See LANDLORD AND TENANT vol 27(1) (Reissue) paras 466–492. As to the transmission of the benefit and burden of covenants in leases beginning on or after 1 January 1996 see the Landlord and Tenant (Covenants) Act 1995; and LANDLORD AND TENANT vol 27(1) (Reissue) paras 466–492.

2   See para 60 post. As to the vendor's duty to reveal whether he holds the property by lease or underlease see para 59 post.

3   As to the vendor's duty to obtain such a licence see para 25 post.

4   It is usual to ask to see the last receipt. As to the production of a receipt for rent as evidence of the performance of covenants at the time of completion see para 98 post.

5   Ie notices under the Law of Property Act 1925 s 146: see LANDLORD AND TENANT vol 27(1) (Reissue) para 513. As to the necessity for the service of such a notice and default under it before the enforcement of a forfeiture for breach of covenant, and as to the tenant's right to apply to the court for relief see LANDLORD AND TENANT vol 27(1) (Reissue) para 513 et seq.

6   As to conditions on the sale of leaseholds out of repair see para 99 post.

7   Such inquiries are necessary because, in general, the fact of occupation is notice of a tenant's rights: see para 329 post. As to the necessity of inspection of the property by the purchaser and inquiries of the tenant see para 6 ante; and as to inquiries in relation to agricultural holdings see para 9 post.

8   See LANDLORD AND TENANT vol 27(1) (Reissue) para 655 et seq. Cf *Goody v Baring* [1956] 2 All ER 11, [1956] 1 WLR 448, where the purchaser's solicitor was negligent in accepting information supplied by the vendor as to rents actually being paid without ascertaining standard and recoverable rents. It seems that the rights of tenants under the Rent Act 1977 and similar legislation are incidents of tenure which need not be disclosed by the vendor in the absence of inquiry: see para 61 text and notes 1–2 post.

9   See LANDLORD AND TENANT vol 27(1) (Reissue) para 847 et seq.

10   See LANDLORD AND TENANT vol 27(1) (Reissue) para 878 et seq.

11   See LANDLORD AND TENANT vol 27(2) (Reissue) paras 1047 et seq, 1060 et seq.

12   See LANDLORD AND TENANT vol 27(1) (Reissue) para 558 et seq.

13   See LANDLORD AND TENANT vol 27(2) (Reissue) para 1253 et seq.

14   See LANDLORD AND TENANT vol 27(1) (Reissue) para 766.

15   See LANDLORD AND TENANT vol 27(1) (Reissue) para 858.

16   See para 6 ante.

9. Agricultural holdings and land used for growing timber. Where land is let as an agricultural holding[1], statutory provisions apply entitling the landlord or tenant to have the rent determined by arbitration[2], and restrictions are placed on the issue by the landlord of a notice to quit[3]. Further, the tenant, on the termination of the tenancy, has certain rights to compensation[4] of which a purchaser of the land may be deemed to have notice[5], and the landlord may be liable to provide the tenant with fixed equipment necessary to comply with statutory requirements[6].

It is consequently necessary for the purchaser of land which is or may be agricultural land in the occupation of a tenant to inquire whether the land constitutes or comprises any agricultural holding, whether any notice to quit has been served, whether the tenant has any prospective claims for compensation, and whether any direction has been made for the provision by the landlord of fixed equipment[7].

Where land is used for the growing of timber, inquiry should be made whether it is the subject of any forestry dedication covenant, since such a covenant is deemed to have been made on behalf of the covenantor and his successors in title and is enforceable by the Forestry Commissioners against the covenantor's successors in title as if the commissioners had adjacent land benefited by the covenant[8].

Searches for the existence of agricultural charges are mentioned later in this title[9].

1   For the meaning of 'agricultural holding' see AGRICULTURE vol 1(2) (Reissue) para 301.
2   See AGRICULTURE vol 1(2) (Reissue) paras 325–327.
3   See AGRICULTURE vol 1(2) (Reissue) paras 340–364.
4   See AGRICULTURE vol 1(2) (Reissue) para 387 et seq.
5   See para 58 text and note 7 post; and AGRICULTURE vol 1(2) (Reissue) para 378. As to conditions with
     regard to the payment of the outgoing tenant's valuation see para 89 post.
6   See AGRICULTURE vol 1(2) (Reissue) para 324 et seq.
7   See generally AGRICULTURE.
8   See FORESTRY vol 19(1) (Reissue) para 42 et seq. Such a covenant is registrable as a Class D land charge:
     see FORESTRY vol 19(1) (Reissue) para 43; LAND CHARGES vol 26 (Reissue) paras 522, 533–536. As to
     searches for land charges see para 167 post.
9   See para 22 post.

10. Restrictive covenants. Subject to the statutory provisions which render restrictive
covenants entered into after 1925 (unless made between lessor and lessee) void against a
purchaser unless registered as land charges[1], a restrictive covenant binds in equity the
successors in title of the covenantor who purchases the land affected with notice of the
covenant[2]. The vendor should therefore be asked whether all covenants and conditions
restricting the user of the land have been observed and, if they have not, to specify any
breaches of which he is aware[3].

1   See EQUITY vol 16 (Reissue) para 793; LAND CHARGES vol 26 (Reissue) para 535. In the case of registered
     land, notice of a restrictive covenant may be entered on the register, and such a notice takes the place of
     registration as a land charge: see LAND REGISTRATION vol 26 (Reissue) paras 1110–1112.
2   See EQUITY vol 16 (Reissue) para 789 et seq. Registration of a covenant as a land charge constitutes
     notice: see the Law of Property Act 1925 s 198(1) (as amended); and EQUITY vol 16 (Reissue) para 768;
     LAND CHARGES vol 26 (Reissue) para 516. As to the effect of entry of a notice of a restrictive covenant
     in the case of registered land see LAND REGISTRATION vol 26 (Reissue) para 1112. As to the effect of the
     Law of Property Act 1969 s 24 see para 54 post; and EQUITY vol 16 (Reissue) para 768. As to the
     availability of compensation to a purchaser affected by a charge which he was unable to discover because
     it was registered against the name of an estate owner who was not a party to any transaction, or concerned
     in any event, comprised in the relevant title see the Law of Property Act 1969 s 25 (as amended); and
     LAND CHARGES vol 26 (Reissue) para 517.
3   As to the existence of restrictive covenants as a defect in title see para 57 post.

11. Restrictions under planning legislation. The most important legislation
affecting the use of land is the town and country planning legislation, under which the
permission of a local planning authority is in general required for the development of
land[1]. Compliance with planning control may be compelled by means of an enforcement
notice[2], although in certain circumstances a landowner may be entitled to recover
compensation for the refusal or the revocation or modification of planning permission[3],
or to require a local authority to purchase his land after the refusal of permission to
develop on the ground that it is incapable of reasonably beneficial use in its existing state[4].
Where the land proposed to be purchased is, for example, a dwelling house which does
not appear to have been substantially modified since its erection, it may be necessary for
a purchaser to inquire only as to the position under any development plan affecting the
property[5].

     In other cases, however, it may be necessary to ascertain certain matters by inquiries
of the vendor[6] and of the appropriate local authority[7], for example: (1) what is the
present user of the property[8]; (2) whether any development has taken place since that
date; (3) whether any applications for permission to develop have been made and with
what results[9]; (4) whether any permission granted was limited as to time or has since been
revoked[10]; (5) whether any directions restricting permitted development are in force in
the relevant area[11]; (6) whether an established use certificate has been granted[12]; (7)
whether any claims have been made for compensation for loss of development value[13];

(8) whether any claim has been made for compensation for refusal of permission to develop or revocation or modification of permission[14]; (9) whether any notice requiring the local authority to purchase the land has been served and with what result[15]; (10) whether any agreement respecting development has been made with the local planning authority[16]; and (11) whether there is anything on the land which is subject to the special statutory provisions relating to amenities, trees and woodlands, buildings of special architectural or historic interest, industrial or office development, advertisements or waste land[17].

Search must also be made in the registers kept by local planning authorities of applications for development, enforcement notices and stop notices, if inquiry of the appropriate authority reveals that there is a relevant entry[18], and in the part of the local land charges register relating to planning charges[19].

1   See the Town and Country Planning Act 1990 ss 57, 58; and TOWN AND COUNTRY PLANNING vol 46 (Reissue) paras 167–168. Permission can be granted to an intending purchaser even before he enters into the contract of purchase: *Hanily v Minister of Local Government and Planning* [1952] 2 QB 444, [1952] 1 All ER 1293. As to contracts conditional upon planning permission see para 26 post; and as to the certificate which must accompany an application by an intending purchaser see the Town and Country Planning (General Development Procedure) Order 1995, SI 1995/419, art 7; and TOWN AND COUNTRY PLANNING vol 46 (Reissue) para 410. As to the effect of a factually erroneous certificate on the validity of a subsequent grant of planning permission in respect of the planning application see *Main v Swansea City Council* (1984) 49 P & CR 26, [1985] JPL 558, CA.

2   See the Town and Country Planning Act 1990 ss 172–182 (as amended); and TOWN AND COUNTRY PLANNING vol 46 (Reissue) paras 664–675. As to the time limits for breaches of planning control see s 171B (as added); and TOWN AND COUNTRY PLANNING vol 46 (Reissue) para 655. As to stop notices see ss 183–187 (as amended); and TOWN AND COUNTRY PLANNING vol 46 (Reissue) paras 676–681. As to the power to order discontinuance of the use or alteration or the removal of a building or works see s 102 (as amended); and TOWN AND COUNTRY PLANNING vol 46 (Reissue) paras 474–475.

3   See ibid Pt IV (ss 107–118) (as amended); and TOWN AND COUNTRY PLANNING vol 46 (Reissue) paras 695–716. Notices as to apportionment of compensation must be deposited with certain local authorities and are also registrable as local land charges: see s 110 (as amended); the Local Land Charges Rules 1977, SI 1977/985, r 3; and LAND CHARGES vol 26 (Reissue) para 575.

4   See the Town and Country Planning Act 1990 Pt VI Ch I (ss 137–148) (as amended); and TOWN AND COUNTRY PLANNING vol 46 (Reissue) paras 717–728. As to other cases where the owner may compel purchase see Pt VI Ch II (ss 149–171) (as amended); and TOWN AND COUNTRY PLANNING vol 46 (Reissue) paras 729–759. As to the right to require the purchase of land where its value for sale has been adversely affected by planning proposals see para 15 post.

5   See ibid Pt II (ss 10–54A) (as amended); and TOWN AND COUNTRY PLANNING vol 46 (Reissue) para 36 et seq. In *Lake v Bushby* [1949] 2 All ER 964 a solicitor was held to be negligent in failing to communicate to his client (the purchaser) his discovery that plans for a building had not been approved.

6   As to inquiries of vendor see para 5 ante.

7   This will be the local planning authority: see the Town and Country Planning Act 1990 Pt I (ss 1–9) (as amended); and TOWN AND COUNTRY PLANNING vol 46 (Reissue) paras 11–20. Answers to inquiries given by an unidentified officer of the local authority over the telephone cannot be relied upon in a subsequent action in negligence for failure to disclose a planning blight: *JGF Properties Ltd v Lambeth London Borough Council* [1986] 1 EGLR 179, [1986] JPL 839.

8   As to the time limits for breaches of planning control see the Town and Country Planning Act 1990 s 171B (as added); and TOWN AND COUNTRY PLANNING vol 46 (Reissue) para 655. As to the continuance in force of certain schemes and agreements made under earlier planning legislation see the Planning (Consequential Provisions) Act 1990 s 5, Sch 3 (as amended); and see generally TOWN AND COUNTRY PLANNING.

9   As to the power of an intending purchaser to apply for permission see note 1 supra; as to conditions providing for rescission if the permitted user differs from that stated in the contract see para 80 post; and as to contracts conditional upon obtaining permission see para 26 post.

10 As to the duration of planning permission see the Town and Country Planning Act 1990 ss 91–96 (as amended); and TOWN AND COUNTRY PLANNING vol 46 (Reissue) paras 450, 465–469. As to revocation or modification see ss 97–100 (as amended); and TOWN AND COUNTRY PLANNING vol 46 (Reissue) paras 470–473. As to time limits annexed as a condition on the grant of outline permission see *Kent County Council v Kingsway Investments (Kent) Ltd* [1971] AC 72, [1970] 1 All ER 70, HL; *Cardiff Corpn*

v Secretary of State for Wales (1971) 22 P & CR 718; and TOWN AND COUNTRY PLANNING vol 46 (Reissue) para 450.

11 See the Town and Country Planning (General Development Procedure) Order 1995, SI 1995/418, art 4 (as amended), art 5; and TOWN AND COUNTRY PLANNING vol 46 (Reissue) para 137.

12 See the Town and Country Planning Act 1990 ss 191–196 (as amended); and TOWN AND COUNTRY PLANNING vol 46 (Reissue) paras 685–692.

13 See notes 3–4 supra.

14 See note 3 supra.

15 See note 4 supra.

16 See the Town and Country Planning Act 1990 s 106 (as substituted); and TOWN AND COUNTRY PLANNING vol 46 (Reissue) paras 172–173, 182.

17 See ibid Pt VIII (ss 197–225) (as amended); the Planning (Listed Buildings and Conservation Areas) Act 1990; and TOWN AND COUNTRY PLANNING vol 46 (Reissue) paras 492 et seq, 555 et seq, 888 et seq. As to the control of advertisements see para 14 post; and as to the control of pollution and waste see the Environmental Protection Act 1990 Pt I (ss 1–28) (as amended), Pt II (ss 29–78); and see generally PUBLIC HEALTH; WATER. As to the registration of planning matters as local land charges see LAND CHARGES vol 26 (Reissue) para 578; and as to the registration of lists of buildings of special architectural or historic interest see LAND CHARGES vol 26 (Reissue) para 585.

18 See the Town and Country Planning Act 1990 s 69 (as amended), s 188 (as amended); and TOWN AND COUNTRY PLANNING vol 46 (Reissue) paras 406, 1061. Enforcement notices and stop notices seem also to be registrable as local land charges. As to special controls relating to caravan sites see the Caravan Sites and Control of Development Act 1960; the Caravan Sites Act 1968; and TOWN AND COUNTRY PLANNING vol 46 (Reissue) paras 593–627; and as to the protection of residential occupiers of caravans see the Mobile Homes Act 1975; the Mobile Homes Act 1983; and LANDLORD AND TENANT vol 27(1) (Reissue) paras 1118–1124.

19 See LAND CHARGES vol 26 (Reissue) paras 578 (planning charges), 585 (listed building charges). As to the necessity for making searches for local land charges see para 20 post.

12. Particular matters affecting user. Inquiries should be made of local authorities in appropriate cases, according to the nature of the property: (1) whether an order, draft order, scheme or draft scheme affecting the property has been made under the statutory provisions relating to trunk roads or special roads[1]; (2) whether any proposals for road construction or road widening affecting the property have been approved[2]; (3) whether the property is a prospectively maintainable highway for the purpose of the statutory street works code[3]; (4) whether any proceedings have been authorised for breach of building regulations[4]; (5) whether the property is likely to be purchased compulsorily by any local authority or statutory body having powers of compulsory acquisition[5]; and (6) in the case of country property, whether the property is affected by the legislation concerning the designation of national parks and of areas of outstanding natural beauty[6] and access to the countryside[7].

1 See the Highways Act 1980 ss 10(5), 14(4), 18(4), Sch 1 Pts I, III (as amended); and HIGHWAYS, STREETS AND BRIDGES vol 21 (Reissue) para 627 et seq.

2 As to compulsory purchase powers with respect to highway purposes see HIGHWAYS, STREETS AND BRIDGES vol 21 (Reissue) para 800 et seq.

3 See HIGHWAYS, STREETS AND BRIDGES vol 21 (Reissue) para 529. A declaration by the local highway authority, that a street in its area is likely to become a maintainable highway, is registrable as a local land charge: New Roads and Street Works Act 1991 s 87(1), (2).

4 See generally PUBLIC HEALTH.

5 See para 15 post; and COMPULSORY ACQUISITION OF LAND.

6 See OPEN SPACES AND ANCIENT MONUMENTS vol 34 (Reissue) paras 148–199.

7 See OPEN SPACES AND ANCIENT MONUMENTS vol 34 (Reissue) paras 250–284.

13. Restrictions registrable as local land charges. Restrictions as to user imposed or enforceable by a local authority over particular properties, including restrictions embodied in a condition attached to a consent, approval or licence given by a local authority, are in general registrable as local land charges[1]. Such restrictions may be discovered by search in the appropriate part of the local land charges register[2], whether the land is registered land or not[3], and in general no preliminary inquiry is necessary. In certain cases the legislation relating to local land charges is applied to restrictions imposed by authorities other than local authorities[4].

1   See LAND CHARGES vol 26 (Reissue) para 571 et seq. The definition of 'local land charge' excludes a condition in a planning permission granted before 1 August 1977 or deemed to be granted at any time under any statutory provision relating to town and country planning: see LAND CHARGES vol 26 (Reissue) para 573.
2   This will normally be Parts 3 and 4 of the register: see LAND CHARGES vol 26 (Reissue) paras 578–579. As to searches for local land charges generally see para 20 post.
3   See para 20 post.
4   Eg under the Highways Act 1980 ss 73, 74, Sch 9 (all as amended) (improvement and building lines imposed by a highway authority): see HIGHWAYS, STREETS AND BRIDGES vol 21 (Reissue) paras 351–361; LAND CHARGES vol 26 (Reissue) para 572.

14. Control of advertisements. Under regulations made under statutory powers for the control of advertisements[1], the consent of the local planning authority or the Secretary of State[2] is required for the display of advertisements[3], and although consent is not required in the case of certain excepted classes of advertisements[4], the Secretary of State may direct that the exceptions are not to apply in a particular area or in a particular case[5], and the authority may require the discontinuance of the display of advertisements which are within the excepted classes[6]. The authority may define any part of its area as an area of special control within which the display of advertisements is to be specially restricted[7]. A register of applications for consents and decisions on them must be kept by the authority[8]. Inquiries should therefore be made of the appropriate authorities[9] whether any consent is required in respect of the property to be purchased, whether there is any entry regarding any application for consent in the register of applications[10], and whether the property is situated within an area of special control.

1   See the Town and Country Planning Act 1990 ss 220, 333 (both as amended); the Town and Country Planning (Control of Advertisements) Regulations 1992, SI 1992/666 (as amended); and TOWN AND COUNTRY PLANNING vol 46 (Reissue) paras 492–554.
2   Ie one of Her Majesty's Principal Secretaries of State: see the Interpretation Act 1978 s 5, Sch 1. As to the office of Secretary of State see CONSTITUTIONAL LAW AND HUMAN RIGHTS vol 8(2) (Reissue) para 355.
3   See the Town and Country Planning (Control of Advertisements) Regulations 1992, SI 1992/666, reg 5; and TOWN AND COUNTRY PLANNING vol 46 (Reissue) para 500.
4   See ibid reg 6; and TOWN AND COUNTRY PLANNING vol 46 (Reissue) paras 512–538.
5   See ibid reg 7; and TOWN AND COUNTRY PLANNING vol 46 (Reissue) para 537.
6   See ibid reg 8; and TOWN AND COUNTRY PLANNING vol 46 (Reissue) para 538.
7   See ibid regs 18, 19; and TOWN AND COUNTRY PLANNING vol 46 (Reissue) paras 547–549.
8   See ibid reg 21; and TOWN AND COUNTRY PLANNING vol 46 (Reissue) para 544.
9   As to these authorities see para 11 note 7 ante.
10   The register is not normally searched unless the answer to the inquiry reveals that there is an entry: see para 22 post.

15. Compulsory acquisition. Compulsory purchase orders are not, as a rule, registrable as such in the registers of land charges or local land charges[1]. It is therefore necessary to ascertain, by inquiries of the vendor and of the local authorities in the area where the property lies, whether there is any indication in any development plan or otherwise that the property is likely to be the subject of compulsory acquisition and whether any order has been made or resolution passed for its compulsory acquisition[2]. Inquiry should also be made whether any notice has been served in respect of the property under the provisions which entitle owner-occupiers to require the purchase of property which cannot be sold at a reasonable price because of the adverse effect of proposals implying future acquisition[3].

1   Orders which form an exception to the rule and which are registrable in the register of local land charges
    are: (1) orders under the New Towns Act 1981 ss 1, 10–12 (all as amended) (see TOWN AND COUNTRY
    PLANNING vol 46 (Reissue) para 1104 et seq); (2) wayleave orders for government oil pipelines under the
    Requisitioned Land and War Works Act 1948 s 14 (as amended) and under the Land Powers (Defence)
    Act 1958 ss 12(2), 17 (as amended) (see WAR AND ARMED CONFLICT vol 49(1) (Reissue) paras 620–621);
    (3) orders in favour of the Coal Authority and licensed operators in connection with the opencast
    working of coal under the Opencast Coal Act 1958 s 11(1) (as substituted), s 16(6) (as amended) (see
    MINES, MINERALS AND QUARRIES vol 31 (Reissue) para 424 et seq). As to the licensing of coal mining
    operations see the Coal Industry Act 1994 Pt II (ss 25–36); and MINES, MINERALS AND QUARRIES vol
    31 (Reissue) paras 91–106. See LAND CHARGES vol 26 (Reissue) para 574.
2   As to inquiries as to the acquisition of rights over the property see para 17 post; and as to the conditions
    of sale providing against the possibility of compulsory acquisition see para 80 post.
3   See the Town and Country Planning Act 1990 Pt VI Ch II (ss 149–171) (as amended) (interests affected
    by planning proposals: blight); and COMPULSORY ACQUISITION OF LAND vol 8(1) (Reissue) para 88 et
    seq. As to the power of an owner of land to require its purchase on the refusal of permission to develop
    see para 11 ante.

16. Boundaries, easements, local authority charges and sewers. The matters as
to which inquiry should be made of the vendor include the ownership of the walls or
fences bounding the property[1], the liability to repair roads or paths abutting on the
property[2], the means of access to the property, the means of drainage[3] and the existence
of any easements[4], wayleaves, rights of light[5] or similar rights affecting the property or of
any agreements conferring rights, for example a right to lay cables or wires, under or over
the property.

   In order to prevent the acquisition of a right to light by prescription, the owner of a
servient tenement may register a notice in the register of local land charges for the purpose
of preventing access of light to the dominant tenement being taken to be enjoyed without
interruption. The owner of the dominant tenement may in certain circumstances bring
proceedings to have the notice cancelled[6]. The existence of such a notice affecting the
land to be purchased will be revealed on the search of the local land charges register[7].
Where such a notice has been registered, it seems that the purchaser should inquire of the
vendor whether any action has been commenced or is contemplated in respect of the
notice.

   Inquiry should be made of the appropriate local authority whether the highways
abutting on the property are maintainable at the public expense, and, if they are not, as
to the application to the property of the enactments requiring advance payments to be
made, or security to be given, in respect of the expenses of street works, by persons
proposing to erect buildings abutting on private streets[8]. Expenses incurred by local
authorities in making up private streets[9] in cases where the advance payments code does
not apply constitute a charge upon the property affected which is registrable as a local land
charge[10]; but no charge can be registered until money has been actually expended[11], and
resolutions of a local authority to execute works are not registrable. Inquiry should
therefore be made by the purchaser of the vendor and of local authorities whether any
outstanding notices have been served by an authority on the vendor. Inquiries should also
be made of water authorities whether there is a public sewer available to serve the
property[12], whether the owner of the property is liable to contribute to the cost of
maintaining any public sewer[13] and, in the case of property intended to be used for trade,
what right there is to discharge trade effluent from the property into public sewers[14].

1   As to statutory provisions regarding the ownership of party walls see BOUNDARIES vol 4(1) (Reissue)
    paras 964–975.
2   As to inquiries of local authorities as to roads see the text to notes 8–11 infra.
3   As to inquiries of local authorities as to drainage see the text to notes 12–14 infra.

4   As to the existence of an undisclosed easement as a defect in title see para 57 post. Property is usually sold
    subject to easements affecting it: see para 89 post. As to easements generally see EASEMENTS AND PROFITS
    À PRENDRE.
5   As to light obstruction notices see the text to notes 6–7 infra. As to conditions designed to prevent the
    acquisition by the purchaser of rights of light over the vendor's property see para 81 post.
6   See the Rights of Light Act 1959 ss 2, 3 (s 2 as amended); and EASEMENTS AND PROFITS À PRENDRE;
    LAND CHARGES vol 26 (Reissue) paras 574, 586.
7   As to this search generally see para 20 post. The normal rule set out in the Local Land Charges Act 1975
    s 10 (as amended) (see LAND CHARGES vol 26 (Reissue) para 594), that failure to register a local land
    charge does not affect its enforceability but may entitle a purchaser to compensation, does not apply to
    light obstruction notices: see LAND CHARGES vol 26 (Reissue) para 586.
8   See the Highways Act 1980 ss 219–225 (as amended); and HIGHWAYS, STREETS AND BRIDGES vol
    21 (Reissue) para 749 et seq. As to matters under the advance payments code which are registrable in
    the register of local land charges see s 224; and HIGHWAYS, STREETS AND BRIDGES vol 21 (Reissue)
    para 751–752; LAND CHARGES vol 26 (Reissue) para 574.
9   Ie under ibid ss 205–218 (as amended): see HIGHWAYS, STREETS AND BRIDGES vol 21 (Reissue)
    paras 718–741.
10 See para 126 post; and LAND CHARGES vol 26 (Reissue) para 574.
11 See para 126 post.
12 As to the right to drain into public sewers generally see PUBLIC HEALTH.
13 As to contribution to cost of sewering highways see PUBLIC HEALTH.
14 As to restrictions on the discharge of trade effluents see generally PUBLIC HEALTH.

17. Rights in favour of government departments and public authorities.
Certain enactments which authorise government departments or public authorities to
create or require easements, wayleaves or other rights over land provide that the relevant
order must be registered in the register of local land charges[1], and in such cases it is
unnecessary to make a preliminary inquiry. Certain enactments conferring similar
authority do not provide for registration[2], and, in an appropriate case, it may be advisable
to inquire whether any acquisition of a right has taken place or is pending.

1   See eg AVIATION vol 2 (Reissue) paras 1113, 1115; MINES, MINERALS AND QUARRIES vol 31 (Reissue)
    para 424 et seq. As to the registration of wayleave orders relating to oil pipelines see para 15 note 1
    ante; and LAND CHARGES vol 26 (Reissue) para 574; WAR AND ARMED CONFLICT vol 49(1) (Reissue)
    paras 620–621. As to easements etc generally see EASEMENTS AND PROFITS À PRENDRE.
2   See eg the Atomic Energy Act 1946 s 7 (as amended); and FUEL AND ENERGY vol 19(1) (Reissue)
    paras 1194–1195.

18. Outgoings.
The vendor should be asked what is the amount of council tax payable
each year in respect of the property[1], whether the property is subject to any other
outgoings[2], and for particulars of any insurance policy against fire or other damage to the
property[3].

1   As to the amount of council tax payable see RATING AND THE COUNCIL TAX vol 39(1) (Reissue) paras
    835–856; and as to valuation lists see RATING AND THE COUNCIL TAX vol 39(1) (Reissue) paras 857–868.
2   For the meaning of 'outgoings' see para 125 post. Where the property is subject to a ground rent or
    rentcharge and has been part of a larger property which has been developed and sold in lots, inquiry
    should be made as to any liability which may fall on the purchaser to collect apportioned parts of the
    ground rent or rentcharge from adjoining owners and to pay the whole ground rent or rentcharge to the
    freeholder or owner of the rentcharge. As to legal and equitable apportionments see the Rentcharges Act
    1977 ss 4, 13; and RENTCHARGES AND ANNUITIES vol 39(2) (Reissue) para 844 et seq; and as to the
    redemption and extinguishment of existing rentcharges see s 3; and RENTCHARGES AND ANNUITIES vol
    39(2) (Reissue) para 894.
3   As to the respective rights of a vendor and purchaser in relation to an insurance policy effected by the
    vendor see paras 117–118 post.

(ii) Searches

19. The National Conveyancing Protocol. In residential freehold conveyancing the use of preliminary inquiries addressed to the vendor is now regulated by The National Conveyancing Protocol[1], which provides for the vendor and his solicitor[2] to prepare a package of information for the purchaser. The package includes the Seller's Property Information Form, which comprises a standardised set of preliminary inquiries. The first part of the form is to be completed by the vendor and the second part by the vendor's solicitor.

In the case of a leasehold property the package includes a Seller's Leasehold Information Form, again divided into parts to be completed by the vendor and the vendor's solicitor respectively. The leasehold information form is designed to be used in both residential and commercial transactions.

1   See The National Conveyancing Protocol (3rd Edn, 1994), published by The Law Society. The National Conveyancing Protocol was introduced in 1990.
2   See para 3 ante.

20. The local land charges register. The registration of any instrument or matter under the Local Land Charges Act 1975 is deemed to constitute actual notice of the instrument or matter to all persons and for all purposes connected with the land affected[1], and, if any matter has been so registered at the date of a contract for sale, it seems that the purchaser may be bound to complete, even though the vendor has contracted to sell free from incumbrances[2]. Subject to certain exceptions[3], failure to register a local land charge does not affect the enforceability of the charge; but a purchaser who has searched the register and who suffers loss by reason of the non-registration of the charge, or in the case where the register is kept otherwise than in documentary form and entitlement to search in that register was not satisfied, or in the case of an official search by reason of the non-disclosure of the charge, may be entitled to compensation[4]. It is therefore necessary for the purchaser before contract to search[5] the local land charges register[6] for matters registrable in it[7]. The registers are maintained by district councils, London borough councils and the Common Council of the City of London, and the search must be made of the appropriate register for the area or areas in which the land is situated[8]. If the search does not provide sufficient information, the matter must be taken up by further inquiries of the vendor and of the local authority[9].

1   See the Law of Property Act 1925 s 198(1) (as amended); and EQUITY vol 16 (Reissue) para 768; LAND CHARGES vol 26 (Reissue) para 593. As to local land charges affecting registered land see LAND REGISTRATION vol 26 (Reissue) para 709.
2   See para 54 post.
3   See the Local Land Charges Act 1975 s 11 (as amended); and LAND CHARGES vol 26 (Reissue) para 594.
4   See ibid s 10 (as amended); and LAND CHARGES vol 26 (Reissue) para 594.
5   As to the mode of search see LAND CHARGES vol 26 (Reissue) para 605 et seq. Entries in the register of local land charges are against the land affected: see ibid s 5(3); and LAND CHARGES vol 26 (Reissue) para 589. See however, the names register for charges registrable under the Land Charges Act 1972: see para 21 post; and LAND CHARGES vol 26 (Reissue) paras 509, 589.
6   As to the parts into which the register is divided, and the contents of the different parts see LAND CHARGES vol 26 (Reissue) paras 576–587.
7   As to the registration of planning matters see para 11 notes 3, 17, 19 ante; as to the registration of restrictions on user imposed by local authorities and other authorities, local authority charges and rights in favour of government departments see para 13 ante; as to the registration of certain compulsory

purchase orders see para 15 note 1 ante; as to the registration of light obstruction notices see para 16 ante; and as to the full list of matters which are registrable see LAND CHARGES vol 26 (Reissue) para 571 et seq.

8   See the Local Land Charges Act 1975 s 4 (as amended); the Interpretation Act 1978 ss 5, 22, Sch 1, Sch 2 para 6 (as amended); and LAND CHARGES vol 26 (Reissue) para 588.

9   As to preliminary inquiries of vendors and local authorities see generally para 5 ante.

21. The land charges register. Although the entry of a matter in the registers kept at the Land Registry[1] is notice to the purchaser[2], these registers are not normally searched before contract, since it is not known at that time against what names such a search should be made[3].

1   See LAND CHARGES vol 26 (Reissue) para 507.

2   See the Law of Property Act 1925 s 198(1) (as amended); and EQUITY vol 16 (Reissue) para 768; LAND CHARGES vol 26 (Reissue) para 516. See also note 3 infra.

3   See para 167 post. Any question as to the purchaser's knowledge of a centrally registered land charge is to be determined by reference to his actual knowledge and without regard to the actual notice deemed to be given by registration: see the Law of Property Act 1969 s 24; and para 54 post. As to the statutory scheme of compensation for a purchaser who suffers loss because he is bound by a registered charge registered against the names of estate owners undiscoverable from the relevant title see s 25 (as amended); and LAND CHARGES vol 26 (Reissue) para 517. As to searches which in the case of registered land take the place of searches in the register of land charges see para 169 post; and as to searches to see if land is registered see para 2 ante.

22. Searches in other registers. Searches are normally made before contract in the register of agricultural charges[1] if the property to be sold includes farm property, and in the registers kept by the Registrar of Companies[2] where the vendor is a company.

Search must be made in the registers of rents kept by the president of every rent assessment panel under the legislation relating to restricted contracts[3] and the registers of enforcement notices, stop notices, applications for planning permission[4] and applications for consent to the display of advertisements[5] kept under planning legislation, if the preliminary inquiries of local authorities have revealed the existence of an entry affecting the property to be sold. Where the property is vacant land on which no building has ever been erected, a search should be made in the commons register, although there is room for discretion where the property is surrounded by densely built-up land[6].

In areas affected by mining, whether the mining operations are current or not, a search should be made of the Coal Authority[7]. If the property is in the Forest of Dean, inquiries should be made additionally to the Deputy Gaveller and Crown Receiver of the Forestry Commission[8].

1   See AGRICULTURE vol 1(2) (Reissue) para 554; LAND CHARGES vol 26 (Reissue) para 597. Registration constitutes actual notice of the charge: see AGRICULTURE vol 1(2) (Reissue) para 554.

2   See COMPANIES vol 7(2) (1996 Reissue) para 1299 et seq; LAND CHARGES vol 26 (Reissue) paras 506, 597. See also *Property Discount Corpn Ltd v Lyon Group Ltd* [1981] 1 All ER 379, [1981] 1 WLR 300, CA.

3   See para 8 ante. In the case of a protected tenancy, the register of rents is kept by the rent officer and should be searched as appropriate.

4   See para 11 ante.

5   See para 14 ante.

6   See *G & K Ladenbau (UK) Ltd v Crawley and de Reya* [1978] 1 All ER 682, [1978] 1 WLR 266, where a solicitor was negligent in failing to search the commons register. As to commons registration generally see COMMONS vol 6 (Reissue) paras 535, 672–703.

7   See MINES, MINERALS AND QUARRIES vol 31 (Reissue) para 107 et seq; and EF & P vol 35 (1997 Reissue) SALE OF LAND paras 44[74], 170.2.11[208].

8   See MINES, MINERALS AND QUARRIES vol 31 (Reissue) para 600 et seq. For a list of searches see EF & P vol 35 (1997 Reissue) SALE OF LAND para 170.2.

(3) FORMATION OF THE CONTRACT

(i) Requirements for the Existence of the Contract

23. Offer and acceptance. The formation of a contract for the sale of land is governed by the same legal rules as any other contract[1], and it is only necessary to consider here the application of the general law to the particular subject matter of the sale of land. Thus a contract for the sale of land may be made either by private agreement between the parties or by public auction[2]; but, however made, it must contain the ordinary essentials of a contract, namely an offer by one party to the other, and an acceptance of that offer by the party to whom it was made[3]. The acceptance may be subject to the execution of a formal contract in which case there is no binding agreement until formal contracts are exchanged[4].

Subject to any express instructions, a solicitor[5] employed to act in a contract for the sale of land has implied and ostensible authority to effect an exchange of contracts binding his client by any method effective to constitute the exchange, including an exchange agreed by solicitors over the telephone[6] and an exchange effected by means of a document exchange[7].

Where the offer and acceptance are contained in correspondence between the parties, it is a matter of construction whether or not there is a concluded contract[8].

1   See CONTRACT vol 9(1) (Reissue) para 631 et seq. An agreement for the discharge of a debt conditional on the transfer of land is not a contract for the sale of land: *Simpson v Connolly* [1953] 2 All ER 474, [1953] 1 WLR 911.
2   See AUCTION vol 2 (Reissue) para 901 et seq.
3   See CONTRACT vol 9(1) (Reissue) para 631 et seq. A statement that the owner will favourably consider an offer is not an offer in law which can be accepted: *Montreal Gas Co v Vasey* [1900] AC 595, PC. A promise to sell or to purchase at a price to be agreed upon is not enforceable until the price has been agreed: *Loftus v Roberts* (1902) 18 TLR 532, CA. A statement of the lowest price at which a person will sell even if made in answer to an inquiry is not an offer to sell at that price: *Harvey v Facey* [1893] AC 552, PC. An offer to sell at a named price is not necessarily a binding offer to sell: *Clifton v Palumbo* [1944] 2 All ER 497, CA; cf *Bigg v Boyd Gibbins Ltd* [1971] 2 All ER 183, [1971] 1 WLR 913, CA. As to options to purchase see para 27 post. An offer accepted by an agent which requires ratification can be withdrawn at any time before ratification: *Watson v Davies* [1931] Ch 455; and see AGENCY vol 1(2) (Reissue) para 73.
4   See CONTRACT vol 9(1) (Reissue) paras 637, 671; and *Harrison v Battye* [1974] 3 All ER 830, [1975] 1 WLR 58, CA.
5   See para 3 ante.
6   *Domb v Isoz* [1980] Ch 548, [1980] 1 All ER 942, CA. See the alternative formulae recommended by The Law Society in 'Council News *Domb v Isoz* Arrangements for Effecting Exchange of Contracts by Telephone or Telex' (1980) 77 Law Society's Gazette 144; and see the Standard Conditions of Sale (3rd Edn), conditions 1, 2. As to the Standard Conditions of Sale see para 1 note 9 ante.
7   As to the use of a document exchange see 'The Law Society's Formulae for Exchanging Contracts by Telephone/Telex' (1984) 81 Law Society's Gazette 1891.
8   See eg *Bigg v Boyd Gibbins Ltd* [1971] 2 All ER 183, [1971] 1 WLR 913, CA; *Storer v Manchester City Council* [1974] 3 All ER 824, [1974] 1 WLR 1403, CA; *Gibson v Manchester City Council* [1979] 1 All ER 972, [1979] 1 WLR 294, HL; and CONTRACT vol 9(1) (Reissue) paras 637, 671. The contract must be in writing and signed by both parties: see paras 29–40 post. In the case of contracts by correspondence, the statutory conditions of sale apply: see para 76 note 6 post.

24. Offer at auction. On a sale by auction, the offer is made by the purchaser in the form of the bid which is ultimately accepted by the auctioneer as the agent of the vendor[1]. A contract made in the course of a public auction is exempt from the statutory requirement that a contract for the sale of land be in writing[2], and it follows that the contract is complete when the successful bid is accepted by the auctioneer. The advertisement of the sale is not itself an offer, but only a declaration of intention to hold the sale and to allow the public generally to make offers[3].

1   See AUCTION vol 2 (Reissue) paras 906–908. If the auctioneer exceeds his authority by offering rights,
    eg riparian rights, which the vendor did not intend to be included in the sale, there is, it seems, no
    contract which can be specifically enforced: see *Hammond v Chubb* (1915) 138 LT Jo 360. As to the
    auctioneer's authority to sign the contract see para 40 post; and AUCTION vol 2 (Reissue) para 914.
2   See the Law of Property (Miscellaneous Provisions) Act 1989 s 2(5)(b). As to the requirement of a written
    contract see paras 29–40 post.
3   *Harris v Nickerson* (1873) LR 8 QB 286. Hence no action will lie against the proposing vendor for not
    holding the sale: *Harris v Nickerson* supra. As to withdrawal of the property from sale see AUCTION vol 2
    (Reissue) para 947. A bid, like any other offer, may be retracted before it is accepted, ie before the fall of
    the auctioneer's hammer: see *Payne v Cave* (1789) 3 Term Rep 148. As to offer and acceptance see
    CONTRACT vol 9(1) (Reissue) paras 631–675.

25. Consents. If a lease requires the landlord's consent to be obtained to an assignment, it is the duty of the vendor who agrees to assign the lease to obtain the necessary licence[1].

There are statutory restrictions on the disposition of land held by or in trust for a charity[2]. In certain exceptional cases no disposition can be made without the consent of the court or the Charity Commissioners[3]. In such cases, an unconditional contract for the sale of such charity land made before the requisite consent has been obtained is unlawful and void[4], and the purchaser can recover his deposit[5]. Outside those exceptional cases, the land may be disposed of by the charity trustees on compliance with various statutory conditions which must be carried out before entering into an agreement for the sale, or, as the case may be, for a lease or other disposition, of the land, such as obtaining and considering a written report on the proposed disposition from a qualified surveyor instructed by the trustees and acting exclusively for the charity, advertising the proposed disposition for such period and in such manner as the surveyor has advised in his report (unless he has there advised that it would not be in the best interests of the charity to advertise the proposed disposition), and deciding that they are satisfied, having considered the surveyor's report, that the terms on which the disposition is proposed to be made are the best that can reasonably be obtained for the charity[6]. Where the latter restrictions on disposition apply, the contract must be made conditional upon compliance with the statutory restrictions[7].

Many dispositions of land by local authorities are precluded without the necessary consent[8]. However, in favour of a person claiming under the local authority, the lack of consent does not invalidate the transaction, and a person dealing with or claiming under the authority is not concerned to see or inquire whether such consent has been obtained[9].

1   See eg *Ellis v Rogers* (1885) 29 ChD 661, CA; and LANDLORD AND TENANT vol 27(1) (Reissue) para 462.
    See further para 240 post, which also considers the question of the time within which the consent must be
    obtained. As to conditions providing for the possibility of refusal of consent see para 94 post.
2   See the Charities Act 1993 ss 36, 37 (as amended); and CHARITIES vol 5(2) (Reissue) paras 329–330.
3   See ibid s 36(1); and CHARITIES vol 5(2) (Reissue) para 329.
4   See ibid ss 36(1), 37(1); *Bishop of Bangor v Parry* [1891] 2 QB 277; and CHARITIES vol 5(2) (Reissue)
    paras 329–330.
5   See *Milner v Staffordshire Congregational Union Inc* [1956] Ch 275, [1956] 1 All ER 494.
6   See the Charities Act 1993 s 36(3); and CHARITIES vol 5(2) (Reissue) para 329.
7   See ibid s 37(1) (see CHARITIES vol 5(2) (Reissue) para 330); and *Manchester Diocesan Council for Education
    v Commercial and General Investments Ltd* [1969] 3 All ER 1593, [1970] 1 WLR 241; *Michael Richards
    Properties Ltd v Corpn of Wardens of St Saviour's Parish, Southwark* [1975] 3 All ER 416; *Haslemere Estates
    Ltd v Baker* [1982] 3 All ER 525, [1982] 1 WLR 1109.
8   See the Local Government Act 1972 ss 123, 127 (both as amended); and LOCAL GOVERNMENT.
9   See ibid s 128(2); and LOCAL GOVERNMENT.

26. Conditional contracts. Contracts for the sale of land are not infrequently made dependent on the occurrence of some event. The effect of such a qualification may be to deny the existence of any contract at all. The commonest example of this is the phrase 'subject to contract' and its equivalents, which must be distinguished from phrases indicating the existence of a provisional but binding agreement[1]. In the case of qualifications such as 'subject to survey of the property'[2], 'subject to a satisfactory survey'[3], 'subject to a satisfactory mortgage'[4], and 'subject to planning permission to develop'[5], it is a question of construction whether the qualification precludes the existence of a contract, leaving the parties still in negotiation, or whether there is a contract which is concluded but enforceable only on the occurrence of the condition[6]. In the latter case, it follows, inter alia, that neither party can withdraw from the contract pending the occurrence of the condition[7], and that the purchaser immediately acquires an equitable interest in the land[8]. The trend of decisions is in favour of treating such qualifications as not being inconsistent with the existence of a concluded contract, but rather as amounting to a condition precedent upon which the contract depends[9]. In the case of a conditional contract, where one party has the power to decide whether the condition has been fulfilled, it will be implied that such party must act reasonably. Thus if a contract for the sale of land is subject to a satisfactory survey, the purchaser must obtain a survey from a competent person and must act in good faith in considering whether it is satisfactory[10]. Where the condition is for the benefit of one party alone, that party may waive it and enforce the contract[11]. If the condition is unfulfilled the contract will fail. If the condition is void for uncertainty, no contract comes into existence[12].

1   See CONTRACT vol 9(1) (Reissue) para 671.
2   See *Ee v Kakar* (1979) 40 P & CR 223.
3   See *Marks v Board* (1930) 46 TLR 424.
4   See *Lee-Parker v Izzet (No 2)* [1972] 2 All ER 800, [1972] 1 WLR 775.
5   See *Batten v White* (1960) 12 P & CR 66. Where a contract is conditional on the obtaining of planning permission it is a question of construction whether the condition is fulfilled by the obtaining of outline permission: see *Hargreaves Transport Ltd v Lynch* [1969] 1 All ER 455, [1969] 1 WLR 215, CA; *Richard West & Partners (Inverness) Ltd v Dick* [1969] 2 Ch 424, [1969] 1 All ER 943, CA. See further CONTRACT vol 9(1) (Reissue) para 670.
6   See *Batten v White* (1960) 12 P & CR 66; *Ee v Kakar* (1979) 40 P & CR 223.
7   See eg *Smallman v Smallman* [1972] Fam 25, [1971] 3 All ER 717, CA, where it was held that an agreement subject to the approval of the court is binding before such approval is given, and neither party can resile.
8   *Gordon Hill Trust Ltd v Segall* [1941] 2 All ER 379, CA. A conditional contract would, it seems, be registrable as an estate contract under the Land Charges Act 1972 s 2(4) (as amended) (see LAND CHARGES vol 26 (Reissue) paras 528, 532), and in the case of registered land could be protected by a caution under the Land Registration Act 1925 s 54 (as amended) (see LAND REGISTRATION vol 26 (Reissue) paras 1114, 1126). See *Haslemere Estates Ltd v Baker* [1982] 3 All ER 525, [1982] 1 WLR 1109.
9   See *Batten v White* (1960) 12 P & CR 66; *Ee v Kakar* (1979) 40 P & CR 223. Cases which had tended to favour the construction of such qualifications as precluding the existence of a contract (eg *Marks v Board* (1930) 46 TLR 424; *Astra Trust Ltd v Adams and Williams* [1969] 1 Lloyd's Rep 81) may now be taken as disapproved. As to conditional contracts other than in a conveyancing context see *United Dominions Trust (Commercial) Ltd v Eagle Aircraft Services Ltd* [1968] 1 All ER 104 at 109, [1968] 1 WLR 74 at 83, CA, per Diplock LJ; *Wood Preservation Ltd v Prior (Inspector of Taxes)* [1968] 2 All ER 849 at 855, [1969] 1 WLR 1077 at 1090 per Goff J (affd [1969] 1 All ER 364, [1969] 1 WLR 1077 at 1094, CA).
10   *Ee v Kakar* (1979) 40 P & CR 223. See also *100 Main Street Ltd v WB Sullivan Construction Ltd* (1978) 20 OR (2d) 401, 88 DLR (3d) 1, Ont CA, where it was held that where a contract is conditional on the vendor's obtaining the consent of the mortgagee to the sale, there is an implied obligation on the purchaser to co-operate in obtaining the consent; *Sinclair-Hill v Sothcott* (1973) 26 P & CR 490, where the vendor, who had lodged a planning application before contract, was held to be under an implied obligation not to withdraw it after contract without the purchaser's consent.
11   *Heron Garage Properties Ltd v Moss* [1974] 1 All ER 421, [1974] 1 WLR 148; *Ee v Kakar* (1979) 40 P & CR 223, *Balbosa v Ayoub Ali* [1990] 1 WLR 914, 134 Sol Jo 545, PC; *Graham v Pitkin* [1992] 2 All ER 235, [1992] 1 WLR 403, PC; cf *Boobyer v Thornville Properties Ltd* (1968) 19 P & CR 768; *Federated Homes Ltd v Turner* [1975] 1 EGLR 147, (1974) 233 Estates Gazette 845.
12   See eg *Lee-Parker v Izzet (No 2)* [1972] 2 All ER 800, [1972] 1 WLR 775, where a contract for sale 'subject to the purchaser obtaining a satisfactory mortgage' was void for uncertainty; but cf the questioning of that decision in *Graham v Pitkin* [1992] 2 All ER 235 at 237, [1992] 1 WLR 403 at 405, PC. Cf *Lee-Parker v Izzet* [1971] 3 All ER 1099 at 1105, not reported on this point at [1971] 1 WLR

1688, where completion was to be within 28 days of the vendor arranging 'a satisfactory mortgage', and this phrase was construed as a mortgage to the satisfaction of the purchaser acting reasonably, and the contract was valid; and *Janmohamed v Hassam* [1977] 1 EGLR 142, (1976) Times, 10 June. See also CONTRACT vol 9(1) (Reissue) para 672.

27. Option to purchase. An option to purchase is, in effect, an offer to sell, irrevocable for a stated period or until a stated event, made by the grantor of the option to the grantee, which the grantee is entitled to convert into a concluded contract of purchase on giving the prescribed notice and otherwise complying with the conditions on which the option is made exercisable in any particular case[1]. There must be a binding contract to keep the offer open which requires either a deed or valuable consideration. Specific performance will not be granted of a voluntary contract, even if made by deed[2], but the decree may be awarded where the consideration is merely nominal[3]. Where the parties do not stand in the relationship of landlord and tenant, the option will normally be contained in a separate agreement[4]. An option conferred on a tenant to purchase the reversion will normally be contained in the lease; however, such an option is collateral to, and not an incident of, the relationship of landlord and tenant[5]. If the option is phrased so as to be not merely personal to the grantor, and is capable of being enforced by a decree of specific performance, it will create an equitable interest in the land[6]. Such an option is a contract for the sale or other disposition of an interest in land and must therefore satisfy the statutory requirements as to a written contract[7]. However, a notice by the purchaser exercising the option does not create a new contract and therefore there is no need for the statutory requirements to be satisfied a second time[8]. If the option is to purchase a legal estate, it must be protected by registration in order to bind a purchaser of the legal estate[9], although failure to register will not affect the grantor's contractual liability[10].

So far as an option to purchase creates an interest in land, it is governed by the rule against perpetuities[11]. Any terms which are conditions precedent to the exercise of the option must be strictly observed[12].

Prima facie an option to purchase is binding on the grantor's personal representatives; the presumption is rebutted only if the option itself states that it is personal to the grantor, or if the option is of such a nature as to be substantially incapable of vicarious performance[13]. Where the option does bind the grantor's estate, it may be properly exercised by notice to the personal representatives[14]. The question whether the benefit of the option is personal to the grantee or is assignable (and thus on death passes to his personal representatives) is a question of construction in the light of the relevant surrounding circumstances[15]. Like the original grantee, an assignee or personal representative must strictly observe any conditions precedent to the exercise of the option[16].

The exercise of an option to purchase creates the relationship of vendor and purchaser from the date of the expiry of the notice exercising the option[17]. Whether, in the case of a tenant's option to purchase the reversion, the establishment of the relationship of vendor and purchaser also operates to determine the lease depends on the intention of the parties to be ascertained from the terms of the agreement[18]. The contract of sale arising from the exercise of the option will be an open contract unless conditions of sale have been included in the option contract itself[19].

The document creating an option to purchase is liable to ad valorem stamp duty as a conveyance on sale[20].

1   *Griffith v Pelton* [1958] Ch 205 at 225, [1957] 3 All ER 75 at 83, CA, per Jenkins LJ. See also *Stromdale and Ball Ltd v Burden* [1952] Ch 223 at 235, [1952] 1 All ER 59 at 65 per Danckwerts J; *Beesly v Hallwood Estates Ltd* [1960] 2 All ER 314 at 317, [1960] 1 WLR 549 at 556 per Buckley J (not considered on appeal [1961] Ch 105, [1961] 1 All ER 90, CA); *Re Button's Lease, Inman v Button* [1964] Ch 263 at 267, [1963] 3 All ER 708 at 710 per Plowman J; *United Scientific Holdings Ltd v Burnley Borough Council* [1978] AC

904 at 928–929, [1977] 2 All ER 62 at 71, HL, per Lord Diplock, at 945 and at 84 per Lord Simon of Glaisdale, and at 951 and at 88–89 per Lord Salmon; *Mountford v Scott* [1975] Ch 258 at 264, [1975] 1 All ER 198 at 200, CA, per Russell LJ. Cf *Varty v British South Africa Co* [1965] Ch 508 at 522, [1964] 2 All ER 975 at 981, CA, obiter per Diplock LJ (revsd on other grounds [1966] AC 381, [1965] 2 All ER 395, HL). See further CONTRACT vol 9(1) (Reissue) para 640. As to the distinction between an option to purchase and a conditional contract of sale see *Helby v Matthews* [1895] AC 471, HL; *Spiro v Glencrown Properties Ltd* [1991] Ch 537, [1991] 1 All ER 600. For an example of an option terminable by notice given by the grantor see *Re Downes and Lobbs' Contract, Downes v Lobbs* [1937] 4 All ER 324 (affd sub nom *Re Down's Agreement* (1938) 82 Sol Jo 373, CA), where the option was to operate for three years certain and was then determinable by the grantor giving 12 months' notice to terminate at the expiration of the three years or at any later date, and a notice given before the end of the second year to terminate the option at the end of the third year was held to be valid. See also *Westway Homes Ltd v Moores* [1991] 2 EGLR 193, [1991] 31 EG 57, CA (effect of words 'subject to contract' in a notice purporting to exercise an option).

2   See *Jefferys v Jefferys* (1841) Cr & Ph 138; *Mountford v Scott* [1975] Ch 258, [1975] 1 All ER 198, CA; and SPECIFIC PERFORMANCE vol 44(1) (Reissue) para 805.

3   *Mountford v Scott* [1975] Ch 258, [1975] 1 All ER 198, CA, (where an option to purchase a house worth £10,000 was granted in consideration of £1). See also *Midland Bank Trust Co Ltd v Green* [1981] AC 513, [1981] 1 All ER 153, HL, (where an option to purchase land worth at least £40,000 was granted in consideration of £1).

4   See eg *Re Downes and Lobbs' Contract, Downes v Lobbs* [1937] 4 All ER 324 (affd sub nom *Re Down's Agreement* (1938) 82 Sol Jo 373, CA); *Kelly v Enderton* [1913] AC 191, PC. An option may also be granted by will, in which case it operates as a conditional gift: see *Re Armstrong's Will Trusts, Graham v Armstrong* [1943] Ch 400, [1943] 2 All ER 537. If the purchase price stipulated in the option is less than the market value of the land, the grantee of the option must, subject to any contrary direction in the will, pay what is now inheritance tax on the bounty element: see *Re Lander, Lander v Lander* [1951] Ch 546, [1951] 1 All ER 622; and INHERITANCE TAXATION vol 24 (Reissue) para 637; WILLS. Equally, in the case of an option granted inter vivos, a purchase price less than market value may be a transfer of value for the purposes of inheritance tax: see INHERITANCE TAXATION vol 24 (Reissue) paras 442–453, 635. An option may be conferred by a deed on a person who is not a party to the deed: *Stromdale and Ball Ltd v Burden* [1952] Ch 223, [1952] 1 All ER 59 (applying the Law of Property Act 1925 s 56(1)): see DEEDS AND OTHER INSTRUMENTS. As to whether s 56(1) applies to an instrument other than a deed see *Beswick v Beswick* [1968] AC 58 at 104–106, [1967] 2 All ER 1197 at 1222–1224, HL, per Lord Upjohn, at 76 and at 1204 per Lord Reid, and at 94 and at 1216 per Lord Pearce; and CONTRACT vol 9(1) (Reissue) para 617.

5   *Griffith v Pelton* [1958] Ch 205 at 225, [1957] 3 All ER 75 at 84, CA, per Jenkins LJ. Whether the benefit of such an option is assignable is a question of construction. If the benefit is assignable, it may be passed by an assignment of the lease: *Griffith v Pelton* supra; *Re Button's Lease, Inman v Button* [1964] Ch 263, [1963] 3 All ER 708; see further LANDLORD AND TENANT vol 27(1) (Reissue) para 110. An option in a tenancy agreement to purchase the freehold 'at any time' may mean, according to the true construction of the agreement, at any time during the contractual tenancy, not during a subsequent statutory tenancy: *Longmuir v Kew* [1960] 3 All ER 26, [1960] 1 WLR 862. As to the statutory right of a tenant of a dwelling house to acquire the freehold where the lease is a long lease at a low rent, under the Leasehold Reform Act 1967 see LANDLORD AND TENANT vol 27(2) (Reissue) para 1253 et seq.

6   See *Birmingham Canal Co v Cartwright* (1879) 11 ChD 421 at 434–435 per Fry J; and EQUITY vol 16 (Reissue) paras 660–661, 775 et seq; SPECIFIC PERFORMANCE vol 44(1) (Reissue) paras 801 et seq, 825.

7   See the Law of Property (Miscellaneous Provisions) Act 1989 s 2(1); and para 29 et seq post.

8   *Spiro v Glencrown Properties Ltd* [1991] Ch 537, [1991] 1 All ER 600; and see para 30 post.

9   Where the title is unregistered, the option must be registered under the Land Charges Act 1972 s 2(4) (as amended), Class C(iv): see LAND CHARGES vol 26 (Reissue) paras 528, 532. Failure to register renders the option void against a purchaser of a legal estate for money or money's worth: see s 4(6) (as amended) (LAND CHARGES vol 26 (Reissue) para 534); and *Midland Bank Trust Co Ltd v Green* [1981] AC 513, [1981] 1 All ER 153, HL. Where the title is registered, protection is by notice or caution under the Land Registration Act 1925: see Pt IV (ss 48–62) (as amended); and LAND REGISTRATION vol 26 (Reissue) para 1098 et seq. Failure to protect renders the option void against a transferee for value in good faith (see ss 20, 23, 59(6) (all as amended) (see LAND REGISTRATION vol 26 (Reissue) paras 958–962); *Peffer v Rigg* [1978] 3 All ER 745, [1977] 1 WLR 285) unless the option holder is in actual occupation of the land affected, when he will have an overriding interest within the Land Registration Act 1925 s 70(1)(g) (see LAND REGISTRATION vol 26 (Reissue) para 784) (*Webb v Pollmount Ltd* [1966] Ch 584, [1966] 1 All ER 481). Failure by the option holder's solicitor to register the option is capable of constituting negligence actionable in both contract and tort: *Midland Bank Trust Co Ltd v Hett, Stubbs and Kemp (a firm)* [1979] Ch 384, [1978] 3 All ER 571.

For the requirement of certainty in an option to renew see *Brown v Gould* [1972] Ch 53, [1971] 2 All ER 1505, where the option specified factors to be applied in fixing a new rent, but laid down no machinery for fixing the rent; it was held to be valid because, in the absence of agreement between the parties, the court could fix the rent by applying the specified factors.

10 *Wright v Dean* [1948] Ch 686, [1948] 2 All ER 415; *Hollington Bros Ltd v Rhodes* [1951] 2 All ER 578n. In both these cases the grantor was held liable in damages, the option having been defeated by a purchaser for non-registration. It would seem to follow that specific performance could be awarded if the grantor or his estate still held the land. Damages may include loss of profit from an intended development: *Cottrill v Steyning and Littlehampton Building Society* [1966] 2 All ER 295, [1966] 1 WLR 753. The grantor may be entitled to an indemnity from the second purchaser who defeats the option for non-registration: see *Eagon v Dent* [1965] 3 All ER 334, applying what is now the Standard Conditions of Sale (3rd Edn), condition 3.3.2(d). As to the Standard Conditions of Sale see para 1 note 9 ante.

11 *London and South Western Rly Co v Gomm* (1882) 20 ChD 562, CA. In the case of an option created after 15 July 1964, the position is governed by the Perpetuities and Accumulations Act 1964 ss 9, 10: see generally PERPETUITIES AND ACCUMULATIONS vol 35 (Reissue) paras 1037–1039. An option to renew a lease is not affected by the rule against perpetuities: see PERPETUITIES AND ACCUMULATIONS vol 35 (Reissue) para 1039.

12 See eg *West Country Cleaners (Falmouth) Ltd v Saly* [1966] 3 All ER 210, [1966] 1 WLR 1485, CA; *Hare v Nicoll* [1966] 2 QB 130, [1966] 1 All ER 285, CA; cf *United Scientific Holdings Ltd v Burnley Borough Council* [1978] AC 904, [1977] 2 All ER 62, HL. See further LANDLORD AND TENANT vol 27(1) (Reissue) para 111.

13 *Kennewell v Dye* [1949] Ch 517, [1949] 1 All ER 881; and see generally EXECUTORS AND ADMINISTRATORS.

14 *Kennewell v Dye* [1949] Ch 517, [1949] 1 All ER 881, following *Harwood and Bincks v Hilliard* (1677) 2 Mod Rep 268.

15 *Kennewell v Dye* [1949] Ch 517, [1949] 1 All ER 881; *Skelton v Younghouse* [1942] AC 571, [1942] 1 All ER 650, HL; *Re Zerny's Will Trusts, Symons v Zerny* [1968] Ch 415, [1968] 1 All ER 686, CA.

16 *Re Avard, Hook v Parker* [1948] Ch 43, [1947] 2 All ER 548, where a notice exercising an option out of time through no fault of the personal representatives was held to be void.

17 *Raffety v Schofield* [1897] 1 Ch 937; *Cockwell v Romford Sanitary Steam Laundry Ltd* [1939] 4 All ER 370, CA.

18 *Doe d Gray v Stanion* (1836) 1 M & W 695; *Leek and Moorlands Building Society v Clark* [1952] 2 QB 788, [1952] 2 All ER 492, CA; *Nightingale v Courtney* [1954] 1 QB 399, [1954] 1 All ER 362, CA. See also LANDLORD AND TENANT vol 27(1) (Reissue) paras 111, 530. In general, termination of the lease will be inferred only from the date when the landlord shows a good title, ie as from the date that interest becomes payable under the contract of sale: see paras 122, 127 post.

19 *Welchman v Spinks* (1861) 5 LT 385. As to the position of vendor and purchaser under an open contract see para 76 post. It will usually be implied that on the exercise of the option the property is to be conveyed free from incumbrances created after the date of the option: see *Re Crosby's Contract, Crosby v Houghton* [1949] 1 All ER 830; cf *Fowler v Willis* [1922] 2 Ch 514, where the purchaser was not entitled to the discharge of a mortgage affecting the property at the date of the option. However, this decision seems open to criticism on its facts, since the vendor did not disclose the mortgage until after the date of the option. As to the duty of disclosure see para 55 post.

20 *George Wimpey & Co Ltd v IRC* [1975] 2 All ER 45, [1975] 1 WLR 995, CA; and see paras 318–319 post; STAMP DUTIES AND STAMP DUTY RESERVE TAX vol 44(1) (Reissue) para 1027.

28. Right of pre-emption.

An option to purchase must be distinguished from a right of pre-emption, otherwise known as a right of first refusal. A right of pre-emption arises where the owner of land contracts that, if he decides to sell the land, he will first offer it to the other contracting party in preference to any other purchaser. It differs from an option in that it is not an offer to sell, and in itself it imposes no obligation on the owner to sell. He may do so or not as he wishes; but if he does decide to sell, then the holder of the right of pre-emption has the right to receive the first offer, which he also may accept or not as he wishes[1]. It is not yet clear beyond doubt whether a right of pre-emption creates an interest in land or is merely enforceable contractually[2]. On the basis that an interest in land is created, the right is registrable in the same way as an option[3], but registration does not create any priority over subsequent interests which do not make the right of pre-emption exercisable[4]. On the same basis, the right would appear to fall within the statutory provisions relating to a contract in writing[5]. In both its contractual and its proprietary aspects it would appear that the right is subject to the rule against perpetuities[6].

1   This statement is based on *Mackay v Wilson* (1947) 47 SR NSW 315 at 325 per Street J; cited with approval in *Pritchard v Briggs* [1980] Ch 338 at 389, [1980] 1 All ER 294 at 305, CA, per Goff LJ. Since the obligation is merely to offer first refusal, a right of pre-emption 'at a figure to be agreed upon' is not void for uncertainty: *Smith v Morgan* [1971] 2 All ER 1500, [1971] 1 WLR 803. It is a question of construction of the particular contract whether an option or a right of pre-emption has been created: see eg *Woodroffe v Box* [1954] ALR 474, 28 ALJ 90, Aust HC, where a right called in the contract a 'first refusal' was construed as creating an option. A particular contract may create both rights: see *Du Sautoy v Symes* [1967] Ch 1146, [1967] 1 All ER 25, where a right of pre-emption had lapsed through non-exercise, but the option was still subsisting; *Gardner v Coutts & Co* [1967] 3 All ER 1064, [1968] 1 WLR 173, where a right of pre-emption during the owner's lifetime, coupled with an option exercisable at the owner's death, impliedly precluded the owner from giving away the land without first offering it to the other contracting party. See also *Miller v Lakefield Estates Ltd* (1988) 57 P & CR 104, Times, 16 May, CA (court will not necessarily imply a term that the sale was to be for a reasonable or market price). As to whether purchasers are entitled to withdraw an offer to resell before the expiry of an acceptance period see *Tuck v Baker* [1990] 2 EGLR 195, [1990] 32 EG 46, CA. See further CONTRACT vol 9(1) (Reissue) para 641.

2   The contractual effect is that the owner, having put the land on the market at a certain price, must first offer to sell to the other contracting party at that price, and, having received a refusal, the owner cannot then sell to another person at a lower price: *Manchester Ship Canal Co v Manchester Racecourse Co* [1901] 2 Ch 37, CA; *Ryan v Thomas* (1911) 55 Sol Jo 364. See also *Gardner v Coutts & Co* [1967] 3 All ER 1064, [1968] 1 WLR 173. A majority of the Court of Appeal (Templeman and Stephenson LJJ, Goff LJ dissenting) have expressed obiter the view that an interest in land is created but has priority only from the date when the right becomes exercisable: *Pritchard v Briggs* [1980] Ch 338, [1980] 1 All ER 294, CA; followed in *Kling v Keston Properties Ltd* (1983) 49 P & CR 212, (1984) 81 LS Gaz R 1683; cf *Manchester Ship Canal Co v Manchester Racecourse Co* supra; *Murray v Two Strokes Ltd* [1973] 3 All ER 357, [1973] 1 WLR 823; *Imperial Chemical Industries Ltd v Sussman* (28 May 1976, unreported); and see *London and Blenheim Estates Ltd v Ladbroke Retail Parks Ltd* [1993] 4 All ER 157, [1994] 1 WLR 31, CA; *Homsy v Murphy* (1996) 73 P & CR 26, CA; HWRW 'Rights of Pre-emption: Interests in Land?' (1980) 96 LQR 488. As to the contrary view of the Commonwealth courts see *Mackay v Wilson* (1947) 47 SR NSW 315; *Canadian Long Island Petroleums Ltd v Irving Industries (Irving Wire Products Division) Ltd* [1975] SCR 715, 50 DLR (3d) 265, Can SC; *Re Essex County Roman Catholic Separate School Board and Antaya* (1977) 17 OR (2d) 307, 80 DLR (3d) 405.

3   See the Land Charges Act 1972 s 2(4) (as amended), Class C(iv); and LAND CHARGES vol 26 (Reissue) paras 528, 532. As to the registration of an option see para 27 note 9 ante. A right of pre-emption granted to a local authority by the purchaser of a house under the Housing Act 1985 ss 32 (as amended), 33 (see HOUSING vol 22 (Reissue) paras 274–275) is an interest in land and therefore registrable: *First National Securities Ltd v Chiltern District Council* [1975] 2 All ER 766, [1975] 1 WLR 1075. Such a right of pre-emption binds the purchaser and his successors in title (see the Housing Act 1985 s 33(4); and HOUSING vol 22 (Reissue) para 275), and it would appear that the right has priority to all subsequent interests; but cf *Pritchard v Briggs* [1980] Ch 338, [1980] 1 All ER 294, CA.

4   *Pritchard v Briggs* [1980] Ch 338, [1980] 1 All ER 294, CA. Statutory rights of pre-emption derive their force and priority from the statute: *First National Securities Ltd v Chiltern District Council* [1975] 2 All ER 766, [1975] 1 WLR 1075.

5   Ie the Law of Property (Miscellaneous Provisions) Act 1989 s 2 (as amended) (see para 29 post): see *Birmingham Canal Co v Cartwright* (1879) 11 ChD 421. See further paras 29–40 post.

6   See the Perpetuities and Accumulations Act 1964 ss 9, 10; and PERPETUITIES AND ACCUMULATIONS vol 35 (Reissue) paras 1037–1039. Cf however, PERPETUITIES AND ACCUMULATIONS vol 35 (Reissue) para 1038 (rights of pre-emption and repurchase). See s 9(2) proviso, which excepts certain statutory rights of pre-emption, thus implying that other rights are within the rule: see PERPETUITIES AND ACCUMULATIONS vol 35 (Reissue) para 1037.

(ii)   The Requirement of a Written Contract

29.   Contracts required to be in writing. A contract for the sale or other disposition[1] of an interest in land[2] can only be made in writing and only by incorporating all the terms which the parties have expressly agreed in one document or, where contracts are exchanged, in each document[3]. The terms may be incorporated in a document either by being set out in it or by reference to some other document[4]. The document incorporating the terms or, where contracts are exchanged, one of the documents incorporating them (but not necessarily the same one), must be signed by or on behalf of each party to the contract[5]. Where such a contract satisfies these conditions by reason only of the rectification of one or more documents in pursuance of an order of a court, the contract comes into being, or is deemed to come into being, at such time as is specified in the order[6].

These provisions do not apply in relation to a contract to grant a short lease[7], a contract made in the course of a public auction, or a contract regulated under the Financial Services Act 1986[8]; nor do they affect the creation or operation of resulting, implied or constructive trusts[9].

A contract which fails to satisfy the requirement of writing is invalid, and it follows that the intended contract must be set up as a defence to actions in tort which the intended contract would have authorised, and that any deposit, or other money, or indeed any other property, paid or transferred under the intended contract can be recovered back[10].

An oral contract made between two joint tenants for the sale of the beneficial interest of one to the other will sever the beneficial joint tenancy[11].

1   'Disposition' includes a conveyance and also a devise, bequest, or an appointment of property contained in a will: Law of Property Act 1925 s 205(1)(ii); definition applied by the Law of Property (Miscellaneous Provisions) Act 1989 s 2(6).

2   For the meaning of 'interest in land' see para 31 post.

3   Law of Property (Miscellaneous Provisions) Act 1989 s 2(1). See *Take Harvest Ltd v Liu* [1993] AC 552, [1993] 2 All ER 459, PC; *Commission for the New Towns v Cooper (GB) Ltd* [1995] Ch 259, [1995] 2 All ER 929, CA (exchange of letters regarding grant of put option enjoyed by grantee's predecessor not constituting an exchange of contracts for the purposes of the Law of Property (Miscellaneous Provisions) Act 1989 s 2 (as amended)); *Firstpost Homes Ltd v Johnson* [1995] 4 All ER 355, [1995] 1 WLR 1567, CA (a letter purporting to constitute a contract for the sale of land which contained a reference to the plan enclosed with it was a separate document from the plan itself, so the purchaser's signature on the plan alone did not suffice to create a contract).

Nothing in the Law of Property (Miscellaneous Provisions) Act 1989 s 2 (as amended) applies in relation to contracts made before 27 September 1989: s 2(7). Section 2 (as amended) supersedes the Law of Property Act 1925 s 40 (repealed): see the Law of Property (Miscellaneous Provisions) Act 1989 s 2(8). The policy of s 2 (as amended) is to avoid the possibility that one or other party may wish to go behind the written document and introduce oral evidence to establish the terms of the contract. Decisions of the courts based on the Statute of Frauds Act 1677 (repealed) or the Law of Property Act 1925 s 40 (repealed) will in some instances be relevant to the present law, but not where they conflict with the policy of the present law: see *Firstpost Homes Ltd v Johnson* [1995] 4 All ER 355 at 362–363, [1995] 1 WLR 1567 at 1574–1576 per Peter Gibson and Balcombe LJJ.

4   Law of Property (Miscellaneous Provisions) Act 1989 s 2(2). A collateral contract between the parties independent of the contract for sale falls outside the provisions of s 2 (as amended): see *Record v Bell* [1991] 4 All ER 471, [1991] 1 WLR 853; *Tootal Clothing Ltd v Guinea Properties Ltd* (1992) 64 P & CR 452, CA (sub nom *Tootal Clothing v Guinea Properties Management* [1992] 2 EGLR 80, CA). Agreements not to consider further offers for a fixed period (a 'lock-out agreement') also fall outside the provisions of the Law of Property (Miscellaneous Provisions) Act 1989 s 2 (as amended): *Pitt v PHH Asset Management Ltd* [1993] 4 All ER 961, [1994] 1 WLR 327, CA. When such a 'lock-out' or exclusivity agreement is breached, damages will be the appropriate remedy: *Tye v House and Jennings* (1998) 76 P & CR 188.

5   Law of Property (Miscellaneous Provisions) Act 1989 s 2(3). Each party to the contract must write his name on the document in his own handwriting; typed or printed names are insufficient: *Firstpost Homes Ltd v Johnson* [1995] 4 All ER 355, [1995] 1 WLR 1567, CA.

6   Law of Property (Miscellaneous Provisions) Act 1989 s 2(4). For examples of such rectification see *Wright v Robert Leonard Developments Ltd* [1994] NPC 49, [1994] EGCS 69, CA; and *Commission for the New Towns v Cooper (GB) Ltd* [1995] Ch 259, [1995] 2 All ER 929, CA.

7   Ie such a lease as is mentioned in the Law of Property Act 1925 s 54(2): see LANDLORD AND TENANT vol 27(1) (Reissue) para 78. See also *Long v Tower Hamlets London Borough Council* [1998] Ch 197, [1996] 2 All ER 683. The Law of Property Act 1925 s 54(2) applies to the creation of a short lease, not its

assignment: see *Crago v Julian* [1992] 1 All ER 744, [1992] 1 WLR 372, CA (it follows that a contract for the assignment of a short lease is required to be in writing); and *Botting v Martin* (1808) 1 Camp 317; *Poultney v Holmes* (1720) 1 Stra 405; *Barrett v Rolph* (1845) 14 M & W 348.

8   Law of Property (Miscellaneous Provisions) Act 1989 s 2(5)(a)–(c).
9   Ibid s 2(5).
10   Cf *Thomas v Brown* (1876) 1 QBD 714; *Monnickendam v Leanse* (1923) 39 TLR 445; *Jones v Jones* (1840) 6 M & W 84; *Low v Fry* (1935) 152 LT 585 (all decided under previous legislation).
11   See *Burgess v Rawnsley* [1975] Ch 429, [1975] 3 All ER 142, CA (decided under previous legislation).

30.   Transactions to which the requirement of writing applies. The requirement for contracts to be in writing[1] has been held to apply to: (1) a contract to sell or dispose of an interest in land[2] where neither of the contracting parties owns such an interest at the time when the contract is made[3]; (2) a contract granting an option over land[4] (but does not apply to a notice by the purchaser exercising an option to purchase, which then creates a full contract of sale[5]); (3) a contract to surrender a lease for[6] and the creation of an equitable mortgage[7]; (4) contracts concerning land which are incidental to contracts to sell or dispose of an interest in land: for example, an agreement between two persons that, in consideration of one party not competing with the other to purchase a piece of land, the other will transfer to him a part of the land[8]; an agreement between mortgagor and mortgagee that foreclosure proceedings will be brought, the land sold and the proceeds divided between the parties[9]; a submission to arbitration of a dispute relating to land[10]; a relinquishment of possession by a tenant in consideration of a payment towards repairs to the property[11]; an agreement by which the intending vendor of land promises that he will enter into a formal contract of sale, on terms orally agreed, if the purchaser tenders on a certain date his part of the contract on the agreed terms and produces a banker's draft for the agreed deposit[12]; and an agreement made between husband and wife to compromise a maintenance dispute, having as one of its terms a promise to transfer the matrimonial home[13].

On the other hand, the requirement for contracts to be in writing has been held not to apply to: (a) an agreement not to consider further offers for a fixed period (a lock-out agreement)[14]; (b) a collateral contract which is independent of the contract of sale[15]; (c) an agreement as to the purchase price on a compulsory purchase[16]; (d) an agreement to discharge a debt conditional on the transfer of certain land to the creditor[17].

The requirement of writing applies only to an executory contract and not to a contract which has been completed by the execution of the relevant disposition[18].

1   The provision is now contained in the Law of Property (Miscellaneous Provisions) Act 1989 s 2(1); see para 29 ante.
2   For the meaning of 'interest in land' see para 31 post.
3   *Singh v Beggs* (1995) 71 P & CR 120.
4   See *Spiro v Glencrown Properties Ltd* [1991] Ch 537, [1991] 1 All ER 600; *Take Harvest Ltd v Liu* [1993] AC 552, [1993] 2 All ER 459, PC; and *Commission for the New Towns v Cooper (GB) Ltd* [1995] Ch 259, [1995] 2 All ER 929, CA.
5   *Spiro v Glencrown Properties Ltd* [1991] Ch 537, [1991] 1 All ER 600; *Trustees of Chippenham Golf Club v North Wiltshire District Council* (1991) 64 P & CR 527 at 530–531 per Scott LJ. Similarly, where an option to purchase is registered, further registration of the contract of sale envisaged by the option is not required to protect the holder of the option as it would add nothing to the protection already afforded him by registration of the option: see *Armstrong & Holmes Ltd v Holmes* [1994] 1 All ER 826, [1993] 1 WLR 1482.
6   See *Smart v Harding* (1855) 15 CB 652 (decided under previous legislation).
7   See *United Bank of Kuwait plc v Sahib* [1997] Ch 107, [1996] 3 All ER 215, CA.
8   See *Lamas v Bayly* (178) 2 Vern 627 (decided under previous legislation). As to the disposition of registered and unregistered land by transfer see para 262 note 2 post.
9   See *Cox v Peele* (1788) 2 Bro CC 334 (decided under previous legislation).
10 See *Rainforth v Hamer* (1855) 25 LTOS 247 (decided under previous legislation).
11 See *Buttemere v Hayes* (1839) 5 M & W 456 (decided under previous legislation). See also *Griffith v Young* (1810) 12 East 513; *Smith v Tombs* (1839) 3 Jur 72; *Cocking v Ward* (1845) 1 CB 858; *Kelly v Webster*

(1852) 12 CB 283; *Smart v Harding* (1855) 15 CB 652; *Green v Saddington* (1857) 7 E & B 503; *Hodgson v Johnson* (1858) EB & E 685; *Lavery v Turley* (1860) 6 H & N 239; and *Horsey v Graham* (1869) LR 5 CP 9 (all decided under previous legislation).

12 See *Daulia Ltd v Four Millbank Nominees Ltd* [1978] Ch 231, [1978] 2 All ER 557, CA (decided under previous legislation).
13 See *Steadman v Steadman* [1976] AC 536, [1974] 2 All ER 977, HL (decided under previous legislation).
14 See *Pitt v PHH Asset Management Ltd* [1993] 4 All ER 961, [1994] 1 WLR 327, CA.
15 See *Record v Bell* [1991] 4 All ER 471, [1991] 1 WLR 853; *Tootal Clothing Ltd v Guinea Properties Ltd* (1992) 64 P & CR 452, CA, sub nom *Tootal Clothing v Guinea Properties Management* [1992] 2 EGLR 80, CA.
16 Such an agreement is not an ordinary contract but a statutory contract which is not within the provision: see *Munton v Greater London Council* [1976] 2 All ER 815 at 818, [1976] 1 WLR 649 at 653, CA, per Lord Denning MR (decided under previous legislation).
17 See *Simpson v Connolly* [1953] 2 All ER 474, [1953] 1 WLR 911 (decided under previous legislation).
18 See *Tootal Clothing Ltd v Guinea Properties Ltd* (1992) 64 P & CR 452, CA, sub nom *Tootal Clothing v Guinea Properties Management* [1992] 2 EGLR 80, CA.

31. Meaning of 'an interest in land'. The expression 'an interest in land' in the statutory provision requiring writing[1] comprises all proprietary interests in land, whether legal or equitable. 'Interest in land' means any estate, interest or charge in or over land[2].

The following have been held to fall within the provision requiring writing: an agreement to assign a lease, even an informal lease, such as a yearly tenancy[3]; an agreement to create an easement[4]; an agreement to grant a right of shooting and taking away part of the game killed[5]; an agreement to charge rent due under a lease[6]; the creation by debenture of a floating charge comprising land[7]; an agreement relating to fixtures[8], except tenant's fixtures removable during the term[9]; an agreement for the sale and removal of building materials on the demolition of a house, with a time limit for removal[10]; the creation of an option to purchase[11] and a right of pre-emption[12]; an agreement to assign a share in a partnership in land[13]; and an agreement for the sale of the beneficial interest of a co-owner[14].

A sale of growing crops, including timber, where the intention of the parties is that property is to pass before they are severed from the land, is a sale of land within the statutory provision[15] unless the crops are fructus industriales, that is, not the spontaneous produce of the land but produced with human labour[16]. Where the intention is that property is not to pass until severance from the land, there is a sale of goods not within the provision[17]; such an intention may be shown by an agreement that the vendor is to cut the crops and deliver them to the purchaser[18], and by an agreement that the purchaser is to fell the trees and remove them as soon as possible[19].

A contractual licence to occupy land does not create a proprietary interest and therefore does not fall within the provision[20].

1 The provision is now contained in the Law of Property (Miscellaneous Provisions) Act 1989 s 2(1); see para 29 ante.
2 Ibid s 2(6) (amended by the Trusts of Land and Appointment of Trustees Act 1996 s 25(2), Sch 4). 'Land' is not defined by the Law of Property (Miscellaneous Provisions) Act 1989. For the meaning of land see the Interpretation Act 1978 s 5, Sch 1; and REAL PROPERTY vol 39(2) (Reissue) para 76.
3 *Botting v Martin* (1808) 1 Camp 317 (decided under previous legislation). The provision also applies where the residue of the term to be assigned is less than three years: *Poultney v Holmes* (1720) 1 Stra 405; *Barrett v Rolph* (1845) 14 M & W 348 (both decided under previous legislation). Cf *Crago v Julian* [1992] 1 All ER 744, [1992] 1 WLR 372, CA.
4 *Hoare & Co Ltd v Lewisham Corpn* (1901) 85 LT 281; affd (1902) 87 LT 464, CA (decided under previous legislation). See also *McManus v Cooke* (1887) 35 ChD 681 (decided under previous legislation).
5 *Webber v Lee* (1882) 9 QBD 315; *Mason v Clarke* [1955] AC 778, [1955] 1 All ER 914, HL (both decided under previous legislation).
6 *Re Whitting, ex p Hall* (1879) 10 ChD 615, CA (decided under previous legislation).
7 *Driver v Broad* [1893] 1 QB 744, CA (decided under previous legislation).
8 *Jarvis v Jarvis* (1893) 63 LJ Ch 10; *Morgan v Russell & Sons* [1909] 1 KB 357, DC (both decided under previous legislation).

9 *Lee v Gaskell* (1876) 1 QBD 700; *Thomas v Jennings* (1896) 66 LJQB 5 (both decided under previous legislation).

10 *Lavery v Pursell* (1888) 39 ChD 508 (decided under previous legislation). A contract to build a house is not within the provision (*Wright v Stavert* (1860) 2 E & E 721 at 728 per Hill J (decided under previous legislation)); nor is a contract to build a road (*Jameson v Kinmell Bay Land Co Ltd* (1931) 47 TLR 593, CA (decided under previous legislation)).

11 *Birmingham Canal Co v Cartwright* (1879) 11 ChD 421 at 434 per Fry J (decided under previous legislation).

12 *Birmingham Canal Co v Cartwright* (1879) 11 ChD 421; *Pritchard v Briggs* [1980] Ch 338 at 369, [1978] 1 All ER 886 at 905 per Walton J; revsd on another point [1980] Ch 338 at 374, [1980] 1 All ER 294, CA (both decided under previous legislation).

13 *Gray v Smith* (1889) 43 ChD 208 (on appeal (1889) 43 ChD 217, CA); see also *Caddick v Skidmore* (1857) 2 De G & J 52; cf *Forster v Hale* (1800) 5 Ves 308 (all decided under previous legislation).

14 As to the abolition of the equitable doctrine of conversion see the Trusts of Land and Appointment of Trustees Act 1996 s 3; and TRUSTS vol 48 (Reissue) paras 841–842.

As to the law prior to 1997 see *Cooper v Critchley* [1955] Ch 431 at 439, [1955] 1 All ER 520 at 524, CA, obiter per Jenkins LJ, at 440 and 525 obiter per Evershed MR; *Liddell v Hopkinson* (1974) 233 Estates Gazette 513; *Steadman v Steadman* [1974] QB 161, [1973] 3 All ER 977, CA (affd [1976] AC 536, [1974] 2 All ER 977, HL); *McDonald v Windaybank* (1975) 120 Sol Jo 96. See also *Burgess v Rawnsley* [1975] Ch 429, [1975] 3 All ER 142, CA.

15 *Waddington v Bristow* (1801) 2 Bos & P 452; *Crosby v Wadsworth* (1805) 6 East 602; *Emmerson v Heelis* (1809) 2 Taunt 38 (but see note 16 infra); *Teal v Auty and Dibb* (1820) 2 Brod & Bing 99; *Scorell v Boxall* (1827) 1 Y & J 396; *Earl of Falmouth v Thomas* (1832) 1 Cr & M 89; *Carrington v Roots* (1837) 2 M & W 248; *Rodwell v Phillips* (1842) 9 M & W 501 (all decided under previous legislation).

16 *Parker v Staniland* (1809) 11 East 362 (potatoes); *Warwick v Bruce* (1813) 2 M & S 205 (potatoes); *Mayfield v Wadsley* (1824) 3 B & C 357 (wheat); *Evans v Roberts* (1826) 5 B & C 829 (potatoes); *Sainsbury (or Stansbury) v Matthews* (1838) 4 M & W 343 (potatoes); *Jones v Flint* (1839) 10 Ad & El 753 (wheat, barley and potatoes) (all decided under previous legislation). Cf *Emmerson v Heelis* (1809) 2 Taunt 38, where a sale of growing turnips was held to be a sale of an interest in land, although the decision was doubted in *Evans v Roberts* supra, and *Jones v Flint* supra (all decided under previous legislation).

17 *Smith v Surman* (1829) 9 B & C 561; *Washbourn v Burrows* (1847) 1 Exch 107; *Marshall v Green* (1875) 1 CPD 35 (all decided under previous legislation). The statement in the text is based on the proposition that the wide definition of 'goods' in the Sale of Goods Act 1979 s 61 (as amended) (see SALE OF GOODS) cannot have affected the earlier authorities on the Statute of Frauds (1677) (which should apply in the context of the Law of Property (Miscellaneous Provisions) Act 1989 s 2 (as amended) (see para 29 ante): see Hudson 'Goods or Land?' (1958) 22 Conv (NS) 137. In *Lowe v J W Ashmore Ltd* [1971] Ch 545, [1971] 1 All ER 1057, an informal contract for the sale of turves was regarded as a contract for sale of goods.

18 *Washbourn v Burrows* (1847) 1 Exch 107 (decided under previous legislation).

19 *Marshall v Green* (1875) 1 CPD 35, DC (decided under previous legislation).

20 See *Ashburn Anstalt v Arnold* [1989] Ch 1, [1988] 2 All ER 147, CA (rejecting previous authority to the contrary). As to the distinction between a licence to occupy and a lease see LANDLORD AND TENANT vol 27(1) (Reissue) paras 6–16.

32. Contracts partly within the provision requiring writing. Where an agreement is in part for a transaction in land and in part for some other purpose, the question arises whether there is one entire agreement or whether the agreement is divisible. In the former case, the whole contract will fail unless it is in writing[1], whereas in the latter case only that part of the agreement relating to land will fail. The question whether a transaction amounts to one entire contract or is severable into parts depends upon the circumstances of each case[2].

The following contracts have been held to be entire: a promise to pay rent due and to accrue within a certain time, in consideration of a forbearance to distrain[3]; an agreement for the sale of land and chattels[4]; an agreement for a lease with plant to be taken at a valuation[5]; an agreement for a lease with crops and materials at valuation[6]; an agreement for the sale of land with goodwill and stock in trade[7]; an agreement in writing to sell certain land, subsequently extended orally to include additional land[8]; an agreement to let a furnished house with a promise to provide additional furniture[9]; an agreement for the surrender of a lease and the grant of a new lease, with an agreement for a yearly tenancy pending the grant of the new lease[10]; an agreement for the assignment of a tenancy with an undertaking by the assignee to pay the rent and keep the premises in repair[11]; and an agreement for the sale of land with a provision for set-off against the purchase price[12].

The following contracts have been held to be divisible: an agreement for payment for wheat and dead stock divisible from an agreement to give up possession of land[13]; an agreement for the sale of land and a provision for set-off against the purchase price[14]; a landlord's promise to keep down game, which induced the tenant to sign a lease[15]; a landlord's oral warranty that drains were in order, inducing the tenant to sign the lease[16]; a landlord's promise to effect repairs and supply additional furniture within a reasonable time after the tenant's entry, which induced the tenant to sign the lease[17]; an agreement between A and B that if A will purchase certain land from C, B will reimburse to A the amount of the purchase price[18].

Some of the above examples of divisible contracts may also be regarded as cases where the divisible part amounted to a contract collateral to the main agreement[19]. For example, a landlord's oral promise that the drains are in order, inducing the tenant to enter into the lease, may be regarded as a contract collateral to the lease; oral evidence may therefore be given to prove it, and the contract is not within the statutory provision requiring writing[20]. Similarly, where the vendor's letter was an offer of warranty by the vendor's solicitor[21] to the purchaser's solicitor as to the state of the title to induce him to exchange and that offer had been accepted by exchanging contracts, there existed a collateral contract, and it was therefore irrelevant that the warranty was not contained in the contracts which the parties exchanged[22].

1   See now the Law of Property (Miscellaneous Provisions) Act 1989 s 2(1); and para 29 ante.
2   *Bigg v Whisking* (1853) 14 CB 195 (decided under previous legislation).
3   *Thomas v Williams* (1830) 10 B & C 664 (decided under previous legislation).
4   *Cooke v Tombs* (1794) 2 Anst 420; *Lea v Barber* (1794) 2 Anst 425n (both decided under previous legislation).
5   *Hodgson v Johnson* (1858) EB & E 685; doubted in *Pulbrook v Lawes* (1876) 1 QBD 284, DC (both decided under previous legislation).
6   *Earl of Falmouth v Thomas* (1832) 1 Cr & M 89 (decided under previous legislation).
7   *Hawkesworth v Turner* (1930) 46 TLR 389; *Ram Narayan v Rishad Hussain Shah* [1979] 1 WLR 1349, PC (agreement for sale of leasehold farms with livestock and equipment) (both decided under previous legislation).
8   *Bellaney v Knight* (1862) 5 LT 785 (decided under previous legislation).
9   *Mechelen v Wallace* (1837) 7 Ad & El 49; *Vaughan v Hancock* (1846) 3 CB 766; but cf *Angell v Duke* (1875) LR 10 QB 174, where the tenant was induced to agree to the letting by the landlord's promise to effect repairs and supply additional furniture within a reasonable time after entry, and the latter promise was held to be divisible and enforceable without writing (all decided under previous legislation).
10   *Foquet v Moor* (1852) 7 Exch 870 (decided under previous legislation).
11   *Bentham v Hardy* (1843) 6 ILR 179 (decided under previous legislation).
12   *Savage v Canning* (1867) 16 WR 133; cf *Archer v Hall* (1859) 7 WR 222, where the contrary conclusion was reached (both decided under previous legislation).
13   *Mayfield v Wadsley* (1824) 3 B & C 357 (decided under previous legislation).
14   *Archer v Hall* (1859) 7 WR 222; cf *Savage v Canning* (1867) 16 WR 133, cited in note 12 supra (both decided under previous legislation).
15   *Morgan v Griffith* (1871) LR 6 Exch 70 (decided under previous legislation).
16   *De Lassalle v Guildford* [1901] 2 KB 215, CA (decided under previous legislation).
17   *Angell v Duke* (1875) LR 10 QB 174 (decided under previous legislation).
18   *Boston v Boston* [1904] 1 KB 124, CA (decided under previous legislation). See also *Re Banks, Weldon v Banks* (1912) 56 Sol Jo 362 (decided under previous legislation).
19   See generally CONTRACT vol 9(1) (Reissue) para 753.
20   *De Lassalle v Guildford* [1901] 2 KB 215, CA (decided under previous legislation). For an example of the use of the collateral contract device in avoiding the oral evidence rule see *City and Westminster Properties (1934) Ltd v Mudd* [1959] Ch 129, [1958] 2 All ER 733 (decided under previous legislation). It must, of

course, be proved that the promise sued upon was intended to have contractual effect, and was not merely a representation inducing the main contract: *Wells (Merstham) Ltd v Buckland Sand and Silica Ltd* [1965] 2 QB 170, [1964] 1 All ER 41 (decided under previous legislation).

21 See para 3 ante.

22 *Record v Bell* [1991] 4 All ER 471, [1991] 1 WLR 853. 'It would be unfortunate if common transactions of this nature should nevertheless cause the contracts to be avoided. It may, of course, lead to a greater use of the concept of collateral warranties than has hitherto been necessary': *Record v Bell* supra at 479 and 862 per Judge Paul Baker QC. See also *Tootal Clothing Ltd v Guinea Properties Ltd* (1992) 64 P & CR 452, CA, sub nom *Tootal Clothing v Guinea Properties Management* [1992] 2 EGLR 80, CA.

33. The requirement of a signed document. The document for the sale of land[1] incorporating all the terms which the parties have expressly agreed, or where contracts are exchanged, one of the documents incorporating them (but not necessarily the same one) must be signed by or on behalf of each party[2]. Where the contract document incorporates another document by reference, it is essential that the parties' signatures are on the contract document[3]. Where a letter purported to constitute a contract for the sale of land and contained a reference to the plan enclosed with it, the letter was one document and the plan was another (the terms of which were incorporated in the letter); it was the letter and not the plan that needed to be signed. Therefore, the purchaser's signature on the plan alone did not suffice to create a contract[4].

The phrase 'exchange of contracts' refers to the exchange of identical documents which the parties intend as an embodiment of their agreement[5]; it does not include a situation where the parties reach agreement by an exchange of correspondence containing an offer and acceptance[6].

The word 'signed' is to be given its ordinary meaning, and it means 'the document being signed by or on behalf of each party obviously so as to authenticate the document'[7]. Where the purchaser's name had been typed at the top of the letter as addressee and he had not otherwise signed the letter, the signature requirement was not satisfied and no valid contract existed[8].

Where a written contract for the sale of land is subsequently varied, for example where the date for completion is altered, the contract as varied must comply with the statutory requirement, so that it is in writing and incorporated in one document (or each document if contracts were exchanged), and signed by or on behalf of each party to the contract[9]. Presumably it is sufficient to incorporate the original terms by reference to the previous contract[10]. Where the variation does not comply with the statutory requirement, the original contract remains valid and can be enforced[11]. If, however, the oral agreement shows that the parties intend to rescind the original contract in any event, the rescission takes effect, and neither the original nor the subsequent contract can be enforced[12]. A variation involving a definite alteration of the contractual obligations must be distinguished from a mere waiver or forbearance by one party, at the request of the other, to insist on performance of the strict terms of the contract[13]. Such a waiver or forbearance need not be in writing and oral evidence of it is admissible[14].

1 As to the statutory requirement for such contracts to be in writing see the Law of Property (Miscellaneous Provisions) Act 1989 s 2 (as amended); and para 29 ante.

2 See ibid s 2(3); and para 29 ante.

3 See ibid s 2(2); and para 29 ante. The singular 'document' includes the plural, so that a contract document could incorporate terms from more than one other document: see the Interpretation Act 1987 s 6; 503 HL Official Report (5th series), 24 January 1989, col 610.

4 *Firstpost Homes Ltd v Johnson* [1995] 4 All ER 355, [1995] 1 WLR 1567, CA.

5 As to methods of exchange see para 23 ante.

6 *Commission for the New Towns v Cooper (GB) Ltd* [1995] Ch 259, [1995] 2 All ER 929, CA (where a plaintiff confirmed an agreement in a letter and annexed a recommendation to it, which he later confirmed the accuracy of in another letter, the two letters confirming the agreement were insufficient to satisfy the statutory requirement that contracts for the sale or disposition of an interest in land should

be in writing). This decision did not follow the decision in *Hooper v Sherman* [1994] NPC 153, CA, where the exchange of correspondence recorded an oral agreement already reached: see *Commission for New Towns v Cooper (GB) Ltd* supra at 295 and 959 per Evans LJ.

7　*Firstpost Homes Ltd v Johnson* [1995] 4 All ER 355 at 363, [1995] 1 WLR 1567 at 1577, CA, per Balcombe LJ.

8　*Firstpost Homes Ltd v Johnson* [1995] 4 All ER 355, [1995] 1 WLR 1567, not following *Evans v Hoare* [1892] 1 QB 593, and citing with approval (Gibson and Balcombe LJJ) the comments of Evershed MR and Denning LJ in *Goodman v J Eban Ltd* [1954] 1 QB 550 at 555, 561, [1954] 1 All ER 763 at 765, 768. It does not necessarily follow that a handwritten signature will be required in all circumstances: see *Firstpost Homes Ltd v Johnson* [1995] 4 All ER 355 at 362, [1995] 1 WLR 1567 at 1576 per Peter Gibson LJ; and para 39 post.

9　*McCausland v Duncan Lawrie Ltd* [1996] 4 All ER 995, [1997] 1 WLR 38, CA. 'The formalities prescribed by the Law of Property (Miscellaneous Provisions) Act 1989 s 2 must be observed in order to effect a variation of a term material to the contract(it does not follow that s 2 must be observed in order to secure the variation of a term which is immaterial': *McCausland v Duncan Lawrie Ltd* supra at 1006 and 49 per Morritt LJ.

10　See *B Ltd v T Ltd* [1991] NPC 47. See also the text and note 3 supra.

11　See *McCausland v Duncan Lawrie Ltd* [1996] 4 All ER 995, [1997] 1 WLR 38, CA.

12　*Morris v Baron & Co* [1918] AC 1, HL (decided under previous legislation); and see *McCausland v Duncan Lawrie Ltd* [1996] 4 All ER 995 at 1006, [1997] 1 WLR 38 at 48, CA, per Morritt LJ. As to the distinction between variation and rescission see also *GW Fisher Ltd v Eastwoods Ltd* [1936] 1 All ER 421; *United Dominions Corpn (Jamaica) Ltd v Shoucair* [1969] 1 AC 340, [1968] 2 All ER 904, PC; *Marriott v Oxford and District Co-operative Society Ltd* [1970] 1 QB 186, [1969] 3 All ER 1126, CA (all decided under previous legislation).

13　As to the distinction between a variation and a waiver for forbearance see CONTRACT vol 9(1) (Reissue) paras 1019–1029; and as to whether such a waiver is binding see CONTRACT vol 9(1) (Reissue) para 1027.

14　See *Ogle v Earl Vane* (1868) LR 3 QB 272, Ex Ch; *Leather-Cloth Co v Hieronimus* (1875) LR 10 QB 140; *Hickman v Haynes* (1875) LR 10 CP 598; *Morris v Baron & Co* [1918] AC 1 HL; *Besseler, Waechter, Glover & Co v South Derwent Coal Co Ltd* [1938] 1 KB 408, [1937] 4 All ER 552 (all decided under previous legislation); and *McCausland v Duncan Lawrie Ltd* [1996] 4 All ER 995 at 1006, [1997] 1 WLR 38 at 48, CA, per Morritt LJ. For cases where there was held to be a variation rather than a waiver see CONTRACT vol 9(1) (Reissue) paras 1019–1024.

34. The contents of the written contract. In order to be sufficiently certain, the contract must: (1) define the parties and show who is the vendor and who is the purchaser (or lessor and lessee, or mortgagor and mortgagee, as the case may be)[1]; (2) define the property and the interest in it being disposed of, and state what kind of disposition is to be made[2]; and (3) show what is the consideration or how it is to be ascertained[3]. Where these requirements are satisfied, together with the statutory requirement of a signed document, there is a valid open contract; other terms will be implied by the law in order to give business efficacy to the contract. In particular, terms will be implied imposing an obligation on the vendor to make a good title free from incumbrances[4], providing for completion within a reasonable time[5], for vacant possession on completion[6]; and in the case of unregistered land providing for the delivery by the vendor of an abstract of title within a reasonable time[7], and fixing the length of title to be deduced by the vendor[8].

1　As to the identification of the parties see para 35 post.

2　As to the identification of the property and the interest in it see para 36 post.

3　As to the consideration see para 37 post.

4　See *Gray v Smith* (1889) 43 ChD 208 at 214 per Kekewich J (on appeal (1889) 43 ChD 217, CA); and *Johnson v Humphrey* [1946] 1 All ER 460 at 463 per Roxburgh J. The cases cited in this paragraph were all decided under legislation prior to the coming into force of the Law of Property (Miscellaneous Provisions) Act 1989: see para 29 note 3 ante. As to the statutory requirement for such contracts to be in writing see s 2 (as amended); and para 29 ante.

5　See *Green v Sevin* (1879) 13 ChD 589 at 599; *Compton v Bagley* [1892] 1 Ch 313; *Simpson v Hughes* (1897) 66 LJ Ch 334, CA; *Bond v Bassett* (1917) 87 LJ Ch 160; and *Re Bayley and Shoesmith's Contract* (1918) 87 LJ Ch 626.

6　See *Cook v Taylor* [1942] Ch 349 at 354, [1942] 2 All ER 85 at 87 per Simonds J; and *Re Crosby's Contract, Crosby v Houghton* [1949] 1 All ER 830. See further para 123 post.

7   See *Compton v Bagley* [1892] 1 Ch 313. See further para 100 post. As to the need for an abstract of title
     with respect to both unregistered and registered land see paras 138, 141–149 post.
8   See the Law of Property Act 1925 s 44(1) (as amended); and para 139 post. For the provisions as between
     vendor and purchaser on a sale or other disposition of registered land to a purchaser see the Land
     Registration Act 1925 s 110; and LAND REGISTRATION vol 26 (Reissue) paras 925–931.

35. Identification of the parties. In identifying the parties the overriding principle is
that the parties must be so described that their identities cannot fairly be disputed[1]. If the
description of a party is insufficient, oral evidence is inadmissible to show that the other
party knew who he was[2]. In almost all cases, the requirement that the contract be signed
by both parties will, of necessity, define those parties by name, but the signature in itself
may not be sufficient to identify the capacity of each of the parties. Moreover, there may
be exceptional circumstances, for example if the signature is by a mark, where the party
signing is not identified by name. In either case the question may then arise whether some
other form of identification in the contract is sufficient to satisfy the statutory
requirement. It seems likely that expressions such as 'proprietor'[3] or 'owner'[4] of a
specified property will continue to be regarded as adequate[5]. On the other hand,
expressions such as 'vendor'[6] or 'client'[7] are unlikely to be considered adequate, if the
party is not otherwise named or identified[8].

If the contract fails to identify the vendor but is signed by the vendor's agent without
mentioning the agency, then, since the agent incurs personal liability (even though the
purchaser knows of the agency), the contract may be enforced against the vendor as
principal[9].

The description of a limited company by the wrong name does not invalidate the
contract if it is clear from the surrounding circumstances or from facts known to the other
party that the name in the document is merely an inaccurate description[10].

1   See *Potter v Duffield* (1874) LR 18 Eq 4; *Dewar v Mintoft* [1912] 2 KB 373; *Cohen v Roche* [1927] 1 KB
     169. The cases cited in this paragraph were all decided under legislation prior to the coming into force
     of the Law of Property (Miscellaneous Provisions) Act 1989: see para 29 note 3 ante. As to the statutory
     requirement for such contracts to be in writing see s 2 (as amended); and para 29 ante.
2   See *Jarrett v Hunter* (1886) 34 ChD 182. Under the law prior to the coming into force of the Law of
     Property (Miscellaneous Provisions) Act 1989 s 2 (as amended) (see para 29 ante), evidence of
     surrounding circumstances was admitted to resolve an ambiguity: see *Newell v Radford* (1867) LR 3 CP
     52; *Carr v Lynch* [1900] 1 Ch 613; *Stokes v Whicher* [1920] 1 Ch 411. It seems unlikely that those
     authorities would now be followed.
3   *Sale v Lambert* (1874) LR 18 Eq 1; *Rossiter v Miller* (1878) 3 App Cas 1124, HL; *Jarrett v Hunter* (1886) 34
     ChD 182.
4   *Jarrett v Hunter* (1886) 34 ChD 182; *Butcher v Nash* (1889) 61 LT 72; *Walters v Le Blanc* (1900) 16 TLR
     366, CA.
5   Under the law prior to the coming into force of the Law of Property (Miscellaneous Provisions) Act 1989
     s 2 (as amended) (see para 29 ante), the following expressions were also held to be adequate: 'trustee for
     sale' (*Catling v King* (1877) 5 ChD 660, CA; *Butcher v Nash* (1889) 61 LT 72); 'mortgagee' (*Jarrett v Hunter*
     (1886) 34 ChD 182; *AH Allen & Co Ltd v Whiteman* (1920) 89 LJ Ch 534); 'executors' (*Hood v Lord
     Barrington* (1868) LR 6 Eq 218); 'legal personal representative' (*Towle v Topham* (1877) 37 LT 308; *Fay v
     Miller, Wilkins & Co* [1941] Ch 360); a named vendor 'on behalf of himself and all parties interested'
     (*Morgan v Worthington*: (1878) 38 LT 443); 'you' (*Carr v Lynch* [1900] 1 Ch 613); 'I' (*Stokes v Whicher*
     [1920] 1 Ch 411).
6   See *Hood v Lord Barrington* (1868) LR 6 Eq 218; *Potter v Duffield* (1874) LR 18 Eq 4; *Thomas v Brown*
     (1876) 1 QBD 714. Cf *Commins v Scott* (1875) LR 20 Eq 11, followed in *F Goldsmith (Sicklesmere) Ltd v
     Baxter* [1970] Ch 85, [1969] 3 All ER 733.
7   See *Jarrett v Hunter* (1886) 34 ChD 182; *Lovesy v Palmer* [1916] 2 Ch 233; but see *Cropper v Cook* (1868)
     LR 3 CP 194; and cf *AH Allen & Co Ltd v Whiteman* (1920) 89 LJ Ch 534.
8   Under the law prior to the coming into force of the Law of Property (Miscellaneous Provisions) Act 1989
     s 2 (as amended) (see para 29 ante), the following expressions were held to be insufficiently precise:
     'friend' (*Jarrett v Hunter* (1886) 34 ChD 182); 'principal' (*Rossiter v Miller* (1878) 3 App Cas 1124, HL);

'landlord' (*Coombs v Wilkes* [1891] 3 Ch 77 (cf the interpretation of 'tenant' in *Stokell v Niven* (1889) 61 LT 18, CA)); 'proposing and intending lender' (*Pattle v Anstruther* (1893) 69 LT 175, CA).

9   *Davies v Sweet* [1962] 2 QB 300, [1962] 1 All ER 92, CA, applying *Basma v Weekes* [1950] AC 441 (sub nom *Abdual Karim Basma v Weekes* [1950] 2 All ER 146, PC). See also *Filby v Hounsell* [1896] 2 Ch 737, considered in *Lovesy v Palmer* [1916] 2 Ch 233 at 242–244 per Younger J. Quaere whether this principle still applies despite the change in the law (see para 29 note 3 ante), as it depends on the law of agency and does not conflict with any express provision in the Law of Property (Miscellaneous Provisions) Act 1989.

10   See *F Goldsmith (Sicklesmere) Ltd v Baxter* [1970] Ch 85, [1969] 3 All ER 733 (where the plaintiff company, the vendor, contracted in the name of *Goldsmith Coaches (Sicklesmere) Ltd*).

36. Identification of the property and interest disposed of and the nature of the disposition. Where the contract contains a description which renders the property ascertainable, oral evidence has been admitted to complete the identification[1]. 'The property' alone is insufficient[2], but the following incomplete descriptions have sufficed: 'this place'[3], 'property' sold to a named person at a stated auction[4]; 'my house'[5]; 'Mr Ogilvie's house'[6]; 'the house etc in Newport', coupled with a statement that the deeds were in the possession of a named person[7]; 'the intended new public house at Putney'[8]; '24 acres of land, freehold, and all appurtenances at Totmonslow'[9]; 'house being sold for £500 from' the defendant[10]; 'the mill property including cottages in Esher village', even though part of the property was not in Esher village[11]; and 'the Jolly Sailor offices'[12].

It is not generally necessary for the contract to identify the interest disposed of[13]. Where the contract relates to freehold land, there is a presumption that the interest disposed of is the unincumbered fee simple, unless the purchaser knows that the vendor has only a lesser estate, in which case the purchaser is entitled to a transfer of the vendor's whole interest[14]. Where a freehold is, to the purchaser's knowledge, subject to a subsisting lease, it is not necessary for the contract to refer to the lease[15]. If the contract indicates that something less than the vendor's whole interest is to pass, the contract must go on to define that interest. Where there is a sale of a leasehold, the contract must state whether the lease is to be assigned or whether an underlease is to be granted[16], and a contract to grant a lease must state the date of commencement and the duration of the term to be granted[17].

1   See *Ogilvie v Foljambe* (1817) 3 Mer 53; *Shardlow v Cotterell* (1881) 20 ChD 90, CA; *Plant v Bourne* [1897] 2 Ch 281, CA; *Sheers v Thimbleby & Son* (1897) 76 LT 709 at 712 per Chitty J; *Auerbach v Nelson* [1919] 2 Ch 383.

2   See *Vale of Neath Colliery Co v Furness* (1876) 45 LJ Ch 276; cf *Shardlow v Cotterell* (1881) 20 ChD 90, CA.

3   See *Waldron v Jacob and Millie* (1870) IR 5 Eq 131.

4   See *Shardlow v Cotterell* (1881) 20 ChD 90, CA. See also *Bleakley v Smith* (1840) 11 Sim 150; *McMurry v Spicer* (1868) LR 5 Eq 527.

5   See *Cowley v Watts* (1853) 22 LJ Ch 591.

6   See *Ogilvie v Foljambe* (1817) 3 Mer 53.

7   See *Owen v Thomas* (1834) 3 My & K 353.

8   See *Wood v Scarth* (1855) 2 K & J 33.

9   See *Plant v Bourne* [1897] 2 Ch 281, CA.

10   See *Auerbach v Nelson* [1919] 2 Ch 383.

11   See *McMurray v Spicer* (1868) LR 5 Eq 527.

12   See *Naylor v Goodall* (1877) 47 LJ Ch 53.

13   See *Timmins v Moreland Street Property Co Ltd* [1958] Ch 110 at 118–121, [1957] 3 All ER 265 at 269–270, CA, per Jenkins LJ.

14   See *Cox v Middleton* (1854) 2 Drew 209 at 217 per Kindersley V-C. As to the disposition of registered and unregistered land by transfer see para 262 note 2 post.

15   See *Timmins v Moreland Street Property Co Ltd* [1958] Ch 110, [1957] 3 All ER 265, CA.

16   See *Dolling v Evans* (1867) 36 LJ Ch 474.

17   See *Cox v Middleton* (1854) 2 Drew 209; *Dolling v Evans* (1867) 36 LJ Ch 474; *Cartwright v Miller* (1877) 36 LT 398; *Edwards v Jones* (1921) 124 LT 740, CA; *Harvey v Pratt* [1965] 2 All ER 786, [1965] 1 WLR 1025, CA; and *Prudential Assurance Co Ltd v London Residuary Body* [1992] 2 AC 386, [1992] 3 All ER 504, HL.

37. Indication of the price or other consideration. The contract must state the agreed consideration[1] or the agreed means of ascertaining it[2]. In the absence of such indication, the law will not imply a term that a sale is to be for a reasonable price[3]. Any provision as to the method of payment must be specified in the contract[4]. Where land is purchased in three separate lots, at a separate price for each lot, a document setting out merely the total consideration is not a sufficient memorandum in support of any of the transactions[5]. A contract to purchase land 'at a fair price' or 'at a reasonable valuation' is sufficiently certain, and is enforceable[6].

1   See *Elmore v Kingscote* (1826) 5 B & C 583 at 584; *Re Kharaskhoma Exploring and Prospecting Syndicate Ltd* [1897] 2 Ch 451 at 464, CA. The cases cited in this paragraph were all decided under legislation prior to the coming into force of the Law of Property (Miscellaneous Provisions) Act 1989: see para 29 note 3 ante. As to the statutory requirement for such contracts to be in writing see s 2 (as amended); and para 29 ante.
2   See *Milnes v Gery* (1807) 14 Ves 400 at 408; *Wilks v Davis* (1817) 3 Mer 507. See also *Frewen v Hays* (1912) 106 LT 516, PC. Where the means so specified cannot be followed, eg by reason of the death of the person agreed upon as valuer, it was formerly held that there is in effect no agreement as to price, and the court cannot ascertain the price in any other manner and enforce the contract with the price so ascertained, for that would be making a new agreement for the parties: see *Milnes v Gery* supra; *Blundell v Bettargh* (1810) 17 Ves 232; *Gourlay v Duke of Somerset* (1815) 19 Ves 429 at 430; *Wilks v Davis* supra; *Agar v Macklew* (1825) 2 Sim & St 418; *Morgan v Milman* (1853) 3 De GM & G 24 at 34; *Vickers v Vickers* (1867) LR 4 Eq 529; *Firth v Midland Rly Co* (1875) LR 20 Eq 100. However, those authorities must be reconsidered in the light of *Sudbrook Trading Estate Ltd v Eggleton* [1983] 1 AC 444, [1982] 3 All ER 1, HL, where a leasehold option to purchase a freehold reversion provided that the lessee could purchase at such price not being less than £12,000 as might be agreed by two valuers, one appointed by the lessor and one by the lessee, and in default of such an agreement by an umpire appointed by the valuers. The lessor refused to appoint a valuer. It was held that, on its true construction, the agreement was for a sale at a fair and reasonable price, and since the parties' machinery for ascertaining the price had broken down, the court would order an inquiry as to the fair valuation of the reversion. *Agar v Macklew* supra, and *Vickers v Vickers* supra, were specifically overruled. It seems to follow from the decision that, whenever the criteria for fixing the price are sufficiently specified (if they are not, the contract will presumably fail for uncertainty: see note 6 infra) and can be applied objectively, but the stipulated machinery for applying those criteria breaks down for any reason, the court will substitute its own machinery for applying the criteria.
3   *Gourlay v Duke of Somerset* (1815) 19 Ves 429 at 431; *Morgan v Milman* (1853) 3 De GM & G 24 at 37.
4   *Neale v Merrett* [1930] WN 189.
5   *Smith v MacGowan* [1938] 3 All ER 447.
6   *Milnes v Gery* (1807) 14 Ves 400 at 407; *Morgan v Milman* (1853) 3 De GM & G 24 at 34, 37; *Talbot v Talbot* [1968] Ch 1 at 12, [1967] 2 All ER 920 at 922, CA, per Harman LJ; *Brown v Gould* [1972] Ch 53, [1971] 2 All ER 1505. Cf the following cases where the contract was held void for uncertainty: *Courtney and Fairbairn Ltd v Tolaini Bros (Hotels) Ltd* [1975] 1 All ER 716, [1975] 1 WLR 297, CA (building contract provides that the parties should 'negotiate fair and reasonable contract sums'); *King's Motors (Oxford) Ltd v Lax* [1969] 3 All ER 665, [1970] 1 WLR 426 (option to renew lease 'at such rental as may be agreed upon between the parties'); *Bushwall Properties Ltd v Vortex Properties Ltd* [1976] 2 All ER 283 (contract for sale of 51e in instalments, with a provision that on each payment 'a proportionate part of the land shall be released'). See generally CONTRACT vol 9(1) (Reissue) para 672.
    Where the price is to be fixed by a valuer, the valuer's decision is final unless fraud or collusion can be proved, or incorrect or incomplete reasons or calculations are stated by the valuer: *Campbell v Edwards* [1976] 1 All ER 785, [1976] 1 WLR 403, CA; *Baber v Kenwood Manufacturing Co Ltd and Whinney Murray & Co* [1978] 1 Lloyd's Rep 175, CA. A valuer owes a duty of care and may be liable in negligence: *Arensen v Casson Beckman Rutley & Co* [1977] AC 405, [1975] 3 All ER 901, HL. See generally VALUERS AND SURVEYORS vol 49(1) (Reissue) paras 410–411.

38. Specification of other material terms not implied by law. A contract for the sale or other disposition of an interest in land must incorporate all the terms that have been expressly agreed by the parties[1]. Where the defendant alleges that a contract, complete on the face of it, is in fact incomplete, oral evidence is admissible to show that other terms were agreed and have been omitted but the defendant must prove what the other terms were[2]. Thus an agreement that one party is to pay the other's legal fees should be included in the written document[3], as should a provision as to the date for completion and vacant possession[4], an undertaking to make up a road[5] and a provision for the payment of the purchase price in stages[6]. However, it is probably unnecessary for the written document to set out a term which the parties have expressly agreed but which is identical to one which the law will imply[7].

The equitable remedy of rectification may be available if any term has been omitted from a written contract owing to a mistake common to both parties[8]. Such a remedy may be granted if there was a prior concluded agreement or if there was a clear common intention of the parties which had some outward expression of accord[9]. Where the remedy is available the court may in one action both rectify the contract and grant specific performance[10].

1   See the Law of Property (Miscellaneous Provisions) Act 1989 s 2(1); and para 29 ante. For the meaning of 'interest in land' see para 31 ante.
2   See *Gibbins v North Eastern Metropolitan Asylum District* (1847) 11 Beav 1; *Ball v Bridges* (1874) 30 LT 430; *Jones v Daniel* [1894] 2 Ch 332; *Johnson v Humphrey* [1946] 1 All ER 460; *Beckett v Nurse* [1948] 1 KB 535, [1948] 1 All ER 81, CA (all decided under previous legislation).
3   See *North v Loomes* [1919] 1 Ch 378; *Scott v Bradley* [1971] Ch 850, [1971] 1 All ER 583 (both decided under previous legislation).
4   See *Hawkins v Price* [1947] Ch 645, [1947] 1 All ER 689 (decided under previous legislation). Cf *Fowler v Bratt* [1950] 2 KB 96, [1950] 1 All ER 662, CA (decided under previous legislation). The Standard Conditions of Sale (3rd Edn) include conditions providing for completion on a specified date, with a fallback date if no other date is agreed, and for vacant possession on the date of completion: see conditions 6, 7; and para 120 post. There is, therefore, no need to rely on an implied term: cf *Smith v Mansi* [1962] 3 All ER 857, [1963] 1 WLR 26, CA; *Lee-Parker v Izzet* [1971] 3 All ER 1099, [1971] 1 WLR 1688 (both decided under previous legislation). As to the Standard Conditions of Sale see para 1 note 9 ante.
5   See *Tweddell v Henderson* [1975] 2 All ER 1096, [1975] 1 WLR 1496 (decided under previous legislation).
6   See *Tweddell v Henderson* [1975] 2 All ER 1096, [1975] 1 WLR 1496 (decided under previous legislation). Other examples of material terms omitted from the memorandum are a reference to chattels included in the sale (*Blackburn v Walker* (1920) 150 LT Jo 73 (decided under previous legislation)), and a promise to forgo payment of a debt (*P Preece & Co Ltd v Lewis* (1963) 186 Estates Gazette 113 (decided under previous legislation)).
7   See *Farrell v Green* (1974) 232 Estates Gazette 587 (decided under previous legislation).
8   See the Law of Property (Miscellaneous Provisions) Act 1989 s 2(4); and para 29 ante. For examples of rectification following the Law of Property (Miscellaneous Provisions) Act 1989 see *Wright v Robert Leonard Developments Ltd* [1994] NPC 49, [1994] EGCS 69, CA; *Commission for the New Towns v Cooper (GB) Ltd* [1995] Ch 259, [1995] 2 All ER 929, CA.
9   See *Joscelyne v Nissen* [1970] 2 QB 86, [1970] 1 All ER 1213, CA (decided under previous legislation).
10   See *Craddock Bros v Hunt* [1923] 2 Ch 136, CA; *United States of America v Motor Trucks Ltd* [1924] AC 196, PC (both decided under previous legislation). As to the equitable remedy of rectification generally see MISTAKE. As to specific performance see SPECIFIC PERFORMANCE.

39. Writing and signature. The contract must be in writing, signed by or on behalf of each party to the contract[1]. 'Writing' includes typing, printing, lithography, photography and other modes of representing or reproducing words in a visible form[2].

It is immaterial in what part of the document the signature is to be found, provided that it was intended to relate to and does in fact relate to every part of the document, so as to authenticate the whole document[3]. Where the contract consists of more than one document, the signatures must appear on the primary contract document which incorporates terms from another document[4].

A signature in pencil has been held to be sufficient[5], and also a signature by initials[6], or by means of a stamp or a mark[7]. It is not necessary to prove that the person making the mark could not write his name[8]. A letter bearing the handwritten signature of the vendor and the typewritten name and address of the purchaser is not signed by the purchaser[9]. Where an illiterate person held the top of the pen while another person wrote his name, it was held to be a sufficient signature[10], but the mere tracing over a signature with a dry pen is not sufficient[11]. It is also sufficient if a third person writes the signature at the request of the party[12]. There is a sufficient signature where a handwritten contract begins: 'I, John Jones, have agreed...'[13], or 'Mr John Jones has agreed...'[14], and it is sufficient if only the surname is used[15].

It is essential, however, that some indication of a name should appear; a contract signed 'Your affectionate mother' is insufficient[16], as is a document containing the names of the parties and concluding with the words 'As witness our hands', but bearing no signatures[17].

1   See the Law of Property (Miscellaneous Provisions) Act 1989 s 2(1), (3); and paras 29, 33 ante.
2   Interpretation Act 1978 s 5, Sch 1. This would clearly include a contract by telex, as in *Aquis Estates Ltd v Minton* [1975] 3 All ER 1043, [1975] 1 WLR 1452, CA.
3   *Caton v Caton* (1867) LR 2 HL 127; *Evans v Hoare* [1892] 1 QB 593; *Brooks v Billingham* (1912) 56 Sol Jo 503; *Leeman v Stocks* [1951] Ch 941, [1951] 1 All ER 1043 (all decided under previous legislation). A signature on a letter does not extend to a postscript headed 'Supplement' and written on a separate piece of paper which was sent with the letter but was not referred to in it (*Kronheim v Johnson* (1877) 7 ChD 60 (decided under previous legislation)), and a name inserted in the body of an instrument and applicable to particular purposes only is not sufficient (*Stokes v Moore* (1786) 1 Cox Eq Cas 219; *Caton v Caton* supra (both decided under previous legislation)).
4   See the Law of Property (Miscellaneous Provisions) Act 1989 s 2(2); *Firstpost Homes Ltd v Johnson* [1995] 4 All ER 355, [1995] 1 WLR 1567, CA; and para 29 ante.
5   See *Lucas v James* (1849) 7 Hare 410 at 419; and *Geary v Physic* (1826) 5 B & C 234 (both decided under previous legislation).
6   See *Chichester v Cobb* (1866) 14 LT 433; *Caton v Caton* (1867) LR 2 HL 127 at 143 per Lord Westbury (both decided under previous legislation). See also *Re Blewitt* (1880) 5 PD 116 (signature by initials sufficient for a will) (decided under previous legislation).
7   See *Bennett v Brumfitt* (1867) 37 LJCP 25 (decided under previous legislation). See also *Jenkins v Gaisford and Thring* (1863) 3 Sw & Tr 93; *Mcdonald v John Twiname Ltd* [1953] 2 QB 304, [1953] 2 All ER 589, CA; *Goodman v J Eban Ltd* [1954] 1 QB 550, [1954] 1 All ER 763, CA (all decided under previous legislation).
8   See *Baker v Dening* (1838) 8 Ad & El 94 (decided under previous legislation).
9   See *Firstpost Homes Ltd v Johnson* [1995] 4 All ER 355, [1995] 1 WLR 1567, CA, not following *Evans v Hoare* [1892] 1 QB 593 (decided under previous legislation). See also para 33 ante.
    On the other hand, a printed heading of the name of a party is probably a sufficient signature if the remainder of the document is written by him or at his dictation, or is at the time or subsequently acknowledged by him: see *Schneider v Norris* (1814) 2 M & S 286; *Tourret v Cripps* (1879) 48 LJ Ch 567; *Hucklesby v Hook* (1900) 82 LT 117; *Leeman v Stocks* [1951] Ch 941, [1951] 1 All ER 1043 (all decided under previous legislation).
    It has been held (under previous legislation) that if the vendor's agent inserts the vendor's name in a printed agreement and then procures the purchaser's signature, the document is sufficiently signed by the vendor: see *Leeman v Stocks* [1951] Ch 941, [1951] 1 All ER 1043 (decided under previous legislation). See also *Evans v Hoare* [1892] 1 QB 593 (decided under previous legislation).
10 *Helsham v Langley* (1841) 11 LJ Ch 17 (decided under previous legislation).
11 See *Re Maddock* (1874) LR 3 PD 169; *Re Cunningham* (1860) 4 Sw & Tr 194 (both decisions on wills and both decided under previous legislation).
12 *Brooks v Billingham* (1912) 56 Sol Jo 503 (decided under previous legislation).
13 *Knight v Crockford* (1794) 1 Esq 190 (decided under previous legislation). Cf *Wood v Smith* [1993] Ch 90, [1992] 3 All ER 556, CA (testator's signature only at beginning of will).
14 *Propert v Parker* (1830) 1 Russ & M 625; *Johnson v Dodgson* (1837) 2 M & W 653; *Bleakley v Smith* (1840) 11 Sim 150 (all decided under previous legislation).
15 *Lobb v Stanley* (1844) 5 QB 574 (decided under previous legislation).
16 *Selby v Selby* (1817) 3 Mer 2 (decided under previous legislation).
17 *Hubert v Treherne* (1842) 4 Scott NR 486, distinguished in *Leeman v Stocks* [1951] Ch 941, [1951] 1 All ER 1043. See also *Hawkins v Holmes* (1721) 1 P Wms 770, where the defendant altered the draft in his own hand but did not sign it. All the cases cited in this note were decided under previous legislation.

40. Signature by agent. The written contract must be signed by or on behalf of each party to the contract[1]. The contract may be signed by a person who is an agent of both parties[2], for example a contract signed on behalf of both parties by an auctioneer immediately after a sale by auction[3]. The agent must be a third person; a contract cannot be signed by one of the parties to the contract as agent for the other so as to satisfy the statutory requirement[4], although it may be signed on behalf of one party by a person who is already acting as agent of the other party[5].

For the purpose of signing a contract, it has been held that an agent may be authorised orally[6]; and it may be proved by oral evidence that a person who signed a contract did so as agent for a third person[7], so as to make that third person also liable on the contract[8]. It follows that, where an agent for the purchaser appointed by word of mouth purchases in his own name, oral evidence may be given to show that the real purchaser was not the person named in the contract, and the contract may be enforced by the principal against both the agent so appointed and the vendor[9]. In all cases there must be proof that the agent was expressly or impliedly authorised to sign the memorandum, in accordance with the ordinary principles of the law of agency[10]. A limited company must act through an agent, and a contract signed by the company secretary is sufficient[11]. The general authority of an estate agent is not to sell but to find a purchaser, and in such a case he has no implied authority to sign a contract[12]. The authority of an agent to sign a contract may be revoked at any time before it has been exercised, even after the terms of the contract have been agreed[13].

If a party who has contracted as a principal signs a document by which he represents himself merely as the agent of a hitherto undisclosed principal, the document is not a sufficient memorandum, because it sets up a fresh term[14]. On the other hand, where a person known by the vendor to be the agent of the purchaser contracts in his own name, the contract is enforceable even though the real purchaser's name is not mentioned in the contract[15].

An agent cannot without the consent of his principal delegate his authority to sign a contract[16]; thus a signature by an auctioneer's clerk will not bind the vendor[17] unless he assents to the clerk so signing[18]. If the contract is signed by the delegate in the presence of the principal and without objection by him, that will normally be sufficient evidence of his assent[19].

The statutory requirement of a written contract does not apply to a contract made in the course of a public auction[20]. However, it is thought likely that in most cases a written contract will in fact be used. An auctioneer is the agent of both purchaser and vendor for the purpose of signing the contract, and a contract signed by him is sufficient to bind both parties[21], provided that he signs it immediately after the sale or so soon afterwards as to be part of the transaction of sale[22]. It is not sufficient for an auctioneer's name to be printed at the foot of particulars and conditions of sale[23]. The auctioneer's authority is limited to the sale by auction and does not extend to a private sale negotiated after an abortive auction[24].

A solicitor has no general authority to sign a contract on behalf of his client[25]. Thus a solicitor who is merely instructed to draw up a contract has no authority to bind his client by signing the contract[26]. Whether the solicitor has such authority is a question of evidence in the particular case. The following instructions have been held to confer such authority: instructions to settle the terms of a contract[27]; or to perform a contract[28]; or to forward documents relating to a contract[29]. Instructions to deny a contract do not confer authority to sign a contract[30]; nor do instructions to act in a matter which is still in negotiation or subject to contract[31].

1   See the Law of Property (Miscellaneous Provisions) Act 1989 s 1(3); and para 29 ante.
2   See *Heyman v Neale* (1809) 2 Camp 337; *Sievewright v Archibald* (1851) 17 QB 103; *Thompson v Gardiner* (1876) 1 CPD 777. The cases cited in this paragraph were all decided under legislation prior to the coming into force of the Law of Property (Miscellaneous Provisions) Act 1989: see para 29 note 3 ante. As to the statutory requirement for such contracts to be in writing see s 2 (as amended); and para 29 ante.

3   *Simon v Motivos* (1766) 3 Burr 1921; *Emmerson v Heelis* (1809) 2 Taunt 38; *Wood v Midgley* (1854) 5 De
    GM & G 41; *Peirce v Corf* (1874) LR 9 QB 210 at 214; *Cohen v Roche* [1927] 1 KB 169; *Richards v Phillips*
    [1969] 1 Ch 39, [1968] 2 All ER 859, CA.
4   *Wright v Dannah* (1809) 2 Camp 203; *Sharman v Brandt* (1871) LR 6 QB 720, Ex Ch. See also *Rayner v
    Linthorne* (1825) 2 C & P 124. Thus an auctioneer cannot sue on a contract signed by himself (see
    Farebrother v Simmons (1822) 5 B & Ald 333), but he may sue on a contract signed by his employee (see
    Wilson & Sons v Pike [1949] 1 KB 176, [1948] 2 All ER 267, CA).
5   *Bird v Boulter* (1833) 4 B & Ad 443; *Murphy v Boese* (1875) LR 10 Exch 126.
6   See *Waller v Hendon and Cox* (1723) 2 Eq Cas Abr 50; *Clinan v Cooke* (1802) 1 Sch & Lef 22; *Wilson v
    Hart* (1817) 7 Taunt 295; *Heard v Pilley* (1869) 4 Ch App 548; *Cave v Mackenzie* (1877) 46 LJ Ch 564;
    James v Smith [1891] 1 Ch 384 (affd 65 LT 544, CA); *Brooks v Billingham* (1912) 56 Sol Jo 503; *North v
    Loomes* [1919] 1 Ch 378.
7   *Heard v Pilley* (1869) 4 Ch App 548; *Cave v Mackenzie* (1877) 46 LJ Ch 564. However, where a contract
    is made between a builder and a person who is described throughout and signs as 'proprietor', oral
    evidence is not admissible to show that he is in fact merely the agent of another: *Formby Bros v Formby*
    [1910] WN 48, CA.
8   *Higgins v Senior* (1841) 8 M & W 834.
9   *Heard v Pilley* (1869) 4 Ch App 548; *Cave v Mackenzie* (1877) 46 LJ Ch 564. The admissibility of oral
    evidence cannot be resisted on the ground that the creation of a trust in land must be proved by writing
    (see the Law of Property Act 1925 s 53(1)(b)), because, inter alia, it would be inequitable in such a case
    for the agent to set up the statute: *Heard v Pilley* (1869) 4 Ch App 548; *Rochefoucauld v Boustead* [1897] 1
    Ch 196, CA. See further AGENCY vol 1(2) (Reissue) paras 23, 51; TRUSTS vol 48 (Reissue) para 543.
10 See generally AGENCY vol 1(2) (Reissue) para 44 et seq. The principle of ratification also applies in this
    context: see *Koenigsblatt v Sweet* [1923] 2 Ch 314, CA; and AGENCY vol 1(2) (Reissue) para 84.
11 *Beer v London and Paris Hotel Co* (1875) LR 20 Eq 412; *John Griffiths Cycle Corpn Ltd v Humber & Co Ltd*
    [1899] 2 QB 414, CA (revsd on another point sub nom *Humber & Co v John Griffiths Cycle Co* (1901) 85
    LT 141, HL). See also *Panorama Developments (Guildford) Ltd v Fidelis Furnishing Fabrics Ltd* [1971] 2 QB
    711, [1971] 3 All ER 16, CA.
12 *Godwin v Brind* (1868) LR 5 CP 299n; *Wire v Pemberton* (1854) 23 LTOS 345; *Hamer v Sharp* (1874) LR
    19 Eq 108; *Vale of Neath Colliery Co v Furness* (1876) 45 LJ Ch 276; *Prior v Moore* (1887) 3 TLR 624;
    Chadburn v Moore (1892) 61 LJ Ch 674; *Keen v Mear* [1920] 2 Ch 574; *Lewcock v Bromley* (1920) 127 LT
    116; *Wragg v Lovett* [1948] 2 All ER 968, CA. See further AGENCY vol 1(2) (Reissue) para 56.
13 *Farmer v Robinson* (1805) 2 Camp 339n; *Warwick v Slade* (1811) 3 Camp 127. However, the auctioneer's
    implied authority cannot be revoked after the fall of the hammer: *Phillips v Butler* [1945] Ch 358, [1945]
    2 All ER 258; and see AUCTION vol 2 (Reissue) para 914.
        It has been held (under previous legislation) that the signature of an agent may bind his principal even
    though the agent signs only in the character of witness: see *Wallace v Roe* [1903] 1 IR 32.
14 *Re Cox, McEven & Co and Hoare Marr & Co* (1907) 96 LT 719, CA; *Lovesey v Palmer* [1916] 2 Ch 233;
    Keen v Mear [1920] 2 Ch 574.
15 *Basma v Weekes* [1950] AC 441, sub nom *Abdul Karim Basma v Weekes* [1950] 2 All ER 146, PC,
    disapproving a dictum of Luxmoore LJ to the contrary in *Smith-Bird v Blower* [1939] 2 All ER 406 at 407.
    That dictum was again disapproved in *Davies v Sweet* [1962] 2 QB 300, [1962] 1 All ER 92, CA.
16 *Henderson v Barnewall* (1827) 1 Y & J 387; *Blore v Sutton* (1817) 3 Mer 237.
17 *Bell v Balls* [1897] 1 Ch 663; *Gosbell v Archer* (1835) 2 Ad & El 500.
18 *Coles v Trecothick* (1804) 9 Ves 234; *Dyas v Stafford* (1882) 7 LR Ir 520, Ir CA.
19 *Bird v Boulter* (1833) 4 B & Ad 443; *Sims v Landray* [1894] 2 Ch 318; *Brooks v Billingham* (1912) 56 Sol Jo 503.
20 See the Law of Property (Miscellaneous Provisions) Act 1989 s 2(5)(b).
21 *Simon v Motivos* (1766) 3 Burr 1921; *Emmerson v Heelis* (1809) 2 Taunt 38; *Wood v Midgley* (1854) 5 De
    GM & G 41; *Peirce v Corf* (1874) LR 9 QB 210 at 214; *Cohen v Roche* [1927] 1 KB 169; *Richards v Phillips*
    [1969] 1 Ch 39, [1968] 2 All ER 859, CA.
22 *Matthews v Baxter* (1873) LR 8 Exch 132 (signature eight days after sale too late); *Bell v Balls* [1897] 1 Ch
    663 (signature one week after sale too late); *Chaney v Maclow* [1929] 1 Ch 461, CA (signature on day of
    auction sufficient). See also *Phillips v Butler* [1945] Ch 358 at 363, [1945] 2 All ER 258 at 263.
23 *Dyas v Stafford* (1882) 7 LR Ir 520, CA.
24 *Mews v Carr* (1856) 1 H & N 484.
25 *Forster v Rowland* (1861) 7 H & N 103; *Matthews v Baxter* (1873) LR 8 Exch 132; *Smith v Webster* (1876)
    3 ChD 49, CA. This must equally be true of a licensed conveyancer: see para 3 ante.
26 *Forster v Rowland* (1861) 7 H & N 103; *Smith v Webster* (1876) 3 ChD 49, CA; *Bowen v Duc d'Orléans*
    (1900) 16 TLR 226, CA; *Goodall v Harding* (1884) 52 LT 126.
27 *Jolliffe v Blumberg* (1870) 18 WR 784.

28 *North v Loomes* [1919] 1 Ch 378; *Horner v Walker* [1923] 2 Ch 218; *Gavaghan v Edwards* [1961] 2 QB 220, [1961] 2 All ER 477, CA.
29 *Daniels v Trefusis* [1914] 1 Ch 788. As to the authority of a solicitor to effect an exchange of contracts see *Domb v Isoz* [1980] Ch 548, [1980] 1 All ER 942, CA; and para 23 ante.
30 *Thirkell v Cambi* [1919] 2 KB 590, CA.
31 *D'silva v Lister House Development Ltd* [1971] Ch 17 at 28, 29, [1970] 1 All ER 858 at 866, per Buckley J; *Griffiths v Young* [1970] Ch 675 at 685, [1970] 3 All ER 601 at 607, CA, per Widgery LJ; and see *Tiverton Estates Ltd v Wearwell Ltd* [1975] Ch 146, [1974] 1 All ER 209, CA.

(4) DISCLOSURE OF MATERIAL FACTS

(i) In general

41. Avoidance of contract. In certain cases a contract may be avoided on the ground that the consent of one of the parties was given in ignorance of material facts which were within the knowledge of the other party[1]. A contract for the sale of land is not a contract of the utmost good faith in which there is an absolute duty upon each party to make full disclosure to the other of all material facts of which he has full knowledge[2], but the contract may be avoided on the ground of misrepresentation, fraud or mistake in the same way as any other contract[3], and also on the ground of non-disclosure of latent defects of title[4].

1 See CONTRACT vol 9(1) (Reissue) para 701; MISREPRESENTATION AND FRAUD vol 31 (Reissue) para 701; MISTAKE.
2 See eg INSURANCE vol 25 (Reissue) para 349 et seq; PARTNERSHIP vol 35 (Reissue) paras 93–96.
3 See CONTRACT vol 9(1) (Reissue) para 701 et seq; MISREPRESENTATION AND FRAUD vol 31 (Reissue) para 814 et seq; MISTAKE.
4 As to the duty to disclose defects in title see paras 54–61 post.

42. Damages for misrepresentation. Innocent misrepresentation may be a ground for avoiding a contract and may be a defence to an action for specific performance[1]. Prior to the enactment of the Misrepresentation Act 1967[2], damages could only be awarded if the misrepresentation were fraudulent[3], negligent[4] or a breach of fiduciary duty[5]. Damages could not, therefore, be awarded for a purely innocent misrepresentation[6], nor could the purchaser be granted specific performance with abatement of price[7]. The Misrepresentation Act 1967 provides that damages for misrepresentation are available as of right unless the person making the misrepresentation proves that he believed, on reasonable grounds, in the truth of the facts represented up to the time when the contract was made[8]. Such damages are assessed on the tortious basis and will not include damages for loss of a bargain[9]. Where a person has entered into a contract after a misrepresentation has been made to him otherwise than fraudulently, the court has a discretion to award damages in lieu of rescission if it is equitable to do so having regard to the nature of the misrepresentation and the loss that would be caused by it if the contract were to be upheld, as well as to the loss that rescission would cause to the other party[10].

The vendor's solicitor[11] does not normally owe a duty of care to the purchaser[12]. Where the misrepresentation relates to the vendor's title, damages may be awarded for loss of a bargain[13]. The right to rescind does not run with the land, so a sub-purchaser has no right to rescind as against the original vendor, even if the transfer is made by the original vendor direct to the sub-purchaser[14].

1   See MISREPRESENTATION AND FRAUD vol 31 (Reissue) paras 782–788. As to specific performance see SPECIFIC PERFORMANCE.

2   Ie prior to the Misrepresentation Act 1967: see generally MISREPRESENTATION AND FRAUD.

3   *Derry v Peek* (1889) 14 App Cas 337, HL; *Akerhielm v de Mare* [1959] AC 789, [1959] 3 All ER 485, PC.

4   *Hedley Byrne & Co Ltd v Heller & Partners Ltd* [1964] AC 465, [1963] 2 All ER 575, HL; *WB Anderson & Sons Ltd v Rhodes (Liverpool) Ltd* [1967] 2 All ER 850, 31 MLR 322; *Esso Petroleum Co Ltd v Mardon* [1976] QB 801, [1976] 2 All ER 5, CA.

5   *Nocton v Lord Ashburton* [1914] AC 932, HL; *Woods v Martins Bank Ltd* [1959] 1 QB 55, [1958] 3 All ER 166.

6   See eg *Lawrence v Hull* (1924) 41 TLR 75; *Terrene Ltd v Nelson* [1937] 3 All ER 739. On rescission a financial indemnity may be awarded in respect of obligations created by the contract, such as the costs attending on purchase: see *Hart v Swaine* (1877) 7 ChD 42; *Whittington v Seale-Hayne* (1900) 82 LT 49. See also CONTRACT vol 9(1) (Reissue) paras 986–987; MISREPRESENTATION AND FRAUD vol 31 (Reissue) para 812 et seq. As to the distinction between terms and representations see CONTRACT vol 9(1) (Reissue) para 767; MISREPRESENTATION AND FRAUD vol 31 (Reissue) para 704.

7   *Gilchester Properties Ltd v Gomm* [1948] 1 All ER 493 (incorrect reply to preliminary inquiries regarding rents at which properties were let). An innocent misrepresentation may, however, give rise to an estoppel: *Oades v Spafford* [1948] 2 KB 74, [1948] 1 All ER 607, CA; see generally ESTOPPEL vol 16 (Reissue) para 1038 et seq.

8   See the Misrepresentation Act 1967 s 2(1); and MISREPRESENTATION AND FRAUD vol 31 (Reissue) para 801. As to availability of defence of *ex turpi causa non oritur actio* to claim for damages see *Saunders v Edwards* [1987] 2 All ER 651, [1987] 1 WLR 1116, CA.

9   See *Royscot Trust Ltd v Rogerson* [1991] 2 QB 297, [1991] 3 All ER 294, CA; *Cemp Properties (UK) Ltd v Dentsply Research and Development Corpn (Denton, Hall & Burgin (Third Parties)* [1991] 2 EGLR 197; *William Sindall plc v Cambridgeshire County Council* [1994] 3 All ER 932, [1994] 1 WLR 1016, CA.

10 See the Misrepresentation Act 1967 s 2(2); and MISREPRESENTATION AND FRAUD vol 31 (Reissue) para 834. See also *William Sindall plc v Cambridgeshire County Council* [1994] 3 All ER 932 at 952–995, [1994] 1 WLR 1016 at 1035–1038, CA, per Hoffmann LJ. The completion of a contract for the sale of land is not a bar to rescission (see the Misrepresentation Act 1967 s 1(b)), but if rescission would upset a chain of transactions the court might well award damages in lieu of rescission. As to contractual provisions purporting to restrict or exclude liability for misrepresentation see para 116 post.

11 See para 3 ante.

12 See *Gran Gelato Ltd v Richcliff (Group) Ltd* [1992] Ch 560, [1992] 1 All ER 865. See also *Al-Kandari v JR Brown & Co (a firm)* [1988] QB 665, [1988] 1 All ER 833, CA; and cf *Wilson v Bloomfield* (1979) 123 Sol Jo 860, CA. As to the duty of care generally see NEGLIGENCE.

13 *Watts v Spence* [1976] Ch 165, [1975] 2 All ER 578. See further para 256 post.

14 *Gross v Lewis Hillman Ltd* [1970] Ch 445, [1969] 3 All ER 1476, CA. The position would be different if the original purchaser were authorised or intended to pass on the representation to the sub-purchaser: see *Gross v Lewis Hillman Ltd* supra; para 359 post; and MISREPRESENTATION AND FRAUD vol 31 (Reissue) para 737. As to the disposition of registered and unregistered land by transfer see para 262 note 2 post.

43.   What amounts to a representation. Representations of fact as to the quality of the subject matter of a contract must be distinguished from such expressions of opinion as to its value or desirability as do not involve any representation of fact. A purchaser cannot avoid liability to perform his contract on the ground that he has been misled by statements which are mere puffing. It has been held to be puffing to describe property as a desirable residence for a family of distinction, when in fact it is a small farmhouse[1], or (formerly) to describe renewable leaseholds as nearly equal to freehold[2], or to describe a house as substantial and convenient[3], or well built[4], or eligible[5]. Where, however, a landlord who has the means of knowing the character of his tenant describes him to an intending purchaser as a most desirable tenant, this is a representation of fact, and the purchaser has a remedy if it turns out that the tenant has paid his last quarter's rent by driblets under pressure[6].

A statement of belief may amount to an implied representation that there are reasonable grounds for that belief, and is actionable by a purchaser if he has been induced to enter the contract by the representation and it is untrue[7]. Even where a vendor's replies to preliminary inquiries are qualified by the phrase 'so far as the vendor is aware', liability for misrepresentation may arise, since such a qualifying statement amounts to an implied representation that such inquiries have been made to determine the truth of the matter as would have been made by a prudent conveyancer[8].

1 *Magennis v Fallon* (1828) 2 Mol 561 at 589.
2 *Fenton v Browne* (1807) 14 Ves 144 at 149. Perpetually renewable leaseholds cannot now exist: see LANDLORD AND TENANT vol 27(1) (Reissue) para 453.
3 *Johnson v Smart* (1860) 2 Giff 151; affd 2 LT 783.
4 *Kennard v Ashman* (1894) 10 TLR 213; affd 10 TLR 447, CA. However, a house of which the external walls are composed partly of brick and partly of lath and plaster must not be described as brick built: see *Powell v Doubble* (1832), cited in Sugden's Law of Vendors and Purchasers (14th Edn, 1862) 29.
5 *Hope v Walter* [1900] 1 Ch 257 at 258, CA, per Lindley MR. It has also been held to be mere puffing to describe an imperfectly watered piece of land as uncommonly rich water meadow land (*Scott v Hanson* (1826) 1 Sim 13; affd (1829) 1 Russ & M 128), or land as fertile and improvable when part of it has been abandoned as useless (*Dimmock v Hallett* (1866) 2 Ch App 21 at 27 per Turner LJ); but these cases seem to involve misrepresentations of fact. Cf *Robinson v Musgrove* (1838) 8 C & P 469; and see further MISREPRESENTATION AND FRAUD vol 31 (Reissue) paras 709–710, 715–716.
6 *Smith v Land House Property Corpn* (1884) 28 ChD 7 at 15–16, CA, per Bowen LJ. See also *Bisset v Wilkinson* [1927] AC 177 at 182, PC.
7 *Brown v Raphael* [1958] Ch 636, [1958] 2 All ER 79, CA (statement as to prospective liability to death duty in the words that an annuitant 'is believed to have no aggregable estate'); *Goff v Ganthier* (1991) 62 P & CR 388 (untrue statement of intention to offer contract to another prospective purchaser at a higher price). See also MISREPRESENTATION AND FRAUD vol 31 (Reissue) para 710.
8 See *William Sindall plc v Cambridgeshire County Council* [1994] 3 All ER 932, [1994] 1 WLR 1016, CA; and see also *Cremdean Properties Ltd v Nash* (1977) 244 Estates Gazette 547 at 551, CA, per Bridge LJ; *Gran Gelato Ltd v Richcliff (Group) Ltd* [1992] Ch 560, [1992] 1 All ER 865; and cf *Gilchester Properties Ltd v Gomm* [1948] 1 All ER 493 at 495, [1948] WN 71, per Romer J. A solicitor's knowledge will be imputed to his client: *Strover v Harrington* [1988] Ch 390, [1988] 1 All ER 769.

44. Removable and irremovable defects. Where a defect of title is removable by the vendor, for example a mortgage which can be paid off, the purchaser cannot repudiate the contract on the ground of non-disclosure[1]. However, an irremovable, latent and undisclosed defect, such as a binding restrictive covenant, entitles the purchaser to refuse to complete[2], unless he actually knew of the defect at the time of entering into the contract[3]. The vendor need not disclose matters which are necessarily incident to his tenure of the property[4].

1 Cf *Brickles v Snell* [1916] 2 AC 599, PC. There is no need to mention such an incumbrance in the conditions of sale: see para 91 post.
2 See eg *Nottingham Patent Brick and Tile Co v Butler* (1886) 16 QBD 778, CA; and para 54 et seq post. The distinction between removable and irremovable defects has never been very clearly defined. A usual illustration of a removable defect is a covenant to repair which has not been complied with. 'Irremovable' in this context means irremovable by the vendor, with or without the parties upon whose concurrence in the removal he is entitled to insist. The fact that a defect can be removed by a third person or a local or public authority does not make it any the less irremovable in the sense in which that word is here used unless the vendor can insist upon its removal. As to the vendor's obligations with respect to a spouse's statutory rights of occupation of the matrimonial home see the Family Law Act 1996 s 32, Sch 4 para 3; and para 123 post.
3 So far as concerns incumbrances registered under the Land Charges Act 1972, the question whether the purchaser had knowledge is to be determined without reference to the provisions under which registration constitutes actual notice (ie the Law of Property Act 1925 s 198 (as amended) (see EQUITY vol 16 (Reissue) para 768)): see the Law of Property Act 1969 s 24; and para 54 post.
4 See para 61 post. See also *Re City of London Real Property Co Ltd's Appeal* [1949] Ch 581 at 588, [1949] 1 All ER 763 at 766 per Vaisey J, where the distinction between general restrictions on property and particular restrictions on property to be sold is stated.

(ii) Disclosure by the Vendor

45. Patent defects of quality. Defects of quality may be either patent or latent. Patent defects are such as are discoverable by inspection and ordinary vigilance on the part of a purchaser[1], and latent defects are such as would not be revealed by any inquiry which a purchaser is in a position to make before entering into the contract for purchase[2].

The vendor is not bound to call attention to patent defects; the rule is 'caveat emptor'[3]. Therefore, a purchaser should make inspection and inquiry as to what he is proposing to buy[4]. If he omits to ascertain whether the land is such as he desires to acquire, he cannot complain afterwards on discovering defects of which he would have been aware if he had taken ordinary steps to ascertain its physical condition[5]; and, although as a general rule a vendor must deliver property corresponding to the description contained in the contract[6], yet an error in the particulars or description of the property in the contract is not a ground of objection if it is readily corrected on inspection[7].

1   In order to be a patent defect, the defect must either be visible to the eye, or arise by necessary implication from something visible to the eye: *Yandle & Sons v Sutton* [1922] 2 Ch 199. See also *Ashburner v Sewell* [1891] 3 Ch 405 at 408; *Simpson v Gilley* (1922) 92 LJ Ch 194. A defect is not patent if it can only be discovered by minute inspection such as a purchaser cannot be reasonably expected to make: *Shepherd v Croft* [1911] 1 Ch 521 at 529.

2   As to latent defects of quality see para 48 post.

3   See EQUITY vol 16 (Reissue) para 663; MISREPRESENTATION AND FRAUD vol 31 (Reissue) paras 748–751.

4   *Lowndes v Lane* (1789) 2 Cox Eq Cas 363; *Edwards-Wood v Marjoribanks* (1860) 7 HL Cas 806 at 809–811; *Cook v Waugh* (1860) 2 Giff 201 at 206; Sugden's Law of Vendors and Purchasers (14th Edn, 1862) 328; and see EQUITY vol 16 (Reissue) para 663; MISREPRESENTATION AND FRAUD vol 31 (Reissue) paras 748–751. As to preliminary inquiries generally see para 4 et seq ante; as to inquiries of tenants see para 6 ante; and as to the rule that occupation is notice of a tenant's rights see para 329 post.

5   *Oldfield v Round* (1800) 5 Ves 508, where the contract was for the sale of a meadow without mention of a road across it, the road being obviously a road used either by third persons or by the public in general. See also *Ashburner v Sewell* [1891] 3 Ch 405 at 409; *Yandle & Sons v Sutton* [1922] 2 Ch 199; *Simpson v Gilley* (1922) 92 LJ Ch 194. See also *Keates v Earl of Cadogan* (1851) 10 CB 591 at 600 (agreement for tenancy of a dwelling house in an obviously ruinous and unsafe condition); *Cook v Waugh* (1860) 2 Giff 202 (agreement to take a lease of a house with a cracked wall and otherwise greatly out of repair). After personal inspection, the purchaser cannot contradict his own view as to the state of repair on the ground that he is not a surveyor: *Haywood v Cope* (1858) 25 Beav 140 at 148. As to the advisability of the purchaser having the property surveyed and his position where the property has been surveyed on behalf of a mortgagee see para 7 ante.

6   See *Flight v Booth* (1834) 1 Bing NC 370 at 377.

7   *Dyer v Hargrave, Hargrave v Dyer* (1805) 10 Ves 505 at 508, where a farm was described as being 'within a ring fence'; *White v Bradshaw* (1851) 16 Jur 738, where a house in Brighton was described as '39 Regency Square', its usual description, although it was not actually in Regency Square. It is otherwise where the description is substantially wrong: *Stanton v Tattersall* (1853) 1 Sm & G 529; and see para 52 note 11 post.

46. Concealment by the vendor. A representation as to the property which is contradicted by its obvious physical condition does not enable the purchaser to repudiate the contract or obtain compensation, unless, in reliance on the representation, he abstains from inspecting it[1]. However, any active concealment by the vendor of defects which would otherwise be patent is treated as fraudulent, and the contract is voidable by the purchaser[2] if he has been deceived by it[3]. Any conduct calculated to mislead a purchaser or lull his suspicions with regard to a defect known to the vendor has the same effect[4].

1   *Grant v Munt* (1815) Coop G 173. Cf *Denny v Hancock* (1870) 6 Ch App 1, where inspection of the
    property did not reveal the fact that a plan was misleading; *Re Arnold, Arnold v Arnold* (1880) 14 ChD
    270, CA.
2   Sugden's Law of Vendors and Purchasers (14th Edn, 1862) 2, 333–335; *Shirley v Stratton* (1785) 1 Bro
    CC 440; *Pickering v Dowson* (1813) 4 Taunt 779 at 785; *Small v Attwood* (1832) You 407 at 490 (on appeal
    Attwood v Small (1838) 6 Cl & Fin 232, HL). This is so notwithstanding that the property is sold with all
    faults: *Baglehole v Walters* (1811) 3 Camp 154 at 156; *Schneider v Heath* (1813) 3 Camp 506. See
    MISREPRESENTATION AND FRAUD vol 31 (Reissue) paras 720, 750–751.
3   In *Horsfall v Thomas* (1862) 1 H & C 90, a vendor of a gun which he had made to the purchaser's order
    concealed a defect, but as the purchaser never inspected the gun the concealment had no operation on
    his mind or conduct, and he was not allowed to avoid the contract on the ground of the vendor's fraud.
    This decision was dissented from by Cockburn CJ in *Smith v Hughes* (1871) LR 6 QB 597 at 605, but
    appears to be correct: see *Coaks v Boswell* (1886) 11 App Cas 232 at 236, HL; *Shepherd v Croft* [1911] 1
    Ch 521 at 530; and MISREPRESENTATION AND FRAUD vol 31 (Reissue) para 765 et seq.
4   See *Small v Attwood* (1832) You 407 (revsd *Attwood v Small* (1838) 6 Cl & Fin 232, HL, on the grounds
    that fraud had not been proved and that the purchasers had not relied on the representations made). See
    also MISREPRESENTATION AND FRAUD vol 31 (Reissue) para 742 et seq.

47. Purchaser's erroneous opinion. If the purchaser has an opportunity of forming
an independent opinion, he alone is responsible for the opinion that he forms, whether
in fact he uses the opportunity or not, and the vendor is not bound to correct the opinion
if erroneous[1]. It makes no difference that the vendor knows or believes that the purchaser
contracts in reliance upon his erroneous opinion[2]. There is an exception where a
purchaser mistakenly believes that the vendor is in effect giving a warranty as to quality
and enters into the contract on that footing, and the vendor is aware of the mistake. It is
then the vendor's duty to correct the mistake, and, if he fails to do so, the contract is not
binding on the purchaser[3].

1   *Smith v Hughes* (1871) LR 6 QB 597; cf *Lowndes v Lane* (1789) 2 Cox Eq Cas 363. See
    MISREPRESENTATION AND FRAUD vol 31 (Reissue) para 751.
2   *Smith v Hughes* (1871) LR 6 QB 597 at 607 per Blackburn J.
3   *Smith v Hughes* (1871) LR 6 QB 597 at 610 per Hannen J.

48. Latent defects of quality. Prima facie the rule 'caveat emptor'[1] applies also to
latent defects of quality or other matters (not being defects of title) which affect the value
of the property sold, and the vendor, even if he is aware of any such matters, is under no
general obligation to disclose them[2]. There is no implied warranty that land agreed to be
sold is of any particular quality or suitable for any particular purpose[3]. The vendor of a
house who sells it after it has been completed gives no implied warranty to the purchaser
that it is safe, even if he is also its builder[4]; and, although a vendor, and a builder, owes a
duty of care in negligence with regard to defects created by him, the potential liability
extends only to damage causing physical injury to persons or damage to other property[5].
Where a house in course of erection is sold by the builder there is an implied warranty
that it will be completed in a proper and workmanlike manner and will be reasonably fit
for human habitation[6]; but, even in such a case, no implied warranty is applicable if there
is an express contract between the parties as to the way in which the building is to be
completed[7] or a covenant by the purchaser that, having inspected the property, he is
satisfied with it and agrees to pay for any alterations required by him[8].

The implied warranty applies where the builder departs from an agreed specification,
even by improving on it[9]; and where there is an express undertaking to complete the
house in a proper and workmanlike manner in accordance with an agreed specification,
the builder is liable for using defective materials even though they accord with the
specification[10].

1   See para 45 ante. A contract of sale of land is different from a contract of insurance which is a contract
    of the utmost good faith: see *Turner v Green* [1895] 2 Ch 205 at 208; and INSURANCE vol 25 (Reissue)
    para 349 et seq. The rule 'caveat emptor' does not, however, apply where there has been a
    misrepresentation by the vendor (*Colby v Gadsden* (1867) 17 LT 97; see also *Mills v Oddy* (1835) 2 Cr
    M & R 103), although silence by itself does not amount to misrepresentation (*Seddon v North Eastern
    Salt Co Ltd* [1905] 1 Ch 326 at 335); cf para 46 ante.

2   There is no fiduciary relationship between vendor and purchaser in the negotiation of the agreement:
    Walters v Morgan (1861) 3 De GF & J 718 at 723; *Turner v Green* [1895] 2 Ch 205 at 209. Thus mere silence
    as regards a material fact which the one party is not bound to disclose to the other is not a ground for
    rescission of the contract, or a defence to specific performance: *Turner v Green* supra at 208 (non-disclosure
    of a fact likely to influence the other party not to compromise proceedings). See also *Greenhalgh v Brindley*
    [1901] 2 Ch 324 (non-disclosure of deed preventing acquisition of easement of light); *Re Ward and Jordan's
    Contract* [1902] 1 IR 73 (non-disclosure on sale of licensed premises of fact that a conviction has been
    indorsed on the licence); *Percival v Wright* [1902] 2 Ch 421 (purchase of shares in a company by directors
    without disclosing pending negotiations for sale of the company's undertaking).

3   *Miller v Cannon Hill Estates Ltd* [1931] 2 KB 113 at 120 per Swift J; *Otto v Bolton and Norris* [1936] 2 KB
    46 at 52, [1936] 1 All ER 960 at 965. See also para 353 post.

4   *Bottomley v Bannister* [1932] 1 KB 458, CA; *Otto v Bolton and Norris* [1936] 2 KB 46, [1936] 1 All ER 960.

5   *Murphy v Brentwood District Council* [1991] 1 AC 398, [1990] 2 All ER 908, HL (local authority not liable
    for cost of repairing defect if discovered before harm caused by it); and see *Department of the Environment
    v Thomas Bates & Son* [1991] 1 AC 499, [1990] 2 All ER 943, HL (builder was not liable in tort for the
    cost of remedying defects in a building in order to make it safe and suitable for its intended purpose where
    there was no damage to the building and no imminent danger to personal safety and health). After these
    decisions it is uncertain whether a similar duty of care is owed by a local authority which exercises its
    statutory power to inspect a building in course of erection. The duty is not abated by the subsequent
    disposal of the premises by the person who owed the duty: see the Defective Premises Act 1972 s 3. A
    valuer who prepares a valuation report for a mortgagee owes a duty of care to the purchaser: *Yianni v
    Edwin Evans & Sons* [1982] QB 438, [1981] 3 All ER 592; *Smith v Eric S Bush (a firm)*, *Harris v Wyre Forest
    District Council* [1990] 1 AC 831, [1989] 2 All ER 514, HL; and see VALUERS AND SURVEYORS vol 49(1)
    (Reissue) para 416. As to the duty of care generally see NEGLIGENCE.

6   *Miller v Cannon Hill Estates Ltd* [1931] 2 KB 113; *Perry v Sharon Development Co Ltd* [1937] 4 All ER 390,
    CA, where the distinction between a completed house and one in course of erection is considered;
    Hoskins v Woodham [1938] 1 All ER 692, where the house was held to be complete at the time of the
    sale. The implied warranty extends to the foundations: *Jennings v Tavener* [1955] 2 All ER 769, [1955] 1
    WLR 932; *Hancock v BW Brazier (Anerley) Ltd* [1966] 2 All ER 901, [1966] 1 WLR 1317, CA. The
    question whether a house is a completed house or in course of erection is a question of fact: *Brown v
    Norton* [1954] 1 IR 34.

7   *Lynch v Thorne* [1956] 1 All ER 744, [1956] 1 WLR 303, CA; cf *Basildon District Council v JE Lesser
    (Properties) Ltd* [1985] QB 839, [1985] 1 All ER 20. The warranty may also be excluded by the
    surrounding circumstances: *Young and Marten Ltd v McManus Childs Ltd* [1969] 1 AC 454, [1968] 2 All
    ER 1169, HL; *Gloucestershire County Council v Richardson* [1969] 1 AC 480, [1968] 2 All ER 1181, HL.

8   *Brown v Norton* [1954] IR 34.

9   *King v Victor Parsons & Co* [1972] 2 All ER 625, [1972] 1 WLR 801 (not challenged on appeal [1973] 1
    All ER 206, [1973] 1 WLR 29, CA).

10 *Hancock v BW Brazier (Anerley) Ltd* [1966] 2 All ER 901, [1966] 1 WLR 1317, CA.

49. Statutory duty as to defective premises. A person who takes on work[1] for or
in connection with the building, conversion or enlargement of a dwelling owes a
statutory duty (additional to any duty imposed at common law[2]) to the person ordering
the work[3], and to every other person who acquires a legal or equitable interest in the
dwelling[4], to see that the work is done in a workmanlike or, as the case may be,
professional manner, with proper materials, so that the dwelling will be fit for habitation
when completed[5].

A person who takes on such work for another on terms that he is to do it in
accordance with instructions given by or on behalf of that other is, to the extent to which
he does it properly in accordance with those instructions, to be treated as discharging the
duty, except where he owes a duty to that other to warn him of any defects in the
instructions and fails to discharge that duty[6]. For this purpose a person is not treated as

having given instructions for the doing of work merely because he has agreed to the work being done in a specified manner, with specified materials or to a specified design[7].

The limitation period in respect of any cause of action arising out of any breach of the duty imposed by these provisions runs from the time when the dwelling is completed[8].

Where construction, repair, maintenance, demolition or any other work is done on or in relation to premises, any duty of care owed, because of the doing of the work, to persons who might reasonably be expected to be affected by defects in the state of the premises is not abated by the subsequent disposal[9] of the premises by the person who owed the duty[10].

Many new houses are now guaranteed against defects under the National House Building Council Scheme 1979[11]. Where a standard or common form notice of insurance cover is issued under the scheme, the statutory duty is excluded[12].

1   A person who (1) in the course of a business consisting of or including providing or arranging for the provision of dwellings or installations in them; or (2) in the exercise of a power of making such provision or arrangements conferred by or by virtue of any enactment, arranges for another to take on work for or in connection with the provision of a dwelling is treated for these purposes as included among the persons who have taken on the work: Defective Premises Act 1972 s 1(4). These provisions apply not only where a contractual obligation to work exists but also where the work is done without contractual obligation, or done voluntarily or done by the building owner himself: *Alexander v Mercouris* [1979] 3 All ER 305, [1979] 1 WLR 1270, CA.
2   Defective Premises Act 1972 s 6(2).
3   Ibid s 1(1)(a).
4   Ibid s 1(1)(b).
5   Ibid s 1(1). Any term of an agreement purporting to exclude or restrict the operation of any provision of the Defective Premises Act 1972 or any liability arising by virtue of any such provision is void: s 6(3). As to the limited application of these provisions to the Crown see s 5. See generally BUILDING CONTRACTS, ARCHITECTS, ENGINEERS AND SURVEYORS vol 4(2) (Reissue) para 375 et seq.
6   Ibid s 1(2).
7   Ibid s 1(3).
8   Ibid s 1(5). If any further work has been done to rectify work already done, the cause of action in respect of the further work is deemed to have accrued at the time the further work was finished: s 1(5). As to limitation periods see LIMITATION OF ACTIONS.
9   'Disposal' in relation to premises includes a letting, and an assignment or surrender of a tenancy, of the premises and the creation by contract of any other right to occupy them: ibid s 6(1).
10   Ibid s 3(1). Section 3 does not apply to disposals before 1974: see ss 3(2), 7(2).
11   This scheme comprises the documents listed in the House Building Standards (Approved Scheme etc) Order 1979, SI 1979/381, Schedule: art 2(1).
12   See the Defective Premises Act 1972 s 2; and BUILDING CONTRACTS, ARCHITECTS, ENGINEERS AND SURVEYORS vol 4(2) (Reissue) para 376. As to whether the benefit of the guarantee passes to subsequent purchasers see *Marchant v Caswell and Redgrave Ltd* (1976) 240 Estates Gazette 127 (applying the Law of Property Act 1925 s 78 (see LANDLORD AND TENANT vol 27(1) (Reissue) para 476; EQUITY vol 16 (Reissue) para 791)). It might be wise for the benefit to be expressly assigned.

50. Disclosure by the vendor. In special circumstances it may be the duty of the vendor to disclose matters which are known to himself, but which the purchaser has no means of discovering[1], such as a defect which will render the property useless to the purchaser for the purpose for which, to the vendor's knowledge, he wishes to acquire it[2]; or a notice served in respect of the property, knowledge of which is essential to enable a purchaser to estimate the value[3]. If the vendor fails to make disclosure, he cannot obtain specific performance and may be ordered to return the deposit[4].

1   See *Cook v Waugh* (1860) 2 Giff 201 at 207, where Stuart V–C said that it was a very well established doctrine that if a vendor or lessor is aware of some latent defect, and does not disclose it, the court will consider him as acting in bad faith; and Lord St Leonards treated non-disclosure of a latent defect of which the vendor was aware as preventing the contract from being binding either at law or in equity: see Sugden's Law of Vendors and Purchasers (14th Edn, 1862) 333. This view appears to have been

adopted by Joyce J in *Carlish v Salt* [1906] 1 Ch 335, relied on in *Sakkas v Donford Ltd* (1982) 46 P & CR 290 at 302 per Lord Grantchester. In its full extent, however, the obligation of disclosure exists only as regards latent defects of title: see T Cyprian Williams 'Non-disclosure, Upon the Sale of Land, of a Latent Defect Known to the Vendor' (1905–06) 50 Sol Jo 611. As regards other defects, the duty of disclosure does not arise merely out of the relation of vendor and purchaser; where it exists it arises from the special circumstances of the case, with the result that the court may either rescind the contract, or, without rescission, may refuse specific performance: see Fry *A Treatise on the Specific Performance of Contract* (6th Edn, 1921) 705. As to the return of the deposit where there is no rescission see note 4 infra.

2   See *Lucas v James* (1849) 7 Hare 410 at 418, where the character of the neighbouring houses made it impossible to use the house in question for a family residence. A similar question arose in *Hope v Walter* [1900] 1 Ch 257, CA, where the house was being used as a disorderly house by the tenant. In neither case was non-disclosure made the ground of the decision.

3   See *Carlish v Salt* [1906] 1 Ch 335 (party structure notice under London building legislation); *Beyfus v Lodge* [1925] Ch 350 (where notices to repair with schedules assessing the value of the repairs required to be done had been served under what is now the Law of Property Act 1925 s 146 (as amended) (see LANDLORD AND TENANT vol 27(1) (Reissue) para 513)). In both cases the notices affected the title to the property, and it does not appear to be the law that either vendor or purchaser is bound to disclose facts material to the value unless they relate to the title (see T Cyprian Williams 'Non-disclosure, Upon the Sale of Land, of a Latent Defect Known to the Vendor' (1905–06) 50 Sol Jo 611 at 613; and *Hill v Harris* [1965] 2 QB 601, [1965] 2 All ER 358, CA), but the vendor must be careful not to make any representation or give any warranty affecting the value of the property in the hands of the purchaser. As to other cases where a defect of quality also constituted a defect of title see *Re Puckett and Smith's Contract* [1902] 2 Ch 258, CA; *Shepherd v Croft* [1911] 1 Ch 521; *Re Belcham and Gawley's Contract* [1930] 1 Ch 56.

4   The effect of the non-disclosure may be to deprive the vendor of the special equitable relief of specific performance, but to leave the contract on foot, so that the purchaser cannot as of right recover his deposit: *Beyfus v Lodge* [1925] Ch 350 at 359 (criticised by Harpum 'Selling Without Title: A Vendor's Duty of Disclosure?' (1992) 108 LQR 280 at 328; and Harpum 'Exclusion Clauses and Contracts for the Sale of Land' [1992] 51 CLJ 263 at 300–301); *Re Scott and Alvarez's Contract, Scott v Alvarez* [1895] 2 Ch 603 at 612. However, the court can disregard this distinction and may, when it refuses specific performance, direct the return of the deposit: see the Law of Property Act 1925 s 49(2). When the result of the defect is to deprive the purchaser of the benefit of the property, or to make his enjoyment of it dependent on the payment of money which the vendor declines to pay, and there is no condition covering the defect, the purchaser is entitled to the return of the deposit: *Stevens v Adamson* (1818) 2 Stark 422; *Carlish v Salt* [1906] 1 Ch 335. As to the return of the deposit see paras 245–246 post.

51. Misdescription or misrepresentation as to quality.

The vendor is bound to deliver to the purchaser property corresponding in extent and quality to the property which, either by the description in the contract (including any particulars of sale), or by representations of fact[1] made by the vendor, the purchaser expected to get. Where, owing to a misdescription, the vendor fails to perform this duty, and the misdescription, although not proceeding from fraud, is material and substantial, affecting the subject matter of the contract to such an extent that it may reasonably be supposed that, but for the misdescription, the purchaser might never have entered into the contract at all, the contract may be avoided altogether, and if there is a clause of compensation, the purchaser is not bound to resort to it[2]. Where a representation is true at the time when it is made, but owing to change of circumstances becomes untrue before or at the time of completion, it is the vendor's duty to disclose the change of circumstances[3]. However, where the discrepancy between the property as offered by the vendor and the property which, by reason of the defect, the vendor is able to hand over is not such as to alter substantially the nature of the property, then the contract is enforced subject to payment of compensation by the vendor[4].

1   Ie as distinguished from expressions of opinion: see *Bisset v Wilkinson* [1927] AC 177, PC.

2   *Flight v Booth* (1834) 1 Bing NC 370 at 377 per Tindal CJ, where there was a substantial misdescription of leasehold property as regards permitted trades, and a condition providing compensation for errors, and rescission and recovery of the deposit was ordered. The case is stronger where the misrepresentation is made with intent to deceive and is therefore fraudulent: *Edwards v M'Leay* (1818) 2 Swan 287; *Small v*

Attwood (1832) You 407 at 460 (on appeal *Attwood v Small* (1838) 6 Cl & Fin 232 at 395, HL, per Lord Lyndhurst). As to misrepresentation without fraud see para 42 ante. As to conditions providing against error in description see para 110 et seq post.

3   *With v O'Flanagan* [1936] Ch 575, CA. See also MISREPRESENTATION AND FRAUD vol 31 (Reissue) paras 750, 754, 760. In *Wales v Wadham* [1977] 2 All ER 125, [1977] 1 WLR 199, it was held in a matrimonial case that where the original statement was an honest statement of future intention never to remarry there is no duty to disclose a change of intention. However, it is difficult to see why such facts do not fall within the principle of *With v O'Flanagan* supra.

4   The rule that, in case of substantial misdescription resulting in the purchaser not getting the property he contracted for, he will not be compelled to take compensation, is known as the rule in *Flight v Booth* (1834) 1 Bing NC 370. As to the rule see *Re Davis and Cavey* (1888) 40 ChD 601 at 608; *Jacobs v Revell* [1900] 2 Ch 858 at 864; *Re Puckett and Smith's Contract* [1902] 2 Ch 258 at 264, CA; *Shepherd v Croft* [1911] 1 Ch 521 at 527; *Lee v Rayson* [1917] 1 Ch 613 at 618. As to the principle that equity will interfere and give compensation where the misdescription does not constitute a substantial difference see *Halsey v Grant* (1806) 13 Ves 73 at 77; and SPECIFIC PERFORMANCE vol 44(1) (Reissue) para 959. As to conditions relating to compensation see para 110 et seq post.

52. Examples of misrepresentation or misdescription as to quality. The following have been held to be sufficient misrepresentations or misdescriptions to allow the purchaser to rescind the contract: that land is ripe for immediate development, or suitable for development, when there is a covered culvert running under it[1], or where special expense must be incurred before it can be used for building[2]; that a farm is in a high state of cultivation[3]; that premises are in good repair[4]; that drains are in good order[5]; that a house is not damp[6]; that a farm was lately in the occupation of a particular person at a specified annual rent when in fact the farm could not possibly be let for nearly that rent, and the person had been out of possession for nearly a year and a half[7]; that property has been valued by a certain surveyor at a specified sum[8]; that the timber on a timber estate averages a certain size[9]; that property subject to trading restrictions has been sold as business premises[10]; where property held on an underlease is described as leasehold[11]; and where a three storey building is described as offices when planning permission has been obtained to use only part of the building for office purposes[12]; and where a full description of rooms in a house failed to disclose that some of the rooms were subject to a closing order[13].

Where property described as shop premises was sold subject to the restrictions contained in a particular deed, so far as still subsisting, but the restrictions were not specified, although a copy of them was declared to be open to inspection and the purchaser was to be deemed to purchase with notice of them, whether or not he inspected the copy, an answer to requisitions which constituted an admission that there was a subsisting restriction on the user of the property except as private premises entitled the purchaser to refuse to complete on the ground of misdescription and to recover his deposit[14].

The following are examples of misdescription where the purchaser cannot repudiate the contract but can obtain compensation: where there is a deficiency in the area of the property agreed to be sold, but the purchaser will obtain substantially what he bargained for[15]; where an underground watercourse does not make the description of property as a residential property materially incorrect[16]; where the existence of two sewers running along one side of the premises and along the yard at the back, although materially affecting the description of the property, does not constitute a substantial difference from that agreed to be sold[17].

Compensation cannot be obtained where the misdescription is collateral to the contract and is proved by the vendor to have been made with reasonable grounds for belief in its truth; in such a case the purchaser's only remedy is rescission, unless a court in its discretion awards damages in lieu of rescission[18]. Where a vendor makes a false representation as to a material fact, it is for him to show, if he wishes to enforce the contract, that the purchaser did not rely upon the representation[19].

1   *Re Puckett and Smith's Contract* [1902] 2 Ch 258, CA.

2   *Baker v Moss* (1902) 66 JP 360.

3   *Dyer v Hargrave, Hargrave v Dyer* (1805) 10 Ves 505.

4   *Grant v Munt* (1815) Coop G 173; *Dyer v Hargrave, Hargrave v Dyer* (1805) 10 Ves 505; *Cree v Stone* (1907) Times, 10 May.

5   *Cree v Stone* (1907) Times, 10 May. In *de Lassalle v Guildford* [1901] 2 KB 215, CA, a lessee recovered damages for breach of a collateral warranty as to drains being in order, but dicta in this case as to the test for determining whether a statement amounts to a warranty were disapproved in *Heilbut, Symons & Co Ltd v Buckleton* [1913] AC 30 at 50, HL: see MISREPRESENTATION AND FRAUD vol 31 (Reissue) para 704. As to collateral warranties see CONTRACT vol 9(1) (Reissue) para 627.

6   *Strangways v Bishop* (1857) 29 LTOS 120.

7   *Dimmock v Hallett* (1866) 2 Ch App 21. See also *Lysney v Selby* (1705) 2 Ld Raym 1118; *Price v Macaulay* (1852) 2 De GM & G 339 (misrepresentations as to annual value); *Re Hurlbalt and Chaytor's Contract* (1888) 57 LJ Ch 421, where an honestly estimated annual value was not a misrepresentation. Cf *Re Ryan's Estate* (1868) IR 3 Eq 255.

8   *Buxton v Lister* (1746) 3 Atk 383 at 386. Cf *Abbott v Sworder* (1851) 4 De G & Sm 448 at 457, where the vendor was held not bound to disclose a recent valuation.

9   *Lord Brooke v Rounthwaite* (1846) 5 Hare 298 at 304. Cf *Lowndes v Lane* (1789) 2 Cox Eq Cas 363.

10 *Re Davis and Cavey* (1888) 40 ChD 601; *Charles Hunt Ltd v Palmer* [1931] 2 Ch 287; *Atlantic Estates plc v Ezekiel* [1991] 2 EGLR 202, [1991] EGCS 54, CA.

11 *Re Russ and Brown's Contract* [1934] Ch 34, CA. See also *Stanton v Tattersall* (1853) 1 Sm & G 529, where a house described as '58 Pall Mall, opposite Marlborough House' had no windows or frontage towards Pall Mall and could only be approached by a narrow passage from the street; *Leyland v Illingworth* (186C) 2 De GF & J 248, where the only water on premises described as 'well supplied with water' was that obtained from the local waterworks on payment of the water rate; *Jacobs v Revell* [1900] 2 Ch 858, where title was shown to only part of the premises; and *Lee v Rayson* [1917] 1 Ch 613, where there were misrepresentations as to the leases on which freehold property consisting of several houses was let. See also para 45 note 7 ante. A representation of water supply on the sale plan does not necessarily entitle the purchaser to the supply: *Fewster v Turner* (1842) 11 LJ Ch 161. As to misrepresentations with regard to one lot where a purchaser has separately acquired two lots at an auction see *Holliday v Lockwood* [1917] 1 Ch 47. There can be no rescission unless the purchases in effect form one contract or the enjoyment of the one is affected by the failure to obtain the other: *Holliday v Lockwood* supra.

12 *Laurence v Lexcourt Holdings Ltd* [1978] 2 All ER 810, [1978] 1 WLR 1128, where it was also held that the contract could be rescinded on the ground of fundamental mistake (but see the criticism of this latter ground in *William Sindall plc v Cambridgeshire County Council* [1994] 3 All ER 932, [1994] 1 WLR 1016, CA.

13 See *Registered Holdings Ltd v Kadri* (1972) 222 Estates Gazette 621.

14 *Simmons v Pennington & Son (a firm)* [1955] 1 All ER 240, [1955] 1 WLR 183, CA.

15 *Re Fawcett and Holmes' Contract* (1889) 42 ChD 150.

16 *Shepherd v Croft* [1911] 1 Ch 521, where the vendors waived a clause in the contract excluding compensation.

17 *Re Belcham and Gawley's Contract* [1930] 1 Ch 56, following *Re Brewer and Hankins' Contract* (1899) 80 LT 127, CA, where a public sewer ran under the garden of the property, but no building on it was possible.

18 *Rutherford v Acton-Adams* [1915] AC 866, PC, as modified by the Misrepresentation Act 1967 s 2 (see MISREPRESENTATION AND FRAUD vol 31 (Reissue) para 834). See also para 42 ante.

19 *Redgrave v Hurd* (1881) 20 ChD 1, CA. See also *Attwood v Small* (1838) 6 Cl & Fin 232, HL; *Clapham v Shillito* (1844) 7 Beav 146; *Roots v Snelling* (1883) 48 LT 216. It is insufficient for the vendor to offer the means of verification: *Redgrave v Hurd* supra at 22–23 per Baggallay LJ; *Stanley v M'Gauran* (1882) 11 LR Ir 314 at 331, Ir CA. As to inducement as a factor in misrepresentation see generally MISREPRESENTATION AND FRAUD vol 31 (Reissue) para 765 et seq. As to the extent to which inducement is a question of law or a question of fact see MISREPRESENTATION AND FRAUD vol 31 (Reissue) para 766.

53.   Misrepresentation by agent. The principle underlying liability for misrepresentation by an agent acting in the course of his employment is that the principal and agent are one, and, subject to the qualification mentioned later[1], it does not signify which of them made the misrepresentation or which of them possessed the guilty knowledge[2]. It follows that misrepresentation by an agent in the course of his employment has the same effect as if it were made by the principal, even though made without his knowledge or approval and whether or not made for the principal's benefit[3], for an agent employed to find a purchaser has implied authority to describe the nature and the value of the property[4] and to state the nature of any restrictive covenants which affect it[5]. The purchaser must prove that either the vendor or his agent was aware of the true facts[6], but, in the absence of fraud on the part of the principal, knowledge by him of facts which render false a statement made innocently by his agent does not render the principal guilty of fraudulent misrepresentation[7]. Misrepresentation by the agent as to the identity of his principal will vitiate the contract only where it is of importance to the other party to know with whom he is contracting, so that he would not have entered into the contract if he had known who was the agent's principal[8]. The principal may restrict the implied or ostensible authority which his agent would otherwise have, by bringing the restriction to the notice of the other contracting party. A misrepresentation made by the agent outside his authority as so restricted will not bind the principal[9].

1   See the text and note 7 infra.
2   *S Pearson & Son Ltd v Dublin Corpn* [1907] AC 351 at 354, HL; and see AGENCY vol 1(2) (Reissue) para 164.
3   *Lloyd v Grace Smith & Co* [1912] AC 716, HL.
4   *Mullens v Miller* (1882) 22 ChD 194; *Smith v Land and House Property Corpn* (1884) 28 ChD 7 at 13, CA.
5   *Richardson v Williamson and Lawson* (1871) LR 6 QB 276; *West London Commercial Bank Ltd v Kitson* (1884) 13 QBD 360, CA; *Wauton v Coppard* [1899] 1 Ch 92.
6   *S Pearson & Son Ltd v Dublin Corpn* [1907] AC 351, HL. See also *National Exchange Co of Glasgow v Drew and Dick* (1855) 2 Macq 103 at 145–146; *Ludgater v Love* (1881) 44 LT 694, CA.
7   *Armstrong v Strain* [1952] 1 KB 232, [1952] 1 All ER 139, CA, approving the decision in *Gordon Hill Trust Ltd v Segall* [1941] 2 All ER 379, CA, and observations of Atkinson J in *Anglo-Scottish Beet Sugar Corpn Ltd v Spalding UDC* [1937] 2 KB 607 at 625, [1937] 3 All ER 335 at 345, and criticising *London County Freehold and Leasehold Properties Ltd v Berkeley Property and Investment Co Ltd* [1936] 2 All ER 1039, CA. It is not possible to add to the innocent misstatement of an agent the fact that its falsity is known to another agent or the principal: *Armstrong v Strain* supra. However, this does not prevent its being shown that the agent made the statement without belief in its truth or recklessly, not caring whether it was true or false. It would appear, too, that fraud may be proved where a false statement is handed on by an innocent agent provided that the maker of the statement (who may be either the principal or an agent) knows that it is false and is going to be handed on. See further MISREPRESENTATION AND FRAUD vol 31 (Reissue) para 797.
8   *Archer v Stone* (1898) 78 LT 34; *Nash v Dix* (1898) 78 LT 445; *Said v Butt* [1920] 3 KB 497.
9   *Overbrooke Estates Ltd v Glencombe Properties Ltd* [1974] 3 All ER 511, [1974] 1 WLR 1335. Such a limitation of authority is not affected by the Misrepresentation Act 1967 s 3 (as substituted) (see MISREPRESENTATION AND FRAUD vol 31 (Reissue) para 803): see *Overbrooke Estates Ltd v Glencombe Properties Ltd* supra; *Collins v Howell-Jones* (1980) 259 Estates Gazette 331, CA.

B.   DEFECTS OF TITLE

54.   Vendor's interest. In the absence of any indication to the contrary[1], an agreement to sell land implies that the whole of the vendor's interest in the land is the subject of the agreement[2], and that that interest is an estate in fee simple[3] free from incumbrances[4], unless the purchaser had notice, before entering into the contract, that the title which the vendor was able to give was subject to limitations or incumbrances which the vendor could not remove[5]. Such notice does not affect the liability of a vendor who expressly agrees to show a good title if the notice can be proved only by the admission of oral evidence to contradict the written contract[6].

Where the incumbrance is one (such as a registered local land charge[7]) of which the purchaser is deemed by statute to have actual notice[8], it seems that the purchaser must complete subject to the incumbrance, even though the vendor has contracted to sell free from incumbrances[9], unless the vendor himself, or his solicitor[10], also has actual knowledge of the registered charge[11]. However, in the case of incumbrances registered under the Land Charges Act 1972, the question of the purchaser's knowledge is to be determined without reference to the statutory provision[12] which deems him to have actual notice[13], and where an innocent purchaser would in such a case have a remedy against the vendor, any provision of the contract is void so far as it purports to exclude or restrict the purchaser's remedy[14].

1   If the vendor has sold only such estate and interest as he has in the land, this is all that he can be required to transfer. Hence, if at the date of a lease land is subject to a mortgage, and the lease contains an option for the lessee to purchase for a specified sum all the lessor's estate and interest at the date of the lease, the option extends only to the equity of redemption, and, in exercising the option, the lessee cannot require the lessor to pay off the mortgage: *Fowler v Willis* [1922] 2 Ch 514. As to the distinction between the subject matter of the sale (ie what the vendor has agreed to sell) and the vendor's duty to prove a good title to the sale see *Barclay's Bank plc v Weeks Legg & Dean (a firm)* [1998] 3 All ER 213 at 221–222, [1998] 3 WLR 656 at 666–668, CA, per Millett J.

2   *Bower v Cooper* (1843) 2 Hare 408. On the sale of a leasehold the fact that the vendor's interest has been forfeited before contract entitles the purchaser to treat the contract as repudiated: *Pips (Leisure Productions) Ltd v Walton* (1980) 43 P & CR 415.

3   *Hughes v Parker* (1841) 8 M & W 244; *Cox v Middleton* (1854) 2 Drew 209 at 216.

4   *Phillips v Caldcleugh* (1868) LR 4 QB 159; *Cato v Thompson* (1882) 9 QBD 616, CA.

5   *Cowley v Watts* (1853) 17 Jur 172; *Cox v Middleton* (1854) 2 Drew 209 at 216 per Kindersley V-C; *Re Gloag and Miller's Contract* (1883) 23 ChD 320 at 327 per Fry J; *Ellis v Rogers* (1885) 29 ChD 661, CA; *Timmins v Moreland Street Property Co Ltd* [1958] Ch 110 at 132, [1957] 3 All ER 265 at 277, CA. Evidence of the purchaser's knowledge of an incurable defect of title cannot be given on an inquiry as to title under a vendor's order for specific performance; such evidence can be given only at the trial: *McGrory v Alderdale Estate Co Ltd* [1918] AC 503, HL.

6   *Cato v Thompson* (1882) 9 QBD 616, CA; *Re Gloag and Miller's Contract* (1883) 23 ChD 320. Even if the purchaser agrees to accept a defective title, the vendor is not entitled to have the usual covenants for title restricted: *Re Geraghty and Lyon's Contract* (1919) 53 ILT 57.

7   Registration will be under the Local Land Charges Act 1975: see LAND CHARGES vol 26 (Reissue) para 571 et seq. As to the making of pre-contract searches for such charges see para 13 ante.

8   Ie under the Law of Property Act 1925 s 198(1) (as amended): see LAND CHARGES vol 26 (Reissue) para 516. See also EQUITY vol 16 (Reissue) para 767 et seq.

9   *Re Forsey and Hollebone's Contract* [1927] 2 Ch 379 at 387, obiter, per Eve J (not considered on appeal at [1927] 2 Ch 387, CA), criticised by Millett J in *Rignall Developments Ltd v Halil* [1988] Ch 190 at 194, 203, [1987] 3 All ER 170 at 172, 178. See also para 123 note 5 post.

10 See para 3 ante.

11 See *Rignall Developments Ltd v Halil* [1988] Ch 190, [1987] 3 All ER 170.

12 Ie the Law of Property Act 1925 s 198(1) (as amended): see LAND CHARGES vol 26 (Reissue) para 516. See also EQUITY vol 16 (Reissue) para 767 et seq.

13 Law of Property Act 1969 s 24(1); Land Charges Act 1972 s 18(6). For this purpose the knowledge acquired in the course of a transaction by a person who is acting in it as counsel or as solicitor or other agent for another is to be treated as knowledge of the other: Law of Property Act 1969 s 24(4).

14 See ibid s 24(2).

55. Vendor's duty to disclose defects of title. Since a vendor's title to land is exclusively within his own knowledge, he is bound to disclose all latent defects in his title to an intending purchaser. If a purchaser subsequently becomes aware of an irremovable defect of title[1] which the vendor did not disclose to him before entering into the contract, he may rescind the contract[2] or resist its specific performance on that ground, even though the vendor may have sought to protect himself by imposing misleading conditions as to the title or proof of title to which the purchaser is entitled[3]. Whether the sale is made by auction or by private treaty, the purchaser is under no obligation to make inquiry as to defects in the vendor's title, but it is the vendor's duty to disclose all that is necessary for his own protection[4]. The vendor's disclosure should be frank and full, and it is not sufficient for him to make ambiguous or misleading statements[5]. If he wishes to prevent a purchaser from objecting to a defect he must do so in plain terms, stating clearly the exact nature of the defect to which the purchaser is not to make objection[6].

The Standard Conditions of Sale now in general use limit the vendor's duty of disclosure[7] by providing that the property is sold subject to the following incumbrances[8]: (1) those mentioned in the agreement[9]; (2) those discoverable by inspection of the property before the contract[10]; (3) those the vendor does not and could not know about; (4) entries made before the date of the contract in any public register except those maintained by Her Majesty's Land Registry[11] or its Land Charges Department[12] or by Companies House[13]; (5) any public requirements[14].

In certain cases the contract is deemed to extend beyond the vendor's actual interest. If the vendor of a mortgage term has power to transfer the fee simple, or, in the case of a mortgage sub-term, the leasehold reversion, the contract is deemed to extend to the fee simple or the leasehold reversion[15]. If the vendor of an equitable interest capable of existing as a legal estate has power to vest, or to require to be vested, such a legal estate in himself or in the purchaser[16], the contract is deemed to extend to the legal estate[17]. If the vendor of an entailed interest in possession has power to vest or to require to be vested in himself or in the purchaser the fee simple (or if the entailed interest is an interest in a term of years absolute, the term), the contract is deemed to extend to the fee simple or the term of years absolute[18].

1   As to the distinction between removable and irremovable defects see para 44 ante; and as to the position with regard to defects of which the purchaser is by statute deemed to have actual notice see para 54 ante.
2   See *Peyman v Lanjani* [1985] Ch 457 at 496–497, [1984] 3 All ER 703 at 731, CA, where this passage was cited with approval by Slade LJ. See also paras 44 ante, 57, 174–176 post.
3   See eg *Heywood v Mallalieu* (1883) 25 ChD 357; *Nottingham Patent Brick and Tile Co v Butler* (1886) 16 QBD 778, CA (applied in *Rignall Developments Ltd v Halil* [1988] Ch 190, [1987] 3 All ER 170); *Re Haedicke and Lipski's Contract* [1901] 2 Ch 666; *Becker v Partridge* [1966] 2 QB 155, [1966] 2 All ER 266, CA.
4   *Reeve v Berridge* (1888) 20 QBD 523 at 528, CA; *Re White and Smith's Contract* [1896] 1 Ch 637 at 643. See also dicta in *Carlish v Salt* [1906] 1 Ch 335 at 341. See also *Wilson v Allen* (1820) 1 Jac & W 611 at 623 per Plumer MR; *Flood v Pritchard* (1879) 40 LT 873 at 875 per Fry J; *Brewer v Brown* (1884) 28 ChD 309; *Dougherty v Oates* (1900) 45 Sol Jo 119. If, on a sale of registered land, the title is possessory only, this should be disclosed before the contract: *Re Brine and Davies' Contract* [1935] Ch 388; and see LAND REGISTRATION vol 26 (Reissue) para 740.
5   *Baskcomb v Beckwith* (1869) LR 8 Eq 100 at 109; *Re Banister, Broad v Munton* (1879) 12 ChD 131 at 136 per Fry J (on appeal (1879) 12 ChD 131); *Re Marsh and Earl Granville* (1882) 24 ChD 11 at 15 per Fry J. See also MISREPRESENTATION AND FRAUD vol 31 (Reissue) paras 749–750.
6   As to misleading conditions see para 83 post.
7   See the Standard Conditions of Sale (3rd Edn); and para 1 note 9 ante. As to the duty of the purchaser to satisfy himself as to incumbrances and the vendor's duty of disclosure see *Celsteel Ltd v Alton House Holdings Ltd (No 2)* [1986] 1 All ER 598 at 607 (not reported on this point at [1986] 1 WLR 666); affd [1987] 2 All ER 240, [1987] 1 WLR 291, CA (not mentioning the point).
8   See the Standard Conditions of Sale (3rd Edn), conditions 3.1.1–3.1.2.
9   'Agreement' means the contractual document which incorporates these conditions, with or without amendment: Standard Conditions of Sale (3rd Edn), condition 1.1.1(b).
10 'Contract' means the bargain between the vendor and the purchaser of which these conditions, with or without amendment, form part: Standard Conditions of Sale (3rd Edn), condition 1.1.1(f).
11 As to Her Majesty's Land Registry see LAND REGISTRATION vol 26 (Reissue) para 712.
12 As to Her Majesty's Land Charges Department see LAND CHARGES vol 26 (Reissue) para 502; LAND REGISTRATION vol 26 (Reissue) paras 1201–1211.
13 As to registration of charges at Companies House see COMPANIES vol 7(2) (1996 Reissue) para 1296 et seq.
14 Standard Conditions of Sale (3rd Edn), condition 3.1.2(a)–(e). 'Public requirement' means any notice, order or proposal given or made (whether before or after the date of the contract) by a body acting on statutory authority: condition 1.1.1(j).
15 Law of Property Act 1925 s 42(4)(i).
16 'Purchaser' means a purchaser in good faith for valuable consideration and includes a lessee, mortgagee or other person who for valuable consideration acquires an interest in property except that in ibid Pt I (ss 1–39) (as amended) and elsewhere where so expressly provided 'purchaser' only means a person who acquires an interest in or charge on property for money or money's worth; and in reference to a legal estate includes a

chargee by way of legal mortgage; and where the context so requires 'purchaser' includes an intending purchaser; 'purchase' has a meaning corresponding with that of 'purchaser'; and 'valuable consideration' includes marriage but does not include a nominal consideration in money: s 205(1)(xxi).

17 Ibid s 42(4)(ii).

18 Ibid s 42(4)(iii). See also *Elliott and H Elliott (Builders) Ltd v Pierson* [1948] Ch 452, [1948] 1 All ER 939, where the vendor, who controlled a company as shareholder and sole director, contracted to sell the fee simple when he had only a leasehold interest in the land, the fee simple being vested in the company. The purchaser, on discovering these facts, purported to repudiate, but it was held that, as the vendor could compel the company to transfer, he could obtain specific performance.

56. Purchaser's remedies. The vendor's duty to disclose is absolute, and his ignorance of the defect is no excuse[1]. If the defect is substantial the purchaser may repudiate or obtain specific performance with a reduction in the price[2], whereas the vendor cannot enforce the contract[3]. If the defect is not substantial, the purchaser's remedy is in damages, and the vendor can enforce the contract but with a reduction in the price[4]. If the vendor with intent to defraud conceals from the purchaser any instrument or incumbrance material to the title[5], or falsifies any pedigree upon which the title may depend[6], he commits a criminal offence[7] and is also liable to the purchaser in damages[8].

1   *Re Brewer and Hankins' Contract* (1899) 80 LT 127, CA. Cf the provisions in the Standard Conditions of Sale (3rd Edn): see para 55 ante. As to the Standard Conditions of Sale see para 1 note 9 ante. There are circumstances in which the vendor's knowledge may be material; for example his knowledge may preclude the vendor from relying on a condition of sale covering the defect and entitle the purchaser to rescind (*Re Banister, Broad v Munton* (1879) 12 ChD 131, CA; *Nottingham Patent Brick and Tile Co v Butler* (1886) 16 QBD 778, CA (applied in *Rignall Developments Ltd v Halil* [1988] Ch 190, [1987] 3 All ER 170); and the vendor's knowledge may preclude him from relying on a condition of sale permitting rescission where requisitions are persisted in (see eg *Baines v Tweddle* [1959] Ch 679, [1959] 2 All ER 724, CA; and para 104 post). See also *William Sindall plc v Cambridgeshire County Council* [1994] 3 All ER 932, [1994] 1 WLR 1016, CA.

2   *Rudd v Lascelles* [1900] 1 Ch 815.

3   *Phillips v Caldcleugh* (1868) LR 4 QB 159.

4   *Re Brewer and Hankins' Contract* (1899) 80 LT 127, CA; *Re Belcham and Gawley's Contract* [1930] 1 Ch 56.

5   See the Law of Property Act 1925 s 183(1)(a); and para 149 post.

6   See ibid s 183(1)(b); and para 149 post.

7   See ibid s 183(1); para 149 post; and CRIMINAL LAW, EVIDENCE AND PROCEDURE vol 11(1) (Reissue) para 574. No prosecution under s 183 can be commenced without the leave of the Attorney General: s 183(4). Notice of any application for leave to prosecute must be given to the person intended to be prosecuted: s 183(5).

8   See ibid s 183(2); and para 149 post. In estimating the amount of damages where property is recovered from the purchaser, regard must be had to any expenditure by him in improvements of the land: s 183(3). The action for damages lies only on proof of an intent to defraud: *District Bank Ltd v Luigi Grill Ltd* [1943] Ch 78, [1943] 1 All ER 136.

57. What amounts to a defect of title. Any fact calculated to prevent the purchaser obtaining such a title to the property as he was led to expect constitutes a defect of title[1]. The following are examples of defects of title: where title is to be shown for less than the full statutory period[2], the fact that the deed forming the stipulated root of title is a voluntary one upon which ordinarily there would not have been an investigation of the title[3]; the existence or alleged existence of an easement over the property[4], or of covenants restricting its use and enjoyment[5]; in the case of leasehold property, the onerous or unusual nature of the covenants in the lease under which the property is held[6]; the existence of restrictions as to the use for certain trades of premises described as leasehold business premises[7], or of a covenant to expend a specified sum in building within a limited time on land described in general terms as freehold building land[8], or of a party wall notice[9], and an award made under it imposing a pecuniary liability on the owner of the property sold[10]. Similarly, it is a defect of title if the maxim *cuius est solum* *eius est usque ad coelum et ad inferos*[11] is not applicable to the property sold owing to the vendor's title not extending to an underground cellar[12] or to the subjacent minerals[13], or owing to a third person having a right to overhang part of the property[14]. All such matters must be disclosed by the vendor[15].

On the other hand, a vendor has been held to have shown a good title despite failing to disclose a contract for the sale of the land made some 60 years earlier[16].

1   See *Denne v Light* (1857) 8 De GM & G 774, where it appeared uncertain whether any means of entering at all times upon the piece of agricultural land agreed to be sold would be conferred upon the purchaser; *Langford v Selmes* (1857) 3 K & J 220 at 225, 229 per Page Wood V-C, where the purchaser of freehold ground rents would not have been able to employ the ordinary remedies for their recovery. Cf *Stanton v Tattersall* (1853) 1 Sm & G 529; and see para 52 note 11 ante.

2   Ie 15 years: see para 139 post.

3   *Re Marsh and Earl Granville* (1883) 24 ChD 11, CA.

4   *Heywood v Mallalieu* (1883) 25 ChD 357; *Yandle & Sons v Sutton* [1922] 2 Ch 199. Cf *Burnell v Brown* (1820) 1 Jac & W 168 at 172 (undisclosed reservation of right of sporting); *Gibson v Spurrier* (1795) Peake Add Cas 49 (right of common); *Shackleton v Sutcliffe* (1847) 1 De G & Sm 609 (easement of watercourse).

5   *Nottingham Patent Brick and Tile Co v Butler* (1886) 16 QBD 778, CA. See also *Bristow v Wood* (1844) 1 Coll 480; *Phillips v Caldcleugh* (1868) LR 4 QB 159; *Re Judge and Sheridan's Contract* (1907) 96 LT 451; *Pemsel and Wilson v Tucker* [1907] 2 Ch 191 (covenant with neighbour not to do anything to prejudice the right of light to respective properties); *Re Stone and Saville's Contract* [1963] 1 All ER 353, [1963] 1 WLR 163, CA; and cf *Andrew v Aitken* (1882) 22 ChD 218; *Cato v Thompson* (1882) 9 QBD 616, CA. Restrictive covenants (other than covenants between lessor and lessee) entered into after 1925 are registrable as land charges (see LAND CHARGES vol 26 (Reissue) para 535), and the registration of a restrictive covenant as a land charge constitutes actual notice to all the world (see the Law of Property Act 1925 s 198(1) (as amended); and LAND CHARGES vol 26 (Reissue) para 516; see also EQUITY vol 16 (Reissue) para 767 et seq). Failure to register makes the contract void against a purchaser of the legal estate for money or money's worth: see the Land Charges Act 1972 s 4(6) (as amended); and LAND CHARGES vol 26 (Reissue) para 543. If the agreement states that any part of the property is sold subject to a lease, the purchaser is to indemnify the vendor against all claims arising from the lease after actual completion; this includes claims which are unenforceable against a purchaser for want of registration: Standard Conditions of Sale (3rd Edn), conditions 3.3.1, 3.3.2(d). For the meaning of 'agreement' see para 55 note 9 ante. 'Lease' includes sub-lease, tenancy and agreement for a lease or sub-lease: condition 1.1.1(h). If after completion the vendor will remain bound by any obligation affecting the property, but the law does not imply any covenant by the purchaser to indemnify the vendor against liability for future breaches of it, the purchaser is to covenant in the transfer to indemnify the vendor against liability for any future breach of the obligation and to perform it from then on: condition 4.5.4(a). As to the Standard Conditions of Sale see para 1 note 9 ante.

6   *Reeve v Berridge* (1888) 20 QBD 523, CA; see para 60 post; and LANDLORD AND TENANT vol 27(1) (Reissue) para 62.

7   *Re Davis and Cavey* (1888) 40 ChD 601; *Charles Hunt Ltd v Palmer* [1931] 2 Ch 287; *Atlantic Estates plc v Ezekiel* [1991] 2 EGLR 202, [1991] EGCS 54, CA.

8   *Dougherty v Oates* (1900) 45 Sol Jo 119.

9   See *Carlish v Salt* [1906] 1 Ch 335. As to party wall notices see BOUNDARIES.

10   *Carlish v Salt* [1906] 1 Ch 335; but cf *Re Leyland and Taylor's Contract* [1900] 2 Ch 625, CA, where a notice was served on the vendor by the local highways authority, requiring him to make up a private street. He did not disclose the notice, but the work was not executed or the expense incurred until after completion of the purchase. As to a dormant order for closing a street see *Barnes v Cadogan Developments Ltd* [1930] 1 Ch 479.

11   See MINES, MINERALS AND QUARRIES vol 31 (Reissue) para 20 et seq; REAL PROPERTY vol 39(2) (Reissue) para 76.

12   *Whittington v Corder* (1852) 16 Jur 1034.

13   *Upperton v Nickolson* (1871) 6 Ch App 436 at 444; *Bellamy v Debenham* [1891] 1 Ch 412, CA. Cf *Seaman v Vawdrey* (1810) 16 Ves 390; *Ramsden v Hurst* (1858) 27 LJ Ch 482.

14   *Pope v Garland* (1841) 4 Y & C Ex 394 at 403. Cf *Laybourn v Gridley* [1892] 2 Ch 53.

15   If the vendor states the effect of a deed, he is bound by his statement; if instead of doing so he offers the deed for inspection the risk is on the purchaser: *Cox v Coventon* (1862) 31 Beav 378 at 388.

16   See *MEPC Ltd v Christian-Edwards* [1981] AC 205, [1979] 3 All ER 752, HL.

58. Existing tenancies. In the absence of an intimation to the contrary, a purchaser is entitled to assume that property offered for sale is in hand, so that he will obtain possession of the property on completion[1]; consequently, any existing lease or tenancy must be mentioned in the particulars or referred to in the agreement for sale[2]. The information as to past or existing tenancies must not be misleading[3], for example by stating the rent paid by the last tenant and implying, contrary to the fact, that a similar rent can be obtained at the time of the sale[4], or by stating the existing tenancies without mentioning that the tenants have given notice to quit[5], or by stating that the property is sold with the benefit of leases containing certain covenants without stating that the covenants are not enforceable[6]. On a sale of agricultural land subject to a tenancy, where particulars of the tenancy are given, the fact that the tenant has made improvements which will entitle him to compensation need not be specifically mentioned[7].

1 As to vacant possession see para 123 post.

2 *Hughes v Jones* (1861) 3 De GF & J 307; *Edwards v Wickwar* (1865) LR 1 Eq 68; *Cook v Taylor* [1942] Ch 349 at 352, [1942] 2 All ER 85 at 87; *Re Crosby's Contract, Crosby v Houghton* [1949] 1 All ER 830. Cf *Royal Bristol Permanent Building Society v Bomash* (1887) 35 ChD 390 at 394, where, on a sale by mortgagees, the mortgagor was in possession at the time fixed for completion and remained so until turned out by the sheriff more than a month later.

3 *Lachlan v Reynolds* (1853) Kay 52; *Farebrother v Gibson* (1857) 1 De G & J 602; *Swaisland v Dearsley* (1861) 29 Beav 430; *Re Edwards to Daniel Sykes & Co Ltd* (1890) 62 LT 445; and see *Lee v Rayson* [1917] 1 Ch 613, where an inaccurate statement was made as to the ground rents of leases affecting a number of freehold houses. A certificate of disrepair and consequent abatement of rent must be disclosed: *Re Englefield Holdings Ltd and Sinclair's Contract* [1962] 3 All ER 503, [1962] 1 WLR 1119; but see the Standard Conditions of Sale (3rd Edn) which provide that if the agreement states that any part of the property is sold subject to a lease, the vendor takes no responsibility for what rent is lawfully recoverable, nor for whether or how any legislation affects the lease: condition 3.3.2(e). For the meaning of 'agreement' see para 55 note 9 ante; and for the meaning of 'lease' see para 57 note 5 ante. As to the Standard Conditions of Sale see para 1 note 9 ante.

4 *Dimmock v Hallett* (1866) 2 Ch App 21: see para 52 text and note 7 ante.

5 *Dimmock v Hallett* (1866) 2 Ch App 21 at 28, 30. See also *Re Englefield Holdings Ltd and Sinclair's Contract* [1962] 3 All ER 503 at 505, [1962] 1 WLR 1119 at 1122 per Pennycuick J; and *Pagebar Properties Ltd v Derby Investment Holdings Ltd* [1973] 1 All ER 65 at 68, [1972] 1 WLR 1500 at 1503 per Goulding J.

6 *Flint v Woodin* (1852) 9 Hare 618 at 621.

7 *Re Earl of Derby and Fergusson's Contract* [1912] 1 Ch 479: see AGRICULTURE vol 1(2) (Reissue) para 378. As to conditions as to the payment of the outgoing tenant's valuation see para 89 post.

59. Leasehold property. Where the subject matter of the contract is a leasehold interest, the vendor must make it clear whether the interest he is selling is created by an original lease or an underlease[1], although it does not appear to be material to distinguish between an underlease and a sub-underlease[2]. Where the premises sold are held under a lease comprising other property[3], or are held by underlease derived from a head lease which comprises other property[4], these are material facts which must be disclosed[5]. Further, where the lease contains the usual covenant to deliver up in repair at the expiration of the term, and part of the demised buildings has been demolished[6], or where underleases have been granted not containing the same covenants as the head lease under which the interest agreed to be sold is derived[7], these facts must be stated. A rent review notice served by the lessor must be disclosed[8].

1 *Madeley v Booth* (1848) 2 De G & Sm 718; *Henderson v Hudson* (1867) 15 WR 860; *Re Beyfus and Masters's Contract* (1888) 39 ChD 110, CA. See also *Hayford v Criddle* (1855) 22 Beav 477 at 480 per Romilly MR; *Brumfit v Morton* (1857) 3 Jur NS 1198 at 1200 per Stuart V-C; *Flood v Pritchard* (1879) 40 LT 873; and cf *Bartlett v Salmon* (1855) 6 De GM & G 33; *Camberwell and South London Building Society v Holloway* (1879) 13 ChD 754; *Waring v Scotland* (1888) 57 LJ Ch 1016; *Re Russ and Brown's Contract* [1934] Ch 34, CA; *Cunningham v Shackleton* (1935) 79 Sol Jo 381. In *Jones v Rimmer* (1880) 14 ChD 588, CA, on a sale of

leaseholds held under a corporation which usually reserved only a nominal rent, no mention of the ground rent in fact payable was made, and the purchaser was held entitled to be discharged. Where a head lease has been disclaimed on bankruptcy, an underlease of part of the property comprised in it can still be properly described as an underlease: *Re Thompson and Cottrell's Contract* [1943] Ch 97, [1943] 1 All ER 169.

2 *Becker v Partridge* [1966] 2 QB 155 at 170, [1966] 2 All ER 266 at 270, CA, per Danckwerts LJ.

3 *Sheard v Venables* (1867) 36 LJ Ch 922. Cf *Tomkins v White* (1806) 3 Smith KB 435; *Warren v Richardson* (1830) You 1; *Leuty v Hillas* (1858) 2 De G & J 110 at 122 per Lord Cranworth LC. See also *Re Boulton and Cullingford's Contract* (1893) 37 Sol Jo 248, CA, where six houses, in fact held under one lease at a rent of £24, were described as held at ground rents of £4 each.

4 *Darlington v Hamilton* (1854) Kay 550 at 558; *Creswell v Davidson* (1887) 56 LT 811; *Re Lloyds Bank Ltd, and Lillington's Contract* [1912] 1 Ch 601. See also *Taylor v Martindale* (1842) 1 Y & C Ch Cas 658.

5 Such disclosure may not be necessary where the property sold is part of a house and it is obvious that the whole of the house would almost certainly be comprised in a head lease: *Becker v Partridge* [1966] 2 QB 155, [1966] 2 All ER 266, CA.

6 *Granger v Worms* (1814) 4 Camp 83. Cf *Re Taunton and West of England Perpetual Benefit Building Society and Roberts' Contract* [1912] 2 Ch 381. See also *Re Martin, ex p Dixon (Trustee) v Tucker* (1912) 106 LT 381, where it was held that a lessee who has rendered his lease liable to forfeiture by a continuing breach of covenant cannot make a good title under an open contract even though the landlord has accepted the rent; *Pips (Leisure Productions) Ltd v Walton* (1982) 43 P & CR 415. As to the performance of leasehold covenants see paras 98–99 post.

7 *Waring v Hoggart* (1824) Ry & M 39; *Darlington v Hamilton* (1854) Kay 550 at 559. As to a statutory duty to give certain information about a subtenancy derived out of a tenancy extended under the Leasehold Reform Act 1967 see s 16(6), (8); and LANDLORD AND TENANT vol 27(2) (Reissue) para 1333.

8 See *F and H Entertainments Ltd v Leisure Entertainment Ltd* (1976) 120 Sol Jo 331, 240 Estates Gazette 455.

60. Unusual covenants in leases.

Where leasehold property is held subject to any onerous or unusual covenants[1], the vendor must either disclose to the purchaser their existence and nature or give him a reasonable opportunity of inspecting the lease or other document containing the covenants before he enters into the contract[2]. A stipulation in the contract that the vendor's title is accepted does not enable a vendor to compel a purchaser to complete the contract where neither of these courses has been taken[3]. The question whether in any particular case the vendor has given the purchaser such a reasonable opportunity of inspection as to discharge the duty of disclosure is one of fact[4].

1 As to unusual covenants see LANDLORD AND TENANT vol 27(1) (Reissue) para 62.

2 *Reeve v Berridge* (1888) 20 QBD 523, CA; *Re White and Smith's Contract* [1896] 1 Ch 637; *Re Haedicke and Lipski's Contract* [1901] 2 Ch 666; *Molyneux v Hawtrey* [1903] 2 KB 487, CA. A covenant by the lessee to pay the costs and expenses of a notice prior to re-entry for a forfeiture under the Law of Property Act 1925 s 146 (as amended) (see LANDLORD AND TENANT vol 27(1) (Reissue) para 513), is an onerous covenant in the case of a new house let for a long term at a moderate ground rent: *Allen v Smith* [1924] 2 Ch 308. As to what are usual covenants in a lease see LANDLORD AND TENANT vol 27(1) (Reissue) para 61; and cf *Jones v Edney* (1812) 3 Camp 285, where leasehold premises were described as a 'free public house'; the auctioneer read over the lease at the auction, including a covenant making the premises a tied house, but said that the covenant was not enforceable, and the purchaser was entitled to rescission. See also *Flight v Booth* (1834) 1 Bing NC 370; *Bentley v Craven* (1853) 17 Beav 204, where the lease did not in fact contain a restriction stated in the particulars, and an order for completion was refused until the result of a suit to rectify the lease by introducing the restriction was known.

3 *Re Haedicke and Lipski's Contract* [1901] 2 Ch 666; *Becker v Partridge* [1966] 2 QB 155, [1966] 2 All ER 266, CA; and see para 94 post.

4 *Cosser v Collinge* (1832) 3 My & K 283; *Brumfit v Morton* (1857) 3 Jur NS 1198 at 1202 per Stuart V-C; *Hyde v Warden* (1877) 3 Ex D 72 at 80, CA; *Bank of Ireland v Brookfield Linen Co* (1884) 15 LR Ir 37; *Dougherty v Oates* (1900) 45 Sol Jo 119 at 120, where Buckley J said that a man had not a fair opportunity of ascertaining the contents of deeds if he came into the auction room not even knowing that the deeds existed; *Molyneux v Hawtrey* [1903] 2 KB 487, CA; *Re Childe and Hodgson's Contract* (1905) 54 WR 234. A condition which refers to a particular document and offers inspection of it is not misleading unless it refers to it in such a way as to lead to the belief that everything material to the title is disclosed and nothing further is to be learnt on inspection which is not, in fact, the case: *Blenkhorn v Penrose* (1880) 43 LT 668. In *Simmons v Pennington & Son (a firm)* [1955] 1 All ER 240, [1955] 1 WLR 183, CA, property was sold as shop premises although it was subject to a restrictive covenant which prohibited use otherwise than as a private dwelling house; a provision that a copy of the covenants could be inspected at the offices of the

vendor's solicitors or at the auction room, and that the purchaser whether or not he inspected them should be deemed to purchase with full notice of them, did not prevent the purchaser from repudiating when a requisition stated that the covenant was still subsisting.

61. Matters which need not be disclosed. The vendor need not specifically disclose matters which are necessarily incidental to his tenure of the property[1]. Thus statutory security of tenure conferred on various categories of lessees is not a matter for disclosure[2]. On a sale of mines and minerals, any rights of mining under the local customs of the mining district[3] need not be stated, as such customs are notorious[4]. It is unnecessary to disclose matters which will not affect the purchaser[5], but disclosure must be made where the vendor will remain personally liable and requires the purchaser to enter into an indemnity covenant[6].

1　*Hayford v Criddle* (1855) 22 Beav 477 at 480 per Romilly MR.
2　For example, rights under the Landlord and Tenant Act 1954 (see LANDLORD AND TENANT vol 27(1) (Reissue) para 558 et seq), the Rent Act 1977 (see LANDLORD AND TENANT vol 27(1) (Reissue) para 655 et seq), the Housing Act 1988 (see generally HOUSING), the Leasehold Reform Act 1967 (see LANDLORD AND TENANT vol 27(2) (Reissue) para 1253 et seq), the Landlord and Tenant Act 1987 (see LANDLORD AND TENANT vol 27(1) (Reissue) para 5), the Leasehold Reform (Housing and Urban Development) Act 1993 (see generally HOUSING), and the Rent (Agriculture) Act 1976 (see LANDLORD AND TENANT vol 27(2) (Reissue) para 987 et seq). As to inquiries about such rights see para 8 ante.
3　As to such local customs see MINES, MINERALS AND QUARRIES vol 31 (Reissue) para 578 et seq. As to the vesting of coal in the Coal Authority see MINES, MINERALS AND QUARRIES vol 31 (Reissue) para 67 et seq.
4　Cf *Hayford v Criddle* (1855) 22 Beav 477 at 480. The existence of undisclosed quit rents on the property, being incidents of tenure, is a subject for compensation, not a ground for rescission: see *Esdaile v Stephenson* (1822) 1 Sim & St 122 at 124. As to the extinction of quit rents see generally CUSTOM AND USAGE.
5　*Smith v Colbourne* [1914] 2 Ch 533. An example would be a restrictive covenant already defeated by the vendor through lack of notice: *Wilkes v Spooner* [1911] 2 KB 473, CA. The same principle would apply to a covenant defeated for non-registration under the Land Charges Act 1972: see LAND CHARGES vol 26 (Reissue) para 543.
6　See the Standard Conditions of Sale (3rd Edn), conditions 3.3.2(d), 4.5.4(a); *Eagon v Dent* [1965] 3 All ER 334; and para 308 note 5 post. As to the Standard Conditions of Sale see para 1 note 9 ante.

(iii)　Disclosure by the Purchaser

62. Purchaser's duty generally. A purchaser is under no obligation to disclose to the vendor any fact known to him and not to the vendor which enhances, or appears to the purchaser to enhance, the value of the property[1]. Although simple reticence does not amount to fraud, yet, if the purchaser by any act or word induces the vendor to believe in the existence of a non-existent fact[2], or if he attempts to hurry the vendor into a contract without giving him an opportunity to ascertain the value of the property[3], a court of equity may refuse to order specific performance of the contract at the suit of the purchaser; and the same consequence follows where a purchaser makes false statements of fact which discourage other possible purchasers from competing with him for the property[4].

1　Sugden's Law of Vendors and Purchasers (14th Edn, 1862) 5; *Fox v Mackreth, Pitt v Mackreth* (1788) 2 Bro CC 400 at 419 per Lord Thurlow LC; *Turner v Harvey* (1821) Jac 169 at 178; *Walters v Morgan* (1861) 3 De GF & J 718; *Coaks v Boswell* (1886) 11 App Cas 232 at 235, HL, per Lord Selborne. A purchaser of mines who by trespassing has abstracted some of the property must disclose this fact: *Phillips v Homfray, Fothergill v Phillips* (1871) 6 Ch App 770 at 779 per Lord Hatherley LC; and see MISREPRESENTATION AND FRAUD vol 31 (Reissue) para 751.
2　See the cases cited in note 1 supra. 'A single word, or (I may add) a nod or a wink, or a shake of the head, or a smile from the purchaser, intended to induce the vendor to believe the existence of a non-existent fact, which might influence the price of the subject to be sold, would be sufficient ground for a court of

equity to refuse a decree for a specific performance of the agreement': *Walters v Morgan* (1861) 3 De GF & J 718 at 724 per Lord Campbell LC. See also *Davis v London and Provincial Marine Insurance Co* (1878) 8 ChD 469; *Davies v Ohrly* (1898) 14 TLR 260; and MISREPRESENTATION AND FRAUD vol 31 (Reissue) para 751. As to specific performance generally see SPECIFIC PERFORMANCE.

3 See *Walters v Morgan* (1861) 3 De GF & J 718 at 724 per Lord Campbell LC. Cf *Vernon v Keys* (1810) 12 East 632 at 638 (affd (1812) 4 Taunt 488, Ex Ch), where a purchaser represented that he was buying on behalf of himself and others who would not consent to his offering more than a certain figure.

4 Sugden's Law of Vendors and Purchasers (14th Edn, 1862) 5; *Howard v Hopkyns* (1742) 2 Atk 371. Cf *Fuller v Abrahams* (1821) 3 Brod & Bing 116. As to an action for slander of title see LIBEL AND SLANDER vol 28 (Reissue) para 274 et seq.

63. Purchaser's duty arising out of fiduciary relationship.

Where, during the course of negotiations for the sale and purchase of property, the proposed purchaser, in the name of and purportedly as agent on behalf of the vendor, takes some action in regard to the property (such as the making of a planning application or a contract for the sale of the property) which, if disclosed to the vendor, might reasonably be supposed to be likely to influence him in deciding whether or not to conclude the contract, a fiduciary relationship arises between the two parties. That relationship imposes on the proposed purchaser a duty to disclose to the vendor before the conclusion of the contract what he has done as the vendor's purported agent, and in the event of non-disclosure there is a duty to account to the vendor for any profit made in the course of the purported agency, unless the vendor consents to his retaining it[1].

1 *English v Dedham Vale Properties Ltd* [1978] 1 All ER 382 at 399, [1978] 1 WLR 93 at 111 per Slade J. On the facts, an account of profits was ordered where the proposed purchaser, in the name of but entirely without the knowledge of the vendor, obtained planning permission for the land he was proposing to buy, and failed to disclose that fact before contracts were exchanged.

(5) CAPACITY OF PARTIES

(i) Particular Persons

64. Aliens.

An alien may acquire and dispose of real property in the United Kingdom in the same manner in all respects as a British subject[1].

1 See the Status of Aliens Act 1914 s 17 (amended by the British Nationality Act 1948 s 34(3), Sch 4 Pt II). No right is thereby conferred on aliens to hold real property situate out of the United Kingdom: see the Status of Aliens Act 1914 s 17 proviso (1). See further BRITISH NATIONALITY, IMMIGRATION AND RACE RELATIONS vol 4(2) (Reissue) para 66. As to the effect of an outbreak of war on a contract pending completion see generally WAR AND ARMED CONFLICT.

65. Bankrupts.

The estate of a bankrupt vests in the trustee in bankruptcy when the appointment of the trustee takes effect[1], but this does not include property held by the bankrupt on trust for any other person[2]. In the case of registered land the trustee's title vests without any change in the proprietorship register[3], although the trustee may apply to be registered as proprietor in place of the bankrupt[4]. The power to sell the property is exercisable by the trustee in bankruptcy and not by the bankrupt[5]. Any disposition of property made by the bankrupt after the date of the presentation of the bankruptcy petition and the date of the trustee's appointment is void unless the court consents to or ratifies the disposition[6], except in favour of a purchaser who takes in good faith and without notice of the presentation of the petition[7].

1   See the Insolvency Act 1986 s 306; and BANKRUPTCY AND INSOLVENCY vol 3(2) (Reissue) paras 380–
     381. As to the effect of the bankruptcy of the vendor or purchaser pending completion see para 206 et
     seq post.
2   See ibid s 283(3)(a); and BANKRUPTCY AND INSOLVENCY vol 3(2) (Reissue) paras 417 (trust property),
     460 et seq (disclaimer by trustee).
3   See the Land Registration Act 1925 s 61(5); and LAND REGISTRATION vol 26 (Reissue) para 1021.
4   See ibid s 42(1) (as amended); and LAND REGISTRATION vol 26 (Reissue) para 1021.
5   See BANKRUPTCY AND INSOLVENCY vol 3(2) (Reissue) paras 380–381, 449.
6   See the Insolvency Act 1986 s 284; and BANKRUPTCY AND INSOLVENCY vol 3(2) (Reissue) para 205. On
     a purchase by an undisclosed bankrupt where the purchase price is payable by instalments, non-disclosure
     of the bankruptcy is a ground for rescission by the vendor: *De Choisy v Hynes* [1937] 4 All ER 54.
7   See the Insolvency Act 1986 s 284(4); and BANKRUPTCY AND INSOLVENCY vol 3(2) (Reissue) para 205.
     Both the bankruptcy petition and the bankruptcy order are registrable under the Land Charges Act 1972
     (see ss 5(1)(b), 6(1)(c) (as substituted); and LAND CHARGES vol 26 (Reissue) paras 547, 554), and the
     trustee's title is void against a purchaser of a legal estate in good faith for money or money's worth unless
     the bankruptcy order is registered (see s 6(5), (6); and LAND CHARGES vol 26 (Reissue) para 558).
     Registration under the Land Charges Act 1972 does not give notice to a purchaser of registered land: see
     the Land Registration Act 1925 s 110(7); and LAND REGISTRATION vol 26 (Reissue) para 931.

66.   Corporations. The distinction between the powers of statutory corporations which
can do only such acts as are authorised by the statutes creating them and non-statutory
corporations which have in general the same rights as individuals[1], the rights of
corporations to own land and alienate property[2], and the formalities of contracts with
corporations[3] are dealt with elsewhere in this work.

1   See CORPORATIONS vol 9(2) (Reissue) paras 1136–1137.
2   See CORPORATIONS vol 9(2) (Reissue) para 1153 et seq. As to the acquisition of land by the British
     Railways Board and London Regional Transport see RAILWAYS, INLAND WATERWAYS AND PIPELINES
     vol 39(1) (Reissue) paras 35, 320. As to the sale of Crown land see CROWN PROPERTY vol 12(1)
     (Reissue) para 308.
3   See CORPORATIONS vol 9(2) (Reissue) para 1175. As to contracts by limited companies see COMPANIES
     vol 7(2) (1996 Reissue) paras 1129–1132. Contracts for the sale of land in the case of such companies are
     entered into by an officer of the company acting for and on behalf of the company and signed by the
     officer pursuant to a resolution of the board of directors.

67.   Company liquidators. The liquidator of a company in any winding up has
power, without the sanction of the court, to sell any of the company's property by public
auction or by private contract[1]. The liquidator also has the power, without the sanction
of the court or the liquidation committee, to do all acts and execute, in the name of the
company, all deeds, receipts and other documents and for that purpose to use, when
necessary, the company's seal[2].

1   See the Insolvency Act 1986 ss 165, 167, Sch 4 Pt III para 6; and COMPANIES vol 7(3) (1996 Reissue)
     paras 2337, 2504.
2   See ibid ss 165, 167, Sch 4 Pt III para 7; and COMPANIES vol 7(3) (1996 Reissue) paras 2337, 2504. As
     to the effect of winding up upon a pending contract see para 212 et seq post; as to the form of a transfer
     by a company in liquidation see para 277 post. For an instance in which the dissolution of a company
     was declared void in order to enable a sale to be completed see *M'Call and Stephen Ltd Liquidator* 1920
     37 Sc LR 480; and COMPANIES vol 7(3) (1996 Reissue) para 2696. As to the purchase of a company's
     property by a liquidator or member of the liquidation committee see COMPANIES vol 7(3) (1996
     Reissue) paras 2327, 2403.

68.   Local authorities. Local authorities may acquire land by agreement for the
purpose of any of their functions under any public general Act and may be authorised to
purchase land compulsorily[1], and have wide general powers of disposal, subject, however,
in many cases, to the necessary consent[2].

1   See generally LOCAL GOVERNMENT; LONDON GOVERNMENT. As to acquisitions by local education authorities see EDUCATION vol 15 (Reissue) para 193 et seq.
2   See generally LOCAL GOVERNMENT. As to sales by local education authorities see EDUCATION vol 15 (Reissue) para 196; and as to the position of persons deriving title under transactions requiring ministerial consent see para 25 ante.

69. Ecclesiastical corporations. The Church Commissioners have power to acquire land for the purpose of providing churches and houses of residence[1]. Diocesan boards of finance have statutory powers to sell or otherwise dispose of diocesan glebe land on terms approved by the Church Commissioners[2].

1   See generally ecclesiastical law.
2   See the Endowments and Glebe Measure 1976 s 20(1); and ECCLESIASTICAL LAW. As to the power of ecclesiastical corporations to sell land for the purpose of enlarging cemeteries see generally CREMATION AND BURIAL. As to their power to transfer land to literary and scientific institutions see CHARITIES vol 5(2) (Reissue) para 62; LIBRARIES AND OTHER SCIENTIFIC AND CULTURAL INSTITUTIONS vol 28 (Reissue) para 486.

70. Unincorporated bodies. Unincorporated bodies of persons cannot, as such, acquire land; they can only do so as individuals in their private capacity. Thus, the inhabitants of a place, or parishioners, or the commoners of a waste cannot *eo nomine* purchase land[1].

1   Co Litt 3a.

71. Minors. A minor cannot absolutely bind himself by a contract for the sale or purchase of land[1]. A minor is allowed to ratify an otherwise unenforceable contract on attaining majority[2]. As regards the acquisition or disposal under the contract of an interest in land, the contract, unless it is clearly prejudicial to his interests, is not void but is voidable by the minor on his coming of age or within a reasonable time thereafter, or by his representatives if he dies under age or after attaining full age without having adopted the contract[3]. A minor cannot hold a legal estate in land[4], and where he is entitled to any beneficial interest the legal estate must be vested in persons acting on his behalf on a trust of land[5].

1   See CHILDREN AND YOUNG PERSONS vol 5(2) (Reissue) paras 612 et seq (voidability of minor's contracts at common law), 623 (effect of misrepresentation as to age).
2   See the Minors' Contracts Act 1987 ss 1(a), 4(2). See, however, *Davies v Beynon-Harris* (1931) 47 TLR 424. See further CHILDREN AND YOUNG PERSONS vol 5(2) (Reissue) para 614.
3   See CHILDREN AND YOUNG PERSONS vol 5(2) (Reissue) paras 625, 640.
4   Law of Property Act 1925 s 1(6).
5   See CHILDREN AND YOUNG PERSONS vol 5(2) (Reissue) para 630 et seq. It has been the practice to vest land in trustees for sale to hold the proceeds in trust for the minor, thereby avoiding the provisions of the Settled Land Act 1925. As from 1 January 1997 it is no longer possible to create a strict settlement under the Settled Land Act 1925: see the Trusts of Land and Appointment of Trustees Act 1996 s 2; and SETTLEMENTS para 676 post. By amendments made by the Trusts of Land and Appointment of Trustees Act 1996, all trusts for sale formerly imposed by statute have become trusts of land (without a duty to sell) and land formerly held on such implied trusts for sale is now held in trust for the persons interested in the land: see s 5, Sch 2 paras 1–6 (amending the Law of Property Act 1925 ss 31, 32, 34, 36; the Administration of Estates Act 1925 s 33; and the Reverter of Sites Act 1987 s 1); and REAL PROPERTY vol 39(2) (Reissue) para 66. See also the Trusts of Land and Appointment of Trustees Act 1996 Sch 2 para 7; and REAL PROPERTY vol 39(2) (Reissue) para 56. Where after 1 January 1997 a person purports to transfer a legal estate in land to a minor, the land is held in trust for the minor: see s 2, Sch 1 paras 1, 2. As to the exercise of powers by a minor see CHILDREN AND YOUNG PERSONS vol 5(2) (Reissue) para 655.

72. Persons suffering from mental disorder. A contract for the sale or purchase of land entered into by a person suffering from a mental disorder sufficient to deprive him of contractual capacity is voidable if the other party knew of the disorder, and in such a case the transaction can be set aside by the person himself if he recovers, or by his representatives. If the other party had no knowledge of the disorder or of facts from which such knowledge should be inferred, the contract is valid, and if it is fair it will be enforced against the person suffering from the disorder[1].

The judge[2], with respect to the property and affairs of patients suffering from mental disorder, has power[3] to make orders and give directions and authorities[4] for the sale, exchange, charging of or other disposition of or dealing with a patient's property[5], the carrying out of a contract entered into by the patient[6] or the exercise of any power vested in the patient[7] and to appoint a receiver for the patient who must carry out any such orders or directions[8].

1   *Molton v Camroux* (1848) 2 Exch 487 at 501 (affd (1849) 4 Exch 17); *Elliot v Ince* (1857) 7 De GM & G 475 at 488; *Imperial Loan Co v Stone* [1892] 1 QB 599 at 601, CA; *Baldwyn v Smith* [1900] 1 Ch 588 at 590; *York Glass Co Ltd v Jubb* (1925) 42 TLR 1, CA; *Broughton v Snook* [1938] Ch 505, [1938] 1 All ER 411. As to the contracts of persons suffering from mental disorder generally see MENTAL HEALTH vol 30 (Reissue) para 1389 et seq. As to mental disorder supervening before completion see para 218 post.
2   The functions expressed to be conferred by the Mental Health Act 1983 Pt VII (ss 93–113) (as amended) on 'the judge' are exercisable by the Lord Chancellor or by any nominated judge or, subject to certain qualifications, by the master of the Court of Protection, by the Public Trustee, or by any nominated officer: see s 94(1) (amended by the Public Trustee and Administration of Funds Act 1986 s 2); and MENTAL HEALTH vol 30 (Reissue) para 1433.
3   See the Mental Health Act 1983 s 95; and MENTAL HEALTH vol 30 (Reissue) para 1441.
4   See ibid s 96(1); and MENTAL HEALTH vol 30 (Reissue) para 1442
5   See ibid s 96(1)(b); and MENTAL HEALTH vol 30 (Reissue) para 1442.
6   See ibid s 96(1)(h); and MENTAL HEALTH vol 30 (Reissue) para 1442.
7   See ibid s 96(1)(k); and MENTAL HEALTH vol 30 (Reissue) para 1442.
8   See ibid s 99; and MENTAL HEALTH vol 30 (Reissue) para 1463. The judge also has power to make orders and give directions and authorities for the execution for the patient of a will: see s 96(1)(e); and MENTAL HEALTH vol 30 (Reissue) para 1442.

73. Persons purchasing under compulsory powers. Where an authority is authorised to acquire land compulsorily, the procedure is governed by statute[1], and persons under disability are given special powers of selling and transferring the land to the acquiring authority[2]. The effect of the service of notice to treat is to establish a relation analogous in some respects to that of purchaser and vendor, but the actual relation of vendor and purchaser is not established until the price has been ascertained[3]. The transaction must normally be completed by the execution of a transfer[4].

1   See COMPULSORY ACQUISITION OF LAND vol 8(1) (Reissue) para 33 et seq (compulsory purchase orders), para 93 et seq (purchase by agreement), and para 99 et seq (conditions precedent to exercise of compulsory powers).
2   See COMPULSORY ACQUISITION OF LAND vol 8(1) (Reissue) para 96 (persons entitled to sell), and para 98 (payment of purchase money into court).
3   See COMPULSORY ACQUISITION OF LAND vol 8(1) (Reissue) para 115.
4   See COMPULSORY ACQUISITION OF LAND vol 8(1) (Reissue) para 139. As to the costs of the transfer see para 325 post; and COMPULSORY ACQUISITION OF LAND vol 8(1) (Reissue) para 140; as to the execution of a deed poll on the owner's default or absence see COMPULSORY ACQUISITION OF LAND vol 8(1) (Reissue) para 142 et seq; and as to the expedited procedure by way of vesting declaration see COMPULSORY ACQUISITION OF LAND vol 8(1) (Reissue) para 168 et seq. As to the disposition of registered and unregistered land by transfer see para 262 note 2 post.

(ii) Fiduciary and other Vendors

74. Beneficial joint tenants. A legal estate in land beneficially limited to or held on trust for joint tenants[1] is held on a trust of land[2]. Where a transfer is made to two persons without any further words, a purchaser can assume that they are beneficial joint tenants or, at any rate, it is safe for him to deal with the title on that assumption[3]. For the purpose of exercising their functions as trustees, the trustees of land have in relation to the land subject to the trust all the powers of an absolute owner[4].

Where a transfer is made by the survivor of two or more joint tenants he is deemed, in favour of a purchaser of the legal estate, to be solely and beneficially interested if the transfer includes a statement that he is so interested[5]. However, the purchaser is not protected if at any time before the date of the disposition by the survivor a memorandum of severance[6] had been indorsed on or annexed to the conveyance by virtue of which the legal estate vested in the joint tenants[7], or if a bankruptcy order, or a petition for such an order, made against any of the joint tenants, had been registered under the Land Charges Act 1972, being an order or petition of which the purchaser had notice, by virtue of the registration, on the date of the transfer by the survivor[8].

1   As to a joint tenancy see REAL PROPERTY vol 39(2) (Reissue) para 190 et seq.
2   See the Law of Property Act 1925 s 36(1) (amended by the Trusts of Land and Appointment of Trustees Act 1996 s 5(1), Sch 2 para 4).
3   *Re Soden and Alexander's Contract* [1918] 2 Ch 258. As to the disposition of registered and unregistered land by transfer see para 262 note 2 post.
4   Trusts of Land and Appointment of Trustees Act 1996 s 6(1). However, such powers may be excluded or restricted, and may be made subject to the obtaining of any consent: see s 8; and TRUSTS vol 48 (Reissue) paras 894, 908. As to the protection of purchasers where trustees of land transfer land in contravention of their powers and duties see s 16 (s 16 does not apply to registered land: s 16(7)); and TRUSTS vol 48 (Reissue) paras 894–895, 908. As to the consequences of this limitation see Ferris and Battersby 'The Impact of the Trusts of Land and Appointment of Trustees Act 1996 on Purchasers of Registered Land' [1998] Conv 168.
5   See the Law of Property (Joint Tenants) Act 1964 s 1(1) (amended by the Law of Property (Miscellaneous Provisions) Act 1994 s 21, Sch 1 para 3, Sch 2), which also applies, with the necessary modifications, to a transfer by the personal representatives of the survivor of joint tenants: see the Law of Property (Joint Tenants) Act 1964 s 1(2). Where the transfer was made on or before 1 July 1995, the deeming provision applies where the vendor transferred as beneficial owner: see s 1(1) (as originally enacted). Section 1 (as originally enacted) is deemed to have come into operation on 1 January 1926, and for the purposes of s 1 (as originally enacted) in its application to a conveyance executed before 31 July 1964 a statement signed by the vendor or by his personal representatives that he was solely and beneficially interested is to be treated as if it had been included in the conveyance: s 2. The Act does not apply to registered land: s 3 (there is a possibility that, severance having taken place, the former joint tenant might be in actual occupation and thus have an overriding interest binding on the purchaser: cf *Williams and Glyn's Bank Ltd v Boland* [1981] AC 487, [1980] 2 All ER 408, HL).
6   Ie a note or memorandum signed by the joint tenants or one of them recording that the joint tenancy was severed in equity on a date specified in it: Law of Property (Joint Tenants) Act 1964 s 1(1) proviso (a).
7   Ibid s 1(1) proviso (a). As to severance generally see REAL PROPERTY vol 39(2) (Reissue) paras 198–206.
8   Law of Property (Joint Tenants) Act 1964 s 1(1) proviso (b) (amended by the Insolvency Act 1985 s 235(1), Sch 8 para 13); Land Charges Act 1972 s 18(6). As to the registration of a bankruptcy order, or a petition for such an order see BANKRUPTCY AND INSOLVENCY vol 3(2) (Reissue) para 184; LAND CHARGES vol 26 (Reissue) paras 547, 554. As to registration as notice see LAND CHARGES vol 26 (Reissue) para 516.

75. Fiduciary vendors, limited owners and mortgagees. Sales of land by persons acting in a fiduciary capacity, such as trustees under private trusts[1], trustees of charity land[2], and the personal representatives of a deceased person[3], sales by limited owners under the Settled Land Act 1925[4], and sales by mortgagees under express or statutory powers[5] are dealt with elsewhere in this work[6].

1   As to the use of depreciatory conditions see EXECUTORS AND ADMINISTRATORS; SETTLEMENTS para 906 post; TRUSTS vol 48 (Reissue) para 906. In *Micholls v Corbett* (1865) 3 De GJ & Sm 18, a purchaser who had been required by conditions to take the risk of a breach of trust and make no objections to it was precluded from objecting to the title on the ground of concurrence in such breach. As to the powers and duties of trustees purchasing land for the purposes of the trust, and as to the disability of a trustee to purchase the trust property himself see EQUITY vol 16 (Reissue) para 908; TRUSTS vol 48 (Reissue) para 816. As to purchases by solicitors see SOLICITORS vol 44(1) (Reissue) para 138.

2   See CHARITIES vol 5(2) (Reissue) para 329 et seq. As to the effect of failure to obtain a necessary consent
     to a contract for the sale of charity land see para 25 ante.
3   See generally EXECUTORS AND ADMINISTRATORS. Trustees and personal representatives have also a
     statutory power of sale for the purpose of raising inheritance tax, whether the property is or is not vested
     in them: see generally EXECUTORS AND ADMINISTRATORS; INHERITANCE TAXATION vol 24 (Reissue)
     para 652. As to the power of personal representatives to complete a contract, in the event of the death of
     a vendor or purchaser pending completion see paras 202–205 post; and EXECUTORS AND
     ADMINISTRATORS.
4   See SETTLEMENTS para 827 et seq post.
5   See generally MORTGAGE. As to the aiding of sales under express powers where the terms of the power
     are imperfectly complied with see generally POWERS. Express powers (other than powers vested in legal
     mortgagees or estate owners in right of their estates) operate only in equity: see the Law of Property Act
     1925 s 1(7); and POWERS.
6   See also MINES, MINERALS AND QUARRIES vol 31 (Reissue) para 286 et seq.

(6) CONDITIONS OF SALE AND SPECIAL CONDITIONS

(i) In general

76. Conditions in general. An agreement for the sale of land which merely satisfies
the formal requirements of a written contract[1], leaving all other terms to be implied by
law, is called an 'open contract'[2]. The vendor usually desires to exclude or modify the
terms which would be implied by law, and provisions for this purpose are inserted in a
formal contract or in conditions of sale[3]. Printed forms of such conditions are in general
use[4], and for contracts by correspondence[5] there is a statutory form, which may also be
applied to other contracts[6].

1   As to the matters which must be contained in a contract for the sale of land see paras 29–40 ante.
2   See para 137 note 1 post. As to the statutory provisions which apply to such a contract see the Law of
     Property Act 1925 ss 42–45 (as amended), 47; the Law of Property Act 1969 s 23; and paras 139–140,
     142, 150, 171–173 post.
3   See *Hyde v Dallaway* (1842) 4 Beav 606; *Re Priestley's Contract* [1947] Ch 469, [1947] 1 All ER 716
     (deletion of one or a part of one of printed conditions having unnoticed effect upon another condition).
     As to a condition designed to exclude or restrict liability for a misrepresentation see para 111 post; and
     MISREPRESENTATION AND FRAUD vol 31 (Reissue) paras 803, 828.
4   The Standard Conditions of Sale (3rd Edn) are in general use and form the basis of the great majority of
     residential and commercial conveyancing transactions. As to the Standard Conditions of Sale see para 1
     note 9 ante. Where a lessee is acquiring the freehold under the Leasehold Reform Act 1967, the statutory
     conditions of sale prescribed by that Act will apply in the absence of agreement to the contrary: see s 22(2)
     (as amended); the Leasehold Reform (Enfranchisement and Extension) Regulations 1967, SI 1967/1879;
     and LANDLORD AND TENANT vol 27(2) (Reissue) para 1295.
5   As to such contracts see para 23 ante. Oral acceptance of an offer by letter, or acceptance by letter of an
     offer made orally, does not constitute a contract by correspondence; there must be an exchange of letters:
     Stearn v Twitchell [1985] 1 All ER 631, [1985] NLJ Rep 128. However, in view of the statutory
     requirement that the contract should be in a written document signed by both parties (see para 29 et seq
     ante), it seems doubtful whether a contract by correspondence could now arise.
6   See the Statutory Form of Conditions of Sale 1925, SR & O 1925, 1925/779. These conditions apply,
     subject to any modification, or any intention to the contrary expressed in the correspondence, and they
     may by express reference be made to apply to any other contract for the sale of land: see the Law of
     Property Act 1925 s 46. These statutory conditions are very short and it should be considered whether it
     is necessary to add to them or to substitute one of the usual sets of printed conditions. There are also
     various statutory conditions contained in the Law of Property Act 1969 s 23. Where, after an abortive
     auction, the property is sold by private treaty, the conditions of sale which were to have applied at the
     auction will not be incorporated unless referred to in the contract: *Cowley v Watts* (1853) 17 Jur 172; cf
     Dewar v Mintoft [1912] 2 KB 373.

77. General and special conditions. The modern printed conditions are general conditions, which are intended to be applicable to all transactions. Where, in a particular transaction, it is necessary to vary or supplement the general conditions, that matter should be made a special condition. For example, if the purchaser is to enter into a restrictive covenant with the vendor, that intention, with the wording of the intended covenant, should be stated in a special condition[1]. In the event of inconsistency between the general and the special conditions, the special conditions will prevail[2]. The principles of construction stated subsequently are applicable to all conditions, but their application is principally of importance in the case of conditions restricting the title to be shown, which may be misleading conditions[3].

1 See para 81 post.
2 See the Standard Conditions of Sale (3rd Edn), Special Condition 1(a). As to the Standard Conditions of Sale see para 1 note 9 ante.
3 See para 83 post.

78. Construction of conditions. Conditions must be expressed in clear and unambiguous language[1]. In accordance with the general rule of construction, in the case of ambiguity a condition will be construed most strongly against the grantor, namely the vendor who is the framer of the condition[2]. In considering the effect of a condition it may be material that the purchaser is a lawyer[3].

1 *Symons v James* (1842) 1 Y & C Ch Cas 487 at 490; *Taylor v Martindale* (1842) 1 Y & C Ch Cas 658; *Williams v Wood* (1868) 16 WR 1005.
2 *Greaves v Wilson* (1858) 25 Beav 290; *Re Terry and White's Contract* (1886) 32 ChD 14 at 28 per Lindley LJ; and see DEEDS AND OTHER INSTRUMENTS. The proposition is sometimes stated in the case of conditions of sale as construction in favour of the party whose rights are restricted, ie the purchaser: *Osborne v Harvey* (1842) 12 LJ Ch 66; *Seaton v Mapp* (1846) 2 Coll 556 at 562; *Rhodes v Ibbetson* (1853) 4 De GM & G 787; *Drysdale v Mace* (1854) 5 De GM & G 103; *Cruse v Nowell* (1856) 25 LJ Ch 709; *Brumfit v Morton* (1857) 30 LTOS 98; *Allmann v McDaniel* [1912] 1 IR 467. See also Harpum 'Exclusion Clauses and Contracts for the Sale of Land' [1992] CLJ 263, 284–294. It is arguable that the Unfair Terms in Consumer Contracts Regulations 1994, SI 1994/3159 (see CONTRACT vol 9(1) (Reissue) paras 790–796), apply to contracts for the sale of land (unlike the Unfair Contract Terms Act 1977): see Bright and Bright 'Unfair Terms in Land Contracts: Copy Out or Cop Out?' (1995) 111 LQR 655. See also para 166 post.
3 *Minet v Leman* (1855) 7 De GM & G 340 at 352. As to the contra proferentem rule see CONTRACT vol 9(1) (Reissue) para 776.

79. Particulars. Attached to the conditions of sale are particulars which describe the property to be sold, whereas the conditions of sale state the terms on which it is to be sold[1]. The particulars must be accurate[2]. The property may be described in any way sufficient to identify it[3]. Any covenants, rights to minerals or other rights which it is intended to except or reserve on the sale, and any easements or rights which it is intended to confer expressly on the purchaser, must be mentioned, as must any subsisting incumbrances, easements, restrictive covenants or other matters affecting the value of the property subject to which the property is to be sold[4]. The tenure of the property should be stated; for example if it is leasehold and is held by an underlease, that fact should be specified[5].

An oral correction of the particulars made by an auctioneer at a sale cannot be admitted to vary the written contract, but it usually prevents the purchaser from obtaining specific performance without the correction[6].

1 *Torrance v Bolton* (1872) LR 14 Eq 124 at 130; affd 8 Ch App 118. See also para 114 note 2 post.
2 See eg *Calverley v Williams, Williams v Calverley* (1790) 1 Ves 210; and BOUNDARIES vol 4(1) (Reissue) para 907. The parcels in the transfer must normally correspond with the particulars in the contract: see

generally DEEDS AND OTHER INSTRUMENTS. As to the disposition of registered and unregistered land by transfer see para 262 note 2 post.

3   See BOUNDARIES vol 4(1) (Reissue) para 904. As to the rule that a sale of land prima facie includes fixtures and growing timber see para 88 post; and as to conditions as to identity see paras 109–116 post.

4   See eg *Burnell v Brown* (1820) 1 Jac & W 168; *Nottingham Patent Brick and Tile Co v Butler* (1886) 16 QBD 778, CA; *Torrance v Bolton* (1872) 8 Ch App 118; and para 81 post. As to the position of a purchaser who is deemed by statute to have had actual notice of a local land charge see para 54 ante.

5   *Re Russ and Brown's Contract* [1934] Ch 34, CA. Cf *Re Thompson and Cottrell's Contract* [1943] Ch 97, [1943] 1 All ER 169 (cited in para 59 note 1 ante). It seems, however, to be unnecessary to distinguish between an underlease and a sub-underlease: *Becker v Partridge* [1966] 2 QB 155 at 170, [1966] 2 All ER 266 at 270, CA.

6   *Manser v Back* (1848) 6 Hare 443; *Re Hare and O'More's Contract* [1901] 1 Ch 93. See also 1 Dart's Law relating to Vendors and Purchasers (8th Edn, 1929) 104; and AUCTION vol 2 (Reissue) para 941.

80.   Compulsory purchase and planning restrictions. The position as to possible compulsory purchase of the property will have been examined when the preliminary inquiries before contract were made[1], but in some circumstances the position may be left in some doubt and then the conditions may include a provision giving the purchaser an option, to be exercised on notice, to rescind the contract with repayment of the deposit without interest or to complete the contract[2]. If a compulsory purchase order is made pending completion where there is no such condition, the purchaser must complete, but he is entitled to the compensation money[3].

Questions relating to the position under planning legislation should be dealt with when the preliminary inquiries are made[4]. A condition now often inserted provides for rescission if the permitted use of the property is not that which has been stated in the particulars or the contract[5]. Where a contract is conditional upon the obtaining of planning permission, it is a question of construction of the particular contract whether the condition is fulfilled by the obtaining of outline planning permission[6]. Where a planning application is made by the vendor before contract, he is under an implied obligation not to withdraw the application after contract without the purchaser's consent[7].

1   See para 15 ante.
2   Unlike previous sets of general conditions, the Standard Conditions of Sale (3rd Edn), do not contain such a provision. As to the Standard Conditions of Sale see para 1 note 9 ante.
3   *Hillingdon Estates Co v Stonefield Estates Ltd* [1952] Ch 627, [1952] 1 All ER 853, where a contract was held not to have been frustrated by a compulsory purchase order or the service of a notice to treat. As to the effect of a notice to treat generally see para 73 ante; and COMPULSORY ACQUISITION OF LAND vol 8(1) (Reissue) para 115 et seq. See also *Amalgamated Investment and Property Co Ltd v John Walker & Sons Ltd* [1976] 3 All ER 509, [1977] 1 WLR 164, CA (building listed two days after contract for sale); *E Johnson & Co (Barbados) Ltd v NSR Ltd* [1997] AC 400, [1996] 3 WLR 583, PC (contract not frustrated by notice of intention to acquire the land compulsorily).
4   See para 11 et seq ante.
5   See The Law Society's General Conditions of Sale (1980 Edn), condition 4(3)(b); and the National Conditions of Sale (20th Edn), condition 17; and cf the Conveyancing Lawyers' Conditions of Sale, condition 5.
6   *Hargreaves Transport Ltd v Lynch* [1969] 1 All ER 455, [1969] 1 WLR 215, CA; *Richard West & Partners (Inverness) Ltd v Dick* [1969] 2 Ch 424, [1969] 1 All ER 943, CA. See also para 26 ante.
7   *Sinclair-Hill v Sothcott* (1973) 26 P & CR 490.

81.   Covenants and other provisions. References to covenants and other provisions to be inserted in the transfer will appear both in the particulars and the conditions[1]. It is important that these should as far as possible be in the precise terms in which they are to be inserted in the transfer[2]. Where the vendor is under a continuing liability under a subsisting covenant, he will be entitled to an indemnity[3]. Where it is intended to impose restrictive covenants, their precise form should appear in the contract which should be drafted with a view to the covenants running with the land[4]. A condition giving an option or a right of pre-emption to the vendor, if required, must be drafted with particular care, stating all the terms under which the repurchase is to be exercisable and, where necessary, must be limited within the time allowed by the rule against perpetuities[5]. Further, since such a right, so far as it creates a proprietary interest, is registrable as an estate contract[6], provision should be made for the vacation of the charge if that becomes necessary[7]. The conditions should also define the title to be required on repurchase and should contain definite provisions as to notices and the service of notices. Where the vendor retains adjoining land, it might be stipulated that the transfer is to contain a covenant that all lights and windows are opened with the express consent of the vendor and no length of enjoyment by the purchaser or his successors in title is to give an indefeasible right to light or air or to any right to impede or control the erection of buildings on the retained land[8] and that the purchaser is to take no action in respect of any registration of a light obstruction notice[9] by the vendor. Since, as a general rule and apart from express provision to the contrary, conditions merge in the transfer[10], these terms must also appear in the transfer.

It seems desirable to provide[11] that if the purchaser registers the contract as an estate contract[12] and it is rescinded by the vendor, the purchaser must at his own expense procure the vacation of the register[13].

1   As to the particulars see para 79 ante. As to the disposition of registered and unregistered land by transfer see para 262 note 2 post.
2   As to descriptions see DEEDS AND OTHER INSTRUMENTS.
3   See the Standard Conditions of Sale (3rd Edn), conditions 3.3.2(d), 4.5.4; and para 57 ante. As to the Standard Conditions of Sale see para 1 note 9 ante.
4   As to covenants running with the land see para 331–335 post; and EQUITY vol 16 (Reissue) para 787 et seq.
5   See eg *London and South Western Rly Co v Gomm* (1882) 20 ChD 562, CA; para 27 ante; and PERPETUITIES AND ACCUMULATIONS vol 35 (Reissue) para 1038.
6   Ie under the Land Charges Act 1972 s 2(4) (as amended), Class C(iv): see LAND CHARGES vol 26 (Reissue) paras 528, 532.
7   See note 13 infra.
8   See the Standard Conditions of Sale (3rd Edn) which provide that the purchaser will have no right of light or air over the retained land, but otherwise the vendor and the purchaser will each have the rights over the land of the other which they would have had if they were two separate purchasers to whom the vendor had made simultaneous transfers of the property and the retained land: condition 3.4.2. See also *Squarey v Harris-Smith* (1981) 42 P & CR 118, CA; and cf *Lyme Valley Squash Club Ltd v Newcastle-under-Lyme Borough Council* [1985] 2 All ER 405 (this latter decision, that the purchaser acquired an easement of light despite a condition to the contrary seems very questionable).
9   See the Rights of Light Act 1959 ss 2 (as amended), 3; and EASEMENTS AND PROFITS À PRENDRE.
10   See para 293 post; and DEEDS AND OTHER INSTRUMENTS.
11   If either party rescinds the contract the buyer is to return any documents he received from the seller and is to cancel any registration of the contract: Standard Conditions of Sale (3rd Edn), condition 7.2(b). For the meaning of 'contract' see para 55 note 10 ante. Where the rescission is by the vendor on the ground of his inability or unwillingness to satisfy a requisition (see para 104 post), it seems desirable that the vendor should indemnify the purchaser against the expense of procuring the vacation of the register.
12   See note 6 supra.
13   The provisions as to vacation are such that without the aid of such a condition the vacation might need an application to the court or even proceedings to enforce or rescind the contract: see eg *Re Engall's Agreement* [1953] 2 All ER 503, [1953] 1 WLR 977; *Heywood v BDC Properties Ltd* [1963] 2 All ER 1063, [1963] 1 WLR 975, CA; *Hooker v Wyle* [1973] 3 All ER 707, [1974] 1 WLR 235; and LAND CHARGES vol 26 (Reissue) paras 519, 545.

82. Sale of life interests and remainders. In general, sales of life interests and remainders are made to relatives of the vendor who are in possession of the relevant facts affecting the value of the interest to be sold, or to insurance companies which have their own forms of conditions and inquiries. In other cases it is necessary in the first place to require evidence of the age of the tenant for life. A purchaser must be satisfied that this is accurately stated. Usually a birth certificate is available. In its absence a statutory declaration by a member of the family is generally accepted. Where the remainderman's pedigree is material to the title the vendor normally offers such certificates of birth, death and marriage as are in the vendor's possession or can be obtained at the purchaser's expense[1]. The purchaser must obtain sufficient evidence to enforce his rights after completion against the trustees. Where the death of the testator under whose will the interest sold arises is recent, there is usually a condition that it is to be assumed that all debts, legacies, taxes and liabilities have been duly discharged. A further usual condition is that a statement by the trustees that they have not received notice of any incumbrance is to be accepted as conclusive evidence. Provision must be made for the incidence of future inheritance tax[2].

1   As to such certificates as evidence see generally EVIDENCE. As to registration concerning the individual see REGISTRATION CONCERNING THE INDIVIDUAL.

2   As to the inheritance tax implications of sales of life interests and remainders see INHERITANCE TAXATION vol 24 (Reissue) para 486 et seq.

83. Misleading conditions. Conditions restricting the title or proof of title to which the purchaser is entitled must neither state nor suggest things which to the vendor's knowledge are incorrect. A condition is misleading, and therefore not binding, if it requires the purchaser to assume that which the vendor knows to be false, or if it affirms that the state of the title is not accurately known to the vendor when in fact it is known[1]. Similarly, a condition will not be binding if it stipulates for the commencement of the title within the period of 15 years[2] with a certain transfer simpliciter, without disclosing, as is the fact, that the transfer is a voluntary one[3], or if it is used by a vendor who knows that he has a bad title in order to palm that title off upon the purchaser[4]. However, a slight inaccuracy which has not misled the purchaser is immaterial[5].

1   *Edwards v Wickwar* (1865) LR 1 Eq 68; *Re Banister, Broad v Munton* (1879) 12 ChD 131 at 143, CA. See also *Harnett v Baker* (1875) LR 20 Eq 50; *Boyd v Dickson* (1876) IR 10 Eq 239; *Heywood v Mallalieu* (1883) 25 ChD 357; *Re Haedicke and Lipski's Contract* [1901] 2 Ch 666; *Becker v Partridge* [1966] 2 QB 155, [1966] 2 All ER 266, CA; *Faruqi v English Real Estates Ltd* [1979] 1 WLR 963; *Walker v Boyle* [1982] 1 All ER 634, [1982] 1 WLR 495; *Sakkas v Donford Ltd* (1982) 46 P & CR 290; *Rignall Developments Ltd v Halil* [1988] Ch 190, [1987] 3 All ER 170. The vendor must tell the truth and all the truth which is relevant to the matter in hand: *Martin v Cotter* (1846) 3 Jo & Lat 496; *Nottingham Patent Brick and Tile Co v Butler* (1886) 16 QBD 778, CA. It is the vendor's duty to make himself acquainted with all the peculiarities and incidents of the property: *Brandling v Plummer* (1854) 2 Drew 427 at 430. If, however, the vendor believes the truth of the facts which the purchaser is required to assume, the condition is not misleading, even if it precludes the purchaser from requiring evidence which is essential to the title; and it is not necessary to state in the condition the specific defect which the condition is intended to cover: *Re Sandbach and Edmondson's Contract* [1891] 1 Ch 99, CA. Cf *Nash v Browne* (1863) 9 Jur NS 431(which seems questionable); and see *Blenkhorn v Penrose* (1880) 29 WR 237; *Blaiberg v Keeves* [1906] 2 Ch 175. See also *Beyfus v Lodge* [1925] Ch 350. A condition which refers to a particular document and offers an opportunity of inspecting it is not misleading unless it refers to the document in such a way as to lead to the belief that all which is material for the purchaser to know is disclosed in the condition and nothing further is (contrary to the fact) to be learnt on inspection: *Blenkhorn v Penrose* supra. In the case of such a condition, so long as the vendor has stated what he believes to be true, the condition is binding, even if the purchaser proves that the title is wholly bad; but the court will not grant the vendor specific performance and will leave him to his remedy at law in damages: *Re Scott and Alvarez's Contract, Scott v Alvarez* [1895] 2 Ch 603, CA.

2   See para 139 post. If a title for the full 15 years is shown, commencing with a conveyance inter vivos, it is not necessary that this be for value: see para 142 post; and 1 Williams Law relating to Vendors and Purchasers of Real Estate and Chattels Real (4th Edn, 1936) 236.

3   *Re Marsh and Earl Granville* (1882) 24 ChD 11, CA; and see para 142 post. As to the disposition of registered and unregistered land by transfer see para 262 note 2 post.

4   *Re Scott and Alvarez's Contract, Scott v Alvarez* [1895] 1 Ch 596 at 605, CA. A fortiori, in the case of a sale by the court, the utmost good faith must be shown: *Else v Else* (1872) LR 13 Eq 196 at 201; *Manifold v Johnston* [1902] 1 IR 7. See also para 133 note 6 post. As to a condition limiting the time for requisitions or objections see paras 102–103 post.

5   *Re Ossemsley Estates Ltd* [1937] 1 All ER 782, not considered on appeal [1937] 3 All ER 774, CA.

(ii) Rights under Particular Conditions

A. BIDDING AT AUCTION

84. Bidding. On a sale by auction the conditions usually state that the sale of the property and of each lot is subject to a reserve price[1], and that the vendor or his agent may bid up to that reserve[2]. It is provided that the auctioneer may refuse any bid[3] and that, the auctioneer may determine any dispute as to a bid[4] or restart the auction at the last undisputed bid[5].

A contract made at a public auction is not subject to the statutory requirement as to writing[6].

1   See the Standard Conditions of Sale (3rd Edn), conditions 2.3.1, 2.3.2. As to the Standard Conditions of Sale see para 1 note 9 ante. As to a sale by auction see generally AUCTION.

2   See the Standard Conditions of Sale (3rd Edn), condition 2.3.3.

3   See the Standard Conditions of Sale (3rd Edn), condition 2.3.4.

4   See the Standard Conditions of Sale (3rd Edn), condition 2.3.5. This power may be exercised where the dispute concerns whether a bid had been communicated to the auctioneer: *Richards v Phillips* [1969] 1 Ch 39, [1968] 2 All ER 859, CA.

5   See the Standard Conditions of Sale (3rd Edn), condition 2.3.5. Under the general law a bidder may retract a bid at any time until its acceptance (see *Payne v Cave* (1789) 3 Term Rep 148; *Jones v Nanney* (1824) 13 Price 76 at 103; Sugden's Law of Vendors and Purchasers (14th Edn, 1862) 14), but under special circumstances a bidder may be unable to retract (see *Freer v Rimner* (1844) 14 Sim 391).

6   See the Law of Property (Miscellaneous Provisions) Act 1989 s 2(5)(b); and para 29 ante.

85. Sale subject to reserve or vendor's right to bid. The particulars or conditions of sale must state whether the land will be sold without reserve, or subject to a reserve price, or whether a right to bid is reserved, and, if the sale is without reserve, the vendor may not employ any person to bid at the sale, nor may the auctioneer knowingly accept any bidding from such a person[1].

A sale subject to a reserve price and the reservation of a right to bid are distinct matters[2], and a sale expressed to be subject to a reserve price or to a reserved bidding[3] does not give the vendor the right to bid by himself or his agent up to the reserve price[4]. Where the conditions expressly reserve the right to bid without further defining it, the vendor may bid himself or employ any one person to do so on his behalf[5], and, if the vendor or his agent is to be at liberty to bid more than once[6] and beyond the reserve price, this should be expressly stated[7].

1   Sale of Land by Auction Act 1867 s 5; and see AUCTION vol 2 (Reissue) para 940. The particulars or conditions need not use the words 'with reserve' or 'without reserve'; it is sufficient if it is made plain by the words used that the sale is subject to a reserve price: *Hills and Grant Ltd v Hodson* [1934] Ch 53.

2   Although the Sale of Land by Auction Act 1867 s 5 (as amended) is expressed in the alternative, the conditions may state that the sale is subject both to a reserve price and to a right to bid (*Gilliat v Gilliat* (1869) LR 9 Eq 60), and this is usually done: see para 84 ante.

3   *Gilliat v Gilliat* (1869) LR 9 Eq 60. See also *Notley v Salmon* (1853) 1 WR 240.

4   *Gilliat v Gilliat* (1869) LR 9 Eq 60.

5   See the Sale of Land by Auction Act 1867 s 6; and AUCTION vol 2 (Reissue) para 940. As to a condition reserving such a right see the Standard Conditions of Sale (3rd Edn), condition 2.3.3; and para 84 ante. As to the Standard Conditions of Sale see para 1 note 9 ante. Formerly a puffer (ie an agent to bid on behalf of the vendor) was not allowed at law, unless the sale was stated to be subject to a reserve. Whether it was stated to be without reserve, or whether the conditions were silent as to reserve, the employment of a puffer made the sale fraudulent and therefore voidable (*Howard v Castle* (1796) 6 Term Rep 642; *R v Marsh* (1829) 3 Y & J 331 (sale on behalf of Crown); *Thornett v Haines* (1846) 15 M & W 367 at 371; *Green v Baverstock* (1863) 10 Jur NS 47; *Mainprice v Westley* (1865) 11 Jur NS 975; *Mortimer v Bell* (1865) 1 Ch App 10), and it was the same in equity where the sale was stated to be without reserve (*Meadows v Tanner* (1820) 5 Madd 34; *Thornett v Haines* supra; *Robinson v Wall* (1847) 2 Ph 372). However, if the conditions were silent as to reserve, then, in equity, one puffer was allowed in order to prevent a sale at an under value: *Woodward v Miller* (1845) 2 Coll 279; *Flint v Woodin* (1852) 9 Hare 618; *Mortimer v Bell* supra; and see *Smith v Clarke* (1806) 12 Ves 477. Only one puffer was permitted since the employment of more could not be intended for protection against undervalue merely, but to enhance the price: *Smith v Clarke* supra; *Thornett v Haines* supra; *Mortimer v Bell* supra. Statutory form was given to the common law rule by the Sale of Land by Auction Act 1867 s 4, which provides that a sale of land by auction which would be invalid at law owing to the employment of a puffer is to be deemed invalid also in equity.

6   See *Parfitt v Jepson* (1877) 46 LJQB 529. The Standard Conditions of Sale (3rd Edn), condition 2.3.3, gives the right to bid up to the reserve price, which seems to imply the right to bid more than once: see para 84 ante.

7   See the Sale of Land by Auction Act 1867 s 6; and *Parfitt v Jepson* (1877) 46 LJQB 529 at 533 per Lindley J. Cf the Standard Conditions of Sale (3rd Edn), condition 2.3.3, which limits the right to bid to the reserve price: see para 84 ante.

B.   DEPOSITS

86. Payment of deposit. The Standard Conditions of Sale provide for a deposit of 10 per cent to be paid, no later than the date of the contract, to the vendor's solicitor as stakeholder[1]. If the payment is not made to the solicitor as stakeholder he receives it as agent for the vendor. Thus the payment is in effect payment to the vendor[2], and cannot be recovered from the solicitor personally[3]. The deposit is not merely part payment, but a guarantee of the due performance of the contract[4] by the purchaser. Hence it may be forfeited if the sale goes off owing to his default[5]. Interest on a deposit can be ordered where the court orders its return, but it may be refused by reason of the purchaser's conduct[6]. Failure by the purchaser to pay the deposit required by the contract entitles the vendor to repudiate the contract[7]. Despite such repudiation, the vendor may recover the unpaid deposit[8]. Where an estate agent receives a deposit before a contract has been concluded, he does not, in the absence of actual authority, receive it on the vendor's behalf; the vendor will not, normally, therefore, be liable for the agent's default[9].

1   See the Standard Conditions of Sale (3rd Edn), condition 2.2.1. As to the Standard Conditions of Sale see para 1 note 9 ante. For the meaning of 'contract' see para 55 note 10 ante. 'Solicitor' includes barrister, duly certificated notary public, recognised licensed conveyancer and recognised body under the Administration of Justice Act 1985 s 9 or s 32: Standard Conditions of Sale (3rd Edn), condition 1.1.1(l); and see para 3 ante. See also *Wiggins v Lord* (1841) 4 Beav 30; *Ellis v Goulton* [1893] 1 QB 350, CA. Without such a stipulation no deposit could be demanded lawfully, as the whole consideration is not payable until completion, when the vendor has shown good title: *Binks v Lord Rokeby* (1818) 2 Swan 222. Payment of the deposit is not a condition precedent to the contract taking effect, but is a fundamental term of the contract, breach of which entitles the vendor to treat the contract as discharged: see *Millichamp v Jones* [1983] 1 All ER 267, [1982] 1 WLR 1422; *Damon Cia Naviera SA v Hapag-Lloyd International SA* [1985] 1 All ER 475, [1985] 1 WLR 435, CA; cf *Myton Ltd v Schwab-Morris* [1974] 1 All ER 326, [1974] 1 WLR 331. As to the authority of an auctioneer to receive the deposit see AUCTION vol 2 (Reissue) para 909. In the absence of special agreement an auctioneer receives the deposit as stakeholder: see *Harington v Hoggart* (1830) 1 B & Ad 577; and AUCTION vol 2 (Reissue) para 948. He is not justified in taking an IOU in payment of the deposit: see *Hodgens v Keon* [1894] 2 IR 657, Ir CA. As to payment by cheque or bill see *Morrow v Carty* [1957] NI 174 (where it was held that non payment of a deposit payable in cash justified a resale at the same auction); and AUCTION vol 2 (Reissue) para 909. Trustees who are selling are justified in allowing the deposit to be paid to the auctioneer as stakeholder: see 1 Williams Law

relating to Vendors and Purchasers of Real Estate and Chattels Real (4th Edn, 1936) 326. The Standard Conditions of Sale (3rd Edn) provide that, except on a sale by auction, payment is to be made by banker's draft or by a cheque drawn on a solicitors' clearing bank account: condition 2.2.1. 'Banker's draft' means a draft drawn by and on a clearing bank: condition 1.1.1(c). 'Clearing bank' means a bank which is a member of CHAPS Limited: condition 1.1.1(d). As to interest on the deposit see *Townshend v Townshend* (1826) 2 Russ 303; and the Standard Conditions of Sale (3rd Edn), condition 2.2.3. As to investment of the deposit see para 235 post.

Under the Standard Conditions of Sale (3rd Edn), if before the completion date the vendor agrees to buy another property in England and Wales for his residence, he may use all or any part of the deposit as a deposit in that transaction to be held on terms to the same effect as this condition and the Standard Conditions of Sale (3rd Edn), condition 2.2.3: condition 2.2.2. For the meaning of 'completion date' see para 102 note 5 post. Any deposit or part of a deposit not being used in accordance with condition 2.2.2 is to be held by the vendor's solicitor as stakeholder on terms that on completion it is paid to the vendor with accrued interest: condition 2.2.3. 'Accrued interest' means: (1) if money has been placed on deposit or in a building society share account, the interest actually earned; (2) otherwise, the interest which might reasonably have been earned by depositing the money at interest on seven days' notice of withdrawal with a clearing bank, less, in either case, any proper charges for handling the money: condition 1.1.1(a).

As to the position of a stakeholder see CONTRACT vol 9(1) (Reissue) para 1143. A solicitor may not pay rent out of a deposit held as stakeholder: *Dimurro v Charles Caplin & Co* (1969) 211 Estates Gazette 31.

2 *Bamford v Shuttleworth* (1840) 11 Ad & El 926; *Edgell v Day* (1865) LR 1 CP 80; *Ellis v Goulton* [1893] 1 QB 350, CA. See also CONTRACT vol 9(1) (Reissue) para 1143; and SOLICITORS vol 44(1) (Reissue) para 126.

3 *Ellis v Goulton* [1893] 1 QB 350, CA. As to judicial definitions of the distinction between stakeholders and agent for the vendor see also *Burt v Claude Cousins & Co Ltd* [1971] 2 QB 426 at 435–436, [1971] 2 All ER 611 at 615, CA, per Lord Denning MR; *Potters (a firm) v Loppert* [1973] Ch 399 at 409, [1973] 1 All ER 658 at 664 per Pennycuick V-C; *Tudor v Hamid* [1988] 1 EGLR 251, [1987] NLJ Rep 79, CA.

4 Ie a completed contract: see CONTRACT vol 9(1) (Reissue) para 1134; *Myton Ltd v Schwab-Morris* [1974] 1 All ER 326, [1974] 1 WLR 331.

5 See text and notes 6–8 infra; and para 234 et seq post.

6 See the Law Reform (Miscellaneous Provisions) Act 1934 s 3 (as amended) (see PRACTICE AND PROCEDURE); *Ryan v Pilkington* (1959) as reported in 173 Estates Gazette 487 at 493, CA. As to interest generally see MONEY. In *Public Trustee v Pearlberg* [1940] 2 KB 1 at 22, 25, [1940] 2 All ER 270 at 282, 284, CA, per Luxmoore LJ, the court refused to award interest by reason of the purchaser's conduct.

7 The payment of the deposit is a fundamental term of the contract (*Millichamp v Jones* [1983] 1 All ER 267, [1982] 1 WLR 1422; *Damon Cia Naviera SA v Hapag-Lloyd International SA* [1985] 1 All ER 475, [1985] 1 WLR 435, CA), not a condition precedent as held in *Myton Ltd v Schwab-Morris* [1974] 1 All ER 326, [1974] 1 WLR 331; See also *Pollway Ltd v Abdullah* [1974] 2 All ER 381, [1974] 1 WLR 493, CA; and the Standard Conditions of Sale (3rd Edn), condition 2.2 (see the text and note 1 supra, note 8 infra).

8 *Millichamp v Jones* [1983] 1 All ER 267, [1982] 1 WLR 1422; *Damon Cia Naviera SA v Hapag-Lloyd International SA* [1985] 1 All ER 475, [1985] 1 WLR 435, CA; and see *Lowe v Hope* [1970] Ch 94, [1969] 3 All ER 605, which is now discredited on this point. The Standard Conditions of Sale (3rd Edn) provide that, if a cheque tendered in payment of all or part of the deposit is dishonoured when first presented, the vendor may, within seven working days of being notified that the cheque has been dishonoured, give notice to the purchaser that the contract is discharged by the purchaser's breach: condition 2.2.4.

9 *Sorrell v Finch* [1977] AC 728, [1976] 2 All ER 371, HL.

87. Forfeiture of deposit and resale. The conditions of sale usually expressly provide that, where the purchaser fails to comply with the conditions, then, unless the court otherwise directs[1], his deposit is to be forfeited[2] and the vendor is at liberty to resell the property and to recover from the original purchaser[3] any deficiency in price on a resale and also the costs of the resale or any attempted resale. Under such a condition the purchaser cannot call for an account of the surplus if a larger price is obtained on the resale[4], and where the vendor does not succeed in reselling the property he can forfeit the deposit and recover the expenses of the abortive sale[5]. If the vendor seeks to recover the deficiency on the resale, he must bring into account the forfeited deposit[6]. Conditions are commonly inserted providing for the forfeiture of the deposit and resale on the purchaser's failure to comply with a notice to complete[7].

1   See the Law of Property Act 1925 s 49(2); and para 246 post.
2   As to the right to forfeit a deposit in the absence of an express condition and the time when the right of forfeiture arises see paras 234–238 post.
3   See the Standard Conditions of Sale (3rd Edn), condition 7.2(a). As to the Standard Conditions of Sale see para 1 note 9 ante. It has been held that the vendor has a right of resale in the absence of express stipulation (*Noble v Edwardes, Edwardes v Noble* (1877) 5 ChD 378 at 388, CA), and the vendor must have a common law right of resale where he accepts a repudiatory breach by the purchaser (see *Johnson v Agnew* [1980] AC 367, [1979] 1 All ER 883, HL). The omission by a trustee to resell is not necessarily a breach of trust: *Thomson v Christie* (1852) 1 Macq 236 at 240, HL. A provision for forfeiture of instalments already paid is a penalty against which relief may be given: *Kilmer v British Columbia Orchard Lands Ltd* [1913] AC 319, PC; *Steedman v Drinkle* [1916] 1 AC 275, PC; and see *Brickles v Snell* [1916] 2 AC 599 at 605, PC. Relief was refused in *Mussen v Van Diemen's Land Co* [1938] Ch 253, [1938] 1 All ER 210; *Stockloser v Johnson* [1954] 1 QB 476, [1954] 1 All ER 630, CA. See also *Galbraith v Mitchenall Estates Ltd* [1965] 2 QB 473, [1964] 2 All ER 653; *Starside Properties Ltd v Mustapha* [1974] 2 All ER 567, [1974] 1 WLR 816, CA; and para 232 post.
     An attempt to forfeit a deposit of 25% has been held void as a penalty: see *Workers Trust and Merchant Bank Ltd v Dojap Investments Ltd* [1993] AC 573, [1993] 2 All ER 370, PC (the entire deposit was ordered to be returned, the court rejecting the argument that the vendor should be allowed to retain 10%; the vendor's remedy was damages to be assessed).
4   *Ex p Hunter* (1801) 6 Ves 94 at 97.
5   *Essex v Daniell, Daniell v Essex* (1875) LR 10 CP 538 at 548.
6   See para 233 post. After the resale he cannot sue the purchaser for the original purchase money: *Lamond v Davall* (1847) 9 QB 1030.
7   See the Standard Conditions of Sale (3rd Edn), condition 7.2(a), impliedly referring to condition 6.8.

C. FIXTURES, LEASES AND EASEMENTS

88. Timber and fixtures. In the absence of special provision, a sale of land includes the fixtures and growing timber on it at the time of the sale[1]. Hence it is common, both in private sales and on sales by auction, to insert a condition that the fixtures and timber are to be taken at a price stated in the particulars or at a valuation to be made in a specified manner[2]. It is sometimes further provided that, failing such valuation, they are to be taken at a fair valuation or price. This last provision enables the court to direct a reference to ascertain the price[3]. In the absence of such a provision, it was formerly held that if the valuation could not be made in the manner specified the court would not interfere, since that would be to make a new contract for the parties[4], but now it would seem that if the criteria for valuation are objectively applicable the court may, on failure of the stipulated machinery for valuation, substitute its own machinery[5].

Under The National Conveyancing Protocol[6] the vendor must complete a detailed questionnaire[7], specifying which items are to be included in the sale and which excluded[8]. Excluded chattels should then be specified and there is provision for a price to be attached to those chattels. Whether or not a separate price is to be paid for the chattels, the contract takes effect as a contract for the sale of goods[9], and ownership of the chattels passes to the purchaser on actual completion[10].

1   See *Colegrave v Dias Santos* (1823) 2 B & C 76. As to timber see FORESTRY vol 19(1) (Reissue) para 32; LANDLORD AND TENANT vol 27(1) (Reissue) para 157 et seq. As to fixtures see LANDLORD AND TENANT vol 27(1) (Reissue) para 143 et seq.
2   It used to be held that trustees cannot contract to sell property at a price to be fixed by valuation, since this is a delegation of their authority (*Peters v Lewes and East Grinstead Rly Co* (1880) 16 ChD 703 at 713 (on appeal (1881) 18 ChD 429 at 437, CA); *Re Earl of Wilton's Settled Estates* [1907] 1 Ch 50 at 55), but trustees of land now have in relation to the land subject to the trust, for the purpose of exercising their function as trustees, all the powers of an absolute owner (Trusts of Land and Appointment of Trustees Act 1996 s 6(1)). However, the powers of the trustees can be restricted or excluded, or made subject to a consent: see s 8(1), (2); and TRUSTS vol 48 (Reissue) para 894. See also the Settled Land Act 1925 s 49(2); and SETTLEMENTS para 832 post. The word 'timber' in the contract is to be taken as meaning timber properly so called: *Re Tower's Contract* [1924] WN 331; see FORESTRY vol 19(1) (Reissue) para 32. As to felling licences see FORESTRY vol 19(1) (Reissue) para 46 et seq.

3   See *Wilks v Davis* (1817) 3 Mer 507; *Morgan v Milman* (1853) 3 De GM & G 24.
4   See *Milnes v Gery* (1807) 14 Ves 400; *Blundell v Brettargh* (1810) 17 Ves 232; *Gourlay v Duke of Somerset* (1815) 19 Ves 429 at 430; *Wilks v Davis* (1817) 3 Mer 507; *Agar v Macklew* (1825) 2 Sim & St 418; *Morgan v Milman* (1853) 3 De GM & G 24; *Collins v Collins* (1858) 26 Beav 306; *Vickers v Vickers* (1867) LR 4 Eq 529; *Firth v Midland Rly Co* (1875) LR 20 Eq 100.
5   See *Sudbrook Trading Estate Ltd v Eggleton* [1983] 1 AC 444, [1982] 3 All ER 1, HL, specifically overruling *Agar v Macklew* (1825) 2 Sim & St 418, and *Vickers v Vickers* (1867) LR 4 Eq 529; see para 37 note 2 ante.
6   See para 19 ante.
7   This questionnaire is known as the Fixtures, Fittings and Contents Form. See the Standard Conditions of Sale (3rd Edn), Special Condition 4, which makes reference to this form. As to the Standard Conditions of Sale see para 1 note 9 ante.
8   See The National Conveyancing Protocol (3rd Edn, 1994), procedure 2.5; and para 19 ante.
9   See the Standard Conditions of Sale (3rd Edn), conditions 9.1, 9.2. For the meaning of 'contract' see para 55 note 10 ante.
10 See the Standard Conditions of Sale (3rd Edn), conditions 9.1, 9.3.

89. Tenancies and easements. It is usual to provide that the property is sold subject to the existing tenancies and to the rights of tenants under them[1], to rights of way and water and other easements affecting it, and to other liabilities of a permanent or irremovable nature, such as restrictive covenants or rentcharges[2]. This condition does not absolve the owner from his duty to disclose to the purchaser all matters affecting the property which are within his knowledge[3], and matters of the nature in question should, as far as practicable, be stated in the particulars, but such a condition does operate as a protection to the vendor if it subsequently appears that there is some right in favour of a third person of which he was ignorant at the date of the contract[4].

In the case of a sale of agricultural land a condition should be included for the payment, in addition to the balance of the purchase money, of the outgoing valuation if the tenant is quitting at or near the time of completion[5].

1   See *Re Earl of Derby and Fergusson's Contract* [1912] 1 Ch 479. As to notice of a tenant's claim to compensation under the Agricultural Holdings Act 1986 see AGRICULTURE vol 1(2) (Reissue) para 378; and as to conditions relating to such claims see the text and notes 3–5 infra.
2   As to matters affecting the property see the Standard Conditions of Sale (3rd Edn), condition 3; and para 55 ante. As to the Standard Conditions of Sale see para 1 note 9 ante. As to party walls see *Apostal v Simons* [1936] 1 All ER 207, CA; and BOUNDARIES vol 4(1) (Reissue) para 964 et seq.
3   *Heywood v Mallalieu* (1883) 25 ChD 357; *Nottingham Patent Brick and Tile Co v Butler* (1886) 16 QBD 778 at 786, CA. As to such duty of disclosure see *Dougherty v Oates* (1900) 45 Sol Jo 119; *Simpson v Gilley* (1922) 92 LJ Ch 194; *Re Englefield Holdings Ltd and Sinclair's Contract* [1962] 3 All ER 503, [1962] 1 WLR 119; and paras 50, 55 ante. See also *William Sindall plc v Cambridgeshire County Council* [1994] 3 All ER 932, [1994] 1 WLR 1016, CA.
4   *Russell v Harford* (1866) LR 2 Eq 507 at 512. However, the condition only applies to rights available against the vendor; hence, where two lots are sold subject to the condition, a right of way acquired by the tenant of one lot against the tenant of the other is not by virtue of the condition perpetuated in favour of the purchaser of the former lot: *Daniel v Anderson* (1862) 31 LJ Ch 610; and see *Fahey v Dwyer* (1879) 4 LR Ir 271; *Delaparelle v St Martin-in-the-Fields Vestry* (1890) 34 Sol Jo 545.
5   See AGRICULTURE vol 1(2) (Reissue) para 378. On the determination of an agricultural tenancy, there may be payments both by the landlord and by the tenant, and it is the balance of these that is the outgoing valuation. If it is in favour of the landlord, the condition will not apply: see AGRICULTURE vol 1(2) (Reissue) para 378.

D. TITLE TO FREEHOLDS

90. Commencement of title. It is usual to specify the instrument with which the title is to commence[1], and it is necessary to do so if the vendor wishes to deduce a title for less than the statutory period of 15 years[2], or to commence his abstract within that period with an instrument which is not otherwise a good root of title[3]. A purchaser should, however, insist as far as possible on having the full statutory length of title, since he is deemed to have notice of everything that he would have discovered if he had insisted on and investigated the title for the statutory period[4].

A condition that the abstract is to commence with a specified document does not preclude the purchaser from investigating the earlier title by another means if he can[5]. However, if the condition stipulates that the earlier title, whether appearing in any abstracted documents or not, is not to be required, investigated or objected to, this precludes inquiry and investigation for every purpose[6], although if the vendor allows the purchaser to inspect the deeds relating to the earlier title, and thus discloses to the purchaser some blot on the title, the purchaser is not precluded from raising the objection[7].

1   In the Standard Conditions of Sale (3rd Edn), the root of title is to be specified in the special conditions: see Special Condition 3. As to the Standard Conditions of Sale see para 1 note 9 ante.
2   See para 139 post. As to the necessity of expressing such a condition in clear and unambiguous terms see para 78 ante.
3   See para 83 note 2 ante. As to the need for an abstract of title with respect to both unregistered and registered land see paras 138, 141–149 post.
4   *Re Cox and Neve's Contract* [1891] 2 Ch 109; *Re Nisbet and Potts' Contract* [1905] 1 Ch 391 (affd [1906] 1 Ch 386, CA). A purchaser is not deemed to be affected with notice of matters beyond the statutory period unless the purchaser has actually made investigation or inquiries (Law of Property Act 1925 s 44(8)), but it seems that this protection does not extend to matters of which he is to be treated as having actual notice by virtue of s 198(1) (as amended) (see EQUITY vol 16 (Reissue) para 768; LAND CHARGES vol 26 (Reissue) para 593) (see the *Report of the Committee on Land Charges* (Cmd 9825) (1956) para 3; and cf *White v Bijou Mansions Ltd* [1937] Ch 610, [1937] 3 All ER 269 (affd on other grounds [1938] Ch 351, [1938] 1 All ER 546, CA)). As to the desirability of insisting on the full length of title where the property is to be mortgaged see para 1 note 12 ante.
5   *Sellick v Trevor* (1843) 11 M & W 722 at 728; *Darlington v Hamilton* (1854) Kay 550 at 558. This is so notwithstanding that the purchaser is prevented by the Law of Property Act 1925 s 45(1) (see paras 142, 150 post), from requiring production of documents dated or made before the time prescribed by law or fixed by agreement for the commencement of the title: see *Nottingham Patent Brick and Tile Co v Butler* (1885) 15 QBD 261 at 272 (affd (1886) 16 QBD 778, CA); *Re Nisbet and Potts' Contract* [1905] 1 Ch 391 (affd [1906] 1 Ch 386, CA).
6   *Hume v Bentley* (1852) 5 De G & Sm 520; *Re National Provincial Bank of England and Marsh* [1895] 1 Ch 190; *Re M'Lure and Garrett's Contract* [1899] 1 IR 225; *Re Earl of Arran and Knowlesden and Creer's Contract* [1912] 2 Ch 141. Such a condition is construed strictly, and its terms must be clear and unambiguous: *Waddell v Wolfe* (1874) LR 9 QB 515, where the language was held not sufficient to preclude objection to the earlier title.
7   *Warren v Richardson* (1830) You 1; *Smith v Robinson* (1879) 13 ChD 148. Nor does the condition exclude inquiry into a matter on the earlier title (eg a restrictive covenant) which is incorporated by reference in the title to be shown: *White v Hague* [1921] 1 IR 138. See also para 150 note 7 post.

91. Nature of title. The conditions usually state the nature of the title under which the vendor is selling. He may be selling as absolute owner by virtue of the powers incident to his ownership, and if so, he may be entitled free from incumbrances or subject to incumbrances. If he is entitled subject to incumbrances, but these are to be cleared off on or before completion, there is no need to mention them in the conditions. They need only be mentioned if the purchaser is to take the property subject to them[1].

If the vendor is not absolute owner, he will be selling by virtue of some statutory or other power or trust. If the property is settled land, the vendor will usually be the tenant for life or a person having the powers of a tenant for life, and he will sell under his statutory powers[2]. His right to exercise the statutory powers will, in the ordinary course, appear from a vesting instrument by which the property is declared to be vested in him on the trusts of the settlement[3]. On the other hand, the vendors may be trustees or trustees for sale selling under a trust created by deed or will. If the land is comprised in a personalty settlement, the settlement will usually have been created by a conveyance of the land on trust and a declaration by separate deed of the beneficial interests. The vendors will then make title under the conveyance on trust only and the purchaser will not be concerned with the declaration of trust[4]. If the trust was created by will, the vendors' title may be shown by an assent in their favour on trust, in which case the purchaser must ascertain that no notice of a previous assent or conveyance has been placed on or annexed to the probate, but is not otherwise concerned with the will[5]. The vendors may also be trustees holding on the statutory trusts arising where persons are beneficially entitled to land as tenants in common[6] or as joint tenants[7] or on other statutory or implied trusts[8]. In all cases of a trust of land, unless the trustee is a trust corporation, there must be two trustees to give a receipt for the purchase money[9].

Other capacities in which the vendors may be selling are as personal representatives[10] or mortgagees[11], and there may be other circumstances which affect the nature of the title, such as that the owner is suffering from mental disorder[12] or is a bankrupt[13], or is a company in liquidation[14], or that the property is subject to charitable trusts[15] or is partnership property[16], or that the sale is being made by order of the court[17].

1 As to the sale of incumbered land see para 267 post.
2 See the Settled Land Act 1925 ss 19, 20 (as amended), 38 (as amended); and SETTLEMENTS para 761 et seq, 827 et seq post. A settlement created after 1 January 1997 takes effect as a trust of land and not as a settlement for the purposes of the Settled Land Act 1925: see the Trusts of Land and Appointment of Trustees Act 1996 s 2(1), which is subject to savings in s 2(2), (3). See also SETTLEMENTS para 676 post.
3 See the Settled Land Act 1925 ss 4–6, 13 (as amended); and SETTLEMENTS para 688 et seq post. As to the effectiveness of a vesting deed giving effect to a settlement subsisting on 1 January 1926 see s 110(2) proviso; and SETTLEMENTS para 886 post.
4 As to sales by trustees of land see the Law of Property Act 1925 ss 24, 27, 31, 33 (all as amended); and REAL PROPERTY vol 39(2) (Reissue) para 64 et seq; SETTLEMENTS paras 896, 899–900, 906 post; TRUSTS vol 48 (Reissue) paras 689, 712, 723, 879. As to the disposition of registered and unregistered land by transfer see para 262 note 2 post.
5 See the Administration of Estates Act 1925 s 36 (as amended); and EXECUTORS AND ADMINISTRATORS. The assent is sufficient unless the title as deduced shows the assent to have been wrong: *Re Duce and Boots Cash Chemists (Southern) Ltd's Contract* [1937] Ch 642, [1937] 3 All ER 788. As to assent see EXECUTORS AND ADMINISTRATORS. As to the need for a personal representative who is also a trustee to execute an assent in writing in his own favour see *Re King's Will Trusts, Assheton v Boyne* [1964] Ch 542, [1964] 1 All ER 833; and EXECUTORS AND ADMINISTRATORS. Owing to certain difficulties arising on the use of the statutory form of assent on trust contained in the Law of Property Act 1925 s 206, Sch 5 Form 9, it is the practice to assent to the property vesting in the trustees 'upon the trust in the said will contained'. In strictness this brings the will on the title in so far as it contains a trust, but so long as there is a recital of the will down to the trust and omitting the beneficial interests this raises no practical difficulty. As to the modification of Sch 5 Form 9 (in relation to covenants for title) see the Law of Property (Miscellaneous Provisions) Act 1994 s 9. As to the provisions of the Law of Property (Miscellaneous Provisions) Act 1994 relating to implied covenants for title see paras 349–351 post.
6 See REAL PROPERTY vol 39(2) (Reissue) para 207 et seq.
7 See para 74 ante.
8 See eg the Administration of Estates Act 1925 s 33 (as amended); and EXECUTORS AND ADMINISTRATORS.
9 See the Law of Property Act 1925 s 27(2) (as amended); and TRUSTS vol 48 (Reissue) paras 689, 712. The restriction applies only to the receipt of the purchase money and does not prevent a legal estate vesting in a sole trustee nor his power to convey it if no receipt is required or a receipt is otherwise provided for: *Re Myhill, Hull v Myhill* [1928] Ch 100; *Re Wight and Best's Brewery Co Ltd's Contract* [1929] WN 11. Where land is sold and conveyed by a single trustee, the rights of the beneficiaries under the trust are not overreached, and the purchaser is bound by any such rights of which he has notice (or, in the case of registered land, are protected on the register or are overriding interests): see *Caunce v Caunce* [1969] 1 All ER 722, [1969] 1 WLR 286; *Williams and Glyn's Bank Ltd v Boland* [1981] AC 487, [1980] 2 All ER 408, HL. As to notice generally see EQUITY vol 16 (Reissue) para 767 et seq. As to the position where the title to land is registered see LAND REGISTRATION vol 26 (Reissue) paras 719, 782 et seq.
10 See generally EXECUTORS AND ADMINISTRATORS.
11 See generally MORTGAGE.
12 See para 72 ante.
13 See para 65 ante.

14 See para 67 ante.
15 See CHARITIES vol 5(2) (Reissue) para 329 et seq.
16 See *Re Fuller's Contract* [1933] Ch 652.
17 See paras 133–136 post.

92. Statement that title is to be made in a particular way. A statement that the title is to be made in some particular way is indicative only of the vendor's intention, and is not a warranty to make a good title in that way[1]. Hence, if the vendor cannot make title in the way stated, but has at the time of the contract power to make title in some other way[2], or has such power before the purchaser has repudiated the contract[3], the purchaser cannot object to the title.

1 *Re Spencer and Hauser's Contract* [1928] Ch 598 at 608. As to the avoidance of stipulations that title to the legal estate is to be made with the concurrence of persons entitled to an equitable interest see para 272 post.
2 *Re Spencer and Hauser's Contract* [1928] Ch 598 at 608 (statement that vendors would sell as trustees for sale; title made as personal representatives). See also *Re Baker and Selmon's Contract* [1907] 1 Ch 238 (sale as 'trustee'; no power of sale, but contract entered into at beneficiaries' request); *Re Atkinson and Horsell's Contract* [1912] 2 Ch 1 at 11, CA; *Brickles v Snell* [1916] 2 AC 599 at 608, PC.
3 *Re Hailes and Hutchinson's Contract* [1920] 1 Ch 233 (offer of concurrence of beneficiaries before repudiation by purchaser). A purchaser may object if a new title is offered depending on a conveyance by a person not bound to convey at the vendor's request (*Re Bryant and Barningham's Contract* (1890) 44 ChD 218, CA), and where the offer of the beneficiaries' concurrence is not made until after the time for completion has expired and long after repudiation by the purchaser (*Re Head's Trustees and Macdonald* (1890) 45 ChD 310, CA). Where a condition provides that the vendor is to convey such title as he has, but supported by evidence of 20 years' adverse possession, the condition is not satisfied by showing a good possessory title based on 12 years' possession: *George Wimpey & Co Ltd v Sohn* [1967] Ch 487, [1966] 1 All ER 232, CA. See also para 143 post.

93. Capacity of vendor. It was formerly the practice for the conditions to define the capacity in which the vendor sold, since that capacity would define the extent of the implied covenants for title[1]. In dispositions made on or after 1 July 1995, the vendor will give either a full title guarantee or a limited title guarantee, and the conditions will state which kind of guarantee is given[2].

1 As to covenants for title in general see paras 336–337 post; and as to the old law see paras 338–348 post.
2 As to the new law relating to implied covenants for title see paras 349–351 post.

94. Stipulation for acceptance of vendor's title. A vendor may stipulate that the purchaser is to accept such title as the vendor has[1]. This condition does not relieve the vendor from the obligation of making out the best title he can from the material in his possession[2]. A purchaser is bound by such a condition even if the title proves defective[3]. If the conditions simply state the facts and stipulate that the purchaser is to take such title as the facts give, the purchaser must accept it whatever it be, but, if they go on to state as a positive fact that the vendor has power to sell, the purchaser may make further inquiries[4]. The purchaser is entitled to assume that the vendor has disclosed what it was his duty to disclose, and non-disclosure of the existence of onerous covenants affecting the property prevents the condition from being binding upon him[5].

1 See *Freme v Wright* (1819) 4 Madd 364; *Groom v Booth* (1853) 1 Drew 548; *Tweed v Mills* (1865) LR 1 CP 39.
2 *Keyse v Hayden* (1853) 20 LTOS 244; *Hume v Pocock* (1866) 1 Ch App 379 at 385. Nor does it relieve the vendor of the duty of paying off a mortgage on the property: *Goold v Birmingham, Dudley and District Bank* (1888) 4 TLR 413.
3 *Wilmot v Wilkinson* (1827) 6 B & C 506; *Duke v Barnett* (1846) 2 Coll 337; *Ashworth v Mounsey* (1853) 9 Exch 175. However, although the purchaser is bound at law, and therefore cannot recover his deposit, specific performance will not be ordered against him if he will not get a holding title: *Re Scott and Alvarez's*

Contract, Scott v Alvarez [1895] 2 Ch 603, CA. See also *Re National Provincial Bank of England and Marsh* [1895] 1 Ch 190; cf *Lethbridge v Kirkman* (1855) 2 Jur NS 372. Now, where the court refuses to order specific performance, or in other circumstances where it considers it equitable, it can order the return of the deposit: see the Law of Property Act 1925 s 49(2); and para 246 post.

4   See *Johnson v Smiley* (1853) 17 Beav 223. As to the obligation to show that a trust is being properly exercised see *Re O'Flanagan and Ryan's Contract* [1905] 1 IR 280 (condition stating defect of title; improper delegation of trust; vendor's right to refuse to complete). A condition excluding evidence of payment of a charge, where for more than 12 years there has been no payment or acknowledgment, is valid: *Hopkinson v Chamberlain* [1908] 1 Ch 853.

5   *Re Haedicke and Lipski's Contract* [1901] 2 Ch 666; *Becker v Partridge* [1966] 2 QB 155, [1966] 2 All ER 266, CA. Cf *Blake v Phinn* (1847) 3 CB 976. As to the sale of an underlease see para 59 ante; and as to the duty to disclose see para 55 ante.

95. Title to rentcharges. On the sale of a rentcharge[1] the conditions as to title may be similar to those on the sale of a lease[2], although the purchaser may be required to accept as correct the description of the land out of which the rent issues and to accept counterparts or duplicates of the documents creating the rent and not to require production of the original or require evidence of due execution or stamping. He may also by the conditions be precluded from inquiring into the validity of any previous apportionment of the rentcharge[3]. Apportionment as to time on the sale of the rentcharge must be provided for, and if there are any arrears of the rentcharge these will not pass unless special provision is made in the contract[4]. This provision should include power to recover the arrears in the vendor's name and a covenant that the arrears are due and unpaid. Where property is sold subject to a rentcharge[5], it should be provided that the last receipt is to be conclusive evidence of the payment of the rent and the observance and performance of all the covenants and conditions in the conveyance creating the rentcharge and also that no proof is to be required of the title or authority of the person purporting to give the receipt[6]. The purchaser will be deemed to purchase with full knowledge of such covenants and conditions whether or not he inspects the deed. Where there is an overriding rentcharge not paid by the vendor, any requirement as to the apportionment of the rentcharge should be excluded. Where re-entry has been made upon the property charged with the rentcharge on account of non-payment, the conditions will usually stipulate that there is to be a statutory declaration by the vendor of undisturbed possession since the re-entry and that all questions by the purchaser as to the proper exercise of the power of re-entry are to be excluded. It is generally a term of such a condition that the purchaser is to assume that the re-entry vested in the vendor the interest in the property contracted to be sold.

1   As to rentcharges generally see RENTCHARGES AND ANNUITIES. As to the prohibition on the creation of new rentcharges see the Rentcharges Act 1977 s 2 (as amended); and RENTCHARGES AND ANNUITIES vol 39(2) (Reissue) para 774.

2   See para 98 post. Rentcharges are sometimes sold in lots.

3   As to the apportionment of rentcharges generally see RENTCHARGES AND ANNUITIES vol 39(2) (Reissue) para 839 et seq.

4   *Salmon v Dean* (1851) 3 Mac & G 344.

5   As to implied covenants on the sale of property subject to a rentcharge see para 293 post.

6   The Law of Property Act 1925 s 45(2), which makes corresponding provision, applies only to leaseholds: see para 98 post.

96. Instruments of building and similar societies. Where the title includes an instrument to which a building society, friendly society or industrial and provident society was a party, it may be desirable to provide that no evidence is to be required as to the rules, constitution or incorporation of the society and that the purchaser is to assume without inquiry that any officer or trustee of the society signing a receipt was such an officer as stated and that a receipt so signed is valid in all respects[1]. In some cases the condition is made to refer to receipts in the statutory form[2].

1 There is no such provision in the Standard Conditions of Sale (3rd Edn). As to the Standard Conditions of Sale see para 1 note 9 ante. Where there is no such condition there may be occasions where it is necessary to supply a copy of the rules and of the certification of the rules in order to show that the instrument was duly executed. As to unincorporated building societies (the last of which attained corporate status in 1965) see BUILDING SOCIETIES vol 4(2) (Reissue) paras 701, 728.

2 As to such receipts see BUILDING SOCIETIES vol 4(2) (Reissue) paras 869–870; FRIENDLY SOCIETIES vol 19(1) (Reissue) para 228; INDUSTRIAL AND PROVIDENT SOCIETIES vol 24 (Reissue) para 96; MORTGAGE.

97. Stamping of documents. In the absence of express stipulation, a purchaser is entitled to have all documents forming the vendor's title properly stamped at the vendor's expense[1], and, as regards documents executed since 16 May 1888, any condition excluding this right on the part of the purchaser is void[2]. A stipulation that any unstamped or insufficiently stamped document is not to be stamped at once, but that the vendor will undertake to pay the penalty if it ever becomes necessary to stamp it seems not to be enforceable[3].

1 *Whiting to Loomes* (1880) 14 ChD 822 (affd (1881) 17 ChD 10, CA), distinguished in *Ex p Birkbeck Freehold Land Society* (1883) 24 ChD 119 at 124, where the instrument was unnecessary for the protection of the purchaser's title, the defect being cured by obtaining the concurrence of an additional party. The right extends to a lease or tenancy agreement, subject to which the property is sold: *Smith v Wyley* (1852) 16 Jur 1136; *Coleman v Coleman* (1898) 79 LT 66. In *Re Weir and Pitt's Contract* (1911) 55 Sol Jo 536, it was held that a purchaser was not concerned with the sufficiency of the stamp where the consideration was apparently far less than the value of the property and the conveyance did not bear an adjudication stamp. See also *Lap Shun Textiles Industrial Co Ltd v Collector of Stamp Revenue* [1976] AC 530, [1976] 1 All ER 833, PC, where it was held that an instrument is liable to duty on its full valuation if it is proved to have been made for inadequate consideration, albeit that the purchaser dealt at arm's length and in good faith, but it was emphasised that such a case was exceptional and that there need be no change in the normal procedure for routine stamping on a stated consideration. See generally STAMP DUTIES AND STAMP DUTY RESERVE TAX. Where it appeared from an abstract of title that a deed was insufficiently stamped but on the original deed the consideration was seen to have been altered from an amount for which the deed was sufficiently stamped, the purchaser was held not to be bound to accept a statutory declaration that the alteration was made after the execution of the deed: *Re Spollon and Long's Contract* [1936] Ch 713, [1936] 2 All ER 711. Probates and letters of administration do not bear a stamp in respect of inheritance tax, but a certificate may be obtained showing that tax has been paid, and a purchaser need not question the sufficiency of the payment: *Tyrrell v Imperial Tobacco Co Ltd* [1926] IR 285, Ir CA. A purchaser now takes free from any charge for inheritance tax which is not registered as a land charge, or protected by notice on the register of title: see INHERITANCE TAXATION vol 24 (Reissue) para 686.

2 See the Stamp Act 1891 s 117; and STAMP DUTIES AND STAMP DUTY RESERVE TAX vol 44(1) (Reissue) para 1007.

3 See *Smith v Mawhood* (1845) 14 M & W 452; *Abbot v Stratton* (1846) 3 Jo & Lat 603 at 616; *Nixon v Albion Marine Insurance Co* (1867) LR 2 Exch 338. See also STAMP DUTIES AND STAMP DUTY RESERVE TAX vol 44(1) (Reissue) para 1007. Strictly speaking, a document not duly stamped cannot (except in criminal proceedings) be received in evidence or be available for any other purpose: see the Stamp Act 1891 s 14(4); and *Sun Alliance Insurance Ltd v IRC* [1972] Ch 133, [1971] 1 All ER 135 (court order which ought to have been stamped as a conveyance on sale). In practice, however, documents are usually admitted in evidence upon an undertaking given by the solicitor of the party producing them to have them stamped and to pay the penalty: see generally EVIDENCE.

E. TITLE TO LEASEHOLDS AND PERFORMANCE OF COVENANTS

98. Leaseholds generally. In the absence of any condition to the contrary in the contract of sale, a vendor of leaseholds is bound to produce the lease under which he holds, even though it was granted more than 15 years before the contract, as well as to show the intermediate title for 15 years[1]. If the lease has been lost, the vendor must by special condition relieve himself of the liability to produce the original lease[2]. Although the purchaser is precluded by statute from calling for the title to the freehold reversion in the case of a lease and to the leasehold reversion in the case of an underlease, these statutory provisions are subject to a contrary intention expressed in the contract[3] and may therefore be varied or excluded by a condition in the contract[4]. Conversely, the right of a purchaser who is precluded from calling for the freehold title to show by other means that there is an objection based on that title[5] can be excluded by a condition in the contract. If the property to be assigned is part only of the property comprised in the lease, and that part has not been previously assigned, apportionment of the rent payable must be provided for[6], and, if that part has been previously assigned at an apportioned rent, all objection to such apportionment must be excluded. By a special condition a sale of an apportioned part of the property comprised in a lease can be carried out by underlease[7]. Where the landlord's consent to an assignment of a lease is required[8] the possibility of this being refused should be provided for[9].

Upon production of the receipt for the last payment of rent due under the lease or underlease before the date of actual completion of the purchase, an intending purchaser of leaseholds is entitled to assume, unless the contrary appears, that all covenants and provisions of the lease or underlease have been performed and observed, and in the case of an underlease that all rent due under the underlease and every superior lease has been paid and all covenants and provisions performed and observed[10]. As this assumption is conditional on the contrary not appearing, a special condition to the effect that all breaches have been waived is sometimes inserted in a contract of sale, although on sale by private treaty objection is generally taken to its insertion[11]. Such a condition should be extended to prevent the purchaser requiring any evidence of the right or title of the person by whom the receipt for rent purports to be given[12]. Where the lease does not reserve a rent or reserves only a nominal rent, a condition may be inserted in the contract that possession at the date of completion is to be conclusive evidence of the performance and observance of the lessee's covenants[13]. The conditions normally provide that a purchaser is deemed to have notice of matters contained in particular documents which are open to inspection[14], but this gives only a limited protection[15]. The sale of property out of repair[16] or to a sitting tenant[17] requires additional conditions. Where the lease is made in consideration of the surrender of an earlier lease all questions as to the title to the surrendered lease should be excluded by special condition, because otherwise the vendor may be required not only to produce the surrendered lease on a sale of the new lease but to show that at the date of the grant of the new lease the lessee was entitled to the surrendered term[18].

1   As to title to leaseholds generally see para 140 post. Although the purchaser is entitled to this and no more apart from any special condition, a special condition to this effect is usually inserted in the contract of sale. As to the importance to the purchaser of seeing the lease see para 8 ante.
2   See *Frend v Buckley* (1870) LR 5 QB 213 at 216. The condition should exclude all inquiry as to the terms of the lease otherwise than as they may appear from any abstract of the lease or assignment of the lease in the vendor's possession or can be shown by statutory declaration. Such a statutory declaration is commonly at the purchaser's expense. See the Standard Conditions of Sale (3rd Edn), conditions 8.1.1, 8.1.2; and note 14 infra. As to the Standard Conditions of Sale see para 1 note 9 ante.
3   See the Law of Property Act 1925 s 44(2), (3), (11); and para 140 post.
4   Where the sale is by assignment of an existing lease, the Standard Conditions of Sale (3rd Edn) do not contain any provision for deduction of the superior title. However, if the term of a new lease will exceed 21 years, the vendor must deduce a title which will enable the purchaser to register the lease at HM Land Registry with an absolute title: condition 8.2.4. For the meaning of 'lease' see para 57 note 5 ante.
5   See para 140 post.

6   See the Standard Conditions of Sale (3rd Edn) which provide that the fact that a rent or rent charge, whether payable or receivable by the owner of the property, has been or will on completion be, informally apportioned is not to be regarded as a defect in title: condition 4.4.

7   Except where the property is divided into several parts, recourse to this method is not generally adopted.

8   As to the vendor's duty to obtain any necessary consent see para 25 ante; and as to the time within which consent must be procured see para 240 post.

9   See the Standard Conditions of Sale (3rd Edn), condition 8.3. Where the consent is required by the lease, it is not open to the purchaser to waive that requirement in the expectation of being able to obtain an assignment without consent: see *Lipmans Wallpaper Ltd v Mason and Hodghton Ltd* [1969] 1 Ch 20, [1968] 1 All ER 1123. See also *Bickel v Courtenay Investments (Nominees) Ltd* [1984] 1 All ER 657, [1984] 1 WLR 795; *29 Equities Ltd v Bank Leumi (UK) Ltd* [1987] 1 All ER 108, CA.

10   See the Law of Property Act 1925 s 45(2), (3). Unless the contrary appears the purchaser must also assume that the lease, or the underlease and every superior lease, was duly granted: see s 45(2), (3).

11   See *Bull v Hutchens* (1863) 32 Beav 615; *Lawrie v Less* (1881) 7 App Cas 19 at 32, HL; *Re Highett and Bird's Contract* [1903] 1 Ch 287, CA; *Re Taunton and West of England Perpetual Benefit Building Society and Roberts' Contract* [1912] 2 Ch 381. An assignor cannot make a good title under an open contract where he has not complied with a dilapidation notice: *Re Martin, ex p Dixon (Trustee) v Tucker* (1912) 106 LT 381. If the vendor is aware of any breach of covenant, he should disclose it and expressly stipulate for its waiver to be assumed. As to the difficulties which may arise in the absence of such a stipulation, cf *Simmons v Pennington & Son (a firm)* [1955] 1 All ER 240, [1955] 1 WLR 183, CA; and para 52 ante. A condition requiring that the waiver of breaches be assumed does not cover breaches committed by the vendor after contract: *Howell v Kightley* (1856) 21 Beav 331; affd (1856) 8 De GM & G 325. A vendor who has expressly agreed to make a good title cannot give oral evidence that the purchaser was aware of breaches of covenant existing at the time of the contract: *Barnett v Wheeler* (1841) 7 M & W 364. See also *Re Allen and Driscoll's Contract* [1904] 2 Ch 226, CA, explaining *Re Highett and Bird's Contract* [1903] 1 Ch 287, CA. In the absence of express agreement the vendor can give evidence of the purchaser's knowledge, and then the breaches are not an objection to the title: *Clarke v Coleman* [1895] WN 114, CA. See further para 59 ante. As to the sale of leaseholds out of repair see para 99 post.

12   Without such an extension, the purchaser would be entitled to have the title traced from the original lessor to the person giving the receipt, notwithstanding that he is precluded by statute (see the text and notes 1–9 supra; and para 140 post) from investigating the title to the reversion: cf *Pegler v White* (1864) 33 Beav 403.

13   There is no such provision in the Standard Conditions of Sale (3rd Edn).

14   See the Standard Conditions of Sale (3rd Edn) which provide that, the vendor having provided the purchaser with copies of the documents embodying the lease terms, the purchaser is treated as entering into the contract knowing and fully accepting those terms: condition 8.1.2. For the meaning of 'contract' see para 55 note 10 ante.

15   Cf *Simmons v Pennington & Son (a firm)* [1955] 1 All ER 240, [1955] 1 WLR 183, CA; and para 52 ante.

16   See para 99 post.

17   See para 127 post.

18   See *Hodgkinson v Cooper* (1846) 9 Beav 304.

99. Leaseholds out of repair. Prior to 1 July 1995[1], the covenant implied by the assignment of leaseholds as beneficial owner includes a covenant by the assignor that the covenants in the lease have been performed and observed[2]. After 1 July 1995, where the disposition is of leasehold land and is expressed to be made with full title guarantee or with limited title guarantee, the following covenants are implied: (1) that the lease is subsisting at the time of the disposition; and (2) that there is no subsisting breach of a condition or tenant's obligation, and nothing which at that time would render the lease liable to forfeiture[3]. Where the lease includes a covenant to repair, there will be a breach of the implied covenant if the premises are out of repair. The fact that the purchaser knows of the breach is immaterial as the covenant is unqualified[4]. Where, however, there is a condition that the purchaser is deemed to have notice of the actual condition of the property and is to take it as it is[5], it is clear that the implication that the covenant to repair has been performed is contrary to the intention of the parties and the purchaser is entitled to have the assignment rectified, although if the purchaser has subsequently sold the property the rectification must be without prejudice to the rights of purchasers for value without notice of the right to rectification[6]. There should in such cases be a condition that the transfer is to contain a modification of the implied covenants for title so as to exclude any implication that the lease has not become voidable by reason of the covenants for repair and decoration not having been performed[7].

1   Ie the date on which the Law of Property (Miscellaneous Provisions) Act 1994 came into force: see para 337 post.
2   See para 301 post. As to the power to modify the implied covenants for title see para 294 post.
3   Law of Property (Miscellaneous Provisions) Act 1994 s 4(1). If the disposition is the grant of an underlease, the references to 'the lease' in s 4(1) are references to the lease out of which the underlease is created: s 4(2).
4   *Butler v Mountview Estates Ltd* [1951] 2 KB 563, [1951] 1 All ER 693; and see LANDLORD AND TENANT vol 27(1) (Reissue) para 490.
5   The Standard Conditions of Sale (3rd Edn) provide that the purchaser accepts the property in the physical state it is in at the date of the contract unless the vendor is building or converting it (condition 3.2.1), and a leasehold property is sold subject to any subsisting breach of a condition or tenant's obligation relating to the physical state of the property which renders the lease liable to forfeiture (condition 3.2.2). For the meaning of 'contract' see para 55 note 10 ante; and for the meaning of 'lease' see para 57 note 5 ante.
6   *Butler v Mountview Estates Ltd* [1951] 2 KB 563, [1951] 1 All ER 693.
7   As to the disposition of registered and unregistered land by transfer see para 262 note 2 post.

F. ABSTRACT OF TITLE

100. Delivery of abstract. Although, independently of any condition for that purpose, a vendor of unregistered land[1] is bound to deliver an abstract of title[2], and to do so within a reasonable time[3], the Standard Conditions of Sale provide for the delivery of an abstract to the purchaser or his solicitor[4], or an epitome of title with photocopies of the relevant documents, immediately after making the contract[5]. Delivery within such time is not of the essence of the contract[6], and it is for the purchaser, on default by the vendor, to insist on the abstract or epitome being sent. If he neglects to apply for it on the day fixed for its delivery[7], or within such a period as will leave time for completion of the contract on the agreed day[8], or if, upon its being tendered after that time, he receives it without demur[9], he will be held to have waived the condition. If, however, the vendor fails to deliver an abstract or epitome on being pressed by the purchaser to do so, the purchaser can treat the contract as at an end as soon as a reasonable time for delivery has expired[10].

1   As to unregistered land see para 138 post.
2   As to the need for an abstract of title with respect to both unregistered and registered land see paras 138, 141–149 post.
3   *Compton v Bagley* [1892] 1 Ch 313. In case of unreasonable delay, the purchaser should give the vendor notice in writing, fixing a reasonable time within which a proper abstract must be delivered, whereupon the vendor's failure to deliver accordingly will entitle the purchaser to rescind the contract and recover his deposit: *Compton v Bagley* supra. See also *Bond v Bassett* (1917) 87 LJ Ch 160; *Re Bayley and Shoesmith's Contract* (1918) 87 LJ Ch 626. As to rescission see further para 232 et seq post. What is a reasonable time is perhaps a matter of doubt as the courts have shown a tendency to require a longer time than was formerly thought to be reasonable: see *Re Barr's Contract, Moorwell Holdings Ltd v Barr* [1956] Ch 551, [1956] 2 All ER 853, decided on the National Conditions of Sale (16th Edn), condition 23. Cf The Law Society's General Conditions of Sale (1980 Edn), condition 23, the National Conditions of Sale (20th Edn), condition 22, and the Conveyancing Lawyers' Conditions of Sale, condition 20. As to the Conditions of Sale see para 1 note 9 ante.
4   See para 3 ante.
5   See *Steer v Crowley* (1863) 14 CBNS 337; and the Standard Conditions of Sale (3rd Edn), conditions 4.1.1, 4.2.2, 4.2.3. As to the Standard Conditions of Sale see para 1 note 9 ante.
6   *Roberts v Berry* (1853) 3 De GM & G 284. Formerly, such time was regarded at law as of the essence of the contract, and non-delivery of the abstract within that time relieved the purchaser from the contract and entitled him to the return of his deposit (*Berry v Young* (1788) 2 Esp 640n; *Wilde v Fort* (1812) 4 Taunt 334),

but now time is not of the essence of the contract unless it would be so treated in equity (see para 120 text and note 2 post). In the case of a willing vendor and purchaser, conditions as to the delivery of the abstract or epitome are commonly disregarded. It is only where difficulties arise that they become of any importance.

7   *Guest v Homfray* (1801) 5 Ves 818.

8   *Jones v Price* (1797) 3 Anst 724.

9   *Smith v Burnam* (1795) 2 Anst 527. Cf *Oakden v Pike* (1865) 34 LJ Ch 620 at 621; *Re Priestley and Davidson's Contract* (1892) 31 LR Ir 122.

10   See *Venn v Cattell* (1872) 27 LT 469. See also *Pincke v Curteis* (1793) 4 Bro CC 329; *Seton v Slade, Hunter v Seton* (1802) 7 Ves 265; *Magennis v Fallon* (1828) 2 Mol 561 at 576; *Hipwell v Knight* (1835) 1 Y & C Ex 401.

101. Effect on requisitions of failure to deliver abstract or epitome. In the absence of contrary provision in a condition, failure to deliver the abstract or epitome in relation to unregistered land within the specified time relieves the purchaser from any condition binding him to make his requisitions or objections within a given period after delivery of the abstract or epitome[1]. The standard conditions provide that the time for written requisitions[2] is six working days[3] after either the date of the contract[4] or the date of delivery of the vendor's evidence of title, whichever is the later[5]. Under such a condition, where the abstract or epitome is not perfect but the deficiencies are unimportant, in the sense that the purchaser ought to assume that the gaps will be filled in a way which he would expect from the information supplied in the abstract or epitome, time begins to run against the purchaser; he must therefore raise what requisitions he can on the abstract submitted, call for the gaps to be filled, and he will then be entitled within the time prescribed by the condition to raise further requisitions on the new material[6].

1   See *Upperton v Nickolson* (1871) 6 Ch App 436; *Re Todd and M'Fadden's Contract* [1908] 1 IR 213. See also *Southby v Hutt* (1837) 2 My & Cr 207 at 211. As to the need for an abstract of title with respect to both unregistered and registered land see paras 138, 141–149 post.

2   'Requisition' includes objection: Standard Conditions of Sale (3rd Edn), condition 1.1.1(k). As to the Standard Conditions of Sale see para 1 note 9 ante.

3   'Working day' means any day from Monday to Friday (inclusive) which is not Christmas Day, Good Friday or a statutory Bank Holiday: Standard Conditions of Sale (3rd Edn), condition 1.1.1(n).

4   For the meaning of 'contract' see para 55 note 10 ante.

5   See the Standard Conditions of Sale (3rd Edn), condition 4.1.1; and para 102 post.

6   See *Ogilvy v Hope-Davies* [1976] 1 All ER 683. See the Standard Conditions of Sale (3rd Edn), condition 4.1.1; and para 102 post.

G.   REQUISITIONS

102. Time for requisitions. The Standard Conditions of Sale provide that any requisition[1] arising on the vendor's evidence of title[2] is to be made within six working days[3] after either the date of the contract[4] or the date of the delivery of the vendor's evidence of title on which the requisitions are raised whichever is the later. The time limit on the vendor's right to raise requisitions applies even where the vendor supplies incomplete evidence of his title, but the purchaser may, within six working days from delivery of any further evidence, raise further requisitions arising from that evidence. On the expiry of the relevant time limit the purchaser loses the right to raise requisitions or make observations. The vendor must reply in writing within four working days after receiving the requisitions, and the purchaser may make written observations on the vendor's replies within three working days after receiving the replies[5]. The purchaser is not precluded from making any requisition as to matters subsequently discovered which were not disclosed on the face of the abstract or epitome, even if the time has expired[6].

Upon the delivery of a supplementary abstract or epitome, a requisition based upon that abstract[7] or epitome is an original requisition for the purposes of these time limits and the time for requisitions starts again[8].

1   For the meaning of 'requisition' see para 101 note 2 ante; and as to the contents of requisitions see paras 163–165 post.
2   As to the root of title see para 142 post.
3   For the meaning of 'working day' see para 101 note 3 ante.
4   For the meaning of 'contract' see para 55 note 10 ante.
5   See the Standard Conditions of Sale (3rd Edn), condition 4.1.1. As to the Standard Conditions of Sale see para 1 note 9 ante. Where the period between the date of the contract and the completion date is less than 15 working days, these time limits are to be reduced proportionately: see condition 4.1.4. See also the Statutory Form of Conditions of Sale 1925, SR & O 1925/779, condition 6(1) (14 days). A condition sometimes provides expressly that every requisition and objection not so stated is to be considered as waived: see *Blackburn v Smith* (1848) 2 Exch 783; *Smithson v Powell, Powell v Smithson* (1852) 20 LTOS 105. However, even without such a condition, the present standard conditions seem strong enough to imply a waiver: see *Sinclair-Hill v Sothcott* (1973) 26 P & CR 490. It has been said that in this condition time is of the essence of the contract without express words to that effect: *Oakden v Pike* (1865) 11 Jur NS 666. As to a consideration of when the law regards time as of the essence of the contract see para 120 post.
    The Standard Conditions of Sale (3rd Edn) provide that the completion date is 20 working days after the date of the contract but time is not of the essence of the contract unless a notice to complete has been served: conditions 1.1.1(e), 6.1.1. It seems arguable that the time limits in condition 4.1 do make time of the essence. 'Notice to complete' means any notice, order or proposal given or made (whether before or after the date of the contract) by a body acting on statutory authority: condition 1.1.1(i).
    If there is no stipulation as to time, the purchaser must make his objections within a reasonable time after the delivery of the abstract: *Spurrier v Hancock* (1799) 4 Ves 667. In the event of unreasonable delay, the vendor can, by notice, limit a reasonable time for sending in objections, and, upon the purchaser's default, rescind the contract (*Taylor v Brown* (1839) 2 Beav 180), or the purchaser may perhaps be assumed to have accepted the title (*Pegg v Wisden* (1852) 16 Beav 239 at 244). As to waiver of the conditions by the vendor see *Cutts v Thodey* (1842) 13 Sim 206 (affd (1844) 1 Coll 223n); *Ogilvy v Hope-Davies* [1976] 1 All ER 683; *Luck v White* (1973) 26 P & CR 89; and as to waiver by the purchaser see *Re Ossemsley Estates Ltd* [1937] 3 All ER 774, CA. If the vendor shows by his conduct that he is unwilling to deal with a substantial requisition, for example by serving a notice to complete by which he impliedly asserts that he has provided a title in accordance with the contract, the purchaser is entitled to repudiate the contract immediately: *Re Stone and Saville's Contract* [1963] 1 All ER 353, [1963] 1 WLR 163, CA.
6   See *Warde v Dixon* (1858) 28 LJ Ch 315. See also *Gray v Fowler* (1873) LR 8 Exch 249 at 267; *Simpson v Gilley* (1922) 92 LJ Ch 194. Consequently, the purchaser is not precluded from taking an objection arising out of evidence called for before, but supplied by the vendor after, the expiration of the time fixed: *Blacklow v Laws* (1842) 2 Hare 40.
7   As to the need for an abstract of title with respect to both unregistered and registered land see paras 138, 141–149 post.
8   See *Re Ossemsley Estates Ltd* [1937] 3 All ER 774, CA; *Ogilvy v Hope-Davies* [1976] 1 All ER 683. See also *Sherwin v Shakspear* (1854) 5 De GM & G 517 at 536. This is so where the supplementary abstract is no more than an answer to a requisition: *Re Ossemsley Estates Ltd* supra.

103. Position where the vendor's title is wholly bad. A condition limiting the time for requisitions or objections does not apply where the vendor's title is wholly bad; it merely applies to such requirements as might have been properly enforced against a vendor who had a valid title[1]. Hence it cannot be used to force a bad title on a purchaser who has made his requisitions as to title too late[2], and he is entitled to recover his deposit[3]. Moreover, such a condition cannot be used where the contract is misleading, for example where a vendor purports to sell registered land without disclosing that his title is only possessory[4].

1   *Want v Stallibrass* (1873) LR 8 Exch 175 at 185.
2   *Re Tanqueray-Willaume and Landau* (1882) 20 ChD 465, CA; *Want v Stallibrass* (1873) LR 8 Exch 175; *Saxby v Thomas* (1890) 64 LT 65 at 67, CA. In *Pryce-Jones v Williams* [1902] 2 Ch 517, a distinction was made between requisitions as to the root of title and requisitions as to the subsequent devolution of the title, and

it was held that the latter cannot be insisted on if made out of time; but it seems that the true distinction is between matters which would vitiate the title and mere technical objections when a good holding title is shown. See also *Cumberland Court (Brighton) Ltd v Taylor* [1964] Ch 29, [1963] 2 All ER 536.

3   *Want v Stallibrass* (1873) LR 8 Exch 175. However, he cannot recover his deposit if he can show the want of title only by means of inquiries which he is precluded by the contract from making: *Rosenberg v Cook* (1881) 8 QBD 162, CA. As to the recovery of the deposit see paras 245–246 post.

4   *Re Brine and Davies' Contract* [1935] Ch 388. As to misleading conditions see para 83 ante.

104. Rescission on requisition being pressed. A condition may provide that, if the purchaser insists on any requisition or objection as to title which the vendor is unable or on some reasonable ground unwilling to remove or comply with, then, notwithstanding any intermediate negotiation or litigation, or any attempt to remove or comply with the same, the vendor may by notice in writing[1] annul the sale upon returning the deposit, and the purchaser is to return the abstract and any other documents furnished to him[2].

When the condition is framed solely in this way, it applies only to objections as to title and not to objections as to conveyance[3]. Thus the condition covers an objection in respect of an undisclosed right of way[4], or for want of title to minerals[5], or a requisition that the land should be released from a rentcharge[6]. However, the condition is frequently framed so as to cover also requisitions and objections as to conveyance, such as an objection to the conveyance being made subject to covenants and restrictions the existence of which did not appear from the particulars or the abstract[7]. Although the condition does not in terms refer to requisitions as to conveyance, yet, if it is expressed to include objections as to the title, particulars, conditions, and any other matter or thing relating to the sale, it is construed to include requisitions as to conveyance[8].

1   A notice to rescind signed 'without prejudice' seems to be void: *Re Weston and Thomas's Contract* [1907] 1 Ch 244 at 248.

2   The Standard Conditions of Sale (3rd Edn) do not contain such a condition. As to the Standard Conditions of Sale see para 1 note 9 ante. A demand for an unincumbered title is not persisting in objection to the title: see *Leominster Properties Ltd v Broadway Finance Ltd* (1981) 42 P & CR 372. See also *M'Culloch v Gregory* (1855) 1 K & J 286. The condition mentioned in the text is not unduly depreciatory (*Falkner v Equitable Reversionary Society* (1858) 4 Drew 352), even if it is unreasonable from the purchaser's point of view (*Moeser v Wisker* (1871) LR 6 CP 120 at 124). A right of rescission reserved by the contract cannot be used to prevent the purchaser enforcing any right conferred by the Law of Property Act 1925 s 42 (as amended) (such as refusing to take a conveyance with the concurrence of the owners of equitable interests): see s 42(8). The right may, however, be reserved in case the vendor is unable to obtain the cancellation of a registered incumbrance or the concurrence of the person entitled: s 43(2). As to rescission apart from condition and as to forfeiture of the deposit see para 232 et seq post; and as to rescission after completion see para 356 et seq post. As to the need for an abstract of title with respect to both unregistered and registered land see paras 138, 141–149 post.

3   As to the distinction see further paras 164–165 post.

4   *Ashburner v Sewell* [1891] 3 Ch 405 at 410. The condition does not, however, cover an objection to a misdescription: *Price v Macaulay* (1852) 2 De GM & G 339.

5   *Mawson v Fletcher* (1870) 6 Ch App 91.

6   *Re Great Northern Rly Co and Sanderson* (1884) 25 ChD 788, where, on the ground of hardship, the court refused to compel the vendor to apply for the discharge of the incumbrance under what is now the Law of Property Act 1925 s 50: see para 268 post. See also *Page v Adam* (1841) 4 Beav 269, where the condition applied to a requisition that annuitants should join in the conveyance. Annuities would now usually be overreached by a transfer: see para 271 post. As to the disposition of registered and unregistered land by transfer see para 262 note 2 post.

7   *Re Monckton and Gilzean* (1884) 27 ChD 555. Formerly the condition was used in order to exclude requisitions as to getting in a legal estate (*Kitchen v Palmer* (1877) 46 LJ Ch 611; and see *Jumpson v Pitchers* (1844) 1 Coll 13); but now the vendor would have to do this, although, perhaps, the condition may still be effective as regards an outstanding day of a term (see *Re Scott and Eave's Contract* (1902) 86 LT 617).

8   *Re Deighton and Harris's Contract* [1898] 1 Ch 458 at 463, CA. For the view that it is improper for a rescission clause to apply to requisitions both as to title and as to conveyance see *Hardman v Child* (1885) 28 ChD 712 at 718 per Pearson J.

105. Circumstances in which right of rescission arises. Where the condition enables the vendor to rescind upon the purchaser insisting upon[1] or persisting in any requisition, there must be: (1) an objection by the purchaser; (2) inability or unwillingness on a reasonable ground on the part of the vendor to remove the objection[2]; (3) communication to the purchaser of the existence of this unwillingness or inability; and (4) insistence by the purchaser upon his objection notwithstanding this communication[3]. When, however, in the condition the words 'make an objection' or 'make or take an objection' are substituted for 'insist upon an objection', the vendor's right to rescind arises directly the requisitions are sent in, and he need not attempt any answer[4].

1   'This reply is unsatisfactory and the purchasers reserve the right to insist' is a sufficient insistence: see *Re Dames and Wood* (1885) 29 ChD 626 at 631, CA.
2   See *Re Stone and Saville's Contract* [1963] 1 All ER 353, [1963] 1 WLR 163, CA.
3   *Duddell v Simpson* (1866) 2 Ch App 102 at 109. The vendor must attempt to answer the requisition so as to give the purchaser the opportunity either of waiving it or of insisting upon it: *Greaves v Wilson* (1858) 25 Beav 290; *Turpin v Chambers* (1861) 29 Beav 104.
4   *Re Starr-Bowkett Building Society and Sibun's Contract* (1889) 42 ChD 375, CA.

106. Exercise of right of rescission. The vendor must exercise the right of rescission reasonably and in good faith, and not arbitrarily or capriciously[1]. However, provided he has a good reason for rescinding, he is not bound to state it to the purchaser[2]. If the requisition is one which the vendor may reasonably be expected to comply with, he cannot resort to his power to rescind[3]. If the vendor has a sufficient reason for rescinding under the condition, but has knowingly or recklessly made a material misrepresentation concerning the property, he cannot rescind so as to deprive the purchaser of his option either to rescind or to enforce the contract with compensation[4].

The right to rescind should be exercised within a reasonable time[5], and, if the vendor seeks to take any unfair advantage of it, for example by delaying to exercise it whilst negotiating for a sale to a third person, he loses his election to affirm the contract and the purchaser may treat it as rescinded[6]. Where the vendor fails to show any title whatever, he cannot rescind under the condition so as to avoid liability to the purchaser[7].

1   *Re Dames and Wood* (1885) 29 ChD 626 at 630, CA; *Re Glenton and Saunders to Haden* (1885) 53 LT 434, CA; *Re Terry and White's Contract* (1886) 32 ChD 14; *Re Simpson and Thomas Moy Ltd's Contract* (1909) 53 Sol Jo 376. The burden of proof seems to lie on the purchaser. Where the vendor states the reasons in his notice, and is not cross examined as to his good faith, to which he has sworn, and there is no evidence imputing bad faith or caprice, the court does not infer against him an unreasonable or capricious use of the power: see *Re Starr-Bowkett Building Society and Sibun's Contract* (1889) 42 ChD 375 at 383–384, CA. If the right to rescind is exercised in pursuance of a clause in the contract or a condition in the standard conditions of sale, any notice to rescind should expressly refer to that clause or condition. As to the Standard Conditions of Sale see para 1 note 9 ante.
2   *Re Glenton and Saunders to Haden* (1885) 53 LT 434, CA. See also *Woolcott v Peggie* (1889) 15 App Cas 42, PC. Any difficulty in which this may place the purchaser is due to his own fault in entering into a contract in such a form: *Re Glenton and Saunders to Haden* supra; *Re Starr-Bowkett Building Society and Sibun's Contract* (1889) 42 ChD 375, CA.
3   *Re Weston and Thomas's Contract* [1907] 1 Ch 244 (requisition for commutation of succession duty); *Quinion v Horne* [1906] 1 Ch 596 (requisition as to child's date of birth). Cf *Selkirk v Romar Investments Ltd* [1963] 3 All ER 994, [1963] 1 WLR 1415, PC, where it was held that rescission was legitimate after reasonable but unsuccessful attempts to find evidence of the date of a death.
4   *Re Great Northern Rly Co and Sanderson* (1884) 25 ChD 788 at 794; *Smith v Wallace* [1895] 1 Ch 385; *Re Jackson and Haden's Contract* [1906] 1 Ch 412, CA; *Baines v Tweddle* [1959] Ch 679, [1959] 2 All ER 724, CA; *Selkirk v Romar Investments Ltd* [1963] 3 All ER 994, [1963] 1 WLR 1415, PC. 'The purchaser is not bound to come in and say 'I will avoid on the terms of the condition and will only take what the condition gives me', but is entitled to say 'I will avoid the contract, condition and all, and will have what the law gives me apart from the condition': *Holliwell v Seacombe* [1906] 1 Ch 426 at 434 per Kekewich J (a sale under the direction of the court). As to the exercise of the right of rescission see *Mawson v Fletcher*

(1870) 6 Ch App 91, where land was sold as containing minerals, but as the title to minerals under part of the land was doubtful the vendor was entitled to rescind; *Merrett v Schuster* [1920] 2 Ch 240, where an untrue statement of fact made by the vendor in good faith with substantial ground was not a bar to rescission, and where it was said that a statement that a third person will concur, made on his promise (but without a contract)to do so was not necessarily 'reckless'; *Re Milner and Organ's Contract* (1920) 89 LJ Ch 315, where, owing to a misinterpretation of a will, the vendor contracted to sell as trustee and the purchaser refused to accept his offer to sell as personal representative and the vendor was entitled to rescind; *Procter v Pugh* [1921] 2 Ch 256, where the vendor, acting reasonably, was unable to remove a difficulty as to restrictive covenants, and was entitled to rescind even though the purchaser had previously repudiated the contract (for criticism of this decision see T Cyprian Williams 'A Purchaser's Right of Repudiation' (1921) 66 Sol Jo 119, 135); *Re Des Reaux and Setchfield's Contract* [1926] Ch 178, where the vendor unreasonably refused to perfect the title where he knew of the defect and acted recklessly; *Baines v Tweddle* supra, where the vendor who did nothing to ascertain whether a mortgagee would concur was held to have acted recklessly and not to be entitled to rescind.

5   *St Leonard's, Shoreditch, Vestry v Hughes* (1864) 17 CBNS 137; *Ker v Crowe* (1873) IR 7 CL 181; *Bowman v Hyland* (1878) 8 ChD 588.

6   *Smith v Wallace* [1895] 1 Ch 385, where the court ordered the return of the deposit with interest. 'In fact, such a condition is only applicable to an honest case': *Re Deighton and Harris's Contract* [1898] 1 Ch 458 at 463, CA, per Lindley MR.

7   See *Bowman v Hyland* (1878) 8 ChD 588, distinguished in *Re Deighton and Harris's Contract* [1898] 1 Ch 458, CA.

107. Waiver of right of rescission. If the condition allows rescission notwithstanding any intermediate negotiation or litigation with respect to the requisition, an attempt by the vendor to comply with the requisition is no waiver of the right to rescind[1]. However, in the absence of such words a vendor who attempts to answer the requisition may lose his right to rescind unless he answers without prejudice[2], or unless the right to rescind only arises on insistence, for that implies the necessity for an answer[3]. Where the condition is so framed, the vendor can rescind at any time before final judgment[4], but after judgment has been given against him he cannot do so[5]. Where, however, he rescinds pending litigation, and the purchaser's conduct has been reasonable, the court may order the vendor to pay the costs of the litigation until rescission, in addition to the costs of investigation of the title and the return of the deposit[6]. If the vendor himself seeks to enforce the contract without including an alternative claim for rescission[7], he waives his right to rescind under the condition, but he may, perhaps, revert to it, on paying the costs, if he afterwards discontinues the proceedings[8].

1   *Duddell v Simpson* (1866) 2 Ch App 102.

2   *Tanner v Smith* (1840) 10 Sim 410 (on appeal 4 Jur 310); *Morley v Cook* (1842) 2 Hare 106 at 115. An argumentative answer is no waiver of the right to rescind: *Morley v Cook* supra. In *Gardom v Lee* (1865) 3 H & C 651, the condition entitled the vendor either to answer or to rescind, and negotiation was not to affect the right to rescind; however, the vendor was not allowed to rescind because he had disputed, not negotiated. See also *M'Culloch v Gregory* (1855) 1 K & J 286.

3   See para 105 note 3 ante.

4   *Isaacs v Towell* [1898] 2 Ch 285 at 290. It appears that although the words 'notwithstanding litigation' are absent, the vendor may still rescind after action brought by the purchaser: *Isaacs v Towell* supra. See also *Hoy v Smythies* (1856) 22 Beav 510.

5   *Re Arbib and Class's Contract* [1891] 1 Ch 601, CA. The court will not read 'litigation' as 'judicial decision': *Re Arbib and Class's Contract* supra at 612. See also *Re Quigley and M'Clay's Contract* [1918] 1 IR 347.

6   *Re Higgins and Hitchman's Contract* (1882) 21 ChD 95 at 99; *Re Spindler and Mear's Contract* [1901] 1 Ch 908 (although the condition stipulated for the return of the deposit 'without any interest, costs of investigating the title, or other compensation or payment whatsoever'); and see *Duddell v Simpson* (1866) 2 Ch App 102 at 108; *Sheard v Venables* (1867) 36 LJ Ch 922 at 924.

7   See *Public Trustee v Pearlberg* [1940] 2 KB 1 at 19–20, [1940] 2 All ER 270 at 281, CA. Accordingly a notice to fix a new time for completion and, if default were made, to rescind, given by the vendor while an action by him for specific performance was continuing, was ineffective: *Public Trustee v Pearlberg* supra.

8   *Warde v Dickson* (1858) 5 Jur NS 698; *Gray v Fowler* (1873) LR 8 Exch 249. Cf *Motor Carriage Supply Co Ltd v British and Colonial Motor Co* (1901) 45 Sol Jo 672; and see *Isaacs v Towell* [1898] 2 Ch 285 at 292.

108. Rescission or compensation. Where the contract contains a condition for rescission, and also a condition for compensation in case of error in the description of the property, and the matter objected to falls within the latter condition, the purchaser cannot insist upon compensation if the vendor chooses to rescind under the former condition[1].

1   *Mawson v Fletcher* (1870) 6 Ch App 91; *Ashburner v Sewell* [1891] 3 Ch 405; *Vowles v Bristol etc Building Society* (1900) 44 Sol Jo 592. In *Re Terry and White's Contract* (1886) 32 ChD 14, CA, there was a condition excluding compensation, and the vendor was held entitled to rescind under a condition in that behalf against a purchaser seeking to enforce the contract with compensation; see also *Molphy v Coyne* (1919) 53 ILT 177. As to compensation generally see paras 111 et seq, 251 et seq post.

H.   IDENTITY AND DESCRIPTION

109. Identity. It is commonly provided that the purchaser is to admit the identity of the property purchased by him with that comprised in the title deeds upon the evidence afforded by comparison of the descriptions in the particulars and in the title deeds, and that no further evidence of identity is to be required[1]. If the comparison affords no evidence that the property sold corresponds with that described in the abstracted documents[2], or if the descriptions in the abstracted documents differ from one another and from those in the particulars[3], even though the purchaser is precluded by this condition from calling for further evidence, yet, in the absence of satisfactory evidence of identity, the vendor's title is not established, and he cannot require the purchaser to complete[4]; and the vendor is not relieved by the condition from pointing out the entire property sold[5].

1   The Standard Conditions of Sale (3rd Edn) provide that the vendor need not: (1) prove the exact boundaries of the property; (2) prove who owns fences, ditches, hedges or walls; (3) separately identify parts of the property with different titles, further than he may be able to do from information in his possession: condition 4.3.1(a)–(c). The purchaser may, if it is reasonable, require the vendor to make or obtain, pay for and hand over a statutory declaration about facts relevant to these matters; the form of the declaration is to be agreed by the purchaser, who must not unreasonably withhold his agreement: see condition 4.3.2. As to the Standard Conditions of Sale see para 1 note 9 ante. See also *Bird v Fox* (1853) 11 Hare 40 at 48. In the case of registered land, if the property is described as that comprised in the title, care must be taken to see that the land intended to be sold or purchased is precisely that included in the title.
2   *Curling v Austin* (1862) 2 Drew & Sm 129; *Re Bramwell's Contract, Bramwell v Ballards Securities Investments Ltd* [1969] 1 WLR 1659. As to the need for an abstract of title with respect to both unregistered and registered land see paras 138, 141–149 post.
3   *Flower v Hartopp* (1843) 6 Beav 476.
4   *Re Bramwell's Contract, Bramwell v Ballards Securities Investments Ltd* [1969] 1 WLR 1659.
5   *Robinson v Musgrove* (1838) 2 Mood & R 92. Difficulties of this nature usually arise where only part of the property included in the title deeds is sold.

110. Misdescription. The conditions usually provide for the case of error in the description of the property, and regulate the right to compensation[1]. Any restrictions on the right to compensation are intended to apply to the case of unintentional errors, and do not therefore apply to cases of actual fraud or of misrepresentation calculated materially to mislead the purchaser[2]. Where the error is immaterial the right to compensation may be restricted[3].

1   As to the vendor's rights where the contract contains conditions both for rescission and for compensation see para 108 ante; and as to compensation under an open contract see para 250 et seq post.
    The Standard Conditions of Sale (3rd Edn) provide that if any plan or statement in the contract, or in the negotiations leading to it, is or was misleading or inaccurate due to an error or omission, the remedies available are as follows (condition 7.1.1): (1) when there is a material difference between the description or value of the property as represented and as it is, the injured party is entitled to damages (condition 7.1.2); (2) an error or omission only entitles the injured party to rescind the contract: (a) where it results

from fraud or recklessness; or (b) where he would be obliged, to his prejudice, to transfer or accept property differing substantially (in quantity, quality or tenure) from what the error or omission had led him to expect (condition 7.1.3(a)–(b)). As to the Standard Conditions of Sale see para 1 note 9 ante. For the meaning of 'contract' see para 55 note 10 ante.

2   *Stewart v Alliston* (1815) 1 Mer 26; *Viscount Clermont v Tasburgh* (1819) 1 Jac & W 112 at 120; *Price v Macaulay* (1852) 2 De GM & G 339; *Dimmock v Hallett* (1866) 2 Ch App 21 at 29, 31; *Re Terry and White's Contract* (1886) 32 ChD 14 at 20. See also *Duke of Norfolk v Worthy* (1808) 1 Camp 337; *Shepherd v Croft* [1911] 1 Ch 521 at 531. The court's jurisdiction is not exercised in favour of a vendor who fails to satisfy the court that he has done all he can to avoid misunderstanding and mistake: *Turquand v Rhodes* (1868) 37 LJ Ch 830. As to the vendor's liability for misrepresentation see para 51 et seq ante.

3   See the Standard Conditions of Sale (3rd Edn), condition 7.1; and note 1 supra.

111. Compensation. In one form of condition it is stipulated that any error or omission in the description of the property is not to annul the sale but, where material, is to be the subject of compensation on either side[1]. Under such a condition the vendor cannot insist on the purchaser taking, with compensation, a property substantially different from that which he agreed to buy[2], but, if there is no substantial difference, the purchaser must complete the purchase and accept compensation for any deficiency even though that deficiency is considerable[3].

On this principle the purchaser is entitled to be relieved from the contract, without resorting to the condition for compensation, if the legal character or incidents of the property sold differ materially from those set out in the particulars[4], or if it is subject to rights of third persons which materially interfere with its enjoyment[5] or value[6], or if a part of the property material to its enjoyment is missing[7] or where an error in quantity is so great as not to be a proper subject for compensation[8]. The condition does not apply to cases where it is impossible to assess the compensation[9].

1   This result is achieved by different wording in the Standard Conditions of Sale (3rd Edn), condition 7.1: see para 110 note 1 ante. As to the Standard Conditions of Sale see para 1 note 9 ante. See also *Leslie v Tompson* (1851) 9 Hare 268 at 273; *Re Belcham and Gawley's Contract* [1930] 1 Ch 56. The Statutory Form of Conditions of Sale 1925, SR & O 1925/779 make no provision as to compensation. For another form of condition see para 115 post. Fiduciary vendors may make use of a condition in this form: see *Hobson v Bell* (1839) 2 Beav 17; *Dunn v Flood* (1885) 28 ChD 586 at 591, CA; *Re Chifferiel, Chifferiel v Watson* (1880) 40 ChD 45. It was formerly held that the court would not decree specific performance with compensation against trustee-vendors who had been grossly negligent, but would leave the purchaser to his remedy at law against the trustees: *White v Cuddon* (1842) 8 Cl & Fin 766 at 787, HL. However, having regard to the larger powers now conferred upon trustees to overreach equitable interests, it is possible that the preference would now be given to the purchaser, and that the beneficiary would have to look to the trustees to make good any loss to the trust estate due to their negligence.

2   This would be contrary to the principle of *Flight v Booth* (1834) 1 Bing NC 370, that where a misdescription is so substantial as in effect to alter the subject matter of the contract, there is no purchase of the thing that is really the subject of sale. See also *Jones v Edney* (1812) 3 Camp 285 (sale of a public house described as 'free,' but in fact tied); and para 51 ante, where the rule in *Flight v Booth* supra, is stated more fully. This principle is reflected in the Standard Conditions of Sale (3rd Edn), condition 7.1.3(b): see para 110 ante.

3   *Re Fawcett and Holmes' Contract* (1889) 42 ChD 150, CA; *Re Brewer and Hankins's Contract* (1899) 80 LT 127, CA; *Re Belcham and Gawley's Contract* [1930] 1 Ch 56. Cf *Shepherd v Croft* [1911] 1 Ch 521, where a condition excluding compensation was waived by the vendors; *Calcraft v Roebuck* (1790) 1 Ves 221; *Drewe v Hanson* (1802) 6 Ves 675 at 679; *Binks v Lord Rokeby* (1818) 2 Swan 222; *Price v Macaulay* (1852) 2 De GM & G 339; *McKenzie v Hesketh* (1877) 7 ChD 675; *English v Murray* (1883) 32 WR 84. As to the case where the property is greater or less than was supposed see note 8 infra.

4   Eg where land is sold as freehold, but, owing to its having formerly been copyhold, the minerals are reserved to the lord of the manor (*Kerr v Pawson* (1858) 25 Beav 394; *Upperton v Nickolson* (1871) 6 Ch App 436; and see *Bellamy v Debenham* [1891] 1 Ch 412, CA), or leaseholds, although held for a long term, are sold as freehold (*Drewe v Corp* (1804) 9 Ves 368), or the length of a term is greatly overstated (*Nash v Wooderson* (1884) 52 LT 49), or an underlease is sold as a lease (*Madeley v Booth* (1848) 2 De G & Sm 718; *Broom v Phillips* (1896) 74 LT 459; and see para 59 ante), or land is sold as building land when subject in

fact to a right of way (*Dykes v Blake* (1838) 4 Bing NC 463), or there is a mistake as to identity (*Leach v Mullett* (1827) 3 C & P 115). As to the rule that a purchaser cannot be granted specific performance with an abatement of price on the ground of an innocent and non-negligent misrepresentation see para 42 ante.

5   Eg as undisclosed easements (*Shackleton v Sutcliffe* (1847) 1 De G & Sm 609), or undisclosed restrictive covenants (*Flight v Booth* (1834) 1 Bing NC 370; *Rudd v Lascelles* [1900] 1 Ch 815; and see *Cato v Thompson* (1882) 9 QBD 616 at 618, CA; *Pemsel and Wilson v Tucker* [1907] 2 Ch 191). The existence of a sewer under the garden attached to a house may, however, be a subject for compensation: *Re Brewer and Hankins's Contract* (1899) 80 LT 127, CA; *Re Belcham and Gawley's Contract* [1930] 1 Ch 56. The effect of such undisclosed matters will usually depend on the purposes for which the land is intended to be used by the purchaser or for which he is entitled to use it under restrictions affecting the property or planning regulations or for which he is likely to obtain planning permission: see *Shepherd v Croft* [1911] 1 Ch 521 at 528.

6   Eg where it was subject to a lease for lives at a low rent: *Hughes v Jones* (1861) 3 De GF & J 307. As to the conversion of leases for lives into leases for 90 years determinable by notice on the dropping of the last life see the Law of Property Act 1925 s 149(6); and LANDLORD AND TENANT vol 27(1) (Reissue) paras 210–211. Where a lease intended to endure for a life is created after 1925, it will be created in the form of a lease for years determinable by notice on the death of the party named as the life.

7   See eg *Dobell v Hutchinson and Holdsworth* (1835) 3 Ad & El 355, where a yard described as part of the property sold was in fact held by the vendor at a yearly rent; *Brewer v Brown* (1884) 28 ChD 309, where a house and garden was described as enclosed by a rustic wall with a tradesmen's entrance, although the wall did not in fact belong to the property and the entrance was used on sufferance; *Stanton v Tattersall* (1835) 1 Sm & G 529, where the situation of a house was misdescribed through the particulars failing to indicate the peculiar nature of the access to it; *Peers v Lambert* (1844) 7 Beav 546, where the sale was to be of a wharf with a jetty, but the jetty was in fact removable at will by a third person.

8   *Earl of Durham v Legard* (1865) 34 Beav 611, where an estate, described as containing 21,750 acres, in fact contained only 11,814 acres, and the purchaser was not entitled to specific performance with a proportionate reduction of price. In this case there was no provision as to compensation, and the purchaser was allowed the option of paying the full price or rescinding. Similarly, where there is a large error to the prejudice of the vendor, the purchaser may be able to rescind instead of paying an increased price as compensation (*Price v North* (1837) 2 Y & C Ex 620); if not, he must give compensation under the condition (*Leslie v Tompson* (1851) 9 Hare 268). In *Orange to Wright* (1885) 54 LJ Ch 590, compensation was refused to the vendor. See also *Bourne v London and County Land and Building Co* [1885] WN 109. The condition is intended for the benefit of each party.

9   See *Shenwood v Robins* (1828) Mood & M 194 (contingency of not having children). The position was similar where, on the sale of a timber estate, particulars of the trees were not sufficiently given (*Lord Brooke v Rounthwaite* (1846) 5 Hare 298); and where the minerals were found to belong to third persons, and the value could not be ascertained (*Smithson v Powell, Powell v Smithson* (1852) 20 LTOS 105). See also *Ridgway v Gray* (1849) 1 Mac & G 109. A clerical error as to property comprised in an underlease (*Grissell v Peto* (1854) 2 Sm & G 39), or an error in the particulars as to occupation which is corrected by information given to the purchaser (*Farebrother v Gibson* (1857) 1 De G & J 602), is not an objection to the title; but in *Ridgway v Gray* supra, a misstatement as to the occupation under a lease was treated as incapable of assessment and the purchaser was entitled to rescind. The existence of undisclosed restrictive covenants has also been said to give rise to difficulties in assessing compensation: see *Cato v Thompson* (1882) 9 QBD 616 at 618, CA; and note 5 supra.

112. Vendor's interest different from that offered. Where the vendor has not got the interest which he has agreed to sell, the purchaser is in general entitled to take such interest as he has, subject to an abatement of the price, notwithstanding that he thus obtains an interest materially different from that which he agreed to buy[1]. Thus the court has assessed compensation in the case of a sale in fee by a vendor who was entitled in remainder and could not get in the life estate[2] or who had only an estate *pur autre vie*[3], on a sale of leaseholds held for a term of years but misdescribed as carrying a right of renewal[4], and on the grant of a lease for a term longer than that which the lessor had power to grant[5].

1   This rule does not apply to a representation about the subject matter made, not in the contract, but collateral to it: *Rutherford v Acton-Adams* [1915] AC 866, PC; *Gilchester Properties Ltd v Gomm* [1948] 1 All ER 493. See also paras 42 ante, 251 post.

2   *Nelthorpe v Holgate* (1844) 1 Coll 203. See, however, *Thomas v Dering* (1837) 1 Keen 729 at 743.

3 *Barnes v Wood* (1869) LR 8 Eq 424. See also *Horner v Williams* (1839) Jo & Car 274.
4 *Painter v Newby* (1853) 11 Hare 26.
5 *Leslie v Crommelin* (1867) IR 2 Eq 134.

113. Recovery of compensation. Unless the condition for compensation is expressly limited to errors pointed out before completion, the purchaser can recover compensation for errors even after completion. In the absence of such express limitation the court does not import into the condition a distinction between errors discovered before, and errors discovered after, execution of the transfer[1].

A purchaser is not necessarily debarred from claiming compensation under the condition because he knew of the error before he entered into the contract[2].

1 *Cann v Cann* (1830) 3 Sim 447; *Bos v Helsham* (1866) LR 2 Exch 72; *Re Turner and Skelton* (1879) 13 ChD 130; *Phelps v White* (1881) 7 LR Ir 160, Ir CA; *Palmer v Johnson* (1884) 13 QBD 351, CA (distinguishing *Joliffe v Baker* (1883) 11 QBD 255 on the ground that there was there no condition providing for compensation). Contrast *Manson v Thacker* (1878) 7 ChD 620. See also *Eastwood v Ashton* [1915] AC 900, HL. Where there is no condition allowing compensation the purchaser cannot claim compensation after conveyance: *Besley v Besley* (1878) 9 ChD 103; *Allen v Richardson* (1879) 13 ChD 524; *Brett v Clowser* (1880) 5 CPD 376; *Joliffe v Baker* supra at 267; *Clayton v Leech* (1889) 41 ChD 103, CA. See also para 250 post. As to the disposition of registered and unregistered land by transfer see para 262 note 2 post.
2 *Lett v Randall* (1883) 49 LT 71; but see *Cobbett v Locke-King* (1900) 16 TLR 379. However, evidence is admissible to show that the purchaser heard the auctioneer correct the misdescription before the sale, in which event he will not be entitled to compensation under the condition: *Re Edwards to Daniel Sykes & Co Ltd* (1890) 62 LT 445; cf *Henderson v Hudson* (1867) 15 WR 860.

114. Defects of title. Where the condition is framed to cover errors in the description of the property, it does not extend to defects in title, but only applies to misdescriptions of the corporeal property[1]. The same principle seems to apply where the condition provides for any error, misstatement or omission in the particulars[2]. The innocent omission by the vendor to disclose the service upon him of a notice by a local authority requiring him to execute certain works in respect of his property is not such an omission in the particulars as would entitle the purchaser to compensation under the usual condition where the expenses of the works do not become a charge on the property until after completion of the sale[3].

It is a general rule with regard to defects in title that the vendor will not be compelled to give, nor the purchaser to take, an indemnity against the defect[4].

1 *Re Beyfus and Master's Contract* (1888) 39 ChD 110, CA; *Debenham v Sawbridge* [1901] 2 Ch 98. A defect in title which the purchaser is precluded from objecting to is not a ground for compensation: *Re Neale and Drew's Contract* (1897) 41 Sol Jo 274.
2 'It is not the function of the particulars to deal with title': *Blaiberg v Keeves* [1906] 2 Ch 175 at 184; and see para 79 ante.
3 *Re Leyland and Taylor's Contract* [1900] 2 Ch 625, CA, where, at 632, it was left undecided whether the omission would enable the purchaser to resist specific performance or obtain rescission. As to a claim by an agricultural tenant to compensation, cf *Re Earl of Derby and Fergusson's Contract* [1912] 1 Ch 479. As to modern conditions relating to local authorities' charges see para 126 post.
4 *Balmanno v Lumley* (1813) 1 Ves & B 224; *Fildes v Hooker* (1818) 3 Madd 193; *Nouaille v Flight* (1844) 7 Beav 521; *Ridgway v Gray* (1849) 1 Mac & G 109. See, however, *Horniblow v Shirley* (1802) 13 Ves 81; *Halsey v Grant* (1806) 13 Ves 73; *Manning v Turner* [1956] 3 All ER 641, [1957] 1 WLR 91, where it was suggested that a contingent liability to estate duty (now inheritance tax) might be provided for by an indemnity policy. As to indemnity where conditions disclose an incumbrance see para 129 note 3 post.

115. Condition allowing no compensation for misdescription. A second form[1] of condition relating to misdescription provides that any error, misstatement or omission is not to annual the sale, nor, unless the error, misstatement or omission is in a written answer and relates to a matter materially affecting the description or value of the property, are any damages to be payable or compensation allowed by either party in respect of it[2]. Such restrictions on the vendor's remedies do not apply where the error, misstatement or omission is fraudulent or reckless, nor to any matter or thing by which the purchaser is prevented from getting substantially what he contracted to buy[3]. Notwithstanding such a condition, the vendor cannot enforce specific performance of the contract, with or without abatement, if the misdescription or omission is material and substantial (that is, such that the purchaser cannot get what he agreed to buy[4]) and in such circumstances the purchaser is entitled to rescind and recover his deposit[5]. On the other hand, the purchaser cannot enforce the contract against the vendor with compensation, although he may, of course, take the property without compensation[6].

The condition in the second form does not apply to latent defects in the property, but only to such matters as might be discovered by an inspection of the property with reasonable care[7], and it does not apply to errors which are known to the vendor when the conditions are prepared[8]. It does not exclude recovery of damages on the covenant for title where a title is not given to part of the property[9].

1   As to the effect of the first form see para 111 ante.
2   A condition in this form was included in the National Conditions of Sale (20th Edn), condition 17(1). This condition was redrafted in response to the criticisms expressed in *Walker v Boyle* [1982] 1 All ER 634, [1982] 1 WLR 495: see para 116 note 4 post. The errors and omissions are not confined to physical misdescriptions: *Re Courcier and Harrold's Contract* [1923] 1 Ch 565 (error in statement of restrictive covenants); *Curtis v French* [1929] 1 Ch 253, where, on a sale with vacant possession, an error in the statement of the tenant's rights by which vacant possession could not be given was held to be an error or misstatement within a condition excluding compensation. As to the Standard Conditions of Sale see para 1 note 9 ante.
3   See the National Conditions of Sale (20th Edn), condition 17(2); and note 2 supra. See also the Standard Conditions of Sale (3rd Edn), condition 7.1; and para 110 ante.
4   *Jacobs v Revell* [1900] 2 Ch 858, where it was said, at 865, that a condition excluding compensation applies to all errors, whether great or small, but only within the limit laid down in *Flight v Booth* (1834) 1 Bing NC 370 at 377; and see para 51 ante. See also *Portman v Mill* (1826) 2 Russ 570; *Cordingley v Cheeseborough* (1862) 4 De GF & J 379 (deficiency in quantity of nearly one half); *Whittemore v Whittemore* (1869) LR 8 Eq 603 (large deficiency of acreage not covered by 'more or less'); *Re Arnold, Arnold v Arnold* (1880) 14 ChD 270, CA (sale of field as a four acre field, but in fact four undivided sevenths of a seven acre field). 'Notwithstanding such a condition, the court will not decree specific performance at the instance of the vendor, if he has materially misled the purchaser, and it is well known that a less serious misleading is sufficient to enable a purchaser to resist specific performance than is required to enable him to rescind the contract': *Re Terry and White's Contract* (1886) 32 ChD 14 at 29, CA, per Lindley LJ. See also *Re Courcier and Harrold's Contract* [1923] 1 Ch 565; *Watson v Burton* [1956] 3 All ER 929, [1957] 1 WLR 19 (misdescription in contract; area stated as 3,920 in fact 2,360 sq yds).
5   *Heywood v Mallalieu* (1883) 25 ChD 357; *Nottingham Patent Brick and Tile Co v Butler* (1886) 16 QBD 778 at 786, CA; *Lee v Rayson* [1917] 1 Ch 613. As to the recovery of the deposit see paras 245–246 post.
6   *Cordingley v Cheeseborough* (1862) 4 De GF & J 379; *Re Terry and White's Contract* (1886) 32 ChD 14, CA. See also *Nicoll v Chambers* (1852) 11 CB 996; *Molphy v Coyne* (1919) 53 ILT 177.
7   *Re Puckett and Smith's Contract* [1902] 2 Ch 258, CA (underground culvert).
8   *Simpson v Gilley* (1922) 92 LJ Ch 194. See also *Re Tower's Contract* [1924] WN 331. Both forms of condition are now drafted so as to relate also to precontractual misrepresentations: cf *Bellotti v Chequers Developments Ltd* [1936] 1 All ER 89; and para 116 post.
9   *Eastwood v Ashton* [1915] AC 900, HL.

116. Statutory regulation of condition excluding or restricting liability for misrepresentation. The two forms of condition[1] relating to compensation are designed to apply to both precontractual misrepresentations and contractual misdescriptions. In so far as they purport to restrict the purchaser's remedies for misrepresentation[2] they cannot be relied on by the vendor unless he proves in a particular case that the condition satisfies a statutory test of reasonableness[3], that is that the condition is a fair and reasonable one to be included in the contract having regard to the circumstances which were, or ought reasonably to have been, known to or in the contemplation of the parties when the contract was made[4]. Moreover, such a condition is inapplicable where the vendor has, even innocently, made a misrepresentation when the true facts are within his own knowledge[5].

1 Ie those discussed in paras 111, 115 ante.
2 See also MISREPRESENTATION AND FRAUD vol 31 (Reissue) para 803.
3 See the Misrepresentation Act 1967 s 3 (as substituted); and MISREPRESENTATION AND FRAUD vol 31 (Reissue) paras 803, 828.
4 See the Unfair Contract Terms Act 1977 s 11(1). There is no similar regulation of conditions restricting liability for breach of contract, since the more general provisions of the Unfair Contract Terms Act 1977 do not apply to contracts for the creation, transfer or termination of an interest in land: s 1(2), Sch 1 para 1(b). It is arguable, however, that land contracts fall within the Unfair Terms in Consumer Contracts Regulations 1994, SI 1994/3159 (see CONTRACT vol 9(1) (Reissue) paras 790–796): see Bright and Bright 'Unfair Terms in Land Contracts: Copy Out or Cop Out?' (1995) 111 LQR 655; and para 78 note 2 ante. The conditions referred to above may be considered as severable, so that the restrictions are wholly effective in relation to the breach of contract and subject to the test of reasonableness in relation to misrepresentation: see *Cremdean Properties v Nash* (1977) 241 Estates Gazette 837. See also *Walker v Boyle* [1982] 1 All ER 634, [1982] 1 WLR 495, where the vendor in his replies to precontractual inquiries had innocently misrepresented that he was unaware of any boundary dispute, and it was held that the National Conditions of Sale (19th Edn), condition 17, was invalid (see now the National Conditions of Sale (20th Edn), condition 17; the Standard Conditions of Sale (3rd Edn), condition 7; and para 115 ante). The reasonableness test is not applicable to a provision by which an agent's authority to make representations is excluded or restricted: *Overbrooke Estates Ltd v Glencombe Properties Ltd* [1974] 3 All ER 511, [1974] 1 WLR 1335; *Collins v Howell-Jones* [1981] 2 EGLR 108, 259 Estates Gazette 331, CA. As to remedies for errors and omissions in the Standard Conditions of Sale (3rd Edn) see condition 7; and para 110 ante. As to the Standard Conditions of Sale see para 1 note 9 ante.
5 *Walker v Boyle* [1982] 1 All ER 634, [1982] 1 WLR 495, applying by analogy the principles relating to misleading conditions: see para 83 ante.

I. INSURANCE

117. Common law position as to insurance. A vendor retains an insurable interest in land until transfer[1], and the position at common law, in default of express provision in the contract of sale, was that he was entitled against the purchaser to retain payments made after the date of the contract under a fire insurance policy which he had effected, even though the property was at the purchaser's risk pending completion[2]. Moreover, the vendor was not bound to keep the policy in force pending completion or to inform the purchaser of its lapse[3].

1 See INSURANCE vol 25 (Reissue) para 608. As to the disposition of registered and unregistered land by transfer see para 262 note 2 post.
2 See *Rayner v Preston* (1881) 18 ChD 1, CA; and INSURANCE vol 25 (Reissue) para 608. In *Rayner v Preston* supra, at 15, James LJ expressed the opinion that, where the insurance money had not yet been paid over to the vendor, the purchaser could compel the insurance company to expend it on reinstating the property by virtue of the provisions of the Fires Prevention (Metropolis) Act 1774 s 83 (see INSURANCE vol 25 (Reissue) paras 637–639).
3 *Paine v Meller* (1801) 6 Ves 349; *Dowson v Solomon* (1859) 1 Drew & Sm 1 at 12. See also INSURANCE vol 25 (Reissue) para 625.

118. Effect of statute and conditions of sale. By statute any payment made after the contract under an insurance policy maintained by the vendor in respect of damage to, or the destruction of, the property sold must on completion be paid to the purchaser; but this is subject to any stipulation to the contrary in the contract, any requisite consent of the insurers, and the payment by the purchaser of the proportionate part of the premium from the date of the contract[1]. The matter is now usually provided for in the conditions of sale.

The Standard Conditions of Sale[2] reverse the common law position as to risk and exclude the statutory provision outlined above[3]. The vendor must transfer[4] the property in the same physical state as it was at the date of the contract[5] (except for fair wear and tear), which means that the vendor retains the risk until completion[6]. If at any time before completion the physical state of the property makes it unusable for its purpose at the date of the contract (1) the purchaser may rescind the contract[7]; (2) the vendor may rescind the contract where the property has become unusable for that purpose as a result of damage against which the vendor could not reasonably have insured, or which it is not legally possible for the vendor to make good[8]. The vendor is under no obligation to the purchaser to insure the property[9].

Where the vendor is unwilling to bear the risk in this way, consideration should be given to using conditions which were formerly in general use. These conditions may provide that the vendor is not liable to the purchaser to keep the insurance on foot or to notify the purchaser that a premium is due[10], although he may be required to obtain an indorsement on the policy of the purchaser's interest[11]. Despite this condition, a purchaser should generally effect his own insurance on executing the contract[12], and, where he is mortgaging the property to secure part of the purchase money, he will probably have to effect the insurance with such office as the mortgagee requires[13].

If both the vendor and the purchaser have effected insurance, the conditions may provide that if the property is damaged before completion and the proceeds of the purchaser's policy are reduced by reason of the existence of the vendor's policy, the purchase price is to be abated by the amount of the reduction[14].

1   Law of Property Act 1925 s 47(1), (2). Section 47, also applies, subject to necessary modifications, to sales by the court: s 47(3).
2   See the Standard Conditions of Sale (3rd Edn); and para 1 note 9 ante.
3   See the Standard Conditions of Sale (3rd Edn), condition 5.1.4.
4   'Transfer' includes conveyance and assignment: Standard Conditions of Sale (3rd Edn), condition 1.1.1(m). As to the disposition of registered and unregistered land by transfer see para 262 note 2 post.
5   For the meaning of 'contract' see para 55 note 10 ante.
6   Standard Conditions of Sale (3rd Edn), condition 5.1.1.
7   Standard Conditions of Sale (3rd Edn), condition 5.1.2(a).
8   Standard Conditions of Sale (3rd Edn), condition 5.1.2(b).
9   Standard Conditions of Sale (3rd Edn), condition 5.1.3. There may well be circumstances where the purchaser wishes the vendor to maintain the insurance policy, and such an obligation can be created by a special condition, which may give the purchaser the right to inspect the policy and to have his interest noted on the policy, and may also, where appropriate, oblige the purchaser to pay a proportionate part of the premium. For an alternative form of condition containing the latter obligation see Precedents for the Conveyancer, p 8217, clause 16–62. It is suggested that consideration be given to inserting a time limit for rescission. Where the property is in the course of construction, careful thought must be given to the contractual provisions. A special condition requiring the vendor to complete the building works in accordance with agreed plans will override Standard Conditions of Sale (3rd Edn), condition 5.1.1 (see the text to note 7 supra), and it might then be appropriate for the purchaser to bear the risk until completion, in which case the purchaser is to insure and the vendor need not.
10 See The Law Society's General Conditions of Sale (1984 Revision), condition 11(4) (unless the property is leasehold and the vendor has an obligation to insure); and the National Conditions of Sale (20th Edn), condition 21(1). The purchaser may be allowed to inspect the policy: see the National Conditions of Sale (20th Edn), condition 21(2).
11 See the National Conditions of Sale (20th Edn), condition 21(3). In such a case the vendor may require the purchaser to pay on completion a proportionate part of the premium from the date of the contract.
12 This is usually necessary owing to delay in obtaining the insurers' consent to any indorsement or transfer of the benefit to the purchaser.
13 Building societies usually require the insurance to be with a company of their choice and often require the premiums to be paid to them. Insurance companies financing house purchase usually require the

insurance to be with the company. In the case of an owner-occupier the premises are often insured together with the furniture on the premises and many other risks in a comprehensive policy. This policy may be determined if the owner-occupier vacates the premises before completion. Inquiry should therefore be made before contract as to the position as regards insurance, and it may sometimes be necessary for the purchaser to obtain cover before completion of the contract, or the issue of a new policy. As to inquiries before contract generally see para 4 et seq ante.

14 See The Law Society's General Conditions of Sale (1984 Revision), condition 11(1), which does not apply where the proceeds of the vendor's policy are applied towards the reinstatement of property in pursuance of any statutory or contractual obligation: The Law Society's General Conditions of Sale (1980 Edn), condition 11(2). It is therefore desirable that the purchaser should effect his own insurance.

J. COMPLETION

119. Occupation before completion. The Standard Conditions of Sale provide for the situation where the vendor allows the purchaser into occupation before completion[1]. The general effect of these conditions is that the purchaser is to be a licensee and not a tenant of the vendor[2]. The terms of the licence are that the purchaser: (1) cannot transfer the licence[3]; (2) may permit members of his household to occupy the property[4]; (3) is to pay or indemnify the vendor against all outgoings[5] and other expenses in respect of the property[6]; (4) is to pay the vendor a fee calculated at the contract rate[7] on the purchase price (less any deposit paid) for the period of the licence[8]; (5) is entitled to any rents and profits from any part of the property which he does not occupy[9]; (6) is to keep the property in as good a state of repair as it was in when he went into occupation (except for fair wear and tear) and is not to alter it[10]; (7) is to insure the property in a sum which is not less than the purchase price against all risks in respect of which comparable premises are normally insured[11]; and (8) is to quit the property when the licence ends[12], which is on the earliest of completion date[13], rescission of the contract[14], or when five working days'[15] notice given by one party to the other takes effect[16]. If the purchaser is in occupation of the property after his licence has come to an end and the contract is subsequently completed, he must pay the vendor compensation for his continued occupation calculated at the same rate as the fee mentioned in head (4) above[17]. The purchaser is not in occupation for the purposes of this condition if he merely exercises rights of access given solely to do work agreed by the vendor[18]. The purchaser's right to raise requisitions[19] is unaffected by the fact that he is in occupation[20]. Where the vendor unlawfully allows the purchaser into possession, for example contrary to a covenant in the lease, the entry into possession does not make the purchaser liable for interest on the purchase money[21].

1 See the Standard Conditions of Sale (3rd Edn), condition 5.2.1. As to the Standard Conditions of Sale see para 1 note 9 ante. As to power of entry before completion in the case of purchase under compulsory powers see COMPULSORY ACQUISITION OF LAND vol 8(1) (Reissue) para 122 et seq.
2 See the Standard Conditions of Sale (3rd Edn), condition 5.2.2. On the creation of the purchaser's licence, condition 5.1 (see para 118 ante) ceases to apply, which means that the purchaser then assumes the risk until completion: condition 5.2.3.
    These provisions are important, since otherwise there would be a danger that the purchaser would acquire a protected tenancy: see *Francis Jackson Developments Ltd v Stemp* [1943] 2 All ER 601, CA; *Chamberlain v Farr* [1942] 2 All ER 567, 112 LJKB 206, CA; *Bretherton v Paton* [1986] 1 EGLR 172, 18 HLR 257, CA. The efficacy of such a contractual provision must be doubtful after *Street v Mountford* [1985] AC 809, [1985] 2 All ER 289, HL (though see Lord Templeman at 819, 821, and 294, 296); cf *Dunthorne and Shore v Wiggins* [1943] 2 All ER 678, CA; and see LANDLORD AND TENANT vol 27(1) (Reissue) para 170. Where the agreement is for the grant of a lease at a rent, and the intending lessee is allowed into possession before completion and starts to pay rent, the situation is inconsistent with a provision in the conditions that he is to be only a licensee: *Joel v Montgomery and Taylor Ltd* [1967] Ch 272, [1966] 3 All ER 763. In *Hyde v Pearce* [1982] 1 All ER 1029, [1982] 1 WLR 560, CA, where a purchaser had gone into possession before completion but his licence to occupy had been terminated in

1958, it was held that he had not acquired a possessory title by 1972 because he had not made it clear that he was no longer bound by the contract (but see Dockray 'What is Adverse Possession: Hyde and Seek' (1983) 46 MLR 89; and cf *Bridges v Mees* [1957] Ch 475, [1957] 2 All ER 577, not cited).

3   Standard Conditions of Sale (3rd Edn), condition 5.2.2(a). As to the disposition of registered and unregistered land by transfer see para 262 note 2 post.

4   Standard Conditions of Sale (3rd Edn), condition 5.2.2(b).

5   The purchaser cannot recover his expenditure on improvements, even where the sale goes off owing to the vendor's default: see *Worthington v Warrington* (1849) 8 CB 134; *Lloyd v Stanbury* [1971] 2 All ER 267, [1971] 1 WLR 535; *Lee-Parker v Izzet* [1971] 3 All ER 1099, [1971] 1 WLR 1688. Where the purchaser is in default, it seems that the vendor can recover an amount necessary to restore the property to a habitable condition: cf *Crisp v Fox* (1967) 201 Estates Gazette 769. Where the vendor seeks specific performance, the purchaser is usually given the option either to relinquish occupation or to pay into court the balance of the purchase money with interest: *Greenwood v Turner* [1891] 2 Ch 144; *Attfield v DJ Plant Hire & General Contractors Co Ltd* [1987] Ch 141, [1986] 3 All ER 273. This option may be granted even where he has extensively altered the property but probably not where he has caused great and lasting damage: see *Maskell v Ivory* [1970] Ch 502, [1970] 1 All ER 488. In working out these remedies, account must be taken of the fact that, under the present form of the Standard Conditions of Sale (3rd Edn), condition 5.2 it is a specific term of the purchaser's licence that he is not to alter the property: see condition 5.2.2(f); and the text to note 10 infra.

6   Standard Conditions of Sale (3rd Edn), condition 5.2.2(c).

7   'Contract rate', unless defined in the agreement, is The Law Society's interest rate from time to time in force: Standard Conditions of Sale (3rd Edn), condition 1.1.1(g). This rate is published at regular intervals in The Law Society's Gazette.

8   Standard Conditions of Sale (3rd Edn), condition 5.2.2(d).

9   Standard Conditions of Sale (3rd Edn), condition 5.2.2(e).

10 Standard Conditions of Sale (3rd Edn), condition 5.2.2(f).

11 Standard Conditions of Sale (3rd Edn), condition 5.2.2(g).

12 Standard Conditions of Sale (3rd Edn), condition 5.2.2(h).

13 For the meaning of 'completion date' see para 102 note 5 ante.

14 For the meaning of 'contract' see para 55 note 10 ante.

15 For the meaning of 'working day' see para 101 note 3 ante.

16 Standard Conditions of Sale (3rd Edn), condition 5.2.5.

17 Standard Conditions of Sale (3rd Edn), condition 5.2.6.

18 Standard Conditions of Sale (3rd Edn), condition 5.2.4.

19 For the meaning of 'requisition' see para 101 note 2 ante.

20 Standard Conditions of Sale (3rd Edn), condition 5.2.7.

21 *Cantor Art Services Ltd v Kenneth Bieber Photography Ltd* [1969] 3 All ER 843, [1969] 1 WLR 1226, CA.

120. Contractual date for completion. A date is usually fixed by the conditions of sale for the completion of the purchase[1], but, in the absence of express stipulation to that effect, or unless an intention that it should be so can be implied from the circumstances, that date is not of the essence of the contract[2]. However, although time is not originally of the essence of the contract in this respect, it may be made so by either party giving proper notice to the other to complete within a reasonable time[3], and such a notice may be served immediately after the contractual date for completion has passed[4]. Even where time is not originally of the essence, a party who through his own default fails to complete on the contractual date commits a breach of the contract and is liable in damages[5]. In a suitable case, a decree of specific performance can also be obtained before the contractual date for completion if the other party repudiates the contract[6].

Where time is or has been made of the essence, any extension of the time for completion to a new date makes that new date of the essence[7]; so too if the extension to a new date is granted to a third person who wishes to take over the contract[8]. Time will cease to be of the essence only if the party granting the extension leads the other party to think that he will be given time indefinitely and will not be cut off without further notice[9]. Merely standing by and failing to insist on punctual performance, at all events unless it continues for an unreasonably long time, does not amount to waiver[10].

1   For the meaning of 'completion date' in the Standard Conditions of Sale (3rd Edn) see para 102 note 5 ante. As to the Standard Conditions of Sale see para 1 note 9 ante. See also the Statutory Form of Conditions of Sale 1925, SR & O 1925/779, condition 1 (unless otherwise agreed, the first working day after the expiration of seven weeks from the date of the contract). The '28th day of December next' in a contract made on 15 December referred to that December: *Dawes v Charsley* (1866) 2 TLR 530, CA. The date cannot be waived and another day substituted orally: *Stowell v Robinson* (1837) 3 Bing NC 928. Even though no time is fixed the contract is none the less enforceable (*Gray v Smith* (1889) 43 ChD 208 at 214; affd (1889) 43 ChD 208, CA), and the vendor must make out his title within a reasonable time (*Simpson v Hughes* (1897) 66 LJ Ch 334, CA; see also *Green v Sevin* (1879) 13 ChD 589 at 599). On a sale of land used for sheep farming a term that a completion date would be agreed did not render the contract void for uncertainty as it could be implied that completion would take place at the end of a reasonable period after the lambing season: *Walters v Roberts* (1980) 41 P & CR 210. As to delay in completion after the conveyance has been executed and delivered in escrow see *Kingston v Ambrian Investment Co Ltd* [1975] 1 All ER 120, [1975] 1 WLR 161, CA; *Glessing v Green* [1975] 2 All ER 696, [1975] 1 WLR 863, CA. As to completion generally see para 262 et seq post.

2   See the Standard Conditions of Sale (3rd Edn) which provide that time is not of the essence of the contract unless a notice to complete has been served (condition 6.1.1); and the Law of Property Act 1925 s 41, applying the rules of equity to the common law. For the meaning of 'contract' see para 55 note 10 ante. See also *United Scientific Holdings Ltd v Burnley Borough Council* [1978] AC 904, [1977] 2 All ER 62, HL; *Raineri v Miles (Wiejski, third party)* [1981] AC 1050, [1980] 2 All ER 145, HL. In the particular circumstances of the contract the time for completion may be of the essence: *Levy v Lindo* (1817) 3 Mer 81 at 84; *Coslake v Till* (1826) 1 Russ 376 (sale of public house); *Tilley v Thomas* (1867) 3 Ch App 61 (sale of house intended for immediate occupation); *Tadcaster Tower Brewery Co v Wilson* [1897] 1 Ch 705 (sale of public house); *Bernard v Williams* (1928) 139 LT 22, DC; *Lock v Bell* [1931] 1 Ch 35 (sale of licensed premises); *Harold Wood Brick Co Ltd v Ferris* [1935] 2 KB 198, CA; *Pips (Leisure Productions) Ltd v Walton* (1982) 43 P & CR 415 (sale of lease with 15-and-a-half years to run). Cf *Williams v Greatrex* [1956] 3 All ER 705, [1957] 1 WLR 31, CA, where, in special circumstances, a ten year delay was no bar to specific performance; *Lazard Bros & Co Ltd v Fairfield Properties Co (Mayfair) Ltd* (1977) 121 Sol Jo 793, where a three year delay was no bar to specific performance; *Behzadi v Shaftesbury Hotels Ltd* [1992] Ch 1, [1991] 2 All ER 477, CA. The express terms of the contract may prevent time being of the essence where otherwise it would have been: see *Ellis v Lawrence* (1969) 210 Estates Gazette 215; *F and B Entertainments Ltd v Leisure Enterprises Ltd* (1976) 240 Estates Gazette 455, (1976) EGLR 79; *British and Commonwealth Holdings plc v Quadrex Holdings Inc* [1989] QB 842, [1989] 3 All ER 492, CA. The date fixed for completion is no less a part of the contract than any other clause, but equity will grant relief where an unfair use is made of its literal terms: *Stickney v Keeble* [1915] AC 386, HL; and see *Jamshed Khodaram Irani v Burjorji Dhunjibhai* (1915) 32 TLR 156, PC. See also paras 100, 102 ante, 185 post; and CONTRACT vol 9(1) (Reissue) paras 931–932; EQUITY vol 16 (Reissue) para 901; SPECIFIC PERFORMANCE vol 44(1) (Reissue) para 899 et seq. As to waiver of a condition that time is to be of the essence see *Dyas v Rooney* (1890) 25 LR Ir 342; and CONTRACT vol 9(1) (Reissue) para 936.

3   *King v Wilson* (1843) 6 Beav 124 at 126; *United Scientific Holdings Ltd v Burnley Borough Council* [1978] AC 904 at 946, [1977] 2 All ER 62 at 85, HL. As to what is a reasonable time see *Wells v Maxwell* (1863) 33 LJ Ch 44. Reasonableness must be judged as at the date when notice is given: *Crawford v Toogood* (1879) 13 ChD 153; and see *Smith v Batsford* (1897) 76 LT 179, where notice was held to be reasonable, even though after the time for completion. In considering reasonableness the vendor's previous delay and the purchaser's attitude to it must be considered: *Stickney v Keeble* [1915] AC 386 at 418–419, HL. A vendor who has put it out of his own power to complete, or who has by his conduct lost the right to specific performance, has no equity to restrain proceedings at law based on non-observation of the stipulation as to time: *Stickney v Keeble* supra, at 416. Even where a condition provides for giving notice to complete within 28 days, that period may not be reasonable: see *Re Barr's Contract, Moorwell Holdings Ltd v Barr* [1956] Ch 551, [1956] 2 All ER 853. However, the standard conditions of sale now in general use provide for the service of a notice to complete of prescribed length, in respect of which time is of the essence: see para 121 post.

4   See *Behzadi v Shaftesbury Hotels* Ltd [1992] Ch 1, [1991] 2 All ER 477, CA (reviewing previous authorities and overruling *Smith v Hamilton* [1951] Ch 174, [1950] 2 All ER 928). The party serving the notice must not himself be responsible for the delay: *Schindler v Pigault* (1975) 30 P & CR 328, where the vendor, who failed to give access to a sub-purchaser of whom he knew, was unable to rely on a notice to complete. See also *Re Stone and Saville's Contract* [1963] 1 All ER 353, [1963] 1 WLR 163, CA, where a notice to complete was served by a vendor who could not show a good title, and the purchaser was entitled to rescind without first serving notice.

5   *Raineri v Miles (Wiejski, third party)* [1981] AC 1050, [1980] 2 All ER 145, HL, approving *Phillips v Lamdin* [1949] 2 KB 33, [1949] 1 All ER 770. The claim may be by the vendor or the purchaser and in either case the damages may be substantial. In relation to contracts made after 27 September 1989 (ie the date

of commencement of the Law of Property (Miscellaneous Provisions) Act 1989 s 3: see s 5(3), (4)), in the case of a purchaser's claim, the vendor can no longer limit his damages under the rule in *Bain v Fothergill* (1874) LR 7 HL 158: see the Law of Property (Miscellaneous Provisions) Act 1989 s 3; para 256 post; and DAMAGES vol 12(1) (Reissue) para 1059.

6   *Hasham v Zenab* [1960] AC 316, [1960] 2 WLR 374, PC. See also *Marks v Lilley* [1959] 2 All ER 647, [1959] 1 WLR 749, where the purchaser did not make time of the essence, but 33 days after the contractual date for completion he issued a writ claiming specific performance; ten days later the vendor completed but the purchaser was entitled to the taxed costs of his action.

7   *Howe v Smith* (1884) 27 ChD 89, CA; *Lock v Bell* [1931] 1 Ch 35. However, see *Chancery Lane Developments Ltd v Wades Departmental Stores Ltd* (1986) 53 P & CR 306, CA, (The Law Society's Conditions of Sale (1984 Revision), condition 23(7) held to provide, by necessary implication, that time not of essence for purpose of extended date for completion).

8   *Buckland v Farmer and Moody (a firm)* [1978] 3 All ER 929, [1979] 1 WLR 221, CA.

9   *Luck v White* (1973) 26 P & CR 89; *Buckland v Farmer and Moody (a firm)* [1978] 3 All ER 929, [1979] 1 WLR 221, CA.

10 *Buckland v Farmer and Moody (a firm)* [1978] 3 All ER 929 at 942, [1979] 1 WLR 221 at 236, CA, per Goff LJ.

121. Notice to complete. The Standard Conditions of Sale[1] contain a condition by which, if completion has not taken place by the contractual date for completion, either party may serve on the other a notice to complete[2] within a period of ten working days[3] from the giving of the notice, excluding the day on which the notice is given, and that period of time will then be of the essence of the contract[4]. Such a condition makes time automatically of the essence of the notice, whether or not the period prescribed is itself reasonable[5]. The notice need not refer expressly to the condition under which it is served, but it must be clear as a matter of construction that the notice is served under the relevant condition[6].

The person serving the notice must himself not only be ready, able and willing to complete at the date when the notice is served, but must remain so throughout the period of the notice[7]. The notice binds the person serving it as well as the other party[8], and if the person serving it is no longer ready and willing to complete at the date of expiration, the other party may then repudiate the contract[9]. However, time is not of the essence within the period of the notice, and therefore, if the recipient of the notice nominates a day for completion within the period, but in fact is not ready for completion on that date, that party is not in fundamental breach; but the same applies to the server of the notice if that party is not ready to complete on the nominate day[10]. A person cannot serve a notice when he is himself responsible for the delay[11].

Where a conditional contract fixes a date for completion, a notice to complete can be served even though a condition has not yet been fulfilled[12]. When a notice to complete has expired, the party not in default may elect either to affirm or rescind the contract. On affirmation, damages will be available to compensate for loss caused by the delay, and may be claimed even after completion[13]. On rescission by the vendor, he may forfeit the deposit[14] and resell the property[15], claiming as damages his expenses on the resale, together with any deficiency in the resale price as compared with the contract price[16]. He may also apply for vacation of the purchaser's registration of an estate contract[17]. On rescission by the purchaser, he may reclaim his deposit and accrued interest[18] and claim damages for any consequential loss[19]. The rights and remedies available under such conditions of sale are additional to those provided by the general law[20]. Such conditions do not apply after the award of a full decree of specific performance, unless the court so orders in working out the decree[21].

1   See the Standard Conditions of Sale (3rd Edn), condition 6.8; and the text and notes 2–4, 7 infra. As to the Standard Conditions of Sale see para 1 note 9 ante. Where there are joint vendors the notice must be served by all of them: *Woods v Mackenzie Hill Ltd* [1975] 2 All ER 170, [1975] 1 WLR 613. Presumably where there are joint purchasers it must be served on all of them.

2   For the meaning of 'notice to complete' see para 102 note 5 ante.

3   This is applied strictly so that an insufficient notice period invalidates the notice itself: *Country and Metropolitan Homes Surrey Ltd v Topclaim Ltd* [1996] Ch 307, [1997] 1 All ER 254. For the meaning of 'working day' see para 101 note 3 ante.

4   See the Standard Conditions of Sale (3rd Edn), conditions 6.8.1, 6.8.3. For the meaning of 'contract' see para 55 note 10 ante. See also *Behzadi v Shaftesbury Hotels Ltd* [1992] Ch 1, [1991] 2 All ER 477, CA.

5   *Innisfail Laundry Ltd v Dawe* (1963) 107 Sol Jo 437; *Cumberland Court (Brighton) Ltd v Taylor* [1964] Ch 29, [1963] 2 All ER 536.

6   *Babacomp Ltd v Rightside Properties Ltd* [1974] 1 All ER 142, CA, where notice to complete the contract 'according to its terms' was sufficient. It has been said that, if a person purports to serve a notice under a particular contractual condition, and that notice is invalid, it is not open to him to claim that the notice may take effect under the general law: *Rightside Properties Ltd v Gray* [1975] Ch 72, [1974] 2 All ER 1169; and see *Delta Vale Properties Ltd v Mills* [1990] 2 All ER 176 at 181, [1990] 1 WLR 445 at 452, CA, per Slade LJ; *Country and Metropolitan Homes Surrey Ltd v Topclaim Ltd* [1996] Ch 307, [1997] 1 All ER 254; but cf *Woods v Mackenzie Hill Ltd* [1975] 2 All ER 170, [1975] 1 WLR 613; *Dimsdale Developments (South East) Ltd v De Haan* (1983) 47 P & CR 1 (criticised in Thompson 'Case Notes. Notices to Complete and Associated Remedies' [1984] Conv 311). See also note 20 infra.

7   See the Standard Conditions of Sale (3rd Edn), condition 6.8.1, which makes such provision, but this requirement would be implied in any event: see *Finkielkraut v Monohan* [1949] 2 All ER 234; *Re Stone and Saville's Contract* [1963] 1 All ER 353, [1963] 1 WLR 163, CA; *Horton v Kurzke* [1971] 2 All ER 577, [1971] 1 WLR 769; *Pagebar Properties Ltd v Derby Investment Holdings Ltd* [1973] 1 All ER 65, [1972] 1 WLR 1500; *Quadrangle Development and Construction Co Ltd v Jenner* [1974] 1 All ER 729, [1974] 1 WLR 68, CA; *Cole v Rose* [1978] 3 All ER 1121. The requirement is that the person serving the notice must, within his own knowledge, be ready to complete (*Cole v Rose* supra), but an exception is made for purely administrative matters, such as the preparation of a completion statement (which is, in any event, not a legal requirement: see *Carne v Debono* [1988] 3 All ER 485, [1988] 1 WLR 1107, CA), or arranging the time and place of completion, and arranging for the discharge of mortgages (*Cole v Rose* supra at 1128; *Edwards v Marshall-Lee* (1975) 235 Estates Gazette 901, CA). A vendor may be ready to complete even if he is in breach of his duty of trusteeship, which sounds only in damages: *Prosper Homes Ltd v Hambros Bank Executor and Trustee Co Ltd* (1979) 39 P & CR 395.

For cases on the validity of the notice to complete see *McGrath v Shah* (1987) 57 P & CR 452 (purchaser claimed misrepresentation by vendor), applied in *Bechal v Kitsford Holdings Ltd* [1988] 3 All ER 985, [1989] 1 WLR 105 (purchaser claimed material misdescription of property in conditions of sale). See also *Delta Vale Properties Ltd v Mills* [1990] 2 All ER 176, [1990] 1 WLR 445, CA (notice requiring completion in conformity with contract, ie within 15 working days of service, was not invalid although it went on to state consequences of failure to complete within 28 days of service. It operated as a contractual notice to complete, but subject to the time for completion being extended to 28 days after service). See also *Brickwoods Ltd v Butler and Walters* (1970) 23 P & CR 317, CA, where the purchasers' right to rescind under an escape clause did not preclude the vendor from serving notice to complete.

Under the Standard Conditions of Sale (3rd Edn), a party is ready, able and willing: (1) if he could be, but for the default of the other party; and (2) in the case of the vendor, even though a mortgage remains secured on the property, if the amount to be paid on completion enables the property to be transferred freed of all mortgages (except those to which the sale is expressly subject): condition 6.8.2(a), (b). This is designed to reverse the effect of *Cole v Rose* supra.

8   *Quadrangle Development and Construction Co Ltd v Jenner* [1974] 1 All ER 729, [1974] 1 WLR 68, CA.

9   *Re Stone and Saville's Contract* [1963] 1 All ER 353, [1963] 1 WLR 163, CA; *Rightside Properties Ltd v Gray* [1975] Ch 72, [1974] 2 All ER 1169. The clarity of the proposition in the text is perhaps clouded by *Woodar Investment Development Ltd v Wimpey Construction UK Ltd* [1980] 1 All ER 571, [1980] 1 WLR 277, HL, where it was held that unjustified rescission of a contract does not necessarily amount to repudiation of the contract, where the whole circumstances, including the conduct of the party purporting to rescind, do not evidence his intention to abandon the contract. However, that was a rather unusual case where, before the purported notice of rescission was served, there was a disagreement between the parties as to whether the purchasers were entitled to rescind, and the purchasers' service of a rescission notice could plausibly be regarded as without prejudice to their future performance of the contract, if (as happened) the notice should be held invalid.

10   See *Oakdown Ltd v Bernstein & Co (a firm)* (1984) 49 P & CR 282 at 294–296 per Scott J; but see 'Hold Everything' [1985] Conv 309.

11   *Schindler v Pigault* (1975) 30 P & CR 328, where the vendor was unable to rely on his notice to complete, when the delay was caused by his failure to give access to a sub-purchaser of whom he knew. A vendor whose failure to deduce title is the cause of a delayed completion cannot, at a later date, serve a valid notice to complete on a non-defaulting purchaser: *Country and Metropolitan Homes Surrey Ltd v Topclaim Ltd* [1996] Ch 307, [1997] 1 All ER 254.

12   *Carne v Debono* [1988] 3 All ER 485, [1988] 1 WLR 1107, CA.

13 *Phillips v Lamdin* [1949] 2 KB 33, [1949] 1 All ER 770; *Raineri v Miles (Wiejski, third party)* [1981] AC
    1050, [1980] 2 All ER 145, HL; *Oakacre Ltd v Claire Cleaners (Holdings) Ltd* [1982] Ch 197, [1981] 3 All
    ER 667.
        Under the Standard Conditions of Sale (3rd Edn), compensation is calculated at the contract rate on
    the purchase price, or (where the purchaser is the paying party) the purchase price less any deposit paid,
    for the period by which the paying party's default exceeds that of the receiving party, or, if shorter, the
    period between completion date and actual completion: condition 7.3.2. Any claim for loss resulting from
    delayed completion is to be reduced by any compensation payable under this condition: see condition
    7.3.3. Where the purchaser holds the property as tenant of the vendor and completion is delayed, the
    vendor may give notice to the purchaser, before the date of actual completion, that he intends to take the
    net income from the property until completion; if he does so, he cannot claim compensation under
    condition 7.3.1 as well: condition 7.3.4. For the meaning of 'contract rate' see para 119 note 7 ante; and
    for the meaning of 'completion date' see para 102 note 5 ante. As to claims after completion see condition
    7.4; and para 123 post.
14 See the Standard Conditions of Sale (3rd Edn), condition 7.5.2(a). This is subject to the court's
    unfettered power to order the return of the deposit under the Law of Property Act 1925 s 49(2): see
    further para 246 post.
15 See the Standard Conditions of Sale (3rd Edn), condition 7.5.2(b).
16 See the Standard Conditions of Sale (3rd Edn), condition 7.5.2(c); and para 232 et seq post.
17 *Hooker v Wyle* [1973] 3 All ER 707, [1974] 1 WLR 235, where vacation was ordered on summary
    proceedings. Cf *Clearbrook Property Holdings Ltd v Verrier* [1973] 3 All ER 614, [1974] 1 WLR 243 (triable
    issue where purchaser alleged oral extension of period of notice). As to vacation of the register generally
    see LAND CHARGES vol 26 (Reissue) paras 545–546.
18 See the Standard Conditions of Sale (3rd Edn), condition 7.6.2(a).
19 In relation to contracts made after 27 September 1989 (ie the date of commencement of the Law of
    Property (Miscellaneous Provisions) Act 1989 s 3: see s 5(3), (4)), damages are no longer limited under
    the rule in *Bain v Fothergill* (1874) LR 7 HL 158: see the Law of Property (Miscellaneous Provisions) Act
    1989 s 3; para 256 post; and DAMAGES vol 12(1) (Reissue) para 1059.
20 *Woods v Mackenzie Hill Ltd* [1975] 2 All ER 170, [1975] 1 WLR 613, where the vendors' contractual
    notice to complete was invalid, but the purchaser had still not completed some four months after the
    contractual date for completion; it was held that the delay was substantially more than a reasonable time,
    and the vendors' action for specific performance succeeded. This seems to cast doubt on the general
    proposition stated in *Rightside Properties Ltd v Gray* [1975] Ch 72, [1974] 2 All ER 1169, that a notice
    shorter than that provided for in the conditions of sale cannot be valid under the general law. In *Dimsdale
    Developments (South East) Ltd v De Haan* (1983) 47 P & CR 1, such a notice, invalid under the condition,
    was expressly held to be valid under the general law (but see the criticism by Thompson 'Case Notes.
    Notices to Complete and Associated Remedies' [1984] Conv 311). See also note 6 supra. In *Raineri v
    Miles (Wiejski, third party)* [1981] AC 1050, [1980] 2 All ER 145, HL, service of a contractual notice to
    complete after the date fixed for completion had passed did not divest the right to damages which accrued
    on the contractual date for completion.
21 *Sudagar Singh v Nazeer* [1979] Ch 474, [1978] 3 All ER 817.

122. Interest on purchase money. The conditions of sale may provide for payment
of interest on the balance of the purchase money from the date fixed for completion until
the actual date of payment, if the purchase is not completed at the date fixed[1]. The
payment of interest varies according to the form of the condition; it may be payable if the
delay arises (1) from any cause whatever[2]; (2) from any cause whatever other than the
vendor's wilful default; or (3) from the purchaser's default.

Whether the agreement for the payment of interest makes it payable in case of delay
from any cause whatever[3], or from any cause other than the vendor's wilful default[4], the
effect is the same, since even under the former words the purchaser is not bound to pay
interest during delay due to the vendor's wilful default[5], and such conditions are binding
and compel the purchaser to pay interest unless he can bring the delay within the
exception[6]. If the condition is framed under head (3) above, the purchaser is liable to pay
interest only if the delay is attributable to him, and not if it is due to the state of the
vendor's title[7].

It is for the purchaser to show that the vendor was guilty of wilful default[8], and that
this wilful default was the cause of the non-completion of the contract on the date fixed[9].

Delay occasioned merely by the state of the title and not wilful on the part of the vendor does not relieve the purchaser from paying interest[10].

Unless the contract provides otherwise, a purchaser cannot evade payment of interest under a condition by depositing the purchase money at a bank and giving notice to the vendor that he will only be liable for deposit interest[11]. Where the purchase money is paid into court in a specific performance action it still attracts interest while lodged in court[12].

One form of standard condition provides that the purchaser is to pay interest at a specified rate[13] from the contractual completion date until the purchase is actually completed, unless the vendor is in default[14]. The vendor may instead elect to take the income (less outgoings) of the land[15]. Under this form of condition the vendor's right to take the income is dependent upon his right to charge interest, so that, if the delay is caused by his default, he may have neither interest nor income[16]. Where the delay arises from any cause other than the purchaser's neglect or default, he may place the balance of the purchase money on a deposit account and give notice to the vendor or his solicitor[17], and the interest yielded by such deposit must be accepted by the vendor[18].

The standard condition now in general use makes the payment of interest part of a more general condition relating to compensation for late completion[19].

Both forms of condition have independent provisions regulating the payment of interest by a purchaser in possession before completion[20].

1   See the Statutory Form of Conditions of Sale 1925, SR & O 1925/779, condition 4. Interest may be reserved at an increasing rate: *Herbert v Salisbury and Yeovil Rly Co* (1866) LR 2 Eq 221. This condition will not necessarily be read into a contract for sub-purchase in the same terms: *Re Keeble and Stillwell's Fletton Brick Co* (1898) 78 LT 383. As to the payment of interest where it is not expressly provided for see para 194 et seq post. Where there was a mere agreement to pay interest from the day fixed for completion without adding 'in case of delay from any cause whatever' the purchaser was allowed to avoid payment of interest by appropriating money to meet the purchase money: *Kershaw v Kershaw* (1869) LR 9 Eq 56; but see *Re Riley to Streatfield* (1886) 34 ChD 386; and para 197 post. A special condition merely providing for interest from the date for completion has been held not to be a variation of, or inconsistent with, a clause in the general conditions which contains a similar provision and also further terms relating to interest: *Re Debenham and Mercer's Contract* [1944] 1 All ER 364.

2   Formerly the condition seems to have been regarded as fixing only the rate of interest and leaving the actual payment to begin when the title was made: *Monk v Huskisson* (1827) 4 Russ 121n. Where the purchaser insisted on taking the rents and profits from the date fixed for completion and he conceded that he had to pay interest, but the vendor was in wilful default, the interest was chargeable at the court rate of 4% and not at the contract rate of 6%: *Manton v Mannion* [1958] IR 324.

3   *Vickers v Hand* (1859) 26 Beav 630; *Williams v Glenton* (1866) 1 Ch App 200.

4   *Re Riley to Streatfield* (1886) 34 ChD 386.

5   *Williams v Glenton* (1866) 1 Ch App 200 at 210; *Re Woods and Lewis' Contract* [1898] 1 Ch 433 at 436 (affd [1898] 2 Ch 211, CA) where, the word 'wilful' being omitted, the court held nevertheless that 'default' must be construed as 'wilful default' and not in the sense of mere failure to perform. See also *Bennett v Stone* [1903] 1 Ch 509 at 525, CA; *Re Kissock and Taylor's Contract* [1916] 1 IR 393.

6   See the cases cited in notes 3–4 supra.

7   *Jones v Gardiner* [1902] 1 Ch 191. See also *Perry v Smith* (1842) Car & M 554; *Denning v Henderson* (1847) 1 De G & Sm 689.

8   A vendor is guilty of wilful default if he goes abroad on holiday two days before the date fixed for completion (*Re Young and Harston's Contract* (1885) 31 ChD 168, CA, where 'wilful' and 'default' were considered at 175 per Bowen LJ), or neglects to obtain the concurrence of necessary parties (*Re Earl of Strafford and Maples* [1896] 1 Ch 235 (on appeal [1896] 1 Ch 235 at 240, CA)), or, owing to his misinterpretation of the conditions of sale, refuses to deliver an abstract of title (*Re Pelly and Jacob's Contract* (1899) 80 LT 45), or, under a mistake of law, omits to obtain a conveyance from one of two trustee-mortgagees (*Re Hetling and Merton's Contract* [1893] 3 Ch 269 at 281, CA; *Re Postmaster-General and Colgan's Contract* [1906] 1 IR 287 (on appeal [1906] 1 IR 477, Ir CA), where the delay was due to the vendor's mistake as to the length of the tenancy of a party in possession), or underestimates the time necessary for completion (*Re Hewitt's Contract* [1963] 3 All ER 419, [1963] 1 WLR 1298), or, under the former law, if he neglected to procure admittance to copyholds (*Re Wilsons and Stevens' Contract* [1894] 3 Ch 546).

On the other hand, the vendor's oversight or honest mistake of fact is not wilful default, at least if not persisted in (*Bennett v Stone* [1902] 1 Ch 226 at 232; affd [1903] 1 Ch 509 at 520, 526, CA), nor is his repudiation of the contract and unsuccessful resistance to the purchaser's action for specific performance (*North v Percival* [1898] 2 Ch 128 where, at 135, Kekewich J defined 'wilful default' as obstruction in the completion of the contract). 'The honest belief of either party in the validity of his own view will not prevent such party being in default, though it may prevent such default being a wilful default within the meaning of the contract': *Re Bayley-Worthington and Cohen's Contract* [1909] 1 Ch 648 at 657 per Parker J, where earlier cases are considered.

9   *Re London Corpn and Tubbs' Contract* [1894] 2 Ch 524 at 529, CA. The default must be the *causa causans* of the delay: *Bennett v Stone* [1902] 1 Ch 226 at 236; affd [1903] 1 Ch 509, CA.

10 *Sherwin v Shakspear* (1854) 5 De GM & G 517, where the condition read 'from any cause whatever'; *Vickers v Hand* (1859) 26 Beav 630 (overruling *De Visme v De Visme* (1849) 1 Mac & G 336); *Lord Palmerston v Turner* (1864) 33 Beav 524; *Williams v Glenton* (1865) 34 Beav 528 at 531 (affd (1866) 1 Ch App 200 at 206). In *Re Kissock and Taylor's Contract* [1916] 1 IR 393, Ir CA, however, a vendor who entered into the contract knowing that litigation into the title was pending by which completion was delayed by seven months was held to be guilty of wilful default notwithstanding that he had acted on counsel's opinion.

11 *Re Riley to Streatfield* (1886) 34 ChD 386. See also *Vickers v Hand* (1859) 26 Beav 630; and cf paras 196–197 post. In a vendor's action for specific performance, if the purchaser is in possession, he may be allowed the option of paying the purchase money and interest into court or giving up possession and paying the interest into court: *Greenwood v Turner* [1891] 2 Ch 144; *Re Cassano and Mackay's Contract* [1920] WN 7. As to the position of the parties pending completion see para 177 et seq post; and as to completion generally see para 262 et seq post.

12 *Pearlberg v May* [1951] Ch 699, [1951] 1 All ER 1001, CA.

13 The rate should be fixed as a percentage by a special condition. For the meaning of 'contract rate' in the Standard Conditions of Sale (3rd Edn) see para 119 note 7 ante. As to the Standard Conditions of Sale see para 1 note 9 ante.

14 See the National Conditions of Sale (20th Edn), condition 7(1). These conditions are no longer in general use, having been largely superseded by the Standard Conditions of Sale (3rd Edn): see para 1 note 9 ante.

15 See the National Conditions of Sale (20th Edn), condition 7(1)(i); and note 14 supra.

16 *Re Hewitt's Contract* [1963] 3 All ER 419, [1963] 1 WLR 1298, where the delay was attributable to the vendor's default when he underestimated the time necessary for completion.

17 See para 3 ante.

18 See the National Conditions of Sale (20th Edn), condition 7(1)(ii); and note 14 supra.

19 See the Standard Conditions of Sale (3rd Edn), condition 7.3; and para 121 ante.

20 See para 119 ante; cf *Re Priestley's Contract* [1947] Ch 469, [1947] 1 All ER 716. As to the liability under the general law of the vendor in occupation to pay a fair occupation rent see para 191 post.

123. Vacant possession. The special conditions usually state whether or not the property is sold with vacant possession[1]. If no tenancies are disclosed and no statement is made as to possession, the implication is that the purchaser is to have vacant possession[2]. If printed conditions incorporate the particulars and the particulars state that vacant possession will be given on completion, the purchaser is entitled to such possession[3]. Since special conditions prevail over general conditions[4], and since the provision for vacant possession is usually stated in the special conditions, it is essential that any qualification of that provision should also be stated in the special conditions[5]. Where a joint lessee has contracted to purchase the freehold and to resell it, he must obtain the consent of all other joint lessees before he can give vacant possession to the sub-purchaser[6].

In order to give vacant possession, the vendor must eject not only those lawfully in possession but also any person who has no claim of right[7]. The right of a third person to take possession constitutes a breach[8], as does a notice of intention to enter given by an authority exercising powers of compulsory purchase[9]. Subject to the de minimis rule, the vendor must remove all his goods from the premises[10]. The meaning of 'vacant possession' may vary with the context, but where a house is adapted for occupation by two households and the contract discloses a tenancy of the first floor but provides for vacant possession of the ground floor, a direction by the local authority that the house should be occupied by only one household precluded the vendors from giving vacant possession of the ground floor[11].

A provision for vacant possession does not merge into the transfer on completion[12]. Where a spouse's matrimonial home rights are a registered charge on the estate of the other spouse[13], any contract for the sale of that estate by which the vendor agrees to give vacant possession will, subject to any contrary intention being expressed, contain a term requiring the vendor at his own expense to procure the cancellation of the registration of the charge[14]. This does not apply to any such contract made by a vendor who is entitled to sell the estate in the dwelling house freed from any such charge[15].

1   See the Standard Conditions of Sale (3rd Edn), Special Condition 5. As to the Standard Conditions of Sale see para 1 note 9 ante.

2   *Cook v Taylor* [1942] Ch 349 at 354, [1942] 2 All ER 85 at 87; *Re Crosby's Contract, Crosby v Houghton* [1949] 1 All ER 830.

3   *Cook v Taylor* [1942] Ch 349, [1942] 2 All ER 85, where the particulars referring to vacant possession were supplied by the vendor's agent in the course of negotiations and not included in the contract.

4   See para 77 ante.

5   Cf *Korogluyan v Matheou* (1975) 30 P & CR 309; *Topfell Ltd v Galley Properties Ltd* [1979] 2 All ER 388, [1979] 1 WLR 446. In neither case did the judge advert expressly to the superior status of special conditions. Where the breach of the condition for vacant possession arises by virtue of a local land charge registered before the contract, it would seem that there is no need for an express qualification: see para 54 ante.

6   *Leek and Moorlands Building Society v Clark* [1952] 2 QB 788, [1952] 2 All ER 492, CA, where it was held that a surrender of a joint tenancy must be by all joint tenants.

7   *Cumberland Consolidated Holdings Ltd v Ireland* [1946] KB 264 at 270, [1946] 1 All ER 284 at 287, CA.

8   *Engell v Fitch* (1869) LR 4 QB 659, Ex Ch; *James Macara Ltd v Barclay* [1945] KB 148, [1944] 2 All ER 589, CA.

9   *Korogluyan v Matheou* (1975) 30 P & CR 309.

10 *Cumberland Consolidated Holdings Ltd v Ireland* [1946] KB 264, [1946] 1 All ER 284, CA (cellar full of rubbish); *Norwich Union Life Insurance Society v Preston* [1957] 2 All ER 428, [1957] 1 WLR 813 (furniture left on premises). See also *Hynes v Vaughan* (1985) 50 P & CR 444 (rubbish piles in garden and stables).

11 *Topfell Ltd v Galley Properties Ltd* [1979] 2 All ER 388, [1979] 1 WLR 446.

12 *Hissett v Reading Roofing Co Ltd* [1970] 1 All ER 122, [1969] 1 WLR 1757. The Standard Conditions of Sale (3rd Edn) provide that completion does not cancel liability to perform any outstanding obligation under the contract: condition 7.4. For the meaning of 'contract' see para 55 note 10 ante. See also para 293 post. As to the disposition of registered and unregistered land by transfer see para 262 note 2 post.

13 See the Family Law Act 1996 ss 30 (as amended), 31; and HUSBAND AND WIFE.

14 See ibid Sch 4 para 3(1); and LAND CHARGES vol 26 (Reissue) para 538. It is the duty of the vendor to obtain necessary consents to a sale and, if he has sold with vacant possession, to take proceedings to obtain possession from any person in possession who has no right to be there, although he would not usually be required to undertake difficult or uncertain litigation in order to secure any requisite consent or obtain vacant possession: see *Wroth v Tyler* [1974] Ch 30, [1973] 1 All ER 897 (spouse's charge registered after the date of the contract for sale). The term is deemed to have been performed by the delivery to the purchaser or his solicitor of an application by the spouse entitled to the charge for the cancellation of its registration: see the Family Law Act 1996 Sch 4 para 3(3); and LAND CHARGES vol 26 (Reissue) para 538. As to the release of the statutory rights of occupation see para 6 ante. As to the consequences where cancellation of the registration is refused by the spouse entitled to the charge see *Wroth v Tyler* supra. See further paras 248, 252 post.

15 Family Law Act 1996 Sch 4 para 3(2).

124. Entry into possession or receipt of rents. It is usual to provide that upon completion of the purchase the purchaser is entitled to possession[1] or receipt of the rents and profits and that the income and outgoings of the property are to be apportioned either as from the day fixed for completion or from the date of actual completion[2]. In the absence of stipulation the time fixed for completion is not the crucial date, and if a title has not been shown by that date, and there is no stipulation making the time fixed for completion the crucial date, the purchaser does not become entitled to the rents and profits and bound to discharge the outgoings until a good title is shown[3].

1   As to what is vacant possession see para 123 ante.
2   The provisions of the standard conditions are complex and diverse: see the Statutory Form of Conditions of Sale 1925, SR & O 1925/779, condition 3; the Standard Conditions of Sale (3rd Edn), condition 6; the National Conditions of Sale (20th Edn), condition 6; and para 121 ante. As to the Conditions of Sale see para 1 note 9 ante. As to rents, profits, receipts and outgoings generally see para 188 et seq post. 'Possession' does not mean personal occupation if the purchaser has notice of a tenancy: *Lake v Dean* (1860) 28 Beav 607. As to the right to possession see further paras 185–186 post. Without a stipulation for apportionment, such outgoings can be apportioned as are apportionable at law: *Midgley v Coppock* (1879) 4 Ex D 309 at 313, CA. As to rents and other periodical payments see the Apportionment Act 1870 ss 3, 4; and LANDLORD AND TENANT vol 27(1) (Reissue) paras 245–247. Rents should be made apportionable whether payable in advance or in arrear, for rent in advance is not apportionable except under special condition: *Ellis v Rowbotham* [1900] 1 QB 740, CA. It must be noted that under the Apportionment Act 1870 apportionment can only be in respect of time. Any apportionment between property conveyed and property not conveyed or upon any other basis than time must be specially provided for: *Coal Commission v Earl Fitzwilliam's Royalties Co* [1942] Ch 365, [1942] 2 All ER 56.
3   *Carrodus v Sharp* (1855) 20 Beav 56; *Barsht v Tagg* [1900] 1 Ch 231 at 234, 235; *Re Highett and Bird's Contract* [1902] 2 Ch 214 at 217 (affd [1903] 1 Ch 287, CA); *Bennett v Stone* [1903] 1 Ch 509 at 524, CA. See also para 188 et seq post. As to completion see further para 262 et seq post.

125. Meaning of 'outgoings'. The term 'outgoings' is of very wide import[1], and includes not merely business rates[2], rent, service charges, repairs and the ordinary expenses of cultivating or managing the property[3] but also expenses, even if of a capital nature, of works executed by local authorities under their public health, highway and other powers which are recoverable from the owner, and which are also, in general, charged on the property[4].

1   See eg *Aldridge v Ferne* (1886) 17 QBD 212, DC; and LANDLORD AND TENANT vol 27(1) (Reissue) para 430. 'Outgoings' includes payments which the purchaser would have to meet if completion had taken place; in the case of a contract to grant a lease, it includes the rent to be reserved by the lease, but in the case of a contract to grant an underlease it does not include the head rent which would continue to be payable to the vendor: *Vangeen v Benjamin* (1976) 239 Estates Gazette 647.
2   The general rate is normally charged on the occupier, although in certain cases the owner may be liable: see RATING AND COUNCIL TAX vol 39(1) (Reissue) para 613 et seq. As to the liability of occupiers who are in occupation for part only of a rate period see RATING AND COUNCIL TAX vol 39(1) (Reissue) paras 627, 660–678 (non-domestic rating), 823, 835–856 (council tax). If the rate has not been made when the apportionment is made, the calculation should be made according to the old rate: see the Statutory Form of Conditions of Sale 1925, SR & O 1925/779, condition 3(2); 1 Williams Law relating to Vendors and Purchasers of Real Estate and Chattels Real (4th Edn, 1936) 60 note (s); 2 Williams Law relating to Vendors and Purchasers of Real Estate and Chattels Real (4th Edn, 1936) 1232 note (i).
3   *Carrodus v Sharp* (1855) 20 Beav 56. See also *Belfast Bank v Callan* [1910] 1 IR 38. As to the recovery from a subsequent occupier of unpaid arrears for the supply of electricity see FUEL AND ENERGY vol 19(2) (Reissue) para 907.
4   Examples are expenses incurred by local authorities under the provisions now embodied in the Highways Act 1980 ss 205–218 (as amended) (replacing the Private Street Works Act 1892) (see HIGHWAYS, STREETS AND BRIDGES vol 21 (Reissue) para 718 et seq) (see *Stock v Meakin* [1900] 1 Ch 683, CA, followed in *Surtees v Woodhouse* [1903] 1 KB 396, CA) or under local improvement Acts (see *Midgley v Coppock* (1879) 4 Ex D 309, CA), the expenses of abating a nuisance under public health legislation (see *Barsht v Tagg* [1900] 1 Ch 231) or of pulling down dangerous structures under the London Building Acts (Amendment) Act 1939 (repealed in part) (see *Tubbs v Wynne* [1897] 1 QB 74; and as to the recovery of such expenses generally see PUBLIC HEALTH).

126. Expenses charged on the property. Unless the conditions of sale provide to the contrary[1], capital expenses incurred by and payable to a local authority in respect of work done are not apportionable. Under the general law, the liability for those expenses as between vendor and purchaser depends on whether or not they are charged on the property, and, if so charged, when the charge was created. Where a charge is created[2] it usually attaches to the premises on the execution of the works, and not at the time when the apportionment is made by the local authority among the various premises affected, and the expenses must be borne by the vendor or purchaser according to whether the works are completed before or after the date fixed for completion[3]. If the expenses are not a charge upon the premises but the contract for sale contains a condition rendering the vendor liable to pay outgoings up to the date fixed for completion and the purchaser liable after that date, the expenses under the condition fall upon the vendor or the purchaser according to whether they become payable before or after the date for completion[4]. In the absence of conditions, it seems that the vendor is liable for expenses which become payable up to the time when a good title is shown[5], but a purchaser who pays by reason of his liability as owner for the time being cannot recover the amount from the vendor on the vendor's covenants for title where the expenses are not a charge on the property[6].

Charges acquired by local authorities or certain other authorities in respect of such expenses, and sums recoverable by them from various owners of property, are in general registrable as local land charges[7]. However, failure to register does not make the charge void against a purchaser, but the purchaser may be entitled to compensation[8]. A general charge not specifying any amount may be registered as soon as the authority has expended money for any purpose which, when the work is completed and any requisite resolution passed or order made, will confer a charge on the land[9]. This will be replaced in due course by a specific charge specifying the amount secured[10]. The standard conditions now in general use provide that the property is sold subject to certain incumbrances[11], including registered local land charges[12] and 'public requirements'[13].

1   As to the position under the Standard Conditions of Sale (3rd Edn) see the text and notes 11–13 infra. As to the Standard Conditions of Sale see para 1 note 9 ante.
2   Eg under the Highways Act 1980 ss 212, 305: see para 125 note 4 ante; and HOUSING vol 22 (Reissue) para 333 et seq; PUBLIC HEALTH.
3   *Stock v Meakin* [1900] 1 Ch 683, CA; *Re Waterhouse's Contract* (1900) 44 Sol Jo 645; *Re Allen and Driscoll's Contract* [1904] 2 Ch 226 at 230, CA; *Millard v Balby-with-Hexthorpe Urban Council* [1905] 1 KB 60, CA. Under a particular statute the expenses may become a charge on the land upon the local authority approving the assessment, notwithstanding that the work has been completed earlier: *Re Farrer and Gilbert's Contract* [1914] 1 Ch 125, CA.
4   *Midgley v Coppock* (1879) 4 Ex D 309, CA; *Tubbs v Wynne* [1897] 1 QB 74; and see *Barsht v Tagg* [1900] 1 Ch 231.
5   *Barsht v Tagg* [1900] 1 Ch 231.
6   *Egg v Blayney* (1888) 21 QBD 107, DC (expenses arising under the Metropolis Management Amendment Act 1862 s 77 (repealed)).
7   See the Local Land Charges Act 1975 s 1(1) (as amended); and LAND CHARGES vol 26 (Reissue) paras 576–577.
8   See ibid s 10 (as amended); and LAND CHARGES vol 26 (Reissue) para 594.
9   See ibid s 6(1), (2); the Local Land Charges Rules 1977, SI 1977/985, r 2(2); and LAND CHARGES vol 26 (Reissue) para 576. A general charge is in effect a memorandum that at some future date there may be a charge on the property: *Re Middleton and Young's Contract* [1929] WN 70. See also note 12 infra.
10 See the Local Land Charges Act 1975 s 1(1)(a) (as amended); the Local Land Charges Rules 1977/985, r 2(2); and LAND CHARGES vol 26 (Reissue) para 577.
11 See the Standard Conditions of Sale (3rd Edn), condition 3.1; and para 55 ante.
12 See the Standard Conditions of Sale (3rd Edn), condition 3.1.2(d); and para 55 ante. After the contract is made, the vendor is to give the purchaser written details without delay of any new public requirement and of anything in writing which he learns about concerning any incumbrances subject to which the property is sold: condition 3.1.3. For the meaning of 'contract' see para 55 note 10 ante; and for the meaning of 'public requirement' see para 55 note 14 ante.
    See also the National Conditions of Sale (20th Edn), condition 16, under which the purchaser must at his own expense comply with any 'requirement' made by a local authority after the date of the contract. See also *Re Leyland and Taylor's Contract* [1900] 2 Ch 625, CA. Where before the date of the

contract a local authority registered as a local land charge a resolution approving plans and a provisional apportionment under what is now the Highways Act 1980 s 205 (as amended) (see para 125 note 4 ante), and also served notice of the resolution and apportionment on the vendor, the entry was held not to be a 'local land charge required to be registered' (since registration was voluntary) but to be an 'other local land charge' for the purpose of the condition requiring the vendor to indemnify the purchaser against local land charges required to be registered, and duly registered, before the date of the contract or other local land charges of which he had notice before that date: *Re Middleton and Young's Contract* [1929] WN 70, where the charge appears to have been registered as a general charge. Such a charge cannot be registered until money has been expended (see the text and note 9 supra), and a mere resolution or notice issued in respect of it is not registrable: see para 16 ante. Conditions sometimes provide that money becoming receivable or payable under an Act or a planning or other scheme is to be receivable or payable by the vendor if it has become receivable or payable before the date of the contract, and by the purchaser if it becomes receivable or payable after that date. Such a condition will cover eg compensation for refusal or revocation of planning permission under the Town and Country Planning Act 1990 Pt III (ss 55–106B) (as amended), Pt IV (ss 107–118) (as amended) (see TOWN AND COUNTRY PLANNING vol 46 (Reissue) para 697 et seq), or refund of advance payments made by owners of new buildings in respect of street works (see the Highways Act 1980 s 219 (as amended); and HIGHWAYS, STREETS AND BRIDGES vol 21 (Reissue) para 751 et seq).

13 See the Standard Conditions of Sale (3rd Edn), condition 3.1.2(e); and para 55 ante. The purchaser is to bear the cost of complying with any outstanding public requirement and is to indemnify the vendor against any liability resulting from a public requirement: condition 3.1.4.

127. Sale to sitting tenant. Where a tenant, under any kind of lease or tenancy, enters into an agreement with his landlord to purchase the premises in which he is residing, and thereby acquires an immediate equitable interest in the demised premises which is inconsistent with the continuance of the lease, there is no presumption that upon the conclusion of the agreement the lease is determined by surrender or otherwise and the effect of the agreement depends in all cases upon its particular terms[1]. Where the terms of the agreement are such as to render its performance incompatible with a continuance of the lease, it operates to determine the lease[2].

The vendor cannot in any case be entitled both to the rent and to interest on the purchase money[3], and a condition should be inserted to make it clear to what he is entitled. A condition avoiding such difficulties is one providing that nothing contained in the contract (or in the option where the purchase is in exercise of an option in the lease) is to operate to determine the tenancy until the purchase money has been paid in full. Such a special condition seems desirable, since problems might otherwise occur if, for any reason, the purchaser failed to complete.

Where the sale is to a sitting tenant exercising his statutory right of enfranchisement[4] the conditions of sale provide, subject to contrary agreement, that rent continues to be payable until actual completion, unless the landlord elects to receive interest instead of rent[5].

1 *Doe d Gray v Stanion* (1836) 1 M & W 695 at 701; *Tarte v Darby* (1846) 15 M & W 601; *Ellis v Wright* (1897) 76 LT 522; *Leek and Moorlands Building Society v Clark* [1952] 2 QB 788, [1952] 2 All ER 492, CA; *Nightingale v Courtney* [1954] 1 QB 399, [1954] 1 All ER 362, CA; *Watney v Boardley* [1975] 2 All ER 644, [1975] 1 WLR 857. See also para 195 note 11 post; and LANDLORD AND TENANT vol 27(1) (Reissue) paras 534–535. A provision for rescission of the agreement by the vendor may be sufficient to prevent termination of the lease: see *Raffety v Schofield* [1897] 1 Ch 937.

2 *Turner v Watts* (1928) 97 LJKB 403, CA, where interest was payable from the date of the agreement; *Cockwell v Romford Sanitary Steam Laundry Ltd* [1939] 4 All ER 370, CA, where interest was payable from the expiration of the notice exercising an option to purchase; *Watney v Boardley* [1975] 2 All ER 644, [1975] 1 WLR 857, where the purchase price was due on the date of exercise of an option, with interest from that date until payment together with arrears of rent up to that date.

3 See *Brooke v Champernowne* (1837) 4 Cl & Fin 589 at 611, HL.

4 Ie under the Leasehold Reform Act 1967 Pt I (ss 1–37) (as amended): see LANDLORD AND TENANT vol 27(2) (Reissue) para 1253 et seq.

5 Leasehold Reform (Enfranchisement and Extension) Regulations 1967, SI 1967/1879, reg 2, Schedule, Pt I paras 7, 8.

128. Payment of purchase money by instalments. A condition for the payment of the purchase money by instalments should provide for the insurance and repair of the property and for forfeiture on failure to pay any instalment[1]. The vendor will have a lien on the property for unpaid instalments of the purchase price[2]. Such a lien is registrable as a land charge[3], but where the vendor retains (as he usually does) the documents of title of the property pending completion of payment by instalments, this retention of documents probably prevents the registration of the lien[4]. On the other hand, the purchaser can protect his position by a registration of the contract as an estate contract[5]. He should require the condition to provide for at least the form of the transfer[6] to be settled and scheduled to the agreement, for if this is left until all the instalments have been paid he will be in no position to negotiate its contents. If he is to be let into possession before completion, care should be taken not to create a tenancy which might enjoy statutory protection[7]. It must be clearly stated in the condition who is to pay any outgoing, whether of a periodic or capital nature, and who is to receive any payment of a similar nature during the continuance of the agreement[8].

1   As to the operation of such a condition see para 232 note 9 post. The condition takes the form of a power for the vendor to resell on default.
2   See LIEN vol 28 (Reissue) para 758 et seq.
3   See the Land Charges Act 1972 s 2(4) (as amended), Class C(iii); and LAND CHARGES vol 26 (Reissue) para 531; LIEN vol 28 (Reissue) para 758. In the case of registered land, the lien may be protected by a notice or caution, but if the vendor is in actual occupation the lien is an overriding interest under the Land Registration Act 1925 s 70(1)(g): *London and Cheshire Insurance Co Ltd v Laplagrene Property Co Ltd* [1971] Ch 499, [1971] 1 All ER 766; and see LAND REGISTRATION vol 26 (Reissue) para 784. Where the vendor is a limited company, the lien is not registrable under what is now the Companies Act 1985 s 395 (see COMPANIES vol 7(2) (1996 Reissue) para 1299): *London and Cheshire Insurance Co Ltd v Laplagrene Property Co Ltd* supra.
4   See the Land Charges Act 1972 s 2(4)(iii) proviso (a), which excepts a charge protected by the deposit of documents relating to the legal estate. The Law of Property Act 1925 does not prejudicially affect the right or interest of any person arising out of or consequent on the possession of any such document: s 13.
5   See the Land Charges Act 1972 s 2(4) (as amended), Class C(iv); and LAND CHARGES vol 26 (Reissue) paras 528, 532. In the case of registered land, the contract may be protected by an entry on the register, but if the purchaser is in actual occupation the contract will be an overriding interest: see LAND REGISTRATION vol 26 (Reissue) paras 784, 922.
6   As to the disposition of registered and unregistered land by transfer see para 262 note 2 post.
7   See para 119 ante.
8   See eg *Re Watford Corpn's and Ware's Contract* [1943] Ch 82, [1943] 1 All ER 54, where, under an agreement made in 1927, it was held that instalments of the war damage contribution fell on the vendor in the absence of a provision to the contrary.

K. TRANSFER AND CUSTODY OF TITLE DEEDS

129. Expenses of preparing transfer. In the absence of conditions, the purchaser prepares the draft transfer at his own expense[1], but the expense of perusal and execution by the vendor and all other necessary parties falls on the vendor[2], who also bears the expense of any act necessary for completing his own title[3]. The conditions do not in general vary this practice as regards the preparation of the draft transfer[4] and the perusal and execution by the vendor, but a provision is sometimes inserted that the purchaser is to meet the cost of every act or thing required for perfecting or completing the vendor's title except the expenses of tracing and getting in any outstanding legal estate[5]. The purchaser is not bound to take a transfer with the concurrence of persons entitled to an equitable interest if the title can be discharged from the interest under a trust[6], or the Settled Land Act 1925[7] or other statute[8]. If the transfer is made with the concurrence of a person entitled to a registered incumbrance, where the registration is not cancelled, the concurrence must be free of expense to the purchaser[9]. Formerly the conditions might provide that the expense of getting in an outstanding legal estate should be borne by the purchaser[10], but a stipulation to this effect is now void[11]. Where the purchaser is bound to execute the transfer, it may be desirable to provide that a duplicate transfer or a separate acknowledgment of the vendor's right to production and an undertaking for safe custody is to be prepared, engrossed and stamped by and at the vendor's expense and that for the purpose of denoting the stamp the purchaser must produce the original[12].

1   As to the preparation of the transfer generally see para 262 post. As to the disposition of registered and unregistered land by transfer see para 262 note 2 post.
2   *Poole v Hill* (1840) 6 M & W 835; and see para 324 post.
3   See *Reeves v Gill* (1838) 1 Beav 375. As to the expense of getting in an outstanding legal estate see the text and notes 10–11 infra. On a sale of an estate in lots under conditions which throw a common incumbrance on one lot exclusively, the other purchasers are entitled to an indemnity from the purchaser of that lot: *Casamajor v Strode* (1819) 2 Swan 347; affd (1821) Jac 630.
4   See para 262 note 6 post.
5   Cf the Standard Conditions of Sale (3rd Edn), conditions 4.1.2, 4.5. As to the Standard Conditions of Sale see para 1 note 9 ante. Under a condition that the transfer is to be made at the purchaser's expense, the purchaser is not liable for the expense of procuring the concurrence of necessary parties other than the vendor: *Paramore v Greenslade* (1853) 1 Sm & G 541 at 544.
6   See para 146 post.
7   See the Settled Land Act 1925 s 72(2); and SETTLEMENTS para 874 post.
8   See the Law of Property Act 1925 s 42(1) (as amended); and paras 147, 271–273 post.
9   See ibid s 43(1).
10 If the condition merely aimed at the getting in of an outstanding legal estate, it did not apply to an unsatisfied mortgage estate or term (*Stronge v Hawkes* (1856) 2 Jur NS 388; cf *Hopkinson v Chamberlain* [1908] 1 Ch 853), but if the purchaser agreed to bear the expense of 'preparing, obtaining, making, and doing every assurance and every act and thing necessary for perfecting or completing the vendor's title', he had to bear the whole expense of procuring the concurrence of the vendor's mortgagees (*Re Willett and Argenti* (1889) 60 LT 735; cf *Re Sander and Walford's Contract* (1900) 83 LT 316, where the words were not so wide and did not extend to the costs of perusal and execution of the conveyance by a mortgagee), or of the execution of a deed to confirm an imperfectly executed conveyance to the vendor himself (*Re Woods and Lewis' Contract* [1898] 1 Ch 433 at 437). However, such a condition did not absolve the vendor from his duty of deducing, at his own expense, a title to any outstanding legal estate: *Re Adams' Trustees' and Frost's Contract* [1907] 1 Ch 695 at 703; cf *Sheerness Waterworks Co (Official Manager) v Polson* (1861) 3 De GF & J 36.
11 See the Law of Property Act 1925 s 42(3). As to the operation of the Limitation Act 1980 s 17 in extinguishing an outstanding legal estate in unregistered land cf LIMITATION OF ACTIONS vol 28 (Reissue) para 844; and LAND REGISTRATION vol 26 (Reissue) paras 760–761 (effect of acquisition of title by possession in the case of registered land). See also *Jessamine Investment Co v Schwartz* [1978] QB 264, [1976] 3 All ER 521; *Spectrum Investment Co v Holmes* [1981] 1 All ER 6, [1981] 1 WLR 221; *Central London Commercial Estates Ltd v Kato Kagaku Co Ltd* [1998] 4 All ER 948, [1998] TLR 475. Many outstanding legal estates were got in on 1 January 1926 by the operation of the Law of Property Act 1925 s 39 (as amended), Sch 1, Pt II para 3.
12 As to the stamp duty on a duplicate see STAMP DUTIES AND STAMP DUTY RESERVE TAX vol 44(1) (Reissue) para 1079.

130. Free transfer. A provision is sometimes inserted in a contract for sale entitling the purchaser to a free transfer on his submitting to certain restrictions on the proof of title. Certain restrictions have been placed by statute on the terms of such a condition. Any stipulation is void which provides for the transfer or the registration of the purchaser's title to be prepared or carried out at the purchaser's expense by a solicitor appointed by or acting for the vendor or which might restrict a purchaser in selecting a solicitor to act on his behalf[1]. It is, however, lawful for the vendor to reserve the right to furnish a form of transfer from which a draft can be prepared, and to charge a reasonable fee for it[2]. The condition for a free transfer usually stipulates that the purchaser is to make no investigation of title and, provided he is not excluded from employing a solicitor of his own choice, this does not appear to be contrary to statute[3]. A purchaser who is given a right to a free transfer does not thereby without more lose his right to receive an abstract of title, and, if he is to be debarred from receiving an abstract, this must be specifically stated[4].

1 Law of Property Act 1925 s 48(1). In s 48 a reference to a solicitor includes a licensed conveyancer within the Administration of Justice Act 1985 s 11(2) (see SOLICITORS vol 44(1) (Reissue) para 550) or a recognised body within s 9 (see SOLICITORS vol 44(1) (Reissue) para 383) and s 32 (see SOLICITORS vol 44(1) (Reissue) para 610): see s 34(2), Sch 2 para 37. See also para 3 ante. If the sale is effected by demise or sub-demise, the instrument giving effect to the transaction is deemed to be a transfer for this purpose, but the law relating to the preparation of a lease or underlease is not otherwise affected: Law of Property Act 1925 s 48(1), (3). It seems that a condition which merely provides that on a sale effected by demise or sub-demise the lease or underlease is to be prepared by the vendor's solicitor is valid. For an example of such a condition see the National Conditions of Sale (20th Edn), condition 19(1). As to the Conditions of Sale see para 1 note 9 ante. Any stipulation which provides that an assignment of a lease or underlease is to be prepared by the lessor, underlessor or his solicitor at the purchaser's expense is void (see the Law of Property Act 1925 s 48(2), (4)), but where such a stipulation is void a covenant is implied in lieu of it that the lessee or underlessee will register assignments (including probates and letters of administration) with the lessor or his solicitor and will pay a fee in respect of such registration, and the power of re-entry, if any, applies to a breach of such an implied covenant (see s 48(2) proviso). As to the disposition of registered and unregistered land by transfer see para 262 note 2 post.
2 Ibid s 48(1) proviso. Where the only consideration is the reservation of a perpetual rentcharge, the vendor may stipulate that the draft transfer is to be prepared by his solicitor at the purchaser's expense: s 48(1) proviso. This seems unlikely to be used now, however, since the exceptional cases where a rentcharge may be validly created after 22 August 1977 seem unlikely to fall within the statutory provision: see the Rentcharges Act 1977 s 2 (as amended); and RENTCHARGES AND ANNUITIES vol 39(2) (Reissue) para 774 et seq. As to the execution of the transfer in duplicate see para 262 note 5 post.
3 Such conditions are usually employed where an estate is sold in lots. Such transactions are now, however, greatly simplified and cheapened by registering the title at the Land Registry and selling the individual lots as registered land. As to the registration of the lots under different numbers with a view to facilitating future transactions see LAND REGISTRATION vol 26 (Reissue) para 801. Advantage may also be taken of the Land Registry's Title Shown Procedure: see Ruoff and Roper, Registered Conveyancing (Looseleaf Edn) paras 12–63.
4 *Re Pelly and Jacob's Contract* (1899) 80 LT 45. As to the need for an abstract of title with respect to both unregistered and registered land see paras 138, 141–149 post.

131. Transfer and retention of title deeds. Since the owner of the land is entitled to possession of the title deeds[1], the vendor must hand over all documents of title which are in his possession and relate exclusively to the property sold, and in the absence of stipulation to the contrary he must bear the cost of obtaining them if they are not in his possession[2]. However, where the vendor retains part of the land to which any documents of title relate, he is entitled to retain such documents[3]. He is also entitled to retain a document of title which is a trust instrument or other instrument creating a trust which is still subsisting, or an instrument relating to the appointment or discharge of a trustee of a subsisting trust[4]. Where land is sold in lots, the purchaser whose purchase price is the largest is entitled to the deeds relating to the several lots[5]. It is the practice to provide expressly to the same effect. Thus a usual condition of sale stipulates, with respect to common title deeds, that the vendor is to retain them if any lots are unsold, and that as between different purchasers they are to go to the purchaser who pays in the aggregate the largest purchase price, and that he is to give an acknowledgment of right to production and undertaking for safe custody to each of the other purchasers at their expense[6].

1 *Austin v Croome* (1842) Car & M 653; *Re Williams and Duchess of Newcastle's Contract* [1897] 2 Ch 144 at 148; *Clayton v Clayton* [1930] 2 Ch 12. As to the right of a mortgagee to title deeds see MORTGAGE. As to the custody of title deeds in general and the right of a tenant for life to custody see REAL PROPERTY vol 39(2) (Reissue) paras 86–87. Title deeds are property within the Married Women's Property Act 1882 s 17 (as amended): *Re Knight's Question* [1959] Ch 381, [1958] 1 All ER 812; and see HUSBAND AND WIFE.

2   *Re Duthy and Jesson's Contract* [1898] 1 Ch 419. Cf the National Conditions of Sale (20th Edn), condition
     12(3). As to the Conditions of Sale see para 1 note 9 ante. An agreement to give 'real security' against loss
     of title deeds will be specifically enforced: *Walker v Barnes* (1818) 3 Madd 247. The fact that the
     consideration is a rentcharge does not, apparently, entitle the vendor to retain the deeds: 1 Dart's Law
     relating to Vendors and Purchasers (8th Edn, 1929) 582. As to the production of title deeds for proof of
     title see para 150 post.
3   Law of Property Act 1925 s 45(9)(a). Hence, on a sale of land by a mortgagee whose security also includes
     personal property, the purchaser is, in the absence of a special condition, entitled to the mortgage deed,
     notwithstanding that the mortgagee retains the personal property (*Re Williams and Duchess of Newcastle's
     Contract* [1897] 2 Ch 144 at 148), unless the instrument relates to a trust and can be retained under the
     Law of Property Act 1925 s 45(9)(b). Documents showing the extinguishment of an easement in regard
     to which land retained by the vendor was the servient tenement and land sold was the dominant tenement
     are properly retained by the vendor: *Re Lehmann and Walker's Contract* [1906] 2 Ch 640. Since 'land' is
     defined in the Law of Property Act 1925 s 205(1)(ix) (as amended), to include an easement, it would
     appear that documents relating solely to easements are in the same position as the documents relating to
     the land itself.
4   Ibid s 45(9)(b). As to the purchaser's right to have notice of restrictive covenants indorsed on or
     permanently annexed to a document of title retained by the vendor see s 200; and para 298 post. The
     Standard Conditions of Sale (3rd Edn) do not contain any provision entitling the purchaser to
     indorsement of a sale of part of the vendor's land. There should be no problem if the vendor's title is
     registered, but if it is not registered a special condition should provide for indorsement. As to the Standard
     Conditions of Sale see para 1 note 9 ante.
5   *Griffiths v Hatchard* (1854) 1 K & J 17.
6   See *Strong v Strong* (1858) 6 WR 455. Under a condition that the deeds are to go to the purchaser of 'the
     largest lot', the purchaser of the largest single lot in extent takes them, even though the purchase money
     paid by another purchaser may be greater (*Griffiths v Hatchard* (1854) 1 K & J 17) and, a fortiori, the
     purchaser of the largest single lot both in extent and value (*Scott v Jackman* (1855) 21 Beav 110; and see
     Cunnyngham v Hume (1839) 1 I Eq R 150). As to successive sales see *Re Lowe, Capel v Lowe* (1901) 36 L
     Jo 73. The purchaser of part of the property under an open contract is not entitled to title deeds which
     relate to the whole property even if the deeds are in the hands of persons who have ceased to have any
     title to any part of the property, and he must rely upon his equitable right to production: *Re Jenkins and
     Commercial Electric Theatre Co's Contract* (1917) 61 Sol Jo 283.

132. Right to production of deeds. Where documents of title are retained by the
vendor, the purchaser is, in the absence of stipulation to the contrary, entitled at his own
expense to have attested copies of them[1]. He is also entitled at his own expense[2] to a
covenant for, or an acknowledgment of his right to, production, and, unless the vendor
is a trustee or mortgagee, an undertaking for their safe custody[3]. The vendor's inability to
furnish the purchaser with a legal covenant or acknowledgment for production is not an
objection to his title if the purchaser will, on completion, have an equitable right to
production[4]. Where the vendor is a personal representative, the purchaser is entitled to
an acknowledgment for production of the grant of probate or letters of administration[5]
and to have a memorandum of the transfer indorsed on the grant[6].

1   See the Law of Property Act 1925 s 45(4); *Dare v Tucker* (1801) 6 Ves 460; *Boughton v Jewell* (1808) 15
     Ves 176. The purchaser is not entitled to copies of deeds which are produced as negative evidence that
     the property was not comprised in them: Sugden's Law of Vendors and Purchasers (14th Edn, 1862) 436.
2   See the Law of Property Act 1925 s 45(8); and para 323 post.
3   See ibid s 64; and para 299 post. Cf *Yates v Plumbe* (1854) 2 Sm & G 174. The right to an acknowledgment
     replaces in practice the former right to a covenant for production: *Cooper v Emery* (1844) 1 Ph 388 at 390.
4   Law of Property Act 1925 s 45(7); and see para 299 post.
5   *Re Miller and Pickersgill's Contract* [1931] 1 Ch 511.
6   See the Administration of Estates Act 1925 s 36(5); and EXECUTORS AND ADMINISTRATORS. As to the
     disposition of registered and unregistered land by transfer see para 262 note 2 post.

(7) SALES UNDER ORDERS OF THE COURT

133. Power to order sale of land. Where in any cause or matter in the Chancery Division relating to any land[1] it appears necessary or expedient for the purposes of the cause or matter that the land or any part of it should be sold, the court may order that land or part to be sold[2]. The effect of the order is to bind the legal and equitable interests in the land sold of all persons who are either parties to or bound by the proceedings in which the order is made[3], and on a transfer of the legal estate to the purchaser the concurrence of persons who have only equitable interests is not necessary[4]. Any party bound by the order and in possession of the land or part, or in receipt of the rents and profits of it, may be compelled to deliver up that possession or receipt to the purchaser or to such other person as the court may direct[5]. The order cannot be invalidated as against a purchaser on the ground of want of jurisdiction or of any concurrence, consent, notice or service, whether or not the purchaser has notice of any such want[6]. Where an order for sale has been made, a sale otherwise than under the order will not be permitted[7].

The county court has a corresponding jurisdiction where the matter falls within the financial limits of its jurisdiction[8] or where the parties consent[9].

1 'Land' includes any interest in or right over land: CPR Sch 1 RSC Ord 31 r 1. This now includes an interest under a trust for sale: see the Trusts of Land and Appointment of Trustees Act 1996 s 3; and TRUSTS vol 48 (Reissue) paras 841–842.

As from 26 April 1999, the Civil Procedure Rules (CPR) replace the Rules of the Supreme Court and the County Court Rules. Certain provisions of the RSC and CCR are saved in a modified form in CPR Schs 1 and 2 respectively. The CPR apply to proceedings issued on or after 26 April 1999, and new steps taken in existing proceedings, as prescribed: CPR 51; *Practice Direction—Transitional Arrangements* (1999) PD51. As to the principles underlying the new rules see CPR Pt 1.

At the date at which this volume states the law, the extent, if any, to which cases decided under RSC or CCR may be cited in relation to CPR, is unclear. It is thought that they will be persuasive where the same word or concept is used (and binding if subsequently adopted by the court), but in relation to the exercise of a discretion will be of less value in the light of the overriding objective. See further the introduction to Civil Court Practice 1999. Accordingly, cases cited in this title in amplification or explanation of the former rules will be binding over proceedings conducted under those rules, but should be viewed with caution in relation to proceedings conducted under the new regime.

2 CPR Sch 1 RSC Ord 31 r 1. The original jurisdiction of the Court of Chancery seems to have extended only to: (1) sales in satisfaction of creditors' claims enforceable in equity against the land; (2) sales in execution of valid trusts for sale; (3) sales for the purpose of enforcing equitable liens; and (4) sales of partnership land on dissolution: see *Mackreth v Symmons* (1808) 15 Ves 329; *Featherstonhaugh v Fenwick* (1810) 17 Ves 298; *Lechmere v Brasier* (1821) 2 Jac & W 287; *Calvert v Godfrey* (1843) 6 Beav 97. See also LIEN vol 28 (Reissue) para 779; PARTNERSHIP vol 35 (Reissue) paras 195–197; TRUSTS vol 48 (Reissue) para 767. This original jurisdiction and the statutory jurisdiction conferred by 15 & 16 Vict c 86 (Court of Chancery Procedure) (1852) passed to the High Court under the Supreme Court of Judicature Act 1873 s 16 (repealed), and was mainly exercisable in the Chancery Division (s 34(3) (repealed)), which now has jurisdiction by virtue of the Supreme Court Act 1981 ss 19, 61(1), Sch 1 para 1(a): see PRACTICE AND PROCEDURE. Power to order the sale of land delivered to a judgment creditor by way of execution was conferred by the Judgments Act 1864 s 4 (repealed), but this power has been replaced by the power to charge the land of judgment debtors under the Charging Orders Act 1979 s 1(1): see EXECUTION. Power to order a sale in redemption or foreclosure actions conferred by the Law of Property Act 1925 s 91 (as amended) (see MORTGAGE) is supplemented by CPR Sch 1 RSC Ord 31 r 1, which enables the court to make an order for sale in a debenture holder's action: see *Re Crigglestone Coal Co, Stewart v Crigglestone Coal Co* [1906] 1 Ch 523; and COMPANIES vol 7(2) (1996 Reissue) para 1365. As to the court's power to make an order relating to the exercise by trustees of land of any of their functions, including their powers of sale, see the Trusts of Land and Appointment of Trustees Act 1996 s 14; and SETTLEMENTS para 905 post.

3 As to who is bound by an order made in representative proceedings see CPR Sch 1 RSC Ord 15 rr 12(3), 13(3), (4), 14(1), 15(1); EXECUTORS AND ADMINISTRATORS; PRACTICE AND PROCEDURE.

4 *Massy v Batwell* (1843) 4 Dr & War 58; *Cole v Sewell* (1849) 17 Sim 40; *Re Williams' Estate* (1852) 5 De G & Sm 515; *Cottrell v Cottrell* (1866) LR 2 Eq 330; *Basnett v Moxon* (1875) LR 20 Eq 182; *Re Whitham, Whitham v Davies* (1901) 84 LT 585. As to the overriding effect of a sale under court order see the Law

of Property Act 1925 s 2(1)(iv); and REAL PROPERTY vol 39(2) (Reissue) para 251. The order does not, however, affect either the legal or the equitable interests in the land of persons who are neither parties nor bound by the proceedings in which the order is made: *Craddock v Piper* (1844) 14 Sim 310; *Grey Coat Hospital Governors v Westminster Improvement Comrs* (1857) 1 De G & J 531; *Freeland v Pearson* (1869) LR 7 Eq 246. As to the proper persons to transfer see para 274 post. As to the court's power to make a vesting order in favour of a purchaser or to appoint a person to transfer see para 266 post. As to the disposition of registered and unregistered land by transfer see para 262 note 2 post.

5   CPR Sch 1 RSC Ord 31 r 1.

6   Law of Property Act 1925 s 204 (reproducing the Conveyancing Act 1881 s 70 (repealed)); see *Re Hall Dare's Contract* (1882) 21 ChD 41, CA; *Mostyn v Mostyn* [1893] 3 Ch 376, CA; *Re Bridgett and Hayes' Contract* [1928] Ch 163. This provision does not confer a good title on the purchaser as against perfect strangers to the proceedings who were not in the contemplation of the court when it made the order for sale: *Jones v Barnett* [1899] 1 Ch 611; affd [1900] 1 Ch 370, CA. As to misrepresentation on sales by court order see *Mahomed Kala Mea v Harperink* (1908) 25 TLR 180, PC; and para 83 note 4 ante.

7   *Annesley v Ashurst* (1734) 3 P Wms 282.

8   See the County Courts Act 1984 s 23, Sch 2 (as amended); and COUNTY COURTS.

9   See the County Courts Act 1984 s 24 (as amended); and COUNTY COURTS.

134. Manner of carrying out the sale. The sale may be made either in court or out of court. Where an order is made, whether in court or in chambers, directing land to be sold[1], the court appoints the party or person who is to have the conduct of the sale[2], and may permit him to sell the land in such manner as he thinks fit, or may direct that the land be sold in such manner as the court directs, either by the order or subsequently[3], for the best price that can be obtained[4]. The court usually directs that the sale be effected out of court.

The court may direct that the land be sold by contract conditional on the approval of the court (in which case the sale is effected in court[5]), or by private treaty, or by public auction[6] (although an auction may be dispensed with if a reserve price can be agreed between the parties), by tender or in some other manner[7]. The court may fix a reserve or minimum price[8], may direct the payment of the purchase money into court or to trustees or other persons[9], and may give directions for settling the particulars and conditions of sale[10], for obtaining evidence of the value of the property[11] and for requiring the abstract of title to be referred to conveyancing counsel of the court[12] or some other conveyancing counsel for his opinion on it and to settle the particulars and conditions of sale[13].

1   So far as applicable, CPR Sch 1 RSC Ord 31 rr 2, 3, apply also, with the necessary modifications, in relation to the mortgage, exchange or partition of any land under an order of the court: CPR Sch 1 RSC Ord 31 r 4. CPR Sch 1 RSC Ord 31 r 1 (power to order sale of land) also applies to applications for ancillary relief in family proceedings: see the Family Proceedings Rules 1991, SI 1991/1247, r 2.64(3). As to the CPR see para 133 note 1 ante.

2   CPR Sch 1 RSC Ord 31 r 2(2)(a). See further para 135 post.

3   The court's directions as to the manner of sale may be contained in the order for sale; if they are not, directions may be given in proceedings under CPR Sch 1 RSC Ord 44 in chambers under the order. The order for sale may contain directions for the conduct of the proceedings under the order: see CPR Sch 1 RSC Ord 44 r 3. It is not necessary to issue a further summons to proceed; as the procedure is now as directed by the court, which will fix a day for the further attendance of the parties: CPR Sch 1 RSC Ord 44 r 3(1)(f).

4   CPR Sch 1 RSC Ord 31 r 2(1).

5   Thus all the steps are taken under the court's directions. Where the action is begun in a district registry, it is in the judge's discretion whether the sale will take place there or in his chambers: *Macdonald v Foster* (1877) 6 ChD 193, CA.

6   In the case of a sale by auction the court may give directions as to any security to be given by the auctioneer, and as to his remuneration: CPR Sch 1 RSC Ord 31 r 2(2)(g). As to the scales of remuneration usually allowed to estate agents and auctioneers see *Practice Direction* [1983] 1 All ER 160, [1983] 1 WLR 86.

7   CPR Sch 1 RSC Ord 31 r 2(2)(b). The court has power to direct a sale before a master in chambers: *Waterhouse v Wilkinson* (1864) 1 Hem & M 636; *Barlow v Osborne* (1858) 6 HL Cas 556 at 571, 572; *Pemberton v Barnes* (1872) LR 13 Eq 349.

8   CPR Sch 1 RSC Ord 31 r 2(2)(c).
9   CPR Sch 1 RSC Ord 31 r 2(2)(d). In this case the result of the sale must be certified by the solicitor for
     the party or person having the conduct of the sale or, if the sale is by public auction, by the auctioneer,
     and the court may require the certificate to be verified by the witness statement or affidavit by the solicitor
     or auctioneer, as the case may be: CPR Sch 1 RSC Ord 31 r 3(1). The solicitor must file the certificate
     and any witness statement or affidavit in the office of the court dealing with the proceedings: CPR Sch 1
     RSC Ord 31 r 3(2).
10   CPR Sch 1 RSC Ord 31 r 2(2)(e). As to conditions of sale see para 76 et seq ante.
11   CPR Sch 1 RSC Ord 31 r 2(2)(f).
12   As to conveyancing counsel of the court see para 136 post. As to the need for an abstract of title with
     respect to both unregistered and registered land see paras 138, 141–149 post.
13   CPR Sch 1 RSC Ord 31 r 2(2)(h). See further para 136 post.

135. Conduct of the sale. The conduct of a sale of land under an order of the court is usually committed to the plaintiff or other person having the carriage of the order[1], but the court has a discretion in the matter and will give the conduct of the sale to another party or person if such a course is shown to be for the benefit of those interested[2]. As between the vendor and the purchaser, the solicitor for the party or person having the conduct of the sale is deemed to be the agent of all parties to the action[3].

Leave to bid may be given to the parties to the action by the order for sale[4], or may be applied for by summons in chambers, but none of the parties ought to bid without leave[5]. If all obtain leave to bid, the conduct of the sale may be given to an independent solicitor[6].

On a sale by auction the highest bona fide bidder at or above the reserve price, if any, is to be declared to be the purchaser[7]. The same rule applies to a sale by private tender[8].

The result of the sale is stated in the form of a master's order[9], which has effect as a final order disposing of the proceedings in which it is made[10], subject to such directions as the master thinks fit to include in the order as to the further consideration of the proceedings either at a public or private hearing[11], and the order has immediate binding effect on the parties[12], although it is subject to appeal in the usual way[13].

1   *Dale v Hamilton* (1853) 10 Hare App I, vii. This is so notwithstanding that, as between the parties, the
     plaintiff, if there were no action, would not be entitled to interfere with the sale: *Dale v Hamilton* supra. As
     to the court's power to direct who is to have the conduct of the sale see CPR Sch 1 RSC Ord 31 r 2(2)(a).
     As to the CPR see para 133 note 1 ante.
2   *Dixon v Pyner* (1850) 7 Hare 331; *Hewitt v Nanson* (1858) 28 LJ Ch 49; *Knott v Cottee (No 4)* (1859) 27
     Beav 33; *Re Gardner, Gardner v Beaumont* (1879) 48 LJ Ch 644; *Davies v Wright* (1886) 32 ChD 220. The
     Court of Appeal will not interfere with the exercise of the discretion: *Re Love, Hill v Spurgeon* (1885) 29
     ChD 348, CA. Where in an administration claim an order is made for the sale of any property vested in
     executors, administrators or trustees, unless otherwise ordered, the conduct of the sale will be given to
     those executors, administrators or trustees: CPR Sch 1 RSC Ord 85 r 6; and see EXECUTORS AND
     ADMINISTRATORS; TRUSTS vol 48 (Reissue) para 935.
3   *Dalby v Pullen* (1830) 1 Russ & M 296. So also is the conveyancing counsel of the court (as to whom see
     para 136 post): *Re Banister, Broad v Munton* (1879) 12 ChD 131, CA. As to the relations of solicitor and
     client generally see SOLICITORS vol 44(1) (Reissue) para 99 et seq. See also para 3 ante.
4   As to a form of order see 1 Seton's Form of Decrees, Judgments and Orders (7th Edn, 1912) 324.
5   *Elworthy v Billing* (1841) 10 Sim 98. However, if a party bids without leave the purchase may be allowed
     to stand: *Elworthy v Billing* supra. The person having the conduct of the sale will not be allowed to bid:
     Sidny v Ranger (1841) 12 Sim 118; see 2 Dart's Law relating to Vendors and Purchasers (8th Edn, 1929)
     893. A person to whom leave to bid has been given is under no greater obligations as to disclosure and
     good faith than those imposed on ordinary purchasers (see para 62 ante): *Coaks v Boswell* (1886) 11 App
     Cas 232, HL.
6   *Dean v Wilson* (1878) 10 ChD 136.
7   See the Sale of Land by Auction Act 1867 s 7 (as amended). See also *Guest v Smythe* (1870) 5 Ch App
     551; *Delves v Delves* (1875) LR 20 Eq 77; *Union Bank of London v Munster* (1887) 37 ChD 51; *Re Bartlett,
     Newman v Hook* (1880) 16 ChD 561. The practice of opening biddings was abolished by the Sale of Land
     by Auction Act 1867 s 7 (as amended), except in case of fraud or improper conduct bordering on fraud
     in the management of the sale. A mistake in chambers as regards the reserve price, or a misstatement by

the auctioneer affecting the value of the property, is a reason for opening the bidding or refusing to sell to a bidder: see *Re Longvale Brick and Lime Works Ltd* [1917] 1 IR 321, Ir CA; *Re Joseph Clayton Ltd, Smith v The Company* [1920] 1 Ch 257. Where an interested party bought in a sale improperly, resale was ordered and, on no higher bid being made, the original purchaser was held to his purchase: *Re Dumbell, ex p Hughes, ex p Lyon* (1802) 6 Ves 617.

8   *Munster and Leinster Bank v Munster Motor Co* [1922] 1 IR 15.

9   CPR Sch 1 RSC Ord 44 r 11(1).

10   CPR Sch 1 RSC Ord 44 r 11(2). Strictly speaking, it is only at this stage that the contract is concluded with the purchaser: see *Ex p Minor* (1805) 11 Ves 559; and see also *Twigg v Fifield* (1807) 13 Ves 517 at 518. When these cases were decided the decisive time was when the master's certificate became absolute, but the procedure has now changed, and the master's order takes the place of the master's certificate. On a subsale at a profit before the master's certificate became absolute, the profit went to the parties to the original action (*Hodder v Ruffin* (1830) Taml 341), but on a subsale afterwards the original purchaser took the profit (*Dewell v Tuffnell* (1855) 1 K & J 324).

11   CPR Sch 1 RSC Ord 44 r 11(3).

12   CPR Sch 1 RSC Ord 44 r 11(4). Copies of the order must be served on such of the parties as the master directs: CPR Sch 1 RSC Ord 44 r 11(4).

13   See CPR Sch 1 RSC Ord 44 r 12. The appeal lies to the judge in chambers under CPR Sch 1 RSC Ord 58 r 1 (which now extends to appeals from orders of Chancery masters, the former practice of seeking an adjournment to the judge having been discontinued). As to appeals under CPR Sch 1 RSC Ord 58 r 1 see PRACTICE AND PROCEDURE.

136. Preparation of conditions and references to conveyancing counsel.

The solicitor for the party having the conduct of the sale prepares the particulars, which must be entitled in the cause or matter and must state that the sale is made under an order of the court, and that solicitor also prepares the abstract of title.

The court may require the abstract to be referred to conveyancing counsel of the court[1] or some other conveyancing counsel for his opinion on it and to settle the particulars and conditions of sale[2]; and may itself refer to conveyancing counsel of the court (1) any matter relating to the investigation of the title to any property with a view to its sale[3]; (2) any other matter relating to the settlement of a draft of the transfer[4]; and (3) any other matter it may think fit[5]. The court may act upon his opinion in the matter referred[6]. Any party may object to the opinion, whereupon the point in dispute is decided by the judge, either in chambers or in court as he thinks fit[7].

1   The conveyancing counsel of the court are conveyancing counsel in actual practice who have practised as such for not less than ten years: Supreme Court Act 1981 s 131(1). They are appointed by the Lord Chancellor, and are not more than six nor less than three in number: s 131(2). An order referring any matter to conveyancing counsel of the court must be recorded in the books of the court, and a copy of the order must be sent by the court to counsel, and constitutes sufficient authority for him to proceed with the reference: CPR Sch 1 RSC Ord 31 r 8. As to the CPR see para 133 note 1 ante. As to the need for an abstract of title with respect to both unregistered and registered land see paras 138, 141–149 post.

2   CPR Sch 1 RSC Ord 31 r 2(2)(h). It is unclear whether the master has a right to refer a matter to conveyancing counsel: *Flower v Walker* (1826) 1 Russ 408.

3   CPR Sch 1 RSC Ord 31 r 5(a). The power is expressed to extend also to the investigation of the title to any property with a view to the investment of money in its purchase or on its mortgage: see CPR Sch 1 RSC Ord 31 r 5(a).

4   CPR Sch 1 RSC Ord 31 r 5(b). The power is expressed to extend also to the settlement of a draft mortgage or settlement or other instrument: see CPR Sch 1 RSC Ord 31 r 5(b). As to the disposition of registered and unregistered land by transfer see para 262 note 2 post.

5   CPR Sch 1 RSC Ord 31 r 5(c).

6   CPR Sch 1 RSC Ord 31 r 5.

7   CPR Sch 1 RSC Ord 31 r 6.

2. RIGHTS AND DUTIES PRIOR TO COMPLETION

(1) PROOF AND INVESTIGATION OF TITLE

(i) Vendor's Obligation and Length of Title

137. Obligation as to title. In the absence of any express stipulation as to title[1], a contract for the sale of land[2] implies an agreement on the part of the vendor to make a good, that is, a marketable[3] title to the property sold[4]. He discharges this obligation when he shows that he, or some person or persons whose concurrence he can require, can transfer to the purchaser the whole legal and equitable interest in the land sold[5].

In general, it is sufficient if the vendor shows that he has a good title by the time fixed for completion[6], but, if it appears before that time that he has not a title, and is not in a position to obtain one, the purchaser may repudiate the contract[7].

---

1   A contract containing no stipulation restricting the title to be shown by the vendor is called 'an open contract', but the vendor usually protects himself by inserting special stipulations as to title (see para 76 et seq ante), and also by reserving a right of rescission (see para 104 ante).

2   As to the formation of the contract see paras 23–40 ante.

3   A marketable title is one which at all times and under all circumstances can be forced on an unwilling purchaser: *Pyrke v Waddingham* (1853) 10 Hare 1 at 8. See also *Maconchy v Clayton* [1898] 1 IR 291 (Ir CA); *Darvell v Basildon Development Corpn* (1969) 211 Estates Gazette 33; *MEPC Ltd v Christian-Edwards* [1981] AC 205, [1979] 3 All ER 752, HL; *Barclays Bank plc v Weeks Legg & Dean (a firm)* [1999] QB 309 at 324, [1998] 3 All ER 213 at 221, CA, per Millett LJ; and SPECIFIC PERFORMANCE vol 44(1) (Reissue) para 878. Even if it is not marketable a title may be a good holding title (ie one which presents no probability of an adverse claim being made) and can usually be sold under suitable conditions as to title. Such a title can be registered under the Land Registration Act 1925 as absolute: see s 13 proviso (c); para 336 note 1 post; and LAND REGISTRATION vol 26 (Reissue) para 821. As to the vendor's obligations see Harpum 'Selling Without Title: A Vendor's Duty of Disclosure?' (1992) 108 LQR 280; Harpum 'Exclusion Clauses and Contracts for the Sale of Land' [1992] CLJ 263. See also Rudden 'The Terminology of Title' (1964) 80 LQR 63.

4   In *Ogilvie v Foljambe* (1817) 3 Mer 53 at 64, the purchaser's right to a good title was spoken of as 'a right not growing out of the agreement between the parties, but which is given by law'. In this view the right is collateral to and not an implied term of the contract (*Ellis v Rogers* (1885) 29 ChD 661 at 670, CA) but usually it is treated as an implied term of the contract (*Flureau v Thornhill* (1776) 2 Wm Bl 1078; *Duke of St Alban's v Shore* (1789) 1 Hy Bl 270 at 280; *Doe d Gray v Stanion* (1836) 1 M & W 695 at 701). See also para 336 post. The vendor's obligation is the same whether the question arises in an action for specific performance or in one for damages for breach of contract (see *Purvis v Rayer* (1821) 9 Price 488; *Souter v Drake* (1834) 5 B & Ad 992 at 1002) or for a declaration that a good title has been shown under a vendor and purchaser summons (see *MEPC Ltd v Christian-Edwards* [1981] AC 205, [1979] 3 All ER 752, HL). The vendor's obligation to show a title may, however, be excluded by the circumstances as well as by special stipulation (see *Turner v Turner* (1852) 2 De GM & G 28 at 46; *Richardson v Eyton* (1852) 2 De GM & G 79) and if the vendor's interest is limited and the contract shows this, he need not make a title except to the limited interest (*Worthington v Warrington* (1848) 5 CB 635). See also *Re Judge and Sheridan's Contract* (1907) 96 LT 451; and *Hall v Betty* (1842) 4 Man & G 410.

5   See *Lord Braybroke v Inskip* (1803) 8 Ves 417 at 436; *Re Stirrup's Contract* [1961] 1 All ER 805, [1961] 1 WLR 449. It is sufficient if the vendor shows that he has a good equitable title and power to get in the legal estate: *Camberwell and South London Building Society v Holloway* (1879) 13 ChD 754 at 763. The getting in of the legal estate is a matter of conveyance, and not of title: *Avarne v Brown* (1844) 14 Sim 303; *Kitchen v Palmer* (1877) 46 LJ Ch 611; and see *Smith v Ellis* (1850) 14 Jur 682; *Elliot and H Elliot (Builders) Ltd v Pierson* [1948] Ch 452, [1948] 1 All ER 939. However, good equitable title is not sufficient if it is uncertain in whom the legal estate is vested: *Wynne v Griffith* (1826) 1 Russ 283. Where an appointment of trustees is necessary, the execution of such an appointment is a matter of title and not of conveyance: *Re Priestley's Contract* [1947] Ch 469, [1947] 1 All ER 716. Under the system of conveyancing established by the Law of Property Act 1925, equitable interests are, as far as possible, kept off the title, and the title in its simplest form consists only of instruments conveying a legal estate: see s 10; and para 146 post. As

to the duty of a vendor of registered land who is not himself registered as proprietor see LAND REGISTRATION vol 26 (Reissue) para 929. As to the disposition of registered and unregistered land by transfer see para 262 note 2 post.

6   *Boehm v Wood* (1820) 1 Jac & W 419 at 421.

7   *Forrer v Nash* (1865) 35 Beav 167. Cf *Re Head's Trustees and Macdonald* (1890) 45 ChD 310, CA; *Re Cooke and Holland's Contract* (1898) 78 LT 106; *Re Bryant and Barningham's Contract* (1890) 44 ChD 218, CA; *Re Baker and Selmon's Contract* [1907] 1 Ch 238; *Re Hucklesby and Atkinson's Contract* (1910) 102 LT 214; *Pips (Leisure Productions) Ltd v Walton* (1982) 43 P & CR 415; *Pinekerry Ltd v Kenneth Needs (Contractors) Ltd* (1992) 64 P & CR 245, CA. See also paras 239–240 post.

138. Abstract of title. In the case of unregistered land, the vendor shows his title by delivering an abstract of it to the purchaser and makes his title by proving the contents of the abstract by proper evidence[1].

In the case of registered land, subject to any stipulation to the contrary, the vendor must furnish such abstracts and evidence in respect of rights and interests appurtenant to the land as to which the register is not conclusive and matters excepted from the effect of registration as a purchaser is entitled to on a sale of unregistered land, but he cannot be required to furnish any other abstract or written evidence of title[2]. Where the title to the land is registered with an absolute title or good leasehold title, no abstract of title can normally be required[3]. However, where the land is registered with a possessory or qualified title, the title prior to registration must be abstracted and inquired into in the same way as the title to unregistered land, because neither the initial registration nor any disposition of the registered land affects rights adverse to those of the proprietor registered with the possessory title, or rights excepted from the effect of the qualified registration, as the case may be[4].

1   *Parr v Lovegrove* (1858) 4 Drew 170 at 181; *Games v Bonnor* (1884) 54 LJ Ch 517, CA. Cf *Mullings v Trinder* (1870) LR 10 Eq 449 at 455. See also *Horne v Wingfield* (1841) 3 Scott NR 340; and Sugden's Law of Vendors and Purchasers (14th Edn, 1862) 406. As to the nature of the abstract of title see paras 141–149 post. Under the Standard Conditions of Sale (3rd Edn), the vendor's obligation is to produce to the purchaser (without cost to the purchaser) the original of every relevant document, or an abstract, epitome or copy with an original marking by a solicitor of examination either against the original or against an examined abstract or against an examined copy: condition 4.2.3. As to the Standard Conditions of Sale see para 1 note 9 ante. The statements in the text should be read subject to this contractual provision. The law relating to abstracts of title developed before the use of the photocopier, so, the expertise to produce a traditional abstract is unlikely to be found in the office of a present day conveyancer. Therefore, a recently prepared abstract is unlikely to exist and an epitome of title accompanied by certified photocopies is regarded as an acceptable alternative. As to conveyancers see para 3 ante.

2   See LAND REGISTRATION vol 26 (Reissue) paras 926–927.

3   See LAND REGISTRATION vol 26 (Reissue) paras 739 (effect of first registration with absolute title), 747–748 (effect of first registration with absolute leasehold title or good leasehold title), 958 (effect of disposition where absolute freehold title is registered), 962–963 (effect of disposition where title is absolute leasehold title or good leasehold title). It is normal, however, for the conditions of sale to require the vendor to produce office copies of entries in the register and of any filed plans and documents: see the Standard Conditions of Sale (3rd Edn), condition 4.2.1; the Land Registration Act 1925 s 110(1), (2) (s 110(1) as amended); and LAND REGISTRATION vol 26 (Reissue) paras 925–926. See also *Wood v Berkeley Homes (Sussex) Ltd* (1992) 64 P & CR 311, CA (where it was held that the Land Registration Act 1925 s 110(3) does not invalidate a condition requiring the vendor to produce office copies of documents stipulated in s 110(1) (as amended)). As to the effect of s 110(5) on conditions of sale see *Urban Manor Ltd v Sadiq* [1997] 1 WLR 1016, [1997] 12 LS Gaz R 22 CA; and LAND REGISTRATION vol 26 (Reissue) para 929. As to overriding interests see *Williams and Glyn's Bank Ltd v Boland* [1981] AC 487, [1980] 2 All ER 408, HL; and LAND REGISTRATION vol 26 (Reissue) para 782 et seq. The property is sold subject to incumbrances discoverable by inspection of the property before the contract: see the Standard Conditions of Sale (3rd Edn), condition 3.1.2; and para 55 ante. This condition may be wide enough to cover virtually all rights protected as overriding interests under the Land Registration Act 1925 s 70(1)(g): see LAND REGISTRATION vol 26 (Reissue) para 784.

4   See LAND REGISTRATION vol 26 (Reissue) paras 740, 742, 749, 751 (effect of registration), 959–960, 964–965 (effect of disposition).

139. Length of title. On a sale of unregistered land[1] the vendor must deduce a title for a period of at least 15 years preceding the sale[2] unless a contrary intention is expressed in the contract[3]. Fifteen years is only the minimum period, and in fact the title must be deduced for 15 years and so much longer as it is necessary to go back in order to arrive at a proper root of title[4]. Except in so far as a contrary intention is expressed in the contract, a longer title than 15 years can be required in cases where before 1926 a title longer than 40 years[5] could have been required, and as to such cases the former practice still prevails[6]. Thus in the case of a reversionary interest the title must be carried back at least as far as the instrument creating it[7]; and on the sale of a term of years more than 15 years old, the lease creating the term must be produced[8], unless the vendor has protected himself by the contract against production being required[9]. It is sufficient both in the case of reversions, terms of years and rentcharges if the intermediate title is carried back for 15 years only[10] from the date at which title has to be shown; and it seems that the same rule applies in other cases where the title to the property depends on an original grant, such as property held under grant from the Crown: the original grant must be shown, but the subsequent title only for the last 15 years[11].

1 'Land' includes land of any tenure, and mines and minerals, whether or not held apart from the surface, buildings or parts of buildings (whether the division is horizontal, vertical or made in any other way) and other corporeal hereditaments; also a manor, an advowson, and a rent and other incorporeal hereditaments, and an easement, right, privilege or benefit in, over, or derived from land: Law of Property Act 1925 s 205(1)(ix) (definition amended by the Trusts of Land and Appointment of Trustees Act 1996 s 25(2), Sch 4). As to registered land see para 138 ante.

2 See the Law of Property Act 1925 s 44(1) (amended by the Law of Property Act 1969 s 23). 'Sale' includes an extinguishment of manorial incidents, but in other respects means a sale properly so called: Law of Property Act 1925 s 205(xxiv). Section 44(1) (as amended) applies to contracts of sale of land made after 1 January 1970: see the Law of Property Act 1969 ss 23, 31(2). When freehold land was formerly copyhold, the purchaser cannot call for the title to make any enfranchisement (see the Law of Property Act 1925 s 44(6)); nor, in the absence of a contrary intention expressed in the contract, can he call for the title of any person to enter into a compensation agreement (see s 44(7)). As to land formerly copyhold see CUSTOM AND USAGE; REAL PROPERTY.

3 See ibid s 44(11). As to titles for less than the statutory period see para 90 ante; and as to the landlord's title where leasehold land is enfranchised under the Leasehold Reform Act 1967 see the Leasehold Reform (Enfranchisement and Extension) Regulations 1967, SI 1967/1879, reg 2, Schedule Pt I para 3; and LANDLORD AND TENANT vol 27(2) (Reissue) para 1295.

4 *Re Cox and Neve's Contract* [1891] 2 Ch 109 at 118. As to the meaning of 'root of title' see para 142 post. So, under the former law, it might be necessary to carry back the title beyond 40 or 60 years: see *Phillips v Caldcleugh* (1868) LR 4 QB 159.

5 See note 2 supra.

6 See the Law of Property Act 1925 s 44(1), (11) (s 44(1) as amended); and LAND REGISTRATION vol 26 (Reissue) para 1031.

7 See 1 Dart's Law relating to Vendors and Purchasers (8th Edn, 1929) 293. In order to avoid any question as to possession of the land when the interest falls into possession, it must be shown that it is being enjoyed at the time of the sale by the owner of the immediate estate. A reversionary interest, other than a reversion on a lease for years, will now be equitable: see REAL PROPERTY vol 39(2) (Reissue) para 162 et seq.

8 *Frend v Buckley* (1870) LR 5 QB 213, Ex Ch. Where a contract for the assignment of a lease entitled a purchaser to a title commencing from the freeholder, but provided that no title should be called for prior to the lease, the purchaser was entitled to investigate dealings with an agreement in pursuance of which the lease had been granted: *Rhodes v Ibbetson* (1853) 4 De GM & G 787.

9 As to conditions protecting vendors against liability to produce see para 98 ante.

10 *Williams v Spargo* [1893] WN 100. There are now statutory restrictions on the creation of rentcharges, and many existing rentcharges are by statute terminable: see the Rentcharges Act 1977 ss 2 (as amended), 3; and RENTCHARGES AND ANNUITIES.

11 See *Pickering v Lord Sherbourne* (1838) 1 Craw & D 254; Sugden's Law of Vendors and Purchasers (14th Edn, 1862) 367; and 1 Williams Law relating to Vendors and Purchasers of Real Estate and Chattels Real (4th Edn, 1936) 119.

140. Title to leaseholds. On a sale of leaseholds it is sufficient if the vendor produces the lease under which he holds and shows a title to it for at least 15 years, or for the whole existence of the lease if less than 15 years old[1]. Unless a contrary intention is expressed in the contract[2], the purchaser[3] under a contract to sell a term of years, whether derived out of freehold or leasehold land[4], may not call for the title to the freehold[5], or, if the lease is derived out of a leasehold estate, the title to the leasehold reversion[6]. Before 1926 such a purchaser, although precluded from calling for the title to the freehold or leasehold reversion, was nevertheless affected with constructive notice of that title[7]. In the case of contracts made after 1925 he is not affected with notice of any matter or thing of which he might have had notice if he had contracted that the title to the freehold or the leasehold reversion should be furnished[8], but it seems that, in the case of unregistered land, this protection does not extend to matters registered under the Land Charges Act 1972 or the Local Land Charges Act 1975 of which the purchaser is by statute deemed to have actual notice[9], and that the protection has no application to registered land where the matter is an overriding interest or a minor interest protected on the register[10].

1 See para 139 ante.
2 See the Law of Property Act 1925 s 44(11); and para 139 note 6 ante. On the grant of a new lease exceeding 21 years (ie a lease which will be registrable under the Land Registration Act 1925), the vendor must deduce a title which will enable the purchaser to register the lease with an absolute title: see the Standard Conditions of Sale (3rd Edn), condition 8.2.4; and para 98 note 4 ante. As to the Standard Conditions of Sale see para 1 note 9 ante.
3 For the meaning of 'purchaser' see para 55 note 16 ante.
4 For the meaning of 'land' see para 139 note 1 ante.
5 Law of Property Act 1925 s 44(2). A purchaser may, however, raise by other means an objection that the title to the freehold is bad and will thus have the usual right of a litigant to production of the relevant documents: see *Jones v Watts* (1890) 43 ChD 574, CA. As to conditions excluding the right to raise such objections see para 98 ante. In the case of land held on lease or underlease, the purchaser must assume that the lease or underlease was duly granted: see the Law of Property Act 1925 s 45(2), (3). A similar restriction as to title is imposed in the case of a contract to grant a lease: see s 44(2), (4); and LANDLORD AND TENANT vol 27(1) (Reissue) para 67. As to the description in particulars of sale see para 79 ante. A contract to sell a lease is not satisfied by the grant of an underlease: see para 59 ante.
6 Ibid s 44(3). Dicta in *Drive Yourself Hire Co (London) Ltd v Strutt* [1954] 1 QB 250 at 263, [1953] 2 All ER 1475 at 1485, CA, per Romer LJ, suggesting that an assignee of a sub-lease is entitled to see the head lease, and citing *Gosling v Woolf* [1893] 1 QB 39, appear to have been uttered per incuriam; cf *Gosling v Woolf* supra as reported in 68 LT 89, 41 WR 106. From these reports it appears that *Gosling v Woolf* supra, was a case of a grant, not an assignment of an underlease. See also *Becker v Partridge* [1966] 2 QB 155 at 169, [1966] 2 All ER 266 at 268, CA, per Dankwerts LJ.
7 Cf *Patman v Harland* (1881) 17 ChD 353.
8 See the Law of Property Act 1925 s 44(5).
9 See ibid s 198(1) (as amended); and LAND CHARGES vol 26 (Reissue) para 516. See also paras 20–21, 55 ante.
10 See *White v Bijou Mansions Ltd* [1937] Ch 610 at 619–622, [1937] 3 All ER 269 at 272–275 (affd on other points [1938] Ch 351, [1938] 1 All ER 546, CA); the *Report of the Committee on Land Charges* (Cmnd 9825) (1956) paras 34–42; and EQUITY vol 16 (Reissue) para 774; LAND REGISTRATION vol 26 (Reissue) paras 747, 1101; LANDLORD AND TENANT vol 27(1) (Reissue) para 67. A purchaser of unregistered land cannot investigate the superior title so he may be unable to discover the names of previous estate owners against whom charges are registered under the Land Charges Act 1972; and a purchaser so prejudiced is not entitled to compensation under the Law of Property Act 1969 s 25: see s 25(9), (10); and LAND CHARGES vol 26 (Reissue) para 517. A purchaser of registered land may investigate the superior title, since the register is open to public inspection: see the Land Registration Act 1925 s 112 (as substituted); the Land Registration (Open Register) Rules 1991, SI 1992/122, rr 4, 4A (as added), 4B (as added); and LAND REGISTRATION vol 26 (Reissue) para 877.

(ii) The Abstract of Title

141. Contents of abstract. The abstract of title[1] is a summary of the documents by which any dispositions of the property have been made during the period for which title has to be shown, and of all the facts, such as births, marriages, deaths or other matters affecting the devolution of the title during the same period[2]. As far as possible it is (as regards transactions dated since 1925) confined to dispositions of a legal estate[3].

1   As to the need for an abstract of title with respect to both unregistered and registered land see para 138 ante.
2   As to the vendor's obligation to deliver an abstract see para 100 ante; and *Re Priestley and Davidson's Contract* (1892) 31 LR Ir 122.
3   See the Law of Property Act 1925 s 10; and para 146 note 9 post.

142. Root of title. The abstract must commence with a good root of title, that is, in the absence of contrary stipulation, with some document purporting to deal with the entire legal and equitable estate in the property sold, not depending for its validity upon any previous instrument, and containing nothing to throw any suspicion on the title of the disposing parties[1]. The best root of title is a conveyance in fee on sale or a freehold mortgage[2]. A general devise by will is insufficient, as there is nothing to show that the property passed by it[3], and there must, in any event, be proof of the testator's seisin at his death[4]. A specific devise to a beneficiary for his own use and benefit was a proper root of title[5], but, since 1925, such a devise operates only in equity[6], and the root of title is the assent by the executor or executors to such a specific devise, which is a good root of title provided no doubt is cast upon its operation by recital or otherwise[7]. An instrument the effect of which depends on some earlier instrument is prima facie an insufficient root of title, and it is necessary to go back to the earlier instrument; for example, a title depending on an appointment under a power or on a disentailing deed must be carried back to the instrument creating the power or the entail[8]. If, however, it has been expressly agreed that an instrument of appointment or disentailing deed is to form the root of title, the purchaser[9] cannot require the production, nor an abstract, of the document creating the power, nor, it seems, the entail, unless the documents as abstracted throw doubt on the earlier title, in which event the purchaser can resist specific performance unless the vendor abstracts the earlier document so far as is necessary to remove the doubt, and produces it[10].

A voluntary conveyance is a proper root of title under an open contract[11], but if it is made a root of a good title at a shorter period than 15 years the conditions must clearly state its nature[12].

1   See *Re Cox and Neve's Contract* [1891] 2 Ch 109 at 118. The statement that the document must purport to deal with the entire legal and equitable interest appears to be correct, notwithstanding that equitable interests are in general kept off the title. Where intended, the legal estate carries the equivalent equitable interest: see 1 Williams Law relating to Vendors and Purchasers of Real Estate and Chattels Real (4th Edn, 1936) 47 note (u); *Vandervell v IRC* [1967] 2 AC 291 at 311, [1967] 1 All ER 1 at 7, HL, per Lord Upjohn. A conveyance which overreaches equitable interests will form a good root: see LAND REGISTRATION vol 26 (Reissue) paras 717, 719. As to overreaching see the Law of Property Act 1925 s 10; and para 146 note 9 post. As to the need for an abstract of title with respect to both unregistered and registered land see para 138 ante.
2   Since 1925 a freehold mortgage must take effect either by demise for a term of years or by legal charge, and in either case does not in itself dispose of the legal fee simple (see ibid ss 85, 87; and MORTGAGE), but where the mortgagor's title to the fee simple is recited, a mortgage deed is in practice accepted as a good root of title (see 1 Williams Law relating to Vendors and Purchasers of Real Estate and Chattels Real (4th Edn, 1936) 124).
3   Where it is intended that the title is to commence with a general devise, this is always expressly stipulated, and the purchaser is required to assume the seisin of the testator at the time of his death; otherwise the title must commence with the conveyance to the testator or, if there is no conveyance, with evidence of

his seisin at the date of his death. A statutory declaration showing collection of rents on his behalf for more than 20 years is not sufficient: *Re Gilbert and Foster's Contract* (1935) 52 TLR 4.

4   As to a condition requiring seisin to be assumed see *Re Banister, Broad v Munton* (1879) 12 ChD 131, CA (only matters of which vendor knows nothing).

5   This was so, it is believed, in practice, but a specific devise had been said not to be an eligible root of title (see *Parr v Lovegrove* (1858) 4 Drew 170 at 177), and it was better to specify the nature of the document in the contract (see 1 Williams Law relating to Vendors and Purchasers of Real Estate and Chattels Real (4th Edn, 1936) 127).

6   See the Law of Property (Amendment) Act 1924 s 9, Sch 9 para 3.

7   See the Administration of Estates Act 1925 s 36(7). As to doubt being cast upon such an assent see *Re Duce and Boots Cash Chemists (Southern) Ltd's Contract* [1937] Ch 642, [1937] 3 All ER 788.

8   See eg *Re Copelin's Contract* [1937] 4 All ER 447, 54 TLR 130; *Re W & R Holmes and Cosmopolitan Press Ltd's Contract* [1944] Ch 53, [1943] 2 All ER 716. If the deed has been lost, and the possession of the land has been for a considerable time in accordance with the estates purporting to have been created under it, the loss of the deed and the absence of evidence of its contents are not objections to the title: see *Coussmaker v Sewell* (1791), cited in Sugden's Law of Vendors and Purchasers (14th Edn, 1862) 366; *Nouaille v Greenwood* (1822) Turn & R 26.

9   For the meaning of 'purchaser' see para 55 note 16 ante.

10   See the Law of Property Act 1925 s 45(1), (10), (11). This exclusion of documents dated before the commencement of title does not extend to: (1) any power of attorney under which an abstracted document is executed (s 45(1) proviso (i)); or (2) any document creating or disposing of an interest, power or obligation which is not shown to have ceased or expired, and subject to which any part of the property is disposed of by an abstracted document (s 45(1) proviso (ii)); or (3) any document creating any limitation or trust by reference to which any part of the property is disposed of by an abstracted document (s 45(1) proviso (iii)); and where a lease is made under a power contained in a settlement, will, Act of Parliament or other instrument, any preliminary contract for or relating to the lease does not, for the purpose of the deduction of title to a purchaser, form part of the title, or evidence of the title, to the lease (s 44(9)).

11   *Re Marsh and Earl Granville* (1883) 24 ChD 11 at 24, CA, per Cotton LJ. A voluntary deed as a link in the title is not a defect in title, since a purchaser gets a good title under it (see BANKRUPTCY AND INSOLVENCY vol 3(2) (Reissue) para 642 et seq) provided the purchaser has no notice of its being impeachable. As to transactions at an undervalue and preferences where an individual is adjudged bankrupt see the Insolvency Act 1986 ss 339–342 (as amended); and BANKRUPTCY AND INSOLVENCY vol 3(2) (Reissue) para 642 et seq. As to transactions at undervalue and preferences where a company goes into liquidation or an administration order is made see ss 238–241 (as amended); and COMPANIES vol 7(2) (1996 Reissue) para 2602 et seq. As to the protection of purchasers for value without notice in a case where a transaction is impeachable on the ground of undue influence see MISREPRESENTATION AND FRAUD vol 31 (Reissue) para 839 et seq. As to the meaning of 'open contract' see para 76 ante.

12   *Re Marsh and Earl Granville* (1883) 24 ChD 11, CA. See also *Noyes v Paterson* [1894] 3 Ch 267; and para 83 ante.

143. Possessory title. A title gained by the operation of the Limitation Act 1980[1] is a good title and will be forced by the court on an unwilling purchaser[2]. However, proof that a vendor and those through whom he claims have had independent possession of an estate for 12 years[3] will not be sufficient to establish a saleable title without evidence to show the state of the title at the time the possession commenced. If the contract for sale is an open one possession for 15 years must be shown[4]. A condition of sale may be so drawn as to enable a vendor to force the purchaser to accept a title resting on mere possession[5].

1   As to the application of the Limitation Act 1980 to registered land see LAND REGISTRATION vol 26 (Reissue) paras 760–761. As to limitation periods generally see LIMITATION OF ACTIONS.

2   See eg *Games v Bonnor* (1884) 54 LJ Ch 517, CA; *Re Cussons Ltd* (1904) 73 LJ Ch 296; and see LIMITATION OF ACTIONS vol 28 (Reissue) para 996.

3   This is the normal period of limitation for an action to recover land: see the Limitation Act 1980 ss 15(1), 17; and cf LIMITATION OF ACTIONS vol 28 (Reissue) paras 928, 994.

4   *Jacobs v Revell* [1900] 2 Ch 858. See also *Cottrell v Watkins* (1839) 1 Beav 361; *Moulton v Edmonds* (1859) 1 De GF & J 246 at 250; *Re Nisbet and Potts' Contract* [1906] 1 Ch 386, CA; *Re Atkinson and Horsell's Contract* [1912] 2 Ch 1 at 11, CA. Cf the Limitation Act 1980 s 28(4) (see LIMITATION OF ACTIONS vol

28 (Reissue) paras 1069–1070), by which 30 years is the maximum to which the period of limitation for the recovery of land can be extended on the ground that a person entitled to recover has been under a disability. As to the disposition of land registered with a possessory title see para 138 ante.

5   See *Rosenberg v Cook* (1881) 8 QBD 162, CA, where the sale of the land to the vendor by a railway company had been ultra vires; and cf *George Wimpey & Co Ltd v Sohn* [1967] Ch 487, [1966] 1 All ER 232, CA, where the vendor's contractual obligation to show 20 years' undisputed possession was not satisfied by a 12 year possessory title.

144. Documents to be abstracted. The document forming the root of title and all subsequent documents dealing with the legal estate (except documents relating to estates which will be overreached by the conveyance to the purchaser[1]), and also any prior documents or parts of them incorporated by reference in documents subsequent to the commencement of title[2], should be abstracted in chief in date order[3], including mortgages, even if satisfied[4], but not leases which have expired[5]. Similarly, all material facts, such as births, deaths, grants of probate or administration, or other matters, should be stated in date order[6].

1   See the Law of Property Act 1925 s 10, under which documents relating to interests or powers which will be overreached by the conveyance to the purchaser need not be abstracted. Usually these will be equitable interests and powers, but it is possible for legal interests and powers to be overreached, such as a puisne mortgage and the powers incident to it: see MORTGAGE. As to the powers of a legal mortgagee in right of his estate being legal powers see s 1(7); and POWERS; and as to the concealment of incumbrances see s 183; and para 149 post. As to the disposition of registered and unregistered land by transfer see para 262 note 2 post.
2   See paras 142 note 10 ante, 150 note 7 post.
3   This should be done notwithstanding their subsequent recital in the abstracted documents: *Re Ebsworth and Tidy's Contract* (1889) 42 ChD 23 at 34, CA; *Re Stamford, Spalding and Boston Banking Co and Knight's Contract* [1900] 1 Ch 287.
4   See *Heath v Crealock* (1874) 10 Ch App 22; cf *Gray v Fowler* (1873) LR 8 Exch 249 at 265.
5   As to abstracting leases see *Bond v Bassett* (1917) 87 LJ Ch 160, where counterparts of leases and drafts of conveyances were admitted in wartime. As to a document of union of two building societies see *Re Fryer and Hampson's Contract* [1929] WN 45, CA; and BUILDING SOCIETIES vol 4(2) (Reissue) para 779.
6   In the case of deaths before 1926, it was necessary to abstract receipts and other documents showing that death duties payable within 12 years of the date had been discharged. In the case of deaths after 1925 a purchaser of a legal estate took free from a charge in respect of death duties unless the charge was registered as a land charge, and the same is now true of a charge in respect of what is now inheritance tax: see INHERITANCE TAXATION vol 24 (Reissue) para 683; LAND CHARGES vol 26 (Reissue) para 534; LAND REGISTRATION vol 26 (Reissue) para 836.

    It would be desirable also to abstract certificates of search under the Land Charges Act 1972 which would avoid, or mitigate, the problem of land charges which are undiscoverable because the charge is registered against the name of an estate owner whose name is not disclosed by the abstract: see LAND CHARGES vol 26 (Reissue) para 517. In practice, however, search certificates are seldom abstracted (though copies are often kept with the documents of title).

145. Equitable interests. The abstracting [1] of documents relating to equitable interests depends on two considerations: (1) the effect of the conveyance of the legal estate to a purchaser for value without notice; and (2) the effect of the conveyance in overreaching the equitable interests. A purchaser taking the legal estate without notice of any equitable interests affecting it is protected[2]. Thus equitable interests are immaterial to his title and in practice are frequently suppressed. This is always the case where the legal estate has been vested in trustees who are intended to stand as absolute owners as regards third persons. In such cases the conveyance to the trustees is framed so as to keep the trusts off the title, and this object would be defeated if dealings with the beneficial interest were disclosed[3].

1   As to the need for an abstract of title with respect to both unregistered and registered land see para 138 ante.
2   As to the circumstances in which a purchaser will be protected see *Jared v Clements* [1902] 2 Ch 399
      (affd [1903] 1 Ch 428, CA); and EQUITY vol 16 (Reissue) para 761.
3   See *Re Harman and Uxbridge and Rickmansworth Rly Co* (1883) 24 ChD 720; *Carritt v Real and Personal
      Advance Co* (1889) 42 ChD 263 at 272; *Re Soden and Alexander's Contract* [1918] 2 Ch 258. In *Re Blaiberg
      and Abrahams* [1899] 2 Ch 340, trusts of mortgage money were inadvertently disclosed, but the
      inconvenience resulting from such a disclosure has been removed by the Law of Property Act 1925 s 113
      (see LAND REGISTRATION vol 26 (Reissue) para 885). See also *Re Pope's Contract* [1911] 2 Ch 442.

146.   Overreaching of equitable interests. The ordinary effect of a conveyance[1] on
a sale by trustees is that it overreaches the equitable interests[2] of the persons beneficially
entitled, and in certain cases by statute the conveyance overreaches equitable interests
prior to the trust of land[3]. A similar effect is given to a conveyance made by a tenant for
life under his statutory powers, and such a conveyance may also overreach certain legal
estates[4]. An overreaching effect is also given to a conveyance of the legal estate[5] in certain
other cases[6]. Where an equitable interest or a legal estate will be so overreached, a
purchaser[7] is not concerned with it, and where title is shown to a legal estate in land, it is
not necessary or proper to include in the abstract[8] an instrument relating only to interests
or powers which will be overreached by the conveyance of the estate to which title is
being shown[9].

1   'Conveyance' includes a mortgage, charge, lease, assent, vesting declaration, vesting instrument,
      disclaimer, release and every other assurance of property or of an interest therein by any instrument,
      except a will: Law of Property Act 1925 s 205(ii). As to the disposition or assurance of registered or
      unregistered land by transfer see para 262 note 2 post.
2   'Equitable interests' mean all the other interests and charges in or over land: ibid s 205(x); definition
      amended by the Trusts of Land and Appointment of Trustees Act 1996 s 25(2), Sch 4.
3   See the Law of Property Act 1925 s 2(2) (amended by the Law of Property (Amendment) Act 1926 s 7,
      Schedule; and the Trusts of Land and Appointment of Trustees Act 1996 s 25(1), Sch 3 para 4(2)); and
      REAL PROPERTY vol 39(2) (Reissue) para 249. 'Trust of land' means any trust of property which consists
      of or includes land: Trusts of Land and Appointment of Trustees Act 1996 s 1(1)(a); Interpretation Act
      1978 s 5, Sch 1 (definition added by the Trusts of Land and Appointment of Trustees Act 1996 s 25(1),
      Sch 3 para 16).
4   See the Settled Land Act 1925 s 72; and REAL PROPERTY vol 39(2) (Reissue) para 787; SETTLEMENTS
      para 874 post.
5   'Legal estates' mean the estates, interests and charges, in or over land (subsisting or created at law) which
      are by the Law of Property Act 1925 authorised to subsist or to be created as legal estates: s 205(x).
6   See ibid s 2(1) (as amended); paras 282–283 post; and REAL PROPERTY vol 39(2) (Reissue) para 247 et seq.
7   For the meaning of 'purchaser' see para 55 note 16 ante.
8   As to the need for an abstract of title with respect to both unregistered and registered land see para 138 ante.
9   See the Law of Property Act 1925 s 10(1). Solicitors who omit to include in an abstract framed in
      accordance with Pt I (ss 1–39) (as amended) instruments which under s 10 need not be included, or who
      include any such instrument, are protected from liability: s 10(2). This protection extends to a licensed
      conveyancer (see the Administration of Justice Act 1985 s 11(2); and SOLICITORS vol 44(1) (Reissue) paras
      550, 623) and recognised bodies (see s 39(1); and SOLICITORS vol 44(1) (Reissue) para 610): see s 34(2)(a);
      and SOLICITORS vol 44(1) (Reissue) para 623. As to licensed conveyancers see SOLICITORS vol 44(1)
      (Reissue) para 550 et seq. See also para 3 ante. It has always been the practice not to abstract the equitable
      interests where title is being made under a trust. The Law of Property Act 1925 s 10 makes the practice
      apply generally in cases where equitable interests (and, it would seem, legal estates) are overreached by a
      conveyance of the legal estate in question. It introduces no new rule and may be regarded as declaratory
      only, but it emphasises the principle that title is in general to be made by showing devolutions and
      dispositions of the legal estate.
           The term 'overreaching' ordinarily refers to the effect of conveyances under trusts of land and under
      the statutory powers of a tenant for life (see s 2(1), (2) (as amended); the Settled Land Act 1925 s 72; and
      para 144 note 1 ante) where the interest which is overreached is not destroyed in value, but is transferred
      to the proceeds of sale (see REAL PROPERTY vol 39(2) (Reissue) para 247 et seq). However, overreaching
      can apply to transactions where no capital money arises: *State Bank of India v Sood* [1997] Ch 276, [1997]
      1 All ER 169, CA. The term is sometimes used to denote the effect of a conveyance by a mortgagee
      under his statutory power of sale. In that case, however, the mortgagor's estate is transferred to the

purchaser and the estates of subsequent legal incumbrancers are extinguished (see the Law of Property Act 1925 ss 88(1), 89(1); and MORTGAGE), and whether they are covered by s 10(1) or not, it would be contrary to conveyancing practice to abstract them. The term 'overreaching' may also be applied to the leasing powers of a mortgagor and mortgagee in possession: see s 99 (amended by the Agricultural Tenancies Act 1995 s 31(1)–(3)). See also Harpum 'Overreaching Trustees' Powers and the Reform of the 1925 Legislation' [1990] 49 CLJ 277.

Dealings with the equity of redemption, even though they take the form of a legal mortgage, are no part of the mortgagee's title, and do not require to be abstracted, even if he is aware of them. A legal mortgage which may be defeated for want of registration is not within the Law of Property Act 1925 s 10(1), since, until the conveyance is completed, the mortgage may be registered (see MORTGAGE). The purchaser can, however, protect himself against registration within the 15 days preceding completion by obtaining a certificate of search: see LAND CHARGES vol 26 (Reissue) para 601.

147. Abstracting equitable interests. Nothing in the general statutory provisions relating to the subsistence of legal estates[1] and equitable interest[2] affects the liability of any person to disclose an equitable interest or power[3] which will not be overreached by the conveyance[4] of the legal estate to which title is being shown, or to furnish an abstract of any instrument creating or affecting it[5]. However, the abstract not uncommonly omits documents creating equitable charges which have been paid off or, if still subsisting, are intended to be paid off on completion[6].

Subject to the foregoing rule for excluding documents from the abstract[7] in certain cases, any documents which affect equitable interests should be abstracted, and this is necessary where it is proposed to make a title with the concurrence of the owner or owners of equitable interests[8]. In the case of a subsale, the sub-purchaser is entitled to an abstract of the original contract[9].

1 For the meaning of 'legal estates' see para 146 note 5 ante.
2 Ie under the Law of Property Act 1925 Pt I (ss 1–39) (as amended): see s 10(1). For the meaning of 'equitable interest' see para 146 note 2 ante.
3 'Equitable powers' means all the powers in or over land under which equitable interests or powers only can be transferred or created: ibid s 205(xi).
4 For the meaning of 'conveyance' see para 146 note 1 ante.
5 Law of Property Act 1925 s 10(1).
6 In *Drummond v Tracy* (1860) John 608 at 612, where a letter creating an equitable charge which was intended to be paid off out of the purchase money had been suppressed, Wood V-C thought that this course was wrong, and would not have been justifiable even if the charge had no longer been subsisting. In the practice of conveyancers, however, this strict rule is not observed: see 1 Dart's Law relating to Vendors and Purchasers (8th Edn, 1929) 298; 1 Williams Law relating to Vendors and Purchasers of Real Estate and Chattels Real (4th Edn, 1936) 129. As to the concealment of incumbrances see the Law of Property Act 1925 s 183; and para 149 post. As to conveyancers see para 3 ante.
7 As to the need for an abstract of title with respect to both unregistered and registered land see para 138 ante.
8 As a rule, a purchaser is not bound to accept a conveyance made with the concurrence of the owners of equitable interests (see ibid s 42(1) (as amended); and para 272 post), but the rule is not absolute (see s 43(1); and para 129 ante) and to take a conveyance in this form may be the convenient course (see para 273 post). Generally any documents which, although primarily affecting equitable interests, may affect the legal estate should be abstracted: see *Palmer v Locke* (1881) 18 ChD 381, CA; 1 Dart's Law relating to Vendors and Purchasers (8th Edn, 1929) 299.
9 *Re Hucklesby and Atkinson's Contract* (1910) 102 LT 214.

148. Form of abstract. The abstract[1] should set out the contents of every material part of the abstracted documents according to their tenor, and not give merely a statement of their effect.

The parcels as described in the first abstracted deed should be set out verbatim; in the abstracts of subsequent deeds which repeat the same description they are referred to as the abstracted premises. Tracings of plans indorsed on or annexed to the deeds, and referred to in the description of the parcels, should accompany the abstract, and where, as is usually the case, the plans form an essential part of the description of the premises, tracings of them can be insisted on[2].

1   As to the need for an abstract of title with respect to both unregistered and registered land see para 138 ante.
2   See 1 Dart's Law relating to Vendors and Purchasers (8th Edn, 1929) 300. As to the right of a purchaser to have the premises conveyed by reference to a plan see *Re Sansom and Narbeth's Contract* [1910] 1 Ch 741; *Re Sharman and Meade's Contract* [1936] Ch 755, [1936] 2 All ER 1547; and DEEDS AND OTHER INSTRUMENTS. See also BOUNDARIES vol 4(1) (Reissue) para 904. The tracings should show the compass marks (an essential matter which is frequently overlooked) and should be indorsed with the date of the conveyance to which they belong. Where there are several plans and the land has been altered by division, the plans should be detachable for comparison, especially if the direction of the compass marks has been altered.

149. Fraudulent concealment of documents and falsification of pedigrees.
Any person disposing of property or any interest in it for money or money's worth to a purchaser[1], or the solicitor[2] or other agent of any such person, who, with intent to defraud (1) conceals from the purchaser any instrument or incumbrance[3] material to the title[4]; or (2) falsifies any pedigree upon which the title may depend in order to induce the purchaser to accept the title offered or produced[5], is guilty of an offence[6] punishable by fine or imprisonment for a term not exceeding two years or both[7].

Any such person or his solicitor or agent is also liable to an action for damages[8] by the purchaser[9] or persons deriving title under him for any loss sustained by reason of (a) the concealment of the instrument of incumbrance[10]; or (b) any claim made by a person under such pedigree whose right was concealed by the falsification[11].

1   For the meaning of 'purchaser' see para 55 note 16 ante.
2   See para 3 ante.
3   'Incumbrance' includes a legal or equitable mortgage and a trust for securing money, and a lien, and a charge of a portion, annuity, or other capital or annual sum: Law of Property Act 1925 s 205(vii).
4   Ibid s 183(1)(a). Suppression of a document is an offence: see the Theft Act 1968 s 20(1); and CRIMINAL LAW, EVIDENCE AND PROCEDURE vol 11(1) (Reissue) para 573.
5   Law of Property Act 1925 s 183(1)(b).
6   No prosecution is to be commenced without the leave of the Attorney General (ibid s 183(4)) and before leave is granted the person intended to be prosecuted must be given such notice of the application for leave as the Attorney General may direct (s 183(5)). As to the power of the Solicitor General to act in his place see CONSTITUTIONAL LAW AND HUMAN RIGHTS vol 8(2) (Reissue) para 529.
7   Ibid s 183(1).
8   Where the property or any interest in it is recovered from the purchaser or the persons deriving title under him, regard must be had, in estimating damages, to any expenditure by him or them in improvements of any land: ibid s 183(3). For the meaning of 'land' see para 139 note 1 ante. The purchaser must prove an intent to defraud: *District Bank Ltd v Luigi Grill Ltd* [1943] Ch 78, [1943] 1 All ER 136.
9   As to the purchaser's remedies generally see para 56 ante.
10   Law of Property Act 1925 s 183(2)(a). It seems that this does not apply to concealment of an incumbrance prior to the commencement of title: see *Smith v Robinson* (1879) 13 ChD 148.
11   Law of Property Act 1925 s 183(2)(b).

(iii) Proof of Title

A. IN GENERAL

150. Proof of title shown by abstract.
The vendor must prove by production of the proper evidence the title shown by the abstract[1]. In the absence of a contrary stipulation[2], recitals, statements and descriptions of facts, matters and parties contained in deeds, instruments[3], Acts of Parliament or statutory declarations, 20 years old at the date of the contract, are taken to be sufficient evidence (except so far as they can be proved to be

inaccurate) of the truth of such facts, matters and descriptions[4]. Unless the contrary appears, the purchaser[5] must assume that recitals contained in the abstracted instruments of any deed, will or other document forming part of the title prior to the time prescribed by law or stipulated for the commencement of title[6] are correct and give all the material contents of the deed, will or other document so recited, and that every document so recited was duly executed and perfected, if and as required, by fine, recovery, acknowledgment, enrolment or otherwise[7].

1   As to how far the evidence must be such as would be admissible in litigation see para 161 note 8 post. 'I do not entirely assent to the proposition that a vendor is in every case bound to supply evidence which would be admissible in an action for ejectment': *Halkett v Earl of Dudley* [1907] 1 Ch 590 at 604 per Parker J. As to the need for an abstract of title with respect to both unregistered and registered land see paras 138, 141–149 ante.

2   Ie under the Law of Property Act 1925 s 45(10) proviso: see s 45(6).

3   Copies of entries in court rolls of admittances or surrenders seem not to be instruments, since they are records of operative acts and are not operative themselves; consequently recitals in such documents are, it is believed, not within this statutory rule. As to the admissibility of court rolls as evidence see generally CUSTOM AND USAGE; and as to the proof of entries in rolls see para 158 post.

4   Law of Property Act 1925 s 45(6). The decision of Malins V-C in *Bolton v London School Board* (1878) 7 ChD 766, that a recital of a seisin in fee contained in a deed 20 years old at the time of the contract was held to be evidence of such seisin, except so far as it was proved inaccurate by the purchaser, and that no prior title could be required, is not good law: see *Re Wallis and Grout's Contract* [1906] 2 Ch 206 at 210 per Swinfen Eady J. As to the effect of conditions making recitals and statements in deeds evidence see *Goold v White* (1854) Kay 683; *Drysdale v Mace* (1854) 5 De GM & G 103; *Poppleton v Buchanan* (1858) 4 CBNS 20. As to the effect of a recital of an earlier deed as evidence of that deed see *Gillett v Abbott* (1838) 7 Ad & El 783; *Bringloe v Goodson* (1839) 5 Bing NC 738. See further *Shrinivasdas Bavri v Meherbai* (1916) 33 TLR 106, PC (sale of land in India). As to a recital that the grantee is entitled in equity see *Re Chafer and Randall's Contract* [1916] 2 Ch 8, CA (declaration of trust); *Re Soden and Alexander's Contract* [1918] 2 Ch 258 (not sufficient as notice of trust); *Re Balen and Shepherd's Contract* [1924] 2 Ch 365 (recital differing from state of affairs appearing on face of abstract).

5   For the meaning of 'purchaser' see para 55 note 16 ante.

6   As to root of title see para 142 ante.

7   Law of Property Act 1925 s 45(1). This does not preclude the calling for documents prior to the commencement of title which are incorporated by reference in a document subsequent to such commencement: see s 45(1) proviso (iii) (in effect overruling *Re Earl of Arran and Knowlesden and Creer's Contract* [1912] 2 Ch 141). See also para 142 note 11 ante; and TC Williams 'The Abstracting and Production of Documents Incorporated by Reference in a Title Deed' (1919) 63 Sol Jo 406.

151. Proof of abstracted documents. Abstracted documents[1] are proved by production of the originals. If a document comes from the proper custody[2], and there is no cause for suspecting its authenticity, proof of due execution is not required, and it is presumed to have been executed or signed as appears on its face[3].

1   As to the need for an abstract of title with respect to both unregistered and registered land see paras 138, 141–149 ante.

2   Ie if it comes from a place where it might reasonably be expected to be found: see *Croughton v Blake* (1843) 12 M & W 205 at 208; *Doe d Jacobs v Phillips* (1845) 8 QB 158; *Bishop of Meath v Marquis of Winchester* (1836) 3 Scott 561 at 577, HL.

3   Such proof probably cannot be required (even if the document is less than 20 years old) unless there are circumstances of suspicion: see 1 Dart's Law relating to Vendors and Purchasers (8th Edn, 1929) 309. As to the presumption in favour of documents not less than 20 years old see *Re Airey, Airey v Stapleton* [1897] 1 Ch 164 (presumption applies to deeds etc more than 30 years old); and EVIDENCE. The purchaser is entitled to an explanation of any erasures which cause suspicion: *Hobson v Bell* (1839) 8 LJ Ch 241.

152. Lost documents of title. When a deed or other document of title has been lost or destroyed, secondary evidence of its contents and execution may be given upon proof of loss or destruction, and, if that evidence is clear and cogent, a purchaser cannot object to a title depending on the lost document[1].

1   *Re Halifax Commercial Banking Co Ltd and Wood* (1898) 79 LT 536 at 539–540, CA. See also *Bryant v Busk* (1827) 4 Russ 1; *Hart v Hart* (1841) 1 Hare 1; *Moulton v Edmonds* (1859) 1 De GF & J 246 at 251. If due execution is proved its due stamping will be presumed (see *Hart v Hart* supra; and EVIDENCE) but this presumption is rebutted by evidence showing that at a particular time the document was unstamped (*Marine Investment Co v Haviside* (1872) LR 5 HL 624). As to what constitutes secondary evidence of a document see generally EVIDENCE. As to the proof of instruments creating powers of attorney see AGENCY vol 1(2) (Reissue) para 22.

153. Proof of enrolment and acknowledgment of deeds. The enrolment of deeds is now required only in a limited number of cases[1]. Where deeds are required to be enrolled, enrolment is usually proved by memorandum of enrolment indorsed on the deed by the proper officer without proof of his signature or official character[2].

The registration of assurances which were formerly required to be registered in a Yorkshire deeds registry is proved by the certificate indorsed on the assurance by the registrar[3].

1   As to conveyances which must or may be enrolled see para 316 post.
2   *Doe d Williams v Lloyd* (1840) 1 Man & G 671. The necessity for the acknowledgment of deeds by married women was abolished as regards deeds executed after 1925 by the Law of Property Act 1925 s 167(1) (repealed): see REAL PROPERTY vol 39(2) (Reissue) para 230. In the case of acknowledgment of deeds made after 1882 and before 1926, the memorandum indorsed on the deed was sufficient: Conveyancing Act 1882 s 7(2) (repealed).
3   See the Law of Property Act 1969 s 22(1). The Yorkshire deeds registries are now all closed (the last, at Beverley, closing on 31 March 1976) and all the governing legislation has been repealed: see the Law of Property Act 1969 ss 16–19 (as amended), 21, 22; and LAND REGISTRATION vol 26 (Reissue) para 707.

B. PROOF OF PARTICULAR MATTERS

154. Seisin. Seisin[1] may be proved by showing acts of ownership done with respect to the land, such as the grant of a lease under which possession has been taken by the lessee and rent paid[2]. However, mere possession, although sufficient to give a prima facie title in ejectment, raises no presumption of seisin in fee simple as between vendor and purchaser[3].

1   As to seisin see REAL PROPERTY vol 39(2) (Reissue) para 167.
2   *Clarkson v Woodhouse* (1782) 5 Term Rep 412n (affd (1786) 3 Doug KB 194, Ex Ch); *Welcome v Upton* (1840) 6 M & W 536. Cf *Foljambe v Smith's Tadcaster Brewery Co* (1904) 73 LJ Ch 722; and EVIDENCE. As to admissions to the legal estate see *Doe d Daniel v Coulthred* (1837) 7 Ad & El 235 at 239.
3   See *Clibborn v Horan* [1921] 1 IR 93; *Re Gilbert and Foster's Contract* (1935) 52 TLR 4. However, conditions often provide that in the case of a death more than 12 years before contract it is to be presumed that the deceased died seised in fee simple free from incumbrances unless the contrary is shown. As to possessory title see para 143 ante.

155. Enfranchisement award. Awards of enfranchisement of copyholds and voluntary enfranchisements (which must have been made before 1 January 1926[1]) are proved by production of the award or deed of enfranchisement respectively. Confirmation or execution by the minister is conclusive evidence of all necessary formalities having been complied with[2].

1   Ie the date when all copyhold land was enfranchised: see the Law of Property Act 1922 s 128 (repealed); and REAL PROPERTY vol 39(2) (Reissue) paras 31 (abolition of copyhold tenure), 34–35 (extinguishment of manorial incidents). In the absence of agreement to the contrary, a purchaser is not entitled to call for the title of the person entering into a compensation agreement: Law of Property Act 1925 s 44(7); and see para 139 note 2 ante.

2   Copyhold Act 1894 s 61(1) (repealed). An award under the Copyhold Act 1852 may be proved by a copy
      under the seal of the commissioners for the purposes of that Act: see s 49 (repealed). Copies of awards
      were required to be sent, sealed or stamped, to the lord of the manor and entered on the court rolls: see
      the Copyhold Act 1887 s 22 (repealed).

156. Inclosure awards. An award made under the Inclosure Act 1845 may be proved
by a copy or extract signed by the proper officer of the county council, purporting to be
a true copy[1].

1   See the Inclosure Act 1845 s 146 (amended by the Statute Law Revision Act 1891); the Local
      Government Act 1972 s 251(1), Sch 29 para 4(1)(b); and COMMONS vol 6 (Reissue) para 751. The award
      is not conclusive as to the title of the allottee: *Jacomb v Turner* [1892] 1 QB 47.

157. Bankruptcy proceedings. A copy of the London Gazette containing a notice of
a bankruptcy order is conclusive evidence both of the making and of the date of the
order[1].

1   See the Insolvency Rules 1986, SI 1986/1925, r 12.20(2); and BANKRUPTCY AND INSOLVENCY vol 3(2)
      (Reissue) para 770. As to the registration of a bankruptcy order see BANKRUPTCY AND INSOLVENCY vol
      3(2) (Reissue) para 408.

158. Manorial court rolls. Entries in the court rolls of a manor may be proved by
production of the rolls[1], or by examined copies[2], or by copies purporting to be signed and
certified by the steward[3].

The last-mentioned copies are usually accepted without proof of the steward's
handwriting in the absence of any cause for suspecting their genuineness[4].

1   *Doe d Bennington v Hall* (1812) 16 East 208. However, since deposit of the copies originally delivered by
      the steward might create an equitable charge (*Whitbread v Jordan* (1835) 1 Y & C Ex 303), their absence
      must be accounted for if the court rolls themselves are offered as evidence. As to inspection of the rolls
      see generally CUSTOM AND USAGE.
2   *Doe d Cawthorn v Mee* (1833) 4 B & Ad 617; *Doe d Burrows v Freeman* (1844) 12 M & W 844. See also
      Breeze v Hawker (1844) 14 Sim 350; and EVIDENCE.
3   See the Evidence Act 1851 s 14.
4   1 Dart's Law relating to Vendors and Purchasers (8th Edn, 1929) 307–308. As to the admissibility of court
      rolls in evidence see generally CUSTOM AND USAGE.

159. Litigious documents. Court documents are not exhibited since official copies of
such documents prove themselves[1].

1   See CPR Pt 32 *Practice Direction—Written Evidence* (1999) PD 32 para 13.2. As to the CPR see para 133
      note 1 ante.

160. Wills, probate and letters of administration. In the case of deaths after 1925
all enactments and rules of law relating to the effect of probate or letters of
administration as respects chattels real apply to the real estate of the deceased[1], and
consequently the rule that a probate while unrevoked is conclusive evidence of the
validity and contents of a will and that letters of administration are similarly conclusive
of the intestacy of the deceased applies in relation to real estate as well as personal estate[2].
Probates and letters of administration and copies of them purporting to be sealed with
the official seal will be received in evidence in all parts of the United Kingdom without
further proof[3].

1   See the Administration of Estates Act 1925 s 2(1); and EXECUTORS AND ADMINISTRATORS.

2   See EXECUTORS AND ADMINISTRATORS.

3   See EXECUTORS AND ADMINISTRATORS. In showing title to a legal estate a will is usually abstracted only
     as to the appointment of executors; but where there has been an assent vesting property in trustees upon
     the trust contained in the will, it may be necessary to show that the property was left upon trust: see
     generally EXECUTORS AND ADMINISTRATORS.

161. Births, marriages, deaths and other matters of pedigree. A birth[1] is sufficiently
proved either by a certificate of baptism[2] or by a certificate of birth[3]. A marriage is
sufficiently proved by a certified extract from the parochial or general register[4]; and a
death is sufficiently proved by a certificate of burial or by a certificate of death[5]. Evidence
is not usually required of the identity of the parties named in such certificates; when it is
required, it can be given by means of a statutory declaration. Matters of pedigree may also
be proved by the statutory declarations of living members of the family or of other persons
acquainted with the family[6]. In the absence of formal evidence or of a statutory
declaration, the proof of facts may sometimes be assisted by presumption[7]; it has been
held, for example, that persons who have lived together as husband and wife were legally
married (the presumption being supported by proof of general repute[8]), and a purchaser
must in suitable cases be satisfied with such proof[9].

1   As to evidence of pedigree generally see EVIDENCE; and as to evidence which has been tendered in
     peerage claims see eg the *Shrewsbury Peerage Case* (1858) 7 HL Cas 1; and PEERAGES AND DIGNITIES vol
     35 (Reissue) para 957 et seq.

2   Ie a certified copy of the entry in the appropriate parochial register: see ECCLESIASTICAL LAW; EVIDENCE.

3   Ie a certified extract from the general register of births: see EVIDENCE; REGISTRATION CONCERNING
     THE INDIVIDUAL. A birth certificate is not alone sufficient evidence of the parents' marriage expressly or
     impliedly stated in it: *Re Stollery, Weir v Treasury Solicitor* [1926] Ch 284, CA.

4   As to the appropriate parochial register see ECCLESIASTICAL LAW; EVIDENCE; and as to the general
     register and the particulars in it see EVIDENCE; REGISTRATION CONCERNING THE INDIVIDUAL. As to
     non-parochial registers as evidence see 1 Williams Law relating to Vendors and Purchasers of Real Estate
     and Chattels Real (4th Edn, 1936) 189; and EVIDENCE.

5   Ie a certified extract from the general register of deaths: see EVIDENCE; REGISTRATION CONCERNING
     THE INDIVIDUAL. In practice, probate or letters of administration are usually accepted as sufficient
     evidence of death. As to parochial registers of burials as evidence see EVIDENCE; and as to the presumption
     of death see EVIDENCE; EXECUTORS AND ADMINISTRATORS.

6   All statutory declarations should be made by a person having the requisite knowledge and, where possible,
     by an independent person: see *Hobson v Bell* (1839) 2 Beav 17 at 22; *Nott v Riccard* (1856) 22 Beav 307;
     and 1 Dart's Law relating to Vendors and Purchasers (8th Edn, 1929) 329. As to the presumption of
     legitimacy see CHILDREN AND YOUNG PERSONS vol 5(2) (Reissue) para 708 et seq; as to procedures for
     the judicial determination of parentage see CHILDREN AND YOUNG PERSONS vol 5(2) (Reissue) para 667
     et seq; and as to proof of adoption see CHILDREN AND YOUNG PERSONS vol 5(2) (Reissue) para 1096.

7   As to a presumption that a woman is past child-bearing see *Browne v Warnock* (1880) 7 LR Ir 3; *Re
     Westminster Bank Ltd's Declaration of Trust* [1963] 2 All ER 400n, [1963] 1 WLR 820; the Perpetuities and
     Accumulations Act 1964 s 2(1)(a); and EVIDENCE.

8   See *Re Shephard, George v Thyer* [1904] 1 Ch 456; *Re Haynes, Haynes v Carter* (1906) 94 LT 431. The
     presumption applies even where registration of marriage is compulsory: *Re Taplin, Watson v Tate* [1937]
     3 All ER 105. The limits within which presumptions hold as between vendor and purchaser were defined
     thus in the days of jury trials: 'If the case be such that sitting before a jury it would be the duty of a judge
     to give a clear direction in favour of the fact, then it is to be considered as without reasonable doubt; but
     if it would be the duty of a judge to leave it to a jury to pronounce upon the effect of the evidence, then
     it is to be considered as too doubtful to conclude a purchaser': *Emery v Grocock* (1821) 6 Madd 54 at 57
     per Leach V-C. See also *England d Syburn v Slade* (1792) 4 Term Rep 682; *Doe d Bowerman v Syburn*
     (1796) 7 Term Rep 2; *Hillary v Waller* (1806) 12 Ves 239 at 254, 270; *MEPC Ltd v Christian-Edwards*
     [1981] AC 205, [1979] 3 All ER 752, HL; and EVIDENCE.

9   See 1 Williams Law relating to Vendors and Purchasers of Real Estate and Chattels Real (4th Edn, 1936) 190.

162. Payment of inheritance tax. Payment of inheritance tax is proved by the certificate of discharge of the Commissioners of Inland Revenue[1].

1   See the Inheritance Tax Act 1984 s 239(1); and INHERITANCE TAXATION vol 24 (Reissue) paras 687–688. Receipts for inheritance tax are not required in the case of deaths after 1925, since for the Inland Revenue charge to be effective against a purchaser it must be registered as a land charge: see INHERITANCE TAXATION vol 24 (Reissue) para 686; LAND CHARGES vol 26 (Reissue) para 534; LAND REGISTRATION vol 26 (Reissue) para 836. See also paras 144 note 6 ante, 164 note 9 post.

(iv) Requisitions on Title

163. Examination of deeds. On receipt of the abstract the purchaser's solicitor[1] peruses it and examines it with the original documents[2]. This examination is directed (1) to the substance of the documents; (2) to formal matters; and (3) to any incidental matters relevant to the title which do not appear on the abstract. As to substance, it must be ascertained that the abstract, so far as it purports to give the contents of the documents, gives them correctly and with sufficient fullness, and that no material part of any document is omitted. As to formal matters, it is necessary to ensure that the documents are correctly stamped, properly executed and duly indorsed with any necessary memoranda of acknowledgment, registration, enrolment or other requirement. As to incidental matters the solicitor must make certain that there are no notices or memoranda with the documents, or annexed to or indorsed upon them, or any suspicious matters as regards execution or otherwise, or as regards the custody of the deeds, from which it may be inferred that the vendor's title is subject to rights of third persons[3].

1   See para 3 ante. As to the need for an abstract of title with respect to both unregistered and registered land see paras 138, 141–149 ante.
2   As to notice to the purchaser of matters discoverable by the usual inquiries and inspections see the Law of Property Act 1925 s 199(1)(ii); and EQUITY vol 16 (Reissue) para 767 et seq. Recitals may be framed with the highly desirable and perfectly honest object of keeping a trust off the title: see *Re Chafer and Randall's Contract* [1916] 2 Ch 8 at 19, CA.
3   As to suspicions raised by the position of the receipt on a deed under the old practice see *Kennedy v Green* (1834) 3 My & K 699; and cf *Greenslade v Dare* (1855) 20 Beav 284, where there was no receipt. The receipt is now embodied in the deed: see the Law of Property Act 1925 s 67, applying to deeds executed after 31 December 1881; and paras 309–310 post. As to a case where the purchaser's solicitor was directed, but neglected, to examine a will, and the purchaser was discharged but made liable in costs see *M'Culloch v Gregory* (1855) 1 K & J 286 at 293. A will now takes effect in equity only, and in general a purchaser is only concerned with the probate, if he takes a title direct from the executor, or with the probate followed by an assent, where an assent has been made. It seems, however, that if the will is brought on the title, the purchaser can make a requisition in respect of an assent not made in accordance with the will: *Re Duce and Boots Cash Chemists (Southern) Ltd's Contract* [1937] Ch 642, [1937] 3 All ER 788. See also EXECUTORS AND ADMINISTRATORS.

164. Nature of requisitions. After perusing the abstract and examining the deeds, the purchaser's solicitor[1] prepares his requisitions on the title and conveyance[2]. Where there have been preliminary inquiries, few requisitions other than those strictly on title are now necessary, but it is still his duty to make any appropriate requisitions, even if the preliminary inquiries have been so complete that it is only necessary to ask whether the answers to them are still complete and accurate[3]. The requisitions on title fall generally under the following heads: (1) that the abstracted documents, though efficacious, do not show the title which the purchaser is entitled to obtain, having regard to any special stipulations in the contract[4] (in which case a further abstract is asked for[5]); (2) that particular documents do not have the effect required in order to make out the vendor's title; (3) that there are incumbrances on the property remaining unsatisfied[6]; (4) that the identity of the property is not shown[7]; (5) that the documents are not in order as to stamping, execution or other formal matters[8]; and (6) that evidence additional to that already furnished is required as to matters of pedigree or otherwise[9].

1   See para 3 ante. As to the need for an abstract of title with respect to both unregistered and registered land see paras 138, 141–149 ante.

2   See *Re Ossemsley Estates Ltd* [1937] 3 All ER 774, 81 Sol Jo 683, CA. As to the disposition of registered and unregistered land by transfer see para 262 note 2 post.

3   *Goody v Baring* [1956] 2 All ER 11 at 16–17, [1956] 1 WLR 448 at 456 per Danckwerts J. As to inquiries see para 4 et seq ante.

4   As to the title which the purchaser can require under an open contract see para 137 ante; and as to special restrictions imposed by the contract see para 90 et seq ante. See also the cases cited in para 226 note 3 post.

5   A perfect abstract, in the strict sense of the term, is an abstract which shows a good title (*Morley v Cook* (1842) 2 Hare 106 at 111), but for particular purposes it may mean the most perfect abstract in the vendor's possession, actual or constructive at the time of his delivering it (*Morley v Cook* supra at 112). Cf *Blackburn v Smith* (1848) 2 Exch 783; *Want v Stallibrass* (1873) LR 8 Exch 175 at 179; and *Gray v Fowler* (1873) LR 8 Exch 249 at 279 ('full and sufficient abstract'). The abstract is not perfect if it does not show the true state of the title: *Steer v Crowley* (1863) 14 CBNS 337 at 359. See also paras 100–101 ante.

6   See para 89 ante.

7   See para 109 ante.

8   See para 97 ante.

9   It has been usual also to require evidence as to payment of death duties (now inheritance tax), but this is now only necessary in exceptional cases. Death duties in the case of persons who died before 1926 will usually be barred by the lapse of 12 years, and in cases of death since 1925 the land charges register or the register of title will show whether a charge for death duties (or inheritance tax) has been registered; if not, a purchaser takes free from these: see paras 144 note 6, 162 note 1 ante; and 2 Williams Law relating to Vendors and Purchasers of Real Estate and Chattels Real (4th Edn, 1936) 1185 et seq, 1201 et seq.

165.   Requisitions as to the conveyance. The purchaser may make requisitions as to the conveyance[1]. These assume that the vendor has shown that he can either alone, or jointly with other persons whose concurrence he can require, make a title to the property, and the only question is as to the persons to make the conveyance and the form which it is to take[2].

1   As to the distinction between requisitions as to title and requisitions as to conveyance see para 104 ante.

2   As to the parties to make the conveyance and its form see para 269 et seq post. As to the disposition of registered and unregistered land by transfer see para 262 note 2 post.

166.   Vendor's right of rescission. The conditions of sale may give the vendor the right to rescind the contract in the event of any requisition or objection being made which he is unable or unwilling to comply with, and it is then necessary for the purchaser to take care that he does not, by making a requisition not really essential, run the risk of losing the purchase. More usually the right of rescission is made to arise only when a requisition is persisted in, and the purchaser runs no such risk in making the requisition in the first instance[1]. Requisitions should, however, never be frivolous or unnecessary. They should either call attention to a real or apprehended defect in the title, or ask for relevant information[2].

1   However, the Standard Conditions of Sale (3rd Edn) do not contain any such provision; cf the National Conditions of Sale (20th Edn), condition 10. See also para 104 et seq ante. As to the Conditions of Sale see para 1 note 9 ante.

2   As to searching requisitions regarding possible defects not disclosed by the title or otherwise known to the purchaser, which the vendor need not answer see *Re Ford and Hill* (1879) 10 ChD 365, CA; *Taylor v London and County Banking Co* [1901] 2 Ch 231 at 258, CA; and *Luff v Raymond* [1982] LS Gaz R 1330.

(v) Searches

167. Searches for land charges. In the case of unregistered land[1], searches in the registers kept at the Land Registry[2] are normally deferred until after the purchaser has entered into a binding contract, unless there is reason to suppose that they will reveal some matter requiring explanation or causing difficulty, because the entries in these registers are against the names of the owners from time to time of the land and not against the land itself[3], and, until the abstract of title has been delivered, it is not normally known against what names searches should be made[4]. These searches should be made within 15 days of the date on which completion is to take place in order that the protection given by the official certificate of search may extend up to that date[5]. A search of the local land charges register[6] does not protect the purchaser against unregistered charges[7], but a purchaser who has thus been misled by the result of the search will normally be entitled to compensation out of public funds[8].

1   As to searches in the case of registered land see para 169 post; as to searches to ensure that land has never been registered see para 2 ante; and as to the Land Registry see LAND REGISTRATION vol 26 (Reissue) para 1201 et seq.
2   See LAND CHARGES vol 26 (Reissue) para 522 et seq.
3   See LAND CHARGES vol 26 (Reissue) para 509.
4   As to the right to search and the mode of search see LAND CHARGES vol 26 (Reissue) para 596 et seq. As to the need for an abstract of title with respect to both unregistered and registered land see paras 138, 141–149 ante.
5   See LAND CHARGES vol 26 (Reissue) para 601.
6   As to the local land charges register see LAND CHARGES vol 26 (Reissue) paras 571–572.
7   Ie other than a light obstruction notice: see LAND CHARGES vol 26 (Reissue) para 594.
8   In the case of a contract which is dependent upon or avoidable by reference to a search for local land charges, the search must be timed to coincide with completion; in other cases, the search must be before the date of the contract: see LAND CHARGES vol 26 (Reissue) para 594.

168. Searches in respect of farms and companies. Searches may need to be made or repeated, where the land includes farm property, in the register of agricultural charges[1], or, where the vendor is a company, in the registers kept by the Registrar of Companies[2].

1   See para 22 ante; and AGRICULTURE vol 1(2) (Reissue) para 554.
2   See para 22 ante; and COMPANIES vol 7(2) (1996 Reissue) para 1299 et seq. As to the Registrar of Companies see COMPANIES vol 7(1) (1996 Reissue) para 60.

169. Searches in the case of registered land. In the case of land registered with an absolute title, searches under the Land Charges Act 1972 are not required[1] and are replaced by an official search against the title in question[2], but where the registration is of a possessory or qualified title, the same searches must be made as in the case of unregistered land so far as matters are excepted from the registration[3].

1   See LAND CHARGES vol 26 (Reissue) para 505; LAND REGISTRATION vol 26 (Reissue) para 709 (inapplicability of the Land Charges Act 1972 to registered land), para 715 (conclusiveness of register), para 931 (purchaser not affected by notice of land charges capable of being protected under the Land Registration Act 1925).
2   See LAND REGISTRATION vol 26 (Reissue) para 837 et seq (official search).
3   See LAND REGISTRATION vol 26 (Reissue) paras 740–742 (effect of first registration of freehold land), paras 749–751 (effect of first registration of leasehold land), para 926 (information supplied where register not conclusive).

(vi) Expenses

170. Expense of making abstract. The vendor is bound to make and deliver, at his own expense, a perfect abstract[1], that is, an abstract showing such a title as the purchaser is entitled to obtain under the contract[2]. If the documents of title are not in his possession, he must himself bear the cost of procuring them for the purpose of furnishing the abstract[3]. The vendor is not relieved from the expense of delivering a proper abstract by the mere fact that the purchaser is entitled under his contract to a free conveyance[4].

1   *Re Johnson and Tustin* (1885) 30 ChD 42, CA; *Re Stamford, Spalding and Boston Banking Co and Knight's Contract* [1900] 1 Ch 287. However, in sales under the Lands Clauses Consolidation Act 1845 s 82, or the Compulsory Purchase Act 1965 s 23(1), the costs of the abstract, in the absence of agreement, are thrown on the purchaser: see COMPULSORY ACQUISITION OF LAND vol 8(1) (Reissue) para 140. As to the need for an abstract of title with respect to both unregistered and registered land see paras 138, 141–149 ante.
2   See *Morley v Cook* (1842) 2 Hare 106 at 111; and paras 90, 137 et seq, 164 note 5 ante.
3   See the Law of Property Act 1925 s 45(4) (see paras 171–172 post), which does not apply to a document in the chain of title. It assumes that a perfect abstract has been delivered, and deals entirely with matters subsequent to that: *Re Stamford, Spalding and Boston Banking Co and Knight's Contract* [1900] 1 Ch 287 at 291 per North J.
4   *Re Pelly and Jacob's Contract* (1899) 80 LT 45. It is, however, usual to stipulate in such cases that there is to be no investigation of title: see para 130 ante.

171. Expense of certificates and other evidence. On a sale[1] of land[2] under an open contract, the expenses of the production and inspection of all documents of title not in the possession of the vendor or his mortgagee or trustee, and the expenses of all journeys incidental to such production or inspection, fall on the purchaser[3] where he requires such expenses to be incurred for the purpose of verifying the abstract or for any other purpose[4], unless the contract otherwise stipulates[5].

Where the documents are in the vendor's possession and are produced at the proper place for inspection, that is to say either at the office of the vendor's solicitor[6], or near the land sold, or in London[7], the purchaser must pay the cost of their inspection by his own solicitor, but if they are produced elsewhere the vendor must defray any extra costs arising[8]. Documents in the possession of the vendor's mortgagee must in like manner be produced by the mortgagee, usually at the office of the mortgagee's solicitor. The purchaser must pay the costs of their inspection by his own solicitor but not the costs of the mortgagee[9].

1   For the meaning of 'sale' see para 139 note 2 ante.
2   For the meaning of 'land' see para 139 note 1 ante.
3   For the meaning of 'purchaser' see para 55 note 16 ante.
4   Law of Property Act 1925 s 45(4)(a), replacing the Conveyancing Act 1881 s 3(6) (repealed), in an amended form so as to relieve the purchaser of the expense of production of documents in the possession of the vendor's mortgagee or trustee. Under the earlier enactment the purchaser had to pay the costs of procuring the production of title deeds in the hands of the vendor's mortgagee (*Re Willett and Argenti* (1889) 60 LT 735) or trustees (*Re Ebsworth and Tidy's Contract* (1889) 42 ChD 23 at 27, CA). See further para 172 note 2 post. However, the purchaser must pay the costs of procuring the production even of a deed which is the root of the vendor's title, if it is not in the vendor's possession: *Re Stuart and Olivant and Seadon's Contract* [1896] 2 Ch 328, CA. As to the former practice, cf Sugden's Law of Vendors and Purchasers (14th Edn, 1862) 431; and as to the effect of the Law of Property Act 1925 s 45(4) see para 170 note 3 ante. As to the need for an abstract of title with respect to both unregistered and registered land see paras 138, 141–149 ante.
5   Ibid s 45(10) proviso.
6   See para 3 ante.
7   1 Dart's Law relating to Vendors and Purchasers (8th Edn, 1929) 415; 1 Williams Law relating to Vendors and Purchasers of Real Estate and Chattels Real (4th Edn, 1936) 164. Strictly the rule refers to the vendor's residence, but this means in practice his solicitors' office. Arguably, the rule is obsolete; the current practice is for production to be at the office of the vendor's solicitor or his mortgagee's solicitor.

8   *Hughes v Wynne* (1836) 8 Sim 85; affd (1837) 1 Jur 720. If the vendor has the option of producing them
    at any one of several specified places, the purchaser is entitled to reasonable notice of the place selected:
    Rippinghall v Lloyd (1833) 5 B & Ad 742. As a rule, a country solicitor is not allowed the cost of journeys
    to London for the purpose of examining title deeds except in special circumstances (*Re Tryon* (1844) 7
    Beav 496), and it is immaterial that he makes the journey at the request of his client, unless he has first
    explained to him the usage of the profession to dispense with such attendance (*Alsop v Lord Oxford* (1833)
    1 My & K 564; *Horlock v Smith* (1837) 2 My & Cr 495 at 523). A London solicitor is not bound to employ
    a country agent, but may send his clerk to examine the deeds: *Hughes v Wynne* supra.
9   See note 4 supra.

172. Expense of producing deeds. In the absence of any stipulation or contrary
intention expressed in the contract[1] (1) the expenses of searching for, procuring, making,
verifying and producing all certificates, declarations, evidence and information not in the
possession of the vendor or his mortgagee or trustee must be borne by the purchaser[2];
(2) all copies or abstracts[3] of or extracts from documents of title not in the possession of
the vendor or his mortgagee or trustee, and required by the purchaser for whatever
purpose, must be made at the expense of the purchaser[4]; and (3) the expenses of copying
any documents in the possession of the vendor or his mortgagee or trustee, which the
purchaser requires to be delivered to him, must be borne by the purchaser[5].

1   Law of Property Act 1925 s 45(10) proviso.
2   Ibid s 45(4)(b), reproducing the Conveyancing Act 1881 s 3(6), (9) (repealed), with amendment so as to
    include documents in the possession of the vendor's mortgagee or trustee. For the meaning of 'purchaser'
    see para 55 note 16 ante. Apart from statute, all the expense of procuring the evidence necessary for
    verifying the abstract falls on the vendor. Where lessees covenant to finish a house to the satisfaction of
    the lessor's surveyor, the certificate of the surveyor's approval is neither a 'certificate' nor an 'evidence'
    within the statutory provision; it is not like a certificate of a pre-existing fact, such as a birth, a marriage
    or a death, but it is the fact itself and forms part of the vendors' title, which must be procured at their
    expense: *Re Moody and Yates' Contract* (1885) 30 ChD 344 at 349, CA, per Fry LJ. Where a fact is stated
    in the abstract, but the evidence of it is not in the vendor's possession, the expense of procuring the
    evidence falls on the purchaser: *Re Conlon and Faulkener's Contract* [1916] 1 IR 241; *Re Wright and
    Thompson's Contract* [1920] 1 Ch 191; *Hopkins v Geoghegan* [1931] IR 135. Cf *Re Edwards and Rudkin to
    Green* (1888) 58 LT 789.
3   As to the need for an abstract of title with respect to both unregistered and registered land see paras 138,
    141–149 ante.
4   Law of Property Act 1925 s 45(4)(b), reproducing the Conveyancing Act 1881 s 3(6), (9) (repealed), in
    an amended form: see note 2 supra. Notwithstanding the wide language of the statutory provision, it does
    not relieve the vendor from making a proper abstract and procuring the necessary documents for making
    it at his own expense (see para 170 ante); nor does it affect the ordinary right of the purchaser to have the
    title deeds handed over on completion, and any expenses incurred in obtaining them for that purpose, if
    they are not in the vendor's possession, must be borne by the vendor: *Re Duthy and Jesson's Contract* [1898]
    1 Ch 419.
5   Law of Property Act 1925 s 45(4).

173. Sale in lots. Subject to any stipulation or contrary intention expressed in the
contract[1], on a sale[2] of property in lots, the purchaser[3] of two or more lots held wholly
or in part under the same title is not entitled to more than one abstract[4] of the common
title, except at his own expense[5].

1   Law of Property Act 1925 s 45(10) proviso.
2   For the meaning of 'sale' see para 139 note 2 ante.
3   For the meaning of 'purchaser' see para 55 note 16 ante.
4   As to the need for an abstract of title with respect to both unregistered and registered land see paras 138,
    141–149 ante.
5   Law of Property Act 1925 s 45(5), reproducing the Conveyancing Act 1881 s 3(7) (repealed). See also
    Re Simmons' Contract [1908] 1 Ch 452.

(2) ACCEPTANCE OF TITLE BY THE PURCHASER

174. Acceptance of title. A purchaser is deemed to have accepted the title when the last outstanding requisition has been answered to his satisfaction by the vendor. Acceptance need not be notified to the vendor[1].

If the purchaser fails to send in requisitions or objections within the time fixed by the contract for that purpose[2], or if, although not satisfied with the vendor's replies to any requisitions or objections, he does not insist upon satisfactory answers, he may be held to have waived his right to make requisitions or objections, or to insist on those which he has made, and he is then deemed to have accepted the title[3]. If the purchaser enters into possession, or pays the whole or part of the purchase money, or does other acts which a purchaser is not bound to do until a good title has been made, he may be deemed to have waived objections to the title[4]. However, this is not the case if the purchaser has entered into possession under an express condition in the contract enabling him to do so before completion[5], or where the vendor has consented to his doing so without prejudice to his right to require a good title[6], nor where the purchaser was already in possession at the time of the sale, unless he has remained for a long time without raising objections as to title[7].

1   *Re Highett and Bird's Contract* [1902] 2 Ch 214; affd [1903] 1 Ch 287, CA. See the Statutory Form of Conditions of Sale 1925, SR & O 1925/779, condition 6(1), (2); the Standard Conditions of Sale (3rd Edn), condition 4.1.1; and paras 76, 101–102 ante. Under the Standard Conditions of Sale (3rd Edn), a leasehold property is sold subject to any subsisting breach of a condition or tenant's obligation relating to the physical state of the property which renders the lease liable to forfeiture (condition 3.2.2), and a sublease is granted subject to any subsisting breach of a condition or tenant's obligation relating to the physical state of the property which renders the vendor's own lease liable to forfeiture (condition 3.2.3). As to the Standard Conditions of Sale see para 1 note 9 ante.

2   See para 102 ante. As to discovery of a mistake in the abstract after acceptance of the title see *M'Culloch v Gregory* (1855) 1 K & J 286, where a will, which the purchaser's solicitor neglected to examine, was misstated in the abstract. The mistake was discovered after the acceptance of title, and the purchaser was discharged on return of the purchase money, but with loss of interest on his deposit and on the payment of costs. As to the effect of the delivery of a supplementary abstract upon the time limit for requisitions see para 102 ante; and as to the formation of the contract see paras 23–40 ante. As to the need for an abstract of title with respect to both unregistered and registered land see paras 138, 141–149 ante.

3   *Burroughs v Oakley* (1819) 3 Swan 159 at 171. Cf *Flexman v Corbett* [1930] 1 Ch 672; and see para 102 note 5 ante.

4   *Fludyer v Cocker* (1805) 12 Ves 25 at 27; *Fleetwood v Green* (1809) 15 Ves 594; *Binks v Lord Rokeby* (1818) 2 Swan 222; *Hall v Laver* (1838) 3 Y & C Ex 191; *Haydon v Bell* (1838) 1 Beav 337; *Sibbald v Lowrie* (1853) 23 LJ Ch 593; *Wallis v Woodyear* (1855) 2 Jur NS 179; *Deller v Simonds* (1859) 5 Jur NS 997 at 1002. As to letting the property cf *Re Barrington, ex p Sidebotham* (1834) 1 Mont & A 655 at 663 (affd (1835) 4 Deac & Ch 461); and *Simpson v Sadd* (1854) 4 De GM & G 665. Delivery of the keys of a house is equivalent to giving possession: *Guest v Homfrey* (1801) 5 Ves 818. However, these acts do not give rise to such implication where they are accompanied by continued negotiations as to the title: *Knatchbull v Grueber* (1815) 1 Madd 153 at 170 (affd (1817) 3 Mer 124); *Burroughs v Oakley* (1819) 3 Swan 159. See also *Rellie v Pyke* [1936] 1 All ER 345 (entry into possession without waiver).

5   See *Bolton v London School Board* (1878) 7 ChD 766. The ordinary provision as to possession on the day fixed for completion does not have the same effect: *Bown v Stenson* (1857) 24 Beav 631. Under the Standard Conditions of Sale (3rd Edn), entry into occupation by the purchaser pending completion does not affect his right to raise requisitions: see conditions 5.2.1, 5.2.7; and para 119 ante. Strictly, title should not be accepted until the deeds and facts appearing on the abstract are proved by proper evidence (see *Newall v Smith* (1820) 1 Jac & W 263), but since evidence not in the vendor's possession must be procured at the purchaser's expense (see para 171 ante), it is usual to assume, without strict proof, facts as to which there is no substantial doubt. As to completion see paras 262–325 post.

6   See *Burroughs v Oakley* (1819) 3 Swan 159.

7   *Stevens v Guppy* (1828) 3 Russ 171. See also *Vancouver v Bliss* (1805) 11 Ves 458 at 464; *Dixon v Astley* (1816) 1 Mer 133.

175. Effect of submitting draft conveyance or transfer. The submission by the purchaser of the draft conveyance or transfer to the vendor for his approval does not necessarily operate as an acceptance of the title[1], but it is a circumstance from which the inference may be drawn that outstanding objections or requisitions have been waived and the title accepted[2].

1   Sugden's Law of Vendors and Purchasers (14th Edn, 1862) 345; *Burroughs v Oakley* (1819) 3 Swan 159 at 171; *Hanwood v Bland* (1842) Fl & K 540; *Lukey v Higgs* (1855) 24 LJ Ch 495. See also para 174 ante; and *Re Perriam, Perriam v Perriam* (1883) 32 WR 369, where the taking of a conveyance of property by the correct description and payment of the purchase money into court were held not to waive a claim to compensation for misdescription in the particulars. As to the disposition of registered and unregistered land by transfer see para 262 note 2 post.

2   See *Clive v Beaumont* (1848) 1 De G & Sm 397 at 406; *Smith v Capron* (1849) 7 Hare 185 at 191; and *Sweet v Meredith* (1862) 8 Jur NS 637 (subsequent proceedings (1863) 9 Jur NS 569). In practice, the draft conveyance is frequently submitted along with the requisitions, and its delivery is made subject to outstanding questions of title, examination of the deeds and searches. As to preparation of the conveyance or transfer see para 262 post.

176. Extent of acceptance of title. In whatever manner an acceptance of title has taken place, it is an acceptance only of the title shown by the abstract[1], and does not preclude the purchaser from taking objections, not precluded by the contract, by reason of defects not disclosed by the abstract which he subsequently discovers[2]. Such acceptance does not operate as a waiver of the purchaser's right to have the abstract verified[3]; nor does it preclude objections to matters which are matters of conveyance rather than of title, such as the existence of charges upon the property which are removable by the vendor[4]. If a purchaser is willing to accept the title upon a specific objection being removed, and to waive all other objections, the waiver is conditional only on the removal of that specific objection[5].

1   As to the need for an abstract of title with respect to both unregistered and registered land see paras 138, 141–149 ante.

2   *Blacklow v Laws* (1842) 2 Hare 40 at 47.

3   *Southby v Hutt* (1837) 2 My & Cr 207; *Turquand v Rhodes* (1868) 37 LJ Ch 830.

4   *Re Gloag and Miller's Contract* (1883) 23 ChD 320. As to objections to matters of conveyance see para 165 ante.

5   *Lesturgeon v Martin* (1834) 3 My & K 255.

(3) RIGHTS AND DUTIES WITH RESPECT TO THE PROPERTY

(i) Purchaser's Beneficial Ownership; Vendor's Trusteeship

177. Effect of agreement for sale. An agreement for the sale of land, of which specific performance can be ordered[1], operates as an alienation by the vendor of his beneficial proprietary interest in the property[2]. As from the date of the contract[3], his beneficial interest is transferred from the land to the purchase money, and, if his interest was of the nature of realty, it is from that date converted into personalty[4]. As regards the land, he becomes, as between himself and the purchaser, a constructive trustee for the purchaser[5], with the right as trustee to be indemnified by the purchaser against the liabilities of the trust property[6]. Thus the purchaser becomes beneficial owner, with the right to dispose of the property by sale, mortgage or otherwise, and to devise it by will[7], and on his death intestate it devolves on his legal personal representatives, who hold it, subject to the requirements of administration, on trust with a power of sale for the persons entitled on intestacy[8].

1   See paras 247–248 post; and *Cornwall v Henson* [1899] 2 Ch 710 at 714 (revsd on the facts [1900] 2 Ch 298, CA). There must be a binding contract for sale: see para 29 ante.

2   *Wall v Bright* (1820) 1 Jac & W 494 at 500 per Plumer MR. The contract must be one for immediate sale: *Rose v Watson* (1864) 10 HL Cas 672 at 678. As to a sale under court order see para 133–136 ante.

3   As to the formation of the contract see paras 23–40 ante.

4   See EQUITY vol 16 (Reissue) para 819. As to the effect of the exercise of an option to purchase see EQUITY vol 16 (Reissue) para 833; LANDLORD AND TENANT vol 27(1) (Reissue) para 110 et seq.

5   *Wall v Bright* (1820) 1 Jac & W 494; *Shaw v Foster* (1872) LR 5 HL 321 at 333. This is the case if specific performance of the contract would be ordered: *Howard v Miller* [1915] AC 318, PC. Before the coming into effect of the statutory provisions by which real estate held by a deceased person in trust devolves on his personal representative (see EXECUTORS AND ADMINISTRATORS), the property would have passed under a devise by the vendor of trust estates: *Lysaght v Edwards* (1876) 2 ChD 499. As to the devolution of real estate generally see EXECUTORS AND ADMINISTRATORS.

6   *Dodson v Downey* [1901] 2 Ch 620 at 623. See also *Golden Bread Co Ltd v Hemmings* [1922] 1 Ch 162.

7   *Paine v Meller* (1801) 6 Ves 349 at 352; *Shaw v Foster* (1872) LR 5 HL 321 at 333, 338; *Gordon Hill Trust Ltd v Segall* [1941] 2 All ER 379, CA; and see MORTGAGE; WILLS vol 50 (Reissue) para 530.

8   *Paine v Meller* (1801) 6 Ves 349; *Broome v Monck* (1805) 10 Ves 597 at 620. It passes under a general devise of land or real estate: *Broome v Monck* supra. See also *Greenhill v Greenhill* (1711) Prec Ch 320; *Potter v Potter* (1750) 1 Ves Sen 437; *Capel v Girdler* (1804) 9 Ves 509 at 510; *Marston v Roe d Fox* (1838) 8 Ad & El 14 at 63, Ex Ch; and EXECUTORS AND ADMINISTRATORS; WILLS vol 50 (Reissue) paras 265, 279, 494–496. As to the devolution of real estate upon personal representatives and the distribution of the residuary estate on intestacy see the Administration of Estates Act 1925 s 33 (as amended); and EXECUTORS AND ADMINISTRATORS.

178. Nature of vendor's trusteeship. The vendor's trusteeship is in the first place limited to the precise property contracted to be sold. Formerly a contract to sell property did not (apart from special stipulation) include the benefit of the insurance policy relating to the property[1], but this position has been modified by statute[2]. Similarly, a contract to sell a property with vacant possession does not entitle the purchaser to receive a payment in respect of dilapidations payable under a lease which terminates between the date of the contract and the date of completion[3], and the same rule applies to a payment of compensation on the derequisition of requisitioned property[4].

In the second place the vendor is not a bare trustee. Until payment he retains a personal and substantial interest in the property, a right to protect that interest, and an active right to assert it if anything in derogation of it should be done, and the relation of trustee and beneficiary is subject to the trustee's paramount right to protect his own interest as vendor[5]. There is, in fact, only a qualified trusteeship until the price is paid and nothing remains to be done by either party except the execution of the transfer[6]. When that stage has been reached, the full relation of trustee and beneficiary thereby established relates back to the formation of the contract[7].

The vendor's trusteeship and the purchaser's beneficial ownership are, moreover, conditional upon the performance of the contract[8]. If the contract is rescinded, or if, from want of title on the part of the vendor[9] or otherwise, the contract is such that specific performance could not be obtained, and the defect is not waived by the purchaser, the position is the same as regards the interests in the property as though the relation of vendor and purchaser had never arisen. The vendor is treated as if he had never been trustee, and the purchaser as if he had never been equitable owner[10].

The vendor's breach of his obligations as trustee does not prevent him from serving a notice to complete[11].

1   *Rayner v Preston* (1881) 18 ChD 1, CA. As to the formation of the contract see paras 23–40 post.

2   See paras 117–118 ante, 184 post.

3   As to the date of completion see para 185 post.

4   See para 192 post.

5   *Shaw v Foster* (1872) LR 5 HL 321 at 338. See also *Lysaght v Edwards* (1876) 2 ChD 499 at 506–507 per Jessel MR; *Raffety v Schofield* [1897] 1 Ch 937 at 943; *Ecclesiastical Comrs v Pinney* [1899] 2 Ch 729 at 735,

CA; *Re Stucley, Stucley v Kekewich* [1906] 1 Ch 67 at 78, CA; and *Allen v IRC* [1914] 1 KB 327 at 334 (affd [1914] 2 KB 327, CA).

6   As to the disposition of registered and unregistered land by transfer see para 262 note 2 post.

7   *Rayner v Preston* (1881) 18 ChD 1 at 13, CA, per James LJ. See also *Wall v Bright* (1820) 1 Jac & W 494 at 503 per Plumer MR; *Shaw v Foster* (1872) LR 5 HL 321 at 356 per Lord Hatherley; and *Ridout v Fowler* [1904] 1 Ch 658 at 661. The vendor is not a trustee within the meaning of the Trustee Act 1925 (see TRUSTS vol 48 (Reissue) para 501), at any rate until the purchase money is paid: *Re Carpenter* (1854) Kay 418; *Re Colling* (1886) 32 ChD 333, CA; cf *Re Cuming* (1869) 5 Ch App 72; *Re Pagani, Re Pagani's Trust* [1892] 1 Ch 236, CA; *Re Beaufort's Will* (1898) 43 Sol Jo 12.

8   See *Rayner v Preston* (1881) 18 ChD 1, CA.

9   *Broome v Monck* (1805) 10 Ves 597; *Lysaght v Edwards* (1876) 2 ChD 499 at 507; *Re Thomas, Thomas v Howell* (1886) 34 ChD 166.

10   *Cornwall v Henson* [1899] 2 Ch 710 (revsd on another ground [1900] 2 Ch 298, CA); *Plews v Samuel* [1904] 1 Ch 464; *Ridout v Fowler* [1904] 1 Ch 658 at 662 (affd on other grounds [1904] 2 Ch 93, CA). While it is still uncertain whether the contract will be performed, the vendor is only a trustee under a condition, and if the contract is not performed he again becomes absolute owner: see *Wall v Bright* (1820) 1 Jac & W 494 at 501.

11   *Prosper Homes Ltd v Hambros Bank Executor and Trustee Co Ltd* (1979) 39 P & CR 395. As to a notice to complete see para 121 ante.

179. Rights against third persons. Until the contract is completed[1] by transfer of the legal estate to the purchaser, the vendor continues to be the proper person to enforce any rights in respect of the property which depend on the possession of the legal estate[2]. Subject to ultimate completion, the purchaser's interest ranks as against third persons like any other equitable interest, and it is subject to equities prior in date and, subject to any requirement of registration[3], has priority over subsequent equitable and legal interests, except a legal interest taken for value and without notice of the contract[4]. However, the purchaser is not, in general, entitled to enforce his interest against third persons until he has completed his title by transfer[5], but if he pays his purchase money and takes a transfer of the legal estate without notice of an existing equity, subject to any requirement of registration he gains priority over it[6]. Since 1925 the purchaser has been able to register his contract as an estate contract[7], and from the time he does so, no third person can obtain any interest in the property without notice of the purchaser's rights[8]. A purchaser is under no duty to register a contract for sale[9].

Where the purchaser (A) loses his interest to a subsequent purchaser of the legal estate (B) through the operation of the registration provisions, the vendor holds the purchase money or other property received from (B) on trust for (A)[10].

1   As to the formation of the contract see paras 23–40 ante; and as to the completion of the contract see paras 262–325 post.

2   This rule is sometimes expressed by saying that the doctrine of trusteeship applies only as between the parties to the contract of sale: see note 5 infra. The vendor is the proper person to give notice to quit to a tenant and this applies until the purchase money is paid even though a conveyance is executed before the payment: *Thompson v McCullough* [1947] KB 447, [1947] 1 All ER 265, CA. See generally *Leigh and Sillavan Ltd v Aliakmon Shipping Co Ltd* [1986] AC 785, [1986] 2 All ER 145, HL; *MCC Proceeds Inc v Lehman Bros International (Europe)* [1998] 4 All ER 675, [1998] 2 BCLC 659, CA; and Goode 'Ownership and Obligation in Commercial Transactions' (1987) 103 LQR 433 at 455–458.

     As to the disposition of registered and unregistered land by transfer see para 262 note 2 post.

3   As to the requirement of registration of an interest in land see LAND CHARGES vol 26 (Reissue) para 505; LAND REGISTRATION vol 26 (Reissue) paras 712 et seq, 779 et seq.

4   See EQUITY vol 16 (Reissue) para 786.

5   See *Tasker v Small* (1837) 3 My & Cr 63 at 70–71 per Lord Cottenham LC. The rule that, by a contract of purchase, the purchaser becomes in equity the owner of the property applies only as between the parties to the contract: *Tasker v Small* supra at 70 per Lord Cottenham LC. A conveyance without payment in full of the purchase money operates as an escrow: *Thompson v McCullough* [1947] KB 447, [1947] 1 All ER 265, CA (see note 6 infra). See also *Goodwin v Fielding* (1853) 4 De GM & G 90.

6   Where the conveyance and the payment of the purchase money are not simultaneous it would appear that the purchaser must be without notice both at the date of conveyance and the date of payment,

whichever is later: see *Tildesley v Lodge* (1857) 3 Sm & G 543; and *Wigg v Wigg* (1739) 1 Atk 382. If the purchaser has notice of an equitable mortgage, he must ascertain for himself that it has been discharged. His acquisition of the legal estate is no protection if a receipt tendered by the vendor is a forgery: *Jared v Clements* [1903] 1 Ch 428, CA. If the equitable interest is registered as a land charge, the registration will operate as notice (see para 21 ante; and EQUITY vol 16 (Reissue) para 768; LAND CHARGES vol 26 (Reissue) para 516), but if it is capable of registration and is not registered, it will be void against the purchaser (see LAND CHARGES vol 26 (Reissue) para 543) and the purchaser will not be prejudicially affected by any notice which he may have of its existence (see *Midland Bank Trust Co Ltd v Green* [1981] AC 513, [1981] 1 All ER 153, HL; and EQUITY vol 16 (Reissue) para 774; LAND CHARGES vol 26 (Reissue) para 516).

7   See the Land Charges Act 1972 s 2(4) Class C(iv) (as amended); and LAND CHARGES vol 26 (Reissue) para 528. However, it is not the practice to register an ordinary contract for sale unless completion is to be delayed for a long period, although a solicitor who fails to protect his purchaser client's interest by registering the contract might well be liable in negligence: cf *Midland Bank Trust Co Ltd v Hett, Stubbs and Kemp (a firm)* [1979] Ch 384, [1978] 3 All ER 571, where the solicitor was liable in both contract and tort for failing to register a ten year option to purchase. As to the position in relation to registered land see *Bridges v Mees* [1957] Ch 475, [1957] 2 All ER 577 (contractual purchaser in actual occupation has overriding interest); and LAND REGISTRATION vol 26 (Reissue) para 922.

8   See para 21 ante; and EQUITY vol 16 (Reissue) para 768; LAND CHARGES vol 26 (Reissue) para 516.

9   *Wright v Dean* [1948] Ch 686, [1948] 2 All ER 415; *Hollington Bros Ltd v Rhodes* [1951] 2 All ER 578n, [1951] WN 437.

10   *Lake v Bayliss* [1974] 2 All ER 1114, [1974] 1 WLR 1073.

180. Maintenance of property. Because the vendor, while remaining in possession, is in a sense a trustee for the purchaser[1], he is bound to take reasonable care that the property does not deteriorate between the date of the contract[2] and the time when possession is delivered to the purchaser[3], and even where the delay in completion is due to the purchaser[4], this duty remains binding on the vendor so long as he treats his possession as a security for the purchase money[5].

1   See paras 177–178 ante.
2   As to the formation of the contract see paras 23–40 ante.
3   *Clarke v Ramuz* [1891] 2 QB 456 at 462, CA; *Phillips v Lamdin* [1949] 2 KB 33, [1949] 1 All ER 770 (removal of valuable door; order for replacement). The measure of liability is the same as in the case of any other trustee: *Phillips v Silvester* (1872) 8 Ch App 173 at 177; *Earl of Egmont v Smith, Smith v Earl of Egmont* (1877) 6 ChD 469 at 475; *Royal Bristol Permanent Building Society v Bomash* (1887) 35 ChD 390 at 398 per Kekewich J (see TRUSTS vol 48 (Reissue) para 519). The substitution of a contractual tenant for a statutory tenant has been treated as deterioration: *Reehold Properties Ltd v Peacock* (1955) 165 Estates Gazette 114. See also *Abdulla v Shah* [1959] AC 124, [1959] 2 WLR 12, PC; and para 181 post. The vendor's duty is to make title and to look after the property as it is at the date of the contract, and therefore his duty as trustee does not extend to matters arising before the date of the contract: *Prosper Homes Ltd v Hambros Bank Executor and Trustee Co Ltd* (1979) 39 P & CR 395 at 400. The vendor may be liable for the acts of third parties, if the damage caused is the result of the vendor's failure to take reasonable care: see *Clarke v Ramuz* [1891] 2 QB 456, CA; *Davron Estates Ltd v Turnshire Ltd* (1982) 133 NLJ 937, CA (trespassers); *Royal Bristol Permanent Building Society v Bomash* (1887) 35 ChD 390 (outgoing tenant); and *Ware v Verderber* (1978) 247 Estates Gazette 1081 (furniture removers).
4   As to notice to complete see para 121 ante.
5   *Phillips v Silvester* (1872) 8 Ch App 173: see para 178 ante.

181. Repairs and preservation. In pursuance of his duty to preserve the property from deterioration, the vendor must act in regard to it as a provident beneficial owner[1]. If the property is leasehold, the vendor must perform all the covenants of the lease up to the time when the purchaser should take possession[2]. If the property is freehold, the vendor must keep it in repair so far as this can be done by ordinary expenditure[3]. He must not damage it himself[4], and must prevent its being damaged by trespassers[5], and, in the case of agricultural land, must maintain it in a proper state of management and cultivation[6], and if the tenancy determines before completion he must, if he can, relet the land on a yearly tenancy so as to keep it full[7]. On the other hand, where premises are let at the date of the contract[8] and the tenant subsequently surrenders his tenancy, the vendor must not, without consulting the purchaser, relet the premises on a protected or otherwise disadvantageous tenancy[9].

If damage is caused by the vendor's failure to perform any of these duties, the purchaser is entitled to have the amount of the loss deducted from the purchase money[10] or, if he has completed the purchase, he can recover the amount by way of damages[11].

The maintenance of the property is a current expense which should be paid out of the rents and profits, and it is borne by the vendor so long as he is entitled to receive the rents and profits for his own benefit[12]. After that time it must be borne by the purchaser[13].

1   *Wilson v Clapham* (1819) 1 Jac & W 36 at 38; *Sherwin v Shakspear* (1854) 5 De GM & G 517 at 537. Cf *Krehl v Park* (1874) 31 LT 325.

2   See *Palmer v Goren* (1856) 25 LJ Ch 841; *Dowson v Solomon* (1859) 1 Drew & Sm 1 at 10–11; *Newman v Maxwell* (1899) 80 LT 681. A breach of the covenant to repair is a defect of title: *Re Highett and Bird's Contract* [1902] 2 Ch 214 at 215; affd [1903] 1 Ch 287, CA. See also *Re Edie and Brown's Contract* (1888) 58 LT 307; *Re Lyne-Stephens and Scott-Miller's Contract* [1920] 1 Ch 472. Where purchasers contracted to take leaseholds in their existing state of disrepair the purchasers were held to have assumed liability for, and to agree to indemnify the vendor against, the cost of subsequent repairs: *Lockharts v Bernard Rosen & Co* [1922] 1 Ch 433; and see *Butler v Mountview Estates Ltd* [1951] 2 KB 563, [1951] 1 All ER 693. As to conditions of sale intended to protect the vendor see para 99 ante.

3   *Ferguson v Tadman* (1827) 1 Sim 530; *Regent's Canal Co v Ware* (1857) 23 Beav 575 at 588; *Royal Bristol Permanent Building Society v Bomash* (1887) 35 ChD 390 at 397.

4   *Phillips v Lamdin* [1949] 2 KB 33, [1949] 1 All ER 770 (replacement of Adam door by one of plain wood); *Lucie-Smith v Gorman* [1981] CLY 2866 (vacating house in mid–winter without turning off water supply).

5   *Royal Bristol Permanent Building Society v Bomash* (1887) 35 ChD 390 at 398; *Clarke v Ramuz* [1891] 2 QB 456, CA. Cf *Cedar Transport Group Ltd v First Wyvern Property Trustees Co Ltd* (1980) 258 Estates Gazette 1077 (on sale of empty warehouse, vendor's duty discharged by putting property in care of architects and builders).

6   *Foster v Deacon* (1818) 3 Madd 394; *Lord v Stephens* (1835) 1 Y & C Ex 222.

7   *Phillips v Silvester* (1872) 8 Ch App 173; *Earl of Egmont v Smith, Smith v Earl of Egmont* (1877) 6 ChD 469 at 475; *Raffety v Schofield* [1897] 1 Ch 937 at 944. See also para 191 note 3 post.

8   As to the formation of the contract see paras 23–40 ante.

9   *Abdulla v Shah* [1959] AC 124, [1959] 2 WLR 12, PC. Where premises are sold subject to an existing lease, the vendor may owe a duty to the purchaser to remedy a breach of covenant committed by the lessee after the date of the contract: *Prosper Homes Ltd v Hambros Bank Executor and Trustee Co Ltd* (1979) 39 P & CR 395.

10   For a form of order directing such deduction see Seton's Form of Decrees, Judgments and Orders in Equity (7th Edn, 1912) 2174.

11   *Clarke v Ramuz* [1891] 2 QB 456, CA.

12   As to the right to rents and profits see paras 188–193 post.

13   The rule in this respect is the same as that with regard to outgoings generally: see para 193 post. As to damages generally see DAMAGES.

182. Improvements. Where an extraordinary outlay in permanent repairs is necessary for the preservation of the property, the vendor is apparently entitled to be allowed as against the purchaser the amount so expended[1]. The vendor's duty in respect of the property does not extend to making improvements, for instance in expending money in building or in obtaining a renewal of a lease, and he cannot recover from the purchaser money so spent[2].

1   See *Sherwin v Shakspear* (1854) 5 De GM & G 517 at 532; *Phillips v Silvester* (1872) 8 Ch App 173 at 176; *Bolton Partners v Lambert* (1888) 41 ChD 295 (on appeal (1889) 41 ChD 302, CA).

2   *Monro v Taylor* (1848) 8 Hare 51 at 60; cf *Master etc of Clare Hall v Harding* (1848) 6 Hare 273 at 296.

(ii) Particular Rights and Liabilities

183. Vendor's rights and duties. Pending the completion of the contract[1], the rights of the vendor consist generally in (1) the right to retain possession until the purchase money has been paid[2]; (2) a lien on the property for the amount of the unpaid purchase money[3]; (3) a right until the proper time for completion to receive the rents and profits for his own benefit[4] and sums paid in respect of dilapidations on the expiry of a lease or a requisition[5]; and (4) a right after the proper time for completion, to interest on the unpaid purchase money until payment[6]. However, the vendor must preserve the property from deterioration and must pay the current outgoings[7].

1   As to the formation of the contract see paras 23–40 ante; and as to the completion of the contract see paras 262–325 post.
2   See paras 185–186 post.
3   See para 187 post. As to the meaning of 'rents and profits' see para 189 post.
4   See para 188 post.
5   See para 192 post.
6   See paras 194, 197 post.
7   See paras 180–181 ante, 193 post.

184. Purchaser's risk and rights. Subject to the vendor's duty to take reasonable care to prevent the deterioration of the property[1], the property is at the risk of the purchaser[2]. The circumstances in which the purchaser may be entitled to the benefit of payments under any insurance policy effected by the vendor have already been mentioned[3]. The purchaser is entitled to any accretion to the value of the property[4]. From the proper time for completion[5] he is entitled to be credited with rents and profits, and is liable to be charged with outgoings[6]. If he has paid the purchase money or any part of it, and the purchase ultimately goes off without his default, he is entitled to a lien on the land for the amount which he has paid[7].

1   See paras 180–181 ante.
2   *White v Nutts* (1702) 1 P Wms 61; *Paine v Meller* (1801) 6 Ves 349 at 352; *Harford v Purrier* (1816) 1 Madd 532 at 539; *Acland v Cuming, Gaisford v Acland* (1816) 2 Madd 28 at 32. See also *Amalgamated Investment and Property Co Ltd v John Walker & Sons Ltd* [1976] 3 All ER 509, [1977] 1 WLR 164, CA (post-contractual listing of buildings as of special historic interest no defence to specific performance); cf para 248 note 7 post. Where an accident to the premises brings with it a legal obligation which must be satisfied immediately, eg when the premises fall down and injure adjoining property, the case falls within the same principle and the expense must be borne by the purchaser: *Robertson v Skelton* (1849) 12 Beav 260.
3   See paras 117–118 ante.
4   *Vesey v Elwood* (1842) 3 Dr & War 74 at 79. Thus if an interest for life is sold and the tenant for life dies before completion, the loss falls on the purchaser, but if it is a reversion that is sold, the benefit belongs to the purchaser: *White v Nutts* (1702) 1 P Wms 61; *Ex p Manning* (1727) 2 P Wms 410. If after the contract the estate is improved in the interval, or if the value is lessened by the failure of tenants or otherwise, and there is no fault on either side, the purchaser has the benefit or sustains the loss: *Harford v Purrier* (1816) 1 Madd 532 at 539. Similarly, the purchaser has the benefit of any unexpected diminution in the value of the consideration, where, for example, part of the consideration is an annuity on the vendor's life and the vendor dies immediately after the contract: *Mortimer v Capper* (1782) 1 Bro CC 156. See also 1 Dart's Law relating to Vendors and Purchasers (8th Edn, 1929) 269.
5   As to completion see paras 262–325 post.
6   See paras 188–193 post.
7   As to the purchaser's lien see *Hick v Phillips* (1721) Prec Ch 575; *Lee-Parker v Izzet* [1971] 3 All ER 1099, [1971] 1 WLR 1688; and LIEN vol 28 (Reissue) para 763 et seq. Unless the purchaser has custody of the title deeds, the lien is registrable under the Land Charges Act 1972 s 2(4) Class C(iii) (as amended): see paras 128 ante, 187 post; and LAND CHARGES vol 26 (Reissue) para 531. The lien extends to the costs of investigating title: *Kitton v Hewett* [1904] WN 21; *Re Furneaux and Aird's Contract* [1906] WN 215.

(iii) Possession and the Vendor's Lien

185. Material dates for completion of the contract. Three dates are material in regard to the completion of the contract[1]: (1) the date, if any, fixed by the contract for completion; (2) the date when the vendor shows and verifies such a title as the purchaser can require; and (3) the date of actual completion. In the ordinary course, completion consists of the purchaser paying the purchase money, or the balance[2], and the vendor at the same time executing a transfer and delivering possession to the purchaser[3]. When these incidents are separated, the construction to be put upon a reference in the contract to the date for completion depends upon the terms and subject matter of the contract, although it seems that the reference is as a general rule to be taken to be a reference to the complete transfer of the estate and the final settlement of the business[4].

The completion of the contract is conditional on the vendor making out his title[5]. Until the vendor makes out his title, the purchaser is not safe in paying the purchase money and taking possession[6]. Hence the date when the vendor makes out his title is the earliest date at which completion should take place, and it is the proper date for completion if no date is fixed by the contract[7].

If the contract fixes a date for completion, this is the proper date, and if this stipulation is of the essence of the contract[8], the vendor must make out his title by that date, otherwise the purchaser cannot be required to complete either then or subsequently[9]. If it is not of the essence of the contract, and the title has not then been made out, the purchaser can be required to complete as soon as the title has been made out. In case of undue delay, either party may fix a reasonable time for completion, and this time then becomes of the essence of the contract[10].

1   As to the formation of the contract see paras 23–40 ante; and as to the completion of the contract see paras 262–325 post.

2   There will usually be an adjustment for outgoings etc: see para 2 note 8 ante.

3   In addition, the purchaser must, in virtually all cases of a sale of a legal estate, apply to become the registered proprietor of that estate, whether as the first registered proprietor (see the Land Registration Act 1925 ss 123 (as substituted), 123A (as added); and LAND REGISTRATION vol 26 (Reissue) paras 727, 1196 et seq) or as the new registered proprietor of an already registered estate (see ss 19, 22 (both as amended); and LAND REGISTRATION vol 26 (Reissue) paras 911, 918). The exceptions are that first registration is not required on: (1) the grant of a lease not exceeding 21 years; (2) the assignment of a lease which does not have more than 21 years to run; or (3) a first legal mortgage supported by a deposit of the documents of title of a lease which does not have more than 21 years to run: see s 123(1), (2) (s 123 as substituted); and LAND REGISTRATION vol 26 (Reissue) para 1196 et seq. Where the title is already registered, the only exception is the grant of a lease for a term not exceeding 21 years, or the assignment of such a lease (or a sublease derived out of it); such leases are overriding interests within s 70(1)(k) (as substituted) (see LAND REGISTRATION vol 26 (Reissue) para 784): see ss 19, 22 (both as amended); and LAND REGISTRATION vol 26 (Reissue) paras 911, 918.

    On a sale or other disposition of registered land to a purchaser other than a lessee or chargee, where the vendor is not himself registered as proprietor of the land or the charge giving a power of sale over the land, he must, at the request of the purchaser and at his own expense, and notwithstanding any stipulation to the contrary (ie in the conditions of sale), either procure the registration of himself as proprietor of the land or of the charge, as the case may be, or procure a disposition from the registered proprietor to the purchaser: s 110(5). Where, under the conditions of sale, the purchaser accepts the title before making a request under s 110(5), but then refuses to complete, the vendor is entitled to rescind the contract and forfeit the deposit: *Urban Manor Ltd v Sadiq* [1997] 1 WLR 1016, CA. As to other conveyancing problems that may be created by the 'registration gap' (ie the interval between completion and registration) see *Brown & Root Technology Ltd v Sun Alliance & London Assurance Co Ltd* (1996) 75 P & CR 223, CA; cf *Pinekerry Ltd v Kenneth Needs Contractors Ltd* (1992) 64 P & CR 245, CA; *Abbey National Building Society v Cann* [1991] 1 AC 56, [1990] 1 All ER 1085, HL (closing the 'gap' with regard to overriding interests under the Land Registration Act 1925 s 70(1)(g)). As to the date of completion see para 120 ante. As to the disposition of registered and unregistered land by transfer see para 262 note 2 post.

4   See *Killner v France* [1946] 2 All ER 83, 175 LT 377, where the purchase money was paid and the purchaser let into possession, but the property was destroyed by enemy action before the date fixed by

the contract for completion, and it was held that there was no completion and the purchaser was entitled to rescind. *Killner v France* supra approved a dictum in *Lewis v South Wales Rly Co* (1852) 10 Hare 113 at 119, where, however, in the circumstances of the case the reference was held to be to the payment of the purchase money. See also paras 179 note 6 ante, 262 post.

5   *Doe d Gray v Stanion* (1836) 1 M & W 695 at 701; and see para 137 ante.

6   *Binks v Lord Rokeby* (1818) 2 Swan 222 at 225; *Wilson v Clapham* (1819) 1 Jac & W 36 at 37. As to provisions in the conditions of sale see para 124 ante.

7   See 1 Williams Law relating to Vendors and Purchasers of Real Estate and Chattels Real (4th Edn, 1936) 29. Where no date is fixed completion must be within a reasonable time (see *Simpson v Hughes* (1897) 66 LJ Ch 334, CA; *Nosotti v Auerbach* (1898) 79 LT 413 (affd (1899) 15 TLR 140, CA)), but as soon as the vendor has made out his title the purchaser should be ready to complete (see para 120 ante). As to possession upon a sale under order of the court, where no date is fixed see 2 Dart's Law relating to Vendors and Purchasers (8th Edn, 1929) 1000. Where completion was to take place on possession being given and it was stated orally that the vendor would not give possession until other accommodation was obtained, there was no enforceable contract; it could not be implied that possession must be given, and therefore completion take place, in a reasonable time: *Johnson v Humphrey* [1946] 1 All ER 460, 90 Sol Jo 211.

8   Ie if it is made so by the express terms of the contract, the nature of the property or the surrounding circumstances: see para 120 note 2 ante.

9   *Tilley v Thomas* (1867) 3 Ch App 61; *Lock v Bell* [1931] 1 Ch 35. As to the effect of non-completion on the day fixed on the liability to pay interest see paras 122 ante, 194 et seq post.

10 *Stickney v Keeble* [1915] AC 386 at 418, HL. See also para 120 ante. As to provisions in the standard conditions of sale for service of a notice to complete see para 122 ante.

186. Time for transfer of possession.

The contract[1] may contain express provision showing that possession is to be given at a fixed date, even if the sale is not then otherwise completed[2]. Under such a provision the vendor may be required to give possession before the purchase money is paid[3], or the purchaser to take possession before the vendor has made out his title[4]. Otherwise either party can insist on delivery of possession being treated as part of the completion of the contract[5], and, in particular, the vendor is entitled to the actual possession of the property or the actual receipt of rents and profits[6] until the whole of the purchase money has been paid[7].

1   As to the formation of the contract see paras 23–40 ante.

2   *Tilley v Thomas* (1867) 3 Ch App 61 at 66. As to occupation before completion see para 119 ante.

3   *Gedye v Duke of Montrose* (1858) 26 Beav 45.

4   See *Tilley v Thomas* (1867) 3 Ch App 61 at 66. Ordinarily, where possession is to be given at a specified date, this means that the vendor must then have shown such a title that possession can safely be taken: *Tilley v Thomas* supra at 66; and see *Boehm v Wood* (1820) 1 Jac & W 419. These matters are generally the subject of a special condition: see para 119 ante.

5   As to the completion of the contract see paras 262–325 post.

6   As to right of possession or to rents and profits see para 188 post; and as to the meaning of 'rents and profits' see para 189 post.

7   *Acland v Cuming, Gaisford v Acland* (1816) 2 Madd 28. As to the payment of interest on failure to complete on the day fixed for completion see paras 122 ante, 194 et seq post. As to what constitutes possession see REAL PROPERTY vol 39(2) (Reissue) para 167; and cf PERSONAL PROPERTY vol 35 (Reissue) para 1211. As to the meaning of 'vacant possession' see para 123 ante; and as to the possibility that more importance may be attached to vacant possession at a time of housing shortage, cf *Johnson v Humphrey* [1946] 1 All ER 460 at 463.

187. Vendor's lien.

The vendor's right to receive the purchase money is secured, first, by a lien upon the property[1], and secondly, by his right, in the absence of express stipulation as to the time of delivering possession, to retain possession until the purchase money is paid[2]. The vendor's lien is a legal lien on the land and the title deeds or land certificate while in his possession, and in equity the lien subsists until actual payment[3]. In the case of unregistered land, the equitable lien is registrable under the Land Charges Act 1972, unless, presumably, the vendor retains custody of the title deeds[4]. In the case of registered land, the lien should be protected by an entry on the register, unless the vendor is in actual occupation, when the lien constitutes an overriding interest[5]. The lien exists whether the consideration is a sum in gross, an annuity for the vendor's life or a sum payable by instalments[6], but no lien arises in favour of a vendor who agrees to sell in consideration of a life annuity to be secured by bond[7] or where the consideration is otherwise secured[8]. The vendor's lien is a charge upon the property subject to which a beneficiary under a will takes a property under a contract for sale uncompleted at the death of the testator[9].

A person other than the purchaser who pays or provides the purchase money or any part of it may become entitled by subrogation to the vendor's lien[10]. This right arises only where it is the common intention of the purchaser and the third person that the money is used to pay the unpaid vendor[11]. The lien by subrogation is not available where the money is provided by a mortgage[12], or where it is established that the true nature of the advance by the other person is merely an unsecured loan[13].

1   See LIEN vol 28 (Reissue) para 758 et seq. As to the date when the vendor's right to receive the purchase money accrues for the purposes of the rules on limitation of actions see the Limitation Act 1980 s 20(1); and cf LIMITATION OF ACTIONS vol 28 (Reissue) para 1009.

2   *Lysaght v Edwards* (1876) 2 ChD 499 at 506.

3   See LIEN vol 28 (Reissue) para 758.

4   See the Land Charges Act 1972 s 2(4) Class C(iii) (as amended); and LAND CHARGES vol 26 (Reissue) para 531. The lien is not registrable under the Companies Act 1985 s 395 (as amended) (see COMPANIES vol 7(2) (1996 Reissue) para 1299): see *London and Cheshire Insurance Co Ltd v Laplagrene Property Co Ltd* [1971] Ch 499, [1971] 1 All ER 766. See LIEN vol 28 (Reissue) para 759.

5   See *London and Cheshire Insurance Co Ltd v Laplagrene Property Co Ltd* [1971] Ch 499, [1971] 1 All ER 766; *Barclays Bank plc v Estates & Commercial Ltd* [1997] 1 WLR 415, 74 P & CR 30, CA; *UCB Bank plc v Beasley and French* [1995] NPC 144, CA; *Nationwide Anglia Building Society v Ahmed* (1995) 70 P & CR 381, CA. As to registered land generally see LAND REGISTRATION.

6   See LIEN vol 28 (Reissue) para 758.

7   *Dixon v Gayfere* (1857) 1 De G & J 655. Where land was agreed to be sold to a company in consideration of a rentcharge and before conveyance the rentcharge fell into arrear, the vendor had no lien on the land for the arrears: *Earl of Jersey v Briton Ferry Floating Dock Co* (1869) LR 7 Eq 409. On the other hand, where after conveyance the rentcharge fell into arrear, the vendor was allowed, notwithstanding the appointment of a receiver of the tolls, profits and income of the undertaking, to distrain for the arrears upon the land, both where a power to distrain was expressly given by the conveyance (*Eyton v Denbigh, Ruthin and Corwen Rly Co* (1868) LR 6 Eq 14), and where it arose under the Landlord and Tenant Act 1730 s 5 (*Eyton v Denbigh, Ruthin and Corwen Rly Co, Rickman v Johns* (1868) LR 6 Eq 488). As to the power of distress conferred by the Landlord and Tenant Act 1730 see RENTCHARGES AND ANNUITIES vol 39(2) (Reissue) paras 865, 870.

8   For a review of the authorities see *Barclays Bank plc v Estates & Commercial Ltd* [1997] 1 WLR 415 at 419–424, 74 P & CR 30 at 34–39, CA, per Millett LJ; and LIEN vol 28 (Reissue) para 783.

9   *Re Birmingham, Savage v Stannard* [1959] Ch 523, [1958] 2 All ER 397.

10   See eg *Boodle Hatfield & Co (a firm) v British Films Ltd* [1986] FLR 134, (1986) 136 NLJ 117; *Boscawen v Bajwa* [1995] 4 All ER 769, [1996] 1 WLR 328, CA; *Banque Financière de la Cité v Parc (Battersea) Ltd* [1998] 1 All ER 737, [1998] 2 WLR 475, HL; and LIEN vol 28 (Reissue) para 773.

11   *Orakpo v Manson Investments Ltd* [1978] AC 95, [1977] 3 All ER 1, HL.

12   *Burston Finance Ltd v Speirway Ltd* [1974] 3 All ER 735, [1974] 1 WLR 1648, disapproving *Coptic Ltd v Bailey* [1972] Ch 446, [1972] 1 All ER 1242.

13   *Paul v Speirway Ltd (in liquidation)* [1976] Ch 220, [1976] 2 All ER 587.

(iv) Rents, Profits, Receipts and Outgoings

188. Right to possession or to rents and profits. Although the vendor is entitled to possession or to receipt of rents and profits[1] until payment of the purchase money, his beneficial title does not extend beyond the time when completion ought to take place, that is, if no day is fixed for completion, the time when he first makes out his title, or, if a day is fixed for completion, then the day so fixed[2]. Until the proper time for completion, he occupies the property or receives the rents and profits for his own benefit[3]; after that time they belong to the purchaser[4], and the vendor receives them until actual completion as trustee for the purchaser and must account to him accordingly[5]. If the vendor is in occupation, he may be charged with an occupation rent[6].

1   As to the meaning of 'rents and profits' see para 189 post.
2   As to the date for completion see paras 120, 185 ante; and as to the completion of the contract see paras 262–325 post.
3   *Garrick v Earl Camden* (1790) 2 Cox Eq Cas 231; *Cuddon v Tite* (1858) 1 Giff 395. On his death before the day for completion the intermediate rents formerly went to his heir or devisee (*Lumsden v Fraser* (1841) 12 Sim 263; and see *Watts v Watts* (1873) LR 17 Eq 217), but subject to the rights of his personal representatives.
4   *Paine v Meller* (1801) 6 Ves 349 at 352; *Monro v Taylor* (1848) 8 Hare 51 at 70 (affd (1852) 3 Mac & G 713); *De Visme v De Visme* (1849) 1 Mac & G 336 at 346; *Plews v Samuel* [1904] 1 Ch 464 at 468.
5   *M'Namara v Williams* (1801) 6 Ves 143; *Wilson v Clapham* (1819) 1 Jac & W 36; *Plews v Samuel* [1904] 1 Ch 464 at 468. The vendor is not entitled to retain rents received by him after the date for completion in satisfaction of rents accrued due before that date: *Plews v Samuel* supra. Where, on a sale of a business as a going concern, completion is delayed owing to the purchaser's default, the vendor is entitled to carry on the business at the purchaser's risk, but he must inform the purchaser of what he is doing: *Golden Bread Co Ltd v Hemmings* [1922] 1 Ch 162.
6   See para 191 post.

189. Meaning of 'rents and profits'. For the purpose of the rule as to the right to receive rents and profits[1], the rents and profits of the land include the rents of the land, and also all the profits accruing from the use or working of the land in the state in which it exists at the date of the contract[2]. Thus, if it is agricultural land, the vendor, as long as he is entitled to the profits, can get in and dispose of the crops in a proper course of husbandry and retain the proceeds for his own benefit[3]. If the land has an open mine or quarry upon it, the vendor, if the mine is let, takes the rents and royalties accruing due during the same period, notwithstanding that they represent part of the substance of the land, and, if it is not let but is being worked, he takes, apparently, for his own benefit the proceeds of working[4].

However, the vendor is not entitled to take under the guise of profits what is in fact part of the inheritance, and the purchaser may obtain an injunction to prevent him doing anything likely to destroy or depreciate the property sold or to prevent the property being assured to the purchaser[5], although where the vendor disputes the existence of an enforceable contract for sale such an injunction will not be granted unless the balance of convenience requires it[6].

1   As to this rule see paras 188 ante, 190 post.
2   As to the formation of the contract see paras 23–40 ante; and as to the completion of the contract see paras 262–325 post.
3   See *Webster v Donaldson* (1865) 34 Beav 451.
4   *Leppington v Freeman* (1891) 66 LT 357, CA. In this respect the vendor and purchaser appear to be in the same position as lessor and lessee, or tenant for life impeachable for waste and remainderman: *Leppington v Freeman* supra; and see 1 Williams Law relating to Vendors and Purchasers of Real Estate and Chattels Real (4th Edn, 1936) 548. Cf *Nelson v Bridges* (1839) 2 Beav 239, where a purchaser who had been let into possession of quarries and was wrongfully evicted by the vendor was entitled to the proceeds of the quarries from the time of his first possession. As to mining royalties see MINES, MINERALS AND QUARRIES vol 31 (Reissue) para 367. On the sale of a manor the vendor took fines accruing due on admittances before the proper day for completion (*Cuddon v Tite* (1858) 1 Giff 395), and, perhaps, where the event causing the change of tenant was prior to the day for completion, even though the admittance was after that day (*Garrick v Earl Camden* (1790) 2 Cox Eq Cas 231): see 1 Williams Law relating to Vendors and Purchasers of Real Estate and Chattels Real (4th Edn, 1936) 557 note (m).
5   *Spiller v Spiller* (1819) 3 Swan 556, explained in *Hadley v London Bank of Scotland Ltd* (1865) 3 De GJ & Sm 63 at 70–71 per Turner LJ. See also *Echliff v Baldwin* (1809) 16 Ves 267; *Curtis v Marquis of Buckingham* (1814) 3 Ves & B 168; *Shrewsbury and Chester Rly Co v Shrewsbury and Birmingham Rly Co* (1851) 15 Jur 548 at 550; *London and County Banking Co v Lewis* (1882) 21 ChD 490, CA; *Phillips v Lamdin* [1949] 2

KB 33, [1949] 1 All ER 770 (order for restoration of property). As to the destruction of ornamental timber see *Magennis v Fallon* (1828) 2 Mol 561 at 590 (repudiation where material alteration in the property sold).

6   *Turner v Wight* (1841) 4 Beav 40; *Hadley v London Bank of Scotland Ltd* (1865) 3 De GJ & Sm 63 at 70–71. See also INJUNCTIONS vol 24 (Reissue) para 920.

190. Rights of purchaser in possession. If the purchaser is let into possession before the proper time for completion[1], then, unless the contract otherwise provides, he is entitled to the rents and profits[2] from the time of taking possession[3], he is entitled to do all acts ordinarily incident to an estate in possession, and is entitled to gather crops or cut underwood in a proper course of husbandry in the same way as a tenant for life[4]. As, however, the vendor is still entitled to a lien on the estate for his purchase money[5], the purchaser may not do any acts which tend to depreciate the vendor's security for his money, such as cutting timber or otherwise committing waste[6], and, except where the amount of depreciation threatened leaves the vendor with an adequate security for the amount unpaid, he may obtain an injunction to restrain such acts[7].

1   As to occupation before completion see para 119 ante.
2   As to the meaning of 'rents and profits' see para 189 ante.
3   *Powell v Martyr* (1803) 8 Ves 146 at 148; *Fludyer v Cocker* (1805) 12 Ves 25; *A-G v Dean and Chapter of Christ-Church, Oxford, ex p Maddock* (1842) 13 Sim 214; *Birch v Joy* (1852) 3 HL Cas 565 at 591; *Ballard v Shutt* (1880) 15 ChD 122, where the purchaser was held liable for interest from the date when he exercised certain acts of ownership over the land, although under the circumstances there were no rents and profits received by him; *Leppington v Freeman* (1891) 66 LT 357, CA; *Fletcher v Lancashire and Yorkshire Rly Co* [1902] 1 Ch 901 at 908.
4   *Burroughs v Oakley* (1819) 3 Swan 159 at 170; cf *Poole v Shergold* (1786) 1 Cox Eq Cas 273. See also SETTLEMENTS para 986 post.
5   See *Smith v Hibbard* (1789) 2 Dick 730; *Ecclesiastical Comrs v Pinney* [1899] 2 Ch 729 at 735; and para 187 ante.
6   *Crockford v Alexander* (1808) 15 Ves 138, where it was said that the vendor is in the situation of an equitable mortgagee. As to waste see INJUNCTIONS vol 24 (Reissue) paras 890–892; LANDLORD AND TENANT vol 27(1) (Reissue) paras 345–349; SETTLEMENTS para 986 et seq post.
7   See *Humphreys v Harrison* (1820) 1 Jac & W 581; *Hippesley v Spencer* (1820) 5 Madd 422; *King v Smith* (1843) 2 Hare 239. These cases were all between mortgagee and mortgagor in possession. As to injunctions generally see INJUNCTIONS.

191. Rents and profits to be taken into account. Under the ordinary judgment requiring a vendor to account for rents and profits[1] from the proper time for completion[2], he is chargeable only with rents and profits actually received by him or by other persons for his use[3]. However, if it is proved that rents and profits have not been received owing to neglect or improper conduct on the part of the vendor, the order is that he must account for rents and profits received or which, but for his wilful neglect or default, might have been received by him[4].

If it appears that he has been in occupation of the property, a direction may be given that he is to be charged with an occupation rent[5]. An occupation rent is usually allowed if the possession has been beneficial to the vendor[6], but not if the vendor has against his own wish been compelled to remain in possession of business premises[7].

1   As to the meaning of 'rents and profits' see para 189 ante.
2   As to the time for completion see paras 120, 185 ante.
3   *Howell v Howell* (1837) 2 My & Cr 478 at 486. See the form of judgment in 3 Seton's Form of Decrees, Judgments and Orders in Equity (7th Edn, 1912) 2170. This is the usual form in cases of account of rents and profits except as against a mortgagee in possession, who is always charged on the footing of wilful default (see MORTGAGE), and a trustee against whom a breach of trust is proved (see TRUSTS vol 48 (Reissue) para 960). An unpaid vendor, since he has a lien on the land, is in a position analogous to that of a mortgagee in possession, but it seems that he is not, merely on that ground, chargeable on the footing of wilful default: *Sherwin v Shakspear* (1854) 5 De GM & G 517 at 531–532; *Regent's Canal Co v Ware*

(1857) 23 Beav 575 at 588. In *Phillips v Silvester* (1872) 8 Ch App 173, which seems to lay down a contrary rule, there was in fact wilful default: see EQUITY vol 16 (Reissue) paras 693, 785. A vendor of a farm is charged with the proceeds of crops actually realised, subject to deduction of expenses of realisation, but under the ordinary judgment he is not allowed losses incurred in farming: *Bennett v Stone* [1902] 1 Ch 226; affd [1903] 1 Ch 509, CA.

4   *Howell v Howell* (1837) 2 My & Cr 478. See 3 Seton's Form of Decrees, Judgments and Orders in Equity (7th Edn, 1912) 2173. This is done, for instance, where the vendor has, by his neglect, allowed the rents to fall into arrear (see *Wilson v Clapham* (1819) 1 Jac & W 36; and *Acland v Cuming, Gaisford v Acland* (1816) 2 Madd 28, where the account was specifically directed to arrears of rent), or, apparently, where he omits, without the purchaser's assent, to relet on a yearly tenancy agricultural land which falls vacant before completion (see *Earl of Egmont v Smith, Smith v Earl of Egmont* (1877) 6 ChD 469). The fact that the vendor, in common with other landowners in the neighbourhood, has reduced the rents, there being nothing to show that this was not done in the ordinary course of management by a prudent owner, is, however, not a ground for an order to account on the footing of wilful default (*Sherwin v Shakspear* (1854) 5 De GM & G 517); nor is it wilful default to allow a tenant to continue at a low rent when the purchaser has not required him to be turned out (*Crosse v Duke of Beaufort* (1851) 5 De G & Sm 7).

5   See 3 Seton's Form of Decrees, Judgments and Orders in Equity (7th Edn, 1912) 2178; and *Dyer v Hargrave, Hargrave v Dyer* (1805) 10 Ves 505 at 511. In order to charge the vendor with an occupation rent the judgment must be specially framed (see *Bennett v Stone* [1902] 1 Ch 226 at 237, where it was stated that an occupation rent might be charged under a decree on the footing of wilful default), but wilful default is not appropriate to the case of a vendor continuing in occupation, and the judgment should specially refer to that circumstance (see *Sherwin v Shakspear* (1854) 5 De GM & G 517 at 539; *Krehl v Park* (1874) 31 LT 325).

6   *Sherwin v Shakspear* (1854) 5 De GM & G 517; *Metropolitan Rly Co v Defries* (1877) 2 QBD 189 (on appeal (1877) 2 QBD 387); *Halkett v Earl of Dudley* [1907] 1 Ch 590.

7   *Leggott v Metropolitan Rly Co* (1870) 5 Ch App 716.

192. Payments accruing due between contract and completion. Where land is sold subject to a lease which terminates at a date between contract and completion or even on the date fixed for completion[1], and the sale is with vacant possession, the vendor is entitled to any sum paid in respect of dilapidations at the end of the term[2]. The same rule applied where between the date of contract and completion property was requisitioned[3] and a payment was made in respect of damage during the requisition[4].

1   As to the formation of the contract see paras 23–40 ante; as to the completion of the contract see paras 262–325 post. As to the date of completion see paras 120, 185 ante.

2   *Re Lyne-Stephens and Scott-Miller's Contract* [1920] 1 Ch 472, CA. The position may be different if the sale is subject to and with the benefit of the lease: *Re Lyne-Stephens and Scott-Miller's Contract* supra at 486.

3   See COMPULSORY ACQUISITION OF LAND vol 8(1) (Reissue) para 1; and WAR AND ARMED CONFLICT vol 49(1) (Reissue) para 601. As to requisitions see paras 102–108 ante.

4   *Re Hamilton-Snowball's Conveyance* [1959] Ch 308, [1958] 2 All ER 319. Cf *Re Armitage's Contract, Armitage v Inkpen* [1949] Ch 666, [1949] LJR 1511, where the matter was subject to a special condition. As to special conditions see paras 76–77 ante.

193. Vendor's liability for outgoings. In a formal contract it is usually provided that the vendor is to pay all the outgoings until the day fixed for completion, and that for this purpose all necessary apportionments are to be made[1]. In the absence of any such stipulation the vendor must, for the period during which he is entitled to take the rents and profits for his own benefit[2], bear all outgoings[3], and of those which are current at the end of the period and are legally apportionable he bears the part attributable to the period[4].

1   For the meaning of 'outgoings' see para 125 ante. As to apportionment see para 125 et seq ante. As to the formation of the contract see paras 23–40 ante; and as to the completion of the contract see paras 262–325 post. As to the date of completion see paras 120, 185 ante.

2   Ie until the proper date for completion: see para 185 ante. As to the meaning of 'rents and profits' see para 189 ante.

3   *Carrodus v Sharp* (1855) 20 Beav 56. See also *Golden Bread Co Ltd v Hemmings* [1922] 1 Ch 162. As to a vendor's liability for war damage contributions under the legislation subsequently embodied in the War Damage Act 1943 ss 36, 39, 45, 66 (all repealed) see *Re Jacobs' and Stedman's Contract* [1942] Ch 400, [1942] 2 All ER 104; *Re Watford Corpn's and Ware's Contract* [1943] Ch 82, [1943] 1 All ER 54, where the purchase price was payable by instalments; and para 128 ante. As to the wartime emergency legislation see WAR AND ARMED CONFLICT vol 49(1) (Reissue) para 597 et seq.

4   See para 124 note 2 ante.

(v) Interest on Purchase Money

194. Vendor's right to interest. As a general rule, as soon as the vendor ceases to be entitled to receive the rents and profits[1] for his own benefit, he becomes entitled to interest on the unpaid purchase money until actual payment[2]. The right to interest may be either an implied or an express term of the contract[3].

1   As to the meaning of 'rents and profits' see para 189 ante.

2   See *Burton v Todd, Todd v Gee* (1818) 1 Swan 255 at 260; *Leggott v Metropolitan Rly Co* (1870) 5 Ch App 716 at 719; *Toronto City Corpn v Toronto Rly Corpn* [1925] AC 177, PC (compulsory purchase). The rule applies generally, and is not confined to the sale of land: *International Rly Co v Niagara Parks Commission* [1941] AC 328 at 344–345, [1941] 2 All ER 456 at 463–464, PC. Interest is not payable on the deposit: *Bridges v Robinson* (1811) 3 Mer 694. The purchaser, however, pays interest on purchase money which he retains to meet incumbrances: *Hughes v Kearney* (1803) 1 Sch & Lef 132 at 134.

3   As to the case where the right to interest is an express term of the contract or conditions of sale see para 122 ante; and as to the contents of the written contract see para 34 ante.

195. Interest when time for completion is not fixed. Where the contract is silent as to the time for completion and payment of interest, interest is payable from the time when the vendor has so made out his title that the purchaser could safely take possession[1]. When the title is proved in an action for specific performance, interest runs from the date of the master's order that a good title has been made out[2]. The rate of interest formerly allowed was 4 per cent per annum[3], but it now seems that more realistic rates will be awarded[4]. These principles also apply in the case of land acquired compulsorily under statutory powers, and interest at the appropriate rate is normally payable from the date when the vendor makes out his title[5], but not before the purchase money has been ascertained[6]. Where an acquiring authority is entitled to enter on the land before completion[7], interest runs from the date of entry[8], at a rate prescribed by statutory regulations[9].

If the purchaser is let into possession, either immediately at the date of the contract or subsequently, interest begins to run on the unpaid purchase money from the time of possession, unless otherwise agreed[10]. If he is already in possession as tenant, it runs from the date of the contract, and he is from that date entitled to the rents and profits[11].

1   *Carrodus v Sharp* (1855) 20 Beav 56 at 58; *Wells v Maxwell (No 2)* (1863) 32 Beav 550; *Re Pigott and Great Western Rly Co* (1881) 18 ChD 146 at 150; *Re Keeble and Stillwell's Fletton Brick Co* (1898) 78 LT 383 at 384. See also *Binks v Lord Rokeby* (1818) 2 Swan 222 at 226. As to the payment of interest where the contract or conditions expressly provide for it see para 122 ante; and as to completion of the contract see paras 262–325 post.

2   *Halkett v Earl of Dudley* [1907] 1 Ch 590. See also *Pincke v Curteis* (1793) 4 Bro CC 333n (Belt's Edn); and *Enraght v Fitzgerald* (1839) 2 I Eq R 87. As to specific performance see paras 247–253 post; and SPECIFIC PERFORMANCE. As to the master's order (formerly the master's certificate) see CPR Sch 1 RSC Ord 44 r 11. As to the CPR see para 133 note 1 ante.

3   See eg *Calcraft v Roebuck* (1790) 1 Ves 221 at 226; *Halkett v Earl of Dudley* [1907] 1 Ch 590 at 606; *Re Davy, Hollingsworth v Davy* [1908] 1 Ch 61, CA. As to interest see MONEY.

4   See eg *Wallersteiner v Moir (No 2)* [1975] QB 373, [1975] 1 All ER 849, CA, where interest at 1% above minimum lending rate was awarded against a fiduciary. It would appear that the same principle could

apply to the sale of land: see *Wallersteiner v Moir (No 2)* supra at 399 and 865 per Buckley LJ. See also *Bartlett v Barclays Bank Trust Co Ltd (No 2)* [1980] Ch 515 at 546–547, [1980] 2 All ER 92 at 97–98 per Brightman LJ. The matter is now usually provided for in conditions of sale: see the Standard Conditions of Sale (3rd Edn), condition 1.1.1(g); and para 119 note 7 ante. As to the Standard Conditions of Sale see para 1 note 9 ante.

5   *Re Pigott and Great Western Rly Co* (1881) 18 ChD 146. See also COMPULSORY ACQUISITION OF LAND vol 8(1) (Reissue) para 95.

6   *Catling v Great Northern Rly Co* (1869) 18 WR 121 at 122. In *Re Eccleshill Local Board* (1879) 13 ChD 365, it was held that interest ran as soon as the purchase price was ascertained, but, although this is the earliest possible date, interest does not necessarily then commence: see *Re Pigott and Great Western Rly Co* (1881) 18 ChD 146 at 154.

7   See COMPULSORY ACQUISITION OF LAND vol 8(1) (Reissue) para 122 et seq.

8   See COMPULSORY ACQUISITION OF LAND vol 8(1) (Reissue) paras 129, 226.

9   The regulations are made under the Land Compensation Act 1961 s 32: see COMPULSORY ACQUISITION OF LAND vol 8(1) (Reissue) para 125.

10   *Fludyer v Cocker* (1805) 12 Ves 25; *Powell v Martyr* (1803) 8 Ves 146 at 148. See also *Portman v Mill* (1839) 3 Jur 356; *Beresford v Clarke* [1908] 2 IR 317; *Glasgow and South Western Rly Co v Greenock Port and Harbour Trustees* [1909] WN 152, HL; and *Re Cassano and Mackay's Contract* [1920] WN 7. A purchaser who obtains possession before completion without the vendor's consent and without any provision in the contract authorising him to do so, is a mere trespasser: *Crockford v Alexander* (1808) 15 Ves 138. As to the position under conditions of sale see para 119 ante.

11   *Townley v Bedwell* (1808) 14 Ves 591 at 597; *Daniels v Davison* (1809) 16 Ves 249 at 253; cf *Mills v Haywood* (1877) 6 ChD 196. The contract for purchase does not necessarily effect a surrender of the tenancy (see para 127 ante), although in equity the tenant has the ordinary rights of a purchaser, subject always to the terms of the contract, express or implied: *Daniels v Davison* supra; and see *Raffety v Schofield* [1897] 1 Ch 937. However, a mere tenancy at will is determined by the contract: *Daniels v Davison* supra at 252.

196. Interest when time for completion is fixed. When the contract fixes a time for completion[1], but is silent as to the payment of interest, interest at the appropriate rate[2] is as a general rule payable as from the date so fixed[3]. However, if the delay in completion is caused by the vendor[4], he is not allowed to profit by his own default, and, if the interest exceeds the rents and profits[5], he takes the rents and profits, and interest does not run until he is ready to give a good title to the purchaser, or until the purchaser may first safely take possession[6]. If the contract, although silent as to interest, gives the vendor the rents and profits until a specified date, any implied right to interest during the same period is excluded[7].

1   As to the formation of the contract see paras 23–40 ante; and as to the completion of the contract see paras 262–325 post. As to the date of completion see paras 120, 185 ante.

2   As to this rate see para 195 text and notes 3–4 ante.

3   *Calcraft v Roebuck* (1790) 1 Ves 221 at 226; *Acland v Cuming, Gaisford v Acland* (1816) 2 Madd 28; *Esdaile v Stephenson* (1822) 1 Sim & St 122 at 123; *Grove v Bastard* (1851) 1 De GM & G 69 at 79; *Collard v Roe* (1859) 4 De G & J 525; *Catling v Great Northern Rly Co* (1869) 21 LT 17 at 19 (revsd on the facts 21 LT 769). See also *Monro v Taylor* (1852) 3 Mac & G 713 at 725.

4   As to delay in completion see para 121 ante.

5   As to rents and profits see paras 188–193 ante.

6   *Pincke v Curteis* (1793) 4 Bro CC 329; *Esdaile v Stephenson* (1822) 1 Sim & St 122; *Paton v Rogers* (1822) 6 Madd 256 at 257; *Jones v Mudd* (1827) 4 Russ 118. Under the earlier practice interest was charged more strictly against the purchaser: see *Burton v Todd, Todd v Gee* (1818) 1 Swan 255 at 260; *Wilson v Clapham* (1819) 1 Jac & W 36 at 38. Where under a stipulation in the contract a vendor elects to take interest in lieu of rents, he is not at liberty, as against the purchaser, to allocate any part of those rents to arrears of rents due to himself from tenants either at the date of the contract or subsequently before the day fixed for completion: *Plews v Samuel* [1904] 1 Ch 464.

7   See *Brooke v Champernowne* (1837) 4 Cl & Fin 589 at 611, HL.

197. Appropriation to meet purchase money. Where there is no express agreement for the payment of interest, the purchaser, if he is not responsible for the delay, can avoid payment of interest by appropriating money to meet the purchase money[1], and giving notice of the appropriation to the vendor[2]. The money should either be placed on deposit[3], or otherwise kept available at the purchaser's bank[4]. This does not interfere with the purchaser's right to the rents and profits[5], but any interest which is actually made by the money belongs to the vendor[6].

1 See *Powell v Martyr* (1803) 8 Ves 146; *Dyson v Hornby, ex p Markwell* (1851) 4 De G & Sm 481 at 484; *Regent's Canal Co v Ware* (1857) 23 Beav 575 at 587. Cf *Howland v Norris* (1784) 1 Cox Eq Cas 59, where the purchaser was allowed compensation in respect of the time down to which the purchase money was unproductive. See also *Bennett v Stone* [1903] 1 Ch 509 at 524, CA. As to appropriation where the payment of interest is provided for see para 122 ante.

2 Notice to the vendor is essential: *Powell v Martyr* (1803) 8 Ves 146. The effect of the appropriation is only to stop interest; the money remains at the purchaser's risk: *Roberts v Massey* (1807) 13 Ves 561. But if the vendor is in default, interest does not run (see para 122 ante), so that appropriation seems only to be necessary where there is delay for which neither vendor nor purchaser is to blame.

3 See *Kershaw v Kershaw* (1869) LR 9 Eq 56.

4 *Dyson v Hornby, ex p Markwell* (1851) 4 De G & Sm 481 at 484. However, interest does not stop as to any part of the sum which is in fact used for the purpose of maintaining the purchaser's usual credit balance: *Winter v Blades* (1825) 2 Sim & St 393.

5 *Regent's Canal Co v Ware* (1857) 23 Beav 575 at 587. As to rents and profits see paras 188–193 ante.

6 *Dyson v Hornby, ex p Markwell* (1851) 4 De G & Sm 481 at 485; *Kershaw v Kershaw* (1869) LR 9 Eq 56; *Re Golds' and Norton's Contract* (1885) 33 WR 333.

(4) ASSIGNMENT AND DEVOLUTION OF RIGHTS

(i) Assignment of Rights

198. Disposition by the purchaser. Upon the making of an enforceable contract for sale[1] the purchaser becomes the owner of the land in equity[2], and can dispose of his equitable interest to a third person[3].

1 As to the formation of the contract see paras 23–40 ante; and as to the completion of the contract see paras 262–325 post.

2 As to the effect of a contract for sale see para 177 ante.

3 *Paine v Meller* (1801) 6 Ves 349 at 352; and see para 177 ante. Such dispositions are usually made by subsale.

199. Disposition by the vendor. Since the vendor becomes a trustee for the purchaser[1], he is not entitled to dispose of the property to any person other than the purchaser. Where there is a clear contract for sale, any such intended disposition entitles the purchaser to an injunction to prevent the disposition from being carried into effect[2], and if it has been validly carried into effect, the purchaser can forthwith sue the vendor for damages on the ground that the vendor has incapacitated himself from performing the contract[3].

1 See para 177 ante.

2 *Hadley v London Bank of Scotland Ltd* (1865) 3 De GJ & Sm 63 (confining *Spiller v Spiller* (1819) 3 Swan 556 (where Lord Eldon LC stated that in general the purchaser was not entitled to an injunction) to cases of doubt as to the contract being enforceable). See *Echliff v Baldwin* (1809) 16 Ves 267; *Curtis v Marquis of Buckingham* (1814) 3 Ves & B 168; and INJUNCTIONS vol 24 (Reissue) para 920. The original contract must be specifically enforceable: *Goodwin v Fielding* (1853) 4 De GM & G 90; *De Hoghton v Money* (1866) 2 Ch App 164. See also *Potter v Sanders* (1846) 6 Hare 1; and *Trinidad Asphalte Co v Coryat* [1896] AC 587, PC.

3 *Main's Case* (1596) 5 Co Rep 20 b; *Lovelock v Franklyn* (1846) 8 QB 371. See also *Synge v Synge* [1894] 1 QB 466 at 471, CA, per Kay LJ. A dictum of Moulton LJ in *Re Taylor, ex p Norvell* [1910] 1 KB 562 at 573, CA, affirming the vendor's right of transfer, seems erroneous if taken literally. See also CONTRACT vol 9(1) (Reissue) paras 1000–1001; DAMAGES vol 12(1) (Reissue) para 1059. The purchaser could by registration protect his contract as against an alienee from the vendor (see paras 179 ante, 200 post); but the purchaser's failure to register does not give the vendor a defence to an action for damages

(see *Hollington Bros Ltd v Rhodes* [1951] 2 All ER 578n, [1951] WN 437; and *Wright v Dean* [1948] Ch 686, [1948] 2 All ER 415), nor to an action for breach of trust (see *Lake v Bayliss* [1974] 2 All ER 1114, [1974] 1 WLR 1073). As to the possibility of a claim by the purchaser against his solicitor for negligence in failing to register see *Midland Bank Trust Co Ltd v Hett, Stubbs and Kemp (a firm)* [1979] Ch 384, [1978] 3 All ER 571; and para 179 note 7 ante.

200. Position of an alienee from the vendor. The position of an alienee to whom the vendor alienates the property after he has entered into an enforceable contract with the purchaser is governed by statutory provisions[1]. In the case of unregistered land, these enable an estate contract to be registered by the purchaser[2] and, whether or not the alienee from the vendor searches the register, make registration notice to him of the purchaser's contract[3], so that if the contract is registered, the second alienee cannot be a purchaser without notice. On the other hand, if the contract is not registered it is void against the second alienee if he is a purchaser of the legal estate for money or money's worth[4], and he is not prejudicially affected by any notice which he may have of it[5].

1   Ie the Law of Property Act 1925 s 198(1) (as amended) (see LAND CHARGES vol 26 (Reissue) para 516); and the Land Charges Act 1972 s 2(4) (as amended) Class C(iv) (see LAND CHARGES vol 26 (Reissue) para 532). As to the creation and enforcement of contracts see the Land Registration Act 1925 s 107(1); and LAND REGISTRATION vol 26 (Reissue) para 922.
2   As to estate contracts see the Land Charges Act 1972 s 2(4) (as amended) Class C(iv); and LAND CHARGES vol 26 (Reissue) para 532. Registration must be in the name of the legal estate owner whose land is affected (Land Charges Act 1972 s 3(1) (see LAND CHARGES vol 26 (Reissue) para 539)), and therefore, where there is a subsale, the sub-purchaser's contract must be registered in the name of the head vendor (*Barrett v Hilton Developments Ltd* [1975] Ch 237, [1974] 3 All ER 944, CA (see LAND CHARGES vol 26 (Reissue) para 509)).
3   See para 21 ante; and EQUITY vol 16 (Reissue) para 768; LAND CHARGES vol 26 (Reissue) para 516. In favour of a purchaser or intending purchaser, an official certificate of search is conclusive: see the Land Charges Act 1972 s 10(4); and LAND CHARGES vol 26 (Reissue) para 601.
4   See LAND CHARGES vol 26 (Reissue) para 543.
5   See *Midland Bank Trust Co Ltd v Green* [1981] AC 513, [1981] 1 All ER 153, HL; and EQUITY vol 16 (Reissue) para 768; LAND CHARGES vol 26 (Reissue) para 516. As to the protection of a purchaser of registered land against matters not entered on the register see LAND REGISTRATION vol 26 (Reissue) para 958 et seq. A purchaser under an uncompleted contract who is in actual occupation has an overriding interest: *Bridges v Mees* [1957] Ch 475, [1957] 2 All ER 577; and see LAND REGISTRATION vol 26 (Reissue) para 784.

201. Transfer of benefit of contract. Unless the contract provides to the contrary[1], either party may dispose of the benefit of the contract in favour of another person[2], either by way of absolute assignment of the whole contract, or of partial assignment, where, for instance, the contract is charged in favour of another[3], or by an assignment of the contract as to part of the property. The assignee may enforce the contract against the other party to it in an action for specific performance[4], provided that he assumes the position of his assignor and either fulfils or secures the fulfilment of all his liabilities under the contract[5].

The assignee may sue in his own name if the other party has recognised the assignment so as to effect a novation of the contract[6], or if the assignment is of the entire contract[7] and fulfils certain statutory requirements[8]. Otherwise he must either sue in the name of the assignor or make the assignor a party[9]. The assignor remains liable to be sued on the contract unless by novation the assignee has been substituted in his place[10]. Apart from the statutory notice[11], notice of assignment should be given to the other party to the contract, so that he may shape his course of action accordingly[12].

1   Where the contract provides that the benefit is not to be assigned, any purported assignment is invalid: *Helstan Securities Ltd v Hertfordshire County Council* [1978] 3 All ER 262, 76 LGR 735; *Linden Gardens Trust Ltd v Lenesta Sludge Disposals Ltd* [1994] 1 AC 85, [1993] 3 All ER 417, HL; *Don King Productions Inc v Warren* [1998] 2 All ER 608, [1998] 2 Lloyd's Rep 176 (affd [1999] 2 All ER 218, CA). A

prohibition on assignment does not necessarily preclude a declaration of trust: *Don King Productions Inc v Warren* supra. As to limited restrictions on assignment see the Standard Conditions of Sale (3rd Edn), conditions 8.2.5, 8.3.3. As to the Standard Conditions of Sale see para 1 note 9 ante.

2   *Wood v Griffith* (1818) 1 Swan 43 at 55–56; *Shaw v Foster* (1872) LR 5 HL 321 at 349–350; *Tolhurst v Associated Portland Cement Manufacturers (1900) Ltd* [1903] AC 414 at 420, HL; *Dawson v Great Northern and City Rly Co* [1905] 1 KB 260 at 270, CA. The right to make a contract by acceptance of an offer is not assignable: see *Meynell v Surtees* (1854) 3 Sm & G 101 at 116–117 (affd (1855) 25 LJ Ch 257); and CHOSES IN ACTION vol 6 (Reissue) para 9 et seq.

3   See *Browne v London Necropolis and National Mausoleum Co* (1857) 6 WR 188; and *Durham Bros v Robertson* [1898] 1 QB 765, CA.

4   As to specific performance see paras 247–253 post; and SPECIFIC PERFORMANCE.

5   *Dyer v Pulteney* (1740) Barn Ch 160 at 169–170; *Shaw v Foster* (1872) LR 5 HL 321 at 350, 354 per Lord O'Hagan; *Manchester Brewery Co v Coombs* [1901] 2 Ch 608 at 616. See also *Crabtree v Poole* (1871) LR 12 Eq 13.

6   As to novation see CONTRACT vol 9(1) (Reissue) paras 1036–1042. As to whether a subpurchaser may sue the original vendor where there has been no assignment of the head contract see *Berkley v Poulett* (1976) 120 Sol Jo 836, CA. As to the registration of the contract for a subsale see para 200 note 2 ante.

7   See *Forster v Baker* [1910] 2 KB 636, CA. As to transfer of rights and remedies see CHOSES IN ACTION vol 6 (Reissue) paras 21–22; and as to assignee's right to sue see CHOSES IN ACTION vol 6 (Reissue) para 69.

8   Ie the Law of Property Act 1925 s 136(1): see *Torkington v Magee* [1902] 2 KB 427, DC (revsd on another ground [1903] 1 KB 644, CA); and see CHOSES IN ACTION vol 6 (Reissue) para 12 et seq.

9   *Nelthorpe v Holgate* (1844) 1 Coll 203 at 217; *Durham Bros v Robertson* [1898] 1 QB 765 at 769–770, CA, per Chitty LJ. This may not, however, be necessary if there are no equities subsisting between the original parties to the contract and no suggestion of any reason for making the original contractor a party: *Manchester Brewery Co v Coombs* [1901] 2 Ch 608 at 617; but see *Warner Bros Records Inc v Rollgreen Ltd* [1976] QB 430, [1975] 2 All ER 105, CA; and *Three Rivers District Council v Bank of England* [1996] QB 292, [1995] 4 All ER 312, CA.

10 *Tolhurst v Associated Portland Cement Manufacturers (1900) Ltd, Associated Portland Cement Manufacturers (1900) Ltd v Tolhurst* [1902] 2 KB 660 at 668, CA, per Collins MR; *Linden Gardens Trust Ltd v Lenesta Sludge Disposals Ltd* [1994] 1 AC 85 at 103, [1993] 3 All ER 417 at 427 per Lord Browne-Wilkinson, HL. See also *Holden v Hayn and Bacon* (1815) 1 Mer 47; *Chadwick v Maden* (1851) 9 Hare 188; and *Fenwick v Bulman* (1869) LR 9 Eq 165 at 168. As to the assignment of contracts generally see CHOSES IN ACTION vol 6 (Reissue) para 9 et seq; and as to parties to an action for specific performance see SPECIFIC PERFORMANCE vol 44(1) (Reissue) para 911 et seq.

11 Ie under the Law of Property Act 1925 s 136(1): see note 8 supra.

12 *Shaw v Foster* (1872) LR 5 HL 321 at 339 per Lord Cairns. Notice to the other party is essential in order to make the assignee's title effective against that other party and third persons: see *Warner Bros Records Inc v Rollgreen Ltd* [1976] QB 430, [1975] 2 All ER 105, CA; and CHOSES IN ACTION vol 6 (Reissue) para 42.

(ii)   Death or Change in Position of Parties

A. DEATH

202.   Contract not avoided by death. A valid and enforceable contract for the sale of land[1] is not avoided by the death of either or both parties before completion[2], but remains enforceable both at law and in equity by and against the personal representatives of the party or parties so dying[3].

1   As to the formation of the contract see paras 23–40 ante.

2   As to completion of the contract see paras 262–325 post.

3   Sugden's Law of Vendors and Purchasers (14th Edn, 1862) 177; *Roberts v Marchant* (1843) 1 Ph 370; *Hoddel v Pugh* (1864) 33 Beav 489. As to the form in which the vendor's interest passes see *A-G v Day* (1749) 1 Ves Sen 218 at 220 per Lord Hardwicke LC; and EQUITY vol 16 (Reissue) para 832. The personal representatives can carry out the sale under their general powers over the real and leasehold estate of the deceased; and in exercising the power under the Administration of Estates Act 1925, it is sufficient if the executors to whom probate is granted join in the sale: see EXECUTORS AND ADMINISTRATORS. As to a vendor who has received the purchase money before his death see *Re Pagani, Re Pagani's Trust* [1892] 1 Ch 236, CA; para 178 note 7 ante; and EXECUTORS AND ADMINISTRATORS.

203. Parties to action on vendor's death. In proceedings by or against the vendor's personal representatives for specific performance of the contract[1], the vendor's heir or devisee was formerly a necessary party, since he was interested in the question whether the contract was enforceable or not[2]. The devisee[3] is still a proper party, if the executor has assented[4] to the devise to him, but if there has been no assent, only the executor should be a party and the devisee should not be joined except by court order[5]. If the vendor died intestate, only his administrator is a party.

1 As to specific performance see paras 247–253 post; and SPECIFIC PERFORMANCE.
2 *Roberts v Marchant* (1843) 1 Ph 370.
3 Since 1925 there is in general no descent to the heir: see the Administration of Estates Act 1925 s 45(1)(a); and EXECUTORS AND ADMINISTRATORS.
4 See generally EXECUTORS AND ADMINISTRATORS.
5 See CPR Sch 1 RSC Ord 15 r 14; para 205 post; and SPECIFIC PERFORMANCE vol 44(1) (Reissue) para 913; PRACTICE AND PROCEDURE. As to the CPR see para 133 note 1 ante.

204. Devolution on purchaser's death. On the death of the purchaser before completion[1], his equitable interest in the property vests in his legal personal representatives[2]. If he has devised the property, the devisee will become entitled upon the personal representatives making an assent[3] in his favour, but he will take it subject to any lien which the vendor may have on it for the purchase price[4]. Except where the purchaser by his will or by deed or other documents has signified a contrary intention[5], a specific devisee of the purchaser's interest in the land cannot claim to have the purchase money paid out of any other part of the estate of the deceased purchaser[6]. However, this liability of the land to bear the purchase money does not deprive the vendor of his right to enforce payment of the purchase money out of the purchaser's other assets or otherwise[7]. If the purchaser has died intestate, the equitable interest will be dealt with as part of his estate[8].

1 As to the completion of the contract see paras 262–325 post.
2 See the Administration of Estates Act 1925 ss 1(1), 3(1)(i); and EXECUTORS AND ADMINISTRATORS.
3 See generally EXECUTORS AND ADMINISTRATORS.
4 See the Administration of Estates Act 1925 s 35(1); and EXECUTORS AND ADMINISTRATORS. See also *Re Birmingham, Savage v Stannard* [1959] Ch 523, [1958] 2 All ER 397.
5 As to what amounts to signifying a contrary intention see EXECUTORS AND ADMINISTRATORS.
6 *Re Cockcroft, Broadbent v Groves* (1883) 24 ChD 94. See also *Re Fraser, Lowther v Fraser* [1904] 1 Ch 111 (affd [1904] 1 Ch 726, CA), where the interest agreed to be purchased was a rentcharge issuing out of leasehold land, ie a chattel real passing to the next of kin.
7 See the Administration of Estates Act 1925 s 35(3); and EXECUTORS AND ADMINISTRATORS.
8 See ibid s 33(1) (as substituted); and EXECUTORS AND ADMINISTRATORS.

205. Parties to action on purchaser's death. On the death of the purchaser the contract continues to be binding as between the vendor and the purchaser's personal representatives, and an action by the vendor upon the contract, whether at law to recover damages for breach contract or in equity for specific performance, should be brought against the personal representatives; but if the purchaser has devised the property, the devisee may be made a party by special order[1]. An action against the vendor for damages for breach of the contract should be brought by the personal representatives, and until the purchaser's interest has vested in a devisee by assent or transfer from the personal representatives, the personal representatives are proper plaintiffs in an action for specific performance, and although the equitable interest of a devisee in whose favour an assent has been made would support an action by him, yet in such an action the legal personal representatives should be parties, because they are liable for the purchaser money[2].

1 See CPR Sch 1 RSC Ord 15 r 14; para 203 ante; and SPECIFIC PERFORMANCE vol 44(1) (Reissue) para 913; PRACTICE AND PROCEDURE. As to the nature of specific performance see paras 247–253 post; and SPECIFIC PERFORMANCE vol 44(1) (Reissue) paras 801–804. As to the CPR see para 133 note 1 ante.
2 This is so even where the ultimate liability is on the land. As to the parties to the action see further SPECIFIC PERFORMANCE vol 44(1) (Reissue) para 911 et seq. As to assents by personal representatives see EXECUTORS AND ADMINISTRATORS.

B. BANKRUPTCY

206. Bankruptcy of vendor. Where the vendor under an uncompleted contract becomes bankrupt, on the court's making a bankruptcy order[1], the appointment of the trustee in bankruptcy automatically vests the vendor's legal estate in the property to be sold in the trustee in bankruptcy[2], subject, nevertheless, to the equitable title of the purchaser to have the estate transferred to him on payment of the purchase price[3]. This is so if the purchase money is still unpaid, so that the vendor has a lien on the land for the amount[4], or if he has otherwise any beneficial interest in the property or the possibility of a beneficial interest[5].

Where, however, the title has been accepted and the whole purchase money paid to the vendor before the commencement of the bankruptcy[6], so that the vendor is then a mere trustee for the purchaser with no beneficial interest in the property sold, the property is not divisible among the vendor's creditors and does not pass to the trustee in bankruptcy[7].

1 As to the making of a bankruptcy order see BANKRUPTCY AND INSOLVENCY vol 3(2) (Reissue) para 194 et seq.
2 Ie under the Insolvency Act 1986 s 306: see BANKRUPTCY AND INSOLVENCY vol 3(2) (Reissue) para 381.
3 See *Re Pooley, ex p Rabbidge* (1878) 8 ChD 367 at 370, CA; *Re Scheibler, ex p Holthausen* (1874) 9 Ch App 722 at 726 per James LJ. As to the effect of bankruptcy upon a contract see BANKRUPTCY AND INSOLVENCY vol 3(2) (Reissue) paras 407–408; as to its effect upon a power of sale exercisable with the consent of the bankrupt see BANKRUPTCY AND INSOLVENCY vol 3(2) (Reissue) para 393; and as to the transmission of registered land on bankruptcy and the protection of creditors see LAND REGISTRATION vol 26 (Reissue) paras 1021 et seq, 1166 et seq.
4 See *St Thomas's Hospital Governors v Richardson* [1910] 1 KB 271, CA; and LANDLORD AND TENANT vol 27(1) (Reissue) para 496.
5 See *Carvalho v Burn* (1833) 4 B & Ad 382 at 393 per Littledale J. The legal estate of a tenant for life in settled land will not normally vest in his trustee in bankruptcy, notwithstanding that he has an equitable interest in it: see the Settled Land Act 1925 s 103 (as amended); and SETTLEMENTS para 698 post. See also BANKRUPTCY AND INSOLVENCY vol 3(2) (Reissue) para 393. As to the exercise of the statutory powers where the tenant for life unreasonably refuses to exercise them see s 24(1); *Re Cecil's Settled Estates* [1926] WN 262; and SETTLEMENTS para 765 post (contract not to exercise powers is void).
6 Ie the day on which the bankruptcy order is made: see the Insolvency Act 1986 s 278(a); and BANKRUPTCY AND INSOLVENCY vol 3(2) (Reissue) paras 201, 205.
7 See ibid s 283(3)(a); and BANKRUPTCY AND INSOLVENCY vol 3(2) (Reissue) para 417.

207. Remedies against vendor's trustee in bankruptcy. The remedy of the purchaser is either in damages at law for breach of the contract[1] or for specific performance in equity[2]. The former is a claim provable in the vendor's bankruptcy[3], and after the making of the bankruptcy order the purchaser cannot commence an action for the breach without the leave of the court[4]. Without such leave he must prove in the bankruptcy, otherwise the vendor's liability is extinguished by the discharge of the bankrupt[5], or by the acceptance by the creditors and approval by the court of a voluntary arrangement under the bankruptcy legislation[6]. The purchaser's claim for specific performance of the contract is not provable in the bankruptcy[7], and may be enforced against the trustee in bankruptcy either by action or by claim in the bankruptcy[8], and if not enforced during the bankruptcy is not extinguished by the discharge of the vendor or by a composition[9].

1   As to damages for breach of contract see DAMAGES vol 12(1) (Reissue) paras 941–1087.
2   As to the remedy of specific performance generally see SPECIFIC PERFORMANCE.
3   See the Insolvency Act 1986 s 345(3); and BANKRUPTCY AND INSOLVENCY vol 3(2) (Reissue) para 478 et seq.
4   See ibid s 285(3); and BANKRUPTCY AND INSOLVENCY vol 3(2) (Reissue) paras 206, 478. Moreover, at any time after the presentation of a bankruptcy petition the court may stay any proceedings against the property or person of the debtor: see s 285(1); and BANKRUPTCY AND INSOLVENCY vol 3(2) (Reissue) paras 206, 478, 714.
5   As to the effect of discharge see ibid s 281 (as amended); and BANKRUPTCY AND INSOLVENCY vol 3(2) (Reissue) para 617 et seq.
6   As to voluntary arrangements see ibid Pt VIII (ss 252–263); and BANKRUPTCY AND INSOLVENCY vol 3(2) (Reissue) para 75 et seq.
7   *Hardy v Fothergill* (1888) 13 App Cas 351 at 361, HL, per Lord Selborne; *Re Reis, ex p Clough* [1904] 2 KB 769 at 777, 781, 787, CA.
8   *Pearce v Bastable's Trustee in Bankruptcy* [1901] 2 Ch 122 (action); *Freevale Ltd v Metrostore (Holdings) Ltd* [1984] Ch 199, [1984] 1 All ER 495 (action against company in receivership); *Re Taylor, ex p Norvell* [1910] 1 KB 562, CA (claim in the bankruptcy); and see BANKRUPTCY AND INSOLVENCY vol 3(2) (Reissue) para 408. Similarly, the purchaser's lien for his deposit, if he relies on this only, is outside the bankruptcy: *Levy v Stogdon* [1898] 1 Ch 478 at 486; affd on another point [1899] 1 Ch 5, CA.
9   *Re Reis, ex p Clough* [1904] 2 KB 769, CA; affd [1905] AC 442, HL.

208. Disclaimer by vendor's trustee in bankruptcy. The vendor's trustee in bankruptcy may disclaim any onerous property on the ground that it is burdened with onerous covenants, and he may disclaim the contract for sale on the ground that it is unprofitable[1], where, for instance, it binds the vendor to spend money on the property[2]. He must, therefore, either perform the contract and transfer the property, thereby entitling himself to receive the purchase money from the purchaser, or he must disclaim the contract and thereby cease to have any right to enforce it against the purchaser, in which case, although he is no longer bound to perform any onerous obligations, he has no right to receive the purchase money[3], but this does not prejudice the purchaser's interest in the property. No disclaimer can take away the equitable interest which the purchaser has acquired in the property under his contract, or affect his right either to call upon the trustee to transfer the land to him[4], or to apply for an order vesting the property in himself[5].

1   See the Insolvency Act 1986 s 315(1); and BANKRUPTCY AND INSOLVENCY vol 3(2) (Reissue) paras 460–461. As to the disclaimer of leasehold property see s 317; and BANKRUPTCY AND INSOLVENCY vol 3(2) (Reissue) para 469. As to the disclaimer of property in a dwelling house see s 318; and BANKRUPTCY AND INSOLVENCY vol 3(2) (Reissue) para 470. As to the disclaimer of land subject to a rentcharge see s 319; and BANKRUPTCY AND INSOLVENCY vol 3(2) (Reissue) para 471. As to disclaimer generally see BANKRUPTCY AND INSOLVENCY vol 3(2) (Reissue) para 460 et seq.
2   *Re Bastable, ex p Trustee* [1901] 2 KB 518 at 529, CA.
3   *Re Bastable, ex p Trustee* [1901] 2 KB 518 at 529, CA.
4   *Re Bastable, ex p Trustee* [1901] 2 KB 518 at 529, CA.
5   Ie under the Insolvency Act 1986 ss 320, 321: see BANKRUPTCY AND INSOLVENCY vol 3(2) (Reissue) paras 473–474.

209. Registration of bankruptcy petitions and orders. A bankruptcy petition may be registered in the register of pending actions[1], and a bankruptcy order may be registered in the register of writs and orders affecting land[2]. The omission of the trustee in bankruptcy to register the petition as a pending action, and subsequently to register the bankruptcy order, renders the title of the trustee in bankruptcy void against a purchaser of the legal estate in good faith for money or money's worth[3].

1   See the Land Charges Act 1972 s 5(1)(b); and LAND CHARGES vol 26 (Reissue) para 547. The registration
     ceases after five years unless renewed: see s 8; and LAND CHARGES vol 26 (Reissue) para 552.
2   See ibid s 6(1)(c) (as substituted); and LAND CHARGES vol 26 (Reissue) para 554. The registration ceases after
     five years but may be renewed from time to time: see s 8; and LAND CHARGES vol 26 (Reissue) para 560.
     As to delay in renewal see *Re A Receiving Order in Bankruptcy* [1947] Ch 498, [1947] 1 All ER 843.
3   See the Land Charges Act 1972 ss 5(8) (as amended), 6(5) (as substituted), 6(6) (as amended); and LAND
     CHARGES vol 26 (Reissue) paras 550, 558. In order to obtain this protection against the trustee's title, the
     purchaser must have taken a conveyance of the legal estate; if he pays the purchase money without having
     a conveyance he may have to pay it over again to the trustee: *Re Pooley, ex p Rabbidge* (1878) 8 ChD 367,
     CA; *Powell v Marshall, Parkes & Co* [1899] 1 QB 710 at 713, CA. See also *Re Taylor, ex p Norvell* [1910]
     1 KB 562, CA. As to the effect of completion before the date of the bankruptcy order see BANKRUPTCY
     AND INSOLVENCY vol 3(2) (Reissue) paras 380 et seq, 406. As to the equivalent machinery in the case of
     registered land see LAND REGISTRATION vol 26 (Reissue) para 1021.

210. Bankruptcy of purchaser.

If the purchaser becomes bankrupt pending completion[1], his trustee in bankruptcy may either elect within a reasonable time to pay the purchase price and complete the contract[2], or may disclaim the contract as unprofitable[3]. The vendor cannot obtain specific performance against the purchaser's trustee in bankruptcy[4]. He may apply in writing to the trustee requiring him to decide whether he will disclaim or not[5], or to the court for an order discharging obligations under the contract on such terms as to payment of damages (which would be provable as a debt in the bankruptcy) or otherwise as may seem equitable to the court[6].

1   As to completion of the contract see paras 262–325 post.
2   *Re Nathan, ex p Stapleton* (1879) 10 ChD 586 at 590, CA. See also BANKRUPTCY AND INSOLVENCY vol
     3(2) (Reissue) paras 407–408. As to the trustee's right of action in respect of the contract see
     BANKRUPTCY AND INSOLVENCY vol 3(2) (Reissue) para 406 et seq.
3   See BANKRUPTCY AND INSOLVENCY vol 3(2) (Reissue) para 460 et seq. If the trustee does not disclaim
     and does not elect to complete within a reasonable time, the vendor may prove in the bankruptcy for any
     loss: *Re Nathan, ex p Stapleton* (1879) 10 ChD 586, CA.
4   *Holloway v York* (1877) 25 WR 627; *Pearce v Bastable's Trustee in Bankruptcy* [1901] 2 Ch 122 at 125 per
     Cozens-Hardy J. Specific performance may perhaps be decreed where the trustee has adopted the
     contract: see note 5 infra. As to specific performance generally see SPECIFIC PERFORMANCE.
5   As to notice requiring the trustee's decision see the Insolvency Act 1986 s 316; and BANKRUPTCY AND
     INSOLVENCY vol 3(2) (Reissue) para 468. As to the power to make such an application and the rule that
     a trustee who does not disclaim within the statutory period is deemed to have adopted the contract see
     BANKRUPTCY AND INSOLVENCY vol 3(2) (Reissue) para 468. It is not clear whether such adoption
     renders the trustee personally liable as a contracting party; probably he only adopts on behalf of the estate,
     and gives the vendor the right at his election to specific performance or damages: see Williams and Muir
     Hunter on Bankruptcy (19th Edn) 395.
6   See the Insolvency Act 1986 s 345; and BANKRUPTCY AND INSOLVENCY vol 3(2) (Reissue) para 662.

211. Purchaser an undischarged bankrupt.

Where the purchaser is an undischarged bankrupt, the vendor cannot safely complete unless the purchaser can show to his satisfaction that the purchase money has been acquired by the purchaser after the commencement of the bankruptcy, and that his trustee in bankruptcy has not intervened to claim it[1].

1   *Re Vanlohe, ex p Dewhurst* (1871) 7 Ch App 185; *Dyster v Randall & Sons* [1926] Ch 932, CA; and see
     BANKRUPTCY AND INSOLVENCY vol 3(2) (Reissue) para 406. As to the trustee in bankruptcy's power to
     claim after-acquired property see the Insolvency Act 1986 s 307; and BANKRUPTCY AND INSOLVENCY vol
     3(2) (Reissue) para 433; and as to a debtor against whom a bankruptcy order has been made obtaining a
     release of his liabilities under a voluntary arrangement or scheme approved by the court see BANKRUPTCY
     AND INSOLVENCY vol 3(2) (Reissue) para 100. If a bankrupt purchaser by the terms of the contract
     becomes entitled to receive from the vendor credit to the extent of a prescribed amount or upwards,
     without disclosing the fact that he is an undischarged bankrupt, as required by s 360 (see BANKRUPTCY
     AND INSOLVENCY vol 3(2) (Reissue) para 706), the contract is unenforceable by the purchaser, and the
     vendor, on discovering the facts, may obtain an order for rescission of the contract: see *De Choisy v Hynes*
     [1937] 4 All ER 54, 81 Sol Jo 883.

C. WINDING UP

212. Effect of winding-up petition. In the case of a winding up by the court, every disposition of the company's property made after the commencement of the winding up is void unless the court otherwise orders[1]. Hence a contract for the purchase of land from a company cannot safely be completed after the presentation of the petition, since it involves the disposition of the company's land. Similarly, a contract for the sale of land to a company should not be completed, since it involves the disposition of the company's money[2].

1 See the Insolvency Act 1986 s 127; and COMPANIES vol 7(3) (1996 Reissue) para 2460. As to the commencement of the winding up see COMPANIES vol 7(3) (1996 Reissue) para 2249.
2 If the contract is for sale by the company, and is specifically enforceable, the equitable interest is already in the purchaser, and the company on completion only disposes of the legal interest, and the court, if the transaction is in good faith, will probably validate the disposition. If the contract is for purchase by the company, the payment of the purchase money by the company involves more risk: see *Re Civil Service and General Store Ltd* (1887) 57 LJ Ch 119. In either case completion should be postponed until the winding-up petition has been dealt with. The court will validate transactions entered into in the ordinary course of business and completed before the winding-up order (*Re Wiltshire Iron Co, ex p Pearson* (1868) 3 Ch App 443 at 447: see COMPANIES vol 7(3) (1996 Reissue) para 2460), but this rule would apply only in exceptional cases apply to a sale or purchase of land.

213. Completion by liquidator. After the winding-up order has been made[1], or on the appointment of the liquidator in a voluntary winding up[2], the powers of the directors normally cease[3], and the completion of a pending contract rests with the liquidator, subject to the control of the court[4]. The liquidator in the exercise of his power to realise the company's assets[5] can adopt and carry into effect a contract of sale. Apart from this, it is the duty of the liquidator, if the contract is specifically enforceable, to complete the purchaser's title by affixing the company's common seal to a transfer of the legal estate and to receive the purchase money[6]. In the case of a contract for purchase, he can, with the vendor's concurrence, resell the land and pay the vendor pro tanto out of the proceeds, leaving the vendor to prove in the winding up for any deficiency in the price[7].

1 As to winding up by the court generally see COMPANIES vol 7(3) (1996 Reissue) para 2196 et seq.
2 As to voluntary winding up generally see COMPANIES vol 7(3) (1996 Reissue) para 2698 et seq.
3 See the Insolvency Act 1986 s 91(2); and COMPANIES vol 7(3) (1996 Reissue) para 2756.
4 See ibid s 167(1)(b), (3), Sch 4 para 6; and COMPANIES vol 7(3) (1996 Reissue) paras 2338, 2340. The liquidator is an officer of the court: see the Insolvency Rules 1986, SI 1986/1925, r 4.179(1); and COMPANIES vol 7(3) (1996 Reissue) para 2334). As to the liquidator's duties in a voluntary winding up see *Re TH Knitwear (Wholesale) Ltd* [1988] Ch 275, [1988] 1 All ER 860, CA; and COMPANIES vol 7(3) (1996 Reissue) para 2331.
5 See the Insolvency Act 1986 Sch 4 Pt III; and COMPANIES vol 7(3) (1996 Reissue) para 2337.
6 Under such circumstances the land is not the property of the company; the company's interest is transferred by the contract to the purchase money: see para 177 ante. As to transfer by a company in liquidation see para 277 post. As to the disposition of registered and unregistered land by transfer see para 262 note 2 post.
7 See *Thames Plate Glass Co v Land and Sea Telegraph Co* (1870) LR 11 Eq 248 at 250.

214. Liquidator's refusal to complete. If the liquidator under a compulsory or voluntary winding up declines to complete the contract, the other party may either prove in the winding up for any loss which he has sustained[1] or bring an action for specific performance[2]. Where judgment is given for specific performance and the company is the vendor, completion will follow by transfer by the company and payment of the purchase money to the liquidator[3]. If the company is the purchaser, the vendor's claim, as the result of specific performance, is a money claim in the winding up for the deficiency in the purchase money left after resale of the land and payment of the proceeds to the vendor[4].

1   Alternatively, if the claim or the amount of damages is likely to be disputed, he can bring an action for breach of contract (see *Currie v Consolidated Kent Collieries Corpn Ltd* [1906] 1 KB 134, CA; and COMPANIES vol 7(3) (1996 Reissue) para 2652), and then prove for the damages. As to the measure of damages see paras 254–258 post.

2   See *Thames Plate Glass Co v Land and Sea Telegraph Co* (1870) LR 11 Eq 248 at 250. As to obtaining leave to bring the action see COMPANIES vol 7(3) (1996 Reissue) para 2652 et seq. There may be an order to stay the proceedings, save so far as necessary to determine the point in dispute: see *Thames Plate Glass Co v Land and Sea Telegraph Co* supra. As to specific performance see paras 247–253 post; and SPECIFIC PERFORMANCE.

3   See para 213 ante. As to the disposition of registered and unregistered land by transfer see para 262 note 2 post.

4   See *Thames Plate Glass Co v Land and Sea Telegraph Co* (1870) LR 11 Eq 248.

215. Action by the liquidator. Where the other party to the contract refuses to complete, the liquidator may bring an action in the name of the company either for damages or for specific performance[1].

1   See COMPANIES vol 7(3) (1996 Reissue) para 2337. As to the completion of the contract see paras 262–325 post. As to specific performance see paras 247–253 post; and SPECIFIC PERFORMANCE. As to damages see paras 254–261 post; and DAMAGES.

D. EXECUTION

216. Effect of charging order. A charging order made in favour of a judgment creditor upon land or an interest in land belonging to the debtor is registrable in the same way as other orders or writs for enforcing judgments[1], and has otherwise the same effect as an equitable charge created by the debtor[2]. It seems that the charge created by such an order takes effect subject to the equitable interest of a purchaser in the land under a prior contract for sale[3]. Unless protected by registration, such a charge, in the case of unregistered land, is void against a subsequent purchaser for valuable consideration[4] and, in the case of registered land, a person taking under a registered disposition is not concerned with the charge[5]. Where such a charge has been registered, a person who subsequently enters into a contract to purchase the land cannot safely pay his purchase money to the vendor without either satisfying the judgment creditor out of the purchase money or obtaining his consent to payment to the vendor[6].

1   See the Charging Orders Act 1979 s 3(2); and LAND CHARGES vol 26 (Reissue) para 555; EXECUTION. Registration against a company under what is now the Companies Act 1985 s 395 (as amended) (see COMPANIES vol 7(2) (1996 Reissue) para 1299) is not necessary: *Re Overseas Aviation Engineering (GB) Ltd* [1963] Ch 24, [1962] 3 All ER 12, CA. See also LAND CHARGES vol 26 (Reissue) paras 554–555; LAND REGISTRATION vol 26 (Reissue) para 1158. As to charging orders generally see the Charging Orders Act 1979 ss 1 (as amended), 2; and EXECUTION.

2   Ibid s 3(4). As to the property which may be charged see s 2; and EXECUTION.

3   Cf *Prior v Penpraze* (1817) 4 Price 99; *Lodge v Lyseley* (1832) 4 Sim 70; and MORTGAGE.

4   See LAND CHARGES vol 26 (Reissue) para 558.

5   See LAND REGISTRATION vol 26 (Reissue) para 958 et seq. As to the effect where a charging order is protected by a caution see *Clark v Chief Land Registrar* [1994] Ch 370, [1994] 4 All ER 96, CA.

6   See the note to *Forth v Duke of Norfolk* (1820) 4 Madd 503 at 506; and para 314 post.

217. Appointment of receiver. The appointment of a receiver of the vendor's interest in unpaid purchase money, or of the purchaser's interest in the land, is ineffectual if for any reason the contract is not completed so that the money or land, as the case may be, does not come into the debtor's hands[1].

1   *Ridout v Fowler* [1904] 2 Ch 93, CA. As to the effect of the appointment of a receiver generally see generally EXECUTION; RECEIVERS. Where a charging order has been registered as a land charge, an order subsequently appointing a receiver is not void against a purchaser even though not itself registered: see

the Supreme Court Act 1981 s 37(5); County Courts Act 1984 s 107(3); Land Charges Act 1972 ss 6(4) (as amended), 18(6); and LAND CHARGES vol 26 (Reissue) para 558.

E. MENTAL DISORDER

218. Contract not avoided by subsequent mental disorder. A contract for the sale of land made between parties capable of contracting at the time is not avoided by the fact that either party becomes mentally disordered before completion[1].

1   See eg *Hall v Warren* (1804) 9 Ves 605; and MENTAL HEALTH vol 30 (Reissue) para 1390. As to sales and purchases on behalf of mentally disordered persons generally see MENTAL HEALTH vol 30 (Reissue) para 1431 et seq.

219. Vesting order. Where a vendor becomes mentally disordered after the purchase money has been paid, or the contract has been so far performed that a decree for specific performance would be a matter of course, and the purchase money or the balance due is ready to be paid, the purchaser can obtain a High Court order vesting the property in him[1].

1   Ie under the Trustee Act 1925 s 44(ii): see para 266 post; and TRUSTS vol 48 (Reissue) para 760. As to the vendor becoming a constructive trustee for the purchaser see para 177 ante. The High Court and the judge or master concerned with the management of the property of mental patients have concurrent jurisdiction to make a vesting order in this case: see s 54(2)(c) (substituted by the Mental Health Act 1959 s 149(1), Sch 7 Pt 1); and TRUSTS vol 48 (Reissue) para 736. See also *Re Cuming* (1869) 5 Ch App 72; *Re Pagani, Re Pagani's Trust* [1892] 1 Ch 236, CA; and MENTAL HEALTH vol 30 (Reissue) para 1480.

(5) APPLICATIONS BY VENDOR OR PURCHASER FOR SUMMARY ORDER

(i) Jurisdiction

220. Application for summary order. A vendor or purchaser[1] of any interest in land[2], or their representatives respectively, may apply[3] in a summary way to the court[4] in respect of any requisitions or objections, or any claim for compensation, or any other question arising out of or connected with the contract (not being a question affecting the existence or validity of the contract), and the court may make such order upon the application as may appear just, and may order how and by whom all or any of the costs of and incident to the application are to be borne and paid[5].

In cases where this procedure is available it must be adopted in preference to bringing an action[6].

1   For the meaning of 'purchaser' see para 55 note 16 ante.
2   For the meaning of 'land' see para 139 note 1 ante.
3   As to the procedure for making an application see para 227 post.
4   For these purposes, unless the contrary intention appears, 'the court' means the High Court or the county court, where those courts respectively have jurisdiction: Law of Property Act 1925 s 203(3) (amended by the Courts Act 1971 s 56(4), Sch 11 Pt II). Proceedings in the High Court are assigned to the Chancery Division: see the Law of Property Act 1925 s 203(4); and the Supreme Court Act 1981 s 61(1), Sch 1 para 1(a). The county court has jurisdiction where the land does not exceed £30,000 in capital value: Law of Property Act 1925 s 49(4) (added by the County Courts Act 1984 s 148(1), Sch 2 Pt II para 2(1), (3); and amended by the High Court and County Courts Jurisdiction Order 1991, SI 1991/754, art 2(8), Schedule). In any event the parties may agree that a county court is to have jurisdiction: see the County Courts Act 1984 s 24 (as amended); and COUNTY COURTS.

5   Law of Property Act 1925 s 49(1). Section 49 (as amended) applies to a contract for the sale or exchange
     of any interest in land: s 49(3). The jurisdiction has been exercised in respect of contracts to create, as
     well as contracts to assign, leasehold interests (see *Re Anderton and Milner's Contract* (1890) 45 ChD 476;
     Re Lander and Bagley's Contract [1892] 3 Ch 41; and *Re Stephenson and Cox* (1892) 36 Sol Jo 287, CA),
     and has even been applied to a voluntary grant on counsel for each side admitting a contract for a nominal
     consideration (*Re Marquis of Salisbury* (1875) as reported in 23 WR 824; revsd on another point (1876)
     2 ChD 29, CA). As to the application of the procedure to the acquisition of the freehold or an extended
     lease under the Leasehold Reform Act 1967 see s 22; and LANDLORD AND TENANT vol 27(2) (Reissue)
     para 1295. As to summary judgment under the Civil Procedure Rules 1998, which came into force on
     26 April 1999, see CPR Pt 24. As to the CPR see para 133 note 1 ante.
6   See *King v Chamberlayn* [1887] WN 158 at 159, where North J said that if the plaintiff had deliberately
     adopted the more expensive mode of proceeding by action, he would not have allowed any more costs
     than the costs of what is now an application under the Law of Property Act 1925 s 49 (as amended). A
     judge sitting in bankruptcy may for convenience and with the consent of the parties decide a point which
     would ordinarily be decided on what is now an application under s 49 (as amended): *Re Martin, ex p Dixon
     (Trustee) v Tucker* (1912) 106 LT 381.

221. Scope of jurisdiction. An application by vendor or purchaser for a summary
order[1] puts the parties in the same position in chambers in which they would have been,
and with all the rights which they would have had, under a judgment for specific
performance[2]. Hence, whatever could be done in chambers upon a reference as to title
under such a judgment, where the contract has been established, can be done on such an
application[3]. The procedure is not, however, intended to enable the court to try
summarily disputed questions of fact[4], and an application under these provisions[5] cannot
be treated as if it were an action for specific performance, or for rescission, or for any other
purpose[6]. It enables either party to the contract to obtain a decision upon some isolated
point, or points, without having recourse to an action for specific performance[7], such as
whether a requisition has been sufficiently answered, or whether a requisition is
precluded by the conditions[8], or any short point of law or construction arising on the
abstract, contract or requisitions[9].

1   Ie under the Law of Property Act 1925 s 49 (as amended): see para 220 ante.
2   As to specific performance see paras 247–253 post; and SPECIFIC PERFORMANCE.
3   See *Re Burroughs, Lynn and Sexton* (1877) 5 ChD 601 at 604, CA, per James LJ. The particular point in
     that case was that affidavit evidence could be admitted and the deponents cross-examined. As to
     references to title see SPECIFIC PERFORMANCE vol 44(1) (Reissue) para 934 et seq.
4   See *Re Burroughs, Lynn and Sexton* (1877) 5 ChD 601 at 603, CA; *Re Popple and Barratt's Contract* (1877)
     25 WR 248, CA; *Re Gray and Metropolitan Rly Co* (1881) 44 LT 567. Questions of fraud cannot be
     entertained on an application under the Law of Property Act 1925 s 49 (as amended): see para 224 post.
5   See note 1 supra.
6   See *Re Hargreaves and Thompson's Contract* (1886) 32 ChD 454 at 456, CA, per Cotton LJ. See also *Re
     South Eastern Rly Co and London County Council's Contract, South Eastern Rly Co v LCC* [1915] 2 Ch 252,
     CA.
7   See *Re Hargreaves and Thompson's Contract* (1886) 32 ChD 454 at 459, CA, per Lindley LJ; *Re Wallis and
     Barnard's Contract* [1899] 2 Ch 515 at 519.
8   See *Re Burroughs, Lynn and Sexton* (1877) 5 ChD 601 at 603, CA.
9   See *Re Popple and Barratt's Contract* (1877) 25 WR 248 at 249, CA, per James LJ. Cf *Re Wallis and
     Barnard's Contract* [1899] 2 Ch 515 at 520–521, where Kekewich J deprecated the making on such
     applications of declarations that the vendor has or has not shown a good title or a title which cannot be
     forced on the purchaser, ie embracing the whole title instead of dealing with isolated questions. As to the
     need for an abstract of title with respect to both unregistered and registered land see paras 138, 141–149
     ante. As to the vendor's obligation to show and prove a good title see para 137 ante. As to the formation
     of the contract see paras 23–40 ante; as to requisitions on title see paras 163–166 ante; and as to the
     questions which can be decided on an application under the Law of Property Act 1925 s 49 (as amended)
     see paras 220 note 5 ante, 225–226 post.

222. Consequential relief. The jurisdiction to make such order as appears just[1] enables the judge to give relief which is the ordinary consequence of the decision of the point submitted to him[2]. Thus when the decision of the point raised necessarily involves a determination that the vendor has not made a good title, an order may be made for the return of the deposit with interest, and payment by the vendor of the purchaser's costs of investigating title, whether the application was taken out by the vendor or the purchaser[3]. An order for payment of unliquidated damages as compensation for a vendor's delay, or of any sum which entails an inquiry and is not merely a matter for computation or taxation, cannot, however, be made on an application under these provisions[4], as such an application cannot be treated as an action for damages[5].

1 See the Law of Property Act 1925 s 49 (as amended); and para 220 ante.
2 See *Re Hargreaves and Thompson's Contract* (1886) 32 ChD 454, CA.
3 See *Re Hargreaves and Thompson's Contract* (1886) 32 ChD 454, CA. See also *Re Metropolitan District Rly Co and Cosh* (1880) 13 ChD 607, CA; *Re Higgins and Hitchman's Contract* (1882) 21 ChD 95; *Re Smith and Stott* (1883) 48 LT 512; *Re Yeilding and Westbrook* (1886) 31 ChD 344; *Re Ebsworth and Tidy's Contract* (1889) 42 ChD 23 at 53, CA; *Re Bryant and Barningham's Contract* (1890) 44 ChD 218 at 222, CA; *Re Marshall and Salt's Contract* [1900] 2 Ch 202 at 206; *Re Hare and O'More's Contract* [1901] 1 Ch 93 at 96; *Re Haedicke and Lipski's Contract* [1901] 2 Ch 666 at 670. Cf *Furneaux and Aird's Contract* [1906] WN 215. Such orders were made on a vendor's application in *Re Higgins and Percival* (1888) 59 LT 213; and *Re Walker and Oakshott's Contract* [1901] 2 Ch 383 at 387.
     As to the vendor's obligation to show and prove a good title see para 137 ante; as to the purchaser's right to recover the deposit with interest see paras 245–246 post; as to the purchaser's expenses recoverable by way of damages see para 257 post; as to the usual costs paid by the purchaser see para 323 post; and as to when an application under the Law of Property Act 1925 s 49 (as amended) is or is not the proper proceeding see paras 225–226 post.
4 Ie an application under the Law of Property Act 1925 s 49 (as amended): see para 220 ante. See also *Re Wilsons and Stevens' Contract* [1894] 3 Ch 546 at 552.
5 See *Re Hargreaves and Thompson's Contract* (1886) 32 ChD 454, CA. As to damages see paras 254–261 post; and DAMAGES.

223. Doubtful title. The court may decide that the title is too doubtful to be forced on a purchaser[1]. In particular, although the court may be prepared on an application[2] to decide a point of construction of a will or document[3], yet where there is real difficulty or doubt in construing a will, the court will not force the title on the purchaser, for that might result in his buying a lawsuit[4]. So, too, it seems that the court would not decide a question of latent ambiguity in the description of a beneficiary under a will, for on such a question evidence from beneficiaries may be needed and all beneficiaries should be before the court[5].

1 *Re Thackwray and Young's Contract* (1888) 40 ChD 34; *Re New Land Development Association and Gray* [1892] 2 Ch 138, CA; *Re Hollis' Hospital Trustees and Hague's Contract* [1899] 2 Ch 540 at 555; *Re Marshall and Salt's Contract* [1900] 2 Ch 202; *Re Handman and Wilcox's Contract* [1902] 1 Ch 599, CA. Cf *Re Wallis and Barnard's Contract* [1899] 2 Ch 515 at 521 (cited in para 221 note 9 ante).
2 Ie an application under the Law of Property Act 1925 s 49 (as amended): see para 220 ante.
3 See *Re Hill to Chapman* (1885) 54 LJ Ch 595, CA; *Re Bishop and Richardson's Contract* [1899] 1 IR 71; *Re Guyton and Rosenberg's Contract* [1901] 2 Ch 591; *Re Murphy and Griffin's Contract* [1919] 1 IR 187.
4 See *Re Nichols' and Von Joel's Contract* [1910] 1 Ch 43 at 46–47, CA, where the vendor should have taken out an originating summons for construction, the decision upon which would have bound all parties concerned. Cf *Smith v Colbourne* [1914] 2 Ch 533 at 544, CA; *Johnson v Clarke* [1928] Ch 847 at 854. A vendor in such a case who nevertheless proceeds by an application under the Law of Property Act 1925 s 49 (as amended) may even though successful be ordered to pay costs: *Re Nichols' and Von Joel's Contract* supra; *Re Hogan and Marnell's Contract* [1919] 1 IR 422; *Wilson v Thomas* [1958] 1 All ER 871, [1958] 1 WLR 422. An application under the Law of Property Act 1925 s 49 (as amended) can be amended so as to make it also an application for construction: see *Re Tippett's and Newbould's Contract* (1888) 37 ChD 444, CA. As to the court's duty to construe wills see WILLS vol 50 (Reissue) para 429.
5 See *Wilson v Thomas* [1958] 1 All ER 871 at 878, 880, [1958] 1 WLR 422 at 431, 433 per Roxburgh J. This was an action, not an application under the Law of Property Act 1925 s 49 (as amended), but the

court followed *Re Nichols' and Von Joel's Contract* [1910] 1 Ch 43, CA, which was decided on such an application, stating that the case before it was stronger. As to the misdescription of donees under a will see WILLS vol 50 (Reissue) para 567 et seq.

224. Question of validity of contract excluded. Owing to the express exclusion of the power to decide on an application under these provisions[1] questions affecting the existence or validity of the contract[2], the question whether the contract is fraudulent cannot be so decided[3]. However, the exception relates to the existence or validity of the contract in its inception, and does not preclude the court from deciding the validity of a vendor's notice to rescind the contract[4]. The fact that the existence or validity of the contract, or the right of one party or the other to rescind it, is or may be the subject of dispute between the parties does not preclude the court from deciding a point properly raised by the application[5].

1   Ie the Law of Property Act 1925 s 49 (as amended): see para 220 ante.
2   See ibid s 49(1); and para 220 ante.
3   See *Re Hargreaves and Thompson's Contract* (1886) 32 ChD 454 at 459, CA; *Re Davis and Cavey* (1888) 40 ChD 601 at 608; *Re Sandbach and Edmondson's Contract* [1891] 1 Ch 99 at 102, CA; *Re Delany and Deegan's Contract* [1905] 1 IR 602. As to contracts induced by misrepresentation see MISREPRESENTATION AND FRAUD vol 31 (Reissue) paras 704, 783 et seq, 812 et seq; CONTRACT vol 9(1) (Reissue) paras 767–768, 987.
4   See *Re Jackson and Woodburn's Contract* (1887) 37 ChD 44, following *Re Dames and Wood* (1885) 29 ChD 626, CA. As to the formation of the contract see paras 23–40 ante; and as to rescission of the contract by the vendor see paras 232–233 post.
5   See *Re Wallis and Barnard's Contract* [1899] 2 Ch 515; *Re Hughes and Ashley's Contract* [1900] 2 Ch 595, CA. Cf *Re Lander and Bagley's Contract* [1892] 3 Ch 41, where, upon a question of construction, it was decided that there was a valid subsisting agreement to grant a lease.

(ii) Questions Determinable

225. Questions as to the meaning and effect of the contract. The questions which may properly be raised and decided on an application under these provisions[1] include the following questions with regard to the meaning and effect of the contract for sale:

(1)   whether a perpetual rent agreed to be sold was properly described in the contract as a rentcharge[2];

(2)   whether under the terms of the contract the purchaser was entitled to a right of way to the land sold[3];

(3)   the effect of a plan upon the construction of expressions in particulars of sale[4];

(4)   the effect of conditions of sale limiting a purchaser's right to investigate or raise objections to the vendor's title[5], or precluding[6] or providing[7] for compensation for errors of description;

(5)   whether a condition is misleading[8];

(6)   whether in particular circumstances a vendor has, under the conditions, a right to rescind[9], and, if so, upon what terms[10];

(7)   whether a purchaser is entitled to repudiate the contract[11];

(8)   whether, and as from what date, a purchaser is liable to pay interest on his purchase money[12];

(9)   whether, on a sale of premises with possession, the property sold includes a claim for dilapidations against an outgoing tenant[13]; and

(10)   whether there is any statutory claim for compensation[14].

1   Ie the Law of Property Act 1925 s 49 (as amended): see para 220 ante.
2   See *Re Lord Gerard and Beecham's Contract* [1894] 3 Ch 295, CA. As to perpetual rent see RENTCHARGES
    AND ANNUITIES vol 39(2) (Reissue) para 780.
3   See *Re Lavery and Kirk* (1888) 33 Sol Jo 127; *Re Hughes and Ashley's Contract* [1900] 2 Ch 595 at 600, CA;
    Re Walmsley and Shaw's Contract [1917] 1 Ch 93. As to rights of way see EASEMENTS AND PROFITS À
    PRENDRE.
4   See *Re Lindsay and Forder's Contract* (1895) 72 LT 832; *Re Wellings and Parsons' Contract* (1906) 97 LT 165;
    Re Freeman and Taylor's Contract (1907) 97 LT 39.
5   See *Re Cox and Neve's Contract* [1891] 2 Ch 109 at 118; *Re National Provincial Bank of England and Marsh*
    [1895] 1 Ch 190; *Re Scott and Alvarez's Contract, Scott v Alvarez* [1895] 1 Ch 596, CA (subsequent
    proceedings [1895] 2 Ch 603, CA); *Re Englefield Holdings Ltd and Sinclair's Contract* [1962] 3 All ER 503,
    [1962] 1 WLR 1119.
6   See *Re Beyfus and Masters's Contract* (1888) 39 ChD 110, CA.
7   See *Re Leyland and Taylor's Contract* [1900] 2 Ch 625, CA.
8   See *Re Marsh and Earl Granville* (1883) 24 ChD 11, CA; *Re Sandbach and Edmondson's Contract* [1891] 1
    Ch 99, CA; *Re Turpin and Ahern's Contract* [1905] 1 IR 85; *Faruqi v English Real Estates Ltd* [1979] 1 WLR
    963, 38 P & CR 318.
9   See *Re Jackson and Oakshott* (1880) 14 ChD 851; *Re Great Northern Rly Co and Sanderson* (1884) 25 ChD
    788; *Re Monckton and Gilzean* (1884) 27 ChD 555; *Re Dames and Wood* (1885) 29 ChD 626, CA; *Re Jackson
    and Woodburn's Contract* (1887) 37 ChD 44; *Re Arbib and Class's Contract* [1891] 1 Ch 601, CA; *Re Deighton
    and Harris's Contract* [1898] 1 Ch 458, CA; *Re Jackson and Haden's Contract* [1906] 1 Ch 412, CA; *Re Weston
    and Thomas's Contract* [1907] 1 Ch 244. As to the vendor's right to rescind the contract see paras 232–233
    post.
10 See *Re Spindler and Mear's Contract* [1901] 1 Ch 908.
11 See *Re White and Smith's Contract* [1896] 1 Ch 637; *Re Haedicke and Lipski's Contract* [1901] 2 Ch 666; *Re
    Stone and Saville's Contract* [1963] 1 All ER 353, [1963] 1 WLR 163, CA. As to repudiation by the
    purchaser see paras 239–244 post.
12 See *Re Pigott and Great Western Rly Co* (1881) 18 ChD 146; *Re Riley to Streatfield* (1886) 34 ChD 386;
    Re Hetling and Merton's Contract [1893] 3 Ch 269, CA; *Re London Corpn and Tubbs' Contract* [1894] 2 Ch
    524, CA; *Re Wilsons and Stevens' Contract* [1894] 3 Ch 546; *Re Earl of Strafford and Maples* [1896] 1 Ch
    235, CA; *Re Woods and Lewis' Contract* [1898] 2 Ch 211, CA. See also *Re Young and Harston's Contract*
    (1885) 31 ChD 168, CA, where the court ordered a vendor to repay an excess of interest paid under
    protest and without prejudice. As to the vendor's right to interest on purchase money see paras 194–197
    ante.
13 See *Re Edie and Brown's Contract* (1888) 58 LT 307. See also *Re Earl of Derby and Fergusson's Contract* [1912]
    1 Ch 479 (sale of agricultural land where tenant entitled to compensation for improvements); *Re Lyne-
    Stephens and Scott-Miller's Contract* [1920] 1 Ch 472, CA (purchaser's claim to dilapidations). As to the
    vendor's entitlement to any sum paid in respect of dilapidations at the end of the tenancy see para 192
    ante.
14 See *Re Armitage's Contract, Armitage v Inkpen* [1949] Ch 666 (compensation in respect of war damage)
    (see WAR AND ARMED CONFLICT vol 49(1) (Reissue) para 625 et seq); *Re Hamilton-Snowball's
    Conveyance* [1959] Ch 308, [1958] 2 All ER 319 (compensation in respect of requisition) (see WAR AND
    ARMED CONFLICT vol 49(1) (Reissue) para 600 et seq).

226. Other questions determinable. Other questions which may be determined on
an application under these provisions[1] are:

(1) questions as to the abstract, such as whether the abstract is complete
     notwithstanding that a particular document is not abstracted in chief[2];

(2) questions whether the vendor has discharged his obligation to show and prove a
     good title in accordance with the contract[3]; as to the title of persons filling a
     particular capacity[4]; and whether the vendor is bound to answer or comply with
     a particular requisition[5];

(3) questions as to the interpretation and effect of Acts of Parliament, if they arise out
     of, or are connected with, the contract[6];

(4) questions as to the incidence of and liability for expenses, such as stamps[7], the cost
     of searching for and obtaining title deeds not in the vendor's possession[8], of the
     perusal and execution of the transfer by concurring parties[9], or of obtaining a
     surveyor's certificate to prove performance of a building covenant in a lease[10];

(5) questions as to the payment of compensation[11];

(6)   questions as to the form of the assurance to the purchaser, including questions as to the proper parties to concur in the transfer[12], as to the form of the transfer[13], and as to the insertion in it of restrictions or of covenants on the part of the purchaser[14] or the vendor[15]; and

(7)   questions as to the right to the title deeds of the property sold[16].

1   Ie the Law of Property Act 1925 s 49 (as amended): see para 220 ante.

2   See *Re Stamford, Spalding and Boston Banking Co and Knight's Contract* [1900] 1 Ch 287; cf *Re Ebsworth and Tidy's Contract* (1889) 42 ChD 23 at 31, 34, CA, per North J. As to the need for an abstract of title with respect to both unregistered and registered land see paras 138, 141–149 ante.

3   Such questions, being the subject of requisitions or objections, are necessarily within the scope of an application under the Law of Property Act 1925 s 49 (as amended) (see para 220 ante): see *Re Coward and Adam's Purchase* (1875) LR 20 Eq 179 (receipt by married woman for legacy); *Re Packman and Moss* (1875) 1 ChD 214; *Re Brown and Sibly's Contract* (1876) 3 ChD 156; *Re Coleman and Jarrom* (1876) 4 ChD 165; *Re Frith and Osbourne* (1876) 3 ChD 618 (power to partition); *Re Foster and Lister* (1877) 6 ChD 87 (validity of post-nuptial settlement); *Re White and Hindle* (1877) 7 ChD 201; *Re Hutchinson and Tenant* (1878) 8 ChD 540; *Sturge and Great Western Rly Co* (1881) 19 ChD 444 (construction of a will); *Re Bellamy and Metropolitan Board of Works* (1883) 24 ChD 387, CA; *Hallett to Martin* (1883) 24 ChD 624 (power to grant lease); *Re Walker and Hughes' Contract* (1883) 24 ChD 698; *Re Harman and Uxbridge and Rickmansworth Rly Co* (1883) 24 ChD 720; *Re Glenny and Hartley* (1884) 25 ChD 611; *Re Great Northern Rly Co and Sanderson* (1884) 25 ChD 788 (removal of incumbrances); *Re Tweedie and Miles* (1884) 27 ChD 315 (continuance of trust for sale); *Re Flower and Metropolitan Board of Works* (1884) 27 ChD 592 (payment of purchase money to trustee-vendors personally); *Re Horne and Hellard* (1885) 29 ChD 736 (proof that charge in debentures has not crystallised); *Nichols to Nixey* (1885) 29 ChD 1005 (as to power of appointment not vesting in trustee in bankruptcy); *Re Naylor and Spendla's Contract* (1886) 34 ChD 217, CA (as to fine and fees payable to lord and steward in respect of copyholds); *Re Coates to Parsons* (1886) 34 ChD 370 (as to validity of appointment of trustees); *Re Lidiard and Jackson's and Broadley's Contract* (1889) 42 ChD 254 (presumption as to enfranchisement of copyholds); *Re New Land Development Association and Gray* [1892] 2 Ch 138, CA (bankrupt's power to dispose of after-acquired property); *Re Lord Sudeley and Baines & Co* [1894] 1 Ch 334; *Re Clayton and Barclay's Contract* [1895] 2 Ch 212 (bankrupt's power to dispose of after-acquired property); *Re Lord and Fullerton's Contract* [1896] 1 Ch 228, CA (as to effect of disclaimer by trustee); *Re Dyson and Fowke* [1896] 2 Ch 720 (validity of power of sale given by will); *Re Carter and Kenderdine's Contract* [1897] 1 Ch 776, CA (effect of bankruptcy on voluntary settlement); *Re Rumney and Smith* [1897] 2 Ch 351, CA (power of sale by transferee of mortgage); *Re Calcott and Elvin's Contract* [1898] 2 Ch 460, CA (registration of adjudication in bankruptcy in the former Middlesex Deeds Registry); *Re Blaiberg and Abrahams* [1899] 2 Ch 340 (notice of trusts); *Re Hollis' Hospital Trustees and Hague's Contract* [1899] 2 Ch 540 (application of rule against perpetuities); *Re Marshall and Salt's Contract* [1900] 2 Ch 202 (power to assign leaseholds without lessor's consent); *Re Judd and Poland and Skelcher's Contract* [1906] 1 Ch 684, CA (sale of leaseholds in lots by trustees by means of underleases); *Re Lloyds Bank Ltd and Lillington's Contract* [1912] 1 Ch 601 (sale as 'leasehold' of property held on underlease and forming part of property comprised in two head leases); *Re Morrell and Chapman's Contract* [1915] 1 Ch 162 (whether trustees could release from trust legacies: held not a question of title); *Re Kissock and Currie's Contract* [1916] 1 IR 376, Ir CA; *Re Murphy and Griffin's Contract* [1919] 1 IR 187; *Re W & R Holmes and Cosmopolitan Press Ltd's Contract* [1944] Ch 53, [1943] 2 All ER 716 (validity of exercise of power of sale under will); *Horton v Kurzke* [1971] 2 All ER 577, [1971] 1 WLR 769; *MEPC Ltd v Christian-Edwards* [1981] AC 205, [1979] 3 All ER 752, HL (whether, on sale in 1973, there was any likelihood of enforcement of contract of sale made in 1912); *Walia v Michael Naughton Ltd* [1985] 3 All ER 673, [1985] 1 WLR 1115 (whether a general power of attorney entitled donee of the power to transfer as trustee). As to the vendor's obligation to show and prove a good title see para 137 ante.

4   See *Re Waddell's Contract* (1876) 2 ChD 172 (survivor of two trustees in bankruptcy); *Re Metropolitan Bank and Jones* (1876) 2 ChD 366 (survivor of two liquidators of a company); *Re Kearley and Clayton's Contract* (1878) 7 ChD 615 (debtor who had entered into composition with his creditors); *Osborne to Rowlett* (1880) 13 ChD 774; *Re Morton and Hallett* (1880) 15 ChD 143, CA (heir of last surviving trustee); *Re Tanqueray-Willaume and Landau* (1882) 20 ChD 465, CA (executor selling freeholds); *Re Whistler* (1887) 35 ChD 561; *Re Venn and Furze's Contract* [1894] 2 Ch 101; *Re Maskell and Goldfinch's Contract* [1895] 2 Ch 525 (assurance of gavelkind land by infant); *Re Verrell's Contract* [1903] 1 Ch 65 (executor selling leaseholds); *Re Crunden and Meux's Contract* [1909] 1 Ch 690 (devisee or executor of last surviving trustee); *Re Cavendish and Arnold's Contract* [1912] WN 83 (executor selling with reservation of minerals).

5   See *Re Ford and Hill* (1879) 10 ChD 365, CA; cf *Re Glenton and Saunders to Haden* (1885) 53 LT 434, CA. As to requisitions on title see paras 163–166 ante.

6   See *Re Dudson's Contract* (1878) 8 ChD 628, CA (Fines and Recoveries Act 1833); *Re Bowling and Welby's Contract* [1895] 1 Ch 663, CA (Companies Act 1862 (repealed)); *Re Smith and Stott* (1883) 29 ChD 1009n; *Re Chapman and Hobbs* (1885) 29 ChD 1007; *Re Highett and Bird's Contract* [1903] 1 Ch 287, CA; *Re Taunton and West of England Perpetual Benefit Building Society and Roberts' Contract* [1912] 2 Ch 381 (Conveyancing Act 1881 (repealed)); *Re Harkness and Allsopp's Contract* [1896] 2 Ch 358; *Re Brooke and Fremlin's Contract* [1898] 1 Ch 647 (Married Women's Property Act 1882); *Re Earle and Webster's Contract* (1883) 24 ChD 144; *Re Earl of Strafford and Maples* [1896] 1 Ch 235, CA; *Re Pocock and Prankerd's Contract* [1896] 1 Ch 302; *Re Fisher and Grazebrook's Contract* [1898] 2 Ch 660; *Re Mundy and Roper's Contract* [1899] 1 Ch 275, CA (Settled Land Acts (see generally SETTLEMENTS para 601 et seq post)); *Re Pawley and London and Provincial Bank* [1900] 1 Ch 58; *Re Cary and Lott's Contract* [1901] 2 Ch 463; *Re Cohen's Executors and LCC* [1902] 1 Ch 187; *Re Cavendish and Arnold's Contract* [1912] WN 83 (Land Transfer Act 1897 (repealed)); *Re Baroness Bateman and Parker's Contract* [1899] 1 Ch 599 (Consecration of Churchyards Act 1867); *Re Ponsford and Newport District School Board* [1894] 1 Ch 454, CA; *Re Ecclesiastical Comrs and New City of London Brewery Co's Contract* [1895] 1 Ch 702 (Disused Burial Grounds Act 1884); *Corpn of the Sons of the Clergy and Skinner* [1893] 1 Ch 178 (Charitable Trusts Act 1853 (repealed); Charitable Trusts Amendment Act 1855 (repealed)). As to the relationship of statutes to contracts see STATUTES vol 44(1) (Reissue) para 1367; CONTRACT vol 9(1) (Reissue) para 867 et seq.

7   See *Whiting to Loomes* (1881) 17 ChD 10, CA.

8   See *Re Johnson and Tustin* (1885) 30 ChD 42, CA (deeds required for purpose of making proper abstract); *Re Willett and Argenti* (1889) 60 LT 735; *Re Stuart and Olivant and Seadon's Contract* [1896] 2 Ch 328, CA (deeds required to verify abstract); *Re Duthy and Jesson's Contract* [1898] 1 Ch 419 (deeds required for purpose of being handed over to purchaser on completion). As to the expenses of the production and inspection of all documents of title not in the possession of the vendor see para 171 ante.

9   See *Re Willett and Argenti* (1889) 60 LT 735; *Re Sander and Walford's Contract* (1900) 83 LT 316. As to the disposition of registered and unregistered land by transfer see para 262 note 2 post. As to the expenses of preparing the transfer see para 129 ante.

10   See *Re Moody and Yates' Contract* (1885) 30 ChD 344, CA. As to obtaining a surveyor's certificate to prove performance of a building covenant in a lease see BUILDING CONTRACTS, ARCHITECTS, ENGINEERS AND SURVEYORS vol 4(2) (Reissue) para 542; LANDLORD AND TENANT vol 27(1) (Reissue) para 362.

11   See *Re Orange and Wright's Contract* (1885) 52 LT 606 (claim by vendor for increase of price due to mistake in quantities); *Re Terry and White's Contract* (1886) 32 ChD 14, CA; *Aspinalls to Powell and Scholefield* (1889) 60 LT 595; *Re Fawcett and Holmes' Contract* (1889) 42 ChD 150, CA; *Re Laitwood's Contract* (1892) 36 Sol Jo 255 (compensation for delay in delivery of possession, and for injury to and deterioration of premises by removal of fixtures and fittings sold with the premises); *Re Hare and O'More's Contract* [1901] 1 Ch 93 (compensation to purchaser for deficiency in quantity). See also *Re Turner and Skelton* (1879) 13 ChD 130 (compensation after completion); cf *Re Leyland and Taylor's Contract* [1900] 2 Ch 625, CA. Damages for the vendor's delay in completion are not 'compensation', and cannot be recovered on an application under the Law of Property Act 1925 s 49 (as amended): see *Re Wilsons and Stevens' Contract* [1894] 3 Ch 546; and para 256 post. As to damages generally see DAMAGES.

12   See *Re Cookes' Contract* (1877) 4 ChD 454; *Davies to Jones and Evans* (1883) 24 ChD 190 (beneficiaries on sale by trustees or executors); *Royal Society of London and Thompson* (1881) 17 ChD 407; *Finnis and Young to Forbes and Pochin (No 2)* (1883) 24 ChD 591 (Charity Commissioners); *Re Thompson and Curzon* (1885) 29 ChD 177; *Re Brooke and Fremlin's Contract* [1898] 1 Ch 647 (husband of married woman); *Re Bedingfeld and Herring's Contract* [1893] 2 Ch 332 (incumbrancers and trustee in bankruptcy of tenant for life consenting to sale by trustees); *Re Morrell and Chapman's Contract* [1915] 1 Ch 162 (release from trust legacies). As to parties by whom the assurance is made see para 269 post.

13   See *Re Pigott and Great Western Rly Co* (1881) 18 ChD 146. See also *Re Agg-Gardner* (1884) 25 ChD 600 (purchaser's right to acknowledgment and undertaking as to documents); *Re Walmsley and Shaw's Contract* [1917] 1 Ch 93 (insertion of general words). As to the form of transfer see para 265 post.

14   See *Re Gray and Metropolitan Rly Co* (1881) 44 LT 567; *Re Monckton and Gilzean* (1884) 27 ChD 555; *Re Mordy and Cowman* (1884) 51 LT 721, CA; *Re Wallis and Barnard's Contract* [1899] 2 Ch 515; *Re Hughes and Ashley's Contract* [1900] 2 Ch 595, CA. As to the proper form of covenant by a purchaser buying subject to restrictions see *Re Poole and Clarke's Contract* [1904] 2 Ch 173, CA; and as to covenants made by the vendor and the purchaser in the transfer generally see paras 81 ante, 293 post.

15   See *Re Birmingham and District Land Co and Allday* [1893] 1 Ch 342. See note 13 supra.

16   See *Re Williams and Duchess of Newcastle's Contract* [1897] 2 Ch 144; *Re Jenkins and Commercial Electric Theatre Co's Contract* (1917) 61 Sol Jo 283 (title deeds not in vendor's possession). As to the right to the title deeds of the property sold see para 299 post; and as to title deeds not in the vendor's possession see para 171 ante.

(iii) Procedure

227. The application. Application under the summary procedure[1] may be made to the court[2]. On such an application, the judge may make such an order as he thinks just, and he can also order how and by whom all or any of the costs[3] of and incident to the application are to be borne and paid[4].

1 Ie under the Law of Property Act 1925 s 49 (as amended): see para 220 ante.
2 As to the jurisdiction of the courts see para 220 note 6 ante. As from 26 April 1999, proceedings are started by the issue of a claim form: see CPR Pts 7, 8. As to the CPR see para 133 note 1 ante. As to summary judgment see CPR Pt 24. As to the procedure before that date see RSC Ord 5 r 3; and *Practice Note* [1959] 2 All ER 629, sub nom *Practice Direction* [1959] 1 WLR 743. See also *Re Cooper and Allen's Contract for Sale to Harlech* (1876) 4 ChD 802 at 827 per Jessel MR; *Re Coleman and Jarrom* (1876) 4 ChD 165 at 168; *Re Burroughs, Lynn and Sexton* (1877) 5 ChD 601, CA; *Osborne to Rowlett* (1880) 13 ChD 774 at 781 per Jessel MR; *Re Warner's Settled Estates, Warner to Steel* (1881) 17 ChD 711; *Re Naylor and Spendla's Contract* (1886) 34 ChD 217, CA; *Re Jackson and Woodburn's Contract* (1887) 37 ChD 44 at 47; *Re Bartlett and Berry's Contract* (1897) 76 LT 751; *MEPC Ltd v Christian-Edwards*, [1981] AC 205, [1979] 3 All ER 752, HL. See generally PRACTICE AND PROCEDURE.
3 As to costs see para 228 post.
4 See the Law of Property Act 1925 s 49(1); and para 220 ante. The judge may direct a reference to chambers as to the form of conveyance (*Re Monckton and Gilzean* (1884) 27 ChD 555 at 564) or the amount of compensation payable (*Aspinalls to Powell and Scholefield* (1889) 60 LT 595).

228. Costs. As a general rule, the costs of the application are ordered to be paid by the party whose contention has not been upheld by the court[1]. If it is decided that the title is good, the purchaser must pay the costs, even though the title is not such as a conveyancer would advise a purchaser to accept without a decision of the court upon it[2]. A vendor who does not exercise his right to rescind directly the application is issued, but does so at a later stage before the hearing, may be ordered to pay the costs of the proceedings, even if the condition giving the right to rescind provides for the return of the deposit without any interest, costs of investigating title, or other compensation or payment whatsoever[3]. Where a vendor is ordered to pay costs, they may be made a charge upon his interest in the property[4].

1 See *Re Packman and Moss* (1875) 1 ChD 214 at 217; *Re Waddell's Contract* (1876) 2 ChD 172 at 176; *Re Cookes' Contract* (1877) 4 ChD 454 at 463; *Re Ford and Hill* (1879) 10 ChD 365 at 367, 371, CA; *Re Johnson and Tustin* (1885) 30 ChD 42 at 49, CA; *Re Davis and Cavey* (1888) 40 ChD 601 at 609; *Re Ebsworth and Tidy's Contract* (1889) 42 ChD 23 at 53, CA; *Re Starr-Bowkett Building Society and Sibun's Contract* (1889) 42 ChD 375 at 386, CA. As to the liability for costs of a vendor who insists on proceeding by an application under the Law of Property Act 1925 s 49 (as amended) (see para 220 ante), although the proper procedure is by application for construction see para 223 note 4 ante.
2 See *Osborne to Rowlett* (1880) 13 ChD 774 at 798; *Re Tanqueray-Willaume and Landau* (1882) 20 ChD 465 at 483, CA. Sometimes, however, the purchaser has not been made to pay costs where the question was proper to be submitted to the court (*Re Coward and Adam's Purchase* (1875) LR 20 Eq 179; *Finch v Jukes* [1877] WN 211; *Re Metropolitan District Rly Co and Cosh* (1880) 13 ChD 607 at 613, CA; *Re Great Northern Rly Co and Sanderson* (1884) 25 ChD 788 at 794), or where it is one on which there have been conflicting decisions (*Osborne to Rowlett* supra at 798). As to the vendor's obligation to show and prove a good title see para 137 ante. As to conveyancers see para 3 ante.
3 See *Re Spindler and Mear's Contract* [1901] 1 Ch 908. As to the vendor's right to rescission see paras 232–233 ante; as to the vendor's right to interest on the purchase money see paras 194–197 ante; and as to proof of title see paras 137–173 ante.
4 See *Re Yeilding and Westbrook* (1886) 31 ChD 344; *Re Higgins and Percival* (1888) 59 LT 213 at 214. As to the purchaser's lien in the property see LIEN vol 28 (Reissue) para 763.

229. Appeal. Appeal from an order made on an application under these provisions[1] lies to the Court of Appeal[2], and must be brought within four weeks from the date when the order was sealed or otherwise perfected[3].

1   Ie the Law of Property Act 1925 s 49 (as amended): see para 220 ante.
2   See the Supreme Court Act 1981 s 16(1). See also PRACTICE AND PROCEDURE.
3   See CPR Sch 1 RSC Ord 59 rr 1, 4(1). As to the CPR see para 133 note 1 ante. As to appeals to the Court of Appeal generally see PRACTICE AND PROCEDURE.

230. Enforcement of order. Where a party has obtained an order on an application under these provisions[1] which requires something to be done by the other party, and the other party fails to comply, it is usually proper to apply to the court for enforcement of the order, and not to commence an action for specific performance[2]. Where, however, the order does not contain any direction with which a party fails to comply, but merely decides the rights of one or both parties under the contract, an action for specific performance is, it seems, the only remedy open if one party declines to complete the contract[3].

1   Ie the Law of Property Act 1925 s 49 (as amended): see para 220 ante.
2   See *Thompson v Ringer* (1880) 44 LT 507. As to the mode of enforcing orders see CONTEMPT OF COURT; JUDGMENTS AND ORDERS. As to specific performance see paras 247–253 post; and SPECIFIC PERFORMANCE.
3   See *Re Scott and Alvarez's Contract, Scott v Alvarez* [1895] 1 Ch 596 at 610, CA, where this course was adopted, and its propriety does not appear to have been questioned. As to completion of the contract see paras 262–325 post.

231. Review of order. In a proper case where, after an order on an application under these provisions[1] is made, fresh matter is for the first time discovered which is material to the questions raised on the application and which could not be produced or used by the party claiming the benefit of it at the time when the order on the application was made, the order may be reviewed, and the question decided on the application reopened. In such circumstances, a judge of the Chancery Division has jurisdiction to review an order of the Court of Appeal[2].

1   Ie the Law of Property Act 1925 s 49 (as amended): see para 220 ante.
2   See *Re Scott and Alvarez's Contract, Scott v Alvarez* [1895] 1 Ch 596 at 610, 622, CA, per Kekewich J; subsequent proceedings [1895] 2 Ch 603 at 611, CA. See also ESTOPPEL vol 16 (Reissue) para 981.

(6) REMEDIES UNDER AN UNCOMPLETED CONTRACT

(i) Rescission and Resale by the Vendor

232. Rescission. If the contract contains a condition entitling the vendor to rescind on the happening of certain events and those events happen, the vendor may rescind[1]. In the absence of such a condition, the vendor may rescind only if the purchaser's conduct is such as to amount to a repudiation of the contract[2] and the parties can be restored to their former position[3]. A vendor who has claimed rescission and specific performance in the alternative can elect at the hearing for which remedy he will ask[4].

If the vendor, acting within his rights, rescinds the contract, he may resell the property as owner[5] and retain any excess of price obtained on the resale beyond that fixed by the contract[6]. If the rescission follows a repudiatory breach by the purchaser, the vendor may recover damages[7], including, if the purchaser has been in possession, an occupation rent[8]. Where the vendor rescinds the contract and resells under his absolute title, the purchaser forfeits the deposit whatever the result of the resale. Any deficiency in the resale price may be recovered by the vendor as damages consequential on a repudiatory breach by the purchaser[9], but the deposit must be brought into account[10].

1   See paras 87, 104–108, 121 ante. As to the formation of the contract see paras 23–40 ante.
2   *Howe v Smith* (1884) 27 ChD 89 at 95, CA, per Cotton LJ. Conduct which would disentitle the purchaser
      to specific performance does not necessarily amount to a repudiation of the contract. Even though the
      purchaser has lost his equitable right to specific performance, he may be entitled to treat the contract as
      subsisting and recover damages for breach of it: *Cornwall v Henson* [1900] 2 Ch 298, CA. If, after an order
      for specific performance, the purchaser defaults in paying the purchase money, the vendor is entitled to
      an order for rescission (*Foligno v Martin* (1853) 16 Beav 586; *Watson v Cox* (1873) LR 15 Eq 219; *Hall v
      Burnell* [1911] 2 Ch 551) and may recover damages for any loss (*Johnson v Agnew* [1980] AC 367, [1979]
      1 All ER 883, HL). As to conduct amounting to repudiation see CONTRACT vol 9(1) (Reissue) para 997
      et seq. As to rescission for misrepresentation or mistake see MISREPRESENTATION AND FRAUD vol 31
      (Reissue) para 814 et seq; MISTAKE. As to rightful repudiation by the purchaser see paras 239–244 post.
3   *Thorpe v Fasey* [1949] Ch 649, [1949] 2 All ER 393.
4   *Farrant v Olver* (1922) 91 LJ Ch 758.
5   *Howe v Smith* (1884) 27 ChD 89, CA.
6   *Ex p Hunter* (1801) 6 Ves 94. As to retention of the deposit see paras 234–238 post.
7   *Johnson v Agnew* [1980] AC 367, [1979] 1 All ER 883, HL, overruling the following cases: *Henty v Schröder*
      (1879) 12 ChD 666; *Hutchings v Humphreys* (1885) 54 LJ Ch 650; *Jackson v de Kadich* [1904] WN 168;
      Barber v Wolfe [1945] Ch 187, [1945] 1 All ER 399; *Horsler v Zorro* [1975] Ch 302, [1975] 1 All ER 584;
      and *Capital and Suburban Properties Ltd v Swycher* [1976] Ch 319, [1976] 1 All ER 881, CA. See also *Ogle
      v Comboyuro Investments Pty Ltd* (1976) 136 CLR 444, Aust HC. As to the measure of damages see paras
      254–261 post; and as to damages generally see DAMAGES.
8   Cf *Barber v Wolfe* [1945] Ch 187, [1945] 1 All ER 399, overruled in *Johnson v Agnew* [1980] AC 367, [1979]
      1 All ER 883, HL. As to rents and profits see para 189 ante; and as to occupation rent see para 191 ante.
9   *Johnson v Agnew* [1980] AC 367, [1979] 1 All ER 883, HL. Where the purchase money is payable by
      instalments with provision for forfeiture of all the instalments paid on failure to pay any instalment, the
      provision is in the nature of a penalty, from which relief can be granted (*Kilmer v British Columbia Orchard
      Lands Ltd* [1913] AC 319, PC), provided the purchaser is ultimately prepared to make good the default
      and complete the contract. In *Mussen v Van Diemen's Land Co* [1938] Ch 253, [1938] 1 All ER 210, the
      purchaser was not prepared to make good the default and relief was refused; and in *Stockloser v Johnson*
      [1954] 1 QB 476, [1954] 1 All ER 630, CA, the purchaser could not recover instalments of the purchase
      price because he could not satisfy the court that it was unconscionable of the vendor to retain them. See
      also *Galbraith v Mitchenall Estates Ltd* [1965] 2 QB 473, [1964] 2 All ER 653; *Starside Properties Ltd v
      Mustapha* [1974] 2 All ER 567, [1974] 1 WLR 816, CA; *Hyundai Shipbuilding and Heavy Industries Co Ltd
      v Pournaras* [1978] 2 Lloyd's Rep 502, CA; and CONTRACT vol 9(1) (Reissue) para 985. If time is of the
      essence of the contract, the court will not order specific performance unless the condition as to time has
      been waived: see *Steedman v Drinkle* [1916] 1 AC 275 at 279, PC, explaining *Kilmer v British Columbia
      Orchard Lands Ltd* [1913] AC 319, PC; and see 'A Conveyancer's Letter: Forfeiture of Instalments of
      Purchase Money' (1938) 85 Law Journal 169.
10   *Howe v Smith* (1884) 27 ChD 89 at 105, CA, per Fry LJ; *Ockenden v Henly* (1858) EB & E 485. See also
      para 233 note 1 post.

233. Deficiency on resale. In calculating the deficiency on a resale under a power
contained in the contract the purchaser is entitled to be credited with the amount of the
deposit[1]. However, this rule only applies where the power of resale is exercised[2].

1   *Ockenden v Henly* (1858) EB & E 485; *Howe v Smith* (1884) 27 ChD 89, CA; *Shuttleworth v Clews* [1910]
      1 Ch 176, pointing out the error in this respect in the order in *Griffiths v Vezey* [1906] 1 Ch 796. See also
      Lamond v Davall (1847) 9 QB 1030; *Catton v Bennett* (1884) 51 LT 70. As to the formation of the contract
      see paras 23–40 ante; and as to the completion of the contract see paras 262–325 post.
2   *Essex v Daniell, Daniell v Essex* (1875) LR 10 CP 538 at 550.

(ii) Forfeiture of Deposit

234. Deposit. A deposit paid under a contract of sale[1] serves two purposes: if the sale is
completed it counts as part payment of the purchase money, but primarily it is a security
for the performance of the contract[2], and it is usual to provide expressly that, if the
purchaser fails to observe the conditions of the contract, the deposit is to be forfeited to
the vendor[3]. However, such a provision is not necessary, and, unless the contract taken
as a whole shows an intention to exclude forfeiture[4], the vendor is entitled, by virtue of

the purpose of the deposit, to retain it as forfeited, if the contract goes off due to the purchaser's default[5]. If the deposit has been paid to a stakeholder, the vendor can require it to be paid over to himself[6]. The rule as to retention by the vendor applies only to money paid as a deposit, not to instalments of purchase money[7]. By custom, the usual deposit paid is 10 per cent of the purchase price[8]. Forfeiture of a higher deposit may be held void as a penalty[9].

Where agreement has been reached subject to contract and a deposit has been paid, the deposit must be repaid if no binding contract is executed[10]. An estate agent does not have implied or ostensible authority to receive such a pre-contractual deposit on behalf of the proposed vendor; in the absence of actual authority, therefore, the proposed vendor is not liable for the agent's default in failing to repay the deposit[11].

1   As to the formation of the contract see paras 23–40 ante; and as to the completion of the contract see paras 262–325 post.
2   *Depree v Bedborough* (1863) 4 Giff 479 (a sale by auction by court order); *Collins v Stimson* (1883) 11 QBD 142, DC; *Howe v Smith* (1884) 27 ChD 89 at 95, 98, CA; *Soper v Arnold* (1889) 14 App Cas 429 at 435, HL, per Lord Macnaghten; *Levy v Stogdon* [1898] 1 Ch 478 at 485 (affd [1899] 1 Ch 5, CA); *Hall v Burnell* [1911] 2 Ch 551; *Lowe v Hope* [1970] Ch 94 at 97–98, [1969] 3 All ER 605 at 607 per Pennycuick J (approving the statement in the text). See also *Re A Solicitor* [1966] 3 All ER 52 at 57, [1966] 1 WLR 1604 at 1610 per Pennycuick J. As to the payment of a deposit see paras 86–87 ante; and CONTRACT vol 9(1) (Reissue) para 1134. Sometimes an insurance backed deposit guarantee scheme is now used instead of a cash deposit.
3   *Gee v Pearse* (1848) 2 De G & Sm 325 at 341. See also para 97 ante. If the vendor is a tenant for life selling under his statutory powers, a forfeited deposit is capital money: *Re Ward's Settled Estate* (1919) 63 Sol Jo 319; and see SETTLEMENTS para 944 post. Presumably the same would apply to trustees of land, holding for successive beneficiaries, who sell under the powers conferred by the Trusts of Land and Appointment of Trustees Act 1996 s 6: see SETTLEMENTS para 903 post; TRUSTS vol 48 (Reissue) para 894.
4   See *Palmer v Temple* (1839) 9 Ad & El 508, where a provision for payment of £1,000 as liquidated damages by either party in default was held to show an intention against forfeiture of a deposit of £300. It was there said that the question of forfeiture depends on the intention of the parties to be collected from the whole instrument (see *Howe v Smith* (1884) 27 ChD 89 at 97, CA), but in practice an exclusion of forfeiture is never intended. Either there is an express clause of forfeiture, or there is simply a payment by way of deposit, and this implies liability to forfeiture (see the Standard Conditions of Sale (3rd Edn), condition 2.2; and para 86 ante). As to the Standard Conditions of Sale see para 1 note 4 ante.
5   According to the law of vendor and purchaser the inference is that such a deposit (ie a payment of money simply as a 'deposit') is paid as a guarantee for the performance of the contract, and where the contract goes off by default of the purchaser, the vendor is entitled to retain the deposit: *Collins v Stimson* (1883) 11 QBD 142 at 143, DC, per Pollock B. See also *Howe v Smith* (1884) 27 ChD 89, CA; *Levy v Stogdon* [1898] 1 Ch 478; *Sprague v Booth* [1909] AC 576 at 580, PC. The law as to forfeiture of deposits applies to sales by the court: *Depree v Bedborough* (1863) 4 Giff 479.
6   The nature of the deposit and the implied terms on which, in the absence of express terms, it is paid, are not affected by the fact that it is paid to a stakeholder instead of to the vendor: *Hall v Burnell* [1911] 2 Ch 551; *Collins v Stimson* (1883) 11 QBD 142 at 143, DC; *Hart v Porthgain Harbour Co Ltd* [1903] 1 Ch 690 at 696. As to payment to a stakeholder see para 86 note 1 ante. When the deposit is recovered from the vendor, the court has a discretion to award interest: see para 86 text and note 6 ante. As to sales under the Settled Land Act 1925 see 1 Williams Law relating to Vendors and Purchasers of Real Estate and Chattels Real (4th Edn, 1936) 364; and SETTLEMENTS para 827 et seq post. If an IOU has been given for the deposit, and the deposit is forfeited, the IOU is evidence to support an action for its recovery by the vendor: *Hinton v Sparkes* (1868) LR 3 CP 161. See also *Cleave v Moore* (1857) 3 Jur NS 48; *Hodgens v Keon* [1894] 2 IR 657, Ir CA; and AUCTION vol 2 (Reissue) para 995.
7   See *Cornwall v Henson* [1900] 2 Ch 298 at 302, 305, CA. This distinction between a deposit which is forfeitable on the purchaser's default and a part payment which is returnable is not confined to sales of land: see *Dies v British and International Mining and Finance Corpn Ltd* [1939] 1 KB 724; and CONTRACT vol 9(1) (Reissue) para 1134. Cf *Hyundai Heavy Industries Co Ltd v Papadopoulos* [1980] 2 All ER 29, [1980] 1 WLR 1129, HL; *Stocznia Gdanska SA v Latvian Shipping Co* [1998] 1 All ER 883, [1998] Lloyd's Rep 609, HL. Subject to his right to retain money paid as a deposit, the vendor on rescinding the contract must give up all benefits which he has enjoyed under it. He must therefore return money paid as part of the purchase money: see *Harrison v Holland* [1922] 1 KB 211, CA; *Mayson v Clouet* [1924] AC 980 at 987, PC, where the contract specially distinguished between deposit and instalments. As to the forfeiture of instalments see para 232 note 9 ante.

8 See the Standard Conditions of Sale (3rd Edn), condition 2.2.1; and para 86 ante.
9 *Workers Trust and Merchant Bank Ltd v Dojap Investments Ltd* [1993] AC 573, [1993] 2 All ER 370, PC (attempt to forfeit 25% deposit void as penalty; court would not allow retention of 10%).
10 *Chillingworth v Esche* [1924] 1 Ch 97, CA. As to the practice of paying a nominal deposit on the signing of a preliminary agreement see para 1 ante.
11 *Sorrell v Finch* [1977] AC 728, [1976] 2 All ER 371, HL, overruling *Burt v Claude Cousins & Co Ltd* [1971] 2 QB 426, [1971] 2 All ER 611, CA; *Barrington v Lee* [1972] 1 QB 326, [1971] 3 All ER 1231, CA. As to the duties and liabilities of estate agents see the Estate Agents Act 1979 ss 12–17 (as amended); and AGENCY vol 1(2) (Reissue) paras 14–17, 56.

235. Investment of deposit. Where in accordance with the contract the deposit is invested between the dates of sale and completion, the vendor is entitled to any increase, and must bear the loss, if any, in the value of the securities[1].

1 *Burroughes v Browne* (1852) 9 Hare 609. As to putting the unpaid balance of purchase money on deposit see paras 122, 197 ante. Where a deposit is paid to an agent, including an auctioneer, as stakeholder, it is apparently at the risk of whichever party is ultimately entitled to it; but if the agent receives the deposit as agent for the vendor, it is at the risk of the vendor: see AGENCY vol 1(2) (Reissue) para 56; AUCTION vol 2 (Reissue) para 949; but see *Fenton v Browne* (1807) 14 Ves 144 at 150. As to the risk in relation to pre-contractual deposits see para 234 text and note 11 ante. As to the formation of the contract see paras 23–40 ante; and as to the completion of the contract see paras 262–325 post. As to the date of completion see paras 120, 185 ante.

236. When right of forfeiture arises. Where the contract gives the vendor an express right of forfeiture on non-performance of the contract or non-observance of its conditions[1], the right is exercisable when such non-performance or non-observance is finally ascertained, that is, at the date for performance or observance named in the contract if, but only if[2], time is of the essence of the contract[3].

Where the contract gives the vendor no express right of forfeiture, the right is exercisable when, without default on the vendor's part, the purchaser has expressly or impliedly repudiated the contract[4]. An express repudiation gives the vendor an immediate right to retain the deposit as forfeited. There is an implied repudiation if the purchaser fails to complete on the day when he is bound to complete[5]. This is the day, if any, fixed by the contract for completion[6], if time in this respect is of the essence of the contract[7]. Otherwise, if the purchaser is in default, the vendor can make time of the essence of the contract by giving the purchaser notice to complete at a reasonable date and threatening forfeiture of the deposit on non-completion on that date[8].

1 As to the formation of the contract see paras 23–40 ante.
2 See *Sprague v Booth* [1909] AC 576 at 581, PC.
3 *Lennon v Napper* (1802) 2 Sch & Lef 682. See also *Roberts v Berry* (1853) 3 De GM & G 284; *Tilley v Thomas* (1867) 3 Ch App 61 at 67. As to when time is of the essence of the contract see para 120 ante. Where a contract expressly stipulated that the deposit was to be forfeited if the balance of the purchase money was not paid by the date for completion, the purchaser's failure to pay by that date resulted in the loss of the deposit even though time had not been made of the essence: *Warren v Tay Say Geok* (1964) 108 Sol Jo 819, PC.
4 This gives the vendor the right to rescind the contract: see para 232 ante.
5 See *Howe v Smith* (1884) 27 ChD 89 at 95, 103, CA; and *Universal Corpn v Five Ways Properties Ltd* [1979] 1 All ER 552, 38 P & CR 687, CA. As to completion of the contract see paras 262–325 post.
6 As to the date of completion see paras 120, 185 ante.
7 See para 120 ante.
8 See *Cornwall v Henson* [1900] 2 Ch 298, CA; *Green v Sevin* (1879) 13 ChD 589; *Howe v Smith* (1884. 27 ChD 89, CA; *Soper v Arnold* (1889) 14 App Cas 429, HL. It is not enough that, by delay or otherwise, the purchaser has lost the right to specific performance; his conduct must amount to repudiation of the contract on his part (*Howe v Smith* supra at 95 per Cotton LJ), involving the loss of his right to maintain an action for damages (*Howe v Smith* supra at 104 per Fry LJ; see also *Levy v Stogdon* [1898] 1 Ch 478 at 485). Three weeks' notice after two years' delay by the vendors has been held unreasonably short: *Green v Sevin* (1879) 13 ChD 589. See also *Stickney v Keeble* [1915] AC 386, HL, where the vendor, who had

caused the delay, was not entitled to forfeit the deposit. Where performance has been long refused, it is not necessary for time to be made of the essence of the contract: *Farrant v Olver* (1922) 91 LJ Ch 758. Cf *Graham v Pitkin* [1992] 2 All ER 235, [1992] 1 WLR 403, PC, where it was held that unreasonable delay is only one factor in determining whether a party in default had repudiated the contract; but see Harpum 'The Construction of Conditional Contracts and the Effect of Delay in Completion' [1992] Conv 318 at 324–329; Barnsley 'Delayed Completions' [1994] Conv 342; Harpum 'Delayed Completions' [1995] Conv 83. See also *Behzadi v Shaftesbury Hotels Ltd* [1992] Ch 1, [1991] 2 All ER 477, CA. In *Re Barr's Contract, Moorwell Holdings Ltd v Barr* [1956] Ch 551, [1956] 2 All ER 853, 28 days' notice was considered too short where a purchaser had to find £45,000 to complete the purchase. As to the effect of the current standard conditions of sale see para 120 ante; as to the measure of damages see paras 254–261 post; and as to damages generally see DAMAGES.

237. Rights to rescind and retain deposit. If the vendor becomes entitled to rescind the contract owing to the purchaser's default, he may both rescind and retain the deposit[1]. The contract being thus at an end, the forfeiture of the deposit is not strictly in the nature of damages for breach of contract, although it has been said to be in the nature of liquidated damages and not a penalty[2]. The purchaser is not entitled to terminate the contract by giving up the deposit. Notwithstanding the deposit the vendor can insist on the contract, and sue either for specific performance[3] or for damages beyond the deposit[4].

Where the purchaser has failed to pay the deposit (or any part of it) before the vendor rescinds the contract, it is uncertain whether the vendor may demand payment of the deposit with a view to its forfeiture[5].

1   Consequently, upon the purchaser failing to complete in pursuance of a judgment for specific performance, the vendor can obtain an order for rescission of the contract and for forfeiture of the deposit: *Hall v Burnell* [1911] 2 Ch 551 at 555–556, not following *Jackson v De Kadich* [1904] WN 168. See also *Dunn v Vere* (1870) 19 WR 151; *Re Parnell, ex p Barrell* (1875) 10 Ch App 512 (bankruptcy of purchaser); *Olde v Olde* [1904] 1 Ch 35; *Holford v Trim* [1921] WN 243; *Glover v Broome* [1926] WN 46. The court's discretion under the Law of Property Act 1925 s 49(2) seems wide enough to include such a case: see para 246 post. If the vendor himself is not ready to complete at the date of the service of a notice, he cannot forfeit the deposit relying on the purchaser's failure: *Cole v Rose* [1978] 3 All ER 1121, DC.

2   *Hinton v Sparkes* (1868) LR 3 CP 161; *Collins v Stimson* (1883) 11 QBD 142 at 144, DC; *Wallis v Smith* (1882) 21 ChD 243 at 258, CA. As to the distinction between a penalty and liquidated damages see *Workers Trust and Merchant Bank Ltd v Dojap Investments Ltd* [1993] AC 573, [1993] 2 All ER 370, PC; paras 254–261 post; and DAMAGES vol 12(1) (Reissue) para 1065 et seq.

3   *Crutchley v Jerningham* (1817) 2 Mer 502 at 506. See also *Palmer v Temple* (1839) 9 Ad & El 508. As to specific performance generally see SPECIFIC PERFORMANCE.

4   *Icely v Grew* (1836) 6 Nev & MKB 467. As to resale where a purchaser on a sale by the court fails to complete see 2 Dart's Law relating to Vendors and Purchasers (8th Edn, 1929) 1007. As to damages generally see DAMAGES.

5   See *Lowe v Hope* [1970] Ch 94, [1969] 3 All ER 605 (vendor cannot demand payment), disapproving *Dewar v Mintoft* [1912] 2 KB 373. See also *Johnson v Jones* [1972] NZLR 313. However, as the vendor's rescission operates only prospectively and does not affect accrued rights (see *Johnson v Agnew* [1980] AC 367, [1979] 1 All ER 883, HL), it is now clear that the unpaid deposit remains payable: *Damon Cia Naviera SA v Hapag-Lloyd International SA* [1985] 1 All ER 475, [1985] 1 WLR 435, CA (cf *Hyundai Shipbuilding and Heavy Industries Co Ltd v Pournaras* [1978] 2 Lloyd's Rep 502, , CA; *Hyundai Heavy Industries Co Ltd v Papadopoulos* [1980] 2 All ER 29, [1980] 1 WLR 1129, HL; *Stocznia Gdanska SA v Latvian Shipping Co* [1998] 1 All ER 883, [1998] Lloyd's Rep 609, HL). See also *Bot v Ristevski* [1981] VR 120, Vict SC.

238. Rescission after title is accepted. If, by his default in completion after he has accepted the title, the purchaser has given the vendor the right to rescind the contract and retain the deposit as forfeited, and the right has been exercised, the forfeiture is final, and the purchaser cannot recover the deposit on the ground that the vendor's title is subsequently discovered to be defective[1].

1   *Soper v Arnold* (1889) 14 App Cas 429, HL. As to the completion of the contract see paras 262–325 post.

(iii) Repudiation by the Purchaser

239. Repudiation for defect of title or in parcels. The purchaser has the right to repudiate the contract immediately upon failure by the vendor to perform something which goes to the root of the contract[1]. The right usually arises upon the vendor's failure to perform his obligation to show and prove a good title[2]. Thus, where the vendor does not deliver a proper abstract[3], and the purchaser has given reasonable notice fixing a time for its delivery, he can repudiate the contract if the vendor is still in default on the expiration of the notice[4]. Where the vendor shows that he has no intention of answering a requisition going to the root of the title, it is not necessary for the purchaser to give notice making time of the essence of the contract before repudiating[5]. The purchaser may also repudiate as soon as he finds that the vendor is able neither to transfer the property himself, nor to compel any other person to do so, and the purchaser is not bound to wait to see whether the vendor can induce some third person, who has the power, to join in making a good title to the property[6]. The rule does not apply to a defect of conveyance as distinguished from a defect of title[7].

Similarly, where the property which the vendor can transfer is not substantially the same as the property contracted to be sold[8], the purchaser can repudiate. Trifling defects in the property may be regarded by the court merely as matters for compensation[9].

1   This is in accordance with the rule applicable to contracts generally: *Mersey Steel and Iron Co v Naylor, Benzon & Co* (1884) 9 App Cas 434 at 443, HL; *Johnson v Agnew* [1980] AC 367, [1979] 1 All ER 883, HL. See also *Re McLoughlin and M'Grath's Contract* (1914) 48 ILT 87, Ir CA; and CONTRACT vol 9(1) (Reissue) para 997 et seq. A purchaser cannot both repudiate and insist on the contract: *Smith v Butler* [1900] 1 QB 694 at 698, CA. The purchaser cannot terminate the contract by giving up the deposit: see para 237 ante. As to wrongful repudiation by the purchaser see paras 232, 236 ante; and as to the rule that the purchaser cannot repudiate without the leave of the court after a judgment for specific performance see para 242 note 2 post.

2   As to this obligation see paras 137–173 ante. The title to be shown by the vendor must be such as was stipulated, ie it must commence with the specified document or at the specified date: *Re Head's Trustees and Macdonald* (1890) 45 ChD 310, CA; *Bellamy v Debenham* [1891] 1 Ch 412, CA; and see para 90 ante. However, the vendor is not restricted by the contract as to the mode of making title if another mode is equally efficacious: *Re Spencer and Hauser's Contract* [1928] Ch 598; and see para 92 ante. A proviso that, if the vendor cannot deduce a good title or the purchaser does not pay the purchase money on the appointed day, the contract is to be void gives the vendor an option to rescind on non-payment and the purchaser an option to rescind on the vendor's failure to make good title, but not vice versa: *Roberts v Wyatt* (1810) 2 Taunt 268. As to the purchaser being bound to take a possessory title see para 143 ante. As to the vendor's duty to disclose material facts see paras 41–44 ante. As to misdescription and misrepresentation see paras 51–52, 109–116 ante.

3   See *Re Priestley and Davidson's Contract* (1892) 31 LR Ir 122. As to the need for an abstract of title with respect to both unregistered and registered land see paras 138, 141–149 ante.

4   *Venn v Cattell* (1872) 27 LT 469; *Compton v Bagley* [1892] 1 Ch 313, where 14 days was held to be a reasonable time, having regard to previous requests for the delivery of the abstract, and to the nature of the property (a farm of which the purchaser was to have early possession). See also *Stickney v Keeble* [1915] AC 386, HL; and *Re Bayley and Shoesmith's Contract* (1918) 87 LJ Ch 626. The purchaser cannot repudiate if, after such notice, he receives the abstract and keeps it without objection: *Seton v Slade, Hunter v Seton* (1802) 7 Ves 265.

5   *Re Stone and Saville's Contract* [1963] 1 All ER 353, [1963] 1 WLR 163, CA.

6   *Forrer v Nash* (1865) 35 Beav 167; *Brewer v Broadwood* (1882) 22 ChD 105; *Wylson v Dunn* (1887) 34 ChD 569 at 577; *Lee v Soames* (1888) 36 WR 884; *Re Bryant and Barningham's Contract* (1890) 44 ChD 218, CA; *Re Head's Trustees and Macdonald* (1890) 45 ChD 310, CA; *Bellamy v Debenham* [1891] 1 Ch 412 at 420, CA; *Warren v Moore* (1897) 14 TLR 138 (affd (1898) 14 TLR 497, CA); *Re Cooke and Holland's Contract* (1898) 78 LT 106; *Powell v Marshall, Parkes & Co* [1899] 1 QB 710, CA; *Smith v Butler* [1900] 1 QB 694 at 700, CA; *Re Hucklesby and Atkinson's Contract* (1910) 102 LT 214 at 217. The right to repudiate applies both at law and in equity: *Pips (Leisure Productions) Ltd v Walton* (1982) 43 P & CR 415; and see para 243 post. Cf *Boehm v Wood* (1820) 1 Jac & W 419 at 421; *Forster v Hoggart* (1850) 15 QB 155. The purchaser may not repudiate when the vendor, as and when he pleases, can compel others to perfect his

title: see *Elliott and H Elliott (Builders) Ltd v Pierson* [1948] Ch 452, [1948] 1 All ER 939, where title to the leasehold was shown, but the vendor could compel the freeholder to join in.

As to the disposition of registered and unregistered land by transfer see para 262 note 2 post.

7   *Hatten v Russell* (1888) 38 ChD 334 at 347 (cited in SETTLEMENTS para 775 post); *Re Hucklesby and Atkinson's Contract* (1910) 102 LT 214; *Brickles v Snell* [1916] 2 AC 599, PC (where the mortgagee was willing to receive the mortgage money on completion, and the vendor was held to be ready (ie able) to convey); and see para 245 note 1 post. As to what amounts to a defect of title see para 57 ante.

8   *Portman v Mill* (1826) 2 Russ 570; *Flight v Booth* (1834) 1 Bing NC 370; *Re Arnold, Arnold v Arnold* (1880) 14 ChD 270, CA; *Re Fawcett and Holmes' Contract* (1889) 42 ChD 150, CA; *Jacobs v Revell* [1900] 2 Ch 858; *Lee v Rayson* [1917] 1 Ch 613. See *Hearn v Tomlin* (1793) Peake 253; *Gardiner v Tate* (1876) IR 10 CL 460; paras 51–52, 109–116 ante; and SPECIFIC PERFORMANCE vol 44(1) (Reissue) paras 894, 898, 922.

9   *Shepherd v Croft* [1911] 1 Ch 521 (latent defect: watercourse under property). Cf *Re Brewer and Hankins's Contract* (1899) 80 LT 127, CA; *Re Puckett and Smith's Contract* [1902] 2 Ch 258, CA; and see *Carlish v Salt* [1906] 1 Ch 335. See further paras 51–52 ante. But a possible liability to what is now inheritance tax is not a trifling defect: *Manning v Turner* [1956] 3 All ER 641, [1957] 1 WLR 91 (estate duty). As to inheritance tax see generally INHERITANCE TAXATION.

240. Completion depending on third person. Where the completion of the contract[1] depends on the consent of a third person (where, for instance, the vendor of leasehold property requires a licence to assign[2]), the vendor is not bound to procure the consent before the date for completion[3], and the purchaser cannot repudiate earlier on the ground that the consent has not been obtained unless there are special circumstances entitling him to treat the contract as at an end (if, for instance, he can prove, or the vendor has admitted, that the consent cannot be obtained by the due date[4]). If the date by which a condition is to be fulfilled is fixed, either specifically by the contract or impliedly by reference to the date fixed for completion, the time allowed for fulfilling the condition will not be extended by the equitable principles which can apply to extending the time for the general completion of the contract[5]. If there is no fixed date, a reasonable time must be allowed for the fulfilment of the condition[6].

1   As to the formation of the contract see paras 23–40 ante; and as to the completion of the contract see paras 262–325 post.

2   As to the vendor's duty to obtain the necessary licence and the unenforceability of the contract if he fails in his duty see para 25 ante; and LANDLORD AND TENANT vol 27(1) (Reissue) para 462. As to damages to the purchaser for loss of his bargain on the vendor's default in procuring consent see para 256 post. See, however, the Standard Conditions of Sale (3rd Edn), which states that unless there has been a breach of obligation in relation to the obtaining of the licence (see condition 8.3.2(a), (b)), either party may rescind the contract by notice to the other party if three working days before completion date (1) the consent has not been given; or (2) the consent has been given subject to a condition to which the purchaser reasonably objects: see condition 8.3.4. In that case, neither party is to be treated as in breach of contract (see condition 8.3.4) and either may rescind the contract (a) unless the rescission is a result of the purchaser's breach of contract the deposit is to be repaid to the purchaser with accrued interest (see condition 7.2(a)); and (b) the buyer is to return any documents he received from the vendor and is to cancel any registration of the contract (see condition 7.2(b)). Condition 8.3.4 in effect neutralises *29 Equities Ltd v Bank Leumi (UK) Ltd* [1987] 1 All ER 108, [1986] 1 WLR 1490, CA. As to the Standard Conditions of Sale see para 1 note 9 ante.

3   *Ellis v Rogers* (1885) 29 ChD 661 at 671–672, CA. See also *Stowell v Robinson* (1837) 3 Bing NC 928; and *Property and Bloodstock Ltd v Emerton* [1968] Ch 94, [1967] 3 All ER 321, CA. Cf *Dotesio v Biss* (1912) 56 Sol Jo 612, CA. As to the date for completion see paras 120, 185 ante.

4   *Smith v Butler* [1900] 1 QB 694 at 699, CA. Where the sanction of the court is required, and no date is fixed for obtaining the sanction, it must be obtained before the time fixed for completion: *Re Sandwell Park Colliery Co, Field v Sandwell Park Colliery Co* [1929] 1 Ch 277.

5   *Aberfoyle Plantations Ltd v Cheng* [1960] AC 115, [1959] 3 All ER 910, PC (purchase conditional on renewal of leases).

6   *Re Longlands Farm, Long Common, Botley, Hants, Alford v Superior Developments Ltd* [1968] 3 All ER 552, 20 P & CR 25.

241. When right to repudiate must be exercised. Where a purchaser desires to exercise his right of repudiation, which arises as soon as the vendor's defect of title is ascertained either from the abstract or from his replies to the purchaser's requisitions[1], then, unless the defect is slight and can be properly met by compensation[2], he must indicate his election to do so with every reasonable dispatch[3]. If the purchaser continues in negotiation as to the title, and thus treats the contract as subsisting[4], he cannot repudiate at any subsequent moment he may choose[5], but must give the vendor a reasonable time to remedy the defect[6]. Where the defect is irremovable, but the purchaser treats the contract as subsisting, he waives his right to repudiate and his only remedy is in damages[7].

1   See *Lee v Soames* (1888) 36 WR 884; *Weston v Savage* (1879) 10 ChD 736; *Maconchy v Clayton* [1898] 1 IR 291 at 306, Ir CA; *Re Stone and Saville's Contract* [1963] 1 All ER 353, [1963] 1 WLR 163, CA; and *Pips (Leisure Productions) Ltd v Walton* (1982) 43 P & CR 415. As to rescission on the vendor's refusal to comply with a requisition as to conveyance see *Denny v Hancock* (1870) 6 Ch App 1 at 13. The purchaser may repudiate even if the answer to a requisition is in accordance with conveyancing practice: *Simmons v Pennington & Son (a firm)* [1955] 1 All ER 240, [1955] 1 WLR 183, CA. As to the need for an abstract of title with respect to both unregistered and registered land see paras 138, 141–149 ante. As to requisitions on title see paras 163–166 ante.

2   *Halkett v Earl of Dudley* [1907] 1 Ch 590 at 596. See also *Rudd v Lascelles* [1900] 1 Ch 815; *Jacobs v Revell* [1900] 2 Ch 858; and para 239 ante.

3   *Berners v Fleming* [1925] Ch 264, CA.

4   As to the formation of the contract see paras 23–40 ante; and as to the completion of the contract see paras 262–325 post.

5   *Hoggart v Scott* (1830) 1 Russ & M 293; *Eyston v Simonds* (1842) 1 Y & C Ch Cas 608; *Salisbury v Hatcher* (1842) 2 Y & C Ch Cas 54 at 66; *Murrell v Goodyear* (1860) 1 De GF & J 432; *Halkett v Earl of Dudley* [1907] 1 Ch 590 at 596; *Berners v Fleming* [1925] Ch 264, CA; *Elliott and H Elliott (Builders) Ltd v Pierson* [1948] Ch 452, [1948] 1 All ER 939.

6   *Murrell v Goodyear* (1860) 1 De GF & J 432 at 450 per Turner LJ. See also *Thomson v Miles* (1794) 1 Esp 184; *Manning v Turner* [1956] 3 All ER 641, [1957] 1 WLR 91 (liability to death duty). As to making time of the essence of the contract by notice see *Taylor v Brown* (1839) 2 Beav 180; *Wood v Machu* (1846) 5 Hare 158; *Nott v Riccard* (1856) 22 Beav 307; and para 120 ante. See further *Royou v Paul* (1858) 28 LJ Ch 555; *Laughton v Port Erin Comrs* [1910] AC 565 at 569, PC.

7   See eg *Aquis Estates Ltd v Minton* [1975] 3 All ER 1043, [1975] 1 WLR 1452, CA. As to the damages recoverable by the purchaser see paras 256–258 post; and as to damages generally see DAMAGES.

242. Restrictions on repudiation. The purchaser may not repudiate the contract if he has been informed by the vendor of the defect in the title, and that it will not be cured without some delay[1].

After a judgment for specific performance the purchaser may not repudiate the contract without the leave of the court[2]. In such circumstances, on the discovery of the defect in title, he should move to be discharged from the contract[3]. The court's jurisdiction is discretionary and, where the defect is one capable of being remedied, the court will not as a rule make a final declaration of the vendor's inability to make a good title or discharge the purchaser from the contract without first affording to the vendor a reasonable time to remedy the defect[4].

1   *Wylson v Dunn* (1887) 34 ChD 569 at 578. See also *Hoggart v Scott* (1830) 1 Russ & M 293; *Weston v Savage* (1879) 10 ChD 736.

2   *Halkett v Earl of Dudley* [1907] 1 Ch 590. Similarly, after a full decree of specific performance a contractual notice to complete may not be served: *Sudagar Singh v Nazeer* [1979] Ch 474, [1978] 3 All ER 817. See also SPECIFIC PERFORMANCE vol 44(1) (Reissue) para 922. As to a notice to complete see para 121 ante.

3   *Halkett v Earl of Dudley* [1907] 1 Ch 590 at 601.

4   *Cleadon Trust Ltd v Davis* [1940] Ch 940, [1940] 3 All ER 648, CA, where the vendor was allowed a limited time to obtain the release of restrictions (applying principles stated in *Halkett v Earl of Dudley* [1907] 1 Ch 590 at 601–602; *Coffin v Cooper* (1807) 14 Ves 205). See also *Jenkins v Hiles* (1802) 6 Ves 646; and *Wynn v Morgan* (1802) 7 Ves 202.

243. Nature of right to repudiate. Rightful repudiation by the purchaser is available as a defence to an action by the vendor for specific performance[1], and in this aspect it depends on the doctrine of mutuality in the contract[2]. However, in accordance with general contractual principles[3], the repudiation appears also to operate as a rescission of the contract at law so as to entitle the purchaser to maintain an action for a declaration of rescission and the return of the deposit[4], and to be available as a defence to the vendor's action for breach of contract on non-completion at the proper time[5].

1   *Bellamy v Debenham* [1891] 1 Ch 412 at 420, CA. See also *Royou v Paul* (1858) 28 LJ Ch 555. As to the remedy of specific performance see paras 247–253 post; and as to defences to an action of specific performance generally see SPECIFIC PERFORMANCE vol 44(1) (Reissue) para 841 et seq.
2   *Wylson v Dunn* (1887) 34 ChD 569 at 577; *Bolton Partners v Lambert* (1888) 41 ChD 295 (on appeal (1889) 41 ChD 302, CA); *Halkett v Earl of Dudley* [1907] 1 Ch 590 at 596. See also SPECIFIC PERFORMANCE vol 44(1) (Reissue) paras 809–910.
3   See *Johnson v Agnew* [1980] AC 367, [1979] 1 All ER 883, HL; and CONTRACT vol 9(1) (Reissue) para 997 et seq.
4   *Weston v Savage* (1879) 10 ChD 736 at 741; *Lee v Soames* (1888) 36 WR 884; and see paras 245–246 post. In *Procter v Pugh* [1921] 2 Ch 256, the vendor was allowed to take advantage of a clause enabling him to rescind the contract, notwithstanding that the purchaser had previously repudiated it for defect of title. See the criticism of this decision in Williams 'A Purchaser's Right of Repudiation' (1921) 66 Sol Jo 135–138.
5   *Brewer v Broadwood* (1882) 22 ChD 105; *Pips (Leisure Productions) Ltd v Walton* (1982) 43 P & CR 415 (discussing, inter alia, *Bellamy v Debenham* [1891] 1 Ch 412, CA); *Halkett v Earl of Dudley* [1907] 1 Ch 590. See also *Proctor v Pugh* [1921] 2 Ch 256 at 268; 1 Williams Law relating to Vendors and Purchasers of Real Estate and Chattels Real (4th Edn, 1936) 203 note (k); and see generally Harpum 'Selling without Title: A Vendor's Duty of Disclosure' (1992) 108 LQR 280. As to completion of the contract see paras 262–325 post.

244. Restitutio in integrum. Unless restitutio in integrum can substantially be made, the purchaser cannot exercise his right of rescission on the ground of the vendor's default[1]. Thus a lessee of mines who continues to work the mines after warning of circumstances which would entitle him to set aside the lease cannot exercise such right[2].

1   *Erlanger v New Sombrero Phosphate Co* (1878) 3 App Cas 1218, HL; *Thorpe v Fasey* [1949] Ch 649, [1949] 2 All ER 393.
2   *Vigers v Pike* (1842) 8 Cl & Fin 562 at 650, HL.

(iv) Recovery of Deposit by the Purchaser

245. Right to recover deposit. Where the vendor makes a default in performing his part of the contract[1] which entitles the purchaser to rescind the contract[2], the purchaser can recover the deposit with interest at an appropriate rate fixed by the conditions of sale[3], or, in default, determined by the court, or such other rate as may be agreed[4]. In addition, the purchaser can obtain damages[5], which will include his expenses to date[6], the costs of the agreement itself[7] and the costs of investigating the title[8]. The fact that the purchaser has by delay lost the right to specific performance does not prevent him from recovering the deposit[9]. Where a deposit has been paid to a third person as agent for the vendor and not as stakeholder, it can be recovered only from the vendor and not from the third person personally[10].

1   Eg by not performing, before the date fixed for completion, work of such a nature as to make time of the essence of the contract (*Bernard v Williams* (1928) 139 LT 22, DC), or by failing to make a good title (*Edwards v Hodding* (1814) 5 Taunt 815; *Gray v Gutteridge* (1828) 1 Man & Ry KB 614; *Want v Stallibrass* (1873) LR 8 Exch 175; *Hone v Gakstatter* (1909) 53 Sol Jo 286 (failure to disclose restrictive covenants) (see para 137 ante)). If the vendor has a good title, but has not satisfied the purchaser that he can transfer (where eg he himself is entitled under an uncompleted contract), this does not enable the purchaser to repudiate the contract and recover his deposit: *Re Hucklesby and Atkinson's Contract* (1910) 102 LT 214;

Gordon Hill Trust Ltd v Segall [1941] 2 All ER 379, CA. To repudiate the contract for the vendor's want of title, it must appear that the vendor has no title in himself, and cannot compel third persons to supply him with a title: *Re Hucklesby and Atkinson's Contract* supra. See also para 239 ante. As to the formation of the contract see paras 23–40 ante.

2 See paras 239–244 ante. See also *Schindler v Pigault* (1975) 30 P & CR 328, where the vendor refused to allow access to the sub-purchaser until after the date for completion and then refused to complete late, and it was held that the purchaser was entitled to rescind and to recover his deposit. As to repudiation operating as a rescission of contract see para 243 ante. An omission by the vendor to disclose a material fact may deprive him of his right to specific performance, but, unless the purchaser is entitled to rescind, the contract will stand at law and the purchaser will not be able to recover his deposit: *Beyfus v Lodge* [1925] Ch 350. As to the date for completion see paras 120, 185 ante; and as to completion see paras 262–325 post.

3 As to the contract rate see the Standard Conditions of Sale (3rd Edn), condition 1.1.1(g); and para 119 note 7 ante. As to the Standard Conditions of Sale see para 1 note 9 ante.

4 *Day v Singleton* [1899] 2 Ch 320 at 327, CA; *Powell v Marshall, Parkes & Co* [1899] 1 QB 710, CA; *Warren v Moore* (1898) 14 TLR 497, CA. In *Weston v Savage* (1879) 10 ChD 736, interest was allowed at 5% per annum, but 4% was the usual rate: *Re Bryant and Barningham's Contract* (1890) 44 ChD 218 at 222, CA, per Kay J. However, a more realistic rate would probably now be awarded: see *Wallersteiner v Moir (No 2)* [1975] QB 373, [1975] 1 All ER 849, CA; *Bartlett v Barclays Bank Trust Co Ltd (No 2)* [1980] Ch 515 at 547, [1980] 2 All ER 92 at 98 per Brightman LJ; and para 195 text and notes 3–4 ante. In equity no prior demand is necessary for the recovery of interest: see 2 Williams Law relating to Vendors and Purchasers of Real Estate and Chattels Real (4th Edn, 1936) 1005 note (p). As to repayment of the deposit where the vendor has a bad title see para 103 ante; and as to the purchaser's lien for his deposit see para 184 ante; and LIEN vol 28 (Reissue) paras 763–764.

5 See *Johnson v Agnew* [1980] AC 367, [1979] 1 All ER 883, HL; and DAMAGES.

6 See *Gosbell v Archer* (1835) 2 Ad & El 500.

7 See *Pearl Life Assurance Co v Buttenshaw* [1893] WN 123.

8 *Re Bryant and Barningham's Contract* (1890) 44 ChD 218, CA; *Re Hare and O'More's Contract* [1901] 1 Ch 93 at 96; *Re Walker and Oakshott's Contract* [1901] 2 Ch 383 at 387 (affd [1902] WN 147, CA); and see para 222 text and note 3 ante. *Re Walker and Oakshott's Contract* supra was overruled on another point by *Re Judd and Poland and Skelcher's Contract* [1906] 1 Ch 684, CA. See also para 257 post. As to whether the purchaser can recover substantial damages for loss of bargain see para 258 post.

9 *Levy v Stogdon* [1898] 1 Ch 478; affd [1899] 1 Ch 5, CA.

10 See *Ellis v Goulton* [1893] 1 QB 350, CA; and para 86 ante. Where, however, the third person received the money as stakeholder, the deposit can be recovered from the third person if the purchaser has become entitled to its return: see *Ryan v Pilkington* [1959] 1 All ER 689, [1959] 1 WLR 403, CA; and *Goding v Frazer* [1966] 3 All ER 234, [1967] 1 WLR 286. A vendor who has not authorised his agent to employ a sub-agent will not be liable for the defaults of the sub-agent: *Maloney v Hardy and Moorshead* (1970) 216 Estates Gazette 1582, CA. As to the recovery of a deposit from an auctioneer see AUCTION vol 2 (Reissue) paras 948–949. As to the capacity in which a solicitor receives a deposit see para 86 ante; and CONTRACT vol 9(1) (Reissue) para 1143; SOLICITORS vol 44(1) (Reissue) para 126.

246. When the right to recover the deposit arises. The purchaser's right to recover his deposit is a legal right which springs out of breach of contract by the vendor[1]. Formerly, where there had been no breach of contract, the vendor was not liable to return the deposit[2], notwithstanding that he was not entitled to specific performance[3]. Thus a defect in title to which the purchaser was by the conditions precluded from objecting[4], or mere delay[5], might prevent the vendor from obtaining specific performance without rendering him liable to return the deposit[6]. Now, however, where the court refuses to grant specific performance of a contract for the sale or exchange of any interest in land[7], or in any action for the return of a deposit, the court may, if it thinks fit, order the repayment of any deposit[8]. Thus the court is no longer bound to refuse to order the return of the deposit if the vendor is at law protected by the conditions of sale, but may exercise its discretion in the matter[9]. However, the court's discretion is not limited to such a case; there is an unqualified discretion to order the return of the deposit where that is the fairest course between the two parties[10]. The factors to be taken into account include a general consideration of the conduct of the parties (and especially the applicant), the gravity of the matters in question, and the amounts at stake[11]. The court's order for the return of the deposit does not extinguish the vendor's right to claim damages for breach of contract[12].

1   Cf *Howe v Smith* (1884) 27 ChD 89, CA; and see *Farrer v Nightingal* (1798) 2 Esp 639. As to the formation of the contract see paras 23–40 ante. As to discharge of contractual promises generally see CONTRACT vol 9(1) (Reissue) para 920 et seq.
2   *Best v Hamand* (1879) 12 ChD 1, CA.
3   *Re Davis and Cavey* (1888) 40 ChD 601 at 607. As to the remedy of specific performance see paras 247–253 post; and SPECIFIC PERFORMANCE.
4   *Re Scott and Alvarez's Contract, Scott v Alvarez* [1895] 2 Ch 603, CA. See also *Re National Provincial Bank of England and Marsh* [1895] 1 Ch 190.
5   *Southcomb v Bishop of Exeter* (1847) 6 Hare 213 at 227.
6   Before the union of the courts of law and equity (see EQUITY vol 16 (Reissue) para 651), a court of equity, on dismissing the vendor's suit for specific performance, would order a return of the deposit if it was clear that the vendor had lost his legal rights under the contract, but not otherwise (*Southcomb v Bishop of Exeter* (1847) 6 Hare 213), and a decree might be made for specific performance even after the purchaser had recovered the deposit at law (*Hoggart v Scott* (1830) 1 Russ & M 293, where at the date of the contract the vendor had no title, but the purchaser did not at once repudiate, and the title was subsequently completed).
7   For the meaning of 'land' see para 139 note 1 ante.
8   Law of Property Act 1925 s 49(2), (3). It has been questioned whether the court can order the return of part of the deposit: see *James Macara Ltd v Barclay* [1944] 2 All ER 31 at 32 (affd without reference to this point [1945] KB 148, [1944] 2 All ER 589, CA); and see *Dimsdale Developments (South East) Ltd v De Haan* (1983) 47 P & CR 1, [1984] Conv 312 (showing how this limitation can, in appropriate circumstances, be avoided). Where a contract expressly excludes the operation of the Law of Property Act 1925 s 49(2), the vendor cannot automatically claim forfeiture of the purchaser's deposit: see *Country and Metropolitan Homes Surrey Ltd v Topclaim Ltd* [1996] Ch 307, [1997] 1 All ER 254.
9   The effect of *Charles Hunt Ltd v Palmer* [1931] 2 Ch 287 is to overrule *Re Scott and Alvarez's Contract, Scott v Alvarez* [1895] 2 Ch 603, CA, which was a striking instance of the unfairness of the former doctrine: see Williams on Contract of Sale of Land (1930 Edn) XV, 93–94. See also *Faruqi v English Real Estates Ltd* [1979] 1 WLR 963, 38 P & CR 318.
10 *Schindler v Pigault* (1975) 30 P & CR 328; *Universal Corpn v Five Ways Properties Ltd* [1979] 1 All ER 552, 38 P & CR 687, CA; *Maktoum v South Lodge Flats Ltd* (1980) Times, 22 April.
11 See *Schindler v Pigault* (1975) 30 P & CR 328 (where the vendor, who had not afforded access to the sub-purchaser, could not rely on the purchaser's failure to complete by the specified date as a defence to the purchaser's action for rescission, and it was just and equitable for the deposit to be returned); *Universal Corpn v Five Ways Properties Ltd* [1979] 1 All ER 552, 38 P & CR 687, CA (where the purchaser had an arguable case for the return of the deposit where failure to complete was due to a change in Nigerian exchange control regulations which delayed transmission of the purchase money); *Maktoum v South Lodge Flats Ltd* (1980) Times, 22 April (where the purchaser failed to execute underleases within the time for completion, and the deposit was repaid without interest). Cf *Cole v Rose* [1978] 3 All ER 1121 at 1130, DC; *Safehaven Investments Inc v Springbok Ltd* (1995) 71 P & CR 59.
12 *Dinsdale Developments (South East) Ltd v De Haan* (1983) 47 P & CR 1. As to an action for damages see paras 254–261 post; and as to damages generally see DAMAGES.

(v) Specific Performance

247. Remedy of specific performance. Specific performance[1] of a contract is ordered at the court's discretion[2] where damages do not afford a complete remedy[3]. Although, since a vendor's claim is, strictly speaking, merely a pecuniary demand, damages would sufficiently compensate him, the court acts on the principle that the remedy must be mutual, and, therefore, specifically enforces the contract at the suit of the vendor in every case where a similar remedy is open to the purchaser[4]. In an action for specific performance, the court will decide questions which are mere questions of the construction of a document and will not refuse to do so on the ground that the title is too doubtful to force on a purchaser[5]. However, the court will not decide such questions where they can be decided only on the receipt of the evidence of witnesses unknown to the purchaser[6]. An agreement can be rectified on the ground of mistake and in the same action specific performance ordered of the agreement as rectified[7]. Where the circumstances justify equity's intervention, specific performance may be granted in an action begun before the date for completion[8]. Once that date has passed, the claimant may commence the action without serving a notice to complete[9].

A party who obtains an order for specific performance does not elect irrevocably to affirm the contract, for, if it becomes impossible to enforce it, that party may ask the court to discharge the order and terminate the contract and damages may then be awarded[10].

The court does not specifically enforce an agreement to enter into a contract for the sale of land[11].

Where a contract is made between two parties for the benefit of a third person, in an action by one of the contracting parties specific performance may be decreed in favour of the third person[12].

In an action for specific performance where there is also a claim for damages the court may award damages for delay in completion even though the action was begun before the date for completion and thus before the cause of action in damages had accrued[13].

1   As to specific performance generally see SPECIFIC PERFORMANCE. See also para 248 et seq post. As to the specific performance of a contract relating to registered land see LAND REGISTRATION vol 26 (Reissue) para 923.
2   *Cox v Middleton* (1854) 2 Drew 209; *Haywood v Cope* (1858) 25 Beav 140 at 151; *Re Scott and Alvarez's Contract, Scott v Alvarez* [1895] 2 Ch 603 at 615, CA, per Rigby LJ. As to the form of order in an action for specific performance see *Cooper v Morgan* [1909] 1 Ch 261; *Palmer v Lark* [1945] Ch 182, [1945] 1 All ER 355; and SPECIFIC PERFORMANCE vol 44(1) (Reissue) para 933. The appointment of a receiver does not of itself afford a vendor company a defence to a claim by the purchaser for specific performance: *Freevale Ltd v Metrostore (Holdings) Ltd* [1984] Ch 199, [1984] 1 All ER 495.
3   *Adderley v Dixon* (1824) 1 Sim & St 607 at 610; *Re Scott and Alvarez's Contract, Scott v Alvarez* [1895] 2 Ch 603, CA. See also SPECIFIC PERFORMANCE vol 44(1) (Reissue) paras 813–814. As to the measure of damages see paras 254–261 post; and as to damages generally see DAMAGES.
4   *Adderley v Dixon* (1824) 1 Sim & St 607; *Regent's Canal Co v Ware* (1857) 23 Beav 575; *Cogent v Gibson* (1864) 33 Beav 557. As to mutuality see *Price v Strange* [1978] Ch 337, [1977] 3 All ER 371, CA (relevant date for considering defence of want of mutuality is date of hearing, not date of contract); and SPECIFIC PERFORMANCE vol 44(1) (Reissue) para 809.
5   *Johnson v Clarke* [1928] Ch 847; *Smith v Colbourne* [1914] 2 Ch 533 at 544–545, CA; and see SPECIFIC PERFORMANCE vol 44(1) (Reissue) para 878. A vendor who claims specific performance according to a wrong interpretation of the contract does not forfeit his right to specific performance on the right interpretation: *Berners v Fleming* [1925] Ch 264, CA.
6   *Wilson v Thomas* [1958] 1 All ER 871, [1958] 1 WLR 422, where a deed of family arrangement provided that the words 'Allan Hewit' in a will should be read as 'Frederick Allan Wilson and Henry Hewitt Wilson' but it was not stated that there was no such person as Allan Hewit. As to defences to claims for specific performance see SPECIFIC PERFORMANCE vol 44(1) (Reissue) para 840 et seq; and as to the duty of the court to declare the meaning of a will see WILLS vol 50 (Reissue) para 429.
7   *Craddock Bros v Hunt* [1923] 2 Ch 136, CA; *United States of America v Motor Trucks Ltd* [1924] AC 196, PC. See also *Forgione v Lewis* [1920] 2 Ch 326; and MISTAKE; SPECIFIC PERFORMANCE vol 44(1) (Reissue) para 876.
8   *Hasham v Zenab* [1960] AC 316, [1960] 2 WLR 374, PC, where the vendor tore up the contract within a few minutes of signing it. See also *Marks v Lilley* [1959] 2 All ER 647, [1959] 1 WLR 749; *Oakacre Ltd v Claire Cleaners (Holdings) Ltd* [1982] Ch 197, [1981] 3 All ER 667. As to the completion of the contract see paras 262–325 post; and as to the date of completion see paras 120, 185 post.
9   *Marks v Lilley* [1959] 2 All ER 647, [1959] 1 WLR 749. See also *Woods v Mackenzie Hill Ltd* [1975] 2 All ER 170, [1975] 1 WLR 613. As to notice to complete see para 121 ante.
10 *Johnson v Agnew* [1980] AC 367, [1979] 1 All ER 883, HL, overruling *Capital and Suburban Properties Ltd v Swycher* [1976] Ch 319, [1976] 1 All ER 881, CA, and approving *Biggin v Minton* [1977] 2 All ER 647, [1977] 1 WLR 701. As to remedies after the decree of specific performance see para 253 post.
11 *Johnston v Boyes* (1898) 14 TLR 475. See also *Von Hatzfeldt-Wildenburg v Alexander* [1912] 1 Ch 284 at 289 per Parker J; and cf *Daulia Ltd v Four Millbank Nominees Ltd* [1978] Ch 231, [1978] 2 All ER 557, CA.
12 See *Beswick v Beswick* [1968] AC 58, [1967] 2 All ER 1197, HL.
13 *Oakacre Ltd v Claire Cleaners (Holdings) Ltd* [1982] Ch 197, [1981] 3 All ER 667; *Pinekerry Ltd v Needs (Kenneth) (Contractors) Ltd* (1992) 64 P & CR 245, [1992] NPC 15, CA.

248. When specific performance will be refused. The claimant is not entitled to the remedy of specific performance if there has been conduct on his part, such as misrepresentation, disentitling him to the relief in equity, and the remedy may be refused if it would impose great hardship on an innocent vendor, where, for instance, he has entered into the contract under mistake, although the other party has not contributed to it[1]. Delay in itself is not a bar to the award of specific performance; the question is whether, in all the circumstances it would be unjust to the defendant to grant the decree[2]. Where by notice or otherwise time is of the essence of the contract, a party who is unable or unwilling to complete on the completion date is not entitled to specific performance[3].

Specific performance will be refused to a vendor who has made title strictly in accordance with the contract but who has failed to disclose a known defect in the title[4]. It will not be awarded to a purchaser where the property is subject to a spouse's matrimonial home rights[5], since the effect of the decree would be to compel the vendor to embark on speculative litigation to terminate those rights[6].

Similarly, specific performance is not available to a purchaser when the vendor is in truth a joint tenant but has purported to sell as sole legal and beneficial owner, as specific performance cannot be ordered against the other joint tenant, and the effect of the decree would therefore be the transfer of the vendor's beneficial half share, which is something quite different from the interest he had contracted to sell[7].

1   See *Hexter v Pearce* [1900] 1 Ch 341 at 346 per Farwell J; *Patel v Ali* [1984] Ch 283, [1984] 1 All ER 978. See generally *Co-operative Insurance Society Ltd v Argyll Stores (Holdings) Ltd* [1996] Ch 286 at 304–305, [1996] 3 All ER 934 at 949, CA, per Millett LJ (dissenting); on appeal [1998] AC 1 at 18, [1997] 3 All ER 297 at 307–308, HL, per Lord Hoffmann. The remedy will be refused where in the circumstances there is no contract: *Hammond v Chubb* (1915) 138 LT Jo 360. Unless the vendor has expressly agreed to make out a good title, he can, in an action for specific performance, show that the purchaser bought with notice that a good title could not be made (*Ellis v Rogers* (1885) 29 ChD 661, CA), but he can only produce evidence of this at the trial of the action; if not produced then, it cannot be used on the inquiry into title (*McGrory v Alderdale Estate Co Ltd* [1918] AC 503, HL). See also 1 Williams Law relating to Vendors and Purchasers of Real Estate and Chattels Real (4th Edn, 1936) 241. As to the vendor's obligation to show and prove a good title see para 137 ante. As to defences against specific performance see MISREPRESENTATION AND FRAUD vol 31 (Reissue) para 1086; MISTAKE; SPECIFIC PERFORMANCE vol 44(1) (Reissue) para 840 et seq. Where after a vendor has begun proceedings for specific performance the contract is completed, the vendor can recover the costs of the specific performance proceedings: *Marks v Lilley* [1959] 2 All ER 647, [1959] 1 WLR 749.

2   *Lazard Bros & Co Ltd v Fairfield Properties Co (Mayfair) Ltd* (1977) 121 Sol Jo 793, where three years had elapsed since the contract, but both parties had approached the transaction in a leisurely way; specific performance was nevertheless granted, because it would cause no injustice to the defendants, and to refuse the decree would be merely to punish the claimants. See also *Williams v Greatrex* [1956] 3 All ER 705, [1957] 1 WLR 31, CA; *Du Sautoy v Symes* [1967] Ch 1146, [1967] 1 All ER 25; cf *Glasbrook v Richardson* (1874) 23 WR 51 (decree refused after delay of three calendar months and 13 days on sale of leasehold colliery). As to the effect of delay in enforcing a decree of specific performance see *Easton v Brown* [1981] 3 All ER 278. As to the effect of possession by the purchaser see *Sharp v Milligan* (1856) 22 Beav 606; and SPECIFIC PERFORMANCE vol 44(1) (Reissue) para 904. As to delay in completion see para 121 ante.

3   *Finkielkraut v Monohan* [1949] 2 All ER 234, [1949] WN 298; *Maktoum v South Lodge Flats Ltd* (1980) Times, 22 April. As to the date of completion see paras 120, 185 ante; and as to completion of the contract see paras 262–325 post.

4   *Faruqi v English Real Estates Ltd* [1979] 1 WLR 963, 38 P & CR 318. As to the formation of the contract see paras 23–40 ante.

5   Ie under the Family Law Act 1996 Pt IV (ss 30–63) (as amended): see LAND CHARGES vol 26 (Reissue) para 538.

6   See *Wroth v Tyler* [1974] Ch 30, [1973] 1 All ER 897 (where the purchaser could not obtain specific performance with compensation); and para 252 post.

7   *Watts v Spence* [1976] Ch 165, [1975] 2 All ER 528. See also *Cedar Holdings Ltd v Green* [1981] Ch 129, [1979] 3 All ER 117, CA, disapproved in *Williams and Glyn's Bank Ltd v Boland* [1981] AC 487 at 507, [1980] 2 All ER 408 at 415, HL, per Lord Wilberforce. The decision in *Cedar Holdings Ltd v Green* supra was in part based on the equitable doctrine of conversion, which has been abolished by the Trusts of Land and Appointment of Trustees Act 1996 s 3: see REAL PROPERTY vol 39(2) (Reissue) para 77. See also

Basma v Weekes [1950] AC 441, [1950] 2 All ER 146, PC; *Warmington v Miller* [1973] QB 877, [1973] 2 All ER 372, CA, where specific performance of an agreement for an underlease was refused where it would cause a breach of the head lease. As to hardship as a defence to an action for specific performance see SPECIFIC PERFORMANCE vol 44(1) (Reissue) para 869 et seq. In *Amalgamated Investment and Property Co Ltd v John Walker & Sons Ltd* [1976] 3 All ER 509, [1977] 1 WLR 164, CA, the vendor obtained specific performance of a contract to sell a building at a price of £1,700,000, although after contract the building was listed as of historic interest and was then worth only £200,000. It was held inter alia that the contract was not frustrated. Cf *Capital Quality Homes Ltd v Colwyn Construction Ltd* (1975) 9 OR (2d) 617, 61 DLR (3d) 385 Ont CA, and the cases there cited, distinguished in *Victoria Wood Development Corpn Inc v Ondrey* (1978) 22 OR (2d) 1, 92 DLR (3d) 229, Ont CA; and see *Witwicki v Midgley* [1979] 5 WWR 242, 101 DLR (3d) 430, Man CA. Cf also *National Carriers Ltd v Panalpina (Northern) Ltd* [1981] AC 675, [1981] 1 All ER 161, HL (frustration of lease).

249. Effect of order for specific performance. After an order for specific performance the contract continues in existence[1], but the court controls the manner in which the contract will be performed. A contractual provision for service of a notice to complete, even if on its true construction designed to apply after a full decree of specific performance, may not be invoked unless the court so orders in working out the decree[2].

1 As to the formation of the contract see paras 23–40 ante; and as to specific performance generally see SPECIFIC PERFORMANCE.
2 *Sudagar Singh v Nazeer* [1979] Ch 474, [1978] 3 All ER 817. As to notice to complete see para 121 ante; and as to the completion of the contract see paras 262–325 post.

250. Effect of misdescription in open contract. Where there is a material defect in the quantity or quality of the property which the vendor has contracted to transfer, and there is no condition giving or excluding compensation[1], the vendor cannot enforce the contract and compel the purchaser to accept compensation for the deficiency[2]. Where, however, the error in description or the defect is trivial and innocently[3] made, the purchaser may be forced to take the property with compensation[4]. It seems that a vendor cannot enforce specific performance with compensation in his own favour[5].

1 As to the formation of the contract see paras 23–40 ante; and as to conditions giving or excluding compensation see para 110 et seq ante. Where there is no provision for compensation, this cannot be obtained after transfer: see para 113 note 1 ante. As to the disposition of registered and unregistered land by transfer see para 262 note 2 post.
2 *Drewe v Hanson* (1802) 6 Ves 675 at 679; *Halsey v Grant* (1806) 13 Ves 73 at 77, 79; *Binks v Lord Rokeby* (1818) 2 Swan 222 at 225; *Cox v Conventon* (1862) 31 Beav 378; *Re Arnold, Arnold v Arnold* (1880) 14 ChD 270 at 279, CA; *Rudd v Lascelles* [1900] 1 Ch 815 at 819; *Watson v Burton* [1956] 3 All ER 929, [1957] 1 WLR 19. Even where there is a condition for compensation (see para 111 ante), the court does not compel the purchaser to take property substantially different from that which he contracts to buy: *Flight v Booth* (1834) 1 Bing NC 370 at 377; *Re Fawcett and Holmes' Contract* (1889) 42 ChD 150, CA. Where there is a clause excluding compensation (see para 115 ante), the case is a stronger one in favour of the purchaser: *Jacobs v Revell* [1900] 2 Ch 858 at 864; *Re Puckett and Smith's Contract* [1902] 2 Ch 258, CA.
3 It is otherwise where the misdescription is dishonest (*Viscount Clermont v Tasburgh* (1819) 1 Jac & W 112), notwithstanding that there is a condition allowing compensation (*Re Terry and White's Contract* (1886) 32 ChD 14 at 29, CA. See also *Dimmock v Hallett* (1866) 2 Ch App 21 at 28, 31.
4 See *Howland v Norris* (1784) 1 Cox Eq Cas 59 (where an estate was sold with unlimited right of common, although in fact the right only extended to sheep); *Calcraft v Roebuck* (1790) 1 Ves 221 (where the land was described as freehold although a small part was held at will); *Cuthbert v Baker* (1790) Sugden's Law of Vendors and Purchasers (14th Edn, 1862) 313; *Esdaile v Stephenson* (1822) 1 Sim & St 122; *Prendergast v Eyre* (1828) 2 Hog 78 at 81, 94 (where there were undisclosed quitrents or rentcharges of trifling amounts); *King v Wilson* (1843) 6 Beav 124 (error in measurement); *Powell v Elliot* (1875) 10 Ch App 424; and cf *Shepherd v Croft* [1911] 1 Ch 521 (watercourse under property where vendor waived a condition excluding compensation). See also para 52 ante; and SPECIFIC PERFORMANCE vol 44(1) (Reissue) para 948. A purchaser who has precluded himself from repudiating the contract may nevertheless be entitled to compensation: *Hughes v Jones* (1861) 3 De GF & J 307 at 316.
5 *Manser v Back* (1848) 6 Hare 443 at 447; and see 1 Williams Law relating to Vendors and Purchasers of Real Estate and Chattels Real (4th Edn, 1936) 725.

251. Purchaser's right to specific performance with compensation. Where the vendor has either expressly, or impliedly by his conduct, represented that he can transfer a certain property and is entitled to a certain interest in it[1], and it appears that there is a deficiency either in the quantity or quality of the property[2] or in his interest or title[3], and that the deficiency is capable of pecuniary assessment[4], the purchaser can compel the vendor to transfer what he has got and submit to a reduction of the purchase money[5]. It is immaterial that the representation is honestly believed in by the vendor or his agent, provided that it is erroneous and the purchaser relies on it[6]. The misdescription must be contained in the contract. The purchaser cannot obtain compensation for a misrepresentation made collaterally to the contract[7].

1   See *Price v Griffith* (1851) 1 De GM & G 80; *Rudd v Lascelles* [1900] 1 Ch 815 at 819. As to the disposition of registered and unregistered land by transfer see para 262 note 2 post.

2   *Hill v Buckley* (1811) 17 Ves 394 (where the area which the vendor was able to sell was less than the amount stated in the contract); *McKenzie v Hesketh* (1877) 7 ChD 675; *Connor v Potts* [1897] 1 IR 534; *Topfell Ltd v Galley Properties Ltd* [1979] 2 All ER 388, [1979] 1 WLR 446 (where the vendor was unable to give vacant possession of part of the premises).

3   Eg where a vendor who purports to sell the fee simple has no title to part of the land (*Western v Russell* (1814) 3 Ves & B 187), or (formerly) had title only to an undivided moiety (*Mortlock v Buller* (1804) 10 Ves 292 at 315–316; *Hooper v Smart, Bailey v Piper* (1874) LR 18 Eq 683; *Horrocks v Rigby* (1878) 9 ChD 180; *Burrow v Scammell* (1881) 19 ChD 175), or is entitled only as tenant for life (*Cleaton v Gower* (1674) Cas *temp* Finch 164), or pur autre vie (*Barnes v Wood* (1869) LR 8 Eq 424), or in remainder (*Lord Bolingbroke's Case* (circa 1787) 1 Sch & Lef 19n; *Nelthorpe v Holgate* (1844) 1 Coll 203; *Barker v Cox* (1876) 4 ChD 464) (although these interests would now be equitable only; see REAL PROPERTY vol 39(2) (Reissue) para 46). The court also assesses the want of a right to renewal of a lease (*Painter v Newby* (1853) 11 Hare 26), a deficiency in the length of a term (*Leslie v Crommelin* (1867) IR 2 Eq 134; *Dale v Lister* (circa 1800), cited in 16 Ves at 7) or in the parcels agreed to be leased (*McKenzie v Hesketh* (1877) 7 ChD 675), the amount of compensation payable for outstanding leases (*Besant v Richards* (1830) Taml 509; cf *Linehan v Cotter* (1844) 7 I Eq R 176); or (formerly) the possibility of a wife becoming entitled to dower (*Wilson v Williams* (1857) 3 Jur NS 810). As to specific performance generally see SPECIFIC PERFORMANCE.

4   It is otherwise where compensation is impossible or extremely difficult of assessment, as in the case of partial interests (*Thomas v Dering* (1837) 1 Keen 729 at 746) or of restrictive covenants (*Cato v Thompson* (1882) 9 QBD 616 at 618, CA; *Rudd v Lascelles* [1900] 1 Ch 815, criticised by Harpum 'Specific Performance with Compensation as a Purchaser's Remedy: A Study in Contract and Equity' [1981] CLJ 47 at 59–67). The court cannot, it seems, as a rule assess compensation for the existence of sporting rights (*Earl of Durham v Sir Francis Legard* (1865) 34 Beav 611; in *Burnell v Brown* (1820) 1 Jac & W 168, the purchaser had waived his objection to the title on this ground), or (formerly) for the difference of tenure between copyhold and freehold property (*Ayles v Cox* (1852) 16 Beav 23, where there was a condition for compensation). However, in *Barnes v Wood* (1869) LR 8 Eq 424, James V-C considered that the court must assess compensation in the best way it can: see para 112 ante.

5   *Mortlock v Buller* (1804) 10 Ves 292 at 315; *Milligan v Cooke* (1808) 16 Ves 1; *Powell v Elliot* (1875) 10 Ch App 424 (explained in *Gilchester Properties Ltd v Gomm* [1948] 1 All ER 493 at 497–498, [1948] WN 71 at 72 per Romer J).

6   *Hill v Buckley* (1811) 17 Ves 394; *Hooper v Smart, Bailey v Piper* (1874) LR 18 Eq 683; *Burrow v Scammell* (1881) 19 ChD 175; *Connor v Potts* [1897] 1 IR 534. See also *Castle v Wilkinson* (1870) 5 Ch App 534; and para 252 note 5 post.

7   *Rutherford v Acton-Adams* [1915] AC 866, PC; *Gilchester Properties Ltd v Gomm* [1948] 1 All ER 493, [1948] WN 71. As to the remedies available for misrepresentation see para 51 ante; and MISREPRESENTATION AND FRAUD vol 31 (Reissue) para 781 et seq. Where the misrepresentation is collateral, the purchaser's remedy is rescission (or damages in lieu of it), and damages for deceit, negligence or breach of fiduciary duty, or for breach of a collateral contract, if there has been such a contract: see *Rutherford v Acton-Adams* supra at 870. As to an action for damages see 254–261 post; and as to damages generally see DAMAGES.

252. When specific performance with compensation will not be granted. Specific performance with compensation is not decreed at the instance of the purchaser (1) where there is a substantial difference between the property agreed to be sold and that which the vendor can transfer[1] and partial performance would inflict real hardship on the vendor[2]; or (2) where it would be unjust to third persons[3]; or (3) where the purchaser was aware of the defect or misrepresentation when he entered into the contract[4], or did not rely on the vendor's representation[5].

1   *Earl of Durham v Sir Francis Legard* (1865) 34 Beav 611, where the vendor had 11,814 acres and contracted to sell 21,750. Cf *Connor v Potts* [1897] 1 IR 534. See also *Castle v Wilkinson* (1870) 5 Ch App 534; *Rudd v Lascelles* [1900] 1 Ch 815 (criticised by Harpum 'Specific Performance with Compensation as a Purchaser's Remedy: A Study in Contract and Equity' [1981] CLJ 47 at 59–66); *Watson v Burton* [1956] 3 All ER 929, [1957] 1 WLR 19, where the area was stated as 3,920 square yards; in fact it was only 2,360; *Watts v Spence* [1976] Ch 165, [1975] 2 All ER 528; and para 52 ante. As to specific performance generally see SPECIFIC PERFORMANCE.
      As to the disposition of registered and unregistered land by transfer see para 262 note 2 post.
2   See *Price v Griffith* (1851) 1 De GM & G 80 at 86; *Lumley v Ravenscroft* [1895] 1 QB 683, CA; *Hexter v Pearce* [1900] 1 Ch 341 at 345; *Wroth v Tyler* [1974] Ch 30, [1973] 1 All ER 897, where specific performance subject to the spouse's statutory rights of occupation (now matrimonial home rights): see now the Family Law Act 1996 Pt IV (ss 30–63) (as amended); and LAND CHARGES vol 26 (Reissue) para 538) might have had the effect of splitting the family.
3   *Thomas v Dering* (1837) 1 Keen 729 at 747; *Naylor v Goodall* (1877) 47 LJ Ch 53; *Willmott v Barber* (1880) 15 ChD 96 (on appeal (1881) 17 ChD 772, CA); *Basma v Weekes* [1950] AC 441, sub nom *Abdul Karim Basma v Weekes* [1950] 2 All ER 146, PC; *Cedar Holdings Ltd v Green* [1981] Ch 129, [1979] 3 All ER 117, CA (disapproved in *Williams and Glyn's Bank Ltd v Boland* [1981] AC 487 at 507, [1980] 2 All ER 408 at 415, HL, per Lord Wilberforce (see para 248 note 7 ante)); *Thames Guaranty Ltd v Campbell* [1985] QB 210, [1984] 2 All ER 585, CA; cf *Ahmed v Kendrick and Ahmed* (1987) 56 P & CR 120, [1988] 2 FLR 22, CA.
4   *Hopcraft v Hopcraft* (1897) 76 LT 341. Compensation is not payable in respect of patent defects: see *Cobbett v Locke-King* (1900) 16 TLR 379; *Oldfield (or Bowles) v Round* (1800) 5 Ves 508; and para 45 ante. The fact that the purchaser is acquainted with the property does not, however, affect him with notice of easements of water: *Shackleton v Sutcliffe* (1847) 1 De G & Sm 609.
5   *Rudd v Lascelles* [1900] 1 Ch 815 at 818. See also *Thomas v Dering* (1837) 1 Keen 729 at 747; and *Lord Bolingbroke's Case* (circa 1787) 1 Sch & Lef 19n, where the purchaser who, it would seem, knew of the vendor's limited interest but had, with the vendor's consent, expended money on the property was awarded compensation.

253. Remedies after decree of specific performance. Where the vendor fails to comply with the decree of specific performance[1], the most powerful remedy available to the purchaser is to apply to the court for an order vesting the land in him, or appointing some person to transfer it to him[2]. Where the party in default is the purchaser, the vendor may apply for an order rescinding the contract and forfeiting the deposit[3]. For any further loss the vendor may recover damages for breach of contract or damages in lieu of specific performance[4].

1   As to specific performance generally see SPECIFIC PERFORMANCE.
2   See the Trustee Act 1925 ss 48–50; para 266 post; and TRUSTS vol 48 (Reissue) paras 531, 754 et seq. Alternatively, the purchaser could apply for an order rescinding the contract and ordering the return of the deposit, and seek compensation for any further loss by way of damages for breach of contract or damages in lieu of specific performance: see the text and note 4 infra. As to recovery of the deposit by the purchaser see paras 245–246 ante; as to the measure of damages see paras 254–261 post; and as to damages generally see DAMAGES.
      As to the disposition of registered and unregistered land by transfer see para 262 note 2 post.
3   *Foligno v Martin* (1853) 16 Beav 586; *Simpson v Terry* (1865) 34 Beav 423; *Clark v Wallis* (1866) 35 Beav 460; *Henty v Schröder* (1879) 12 ChD 666. As to forfeiture of the deposit to the vendor see paras 234–238 ante; and as to rescission see paras 232–233 ante.
4   *Johnson v Agnew* [1980] AC 367, [1979] 1 All ER 883, HL, overruling a line of cases: see para 232 note 7 ante. As to when damages are awarded in lieu of specific performance see SPECIFIC PERFORMANCE vol 44(1) (Reissue) para 960.

(vi) Damages

254. Action for damages. Either the vendor[1] or the purchaser[2] can maintain an action for damages for breach of the contract by the other party, but for this purpose there must be a contract enforceable at law[3]. The claim may be made by a party who has elected to rescind the contract following a repudiatory breach by the other party[4]. On the other hand, a party who elects to affirm the contract may claim in the alternative for specific performance or damages[5].

1   *Laird v Pim* (1841) 7 M & W 474.
2   *Williams v Glenton* (1866) 1 Ch App 200 at 209.
3   As to a claim for damages for delay in completion see *Raineri v Miles (Wiejski, third party)* [1981] AC 1050, [1980] 2 All ER 145, HL; and para 120 ante. As to damages for breach of contract see DAMAGES vol 12(1) (Reissue) paras 941 et seq, 1059.
4   *Johnson v Agnew* [1980] AC 367, [1979] 1 All ER 883, HL.
5   *Cornwall v Henson* [1900] 2 Ch 298, CA; *Hipgrave v Case* (1885) 28 ChD 356, CA; *Ellis v Rogers* (1885) 29 ChD 661 at 663, CA; *Nicholson v Brown* [1897] WN 52. Formerly only one of these remedies could be obtained (*Orme v Broughton* (1834) 10 Bing 533 at 539; *Sainter v Ferguson* (1849) 1 Mac & G 286 at 290); but, on the claim for specific performance, the court can now give damages either in lieu of, or in addition to, specific performance (see DAMAGES vol 12(1) (Reissue) para 1127; EQUITY vol 16 (Reissue) para 660). In some instances, a claim for specific performance and damages may be cumulative, not alternative; for example specific performance with damages for delay: see DAMAGES vol 12(1) (Reissue) para 1129; SPECIFIC PERFORMANCE vol 44(1) (Reissue) para 959. Such a claim may be made before the date for completion and, if the land is transferred without a court order so that the specific performance action lapses, the court may still award damages: see *Oakacre Ltd v Claire Cleaners (Holdings) Ltd* [1982] Ch 197, [1981] 3 All ER 667; and *Pinekerry Ltd v Needs (Kenneth) (Contractors) Ltd* (1992) 64 P & CR 245, [1992] NPC 15, CA. As to specific performance see paras 247–253 ante; and SPECIFIC PERFORMANCE. As to the date for completion see paras 120, 185 ante; and as to completion see paras 262–325 post. As to the disposition of registered and unregistered land by transfer see para 262 note 2 post.

255. Vendor's action for damages. Damages for breach of contract are in the nature of compensation, not of punishment[1], and the measure of damages is the amount of injury sustained by reason of the breach of contract[2]. This principle applies in the case of a sale of land where the contract is broken by the purchaser[3] even if he is later found to be suffering from mental disorder, provided that the vendor did not know and had no reason to suppose that the purchaser was so suffering[4]. Where no date is fixed for completion the amount of the damages is generally ascertained when the purchaser finally repudiates the contract[5]. Hence the vendor cannot recover the purchase money, notwithstanding that the purchaser has been let into possession[6], unless the transfer has been executed[7]. However, on a resale at a lower price, the vendor can recover the difference in price and the expenses of the resale[8].

1   *Addis v Gramophone Co Ltd* [1909] AC 488 at 494–495, HL. As to damages for breach of contract see DAMAGES vol 12(1) (Reissue) paras 941 et seq, 1059.
2   See *Robinson v Harman* (1848) 1 Exch 850 at 855 per Parke B, who held that a party who has sustained loss by reason of a breach of contract is, with respect to damages, to be placed in the same position as he would have been if the contract had been performed; *Wall v City of London Real Property Co Ltd* (1874) LR 9 QB 249 at 253.
3   *Laird v Pim* (1841) 7 M & W 474.
4   *York Glass Co Ltd v Jubb* (1925) 134 LT 36, CA. As to the subsequent mental disorder of either party see para 218 ante; and as to sales and purchases on behalf of mentally disordered persons generally see MENTAL HEALTH vol 30 (Reissue) para 1431 et seq.
5   *York Glass Co Ltd v Jubb* (1925) 134 LT 36 at 37, CA. As to the date of completion of the contract see paras 120, 185 ante; as to completion of the contract see paras 262–325 post; and as to the date when damages are assessed see para 260 post.

6   *Laird v Pim* (1841) 7 M & W 474 at 478; *Moor v Roberts* (1858) 3 CBNS 830 at 844. As to the recovery of interest on the purchase money see paras 122, 194–197 ante; and as to possession prior to completion of the contract see para 186 ante.

7   See *Laird v Pim* (1841) 7 M & W 474; *East London Union v Metropolitan Rly Co* (1869) LR 4 Exch 309; *Leader v Tod-Heatly* [1891] WN 38. It would appear that, notwithstanding repudiation of the contract by the purchaser, the vendor could unilaterally execute the conveyance and then recover the purchase money: see *White and Carter (Councils) Ltd v McGregor* [1962] AC 413, [1961] 3 All ER 1178, HL; and CONTRACT vol 9(1) (Reissue) paras 1004, 1006. Unilateral execution was successfully achieved in *Tudor v Hamid* [1988] 1 EGLR 251, [1987] NLJ Rep 79, CA. As to the disposition of registered and unregistered land by transfer see para 262 note 2 post.

8   *Noble v Edwardes, Edwardes v Noble* (1877) 5 ChD 378, CA; *Barrow v Arnaud* (1846) 8 QB 604 at 609–610, Ex Ch. The measure of damages is the difference between the contract price and the value of the property. This is determined by the price obtained or obtainable on a resale within a reasonable time of the breach, and not by the price to be obtained by nursing the property: see *Keck v Faber, Jellett and Keeble* (1915) 60 Sol Jo 253; and DAMAGES vol 12(1) (Reissue) para 1059. Any deposit must be taken into account: see *Ockenden v Henly* (1858) EB & E 485; and para 233 ante.

256. Purchaser's action. In relation, to contracts made on or before 27 September 1989[1], at common law the damages which a purchaser of realty[2] can recover for a breach of contract[3] by the vendor are, in general, limited to the expenses which he has incurred[4]. This rule forms an exception to the ordinary law of contract that an injured person is entitled to be placed in the same position as if the contract had been performed[5]. Thus if a vendor who has not expressly undertaken to deduce a good title[6] is unable, acting in good faith[7], and without committing a breach of trust[8], to make a title, the purchaser, in an action for breach of contract, can recover only the expenses which he has incurred[9], but not damages for the loss of his bargain[10]. This is an exceptional rule which applies only if the vendor, through no default of his own, is unable to carry out his contractual obligation to make a good title. In order to obtain the benefit of the rule, the vendor must prove that he has used his best endeavours to make a good title, including a proper attempt to obtain any necessary consent of a third person[11]. If the vendor fails to discharge this burden of proof, the purchaser is entitled to substantial damages[12], which will be assessed according to the normal rule applicable to damages in contract[13]. In such a case the purchaser is entitled to damages for such consequences of the vendor's breach of contract as follow in the usual course from the breach or may reasonably be supposed to have been in the contemplation of both parties at the time of contract[14]. Where there is merely a delay in completion, the purchaser is entitled to recover damages for the delay[15], and where there is a failure to complete, he can recover damages for loss of his bargain[16]. Damages for loss of bargain can be obtained if on the sale of leaseholds the vendor is in default in failing to obtain any necessary consent of the lessor[17]. A spouse's matrimonial home right[18] is not a defect of title within the exceptional rule[19]. It seems that the purchaser may be granted a lien on the land for the damages if he formally claims it[20].

1   In relation to contracts made after 27 September 1989, damages are no longer limited under the rule in *Bain v Fothergill* (1874) LR 7 HL 158: see the Law of Property (Miscellaneous Provisions) Act 1989 s 3; and DAMAGES vol 12(1) (Reissue) para 1059.

2   This includes incorporeal hereditaments (*Pounsett v Fuller* (1856) 17 CB 660), and contracts to grant leases of land (*Pease v Courtney* [1904] 2 Ch 503 at 511–512). See also *Robinson v Harman* (1848) 1 Exch 850; *Hanslip v Padwick* (1850) 5 Exch 615; *Gas Light and Coke Co v Towse* (1887) 35 ChD 519 at 543; *Rowe v London School Board* (1887) 36 ChD 619; and LANDLORD AND TENANT vol 27(1) (Reissue) para 72. As to incorporeal hereditaments see REAL PROPERTY vol 39(2) (Reissue) para 81.

3   The rule applies only to a broken contract, not to a breach of covenant in a conveyance: *Lock v Furze* (1866) LR 1 CP 441. Upon the death of the purchaser, the right to sue for damages passes to his personal representatives: *Orme v Broughton* (1834) 10 Bing 533; Sugden's Law of Vendors and Purchasers (14th Edn, 1862) 238; and see EXECUTORS AND ADMINISTRATORS.

4   See *Grant v Dawkins* [1973] 3 All ER 897, [1973] 1 WLR 1406; and DAMAGES vol 12(1) (Reissue) para 1059. See also note 1 supra.

5   See DAMAGES vol 12(1) (Reissue) paras 1015 et seq, 1059. This exceptional rule is based upon the uncertainty of making out a good title owing to the complexity of the English law of real property: see *Day v Singleton* [1899] 2 Ch 320 at 329, CA; *Malhotra v Choudhury* [1980] Ch 52, [1979] 1 All ER 186, CA. The rule does not apply to damages for misrepresentation: see para 259 post; and DAMAGES vol 12(1) (Reissue) paras 1109–1110.

6   See para 137 ante; and Farrer's Conditions of Sale (2nd Edn, 1909) 9–10. As to the vendor's obligation to show and prove a good title see para 137 ante.

7   *Jones v Gardiner* [1902] 1 Ch 191 at 195 per Byrne J; *Walker v Moore* (1829) 10 B & C 416 at 421. As to the requirements of good faith see paras 41, 48 ante.

8   *Wall v City of London Real Property Co Ltd* (1874) LR 9 QB 249.

9   *Flureau v Thornhill* (1776) 2 Wm Bl 1078; *Bain v Fothergill* (1874) LR 7 HL 158 at 207, 210; and see note 1 supra. See also *Sikes v Wild* (1861) 1 B & S 587 (affd (1863) 4 B & S 421, Ex Ch); *Hyam v Terry* (1881) 25 Sol Jo 371, CA; *Rowe v London School Board* (1887) 36 ChD 619; *Re Daniel, Daniel v Vassall* [1917] 2 Ch 405 at 408; *Braybrooks v Whaley* [1919] 1 KB 435 at 438, DC; *Keen v Mear* [1920] 2 Ch 574 at 581; *Barnes v Cadogan Developments Ltd* [1930] 1 Ch 479 at 488; *JW Cafés Ltd v Brownlow Trust Ltd* [1950] 1 All ER 894, [1950] WN 191 (where a contract to grant a lease in a particular form was prevented by covenants as to user); and *Seven Seas Properties Ltd v Al-Essa* [1989] 1 All ER 164, [1988] 1 WLR 1272 (purchaser given no opportunity to use best endeavours to obtain good title). As to what expenses come within this description see para 257 post.

10   *Bain v Fothergill* (1874) LR 7 HL 158; *Williams v Glenton* (1866) 1 Ch App 200 at 209; *Morgan v Russell & Sons* [1909] 1 KB 357, DC. See note 1 supra.

11   *Malhotra v Choudhury* [1980] Ch 52, [1979] 1 All ER 186, CA, where the vendor and his wife were joint tenants, and there was no evidence that the vendor had tried to persuade his wife to consent. Substantial damages were awarded.

12   *Engell v Fitch* (1869) LR 4 QB 659, Ex Ch (sale by mortgagees with vacant possession who deliberately omitted to eject mortgagor); *Godwin v Francis* (1870) LR 5 CP 295 at 306, 308; *Jaques v Millar* (1877) 6 ChD 153 (overruled on another point by *Marshall v Berridge* (1881) 19 ChD 233, CA); *Royal Bristol Permanent Building Society v Bomash* (1887) 35 ChD 390; *Jones v Gardiner* [1902] 1 Ch 191; *Re Daniel, Daniel v Vassall* [1917] 2 Ch 405 (vendor's inability to complete due to mortgagee's refusal to release the property); *Braybrooks v Whaley* [1919] 1 KB 435, DC (mortgagee's omission to obtain leave of court to sell, where leave required); *Thomas v Kensington* [1942] 2 KB 181, [1942] 2 All ER 263 (vendor unwilling to redeem mortgage: purchaser entitled to damages although he knew of the mortgage at the time of the contract); *Phillips v Lamdin* [1949] 2 KB 33, [1949] 1 All ER 770 (mere delay by the vendor); *Malhotra v Choudhury* [1980] Ch 52, [1979] 1 All ER 186, CA (failure of one joint tenant to obtain consent of the other (his wife)); *Sharneyford Supplies Ltd v Edge* [1987] Ch 305, [1987] 1 All ER 588, CA (failure by vendor to give notice to quit to periodic tenant). See also *AVG Management Science Ltd v Barwell Developments Ltd* [1979] 1 WWR 330, 92 DLR (3d) 289, Can SC (where the vendor, in breach of contract with the purchaser, accepted an offer from a second purchaser); *Strutt v Whitnell* [1975] 2 All ER 510, [1975] 1 WLR 870, CA. As to the recovery of expenses as well as damages see para 257 post. See further *Gedye v Duke of Montrose* (1858) 26 Beav 45; *Lehmann v McArthur* (1868) 3 Ch App 496 at 500; *Wesley v Walker* (1878) 26 WR 368. As to the vendor's duty to do all he reasonably can to perfect his title see *Costigan v Hastler* (1804) 2 Sch & Lef 160 at 166; *Day v Singleton* [1899] 2 Ch 320 at 332, CA, per Jeune P; and para 137 et seq ante. Where the vendor's abstract, which was negligently but not fraudulently prepared, showed a good title, and the purchaser resold without comparing it with the deeds, he did not obtain damages: *Walker v Moore* (1829) 10 B & C 416 at 423. Where the purchaser has resold at a profit, and the vendor by his own default has rendered himself unable to complete the contract, the damages recoverable by the purchaser will be the amount of the profit which would have been made on such resale: *Goffin v Houlder* (1920) 90 LJ Ch 488, applied in *Wright v Dean* [1948] Ch 686, [1948] 2 All ER 415, to an option to purchase in a lease.

13   As to damages in contract see DAMAGES vol 12(1) (Reissue) paras 941 et seq, 1059.

14   See eg *Diamond v Campbell-Jones* [1961] Ch 22 at 31–34, [1960] 1 All ER 583 at 588–590 per Buckley J; *Cottrill v Steyning and Littlehampton Building Society* [1966] 2 All ER 295, [1966] 1 WLR 753; *Seven Seas Properties Ltd v Al-Essa (No 2)* [1993] 3 All ER 577, [1993] 1 WLR 1083; and DAMAGES vol 12(1) (Reissue) para 941 et seq. Such damages can include expenditure required by the contract, even though incurred before the contract was formed: see *Lloyd v Stanbury* [1971] 2 All ER 267, [1971] 1 WLR 535; and DAMAGES vol 12(1) (Reissue) paras 994, 996, 1059.

15   *Jones v Gardiner* [1902] 1 Ch 191; *Phillips v Lamdin* [1949] 2 KB 33, [1949] 1 All ER 770. Cf *Jaques v Millar* (1877) 6 ChD 153. As to delay in completion see para 121 ante; and as to completion of the contract see paras 262–325 post.

16   See eg *Braybrooks v Whaley* [1919] 1 KB 435, DC; *Thomas v Kensington* [1942] 2 KB 181, [1942] 2 All ER 263; and para 258 post.

17   *Day v Singleton* [1899] 2 Ch 320, CA. As to the time by which consent must be obtained see para 240 ante.

18   As to a spouses' matrimonial home right see para 248 note 5 ante; and LAND CHARGES.
19   *Wroth v Tyler* [1974] Ch 30, [1973] 1 All ER 897.
20   See LIEN vol 28 (Reissue) para 764.

257. Purchaser's expenses recoverable by way of damages. The expenses which a purchaser, affirming a contract, can recover as damages include the cost of preparing, stamping and executing the contract[1], investigating the title[2], searching for incumbrances[3], examining deeds[4], and, if the vendor's breach took place after the title had been accepted, of preparing the transfer[5], together with interest on the deposit from the time completion should have taken place[6]. These conveyancing costs are recoverable whether they have actually been paid to the purchaser's solicitor or not[7]. In addition, the purchaser can recover compensation for any pre-contract expenditure where this is contemplated by the contract or which would reasonably be in the contemplation of the parties as likely to be wasted if the contract is broken[8].

Subject to this general principle as to wasted expenditure, the purchaser cannot recover money expended in repairs[9] or improvements[10], or the difference between party and party and common fund costs of an action for specific performance[11], or any expenses incurred after he is aware of a definite breach of the contract on the vendor's part[12]. However, on a sale under the direction of the court, the purchaser can recover, in addition to his other expenses, all costs incurred by his having bid for and become the purchaser of the property[13]. If the purchaser treats the contract as repudiated, he cannot recover any expense which he incurred only because he was at that time keeping open his option to sue for specific performance; on the contrary, the purchaser's duty is to mitigate his loss[14], but this duty does not oblige him to accept an offer by the vendor to repurchase the property at the contract price[15].

1   *Hanslip v Padwick* (1850) 5 Exch 615.
2   *Richards v Barton* (1795) 1 Esp 268; *Hanslip v Padwick* (1850) 5 Exch 615; *Compton v Bagley* [1892] 1 Ch 313. See also *Hall v Betty* (1842) 5 Scott NR 508 at 513; *Re Daniel, Daniel v Vassall* [1917] 2 Ch 405. As to the costs of making and verifying the abstract, producing deeds not in the vendor's possession etc see paras 170–173 ante. As to the need for an abstract of title with respect to both unregistered and registered land see paras 138, 141–149 ante.
3   *Hanslip v Padwick* (1850) 5 Exch 615. As to searching for incumbrances see paras 167–169 ante.
4   *Hodges v Earl of Litchfield* (1835) 1 Bing NC 492. As to requisitions on title see paras 163–166 ante.
5   Sugden's Law of Vendors and Purchasers (14th Edn, 1862) 362; 2 Dart's Law relating to Vendors and Purchasers (8th Edn, 1929) 844; 2 Williams Law relating to Vendors and Purchasers of Real Estate and Chattels Real (4th Edn, 1936) 1021. As to the purchaser's acceptance of the title see paras 174–176 ante; and as to the preparation of the transfer see paras 129 ante, 262 et seq post. As to the disposition of registered and unregistered land by transfer see para 262 note 2 post.
6   *De Bernales v Wood* (1812) 3 Camp 258. As to the purchaser's right to recover the deposit with interest see paras 245–246 ante. As to the completion of the contract see paras 262–325 post; and as to the date for completion see paras 120, 185 ante. As to costs generally payable by the purchaser see para 323 post.
7   *Hodges v Earl of Litchfield* (1835) 1 Bing NC 492 at 498; *Richardson v Chasen* (1847) 10 QB 756. As to solicitors' costs see SOLICITORS vol 44(1) (Reissue) para 158 et seq. See also para 3 ante.
8   *Lloyd v Stanbury* [1971] 2 All ER 267, [1971] 1 WLR 535; *Anglia Television Ltd v Reed* [1972] 1 QB 60, [1971] 3 All ER 690, CA. This principle seems to cast doubt on a number of cases which had disallowed various items of pre-contract expenditure: see eg *Flureau v Thornhill* (1776) 2 Wm Bl 1078 (loss incurred by raising purchase money by sale of stock); *Jarmain v Egelstone* (1831) 5 C & P 172 (preparation of conveyance); *Sherry v Oke* (1835) 3 Dowl 349 at 361 (expenses of raising purchase money by borrowing); *Hodges v Earl of Litchfield* (1835) 1 Bing NC 492 (costs of negotiation, survey, valuation and preparation of conveyance prior to acceptance of title); and *Hanslip v Padwick* (1850) 5 Exch 615.
9   *Bratt v Ellis* (1805) Sugden's Law of Vendors and Purchasers (14th Edn, 1862) App V, 812.
10   *Worthington v Warrington* (1849) 8 CB 134; *Lloyd v Stanbury* [1971] 2 All ER 267, [1971] 1 WLR 535. Cf expenditure necessary to preserve the property: see *Lloyd v Stanbury* supra at 275 and 547 per Brightman J.
11   *Hodges v Earl of Litchfield* (1835) 1 Bing NC 492; *Cockburn v Edwards* (1881) 18 ChD 449, CA. See also *Malden v Fyson* (1847) 11 QB 292; *Wood v Scarth* (1855) 2 K & J 33 at 44. As to specific performance see paras 247–253 ante; and SPECIFIC PERFORMANCE.

12 *Pounsett v Fuller* (1856) 17 CB 660; *Sikes v Wild* (1861) 1 B & S 587 at 590 (affd (1863) 4 B & S 421 at 424, Ex Ch).

13 *Holliwell v Seacombe* [1906] 1 Ch 426.

14 *Lloyd v Stanbury* [1971] 2 All ER 267 at 275, [1971] 1 WLR 535 at 546 per Brightman J. As to the duty to mitigate see generally DAMAGES vol 12(1) (Reissue) para 1041 et seq.

15 *Strutt v Whitnell* [1975] 2 All ER 510, [1975] 1 WLR 870, CA.

258. Damages for loss of bargain. The measure of damages for loss of bargain is normally the difference between the contract price and the market value at the date of repudiation[1]. The mere fact that property is obviously ripe for conversion to a more profitable use is not sufficient to justify imputing to the vendor knowledge that the purchaser intended to convert it to such a use, or to entitle the purchaser to recover as damages the profit which he would have realised by such a conversion[2]. Where the purchaser is by profession a dealer in real estate so that the damages recovered by him are liable to attract income tax as part of the profits or gains of his business, he should be awarded a gross sum equal to the difference between the contract price and the market value and not merely a net sum equivalent to the profit remaining after deduction of income tax[3].

Where a purchaser recovers substantial damages for loss of his bargain on account of a breach of the contract by the vendor, he is not, it seems, entitled to his expenses as well. If he were so entitled, he would actually benefit by the breach, since, if the contract had been completed, he would have had to pay the expenses himself[4]. This rule has, however, been varied where a house was sold with vacant possession at a time of housing shortage and, although the sale was completed, vacant possession was not given owing to the existence of a tenancy[5].

1 *Engell v Fitch* (1869) LR 4 QB 659, Ex Ch; *Godwin v Francis* (1870) LR 5 CP 295 at 306, 308; *Re Daniel, Daniel v Vassall* [1917] 2 Ch 405; *Goffin v Houlder* (1920) 90 LJ Ch 488 (difference between price at which property was offered to claimant and that at which he had contracted to resell it); *Brading v F McNeill & Co Ltd* [1946] Ch 145, [1946] WN 20; *Wright v Dean* [1948] Ch 686, [1948] 2 All ER 415; *Diamond v Campbell-Jones* [1961] Ch 22, [1956] 1 All ER 583. If there is no difference between the contract price and market value, the purchaser is entitled to his expenses: *Wallington v Townsend* [1939] Ch 588, [1939] 2 All ER 225. As to the date for assessing damages see para 260 post; and as to the measure of damages in contract see DAMAGES vol 12(1) (Reissue) para 1059.

2 *Diamond v Campbell-Jones* [1961] Ch 22, [1960] 1 All ER 583; *Seven Seas Properties Ltd v Al-Essa (No 2)* [1993] 3 All ER 577, [1993] 1 WLR 1083. Cf *Cottrill v Steyning and Littlehampton Building Society* [1966] 2 All ER 295, [1966] 1 WLR 753, where the vendors knew that the purchasers intended to develop.

3 *Diamond v Campbell-Jones* [1961] Ch 22, [1960] 1 All ER 583, distinguishing *British Transport Commission v Gourley* [1956] AC 185, [1955] 3 All ER 796, HL. As to the income tax liability of dealers in land see INCOME TAXATION vol 23 (Reissue) para 103 et seq.

4 *Re Daniel, Daniel v Vassall* [1917] 2 Ch 405 at 412; 2 Williams Law relating to Vendors and Purchasers of Real Estate and Chattels Real (4th Edn, 1936) 1023–1024. See also *Hopkins v Grazebrook* (1826) 6 B & C 31; *Robinson v Harman* (1848) 1 Exch 850; *Day v Singleton* [1899] 2 Ch 320, CA; *Ridley v De Geerts* [1945] 2 All ER 654, 146 Estates Gazette 390, CA; and cf *Engel v Fitch* (1868) LR 3 QB 314 (on appeal (1869) LR 4 QB 659, Ex Ch); *Godwin v Francis* (1870) LR 5 CP 295, where damages for loss of bargain and expenses were both allowed (*Engel v Fitch* supra and *Godwin v Francis* supra are generally thought to be wrongly decided, for the reason given in the text). See also *Wallington v Townsend* [1939] Ch 588, [1939] 2 All ER 225; and note 1 supra. As to costs generally payable by the purchaser see para 323 post; and as to completion see paras 262–325 post.

5 *Beard v Porter* [1948] 1 KB 321, [1947] 2 All ER 407, CA, where the purchaser was awarded the difference in value between the purchase price and the value of the house subject to the tenancy, and also solicitor's charges and stamp duty incurred in buying another house and the cost of lodgings between the date when vacant possession of the first house should have been given and the date when the purchaser moved into the second house. As to vacant possession see para 123 ante; as to the position of the parties after completion see paras 326–359 post; and as to solicitors' costs see SOLICITORS vol 44(1) (Reissue) para 158 et seq.

259. Vendor's misrepresentation. Where, at the time of entering into the contract, the vendor knows that he has no title and no means of acquiring one, and the circumstances are such as to make his conduct fraudulent, the purchaser can recover substantial damages in an action of deceit[1]. Equally, substantial damages may be awarded to the purchaser where the vendor makes a misrepresentation as to his title not proved to have been made without negligence[2].

1 *Bain v Fothergill* (1874) LR 7 HL 158 at 207. In relation to contracts made after 27 September 1989, damages are no longer limited under the rule in *Bain v Fottergill* (1874) LR 7 HL 158: see the Law of Property (Miscellaneous Provisions) Act 1989 s 3; and DAMAGES vol 12(1) (Reissue) para 1059. See also *Day v Singleton* [1899] 2 Ch 320 at 329, CA. For this purpose the vendor's conduct must amount to actual fraud: *Derry v Peek* (1889) 14 App Cas 337, HL; and see MISREPRESENTATION AND FRAUD vol 31 (Reissue) para 755 et seq. As to the vendor's obligation to show and prove a good title see paras 137–173 ante; and as to the measure of damages in deceit see DAMAGES vol 12(1) (Reissue) para 875.

2 See the Misrepresentation Act 1967 s 2(1) (see MISREPRESENTATION AND FRAUD vol 31 (Reissue) para 801); *Watts v Spence* [1976] Ch 165, [1975] 2 All ER 528; and *Errington v Martell-Wilson* (1980) 130 NLJ 545. In both these cases the mere fact of contracting to sell was held to amount to an implied representation as to title. Where such a representation is false, substantial damages have always been awarded without regard to the rule limiting damages to expenses (see para 257 ante): *Watts v Spence* supra.

260. Date for assessment of damages. The general principle for the assessment of damages is compensatory, that is, that the innocent party is to be placed, so far as money can do so, in the same position as if the contract had been performed[1]. Whether damages are claimed by the vendor or purchaser, the normal date for the assessment of damages is the date of the breach of contract[2]. However, if to follow this rule would cause injustice, the court may fix such other date as may be appropriate to provide proper compensation for the innocent party[3]. Where one party has obtained a decree of specific performance which proves impossible to execute, the innocent party may rescind the contract and seek damages, which will be assessed as at the date the contract is finally abandoned, not the date of the original breach[4]. The damages cannot be enhanced by any delay of that party in bringing or prosecuting his claim for damages[5].

1 See para 255 ante; and DAMAGES vol 12(1) (Reissue) para 941.
2 *York Glass Co Ltd v Jubb* (1925) 134 LT 36, CA; and see DAMAGES vol 12(1) (Reissue) para 950. Date of breach will be the appropriate date where the property depreciates after that date: *Woodford Estates Ltd v Pollack* (1978) 93 DLR (3d) 350. As to the vendor's action for damages see para 255 ante; and as to the purchaser's action for damages see paras 256–258 ante.
3 See *Johnson v Agnew* [1980] AC 367 at 401, [1979] 1 All ER 883 at 896, HL, per Lord Wilberforce (where it was held that if the innocent party tried to continue the contract, damages should be assessed at the date when the contract was finally lost); and DAMAGES vol 12(1) (Reissue) para 951. See also *Ogle v Earl Vane* (1867) LR 2 QB 275 (affd (1868) LR 3 QB 272, Ex Ch) (date when innocent party acting reasonably went into the market); *Hickman v Haynes* (1875) LR 10 CP 598 (reasonable time after defendant's last request to withhold delivery); *Forster v Silvermere Golf and Equestrian Centre Ltd* (1981) 42 P & CR 255; and *Radford v de Froberville* [1978] 1 All ER 33, [1977] 1 WLR 1262 (damages assessed as at date of hearing). See further *Wroth v Tyler* [1974] Ch 30, [1973] 1 All ER 897; *Grant v Dawkins* [1973] 3 All ER 897, [1973] 1 WLR 1406; *Techno Land Improvements Ltd v British Leyland (UK) Ltd* (1979) 252 Estates Gazette 805; *Malhotra v Choudhury* [1980] Ch 52, [1979] 1 All ER 186, CA; *E Johnson & Co (Barbados) Ltd v NSR Ltd* [1997] AC 400, [1996] 3 WLR 583, PC.
4 *Johnson v Agnew* [1980] AC 367, [1979] 1 All ER 883, HL, also holding (contra *Wroth v Tyler* [1974] Ch 30, [1973] 1 All ER 897), that the position is the same in law as in equity (ie where damages in lieu of specific performance are awarded (see EQUITY vol 16 (Reissue) para 660; SPECIFIC PERFORMANCE vol 44(1) (Reissue) para 960)); and see *Domb v Isoz* [1980] Ch 548, [1980] 1 All ER 942, CA.
5 *Malhotra v Choudhury* [1980] Ch 52, [1979] 1 All ER 186, CA; *Hickey v Bruhns* [1977] 2 NZLR 71; and see DAMAGES vol 12(1) (Reissue) para 1128.

261. Procedure. Damages for breach of the contract cannot be recovered on an application by a vendor or purchaser for a summary order[1], although an order can be made for the return of the deposit with interest and for payment by the vendor of the purchaser's costs of investigating title[2]. Substantial damages can, however, be recovered where an action is brought[3].

1   Ie an application under the Law of Property Act 1925 s 49 (as amended): see para 220 ante.
2   See para 222 ante.
3   See *Laird v Pim* (1841) 7 M & W 474; *Leader v Tod-Heatly* [1891] WN 38. In relation to proceedings commenced after 26 April 1999 the procedure for bringing an action is governed by CPR Pts 7, 8. As to the CPR see para 133 note 1 ante. As to the procedure before that date see RSC Ord 5 r 4(1). As to the pleadings to be made in a vendor's action see *Ellis v Rogers* (1885) 29 ChD 661 at 667, CA. See also *Perry v Smith* (1842) Car & M 554; *Johnstone v Milling* (1886) 16 QBD 460, CA; and PLEADING. As to what a purchaser must prove see *Howe v Smith* (1884) 27 ChD 89 at 103, CA, per Fry LJ. See also *Poole v Hill* (1840) 6 M & W 835 at 841; *Lovelock v Franklyn* (1846) 8 QB 371. See further PRACTICE AND PROCEDURE.

3. COMPLETION

(1) ASSURING THE PROPERTY AND DISCHARGING INCUMBRANCES

(i) The Transfer and the Duty to Prepare it

262. Preparation of transfer. The contract is completed by payment of the purchase money[1] by the purchaser, the execution and delivery at the same time of a transfer[2] by the vendor[3] and the handing over of such deeds as relate wholly to the property transferred[4]. In the absence of agreement to the contrary[5], the purchaser prepares the draft transfer and submits it to the vendor for approval[6]. The purchaser should not prepare the draft transfer before production of the deeds[7].

1   There is at the same time payment or allowance of any balance shown on the completion statement (as to which see para 2 note 8 ante), so that the pecuniary position may be adjusted finally and completely.
2   No particular form of assurance is required where unregistered land is to be registered following completion. A conveyance or, in the case of an existing lease, an assignment, in the usual unregistered form will suffice. However, the parties may use a transfer, commonly called a 'rule 72 transfer', that follows the form for registered land subject to certain modifications needed to reflect the fact that the land is not already registered. The use of transfers in respect of unregistered land is made possible by the Land Registration Rules 1925, SI 1925/1093, r 72(1), which provides that a person having the right to apply for registration as first proprietor who desires to deal with the land in any way permitted by the Land Registration Act 1925 before he himself is registered as proprietor may do so in the manner, and subject to the conditions, which would be applicable if he were in fact the registered proprietor. This means that a transfer in the form used for registered land may be used rather than an unregistered form of conveyance on the sale of unregistered land, because registration of title on sale is compulsory throughout England and Wales. As to persons entitled to be registered as proprietors of registered land see the Land Registration Act 1925 s 37(1); and LAND REGISTRATION vol 26 (Reissue) para 901. As to compulsory registration see LAND REGISTRATION vol 26 (Reissue) paras 727, 1196 et seq.
3   In strictness a conveyance may not be necessary in the case of the purchase of an equitable interest (see para 179 note 5 ante), but it is usual to have a formal conveyance: cf *Fenner v Hepburn* (1843) 2 Y & C Ch Cas 159; and see 1 Dart's Law relating to Vendors and Purchasers (8th Edn, 1929) 459. As to a condition providing for a free transfer see para 130 ante.
4   See paras 131–132 ante.

5 As to provisions for the granting of a free transfer and statutory restrictions relating to the preparation of transfers by the vendor's solicitor see para 130 ante. See also para 3 ante. As to restrictions on the creation of rentcharges see the Rentcharges Act 1977 s 2 (as amended); and RENTCHARGES AND ANNUITIES vol 39(2) (Reissue) para 774 et seq.

6 Sugden's Law of Vendors and Purchasers (14th Edn, 1862) 240–241. Cf the Statutory Form of Conditions of Sale 1925, SR & O 1925/779, condition 8(1); the Standard Conditions of Sale (3rd Edn), condition 4.1.2, which provide expressly for preparation of the transfer by the purchaser. The latter set of conditions makes special provision for sale by way of lease or underlease: see condition 8. As to the Standard Conditions of Sale see para 1 note 9 ante. A transfer in pursuance of the Leasehold Reform Act 1967 will be prepared by the tenant, unless the parties have agreed otherwise: see the Leasehold Reform Act (Enfranchisement and Extension) Regulations 1967, SI 1967/1879, Schedule, Pt I para 9(1). As to matters to be included in and the effect of a conveyance or transfer executed to give effect to a landlord's obligation to enfranchise see the Leasehold Reform Act 1967 ss 8–13 (as amended); and LANDLORD AND TENANT vol 27(1) (Reissue) para 1294 et seq. The 'right to buy' provisions of the Housing Act 1985 (see Pt V (ss 118–188) (as amended); and see LANDLORD AND TENANT vol 27(1) (Reissue) paras 1628–1739) do not state who is to prepare the transfer, so the general law will apply. As to collective enfranchisement under the Leasehold Reform, Housing and Urban Development Act 1993 Pt I Ch I (ss 1–38) (as amended) see LANDLORD AND TENANT vol 27(2) (Reissue) para 1406 et seq. As to settling the transfer on a sale by the court see 2 Dart's Law relating to Vendors and Purchasers (8th Edn, 1929) 1002; and cf para 136 ante.

7 *Jarmain v Egelstone* (1831) 5 C & P 172.

263. Transfer of parts of property by separate deeds. The purchaser of property included in a single contract may divide it into parts, apportioning the purchase money among the parts, and may require the vendor to transfer the several parts by separate deeds[1], provided that this does not impose undue trouble on the vendor, and that the purchaser pays the additional costs occasioned by it to the vendor[2]. Where the land is unregistered, the property is frequently conveyed by separate deeds where it comprises distinct estates or land held under different titles, as the inclusion in one deed would render future dealing with the several parts difficult or expensive[3]. However, it may be advantageous, on first registration of title, to combine the several parts into one registered title.

Where a large property is sold in smaller parts it is essential that each parcel transferred is described with such particularity and precision as to leave no room for doubt as to the boundaries[4].

1 See *Clark v May* (1852) 16 Beav 273.
2 *Earl of Egmont v Smith, Smith v Earl of Egmont* (1877) 6 ChD 469. It is doubtful whether a vendor, in the absence of express stipulation, could be required by the purchaser to transfer the land in parcels by separate transfers at intervals of time. As to the disposition of registered and unregistered land by transfer see para 262 note 2 ante.
3 See 1 Dart's Law relating to Vendors and Purchasers (8th Edn, 1929) 461; 1 Williams Law relating to Vendors and Purchasers of Real Estate and Chattels Real (4th Edn, 1936) 644. However, the purchaser cannot, by having the property transferred to him in separate parts, avoid paying the amount of stamp duty which would be exigible if it were transferred to him as a whole: *A-G v Cohen* [1937] 1 KB 478 at 483, [1937] 1 All ER 27 at 32, CA.
4 See *Scarfe v Adams* [1981] 1 All ER 843 at 845, CA, per Cumming-Bruce LJ; applied in *Mayer v Hurr* (1983) 49 P & CR 56, CA. An Ordnance Survey map of 1:2500 is not adequate for this purpose.

264. Transfer by deed of freeholds and leaseholds. The assurance of freehold property to the purchaser is effected by deed[1], the form of which is settled by him[2]. An assignment of leasehold property is likewise effected by deed[3].

1 See DEEDS AND OTHER INSTRUMENTS; and para 263 text and note 1 ante.
2 See para 262 ante. As to the parties by whom and to whom the assurance is made see para 269 et seq post; as to registered land see para 265 text and note 8 post; as to the formal parts of a deed see generally DEEDS AND OTHER INSTRUMENTS; and as to the desirability of adhering to established forms of words in conveyances, transfers and other deeds see *Bromley v Tryon* [1952] AC 265 at 275, [1951] 2 All ER 1058

at 1065, HL. Where there are several incumbrances on the property, including leases or subleases, and these are to determine or be cleared off at completion, it is advisable to clear them off the title by a separate deed and for the vendor then to transfer as owner in fee simple free from incumbrances: cf para 267 post. As to the disposition of registered and unregistered land by transfer see para 262 note 2 ante.

3　See LANDLORD AND TENANT vol 27(1) (Reissue) para 464. As to the matters to be included in such a deed see para 300 et seq post.

265. Form of transfer. The form of the transfer is primarily for the purchaser to determine, and the vendor is not entitled to raise objections to the draft save as regards matters of substance affecting himself[1]. Special forms of conveyance are authorised by the enactments relating to the acquisition of land under compulsory powers[2] and to grants of sites for schools[3] and certain other enactments[4]. Enactments prescribing such forms are not affected by the Law of Property Act 1925, but remain in full force[5]. Certain forms are also provided by that Act[6], and instruments in the form of, and using the expressions in, these forms, or in the like form and using expressions to the like effect, are sufficient in regard to form and expression[7].

Registered land is transferred to a purchaser by the execution of an instrument of transfer, followed by registration of the purchaser as proprietor of the land[8].

1　*Clark v May* (1852) 16 Beav 273; *Cooper v Cartwright* (1860) John 679 at 685. As to the reserving to the vendor of the right to furnish a draft form of transfer see para 130 text and note 2 ante; and as to the form of assurances of freeholds and leaseholds respectively see paras 269 et seq, 300 et seq post. As to the disposition of registered and unregistered land by transfer see para 262 note 2 ante.
2　See the Lands Clauses Consolidation Act 1845 s 81 (as amended), Schs (A), (B); the Compulsory Purchase Act 1965 s 23(6), Sch 5; and COMPULSORY ACQUISITION OF LAND vol 8(1) (Reissue) para 139. These forms are seldom used in practice. As to covenants for title when land is so acquired or on a sale of superfluous land by the acquiring authority see COMPULSORY ACQUISITION OF LAND vol 8(1) (Reissue) paras 139, 382.
3　See the School Sites Act 1841 s 10 (as amended); and EDUCATION vol 15 (Reissue) para 188. The powers conferred by the Act are no longer necessary and are unlikely to be used in practice.
4　Eg by the Queen Anne's Bounty Act 1838 s 20 (as amended); the Consecration of Churchyards Act 1867 s 5; and the Places of Worship Sites Act 1873 s 4 (as amended): see ECCLESIASTICAL LAW.
5　See the Law of Property Act 1925 s 7(3) (as amended); and REAL PROPERTY vol 39(2) (Reissue) para 246.
6　See ibid s 206(1), Sch 5. As to the modification of the statutory form contained in Sch 5 see the Law of Property (Miscellaneous Provisions) Act 1994 s 9; and as to the provisions of the Law of Property (Miscellaneous Provisions) Act 1994 relating to implied covenants for title see para 336 et seq post.
7　Law of Property Act 1925 s 206(1).
8　See LAND REGISTRATION vol 26 (Reissue) para 937 et seq. As to the protection of minor interests in registered land see LAND REGISTRATION vol 26 (Reissue) para 1098 et seq; as to the necessity for the purchaser of land in an area of compulsory registration to prove himself registered as proprietor see para 317 post; and as to a transfer of registered land being a deed poll see *Chelsea and Walham Green Building Society v Armstrong* [1951] Ch 853, [1951] 2 All ER 250.

266. Vesting order. Where the court[1] gives a judgment or makes an order directing the sale of land, every person who is entitled to or possessed of any interest in the land, or entitled to a contingent interest, and is a party to the proceedings or otherwise bound by the judgment or order, is deemed a trustee for the purposes of the Trustee Act 1925, and the court may, if it thinks expedient, make an order vesting the land in the purchaser[2].

The court may also make a vesting order consequential on a judgment for specific performance of a contract concerning any land[3].

The circumstances in which the court may make vesting orders as to land[4], or may appoint a person to transfer[5], and the power of the court to enforce a judgment or order for the execution of a transfer by directing execution by a nominee[6] are dealt with generally elsewhere.

1 'The court' means the High Court or, where it has jurisdiction, the county court: Trustee Act 1925 s 67(1) (definition amended by the Courts Act 1971 s 56(4), Sch 11 Pt II). The county court has jurisdiction under the Trustee Act 1925 ss 47, 48, where the judgment or order is given or made by the court, and under s 50 where a vesting order can be made by the court: Trustee Act 1925 s 63A(3) (s 63A added by the County Courts Act 1984 s 148(1), Sch 2 para 1). The parties may also consent to jurisdiction: see the County Courts Act 1984 s 24 (as amended); and COUNTY COURTS.

2 Trustee Act 1925 s 47. See also *Re Montagu, Faber v Montagu* [1896] 1 Ch 549 (barring of estate tail). Alternatively, a person may be appointed to transfer the land: Trustee Act 1925 s 50. See also *White v White* (1872) LR 15 Eq 247; *Moorhead v Kirkwood* [1919] 1 IR 225; and TRUSTS vol 48 (Reissue) para 764. As to the disposition of registered and unregistered land by transfer see para 262 note 2 ante.

3 See the Trustee Act 1925 s 48; para 253 ante; and SPECIFIC PERFORMANCE vol 44(1) (Reissue) para 965; TRUSTS vol 48 (Reissue) para 768.

4 See ibid ss 44–49; and TRUSTS vol 48 (Reissue) para 760 et seq. Where a rector died before completion of the sale of his rectory, he was declared to have been a trustee and a vesting order was made: *Re Peek's Contract* (1920) 65 Sol Jo 220. As to vesting orders when an order for sale is made for the purpose of giving effect to an equitable charge see MORTGAGE; and as to vesting orders when a purchaser becomes mentally disordered see para 219 ante.

5 See the Trustee Act 1925 s 50; and note 2 supra. As to the appointment of persons to transfer property of minors to raise money for their maintenance see CHILDREN AND YOUNG PERSONS vol 5(2) (Reissue) para 674.

6 See JUDGMENTS AND ORDERS.

(ii) Discharge of Incumbrances

267. Sale of incumbered land. Where a vendor contracts to sell land which is in fact incumbered, even though this is not shown by the contract, the purchaser may require the vendor at his own expense to obtain the discharge of the incumbrance by separate deed[1]. Before 1926 this right was not usually insisted on[2], and now that mortgages can be discharged by receipt[3] there is usually no need for a separate surrender or release by the incumbrancer. Where there is no discharge of the incumbrance prior to completion, the incumbrancer can join in the transfer to the purchaser[4]. Satisfied terms, whether or not attendant on the inheritance, cease by statute[5], but should it be necessary to procure an assignment of a term, this will be at the vendor's expense[6]. Where there is a registered equitable incumbrance which will not be overreached by the transfer to the purchaser, the purchaser may require the registration to be cancelled, or may require that the person entitled concur in the transfer, and in either case free of expense to himself[7].

Formerly, when an existing incumbrance was to be paid off out of the purchase money, the purchaser was entitled to have it kept on foot for his own protection against subsequent incumbrances[8], although if the vendor was under any personal liability he could insist on this being discharged[9]. Now only a tenant for life or other limited owner can require a mortgage to be kept alive for his benefit; in other cases a mortgage term becomes a satisfied term and ceases when the money secured by the mortgage has been discharged[10].

1 Sugden's Law of Vendors and Purchasers (14th Edn, 1862) 555, 557. See also *Jones v Lewis* (1847) 1 De G & Sm 245; and cf *Reeves v Gill* (1838) 1 Beav 375. A stipulation that an outstanding legal estate is to be got in at the expense of a purchaser is void: see the Law of Property Act 1925 s 42(3); and para 129 ante. As to the meaning of 'incumbrance' see para 346 text to note 6 post.

2 Sugden's Law of Vendors and Purchasers (14th Edn, 1862) 557. It was considered that it was not, as a rule, to the purchaser's advantage to allow the legal estate in incumbered land to become vested in the vendor: 1 Williams Law relating to Vendors and Purchasers of Real Estate and Chattels Real (4th Edn, 1936) 646; and see *General Finance, Mortgage and Discount Co v Liberator Permanent Benefit Building Society* (1878) 10 ChD 15 at 20. However, in view of the changes in the law made by the Law of Property Act 1925, it is not now necessary for the purchaser's protection to prevent the legal estate from vesting in the vendor (1 Williams Law relating to Vendors and Purchasers of Real Estate and Chattels Real (4th Edn, 1936) 648), and it is the practice for the vendor to clear his estate before or on completion so that he will be in a position to transfer an unincumbered legal estate. As to the discharge of incumbrances where the

transfer is in pursuance of the Leasehold Reform Act 1967 see ss 11–13 (as amended); and LANDLORD AND TENANT vol 27(1) (Reissue) paras 1310–1314; and as to a transfer to a tenant exercising his 'right to buy' under the Housing Act 1985 see s 139(1), Sch 6 (as amended); and LANDLORD AND TENANT vol 27(1) (Reissue) paras 1628–1739. As to collective enfranchisement under the Leasehold Reform, Housing and Urban Development Act 1993 Pt I Ch I (ss 1–38) (as amended) see LANDLORD AND TENANT vol 27(2) (Reissue) para 1406 et seq.

As to the disposition of registered and unregistered land by transfer see para 262 note 2 ante.

3   This is usually a statutory receipt, although this is not essential: see MORTGAGE.
4   As to the course to be taken where there are several incumbrances see para 264 note 2 ante.
5   See the Law of Property Act 1925 s 5(1); and REAL PROPERTY vol 39(2) (Reissue) para 113. A term is satisfied when there is no useful purpose to be attained by keeping it on foot: see *Anderson v Pignet* (1872) 8 Ch App 180 at 188.
6   *Stronge v Hawkes* (1856) 2 Jur NS 388.
7   Law of Property Act 1925 s 43(1).
8   *Cooper v Cartwright* (1860) John 679. See also *Barry v Harding* (1844) 1 Jo & Lat 475. As to the method of keeping incumbrances on foot for the benefit of a purchaser see generally MORTGAGE.
9   *Cooper v Cartwright* (1860) John 679.
10 Law of Property Act 1925 s 116. See also *Re Chesters, Whittingham v Chesters* [1935] Ch 77, where a mortgage was kept alive for the protection of a tenant for life in remainder who had paid it off. It follows that an indorsed receipt under the Law of Property Act 1925 s 115 (as amended) (see MORTGAGE), although useful as evidence of the discharge of the mortgage, is not essential for the cessation of the mortgage term: see *Edwards v Marshall-Lee* (1975) 119 Sol Jo 506, CA. In the case of registered land, an application to register a discharge in Form DS1 is made on Form AP1 or on Form DS2: see the Land Registration Rules 1925, SI 1925/1093, r 151 (as substituted); and LAND REGISTRATION vol 26 (Reissue) para 1000.

268. Incumbrances discharged by payment into court. Where it is desired to sell incumbered land freed from incumbrances, but without joining the incumbrancers as parties, either vendor or purchaser may apply to the court[1] to allow payment into court[2] (1) in the case of an annual sum charged on the land, or of a capital sum charged on a determinable interest in the land, of a sum of such amount as when invested in government securities will be sufficient, by means of the dividends thereof, to keep down or otherwise provide for the charge[3]; and (2) in any other case of capital money charged on the land, of an amount sufficient to meet the incumbrance and any interest on it[4]. In either case there must also be paid in an additional amount to meet the contingency of further costs, expenses and interests and any other contingency, except depreciation of investments, not exceeding one-tenth of the original amount to be paid in, unless for special reason the court requires a larger additional amount[5]. Thereupon the court, either after or without notice to the incumbrancer, may declare the land to be freed from the incumbrance, and make any order for transfer, or vesting order, proper for giving effect to the sale[6]. The court may dispense with service of notice on the vendor or purchaser[7].

1   As to application to the court see the Law of Property Act 1925 s 203(2)(a), (4); and CPR Pts 7, 8. As to the CPR see para 133 note 1 ante.
2   As to payment into court generally see PRACTICE AND PROCEDURE. Payment of money into court effectually exonerates therefrom the person making the payment: see the Law of Property Act 1925 s 203(1).
3   Ibid s 50(1)(a).
4   Ibid s 50(1)(b).
5   Ibid s 50(1). See also MORTGAGE. This provision applies to sales or exchanges whenever made, and to incumbrances created by statute or otherwise: see s 50(6). An order for sale in an administration action does not have the effect of payment into court under this provision: *Re Evans and Bettell's Contract* [1910] 2 Ch 438. The court does not compel the vendor to submit to payment into court where this would be a hardship to him, but allows him to rescind the contract under a condition for rescission: *Re Great Northern Rly Co and Sanderson* (1884) 25 ChD 788. On an application under this provision the court has decided a question of the construction of a will affecting the existence or amount of incumbrances: *Re Freme's Contract* [1895] 2 Ch 778 at 780, CA.
6   Law of Property Act 1925 s 50(2). See also MORTGAGE. Other land than that sold can be declared free from the incumbrance, notwithstanding that on a previous occasion an order has been made confined to

the land then sold: see s 50(3). As to a case where an order discharging the rest of the land had been omitted see *Re Ossemsley's Estates Ltd* [1937] 3 All ER 774, CA. The order does not prevent the vendor from alleging that the incumbrance was statute-barred: *Re M'Swiney and Hartnett's Contract* [1921] 1 IR 178. Without an application to the court, certain equitable incumbrances can be overreached and transferred to the purchase money by the creation of a special trust of land under the Law of Property Act 1925 s 2 (as amended) (see para 29 ante), or by a special settlement under the Settled Land Act 1925 s 21: see para 272 post; and REAL PROPERTY vol 39(2) (Reissue) para 247 et seq; SETTLEMENTS para 705 post. In the case of personal representatives, recourse can be had to their overreaching powers: see para 271 post; and EXECUTORS AND ADMINISTRATORS; REAL PROPERTY vol 39(2) (Reissue) para 250.

As to the disposition of registered and unregistered land by transfer see para 262 note 2 ante.

7   Law of Property Act 1925 s 50(4).

(2) FORM OF ASSURANCE OF FREEHOLDS

(i) Parties

A. PARTIES BY WHOM THE ASSURANCE IS MADE

269. Parties by whom the transfer is made. The parties who transfer on the sale of land for an estate in fee simple are determined by the principle that equitable interests are as far as possible kept off the title, and title is made to a purchaser by a transfer of the legal estate[1]. If there are legal mortgages which are not paid off before or on completion, the mortgagees will be parties to surrender or release their incumbrances[2]. Otherwise, the transfer by the person or persons in whom the legal estate in fee simple is vested will in general vest in the purchaser the entire legal and equitable interest in the property.

1   See the Law of Property Act 1925 s 10(1); and paras 145–146 ante. As to the disposition of registered and unregistered land by transfer see para 262 note 2 ante.
2   See para 267 ante; and MORTGAGE.

270. Capacity of vendor. Where the vendor is absolutely entitled to the land, whether freehold or leasehold, both at law and in equity, he can, if of full capacity, transfer it by virtue of his absolute ownership, and he alone is the transferring party[1]. If he is under disability, or has a limited or special capacity, he, or some person on his behalf, may be able to transfer under special statutory or other powers[2].

A sale of an interest less than the fee simple absolute in possession, or term of years absolute, is a sale of an equitable interest[3], and the person entitled to it will be the transferring party.

1   As to the parties to transfer on completion of the contract after the death of the vendor see para 202 et seq ante. As to the disposition of registered and unregistered land by transfer see para 262 note 2 ante.
2   See para 64 et seq ante. As to transfers of the property of a mentally disordered person in whom the legal estate is vested see the Law of Property Act 1925 s 22(1) (as amended); the Mental Health Act 1983 s 96(1)(b); and MENTAL HEALTH vol 30 (Reissue) para 1462; and as to transfer of the property of a bankrupt see para 206 et seq ante.
3   See REAL PROPERTY vol 39(2) (Reissue) para 46.

271. Transfer overreaching equitable interests. Where the vendor, although the owner of the legal estate, is not also solely entitled in equity, he may have power by his transfer to overreach the equitable interests, which thereupon attach to the proceeds of sale. Such overreaching powers exist where the vendor is selling under the powers of the Settled Land Act 1925[1], or where the vendors are trustees of land selling under their statutory powers[2], or are mortgagees[3] or personal representatives[4] selling under their paramount powers[5]. A sale by a mortgagee under his statutory power has a further effect, for while the transfer by him may overreach equitable interests, it also transfers the legal estate of freehold which is vested in the mortgagor and also extinguishes any subsequent mortgage terms or charges[6]. In these cases, therefore, the transfer of the legal estate of freehold by or on behalf of the person or persons in whom it is vested will confer on the purchaser the entire legal and beneficial interest, and that person, or those persons, are alone the transferring party or parties.

1   As to the effect of a transfer under the Settled Land Act 1925 see s 72; and REAL PROPERTY vol 39(2) (Reissue) para 248; SETTLEMENTS para 874 post. As to the disposition of registered and unregistered land by transfer see para 262 note 2 ante.
2   See the Law of Property Act 1925 s 2 (as amended); and REAL PROPERTY vol 39(2) (Reissue) para 249; SETTLEMENTS para 900 et seq post; TRUSTS vol 48 (Reissue) para 904.
3   See MORTGAGE; REAL PROPERTY vol 39(2) (Reissue) para 250.
4   See EXECUTORS AND ADMINISTRATORS; REAL PROPERTY vol 39(2) (Reissue) para 250.
5   See generally the Law of Property Act 1925 s 2(1) (as amended); and REAL PROPERTY vol 39(2) (Reissue) paras 247–252.
6   See generally MORTGAGE.

272. Special settlement or trust of land. Where the person in whom the legal estate is beneficially vested holds it subject to equitable interests, but there is no subsisting statutory power or trust of land under which the equitable interests can be overreached, a special settlement[1] or trust of land[2] can be created for the purpose, and a stipulation that a purchaser of a legal estate in land is to accept a title made with the concurrence of any person entitled to any equitable interest is void, if a title can be made without such concurrence under a trust of land, or under the Settled Land Act 1925 or other statute[3].

1   See the Settled Land Act 1925 s 21; and SETTLEMENTS para 705 post.
2   See the Law of Property Act 1925 ss 2(2) (as amended), 42(1) (as amended); and REAL PROPERTY vol 39(2) (Reissue) para 247. For the meaning of 'trust of land' see para 146 note 3 ante.
3   Ibid s 42(1) (amended by the Trusts of Land and Appointment of Trustees Act 1996 s 25(1), Sch 3 para 4(11)).

273. Concurrence of owner of equitable interest. In general it is possible for the entire legal and equitable interest to be vested in the purchaser by a transfer to which the owner of the legal estate is the only transferring party. Although the scheme of the Law of Property Act 1925 prima facie excludes the concurrence in the transfer of the owners of equitable interests, yet it recognises that such concurrence may be proper[1], and where an equitable interest cannot be discharged before completion, the convenient course may be to make the equitable owner a party to the transfer[2].

1   See the Law of Property Act 1925 s 43(1); and paras 129, 147 ante.
2   Intermediate trustees are not necessary parties to a transfer by the head trustees and the beneficiaries: *Grainge v Wilberforce* (1889) 5 TLR 436. See also *Head v Lord Teynham* (1783) 1 Cox Eq Cas 57, where it was held that trustees of a term who had the legal estate, and the person having the entire beneficial interest, could sell the term without making an intermediate trustee a party, unless they had acquired a lien on the land for costs and expenses, when, it seems, a purchaser could require their concurrence to discharge the lien (1 Williams Law relating to Vendors and Purchasers of Real Estate and Chattels Real (4th Edn, 1936) 641 note (q)). Such a case could rarely now occur. A condition requiring a purchaser to take a transfer from a trustee implies power in the trustee to transfer: see *Mosley v Hide* (1851) 17 QB 91 at 101. As to the position where two persons contract to transfer as trustees, but the deed appointing one of them has not been executed see *Re Priestley's Contract* [1947] 1 All ER 716.
     As to the disposition of registered and unregistered land by transfer see para 262 note 2 ante.

274. Transfer on sale by order of the court. Where a sale takes place by order of the court the persons to transfer are, as a rule, the persons having the legal estate[1]. The concurrence of persons having equitable interests only, who are parties to the action or have been served with notice of the judgment or order, is unnecessary[2]. A direction by the court in an action for specific performance that the vendor is to transfer means that the vendor and all necessary parties are to transfer[3].

1   As to the court's power to make vesting orders or appoint persons to transfer see para 266 ante. As to the disposition of registered and unregistered land by transfer see para 262 note 2 ante.
2   See para 133 text and note 4 ante.
3   See *Minton v Kirwood* (1868) 3 Ch App 614. As to specific performance see paras 247–253 ante; and SPECIFIC PERFORMANCE.

275. Persons joined for collateral purposes. Persons who have no estate or interest to transfer are sometimes joined in the assurance for a collateral purpose. Thus, where on a sale by trustees of land the consent of one or more beneficiaries is required, he or they will usually be joined to give the consent[1]. Where the power of trustees to sell depends on the beneficiaries not having all elected to retain land as an investment, one may be joined to show that there has been no such unanimous election[2].

1   As to the position where the consent of more than two persons is requisite to the execution of a trust of land see the Trusts of Land and Appointment of Trustees Act 1996 ss 10, 11, Sch 4; and TRUSTS vol 48 (Reissue) para 894. For the meaning of 'trust of land' see para 146 note 3 ante.
2   This might formerly, and may perhaps still be necessary where trustees who have purchased land without power to invest the trust funds in that way are reselling: see *Re Jenkins and HE Randall & Co's Contract* [1903] 2 Ch 362; and EQUITY vol 16 (Reissue) para 837. As to the power of trustees of land to invest in land see the Trusts of Land and Appointment of Trustees Act 1996 s 6(3); and TRUSTS vol 48 (Reissue) para 894. As to a sale by a tenant for life under the Settled Land Act 1925 see SETTLEMENTS paras 826–835 post.

276. Vendor's duty to obtain concurrence of necessary persons. The vendor must obtain the concurrence of necessary persons[1], for example trustees of the legal estate[2], but he need not obtain the concurrence of unnecessary persons unless he has expressly contracted to do so[3]. Thus, on a sale by a mortgagee under a power of sale, the purchaser cannot require the vendor to obtain the concurrence of the mortgagor[4], even though the mortgagor has in the mortgage deed agreed to join in any sale if required[5]. A mortgagor vendor who has contracted to sell free from incumbrances must either discharge the mortgage or procure at his own expense the concurrence of the mortgagee[6].

In modern practice, the vendor's mortgage will often be expected to be discharged out of the proceeds of the sale, and the purchaser, and his mortgagee, can safely accept an undertaking by the vendor's solicitor to discharge the mortgage after completion[7].

1   It is the vendor's duty to effect the transfer either by force of his own interests or by force of the interests of others which he can control: *Bain v Fothergill* (1874) LR 7 HL 158 at 209. As to the disposition of registered and unregistered land by transfer see para 262 note 2 ante.
2   *Costigan v Hastler* (1804) 2 Sch & Lef 159 at 166; *Howell v George* (1815) 1 Madd 1 at 11. If they are not bound to transfer at his direction, this, of course, is an objection to the title: see para 137 ante.
3   *Corder v Morgan* (1811) 18 Ves 344; *Benson v Lamb* (1846) 9 Beav 502.
4   *Clay v Sharpe* (1802) 18 Ves 346n; *Allen v Martin* (1841) 5 Jur 239. See also the Law of Property Act 1925 ss 101, 103; and MORTGAGE.
5   *Corder v Morgan* (1811) 18 Ves 344. See also MORTGAGE.
6   Formerly, under a usual condition of sale, the cost of obtaining the mortgagee's concurrence might have to be borne by the purchaser: see *Re Willett and Argenti* (1889) 60 LT 735. Such a condition would now be void under the Law of Property Act 1925 s 42(3): see para 129 ante; and 1 Williams Law relating to Vendors and Purchasers of Real Estate and Chattels Real (4th Edn, 1936) 645 note (p).
7   As to the form of undertaking recommended by The Law Society see 'Council News: Undertaking to Discharge Building Society Mortgages' (1986) 83 LS Gaz 3127. Breach of an undertaking by the solicitor is professional misconduct, and is also a breach of the solicitor's duty as an officer of the court: see SOLICITORS vol 44(1) (Reissue) para 354. A licensed conveyancer is not an officer of the court. See also para 3 ante. It is essential that the redemption monies be paid to the solicitor or licensed conveyancer as

the duly authorised agent of the mortgagee: see *Edward Wong Finance Co Ltd v Johnson, Stokes & Master (a firm)* [1984] AC 296, [1984] 2 WLR 1, PC. As to the interpretation of an undertaking in standard form by the purchaser's solicitor to the purchaser's mortgagee to obtain a good marketable title see *Barclays Bank plc v Weeks Legg & Dean (a firm)* [1999] QB 309, [1998] 3 All ER 213, CA.

277. Transfer by company in liquidation. Where land belonging to a company in liquidation is being transferred[1], the company in which the legal estate, in the absence of a special order[2], remains notwithstanding the liquidation[3] is a necessary party, and the seal is affixed on its behalf by the liquidator[4]. In the absence of a special order the liquidator has no estate or interest, legal or equitable, and is not a necessary party to the transfer, but, unless he is an official receiver, he invariably joins to show his concurrence in the sale and to covenant against incumbrances[5].

1 As to the power of the liquidator of a company to sell its land see para 67 ante; and COMPANIES vol 7(3) (1996 Reissue) paras 2337, 2504; as to the effect of winding up upon a pending contract see paras 212–215 ante; and as to recitals in transfers see paras 284–288 post. As to the disposition of registered and unregistered land by transfer see para 262 note 2 ante.
2 As to the vesting of company property in liquidator see the Insolvency Act 1986 s 145; and COMPANIES vol 7(3) (1996 Reissue) para 2335.
3 See *Re Oriental Inland Steam Co, ex p Scinde Rly Co* (1874) 9 Ch App 557 at 560; *Ayerst v C & K (Construction) Ltd* [1976] AC 167 at 177, [1975] 2 All ER 537 at 541, HL, per Lord Diplock; and COMPANIES vol 7(3) (1996 Reissue) paras 2335, 2505.
4 See COMPANIES vol 7(3) (1996 Reissue) paras 2337, 2504. As to the position of liquidators of unregistered companies see COMPANIES vol 7(3) (1996 Reissue) para 2899 et seq.
5 See COMPANIES vol 7(3) (1996 Reissue) para 2505. The necessity and reason for the liquidator to be joined as a party is challenged by some commentators: see the summary by Adams 'Precedents Editors Notes - What Can One Expect of a Liquidator, After All?' [1983] Conv 177. The company will normally transfer as beneficial owner, but the covenant for title thus implied is likely to be of slight value, in view of the company's impending dissolution: see eg *Butler v Broadhead* [1975] Ch 97, [1974] 2 All ER 401 (no action against contributories after company's dissolution).

B. PARTIES TO WHOM THE ASSURANCE IS MADE

278. Transfer to nominee. As a rule the transfer is made to the purchaser, but, provided the vendor is not prejudiced, the purchaser can direct it to be made to a nominee[1], for such estate and interest, not exceeding the interest purchased, as he pleases[2]. Where the purchaser is to enter into covenants with the vendor, the purchaser cannot substitute a new covenantor for himself without the vendor's consent, and in such a case the nominee must not be a person under disability[3].

1 If the purchaser provides the money on his own account, and not by way of loan to the nominee, and the nominee is a stranger, there is prima facie a resulting trust to the purchaser: see *Dyer v Dyer* (1788) 2 Cox Eq Cas 92 at 93; *Lynch v Clarkin* [1900] 1 IR 178, Ir CA; GIFTS vol 20 (Reissue) para 40 et seq; TRUSTS vol 48 (Reissue) para 607. As a rule there is no resulting trust where the transfer is taken in the name of a wife or child: see *Dyer v Dyer* supra; and GIFTS vol 20 (Reissue) para 43; TRUSTS vol 48 (Reissue) para 609. In the case of family assets, the strength of these presumptions is now greatly diminished: see eg *Pettitt v Pettitt* [1970] AC 777, [1969] 2 All ER 385, HL; *Falconer v Falconer* [1970] 3 All ER 449, [1970] 1 WLR 1333, CA; and HUSBAND AND WIFE.
   As to the disposition of registered and unregistered land by transfer see para 262 note 2 ante.
2 See *Earl of Egmont v Smith, Smith v Earl of Egmont* (1877) 6 ChD 469 at 474 per Jessel MR. However, the vendors are not bound to accept the nominee if the nomination discloses a breach of trust; where, for instance, they are trustees and the nominee is himself one of the trustees: *Delves v Gray* [1902] 2 Ch 606.
3 See further para 280 post.

279. Sub-purchaser. When the purchaser has disposed of the land before the completion of the contract, it is usual, for the purpose of saving the expense of the second transfer and double stamp duty, to make the assurance direct to the second purchaser. The disposition may be either by assignment of the contract or resale of the land[1]. Upon an assignment of the contract the original purchaser is not usually a necessary party to the transfer[2], nor is he a necessary party where there is a resale without increase of price[3].

1 See para 198 et seq ante.
2 It seems, however, that the vendor could require a recital in the conveyance of the original contract and the assignment: see *Hartley v Burton* (1868) 3 Ch App 365. As to the disposition of registered and unregistered land by transfer see para 262 note 2 ante.
3 1 Williams Law relating to Vendors and Purchasers of Real Estate and Chattels Real (4th Edn, 1936) 642–643. As to sale at increased price see para 280 post. Where the sub-contract is for the sale of the land with a building to be erected on it and the original purchaser has become bankrupt, his trustee can disclaim the sub-contract of sale without being obliged to disclaim the contract of purchase: see BANKRUPTCY AND INSOLVENCY vol 3(2) (Reissue) para 460.

280. Where the original purchaser is a necessary party. If the original purchaser was bound by the contract to assume a personal liability under the transfer, the vendor is not bound to accept the liability of another person, as where the property sold is an equity of redemption so that the purchaser can be required to enter into a covenant of indemnity against the mortgage debt[1]. In such a case the original purchaser is a necessary party unless the vendor consents to accept the covenant of the assignee or sub-purchaser[2]. Where there is a resale of the land at an increased price, the transfer states the increased price as the consideration and the original purchaser is joined as the party receiving the increase[3].

1 See para 296 text and note 2 post. As to the disposition of registered and unregistered land by transfer see para 262 note 2 ante.
2 1 Williams Law relating to Vendors and Purchasers of Real Estate and Chattels Real (4th Edn, 1936) 643.
3 The joining of the original purchaser brings onto the title the equitable interest which he obtained under the contract, and any incumbrances created by him on such interest might cause difficulty on a resale: see 1 Dart's Law relating to Vendors and Purchasers (8th Edn, 1929) 465; 1 Williams Law relating to Vendors and Purchasers of Real Estate and Chattels Real (4th Edn, 1936) 642. There would be the same difficulty if the original contract was recited without making the original purchaser a party: see para 279 note 2 ante. It is believed, however, that in practice this risk is treated as negligible, and it is usual to join the original purchaser and, unless there is a big increase in price on the sub-sale, it is the practice for him to transfer as trustee (or now, with limited title guarantee). As to registration of the original contract see paras 179, 200 ante; as to the right of a sub-purchaser to an abstract of the original contract see para 147 ante; and as to a sub-purchaser's right to specific performance see para 201 text and note 5 ante.

281. Land purchased with partnership money. On a purchase of land with partnership money the transfer should be made to the partners as joint tenants holding the land on trust for the partners as part of their partnership property[1], or to trustees on the like trusts[2].

1 As to the presumption that property purchased with partnership money is partnership property see PARTNERSHIP vol 35 (Reissue) para 104. As to oral partnership agreements in the case of a joint purchase of land see *Forster v Hale* (1798) 3 Ves 696 (affd (1800) 5 Ves 308); and PARTNERSHIP vol 35 (Reissue) para 37. As to joint tenancy generally see REAL PROPERTY vol 39(2) (Reissue) para 190 et seq. As to the disposition of registered and unregistered land by transfer see para 262 note 2 ante.
2 If the land is transferred to partners as joint tenants, without any words showing what the equitable interests are, then, in as much as on the face of the transfer there is a beneficial joint tenancy, the land will be subject to a trust of land: see the Law of Property Act 1925 s 36(1) (amended by the Trusts of Land and Appointment of Trustees Act 1996 s 5, Sch 2 para 4(2)); see also *Green v Whitehead* [1930] 1 Ch 38, CA; 1 Williams Law relating to Vendors and Purchasers of Real Estate and Chattels Real (4th Edn, 1936) 501 note (r); and REAL PROPERTY vol 39(2) (Reissue) paras 64–66, 190 et seq. As to the sale of partnership land on the winding up of the partnership see PARTNERSHIP vol 35 (Reissue) para 193 et seq.

282. Transfer to husband and wife. For all purposes of the acquisition of any interest in property under a disposition made after 1925, a husband and wife are treated as two persons[1]. A transfer to a husband and wife should be made to them upon trust for themselves, whether they are intended to hold in equity as joint tenants or tenants in common[2].

1 See the Law of Property Act 1925 ss 37, 209(2) (repealed). For the law before 1926 see generally HUSBAND AND WIFE.
2 Cf ibid ss 34(2), 36(1) (both as amended); and see REAL PROPERTY vol 39(2) (Reissue) para 211. As to the respective rights of the husband and wife in property transferred into their joint names see generally HUSBAND AND WIFE. As to joint tenancies see REAL PROPERTY vol 39(2) (Reissue) paras 190–206; and as to tenancies in common see REAL PROPERTY vol 39(2) (Reissue) paras 207–223. As to the disposition of registered and unregistered land by transfer see para 262 note 2 ante.

283. Right of persons not parties to take interest. An immediate or other interest in land may be taken by a person not named as a party to a disposition[1], if the disposition purports to grant him something[2]. However, a grant cannot be effectually made to persons not in existence at the date of the deed, whether future born persons[3] or persons then dead[4].

1 See the Law of Property Act 1925 s 56(1), replacing in part the Real Property Act 1845 s 5 (repealed); and DEEDS AND OTHER INSTRUMENTS. The Law of Property Act 1925 s 56(1) applies only to land: see *Beswick v Beswick* [1968] AC 58, [1967] 2 All ER 1197, HL. As to the right of persons not parties to take the benefit of covenants see para 335 post.
2 *White v Bijou Mansions Ltd* [1937] Ch 610 at 625, [1937] 3 All ER 269 at 279 (affd [1938] Ch 351, [1938] 1 All ER 546, CA); *Re Ecclesiastical Comrs for England's Conveyance* [1936] Ch 430. See also eg *Stromdale and Ball Ltd v Burden* [1952] Ch 223, [1952] 1 All ER 59, where an option to purchase the reversion was granted to the intended assignee of a tenancy by a deed made between the landlord and tenant, and the assignee was held entitled to enforce the option although not a party to the deed. It is not sufficient in an action under the Law of Property Act 1925 s 56(1) for the plaintiff to show that the deed would benefit him: *White v Bijou Mansions Ltd* supra (where the claim was to the benefit of a restrictive covenant); *Beswick v Beswick* [1968] AC 58, [1967] 2 All ER 1197, HL; *Lyus v Prowsa Developments Ltd* [1982] 2 All ER 953, [1982] 1 WLR 1044; *Pinemain Ltd v Welbeck International Ltd* (1984) 272 Estates Gazette 1166; *Re Distributors and Warehousing Ltd* [1986] 1 EGLR 90, 278 Estates Gazette 1363.
3 *Kelsey v Dodd* (1881) 52 LJ Ch 34 at 39; *Dyson v Forster* [1909] AC 98, HL; *Westhoughton UDC v Wigan Coal and Iron Co Ltd* [1919] 1 Ch 159, CA.
4 *Re Tilt, Lampet v Kennedy* (1896) 74 LT 163; and see GIFTS vol 20 (Reissue) para 19.

(ii) Recitals

284. Nature of recitals. After stating the parties[1], a conveyance of unregistered land usually continues with recitals[2], which are intended either to explain the operation of the deed or to make evidence of matters of fact. Under the former head recitals are introduced to show the interests of the various parties, and the purpose and effect of their concurrence[3]. In consequence, however, of the transfer not disclosing, as a general rule, equitable interests[4], recitals are not so much required as formerly[5].

Where the vendor is absolutely entitled to the whole estate in freehold property his seisin in fee is recited[6], or recitals may be omitted altogether. Where he is not an absolute owner, the recitals show how he is entitled to make the assurance[7]. Where the vendor is a company which is being wound up[8], the winding up and appointment of the liquidator must be recited[9].

1 As to parties see para 269 et seq ante.
2 A vendor is not bound to admit into the deed recitals at variance with the truth, nor can he insist on the insertion of recitals explaining the title of other parties to the deed if, in fact, all necessary persons are parties: *Hartley v Burton* (1868) 3 Ch App 365. Recitals can frequently be avoided or shortened by making

the deed supplemental to a previous deed. The deed then takes effect as if it were indorsed on the previous deed, or contained a full recital of it: see the Law of Property Act 1925 s 58. As to the construction of recitals see generally DEEDS AND OTHER INSTRUMENTS. As to a recital that the grantee is entitled in equity see para 150 note 4 ante; and 1 Williams Law relating to Vendors and Purchasers of Real Estate and Chattels Real (4th Edn, 1936) 298 et seq. As to the reduced need for recitals see para 285 post. As to the disposition of registered and unregistered land by transfer see para 262 note 2 ante.

3   1 Dart's Law relating to Vendors and Purchasers (8th Edn, 1929) 471; 1 Williams Law relating to Vendors and Purchasers of Real Estate and Chattels Real (4th Edn, 1936) 649; Sugden's Law of Vendors and Purchasers (14th Edn, 1862) 558.

4   See para 145 et seq ante.

5   In the case of registered land, because of the statutory provisions relating to the vesting of the legal estate in the registered proprietor, there will be no need for recitals showing the devolution of the legal estate: see LAND REGISTRATION vol 26 (Reissue) paras 713, 779 et seq, 801 et seq, 933.

6   As to seisin see para 154 ante. The recital may be that the vendor is estate owner in respect of the fee simple. As to the effect of the recital see para 150 note 4 ante. Where co-owners in fee are seised of unincumbered land or trustees of land are so entitled under a trust deed framed to keep the equities off the title, it seems not to be technically correct to recite simply that they are so seised, the conveyancing rule being that the origin of every trust or power must be shown by recital. A recital that a vendor is seised in unincumbered fee simple in possession does not negative the possibility of the land being subject to a lease: *District Bank Ltd v Webb* [1958] 1 All ER 126, [1958] 1 WLR 148.

7   The insertion of such recitals is usually required in the interest of the purchaser, and if they are omitted in the draft conveyance the vendor can probably insist on them: see 1 Dart's Law relating to Vendors and Purchasers (8th Edn, 1929) 471.

8   As to the parties to such a transfer see para 277 ante.

9   Where the winding up is voluntary, the resolution for winding up under which the liquidator is appointed must be recited; where the winding up is compulsory, the winding-up order and order appointing the liquidator should be recited. As to voluntary winding up see COMPANIES vol 7(2) (1996 Reissue) para 2698 et seq.

285. Recitals as evidence.

A person is bound by the recitals in a deed to which he is a party, whenever they refer to specific facts and are certain, precise and unambiguous[1]. By statute[2], recitals contained in instruments more than 20 years old are prima facie evidence of the facts recited, and a purchaser must in general assume the correctness of recitals contained in abstracted instruments and relating to documents prior to the commencement of title[3]. Accordingly, facts or events, such as deaths or matters of pedigree, on which the title depends, and which would not otherwise appear from the documents of title, would formerly have been recited with a view to the recitals being used as evidence on a future sale, or to assist a purchaser by giving him information where the proper certificates of those facts may be procured. In order to shorten the recitals, these matters, and also the effect of documents, may have been stated in a schedule. Since, however, most transactions concerning the legal estate now give rise to first registration of title[4], the need for such recitals is greatly reduced, if not entirely eliminated.

1   See ESTOPPEL vol 16 (Reissue) para 1019.

2   Ie by the Law of Property Act 1925 s 45(6): see BOUNDARIES vol 4(1) (Reissue) para 904.

3   See para 150 ante.

4   As to compulsory registration see the Land Registration Act 1925 ss 123 (as substituted), 123A (as added); and LAND REGISTRATION vol 26 (Reissue) para 1196 et seq.

286. Incumbrances.

Where outstanding estates are got in or released by the transfer, or where at the date of the contract[1] the land is subject to incumbrances, and the incumbrancers are paid off on completion[2] and join in the transfer, the recitals[3] show the title of these additional parties[4].

1   As to the formation of the contract see paras 23–40 ante.

2   As to completion of the contract see paras 262–325 ante.

3   As to the nature of recitals see para 284 ante. As to the reduced need for recitals see para 285 ante. As to the disposition of registered and unregistered land by transfer see para 262 note 2 ante.

4   See 1 Williams Law relating to Vendors and Purchasers of Real Estate and Chattels Real (4th Edn, 1936) 650. Formerly, where a transfer was made in exercise of a power, the recitals showed how the power was created, how it had become exercisable and that all necessary consents had been obtained. Perhaps a transfer may still be taken in this way: 1 Dart's Law relating to Vendors and Purchasers (8th Edn, 1929) 472. However, since, in general, powers now operate in equity only (see the Law of Property Act 1925 s 1(7); and POWERS), such a transfer would be unusual.

287. Matters not to be recited. No document or matters which are irrelevant should be recited[1], nor should the preliminary contract be recited as a document[2] save under special circumstances, where, for instance, the contract is in pursuance of an order for sale by the court[3], or one of the parties has died before completion[4].

1   See 1 Williams Law relating to Vendors and Purchasers of Real Estate and Chattels Real (4th Edn, 1936) 650. As to the reduced need for recitals see para 285 ante. As to the disposition of registered and unregistered land by transfer see para 262 note 2 ante.
2   See 1 Dart's Law relating to Vendors and Purchasers (8th Edn, 1929) 475. It is usual to recite that the vendor has agreed to sell and the purchaser to buy, but not to refer to any written contract, since this would bring it on the title. As to subsales see para 279 note 2 ante. As to recitals in the case of a subsale see the forms of transfer referred to in para 280 note 3 ante. As to the formation of the contract see paras 23–40 ante.
3   As to sales under court orders generally see paras 133–136 ante.
4   As to the effect of the death of the vendor or purchaser before completion see paras 202–205 ante; and as to completion of the contract see paras 262–325 ante.

288. Purchase by exercise of option in lease. Where the purchase is in the exercise of an option contained in a lease, the better practice is not to recite the option but to treat the transaction as an ordinary purchase by agreement with the lessor[1].

1   This practice avoids any difficulties arising (1) from the option itself being invalid; (2) from irregularities in the exercise of the option; and (3) from questions whether the option is vested in an assignee of the lease. As to this last point see *Griffith v Pelton* [1958] Ch 205, [1957] 3 All ER 75, CA; *Re Button's Lease, Inman v Button* [1964] Ch 263, [1963] 3 All ER 708. See also para 27 ante; and LANDLORD AND TENANT vol 27(1) (Reissue) para 110. As to the reduced need for recitals see para 285 ante.

(iii) Operative Parts of Transfer

289. Consideration. The consideration for the transfer must be stated in order to prevent the transfer being deemed voluntary[1] and to comply with the statutory provisions as to stamps[2].

1   As to the avoidance in certain circumstances of voluntary transfers see BANKRUPTCY AND INSOLVENCY vol 3(2) (Reissue) para 398 et seq; and as to titles commencing with voluntary conveyances see para 142 text and notes 11–12 ante. As to the disposition of registered and unregistered land by transfer see para 262 note 2 ante.
2   See the Stamp Act 1891 s 5; *Lap Shun Textiles Industrial Co Ltd v Collector of Stamp Revenue* [1976] AC 530, [1976] 1 All ER 833, PC; para 97 ante; and STAMP DUTIES AND STAMP DUTY RESERVE TAX vol 44(1) (Reissue) para 1007. As to the effect of the receipt formerly indorsed on, but now included in, the deed see paras 309–310 post. Before 1926, the statement of the consideration was necessary also in order to prevent a resulting use to the grantor where there was no assurance 'to the use of' the grantee: see generally DEEDS AND OTHER INSTRUMENTS.

290. Operative words. The word 'grant' has been described as one of the largest and most beneficial to the purchaser that can be used[1], but it is not necessary to use it in order to transfer tenements or hereditaments, corporeal or incorporeal; and the words 'convey' or 'transfer' are normally used[2].

1   Co Litt 301b. The Real Property Act 1845 s 2 (repealed), made the word 'grant' appropriate, but not essential, to pass all hereditaments, corporeal and incorporeal. Section 2 was repealed by the Law of Property Act 1925 s 207, Sch 7 (repealed). The use of the word 'grant' is now not necessary to convey land or to create any interest in it: see s 51(2); and REAL PROPERTY vol 39(2) (Reissue) para 239. As to the effect of the word 'grant' in conveyances by undertakers of superfluous land see COMPULSORY ACQUISITION OF LAND vol 8(1) (Reissue) para 382. As to the disposition of registered and unregistered land by transfer see para 262 note 2 ante.

2   See the Law of Property Act 1925 ss 205(1)(ii), 206, Sch 5, Form 3. In relation to covenants implied by virtue of s 76 (repealed) see the Law of Property (Miscellaneous Provisions) Act 1994 s 9; and para 338 post.

291. Parcels. Frequently the property transferred is described both by words[1] and by reference to a plan[2]. A description which is sufficient without reference to a plan may be enough, but the purchaser, at any rate in simple cases, can insist on a plan in order to supplement the general description in the transfer[3]. Land comprised in a registered title[4] is described by reference to a filed plan, usually with a verbal description, and any transfer will be by reference to the particulars in Her Majesty's Land Registry[5]. The description of the parcels in the transfer should correspond with the description in the contract for sale[6]. General words[7] conveying or transferring appurtenances and conveying or creating easements are generally omitted in reliance upon the statutory provisions by which general words are to be implied in transfers[8]. An 'all estates clause' is similarly omitted in reliance upon the statutory provision by which such a clause is implied[9]. Exceptions or reservations out of the property transferred must be specially mentioned[10], unless they are implied by law[11].

1   As to the circumstances in which additions to a description which are at variance with it will be rejected and the circumstances in which effect will be given to them as restrictions of the description see DEEDS AND OTHER INSTRUMENTS; and as to the necessity for accurate description see BOUNDARIES vol 4(1) (Reissue) para 904 et seq. As to the disposition of registered and unregistered land by transfer see para 262 note 2 ante.

2   As to plans generally see DEEDS AND OTHER INSTRUMENTS. The plan should, if possible, be based on the Ordnance Survey map, and reference to the edition, sheet and number is advisable. It is essential that the plan should be on such a large scale as to show clearly where the boundaries run: see *Scarfe v Adams* [1981] 1 All ER 843 at 845, 125 Sol Jo 32 at 32 per Cumming-Bruce LJ, CA, applied in *Mayer v Hurr* (1983) 49 P & CR 56, CA. As to the inference to be drawn from the plan see *AJ Dunning & Sons (Shopfitters) Ltd v Sykes & Son (Poole) Ltd* [1987] Ch 287 at 299, [1987] 1 All ER 700 at 705–706, CA, per Dillon LJ. As to the admissibility of plans and maps generally see BOUNDARIES vol 4(1) (Reissue) para 940; EVIDENCE. A plan may be used to supplement an inadequate description in particulars of sale: *Wigginton and Milner Ltd v Winster Engineering Ltd* [1978] 3 All ER 436, [1978] 1 WLR 1462, CA. A clearly defined boundary on a plan may rebut the hedge and ditch presumption: see *Fisher v Winch* [1939] 1 KB 666, [1939] 2 All ER 144, CA; *Alan Wibberley Building Ltd v Insley* [1998] 2 All ER 82, [1998] 1 WLR 881, CA (revd (1999) Times, 30 April, HL).

3   See note 2 supra. Under the Standard Conditions of Sale (3rd Edn), the vendor need not (1) prove the exact boundaries of the property; (2) prove who owns fences, ditches, hedges or walls; (3) separately identify parts of the property with different titles further than he may be able to do from information in his possession: condition 4.3.1(a)–(c). As to the Standard Conditions of Sale see para 1 note 9 ante.

4   As to registered land generally see LAND REGISTRATION.

5   As to Her Majesty's Land Registry see LAND REGISTRATION vol 26 (Reissue) para 712 et seq.

6   See DEEDS AND OTHER INSTRUMENTS.

7   As to the construction of general words of description see DEEDS AND OTHER INSTRUMENTS.

8   See the Law of Property Act 1925 s 62; the Land Registration Act 1925 ss 19(3), 22(3); and DEEDS AND OTHER INSTRUMENTS; LAND REGISTRATION vol 26 (Reissue) para 937. As to the easements which will be deemed to be included see EASEMENTS AND PROFITS À PRENDRE. The statutory provisions apply only if and so far as a contrary intention is not expressed: Law of Property Act 1925 s 62(4); Land Registration Act 1925 ss 19(3), 22(3). A transfer under which the statutory implication has an unintended effect will be rectified: *Clark v Barnes* [1929] 2 Ch 368. These statutory provisions do not apply on compulsory acquisition: *Sovmots Investments Ltd v Secretary of State for the Environment* [1979] AC 144, [1977] 2 All ER 385, HL. See also *Deen v Andrews* (1986) 52 P & CR 17. As to modifications of the effect of the statutory provisions see the Standard Conditions of Sale (3rd Edn), condition 3.4; and para 81 note 8 ante.

9   See the Law of Property Act 1925 s 63. See however, *Cedar Holdings Ltd v Green* [1981] Ch 129, [1979]
     3 All ER 117, CA, disapproved by Lord Wilberforce in *Williams and Glyn's Bank Ltd v Boland* [1981] AC
     487 at 507, [1980] 2 All ER 408 at 415, HL (see para 248 note 7 ante); *First National Securities Ltd v Hegerty*
     [1985] QB 850, [1984] 3 All ER 641, CA; *Thames Guaranty Ltd v Campbell* [1985] QB 210 at 227–229,
     [1984] 2 All ER 585 at 598–599, CA, per Slade LJ; and *Ahmed v Kendrick* (1987) 56 P & CR 120, (1988)
     Fam Law 201, CA. As to all estates clauses see DEEDS AND OTHER INSTRUMENTS.

10   As to exceptions and reservations see generally DEEDS AND OTHER INSTRUMENTS; EASEMENTS AND
     PROFITS À PRENDRE. Formerly, where there was a reservation to the vendor, the conveyance had to be
     executed by the purchaser for the reservation to take effect at law, but this is not now necessary: see the
     Law of Property Act 1925 s 65(1); and DEEDS AND OTHER INSTRUMENTS. As to a reservation still taking
     effect by way of grant and regrant see *Johnstone v Holdway* [1963] 1 QB 601, [1963] 1 All ER 432, CA;
     and *St Edmundsbury and Ipswich Diocesan Board of Finance v Clark (No 2)* [1975] 1 All ER 772, [1975] 1
     WLR 468, CA. As to the effect of the Law of Property Act 1925 s 65(2) in creating new easements see
     Wiles v Banks (1984) 50 P & CR 80, CA.

11   Eg where a vendor sells part of his land and retains the remainder, there is an implied reservation of such
     rights and easements over the part transferred as are necessary to the enjoyment of the part retained. Unless
     they are easements of necessity they must be expressly reserved: see EASEMENTS AND PROFITS À PRENDRE.
     See however, the Standard Conditions of Sale (3rd Edn), condition 3.4; and para 81 note 8 ante.

292. Habendum. The habendum limits the estate granted and any liabilities or
incidents subject to which the property is transferred[1], but the mere statement that the
property is subject to a restriction is not effective unless there is a corresponding restrictive
covenant[2]. The vendor cannot insist on land being transferred subject to covenants,
conditions or restrictions not mentioned in the contract, or which, although mentioned
there, are not referred to in the particulars or the abstract[3].

1   See DEEDS AND OTHER INSTRUMENTS. Where there are a number of rights etc to which the property
     is subject, it is often convenient to make these the subject of a separate clause in the transfer. It was
     formerly necessary to include the words 'in fee simple' in the transfer because the covenant for right to
     convey implied by the Law of Property Act 1925 s 76(1)(A), Sch 2 Pt I (as amended), extended only to
     the subject matter expressed to be conveyed. As to the reform of the law relating to statutory covenants
     for title see paras 336–337 post; as to covenants for title implied by statute before 1 July 1995 see paras
     338–348 post; and as to covenants implied by statute on or after 1 July 1995 see paras 349–351 post. As
     to the disposition of registered and unregistered land by transfer see para 262 note 2 ante.

2   *Re Rutherford's Conveyance, Goodby v Bartlett* [1938] Ch 396, [1938] 1 All ER 495. As to restrictive
     covenants generally see EQUITY vol 16 (Reissue) para 787 et seq.

3   *Hardman v Child* (1885) 28 ChD 712; *Re Wallis and Barnard's Contract* [1899] 2 Ch 515. As to the
     importance of carefully drafting the particulars see para 89 ante. As to the need for an abstract of title with
     respect to both unregistered and registered land see paras 138, 141–149 ante.

293. Covenants by vendor and purchaser. The vendor's covenants include covenants
for title, express or implied[1], and any special covenants to suit particular circumstances[2].
The purchaser's covenants include covenants, stipulated for in the contract, which restrict
the rights he would otherwise possess over the property, and also covenants indemnifying
the vendor against any incumbrances subject to which it is sold[3].

Where the whole of the land sold is subject to a rentcharge, or a part only of the land
so subject is sold, covenants on the part of the purchaser, or mutual covenants by
purchaser and vendor, are implied by statute for payment of the rentcharge or an
apportioned part of it and for indemnity[4].

Where an executory contract is intended to be carried out by a purchase deed, it is
merged in the deed; the final contract is that which is contained in the deed, and the
executory contract cannot be used for the purpose of enlarging, diminishing or modifying
what is contained in the deed[5]. Accordingly, any obligations of either party which will
not be discharged at the time of completion and which do not from their nature or the
terms of the contract survive after completion must be provided for by the covenants[6]. A
provision for vacant possession on completion does not merge in the transfer[7].

1   As to covenants generally see DEEDS AND OTHER INSTRUMENTS. As to the covenants for title implied
     by statute see paras 336–351 post; as to the covenants for title where the vendor transfers in pursuance of
     an obligation to enfranchise under the Leasehold Reform Act 1967 see s 10 (as amended); and LANDLORD
     AND TENANT vol 27(2) (Reissue) para 1303. As to the position where the transfer is to a tenant exercising
     his right to buy see LANDLORD AND TENANT vol 27(2) (Reissue) para 1666 et seq.

2   As to the benefit and burden of covenants relating to land generally see para 331 et seq post; and as to
     covenants for title see paras 336–351 post.

3   A solicitor is negligent where he allows his client to enter in ignorance into improper covenants: see
     Stannard v Ullithorne (1834) 10 Bing 491; and SOLICITORS vol 44(1) (Reissue) para 155. The Standard
     Conditions of Sale (3rd Edn), provide that if there is more than one vendor or more than one purchaser,
     the obligations which they undertake can be enforced against them all jointly or against each individually:
     condition 1.2. As to the Standard Conditions of Sale see para 1 note 9 ante.

4   See the Law of Property Act 1925 s 77(1) (as amended), Sch 2 Pts VII, VIII; the Rentcharges Act 1977
     s 11 (as amended); and RENTCHARGES AND ANNUITIES vol 39(2) (Reissue) para 776. As to dispositions
     of property made before 1 July 1995 see paras 338–348 post; and as to the dispositions of property made
     on or after 1 July 1995 see paras 349–351 post. Where the rent is apportioned, charges by the vendor and
     purchaser of the apportioned parts on their respective lands are sometimes added, but the contract must
     expressly provide for such an addition. As to apportionment generally see LANDLORD AND TENANT vol
     27(1) (Reissue) para 245.

5   *Leggott v Barrett* (1880) 15 ChD 306 at 309, CA; *Re Cooper and Crondace's Contract* (1904) 90 LT 258; and
     see DEEDS AND OTHER INSTRUMENTS. In the case of registered land, the transfer represents the
     conveyance: *Knight Sugar Co Ltd v Alberta Railway and Irrigation Co* [1938] 1 All ER 266, PC. As to the
     disposition of registered and unregistered land by transfer see para 262 note 2 ante.

6   See *Williams v Morgan* (1850) 15 QB 782; *Teebay v Manchester, Sheffield and Lincolnshire Rly Co* (1883) 24
     ChD 572; *Palmer v Johnson* (1884) 13 QBD 351, CA; *Greville v Hemingway* (1902) 87 LT 443 at 445. See
     also *Barclays Bank Ltd v Beck* [1952] 2 QB 47, [1952] 1 All ER 549, CA. See however, the Standard
     Conditions of Sale (3rd Edn), condition 7.4; and para 123 note 12 ante. As to the date of completion see
     paras 120, 185 ante.

7   *Hissett v Reading Roofing Co Ltd* [1970] 1 All ER 122, [1969] 1 WLR 1757. See also *Hancock v BW Brazier
     (Anerley) Ltd* [1966] 2 All ER 901, [1966] 1 WLR 1317, CA; and *Eagon v Dent* [1965] 3 All ER 334. As
     to vacant possession see para 123 ante.

294. Covenants for title. In the transfer of the property the vendor usually enters into
covenants for title[1], in pursuance of his obligation to give a title clear of defects and
incumbrances, unless otherwise provided by the contract[2].

1   As to the reform of the law relating to statutory covenants for title see paras 336–337 post; as to the old
     law see paras 338–348 post; and as to the new law relating to implied covenants for title see paras 349–351
     post. As to the disposition of registered and unregistered land by transfer see para 262 note 2 ante.

2   See paras 137 ante, 336–337 post.

295. Covenants as to unpaid consideration. Where the consideration is of such a
nature that it is not payable on completion of the contract, the purchaser enters into a
covenant to pay it[1].

1   See eg *Bower v Cooper* (1843) 2 Hare 408 at 410; *Dixon v Gayfere* (1857) 1 De G & J 655. See also
     Remington v Deverall (1795) 2 Anst 550. Where the purchase price is payable by instalments the safer
     course is to postpone completion until all the instalments have been paid: see para 128 ante. As to the
     operation of a condition for the payment of purchase money by instalments see para 232 note 9 ante; and
     as completion see paras 262–325 post.

296. Covenants indemnifying vendor. Where a vendor sells land in respect of
which he is personally subject to some liability or burden, the purchaser must covenant
to indemnify the vendor against his liability[1]. Thus, on the sale of an equity of
redemption, the purchaser must covenant to indemnify the vendor against the mortgage
debt and interest[2].

1   *Moxhay v Inderwick* (1847) 1 De G & Sm 708; *Re Poole and Clarke's Contract* [1904] 2 Ch 173, where the court stated what is now the substance of the usual form of indemnity. Cf *Lukey v Higgs* (1855) 3 Eq Rep 510.

2   *Waring v Ward* (1802) 7 Ves 332 at 337; *Bridgman v Daw* (1891) 40 WR 253; *Adair v Carden* (1892) 29 LR Ir 469. See also *Dodson v Downey* [1901] 2 Ch 620 (sale of partnership share); and MORTGAGE. As to the covenants implied in a transfer of and subject to a rentcharge see para 293 ante; and RENTCHARGES AND ANNUITIES vol 39(2) (Reissue) para 776.

297. Indemnity in respect of restrictive covenants.
Where land is sold subject to restrictive covenants, and the vendor will be under any liability in respect of a breach after the execution of the transfer[1], he is entitled to a covenant of indemnity from the purchaser in case of breach[2]. Nevertheless, where a contract for the sale of land makes no mention that the land is subject to a restrictive covenant, the purchaser may insist on a transfer according to the terms of the contract, and is not bound to have such a restrictive covenant inserted in the transfer[3]; consequently he gives no covenant of indemnity against it. However, in the case of a covenant entered into before 1926, he may be liable to observe it on the ground that he took with notice of its existence[4].

1   In some cases the covenant by its terms does not affect a covenantor who has parted with all his interest in the land, and he is not then entitled to an indemnity. Even where this is not the case, a person who is an assignee of the covenantor is not entitled to an indemnity unless he himself has given an indemnity in the transfer to him. As to restrictive covenants generally see EQUITY vol 16 (Reissue) para 787 et seq. As to the disposition of registered and unregistered land by transfer see para 262 note 2 ante.

2   *Moxhay v Inderwick* (1847) 1 De G & Sm 708; *Re Poole and Clarke's Contract* [1904] 2 Ch 173, CA; *Reckitt v Cody* [1920] 2 Ch 452. Such an indemnity is expressly provided for in the Standard Conditions of Sale (3rd Edn), condition 4.5.4: see para 57 note 5 ante. As to the Standard Conditions of Sale see para 1 note 9 ante. As to covenants of indemnity in relation to assignments of leases see para 302 post; and LANDLORD AND TENANT vol 27(1) (Reissue) para 485 et seq.

3   See para 293 ante.

4   *Re Wallis and Barnard's Contract* [1899] 2 Ch 515 at 522; *Re Gloag and Miller's Contract* (1883) 23 ChD 320 at 327. As to the need to register restrictive covenants, other than those between lessor and lessee, entered into after 1925 see EQUITY vol 16 (Reissue) para 793; LAND CHARGES vol 26 (Reissue) para 535. Where such covenants are first imposed by the transfer, a special condition may be necessary to enable the vendor to secure the priority of the covenants: see eg the National Conditions of Sale (20th Edn), condition 19.4. As to the registration of a priority notice see LAND CHARGES vol 26 (Reissue) para 514; as to restrictive covenants where the land is sold on a building scheme see EQUITY vol 16 (Reissue) para 797 et seq; and as to the liability of a purchaser with knowledge of a covenant for inducement of breach of covenant see *Earl of Sefton v Tophams Ltd* [1965] Ch 1140, [1965] 3 All ER 1, CA (revsd on other grounds sub nom *Tophams Ltd v Earl of Sefton* [1967] 1 AC 50, [1966] 1 All ER 1039, HL); *Esso Petroleum Co Ltd v Kingswood Motors (Addlestone) Ltd* [1974] QB 142, [1973] 3 All ER 1057; *Midland Bank Trust Co Ltd v Green (No 3)* [1982] Ch 529, [1981] 3 All ER 744, CA (tort of conspiracy).

298. Indorsement of notice of restrictive covenants.
Where unregistered land[1] having a common title with other land is disposed of to a purchaser[2] (other than a lessee or mortgagee) who does not hold or obtain possession of the documents forming the common title, then, notwithstanding any stipulation to the contrary, he may require notice of any provision in his conveyance restrictive of the user of, or giving rights over, any other land comprised in the common title to be indorsed on or, where indorsement is impracticable, permanently annexed to, a document selected by him forming part of the common title which is retained by the vendor[3]. However, omission to require such an indorsement or annexation does not affect the title[4].

1   This provision does not apply to dispositions of registered land: see the Law of Property Act 1925 s 200(3). As to registered land see generally LAND REGISTRATION. For the meaning of 'land' see para 139 note 1 ante.

2   For the meaning of 'purchaser' see para 55 note 16 ante.

3   See the Law of Property Act 1925 s 200(1). As to restrictive covenants generally see EQUITY vol 16 (Reissue) para 787 et seq.

4   See ibid s 200(2). The indorsement does not affect the obligation to register the restrictive covenant or agreement affecting freehold land as a land charge: s 200(4)(a). As to the need to register restrictive covenants, other than those between lessor and lessee, entered into after 1925 see LAND CHARGES vol 26 (Reissue) para 535; EQUITY vol 16 (Reissue) para 793.

299. Acknowledgment of right to production; certificate of value. Where any of the documents of title relate to land of the vendor which is not included in the sale to the purchaser, it is the practice for the vendor to retain these documents and give an acknowledgment in writing of the purchaser's right to production and delivery of copies, and also, where he is not a trustee or mortgagee, an undertaking for safe custody, and in such a case certain statutory provisions apply to the acknowledgment[1]. Such an acknowledgment and undertaking are binding on the vendor only while he has possession or control of the documents, and are binding on future possessors of the documents during the period of their possession or control[2]. As a rule, the acknowledgment and undertaking are contained in the transfer, although, where it is desired to keep the documents to which they relate off the title, they are given by a separate document[3]. Apart from the purchaser's rights under an acknowledgment, he has an equitable right to the production of documents in the possession of another person which form the common title to their land[4]. Although a transfer can be made by a person to himself[5], the acknowledgment cannot be included in such a transfer, since the statutory provisions relating to acknowledgments apply only to an acknowledgment given to another[6], but this disability does not apply where the transfer is by a person to himself and other persons[7].

The transfer will generally conclude with a certificate of value[8].

1   See the Law of Property Act 1925 s 64; and para 132 ante. It is the practice for trustees and mortgagees not to give the undertaking (see 1 Williams Law relating to Vendors and Purchasers of Real Estate and Chattels Real (4th Edn, 1936) 702; cf *Re Agg-Gardner* (1884) 25 ChD 600), but the correctness of this practice has been questioned (see (1893) 37 Sol Jo 4, 73–74, 78–79; The Solicitor, February 1947, 28). The Standard Conditions of Sale (3rd Edn), provide that the vendor is to arrange at his expense that, in relation to every document of title which the purchaser does not receive on completion, the purchaser is to have the benefit of (1) a written acknowledgment of his right to production; and (2) a written undertaking for its safe custody (except while it is held by a mortgagee or by somebody in a fiduciary capacity): condition 4.5.5. As to the Standard Conditions of Sale see para 1 note 9 ante. By reason of the notices which may be indorsed upon them (see EXECUTORS AND ADMINISTRATORS), probates and letters of administration are documents of title and should be included in an acknowledgment: *Re Miller and Pickersgill's Contract* [1931] 1 Ch 511.
2   See the Law of Property Act 1925 s 64(2), (9). The statutory obligation imposed by an acknowledgment is (1) to produce the documents at all reasonable times for inspection; (2) to produce the documents for the purposes of litigation; and (3) to deliver copies of them (see s 64(4)); and that imposed by an undertaking is to keep the documents safe, whole, uncancelled and undefaced unless prevented by fire or other inevitable accident (see s 64(9)). See also para 132 ante.
3   This document need only be under hand, and does not attract stamp duty. As to the charge to stamp duty see para 318; and STAMP DUTIES AND STAMP DUTY RESERVE TAX vol 44(1) (Reissue) para 1010 et seq.
4   See *Fain v Ayers* (1826) 2 Sim & St 533; *Re Jenkins and Commercial Electric Theatre Co's Contract* (1917) 61 Sol Jo 283. See also the Law of Property Act 1925 s 45(7) (see para 132 ante); and cf REAL PROPERTY vol 39(2) (Reissue) para 87.
5   See ibid s 72(3); and REAL PROPERTY vol 39(2) (Reissue) para 244.
6   See ibid s 64(1). It seems that at common law a person may contract in his representative capacity with himself as an individual: see *Rowley Holmes & Co v Barber* [1977] 1 All ER 801, [1977] 1 WLR 371, EAT, approving a statement now to be found in CONTRACT vol 9(1) (Reissue) para 604.
7   See the Law of Property Act 1925 s 82; *Rye v Rye* [1962] AC 496 at 512–514, [1962] 1 All ER 146 at 154–155, HL, per Lord Denning; and EQUITY vol 16 (Reissue) para 746. In practice the acknowledgment in such cases is made to the persons other than the grantor.
8   As to the necessity for, and form of, a certificate of value see STAMP DUTIES AND STAMP DUTY RESERVE TAX vol 44(1) (Reissue) para 1028.

(3) FORM OF ASSURANCE OF LEASEHOLDS

300. Recitals in assurance of leaseholds. In an assignment of leaseholds[1] it is customary to recite the lease (defining it as 'the lease') and devolution of title to the vendor, but, where there have been numerous dealings with the property since the granting of the lease, the intermediate dealings are recited generally, and only the ultimate assurance to the vendor is particularly set out[2]. However, such narrative recitals should not be necessary where the title to the leasehold is already registered[3]. The recitals of the lease usually include a verbatim description of the parcels as in the lease, and in the operative part these are referred to as all the premises comprised in and demised by the lease.

1   As to the assignment of leases generally see LANDLORD AND TENANT vol 27(1) (Reissue) para 462 et seq.
2   As to form of assurance of mortgaged leaseholds see *Re National Provincial and Union Bank of England and May's Contract* (1920) 150 LT Jo 262.
3   As to registration of title to leasehold land see LAND REGISTRATION vol 26 (Reissue) paras 743–751.

301. Covenants for title. Covenants for title[1] may be implied by statute into an assignment on a sale of a leasehold property. Dispositions made on or after 1 July 1995 are governed by the new law[2].

1   As to covenants for title see paras 336–351 post.
2   As to the reform of the law relating to statutory covenants for title see para 337 post; as to the old law see paras 338–348 post; and as to the new law relating to implied covenants for title see paras 349–351 post.

302. Indemnity against covenants of lease. Where the vendor as original lessee is liable for the payment of rent or the performance of the covenants under the lease, or is so liable as an assignee who has covenanted to indemnify his assignor in this respect, the purchaser used expressly to covenant for the future to pay the rent and perform and observe the lessee's covenants and to indemnify the vendor against this liability, but until 1 January 1996[1] it was the common practice to rely upon the statutory implied covenant to the like effect[2] in all cases where there is a valuable consideration for the purchase. However, where there is no such consideration, the statutory provision does not apply[3]. This may apply where the rent is a rackrent and the purchaser covenants to pay the rent and observe and perform the covenants, and this is stated to be the consideration for the assignment; but the usual practice in such cases is to include an express covenant.

From 1 January 1996, if a tenant assigns the whole of the premises demised to him under a tenancy, he is released from the tenant covenants of the tenancy and ceases to be entitled to the benefit of the landlord covenants of the tenancy, as from the assignment[4], where on an assignment a tenant is to any extent released from a tenant covenant of a tenancy he may enter into an authorised guarantee agreement with respect to the performance of that covenant by the assignee[5]. Where the assignor is released from liability, no indemnity covenant is necessary.

1   Ie the date the Landlord and Tenant (Covenants) Act 1995 came into force: see s 31(1).
2   See the Law of Property Act 1925 s 77(1)(C), Sch 2 Pt IX (repealed); and the Land Registration Act 1925 s 24(1)(b) (repealed). These provisions are repealed except in relation to tenancies which are not new tenancies: see the Landlord and Tenant (Covenants) Act 1995 s 30(3)(a), (b). For the meaning of a 'new tenancy' see LAND REGISTRATION vol 26 (Reissue) para 950. See also the Standard Conditions of Sale (3rd Edn), condition 4.5.4; and para 57 note 5 ante. As to the Standard Conditions of Sale see para 1 note 9 ante.
3   The Law of Property Act 1925 s 77(1)(C) (repealed) applies only to a transfer for valuable consideration; cf the Land Registration Act 1925 s 24 (repealed). As to the extent of the repeal of these provisions see note 2 supra.

4   See the Landlord and Tenant (Covenants) Act 1995 s 5(1), (2); and LANDLORD AND TENANT. As to the
     release from covenants on assignment of part only of the premises demised see s 5(3), (4); para 303 post;
     and LANDLORD AND TENANT.

5   See ibid s 16; and LANDLORD AND TENANT.

303. Assignment of part of demised premises. In relation to tenancies which are not new tenancies[1], where part only of the property demised by a lease is sold, the total rent is apportioned by the deed of assignment between the vendor and the purchaser, and both parties enter into mutual covenants for payment of their respective shares, and for performance of the lessee's covenants in the lease[2]. However, the assignee of part becomes liable to distress for the rent of the whole of the premises[3]. The transaction may also be carried out by way of underlease, in which case the purchaser incurs no liability under the covenants in the head lease[4].

From 1 January 1996[5], if the tenant assigns part only of the premises demised to him under a tenancy, then as from the assignment he is released from the tenant covenants of the tenancy, and ceases to be entitled to the benefit of the landlord covenants of the tenancy, only to the extent that those covenants fall to be complied with in relation to that part of the demised premises[6].

1   For the meaning of a 'new tenancy' see LAND REGISTRATION vol 26 (Reissue) para 950.

2   The express covenant can be omitted in reliance on the covenant implied under the Law of Property Act
     1925 s 77(1)(D), Sch 2 Pt X (repealed); and the Land Registration Act 1925 s 24(2) (repealed). These
     provisions are repealed except in relation to tenancies which are not new tenancies: see the Landlord and
     Tenant (Covenants) Act 1995 s 30(3)(a), (b). There is now a procedure for making apportionment binding
     on the other party to a lease: see ss 9, 10; and LANDLORD AND TENANT vol 27(1) (Reissue) para 472.

3   See LANDLORD AND TENANT vol 27(1) (Reissue) para 472.

4   See LANDLORD AND TENANT vol 27(1) (Reissue) para 85. A purchaser in such case is not normally liable
     to pay the vendor's costs: *Sims-Clarke v Ilet Ltd* [1953] IR 39.

5   Ie the date the Landlord and Tenant (Covenants) Act 1995 came into force: see s 31(1).

6   See ibid s 5(1), (3); and LANDLORD AND TENANT. See also para 302 ante.

304. Sale in lots. When leasehold property comprised in one lease is sold in lots, the sale is usually effected by an assignment to the purchaser of the largest lot on trust to grant underleases to other purchasers[1].

1   Fiduciary owners may sell in this way: *Re Judd and Poland and Skelcher's Contract* [1906] 1 Ch 684, CA;
     and see TRUSTS vol 48 (Reissue) para 904. See also *Re Braithwaite's Settled Estate* [1922] 1 IR 71 (sale in
     lots by tenant for life); and SETTLEMENTS para 832 note 1 post.

(4) EXECUTION OF ASSURANCE

305. Execution by vendor. When the draft transfer[1] prepared by the purchaser[2] has been approved by the vendor, the purchaser sends an engrossment to him for execution[3]. On a sale, the purchaser[4] is not entitled to require that the transfer to him be executed in his presence, or in that of his solicitor[5]; but he is entitled, at his own cost, to have the execution of the transfer attested by some person appointed by him, who may, if he thinks fit, be his solicitor[6].

1   As to the client's right to drafts see SOLICITORS vol 44(1) (Reissue) para 365; and as to a conveyancer's
     lien on an uncompleted conveyance or transfer see *Esdaile v Oxenham* (1824) 3 B & C 225; *Oxenham v
     Esdaile* (1829) 3 Y & J 262; and LIEN vol 28 (Reissue) para 783. As to conveyancers see para 3 ante. As
     to the disposition of registered and unregistered land by transfer see para 262 note 2 ante.

2   As to the preparation of the transfer see paras 262–266 ante; and as to the expenses of preparing the
     transfer see para 129 ante.

3   As to the formalities necessary for the execution of deeds generally see DEEDS AND OTHER INSTRUMENTS. As to the execution of deeds by individuals see the Law of Property (Miscellaneous Provisions) Act 1989 s 1 (as amended); and DEEDS AND OTHER INSTRUMENTS. As to execution by corporations see the Law of Property Act 1925 s 74 (as amended); and AGENCY vol 1(2) (Reissue) para 60; CORPORATIONS vol 9(2) (Reissue) paras 1021–1022; DEEDS AND OTHER INSTRUMENTS. As to the rights of the purchaser as to execution see s 75; and the text and notes 4–6 infra. As to powers of attorney see the Powers of Attorney Act 1971; the Enduring Powers of Attorney Act 1985; paras 306–307 post; and AGENCY vol 1(2) (Reissue) paras 21–22, 60. The provisions as to the execution of a conveyance contained in the Law of Property Act 1925 (ie ss 74 (as amended), 75) apply, so far as applicable thereto, to transfers on sale of registered land: Land Registration Act 1925 s 38(1); and see LAND REGISTRATION vol 26 (Reissue) para 720.

    As to the delivery of a deed as an escrow see DEEDS AND OTHER INSTRUMENTS. The date properly to be inserted in a deed delivered as an escrow is the date on which the deed is delivered, not the date when the condition is fulfilled: *Alan Estates Ltd v WG Stores Ltd* [1982] Ch 511, [1981] 3 All ER 481, CA. It has also been held, however, that a deed is not 'executed' for the purposes of the Stamp Act 1891 s 14(4) (see EVIDENCE; STAMP DUTIES AND STAMP DUTY RESERVE TAX vol 44(1) (Reissue) para 1007), until the condition has been fulfilled, and therefore that the rates of stamp duty prevailing at this later date, not the date of delivery in escrow, are applicable: *Terrapin International Ltd v IRC* [1976] 2 All ER 461, [1976] 1 WLR 665. As to delay in fulfilling the condition of the escrow see *Kingston v Ambrian Investment Co Ltd* [1975] 1 All ER 120, [1975] 1 WLR 161, CA; *Glessing v Green* [1975] 2 All ER 696, [1975] 1 WLR 863, CA.

4   For the meaning of 'purchaser' see para 55 note 16 ante.

5   See para 3 ante.

6   Law of Property Act 1925 s 75 (replacing the Conveyancing Act 1881 s 8 (repealed)); Land Registration Act 1925 s 38(1); and see note 3 supra. As to the former law see *Viney v Chaplin* (1858) 2 De G & J 468; *Essex v Daniell, Daniell v Essex* (1875) LR 10 CP 538. An alteration in a deed is presumed to have been made before execution: see *Re Spollon and Long's Contract* [1936] Ch 713, [1936] 2 All ER 711. Under an open contract the vendor cannot require the purchaser to accept a statutory declaration to contradict statements appearing in the documents of title: see *Re Spollon and Long's Contract* supra; and see para 97 note 1 ante. As to an open contract see para 76 ante.

306. Execution in person or by attorney. A purchaser may require the transfer to be executed by the vendor and other necessary parties in person where this is practicable[1]. If the transfer cannot be executed otherwise than by attorney the purchaser need only ensure that the power endures beyond the date of actual completion, since, even if the power has been revoked, the purchaser will not be affected by the revocation unless he knew of it[2]. The power of attorney should be handed over on completion, or the right to production acknowledged[3].

1   *Mitchel v Neale* (1755) 2 Ves Sen 679 at 681; *Noel v Weston* (1821) 6 Madd 50; Sugden's Law of Vendors and Purchasers (14th Edn, 1862) 563; 1 Dart's Law relating to Vendors and Purchasers (8th Edn, 1929) 513. In practice, when a deed has to be executed by attorney, the power of attorney is validated by statute (see note 2 infra; and para 307 post), and the former objection to such execution has been in consequence diminished. As to the court's power to make vesting orders or appoint persons to transfer see para 266 ante; and TRUSTS vol 48 (Reissue) paras 724 et seq, 750 et seq, 754–755. As to the disposition of registered and unregistered land by transfer see para 262 note 2 ante.

2   See the Powers of Attorney Act 1971 s 5 (replacing the Law of Property Act 1925 ss 124, 126, 127 (repealed)); the Enduring Powers of Attorney Act 1985 ss 1(1)(c), 9(3); para 307 post; and AGENCY vol 1(2) (Reissue) paras 202–300. As to acknowledgment of the right to production see para 299 ante; as to the revocation of an agency see AGENCY vol 1(2) (Reissue) para 182 et seq; as to the form of execution under a power of attorney see AGENCY vol 1(2) (Reissue) paras 60, 139; and as to the need for the power of attorney to be under seal see AGENCY vol 1(2) (Reissue) paras 20–21.

3   See *Eaton v Sanxter* (1834) 6 Sim 517 at 519. The requirements as to, and the provision for, filing a power of attorney in the Central Office of the Supreme Court have been abolished as from 1 October 1971: see the Powers of Attorney Act 1971 s 2(1) (repealed). However, a file of such instruments continues to be kept, and any person may search it, inspect any such instrument and receive an office copy, which is evidence of its contents: see the Supreme Court Act 1981 s 134; and AGENCY vol 1(2) (Reissue) para 22. As to proof of the contents of powers of attorney by means of copies see the Powers of Attorney Act 1971 s 3 (as amended); and AGENCY vol 1(2) (Reissue) para 22.

307. Acts done under power of attorney. Where a power of attorney[1] has been revoked and a person, without knowledge of the revocation, deals with the donee of the power, the transaction between them is, in favour of that person, as valid as if the power had then been in existence[2]. A person is deemed to know of the revocation of a power if he knows of any event (such as the death or incapacity of the donor) which would revoke the power[3]. Where the interest of a purchaser[4] depends on proof that a previous transaction between the donee of a power of attorney and a third person was valid on the ground that the third person had no knowledge of revocation, the requisite absence of knowledge is conclusively presumed if the third person's transaction was completed within 12 months of the date when the power came into operation, or if the third person makes a statutory declaration, before or within three months after the completion of the purchaser's transaction, that he did not at the material time know of the revocation of the power[5].

Further, where a power of attorney is expressed to be irrevocable and is given to secure a proprietary interest of the donee of the power or the performance of an obligation owed to him, then, so long as the donee has that interest or the obligation remains undischarged, the power may not be revoked by the donor without the donee's consent, or by the death, incapacity or bankruptcy of the donor, or, where the donor is a body corporate, by its winding up or dissolution[6]. Where the power is expressed to be irrevocable and to be given by way of security, then unless the person dealing with the donee knows that it was not in fact given by way of security, he is entitled to assume that the power cannot be revoked except by the donor acting with the donee's consent, and the dealing is valid unless he knows of revocation in that manner[7].

Where an individual creates an enduring power of attorney while of sound mind it will not be revoked by his subsequent mental incapacity[8]. If such a power is registered with the Court of Protection, the purchaser is protected even if he knows of the donor's mental incapacity[9]. The attorney is authorised to execute or exercise all or any of the trusts, powers or discretions vested in the donor as trustee, including the power to give a valid receipt for capital or other money paid[10]. One of two trustees may appoint the other trustee to be the attorney[11].

1 The limits of the power of attorney must be strictly observed: see AGENCY vol 1(2) (Reissue) paras 46–47. As to enduring powers of attorney generally see AGENCY vol 1(2) (Reissue) para 32 et seq.
2 Powers of Attorney Act 1971 s 5(2). Section 5 applies whenever the power of attorney was created, but only to acts and transactions in exercise of the power after 30 September 1971: s 5(7). See also the Enduring Powers of Attorney Act 1985 s 1(1)(c) (applying the Powers of Attorney Act 1971 s 5); and AGENCY vol 1(2) (Reissue) paras 202–300.
3 See ibid s 5(5); and AGENCY vol 1(2) (Reissue) paras 202–300.
4 For the meanings of 'purchaser' and 'purchase' see para 55 note 16 ante; definitions applied by the Powers of Attorney Act 1971 s 5(6); Enduring Powers of Attorney Act 1985 s 9(7).
5 See the Powers of Attorney Act 1971 s 5(4); and the Enduring Powers of Attorney Act 1985 s 9(4).
6 Powers of Attorney Act 1971 s 4(1); and see AGENCY vol 1(2) (Reissue) para 187. Section 4 applies to powers of attorney whenever created: s 4(3); and see *Sowman v David Samuel Trust Ltd* [1978] 1 All ER 616, [1978] 1 WLR 22.
7 Powers of Attorney Act 1971 s 5(3); and see AGENCY vol 1(2) (Reissue) paras 202–300.
8 See the Enduring Powers of Attorney Act 1985 s 1(1)(a); and AGENCY vol 1(2) (Reissue) para 32. As to the characteristics of an enduring power of attorney see s 2; and AGENCY vol 1(2) (Reissue) para 33. The instrument which creates the power must be in the prescribed form: see s 2(1); and the Enduring Powers of Attorney (Prescribed Form) Regulations 1990, SI 1990/1376. As to the subsequent mental disorder of either contracting party see para 218 ante; and as to sales and purchases on behalf of mentally disordered persons generally see MENTAL HEALTH vol 30 (Reissue) para 1431 et seq.
9 See the Enduring Powers of Attorney Act 1985 ss 4, 7 (as amended); and AGENCY vol 1(2) (Reissue) para 39.
10 See ibid s 3(3); and AGENCY vol 1(2) (Reissue) para 34.
11 This overcomes the difficulty revealed by *Walia v Michael Naughton Ltd* [1985] 3 All ER 673, [1985] 1 WLR 1115, but allows the attorney to give what is, in effect, a sole receipt for capital money.

308. Execution by the purchaser. A reservation of an easement for a legal estate, that is for an interest equivalent to an estate in fee simple in possession or a term of years absolute[1], is effectual to give legal effect to the reservation without execution of the transfer by the purchaser[2]. However, if there are covenants by the purchaser, the transfer should be executed by him, even though a purchaser who has not executed the deed but who accepts the benefit of the deed becomes bound in equity to observe and perform the covenants[3]. A transfer of registered land need not be executed by a purchaser except where an entry is to be placed on the register in derogation of the estate passing to him[4]. Where a person fails to comply with a court order directing him to execute a transfer, the court may order the transfer to be executed by a nominee for that purpose[5].

1   See the Law of Property Act 1925 s 1(2)(a); and REAL PROPERTY vol 39(2) (Reissue) para 45.
2   See ibid s 65(1); and DEEDS AND OTHER INSTRUMENTS. As to the disposition of registered and unregistered land by transfer see para 262 note 2 ante.
3   *Willson v Leonard* (1840) 3 Beav 373. See also para 333 post; and DEEDS AND OTHER INSTRUMENTS. Many practitioners, in the case of assignments of leaseholds where the implied covenant of indemnity was relied on, have refused to have the assignment executed by the purchaser. The statutory indemnity is now abolished in relation to leases granted after 1 January 1996, and, where necessary, an indemnity must be by express covenant: see paras 302–303 ante. It is thought that the better practice is, and always has been, for the purchaser to execute the assignment.
4   Eg where the sale is subject to restrictive covenants: see LAND REGISTRATION vol 26 (Reissue) para 920. As to a transfer being a deed poll see *Chelsea and Walham Green Building Society v Armstrong* [1951] Ch 853, [1951] 2 All ER 250; and as to restrictive covenants generally see EQUITY vol 16 (Reissue) para 787 et seq.
5   See para 266 ante; and JUDGMENTS AND ORDERS.

(5) PURCHASE MONEY

(i) Receipt of Purchase Money

309. Form of receipt. The vendor must either himself give, or procure others to give, a valid receipt for the purchase money, and his inability to do so is a defect in the title[1]. In a deed executed after 31 December 1881[2], a receipt in the body of a deed is a sufficient discharge to the person making the payment, without any further receipt being indorsed[3]. It is the practice to insert the receipt in the body of the deed immediately after the statement of the payment of the purchase money[4].

A vendor is not bound to accept payment by cheque[5].

1   *Forbes v Peacock* (1846) 1 Ph 717. On a sale by joint vendors, both should join in the receipt: see *Powell v Brodhurst* [1901] 2 Ch 160. As to repudiation by the purchaser for defect of title see para 239 ante; and as to the purchaser's action for damages see paras 256–258 ante.
2   Ie the date of the commencement of the Conveyancing Act 1881 was 1 January 1882: see s 1(2) (repealed).
3   See the Law of Property Act 1925 s 67 (replacing the Conveyancing Act 1881 s 54 (repealed)); and EQUITY vol 16 (Reissue) para 760.
4   An indorsed receipt is now practically unknown.
5   See *Clarke v King* (1826) 2 C & P 286; *Blumberg v Life Interests and Reversionary Securities Corpn* [1897] 1 Ch 171 (affd [1898] 1 Ch 27, CA); *Johnston v Boyes* [1899] 2 Ch 73. The Standard Conditions of Sale (3rd Edn) require the purchaser to pay the money due on completion in one or more of the following ways: (1) legal tender; (2) a banker's draft (see BANKING vol 3(1) (Reissue) para 227); (3) a direct credit to a bank account nominated by the vendor's solicitor; or (4) an unconditional release of a deposit held by a stakeholder: condition 6.7. As to the Standard Conditions of Sale see para 1 note 9 ante. See also para 315 note 6 post. As to the protection afforded to the vendor if he accepts a marked cheque see BANKING vol 3(1) (Reissue) paras 166, 178; and as to payment to a solicitor by cheque see para 315 post. The usual form of payment is now a banker's draft, but in the case of a substantial company such as an insurance company or a large building society, payment by cheque is often made and, in the absence of prior arrangement, is seldom objected to. Such a cheque given by a mortgagee who is financing the

purchase marked 'not negotiable' raises no difficulty, but, if it is marked 'account payee only' and is made out in the name of the purchaser, difficulties would no doubt arise. See however, BANKING vol 3(1) (Reissue) para 226. Where a mortgagee is financing the purchase, the normal practice is for the mortgagee to send a cheque to the purchaser's solicitor prior to completion upon his giving the necessary undertaking. It is rare for a mortgagee to attend on completion, whether in person or by an agent. As to conveyancing services see para 3 ante.

310. Evidence of receipt. A receipt in the body of a deed executed after 1881[1], or indorsed on it, is conclusive evidence of payment in favour of a subsequent purchaser not having notice of non-payment[2]. However, a subsequent purchaser cannot rely upon such receipt if he was unaware of its existence[3]. Absence of a receipt is presumptive evidence of non-payment of purchase money, and puts a subsequent purchaser upon inquiry as to whether it was paid[4].

1   Ie the date of the commencement of the Conveyancing Act 1881 was 1 January 1882: see s 1(2) (repealed).
2   See the Law of Property Act 1925 s 68 (replacing the Conveyancing Act 1881 s 55 (repealed)); and DEEDS AND OTHER INSTRUMENTS. A statement that the money has been paid is not a receipt within this provision: *Renner v Tolley* (1893) 68 LT 815. As to the form of a receipt see para 309 post; and DEEDS AND OTHER INSTRUMENTS. In the case of registered land, a receipt recorded in the proprietorship register would be sufficient for the purposes of the Law of Property Act 1925 s 68, but the entry of the price paid merely records the amount of the consideration and is not evidence of its payment: see *London and Cheshire Insurance Co Ltd v Laplagrene Property Co Ltd* [1971] Ch 499, [1971] 1 All ER 766.
3   *Lloyds Bank Ltd v Bullock* [1896] 2 Ch 192 at 195.
4   *Kennedy v Green* (1834) 3 My & K 699; *Greenslade v Dare* (1855) 20 Beav 284.

311. Receipt by mortgagee. The written receipt by a mortgagee is a sufficient discharge for any money arising under the statutory power of sale, and a person paying the same to the mortgagee is not concerned to inquire whether any money remains due on the mortgage[1].

1   See the Law of Property Act 1925 s 107(1) (reproducing the Conveyancing Act 1881 s 22(1) (repealed)); and MORTGAGE.

312. Receipt by trustees. A written receipt by a trustee for money payable to him under any trust or power is a sufficient discharge, and exonerates the person making the payment from seeing to its application or being liable for its misapplication[1]. However, unless the trustee is a trust corporation, there must be two trustees to give a receipt for money arising under a trust of land or capital money arising under the Settled Land Act 1925[2]. All trustees who have not disclaimed or retired ought to join[3]. They may appoint a solicitor[4], but not one of themselves, to receive the money[5]. Subject to the restriction on receipts by a sole trustee, a surviving trustee may exercise the powers of the trustees, and accordingly may give a receipt[6].

A purchaser from a tenant for life selling under his statutory power[7] is discharged by the written receipt of the trustees of the settlement, or of a sole trustee where the trustee is a trust corporation, or of the personal representatives of the last surviving or continuing trustee[8].

1   See the Trustee Act 1925 s 14(1); and SETTLEMENTS para 908 post.
2   See the Settled Land Act 1925 s 94(1); the Law of Property Act 1925 s 27(2) (as substituted and amended) (see SETTLEMENTS para 908 post); and the Trustee Act 1925 s 14(2) (as amended) (see TRUSTS vol 48 (Reissue) para 911). The reference to trustees applies to the surviving or continuing trustee or trustees for the time being: Settled Land Act 1925 s 94(2). A beneficiary under a trust for sale may obtain an injunction to restrain sale until the appointment of a second trustee: *Waller v Waller* [1967] 1 All ER 305, [1967] 1 WLR 451 (where it was also held that the position is no different where the property is the

matrimonial home and the parties to the action are husband and wife). As to receipts by trustees see SETTLEMENTS para 785 post; TRUSTS vol 48 (Reissue) para 911. See also para 71 note 5 ante.

3   *Lee v Sankey* (1873) LR 15 Eq 204. See also *Hall v Franck* (1849) 11 Beav 519; *Locke v Lomas* (1852) 5 De G & Sm 326; *Hope v Liddell, Liddell v Norton* (1855) 21 Beav 183; *Re Fryer, Martindale v Picquot* (1857) 3 K & J 317; and TRUSTS vol 48 (Reissue) paras 834, 911.

4   See the Trustee Act 1925 s 23(3)(a); para 315 post; and TRUSTS vol 48 (Reissue) para 858.

5   *Re Flower and Metropolitan Board of Works* (1884) 27 ChD 592. Should there be any difficulty as to the trustees giving a receipt, it seems that the purchase money might be paid into court under the Trustee Act 1925 s 63 (as amended) (see TRUSTS vol 48 (Reissue) para 798): see CPR Sch 1 RSC Ord 92 r 2 (as from 26 April 1999); *Cox v Cox* (1855) 1 K & J 251, (1855) 69 ER 451 (decided under RSC Ord 92 r 2); and PRACTICE AND PROCEDURE. As to the CPR see para 133 note 1 ante. If the amount does not exceed the county court limit it may be paid into a county court: see the Trustee Act 1925 s 63A(3)(d) (as added) (see COUNTY COURTS; TRUSTS vol 48 (Reissue) para 541). The need for payment into court is not, however, likely to arise. As to the county court limit see s 63A(5) (as added); County Court Jurisdiction Order 1981, SI 1981/1123 (as amended); and COUNTY COURTS.

6   See the Trustee Act 1925 s 18(1); and POWERS; TRUSTS vol 48 (Reissue) para 853. As to the powers of the personal representatives of a sole trustee or last surviving trustee see POWERS; TRUSTS vol 48 (Reissue) paras 502, 643, 853.

7   As to these powers see SETTLEMENTS para 827 et seq post.

8   See the Settled Land Act 1925 s 95; and SETTLEMENTS para 785 post.

313. Sale of superfluous land. On a sale of superfluous land under the Lands Clauses Consolidation Act 1845, a receipt under the common seal of the promoters of the undertaking, if a corporation, or the hands of two of the directors or managers acting by the authority of the promoters, is a sufficient discharge for the purchase money[1].

1   Lands Clauses Consolidation Act 1845 s 131; and see COMPULSORY ACQUISITION OF LAND vol 8(1) (Reissue) para 382.

(ii) Payment to Persons other than the Vendor

314. Payment to incumbrancers. Where the property is subject to incumbrances which are to be discharged out of the purchase money, the purchaser must pay the proper amounts to the incumbrancers and the balance to the vendor[1]. A purchaser who disregards an incumbrance of which he has knowledge, and pays the vendor without the incumbrancer's consent, is liable to the incumbrancer to the extent of such payment[2].

1   See Sugden's Law of Vendors and Purchasers (14th Edn, 1862) 552; and 2 Dart's Law relating to Vendors and Purchasers (8th Edn, 1929) 698–699. In practice the solicitor of one of the parties often appoints the solicitor of another as his agent to receive the money due to his client, except where the solicitors are all practising in or near the same town. In some cases an independent solicitor is appointed the agent of one of the parties to attend completion. In the case of some incumbrances, such as those in favour of friendly societies, receipts must be signed by trustees (see FRIENDLY SOCIETIES vol 19(1) (Reissue) para 228), and such trustees must not give a receipt until they have actually received the money. In such cases the vendor's solicitor gives his undertaking to deliver an effectual discharge of the incumbrance within a stated time and the practice is to accept such an undertaking. As to conveyancing services see para 3 ante.

2   See 2 Dart's Law relating to Vendors and Purchasers (8th Edn, 1929) 698–699; *Rayne v Baker* (1859) 1 Giff 241; and *Tildesley v Lodge* (1857) 3 Sm & G 543. As to the equitable rights of a person who pays off a mortgage debt see MORTGAGE.

315. Payment to solicitor or licensed conveyancers. Where a solicitor[1] produces a deed having in the body of the deed or indorsed upon it a receipt for the consideration money or other consideration, and the deed has been executed, or the indorsed receipt signed, by the person entitled to give a receipt, the deed itself authorises payment being made to the solicitor without his producing any separate authority from the person who executed or signed the deed or receipt[2]. This procedure can be adopted by vendors who are trustees[3].

The solicitor producing the deed must be acting for the party to whom the money is expressed to be paid[4], but in the absence of suspicious circumstances the purchaser may assume that the solicitor is so acting[5]. The consideration must be paid in cash, payments by cheque to the statutory agent not being authorised[6], nor is payment by set-off warranted[7].

These provisions also apply to licensed conveyancers[8].

Apart from these provisions as to solicitors and licensed conveyancers, payment should be made to the vendor's agent only when he produces a special authority to receive it[9].

1   See para 3 ante.
2   See the Law of Property Act 1925 s 69(1) (reproducing the Conveyancing Act 1881 s 56 (repealed)); and DEEDS AND OTHER INSTRUMENTS; SOLICITORS vol 44(1) (Reissue) para 123. As to receipt of the purchase money see para 310 et seq ante.
3   See the Trustee Act 1925 s 23(3)(a); and SOLICITORS vol 44(1) (Reissue) para 123; TRUSTS vol 48 (Reissue) para 858. As to receipts by trustees generally see para 312 ante; and TRUSTS vol 48 (Reissue) para 911.
4   *Day v Woolwich Equitable Building Society* (1888) 40 ChD 491 at 494. However, this was questioned in *King v Smith* [1900] 2 Ch 425 at 432.
5   *Re Hetling and Merton's Contract* [1893] 3 Ch 269, CA; *King v Smith* [1900] 2 Ch 425.
6   *Blumberg v Life Interests and Reversionary Securities Corpn* [1897] 1 Ch 171 (affd [1898] 1 Ch 27, CA); *Johnston v Boyes* [1899] 2 Ch 73; and see AGENCY vol 1(2) (Reissue) para 53. As to payment to the vendor by cheque see para 309 note 5 ante.
7   *Coupe v Collyer* (1890) 62 LT 927. As to set-off generally see SET-OFF AND COUNTERCLAIM.
8   See the Administration of Justice Act 1985 s 34(1)(a); para 3 ante; and SOLICITORS vol 44(1) (Reissue) para 623–800.
9   See AGENCY vol 1(2) (Reissue) paras 53, 145. Where the purchase is completed by the vendor's attorney acting under a power of attorney, the power will usually authorise payment of the purchase money to him, and, if it is valid for the purpose of transfer (see paras 306–307 ante), it is valid also for the purpose of payment.

(6) ENROLMENT ETC, STAMPS AND NOTICES

(i) Enrolment and Registration

316. Enrolment of transfer. There are still some exceptional cases where a transfer[1] of land is required to be enrolled. Certain transfers of land by ecclesiastical corporations for the purpose of enlarging a cemetery, churchyard or burying ground must be enrolled[2]. Upon a sale of land to or by the Duchy of Lancaster or of Cornwall, the assurance must be enrolled in the duchy office within six months of its execution[3].

1   As to the disposition of registered and unregistered land by transfer see para 262 note 2 ante.
2   See the Burial Ground Act 1816 s 1 (as amended); and CREMATION AND BURIAL. See also the Supreme Court Act 1981 s 133; and PRACTICE AND PROCEDURE.
3   See CROWN PROPERTY vol 12(1) (Reissue) paras 316 (Duchy of Lancaster), 345 (Duchy of Cornwall). Acquisitions or dispositions of land by the Crown Estate Commissioners are no longer required to be enrolled: see CROWN PROPERTY vol 12(1) (Reissue) para 288.

317. Registration of title. A disposition of a registered estate in land is completed by the registration of the purchaser as proprietor of the estate, and until registration is effected the transferor is deemed to remain the proprietor[1]. Where the land is not already registered, most transactions with the freehold estate, or with a leasehold estate of more than 21 years, will give rise to first registration[2].

1   See LAND REGISTRATION vol 26 (Reissue) paras 1113 (freeholds), 1120 (leaseholds). An unregistered transfer may take effect in equity: see *Mascall v Mascall* (1984) 50 P & CR 119, [1984] LS Gaz R 2218, CA. As to the disposition of registered and unregistered land by transfer see para 262 note 2 ante.

2   See the Land Registration Act 1925 ss 123 (as substituted), 123A (as added); para 185 ante; and LAND
     REGISTRATION vol 26 (Reissue) paras 1196–1200. As to compulsory registration see LAND
     REGISTRATION vol 26 (Reissue) paras 727, 1196 et seq.

(ii) Stamps

318. Charge of stamp duty. A transfer on sale is chargeable with ad valorem stamp
duty at a rate varying according to the amount of the consideration, although where the
consideration is under a specified amount and the transfer contains a certificate of value,
no duty is payable[1]. The amounts of the exemption and the appropriate rates of duty are
dealt with elsewhere in this work[2]. On a transfer on sale of the fee simple of land or of a
lease for a term of seven years or more, it is normally the duty of the purchaser to produce
to the Commissioners of Inland Revenue the instrument by which the transfer is effected,
and, if he fails to do so, he is liable to a fine[3]. For the purposes of stamp duty, a deed
delivered in escrow is not fully executed until the condition is fulfilled, and the applicable
rate of duty is the rate prevailing at that later date[4].

1   See the Stamp Act 1891 s 1, Sch 1 Conveyance or Transfer on Sale (as amended); Finance Act 1963 s 55(1)
     (as amended); and STAMP DUTIES AND STAMP DUTY RESERVE TAX vol 44(1) (Reissue) para 1027 et seq.
     As to partition or division see the Stamp Act 1891 s 73 (as amended) (see STAMP DUTIES AND STAMP DUTY
     RESERVE TAX vol 44(1) (Reissue) para 1080); and cf *IRC v Littlewoods Mail Order Stores Ltd* [1963] AC 135,
     [1962] 2 All ER 279, HL. As to the disposition of registered and unregistered land by transfer see para 262
     note 2 ante.
2   See STAMP DUTIES AND STAMP DUTY RESERVE TAX vol 44(1) (Reissue) paras 1027 et seq, 1082 et seq.
3   See the Finance Act 1931 s 28 (as amended), Sch 2 (as substituted); and STAMP DUTIES AND STAMP DUTY
     RESERVE TAX vol 44(1) (Reissue) para 1026.
4   *Terrapin International Ltd v IRC* [1976] 2 All ER 461, [1976] 1 WLR 665. See also para 305 note 3 ante.

319. Inadmissibility in evidence of unstamped documents. A document requiring
a stamp cannot be admitted in evidence in legal proceedings unless it is duly stamped or
payment of the duty and certain further sums is made or an undertaking to pay is given[1].
The proper stamping of documents of title is an important matter of title because, if the
owner of the property is called upon to defend his right or to attack a wrongdoer with
regard to the property, he must produce his documents of title in evidence and this he
cannot do so long as the requirements for the admission of any deed have not been
complied with[2].

1   See para 97 ante; and EVIDENCE.
2   *Re Spollon and Long's Contract* [1936] Ch 713 at 718, [1936] 2 All ER 711 at 717 per Luxmoore J.

(iii) Notices

320. Notices on purchase of equitable estate. Before 1926 on the purchase of an
equitable interest in land (other than an interest in the proceeds of sale under a trust for
sale), the priority of a purchaser did not depend on his giving notice of his purchase to
the trustees, mortgagees or other persons in whom the legal estate was vested[1]. The rule[2],
which regulates the priorities of assignees and incumbrancers of things in action by the
order in which notice is given to the trustees, has since 1925 applied to dealings with
equitable interests in land[3], and accordingly a purchaser of an equitable interest in land
should give notice to the appropriate person[4]. In the case of a dealing with an equitable
interest in settled land the appropriate persons are the trustees of the settlement[5]; in the
case of a dealing with an equitable interest in land subject to a trust of land, or the
proceeds of the sale of such land, the persons to be served with notice are the trustees[6];
and in any other case the appropriate person is the estate owner of the land affected[7].

1   The doctrine of notice, applicable to equitable interests in trust funds and to choses in action, did not apply to land: see CHOSES IN ACTION vol 6 (Reissue) para 46 et seq; EQUITY vol 16 (Reissue) para 759. Where title deeds are retained by the vendor, notice of the transfer to the purchaser should, by agreement, be indorsed on one of the principal deeds, although in the absence of agreement the purchaser cannot insist on this: see 1 Dart's Law relating to Vendors and Purchasers (8th Edn, 1929) 591. The purchaser can, however, insist on notice of covenants in the transfer to him restricting the use of land retained by the vendor being indorsed upon or annexed to one of the common title deeds: see the Law of Property Act 1925 s 200(1); and para 298 ante. As to the disposition of registered and unregistered land by transfer see para 262 note 2 ante.

2   Ie the rule in *Dearle v Hall* (1828) 3 Russ 1: see CHOSES IN ACTION vol 6 (Reissue) para 42 et seq.

3   See the Law of Property Act 1925 s 137(1); and CHOSES IN ACTION vol 6 (Reissue) para 46.

4   See ibid s 137(2) (as amended); and CHOSES IN ACTION vol 6 (Reissue) para 51.

5   See ibid s 137(2)(i). As to the notice required to be given to the trustees of the settlement by a tenant for life intending to make a sale see SETTLEMENTS para 783 post.

6   Ibid s 137(2)(ii) (amended by the Trusts of Land and Appointment of Trustees Act 1996 s 25(1), Sch 3 para 4(1), (15)(a)). For the meaning of 'trust of land' see REAL PROPERTY vol 39(2) (Reissue) para 207.

7   Law of Property Act 1925 s 137(2)(iii). The estate owner is, as to freehold land, the person who is seised in fee simple absolute, and, as to leasehold land, the person in whom the term of years absolute is vested: see s 1(1), (4); and REAL PROPERTY vol 39(2) (Reissue) paras 45, 47.

321. Notice on purchase of equity of redemption. On the purchase of an equity of redemption in land the purchaser should inquire of the mortgagee as to the amount due to him on the mortgage, and should give him notice of the transfer of the equity. This will prevent the mortgagee from tacking a subsequent advance to the original mortgage, unless that mortgage imposed on him an obligation to make further advances[1].

1   As to the doctrine of tacking see MORTGAGE; as to the risks to a purchaser of an equity of redemption arising from the doctrine of the consolidation of mortgages see MORTGAGE; and as to the notice required to be given by a mortgagee before exercising his statutory power of sale see MORTGAGE.

322. Effect of death of intended recipient of notice. Service of a notice affecting land[1] which would be effective but for the death of the intended recipient is effective despite his death if the person serving the notice has no reason to believe that he has died[2]. Where the person serving a notice affecting land has no reason to believe that the intended recipient has died, the proper address for the service of documents by post[3] is what would be the proper address apart from his death[4]. The above provisions do not apply to a notice authorised or required to be served for the purposes of proceedings before[5] (1) any court[6]; (2) specified tribunals[7]; or (3) the Chief Land Registrar or any district registrar or any assistant district registrar[8]; but this is without prejudice to the power to make provision in relation to such proceedings by rules of court, procedural rules within the meaning of the Tribunals and Inquiries Act 1992[9], or rules under the Land Registration Act 1925[10].

A notice affecting land which would have been authorised or required to be served on a person but for his death is sufficiently served before a grant of representation has been filed if[11]: (a) it is addressed to 'The Personal Representative of' the deceased (naming him) and left at or sent by post to his last known place of residence or business in the United Kingdom[12]; and (b) a copy of it, similarly addressed, is served on the Public Trustee[13]. This method of service is not available where provision is made (i) by or under any enactment; or (ii) by an agreement in writing, requiring a different method of service, or expressly prohibiting this method of service, in the circumstances[14].

1   'Land' includes buildings and other structures, land covered with water, and any estate, interest, easement, servitude or right over land: Interpretation Act 1978 s 5, Sch 1.

2   Law of Property (Miscellaneous Provisions) Act 1994 s 17(1).

3   Ie under the Interpretation Act 1978 s 7 (see STATUTES vol 44(1) (Reissue) paras 1388, 1390): see the Law of Property (Miscellaneous Provisions) Act 1994 s 17(2).

4   Ibid s 17(2).
5   Ibid s 17(3).
6   Ibid s 17(3)(a).
7   Ibid s 17(3)(b). The tribunals are those specified in the Tribunals and Inquiries Act 1992 s 1, Sch 1 (as amended) (see ADMINISTRATIVE LAW vol 1(1) (Reissue) para 49): see the Law of Property (Miscellaneous Provisions) Act 1994 s 17(3)(b).
8   Ibid s 17(3)(c).
9   Ie the Tribunals and Inquiries Act 1992 s 8 (as amended) (see ADMINISTRATIVE LAW vol 1(1) (Reissue) para 48): see the Law of Property (Miscellaneous Provisions) Act 1994 s 17(3).
10 Ie the Land Registration Act 1925 s 144 (see LAND REGISTRATION vol 26 (Reissue) para 1217 et seq): see the Law of Property (Miscellaneous Provisions) Act 1994 s 17(3).
11 Ibid 18(1). The reference to the filing of a grant of representation is to the filing at the Principal Registry of the Family Division of the High Court of a copy of a grant of representation in respect of the deceased's estate or, as the case may be, the part of his estate which includes the land in question: s 18(2). As to the filing of documents served on the Public Trustee, the keeping of a register of details taken from them, and searches of the register see the Public Trustee (Notices Affecting Land) (Title on Death) Regulations 1995, SI 1995/1330; and TRUSTS vol 48 (Reissue) para 657.
12 Law of Property (Miscellaneous Provisions) Act 1994 s 18(1)(a). 'United Kingdom' means Great Britain and Northern Ireland: Interpretation Act 1978 Sch 1. 'Great Britain' means England, Scotland and Wales: Union with Scotland Act 1706, preamble art I; Interpretation Act 1978 s 22(1), Sch 2 para 5(a). Neither the Channel Islands nor the Isle of Man are within the United Kingdom. See further CONSTITUTIONAL LAW AND HUMAN RIGHTS vol 8(2) (Reissue) para 3.
13 Law of Property (Miscellaneous Provisions) Act 1994 s 18(1)(b). As to the fees payable in respect of the function of the Public Trustee see the Public Trustee (Fees) Order 1985, SI 1985/373, art 29A (as added); and TRUSTS vol 48 (Reissue) para 681; and as to the establishment of the office of the Public Trustee see the Public Trustee Act 1906 s 1; and TRUSTS vol 48 (Reissue) para 655.
14 Law of Property (Miscellaneous Provisions) Act 1994 s 18(3).

(7) COSTS

323. Costs payable by the purchaser. In the absence of express stipulation, the purchaser pays the costs of preparing the transfer[1]. Where, however, a sale was carried out by the grant of an underlease, the underlessor was held not entitled to the costs of preparing the underlease[2]. The purchaser pays the costs of registration of a transfer under the Land Registration Act 1925[3]; of an acknowledgment of the right of production of deeds or covenant for production, other than the costs of perusal and execution on behalf of and by the vendor and other necessary parties[4]; and the expense of procuring attested copies of documents retained by the vendor[5].

1   *Poole v Hill* (1840) 6 M & W 835; and see para 262 ante. As to the costs of making and verifying the abstract, producing deeds not in the vendor's possession etc see paras 170–173 ante. As to the need for an abstract of title with respect to both unregistered and registered land see paras 138, 141–149 ante. As to the costs of stamping unstamped or insufficiently stamped deeds see para 97 ante; and as to solicitors' costs see SOLICITORS vol 44(1) (Reissue) para 158 et seq.
2   *Sims-Clarke v Ilet Ltd* [1953] IR 39.
3   See para 265 ante. As to land registration fees generally see LAND REGISTRATION vol 26 (Reissue) para 1217 et seq. As to the disposition of registered and unregistered land by transfer see para 262 note 2 ante.
4   See the Law of Property Act 1925 s 45(8).
5   See ibid s 45(4); and para 132 ante.

324. Costs payable by the vendor. The expense of the perusal and execution of the transfer by all necessary transferring parties[1], of registration of a vendor's title under the Land Registration Act 1925 or of procuring a transfer from the registered proprietor to the purchaser[2] is borne by the vendor, who also pays the expense of discharging incumbrances or getting in outstanding estates[3], or the additional expense occasioned by the incumbrancers, or persons in whom estates are vested, being joined in the transfer[4].

1 Sugden's Law of Vendors and Purchasers (14th Edn, 1862) 561. See also para 276 ante. As to the disposition of registered and unregistered land by transfer see para 262 note 2 ante.
2 See the Land Registration Act 1925 s 110(5); *Urban Manor Ltd v Sadiq* [1997] 1 WLR 1016, [1997] 12 LS Gaz R 22, CA; and LAND REGISTRATION vol 26 (Reissue) para 929.
3 *Esdaile v Oxenham* (1824) 3 B & C 225 at 228–229; *Re Sander and Walford's Contract* (1900) 83 LT 316. Stipulation to the contrary cannot now be made: see para 129 ante.
4 See *Jones v Lewis* (1847) 1 De G & Sm 245; Sugden's Law of Vendors and Purchasers (14th Edn, 1862) 555; and 1 Dart's Law relating to Vendors and Purchasers (8th Edn, 1929) 593. Cf *Reeves v Gill* (1838) 1 Beav 375.

325. Costs of transfer on compulsory purchase. In the case of land purchased under the Lands Clauses Consolidation Act 1845 or the Compulsory Purchase Act 1965, whether compulsorily or by agreement, the vendor's and purchaser's costs of transfer, including getting in outstanding legal estates, terms and interests, and deducing and verifying the title, are paid by the promoters or the acquiring authority[1].

1 See the Lands Clauses Consolidation Act 1845 s 82; the Compulsory Purchase Act 1965 s 23(1); and COMPULSORY ACQUISITION OF LAND vol 8(1) (Reissue) para 140. Preliminary expenses and other costs not covered by statute are usually made the subject of express stipulation on sales by agreement.

4. POSITION OF THE PARTIES AFTER COMPLETION

(1) BENEFITS ENJOYED WITH THE PROPERTY SOLD

(i) Rents and Profits

326. Purchaser's rights after completion. After completion of the purchase by payment of the purchase money[1] and transfer of the property, the purchaser becomes entitled to exercise, in place of the vendor, all such rights of ownership as are incident to the estate transferred, subject, however, to any reservations and liabilities to which it was subject before completion or which are created by the transfer[2].

1 As to the vendor's lien for purchase money when it is not paid on completion see paras 183, 187 ante; and LIEN vol 28 (Reissue) para 758 et seq. As to completion see paras 262–325 ante.
2 As to the rights of an owner in fee simple see REAL PROPERTY vol 39(2) (Reissue) para 94 et seq. As to leaseholds see REAL PROPERTY vol 39(2) (Reissue) para 100 et seq. As to the reservation of easements in the transfer see para 308 ante. As to the disposition of registered and unregistered land by transfer see para 262 note 2 ante.

327. Purchaser's rights against a tenant. If the land sold is in the occupation of a tenant, attornment by the tenant is not necessary to give effect to the transfer of the reversion[1], but notice of the transfer should be given to him in order to prevent any further payment of rent to the vendor[2]. The purchaser, as owner of the reversion, can, in the case of a lease granted before 1 January 1996[3], recover by distress rent which is in arrear at the date of the transfer or which accrues due thereafter[4], and he can sue on the covenant or agreement for payment of rent[5]. In the case of a lease granted on or after 1 January 1996, only rent accruing due after the date of the transfer is recoverable by the purchaser[6]. However, the benefit of a court order for possession made in favour of a landlord against a tenant does not pass merely by transfer of the landlord's estate in the land[7].

1   See the Law of Property Act 1925 s 151(1)(a). As to attornment see LANDLORD AND TENANT vol 27(1) (Reissue) para 3. As to the disposition of registered and unregistered land by transfer see para 262 note 2 ante.

2   Such payment does not prejudice the tenant before he has received notice of the assignment of the reversion: see LANDLORD AND TENANT vol 27(1) (Reissue) paras 3, 231.

3   Ie the date on which the Landlord and Tenant (Covenants) Act 1995 came into force: see the Landlord and Tenant (Covenants) Act 1995 (Commencement) Order 1995, SI 1995/2963.

4   See DISTRESS. As to the reservation of rent, and the running of rent with the reversion see LANDLORD AND TENANT vol 27(1) (Reissue) paras 212 et seq, 482.

5   See the Law of Property Act 1925 s 141; and LANDLORD AND TENANT vol 27(1) (Reissue) paras 479, 482. As to the enforcement of covenants in a lease on the assignment of the reversion generally see para 334 post. An assignee of the reversion on a lease created before 1 January 1996 may sue for rent due and breaches of covenant committed before the assignment (see LANDLORD AND TENANT vol 27(1) (Reissue) para 482); otherwise where the lease is created on or after 1 January 1996 (see the Landlord and Tenant (Covenants) Act 1995 s 23(1)). As to estoppel between the assignee of the reversion and the tenant see ESTOPPEL vol 16 (Reissue) para 1078.

6   See ibid s 23(1). However, the existing rent arrears, though not owed to the purchaser, may still enable the purchaser to forfeit the lease: see *Kataria v Safeland plc* [1998] 05 EG 155, 75 P & CR D30, CA.

7   *Chung Kwok Hotel Co Ltd v Field* [1960] 3 All ER 143, [1960] 1 WLR 1112, CA, where it was expressly left undecided whether the benefit of the order could be expressly assigned. As to actions for possession generally see LANDLORD AND TENANT vol 27(1) (Reissue) para 550 et seq.

328. Apportionment of rent. Where the property sold is only part of the demised premises, the transfer effects a severance of the reversion, and the rent can be apportioned between the part transferred to the purchaser and the remainder of the premises[1]. Usually, on a sale by auction, the particulars show how the rent is to be apportioned and make the apportionment binding between vendor and purchaser; but in order that the apportionment may be binding on the tenant it should be made with his consent or by judicial process[2].

1   As to the apportionment of rent see LANDLORD AND TENANT vol 27(1) (Reissue) para 245 et seq. Under the Law of Property Act 1925 s 141(1), rent goes with the reversionary estate in the land notwithstanding severance of that estate: see LANDLORD AND TENANT vol 27(1) (Reissue) para 484. As to the disposition of registered and unregistered land by transfer see para 262 note 2 ante.

2   See *Walter v Maunde* (1820) 1 Jac & W 181; and LANDLORD AND TENANT vol 27(1) (Reissue) para 484. See also paras 124, 193 ante. As to the effect of particular conditions of sale see para 84 et seq ante.

329. Notice of tenant's interest. From the fact of the tenant's occupation, the purchaser has notice of his interest whatever it may be[1], and he takes, accordingly, subject to the tenant's rights, including not only those which arise out of the tenancy[2], but also those to which the tenant is entitled under any collateral or subsequent agreement, such as an agreement for purchase[3], and he must give effect to such rights[4]. However, a purchaser of unregistered land who does not inquire whether a tenant may have a right to rectification of his lease or tenancy agreement is not bound by any right to rectification which the tenant has, since the purchaser is entitled to assume that a tenancy agreement correctly states the relationship between landlord and tenant[5]. In the case of registered land, a right of rectification belonging to a tenant who is in actual occupation, or in receipt of the rents and profits, constitutes an overriding interest, unless on inquiry the right is not disclosed[6].

1   *Daniels v Davison* (1811) 17 Ves 433; *Meux v Maltby* (1818) 2 Swan 277 at 281; *Lewis v Stephenson* (1898) 67 LJQB 296. See also *Clements v Conroy* [1911] 2 IR 500 at 508, Ir CA; *Poster v Slough Estates Ltd* [1969] 1 Ch 495 at 506, [1968] 3 All ER 257 at 261; and EQUITY vol 16 (Reissue) para 773. As to inquiries of the tenant see para 6 ante.

2   *Taylor v Stibbert* (1794) 2 Ves 437.

3   *Daniels v Davison* (1809) 16 Ves 249 at 254. This, however, has been described as an extreme case: *Jones v Smith* (1841) 1 Hare 43 at 62; affd (1843) 1 Ph 244. See also *Allen v Anthony* (1816) 1 Mer 282 (agreement for sale of timber). To be effective against a purchaser, an agreement or option to purchase

must be registered as an estate contract: see LAND CHARGES vol 26 (Reissue) para 532; LANDLORD AND TENANT vol 27(1) (Reissue) para 110. As to the benefit of the option passing on assignment see *Griffith v Pelton* [1958] Ch 205, [1957] 3 All ER 75, CA; *Re Button's Lease, Inman v Button* [1964] Ch 263, [1963] 3 All ER 708. See also para 27 ante.

4   *Barnhart v Greenshields* (1853) 9 Moo PCC 18 at 32; *Bailey v Richardson* (1852) 9 Hare 734; *Carroll v Keayes, Keayes v Carroll* (1873) IR 8 Eq 97, Ir CA. Possession is prima facie evidence of seisin in fee, and hence the fact of occupation is notice of the possibility of an estate in fee simple: *Jones v Smith* (1841) 1 Hare 43 at 60.

5   *Smith v Jones* [1954] 2 All ER 823, [1954] 1 WLR 1089. This rule does not apply if the purchaser is given notice of the tenant's claim or of facts showing that there is a right of rectification: see *Blacklocks v JB Developments (Godalming) Ltd* [1982] Ch 183 at 195–196, [1981] 3 All ER 392 at 400–401.

6   See the Land Registration Act 1925 s 70(1)(g); and LAND REGISTRATION vol 26 (Reissue) para 784. See also *Blacklocks v JB Developments Ltd* [1982] Ch 183, [1981] 3 All ER 392. Where the vendor has provided the purchaser with copies of the documents embodying the lease terms, the purchaser is treated as entering into the contract knowing and fully accepting those terms (see the Standard Conditions of Sale (3rd Edn), condition 8.1.2; and para 98 ante); but that provision obviously applies only between vendor and purchaser. As to the Standard Conditions of Sale see para 1 note 9 ante.

330. Notice of adverse claims. If the tenant has been paying rent to a person claiming adversely to the vendor, the fact of the tenancy, without actual notice of the adverse claim, is not notice of the title of the adverse claimant[1]. The purchaser is, as between himself and the adverse claimant, not bound to inquire to whom rent has been paid[2]. If, however, the purchaser makes the inquiry and finds that rent is being paid to an adverse claimant, this gives the purchaser notice of his rights[3], although, for this purpose, notice is not imputed from the circumstance that the rents are being paid to an estate agent[4].

The general statutory provisions relating to legal estates, equitable interests and powers[5] do not prejudicially affect the interest of any person in possession[6] or in actual occupation of land to which he may be entitled in right of such possession or occupation[7]. However, the overreaching powers contained in those provisions operate even though the purchaser has failed to make the usual inquiries of the tenant or other person in occupation[8].

1   *Barnhart v Greenshields* (1853) 9 Moo PCC 18 at 34; *Hunt v Luck* [1902] 1 Ch 428 at 432, CA, overruling the dictum to the contrary in *Mumford v Stohwasser* (1874) LR 18 Eq 556 at 562. See also EQUITY vol 16 (Reissue) para 773. Cf, however, the Law of Property Act 1925 s 14 (see the text and note 7 infra); and the Land Registration Act 1925 s 70(1)(g) (see LAND REGISTRATION vol 26 (Reissue) para 784).

2   If, however, the purchaser knows that the rents are being paid to a person other than the vendor, as trustee, he must inquire for whom the trustee receives them: *Knight v Bowyer* (1858) 2 De G & J 421.

3   *Bailey v Richardson* (1852) 9 Hare 734; *Barnhart v Greenshields* (1853) 9 Moo PCC 18; *Hunt v Luck* [1902] 1 Ch 428 at 433, CA.

4   *Hunt v Luck* [1902] 1 Ch 428, CA.

5   Ie the Law of Property Act 1925 Pt I (ss 1–39) (as amended): see REAL PROPERTY vol 39(2) (Reissue) para 91 et seq.

6   'Possession' includes the receipt of rents and profits or the right to receive the same, if any: ibid s 205(1)(xix).

7   Ibid s 14.

8   See ibid s 2 (as amended); paras 271–272 ante; and REAL PROPERTY vol 39(2) (Reissue) para 247 et seq. See also *City of London Building Society v Flegg* [1988] AC 54, [1987] 3 All ER 435, HL, distinguishing *Williams and Glyn's Bank Ltd v Boland* [1981] AC 487, [1980] 2 All ER 408, HL. As to the effect of the Trusts of Land and Appointment of Trustees Act 1996 s 16 on purchasers of registered land see TRUSTS vol 48 (Reissue) paras 894–895, 908.

(ii) Right to Benefit of Covenants running with the Land

331. Covenants running with the land. Upon the sale of land the purchaser is frequently required to enter into covenants, either positive or negative, affecting the enjoyment of the land, or of neighbouring premises. For example, a covenant to lay out money in maintaining roads is a positive covenant of this character, and a covenant not to use premises as a shop is a negative or restrictive covenant. These covenants are binding as between the covenantor and covenantee as the immediate contracting parties. However, the covenants may also be enforceable by the vendor and his successors in title against the purchaser and his successors in title by virtue of their ownership of land, and the benefit and the burden are then said to run with the land, the land being either at the time of sale, or prior to it, land of the vendor, or the land transferred to the purchaser.

The benefit of a covenant may run with the land at law or in equity[1]. In the case of a lease granted before 1 January 1996[2], the burden of covenants between landlord and tenant which touch and concern the demised land will pass on an assignment of the lease[3] or the reversion[4]. Where the lease is granted on or after that date, the requirement that the covenants touch and concern the demised land is abolished, but there is an exclusion for covenants which, in whatever terms, are expressed to be personal to any person[5]. The burden of a covenant between vendor and purchaser does not run at law[6], but will run in equity where the covenants are restrictive[7]. Where the benefit of a restrictive covenant does not run with the land because it has not been annexed to that land, the benefit may be assignable[8].

1 The transmission of the benefit of leasehold covenants depends partly on the common law principle of privity of estate (on the assignment of the lease) (see LANDLORD AND TENANT vol 27(1) (Reissue) para 476), and partly on statute, ie on the Law of Property Act 1925 s 141 (on the assignment of the reversion) (see LANDLORD AND TENANT vol 27(1) (Reissue) paras 479–482).

2 Ie the date on which the Landlord and Tenant (Covenants) Act 1995 came into force: see the Landlord and Tenant (Covenants) Act 1995 (Commencement) Order 1995, SI 1995/2963.

3 Ie on the principle of privity of estate: see LANDLORD AND TENANT vol 27(1) (Reissue) para 469 et seq.

4 See the Law of Property Act 1925 s 142; and LANDLORD AND TENANT vol 27(1) (Reissue) para 483.

5 See the Landlord and Tenant (Covenants) Act 1995 s 3; and LANDLORD AND TENANT.

6 See para 333 post; and EQUITY vol 16 (Reissue) para 787.

7 See para 333 post; and EQUITY vol 16 (Reissue) para 788 et seq. As to the need for registration see EQUITY vol 16 (Reissue) para 793; LAND CHARGES vol 26 (Reissue) para 535; LAND REGISTRATION vol 26 (Reissue) para 1110 et seq.

8 See EQUITY vol 16 (Reissue) para 796; but see *Federated Homes Ltd v Mill Lodge Properties Ltd* [1980] 1 All ER 371, [1980] 1 WLR 594, CA; *Roake v Chadha* [1983] 3 All ER 503, [1984] 1 WLR 40; *J Sainsbury plc v Enfield London Borough Council* [1989] 2 All ER 817, [1989] 1 WLR 590. As to the imposition of restrictive covenants under a scheme of development see EQUITY vol 16 (Reissue) paras 790, 797–799.

332. Circumstances in which benefit will run. In order that the benefit of a covenant may run with the land at law[1] it must be of such a nature as to touch and concern the land[2]; that is, it must either affect the land as regards mode of occupation, or it must be such as in itself, and not merely from collateral circumstances, affects the value of the land[3]. If it fulfils that condition, the benefit of the covenant can run at law with land retained by the vendor and subsequently disposed of by him[4] to successors in title holding the same or a derivative legal estate[5]. If it does not fulfil these conditions, it is a personal covenant, and is binding only between the parties and their personal representatives[6].

A covenant may be expressed so as to be merely personal, and then, whether collateral or not, it binds only the covenantor and his personal representatives[7].

It is not essential to the running of the benefit of a covenant with land that the covenantor should have had an interest in the land to be bound by the covenant[8].

1 In general it is also true of restrictive covenants that the benefit of them will not run with particular land unless they touch and concern the land, in the sense that the land must be capable of being benefited by them: see *Re Ballard's Conveyance* [1937] Ch 473 at 480, [1937] 2 All ER 691 at 696; *Marquess of Zetland v Driver* [1939] Ch 1 at 8, [1938] 2 All ER 158 at 161, CA. There is no difference between law and equity in construing covenants to see whether their benefit is so annexed as to run with land: see *Rogers v*

Hosegood [1900] 2 Ch 388 at 397, CA, per Farwell J. As to the annexation of the benefit of a restrictive covenant to the whole or to each and every part of the land to be benefited see EQUITY vol 16 (Reissue) para 795. As to the running of the benefit of a covenant for title see para 342 post.

2   *Austerberry v Oldham Corpn* (1885) 29 ChD 750 at 776, CA; *Rogers v Hosegood* [1900] 2 Ch 388 at 395, 407, CA; *Re Ballard's Conveyance* [1937] Ch 473 at 480, [1937] 2 All ER 691 at 696; *Marquess of Zetland v Driver* [1939] Ch 1 at 7, [1938] 2 All ER 158 at 161, CA. But see para 331 ante.

3   *Congleton Corpn v Pattison* (1808) 10 East 130 at 135; *Rogers v Hosegood* [1900] 2 Ch 388 at 395, CA; *Smith and Snipes Hall Farm Ltd v River Douglas Catchment Board* [1949] 2 KB 500 at 507, [1949] 2 All ER 179 at 184, CA. A covenant that runs with the land of the covenantee may by virtue of the Law of Property Act 1925 s 78 be enforceable by successors in title, such as, for example, a yearly tenant: see *Smith and Snipes Hall Farm Ltd v River Douglas Catchment Board* supra at 510–511 and at 186; *Williams v Unit Construction Co Ltd* (1951) (unreported; but see 19 Conv NS 262), CA; *Federated Homes Ltd v Mill Lodge Properties Ltd* [1980] 1 All ER 371, [1980] 1 WLR 594, CA; *Roake v Chadha* [1983] 3 All ER 503, [1984] 1 WLR 40; *J Sainsbury plc v Enfield London Borough Council* [1989] 2 All ER 817, [1989] 1 WLR 590. See also EQUITY vol 16 (Reissue) para 791.

4   *Austerberry v Oldham Corpn* (1885) 29 ChD 750, CA; *Rogers v Hosegood* [1900] 2 Ch 388 at 404, CA. See also the seventh resolution in *Spencer's Case* (1583) 5 Co Rep 16a at 17b; 1 Smith LC (13th Edn) 84, 94; and EQUITY vol 16 (Reissue) para 787.

5   *Rogers v Hosegood* [1900] 2 Ch 388 at 404, CA; *Webb v Russell* (1789) 3 Term Rep 393. These cases show that the benefit of a covenant entered into with a mortgagor, who, at that date, had no legal estate, did not run with the land at law, although the position in equity was different: *Smith and Snipes Hall Farm Ltd v River Douglas Catchment Board* [1949] 2 KB 500, [1949] 2 All ER 179, CA; *Williams v Unit Construction Co Ltd* (unreported; but see 19 Conv NS 262), CA.

6   Such a covenant is collateral and personal: *Rogers v Hosegood* [1900] 2 Ch 388 at 407, CA; *Formby v Barker* [1903] 2 Ch 539 at 551, CA.

7   See *Re Fawcett and Holmes' Contract* (1889) 42 ChD 150, CA; *Re Royal Victoria Pavilion, Ramsgate, Whelan v FTS (Great Britain) Ltd* [1961] Ch 581, [1961] 3 All ER 83 (covenant to procure that property should not be used in a particular manner).

8   *Smith and Snipes Hall Farm Ltd v River Douglas Catchment Board* [1949] 2 KB 500 at 505, 512, [1949] 2 All ER 179 at 184, 187, CA.

333. Burden of covenant. Save in cases arising between landlord and tenant, the burden of a covenant relating to the use or enjoyment of land does not run with the land at law[1]. Further, where the covenant is positive in substance, and can only be complied with by the expenditure of money, the burden does not run with the land in equity[2]. The covenantee may validly reserve a right of re-entry exercisable on failure by the original covenantor or his successors to observe the covenant. Such a right of re-entry creates an equitable interest which is not registrable as a land charge affecting unregistered land, and which will be enforceable within the limits prescribed by the rule against perpetuities[3].

Subject to the requirement of registration[4], however, the burden of restrictive covenants runs with the land in equity[5].

An obligation to fulfil the stipulation of a deed, where, for example, contribution to expenses is a corollary of taking benefits, may become binding on successors in title, because it is a principle of law that he who takes the benefit of a deed is bound by a condition contained in the deed[6].

1   *Austerberry v Oldham Corpn* (1885) 29 ChD 750, CA, overruling on this point *Cooke v Chilcott* (1876) 3 ChD 694. Cf *Haywood v Brunswick Building Society* (1881) 8 QBD 403 at 409, CA; *Re Woking UDC (Basingstoke Canal) Act 1911* [1914] 1 Ch 300, CA, where the burden of obligations imposed by a private Act upon a company was held not to run with the land after dissolution of the company; *E and GC Ltd v Bate* (1935) 79 L Jo 203; *Jones v Price* [1965] 2 QB 618, [1965] 2 All ER 625, CA. Exceptionally, a customary duty to maintain fences or walls to keep out animals can exist as an easement and thus bind the land: see *Crow v Wood* [1971] 1 QB 77, [1970] 3 All ER 425, CA; *Egerton v Harding* [1975] QB 62, [1974] 3 All ER 689, CA; and EASEMENTS AND PROFITS À PRENDRE. There are also exceptional instances where by statute positive obligations are made to run with land, for example undertakings given to a London borough council pursuant to the Greater London Council (General Powers) Act 1974 s 16 (as amended): see LONDON GOVERNMENT. A covenant to contribute to the cost of repairs to roads, sea walls and sewers does not run with land so as to bind successors in title: *Halsall v Brizell* [1957] Ch 169 at 182, [1957] 1 All ER 371 at 377. See, however, the text and note 6 infra.

2   *Haywood v Brunswick Building Society* (1881) 8 QBD 403, CA. See also *Smith v Colbourne* [1914] 2 Ch 533,
     CA, where a covenant to remove windows erected under a licence was held unenforceable against
     subsequent purchasers; and a right of entry for the adjoining owner to remove them was apparently void
     for perpetuity. As to the law in Scotland see *Anderson v Dickie* (1915) 84 LJPC 219, HL.
3   *Shiloh Spinners Ltd v Harding* [1973] AC 691, [1973] 1 All ER 90, HL. In the case of registered land, the
     right of re-entry will require to be protected on the register. As to relief against forfeiture for breach of
     covenant see EQUITY vol 16 (Reissue) para 897. As to the rule against perpetuities see PERPETUITIES AND
     ACCUMULATIONS vol 35 (Reissue) para 1040.
4   See EQUITY vol 16 (Reissue) para 793; LAND CHARGES vol 26 (Reissue) para 535; LAND REGISTRATION
     vol 26 (Reissue) para 1110 et seq.
5   See EQUITY vol 16 (Reissue) para 787 et seq. It is doubtful whether or not a covenant restraining
     alienation will run on this principle: see *Caldy Manor Estate Ltd v Farrell* [1974] 3 All ER 753, [1974] 1
     WLR 1303, CA, where this point was left open; and cf *Noble and Wolf v Alley* [1951] SCR 64, [1951] 1
     DLR 321, Can SC, where it was held that such a covenant does not run with the land.
6   *Halsall v Brizell* [1957] Ch 169 at 182, [1957] 1 All ER 371 at 377. See also DEEDS AND OTHER
     INSTRUMENTS. Further, there is also a 'pure' doctrine of benefit and burden, independent of the doctrine
     of conditional benefits and burdens. The pure doctrine will apply, and impose the obligation on a
     successor in title, where the circumstances in which the successor came into the transaction show that the
     doctrine was intended to apply: see *Tito v Waddell (No 2)* [1977] Ch 106 at 289–311, [1977] 3 All ER
     129 at 280–298.

334. Covenants in leases. Where the purchase is of the reversion on a lease, the
purchaser is entitled to enforce the lessee's covenants, and is bound by the lessor's
covenants concerning the land, and may take advantage of the conditions of the lease[1].
Where the assignment to the purchaser comprises part only of the demised premises, so
that the reversion on the term is severed, the purchaser is entitled to enforce the covenants
and take advantage of the conditions so far as they relate to the land assigned[2].

1   See generally LANDLORD AND TENANT vol 27(1) (Reissue) paras 479–482 (benefit of lessee's
     covenants running with reversion), para 483 (burden of lessor's covenants running with reversion). In
     relation to leases created on or after 1 January 1996, these matters are governed by the Landlord and
     Tenant (Covenants) Act 1995: see LANDLORD AND TENANT. As to the purchaser's right to recover
     rent see para 327 ante.
2   See LANDLORD AND TENANT vol 27(1) (Reissue) para 484.

335. Right of persons not parties to take benefit of covenants. A person may
take the benefit of a covenant or agreement respecting land although he may not be
named as a party to the instrument by which the disposition is made[1], provided that he is
a person with whom the covenant or agreement purports to be made[2].

1   See the Law of Property Act 1925 s 56(1), which appears to relate only to covenants of which the benefit
     runs with the land (see generally DEEDS AND OTHER INSTRUMENTS; EQUITY vol 16 (Reissue) para 791)
     and applies only to land (see *Beswick v Beswick* [1968] AC 58, [1967] 2 All ER 1197, HL). As to the right
     of persons not parties to take interests in land see para 283 ante.
2   See *Marquess of Zetland v Driver* [1937] Ch 651 at 657, [1937] 3 All ER 795 at 801; revsd without affecting
     this point [1939] Ch 1, [1938] 2 All ER 158, CA. See also para 283 note 2 ante; and DEEDS AND OTHER
     INSTRUMENTS.

(2) COVENANTS FOR TITLE

(i) In general

336. Protection afforded. In the transfer of the property the vendor usually enters
into covenants for title[1], in pursuance of his obligation to give a title clear of defects and
incumbrances, unless otherwise provided by the contract[2]. While the contract remains

executory, the purchaser can decline to complete unless a proper title is made out[3], but after completion he cannot, on the ground of adverse claims, recover money which has been paid or detain money unpaid, and must rely on the covenants for title[4].

1   See also para 293 et seq ante. The fact that the vendor cannot show a complete chain of previous covenants for title is not an objection to his title: *Re Scott and Alvarez's Contract, Scott v Alvarez* [1895] 1 Ch 596 at 606, CA. The care with which titles are investigated makes it unusual for a purchaser to require to sue on the covenant, and it has been said that more value is attached to covenants for title than they are worth; but at the same time much care is taken to secure the widest covenants which the circumstances permit and even to take an express covenant where no covenant will be implied. The most comprehensive covenants are those implied when the vendor sells with full title guarantee on or after 1 July 1995: see paras 349–351 post. As to covenants for title on the disposition of registered land see LAND REGISTRATION vol 26 (Reissue) paras 948–952. See also *AJ Dunning & Sons (Shopfitters) Ltd v Sykes & Son (Poole) Ltd* [1987] Ch 287, [1987] 1 All ER 700, CA. As to the effect of the word 'grant' in a conveyance or transfer of superfluous land under the Lands Clauses Consolidation Act 1845 see s 132; and COMPULSORY ACQUISITION OF LAND vol 8(1) (Reissue) para 382. As to the disposition of registered and unregistered land by transfer see para 262 note 2 ante.
2   See para 137 ante. An agreement to sell the fee simple, free from incumbrances, carries with it the right of the purchaser to proper covenants: *Church v Brown* (1808) 15 Ves 258 at 263.
3   See para 137 ante.
4   See para 353 post.

337. Reform of the law relating to statutory covenants for title. The law relating to the statutory covenants for title was significantly changed by legislation which came into force on 1 July 1995[1]. Dispositions made before that date continue to be governed by the old law[2]; dispositions made on or after that date are governed by the new law[3].

1   Ie the Law of Property (Miscellaneous Provisions) Act 1994 Pt I (ss 1–13): see paras 349–351 post.
2   Ie the Law of Property Act 1925 s 76 (as amended), Sch 2 Pts I–VI (as amended). These provisions were repealed in relation to dispositions of property made on or after 1 July 1995 by the Law of Property (Miscellaneous Provisions) Act 1994 ss 10(1), 21(2), (3), Sch 2. As to the old law see paras 338–348 post. See also para 349 note 2 post.
3   As to the new law see paras 349–351 post. As to transitional provisions see the Law of Property (Miscellaneous Provisions) Act 1994 ss 10–13; and para 349 note 2 post.

(ii) Dispositions made before 1 July 1995

A. COVENANTS IMPLIED BY STATUTE

338. Implied covenants. It was formerly the practice not to give full express covenants for title in a conveyance[1] but to rely on the covenants on the part of the person conveying which are implied by statute where that person conveys and is expressed to convey as beneficial owner[2], settlor[3], trustee, mortgagee or personal representative of a deceased person, or under an order of the court[4].

On a conveyance of freeholds for valuable consideration, other than a mortgage[5], by a person who conveys and is expressed to convey as beneficial owner[6], the covenants implied by statute are covenants (1) for right to convey[7]; (2) for quiet enjoyment[8]; (3) for freedom from incumbrances[9]; and (4) for further assurance[10]. If the property is leasehold, similar covenants are implied and also covenants that the lease is valid and subsisting, and that the rent and lessee's covenants have been paid and performed to date[11]. The covenants implied by statute on a conveyance by a person conveying as beneficial owner are not absolute, but are limited to acts done by the person who conveys or any one through whom he derives title otherwise than by purchase for value[12]. The express covenants formerly included in conveyances were normally similarly limited[13].

On any conveyance by a person who conveys and is expressed to convey as a trustee[14] or personal representative of a deceased person[15] or under an order of the court or as mortgagee, the only covenant implied is a covenant against incumbrances created by himself[16].

These implied covenants for title may be varied or extended by a deed or assent[17]. Where it is intended to modify them, the modification should be clearly expressed in the conveyance[18]. A proviso destroying and not merely qualifying a covenant is void[19].

Where the sole survivor of joint tenants or his personal representative conveys as beneficial owner or as personal representative, he is deemed in favour of a purchaser to be or to have been solely and beneficially interested[20].

1   For these purposes, 'conveyance' does not include a demise by way of lease at a rent, but does include a charge (Law of Property Act 1925 s 76(5)), as well as a mortgage, any other lease, an assent, vesting declaration, vesting instrument, disclaimer, release and any other assurance of property or an interest in it by any instrument except a will (see s 205(1)(ii)). The provisions of s 76 (as amended) apply to conveyances made after 1881, but only to assents by personal representatives made after 1925: see s 76(8). As to the running of the benefit of a covenant for title see para 342 post.

       As to the repeal of the Law of Property Act 1925 s 76 (as amended), Sch 2 Pts I–VI (as amended) in relation to dispositions of property made on or after 1 July 1995 see para 337 ante. As to dispositions made on or after 1 July 1995 see paras 349–351 post.

       As to the disposition of registered and unregistered land by transfer see para 262 note 2 ante.

2   See ibid s 76(1)(A), Sch 2 Pt I (conveyance for valuable consideration, other than a mortgage: see the text and notes 5–10 infra); s 76(1)(B), Sch 2 Pt II (conveyance of leasehold property for valuable consideration, other than a mortgage: see LANDLORD AND TENANT vol 27(1) (Reissue) para 490); s 76(1)(C), Sch 2 Pt III (conveyance by mortgage or charge: see MORTGAGE); and s 76(1)(D), Sch 2 Pt IV (conveyance by mortgage or charge of freehold property subject to a rent or of leasehold property: see MORTGAGE). As to the significance of the term 'beneficial owner' see note 6 infra.

3   See ibid s 76(1)(E), Sch 2 Pt V (conveyance by way of settlement: see SETTLEMENTS para 690 post).

4   See ibid s 76(1)(F), Sch 2 Pt VI (s 76(1)(F) and Sch 2 Pt VI both amended by the Mental Health Act 1959 s 149(2), Sch 8 Pt I) (any conveyance: see the text and notes 14–16 infra). Where a person is not expressed to convey in any of the capacities mentioned in the text, no covenant as to title is implied by virtue of the Law of Property Act 1925 s 76 (as amended): s 76(4) (amended by the Mental Health Act 1959 Sch 8 Pt I).

5   As to the covenants for title implied in a mortgage see the Law of Property Act 1925 s 76(1)(C), (D), Sch 2 Pts III, IV; note 2 supra; and MORTGAGE.

6   It seems that the covenants are implied only when the grantor is in fact a beneficial owner and conveys as such: see *Pilkington v Wood* [1953] Ch 770 at 777, [1953] 2 All ER 810 at 813 per Harman J. See also *Fay v Miller, Wilkins & Co* [1941] Ch 360 at 362, [1941] 2 All ER 18 at 23, CA, per Greene MR; *Re Robertson's Application* [1969] 1 All ER 257n at 258, [1969] 1 WLR 109 at 112 per Megarry J. A different view was expressed in *Re Ray* [1896] 1 Ch 468 at 474–475, CA, per Kay LJ, who said that such words as 'beneficial owner' were merely a compendious means of bringing particular covenants into a conveyance. See also *David v Sabin* [1893] 1 Ch 523, CA (tenant for life expressed to convey as beneficial owner); *Wise v Whitburn* [1924] 1 Ch 460) (trustees expressed to convey as personal representatives); *Parker v Judkin* [1931] 1 Ch 475, CA (personal representatives expressed to convey as beneficial owners). The practice now, where there is a doubt whether the covenants will be implied, is to insert an express covenant that the covenants are to be implied as if the conveying party were a beneficial owner (or trustee etc) and was expressed to convey and did convey as such. Alternatively, the vendor could covenant in the terms set out in the relevant part of the Law of Property Act 1925 Sch 2 (as amended). A liquidator or receiver is sometimes expressed to convey as trustee (or mortgagee), but it would seem preferable for express covenants to be given. Where a person is expressed to convey by direction of a person expressed to direct as beneficial owner, the person giving the direction is deemed to convey and to be expressed to convey as beneficial owner: s 76(2). Special provision is made for cases where a wife conveys and is expressed to convey as beneficial owner and her husband also conveys and is expressed to convey as beneficial owner (s 76(3)), but this provision is virtually obsolete, since a wife can now dispose of her property without the concurrence of her husband (see HUSBAND AND WIFE).

7   As to the covenant for right to convey see paras 343–344 post.

8   As to the covenant for quiet enjoyment see para 345 post.

9   As to the covenant for freedom from incumbrances see para 346 post.

10   See the Law of Property Act 1925 s 76(1)(A), Sch 2 Pt I; and note 2 supra. As to the covenant for further assurance see paras 347–348 post. As to covenants implied on the sale of land subject to a rentcharge see

para 293 ante. As to restrictions on the creation of rentcharges see the Rentcharges Act 1977 s 2 (as amended); and RENTCHARGES AND ANNUITIES vol 39(2) (Reissue) para 774 et seq.

11 See the Law of Property Act 1925 s 76(1)(A), (B), Sch 2 Pts I, II; note 2 supra; para 301 ante; and LANDLORD AND TENANT vol 27(1) (Reissue) para 490.

12 See ibid Sch 2 Pt I. See also *David v Sabin* [1893] 1 Ch 523 at 531, CA, where it was said that the covenants for right to convey, for quiet enjoyment, for freedom from incumbrances and for further assurance are parts of one entire covenant controlled by the introductory words of the enactment; *Chivers & Sons Ltd v Secretary of State for Air* [1955] Ch 585 at 597–598, [1955] 2 All ER 607 at 611–612. The words 'otherwise than by purchase for value' are not an exception from the covenant, but part of the covenant itself, and in an action for breach of the covenant the onus is on the plaintiff to prove that the act relied on as constituting the breach was done by a person from whom the defendant derived title otherwise than by purchase for value: *Stoney v Eastbourne RDC* [1927] 1 Ch 367, CA. Purchase for value does not include a conveyance in consideration of marriage: see the Law of Property Act 1925 Sch 2 Pt I. The covenants implied in a mortgage are not so limited: see MORTGAGE.

13 *David v Sabin* [1893] 1 Ch 523 at 532, CA. See also eg *Browning v Wright* (1799) 2 Bos & P 13 at 22; *Thackeray v Wood* (1865) 6 B & S 766 at 773, Ex Ch; Sugden's Law of Vendors and Purchasers (14th Edn, 1862) 574; Davidson's Concise Precedents in Conveyancing (21st Edn, 1926) 143; 1 Dart's Law relating to Vendors and Purchasers (8th Edn, 1929) 494–495; 1 Williams Law relating to Vendors and Purchasers of Real Estate and Chattels Real (4th Edn, 1936) 670. For this purpose a settlement on marriage is not treated as made for value; the vendor claiming under such a settlement covenants against the acts of the settlor and his representatives (1 Dart's Law relating to Vendors and Purchasers (8th Edn, 1929) 494), and this is the effect of the covenants implied by statute: see note 12 supra. Where a purchaser decided to accept a defective title, he was held to be entitled to unqualified covenants: see *Re Geraghty and Lyons' Contract* (1919) 53 ILT 57. See also *Page v Midland Rly Co* [1894] 1 Ch 11, CA; *Great Western Rly Co v Fisher* [1905] 1 Ch 316; and para 343 post. Where the covenants in the conveyance are not in accordance with the contract, the conveyance may be rectified: *Strait v Fenner* [1912] 2 Ch 504 at 518. See also *Butler v Mountview Estates Ltd* [1951] 2 KB 563, [1951] 1 All ER 693. As to rectification see paras 354–355 post. The vendor's covenant for title includes the acts and omissions of persons claiming through him: *David v Sabin* supra at 532. A lessee becoming purchaser is entitled as such to require of the vendor only such covenants as are appropriate between vendor and purchaser: *Paton v Brebner* (1819) 1 Bli 42 at 69, HL.

14 Tenants for life and co-owners normally convey as trustees: see paras 339–340 post.

15 The implied covenant applies to assents made after 1925 as well as to conveyances by deed: see the Law of Property Act 1925 s 76(1)(F), (8) (s 76(1)(F) as amended: see note 4 supra). It seems that the covenant is implied only where the vendor both conveys and is expressed to convey as personal representative: see *Fay v Miller, Wilkins & Co* [1941] Ch 360 at 362, [1941] 2 All ER 18 at 23, CA; and note 6 supra. It has been said that because the provisions of the Law of Property Act 1925 s 76(1)(F), Sch 2 Pt VI (both as amended) refer to the personal representative 'of a deceased person', the conveyance should be entered into as personal representative of the particular person deceased, and not merely as personal representative; but objection is not normally taken where the conveyance is simply 'as personal representative'; cf the statutory forms of conveyance and assents by personal representatives contained in Sch 5 Forms 5, 8, 9.

16 See ibid s 76(1)(F), Sch 2 Pt VI (both as amended: see note 4 supra). See also *Wise v Whitburn* [1924] 1 Ch 460 (assent by executors to bequest of premises prior to sale).

17 See the Law of Property Act 1925 s 76(7). As so varied or extended, a covenant is, so far as may be, to operate in the like manner, and with all the like incidents, effects, and consequences, as if the variations or extensions were directed by s 76 (as amended) to be implied: see s 76(7). The text here follows the statute, but the variation or extension is inserted in the actual conveyance or assent and there is no occasion for a separate deed.

18 See *Page v Midland Rly Co* [1894] 1 Ch 11, CA; *May v Platt* [1900] 1 Ch 616.

19 See *Watling v Lewis* [1911] 1 Ch 414; and DEEDS AND OTHER INSTRUMENTS.

20 See the Law of Property (Joint Tenants) Act 1964 s 1 (as amended); and para 74 ante. Where the new law applies (see paras 349–351 post), this provision is modified so that the survivor (or his personal representative) is deemed to be solely and beneficially interested only if the transfer includes a statement that he is so interested: see para 74 ante.

339. Tenant for life. Where a tenant for life sells under his statutory powers[1], he conveys as trustee, since the legal estate is vested in him on the trusts of the settlement[2]. Where an estate owner conveys under a special settlement made to overreach equitable interests, he should convey as beneficial owner[3]. This should also be done, it would appear, under an ordinary settlement where the estate owner is absolutely and beneficially entitled subject only to equitable interests which will be overreached by the conveyance.

1   As to the statutory powers of a tenant for life see SETTLEMENTS para 775 et seq.
2   See SETTLEMENTS para 775 post. Subject to certain exceptions, it has not been possible to create a new settlement under the Settled Land Act 1925 since the coming into force of the Trusts of Land and Appointment of Trustees Act 1996 on 1 January 1997: see REAL PROPERTY vol 39(2) (Reissue) para 65; SETTLEMENTS para 676 et seq post.
3   See para 272 ante.

340. Co-owners etc. Where the vendors are tenants in common or beneficial joint owners, they will be trustees of land and will usually convey as trustees[1]. If, however, being also beneficially entitled, they convey as beneficial owners, the liability may in the case of tenants in common be expressly restricted to their respective shares[2].

In the case of a sub-purchase, the purchaser usually conveys to the sub-purchaser as trustee[3].

1   See REAL PROPERTY vol 39(2) (Reissue) para 189 et seq, 207 et seq.
2   It has been said that in the case of joint tenants such a restriction is not warranted, since if the title of one is invalid the whole conveyance is invalid. As to the interests of the covenantors affecting the construction of the covenant as joint and several see DEEDS AND OTHER INSTRUMENTS.
3   See para 280 note 3 ante.

341. Vendors by whom no covenants for title are given. A purchaser from the Crown cannot require covenants for title[1], and the official custodian for charities enters into no covenants[2]. It is not the general practice to give covenants for title in a voluntary conveyance[3] or in a conveyance where the vendor has only a possessory title[4].

1   See CROWN PROPERTY vol 12(1) (Reissue) para 293.
2   See the Charities Act 1993 ss 2, 21, 22; and CHARITIES vol 5(2) (Reissue) paras 269, 275. Although the official custodian will be named as a party to the conveyance, the managing trustees of the charity will normally execute the conveyance in his name and on his behalf: see s 22(2); and CHARITIES vol 5(2) (Reissue) para 275. As to the official custodian for charities see CHARITIES vol 5(2) (Reissue) para 269. As to the disposition of registered and unregistered land by transfer see para 262 note 2 ante.
3   Where a settlement is created, the grantor may convey as settlor: see para 350 ante; and SETTLEMENTS para 690 post. If no settlement is created, it is doubtful whether the words 'as settlor' will imply any covenant: see para 338 note 4 ante.
    Subject to certain exceptions, it has not been possible to create a new settlement under the Settled Land Act 1925 since the coming into force of the Trusts of Land and Appointment of Trustees Act 1996 on 1 January 1997: see REAL PROPERTY vol 39(2) (Reissue) para 65; SETTLEMENTS para 676 et seq post.
4   Where the contract provides that the purchaser is to accept such title as the vendor has, no action would lie if covenants for title were given and the title proved defective: *May v Platt* [1900] 1 Ch 616; *George Wimpey & Co Ltd v Sohn* [1967] Ch 487 at 509, [1966] 1 All ER 232 at 240, CA, per Russell LJ.

342. Devolution of covenants for title. The burden of the covenants for title falls upon the covenantor (usually the vendor) personally, and after his death is enforceable, like any other liability, against his estate[1]. The benefit of the covenant runs with the purchaser's estate[2] and the covenant is enforceable by subsequent purchasers, provided they take that estate[3]. This is so in the case of express covenants for title[4], and the same rule is applied by statute to the covenants implied[5] by the use of the statutory words[6]. Apparently the statutory covenants given on the conveyance of an equitable estate run with that estate; but express covenants for title only run with the legal estate, and the equitable owner must rely on his right to sue in the name of the covenantee or his assigns[7]. If on a subsequent sale the land has been sub-divided, a purchaser of part of the land who takes the estate of the original purchaser in that part is entitled to sue on the covenants in respect of his part[8]. Where the covenant for right to convey has been broken and the original covenantee has not sued on it, his successors in title may do so notwithstanding that it is not a continuing covenant[9].

1   See 2 Dart's Law relating to Vendors and Purchasers (8th Edn, 1929) 661. See also generally EXECUTORS
     AND ADMINISTRATORS. If the vendor becomes bankrupt, the liability is provable in the bankruptcy and
     if not proved will be discharged: see *Hardy v Fothergill* (1888) 13 App Cas 351, HL; *Davis v Tollemache*
     (1856) 2 Jur NS 1181; and BANKRUPTCY AND INSOLVENCY vol 3(2) (Reissue) para 481. As to the
     covenant for further assurance see para 347 post. Where the vendor is a company, and breach of a
     covenant for title comes to light only after the dissolution of the company, no action lies against the
     contributories: *Butler v Broadhead* [1975] Ch 97, [1974] 2 All ER 401.
2   As to the circumstances in which the benefit of a covenant will run with land generally see paras 331–332
     ante.
3   Where the original conveyance has been obtained by fraud, an assignee for value without notice of the
     fraud can sue on the covenants for title, although the original covenantee could not do so: *David v Sabin*
     [1893] 1 Ch 523, CA. As to the disposition of registered and unregistered land by transfer see para 262
     note 2 ante.
4   *Middlemore v Goodale* (1638) Cro Car 503; *King v Jones* (1814) 5 Taunt 418 (affd sub nom *Jones v King*
     (1815) 4 M & S 188) (covenant for further assurance); *Campbell v Lewis* (1820) 3 B & Ald 392 (covenant
     for quiet enjoyment). See also *Noke v Awder* (1595) Cro Eliz 373 at 436; *Rogers v Hosegood* [1900] 2 Ch
     388 at 396, CA, per Farwell J. The covenantee should, however, have an estate in the land at the time
     of the covenant: 2 Dart's Law relating to Vendors and Purchasers (8th Edn, 1929) 661. As to the necessity
     for the subsequent purchaser to take the estate of the original covenantee so as to create the privity of
     estate which enables the covenant to run with the land see *Roach v Wadham* (1805) 6 East 289 (a sale by
     a person with power to appoint was held to be an appointment and the purchaser's (appointee's) heir was
     not liable therefore on the covenant for rent in arrear); *Onward Building Society v Smithson* [1893] 1 Ch 1,
     CA (a conveyance of land was obtained by fraud and mortgaged to the plaintiffs, who were unable to sue
     the vendors on their covenants). Cf *Webb v Russell* (1789) 3 Term Rep 393 at 402.
5   See para 338 ante.
6   See the Law of Property Act 1925 s 76(6). The benefit of the implied covenant is annexed and incident
     to, and goes with, the estate or interest of the implied covenantee, and is capable of being enforced by
     every person in whom that estate or interest is, for the whole or any part of it, from time to time vested:
     s 76(6). See also *David v Sabin* [1893] 1 Ch 523, CA.
        As to the repeal of the Law of Property Act 1925 s 76 (as amended) in relation to dispositions of
     property made on or after 1 July 1995 see para 337 ante.
7   See 1 Williams Law relating to Vendors and Purchasers of Real Estate and Chattels Real (4th Edn, 1936)
     676; *Rogers v Hosegood* [1900] 2 Ch 388 at 404, CA.
8   *Twynam v Pickard* (1818) 2 B & Ald 105; *Rogers v Hosegood* [1900] 2 Ch 388 at 396, CA. See also the Law
     of Property Act 1925 s 76(6); and note 6 supra.
9   *Kingdon v Nottle* (1815) 4 M & S 53, explained in *Spoor v Green* (1874) LR 9 Exch 99 at 111. See further
     para 343 post.

B. PARTICULAR COVENANTS

(A) Covenant for Right to Convey

343. Nature of the covenant. The covenant for right to convey is a covenant for
title, but the covenant for quiet enjoyment is a covenant relating to possession[1]. This
distinction affects both the date when the covenant is broken and the measure of damages.
A covenant for title is an assurance to the purchaser that the grantor has the very estate in
quantity and quality which he purports to convey[2], and it is broken by the existence of
an adverse right such as a right of way[3], or any outstanding interest, charge or claim[4]
which may prevent the purchaser from enjoying this estate[5]. There is also a breach where,
by the vendor's omission to prevent the acquisition of an adverse title by possession[6], he
has no title to part of the land which he purports to convey[7]. Hence the covenant for
right to convey is not a continuing covenant, but is broken once and for all at the time
of the conveyance if there is then a defect in title which prevents the vendor from
conveying the estate which he purports to convey[8]. Consequently time begins to run
immediately against an action for breach of the covenant[9]. The purchaser can sue on the
covenant notwithstanding that the defect in title is disclosed by a recital in the
conveyance[10]. The purchaser is entitled to a conveyance expressed to be subject to such
incumbrances as are mentioned in the contract[11].

1   See *Howell v Richards* (1809) 11 East 633 at 642. For the early recognition of the distinction between covenants for title and possession see *Gregory v Mayo* (1677) 3 Keb 744 at 755. A covenant for seisin was treated as a covenant for lawful seisin, and was equivalent to a covenant for right to convey the estate expressed to be conveyed: *Gray v Briscoe* (1607) Noy 142; *Cookes v Fowns* (1661) 1 Keb 95; *Nervin v Munns* (1682) 3 Lev 46; *Browning v Wright* (1799) 2 Bos & P 13 at 27.

2   *Howell v Richards* (1809) 11 East 633 at 642. The covenant will not be qualified so as to extend to less than the interest expressed to be conveyed, unless such a qualification is clearly indicated: *May v Platt* [1900] 1 Ch 616, explaining *Delmer v M'Cabe* (1863) 14 ICLR 377.

3   *Turner v Moon* [1901] 2 Ch 825; *Great Western Rly Co v Fisher* [1905] 1 Ch 316 at 321.

4   See 2 Williams Law relating to Vendors and Purchasers of Real Estate and Chattels Real (4th Edn, 1936) 1077–1078.

5   In an action on the covenant, it is necessary to plead the material facts alleged to constitute the breach: see PLEADING.

6   See the Limitation Act 1980 ss 15, 17; and cf LIMITATION OF ACTIONS vol 28 (Reissue) para 919 et seq.

7   *Eastwood v Ashton* [1915] AC 900, HL; *Jackson v Bishop* (1979) 48 P & CR 57, CA; *AJ Dunning & Sons (Shopfitters) Ltd v Sykes & Son (Poole) Ltd* [1987] Ch 287, [1987] 1 All ER 700, CA.

8   *Turner v Moon* [1901] 2 Ch 825. The breach of such a covenant was spoken of as a continuing breach in *Kingdon v Nottle* (1815) 4 M & S 53 at 57; but see *Spoor v Green* (1874) LR 9 Exch 99 at 111 per Bramwell B, explaining *Kingdon v Nottle* supra.

9   *Spoor v Green* (1874) LR 9 Exch 99. See also LIMITATION OF ACTIONS vol 28 (Reissue) para 883.

10   *Page v Midland Rly Co* [1894] 1 Ch 11, CA; *Great Western Rly Co v Fisher* [1905] 1 Ch 316 at 322; *Re Geraghty and Lyons' Contract* (1919) 53 ILT 57. See also DEEDS AND OTHER INSTRUMENTS. Generally, mere notice to the purchaser of a defect in title does not bar his right to recover: *Levett v Withrington* (1688) 1 Lut 317. As to the position in the case of registered land see the Land Registration Rules 1925, SR & O 1925/1093, r 77 (amended by SI 1995/377). As to registered land generally see LAND REGISTRATION.

11   *Re Wallis and Barnard's Contract* [1899] 2 Ch 515. The purchaser is subject to a wide range of incumbrances: see the Standard Conditions of Sale (3rd Edn), condition 3.1.2; and para 55 ante. The transfer is to have effect as if the disposition is expressly made subject to all matters to which the property is sold subject under the terms of the contract: condition 4.5.3. As to the Standard Conditions of Sale see para 1 note 9 ante. As to the disposition of registered and unregistered land by transfer see para 262 note 2 ante.

344. Measure of damages. The measure of damages is the difference between the value of the property as purported to be conveyed and its value as it actually passes to the purchaser[1]. Hence a purchaser who loses the land can only recover the amount of the purchase money and not the value of subsequent improvements[2].

1   *Turner v Moon* [1901] 2 Ch 825; *Eastwood v Ashton* [1913] 2 Ch 39 at 55 (revsd [1914] 1 Ch 68, CA, but restored [1915] AC 900, HL, the question of damages not being discussed on the appeals). In *Gray v Briscoe* (1607) Noy 142, copyhold was conveyed as freehold and the measure of damages was the difference between the values of the copyhold and freehold land. Cf *Wace v Bickerton* (1850) 3 De G & Sm 751. See also *Conodate Investments Ltd v Bentley Quarry Engineering Co Ltd* (1970) 216 Estates Gazette 1407. The value of the property as expressed to be conveyed is usually the amount of the purchase money stated in the conveyance, but this is not so if the purchase money does not correspond to the actual value: see *Jenkins v Jones* (1882) 9 QBD 128, CA. As to conditions providing for compensation for misdescription see para 110 ante.

   As to the disposition of registered and unregistered land by transfer see para 262 note 2 ante.

2   Rawle's A Practical Treatise on the Law of Covenants for Title (5th Edn, 1887) s 158.

(B) Covenants for Quiet Enjoyment and Freedom from Incumbrances

345. Covenant for quiet enjoyment. The covenant for quiet enjoyment is a future covenant[1]. Consequently there is no breach of the covenant until the covenantee is disturbed in his enjoyment[2]. The implied covenant for quiet enjoyment extends to lawful interruption or disturbance by the person who conveys or any person conveying by his direction, or rightfully claiming by, through, under or in trust for the person who conveys or any person conveying by his direction, or by, through or under anyone (not being a person claiming in respect of an estate or interest subject to which the conveyance is expressly made) through whom the person who conveys derives title, otherwise than by purchase for value[3]. A covenant for quiet enjoyment limited to lawful disturbance by the covenantor or any person claiming under or in trust for him[4] is not broken by claims under title paramount to that of the covenantor, or by tortious acts other than those of the covenantor himself[5]. Since the covenant is a future covenant, the damages seem to be measured by the loss to the covenantee when the disturbance takes place. Thus, in case of eviction, the damages include the value of improvements which he has made[6].

1   See *Ireland v Bircham* (1835) 2 Scott 207. The covenant for quiet enjoyment and the covenant for freedom from incumbrances are in effect a single covenant that the covenantee is to enjoy free from incumbrances: see para 346 post.

2   Whereas the covenant for right to convey is a covenant for title (see para 343 ante), that for quiet enjoyment is an assurance against disturbance consequent upon a defective title: *Howell v Richards* (1809) 11 East 633 at 641. See also *Conodate Investments Ltd v Bentley Quarry Engineering Co Ltd* (1970) 216 Estates Gazette 1407; and LIMITATION OF ACTIONS vol 28 (Reissue) para 883.

3   See the Law of Property Act 1925 s 76(1)(A), Sch 2 Pt I; and para 338 ante. As to the repeal of the Law of Property Act 1925 s 76 (as amended), Sch 2 Pts I–VI (as amended) in relation to dispositions of property made on or after 1 July 1995 see para 337 ante.
      As to the implied covenants for title generally see para 338 ante; and as to the disposition of registered and unregistered land by transfer see para 262 note 2 ante.

4   As to the effect of a covenant for quiet enjoyment, and the matters which constitute a breach of the covenant see *Young v Raincock* (1849) 7 CB 310; *Browne v Flower* [1911] 1 Ch 219. See also LANDLORD AND TENANT vol 27(1) (Reissue) para 406 et seq. As to covenants for quiet enjoyment in mining leases see MINES, MINERALS AND QUARRIES vol 31 (Reissue) para 347. A judgment which does not interfere with the possession is not a breach: *Howard v Maitland* (1883) 11 QBD 695, CA; cf *Hunt v Danvers* (1680) T Raym 370. As to arrears of quit rent see *Howes v Brushfield* (1803) 3 East 491; and Sugden's Law of Vendors and Purchasers (14th Edn, 1862) 602. As to disturbance under title paramount see also *Woodhouse v Jenkins* (1832) 9 Bing 431. After conveyance the court does not necessarily interfere by injunction to prevent illegal distress by the vendor on tenants: *Drake v West* (1853) 22 LJ Ch 375. In an action on the covenant for quiet enjoyment the plaintiff must allege the facts constituting the disturbance, and that the disturbance was lawful, with sufficient particularity to show the breach of covenant: *Foster v Pierson* (1792) 4 Term Rep 617. See also *Wotton v Hele* (1670) 2 Wms Saund 175 at 181 note (10).

5   See *Celsteel Ltd v Alton House Holdings Ltd (No 2)* [1987] 2 All ER 240, [1987] 1 WLR 291, CA; LANDLORD AND TENANT vol 27(1) (Reissue) paras 406–407.

6   This is in accordance with the ordinary rule as to damages, and is supported by *Bunny v Hopkinson* (1859) 27 Beav 565. See *Rolph v Crouch* (1867) LR 3 Exch 44; and cf *Duckworth v Ewart* (1863) 10 Jur NS 214. See also 2 Williams Law relating to Vendors and Purchasers of Real Estate and Chattels Real (4th Edn, 1936) 1090. A lessee, in case of eviction, recovers under the covenant for quiet enjoyment the value of the term to him: see LANDLORD AND TENANT vol 27(1) (Reissue) para 417. See also Rawle's A Practical Treatise on the Law of Covenants for Title (5th Edn, 1887) s 169, where the result is explained on grounds peculiar to leases. However, the construction of the covenant should be the same whether it is in a lease or a conveyance on sale; and the rule as to leases supports the statement in the text. Where the improvements effected by the purchaser are in pursuance of the contract of sale (eg where he erects houses out of which the vendor is to receive a rent), there is additional reason for including in the damages the value of the buildings: Rawle's A Practical Treatise on the Law of Covenants for Title (5th Edn, 1887) s 170. In the absence of evidence of increase of value, the damages are the original value: *Jenkins v Jones* (1882) 9 QBD 128, CA. The damages may include the costs of litigation upon an adverse claim: *Sutton v Baillie* (1891) 65 LT 528; and see 2 Dart's Law relating to Vendors and Purchasers (8th Edn, 1929) 674 et seq. See also LANDLORD AND TENANT vol 27(1) (Reissue) para 417. As to mental distress as a head of damage, and as to the possibility of aggravated or exemplary damages where the vendor's wrongful conduct is also a tort, see DAMAGES vol 12(1) (Reissue) para 1113 et seq; LANDLORD AND TENANT vol 27(1) (Reissue) para 417.

346. Covenant for freedom from incumbrances. In the covenants for title implied by statute on a conveyance for valuable consideration as beneficial owner[1], the covenant against incumbrances follows the covenant for quiet enjoyment as part of it[2]. The covenant against incumbrances is consequently a future covenant, like the covenant for quiet enjoyment[3], and the two are in effect a single covenant that the covenantee is to enjoy the land free from incumbrances[4]. The mere existence of an incumbrance does not give the right to sue on the covenant against incumbrances; there must be interruption of enjoyment by a claim or demand on the purchaser[5].

An incumbrance has been said to be every right to or interest in the land which may subsist in third persons to the diminution in the value of the land, but consistent with the passing of the fee in the conveyance[6]. It will include a mortgage[7], charge or lien capable of being enforced against the purchaser, an easement and a subsisting term, unless, in the case of a term, the real subject of the purchase was the reversion on the term[8], and probably also a restrictive covenant enforceable against the purchaser[9]. Apart from the effect of the statutory provisions as to the registration of local land charges or of any relevant conditions contained in the contract for sale[10], the question whether expenses payable to a local authority in respect of work done under statutory powers constitute an incumbrance depends upon whether the expenses are merely a liability of the landowner personally[11] or are charged upon the land and whether, if they are a charge upon the land, the charge attached before completion[12].

1   See para 338 ante. As to the covenants implied on a sale by a trustee, mortgagee, personal representative or settlor see para 338 ante. As to the disposition of registered and unregistered land by transfer see para 262 note 2 ante.
2   See the Law of Property Act 1925 s 76(1)(A), Sch 2 Pt I; and para 338 ante. As to the repeal of the Law of Property Act 1925 s 76 (as amended), Sch 2 Pts I–VI (as amended) in relation to dispositions of property made on or after 1 July 1995 see para 337 ante.
3   As to the covenant for quiet enjoyment see para 345 ante.
4   See *Vane v Lord Barnard* (1708) Gilb Ch 6 at 7; Rawle's A Practical Treatise on the Law of Covenants for Title (5th Edn, 1887) s 73 p 87 note (1).
5   *Nottidge v Dering, Raban v Dering* [1909] 2 Ch 647 at 656 (affd [1910] 1 Ch 297, CA); cf *Turner v Moon* [1901] 2 Ch 825.
6   Rawle's A Practical Treatise on the Law of Covenants for Title (5th Edn, 1887) s 75.
7   See eg *David v Sabin* [1893] 1 Ch 523, CA. As to the mortgages which are registrable as land charges and the effect of failure to register see LAND CHARGES vol 26 (Reissue) paras 529, 543; MORTGAGE.
8   See Rawle's A Practical Treatise on the Law of Covenants for Title (5th Edn, 1887) s 78. See also *Haverington's Case* (1586) Owen 6. If the purchaser has paid off a mortgage or charge, or bought in an easement, he can recover the amount so paid and any expense which he has incurred, but until he has incurred some loss, it seems that he cannot sue on the covenant, since according to the English form, the covenant is a future covenant: see Rawle's A Practical Treatise on the Law of Covenants for Title (5th Edn, 1887) s 188 et seq.
9   See *Cato v Thompson* (1882) 9 QBD 616 at 618, CA; *Ellis v Rogers* (1885) 29 ChD 661 at 665, CA; cf *Phillips v Caldcleugh* (1868) LR 4 QB 159 at 163. As to the registration as land charges of restrictive covenants entered into after 1925 and the effect of failure to register see para 10 ante; and LAND CHARGES vol 26 (Reissue) paras 535, 543.
10   See para 126 ante.
11   See *Egg v Blayney* (1888) 21 QBD 107, DC.
12   See *Re Bettesworth and Richer* (1888) 37 ChD 535; *Stock v Meakin* [1900] 1 Ch 683, CA; *Re Allen and Driscoll's Contract* [1904] 2 Ch 226, CA. See para 126 ante.

(C) Covenant for Further Assurance

347. Effect of covenant for further assurance. Under the covenant for further assurance the vendor is bound to do such further acts for the purpose of perfecting the purchaser's title as the purchaser may reasonably require[1] and the vendor can properly do[2]. The purchaser should tender a draft of the further conveyance to which he considers that he is entitled[3], and should tender or offer to pay the vendor's costs[4]. The vendor is entitled to a reasonable time to procure professional assistance[5]. If the conveyance is proper and the vendor declines to execute it or to do any act which the purchaser can properly require, this constitutes a breach of the covenant[6]. The purchaser cannot, by means of the covenant for further assurance, obtain a greater estate than that which was the subject of the original conveyance[7], although if the vendor's title was defective the vendor may be required to assure an estate which he has got in since, whether by devise[8] or by purchase[9]. No further assurance can be required where there was an estoppel created in favour of the purchaser which is fed by the vendor's subsequent acquisition of the legal estate[10].

1   See Rawle's A Practical Treatise on the Law of Covenants for Title (5th Edn, 1887) s 99. Such acts include the removal of a judgment if charged on the land, or other incumbrance: *King v Jones* (1814) 5 Taunt 418 (affd sub nom *Jones v King* (1815) 4 M & S 188); *Re Jones, Farrington v Forrester* [1893] 2 Ch 461 at 471. As to a request for further assurance see *Bennet's Case* (1582) Cro Eliz 9 ('such assurance as purchaser's counsel should advise'; the vendor must be notified of such advice and given time to consider it). The vendor's death within the time limited ends the covenant: *Nash v Ashton* (1682) T Jo 195. Cf *Blicke v Dymoke* (1824) 2 Bing 105. The assurance must be necessary (*Warn v Bickford* (1819) 7 Price 550; subsequent proceedings (1821) 9 Price 43), and the execution of it possible (*Pet and Cally's Case* (1589) 1 Leon 304 (party mentally disordered); *Nash v Ashton* supra).

2   See *Heath v Crealock* (1874) 10 Ch App 22 at 31.

3   2 Dart's Law relating to Vendors and Purchasers (8th Edn, 1929) 673. The draft is usually settled by counsel and accompanied by counsel's opinion as to the necessity and propriety of the further assurance, although this is not necessary: *Blicke v Dymoke* (1824) 2 Bing 105. Under the early form of covenant, the covenant was to make such assurance as the purchaser's counsel should advise: *Rosewel's Case* (1593) 5 Co Rep 19b; *Bennet's Case* (1582) Cro Eliz 9; *Baker v Bulstrode* (1674) 2 Lev 95; *Lassels v Catterton* (1670) 1 Mod Rep 67. As to the preparation of the conveyance or transfer see para 262 et seq ante. As to the disposition of registered and unregistered land by transfer see para 262 note 2 ante.

4   2 Dart's Law relating to Vendors and Purchasers (8th Edn, 1929) 673. As to the costs of the conveyance see para 323 et seq ante.

5   *Bennet's Case* (1582) Cro Eliz 9.

6   Rawle's A Practical Treatise on the Law of Covenants for Title (5th Edn, 1887) s 99. In an action on the covenant, the facts showing the necessity and propriety for the further assurance, and the defendant's refusal to execute it, should be alleged: see PLEADING.

7   *Davis v Tollemache* (1856) 2 Jur NS 1181.

8   *Smith v Baker* (1842) 1 Y & C Ch Cas 223. The devise would now have to be made effectual by assent: see EXECUTORS AND ADMINISTRATORS.

9   See *Taylor v Debar* (1676) 1 Cas in Ch 274; 2 Cas in Ch 212; *Otter v Lord Vaux* (1856) 6 De GM & G 638; Sugden's Law of Vendors and Purchasers (14th Edn, 1862) 612. It seems that the vendor is under the same liability in equity, even apart from a covenant for further assurance: *Noel v Bewley* (1829) 3 Sim 103; *Smith v Osborne* (1857) 6 HL Cas 375; *Re Bridgwater's Settlement, Partridge v Ward* [1910] 2 Ch 342. See also EQUITY vol 16 (Reissue) para 818; ESTOPPEL vol 16 (Reissue) para 1034. Where, however, the covenant for further assurance is, with the other covenants, limited in the usual way to the acts of the vendor and his predecessors since the last sale, the vendor can, it seems, only be required to assure an after-acquired estate which is necessary to satisfy this limited covenant: Rawle's A Practical Treatise on the Law of Covenants for Title (5th Edn, 1887) s 104. A vendor tenant in tail who has conveyed a base fee (which would now be an equitable interest) may be required to turn it into a fee simple: *Bankes v Small* (1887) 36 ChD 716, CA; and see REAL PROPERTY vol 39(2) (Reissue) para 136. Probably a purchaser who has not obtained the title deeds cannot obtain a covenant for their production under the covenant for further assurance, but his equitable right to production is usually sufficient without a covenant: see *Hallett v Middleton* (1826) 1 Russ 243; *Fain v Ayers* (1826) 2 Sim & St 533; and para 299 ante. The vendor can be required to execute a duplicate of the conveyance if the original has been destroyed through his fault or handed by him to a sub-purchaser of part: see *Bennett v Ingoldsby* (1676) Cas temp Finch 262; *Napper v Lord Allington* (1700) 1 Eq Cas Abr 166. In such cases, either the conveyance should bear an indorsement showing that it is a duplicate, or it should be expressed to be merely a deed of confirmation: see 2 Dart's Law relating to Vendors and Purchasers (8th Edn, 1929) 673. The deed of further assurance should not itself contain additional covenants of title by the vendor: *Coles v Kinder* (1620) Cro Jac 571; *Lassels v Catterton* (1670) 1 Mod Rep 67; Sugden's Law of Vendors and Purchasers (14th Edn, 1862) 615.

10   *Cumberland Court (Brighton) Ltd v Taylor* [1964] Ch 29, [1963] 2 All ER 536.

348. Remedy on the covenant. The purchaser may either bring an action for breach of the covenant for further assurance, or sue for specific performance[1]. In the former case the damages are the loss arising to him from the neglect to execute the assurance[2]. In the event of the vendor's bankruptcy, specific performance of the covenant can be enforced against his trustee in bankruptcy, against the vendor himself after his discharge, and also against his assigns, except such as take the legal estate for value without notice[3].

1   See Sugden's Law of Vendors and Purchasers (14th Edn, 1862) 612. As to the remedy of specific performance see generally SPECIFIC PERFORMANCE.
2   See *King v Jones* (1814) 5 Taunt 418 (affd sub nom *Jones v King* (1815) 4 M & S 188), where the purchaser's heir, who had been evicted, was awarded the amount of the purchase money. However, since there is no breach until the refusal to execute the further assurance, the damages may, perhaps, be the value of the land at this time where that value differs in amount from the purchase money: see para 345 ante. The action may be brought at once upon breach of covenant, but it is better to wait until the ultimate damage has been sustained, provided the statutory time-limit for an action to recover land is not exceeded: *King v Jones* supra at 428. As to the statutory time-limit see the Limitation Act 1980 s 8; and cf LIMITATION OF ACTIONS vol 28 (Reissue) para 881 et seq (action upon a specialty). See also ss 15, 17; and LIMITATION OF ACTIONS vol 28 (Reissue) para 919 et seq (action for recovery of land).
3   *Pye v Daubuz* (1792) 3 Bro CC 595; *Re Phelps, ex p Fripp* (1846) 1 De G 293. See also *Davis v Tollemache* (1856) 2 Jur NS 1181; and cf *Re Reis, ex p Clough* [1904] 2 KB 769 at 777, 781, CA (affd sub nom *Clough v Samuel* [1905] AC 442, HL) (covenant to settle after-acquired property).

(iii)   Dispositions made on or after 1 July 1995

349.   Covenants implied by statute. Covenants for title are no longer implied on the basis of the capacity in which the vendor conveys and is expressed to convey[1]. In dispositions made on or after 1 July 1995 the nature of the covenants implied will depend on whether the disposition is expressed to be made with full title guarantee or with limited title guarantee[2].

1   As to the old law see note 2 infra; and para 338 et seq ante. As to the disposition of registered and unregistered land by transfer see para 262 note 2 ante.
2   See the Law of Property (Miscellaneous Provisions) Act 1994 s 1(1), (2), (3). As to full title guarantee see para 350 post; and as to limited title guarantee see para 351 post. As to the covenants implied see Pt I (ss 1–13); and paras 350–351 post.
      Where a contract was made before 1 July 1995, but completion took place on or after that date, the disposition will normally be governed by the old law contained in the Law of Property Act 1925 s 76 (as amended) and the Land Registration Act 1925 s 24(1)(a) (both repealed in relation to dispositions of property made on or after 1 July 1995): see the Law of Property (Miscellaneous Provisions) Act 1994 s 11; and cf s 12. See also the Land Registration Rules 1925, SR & O 1925/1093, r 77 (amended by SI 1995/377); and LAND REGISTRATION. As to options granted before 1 July 1995 and exercised after that date see the Law of Property (Miscellaneous Provisions) Act 1994 s 13.

350.   Dispositions made with full title guarantee. In an instrument effecting or purporting to effect a disposition of property[1], and made with full title guarantee[2], certain covenants are implied by statute[3].

There is an implied covenant that the person making the disposition[4] (1) has the right (with the concurrence of any other person transferring the property) to dispose of the property as he purports to[5]; and (2) will at his own cost do all that he reasonably can to give the person to whom he disposes of the property the title he purports to give[6]. The latter obligation includes: (a) in relation to a disposition of a registered title, doing all that he can to ensure that the person to whom the disposition is made is entitled to be registered with at least the class of title registered immediately before the disposition; and (b) in relation to a disposition which gives rise to first registration of title, giving all reasonable assistance to establish to the satisfaction of the Chief Land Registrar the right of the person to whom the disposition is made to be registered as proprietor[7]. Subject to the terms of the instrument making the disposition, it is to be presumed (i) where the title to the interest is registered, that the disposition is of the whole of that interest; and

(ii) where the title is not registered, that, if the disposition is of a leasehold interest, the disposition is of the whole unexpired term of the lease and, in any other case, is of the fee simple[8].

There is also an implied covenant that the person making the disposition is disposing of the property free from all charges and incumbrances (whether monetary or not) and from all other rights exercisable by third parties, other than any charges, incumbrances or rights which he does not and could not reasonably be expected to know about[9].

Where the disposition is of leasehold property, there is an implied covenant that the lease is subsisting at the date of the disposition, and that there is no subsisting breach of a condition or tenant's obligation, and nothing which at that time would render the lease liable to forfeiture[10].

Where the disposition is a mortgage[11] of property subject to a rentcharge, or of leasehold land, there is an implied covenant that the mortgagor will fully and promptly observe and perform all the obligations relating to the rentcharge, or the obligations under the lease, as the case may be[12].

The operation of any of these covenants may be limited or extended by a term in the instrument of disposition[13].

The benefit of a covenant implied by virtue of these provisions is annexed and incident to, and goes with, the estate or interest of the person to whom the disposition is made; and is capable of being enforced by every person in whom that estate or interest is (in whole or in part) for the time being vested[14].

1   'Instrument' includes an instrument which is not a deed: Law of Property (Miscellaneous Provisions) Act 1994 s 1(4). 'Disposition' includes the creation of a term of years: s 1(4). The disposition need not be made for valuable consideration: see s 1(1). 'Property' includes a thing in action and any interest in real or personal property: s 1(4). As to the disposition of registered and unregistered land by transfer see para 262 note 2 ante.

2   The Standard Conditions of Sale (3rd Edn), condition 4.5.2 provides for a transfer with full title guarantee unless contrary provision is made. See also Special Condition 3. As to the Welsh equivalent of full title guarantee see the Law of Property (Miscellaneous Provisions) Act 1994 s 8(4)(a). As to the Standard Conditions of Sale see para 1 note 9 ante.

3   Ie by ibid Pt I (ss 1–13). The provisions of the Law of Property Act 1925 ss 81, 83 (s 81 as amended) apply to a covenant implied by virtue of the Law of Property (Miscellaneous Provisions) Act 1994 Pt I as they apply to a covenant implied by virtue of the Law of Property Act 1925): Law of Property (Miscellaneous Provisions) Act 1994 s 8(2).
     As to implied covenants in registered dispositions see the Land Registration Rules 1925, SR & O 1925/1093, rr 76A, 77A (both added by SI 1995/377); and LAND REGISTRATION vol 26 (Reissue) para 948 et seq.

4   Where in an instrument effecting or purporting to effect a disposition of property a person is expressed to direct the disposition, the Law of Property (Miscellaneous Provisions) Act 1994 Pt I applies to him as if he were the person making the disposition: s 8(3).

5   Ibid s 2(1)(a). The person making the disposition is not liable under the covenant implied by virtue of this provision or by virtue of s 3 (see the text and note 9 infra) or s 4 (see the text and note 10 infra) in respect of any particular matter to which the disposition is expressly made subject: s 6(1). Property is sold subject to a range of incumbrances (see the Standard Conditions of Sale (3rd Edn), condition 3.1.2; and para 55 ante), and a transfer has effect as if the disposition is expressly made subject to the incumbrances (see condition 4.5.3; and para 343 note 11 ante).
     Nor is the person making the disposition liable under such a covenant for anything (not falling within s 6(1)) which at the time of the disposition is within the actual knowledge, or which is a necessary consequence of facts that are then within the actual knowledge, of the person to whom the disposition is made: s 6(2). For this purpose, the Law of Property Act 1925 s 198 (as amended) (deemed notice by irtue of registration: see EQUITY vol 16 (Reissue) para 768; LAND CHARGES vol 26 (Reissue) para 516) is to be disregarded: Law of Property (Miscellaneous Provisions) Act 1994 s 6(3).

6   Ibid s 2(1)(b).
7   See ibid s 2(2). As to the Chief Land Registrar see LAND REGISTRATION vol 26 (Reissue) para 1203 et seq.
8   See ibid s 2(3).

9   See ibid s 3(1). See also note 5 supra. The covenant extends to liabilities imposed and rights conferred by or under any enactment, except to the extent that such liabilities and rights are, by reason of (1) being at the time of the disposition only potential liabilities and rights in relation to the property; or (2) being liabilities and rights imposed or conferred in relation to property generally, not such as to amount to defects of title: see s 3(2).

10   See ibid s 4(1). See also note 5 supra. If the disposition is the grant of an underlease, a reference to 'lease' means the lease out of which the underlease is created: see s 4(2).

     In the case of a leasehold property, the operation of this covenant is qualified by the Standard Conditions of Sale (3rd Edn), condition 3.2.2, which provides that the property is sold subject to any subsisting breach of a condition or tenant's obligation relating to the physical state of the property which renders the lease liable to forfeiture. There is a similar qualification where a sub-lease is granted: see condition 3.3.3. See also para 174 ante.

11   For these purposes, 'mortgage' includes charge, and 'mortgagor' is to be construed accordingly: Law of Property (Miscellaneous Provisions) Act 1994 s 5(4).

12   See ibid s 5(1), (2), (3).

13   See ibid s 8(1).

14   Ibid s 7.

351. Dispositions made with limited title guarantee. Where the disposition[1] is expressed to be made with limited title guarantee, the implied covenants are similar to those implied in the case of dispositions made with full title guarantee[2], except that the implied covenant to transfer free from third party rights[3] is modified. The implied covenant is that the person making the disposition has not since the last disposition for value (1) charged or incumbered the property[4] by means of any charge or incumbrance which subsists at the time when the disposition is made, or granted third party rights in relation to the property which so subsist; or (2) suffered the property to be so charged or incumbered or subjected to any such rights, and that he is not aware that anyone else has done so since the last disposition for value[5]. In other words, under this qualified covenant the vendor does not undertake liability for actions of a predecessor in title.

1   For the meaning of 'disposition' see para 350 note 1 ante. As to the disposition of registered and unregistered land by transfer see para 262 note 2 ante.

2   See para 350 ante.

3   See para 350 ante.

4   For the meaning of 'property' see para 350 note 1 ante.

5   Law of Property (Miscellaneous Provisions) Act 1994 s 3(3). As to the Welsh equivalent of limited title guarantee see s 8(4)(b).

(3) PARTIES' REMEDIES AFTER COMPLETION

(i) In general

352. Rectification or rescission. Where, owing to mutual mistake, the transfer does not carry out the intention of the parties, it may be rectified[1]. Where the transaction has been induced by fraud or by mutual mistake of a fundamental character, in a proper case the court will order rescission of the sale even after transfer[2]. Where the transaction has been induced by an innocent misrepresentation, rescission can be ordered after transfer; but the court has a discretion to award damages in lieu of rescission[3].

1   See paras 354–355 post. As to the disposition of registered and unregistered land by transfer see para 262 note 2 ante.

2   See para 356 et seq post. As to the repudiation of a sale before completion under the provisions of conditions of sale see para 239 et seq ante.

3   See the Misrepresentation Act 1967 ss 1(b), 2(2); para 356 post; and MISREPRESENTATION AND FRAUD vol 31 (Reissue) paras 817, 834.

353. Damages, compensation or return of purchase money. After completion
of the contract the transaction is generally at an end between vendor and purchaser, and
no action can be maintained by either party against the other for damages or
compensation on account of errors as to the quantity or quality of the thing sold[1], except
in so far as the purchaser may be entitled to sue on the covenants for title[2], or on any
express provision for compensation for errors of description[3], or in respect of any breach
of a warranty or collateral agreement[4] or for fraudulent or negligent misrepresentation[5].
The purchaser cannot on the ground of adverse claims recover purchase money which
has been paid or detain money unpaid, but must rely on the covenants for title[6]. In the
absence of covenants for title or so far as these do not apply, he is without remedy in
relation to his purchase money[7], unless he can obtain rescission on the ground of
misrepresentation or mistake[8].

1 The purchaser can be compelled to restore land of which he has taken possession and which is in excess
   of that transferred to him, notwithstanding that the error has arisen through the vendor's failure to mark
   out plots: *Marriott v Reid* (1900) 82 LT 369.
2 As to the covenants for title see para 336 et seq ante. As to the measure of damages on the breach of a
   covenant for right to convey see para 344 ante.
3 See paras 110 et seq, 250 ante.
4 See eg *Saunders v Cockrill* (1902) 87 LT 30, DC; *Lawrence v Cassel* [1930] 2 KB 83, CA (breaches of express
   agreements to complete houses in a workmanlike manner); *Miller v Cannon Hill Estates Ltd* [1931] 2 KB
   113; *Jennings v Tavener* [1955] 2 All ER 769, [1955] 1 WLR 932; *Hancock v BW Brazier (Anerley) Ltd*
   [1966] 2 All ER 901, [1966] 1 WLR 1317, CA (breaches of implied warranty of fitness on sale of house
   in course of erection (see para 48 ante)). Cf *De Lassalle v Guildford* [1901] 2 KB 215, CA (oral warranty
   collateral to lease that drains were in order). An award of damages is the proper remedy for a breach of a
   collateral contract: *Rutherford v Acton-Adams* [1915] AC 866 at 870, PC. An answer to a preliminary
   inquiry before contract is not a warranty: see para 5 ante. For the distinction between a warranty and a
   representation see CONTRACT vol 9(1) (Reissue) para 768; MISREPRESENTATION AND FRAUD vol 31
   (Reissue) para 704.
5 As to actions for damages for fraudulent or negligent misrepresentation see MISREPRESENTATION AND
   FRAUD vol 31 (Reissue) para 789 et seq. As to the general principle that the contract merges in the transfer
   on completion see para 293 ante; and DEEDS AND OTHER INSTRUMENTS. See, however, the Standard
   Conditions of Sale (3rd Edn), condition 7.4; and para 123 ante. As to the Standard Conditions of Sale see
   para 1 note 9 ante. As to the disposition of registered and unregistered land by transfer see para 262 note
   2 ante.
6 See *Maynard v Moseley* (1676) 3 Swan 651 at 653, where the point as to detention of unpaid purchase
   money was left open; *M'Culloch v Gregory* (1855) 1 K & J 286 at 291. It seems now to be settled that the
   purchaser can neither recover purchase money paid (*Craig v Hopkins* (1732) Mor Dict 16,623; *Bree v
   Holbech* (1781) 2 Doug KB 654; *Urmston v Pate* (1794) 4 Cru Dig 390; *Wakeman v Duchess of Rutland*
   (1797) 3 Ves 233 at 235 (affd sub nom *Duchess of Rutland v Wakeman* (1798) 8 Bro Parl Cas 145, HL);
   Clare v Lamb (1875) LR 10 CP 334; Sugden's Law of Vendors and Purchasers (14th Edn, 1862) 549),
   nor detain purchase money unpaid (see *Thomas v Powell* (1794) 2 Cox Eq Cas 394, where the court
   declined to prevent payment out of court on the ground of an adverse claim; Sugden's Law of Vendors
   and Purchasers (14th Edn, 1862) 551; Rawle's A Practical Treatise on the Law of Covenants for Title
   (5th Edn, 1887) s 321). Probably, however, the purchaser can apply unpaid purchase money in
   discharging incumbrances which the vendor should have cleared: see *Tourville v Naish* (1734) 3 P Wms
   307; *Lacey v Ingle* (1847) 2 Ph 413; Sugden's Law of Vendors and Purchasers (14th Edn, 1862) 552; and
   cf *Miller v Pridden* (1856) 3 Jur NS 78. As to damages for breach of a covenant for quiet enjoyment see
   para 345 ante.
7 *Bree v Holbech* (1781) 2 Doug KB 654; *Wakeman v Duchess of Rutland* (1797) 3 Ves 233 at 235. The
   purchaser takes the conveyance at his own risk, and upon eviction cannot recover the purchase money
   on the ground of failure of consideration (*Clare v Lamb* (1875) LR 10 CP 334); but he has been allowed
   to do so where the purchase has been completed without conveyance (*Cripps v Reade* (1796) 6 Term Rep
   606, where, on a sale of leaseholds, the lease was handed over without assignment). See also *Johnson v
   Johnson* (1802) 3 Bos & P 162; and cf *Awbry v Keen* (1687) 1 Vern 472.
8 See *Bree v Holbech* (1781) 2 Dough KB 654; *Edwards v M'Leay* (1815) Coop G 308; *Hitchcock v Giddings*
   (1817) 4 Price 135; Co Litt 384a note. As to rescission even after completion and repayment of purchase
   money in cases of misrepresentation and mistake see para 356 et seq post.

(ii) Rectification

354. Rectification in case of mutual mistake. The remedy of rectification is discussed principally elsewhere in this work[1]. Mutual mistake[2] arises where the transfer does not operate to carry out the intentions of the parties, for example where the land transferred is less[3] or more[4] than was comprised in the contract, or there is an error in the limitations[5], or the vendor's covenants for title are wider than the contracting parties intended[6], or the implied covenant for title is not consistent with all the terms of the contract[7], or there has been a common mistake in the description of an easement[8], or a covenant has been inserted to which the parties had not agreed[9]. In such circumstances, upon sufficient evidence of the mistake[10], the court will rectify the transfer[11] and will direct that a copy of the order to rectify be indorsed on the transfer[12]. The fact that rectification would confer a tax advantage on one or other party is not a bar to relief[13]. The right to rectification is a mere equity, which, in the case of registered land, will be defeated by a purchaser for value of any interest without notice[14].

1   See MISTAKE.
2   Rectification can normally be granted only where the mistake is mutual: see MISTAKE.
3   *White v White* (1872) LR 15 Eq 247, where it was held that the order for rectification was sufficient to pass the legal estate in the additional land, without a further conveyance. As to vesting orders see para 266 ante. As to the disposition of registered and unregistered land by transfer see para 262 note 2 ante.
4   *Beaumont v Bramley* (1822) Turn & R 41; *Marquess of Exeter v Marchioness of Exeter* (1838) 3 My & Cr 321; *Mortimer v Shortall* (1842) 2 Dr & War 363; *Beale v Kyte* [1907] 1 Ch 564. See also *Tyler v Beversham* (1674) Cas *temp* Finch 80; *Thomas v Davis* (1757) 1 Dick 301; *Leuty v Hillas* (1858) 2 De G & J 110.
5   *Re Bird's Trusts* (1876) 3 ChD 214; *Hanley v Pearson* (1879) 13 ChD 545. As to the effect of limitations after 1925 see REAL PROPERTY vol 39(2) (Reissue) para 93 (passing of fee simple without words of limitation), para 172 (abolition of rule in *Shelley's Case*, *Wolfe v Shelley* (1581) 1 Co Rep 93b).
6   *Coldcot v Hill* (1662) 1 Cas in Ch 15; *Feilder v Studley* (1673) Cas *temp* Finch 90; *Stait v Fenner* [1912] 2 Ch 504 at 516, 519, sub nom *Fenner v McNab* 107 LT 124.
7   *Butler v Mountview Estates Ltd* [1951] 2 KB 563, [1951] 1 All ER 693, where, on a sale, leaseholds (which by the contract were to be taken with full notice of the actual state and condition of the property as to the state of repair) were conveyed by the vendors 'as beneficial owners' without any modification, and the conveyance was rectified by allowing a modification of the implied covenants.
8   *Cowen v Truefitt Ltd* [1899] 2 Ch 309, CA.
9   *Rob v Butterwick* (1816) 2 Price 190, where the court ordered a fresh conveyance to be executed without the covenant objected to.
10 As to the evidence on which relief will be granted generally see MISTAKE. As to the rectification of a written instrument on oral evidence see para 355 post.
11 *Ellis v Hills and Brighton and Preston ABC Permanent Benefit Building Society* (1892) 67 LT 287.
12 *White v White* (1872) LR 15 Eq 247. The court may in a proper case treat the instrument as though it were already rectified: see MISTAKE.
13 *Re Colebrook's Conveyances, Taylor v Taylor* [1973] 1 All ER 132, [1972] 1 WLR 1397; *Re Slocock's Will Trusts* [1979] 1 All ER 358. As to the rectification of a voluntary transfer see MISTAKE. The negligence of the plaintiff or of his legal adviser in committing the mistake is not a bar to rectification: *Weeds v Blaney* (1977) 247 Estates Gazette 211, CA (citing *Monaghan County Council v Vaughan* [1948] IR 306; *Ball v Storie* (1823) 1 Sim & St 210).
14 *Smith v Jones* [1954] 2 All ER 823, [1954] 1 WLR 1089, where it was held that occupation by a tenant was not sufficient to give notice of his right to rectification of the lease. Cf *Blacklocks v JB Developments (Godalming) Ltd* [1982] Ch 183 at 195–196, [1981] 3 All ER 392 at 400–401 (registered title). In relation to registered title see the Land Registration Act 1925 s 70(1)(g); and LAND REGISTRATION vol 26 (Reissue) para 784.

355. Rectification of contract and transfer. The court may on oral evidence rectify both the written contract and the transfer so as to make them correspond to the true agreement between the parties[1].

1   See DEEDS AND OTHER INSTRUMENTS; MISTAKE. As to the disposition of registered and unregistered land by transfer see para 262 note 2 ante.

(iii) Rescission after Completion

356. Rescission for misrepresentation or mutual mistake. The remedy of rescission is discussed generally elsewhere in this work[1]. If the transaction has been induced by fraud, or misrepresentation amounting to fraud[2], or by mutual mistake of a fundamental character[3], the court will order a re-transfer of the land sold[4], and repayment of the purchase money with interest from the date of payment[5]. The purchaser will be entitled to the costs, charges and expenses incident to the purchase and transfer, including the costs of investigating the title[6], and the costs of the action to set aside the transfer[7]. Where the misrepresentation is innocent, the execution of the transfer is not a bar to rescission[8], but the court may in its discretion award damages in lieu of rescission[9].

1 See CONTRACT vol 9(1) (Reissue) para 986 et seq; MISREPRESENTATION AND FRAUD vol 31 (Reissue) para 812 et seq; MISTAKE.
2 *Bree v Holbech* (1781) 2 Doug KB 654; *Berry v Armistead* (1836) 2 Keen 221; *Wilde v Gibson* (1848) 1 HL Cas 605 at 633; *Brownlie v Campbell* (1880) 5 App Cas 925 at 937, HL, per Lord Selborne LC; *Joliffe v Baker* (1883) 11 QBD 255 at 267, 269. It may be fraud if the vendor knows and conceals a fact material to the validity of the title: *Edwards v M'Leay* (1815) Coop G 308; on appeal (1818) 2 Swan 287. As to the meaning of 'fraud' in connection with representations and the state of mind on the part of the representor required to render a representation fraudulent see MISREPRESENTATION AND FRAUD vol 31 (Reissue) para 755 et seq. The plaintiff cannot obtain rescission if he was from the beginning aware of the matters complained of: see *Vigers v Pike* (1842) 8 Cl & Fin 562 at 650, HL. Rescission of the contract for misrepresentation was refused in *Wilde v Gibson* (1848) 1 HL Cas 605 (revsg *Gibson v D'Este* (1843) 2 Y & C Ch Cas 542 at 581) (right of way not disclosed). Rescission was, however, granted in *Smith v Harrison* (1857) 3 Jur NS 287 (puffer at auction sale); and *Tibbatts v Boulter* (1895) 73 LT 534 (failure to cure defect, for which purpose time had been allowed). See also para 41 et seq ante.
3 *Brownlie v Campbell* (1880) 5 App Cas 925, HL; *Debenham v Sawbridge* [1901] 2 Ch 98, where a portion of the property was discovered to belong to a third person, but the error was not sufficient to justify rescission. Relief has been granted where, for example, it was discovered after completion that the property belonged to the purchaser (*Bingham v Bingham* (1748) 1 Ves Sen 126; *Cooper v Phibbs* (1867) LR 2 HL 149 at 164; *Jones v Clifford* (1876) 3 ChD 779 at 791), or that at the time of completion it had ceased to exist (*Hitchcock v Giddings* (1817) 4 Price 135). Cf *Okill v Whittaker* (1847) 2 Ph 338; *Re Tyrell, Tyrell v Woodhouse* (1900) 82 LT 675. See MISTAKE.
4 *Edwards v M'Leay* (1818) 2 Swan 287. As to rescission after transfer in cases of misrepresentation see MISREPRESENTATION AND FRAUD vol 31 (Reissue) para 817. As to rescission after transfer in cases of mistake see MISTAKE. As to setting aside a transfer in cases of undue influence see MISREPRESENTATION AND FRAUD vol 31 (Reissue) para 839 et seq. As to undue influence see also EQUITY vol 16 (Reissue) para 667 et seq. As to the disposition of registered and unregistered land by transfer see para 262 note 2 ante.
5 *Hart v Swaine* (1877) 7 ChD 42. See also MISREPRESENTATION AND FRAUD vol 31 (Reissue) para 781.
6 *Edwards v M'Leay* (1818) 2 Swan 287 at 289.
7 *Berry v Armistead* (1836) 2 Keen 221.
8 See the Misrepresentation Act 1967 s 1(b); and MISREPRESENTATION AND FRAUD vol 31 (Reissue) para 817.
9 See ibid s 2(2); and MISREPRESENTATION AND FRAUD vol 31 (Reissue) para 834. See also *William Sindall plc v Cambridgeshire County Council* [1994] 3 All ER 932, [1994] 1 WLR 1016, CA. If the misrepresentor is unable to prove that he believed on reasonable grounds the truth of his representation, there is an independent right to damages: see the Misrepresentation Act 1967 s 2(1); and MISREPRESENTATION AND FRAUD vol 31 (Reissue) para 801. As to the measure of damages see paras 42, 256 ante; and MISREPRESENTATION AND FRAUD vol 31 (Reissue) para 811.

357. Purchaser's liability to account. The purchaser must account for rents and profits and, if he has been in possession, is charged with an occupation rent[1]. If the rents and profits exceed the interest, and there are special circumstances to justify this course, the account is directed to be taken with periodical rests[2]. Credit is given to the purchaser for substantial repairs and lasting improvements[3], and he is debited with deterioration[4].

1   *Donovan v Fricker* (1821) Jac 165; *Trevelyan v White* (1839) 1 Beav 588; *Gresley v Mousley* (1859) 4 De G
     & J 78; *Haygarth v Wearing* (1871) LR 12 Eq 320. See also para 191 ante. Except, perhaps, where there
     has been fraud on the part of the purchaser, the account is not taken on the footing of wilful default: see
     Howell v Howell (1837) 2 My & Cr 478; *Parkinson v Hanbury* (1867) LR 2 HL 1 at 14 (the contrary decision
     in *Adams v Sworder* (1864) 2 De GJ & Sm 44 seems to be impliedly overruled).
2   *Donovan v Fricker* (1821) Jac 165; *Neesom v Clarkson* (1845) 4 Hare 97 at 105. See also *Press v Coke* (1871)
     6 Ch App 645 at 651. As to taking accounts with rests see MORTGAGE. Interest on rents and profits is not
     charged: *Silkstone and Haigh Moor Coal Co v Edey* [1900] 1 Ch 167.
3   *Trevelyan v White* (1839) 1 Beav 588; *Neesom v Clarkson* (1845) 4 Hare 97. Old buildings, if incapable of
     repair, are valued as old materials; but otherwise as buildings standing: *Robinson v Ridley* (1821) 6 Madd 2.
4   *Ex p Bennett* (1805) 10 Ves 381 at 400.

358. Time for rescission. The claim to rescind must be made promptly[1], and before
the interests of third persons have intervened[2]. Moreover, it must be possible for the
parties to the contract to be restored to their original position for the purchaser to receive
back his purchase money[3] and for the vendor to receive back the property unimpaired[4].
Depreciation caused by the vendor himself is no bar to rescission[5], nor is depreciation a
bar where it can be made good by compensation[6]. However, the contract cannot be
rescinded in part and stand good for the residue; if it cannot be rescinded as a whole, it
cannot be rescinded at all[7].

1   See EQUITY vol 16 (Reissue) para 932; MISREPRESENTATION AND FRAUD vol 31 (Reissue) para 835.
2   In this respect the principle is the same as where rescission of an executory contract is sought: see *Clough
     v London and North Western Rly Co* (1871) LR 7 Exch 26 at 35; and MISREPRESENTATION AND FRAUD
     vol 31 (Reissue) para 832. The transfer, like the contract, is valid until the injured party elects to avoid
     it: see *United Shoe Machinery Co of Canada v Brunet* [1909] AC 330 at 337, PC; and MISREPRESENTATION
     AND FRAUD vol 31 (Reissue) para 783. The right to rescind is a mere equity, which will be defeated by
     a purchaser for value of any interest without notice: *Latec Investments Ltd v Hotel Terrigal Pty Ltd* (1965)
     113 CLR 265, Aust HC. The claimant's occupation of the land would not usually be sufficient to give
     notice of the claim: cf *Smith v Jones* [1954] 2 All ER 823, [1954] 1 WLR 1089; *Blacklocks v JB Developments
     (Godalming) Ltd* [1982] Ch 183 at 195–196, [1981] 3 All ER 392 at 400–401 (registered land). In relation
     to registered land, however, the Land Registration Act 1925 s 70(1)(g) applies: see LAND REGISTRATION
     vol 26 (Reissue) para 784.
3   *Debenham v Sawbridge* [1901] 2 Ch 98.
4   *Clarke v Dickson* (1858) EB & E 148 at 154–155; *Western Bank of Scotland v Addie, Addie v Western Bank of
     Scotland* (1867) LR 1 Sc & Div 145 at 159, 165, HL; *Urquhart v Macpherson* (1878) 3 App Cas 831 at 837,
     PC; *Erlanger v New Sombrero Phosphate Co* (1878) 3 App Cas 1218 at 1278, HL; *Rees v De Bernardy* [1896] 2
     Ch 437 at 446. If the right of rescission cannot be exercised, the injured party must have recourse to his
     remedy in damages for deceit, negligent misrepresentation at common law, or under the Misrepresentation
     Act 1967 s 2(2): see MISREPRESENTATION AND FRAUD vol 31 (Reissue) para 789 et seq.
5   See *Phosphate Sewage Co v Hartmont* (1877) 5 ChD 394, CA; *Rees v De Bernardy* [1896] 2 Ch 437 at 446.
6   *Lagunas Nitrate Co v Lagunas Syndicate* [1899] 2 Ch 392 at 456, CA. See further MISREPRESENTATION
     AND FRAUD vol 31 (Reissue) para 831.
7   *Sheffield Nickel Co v Unwin* (1877) 2 QBD 214 at 223. As to the form and extent of relief by rescission
     generally see MISREPRESENTATION AND FRAUD vol 31 (Reissue) paras 812–813.

359–400. Parties to rescission. A right to rescind a sale or purchase of land may be
enforced by the personal representatives of a contracting party, or by his trustee in
bankruptcy[1], and, in the case of the vendor, by his personal representatives, or, after
assent[2], his devisee[3], or an assignee of his whole interest in the land[4].

Conversely, a right of rescission may be exercised against the devisees or
representatives[5], the assigns, other than those purchasing for value without notice[6], or the
trustee in bankruptcy[7] of the opposite party[8].

Where a misrepresentation is made to a purchaser who then resells the land and passes
on the representation to the sub-purchaser, rescission is not available to the sub-purchaser
unless it was the intention of the representor that the representation should be passed on[9].

1	As to rights of action vesting in the trustee in bankruptcy see BANKRUPTCY AND INSOLVENCY vol 3(2) (Reissue) para 423 et seq. As to the powers of the trustee in bankruptcy generally see BANKRUPTCY AND INSOLVENCY vol 3(2) (Reissue) para 380 et seq.
2	See EXECUTORS AND ADMINISTRATORS.
3	See *Stump v Gaby* (1852) 2 De GM & G 623 at 630; *Gresley v Mousley* (1859) 4 De G & J 78.
4	See EQUITY vol 16 (Reissue) para 778. As to the avoidance of the assignment of rights of action see *Defries v Milne* [1913] 1 Ch 98, CA; and CHOSES IN ACTION vol 6 (Reissue) paras 87–88; MISREPRESENTATION AND FRAUD vol 31 (Reissue) para 821.
5	*Bridgman v Green* (1757) Wilm 58 at 64–65; *Huguenin v Baseley* (1807) 14 Ves 273 at 289; *Trevelyan v White* (1839) 1 Beav 588; *Charter v Trevelyan* (1844) 11 Cl & Fin 714, HL.
6	*Trevelyan v White* (1839) 1 Beav 588; *Charter v Trevelyan* (1844) 11 Cl & Fin 714, HL. See also para 358 note 2 ante; and EQUITY vol 16 (Reissue) para 758.
7	Cf *Re Shackleton, ex p Whittaker* (1875) 10 Ch App 446; *Re Eastgate, ex p Ward* [1905] 1 KB 465; *Tilley v Bowman Ltd* [1910] 1 KB 745 (cases relating to the sale of goods: see SALE OF GOODS).
8	See further MISREPRESENTATION AND FRAUD vol 31 (Reissue) para 822.
9	*Gross v Lewis Hillman Ltd* [1970] Ch 445, [1969] 3 All ER 1476, CA. See also para 42 ante; and MISREPRESENTATION AND FRAUD vol 31 (Reissue) para 737.

SET-OFF AND COUNTERCLAIM

For actions .... *see*   PRACTICE AND PROCEDURE
       Admiralty counterclaims....................   ADMIRALTY
       administration actions........................   EXECUTORS AND ADMINISTRATORS
       auctioneers..   AUCTION
       choses in action................................   CHOSES IN ACTION
       contract, discharge of ....   CONTRACT
       county courts ....   COUNTY COURTS
       deduction from price..........................   SALE OF GOODS
       deduction from rent ....   LANDLORD AND TENANT
       divorce cross-petitions.......................   DIVORCE
       equitable set-off................................   EQUITY
       executors and administrators.............   EXECUTORS AND ADMINISTRATORS
       mortgage...   MORTGAGE
       payment into court............................   PRACTICE AND PROCEDURE
       set-off by assignee of debt.................   CHOSES IN ACTION
              banker.............................   BANKING
              partner ....   PARTNERSHIP
              purchaser from auctioneer   AUCTION
              solicitor............................   SOLICITORS
              surety...............................   GUARANTEE AND INDEMNITY
              trustee.............................   TRUSTS
          in bankruptcy.......................   BANKRUPTCY AND INSOLVENCY
              company winding up ....   COMPANIES
              equity ....   EQUITY
          of losses for tax purposes.......   INCOME TAXATION
       statute-barred debts ....   LIMITATION OF ACTIONS

1. THE RIGHT OF SET-OFF AND THE RIGHT TO COUNTERCLAIM

(1) INTRODUCTION

(i) In general

401. Scope and significance of title. This title is concerned with the situation where A has a claim against B and B has a cross-claim against A[1]. It deals with the following situations:

(1) B's right, where his cross-claim consists of a money claim, to deduct from the amount paid to A a sum representing his cross-claim[2];

(2) B's right to raise legitimately and successfully such a cross-claim in a claim brought by A, so as to reduce or extinguish A's claim[3] and to establish any right of B to an excess over A's claim[4]; and

(3) B's right to raise a non-pecuniary cross-claim in a claim brought by A[5].

Whilst much of the jurisprudence applicable to this title appears to bear a procedural hallmark[6], the substantial advantage which B derives from the relevant doctrines is that he may defer meeting A's claim, wholly or in part, until a court has adjudicated on his own cross-claim[7]. Typically, the doctrines of set-off, counterclaim and abatement are concerned with deductions made by B. If these are permissible and B has a triable cross-claim, then B is entitled to withhold payment, wholly or pro tanto, until his cross-claim has been resolved by the court. If the deductions are impermissible, B may at best have to meet A's claim at once, the trial of his cross-claim being deferred to a later hearing[8]; at worst, B may have placed himself in breach of a continuing contract thereby entitling A to repudiate[9], or may be met by an applicable time-bar in his later action[10].

---

1   See eg CONTRACT vol 9(1) (Reissue) para 1073.

2   See eg the Sale of Goods Act 1979 s 53(1)(a) (breach of warranty). As to abatement generally see para 411 et seq post.

3   See RSC Ord 15 r 2(1), and PRACTICE AND PROCEDURE.

     As from 26 April 1999, the Civil Procedure Rules (CPR) replace the Rules of the Supreme Court and the County Court Rules. Certain provisions of the RSC and CCR are saved in a modified form in CPR Schs 1 and 2 respectively. The CPR (including Schs 1, 2) apply to proceedings issued on or after 26 April 1999, and new steps taken in existing proceedings, as prescribed: CPR 51; *Practice Direction—Transitional Arrangements* (1999) PD51.

     The CPR have the overriding objective of enabling the court to deal with cases justly: CPR 1.1(1). Dealing with a case justly includes, so far as is practicable, (1) ensuring that the parties are on an equal footing; (2) saving expense; (3) dealing with the case in ways which are proportionate (a) to the amount of money involved, (b) to the importance of the case, (c) to the complexity of the issues, and (d) to the financial position of each party; (4) ensuring that it is dealt with expeditiously and fairly; and (5) allotting to it an appropriate share of the court's resources, while taking into account the need to allot resources to other cases: CPR 1.1(2). The court must seek to give effect to the overriding objective when it exercises any power given to it by the Rules, or interprets any rule: CPR 1.2. The parties are required to help the court to further the overriding objective: CPR 1.3. The court must also further the overriding objective by actively managing cases: CPR 1.4(1). Active case management includes: (i) encouraging the parties to co-operate with each other in the conduct of the proceedings; (ii) identifying the issues at an early stage; (iii) deciding promptly which issues need full investigation and trial and accordingly disposing summarily of the others; (iv) deciding the order in which issues are to be resolved; (v) encouraging the parties to use an alternative dispute resolution procedure if the court considers that appropriate and facilitating the use of such procedure; (vi) helping the parties to settle the whole or part of the case; (vii) fixing timetables or otherwise controlling the progress of the case; (viii) considering whether the likely benefits of taking a particular step justify the cost of taking it; (ix) dealing with as many aspects of the case as it can on the same occasion; (x) dealing with the case without the parties needing to attend at court;

(xi) making use of technology; and (xii) giving directions to ensure that the trial of a case proceeds quickly and efficiently: CPR 1.4(2). The court may act on its own initiative: see CPR 3.3.

At the date at which this volume states the law, the extent, if any, to which cases decided under RSC or CCR may be cited in relation to CPR, is unclear. It is thought that they will be persuasive where the same word or concept is used (and binding if subsequently adopted by the court), but in relation to the exercise of a discretion will be of less value in the light of the overriding objective. See further the introduction to Civil Court Practice 1999. Accordingly, cases cited in this title in amplification or explanation of the former rules will be binding over proceedings conducted under those rules, but should be viewed with caution in relation to proceedings conducted under the new regime.

Provision as to the making of counterclaims is contained in CPR Pt 20 (see para 493 et seq post). The value and complexity of a Part 20 claim (see para 481 note 15 post) must be taken into consideration in deciding which track to allocate a claim to: CPR 26.8(1)(e). As to the allocation of claims to the small claims track, the fast track or the multi-track see CPR Pt 26. See also CPR Pts 27–29.

4   See RSC Ord 15 r 2(4); and note 3 supra.
5   See PRACTICE AND PROCEDURE.
6   See PRACTICE AND PROCEDURE.
7   See eg RSC Ord 14 r 3(2) (execution of summary judgment stayed until trial of counterclaim); and para 402 post.
8   An example is where A has already obtained summary judgment against B, which has been satisfied, and B is then not entitled to counterclaim: *CSI International Co Ltd v Archway Personnel (Middle East) Ltd* [1980] 3 All ER 215, [1980] 1 WLR 1069, CA.
9   Eg a rescission of the contract for an inadequate reason: see CONTRACT vol 9(1) (Reissue) para 1007.
10 As to the limitation of actions as it affects set-off and counterclaim see paras 412, 424, 434 post; and LIMITATION OF ACTIONS vol 28 (Reissue) para 850.

402. Summary judgment. In relation to proceedings begun before 26 April 1999[1], where A seeks summary judgment[2] and B demonstrates a triable cross-claim by way of abatement[3] or set-off[4], the court may give B leave to defend, wholly or in part[5]. Similarly if B demonstrates a counterclaim the court may make the same order or give judgment on the claim, with a stay of execution pending trial of the counterclaim[6]. In neither case does B have to make payment to A until his cross-claim is resolved.

In relation to proceedings begun on or after 26 April 1999, the court may give summary judgment against a claimant or defendant if it considers that the claimant or defendant has no real prospect of succeeding on, or as the case may be, successfully defending, the claim or issue, and there is no other reason why the case or issue should be disposed of at a trial[7].

1   Ie the date on which the CPR came into operation: see para 401 note 3 ante. As to the replacement of the RSC by the CPR, and the transitional arrangements in relation thereto, see para 401 note 3 ante.
2   Ie judgment pursuant to RSC Ord 14 r 1.
3   As to abatement see para 411 et seq post.
4   As to set-off generally see para 420 et seq post.
5   See RSC Ord 14 r 4(3); and JUDGMENTS AND ORDERS; PRACTICE AND PROCEDURE.
6   See RSC Ord 14 r 3(2); and JUDGMENTS AND ORDERS; PRACTICE AND PROCEDURE.
7   CPR 24.2. As to the matters which the court has considered in determining whether a set-off or counterclaim will provide sufficient reason for refusing summary judgment, see *Esso Petroleum Co Ltd v Milton* [1997] 2 All ER 593, [1997] 1 WLR 938, CA. See, however, as to the citation of cases decided before the commencement of the CPR, para 401 note 3 ante.

403. Limitation periods. In some cases a period of limitation[1] affecting B's cross-claim may prevent him from relying on the relevant doctrines[2], so that he must meet A's claim at once, his cross-claim being remitted to a separate claim which A can meet by pleading the limitation period. A period of limitation may apply because English statute law so provides[3] or because the parties to a contract have agreed on a time-limit for initiating proceedings on the cross-claim[4].

1   For the purposes of the Limitation Act 1980, a claim by way of set-off or counterclaim is deemed to be a separate action which commenced on the same date as the original action: s 35(1)(b), (2).

2 As to the situation where B's cross-claim is a true defence see paras 405, 411 et seq post; and LIMITATION OF ACTIONS vol 28 (Reissue) para 850.
3 See the Limitation Act 1980 s 35 (as amended); and para 413 post.
4 See paras 413, 416 post.

404. Rules of court. Rules of court do not define or determine the juridical nature of set-off[1] or counterclaim[2], which is a matter of law for the courts[3].

1 As to set-off see RSC Ord 18 r 17; CPR 16.6; and para 406 post. See also the Supreme Court Practice 1999; and para 401 note 3 ante.
2 As to counterclaims see RSC Ord 15 r 2; CPR Pt 20; para 407 text and note 4 post; and PRACTICE AND PROCEDURE.
3 The question as to what is a set-off is to be determined as a matter of law and is not in any way governed or influenced by the language used by the parties in their pleadings: *Hanak v Green* [1958] 2 QB 9 at 26, [1958] 2 All ER 141 at 152, CA, per Morris LJ.

(ii) Definitions

405. Abatement at common law. Subject to certain exceptions[1], where A has a claim for a sum of money against B for the price of goods or services and B has a cross-claim for a sum of money, whether liquidated or unliquidated, against A, arising out of deficiencies in those goods or services, the general rule is that B is entitled to deduct the amount of his cross-claim and set it up as a true defence at common law in an action by A[2]. This defence is unaffected by any English statute of limitation[3].

1 As to the exceptions to the abatement rule see para 413 et seq post.
2 See para 411 post.
3 See para 412 post; and LIMITATION OF ACTIONS vol 28 (Reissue) para 850.

406. Meaning of 'set-off'. Where A has a claim for a sum of money against B and B has a cross-claim for a sum of money against A[1] such that B is, to the extent of his cross-claim, entitled to be absolved from payment of A's claim, and to plead his cross-claim as a defence to an action by A for the enforcement of his claim[2], then B is said to have a right of set-off against A to the extent of his cross-claim[3].

1 The claim may be for an unascertained amount: RSC Ord 18 r 17; CPR 16.6 (which does not limit the right of set-off to an ascertained amount). As to the replacement of the RSC by the CPR, and the transitional arrangements in relation thereto, see para 401 note 3 ante.
2 RSC Ord 18 r 17; CPR 16.6.
3 See para 420 et seq post.

407. Meaning of 'counterclaim'. When A has a claim of any kind against B and brings an action to enforce that claim, and B has a cross-claim of any kind against A[1] which by law he is entitled to raise and have disposed of in the action brought by A[2], then B is said to have a right of counterclaim[3].

In relation to proceedings begun on or after 26 April 1999, 'counterclaim' means a claim brought by the defendant in response to the claimant's claim, which is included in the same proceedings as the claimant's claim[4].

1 See PRACTICE AND PROCEDURE.
2 See RSC Ord 15 r 2(1).
3 See para 480 et seq post.
4 CPR 2.2(1), Glossary. However, the meaning given to terms in the Glossary is not to be taken as giving those terms any meaning in the CPR which they do not have in the law generally: CPR 2.2(1). As to the replacement of the RSC by the CPR, and the transitional arrangements in relation thereto, see para 401 note 3 ante.

408. Distinction between abatement and set-off. Abatement is a right at common law[1], and is distinct from set-off at law which originated in statute[2] and equitable set-off (or defence)[3].

1   See *Mondel v Steel* (1841) 8 M & W 858; and para 411 post.
2   See the Statutes of Set-off, 2 Geo 2 c 22 (Insolvent Debtors Relief) (1728), and 8 Geo 2 c 24 (Set-off) (1734) (both repealed); and para 426 post.
3   See para 426 post.

409. Distinction between set-off and counterclaim. Set-off is distinguishable from counterclaim both in its application and in its effect. In its application set-off is limited to money claims[1], whereas counterclaim is not so limited. Any claim in respect of which the defendant could bring an independent claim against the plaintiff may be enforced by counterclaim subject only to the limitation that it must be such as can conveniently be tried with the plaintiff's claim[2]. Thus not only claims for money, but also other claims such as a claim for an injunction or for specific performance or for a declaration may be the subject of a counterclaim.

In its effect set-off is essentially different from counterclaim in that set-off is a ground of defence, a shield and not a sword[3], which, if established, affords an answer to the plaintiff's claim wholly or pro tanto, whereas counterclaim as such affords no defence to the plaintiff's claim, but is a weapon of offence which enables a defendant to enforce a claim against the plaintiff as effectually as in an independent action[4]. Where facts pleaded by way of counterclaim constitute a set-off they may be additionally pleaded as such[5].

1   See RSC Ord 18 r 17; CPR 16.6; and para 420 et seq post. See also para 401 et seq ante.
2   See RSC Ord 15 r 2; CPR Pt 20; para 480 post; and PRACTICE AND PROCEDURE.
3   *Stooke v Taylor* (1880) 5 QBD 569 at 575–576, DC, per Cockburn CJ.
4   *Stooke v Taylor* (1880) 5 QBD 569 at 576, DC; applied in *BICC v Burndy Corpn* [1985] Ch 232, [1985] 1 All ER 417, CA; *Re Stahlwerk Becker AG's Patent* [1917] 2 Ch 272 at 276; *Sociedad Financiera de Bienes Raices SA v Agrimpex Hungarian Trading Co for Agricultural Products* [1961] AC 135, [1960] 2 All ER 578, HL. For a modern case in which the distinction between set-off and counterclaim has been considered in a bankruptcy context see *Hofer v Strawson* (1999) Times, 17 April. As to set-off in bankruptcy generally see BANKRUPTCY AND INSOLVENCY vol 3(2) (Reissue) para 535 et seq.
5   See RSC Ord 18 r 17; CPR 16.6; and para 496 post.

410. Distinction between set-off and payment. Set-off is entirely distinct from payment. Payment is satisfaction of a claim made by or on behalf of a person against whom the claim is brought. The person paying performs the obligation in respect of which the claim arises, which thereby becomes extinguished. Set-off exempts a person entitled to it from making any satisfaction of a claim brought against him, or of so much of the claim as equals the amount which he is entitled to set off, and thus to the extent of his set-off he is discharged from performance of the obligation in respect of which the claim arises[1].

Where there has been payment, the party against whom the claim is brought pleads payment or accord and satisfaction[2], which in effect alleges that the claim no longer exists. On the other hand, a plea of set-off in effect admits the existence of the claim, and sets up a cross-claim as being ground on which the person against whom the claim is brought is excused from payment and entitled to judgment on the plaintiff's claim. Until judgment in favour of the defendant on the ground of set-off has been given, the plaintiff's claim is not extinguished[3].

Payment is a good answer to set-off, and a payment made by an unauthorised agent and not ratified until after set-off has been pleaded may be pleaded in defence to a set-off[4].

1   See *Ribblesdale v Forbes* (1916) 140 LT Jo 483, CA. Tender of the balance of a debt due after setting off a sum due from the creditor, without his consent, is not strictly a legal tender, although the same consequences as to costs may follow. See also para 508 et seq post; and CONTRACT vol 9(1) (Reissue) para 974. A defendant who pays into court the difference between the amount of the claim and the set-off he succeeds in establishing is in the same position as a defendant who has paid into court the whole amount recovered.
2   As to accord and satisfaction see CONTRACT vol 9(1) (Reissue) paras 1043–1051. See also PLEADING.
3   *Re Hiram Maxim Lamp Co* [1903] 1 Ch 70. If there is a doubt whether the facts show payment or set-off, both payment and set-off should be pleaded as alternative defences. Both defences must be specially pleaded: see PLEADING; *Fidgett v Penny* (1834) 1 Cr M & R 108; *Cooper v Morecraft* (1838) 3 M & W 500; *Thomas v Cross* (1852) 7 Exch 728.
4   *Eyton v Littledale* (1849) 7 Dow & L 55; *Simpson v Eggington* (1855) 10 Exch 845. This defence must be specially pleaded: see PLEADING.

(2) ABATEMENT AT COMMON LAW

(i) The Rule

411. Origins and nature of abatement. From the early nineteenth century, when A sued B for the cost of goods or for work and labour, B was permitted to deduct from the amount due to A a sum representing the diminution in the value of the goods or services caused by A's breach of contract[1]. This would also give B a true defence at law to A's claim. In the case of breach of warranty on the sale of goods, the defence is now confirmed by statute[2]. Such a defence may, and usually does, rely on an unliquidated cross-claim for damages[3]. Being a true defence it is unaffected by English statutes of limitation[4]. The rule is confined to contracts for the sale of goods and for work and labour[5], and does not extend to contracts generally[6]. For a party to rely on the right of abatement he must establish that the breach of contract directly affected and reduced the actual value of the goods or work, so that any other loss or damage, if it is to be relied on as an answer to a claim for the price, will arise from the principle of equitable set-off[7].

1   The term 'abatement' originated in *Mondel v Steel* (1841) 8 M & W 858 at 871 per Parke B, and was adopted in *Aries Tanker Corpn v Total Transport Ltd* [1977] 1 All ER 398 at 404, [1977] 1 WLR 185 at 190, HL, per Lord Wilberforce, and at 405 and at 192 per Lord Simon of Glaisdale. In early editions of this work the subject was not treated under this title. See also para 433 post.
2   See the Sale of Goods Act 1979 s 53(1); and SALE OF GOODS.
3   *Basten v Butter* (1806) 7 East 479; *Farnsworth v Garrard* (1807) 1 Camp 38; *Mondel v Steel* (1841) 8 M & W 858; *Bright v Rogers* [1917] 1 KB 917; *Hanak v Green* [1958] 2 QB 9, [1958] 2 All ER 141, CA; *Gilbert-Ash (Northern) Ltd v Modern Engineering (Bristol) Ltd* [1974] AC 689, [1973] 3 All ER 195, HL; *Henriksens Rederi A/S v PHZ Rolimpex, The Brede* [1974] QB 233, [1973] 3 All ER 589, CA; *Aries Tanker Corpn v Total Transport Ltd* [1977] 1 All ER 398, [1977] 1 WLR 185, HL.
4   See para 416 post; and LIMITATION OF ACTIONS vol 28 (Reissue) para 850.
5   As to contracts of employment see *Sagar v H Ridehalgh & Son Ltd* [1931] 1 Ch 310, CA; and para 468 post.
6   See *Aries Tanker Corpn v Total Transport Ltd* [1977] 1 All ER 398, [1977] 1 WLR 185, HL.
7   *Mellowes Archital Ltd v Bell Properties Ltd* (1997) 87 BLR 26, CA.

412. Abatement and limitation. The general statutory provisions relating to limitation of actions provide that any claim by way of set-off or counterclaim is to be deemed to be a separate action and to have been commenced on the same date as the action in which the set-off or counterclaim is pleaded[1]. Since the defence of abatement is a true defence rather than a set-off or counterclaim it is not subject to that provision[2].

1   See the Limitation Act 1980 s 35(1). The Limitation Act 1980 does not apply where a period of limitation is prescribed by or under any other enactment: s 39. The Act applies to arbitrations: see the Arbitration Act 1996 ss 13, 14; and ARBITRATION vol 2 (Reissue) paras 649–650. As to international carriage by land or air see para 416 post. As to the carriage of goods by sea see the amended Hague

Rules, art III para 6, set out in the Carriage of Goods by Sea Act 1971, Schedule; para 413 post; and CARRIERS vol 5(1) (Reissue) paras 567, 573.

2　See the cases cited in para 411 note 3 ante, especially *Henriksens Rederi A/S v PHZ Rolimpex, The Brede* [1974] QB 233, [1973] 3 All ER 589, CA; and see LIMITATION OF ACTIONS vol 28 (Reissue) para 850. As to limitation as it affects exceptions to the abatement rule see para 413 note 5 post.

(ii)　Established and Possible Exceptions

413.　The freight exception (voyage charter). It has long been accepted as law, and has now been confirmed[1], that a claim to freight under a voyage charter, where the charterer has a cross-claim concerning deficiencies in the services performed, constitutes an exception to the rule of abatement. Hence, in principle, the charterer cannot deduct anything from the amount due, or raise his cross-claim by way of abatement, but must meet the claim to freight in full, and then raise his cross-claim in a separate action[2]. However, since the cross-claim ranks as a counterclaim, and having regard to the practice and procedure in relation to counterclaim[3], it is rare for the charterer to suffer any disadvantage in practice[4], although where there is a time-limit affecting his cross-claim the exception may result in the charterer being debarred from a remedy[5]. Equity follows the law in applying the freight exception equally to an equitable defence[6].

The freight exception applies to an agent who collects freight on behalf of the shipowner or charterer. The agent must account for it without deduction or set-off[7]. The exception applies also to an assignee of the right to freight, to advance freight and to freight payable on delivery of goods at the port of discharge[8].

1　See *Aries Tanker Corpn v Total Transport Ltd* [1977] 1 All ER 398, [1977] 1 WLR 185, HL.

2　See *Shields v Davis* (1815) 6 Taunt 65 (previous proceedings sub nom *Sheels v Davies* (1814) 4 Camp 119); *Mondel v Steel* (1841) 8 M & W 858 at 871; *Dakin v Oxley* (1864) 15 CBNS 646; *Meyer v Dresser* (1864) 16 CBNS 646; *Henriksens Rederi A/S v PHZ Rolimpex, The Brede* [1974] QB 233, [1973] 3 All ER 589, CA. See also *Kish v Taylor* [1912] AC 604 at 612, HL; *Bede Steam Shipping Co Ltd v Bunge y Born* (1927) 27 Ll L Rep 410.

3　See PRACTICE AND PROCEDURE. The CPR (see para 401 note 3 ante) apply to specialist proceedings, which include admiralty and commercial actions, subject to the provisions of relevant Practice Directions: CPR Pt 49; *Practice Direction—Commercial Court* (1999) PD49D and *Practice Direction—Admiralty* (1999) PD49F.

4　Where the charterer has a triable counterclaim unaffected by a time-bar, the proper order is 'judgment on the claim; stay of execution pending trial of counterclaim'. This has been a practice in the Commercial Court. Hence, in most cases, the question will not arise. See *Henriksens Rederi A/S v PHZ Rolimpex, The Brede* [1974] QB 233 at 257, [1973] 3 All ER 589 at 603, CA, per Roskill LJ.

5　Where the only applicable period of limitation is to be found in the Limitation Act 1980 s 35(1) (see para 412 ante), the exception is unlikely to have practical effect since the charterer has six years in which to initiate his cross-complaint (s 5), and perhaps longer, if he can invoke s 35(1) and date back the initiation of his action to the commencement of the plaintiff's claim. However, where the parties have agreed in the charterparty that complaints by the charterer must be initiated within a certain period, the exception may come into play. For example, the amended Hague Rules art III para 6 (set out in the Carriage of Goods by Sea Act 1971 Schedule), provides that in any event the carrier and the ship are to be discharged from all liability in respect of loss or damage unless suit is brought within one year after delivery of the goods or the date when the goods should have been delivered. If, therefore, the claimant does not bring proceedings within one year, a counterclaim by the charterer is not assisted by the Limitation Act 1980 s 35(1), as his counterclaim is still outside the one-year limit to which he has agreed. Since his cross-complaint does not constitute a defence and since it is out of time, his cross-action must fail: *Henriksens Rederi A/S v PHZ Rolimpex, The Brede* [1974] QB 233, [1973] 3 All ER 589, CA; *Aries Tanker Corpn v Total Transport Ltd* [1977] 1 All ER 398, [1977] 1 WLR 185, HL. Furthermore, the provisions of the Hague Rules (unlike some other statutes of limitation, including the Limitation Act 1980), when incorporated in a contract, operate as a contractual time-bar to the rights of the charterer as well as the remedy. This was the first ground on which the charterers failed in *Aries Tanker Corpn v Total Transport Ltd* supra, the second being general in nature, relying on the exception: see para 418 post. In the case of international carriage of goods by road, the Convention on the Contract for the International Carriage of Goods by Road (CMR) (Geneva, 19 May 1956; TS 90 (1967); Cmnd 3455), art 32, provides a time-limit for claims by the customer and, by art 32(4), a right of action which has become barred by lapse of time may not be exercised by way of counterclaim or set-off. The convention is set out in the Carriage of Goods by Road Act 1965, Schedule. See CARRIERS vol 5(1) (Reissue) para 543 et seq. As to international carriage by air see the Carriage by Air Act 1961 s 1(1), Sch 1 Pt I art 29 (substituted as from a day to be appointed by the Carriage by Air and Road Act 1979 s 1(1), Sch 1); and AVIATION vol 2 (Reissue) paras 1554, 1607. See also para 416 post.

6   *Henriksens Rederi A/S v PHZ Rolimpex, The Brede* [1974] QB 233, [1973] 3 All ER 589, CA; *Aries Tanker Corpn v Total Transport Ltd* [1977] 1 All ER 398, [1977] 1 WLR 185, HL; *Bank of Boston Connecticut v European Grain and Shipping Ltd* [1989] AC 1056, [1989] 1 All ER 545, HL. See also para 426 post.

7   *James & Co Scheepvaart en Handelmij BV v Chinecrest Ltd* [1979] 1 Lloyds Rep 126, CA, but cf *Samuel v West Hartlepool Steam Navigation Co* (1906) 11 Com Cas 115, 12 Com Cas 203, and see *Colonial Bank v European Grain and Shipping Ltd, The Dominique* [1987] 1 Lloyd's Rep 239 at 256–257 (affd sub nom *Bank of Boston Connecticut v European Grain and Shipping Ltd* [1989] AC 1056, [1989] 1 All ER 545, HL); *Wehner v Dene Shipping Co* [1905] 2 KB 92.

8   *Bank of Boston Connecticut v European Grain and Shipping Ltd* [1989] AC 1056, [1989] 1 All ER 545, HL.

414. Bills of exchange. An unliquidated cross-claim[1] cannot be relied upon as an extinguishing set-off against a claim on a bill of exchange[2]. However, as between the immediate parties, a partial failure of consideration may be relied on as a pro tanto defence provided that the amount involved is ascertained and liquidated[3].

1   Ie a cross-claim by way of abatement or equitable defence, as to which see para 431 post.
2   See *James Lamont & Co Ltd v Hyland Ltd* [1950] 1 KB 585, [1950] 1 All ER 341, CA; *Nova (Jersey) Knit Ltd v Kammgarn Spinnerei GmbH* [1977] 2 All ER 463, [1977] 1 WLR 713, HL; considered in *Esso Petroleum Ltd v Milton* [1997] 2 All ER 593 at 600, [1997] 1 WLR 938 at 946, CA; and BILLS OF EXCHANGE AND OTHER NEGOTIABLE INSTRUMENTS vol 4(1) (Reissue) para 497. See also PRACTICE AND PROCEDURE.
3   *Nova (Jersey) Knit Ltd v Kammgarn Spinnerei GmbH* [1977] 2 All ER 463, [1977] 1 WLR 713, HL, considered in *Esso Petroleum Ltd v Milton* [1997] 2 All ER 593 at 600, [1997] 1 WLR 938 at 946, CA.

415. Time charters: a partial exception. Since payment under a time charter partakes of hire, the withholding of payment is not necessarily governed by the same principles as apply to a voyage charter[1]. A wrongful deduction from payment by the charterer may entitle the owner to repudiate[2]; conversely, such a deduction correctly made, to which the owner wrongly reacts by claiming that the contract has been repudiated, entitles the charterer to damages for repudiation by the owner. Where the owner wrongly deprives the charterer of the use of the vessel, or prejudices him in the use of it, the charterer is entitled to deduct the appropriate amount by way of abatement without untoward consequences, but it seems that no such right exists in the case of damage to cargo due to the negligence of the crew. This situation therefore constitutes a partial exception to the abatement rule[3].

1   As to voyage charters see para 413 ante; and SHIPPING AND NAVIGATION.
2   As to the repudiation of contracts generally see CONTRACT vol 9(1) (Reissue) para 997 et seq.
3   *Federal Commerce and Navigation Co Ltd v Molena Alpha Inc* [1978] QB 927, [1978] 3 All ER 1066, CA (affd on other grounds [1979] AC 757, [1979] 1 All ER 307, HL). The many cases considered in this decision are not cited here, because the results of the decision are more apt for consideration of their substantive effect on the law of contract, especially charterparties (see SHIPPING AND NAVIGATION), and because the case was debated under the rubric of equitable estoppel (see para 426 post). However, the decision does have an impact on the predominantly procedural matters considered in this title, and in suitable cases the partial exception could be significant. See also *SL Sethia Lines Ltd v Naviagro Maritime Corpn, The Kostas Melas* [1981] 1 Lloyd's Rep 18.

416. Carriage by land or air. The freight exception[1] applies to a contract for the carriage of goods by road made subject to the Convention on the Contract for the International Carriage of Goods by Road, although certain provisions[2] contemplate the possibility of a set-off or counterclaim[3]. It has been held that the exception applies also to a domestic contract for carriage by land⁴. Otherwise, contracts of carriage by land⁵ or air⁶ have not yet been placed authoritatively either in the category of contracts falling within the abatement rule or within the freight exception⁷. These contracts may, therefore, be considered further in future cases on this subject⁸.

1 See para 413 ante.
2 Ie the Convention on the Contract for the International Carriage of Goods by Road, Schedule arts 32(4), 36; see para 413 note 5 ante.
3 *RH & D International Ltd v IAS Animal Air Services Ltd* [1984] 2 All ER 203, [1984] 1 WLR 573. See also *Impex Transport Aktieselskabet v A G Thames Holdings Ltd* [1982] 1 All ER 897 at 901–902, [1981] 1 WLR 1547 at 1551–1553, where Robert Goff J assumed that a set-off is possible in contracts for the carriage of goods by road, at least when they are subject to the Convention.
4 *United Carriers Ltd v Heritage Food Group (UK) Ltd* [1995] 4 All ER 95 at 102, [1996] 1 WLR 371 at 378, where May J so held 'with unconcealed reluctance'.
5 As to carriage by road and rail generally see CARRIERS vol 5(1) (Reissue) para 425 et seq.
6 As to carriage of goods by air generally see CARRIERS vol 5(1) (Reissue) para 408 et seq.
7 As to these categories see para 411 ante.
8 This caveat is made necessary by an observation of Lord Wilberforce in *Aries Tanker Corpn v Total Transport Ltd* [1977] 1 All ER 398, [1977] 1 WLR 185, HL, that there is no case of the rule of abatement having been extended to contracts of any kind of carriage, and that the rule against deduction in cases of carriage by sea is, in fact, as well settled as any common law rule can be. Lord Wilberforce thus kept open all contracts of carriage for further consideration.

In the case of international carriage, if the application or incorporation of a statute or rules bars the right as well as the remedy, the rule in *Aries Tanker Corpn v Total Transport Ltd*, supra would presumably apply: see para 413 note 5 ante. When rules or standard terms are incorporated into a contract they are to be construed as part of the contract: *Nea Agrex SA v Baltic Shipping Co Ltd* [1976] QB 933, [1976] 2 All ER 842, CA; *Consolidated Investment and Contracting Co v Saponaria Shipping Co Ltd, The Virgo* [1978] 3 All ER 988 at 992, [1978] 1 WLR 968 at 991, CA, per Ormrod LJ. In an arbitration, whether the incorporated contractual clause affects the right or the remedy, the court retains jurisdiction to extend time under the Arbitration Act 1996 s 12: see *Nea Agrex SA v Baltic Shipping Co Ltd* supra; *Consolidated Investment and Contracting Co v Saponaria Shipping Co Ltd, The Virgo* supra; and ARBITRATION vol 2 (Reissue) para 651; LIMITATION OF ACTIONS vol 28 (Reissue) paras 815, 817.

417. Rent. In answer to a claim for rent, a tenant has an ancient common law right¹ to set up by way of defence any sum of money actually expended by him on repairs which the landlord, in breach of covenant, has failed to carry out, or any sum of money actually expended by him at the landlord's request to fulfil the landlord's obligations in respect of the land or to protect the tenant's occupation². Ordinarily the common law right cannot be exercised before the landlord has notice of the want of repair³, though in cases of emergency it may be that the tenant can effect the repairs and recoup the expense from the rent despite lack of notice⁴. The right is a right of recoupment apart from being a defence to an action for rent and, if the rent has been paid, the right may constitute an answer to a claim to distrain⁵. The right is exercisable against arrears of rent as well as future rent⁶. However, the common law right extends no further, and it is said that it does not include cross-claims for an uncertain or unliquidated sum⁷.

1 See *Lee-Parker v Izzet* [1971] 3 All ER 1099 at 1107, [1971] 1 WLR 1688 at 1693 per Goff J; *Connaught Restaurants Ltd v Indoor Leisure Ltd* [1994] 4 All ER 834 at 840, [1994] 1 WLR 501 at 507, CA, per Wait LJ, and at 844, 511 per Neill LJ. See also *Waters v Weigall* (1795) 2 Anst 575.
2 *Federal Commerce and Navigation Co Ltd v Molena Alpha Inc* [1978] QB 927 at 973, [1978] 3 All ER 1066 at 1077, CA, per Lord Denning MR (affd [1979] AC 757, [1979] 1 All ER 307, HL); *British Anzani (Felixstowe) Ltd v International Marine Management (UK) Ltd* [1980] QB 137, [1979] 2 All ER 1063, applying *Taylor v Beal* (1591) Cro Eliz 222, considering *Waters v Weigall* (1795) 2 Anst 575, and following *Lee-Parker v Izzet* [1971] 3 All ER 1099, [1971] 1 WLR 1688. See also *Carter v Carter* (1829) 5 Bing 406 (payment of mesne landlord's ground rent); *Doe v Hare* (1833) 2 Cr & M 145; *Johnson v Jones* (1839) 9 Ad & El 809 (payment of rent to mortgagee); *Boodle v Campbell* (1844) 2 Dow & L 66.

3   *Lee-Parker v Izzet* [1971] 3 All ER 1099 at 1108, [1971] 1 WLR 1688 at 1693, per Goff J; *British Anzani (Felixstowe) Ltd v International Marine Management (UK) Ltd* [1980] QB 137 at 147–148, [1979] 2 All ER 1063 at 1070 per Forbes J.
4   See SR Derham *Set-Off* (2nd edn, 1996) p 119.
5   *Connaught Restaurants Ltd v Indoor Leisure Ltd* [1994] 4 All ER 834 at 844, [1994] 1 WLR 501 at 511, CA; see also *Lee-Parker v Izzet* [1971] 3 All ER 1099 at 1106–1107, [1971] 1 WLR 1688 at 1692–1693.
6   *Asco Developments Ltd v Gordon* [1978] 248 Estates Gazette 683.
7   See *British Anzani (Felixstowe) Ltd v International Marine Management (UK) Ltd* [1980] QB 137 at 148, [1979] 2 All ER 1063 at 1070, obiter per Forbes J; and para 465 post.

418. Contracting out from right to set–off, deduct or abate. Parties may contract out of the right to set–off, deduct or abate, but this can only be done by clear and unequivocal words[1] or at least a clear implication[2].

1   *Gilbert-Ash (Northern) Ltd v Modern Engineering (Bristol) Ltd* [1974] AC 689, [1973] 3 All ER 195, HL. See *Mottram Consultants Ltd v Bernard Sunley & Sons Ltd* [1975] 2 Lloyd's Rep 197, (1974) 118 Sol Jo 808, HL (in which the contract was held to exclude abatement). For instances of strict insistence on clear words see *Acsim (Southern) Ltd v Danish Contracting and Development Co Ltd* (1989) 47 BLR 55, CA; *Connaught Restaurants Ltd v Indoor Leisure Ltd* [1994] 4 All ER 834 at 838, 843–844, [1994] 1 WLR 501 at 505, 510–511, CA; *The Teno* [1977] 2 Lloyd's Rep 289. But a clause excluding set-off is not subject to the requirement that set-off be specifically excluded; such a clause does not exclude liability in the way that a clause excluding liability for negligence does: see *Continental Illinois National Bank & Trust Co of Chicago v Papanicolaou* [1986] 2 Lloyd's Rep 441 at 443–444, 83 LS Gaz R 2569, CA. For instances of 'no set-off' clauses and the application to them of the Unfair Contract Terms Act 1977 s 3 see *Stewart Gill Ltd v Horatio Myer & Co Ltd* [1992] QB 600, [1992] 2 All ER 257, CA; *George Mitchell (Chesterhall) Ltd v Finney Lock Seeds Ltd* [1983] 1 All ER 108, [1982] 3 WLR 1036, CA (affd [1983] 2 AC 803, 2 All ER 737, HL) (clause held to be unfair and unreasonable); *Schenkers Ltd v Overland Shoes Ltd* [1998] 1 Lloyd's Rep 498, CA (clause held to be reasonable); *RW Green Ltd v Cade Bros Farms* [1978] 1 Lloyd's Rep 602 (clause held to be reasonable); *Singer Co (UK) Ltd v Tees and Hartlepool Port Authority* [1988] 2 Lloyd's Rep 164, FTLR 442 (clause held to be fair and reasonable). As to contracts imposing a time-limit for cross-complaints see para 413 note 5 ante; and as to similar principles affecting an equitable defence see paras 432–433 post.
2   *Gilbert-Ash (Northern) Ltd v Modern Engineering (Bristol) Ltd* [1974] AC 689 at 723, [1973] 3 All ER 195 at 220 per Lord Salmon. See also *Connaught Restaurants Ltd v Indoor Leisure Ltd* [1994] 4 All ER 834 at 838, [1994] 1 WLR 501 at 505, CA.

419. The contemporary significance of the right of abatement. It may still be essential to prove a right of abatement at common law in at least two cases: (1) where an equitable defence (set-off) is unavailable because the facts do not disclose the necessary 'equity' in the defendant[1]; and (2) when an equitable defence (set-off) is time-barred by reason of the Limitation Act 1980[2].

1   As to the equitable defence see para 424 et seq post. The necessary equity in the defendant may be lacking because he has contractually agreed to a time-limit on his cross-claim: *Aries Tanker Corpn v Total Transport Ltd* [1977] 1 All ER 398, [1977] 1 WLR 185, HL, where it was held that, if anything, the equity lay with the shipowner, having regard to the terms of the contract; see paras 431, 433 post. It appears to follow that if, for example, a contract of carriage by land is in issue, and it contains a time-limit on a claim by the customer, it may be essential to prove that such a contract is within the rule of abatement, since the necessary equity may be lacking for equitable defence: see the discussion in para 433 post.
2   *Henriksens Rederi A/S v PHZ Rolimpex, The Brede* [1974] QB 233 at 246, [1973] 3 All ER 589, CA, where Lord Denning MR held (obiter) that what is now the Limitation Act 1980 s 35, did not apply to equitable set-off, in which case the point mentioned in the text does not arise. This was a minority view; as to the implications of the contrary view see para 434 note 3 post. It is sufficient to note here that if the contrary view prevailed, there would be cases where proof of a common law right of abatement would be essential.

(3) SET-OFF AT LAW

420. Origin of the right. Set-off at law was the creature of two statutes[1] early in the eighteenth century designed to prevent the imprisonment as a debtor of a person not truly indebted because there was a mutual debt owing by his creditor. Although now repealed, their effect has been preserved[2].

1   The original enabling statutes were 2 Geo 2 c 22 (Insolvent Debtors Relief) (1728), and 8 Geo 2 c 24 (Set-off) (1734) (both repealed), known as the Statutes of Set-off.

2   The Statutes of Set-off were repealed by the Civil Procedure Acts Repeal Act 1879 (repealed), and the Statute Law Revision and Civil Procedure Act 1883 (repealed), but the rights conferred by them were preserved by the Supreme Court of Judicature (Consolidation) Act 1925 s 39(1)(a) (repealed). See now RSC Ord 15 rr 2, 3; Ord 18 r 17; and the Supreme Court Act 1981 ss 49(2), 84(2). See also the County Courts Act 1984 s 38 (substituted by the Courts and Legal Services Act 1990 s 3). As to the replacement of the RSC by the CPR, and the transitional arrangements in relation thereto, see para 401 note 3 ante.

421. Nature of the right. The right conferred by the Statutes of Set-off[1] was a right to set off mutual debts[2] arising from transactions of a different nature[3] which were due and payable[4] and could be ascertained with certainty at the time of pleading[5]. Thus no legal set-off could exist against a claim which sounded in unliquidated or uncertain damages[6], nor could a claim which sounded in such damages be set off at law against a plaintiff's claim[7]. The fact that a claim was framed in damages precluded the raising of a set-off at law, notwithstanding that the claim might have been differently framed in a way which would have permitted such a set-off[8]. Where a claim for a liquidated debt was joined by a plaintiff with a claim for damages, set-off at law might only be pleaded in defence to the former claim[9]. Set-off at law operates as a defence[10].

1   As to these statutes see para 420 notes 1–2 ante.

2   Mutuality does not require that the debts arise at the same time: *Day & Dent Constructions Pty Ltd v North Australian Properties Pty Ltd* (1986) 150 CLR 85. Mutuality requires that the demands be between the same parties and in the same right or interest: *Inca Hall Rolling Mills Co Ltd v Douglas Forge Co* (1882) 8 QBD 179, 183. The suggestion by Lord Denning in the Court of Appeal that the nature of the arrangements may be so special as to deny mutuality (*Halesowen Presswork & Assemblies Ltd v National Westminster Bank* [1971] 1 QB 1 at 36) was criticised on appeal [1972] AC 785 at 812 per Lord Cross of Chelsea; cf at 806 per Viscount Dilhorne, [1972] 1 All ER 641 at 654–655, cf 650.

3   Where there was a running account of connected transactions, the common law regarded the balance as the debt so no question of set-off arose: *Green v Farmer* (1768) 4 Burr 2214 per Lord Mansfield. The third edition of this work gave the impression that Lord Mansfield was referring to a cross-complaint arising out of the transaction which was the subject of the plaintiff's claim, and the passage was adopted in *Henriksens Rederi A/S v PHZ Rolimpex, The Brede* [1974] QB 233, [1973] 3 All ER 589, CA, by Lord Denning MR, who took Lord Mansfield and the learned editor to be distinguishing set-off at law (necessarily separate transactions) from abatement (the same transaction: see para 411 ante). It is respectfully submitted that this was not the case. Abatement was not recognised until later (see para 411 ante) and Lord Mansfield was dealing with separate but connected transactions at common law, and separate but unconnected transactions under the statutes, which permitted set-off 'notwithstanding that such debts are deemed in law to be of a different nature'. It is submitted that if any defendant ever wished to avail himself of a liquidated set-off at law arising out of the transaction on which the plaintiff sues, he is entitled to do so. It is further submitted that the conclusion of Lord Denning MR, that 'set-off' in what is now the Limitation Act 1980 s 35 is confined to set-off at law, is unaffected by the foregoing analysis. See paras 422, 431 post.

4   *Stein v Blake* [1996] AC 243 at 251, [1995] 2 All ER 961 at 964, HL, per Lord Hoffmann. The traditional view was that the mutual debts should be due and payable at the date of commencement of the action: *Pilgrim v Kinder* (1744) 7 Mod 463; *Richards v James* (1848) 2 Exch 471. But now, as a result of rules of court, a right of set-off arising after the action has commenced may be relied upon as a defence: *Stein v Blake* supra at 252 and at 964–965.

5   See *Hanak v Green* [1958] 2 QB 9 at 17, [1958] 2 All ER 141 at 145, CA. Such claims include the amount of a judgment debt or of a verdict for which judgment has not been entered: *Baskerville v Brown* (1761) 2 Burr 1229; *Hawkins v Baynes* (1823) 1 LJOSKB 167; *Russell v May* (1828) 7 LJOSKB 88.

6   *Stooke v Taylor* (1880) 5 QBD 569 at 575 per Cockburn CJ (the plea 'is available only where the claims on both sides are in respect of liquidated debt, or money demands which can be readily and without difficulty ascertained'). If an indemnity is given in respect of a liquidated demand, the liability under the indemnity is liquidated and may be set-off under the Statutes of Set-Off: see *Attwooll v Attwooll* (1853) 2 E & B 23, explained in *Axel Johnson Petroleum AB v MG Mineral Group AG* [1992] 2 All ER 163, [1992] 1 WLR 270, CA; *Crawford v Stirling* (1802) 4 Esp 207; *Cooper v Robinson* (1818) 2 Chit 161; *Morley v Inglis* (1837) 4 Bing NC 58; *Williams v Flight* (1842) 2 Dowl NS 11; *Hutchinson v Sydney* (1854) 10 Exch 438; *Brown v Tibbits* (1862) 11 CBNS 855; *Pellas v Neptune Marine Insurance Co* (1879) 5 CPD 34, CA. The reference in *Stooke v Taylor* supra at 575 to 'money demands' is to demands analogous to debts which can be readily ascertained: *Aectra Refining & Manufacturing Inc v Exmar NV* [1994] 1 WLR 1634 at 1647, [1995] 1 Lloyd's Rep 191 at 199, CA, per Hirst LJ. To generate a set-off, it now seems that the claim and cross-claim need not be debts strictly so called, but may sound in damages: *Axel Johnson Petroleum AB v MG Mineral Group AG* supra at 272 per Leggatt LJ, cited with evident approval in *B Hargreaves Ltd v Action 2000 Ltd* [1993] BCLC 1111 at 1113, CA, per Balcombe LJ. A sum specified as payable by way of demurrage and liquidated damages could ground a set-off: *Axel Johnson Petroleum AB v MG Mineral Group AG* supra. But cf *Seager v Duthie* (1860) 8 CBNS 45 (where a claim for delay in loading a ship was not within the demurrage clause and could not ground a set-off).

7   *Freeman v Hyett* (1762) 1 Wm Bl 394; *Howlet v Strickland* (1774) 1 Cowp 56 (non-delivery of goods); *Weigall v Waters* (1795) 6 Term Rep 488; *Morley v Inglis* (1837) 4 Bing NC 58; *Williams v Flight* (1842) 2 Dowl NS 11; *Newfoundland Government v Newfoundland Rly Co* (1888) 13 App Cas 199 at 213, PC.

8   *Cooper v Robinson* (1818) 2 Chit 161; *Hardcastle v Netherwood* (1821) 5 B & Ald 93; *Thorpe v Thorpe* (1832) 3 B & Ad 580.

9   *Birch v Depeyster* (1816) 4 Camp 385; *Crampton v Walker* (1860) 3 E & E 321.

10 *Re Bankruptcy Notice (No 171 of 1934)* [1934] Ch 431, CA, cited in *Hanak v Green* [1958] 2 QB 9 at 16, [1958] 2 All ER 141 at 145, CA, per Morris LJ.

422. Set-off generated by a claim based on a guarantee. The traditional view was that a claim based on a guarantee cannot give rise to a set-off. This was because it was thought that the obligation undertaken by a guarantor under a contract of guarantee is to see that the debtor performs his obligation to the principal creditor[1]. So even if the guarantee is of the payment of a debt, the creditor's remedy against the guarantor is an action for damages for breach of contract[2]. But now that legal set-off is not confined to debts strictly so called, it is doubtful that the traditional view would prevail. In comparable jurisdictions at least it seems that the guarantor can be sued for the sum which the debtor has failed to pay[3] and, accordingly, that a claim based on a guarantee can give rise to a set-off[4]. In any event, a guarantee may be expressed as a conditional agreement to pay in which event the liability arising upon breach would ground a set-off[5]. It has been held that a guarantor can avail himself of any right of set-off held by the debtor against the creditor[6].

1   *Moschi v Lep Air Services* [1973] AC 331 at 348–349, [1972] 2 All ER 393 at 401–402, HL, per Lord Diplock; see also at 357 and at 409 per Lord Simon of Glaisdale.

2   *Moreley v Inglis* (1837) 4 Bing NC 58.

3   *Sunbird Plaza Pty Ltd v Maloney* (1988) 166 CLR 245 at 255–256 per Mason CJ; *Hawkins v Bank of China* (1992) 26 NSWLR 562.

4   See *National Bank of Australia v Swan* (1872) 3 VR(L) 168; and text and note 6 infra.

5   *Moschi v Lep Air Services* [1973] AC 331 at 344–345, [1972] 2 All ER 393 at 398–399, HL, per Lord Reid; *Sunbird Plaza Pty Ltd v Maloney* (1988) 166 CLR 244 at 256–257 per Mason CJ. See also *The Raven* [1980] 2 Lloyd's Rep 266 at 271–272 per Parker J.

6   *BOC Group plc v Centeon LLC* [1999] 1 All ER (Comm) 53.

423. Claim upon an indemnity as the subject of a set-off. As an indemnity, unlike a guarantee, creates a primary not a secondary liability[1], if the principal obligation is capable of generating a set-off, then so is the indemnity. The critical question is whether the amount of the indemnity is ascertainable with precision at the time of pleading[2]. So, if the indemnity is given in respect of a liquidated demand, liability may be legally set-off[3], but not otherwise[4].

An indemnity in respect of a loss arising out of the occurrence of a particular event can give rise to a set-off, if the loss is ascertainable with precision[5]. It is otherwise in the case of claims on policies of indemnity insurance because they are held to be claims for unliquidated damages[6], even when the loss has been adjusted[7]. However, the correctness of this approach has been doubted[8].

In the case of non-indemnity insurance, it seems that a set-off is available when the liability relates to a liquidated sum due under the contract[9].

1   *Argo Caribbean Group Ltd v Lewis* [1976] 2 Lloyd's Rep 289 at 296, CA, citing *Yeoman Credit Ltd v Latter* [1961] 1 WLR 828 at 830–831, CA.
2   *Axel Johnson Petroleum AB v MG Mineral Group AG* [1992] 2 All ER 163 at 167, [1992] 1 WLR 270 at 274, CA.
3   *Hutchinson v Sydney* (1854) 10 Exch 438.
4   *Cooper v Robinson* (1818) 2 Chit 161; *Hardcastle v Netherwood* (1821) 5 B & Ald 93.
5   *Hutchinson v Sydney* (1854) 10 Exch 438.
6   *Pellas v Neptune Marine Insurance Company* (1879) 5 CPD 34, CA; *William Pickersgill & Sons Ltd v London and Provincial Marine and General Insurance London and Provincial Marine and General Insurance Co Ltd* [1912] 3 KB 614 at 622; *Jabbour v Custodian of Israeli Absentee Property* [1954] 1 WLR 139; *Chandris v Argo Insurance Co Ltd* [1963] 2 Lloyd's Rep 65; *Edmunds v Lloyd's Italico* [1986] 2 All ER 249 at 250, [1986] 1 WLR 492 at 493.
7   *Luckie v Bushby* (1853) 13 B & C 864; *Jabbour v Custodian of Israeli Absentee Property* [1954] 1 WLR 139 at 143.
8   See SR Derham *Set Off* (2nd edn, 1996) p 18.
9   *Blackley v National Mutual Life Association (No 2)* [1973] 1 NZLR 668 at 672.

424. Statutes of limitation. A set-off at law is deemed to be a separate action and to have been commenced on the same date as the action in which it is pleaded[1]. But where a set-off is based on a debt which arose after the commencement of the action, enforceability would be determined when set-off is pleaded[2]

1   Limitation Act 1980 s 35(1)(b), (2), which refers to 'set-off' without further description. It is established that this phrase refers to set-off at law: *Henriksens Rederi A/S v PHZ Rolimpex, The Brede* [1974] QB 233, [1973] 3 All ER 589, CA. A set-off cannot be based on an unenforceable debt: *Walker v Clements* (1850) 15 QB 1046; *Aectra Refining & Manufacturing Inc v Exmar NV* [1994] 1 WLR 1634, 1650–1651 CA ('the cross-claim has to be actionable'). See para 421 note 2 ante. As to whether the statute refers to equitable defence see para 431 post.
2   See SR Derham *Set-off* (2nd edn, 1996) p 27 n 130.

425. Bankruptcy. Bankruptcy may have constituted an exception to principles of common law limiting the right to set off[1]. Set-off in bankruptcy is now governed by special statutory principles[2].

1   *Anon* (1676) 1 Mod Rep 215 per North CJ; *Chapman v Derby* (1689) 2 Vern 117; *Green v Farmer* (1768) 4 Burr 2214 at 2221, note (a).
2   See BANKRUPTCY AND INSOLVENCY vol 3(2) (Reissue) para 535 et seq. For a modern case in which the distinction between set-off and counterclaim has been considered in a bankruptcy context see *Hofer v Strawson* (1999) Times, 17 April.

(4) EQUITABLE DEFENCE

(i) The Right

426. History of the right. The traditional view is that equitable set-off pre-dated the statutes of set-off[1]. But it is difficult to find instances of equitable set-off before 1728[2]. Prior to the Judicature Acts[3], courts of equity admitted cross-complaints by way of defence in actions proceeding in Chancery and would also restrain a plaintiff in an action at law from proceeding or levying execution where there was an equity which went to impeach the title to the legal demand[4]. The right was then usually referred to as 'equitable set-off'. Since 1873, however, the right of equitable set-off previously available in Chancery is available as a defence to an action at law[5]. That is not to say that the legislation of that date, which brought about the fusion of law and equity, extended the right of set-off to cases where it had not previously existed; rather it equated the procedure by which these hitherto separate remedies might henceforth be employed, so that an equitable defence is now available in all circumstances in which before 1873 it might have been raised either in equity as a defence or to restrain an action at law[6]. However, whilst the courts will derive general principles from the practice of the former courts of equity[7], it appears that in making a practical application of principle the courts today are prepared to develop the fused system independently of an inquiry into what might have been done in the nineteenth century in a Court of Chancery[8].

1   *Ex p Stephens* (1805) 11 Ves 24 at 27, 32 ER 996 at 997 per Lord Eldon LC.
2   The cases are discussed in Meagher, Gummow & Lehane *Equity Doctrines and Remedies* (3rd edn, 1992).
3   Ie the Supreme Court of Judicature Act 1873, and the Supreme Court of Judicature Act 1875.
4   *Rawson v Samuel* (1841) Cr & Ph 161 at 178–179 per Lord Cottenham LC, cited by Lord Denning MR in *Federal Commerce Ltd v Molena Alpha Inc* [1978] QB 927 at 974, [1978] 3 All ER 1066 at 1078, CA.
5   See the Supreme Court Act 1981 s 49(2)(a), which specifically refers to 'equitable defences'. In this title 'equitable set-off' and 'equitable defence' are used indiscriminately, as in the decided cases. See also *Coca-Cola Financial Corpn v Finsat International Ltd* [1998] QB 43, [1996] 3 WLR 849, CA.
6   The Judicature Acts did not alter the rights of parties; they only affected procedure: *Stumore v Campbell & Co* [1892] 1 QB 314 at 316, CA, per Lord Esher MR. See also, however, *Bankes v Jarvis* [1903] 1 KB 549, DC, and the cases cited in notes 7–8 infra.
7   *Aries Tanker Corpn v Total Transport Ltd* [1977] 1 All ER 398, [1977] 1 WLR 185, HL; *Federal Commerce and Navigation Co Ltd v Molena Alpha Inc* [1978] QB 927, [1978] 3 All ER 1066, CA (affd on another point [1979] AC 757, [1979] 1 All ER 307, HL).
8   *Federal Commerce and Navigation Co Ltd v Molena Alpha Inc* [1978] QB 927 at 974, [1978] 3 All ER 1066 at 1078, CA, per Lord Denning MR: 'These grounds [of equitable set-off] were never precisely formulated before the Judicature Act 1873. It is now far too late to search through the old books and dig them out... the streams of common law and equity have flown together and combined so as to be indistinguishable... we have to ask ourselves: what should we do now so as to ensure fair dealing between the parties?'. Cf *United Scientific Holdings Ltd v Burnley Borough Council* [1978] AC 904 at 924, [1977] 2 All ER 62 at 68, HL, per Lord Diplock; and see also EQUITY vol 16 (Reissue) para 916 et seq.

427. Nature of the right. Where a right of set-off exists at law, it will be recognised in equity, unless reliance on it is inequitable[1]. Apart from the recognition of a legal set-off, there are now three kinds of equitable set-off: (1) an equitable set-off existing by an analogy with a legal set-off; (2) an equitable set-off arising by agreement; and (3) general equitable set-off, which is much more comprehensive in its scope and arises where the party seeking the benefit of it can show some equitable ground for being protected against his adversary's demand[2].

1   See *Re Whitehouse & Co* (1878) ChD 595 at 597; *Sankey Brook Coal Co Ltd v Marsh* (1871) LR 6 Exch 185.
2   *Rawson v Samuel* (1841) Cr & Ph 161 at 178 per Lord Cottenham LC.

428. Analogy with set-off at common law. Equity developed its jurisdiction by analogy with set-off at common law[1]. Where there are cross-claims of such a nature that if both were reasonable at law they would be the subject of a legal set-off, if either of the claims is equitable only, a set-off will be allowed in equity[2], so when there are mutual liquidated cross-claims one of which is cognisable in equity, an additional equity is not required to support a set-off[3]. But a set-off will not be allowed if special circumstances make it inequitable to do so[4].

1 As to set-off at common law see para 420 et seq ante.

2 *Clark v Cort* (1840) Cr & Ph 154, *Thornton v Maynard* (1875) LR 10 CP 695; *Ex p Mariar* (1879) 12 ChD 491. See also *Tony Lee Motors Ltd v MS MacDonald & Son (1974) Ltd* [1981] 2 NZLR 281 at 286–288 (approving the statement of principle in Meagher, Gummow & Lehane *Equity Doctrines and Remedies* (3rd edn, 1992) para 3707); but cf *Middleton v Pollock, ex p Nugee* (1875) LR 20 Eq 29 at 36–37.

3 See *Tony Lee Motors Ltd v MS MacDonald & Son (1974) Ltd* [1981] 2 NZLR 281, 287–288; but cf *Middleton v Pollock, ex p Nugee* (1875) LR 20 Eq 29 at 36–37.

4 See Spry *Equitable Remedies* (4th edn, 1990) pp 172–173.

429. Equitable set-off arising from agreement. A right of set-off may be created by agreement, and on this ground there may be a set-off of a debt which could not otherwise be so pleaded[1]. Equitable set-off was initially based on an express or implied agreement to that effect[2], though the jurisdiction has been exercised when there was no such agreement[3]. The court has been willing to imply an agreement from slight foundations[4], but there must generally be some evidence on which the court can find an agreement, express or implied[5]. A course of dealing between the parties by which mutual debts have been set off is evidence from which the court will imply such an agreement[6], but a set-off cannot be based on a custom of which the plaintiff was not aware[7]. Set-off by agreement is not allowed if there is no consideration to support the agreement[8].

1 *Wood v Akers* (1797) 2 Esp 594 (claim by husband and set-off of debt owed by wife before marriage); *Kinnerley v Hossack* (1809) 2 Taunt 170.

2 *Downam v Matthews* (1721) Prec Ch 580; *Hawkins v Freeman* (1723) 2 Eq Cas Abr 10.

3 *Arnold v Richardson* (1699) 1 Eq Cas Abr 8.

4 *Jeffs v Wood* (1723) 2 P Wms 128 at 130; *Ex p Prescot* (1753) 1 Atk 230. See also *Downam v Matthews* (1721) Prec Ch 580; *Cuxon v Chadley* (1824) 5 Dow & Ry KB 417 (agreement binding though not in writing); *Unity Joint-Stock Mutual Banking Association v King* (1858) 25 Beav 72.

5 *Freeman v Lomas* (1851) 9 Hare 109; *Hunt v Jessel* (1854) 18 Beav 100.

6 *Jeffs v Wood* (1723) 2 P Wms 128; *Bamford v Harris* (1816) 1 Stark 343. See also CONTRACT vol 9(1) (Reissue) para 944.

7 *Blackburn v Mason* (1893) 68 LT 510, CA.

8 *Birkbeck Building Society v Birkbeck* (1913) 29 TLR 218, DC.

430. General equitable set-off. Where a cross-claim for a sum of money is so closely connected with the claim that it goes to impeach the plaintiff's title to be paid and raises an equity in the defendant, making it unfair that he should pay the plaintiff without deduction, the general rule is that the defendant may deduct with impunity the amount of the cross-claim, or raise it by way of equitable defence when sued[1]. The element of impeachment requires, in the absence of an independent equitable ground, a sufficiently close connection between the claims. This is not necessarily to be equated with a requirement that the claims arose out of the same transactions, though there is some support for such a proposition[2]. If the cross-claims arise out of separate transactions, they may not be sufficiently connected[3]. It is not enough that the claims arise out of the same contract[4]. Nor is it necessarily enough that the cross-claim is related to the transaction on which the claim is based[5]. It has been said that the cross-claim must go to the root of the plaintiff's claim[6] or that it must question, impugn or disparage the title to the claim[7] or that the claims must be interdependent[8]. There is some support for the proposition that equitable set-off is available whenever the cross-claim arises out of the same transaction as the claim or out of a transaction that is closely related to the claim[9]. But the impeachment test was subsequently confirmed at the highest level[10], though it has been linked subsequently to the notion that the cross-claim will impeach the plaintiff's claim if the cross-claim is so closely connected with the claim that it would be unfair not to allow a set-off[11]. Because the impeachment test is unfamiliar to modern lawyers, the House of

Lords has re-stated the test so that an equitable set-off may arise if there is a cross-claim flowing out of and inseparably connected with the dealings and transactions which also give rise to the claim[12].

The cross-claim must be for a sum of money, whether liquidated or unliquidated[13]. As to the claim, it is probable that set-off can only be raised in defence to a money claim[14], and uncertain whether it may be raised only in defence to a liquidated money claim[15].

1   *Piggott v Williams* (1821) 6 Madd 95; *Rawson v Samuel* (1841) Cr & Ph 161 at 165; *Young v Kitchin* (1878) 3 ExD 127; *Newfoundland Government v Newfoundland Rly Co* (1888) 13 App Cas 199, PC; *Bankes v Jarvis* [1903] 1 KB 549; *Morgan & Son Ltd v S Martin Johnson & Co Ltd* [1949] 1 KB 107, [1948] 2 All ER 196, CA; *Hanak v Green* [1958] 2 QB 9, [1958] 2 All ER 141, CA; *Henriksens Rederi A/S v THZ Rolimpex, The Brede* [1974] QB 233, [1973] 3 All ER 589, CA; *Aries Tanker Corpn v Total Transport Ltd* [1977] 1 All ER 398, [1977] 1 WLR 185, HL; *Federal Commerce and Navigation Co Ltd v Molena Alpha Inc* [1978] QB 927, [1978] 3 All ER 1066, CA (affd on another point [1979] AC 757, [1979] 1 All ER 307, HL); *Sim v Rotherham Metropolitan Borough Council* [1987] Ch 216 at 261–262, [1986] 3 All ER 387 at 414–415; *Dole Dried Fruit and Nut Co v Trustin Kenwood Ltd* [1990] 2 Lloyd's Rep 309, CA.

2   *Bank of Boston Connecticut v European Grain & Shipping Ltd* [1989] AC 1056, [1989] 1 All ER 545, HL.

3   *Re Convere Pty Ltd* [1976] VR 345 at 349.

4   *Rawson v Samuel* (1841) Cr & Ph 161.

5   *Hanak v Green* [1958] 2 QB 9 at 23, [1958] 2 All ER 141 at 148, CA.

6   *British Anzani (Felixstowe) Ltd v International Marine Management (UK) Ltd* [1980] 1 QB 137 at 145.

7   *MEK Nominees Pty Ltd v Billboard Entertainments Pty Ltd* (1993) Conv R 54–468.

8   *Grant v NZMC Ltd* [1989] 1 NZLR 8 at 13. The fact that the plaintiff is insolvent is not enough for a set-off : *Rawson v Samuel* (1841) Cr & Ph 162 at 175.

9   *Henriksens Rederi A/S v PHZ Rolimpex, The Brede* [1974] QB 233 at 248, citing *Morgan & Son Ltd v S Martin Johnson & Co Ltd* [1949] 1 KB 407, [1948] 2 All ER 196, CA, and *Hanak v Green* [1958] 2 QB 9, [1958] 2 All ER 141, CA. In *The Brede* supra, at 249, Lord Denning MR asserted 'with any breach by the plaintiff of the self-same contract, the defendant can in equity set up his loan in diminution or extinction of the contract price'. See also *Box v Midland Bank Ltd* [1981] 1 Lloyd's Rep 434 at 437, CA.

10   *Aries Tanker Corpn v Total Transport Ltd* [1977] 1 All ER 398, [1977] 1 WLR 185 HL. See also *Federal Commerce & Navigation Co Ltd v Molena Alpha Inc* [1978] 1 QB 927 (where Lord Denning MR finally acknowledged that there must be an equitable ground to impeach the plaintiff's claim and went on to ask at 974 'what should we do now so as to ensure fair dealing between the parties?'); *AB Contractors Ltd v Flaherty Bros Ltd* (1978) 16 BLR 8 at 14, CA.

11   *Federal Commerce & Navigation Co Ltd v Molena Alpha Inc* [1978] QB 927 at 975, 981, 987, [1978] 3 All ER 1066 at 1078, 1083, 1088, CA; *The Teno* [1977] 2 Lloyd's Rep 289; *Dole Dried Fruit and Nut Co v Trustin Kenwood Ltd* [1990] 2 Lloyd's Rep 309 at 311, CA; *National Westminster Bank plc v Skelton* [1993] All ER 242 at 247, [1993] 1 WLR 72 at 76 CA; *SL Sethia Liners Ltd v Naviagro Maritime Corpn, The Kostas Melas* [1981] 1 Lloyd's Rep 18 at 25; *BICC v Burndy Corpn* [1985] Ch 232 at 250, [1985] 1 All ER 417 at 427, CA; *Sim v Rotherham Metropolitan Borough Council* [1987] Ch 216 at 261–262, [1986] 3 All ER 387 at 414–415.

12   *Bank of Boston Connecticut v European Grain & Shipping Ltd* [1989] AC 1056 at 1102–1103, 1110–1111, [1989] 1 All ER 545 at 552–553, 558–559, HL; *Dole Dried Fruit and Nut Co v Trustin Kenwood Ltd* [1990] 2 Lloyd's Rep 309, CA (where a counterclaim was allowed for damages for breach of agency sales contracts); *Esso Petroleum Ltd v Milton* [1997] 2 All ER 593, [1997] 1 WLR 938, CA (where counterclaim by motor fuel retailer for future loss arising from oil company's repudiation of contract was held not to be sufficiently connected with oil company's claim for payment for past deliveries); see also *Guinness plc v Saunders* [1988] 2 All ER 940 [1988] 1 WLR 863, CA; *Zemco Ltd v Jerrom-Pugh* [1993] BCC 275; *The Aditya Vaibhav* [1991] 1 Lloyd's Rep 573.

13   This is the essential nature of set-off and equitable defence: see RSC Ord 18 r 17; CPR 16.6; and para 401 ante. Other cross-complaints can be raised by way of counterclaim, as to which see para 480 et seq post; and PRACTICE AND PROCEDURE. The view expressed by Dixon J in *MacDonnell & East Ltd v McGregor* (1936) 56 CLR 50 at 62 that an unliquidated demand cannot support a set-off does not apply to an equitable set-off. See *Beasley v Darcy* (1800) 2 Sch & Lef at 403n, HL; *Galambas & Son Pty Ltd v McIntyre* (1974) 5 ACTR 10; *British Anzani (Felixstowe) Ltd v International Marine Management (UK) Ltd* [1980] QB 137 at 145–146, [1979] 2 All ER 1063 at 1068.

14   See eg para 443 post.

15   See *Hanak v Green* [1958] 2 QB 9, [1958] 2 All ER 141, CA, where a customer sued a builder in respect of allegedly defective work (a claim for unliquidated damages in which she recovered much less than the sum claimed) and the builder set up by way of defence the fact that various sums were owing to him. There was a balance due to the builder, and the Court of Appeal awarded him all the costs of the action.

It is submitted that the implication that equitable defence lies against unliquidated claims is sound and consistent with principle, although the contrary was decided in *McCreagh v Judd* [1923] WN 174, DC (not cited in *Hanak v Green* supra). See also *Rawson v Samuel* (1841) Cr & Ph 161; and *Gathercole v Smith* (1881) 7 QBD 626 at 631, CA, per Bramwell LJ. It is also submitted that in general a defendant should be permitted an equitable set-off against an unliquidated money claim. If he is permitted to deduct and defend in respect of a merely triable and unliquidated cross-claim against a plaintiff's otherwise cast-iron liquidated claim, the equities would appear to be still more in his favour if the plaintiff's claim is unliquidated and the defendant's is liquidated and cast-iron. Both *Hanak v Green* supra, and *McCreagh v Judd* supra, concerned the effect of the doctrine on costs. The former result appears just, and the latter indefensible. See also para 514 post. See also *BICC v Burndy Corpn* [1985] Ch 232, [1985] 1 All ER 417, CA; *Aectra Refining & Manufacturing Inc v Exmar NV* [1995] 1 WLR 1634, CA (claim under charterparty for stipulated rate of daily hire in respect of specific off-hire periods is a liquidated debt capable of constituting a legal set-off).

431. Analogy with abatement. In certain cases where the common law would not permit abatement[1] equity follows the law by recognising similar exceptions[2]. However, in other cases equity supplements the law by allowing an equitable defence[3].

1　See para 413 et seq ante.

2　As to the freight exception (voyage charter) see para 413 text and notes 5–6 ante. In the cases there cited it was held that the freight exception operated on an equitable defence as well as on the common law defence of abatement: see especially *Aries Tanker Corpn v Total Transport Ltd* [1977] 1 All ER 398, [1977] 1 WLR 185, HL; *Henriksens Rederi A/S v PHZ Rolimpex, The Brede* [1974] QB 233, [1973] 3 All ER 589, CA. See also para 419 note 1 ante. As to bills of exchange see para 414 ante. As to time-charters see para 415 ante. See also *Santiren Shipping Ltd v Unimarine SA, The Chrysovalandou-Dyo* [1981] 1 All ER 340. As to other contracts of carriage see para 416 ante. It is submitted that whatever may be the status of contracts of carriage generally in relation to abatement, equitable set-off should be generally available: see *Federal Commerce and Navigation Co Ltd v Molena Alpha Inc* [1978] QB 927, [1978] 3 All ER 1066, CA (on appeal on other points [1979] AC 757, [1979] 1 All ER 307, HL); and para 424 note 5 ante. However, where there is a relevant time-limit for a defendant to bring his claim, difficult considerations may arise: see para 433 post. As to contracting out from a right to deduct or abate see para 418 ante; and *Gilbert-Ash (Northern) Ltd v Modern Engineering (Bristol) Ltd* [1974] AC 689, [1973] 3 All ER 195, HL. Although this case was concerned partly with construction of a contract and partly with abatement, it would seem to follow that a defendant may by clear words contractually agree to give up a right to an equitable defence. See paras 432–433 post.

3　As to cross-claims against claims for rent at law see para 417 ante. As to the current position by way of equitable defence see para 465 post. For the general principle see the observations of Lord Denning MR cited in para 426 note 8 ante.

(ii)　Contractual Terms affecting the Right

432. Contracting out of right to deduct. Parties may contract out of the equitable right of set-off, but this can only be done by clear and unequivocal words[1] or a clear implication[2]. A clause which excludes a right of set-off is not subject to the same rule of construction that applies to clauses excluding liability for negligence[3]. It has been suggested that an agreement to submit disputes to arbitration (including the cross-claim) may possibly constitute an agreement to exclude equitable set-off[4]. The suggestion is problematic and depends in any event on the terms of the contract[5]. The Unfair Contract Terms Act 1977 may operate to restrict or exclude a right of set-off in respect of a liability arising under a contract[6].

1　*Gilbert-Ash (Northern) Ltd v Modern Engineering (Bristol) Ltd* [1974] AC 689, [1973] 3 All ER 195, HL (this was concerned with the interpretation of a contract and abatement at common law). See also *The Teno* [1977] 2 Lloyd's Rep 289; *BICC plc v Burndy Corpn* [1985] Ch 232, [1985] 1 All ER 417, CA; *CM Pillings & Co Ltd v Kent Investments Ltd* (1985) 30 BLR 80, CA; *NEI Thompson Ltd v Wimpey Construction UK Ltd* (1987) 39 BLR 65, (1988) 4 Const LJ 46, *Acsim (Southern) Ltd v Danish Contracting & Development Co*

Ltd (1989) 47 BLR 55, CA; *Rosehaugh Stanhope (Broadgate Phase 6) plc v Redpath Dorman Long Ltd* (1990) 50 BLR 75, 26 Con LR 80; *Connaught Restaurants Ltd v Indoor Leisure Ltd* [1994] 4 All ER 834, [1994] 1 WLR 501, CA. As to the overriding effect of clear contractual words see para 433 post.

2   *Gilbert-Ash (Northern) Ltd v Modern Engineering (Bristol) Ltd* [1974] AC 689 at 723, [1973] 3 All ER 195 at 220, HL, per Lord Salmon; *Connaught Restaurants Ltd v Indoor Leisure Ltd* [1994] 4 All ER 834 at 838, [1994] 1 WLR 501 at 505 CA (where a lease provided that rent was to be paid 'without any deduction' and it was held that the expression would not ordinarily exclude a right of equitable set-off arising from the party's own breach of contract); *The Teno* [1977] 2 Lloyd's Rep 289 (where a provision in a time charter that fine was to be paid 'without discount' was held not to exclude an equitable set-off). See also *BOC Group plc v Centeon LLC* [1999] 1 All ER (Comm) 53 (defendant's obligations expressed to be unaffected by '…any other matter whatsoever'; those words did not exclude the right of set-off).

3   *Continental Illinois National Bank & Trust Company of Chicago v Papanicolaou* [1986] 2 Lloyd's Rep 441, 83 LS Gaz R 2569, CA; *Mottram Consultants Ltd v Bernard Sunley & Sons Ltd* [1975] 2 Lloyd's Rep 197, HL.

4   Wood *English and International Set-off* (1989) p 691.

5   See SR Derham *Set-off* (2nd edn, 1996) pp 140–144.

6   See the Unfair Contract Terms Act 1977 s 13; *Stewart Gill Ltd v Horatio Myer & Co Ltd* [1992] QB 600, [1992] 2 All ER 257, CA (where it was held that, in the circumstances of the case, the term was unreasonable). See also *Electricity Supply Nominees Ltd v IAF Group Ltd* [1993] 3 All ER 372, [1993] 1 WLR 1059.

433. Contractual time-bar. The existence of a contractual time-bar is one of the features which renders this subject somewhat complex. Where the defendant has, by the contract, undertaken that any cross-action will be commenced within a certain time, it is a matter of construction whether he has abandoned all right to deduct[1]. If the words are clear and unequivocal in extinguishing his rights, the defendant loses all right to deduct once the period has expired[2]. If, however, the words used are appropriate only to bar the remedy, the defendant may deduct if the general rule of abatement at common law applies[3]. If the rule of abatement does not apply[4] it is uncertain whether the defendant can rely on the equitable defence to allow him to deduct once the period has expired[5].

1   See *Gilbert-Ash (Northern) Ltd v Modern Engineering (Bristol) Ltd* [1974] AC 689, [1973] 3 All ER 195, HL.

2   See *Aries Tanker Corpn v Total Transport Ltd* [1977] 1 All ER 398, [1977] 1 WLR 185, HL; and para 413 note 5 ante.

3   If the time-limit only goes to the remedy this will affect the defendant if, for example, his cross-action is greater than the plaintiff's claim.

4   Eg if the freight exception (as to which see paras 413, 416 ante) operates.

5   The existence of the time-bar will affect the defendant's 'equities': see *Aries Tanker Corpn v Total Transport Ltd* [1977] 1 All ER 398, [1977] 1 WLR 185, HL. However, that case may, arguably, be limited to the situation where the freight exception applies or where the contractual time-bar goes to the cross-claim itself and not merely to the remedy. Where the time-bar applies to the remedy only, there should be no equity against the defendant to prevent him exercising his right to deduct. Reference in that case to 'equities' may, it is submitted, be limited to the two primary findings in that case, that the construction in the text to note 2 supra applied, and that the freight exception applied. If the construction in the text to note 3 supra applies, there would appear to be no equity at all against the defendant. Where the defendant claims in time, whether by separate action or by counterclaim, no problem arises, since a proper order in summary judgment proceedings is 'judgment on the claim; stay pending counter-claim': see paras 416, 418–419 ante.

(iii) Equitable Defence and Limitation

434. English statutes of limitation. It is uncertain whether the equitable defence of set-off operates as a true defence unaffected by the Limitation Act 1980 or whether it is within the description 'set-off' in that Act[1], in which case it is deemed to be a separate action commenced on the same date as the action in which it is pleaded[2]. In the latter case the equitable defence might in some cases become statute-barred[3].

1   See the Limitation Act 1980 s 35(2). As to abatement as a true defence, unaffected by statute, see para 412 ante. As to set-off at law and limitation see para 424 ante.

2   Ibid s 35(1)(b).

3   See *Henriksens Rederi A/S v PHZ Rolimpex, The Brede* [1974] QB 233, [1973] 3 All ER 589, CA; and para 419 note 2 ante. In that case Lord Denning MR (obiter) held that equitable defence was not a 'set-off' within the Limitation Act 1939 s 28 (now the Limitation Act 1980 s 35), and was a defence unaffected by the statute. Cairns LJ (obiter) did not accede to this interpretation and Roskill LJ (obiter and without expressing a final opinion) disagreed. See *Federal Commerce & Navigation Co Ltd v Molena Alpha Inc* [1978] QB 927 at 973–974, [1978] 3 All ER 1066 at 1077, CA (affd [1979] AC 757, [1979] 1 All ER 307); *Westdeutsche Landesbank v Islington Borough Council* [1994] 4 All ER 890 at 943, (1993) 91 LGR 323 at 384, per Hobhouse J. See also *Aries Tanker Corpn v Total Transport Ltd* [1977] 1 All ER 398 at 409–410, [1977] 1 WLR 185 at 196–197 HL, per Lord Salmon. It is submitted that the former view is preferable. Unlike legal set-off, equitable set-off is a substantive defence which would seem to be affected by those statutes which simply bar the remedy but leave the substantive right on foot. By 1939 the nature of equitable set-off as a defence was well recognised (see paras 426, 430 ante) and the courts had established a limitation period for set-off at law: *Walker v Clements* (1850) 15 QB 1046; see para 422 ante. It is submitted that in 1939 it was unlikely that Parliament, in a procedural statute, would have intended to affect adversely the judicial status of equitable defence, but was more likely to be enacting the decision in *Walker v Clements* supra, relating to set-off at law. It is also incongruous to 'deem' equitable defence to be a separate action, since at least in the Courts of Chancery it had always availed as a defence. As to limitation accepted by contract see paras 418, 433 ante.

(5) THE MODERN RIGHT OF SET-OFF

(i) In general

435. When set-off is available. A set-off[1] is available to a defendant only when the rules of procedure of the court in which the plaintiff brings his action allow a set-off to be pleaded[2], and the mode in which a plea of set-off is to be raised is also determined by those rules[3].

A defendant cannot be compelled to plead a set-off; he can, if he wishes, enforce his claim by independent action[4].

1   In this paragraph and in paras 436–479 post, unless specifically stated, no distinction is drawn between authorities based on set-off at law and those based on equitable defence. As to this distinction see paras 421, 426 ante.

2   See RSC Ord 18 r 17; CPR 16.6; and paras 401 note 3 ante, 493 et seq post.

3   This is part of the general rule that the pleadings in a court are governed by the rules of procedure of that court: see PLEADING.

4   *Laing v Chatham* (1808) 1 Camp 252; *Jenner v Morris* (1861) 3 De GF & J 45 at 54; *Davis v Hedges* (1871) LR 6 QB 687; *Re Sturmey Motors Ltd, Rattray v Sturmey Motors Ltd* [1913] 1 Ch 16.

436. Set-off in Crown proceedings. When sued in the name of the Attorney General, the Crown is not entitled to avail itself of any set-off without the leave of the court[1]. When sued in the name of a government department the Crown cannot rely on any set-off without leave, except where the subject matter of the set-off relates to that department; similarly, a person may not, without leave, avail himself of a set-off against the Crown, except where the subject matter of the set-off relates to a government department in whose name proceedings are brought[2]. In any proceedings by the Crown a person may not plead a set-off if the proceedings are for the recovery of, or the set-off arises out of a right or claim to repayment in respect of, any taxes, duties or penalties[3].

1   RSC Ord 77 r 6(2)(b); CPR Sch 1 RSC Ord 77 r 6(2)(b). Application for leave is made by summons (RSC Ord 77 r 6(3)), or in accordance with CPR Pt 23: CPR Sch 1 RSC Ord 77 r 6(3)). RSC Ord 77 r 6 was made pursuant to the Crown Proceedings Act 1947 s 35(2)(g): see CROWN PROCEEDINGS AND CROWN PRACTICE vol 12(1) (Reissue) para 126. These provisions also apply to counterclaims: see para 477 post.

For the similar rules which apply in county court proceedings see CCR 1981 Ord 42 r 9; CPR Sch 2 CCR Ord 42 r 9; and COUNTY COURTS. As to the position before the Crown Proceedings Act 1947 see *A-G v Guy Motors Ltd* [1928] 2 KB 78. As to proceedings by the Crown generally see CROWN PROCEEDINGS AND CROWN PRACTICE vol 12(1) (Reissue) paras 107–109.

As to the modification of the RSC and CCR as scheduled to the CPR see para 401 note 3 ante.

2   RSC Ord 77 r 6(2)(a); CPR Sch 1 RSC Ord 77 r 6(2)(a). See also note 1 supra.
3   RSC Ord 77 r 6(1); CPR Sch 1 RSC Ord 77 r 6(1). See also note 1 supra.

437. Set-off : waiver and estoppel. Old authorities support the view that the right of set-off under the Statutes of Set-off cannot be waived[1]. But, in principle, there is a strong argument that a defendant should be entitled to waive the benefit of a set-off[2]. The modern view is that a person can contract out of the right of set-off[3]. If it is possible to contract out of the right of equitable set-off, then it would seem possible to waive the right to equitable set-off and set-off under the Statutes[4].

A defendant may be estopped by his conduct from relying on a set-off. Thus a defendant to whom the plaintiff had produced an account which the defendant admitted to be correct was not allowed, when sued for a sum debited in the account after a long period of acquiescence, to claim a set-off in respect of a loss as to which he had admitted he had no claim[5]. Similarly, where a defendant, due to a mistake, had given credit in an account with the plaintiff, and, after discovering the mistake, had allowed the plaintiff to remain in ignorance of it, he was not allowed to set off the sum for which credit had been so given when sued by the plaintiff[6].

1   *Lechmere v Hawkins* (1798) 2 Esp 625; *Taylor v Okey* (1896) 13 Ves 180; *McGillivray v Simson* (1826) 9 Dow & Ry KB 35. There are also old cases in which a debtor has been allowed a set-off, although he has contracted to pay in money : *Eland v Karr* (1801) 1 East 375; *Cornforth v Rivett* (1814) 2 M & S 510. As to the Statutes of Set-off see para 420 ante.
2   If the Statutes of Set-off were enacted for the benefit of defendants rather than in the public interest, then there is no strong reason why a defendant should not be entitled to waive the benefit.
3   *Hong Kong & Shanghai Banking Corpn v Kloeckner & Co AG* [1990] 2 QB 514, [1989] 3 All ER 513, applied in *Coca-Cola Financial Corpn v Finsat International Ltd* [1998] QB 43, [1996] 3 WLR 849, CA, and not following *Taylor v Okey* (1806) 13 Ves 180 and *Lechmere v Hawkins* (1798) 2 Esp 625. See also *BICC plc v Burndy Corpn* [1985] Ch 232 at 248, [1985] 1 All ER 417 at 425, CA; and Farrar 'Contracting Out of Set-off' (1970) NLJ 771.
4   *BICC v Burndy Corpn* [1985] Ch 232 at 248, [1985] 1 All ER 417 at 425, CA.
5   *Baker v Langhorn* (1816) 6 Taunt 519.
6   *Skyring v Greenwood* (1825) 4 B & C 281, and cf *R v Blenkinsop* [1892] 1 QB 43 at 46–47. See also ESTOPPEL vol 16 (Reissue) paras 1054, 1064.

438. Claims must arise in the same right. Subject to certain exceptions[1], a set-off may only be maintained where the claims to be set off against each other exist between the same parties and in the same right[2].

1   For these exceptions see para 447 et seq post.
2   See the Statutes of Set-off (2 Geo 2 c 22 (Insolvent Debtors Relief) (1728) s 13; 8 Geo 2 c 24 (Set-off) (1734) s 5 (both repealed)), and paras 420, 421 ante. See also *Freeman v Lomas* (1851) 9 Hare 109; *Richardson v Richardson* (1867) LR 3 Eq 686 at 695; *Stammers v Elliott* (1867) LR 4 Eq 675 at 679, (1868) 3 Ch App 195 at 199; *Middleton v Pollock, ex p Nugee* (1875) LR 20 Eq 29 at 34; *NW Robbie & Co Ltd v Witney Warehouse Co Ltd* [1963] 3 All ER 613, [1963] 1 WLR 1324, CA; *Rother Iron Works Ltd v Canterbury Precision Engineers Ltd* [1974] QB 1, [1973] 1 All ER 394, CA. For example, where a municipal corporation opened three separate accounts with the plaintiff's bank, the first as the corporation, the second as managers of public baths and washhouses, and the third as the local board of health, and was sued for a balance due on the first account, it was held that it could set off sums due to it on the second and third accounts: *Pedder v Preston Corpn* (1862) 12 CBNS 535. However, where a trustee for creditors of a firm to whom an assignment of debts due to the firm had been made sued for a debt owing to him in respect of the business which had accrued since the assignment, it was held that the defendant could not set off a pre-existing debt due from the firm: *Hunt v Jessel* (1854) 18 Beav 100. As to set-off at law and in equity see para 435 note 1 ante.

439. Inalienable claims. Where a claim is based upon a statutory right which, by the terms of the statute, is not transferable to any person other than the claimant, a debt due from the claimant may not be set off against it[1].

1   *Gathercole v Smith* (1881) 17 ChD 1, CA (claim for a pension created by the Incumbents Resignation Act 1871 (repealed)). See also *Gathercole v Smith* (1881) 7 QBD 626, CA. It may be that the decision in this case disallowing set-off turns on the view that allowance of a set-off would have frustrated the object of the statute. As to the transfer and assignment of pensions see CHOSES IN ACTION vol 6 (Reissue) para 83 et seq.

440. Debt due to or by the plaintiff jointly with others. A joint debt and a several debt cannot be set off against each other[1]. Thus in an action for a debt due from the defendant to the plaintiff separately, the defendant cannot set off a debt due from the plaintiff jointly with others who are not co-plaintiffs in the action[2]. However, he may set off a debt due from the plaintiff severally as well as jointly with others[3].

A defendant sued for a debt by two or more plaintiffs jointly cannot set off a debt from one of the plaintiffs separately[4], even though the joint debt was contracted owing to fraud[5].

1   *Ex p Twogood* (1805) 11 Ves 517. This rule applies where the joint debt is a partnership debt, unless one partner has been held out as sole partner: see para 470 post.
2   *Arnold v Bainbrigge* (1853) 9 Exch 153. But if a course of business is shown in which such debts have been set off, then, if the facts are strong enough to raise a presumption of an agreement to set off, the set-off is allowed: *Downam v Matthews* (1721) Prec Ch 580; *Vulliamy v Noble* (1817) 3 Mer 593 at 618. See also *Middleton v Pollock, ex p Knight and Raymond* (1875) LR 20 Eq 515 at 521. See also para 430 ante. Cf *Re Pennington and Owen Ltd* [1925] Ch 825, CA, where the liquidator in the winding up of a company was not allowed to set off a debt of a partnership firm against a separate debt due by the company to one of the partners. As to set-off at law and in equity see para 435 note 1 ante.
3   *Fletcher v Dyche* (1787) 2 Term Rep 32; *Owen v Wilkinson* (1858) 5 CBNS 526.
4   *Crawford v Stirling* (1802) 4 Esp 207; *Gordon v Ellis* (1846) 2 CB 821; *Piercy v Fynney* (1871) LR 12 Eq 69.
5   *Middleton v Pollock, ex p Knight and Raymond* (1875) LR 20 Eq 515.

441. Debt due by or to the defendant jointly with others. If two defendants are sued for a joint debt they cannot set off a debt due to one of them separately[1], and, if a defendant is sued for a separate debt, he cannot set off a debt due to himself and another jointly[2].

A defendant who is sued alone as one of several joint debtors may plead that the debt is due from himself jointly with others, and that he and his co-debtors are entitled to a set-off in respect of a debt owed by the plaintiff to them jointly[3], but he cannot set off a debt due to one of the co-debtors separately, even though the co-debtor has assigned a share of the debt to him[4].

1   *Jones v Fleeming* (1827) 7 B & C 217; *Watts v Christie* (1849) 11 Beav 546.
2   *Ex p Riley* (1731) Kel W 24; *Kinnerley v Hossack* (1809) 2 Taunt 170; *Re Fisher, ex p Ross* (1817) Buck 125; *Toplis v Grane* (1839) 5 Bing NC 636; *Re Willis, Percival & Co, ex p Morier* (1879) 12 ChD 491, CA; and see *Loughnan v O'Sullivan* [1922] 1 IR 103 (Ir CA) (affd [1922] 1 IR 160 (High Court of Appeal)). If the other person is dead the defendant as sole surviving creditor may set off the debt: *Slipper v Stidstone* (1794) 5 Term Rep 493. As to set-off at law and in equity see para 435 note 1 ante.
3   *Stackwood v Dunn* (1842) 3 QB 822.
4   *Bowyear v Pawson* (1881) 6 QBD 540.

442. Set-off as affected by the character in which the claims are made. The Statutes of Set-off applied to cross-debts at law between the parties to an action at law[1]. If there is a lack of mutuality at law, but there is in equity, equity by analogy with the legal right of set-off under the Statutes may allow a set-off[2]. On the other hand, where there is mutuality at law, if one of the debts has been assigned in equity or held in trust for a third party, equity would generally not allow a set-off on the ground that it would be unconscionable to do so[3].

The general rule is that an equitable assignee takes subject to the debtor's right of set-off against the assignor before the debtor receives notice of the assignment[4]. But no set-off is available in relation to a debt arising after notice[5].

1   See *Isberg v Bowden* (1853) 8 Exch 852, discussed in *Watkins v Clark* (1862) 12 CBNS 277 at 281–282 per Keating J ('the statutes of set-off are confined to legal debts set between the parties'); *Wilson v Gabriel* (1863) 8 LT 502; *Bankes v Jarvis* [1903] 1 KB 549, DC. As to set-off at law and in equity see para 435 note 1 ante. As to the Statutes of Set-off see para 420 ante.
2   *Freeman v Lomas* (1851) 9 Hare 109; *Cavendish v Geaves* (1857) 24 Beav 163; *Cochrane v Green* (1860) 9 CBNS 448; *Agra and Masterman's Bank Ltd v Leighton* (1866) LR 2 Exch 56 at 65; *Barclay's Bank Ltd v Aschaffenburger Zellstoffwerke AG* [1967] 1 Lloyd's Rep 387, CA. See also *Winch v Keeley* (1787) 1 Term Rep 619 at 621–622; *Tucker v Tucker* (1833) 4 B & Ad 745.
3   *Re Whitehouse & Co* (1878) 9 ChD 595 at 597; *Re Paraguassu Steam Tramroad Co* (1872) 8 Ch App 254; *Mercer v Graves* (1872) LR 7 QB 499 at 504. It is though that the statements by Jessel MR in *Re Whitehouse* supra, and Lord Selborne LC in *Re Paraguassu* supra that, where cross-claims are mutual at law but not in equity, set-off under the Statutes will not be allowed, are too absolute. The governing principle is that of unconscionability: *Rother Iron Works Ltd v Canterbury Precision Engineers Ltd* [1974] QB 1.
4   *Moore v Jervis* (1845) 2 Coll 60; *Wilson v Gabriel* (1863) 4 B & S 243; but cf *Dixon v Winch* [1900] 1 Ch 736 at 742; *Turner v Smith* [1901] 1 Ch 213 at 219.
5   *Wilson v Gabriel* (1863) 4 B & S 243 at 247–248; *Christie v Taunton, Delmard, Lane & Co* [1893] 2 Ch 175 at 182.

443. Claims which may or may not be pleaded by way of set-off. Modern authority favours the view that in an action for specific performance of a contract for the sale of land the defendant can plead by way of set-off a debt due from the plaintiff to the defendant[1]. A mortgage debt may be set off against a claim for the purchase money[2].

In an action for a sum payable under a contract which contains a provision that in certain events the defendant may claim a deduction to be ascertained by arbitration, a set-off may be pleaded of a sum which the arbitrator has found to be the proper amount of deduction[3].

1   *BICC plc v Burndy Corpn* [1985] Ch 232, [1985] 1 All ER 417, CA (where Dillon and Ackner LJJ considered that both statutory and equitable set-off are a good defence re an action for specific performance; but cf Kerr LJ, who considered that neither is a defence though each is relevant to the exercise of the court's discretion to refuse relief). The view of Kerr LJ may be correct as to legal set-off, but it does not seem to be correct as to equitable set-off. See also *Phipps v Child* (1857) 3 Drew 709. If the vendor's agent without the vendor's knowledge agrees that the purchaser may deduct from the purchase price a debt due from the agent, this agreement does not bind the vendor and affords no ground of set-off, even though completion has taken place: *Young v White* (1844) 7 Beav 506; but see, to the contrary, *Gathercole v Smith* (1881) 7 QBD 626 at 631, CA, per Bramwell LJ. Cf para 425 ante.
2   *Wallis v Bastard* (1853) 4 De GM & G 251 (where the set-off was based on an implied agreement).
3   *Parkes v Smith* (1850) 15 QB 297; *Murphy v Glass* (1869) LR 2 PC 408; *Alcoy and Gandia Rly and Harbour Co Ltd v Greenhill* (1897) 76 LT 542 (on appeal (1898) 79 LT 257, CA). See EQUITY vol 16 (Reissue) para 916. As to set-off at law and in equity see para 435 note 1 ante.

444. When the claim must arise. Under the law as it existed before 1873[1] no debt could be made the subject of a set-off at law unless it was in existence and was an actionable and enforceable debt both at the time when the action was commenced[2] and at the date when the plea was pleaded[3], and had continued unsatisfied up to the trial[4]. It was no objection to a set-off that the debt relied upon accrued due after the plaintiff's cause of action accrued[5]. Nevertheless, a plea of set-off of a debt was bad unless it alleged that the plaintiff was liable to the defendant at the commencement of the action and still was so liable[6]. Equity would appear to have followed the law in refusing to permit such debts to be set off[7].

In relation to proceedings begun before 26 April 1999[8], any party may, in any pleading, plead any matter which has arisen at any time, whether before or after the issue of the writ[9]. However, in relation to actions begun on or after 26 April 1999, a claim (including a counterclaim) must be made by a statement of case, and amendment to such statement may only be made as permitted by the rules of procedure[10].

1   Ie before the passing of the Supreme Court of Judicature Act 1873 (repealed).
2   *Evans v Prosser* (1789) 3 Term Rep 186; *Richards v James* (1848) 2 Exch 471. So a defendant could not set off a sum due on a bill of exchange which was in the hands of a third person at the date the action was brought, and which was subsequently indorsed to the defendant: *Braithwaite v Coleman* (1835) 4 Nev & MKB 654.
3   *Eyton v Littledale* (1849) 7 Dow & L 55.
4   *Eyton v Littledale* (1849) 7 Dow & L 55; *Lee v Lester* (1849) 7 CB 1008 at 1015 per Maule J, arguendo. See also *Loughnan v O'Sullivan* [1922] 1 IR 103, Ir CA (affd [1922] 1 IR 160 (High Court of Appeal).
5   *Lee v Lester* (1849) 7 CB 1008.
6   *Dendy v Powell* (1838) 3 M & W 442.
7   *Whyte v O'Brien* (1824) 1 Sim & St 551; *Green v Darling* 5 Mason's Reps 201 at 212 (US 1828) per Story J; *Maw v Ulyatt* (1861) 31 LJ Ch 33.
8   Ie the date on which the CPR came into operation. As to the replacement of the RSC by the CPR, and the transitional arrangements in relation thereto, see para 401 note 3 ante.
9   RSC Ord 18 r 9. Cf *Beddall v Maitland* (1881) 17 ChD 174 at 181; *Toke v Andrews* (1882) 8 QBD 428, DC; *Wood v Goodwin* [1884] WN 17. As to counterclaims see para 484 post.
10 See CPR Pts 16–18; and paras 493 et seq, 510 post.

445.   Company winding up and bankruptcy. If a company goes into liquidation, debts which accrued due before the winding up may be set off against one another[1], but there is authority for the proposition that a defendant sued for a debt which has accrued since the winding up cannot set off a debt due from the company before the liquidator was appointed[2]. Similar considerations govern set-off in bankruptcy[3].

1   *Re Agra and Masterman's Bank, Anderson's Case* (1866) LR 3 Eq 337; *Christie v Taunton, Delmard, Lane & Co* [1893] 2 Ch 175. As to set-off at law and in equity see para 435 note 1 ante.
2   *Ince Hall Rolling Mills Co v Douglas Forge Co* (1882) 8 QBD 179; *Re Newdigate Colliery Ltd, Newdegate v Newdigate Colliery Ltd* [1912] 1 Ch 468, CA. The decision in *Ince Hall Rolling Mills* supra has been the subject of controversy. The decision is inconsistent with the principle as stated by Dixon J in *Hiley v Peoples Prudential Assurance Co Ltd* (1938) 60 CLR 468 at 497 ('it is enough that at the commencement of the winding-up mutual dealings exist which involve rights and obligations of such a nature that afterwards in the events that happen they mature or develop into pecuniary demands capable of set-off'). See *Re Charge Card Services Ltd* [1987] Ch 150 at 178, [1986] 3 All ER 289 at 310 (where Millett J accepted the statement by Dixon J as correct); affd [1987] Ch 150, [1998] 3 All ER 702, CA. See also *Naoroji v Chartered Bank of India* (1868) LR 3 CP 444 at 451–452; *Gye v McIntyre* (1991) 171 CLR 609 at 624. Compare *Ince Hall Rolling Mills* supra with *Rother Iron Works Ltd v Canterbury Precision Engineers Ltd* [1974] QB 1, [1973] 1 All ER 394, CA (a receivership case in which a set-off was allowed and *Ince Hall Rolling Mills* was distinguished). See also Wood *English and International Set-off* (1989) pp 326, 336; SR Derham *Set-off* (2nd edn, 1996) pp 367–376. A debtor to a company of which a receiver has been appointed cannot set off an amount due to him as holder of second mortgage debentures in the company, as the effect would be to give him a preference over the first debenture holders: see *H Wilkins and Elkington Ltd v Milton* (1916) 32 TLR 618; and COMPANIES vol 7(2) (1996 Reissue) para 1274.
3   But see *Drew v Josolyne* (1887) 18 QBD 590, CA; *Re Tout and Finch Ltd* [1954] 1 WLR 178; *Re Davis & Co, ex p Rawlings* (1888) 22 QBD 193, CA. As to set-off in bankruptcy generally see BANKRUPTCY AND INSOLVENCY vol 3(2) (Reissue) para 535 et seq.

446.   Set-off of costs by solicitor. A solicitor may set off an amount due to him for costs even though he has not complied with the statutory provision[1] which requires the delivery of a bill of costs a month before action[2].

1   Ie the Solicitors Act 1974 s 69(1): see SOLICITORS vol 44(1) (Reissue) para 190.
2   *Harrison v Turner* (1847) 10 QB 482; *Ex p Cooper* (1854) 14 CB 663; *Brown v Tibbits* (1862) 11 CBNS 855; *Currie v Law Society* [1977] QB 990, [1976] 3 All ER 832 (where, however, set-off was refused in the exercise of the judge's discretion). See also *Rawley v Rawley* (1876) 1 QBD 460 at 463; and SOLICITORS. As to set-off at law and in equity see para 435 note 1 ante.

(ii) Set-off in Particular Cases

A. AGENTS AND ASSIGNEES

447. Claim by disclosed principal or by agent. A defendant who is sued by the disclosed principal of an agent cannot set off a debt due from the agent[1], and if the defendant is sued by the agent he cannot set off a debt due from the principal[2], unless it can be shown that the agent has assented to such a set-off[3]. A set-off will not be allowed if it would prejudice an agent's lien for his expenses or any prior charge given him by his principal over the money in respect of which the action is brought[4].

1   *Moore v Clementson* (1809) 2 Camp 22; *Richardson v Stormont, Todd & Co* [1900] 1 QB 701, CA. As to the relationship between principal and agent see AGENCY vol 1(2) (Reissue) para 86 et seq. As to set-off at law and in equity see para 435 note 1 ante.
2   *Atkyns and Batten v Amber* (1796) 2 Esp 491; *Isberg v Bowden* (1853) 8 Exch 852; *Manley & Sons Ltd v Berkett* [1912] 2 KB 329 (set-off of debt due from owner to purchaser against claim by auctioneer for price). As to actions by auctioneers see AUCTION vol 2 (Reissue) para 955.
3   *Jarvis v Chapple* (1815) 2 Chit 387. In such a case the set-off may be considered as based on agreement: see para 429 ante.
4   *Manley & Sons Ltd v Berkett* [1912] 2 KB 329. As to lien generally see LIEN. As to agents' liens see AGENCY vol 1(2) Reissue) paras 126–130

448. Claim by undisclosed principal. A defendant sued on a liquidated claim by an undisclosed principal[1] may set off a debt due to him from the agent of that undisclosed principal[2], provided: (1) that the claim is in respect of a transaction entered into by the agent acting in his own name as principal; (2) that the plaintiff authorised the agent so to act or held him out as principal; (3) that the defendant dealt with the agent in the belief that he was the principal; and (4) that the debt which the defendant seeks to set off accrued due before he knew that the agent was merely an agent[3].

1   As to the enforceability of contracts with undisclosed principals generally see AGENCY vol 1(2) (Reissue) para 137 et seq.
2   *Rabone v Williams* (1785) 7 Term Rep 360n; *George v Clagett* (1797) 7 Term Rep 359; *Carr v Hinchcliff* (1825) 4 B & C 547; *Purchell v Salter* (1841) 1 QB 197 (revsd sub nom *Salter v Purchell* (1841) 1 QB 209, Ex Ch); *Turner v Thomas* (1871) LR 6 CP 610; *Montgomerie v United Kingdom Mutual Steamship Association Ltd* [1891] 1 QB 370; *Re Henley, ex p Dixon* (1876) 4 ChD 133, CA; *Montagu v Forwood* [1893] 2 QB 350, CA; *Browning v Provincial Insurance Co of Canada* (1873) LR 5 PC 263 at 272. As to set-off at law and in equity see para 435 note 1 ante.
3   *Borries v Imperial Ottoman Bank* (1873) LR 9 CP 38; *Cooke & Sons v Eshelby* (1887) 12 App Cas 271 at 275, HL. If the defendant has no belief one way or the other, the right of set-off does not arise: *Cooke & Sons v Eshelby* supra. See also *Carr v Hinchcliff* (1825) 4 B & C 547; *Fish v Kempton* (1849) 7 CB 687; *Kaltenbach, Fischer & Co v Lewis & Peat* (1885) 10 App Cas 617.

449. Mercantile agents. If the defendant knows only that the agent is an agent, for example that he is a broker, without knowing his principal, he is put on inquiry and in an action by the principal cannot set off a debt due from the agent[1], nor can he rely on any custom not known to the plaintiff as giving him the right of set-off[2]. The existence of an authority from the principal to the agent to receive payment from the defendant on behalf of the principal does not enable the defendant to effect payment by a set-off against a debt owing by the agent[3]. However, if the defendant believes that the agent, having the right to do so, for example if he is a factor, has sold in his own name to repay advances made by him to his principal, the defendant is not bound to make further inquiry, and so may set off against a claim by the principal a debt due from the agent[4].

1   *Baring v Corrie* (1818) 2 B & Ald 137 (where a set off was denied to a third party who bought goods from a broker selling in his own name, the broker's authority being confined to selling in the name of the principal); *Fish v Kempton* (1849) 7 CB 687; *Walshe v Provan* (1853) 8 Exch 843; *Dresser v Norwood* (1863) 14 CBNS 574; *Semenza v Brinsley* (1865) 18 CBNS 467; *Pearson v Scott* (1878) 9 ChD 198; *Mildred v Maspons* (1883) 8 App Cas 874, HL; *Knight v Matson & Co* (1902) 22 NZLR 293. In this respect the position of a broker differs from that of a factor. As to set-off at law and in equity see para 435 note 1 ante.
2   *Blackburn v Mason* (1893) 68 LT 510, CA.
3   *Pearson v Scott* (1878) 9 ChD 198.
4   *Warner v McKay* (1836) 1 M & W 591. See also *Hudson v Granger* (1821) 5 B & Ald 27.

450. Defendant contracting by broker. If the claim which the defendant seeks to set off arises out of a transaction with an agent entered into by a broker acting on the defendant's behalf, the knowledge of the broker is the knowledge of the defendant, and if the broker knew that the agent was an agent the defendant cannot set off a debt due from the agent[1].

1   *Dresser v Norwood* (1864) 17 CBNS 466, Ex Ch: see AGENCY vol 1(2) (Reissue) paras 145, 149.

451. Set-off between principal and agent. A broker may set off as against his principal a debt due from the principal[1]. Where, however, a broker, the defendant, had purchased and then resold goods on behalf of the plaintiff he could not set off the price paid by him to the original seller, for whom he sold the goods under a del credere commission, against the claim made by the plaintiff for the proceeds of the resale, even though the plaintiff knew that the defendant had acted throughout as broker[2].

1   *Dale v Sollet* (1767) 4 Burr 2133, which is an authority not on set-off but rather on the common law right of deduction enabling an agent who recovered money for his principal to deduct from the proceeds the amount of his recompense. As to set-off at law and in equity see para 435 note 1 ante.
2   *Morris v Cleasby* (1816) 4 M & S 566 at 575 per Lord Ellenborough CJ. His Lordship thought that the case must be considered on the basis that the principal was disclosed at the sale and went on to say 'the principal must always be debtor, and that, whether he is known in the first instance or not, except where the broker has by the form of the instrument made himself so liable'. As to del credere agents see AGENCY vol 1(2) (Reissue) para 13; SALE OF GOODS.

452. Claims between insurance brokers and underwriters. A claim under an insurance policy is a claim for unliquidated damages, and losses and premiums could not be set off against each other under the Statutes of Set-off[1]. However, the nature of the claim and cross-claim might in appropriate cases permit an equitable defence or counterclaim[2].

1   See paras 420–421 ante. As to the Statutes of Set-off see para 420 note 1 ante. As to set-off at law and in equity see para 435 note 1 ante. A broker who effects a policy of marine insurance on behalf of an insured is responsible as a principal to the underwriter for the premium: Marine Insurance Act 1906 s 53(1). The prima facie rule is that, unless the broker effects the policy on his own account, a set-off of the underwriter's liability to the insured is not available against the broker's liability for unpaid premiums: see *Koster v Eason* (1813) 2 M & S 112; *Wilson v Creighton* (1782) 3 Doug KB 132; *Bell v Auldjo* (1784) 4 Doug KB 48.
2   As to equitable defence see para 426 et seq ante. As to counterclaims see para 480 et seq post.

453. Set-off against assignee of chose in action. In general, a debtor may set off against an assignee of a chose in action any debt that he could have set off against the assignor, provided that it is a debt which accrued due before notice of assignment[1]. The defendant to an action brought by the assignee of a marine insurance policy is entitled to raise any defence, and therefore any set-off, arising out of the contract which he would have been entitled to raise against the assignor[2].

1   For a detailed analysis of this right of set-off see CHOSES IN ACTION vol 6 (Reissue) para 64. There is no right of set-off against the assignee of a debt which had neither accrued due before the date of the assignment nor was connected with the assigned debt, even though it had arisen under a contract which had been made between the debtor and the assignor before the date of the assignment: *Business Computers Ltd v Anglo-African Leasing Ltd* [1977] 2 All ER 741, [1977] 1 WLR 578. See also *Banco Central SA and Trevelan Navigation Inc v Lingoss and Falce Ltd and BFI Line Ltd, The Raven* [1980] 2 Lloyd's Rep 266.
2   See the Marine Insurance Act 1906 s 50(2); and INSURANCE vol 25 (Reissue) para 214. Such a defendant has no greater right of set-off than the assignee of any other chose in action and may not set off a claim for indemnity arising out of a policy other than that on which the plaintiff sues: *Baker v Adam* (1910) 102 LT 248.

B. BANKS AND CUSTOMERS

454. Set-off between bank and customer. A bank is entitled to set off what is due to a customer on one account against what is due from him on another account[1], even if the money due to him may in fact belong to another person[2], unless there is some equity sufficient to bar the legal right of set-off[3]. But a bank has no right to set-off a credit in a customer's account against a debit in a third party's account merely on suspicion that the customer holds as nominee of the third party[4]. Neither is a bank justified of its own motion in transferring a balance from what it knows to be a trust account of its customer to the customer's private account[5], or in setting off against its customer's balance a debt from the customer before it has actually fallen due[6]; nor may it set off any debt from its customer against the holder of a letter of credit given to the customer[7].

A customer has a right to set off a balance due to him from his bank against a debt due to the bank from him[8], unless he has notice that the debt due from him has been assigned to a stranger[9].

1   *Bailey v Finch* (1871) LR 7 QB 34 (which was distinguished in *Re Willis, Percival & Co, ex p Morier* (1879) 12 ChD 491 at 501–502, CA, and has been criticised: see SR Derham *Set-off* (2nd edn, 1996) pp 423–424); *Re European Bank, Agra Bank Claim* (1872) 8 Ch App 41; *Union Bank of Australia Ltd v Murray-Aynsley* [1898] AC 693, PC. See also *Watts v Christie* (1849) 11 Beav 546; *Baker v Lloyds Bank Ltd* [1920] 2 KB 322; and BANKING vol 3(1) (Reissue) paras 166, 191. As to set-off at law and in equity see para 435 note 1 ante.
2   *Bank of New South Wales v Goulburn Valley Butter Co Pty* [1902] AC 543, PC; cf *North and South Wales Bank Ltd v Macbeth, North and South Wales Bank Ltd v Irvine* [1908] AC 137 at 141, HL.
3   *Bailey v Finch* (1871) LR 7 QB 34; *Newell v National Provincial Bank of England* (1876) 1 CPD 496; *Parsons v Sovereign Bank of Canada* [1913] AC 160, PC.
4   *Bhogal v Punjab National Bank* [1988] 2 All ER 296, 1 FTLR 161, CA.
5   *Re Gross, ex p Kingston* (1871) 6 Ch App 632, approved in *Bank of New South Wales v Goulburn Valley Butter Co Pty* [1902] AC 543 at 550, PC. See BANKING vol 3(1) (Reissue) para 173.
6   *Rogerson v Ladbroke* (1822) 1 Bing 93; *Jeffryes v Agra and Masterman's Bank* (1866) LR 2 Eq 674 at 680; cf *Thomas v Howell* (1874) LR 18 Eq 198 (distinguished in *Halse v Rumford* (1878) 47 LJ Ch 559).
7   *Re Agra and Masterman's Bank, ex p Asiatic Banking Corpn* (1867) 2 Ch App 391, explained in *Rainford v James Keith and Blackman Co Ltd* [1905] 1 Ch 296 at 303.
8   *Bailey v Finch* (1871) LR 7 QB 34.
9   *Cavendish v Geaves* (1857) 24 Beav 163.

455. Customer's personal and joint accounts. Where a customer of a bank having an account in his own name also has an account in the name of himself and another jointly[1], a right to set off items in the two accounts will only arise where the customer is so beneficially interested in the balance of the joint account that a court of equity would without terms or inquiry compel a transfer of the account into the customer's name alone[2].

1   As to joint accounts generally see BANKING vol 3(1) (Reissue) para 154.
2   *Watts v Christie* (1849) 11 Beav 546; *Re Willis, Percival & Co, ex p Morier* (1879) 12 ChD 491 at 502, CA, per Brett LJ. As to set-off at law and in equity see para 435 note 1 ante.

C. PERSONAL REPRESENTATIVES; TRUSTEES AND BENEFICIARIES

456. Claims by and against personal representatives. The defendant to a claim by an executor or administrator for a debt which has accrued due to the estate since the death may not set off a debt due to himself from the deceased during the lifetime of the deceased[1]. Nor may a person sued for a debt which accrued due before the death set off a debt which has accrued due from the estate after the death[2]. Similarly, an executor or administrator who is sued for a debt which accrued due from the deceased during his lifetime cannot set off a debt which has accrued due to the estate since the death[3]; but where an executor or administrator can show a debt due from the deceased he may set it off against a debt due to him[4].

1   *Shipman v Thompson* (1738) Willes 103; *Schofield v Corbett* (1836) 11 QB 779; *Rees v Watts* (1855) 11 Exch 410; *Mardall v Thellusson* (1856) 6 E & B 976; *Hallett v Hallett* (1879) 13 ChD 232; *Re Gregson, Christison v Bolam* (1887) 36 ChD 223; *Re Gedney, Smith v Grummitt* [1908] 1 Ch 804 at 810. See further EXECUTORS AND ADMINISTRATORS. As to set-off at law and in equity see para 435 note 1 ante.
2   *Newell v National Provincial Bank of England* (1876) 1 CPD 496. See also *Lambarde v Older* (1851) 17 Beav 542; *Allison v Smith* (1869) 10 B & S 747.
3   *Rees v Watts* (1855) 11 Exch 410 at 416; *Mardall v Thellusson* (1856) 6 E & B 976.
4   *Blakesley v Smallwood* (1846) 8 QB 538, explained in *Rees v Watts* (1855) 11 Exch 410.

457. Set-off against debts due from legatees. An executor can set off against a legatee a debt owed to the testator[1] even though the debt has become statute-barred since the death of the testator[2]. A debtor of a testator who is also the creditor of a legatee cannot, by some interposition of the executors, apply a legacy bequeathed by the testator to the legatee in discharge of the debt, unless there is some contract with the legatee for the purpose[3].

1   *Smith v Smith* (1861) 3 Giff 263. See EQUITY vol 16 (Reissue) para 918; EXECUTORS AND ADMINISTRATORS. As to set-off at law and in equity see para 435 note 1 ante.
2   *Coates v Coates* (1864) 33 Beav 249; *Gee v Liddell (No 2)* (1866) 35 Beav 629.
3   *Smee v Baines* (1861) 4 LT 573, where A bought part of the testator's business in his lifetime for £350 and sold it after his death to a legatee for £350.

458. Claims must exist in the same right. The rule that the debts must accrue in the same right[1] is strictly applied. Therefore, if a plaintiff sues as executor, the defendant cannot set off a debt due from the plaintiff in his personal capacity[2]. If an executor is sued as executor, he cannot set off a claim he has in his personal capacity against the plaintiff[3], and if sued in his personal capacity he cannot set off a claim he has as executor, unless it is such a claim that he can also sue on it in his personal capacity[4]. If the plaintiff sues as assignee, the executor cannot set off a personal claim against the assignor[5].

1   As to this rule see para 438 ante.
2   *Hutchinson v Sturges* (1741) Willes 261; *Bishop v Church* (1748) 3 Atk 691; *Macdonald v Carington* (1878) 4 CPD 28; *Re Dickinson, Marquis of Bute v Walker, ex p Hoyle, Shipley and Hoyle* [1888] WN 94; *Phillips v Howell* [1901] 2 Ch 773. As to set-off at law and in equity see para 435 note 1 ante.
3   *Gale v Luttrell* (1826) 1 Y & J 180.
4   *Bishop v Church* (1748) 3 Atk 691; *Harvey v Wood* (1821) 5 Madd 459; *Macdonald v Carington* (1878) 4 CPD 28; *Re Willis, Percival & Co, ex p Morier* (1879) 12 ChD 491, CA; *Nelson v Roberts* (1893) 69 LT 352, DC.
5   *Bishop v Church* (1748) 3 Atk 691; *Whitaker v Rush* (1761) Amb 407. But cf *Taylor v Taylor* (1875) LR 20 Eq 155; *Re Jones, Christmas v Jones* [1897] 2 Ch 190.

459. Personal representative who is both debtor and creditor. There is no principle which requires a different rule as to set-off to be applied in equity[1] from that to be applied at law. However, where the representative, having discharged all the liabilities of the estate, has, as sole next of kin or residuary legatee, become legally and equitably the absolute owner of a debt due to his testator, the debtor may set off a debt due from the representative personally against a claim for the debt, even though made by the representative in his representative capacity[2]. This equitable exception is not, however, to be extended to a case in which administration accounts require to be taken in order to show that the representative is the beneficial owner of the debt[3].

1 *Newell v National Provincial Bank of England* (1876) 1 CPD 496 at 504 per Lindley J. As to equitable defences see para 426 ante.
2 *Jones v Mossop* (1844) 3 Hare 568. See the discussion of this case in SR Derham *Set-off* (2nd edn, 1996) pp 424–425.
3 *Re Willis, Percival & Co, ex p Morier* (1879) 12 ChD 491, CA, explaining *Bailey v Finch* (1871) LR 7 QB 34.

460. Set-off against claim of next of kin. Where there is a claim in administration proceedings by a next of kin for a sum due in respect of a share of the intestate's estate, the administrator may set off a debt due to himself personally from the next of kin[1] notwithstanding that the share has been paid into court[2] or has been assigned by the next of kin[3] or that the debt is statute-barred[4].

1 *Taylor v Taylor* (1875) LR 20 Eq 155 (there was no fund in existence representing the proceeds of the intestate's estate). See also *Whitaker v Rush* (1761) Amb 407 (where it seems the legatee's claim was for payment out of a particular fund). As to set-off at law and in equity see para 435 note 1 ante.
2 *Taylor v Taylor* (1875) LR 20 Eq 155.
3 *Re Jones, Christmas v Jones* [1897] 2 Ch 190. An executor may set off against a legacy costs which have been ordered to be paid to him by the legatee in probate proceedings: see *Re Knapman, Knapman v Wreford* (1881) 18 ChD 300, CA.
4 *Re Cordwell's Estate, White v Cordwell* (1875) LR 20 Eq 644. The decision in this case was based on the rule in *Cherry v Boultbee* (1839) 4 My & Cr 442 (see BANKRUPTCY AND INSOLVENCY vol 3(2) (Reissue) para 547), rather than set-off.

461. Set-off between trustee and trust estate. A trustee is ordinarily entitled to set off an amount due to him from the trust estate against an amount due to it from him[1]. He can also set off an amount due to the estate from a beneficiary against a sum payable out of the estate to that beneficiary[2].

In garnishee proceedings by a judgment creditor against solicitors for payment of money received by them on trusts which had failed, the solicitors could not set off against the fund the amount of legal costs owed to them by the judgment debtor[3].

1 *McEwan v Crombie* (1883) 25 ChD 175, where, on a sum being found to be due to two trustees from the trust estate and a sum being due to the estate from one of them who was bankrupt, it was held that the portion, if any, of the sum due to the two trustees which, on inquiry, should be found to be due to the bankrupt trustee should be set off against the sum due from him. There is generally no right to set off a gain against a loss arising out of different breaches of trust: see *Adye v Feuilleteau* (1783) 3 Swan 84n; and TRUSTS vol 48 (Reissue) para 954.
2 *Re Harrald, Wilde v Walford* (1884) 53 LJ Ch 505, CA: see para 458 et seq ante. As to the right of trustees to retain trust property against beneficiaries indebted to the trustees as such see *Priddy v Rose* (1817) 3 Mer 86; and TRUSTS vol 48 (Reissue) para 804.
3 *Stumore v Campbell & Co* [1892] 1 QB 314, CA. See also para 475 post.

462. Set-off between trustee and debtors to the trust estate. Where a trustee sues a debtor to the trust estate, the debtor can set off against the trustee's claim an amount due to him from the beneficiary[1], and a person who is sued for a debt can set off a sum due from the plaintiff to a trustee for him[2].

1   *Thornton v Maynard* (1875) LR 10 CP 695 at 698–699. There can be a set-off even if the amount due from the beneficiary is in respect of unliquidated damages: *Bankes v Jarvis* [1903] 1 KB 549, which was approved in *Hanak v Green* [1958] 2 QB 9 at 24, [1958] 2 All ER 141 at 150, CA, per Morris LJ. Note, however, that the statement by Channell J in *Banker v Jarvis* supra at 553 that 'the Judicature Act, and more especially the rules,...put an unliquidated claim on the same footing as a liquidated claim for the purpose of set-off' is difficult to support: *McDonnell & East v McGregor* (1936) 56 CLR 50 at 61–62. But where trustees of a settlement are creditors of a testator under his covenant in the settlement, a legacy left by him to their beneficiary cannot be set off by way of satisfaction against their claim under the settlement: *Smith v Smith* (1861) 3 Giff 263 at 272–273.
2   *Cochrane v Green* (1860) 9 CBNS 448; but see *Middleton v Pollock, ex p Nugee* (1875) LR 20 Eq 29 at 35 et seq per Jessel MR. Trustees of an estate in which they are also beneficiaries cannot set off a debt due to the estate from a person who is insolvent against a debt due from them personally to trustees for that person: *Middleton v Pollock, ex p Nugee* supra. As to set-off at law and in equity see para 435 note 1 ante.

D. HUSBAND AND WIFE

463. Debts of or due to wife in proceedings between husband and third person. Debts incurred by or due to a wife before marriage cannot be set off in proceedings between her husband and a third person[1]. Debts due to a wife after marriage are her separate property and cannot be set off by her husband in an action against him[2], but debts incurred by a wife after marriage may apparently be set off by a defendant to an action by the husband if they were incurred in respect of necessaries[3].

1   See *Wood v Akers* (1797) 2 Esp 594; *Ex p Blagden* (1815) 19 Ves 465; *Burrough v Moss* (1830) 10 B & C 558. As to set-off at law and in equity see para 435 note 1 ante.
2   See HUSBAND AND WIFE. A debt due to a husband in right of his wife before the Married Women's Property Act 1882 could not be set off by him against a debt due from him personally: *Paynter v Walker* (1764) Bull NP 175.
3   *Jenner v Morris* (1860) 1 Dr & Sm 218; affd (1861) 3 De GF & J 45 (advances to deserted wife for purchase of necessaries; held that the lender stood in the shoes of a supplier who had a remedy against the husband and that the lender could set-off against the husband's judgment debt the husband's liability in equity arising from the advances). See *Jenner v Morris, Webster v Jenner* (1863) 11 WR 943; and HUSBAND AND WIFE.

464. Debts between husband and wife. A husband may set off a debt paid by him as surety for his wife against an amount payable by him to trustees for his wife under an agreement[1]. Where a wife was entitled to set off against a debt due from her to her husband the amount ordered to be paid by him by way of maintenance, the amount of set-off was limited to the amount actually paid to the wife under a 'less tax' order and did not include deductions for income tax[2].

1   *Ribblesdale v Forbes* (1916) 140 LT Jo 483, CA. As to set-off at law and in equity see para 435 note 1 ante.
2   *Butler v Butler* [1961] P 33, [1961] 1 All ER 810, CA.

E. LANDLORD AND TENANT

465. Set-off against claims for rent. At common law a tenant's cross-demand for a liquidated sum may be set off against the landlord's claim for rent under the Statutes of Set-off[1]. Although it was thought that a tenant could not set off a cross-claim for unliquidated damages against the landlord's claim for rent[2], it is now recognised that there is nothing in the nature of the landlord's claim for rent that precludes a tenant from setting-off a cross-claim so long as the cross-claim is sufficiently closely connected with the liability to pay rent[3]. Equitable set-off against rent is not confined to a cross-claim for breach of a covenant to repair[4]. However, a cross-claim that would otherwise give rise to an equitable set-off against a claim for the payment of rent by the landlord mortgagor will not do so when the rent is claimed by the mortgagee[5].

The right of set-off is to be distinguished from the lessee's right to recoup from arrears of rent or future payments of rent money expended on repairs where the leased premises have fallen into disrepair and the landlord is in breach of a covenant to repair[6]. The right of set-off is also to be distinguished from rights of abatement[7].

The traditional view is that no right of set-off under the Statutes can affect the landlord's remedy of distress[8]. But where an equitable set-off is available to the tenant he may be entitled to an injunction to restrain the landlord's remedy of distress[9]; and where a sub-tenant is forced by the superior landlord to pay unpaid rent or other charges owing by the immediate landlord, the immediate landlord cannot levy distress on the ground that the sub-tenant is regarded as authorised by the immediate landlord to apply the rent to which he is entitled in this way[10].

A tenant's right of set-off is, of course, not limited to cases in which the landlord seeks to recover rent[11]. Money due from the landlord may also, it seems, be set off against rent where there is an agreement to that effect between the parties[12].

1   *Gower v Hunt* (1734) Barnes 290 at 291; *Brown v Holyoak* (1734) cited in Willes 263; *Cleghorn v Durrant* (1858) 31 LTOS 235; *Hamp v Jones* (1840) 9 LJ Ch 258. As to the Statutes of Set-off see para 420 note 1 ante.

2   *Weigall v Waters* (1795) 6 Term Rep 488; *Hart v Rogers* [1916] 1 KB 646. See also *Taylor v Webb* [1937] 2 KB 283.

3   *British Anzani (Felixstowe) Ltd v International Marine Management (UK) Ltd* [1980] QB 137, [1979] 2 All ER 1063. See also *Melville v Grapelodge Developments Ltd* (1978) 39 P & CR 179. As to equitable set-off see para 426 et seq ante.

4   *British Anzani (Felixstowe) Ltd v International Marine Management (UK) Ltd* [1980] QB 137, [1979] 2 All ER 1063; *Connaught Restaurants Ltd v Indoor Leisure Ltd* [1994] 4 All ER 834, [1994] 1 WLR 501, CA (set-off based on breach of the covenant for quiet enjoyment).

5   *Reeves v Pope* [1914] 2 KB 284, CA. See Wood *English and International Set-off* (1989) pp 886–887; Waite 'Disrepair and Set-off of Damages Against Rent: The Implications of British Anzani' [1983] Conv 373 at 384–386 (as to absolute sale of the reversion); and the discussion in SR Derham *Set-off* (2nd edn, 1996) pp 597–603.

6   *Taylor v Beal* (1591) Cro Eliz; 222; *Watson v Weigall* (1795) 2 Anst 575, *Lee-Parker v Izzet* [1971] 1 WLR 1688; *Connaught Restaurants Ltd v Indoor Leisure Ltd* [1994] 4 All ER 834, [1994] 1 WLR 501, CA; *Asco Developments Ltd v Gordon* [1978] 248 Estates Gazette 683. See LANDLORD AND TENANT vol 27(1) (Reissue) para 376.

7   See para 408 ante; and LANDLORD AND TENANT vol 27(1) (Reissue) para 234.

8   *Absolon v Knight* (1743) Barnes 450; *Townrow v Benson* (1818) 3 Madd 203. See also *Sapsford v Fletcher* (1792) 4 Term Rep 511; *Willson v Davenport* (1833) 5 C & P 531; *Pratt v Keith* (1864) 33 LJ Ch 528; *British Anzani (Felixstowe) Ltd v International Marine Management (UK) Ltd* [1980] QB 137 at 149, [1979] 2 All ER 1063 at 1071 per Forbes J. But see now *Eller v Grovecrest Investments Ltd* [1995] QB 272 at 278, [1994] 4 All ER 845 at 850, CA, per Hoffmann LJ, and at 280 and 852 per Neill LJ (where there are suggestions that the traditional view might be reconsidered). On the other hand, there is still support for a distinction between set-off under the Statutes of Set-off and equitable set-off in relation to distress: see *Aectra Refining & Manufacturing Inc v Exmar NV* [1994] 1 WLR 1634 at 1650, [1995] 1 Lloyd's Rep 191 at 200–201, CA, per Hoffman LJ. As to distress generally see DISTRESS.

9   *Eller v Grovecrest Investments Ltd* [1995] QB 272, [1994] 4 All ER 845, CA.

10   *Sapsford v Fletcher* (1792) 4 Term Rep 511; *Carter v Carter* (1829) 5 Bing 406. See the discussion in SR Derham *Set-off* (2nd edn, 1996) p 117.

11   *Filross Securities Ltd v Midgeley* [1998] EGCS 124, 43 EG 134, CA (where the landlord sued in respect of the tenant's failure to pay service charges).

12   *Willson v Davenport* (1833) 5 C & P 531; *Roper v Bumford* (1810) 3 Taunt 76.

466. Tenant's claims against landlord Where a tenant who had obtained judgment against his landlord became subsequently indebted to him in arrears of rent and for dilapidations, it was held that he could not be restrained from issuing execution against his landlord on the judgment[1].

1   *Maw v Ulyatt* (1861) 31 LJ Ch 33.

467. Assignment of reversion. The rule of equity that to an action by an assignee of a chose in action the defendant may set off a claim for damages against the assignor directly arising out of the same transaction as the subject matter of the assignment[1] does not apply where a mortgagee of a reversion on a lease, being in possession, is claiming rent against which the set-off is claimed in respect of a liability of the mortgagor[2]. But where a mortgagee, having sold the mortgaged property pursuant to a possession order and the sale yielded insufficient funds to satisfy the debt, petitioned for the mortgagor's bankruptcy in respect of the balance, the mortgagor was allowed to counterclaim, on the ground that the mortgagee had negligently failed to obtain the market value of the property[3].

1   As to set-off against assignees generally see para 453 ante and 473 post; and CHOSES IN ACTION vol 6 (Reissue) para 64.
2   *Reeves v Pope* [1914] 2 KB 284, CA. See para 462, ante.
3   *TSB Bank plc v Platts* [1998] 2 BCLC 1, CA (where it was held that it was for the court hearing the petition to ascertain the maximum possible value of the counterclaim and deduct it from the value of the debt on which bankruptcy was sought).

F. EMPLOYER AND EMPLOYEE OR INDEPENDENT CONTRACTOR

468. Proceedings between employer and employee. The right of an employer to make certain deductions from his employee's wages is governed by the contract between them and sometimes by usage, and is controlled by statute[1]. An employee discharged without proper notice may set off a claim for wages in lieu of notice against a claim by the employer for money had and received[2]. However, it has been held that an employer sued for wages cannot set off a sum claimed for the value of goods lost by the negligence of his employee[3] unless there is an agreement between them authorising such sum to be deducted from the wages[4].

1   See EMPLOYMENT vol 16 (Reissue) para 84 et seq. As to deductions in respect of bad work see *Sagar v H Ridehalgh & Son Ltd* [1931] 1 Ch 310 at 326, CA (deduction being permissible in appropriate cases under the principle of abatement). But in later cases the principle of abatement has not been applied and it has been said that the question is whether the employee can make out a case for equitable set-off: see *Miles v Wakefield Metropolitan District Council* [1987] AC 539 at 570, [1987] 1 All ER 1089 at 1105–1106, HL, per Lord Oliver of Aylmerton; *Sim v Rotherham Metropolitan Borough Council* [1987] Ch 216, [1986] 3 All ER 387 (where it was held that the employer can maintain a cross-claim for damages).
2   *East Anglian Rlys Co v Lythgoe* (1851) 10 CB 726.
3   *Le Loir v Bristow* (1815) 4 Camp 134.
4   *Le Loir v Bristow* (1815) 4 Camp 134. See also *Duckworth v Alison* (1836) 1 M & W 412; *Cleworth v Pickford* (1840) 7 M & W 314 (both cases concern independent contractors).

469. Proceedings between employer and independent contractor. Proceedings between an employer and an independent contractor[1], involving as they usually do a contract for services or work and labour, are subject to the rules governing abatement[2] and equitable defence[3].

1   As to rights of set-off arising under building contracts see BUILDING CONTRACTS, ARCHITECTS,
     ENGINEERS AND SURVEYORS vol 4(2) (Reissue) paras 387, 389. See *Sable Contractors Ltd v Bluett Shipping
     Ltd* [1979] 2 Lloyd's Rep 33, CA; *Rapid Building Group Ltd v Ealing Family Housing Association Ltd* (1984)
     29 BLR 5, CA; *Tubeworkers Ltd v Tilbury Construction Ltd* (1985) 30 BLR 67, [1985] Const LJ 385, CA;
     Chatbrown Ltd v Alfred McAlpine Construction (Southern) Ltd (1986) 35 BLR 44, 11 Con LR 1, CA; *Archital
     Luxfer Ltd v AJ Dunning & Sons (Weyhill) Ltd* (1987) 47 BLR 1, [1987] 1 FTLR 372, CA; *NEI Thompson
     Ltd v Wimpey Construction UK Ltd* (1987) 39 BLR 65, (1988) 4 Const LJ 46, CA; *BWP (Architectural) Ltd
     v Beaver Building Systems Ltd* (1988) 42 BLR 86; *Smallman Construction Ltd v Redpath Dorman Long Ltd*
     (1988) 47 BLR 15, CA; *Acsim (Southern) Ltd v Danish Contracting and Development Co Ltd* (1989) 47 BLR
     55, CA; *Mellowes PPG Ltd v Snelling Construction Ltd* (1989) 49 BLR 109, QBD; *MJ Gleeson plc v Taylor
     Woodrow Construction Ltd* (1989) 49 BLR 95, 21 Con LR 71, QBD; *A Cameron Ltd v John Mowlem & Co
     plc* (1990) 52 BLR 24, CA; *RM Douglas Construction Ltd v Bass Leisure Ltd* (1990) 53 BLR 119, 25 Con
     LR 38, QBD; *Hermcrest plc v G Percy Trentham Ltd* (1991) 53 BLR 104, 25 Con LR 78, CA; *B Hargreaves
     Ltd v Action 2000* (1992) 62 BLR 72, [1993] BCLC 1111, CA; *CA Duquemin v Raymond Slater* (1993) 65
     BLR 124.
2   See para 411 et seq ante. The right of set-off may only be taken away by clear and unequivocal words:
     Gilbert-Ash (Northern) Ltd v Modern Engineering (Bristol) Ltd [1974] AC 689, [1973] 3 All ER 195, HL or
     at least by a clear implication: *Gilbert-Ash (Northern) Ltd* supra at 723 and 220 per Lord Salmon; *Connaught
     Restaurants Ltd v Indoor Leisure Ltd* [1994] 4 All ER 834 at 838, [1994] 1 WLR 501 at 505, CA; *RM
     Douglas Construction Ltd v Bass Leisure Ltd* (1990) 53 BLR 124 at 133–134, 25 Con LR 38 at 49.
3   See para 426 et seq ante.

G. PARTNERS; SHAREHOLDERS

470. Partner's joint and separate debts. The law as to set-off between joint debts
and several debts[1] applies when one or more of the parties is a firm. Therefore, where a
defendant is sued by a firm he cannot set off a debt due from one of the partners
individually[2] unless the partners have permitted one of their number to deal as a sole
trader with the defendant and thereby led him to believe that he was dealing with an
individual and not with a firm, and the defendant in this belief has made advances or given
credit to that partner. In such a case the defendant may set off against the firm the debt
due from the individual partner in respect of that advance or as to which the credit has
been given[3]. Similarly, if in like circumstances an individual partner has agreed to allow
a set-off, the agreement is binding on the firm[4] provided the debt is due in respect of a
matter within the scope of the apparent authority given by the firm to the individual
partner[5]. However, if the other party knew that somebody besides the individual partner
had an interest in the debt sued for, he will not be allowed to set off a debt due from the
individual partner, and an agreement to allow him to do so, if made without the authority
of the other partners, is not binding on the firm[6].

1   See paras 441–442 ante.
2   See PARTNERSHIP vol 35 (Reissue) para 76. Where the debt accrued due from the individual partner
     before the firm was constituted, there is no right of set-off even though the firm has since admitted the
     existence of the debt: *France v White* (1839) 6 Bing NC 33.
3   *Stracey and Ross v Deey* (1789) 7 Term Rep 361n; *Gordon v Ellis* (1846) 2 CB 821 (where set-off was
     disallowed because the plea did not allege that the partner appeared as sole owner with the consent or by
     default of his partners). As to set-off at law and in equity see para 435 note 1 ante.
4   *Muggeridge's v Smith & Co* (1884) 1 TLR 166 (where the other party was justified in believing that the
     individual partner was the only partner in the business and was authorised to give the other party credit
     for the amount of his account).
5   *Baker v Gent* (1892) 9 TLR 159 (where the court disallowed a counterclaim for articles supplied by the
     defendant to 'L & Co', the defendant believing L to be the sole partner when the name 'L & Co'
     suggested otherwise).
6   *Piercy v Fynney* (1871) LR 12 Eq 69; but cf *Harper v Marten* (1895) 11 TLR 368. See also PARTNERSHIP
     vol 35 (Reissue) paras 46–55.

471. Firm acting as agent. Where a firm makes a contract as agent for an undisclosed principal, the other party to the contract in an action brought against him by the undisclosed principal may set off a debt due from the firm if the circumstances are such that he would have had a right of set-off if the agent had been a single individual[1]. A similar rule applies where the agent is not really a firm but contracts in a firm name on behalf of one only of the persons acting as agents under that name[2].

1   *Rabone v Williams* (1785) 7 Term Rep 360n. As to claims by undisclosed principals see para 444 ante.
2   *Spurr v Cass, Cass v Spurr* (1870) LR 5 QB 656.

472. Debts owed by and to a firm. A defendant sued for a debt due from himself alone may not set off a debt owing to a firm of which he is a member[1]. Similarly, a debt owed by a firm may not be set off against a claim by an individual partner[2]. However, where all the other partners have died and the right to the firm debts is in the individual partner as survivor, the common law rule was that it could be made the subject of a set-off[3]. In equity, however, the claim is brought to account in ascertaining the entitlement of the deceased partners' estates[4].

1   See the cases cited in para 441 note 2 ante. A person may not be sued alone for a debt on a transaction concluded by him under a firm name unless he alone constituted the firm or so held himself out to the plaintiff: see *Bonfield v Smith* (1844) 12 M & W 405. As to set-off at law and in equity see para 435 note 1 ante.
2   See the cases cited in para 440 note 2 ante.
3   *Golding v Vaughan* (1782) 2 Chit 436; *Slipper v Stidstone* (1794) 5 Term Rep 493; *French v Andrade* (1796) 6 Term Rep 582; *Smith v Parkes* (1852) 16 Beav 115. See also PARTNERSHIP vol 35 (Reissue) para 80.
4   *McClean v Kennard* (1874) 9 Ch App 336.

473. Set-off against assignee of debt. The law as to set-off as against an assignee obtains where any one or more of the parties concerned is a firm[1], and a firm may set off against the assignee of a retiring partner a debt due from the retiring partner at the date of assignment[2]. Similarly, a debtor may set off against the assignee of a firm a debt due from the firm before assignment[3].

1   This is, of course, subject to the limitation as to setting off joint and several debts, as to which see paras 440–441 ante.
2   *Smith v Parkes* (1852) 16 Beav 115. See PARTNERSHIP vol 35 (Reissue) para 113. As to set-off at law and in equity see para 435 note 1 ante.
3   *Puller v Roe* (1793) Peake 198. For a criticism of this decision see SR Derham *Set-off* (2nd edn, 1996) pp 347–348. As to set-off against assignees generally see para 453 ante.

474. Set-off in relation to companies. A shareholder may set off against a call a debt presently due and owing to him by the company while the company is a going concern[1]. However, a set-off made within six months of a winding-up petition may constitute a fraudulent preference[2].

A debenture holder cannot set off a debt due from him to the company against sums due from the company to him on his debentures[3], nor can a company's solicitor set off an unliquidated claim for his costs against calls made in respect of shares in the company held by him[4].

In a winding-up, whether compulsory or voluntary, the ordinary rules of set-off apply in the case of a solvent company[5], but if the company is insolvent the mutual credit provisions of bankruptcy apply[6]. Further in a winding-up a contributory cannot himself set off a debt owed to him by the company, although his trustee in bankruptcy may do so[7]. Where the liability of either the contributory or the company is unlimited the court may allow the contributory to set off money due to him in his personal capacity but not money due to him as a member of the company[8].

1 See COMPANIES vol 7(1) (1996 Reissue) para 424, vol 7(3) (1996 Reissue) paras 2498–2500.
2 See COMPANIES vol 7(3) (1996 Reissue) paras 2605, 2609.
3 See COMPANIES vol 7(2) (1996 Reissue) para 1285.
4 *Johnson v Lyttle's Iron Agency* (1877) 5 ChD 687, CA.
5 See COMPANIES vol 7(3) (1996 Reissue) para 2551.
6 See COMPANIES vol 7(3) (1996 Reissue) para 2551; BANKRUPTCY AND INSOLVENCY vol 3(2) (Reissue) para 535 et seq. In a compulsory winding-up, the Insolvency Rules 1986, SI 1986/1925 (as amended), apply. For the purposes of r 4.90 of those rules, set-off is limited to mutual claims existing at the date of the bankruptcy and there can be no set-off of claims by third parties, even with their consent: *Re Bank of Credit and Commerce International SA (No 8)* [1997] 4 All ER 568, HL.
7 See COMPANIES vol 7(3) (1996 Reissue) para 2498.
8 See COMPANIES vol 7(3) (1996 Reissue) para 2500.

H. SOLICITORS

475. Solicitor's costs. A solicitor is not prevented from setting off a sum due for costs by reason only of the fact that he has not complied with the statutory provision as to the delivery of a bill[1].

Where a claim for costs and disbursements in respect of work done by a solicitor fails because the solicitor has been negligent, and there is joined with that claim a claim to which this defence does not apply, the defendant cannot set off against the second claim money paid to the solicitor and expended by him in doing the work before the negligence occurred[2]. In proceedings where one party is legally aided, the court has a discretion to order a set-off between the legally aided party and the solicitors acting for the other party, despite the existence of a charge in favour of the legal aid fund on property recovered by the legally aided party in the proceedings[3].

1 See para 446 ante.
2 *Lewis v Samuel* (1846) 8 QB 685. As to solicitor-trustees see paras 457–458 ante.
3 See the Legal Aid Act 1988 s 16(6), (8) (amended by the Courts and Legal Services Act 1990 s 125(3), Sch 18 para 63(2); *Rawley v Rawley* (1876) 1 QBD 460 per Mellish LJ; *Currie & Co v Law Society* [1977] QB 990, [1976] 3 All ER 832; and LEGAL AID; PRACTICE AND PROCEDURE.

I. SURETIES

476. Claim against surety by third person. A surety for payment of a sum due under a contract is entitled to be exonerated by his principal, and in an action against himself as surety may therefore set off a debt due from the plaintiff to the principal arising out of the same transaction[1]. If under the contract the principal is entitled to the benefit of a deduction to be ascertained by arbitration, the surety may set off a sum awarded by an arbitrator acting under the contract[2].

1 *Bechervaise v Lewis* (1872) LR 7 CP 372. *Hyundai Shipbuilding and Heavy Industries Co Ltd v Pournaras* [1978] 2 Lloyd's Rep 502 at 508, CA; but cf *National Westminster Bank plc v Skelton* [1993] 1 WLR 72n at 79, CA, per Slade LJ (where doubt is expressed as to this proposition). See the discussion in SR Derham *Set-off* (2nd edn, 1996) pp 642–644. See also GUARANTEE AND INDEMNITY vol 20 (Reissue) para 225.

2 *Parkes v Smith* (1850) 15 QB 297; *Murphy v Glass* (1869) LR 2 PC 408; *Alcoy and Gandia Rly and Harbour Co Ltd v Greenhill* (1897) 76 LT 542 (on appeal (1898) 79 LT 257, CA).

477. Proceedings between surety and principal. A surety sued by his principal may set off sums paid by him as surety[1], and if he is sued by the executor of the principal the right of set-off holds good[2].

1 This is so even if the surety has been sued to judgment and a writ of fieri facias has been issued, and the sum has been paid by the sheriff out of the proceeds of the goods taken in execution: *Rodgers v Maw* (1846) 15 M & W 444. See also GUARANTEE AND INDEMNITY vol 20 (Reissue) paras 216, 225, 254.
2 *Jones v Mossop* (1844) 3 Hare 568. See also *Ribblesdale v Forbes* (1916) 140 LT Jo 483, CA, where a husband who paid a debt as surety for his wife was allowed to set off the amount of the debt against a sum due to trustees for his wife under an agreement.

478. Claim against surety's securities. Where a loan is made by an insurance company to a person on the security of a policy on the life of another, and the latter dies, the company cannot set off a debt due from the deceased against a claim on the policy by a surety who has paid off the loan[1].

1 *Re Jeffery's Policy* (1872) 20 WR 857.

J. BILLS OF EXCHANGE

479. Proceedings by holder of bill of exchange. Actions on bills of exchange constitute an exception to the rights of abatement and equitable defence[1].

1 See para 414 ante.

(6) COUNTERCLAIMS AND ASSOCIATED CLAIMS

480. When a counterclaim is available. A counterclaim[1] is available to a defendant only when the rules of procedure of the court in which the plaintiff brings his action allow a counterclaim to be set up, and the way in which a counterclaim may be brought is determined by those rules[2]. A counterclaim may be set up by or against the Crown, subject to the same limitations as are imposed in the case of a set-off[3]. The Supreme Court of Judicature Act 1873[4] did not give, and the Rules of the Supreme Court[5] have not given, new rights of action, but have only altered the procedure to the extent of allowing a cross-action and an action to be brought and tried in the same proceedings[6]. A person who has a right enforceable not by action, but in some other way, cannot enforce that right by a counterclaim, but is confined to the proper remedy[7].

In relation to proceedings begun on or after 26 April 1999, new rules of procedure govern the making of counterclaims and similar claims[8]. No provision is made limiting the subject matter of a counterclaim.

1 Counterclaim was introduced by the Supreme Court of Judicature Act 1873 s 24(3) (repealed), which was replaced by the Supreme Court of Judicature (Consolidation) Act 1925 s 39(1)(a) (repealed). This was in turn repealed by the Supreme Court Act 1981 which, by s 49(2)(a), preserved the procedure relating to counterclaim prevailing at 1 January 1982: see PRACTICE AND PROCEDURE. Before 1873, a defendant could not raise in the plaintiff's action any claim which could not be made the subject of set-off. A defendant's only remedy was to bring an independent cross-action: *Stooke v Taylor* (1880) 5 QBD 569 at 576, DC; *Stumore v Campbell & Co* [1892] 1 QB 314 at 316, CA. Now by his counterclaim he may raise any claim, whatever its nature, against the plaintiff in the plaintiff's action that might have been the subject of an independent action, subject only to the court's discretionary power to strike out the

counterclaim, order it to be tried separately or make such other order as may be expedient if it appears to the court that the subject matter of the counterclaim ought for any reason to be disposed of by a separate action: see paras 502–503 post.

2   This is part of the general law as to pleading: see RSC Ord 15 r 2; Ord 18 r 17; and PLEADING. Cf *Popi (Owners) v SS Gniezno (Owners), The Gniezno* [1968] P 418, [1967] 2 All ER 738.

3   See the Crown Proceedings Act 1947 ss 1, 35(2)(g); RSC Ord 77 r 6; CPR Sch 1 RSC Ord 77 r 6; and para 436 ante. See also CROWN PROCEEDINGS AND CROWN PRACTICE vol 12(1) (Reissue) para 126. As to the modification of the RSC and CCR as scheduled to the CPR see para 401 note 3 ante.

4   See note 1 supra.

5   Ie RSC Ord 15 r 2, Ord 18 r 7: see PRACTICE AND PROCEDURE. As to the replacement of the RSC by the CPR, and the transitional arrangements in relation thereto, see para 401 note 3 ante. See also para 424 ante.

6   *Re Milan Tramways Co, ex p Theys* (1882) 22 ChD 122 at 126 per Kay J; affd (1884) 25 ChD 587, CA. See also *Stumore v Campbell & Co* [1892] 1 QB 314, CA, per Lord Esher MR, cited in para 426 note 3 ante.

7   *Gaslight and Coke Co v Holloway* (1885) 52 LT 434; *Schofield v Hincks* (1888) 58 LJQB 147; *Lancashire and Yorkshire Rly Co v Greenwood* (1888) 21 QBD 215.

8   See generally CPR Pt 20; and para 493 et seq post.

481. Subject matter of counterclaim.

In relation to proceedings begun on or after 26 April 1999[1], a counterclaim can in general be brought in respect of any claim, or the entitlement to any relief or remedy, against a plaintiff in an existing action in respect of any matter, whenever and however arising, being a claim or entitlement that could be the subject of a separate action[2]. It is not confined to money claims, or to causes of action of the same nature as the original action[3], and, except where a person other than the plaintiff is also made a defendant to it, it need not relate to or be connected with the original subject of the cause or matter[4]. A claim founded on tort may be opposed to one founded on contract[5] and in an action in rem the defendant may set up a counterclaim in personam[6]. The defendant by his counterclaim may ask for any form of relief, for example a declaration[7], a vesting order against forfeiture[8], an injunction[9], the appointment of a receiver[10], specific performance[11], the revocation of a patent[12], an account[13], payment of a money claim or damages[14].

In relation to proceedings begun on or after 26 April 1999, new provision is made as to counterclaims[15].

1   Ie the date on which the CPR came into force. As to the replacement of the RSC by the CPR, and the transitional arrangements in relation thereto, see para 401 note 3 ante.

2   RSC Ord 15 r 2(1); *Birmingham Estates Co v Smith* (1880) 13 ChD 506 at 508. This is, however, subject to the court's power to order separate trials under RSC Ord 15 r 5(2): see paras 502–503 post.

3   *Beddall v Maitland* (1881) 17 ChD 174 at 181; *Gray v Webb* (1882) 21 ChD 802; *Re Richardson, Richardson v Nicholson* [1933] WN 90, CA.

4   See para 483 post.

5   *Besant v Wood* (1879) 12 ChD 605; *Stooke v Taylor* (1880) 5 QBD 569, DC; *Lewin v Trimming* (1888) 21 QBD 230, DC.

6   *The Cheapside* [1904] P 339, CA. See also ADMIRALTY vol 1(1) (Reissue) paras 414–415.

7   *Adams v Adams* (1890) 45 ChD 426 (affd [1892] 1 Ch 369, CA); *Warden etc of Sir Roger Cholmeley's School at Highgate v Sewell* [1893] 2 QB 254, DC.

8   *Warden etc of Sir Roger Cholmeley's School at Highgate v Sewell* [1893] 2 QB 254, DC.

9   See INJUNCTIONS vol 24 (Reissue) para 960.

10 *Carter v Fey* [1894] 2 Ch 541, CA; *Collison v Warren* [1901] 1 Ch 812, CA.

11 *Dear v Sworder, Sworder v Dear* (1876) 4 ChD 476.

12 See PATENTS AND REGISTERED DESIGNS vol 35 (Reissue) paras 649, 651.

13 *Dear v Sworder, Sworder v Dear* (1876) 4 ChD 476; *Mutrie v Binney* (1887) 35 ChD 614, CA.

14 See generally DAMAGES.

15 See CPR Pt 20; and para 493 et seq post. As to the meaning of 'counterclaim' see para 407 ante. No provision is made limiting the subject matter of a counterclaim. As to the power of the court to order that a Part 20 claim be dealt with separately from the original claim see para 502 post.

     A Part 20 claim is any claim other than a claim by a claimant against a defendant, and includes: (1) a counterclaim by a defendant against a claimant or against the claimant and some other person; (2) a claim by a defendant against any person (whether or not already a party) for contribution or indemnity or some other remedy; and (3) where a Part 20 claim has been made against a person who is not already a party, any claim made by that person against any other person (whether or not already a party): CPR 20.2(1). For the meaning of 'contribution' see para 491 note 7 post. For the meaning of 'indemnity' see para 491 note 8 post.

482. Jurisdiction of county courts. A county court has jurisdiction to try counterclaims in the same way as the High Court[1], even if the counterclaim involves matters beyond the jurisdiction[2] of the county court[3], although if a counterclaim involves matters beyond the jurisdiction of the county court, or the court considers that a party is likely to be entitled, in respect of a counterclaim, to an amount exceeding the amount recoverable in the county court, the court may of its own motion or on the application of any party to the proceedings transfer the whole or part of the proceedings to the High Court[4]. The High Court can itself order such a transfer if it thinks it desirable[5]. Similarly, proceedings may be transferred from the High Court to the County Court[6].

1   See the County Courts Act 1984 s 38 (substituted by the Courts and Legal Services Act 1990 s 3); and COUNTY COURTS.
2   As to the monetary jurisdiction of the county court see COUNTY COURTS.
3   See *Hardwicke v Gilroy* [1944] KB 460, [1944] 1 All ER 521, CA.
4   See the County Courts Act 1984 s 42 (substituted by the Courts and Legal Services Act 1990 s 2(3)); and COUNTY COURTS.
     As from 26 April 1999, the matters to which the court must have regard in considering whether to transfer proceedings are set out in CPR Pt 30. See particularly CPR 30.3, where the criteria are listed. The claims which may be so transferred expressly include counterclaims: CPR 30.2(1). As to the replacement of the RSC and CCR by the CPR, and the transitional arrangements in relation thereto, see para 401 note 3 ante.
5   See the County Courts Act 1984 s 41 (as amended); and COUNTY COURTS. As to the procedure on transfer of proceedings begun on or after 26 April 1999 see CPR Pt 30; and note 4 supra.
6   See the County Courts Act 1984 s 40 (substituted by the Courts and Legal Services Act 1990 s 2(1)); and COUNTY COURTS. As to the procedure on transfer of proceedings begun on or after 26 April 1999 see CPR Pt 30; and note 4 supra.

483. Joint claims. A counterclaim cannot be set up in respect of a cause of action or to claim relief which would not be available to the defendant if he was suing in an independent action alone, without a co-plaintiff, and the court will not add a fresh defendant to enable such a counterclaim to be raised[1] unless the relief claimed by the plaintiff in the action is such that the fresh defendant may properly be added having regard to the plaintiff's claim[2].

One of several co-defendants may set up a counterclaim in respect of a several cause of action available to himself alone[3].

1   *Norris v Beazley* (1877) 2 CPD 80; *Pender v Taddei* [1898] 1 QB 798, CA; *McCheane v Gyles (No 2)* [1902] 1 Ch 911.
2   *Montgomery v Foy, Morgan & Co* [1895] 2 QB 321, CA; and see *Dear v Sworder, Sworder v Dear* (1876) 4 ChD 476 at 482. A husband joined as co-defendant with his wife for conformity only could with his wife counterclaim in respect of a cause of action available to them jointly: *Hodson v Mochi* (1878) 8 ChD 569.
3   *Hodson v Mochi* (1878) 8 ChD 569.

484. When cause of action may arise. A defendant may set up by a counterclaim a cause of action which has accrued since the action was begun[1]. A contributory on whom calls have been made in the winding-up of a company can counterclaim for rescission of the contract to take shares, provided he has taken legal steps to have his name removed from the register before the winding-up commenced[2].

A defendant may set up a counterclaim in respect of a cause of action arising after defence, if he amends the defence and states in the counterclaim that it arose after defence[3].

1   See RSC Ord 15 r 2(1); *Beddall v Maitland* (1881) 17 ChD 174 at 180 per Fry J, dissenting from the view taken by Jessel MR in *Original Hartlepool Collieries Co v Gibb* (1877) 5 ChD 713; *Wood v Goodwin* [1884] WN 17; and see *Lowe v Bentley* (1928) 44 TLR 388. As to set-off see para 444 ante. See also PLEADING.
     As to the replacement of the RSC by the CPR, and the transitional arrangements in relation thereto, see para 401 note 3 ante. As to the making of a counterclaim in proceedings begun on or after that date see CPR Pt 20; and para 493 et seq post. The CPR make no mention of whether a cause of action arising after the commencement of the action may be set up as a counterclaim. However, the rules permit the defendant to make a counterclaim after filing his defence with the permission of the court: see *Practice Direction—Counterclaims and other Part 20 Claims* (1999) PD20 paras 2.1–2.3; and para 493 post.
2   *Re General Railway Syndicate, Whiteley's Case* [1900] 1 Ch 365, CA: see COMPANIES vol 7(1) (1996 Reissue) para 328.
3   *Ellis v Munson* (1876) 35 LT 585, CA. See also note 1 supra.

485. Effect of counterclaim. The effect of a counterclaim when raised is to put the plaintiff, together with any third person against whom together with the plaintiff the counterclaim is set up, in the position of defendants to a cross-action[1]. They must defend themselves and show a good answer or suffer judgment, on which execution may issue in respect of the cause or causes of action alleged in the counterclaim[2].

The counterclaim may be proceeded with as an independent action notwithstanding that judgment is given for the plaintiff in the original action or that that action is stayed, discontinued or dismissed[3].

As from 26 April 1999, a counterclaim[4] is treated for most purposes as any other claim[5].

1   See RSC Ord 15 r 2(2).
2   See eg *Stooke v Taylor* (1880) 5 QBD 569 at 576, DC, per Cockburn CJ, and *Amon v Bobbett* (1889) 22 QBD 543, CA. See also JUDGMENTS AND ORDERS. For cases in which application may be made to strike out a counterclaim or order separate trials see paras 503–504 post.
3   RSC Ord 15 r 2(3); *McGowan v Middleton* (1883) 11 QBD 464, CA; and see para 510 post.
4   Counterclaims fall within the category of 'Part 20 claims' under CPR Pt 20 (see para 493 et seq post): see para 481 note 15 ante.
5   See CPR 20.3(1); and para 494 post. As to the replacement of the RSC by the CPR, and the transitional arrangements in relation thereto, see para 401 note 3 ante. No equivalent provision to RSC Ord 15 r 2(3) is made, but it is conceived that since a Part 20 claim is a claim for the purposes of the Rules, no specific provision is necessary to keep a Part 20 claim alive after discontinuance of the original action.

486. Plaintiff must be a party. In relation to proceedings begun before 26 April 1999[1], a counterclaim by a defendant must allege that he has a claim or is entitled to some relief or remedy against a plaintiff in the action[2], either alone[3] or together with some other person, whether or not that other person is a party to the action[4], as defendant or defendants to the counterclaim[5]. A defendant who alleges a claim or the entitlement to some relief or remedy against the plaintiff or plaintiffs together with some other person who is not a plaintiff may join that person as defendant to the counterclaim subject to certain restrictions[6].

In relation to proceedings begun on or after 26 April 1999, a counterclaim may be brought by the defendant against the claimant[7] or against the claimant and some other party[8]. A defendant who wishes to counterclaim against a person other than the claimant must apply to the court for an order that that person be added as defendant to the counterclaim[9].

1   Ie the date on which the CPR came into force. As to the replacement of the RSC by the CPR, and the transitional arrangements in relation thereto, see para 401 note 3 ante.
2   *Harris v Gamble* (1877) 6 ChD 748.
3   RSC Ord 15 r 2(1).
4   RSC Ord 15 r 3(1). Relief claimed only against a person who is not a plaintiff may be claimed only, if at all, in third party proceedings: see PRACTICE AND PROCEDURE.
5   RSC Ord 15 r 2(2). Accordingly a counterclaim cannot be set up by one defendant against his co-defendant only: *Furness v Booth* (1876) 4 ChD 586; *Warner v Twining* (1876) 24 WR 536; *Harris v Gamble* (1877) 6 ChD 748; *McLay v Sharp* [1877] WN 216; *Central African Trading Co v Grove* (1879) 48 LJQB 510, CA. However, a counterclaim can be set up against a defendant by a person served with a third party notice: see para 492 post.
6   See RSC Ord 15 r 3; and para 487 et seq post.
7   Note that in the CPR, the term 'claimant' is used rather than 'plaintiff'. A defendant who brings a counterclaim (or other Part 20 claim: see para 481 note 15 ante) is known as a 'Part 20 claimant': CPR 20.2(2). A person against whom a Part 20 claim is made is a 'Part 20 defendant': see *Practice Direction—Counterclaims and other Part 20 Claims* PD20 para 2.1(4). This is in keeping with the principle that Part 20 claims are claims in their own right: see para 494 post.
8   CPR 20.2(1)(a). A Part 20 defendant who is not already a party may also make a Part 20 claim against any other person (whether or not the latter is also a party): CPR 20.2(1)(c).
9   CPR 20.5(1). An application for such an order may be made without notice unless the court directs otherwise: CPR 20.5(2). If the court makes such an order it will give directions as to the management of the case: CPR 20.5(3).

487. Claim against one or more of several co-plaintiffs. Where there are several co-plaintiffs, a counterclaim may be brought against all of them or against one or some of them only, and in such a case the defendant may in his counterclaim allege separate causes of action against each or any of them[1].

1   *Manchester and Sheffield Rly Co v Brooks* (1877) 2 ExD 243.

488. Claim against plaintiff in different capacity. A counterclaim cannot be brought against a plaintiff personally and also in a representative capacity unless the rules governing joinder of parties[1] would allow the joinder in an independent action[2]. A counterclaim may, however, be brought against a plaintiff in a capacity different from that in which his claim is made[3]. For example, a counterclaim against a plaintiff as administratrix may be set up in opposition to a personal claim by her[4].

1   See RSC Ord 15 r 4; and PRACTICE AND PROCEDURE. As from 26 April 1999 the rules governing joinder of parties are contained in CPR Pt 19. As to the replacement of the RSC by the CPR, and the transitional arrangements in relation thereto, see para 401 note 3 ante.
2   *Macdonald v Carington* (1878) 4 CPD 28; *McEwan v Crombie* (1883) 25 ChD 175 at 177; *Stumore v Campbell & Co* [1892] 1 QB 314, CA.
3   See eg CPR 20.10(2); and para 493 text and note 15 post.
4   *Re Richardson, Richardson v Nicholson* [1933] WN 90, CA. As to the power of the court to order that a claim and counterclaim be heard separately see para 502 post.

489. Claim against plaintiff and another. In relation to proceedings begun before 26 April 1999[1], where a defendant who makes a counterclaim against the plaintiff alleges that any other person (whether or not a party to the action) is liable to him along with the plaintiff in respect of the subject matter of the counterclaim[2], or claims against that other person any relief relating to or connected with the original subject matter of the action, he may join that other person as a party to the counterclaim[3], adding his name to the title of the action, and serving on him a copy of the counterclaim[4], whereupon, if that person is not already a party, he becomes a party to the action[5]. The counterclaim operates as a writ for the purpose of seeking leave to serve out of the jurisdiction[6].

The position after 26 April 1999 has been considered previously[7].

1 Ie the date on which the CPR came into force. As to the replacement of the RSC by the CPR, and the transitional arrangements in relation thereto, see para 401 note 3 ante.

2 See eg *Dear v Sworder, Sworder v Dear* (1876) 4 ChD 476.

3 RSC Ord 15 r 3(1). The right is subject to the court's discretion to order separate trials under Ord 15 r 5(2): see paras 498–499 post.

4 He must also serve a form of acknowledgment of service if the person is not already a party: RSC Ord 15 r 3(2).

5 RSC Ord 15 r 3(2). See further PRACTICE AND PROCEDURE.

6 See RSC Ord 15 r 3(5)(a). As to service out of the jurisdiction see PRACTICE AND PROCEDURE.

7 See para 486 text and notes 7–9 ante.

490. Counterclaim to counterclaim. In relation to proceedings begun before 26 April 1999[1], a plaintiff in reply to a counterclaim may himself counterclaim in respect of any matter whenever or however arising, as if the original counterclaim was a separate action to which the original plaintiff was defendant[2]. A party brought in as defendant to a counterclaim may counterclaim against the defendant[3].

The position after 26 April 1999 has been considered previously[4].

1 Ie the date on which the CPR came into force. As to the replacement of the RSC by the CPR, and the transitional arrangements in relation thereto, see para 401 note 3 ante.

2 See RSC Ord 15 r 2(2). As with the original counterclaim, the plaintiff's counterclaim may have arisen after action brought: see para 481 ante. The rule adopts and possibly extends the previous law: see *Beddall v Maitland* (1881) 17 ChD 174; *Toke v Andrews* (1882) 8 QBD 428, DC; *Renton Gibbs & Co Ltd v Neville & Co* [1900] 2 QB 181, CA; *James v Page* (1888) 85 LT Jo 157, DC; *Lewis Falk Ltd v Jacobwitz* (1944) 171 LT 36.

3 RSC Ord 15 r 3(2), under which the new party has all the rights of a defendant in a separate action. Such cases as *Alcoy and Gandia Rly and Harbour Co v Greenhill* [1896] 1 Ch 19, CA, are thus reversed.

4 See para 486 text and notes 7–9 ante.

491. Third party notice; proceedings for contribution and indemnity. In relation to proceedings begun before 26 April 1999[1], a plaintiff or other person against whom a counterclaim is set up may by leave issue a third party notice against a third person from whom he claims contribution or indemnity in respect of the subject matter of the counterclaim[2]. A person against whom the defendant has issued a third party notice may counterclaim against the defendant[3] but not against the plaintiff[4], and a defendant against whom a counterclaim is made by a third party may counterclaim against the counterclaim[5].

In relation to proceedings begun on or after 26 April 1999, specific provision for third party proceedings is no longer made. However, a defendant who has filed an acknowledgement of service or a defence may make a Part 20 claim[6] for contribution[7] or indemnity[8] against another defendant by filing a notice containing a statement of the name[9] and grounds of his claim, and serving that notice on the other defendant[10].

1 Ie the date on which the CPR came into force. As to the replacement of the RSC by the CPR, and the transitional arrangements in relation thereto, see para 401 note 3 ante.

2 RSC Ord 16 r 11; *Levi v Anglo-Continental Gold Reefs of Rhodesia Ltd* [1902] 2 KB 481, CA. As to third party procedure see PRACTICE AND PROCEDURE vol 37 para 254 et seq.

3 *Barclays Bank v Tom* [1923] 1 KB 221, CA. See also *McCheane v Gyles* [1902] 1 Ch 287, CA.

4 *Eden v Weardale Iron and Coal Co* (1884) 28 ChD 333 at 338, CA.

5 *Normar (Owners) v British Transport Docks Board, The Normar* [1968] P 362, [1968] 1 All ER 753.

6 For the meaning of 'Part 20 claim' see para 481 note 15 ante.

7 'Contribution' means a right of someone to recover from a third person all or part of the amount which he himself is liable to pay: CPR 2.2(1), Glossary. As to the effect of Glossary definitions see para 407 note 4 ante.

8 'Indemnity' means a right of someone to recover from a third party the whole amount which he himself is liable to pay: CPR Glossary. As to the effect of Glossary definitions see para 407 note 4 ante.

9   As to the titles of proceedings where there are Part 20 claims see *Practice Direction—Counterclaims and other Part 20 Claims* (1999) PD20 para 7.
10   CPR 20.6.

492. Enforcement of foreign judgments. A foreign[1] court is deemed to have had jurisdiction to hear an action, and its judgment will be registered[2] and enforced in the United Kingdom[3] if, inter alia, the judgment debtor was the plaintiff in or counterclaimed in the original court[4].

1   For the countries to which the Foreign Judgments (Reciprocal Enforcement) Act 1933 applies see CONFLICT OF LAWS vol 8(1) (Reissue) para 1028.
2   As to registration of foreign judgments see CONFLICT OF LAWS vol 8(1) (Reissue) para 1030.
3   'United Kingdom' means Great Britain and Northern Ireland: Settled Land Act 1925 s 117(1)(xxxii). 'Great Britain' means England, Scotland and Wales: Union with Scotland Act 1706 preamble art I; Interpretation Act 1978 s 22(1), Sch 2 para 5(a). See further CONSTITUTIONAL LAW AND HUMAN RIGHTS vol 8(2) (Reissue) para 3.
4   Foreign Judgments (Reciprocal Enforcement) Act 1933 s 4(2)(a)(ii). See generally CONFLICT OF LAWS vol 8(1) (Reissue) para 1034. As to the effect of the Convention on Jurisdiction and the Enforcement of Judgments in Civil and Commercial Matters (Brussels, 27 September 1968; EC 46 (1978); Cmnd 7395) on the right to counterclaim in proceedings brought in a member state of the European Community see art 6(3); and CONFLICT OF LAWS vol 8(1) (Reissue) para 644. For the application of the counterclaim provisions of the Convention in the specific context of insurance see art 11; and *Jordan Grand Prix Ltd v Baltic Insurance Group* [1999] 1 All ER 289, [1999] 2 WLR 134, HL. The Convention as it applies in the United Kingdom is set out in the Civil Jurisdiction and Judgments Act 1982 Sch 1.

2. PLEADING AND PRACTICE

(1) PLEADING A SET-OFF, COUNTERCLAIM OR ASSOCIATED CLAIM

493. Procedure. In relation to proceedings begun before 26 April 1999[1], a set-off or counterclaim is raised by being specially pleaded in the same document as the defence[2]. In the county court a set-off or counterclaim is raised by completing in the appropriate manner the form appended to the summons or preparing a separate form, and delivering it to the court office[3].

In relation to proceedings begun on or after 26 April 1999, a set-off may be raised as follows. Where a defendant contends that he is entitled to money from the claimant[4], and relies on this as a defence to the whole or part of the claim, the contention may be included in the defence and set off against the claim[5].

In relation to proceedings begun on or after 26 April 1999, a defendant may make a counterclaim against a claimant by filing particulars of the counterclaim[6]. He may make a counterclaim without the permission of the court if he files it with his defence[7], and at any time with the court's permission[8]. Where a counterclaim may be made without the court's permission, the claim form[9] must be served on every other party when the defence is served[10]. Where the court gives permission to make a counterclaim it will at the same time give directions as to service[11].

Where the alternative procedure for claims is followed for the original claim[12], a counterclaim (or other Part 20 claim) may not be made without the permission of the court[13].

A person on whom a Part 20 claim is served becomes a party to the proceedings if he is not a party already[14]. Where a Part 20 claim is served on an existing party for the purpose of requiring the court to decide a question against that party in a further capacity, that party also becomes a party in that further capacity[15].

The contents of a Part 20 claim must be verified by a statement of truth[16].

1   Ie the date on which the CPR came into force. As to the replacement of the RSC by the CPR, and the transitional arrangements in relation thereto, see para 401 note 3 ante.
2   RSC Ord 15 r 2(1); *Graham v Partridge* (1836) 1 M & W 395. See para 496 post. As to pleading a probate counterclaim see RSC Ord 76; and EXECUTORS AND ADMINISTRATORS.
3   See CCR 1981 Ord 9 r 2(1). The procedure discussed in this part of the title is principally the procedure in the High Court.
4   As to the meaning of 'claimant' see para 486 note 7 ante.
5   CPR 16.6. See para 496 post.
6   CPR 20.4(1). The provisions of CPR 7.5, 7.6 (time for serving claim forms) do not apply to Part 20 claims: see para 494 note 7 post. As to procedure for making a probate counterclaim see *Practice Direction—Contentious Probate Proceedings* (1999) PD49A para 8. As to the procedure where a defendant makes a probate counterclaim in proceedings other than probate proceedings see PD49A para 16. For the meaning of 'Part 20 claim' see para 481 note 15 ante. See generally EXECUTORS AND ADMINISTRATORS.
7   CPR 20.4(2)(a). The provisions of Pt 15 (defences) apply to counterclaims: CPR 20.3.
8   CPR 20.4(2)(b). See further para 500 et seq post.
     An application for permission to make a Part 20 claim (including a counterclaim) must be supported by evidence stating: (1) the stage which the action has reached; (2) the nature of the claim to be made by the Part 20 claimant or details of the question or issue which needs to be decided; (3) a summary of the facts on which the Part 20 claim is based; and (4) the name and address of the proposed Part 20 defendant: *Practice Direction—Counterclaims and other Part 20 Claims* (1999) PD20 para 2.1. where delay has been a factor contributing to the need to apply for permission, an explanation of the delay would be given in evidence: para 2.2. Where possible, the applicant should provide a timetable of the action to date: para 2.3. The application notice should be filed together with a copy of the proposed Part 20 claim: para 1.1. For the meanings of 'Part 20 claimant' and 'Part 20 defendant' see para 486 note 7 ante.
     When the court is considering whether to permit a Part 20 claim to be made, it may have regard to the same matters as if it were considering whether to dismiss a Part 20 claim or order it to be tried separately: see CPR 20.9(1); and para 502 text to notes 4–10 post.
     As to the titles of proceedings where there are Part 20 claims see *Practice Direction—Counterclaims and other Part 20 Claims* (1999) PD20 para 7.
9   Ie the Part 20 claim form. As to claim forms see CPR Pt 7.
10   CPR 20.8(1)(a). In the case of any other Part 20 claim, the claim form must be served on the person against whom it is made within 14 days after the date on which the Part 20 claimant files his defence: CPR 20.8(1)(b). This does not, however, apply to a claim for contribution or indemnity made under CPR 20.6 (see para 491 text to note 10 ante): CPR 20.8(2). For the meaning of 'contribution' see para 491 note 7 ante. For the meaning of 'indemnity' see para 491 note 7 ante.
11   CPR 20.8(3).
12   Ie the procedure provided by CPR Pt 8. This procedure is available where a claimant seeks the court's decision which is unlikely to involve a substantial dispute of fact, or where it is provided by a practice direction that the procedure is to apply: CPR 8.1(1), (6).
13   CPR 8.7.
14   CPR 20.10(1). As to procedure for making a counterclaim against a person other than the claimant see CPR 20.5; and para 486 ante.
15   CPR 20.10(2). See also para 488 ante.
16   *Practice Direction—Counterclaims and other Part 20 Claims* (1999) PD20 para 4.1. the form must be as follows: '[I believe] [the Part 20 claimant] believes] that the facts stated in this statement of case are true': para 4.2.
     As to statements of truth generally see CPR Pt 22. If a party fails to verify a statement of case by a statement of truth the statement of case remains effective unless struck out, but the party may not rely on the statement of case as evidence of any of the matters set out in it: CPR 22.2(1). The court may strike out a statement of case which is not verified by a statement of truth: CPR 22.2(2). Any party may apply for an order to strike out the statement of case on that ground: CPR 22.2(3). Note also, however, the court's power to strike out a statement of case on its own initiative for failure to comply with a rule or practice direction: see CPR 3.4; and para 502 note 16 post.

494. Counterclaim as separate action. A counterclaim is for most purposes of procedure, except execution, treated as a separate action to be tried together with the original action[1]. A counterclaim or set-off is specifically included in the word 'action' for the purposes of the Bills of Exchange Act 1882[2] and the Sale of Goods Act 1979[3]. Where a counterclaim operates also as a defence, it should be treated as one, for example when considering security for costs against a defendant[4].

In relation to actions begun on or after 26 April 1999, a counterclaim[5] is to be treated for the purposes of rules of procedure as if it were a claim[6], subject to certain exceptions[7].

A claim for set-off is not an 'action' within the provisions[8] restricting the bringing of an action by a solicitor to recover costs[9]. For the purposes of the Crown Proceedings Act 1947, 'proceedings against the Crown' includes a claim by way of set-off or counterclaim[10].

For limitation purposes a claim by way of set-off or counterclaim is deemed to be a separate action and to have been commenced on the same date as the action in which the set-off or counterclaim is pleaded[11].

1   See RSC Ord 15 r 2(2), (3); *Beddall v Maitland* (1881) 17 ChD 174; *Re Milan Tramways Co, ex p Theys* (1882) 22 ChD 122 (affd (1884) 25 ChD 587, CA); *McGowan v Middleton* (1883) 11 QBD 464, CA; *Sykes v Sacerdoti* (1885) 15 QBD 423, CA; *Levi v Anglo-Continental Gold Reefs of Rhodesia Ltd* [1902] 2 KB 481, CA; *Barclays Bank v Tom* [1923] 1 KB 221, CA. A counterclaim was not an 'action' within the Supreme Court of Judicature (Consolidation) Act 1925 s 225 (repealed), so as to give a counterclaiming defendant the right to trial by jury for libel: *Lord Kinnaird v Field* [1905] 2 Ch 361, CA. As to the court's discretion to order trial by jury see the Supreme Court Act 1981 s 69(1); RSC Ord 33 r 5; and PRACTICE AND PROCEDURE. As to orders for the separate trial of counterclaims see para 498 post.
2   Bills of Exchange Act 1882 s 2.
3   Sale of Goods Act 1979 s 61.
4   Where the counterclaim is in substance a cross-action, security for costs may be ordered (*Sykes v Sacerdoti* (1885) 15 QBD 423, CA), but if the counterclaim is merely a defence security will not be ordered (*Neck v Taylor* [1893] 1 QB 560, CA). The rules as to security for costs apply as if references to a plaintiff and a defendant were references to the person who is in the position of plaintiff or defendant, as the case may be, in the proceedings on a counterclaim: RSC Ord 23 r 1(3); see PRACTICE AND PROCEDURE.
5   For the meaning of 'counterclaim' in the CPR see para 407 ante. As to the replacement of the RSC by the CPR, and the transitional arrangements in relation thereto, see para 401 note 3 ante.
6   CPR 20.3(1).
7   The following provisions of the CPR do not apply to Part 20 claims: 7.5, 7.6 (time for serving a claim form); 16.3(5) (statement of value where claim to be issued in the High Court); and Pt 26 (Case Management: Preliminary Stage): CPR 20.3(2). For the meaning of 'Part 20 claim' see para 481 note 15 ante.
8   Ie the Solicitors Act 1974 s 69 (as amended): see SOLICITORS vol 44(1) (Reissue) para 190 et seq.
9   See para 446 ante.
10 Crown Proceedings Act 1947 s 38(2). As to proceedings against the Crown see CROWN PROCEEDINGS AND CROWN PRACTICE vol 12(1) (Reissue) paras 110–114.
11 Limitation Act 1980 s 35(1), (2). As to whether this provision applies only to set-off at law and not to abatement or equitable defence see paras 412, 424, 434 ante.

495. Counterclaim operating as set-off. As a general rule, when the defendant's cross-claim exceeds the plaintiff's claim and is also effective as a set-off or defence, his cross-claim extinguishes the plaintiff's claim, and he also recovers the excess on his counterclaim[1]. Where the plaintiff sues as an assignee of a debt[2] or the plaintiff is a sovereign prince or state unamenable to English jurisdiction[3], the defendant may still raise his defence but he cannot recover the excess on his counterclaim. If, in either case, the nature of the cross-claim is not such as to make it a defence, the defendant cannot pursue his counterclaim at all in that action[4].

1   See para 494 ante.
2   *Young v Kitchin* (1878) 3 ExD 127; *Newfoundland Government v Newfoundland Rly Co* (1888) 13 App Cas 199, PC; *Banco Central SA and Trevelan Navigation Inc v Lingoss and Falce Ltd and BFI Line Ltd, The Raven* [1980] 2 Lloyd's Rep 266. See also CHOSES IN ACTION vol 6 (Reissue) para 64.

3   *Imperial Japanese Government v Peninsular and Oriental Steam Navigation Co* [1895] AC 644, PC; *South African Republic v Compagnie Franco-Belge du Chemin de Fer du Nord* [1898] 1 Ch 190. As to diplomatic immunity generally see FOREIGN RELATIONS LAW.

4   See para 503 post.

496. Pleading a set-off or counterclaim. In relation to proceedings begun before 26 April 1999[1], where a claim by a defendant to a sum of money (whether ascertained or not) is relied on as a total or partial defence to a claim, the defendant may include it in his defence and claim to set it off against the plaintiff's claim whether or not it is also added as a counterclaim[2]. Where a defendant counterclaims, he must add the counterclaim after his defence[3]. A counterclaim must be pleaded while the action is still in existence, before the plaintiff's claim is satisfied[4]. A defendant who joins as a party a person against whom he makes a counterclaim must add that person's name to the title of the action[5], and must indorse on the copy of the counterclaim served on that person a notice[6] addressed to him requiring him to acknowledge service and state whether he intends to contest the proceedings, and warning him of the consequences of not doing so[7].

In relation to proceedings begun on or after 26 April 1999, where a defendant contends that he is entitled to money from the claimant[8], and relies on this as a defence to the whole or part of the claim, the contention may be included in the defence and set off against the claim[9].

Where a defendant to a claim serves a counterclaim, the defence and counterclaim should normally form one document with the counterclaim following on from the defence[10].

1   Ie the date on which the CPR came into force. As to the replacement of the RSC by the CPR, and the transitional arrangements in relation thereto, see para 401 note 3 ante.

2   RSC Ord 18 r 17. It is usual to plead set-off specifically.

3   RSC Ord 15 r 2(1). For forms of counterclaim see Court Forms. Unlike a set-off, which is pleaded in the defence itself, a counterclaim is pleaded in a separate part of the pleading under the heading 'Counterclaim', the whole pleading being headed 'Defence and Counterclaim' and the defence simpliciter 'Defence'.

4   *CSI International Co Ltd v Archway Personnel (Middle East) Ltd* [1980] 3 All ER 215, [1980] 1 WLR 1069, CA.

5   RSC Ord 15 r 3(2); and see PLEADING.

6   For the form of notice see RSC App A Form 17.

7   RSC Ord 15 r 3(6). As to acknowledgment of service by such a person see para 501 post.

8   As to the meaning of 'claimant' see para 486 note 7 ante.

9   CPR 16.6. The defence of set-off may be included whether or not it is also a Part 20 claim: CPR 16.6. For the meaning of 'Part 20 claim' see para 481 note 15 ante. The statement of value required to be included in the particulars of claim of a claim for money must disregard the possibility that the defendant may make a counterclaim or that the defence may include a set-off: CPR 16.3(6)(c).

     As to the procedure for filing a defence see CPR Pt 15. In relation to contentious probate proceedings, the CPR apply subject to the provisions of the relevant practice direction which applies to such proceedings: CPR 49(1), (2)(g). See *Practice Direction—Contentious Probate Proceedings* (1999) PD49A; and para 493 note 6 ante.

10   *Practice Direction—Counterclaims and other Part 20 Claims* (1999) PD20 para 6.1; *Practice Direction—Defence and Reply* (1999) PD15 para 3.1.

497. Contents of claim. In relation to proceedings begun before 26 April 1999[1], a defendant seeking to avail himself of a set-off or counterclaim must state in his pleading[2] in summary form the material facts on which he relies in support of it[3] with the same particularity[4] as he would if he were a plaintiff in an independent action brought to enforce the subject of the set-off or counterclaim[5]. Set-off should not be pleaded in respect of a sum for which the plaintiff has properly given credit in his claim[6].

In relation to proceedings begun on or after 26 April 1999, a counterclaim is for most purposes a claim in its own right, and, with certain exceptions, subject to the same procedural and evidential requirements as any other claim[7].

1   Ie the date on which the CPR came into force. As to the replacement of the RSC by the CPR, and the transitional arrangements in relation thereto, see para 401 note 3 ante.
2   As to the rules of pleading generally, which apply to a set-off or counterclaim as they apply to other pleadings see RSC Ord 18; and PLEADING.
3   RSC Ord 18 r 7(1).
4   As to the particulars which must be set out in a pleading see RSC Ord 18 r 12.
5   Set-off is a ground of defence, and the facts in support of it are relied upon as showing that the plaintiff's claim is not maintainable and they must therefore be raised by the defendant's pleading: RSC Ord 18 r 8(1)(a). As to pleading a defence generally see PLEADING. A counterclaim, being in effect a cross-action, is as regards the mode of pleading governed by the same rules as a statement of claim: see Ord 18 r 15(1), applied by Ord 18 r 18(a).
6   *Lovejoy v Cole* [1894] 2 QB 861, DC.
7   See CPR 20.3; and para 494 ante.

498. Form of claim. In relation to proceedings begun before 26 April 1999[1], a defendant may plead several grounds of set-off or counterclaim[2], either simply or in the alternative. The several grounds must be pleaded in the same manner as grounds of claim in a statement of claim[3]. A counterclaim may allege more than one cause of action provided the different causes of action are such as could be joined in the same statement of claim in an independent action[4], but the facts relied upon in support of each cause of action must be separately alleged, and if more than one relief or remedy is claimed the forms of relief or remedy must be specifically stated, either simply or in the alternative[5].

In relation to proceedings begun on or after 26 April 1999, a counterclaim is for most purposes a claim in its own right, and, with certain exceptions, subject to the same procedural and evidential requirements as any other claim[6].

1   Ie the date on which the CPR came into force. As to the replacement of the RSC by the CPR, and the transitional arrangements in relation thereto, see para 401 note 3 ante.
2   See RSC Ord 15 rr 1, 2(2); Ord 18 r 18(a).
3   See RSC Ord 18 r 18; and PLEADING.
4   See RSC Ord 15 rr 1, 2(2); *Turner v Hednesford Gas Co* (1878) 3 ExD 145, CA; *Compton v Preston* (1882) 21 ChD 138. Cf *Macdonald v Carington* (1878) 4 CPD 28; and see PRACTICE AND PROCEDURE.
5   RSC Ord 18 rr 15(1), 18(a); and see PLEADING.
6   See CPR 20.3; and para 494 ante.

499. Facts alleged by way of defence, set-off and counterclaim. A defendant relying, in support of a set-off or counterclaim, on facts already alleged by way of defence need not repeat them in full, but may incorporate them in the set-off or counterclaim by way of reference only[1]. Similarly, where the same claim is relied on as a subject both of set-off and counterclaim, the facts, if not already alleged in the defence, may be alleged in the counterclaim and incorporated in the set-off by way of reference.

In relation to proceedings begun on or after 26 April 1999[2], a counterclaim is for most purposes a claim in its own right, and, with certain exceptions, subject to the same procedural and evidential requirements as any other claim[3].

1   *Birmingham Estates Co v Smith* (1880) 13 ChD 506; *Benbow v Low* (1880) 13 ChD 553.
2   Ie the date on which the CPR came into force. As to the replacement of the RSC by the CPR, and the transitional arrangements in relation thereto, see para 401 note 3 ante.
3   See CPR 20.3; and para 494 ante. The CPR are silent on the question whether facts may be incorporated by reference as described in this paragraph. As to the citation of old cases in connection with the new rules of procedure see para 401 note 3 ante.

(2) SERVICE, ACKNOWLEDGMENT, STRIKING OUT ETC

500. Service of set-off or counterclaim. In relation to proceedings begun before 26 April 1999[1], a set-off raised by a defendant against a plaintiff is pleaded in the defence[2]. A counterclaim raised by a defendant against a plaintiff must be added to the defence[3]. A defence containing a set-off or counterclaim against a plaintiff is served on him in the usual way before the expiration of 14 days after the time limited for acknowledging service of the writ[4] or after the statement of claim is served on that defendant, whichever is the later[5].

Where a defendant joins a person as a party against whom he makes a counterclaim, he must serve on him a copy of the counterclaim and, if that person is not already a party to the action, a form of acknowledgment of service with such modifications as the circumstances may require[6]. If that person is already a party the time limited for serving the counterclaim is the same as that stated above in relation to the plaintiff[7]. Where a counterclaim is served on a person who is not already a party, that person becomes a party as from the time of service with the same rights in respect of his defence to the counterclaim[8] and otherwise as if he had been duly served in the ordinary way by the person making the counterclaim[9].

In relation to proceedings begun on or after 26 April 1999, a counterclaim[10] may be filed with the defence[11], in which case it must be served: (1) within 14 days of service of the particulars of claim[12]; or (2) if the defendant has filed an acknowledgement of service[13], within 28 days of service of the particulars of claim[14]. A counterclaim may be made at any other time with the permission of the court[15]. Similarly, a defendant may make any other Part 20 claim[16], other than a claim for contribution[17] or indemnity[18], by filing it with the defence (in which case the above provisions[19] apply), or at any other time with the court's permission[20].

Where a Part 20 claim form[21] is served[22] on a person who is not already a party, it must be accompanied by: (a) a form for defending the claim[23], (b) a form for admitting the claim[24], (c) a form for acknowledging service, and (d) a copy of every statement of case[25] which has already been served in the proceedings and such other documents as the court may direct[26]. A copy of the Part 20 claim form must also be served on every existing party to the proceedings[27].

1   Ie the date on which the CPR came into force. As to the replacement of the RSC by the CPR, and the transitional arrangements in relation thereto, see para 401 note 3 ante.
2   See generally PLEADING.
3   See para 493 ante.
4   As to the time limited for acknowledging service see RSC Ord 12 r 5; and PRACTICE AND PROCEDURE.
5   See RSC Ord 18 r 2(1); and PLEADING. Before serving a defence a defendant must give notice of intention to defend: Ord 18 r 2(1).
6   RSC Ord 15 r 3(1). For the form of acknowledgment of service see App A Form 14. The copy of the counterclaim served on such a person must be indorsed with a notice (see App A Form 14) as to the need to acknowledge service: see Ord 15 r 3(6); and para 496 ante. In these circumstances the provisions of Ord 10 as to service, Ord 11 as to service out of the jurisdiction, Ord 12 as to acknowledging service (subject to Ord 15 r 3(4), for which see para 501 post) and Ord 13 as to failure to give notice of intention to defend apply in relation to the counterclaim and the proceedings arising from it as if the counterclaim were a writ and the proceedings arising from it were an action, and the party counterclaiming were a plaintiff and the party against whom the counterclaim is made a defendant in that action: Ord 15 r 3(5). The name of the new party must be added to the title of the action: see Ord 15 r 3(2); and para 489 ante.
7   RSC Ord 15 r 3(3).
8   As to the defence to a counterclaim see para 505 post.
9   RSC Ord 15 r 3(2).
10   For the meaning of 'counterclaim' see para 407 ante.
11   See CPR 20.4(1), (2); and para 493 text and notes 6–8 ante.

12 As to particulars of claim see CPR 7.4.

13 As to acknowledgement of service see CPR Pt 10, which applies to Part 20 claims unless the claimant wishes to defend a counterclaim: CPR 20.3, 20.4(3). For the meaning of 'Part 20 claim' see para 481 note 15 ante.

14 CPR 15.4(1).

15 See CPR 20.4(2)(b); and para 493 note 8 ante.

16 The claim is made when the court issues a Part 20 claim form: CPR 20.7(2).

17 For the meaning of 'contribution' see para 491 note 7 ante.

18 For the meaning of 'indemnity' see para 491 note 8 ante.

19 See text to note 14 supra.

20 CPR 20.7(3).

21 As to Part 20 claim forms see para 493 note 9 ante. For forms of title of proceedings where there are Part 20 claims see *Practice Direction—Counterclaims and other Part 20 Claims* (1999) PD20 para 7.

22 As to service of the claim form see CPR Pt 6, which applies to Part 20 claims: CPR 20.3.

23 As to defending a claim see CPR Pt 15, which applies to defences to Part 20 claims: CPR 20.3.

24 As to admitting claims see CPR Pt 14, which (except CPR 14.1(1), (2), 14.3) does not apply to Part 20 claims other than counterclaims: CPR 20.3(3)(b).

25 As to statements of case see CPR Pts 16, 17, which (except CPR 16.3(5)) apply to defences to Part 20 claims: CPR 20.3.

26 CPR 20.12(1).

27 CPR 20.12(2).

501. Acknowledgment of service. In relation to proceedings begun before 26 April 1999[1], a person who is not already a party to the action who is served with a counterclaim must acknowledge service of it, as if he were a defendant served with a copy of a writ[2], normally within 14 days after service[3], indicating on his acknowledgment whether he intends to contest the proceedings[4]. The appropriate office for acknowledging service is the Central Office, although if the action is proceeding in a district registry it is that registry, and if the counterclaim is made in an Admiralty action which is not proceeding in a district registry it is the Admiralty Registry[5]. The consequence of failure to give notice of intention to defend may be judgment in default[6].

In relation to proceedings begun on or after 26 April 1999, a counterclaim is for most purposes a claim in its own right, and, with certain exceptions, subject to the same procedural and evidential requirements as any other claim[7]. The consequence of failure to file a defence may be judgment in default[8].

1 Ie the date on which the CPR came into force. As to the replacement of the RSC by the CPR, and the transitional arrangements in relation thereto, see para 401 note 3 ante.

2 RSC Ord 15 r 3(5).

3 See RSC Ord 12 r 5, applied by Ord 15 r 3(5); and PRACTICE AND PROCEDURE.

4 See the form of acknowledgment of service in RSC App A Form 14. If he states that he intends to contest the proceedings he is said to give notice of intention to defend.

5 RSC Ord 15 r 3(4).

6 See RSC Ord 13; and PRACTICE AND PROCEDURE.

7 See CPR 20.3; and para 507 post.

8 CPR 15.3. As to default judgment see now CPR Pt 12.

502. Striking out set-off or counterclaim; order for separate trial. In relation to proceedings begun before 26 April 1999[1], where a defendant sets up a counterclaim[2] and it appears on the application of any person against whom the counterclaim is made that the subject matter of the counterclaim ought for any reason to be disposed of by a separate action, the court may order the counterclaim to be struck out or may order it to be tried separately or may make such other order as may be expedient[3]. If claims in respect of two or more causes of action are included by a defendant in a counterclaim and it appears to the court that the joinder may embarrass or delay the trial or is otherwise inconvenient, the court may order separate trials or make such other order as may be expedient[4].

In relation to proceedings begun on or after 26 April 1999, where the court is considering whether to dismiss a Part 20 claim[5] or to require it to be dealt with separately from the claim by the claimant against the defendant[6], it may have regard to: (1) the connection between the Part 20 claim and the claim made by the claimant against the defendant; (2) whether the Part 20 claimant[7] is seeking substantially the same remedy which some other claimant is claiming from him[8]; (3) whether the Part 20 claimant wants the court to decide any question connected with the subject matter of the proceedings (a) not only between existing parties but also between existing parties and a person not already a party[9], or (b) against a party not only in a capacity in which he is already a party, but also in some further capacity[10].

In relation to proceedings begun prior to 26 April 1999, a set-off or counterclaim may be struck out as one which ought not to be allowed under the rules relating to pleadings generally, for instance because it is embarrassing[11], or tends to delay the fair trial of the action[12], or (in the case of a counterclaim) because it discloses no reasonable cause of action[13]. However, the court will not strike out a counterclaim which in itself is proper to be tried merely because the plaintiff has had to give security but the defendant has not[14]. The defendant may not serve a counterclaim after judgment has been obtained for the plaintiff and has been satisfied[15].

In relation to proceedings begun on or after 26 April 1999, a counterclaim is for most purposes a claim in its own right, and the grounds for striking out a statement of case are the same with regard to counterclaims as to any other claim[16].

1 Ie the date on which the CPR came into force. As to the replacement of the RSC by the CPR, and the transitional arrangements in relation thereto, see para 401 note 3 ante.
2 RSC Ord 15 r 5 does not apply to a set-off.
3 RSC Ord 15 r 5(2): see PRACTICE AND PROCEDURE.
4 RSC Ord 15 r 5(1): see PRACTICE AND PROCEDURE.
5 For the meaning of 'Part 20 claim' see para 481 note 15 ante.
6 As to the court's power to order that part of proceedings be dealt with as separate proceedings see CPR 3.1(2)(e). As to the power to decide the order in which issues are to be tried see CPR 3.1(2)(j).
7 For the meaning of 'Part 20 claimant' see para 486 note 7 ante.
8 As to Part 20 claims for contribution or indemnity see para 491 ante.
9 As to Part 20 claims against a person who is not already a party see para 500 ante.
10 CPR 20.9. As to Part 20 claims against an existing party in a further capacity see para 493 text and note 15 ante. The court has a duty to ensure that, as far as possible, the claim and corresponding Part 20 claim are dealt with together: see CPR 20.13(2); and para 505 text and note 20 post.
11 *Fendall v O'Connell* (1885) 52 LT 538 (on appeal 29 ChD 899, CA). See RSC Ord 18 r 19(1)(c); and PLEADING. The mere fact that a counterclaim sets up a claim in personam against a statement of claim in rem does not make it embarrassing: *The Cheapside* [1904] P 339, CA; and see ADMIRALTY vol 1(1) (Reissue) para 415.
12 *Gray v Webb* (1882) 21 ChD 802; *Normar (Owners) v British Transport Docks Board, The Normar* [1968] P 362, [1968] 1 All ER 753; *Zimmer Orthopaedic Ltd v Zimmer Manufacturing Co* [1968] 3 All ER 449, [1968] 1 WLR 1349, CA. See RSC Ord 18 r 19(1)(c); and PLEADING.
13 *Birmingham Estates Co v Smith* (1880) 13 ChD 506. See RSC Ord 18 r 19(1)(a); and PLEADING.
14 *The Neptune* [1919] P 17 at 20. As to security for costs see para 509 post.
15 *CSI International Co Ltd v Archway Personnel (Middle East) Ltd* [1980] 3 All ER 215, [1980] 1 WLR 1069, CA (where the counterclaim had been foreshadowed but not pleaded before the judgment was satisfied).
16 See CPR 20.3; and para 494 ante. As to the power to strike out a statement of case see CPR 3.4. the grounds for striking out are: (1) that the statement of case discloses no reasonable grounds for bringing or defending the claim; (2) that the statement of case is an abuse of the court's process or is otherwise likely to obstruct the just disposal of the proceedings; or (3) that there has been a failure to comply with a rule, practice direction or court order: CPR 3.4(2). This does not limit any other power of the court to strike out a statement of case: CPR 3.4(5).

503. Particular grounds for striking out counterclaim. In relation to proceedings begun prior to 26 April 1999[1], any counterclaim infringing the rules as to joinder of causes of action or parties[2] may be disallowed[3], although a counterclaim will not be struck out on the ground that the plaintiff is a foreigner who would not be amenable to the jurisdiction as defendant in an independent action[4].

If a plaintiff is entitled to state immunity[5], he will be taken to have submitted to the jurisdiction of the court in respect of a counterclaim only if it arises out of the same legal relationship or facts as the claim[6]. A defendant alien enemy will not be allowed to prosecute a counterclaim so long as he remains an enemy[7].

In an action for the protection of a trust fund in which the plaintiff claimed a beneficial interest, a counterclaim for libel was excluded[8], and in an action for the balance of an account leave to amend by adding a counterclaim for libel was refused[9]. Similarly, a counterclaim not connected with the subject matter of the claim was excluded in an action for rent[10], but a counterclaim will not be struck out merely on the ground that it is brought in the Chancery Division[11].

In an action by a trustee on a covenant of indemnity, the court will not allow a counterclaim involving an administration action, nor one asserting a secret trust in favour of a third person[12]. In an action by a tenant for life for breach of trust the defendant will not be allowed to counterclaim on a bill of exchange[13].

In an action for goods sold and delivered, the defendant may not counterclaim in respect of a totally different transaction against a third person who happens to be the plaintiff's principal[14].

In relation to proceedings begun on or after 26 April 1999, a counterclaim is for most purposes a claim in its own right, and the grounds for striking out a statement of case are the same with regard to counterclaims as to any other claim[15].

If a defendant does not attend a trial, the court may strike out his defence or counterclaim (or both)[16]. If the claimant does not attend, the court may strike out his claim and any defence to counterclaim[17].

1   Ie the date on which the CPR came into operation. As to the replacement of the RSC by the CPR, and the transitional arrangements in relation thereto, see para 401 note 3 ante. As to the grounds for striking out a statement of case under the CPR see para 502 note 16 ante. As to particular grounds for striking out a counterclaim under the CPR see text and notes 16–17 infra.
2   Ie RSC Ord 15 rr 1, 4: see PRACTICE AND PROCEDURE.
3   See RSC Ord 15 r 5(1); and para 502 ante.
4   *Griendtoveen v Hamlyn & Co* (1892) 8 TLR 231, DC.
5   As to the immunity of a foreign or Commonwealth state see the State Immunity Act 1978 s 1(1); and PRACTICE AND PROCEDURE.
6   Ibid s 2(6). In the absence of amendment to contrary effect, this must be taken to apply equally to counterclaims under the CPR. Thus a counterclaim is probably confined to the extent of the plaintiff's claim in such a case and should not extend to matter outside or independent of that claim: see *Strousberg v Costa Rica Republic* (1880) 44 LT 199, CA; *Imperial Japanese Government v Peninsular and Oriental Steam Navigation Co* [1895] AC 644, PC; *Union of Soviet Republics v Belaiew* (1925) 134 LT 64.
7   *Robinson & Co v Continental Insurance Co of Mannheim* [1915] 1 KB 155 at 159 per Bailhache J; see also WAR AND ARMED CONFLICT.
8   *South African Republic v Compagnie Franco-Belge du Chemin de Fer du Nord* [1897] 2 Ch 487, CA.
9   *Factories Insurance Co Ltd v Anglo-Scottish General Commercial Insurance Co Ltd* (1913) 29 TLR 312, CA.
10   *Rotherham v Priest* (1879) 49 LJQB 104.
11   *Lord Kinnaird v Field* [1905] 2 Ch 361, CA.
12   *Padwick v Scott, Re Scott's Estate, Scott v Padwick* (1876) 2 ChD 736.
13   *Fendall v O'Connell* (1885) 52 LT 538.
14   *Tagart & Co v Marcus & Co* (1888) 36 WR 469, DC. As to set-off against principals see paras 447–448 ante.
15   See para 502 text and note 16 ante.
16   CPR 39.3(1)(c). As to the court's power to restore proceedings see CPR 39.3.
17   CPR 39.3(1)(b).

504. Stay on submission to arbitration. A counterclaim in respect of a matter which the parties have agreed to submit to arbitration[1] may be stayed[2].

1   See the Arbitration Act 1996 s 9; and ARBITRATION vol 2 (Reissue) para 616.
2   See *Chappell v North* [1891] 2 QB 252, DC; and ARBITRATION vol 2 (Reissue) para 560 et seq. The plaintiff must not have taken a step in the proceedings to answer the substantive claim since the counterclaim was served: Arbitration Act 1996 s 9(3); see ARBITRATION vol 2 (Reissue) para 627. Merely applying for leave to defend and counterclaim does not constitute a step in the proceedings: *Patel v Patel* (1999) Times, 9 April, CA.

(3) RESPONDING TO A SET-OFF, COUNTERCLAIM OR ASSOCIATED CLAIM

505. Reply and defence to counterclaim. In relation to proceedings begun before 26 April 1999[1], a defence to a set-off is pleaded by way of a reply[2], which must be served on the defendant who pleaded the set-off before the expiration of 14 days after the service of the pleading in which the set-off was alleged[3]. A plaintiff[4] on whom a defendant serves a counterclaim must[5], if he intends to defend it[6], serve on that defendant a defence to counterclaim[7] before the expiration of 14 days after the service of the counterclaim[8] and, if he serves both a reply and a defence to counterclaim, he must include them in the same document[9]. In an Admiralty collision action[10] a reply or defence to counterclaim may be served only with the leave of the court[11].

In relation to proceedings begun on or after 26 April 1999, a counterclaim falls within the category of Part 20 claims[12], and is for most purposes a claim in its own right[13], and the new procedure for entering a defence applies equally to defence to a counterclaim[14], subject to the following. Where in an Admiralty collision claim[15] in rem, a Part 20 claim or a cross claim[16] in rem is made arising out of the same collision or occurrence, and (1) the party bringing the original claim has caused the arrest of a ship or has obtained security in order to prevent such arrest, and (2) the party bringing the Part 20 claim or cross claim is unable to arrest a ship or otherwise to obtain security, then the party bringing the Part 20 claim or cross claim may apply to the Admiralty Court to stay the original claim until sufficient security is given to satisfy any judgment that may be given in favour of that party[17].

Where a claimant serves a reply and defence to counterclaim, the reply and the defence to counterclaim should normally form one document with the defence to counterclaim following on from the reply[18].

Where a defence to a Part 20 claim is filed the court must consider the future conduct of the proceedings and give appropriate directions[19], and in doing so must ensure that, so far as practicable, the Part 20 claim and the main claim are managed together[20].

Where a Part 20 defendant[21] files a defence, other than to a counterclaim, the court will arrange a hearing to consider case management of the Part 20 claim[22]. At that hearing the court may: (a) treat the hearing as a summary judgment hearing[23]; (b) order that the Part 20 proceedings be dismissed; (c) give directions about the way any claim, question or issue set out in or arising from the Part 20 claim should be dealt with; (d) give directions as to the part, if any, the Part 20 defendant will take at the trial of the claim[24]; and (e) give directions about the extent to which the Part 20 defendant is to be bound by any judgment or decision to be made in the claim[25]. The court may make any of these orders either before or after any judgment in the claim has been entered against the defendant[26].

1   Ie the date on which the CPR came into operation. As to the replacement of the RSC by the CPR, and the transitional arrangements in relation thereto, see para 401 note 3 ante.

2   RSC Ord 18 r 3(1). No reply is needed for a general traverse of facts alleged in the defence: see Ord 18 r 14(1); and PLEADING. A reply must be served if needed for compliance with Ord 18 r 8: Ord 18 r 3(1).

3   RSC Ord 18 r 3(4).

4   When a counterclaim is served on a person who is not already a party he becomes in effect a plaintiff for this purpose: see RSC Ord 15 r 3(2); App A Form 14.

5   There can be no joinder of issue, implied or express, on a counterclaim: RSC Ord 18 r 14(3). See, however, note 11 infra. A general denial of the allegations of fact contained in the counterclaim is not sufficient; every allegation of fact made in a counterclaim which the person on whom it is served does not intend to admit must be specifically traversed in his defence to counterclaim: Ord 18 r 13(3).

6   A person not already a party must give notice of intention to defend before serving a defence to counterclaim: see para 502 ante.

7   RSC Ord 18 r 3(2).

8   RSC Ord 18 r 3(4).

9   RSC Ord 18 r 3(3).

10 Ie an action such as is referred to in RSC Ord 75 r 2(1)(a): see ADMIRALTY vol 1(1) (Reissue) para 399.

11 RSC Ord 75 r 20(1). In a collision action where there is a counterclaim there is an implied joinder of issue on the counterclaim even though no defence to counterclaim has been served: Ord 75 r 20(2); see ADMIRALTY vol 1(1) (Reissue) para 416.

12 For the meaning of 'Part 20 claim' see para 481 note 15 ante.

13 See CPR 20.3; and para 494 ante.

14 CPR 20.4(2). For the meaning of 'counterclaim' see para 407 ante. As to procedure for entering a defence see CPR Pt 15.

15 'Collision claim' here means a claim falling within the Supreme Court Act 1981 s 20(3)(b), namely any action to enforce a claim for damage, loss of life or personal injury arising out of: (1) a collision between ships; (2) the carrying out or omission to carry out any manoeuvre in the case of one or more of two or more ships; or (3) non-compliance, on the part of one or more of two or more ships, with the collision regulations: *Practice Direction—Admiralty* (1999) PD49E para 1.4(d). As to the collision regulations see SHIPPING AND NAVIGATION vol 43(1) (Reissue) para 793 et seq.

    The CPR apply to Admiralty proceedings only as indicated in *Practice Direction—Admiralty* PD49E: see CPR Pt 49.

16 'Cross claim' is not defined for these purposes.

17 *Practice Direction—Admiralty* (1999) PD49E para 4.5. As to arrest and detention of ships generally see ADMIRALTY vol 1(1) (Reissue) para 375 et seq.

18 *Practice Direction—Counterclaims and other Part 20 Claims* (1999) PD20 para 6.2; *Practice Direction—Defence and Reply* (1999) PD15 para 3.2.

19 CPR 20.13(1).

20 CPR 20.13(2). As to case management see para 401 note 3 ante.

21 For the meaning of 'Part 20 defendant' see para 486 note 7 ante.

22 *Practice Direction—Counterclaims and other Part 20 Claims* (1999) PD20 para 5.1. The court will give notice of the hearing to each party likely to be affected by any order made at the hearing: para 5.2.

23 As to summary judgment see CPR Pt 24.

24 Ie the original claim rather than the Part 20 claim.

25 *Practice Direction—Counterclaims and other Part 20 Claims* (1999) PD20 para 5.3. 'Claim' in head (e) in the text refers to the original claim.

26 *Practice Direction—Counterclaims and other Part 20 Claims* (1999) PD20 para 5.4.

506. Point of law in reply or defence to counterclaim. In relation to proceedings begun before 26 April 1999[1], where a person against whom a set-off or counterclaim is set up raises by his pleading any point of law[2], the point may be disposed of in the same way as a point of law raised by a defendant in answer to a statement of claim[3]. If the decision of such point of law substantially disposes of any ground of set-off or counterclaim, the court may dismiss it or make such other order as may be just[4].

In relation to proceedings begun on or after 26 April 1999, a counterclaim, along with other Part 20 claims[5], is for most purposes a claim in its own right, and raising a point of law in defence to a Part 20 claim is treated in the same way as in defence to any other claim[6].

1   Ie the date on which the CPR came into operation. As to the replacement of the RSC by the CPR, and the transitional arrangements in relation thereto, see para 401 note 3 ante.
2   See RSC Ord 18 r 11; and PLEADING.
3   The point of law may be tried as a preliminary issue: see RSC Ord 33 r 3; and PRACTICE AND PROCEDURE.
4   RSC Ord 33 r 7.
5   For the meaning of 'Part 20 claim' see para 481 note 15 ante.
6   See CPR 20.3; and para 494 ante. As to raising a point of law in defence see *Practice Direction—Statements of Case* (1999) PD16 para 16.3(1). As to disposal of cases after decisions on preliminary issues see CPR 3.1(2)(l).

(4) INTERLOCUTORY MATTERS

507. Default in pleading; judgment in default of defence or acknowledgement of service. In relation to proceedings begun prior to 26 April 1999[1], for the purpose of default in pleading[2], a counterclaim is treated as a claim[3]. Therefore, if the plaintiff or other person against whom a counterclaim is made fails to serve a defence to counterclaim within the appropriate time[4], the counterclaiming defendant may enter final judgment[5] or apply to the court for judgment[6] according to the nature of the counterclaim.

In relation to proceedings begun on or after 26 April 1999, for the purposes of judgments in default a counterclaim[7] is treated as any other claim[8]. Judgment in default of acknowledgment of service[9] may be obtained where an acknowledgement of service has not been filed within the appropriate time, and judgment in default of defence may be obtained where a defence[10] has not been filed within the appropriate time[11].

In the case of a Part 20 claim[12] which is not a counterclaim or a claim for contribution[13] or indemnity[14] against another defendant[15], where the party against whom the Part 20 claim is made fails to file an acknowledgement of service or a defence, he is deemed to admit[16] the Part 20 claim, and is bound by any judgment or decision in the main proceedings in so far as it is relevant to the Part 20 claim[17]. If default judgment is given[18] against the Part 20 claimant[19], the Part 20 claimant may obtain judgment in respect of the Part 20 claim by filing a request in the relevant practice form[20].

1   Ie the date on which the CPR came into operation. As to the replacement of the RSC by the CPR, and the transitional arrangements in relation thereto, see para 401 note 3 ante.
2   As to judgment in default of defence generally see JUDGMENTS AND ORDERS; PRACTICE AND PROCEDURE.
3   RSC Ord 19 r 8.
4   As to the time for service see para 505 ante.
5   See RSC Ord 19 r 2, applied to counterclaims by Ord 19 r 8.
6   See RSC Ord 19 rr 3–7, applied to counterclaims by Ord 19 r 8.
7   For the meaning of 'counterclaim' see para 407 ante.
8   CPR 20.3(3).
9   As to acknowledgement of service see CPR Pt 10.
10   As to filing a defence see CPR Pt 15.
11   See CPR 12.3(1), (2), 15.3. As to the setting aside of default judgments see CPR Pt 13.
12   For the meaning of 'Part 20 claim' see para 481 note 15 ante.
13   For the meaning of 'contribution' see para 491 note 7 ante.
14   For the meaning of 'indemnity' see para 491 note 8 ante.
15   Ie under CPR 20.6; see para 491 text to note 10 ante.
16   As to admissions generally see CPR Pt 14.
17   CPR 20.11(1), (2)(a).
18   Ie in the trial of the main claim.
19   For the meaning of 'Part 20 claimant' see para 486 note 7 ante.
20   CPR 20.11(2)(b). However, he may not obtain judgment under this provision without the court's permission if: (1) he has not satisfied the default judgment which has been given against him; or (2) he wishes to obtain judgment for any remedy other than a contribution or indemnity: CPR 20.11(3). An application for the court's permission may be made without notice unless the court directs otherwise:

CPR 20.11(4). The court may set aside or vary a judgment entered under CPR 20.11(2)(b): CPR 20.11(5). 'Practice forms' are to be specified in a Practice Direction: CPR 2.2(1), Glossary. As to the effect of Glossary definitions see para 407 note 4 ante.

508. Security for costs. A defendant who sets up a counterclaim may be ordered in a proper case to give security for costs[1].

Whether security for costs should be ordered to be given by a foreigner resident out of the jurisdiction who is making a claim as plaintiff in a cross-action, or is counter-claiming as defendant in an action, is a matter of discretion[2]. There is no hard and fast rule about the circumstances in which an order for security for costs should be made. Generally speaking, if a defendant is in substance setting up the counterclaim by way of defence to the action, he ought not to be required to give security; but, if the counterclaim is really a cross-claim having nothing to do with the subject matter of the plaintiff's claim, then the fact that he is the defendant will not prevent him being ordered to give security for costs[3]. Such a defendant will not be ordered to give security whenever the cross-claim goes beyond mere matter of defence, although if by his counterclaim he is in effect bringing an action quite independent of the transaction out of which the plaintiff's claim arises, he will be ordered to give security for costs[4]. If the only matter really in dispute is that raised by the counterclaim, such a defendant will be ordered to give security[5]. Where a counterclaim is set up in an Admiralty action in rem the party setting it up must in general give security for the costs of the whole action and not merely for the costs of the counterclaim[6].

A defendant who admits the cause of action sued upon and counterclaims against a foreign plaintiff is not entitled to security for costs[7].

A defendant company in liquidation setting up a counterclaim may be ordered to give security for costs in the same way as though it were plaintiff in an independent action[8].

1 RSC Ord 23 r 1(3); CPR Sch 1 RSC Ord 23 r 1(3): see PRACTICE AND PROCEDURE. As to the modification of the RSC and CCR as scheduled to the CPR see para 401 note 3 ante.
2 See RSC Ord 23 r 1(1); CPR Sch 1 RSC Ord 23 r 1(3); and PRACTICE AND PROCEDURE.
3 *Neck v Taylor* [1893] 1 QB 560, CA; *New Fenix Compagnie Anonyme d'Assurances de Madrid v General Accident, Fire and Life Assurance Corpn Ltd* [1911] 2 KB 619, CA; *Visco v Minter* [1969] P 82, [1969] 2 All ER 714; *Samuel J Cohl Co v Eastern Mediterranean Maritime Ltd, The Silver Fir* [1980] 1 Lloyd's Rep 371, CA. For the position where a Mareva injunction has been granted against the counterclaiming defendant see *Hitachi Shipbuilding and Engineering Co Ltd v Viafiel Compania Naviera SA* [1981] 2 Lloyd's Rep 498, CA.
4 *Mapleson v Masini* (1879) 5 QBD 144, DC.
5 *Sykes v Sacerdoti* (1885) 15 QBD 423, CA.
6 *The Julia Fisher* (1877) 2 PD 115. As to the practice in regard to security for damages in cross-actions and counterclaims in Admiralty see ADMIRALTY vol 1(1) (Reissue) para 399.
7 *Winterfield v Bradnum* (1878) 3 QBD 324, CA.
8 Companies Act 1985 s 726(1): see COMPANIES vol 7(2) (1996 Reissue) para 1183.

509. Effect of stay or disposal of action. In relation to proceedings begun before 26 April 1999[1], a counterclaim made by a defendant may be proceeded with notwithstanding that judgment is given for the plaintiff in the action or that the action is stayed, discontinued or dismissed[2]. However, the defendant must have made his counterclaim before the plaintiff has obtained and been paid on his judgment[3].

In relation to proceedings begun on or after 26 April 1999, a counterclaim is for most purposes a claim in its own right, and, with certain exceptions, subject to the same procedural rules as any other claim[4].

1 Ie the date on which the CPR came into operation: see para 401 note 3 ante. As to the replacement of the RSC by the CPR, and the transitional arrangements in relation thereto, see para 401 note 3 ante.
2 RSC Ord 15 r 2(3): see PRACTICE AND PROCEDURE.

3   *CSI International Co Ltd v Archway Personnel (Middle East) Ltd* [1980] 3 All ER 215, [1980] 1 WLR 1069, CA. There is no special rule in Admiralty proceedings permitting the making of a counterclaim otherwise than as contemplated by rules of court: *Popi (Owners) v SS Gniezno (Owners), The Gniezno* [1968] P 418, [1967] 2 All ER 738. See also para 477 ante, and ADMIRALTY vol 1(1) (Reissue) para 414.

4   See CPR 20.3; and para 494 ante. In keeping with this principle, with the overriding objective (see para 401 note 3 ante) and with the court's power to order separate trial of claim and counterclaim, it is conceived that a counterclaim or other Part 20 claim may be proceeded with despite the disposal of the main action. For the meaning of 'counterclaim' see para 407 ante. For the meaning of 'Part 20 claim' see para 481 note 15 ante.

510. Amendment of set-off or counterclaim.

In relation to proceedings begun before 26 April 1999[1], a defendant who has pleaded a set-off or counterclaim may amend his pleading without leave once, before the close of pleadings[2]. The opposite party may, within 14 days of service of the amended pleading, apply to the court to disallow the amendment[3].

Where an amended defence or counterclaim is served on a plaintiff by a defendant, the plaintiff may amend any reply or defence to counterclaim which he has already served[4], and the period for service of his reply or defence to counterclaim is 14 days after the amended defence or counterclaim is served on him[5]. Similarly, where an amended counterclaim is served by a defendant on any party other than the plaintiff, that party may amend any defence he has already served[6] and the period for service of his defence or amended defence is either the normal period for service of a defence[7] or a period of 14 days after the amended counterclaim is served on him, whichever is the later[8]. If the party on whom an amended counterclaim is served does not amend his pleading under these provisions he will be taken to rely on it in answer to the amended counterclaim[9].

A set-off or counterclaim, or reply and defence to counterclaim, may be amended at any time with leave in the same manner as any other pleading[10].

In relation to proceedings begun on or after 26 April 1999, a counterclaim, or any other Part 20 claim, is for most purposes a claim in its own right, and, with certain exceptions, subject to the same procedural rules as any other claim[11]. A party may amend his statement of case[12] at any time before it has been served on any other party[13]. After a statement of case has been served it may be amended only with the written consent of all other parties or with the permission of the court[14]. In a case where permission is not required[15], a party may, within 14 days of service of a copy of the amended statement of case on him, apply to the court to disallow the amendment[16].

An amendment to a statement of case must be verified by a statement of truth unless the court orders otherwise[17].

1   Ie the date on which the CPR came into operation. As to the replacement of the RSC by the CPR, and the transitional arrangements in relation thereto, see para 401 note 3 ante.

2   RSC Ord 20 r 3(1): see PRACTICE AND PROCEDURE. As to the close of pleadings see Ord 20 r 1; and PRACTICE AND PROCEDURE. As to amendment of pleadings generally see PLEADING. The costs of and occasioned by any amendment made without leave in any counterclaim or set-off by a defendant must be borne by the defendant unless the court otherwise orders: Ord 62 r 3(3).

3   RSC Ord 20 r 4(1): see PLEADING.

4   RSC Ord 20 r 3(3)(a), (4).

5   RSC Ord 20 r 3(3)(b), (4).

6   RSC Ord 20 r 3(2)(a), (4), (5).

7   See RSC Ord 18 r 2(1); and para 500 ante.

8   RSC Ord 20 r 3(2)(b), (4), (5).

9   RSC Ord 20 r 3(6). There is then an implied joinder of issue under Ord 18 r 14(2) (see PLEADING): Ord 20 r 3(6).

10   RSC Ord 20 r 5: see PLEADING; PRACTICE AND PROCEDURE.

11   See CPR 20.3; and para 494 ante. For the meaning of 'counterclaim' see para 407 ante. For the meaning of 'Part 20 claim' see para 481 note 15 ante.

12   As to statements of case see CPR Pts 16, 17, which (except CPR 16.3(5)) apply to defences to Part 20 claims: CPR 20.3.

13   CPR 17.1(1).

14   CPR 17.1(2). Where the court gives permission it may give directions as to the amendment of any other statement of case, and service of any amended statement of case: CPR 17.3(1).

15   See text and note 13 supra.

16   See CPR 17.2.

17   CPR 22.1(2). As to statements of truth see para 493 note 16 ante.

(5) JUDGMENT

511. Form of judgment. Where the defendant establishes a set-off equal to or exceeding the plaintiff's claim, judgment is entered in his favour on the claim, because a set-off amounts to an absolute defence[1]. Therefore, if he has also counterclaimed in respect of the matters pleaded by way of set-off, he obtains judgment both on the claim and the counterclaim[2]. If both the claim and the counterclaim fail, judgment is entered for the defendant on the claim and the plaintiff on the counterclaim[3].

In relation to proceedings commenced before 26 April 1999[4], where a defendant establishes a counterclaim against the plaintiff's claim, and there is a balance in favour of one of the parties, the court may give judgment for the balance, although this does not affect the court's discretion[5] as to costs[6].

Where the defendant succeeds in establishing a set-off, but for less amount than the plaintiff recovers on the claim, judgment is given for the plaintiff for the difference between the amount recovered on the claim and the amount in respect of which a set-off has been proved[7]. If in such a case the subject matter of the set-off has also been pleaded by way of counterclaim, the proper course would seem to be to dismiss the counterclaim[8]. Where, however, the plaintiff succeeds upon a claim and the defendant upon a counterclaim, not amounting to a set-off, it is in general more convenient for judgment to be given for the plaintiff upon the claim and the defendant upon the counterclaim rather than for a single judgment to be given upon the balance[9].

In relation to proceedings begun on or after 26 April 1999, where the court gives judgment for specified amounts both for the claimant on his claim and against the claimant on a counterclaim[10], if there is a balance in favour of one of the parties it may order the party whose judgment is for the lesser amount to pay the balance[11]. In such a case the court may make a separate order for costs against each party[12].

1   *Baines v Bromley* (1881) 6 QBD 691, CA; *Lowe v Holme* (1883) 10 QBD 286; *Hanak v Green* [1958] 2 QB 9, [1958] 2 All ER 141, CA; *Henriksens Rederi A/S v PHZ Rolimpex, The Brede* [1974] QB 233, [1973] 3 All ER 589, CA.

2   See the cases cited in para 514 notes 1–2 post; and see para 480 note 1 ante.

3   *Saner v Bilton* (1879) 11 ChD 416; *Mason v Brentini* (1880) 15 ChD 287, CA; *James v Jackson* [1910] 2 Ch 92.

4   Ie the date on which the CPR came into operation. As to the replacement of the RSC by the CPR, and the transitional arrangements in relation thereto, see para 401 note 3 ante.

5   As to this discretion see para 514 post; and PRACTICE AND PROCEDURE.

6   RSC Ord 15 r 2(4); *Provincial Bill Posting Co v Low Moor Iron Co* [1909] 2 KB 344 at 351, CA, per Kennedy LJ. Where a defendant desires judgment in his own favour for a balance in addition to judgment in respect of the plaintiff's claim, he should set up a counterclaim for this as well as pleading a set-off: see *Stooke v Taylor* (1880) 5 QBD 569 at 576, DC; *Stumore v Campbell & Co* [1892] 1 QB 314, CA; but see *Gathercole v Smith* (1881) 7 QBD 626 at 629, CA.

7   *Re Brown, Ward v Morse* (1883) 23 ChD 377, CA.

8   This course was adopted by the county court judge in *Nicholson v Little* [1956] 2 All ER 699, [1956] 1 WLR 829, CA.

9   *Provincial Bill Posting Co v Low Moor Iron Co* [1909] 2 KB 344, CA; *Sharpe v Haggith* (1912) 106 LT 13, CA; *Chell Engineering Ltd v Unit Tool and Engineering Co Ltd* [1950] 1 All ER 378, CA. As to the exercise

of the judicial discretion conferred by RSC Ord 15 r 2, where the same sum was recovered upon the claim and the counterclaim see *Sprange v Lee* [1908] 1 Ch 424, CA. RSC Ord 80 r 12, which provides for control by the court over money recovered by persons under disability, is applied with modifications in relation to counterclaims by RSC Ord 80 r 12(5): see CHILDREN AND YOUNG PERSONS vol 5(2) (Reissue) para 1370; MENTAL HEALTH vol 30 (Reissue) para 1428.

10   For the meaning of 'counterclaim' see para 407 ante.

11   CPR 40.13(1), (2).

12   CPR 40.13(3). As to costs see further para 513 et seq post.

512. Execution. Where a plaintiff obtains judgment on his claim and a defendant on the counterclaim, there are two judgments for all purposes except execution. Execution may not issue for more than the balance, and for this purpose it is immaterial whether judgment has been entered in the one or the other of these forms[1].

1   *Stumore v Campbell & Co* [1892] 1 QB 314 at 317, CA. Where judgment was entered for the plaintiffs with costs on the claim, and judgment for the plaintiffs and other persons (added as defendants to the counterclaim) with costs on the counterclaim, it was held that the judgment debts were separate and could not be the subject of one bankruptcy notice: *Re A Bankruptcy Notice* (1906) 96 LT 133, CA. The claim and counterclaim are treated as one action for the purpose of determining the sum on which a solicitor has a charging order for his costs: *Westacott v Bevan* [1891] 1 QB 774. As to such charging orders see SOLICITORS.

(6) COSTS

513. The court's discretion. In relation to proceedings begun before 26 April 1999[1], in both the High Court and in the county court the costs of proceedings are, subject to the provisions of any Act or rule of court, in the discretion of the court[2]. All orders as to costs in cases concerning set-offs and counterclaims are subject to the discretion so conferred[3] and to the desirability of considering whether a special order should be made because the issues are often very much interlocked[4]. Thus, in the High Court, where a plaintiff succeeds on a claim and a defendant on a counterclaim which is not subject to set-off, the plaintiff will normally recover the costs of the claim and the defendant the costs of the counterclaim[5], although this will not necessarily be the result in all circumstances. Similar considerations apply where in such cases the plaintiff fails on the claim and the defendant on the counterclaim[6]. Where, however, a defendant sued in the High Court succeeds and is awarded costs upon a counterclaim, he will normally be awarded them upon the High Court scale however small the amount recovered by him[7], and when a plaintiff whose claim is within the county court scale successfully defends a counterclaim for an amount beyond that scale, and is awarded costs thereon, they will normally be upon the High Court scale[8].

In relation to proceedings begun on or after 26 April 1999, largely similar provisions apply. The court has discretion as to whether costs are payable by one party to another, the amount of those costs, and when they are to be paid[9]. The general rule is that the unsuccessful party will be ordered to pay the costs of the successful party, but the court may make a different order[10]. In deciding what order to make, the court must have regard to all the circumstances, including: (1) the conduct of all the parties[11]; (2) whether a party has succeeded on part of his case, even if he has not been wholly successful; and (3) any payment into court or admissible offer to settle[12] made by a party which is drawn to the court's attention[13].

Where a party entitled to costs is also liable to pay costs the court may assess the costs which that party is liable to pay and either (a) set off the amount assessed against the amount the party is entitled to be paid and direct him to pay any balance; or (b) delay the issue of a certificate for the costs to which the party is entitled until he has paid the amount which he is liable to pay[14].

Where the court gives judgment for specified amounts both for the claimant on his claim and against the claimant on a counterclaim[15], the court may make a separate order for costs against each party[16].

Where in fast track proceedings[17] a defendant has made a counterclaim against the claimant, and the claimant has succeeded on his claim and the defendant has succeeded on his counterclaim, the court will quantify the amount of the award of fast track trial costs to which (i) but for the counterclaim, the claimant would be entitled for succeeding on his claim; and (ii) but for the claim, the defendant would be entitled for succeeding on his counterclaim, and make one award of the difference, if any, to the party entitled to the higher award of costs[18].

Where in fast track proceedings (A) a defendant has made a counterclaim against the claimant, (B) the counterclaim has a higher value than the claim, and (C) the claimant succeeds at trial both on his claim and the counterclaim, then for the purpose of quantifying fast track trial costs awarded to the claimant, the value of the claim is the value of the defendant's counterclaim[19].

1   Ie the date on which the CPR came into operation. As to the replacement of the RSC by the CPR, and the transitional arrangements in relation thereto, see para 401 note 3 ante.

2   See the Supreme Court Act 1981 s 51(1) (substituted by the Courts and Legal Services Act 1991 s 4(1)); RSC Ord 62 r 2(4); and PRACTICE AND PROCEDURE; and see CCR Ord 38 r 1; and COUNTY COURTS.

3   If an order for costs is made, then, subject to RSC Ord 62, the costs must follow the event unless it appears to the court that, in the circumstances, some other order should be made: Ord 62 r 3(3).
     A judge erred in principle in making an order which at one and the same time struck out part of a defendant's counterclaim, required payment of costs by the defendant and stayed further proceedings on the counterclaim until those costs had been paid: *Theakston v Matthews* (1998) Times, 13 April, CA.

4   See *Chell Engineering Ltd v Unit Tool and Engineering Co Ltd* [1950] 1 All ER 378 at 383, CA, per Denning LJ; *Childs v Blacker, Childs v Gibson* [1954] 2 All ER 243, [1954] 1 WLR 809, CA; *Nicholson v Little* [1956] 2 All ER 699, [1956] 1 WLR 829, CA; *Hanak v Green* [1958] 2 QB 9 at 26, [1958] 2 All ER 141 at 152, CA, per Morris LJ; *Baylis Baxter Ltd v Sabath* [1958] 2 All ER 209 at 216, [1958] 1 WLR 529 at 538, CA, per Parker LJ.

5   See *Wight v Shaw* (1887) 19 QBD 396, CA; *Chell Engineering Ltd v Unit Tool and Engineering Ltd* [1950] 1 All ER 378, CA; and cf *Childs v Blacker, Childs v Gibson* [1954] 2 All ER 243, [1954] 1 WLR 809, CA. The position is now governed by RSC Ord 62 r 3(3), for which see note 2 supra. Costs incurred only by reason of the claim cannot be costs of the counterclaim: see *Saner v Bilton* (1879) 11 ChD 416; and para 515 post.

6   *Saner v Bilton* (1879) 11 ChD 416 at 419 per Fry LJ; *Medway Oil and Storage Co Ltd v Continental Contractors Ltd* [1929] AC 88 at 112, HL, per Lord Blanesburgh. The costs of the counterclaim are the amount by which the whole costs of the proceedings have been increased by reason of it: see para 515 post.

7   *Staples v Young* (1877) 2 ExD 324; *Blake v Appleyard* (1878) 3 ExD 195; *Chatfield v Sedgwick* (1879) 4 CPD 459, CA; *Wood's Patent Brick Co v Cloke* (1896) 40 Sol Jo 390, DC. This is so in the absence of a special order as against a person not a plaintiff made a defendant to the counterclaim: *Lewin v Trimming* (1888) 21 QBD 230, DC.

8   *Amon v Bobbett* (1889) 22 QBD 543, CA.

9   CPR 44.3(1).

10   CPR 44.3(2). The orders which the court may make under this rule include an order that a party must pay: (1) a proportion of another party's costs; (2) a stated amount in respect of another party's costs; (3) costs from or until a certain date only; (4) costs incurred before proceedings have begun; (5) costs relating to particular steps taken in the proceedings; (6) costs relating only to a distinct part of the proceedings; and (7) interest on costs from or until a certain date, including a date before judgment: CPR 44.3(6). Where the court would otherwise consider making an order under head (5) supra, it must instead, if practicable, make an order under head (1) or (3) supra: CPR 44.3(7).

11   The conduct of the parties includes (1) conduct before, as well as during, the proceedings, and in particular the extent to which the parties followed any relevant pre-action protocol; (2) whether it was reasonable for a party to raise, pursue or contest a particular allegation or issue; (3) the manner in which a party has pursued or defended his case or a particular allegation or issue; and (4) whether a claimant who has succeeded in his claim, in whole or in part, exaggerated his claim: CPR 44.3(5).

12 Ie whether or not made in accordance with CPR Pt 36 (as to which see further para 516 post): CPR 44.3(4)(c).
13 CPR 44.3(4).
14 CPR 44.3(9).
15 For the meaning of 'counterclaim' see para 407 ante.
16 CPR 40.13(3). It was established that if the plaintiff obtains judgment for an amount entitling him to High Court costs and the defendant establishes a claim for a less amount by counterclaim, the plaintiff is nevertheless entitled to costs on the claim, however small the amount by which his claim exceeds the defendant's claim: see *Neale v Clarke* (1879) 4 Ex D 286; *Stooke v Taylor* (1880) 5 QBD 569, DC. As to the citation of old cases, however, see para 401 note 3 ante.
17 As to the allocation of proceedings to tracks see para 401 note 3 ante.
18 CPR 46.3(6).
19 CPR 46.2(6). As to the calculation of fast track costs see CPR 46.2.

514. Set-off equalling or exceeding claim. Where a defendant succeeds in establishing a set-off equal to or exceeding the plaintiff's claim, then, in the absence of circumstances which the court may treat as a ground for depriving him of costs, he is entitled to judgment with costs[1], and, if he has also counterclaimed in respect of the matters relied on by way of set-off, he is similarly entitled to the costs of the counterclaim[2]. If he proves a set-off for less than the plaintiff's claim he is held to have succeeded to that extent[3].

1 *Baines v Bromley* (1881) 6 QBD 691, CA; RSC Ord 62 r 3(3). See also CPR 44.3; and para 513 ante.
    As to the replacement of the RSC by the CPR, and the transitional arrangements in relation thereto, and as to the citation of cases decided under the RSC, see para 401 note 3 ante.
2 *Lowe v Holme* (1883) 10 QBD 286; *Lund v Campbell* (1885) 14 QBD 821, CA. Where a defendant recovered on his counterclaim a sum equal to that recovered by a plaintiff on his claim, Neville J ordered the plaintiff to pay the costs of the claim and counterclaim (*Sprange v Lee* [1908] 1 Ch 424 at 432, CA), but it is difficult to see how this order can be supported unless the subject of counterclaim was also a good ground of set-off.
3 *Lund v Campbell* (1885) 14 QBD 821, CA. The word formerly used in the County Courts Act 1984 ss 19, 20 (repealed), was 'recover', and it has been held that the word 'recover' means recover when set-off is allowed: *Ashcroft v Foulkes* (1856) 18 CB 261 at 271; *Beard v Perry* (1862) 2 B & S 493; *Staples v Young* (1877) 2 Ex D 324; *Stooke v Taylor* (1880) 5 QBD 569 at 575, DC. If the plaintiff succeeds on his claim to an extent entitling him to High Court costs, and the defendant succeeds on a counterclaim but not on a set-off, the plaintiff is entitled to costs on the High Court scale as he has 'recovered' the amount of the claim: *Stooke v Taylor* supra.

515. Taxation or detailed assessment of costs. In relation to proceedings begun before 26 April 1999[1], the proper principle of taxation[2] is to take the claim as if it and its issues were an action, and then to take the counterclaim and its issues as if it were an action, and then to give the allocatur for costs for the balance in favour of the litigant in whose favour the balance turns[3]. If all the issues on the claim are found for the plaintiff, he is entitled to all the costs of the claim, but if only some of such issues are found in his favour he will nevertheless obtain the general costs of the action and of the issues on which he succeeds, but the defendant will be awarded the costs of the issues on which the plaintiff fails[4]. Where the claim and the counterclaim both succeed or are both dismissed, the rule is that the claim is to be treated as if it stood alone and the counterclaim is to bear only the amount by which the costs of the proceedings have been increased by it; no costs not incurred by reason of the counterclaim can be costs of the counterclaim[5]. In the absence of special directions by the court there should be no apportionment of the costs of the action, but there may be individual items common to both the claim and the counterclaim, such as a single fee to counsel, which the taxing master may properly divide[6].

Where there is a counterclaim by a minor or a patient on which money is claimed or recovered or agreed to be paid to or for the benefit of the defendant making the counterclaim, solicitor and own client costs[7] are not payable by that defendant to his solicitor except upon taxation[8].

In relation to proceedings begun on or after 26 April 1999, taxation of costs is replaced by assessment of costs, which may be either a summary assessment by the court, or a detailed assessment by a costs officer[9].

1   Ie the date on which the CPR came into operation. As to the replacement of the RSC by the CPR, and the transitional arrangements in relation thereto, see para 401 note 3 ante.
2   As to the taxation of costs generally see PRACTICE AND PROCEDURE.
3   *Baines v Bromley* (1881) 6 QBD 691 at 695, CA, per Brett LJ; *Re Brown, Ward v Morse* (1883) 23 ChD 377, CA; *Hewitt & Co v Blumer & Co* (1886) 3 TLR 221, CA. The costs which that litigant is liable to pay are thus set off against the costs which he is entitled to be paid: see RSC Ord 62 r 23(a). The taxing officer may delay issuing a certificate to a party entitled to receive costs until he has paid or tendered the amount he is liable to pay: Ord 62 r 18(b). See PRACTICE AND PROCEDURE.
4   *Hewitt & Co v Blumer & Co* (1886) 3 TLR 221, CA; *Atlas Metal Co v Miller* [1898] 2 QB 500, CA; *Slatford v Erlebach* [1912] 3 KB 155, CA.
5   *Saner v Bilton* (1879) 11 ChD 416; *Atlas Metal Co v Miller* [1898] 2 QB 500 at 506, CA, per Lindley MR; *Medway Oil and Storage Co Ltd v Continental Contractors Ltd* [1929] AC 88, HL. See also *Mason v Brentini* (1880) 15 ChD 287, CA; *James v Jackson* [1910] 2 Ch 92; *Wilson v Walters* [1926] 1 KB 511, DC; *Amsterdamsche Lucifersfabrieken NV v H and H Trading Agencies Ltd* [1940] 1 All ER 587, CA; *Millican v Tucker* [1980] 1 All ER 1083, [1980] 1 WLR 640, CA, where the counterclaiming defendants were legally aided.
6   *Atlas Metal Co v Miller* [1898] 2 QB 500 at 506, CA, per Lindley MR; *Medway Oil and Storage Co Ltd v Continental Contractors Ltd* [1929] AC 88, HL. See also *Baines v Bromley* (1881) 6 QBD 691, CA, per Brett LJ; *Re Brown, Ward v Morse* (1883) 23 ChD 377, CA; *Shrapnel v Laing* (1888) 20 QBD 334, CA, per Lord Esher MR; *Fox v Central Silkstone Collieries Ltd* [1912] 2 KB 597; *Crean v M'Millan* [1922] 2 IR 105. Cf *Christie v Platt* [1921] 2 KB 17, CA. The whole of the general costs of the action must be paid by a defendant against whom the plaintiff has established his claim; he is not entitled to any deduction on the ground that he has served a counterclaim instead of bringing a separate action: *Atlas Metal Co v Miller* supra; *Re Brown, Ward v Morse* supra.
7   Ie under RSC Ord 62 r 15: see PRACTICE AND PROCEDURE.
8   RSC Ord 62 r 16(2), (6)(a).
9   See CPR 44.7. As to provision for detailed assessment see CPR Pt 47. As to the extent to which the cases cited in the notes supra may be relied on to interpret the CPR see para 401 note 3 ante.

(7) OFFERS AND PAYMENTS INTO COURT

516–600. Offers and payments into court. In relation to proceedings begun on or after 26 April 1999[1], where a party makes an offer to settle (a 'Part 36 offer')[2], the offer must state whether it takes into account any counterclaim[3]. Similarly, where a defendant makes a payment into court in relation to a claim (a 'Part 36 payment')[4], he must file a notice stating whether the payment takes into account any counterclaim[5].

Where the claimant accepts a Part 36 offer or Part 36 payment, his costs will include any costs attributable to the defendant's counterclaim if the Part 36 offer or the Part 36 payment notice states that it takes into account the counterclaim[6].

1   Ie the date on which the CPR came into operation: see para 401 note 3 ante.
2   CPR 36.2(1)(b). As to offers to settle and payments into court generally see CPR Pt 36; and PRACTICE AND PROCEDURE.
3   CPR 36.5(3)(b).
4   CPR 36.2(1)(a).
5   CPR 36.5(3)(b).
6   CPR 36.13(3).

SETTLEMENTS

1. NATURE AND VALIDITY OF SETTLEMENTS

(1) IN GENERAL

(i) Kinds of Settlements

601. Meaning of 'settlement'. Although there is no generally accepted definition of 'settlement', Parliament has from time to time defined the word for the purposes of particular statutes[1]. A possible definition of 'settlement' is any disposition of property, of whatever nature[2], by any instrument or instruments, by which trusts are constituted[3] for the purpose of regulating the enjoyment of the settled property successively among the persons or classes of persons nominated by the settlor[4]. 'Settlement' has two different senses in law: it can mean either the documents which express the dispositions that are the settlement, or the state of affairs which those documents bring about[5].

A single document may create more than one settlement, whereas trusts constituted by more than one document may create a single settlement[6].

The term 'compound settlement' is used to describe a settlement that subsists by virtue of several different instruments, often a series of successive dispositions such as a deed of settlement[7], a disentailing deed[8] and a deed of resettlement[9].

1   For examples of statutory definitions of 'settlement' see the Harbours and Passing Tolls etc Act 1861 s 2; the Settled Land Act 1925 s 1 (as amended), s 117 (see para 678 post); the Land Registration Act 1925 s 88(2) (see LAND REGISTRATION vol 26 (Reissue) para 1037); the Inheritance Tax Act 1984 s 43(2) (see INHERITANCE TAXATION vol 24 (Reissue) para 477); and the Income and Corporation Taxes Act 1988 s 660G (as added) (see INCOME TAXATION vol 23 (Reissue) para 1504). For a corresponding definition of 'settled property' see eg the Taxation of Chargeable Gains Act 1992 s 68 (see para 621 note 3 post). For the meaning of 'settled land' see the Settled Land Act 1925 ss 2, 117(1)(xxiv); and para 677 post.
2   Everything capable of private ownership and alienation may be settled by the owner, but limited interests cannot normally be created in consumable chattels: see para 611 post; EQUITY vol 16 (Reissue) para 782; GIFTS vol 20 (Reissue) para 23; PERSONAL PROPERTY vol 35 (Reissue) para 1230. Real and personal property may be, and frequently is, settled by the same instrument: see para 937 et seq post.
3   See *Re Marshall's Will Trusts* [1945] Ch 217, [1945] 1 All ER 550; and TRUSTS vol 48 (Reissue) para 543 et seq. As to the essentials to validity of trusts see para 614 et seq post.
4   Cf the shorter description given in *Re Symon, Public Trustee v Symon* [1944] SASR 102 at 109 per Mayo J.
5   See *Cook v Cook* [1962] P 181 at 185, [1962] 2 All ER 262 at 265 per Phillimore J; affd [1962] P 235, [1962] 2 All ER 811, CA. See also eg *Re Ogle's Settled Estates* [1927] 1 Ch 229 at 233 per Romer J, referring to the use of the word 'settlement' in the Settled Land Act 1925. An analogous distinction in meaning is borne by the word 'provision', which may refer either to a clause of a written instrument or to the result ensuing from the clause: see *Berkeley v Berkeley* [1946] AC 555 at 580, [1946] 2 All ER 154 at 166, HL, per Lord Simonds. Cf *IRC v Saunders* [1958] AC 285 at 291–292, [1957] 3 All ER 43 at 45–46, HL, per Viscount Simonds ('power to determine settlement or any provision thereof').
6   As to whether a transaction creates more than one settlement see *Roome v Edwards* [1982] AC 279 at 292–293, [1981] 1 All ER 736 at 739–740, HL, per Lord Wilberforce. Cf *Bond v Pickford* [1983] STC 517, 57 TC 301, CA; *Swires v Renton* [1991] STC 490, 64 TC 315.
7   As to deeds of settlement see para 612 post.
8   As to disentailing deeds see REAL PROPERTY vol 39(2) (Reissue) para 121 et seq.
9   As to this use of the term 'compound settlement' see eg *Re Earl of Carnarvon's Chesterfield Settled Estates, Re Earl of Carnarvon's Highclere Settled Estates* [1927] 1 Ch 138 at 143. Cf *Re Byng's Settled Estates* [1892] 2 Ch 219 at 225 per North J; *Re Marquis of Ailesbury and Lord Iveagh* [1893] 2 Ch 345; *Re Lord Monson's Settled Estates* [1898] 1 Ch 427. The term 'compound settlement' is used in, but is not defined by, the Settled Land Act 1925: see s 1(1) proviso; and para 681 post. As to compound settlements see further para 681 et seq post. As to resettlement generally see para 606 post.

602. Kinds of settlement. Settlements may be made on many occasions and for many purposes. Among familiar kinds of settlements are marriage settlements[1] postnuptial settlements[2], settlements for the benefit of children[3], strict settlements and resettlements of land[4], protective settlements[5], settlements made for the purpose of reducing the incidence of tax[6], settlements made on the separation of spouses[7] and settlements made on divorce[8].

Settlements may also be classified according to whether they are made for valuable consideration[9] or are voluntary[10], and according to whether their subject matter consists of realty or personalty[11].

1   See para 603 post.
2   See para 604 post.
3   See para 605 post.
4   See para 606 post.
5   See para 607 post.
6   See para 608 post.
7   See HUSBAND AND WIFE.
8   See DIVORCE.
9   As to consideration for settlements see paras 659–663 post.
10 As to the importance of the distinction between settlements made for valuable consideration and voluntary settlements see para 615 post.
11 As to settlements of realty see para 609 post; and as to settlements of personalty see para 611 post.

603. Marriage settlements. A marriage settlement is a settlement made in consideration of marriage either before or after the marriage, but after the marriage only if made in pursuance of an ante-nuptial agreement to settle[1]. The form of a marriage settlement has to a large extent become stereotyped[2], although not so stereotyped that any particular provision can be presumed to have been inserted in the settlement[3].

1   As to contracts for settlements see para 627 et seq post. As to consideration for settlements see paras 659–663 post. If the court grants a decree of divorce, nullity or judicial separation, it has power to vary an ante-nuptial or post-nuptial settlement for the benefit of the parties to the marriage and of the children of the family, and for this purpose the term 'settlement' has been interpreted as having a wide meaning: see the Matrimonial Causes Act 1973 s 24(1) (as prospectively substituted); and DIVORCE. See also *Brooks v Brooks* [1996] AC 375, [1995] 3 ALL ER 257, HL, where a pension scheme was held to be a post-nuptial settlement for the purposes of that provision.
2   See further para 628 et seq post.
3   See *Re Knapp's Settlement, Cowan v Knapp* [1952] 1 All ER 458n; *Cummins v Hall and Cummins* [1933] IR 419. Marriage settlements, including post-nuptial settlements made in pursuance of an ante-nuptial contract, are not bills of sale within the Bills of Sale Act 1878 s 4 (see BILLS OF SALE vol 4(1) (Reissue) paras 619, 637), but a post-nuptial settlement which is not made in pursuance of such a contract is a bill of sale within that Act, and, if it contains an assurance of chattels by way of security for the payment of money, is a bill of sale within the Bills of Sale Act (1878) Amendment Act 1882: see s 3; and BILLS OF SALE vol 4(1) (Reissue) para 619.

604. Post-nuptial settlements. A post-nuptial settlement usually contains the same provisions as those contained in an ante-nuptial settlement[1]. It will be considered as a voluntary settlement[2] unless either it is made in pursuance of an agreement made prior to the marriage[3], in which event it will be deemed to have been made in consideration of the marriage[4], or it is the result of a bargain made after the marriage between the spouses[5], or it is made for valuable consideration given by some other person[6].

1   As to variations of post-nuptial settlements on divorce, nullity or judicial separation see para 603 note 1 ante. As to marriage settlements generally see para 628 et seq post.
2   See *Goodright d Humphreys v Moses* (1775) 2 Wm Bl 1019; *Evelyn v Templar* (1787) 2 Bro CC 148; *Currie v Nind* (1836) 1 My & Cr 17; *Doe d Barnes v Rowe* (1838) 6 Scott 525; *Shurmur v Sedgwick, Crossfield v Shurmur* (1883) 24 ChD 597; *Re Gillespie, ex p Knapman, Trustee v Gillespie* (1913) 20 Mans 311. See also *Pownall v Anderson* (1856) 2 Jur NS 857, where articles entered into after marriage were held inoperative.
3   As to contracts for settlements see para 627 et seq post.

4   As to marriage as consideration for a settlement see para 660 et seq post. A settlement made after a
marriage in Scotland does not become an ante-nuptial settlement by reason of the recelebration of the
marriage in England: *Ex p Hall* (1812) 1 Ves & B 112.

5   *Teasdale v Braithwaite* (1876) 4 ChD 85 (affd (1877) 5 ChD 630, CA); *Re Foster and Lister* (1877) 6 ChD
87, dissenting from *Butterfield v Heath* (1852) 15 Beav 408; *Re Lynch, Lynch v Lynch* (1879) 4 LR Ir 210,
Ir CA; *Re Bell's Estate* (1882) 11 LR Ir 512; *Schreiber v Dinkel* (1884) 54 LJ Ch 241. See also *Stileman v
Ashdown* (1742) 2 Atk 477; *Brown v Jones* (1744) 1 Atk 188 at 190; *Ramsden v Hylton* (1751) 2 Ves Sen
304; *Parker v Carter* (1845) 4 Hare 400 at 409; *Harman v Richards* (1852) 10 Hare 81; *Hewison v Negus*
(1853) 16 Beav 594; *Carter v Hind* (1853) 22 LTOS 116; *Whitbread v Smith* (1854) 3 De GM & G 727 at
739; *Stephens v Green, Green v Knight* [1895] 2 Ch 148, CA. In this case the consideration does not extend
to the children of the marriage, who are volunteers and cannot enforce the settlement, unless they are
parties to it (see *Joyce v Hutton* (1860) 11 I Ch R 123 (on appeal (1861) 12 I Ch R 71, Ir CA); *Green v
Paterson* (1886) 32 ChD 95, CA; cf *Gandy v Gandy* (1885) 30 ChD 57, CA), or there is an executed trust
in their favour (see *Joyce v Hutton* supra; *Green v Paterson* supra). See further para 615 post.

6   *Bayspoole v Collins* (1871) 6 Ch App 228; cf *Ex p Hall* (1812) 1 Ves & B 112. See also *Ford v Stuart* (1852)
15 Beav 493; *Townend v Toker* (1866) 1 Ch App 446.

605. Settlements for the benefit of children.

In settlements under which a child[1]
has an interest, express powers of maintenance, accumulation or advancement[2] may be
inserted, but, even if there are no such powers, there are, subject to certain limitations,
statutory powers for the same purposes[3]. Land in which a child has a beneficial interest in
possession is in most cases settled land if the settlement was created on or before 1 January
1997[4] and contained no express trust for sale, but is otherwise a trust of land[5]. Whichever
statutory regime applies, the trustees are given special powers for the management of such
land[6]. The court has power to vary settlements for the benefit of children of a marriage
which is dissolved or annulled or in the event of judicial separation[7].

A child cannot be a trustee, but, subject to certain limitations, a child may exercise a
power to appoint a new trustee of a settlement[8].

1   The age of majority, formerly 21, was reduced to 18 with effect from 1 January 1970: see the Family Law
Reform Act 1969 s 1; and CHILDREN AND YOUNG PERSONS vol 5(2) (Reissue) para 601. As to the use
of the word 'child' see CHILDREN AND YOUNG PERSONS vol 5(2) (Reissue) para 603. See *Begg-MacBrearty
(Inspector of Taxes) v Stilwell (Trustee of the GE Coke Settlement)* [1996] 4 All ER 205, [1996] 1 WLR 951,
where the reduced age of majority was held to apply to trusts created in 1975 by the exercise of a special
power of appointment contained in a 1959 settlement.

2   As to powers of maintenance, accumulation and advancement see para 667 post; and CHILDREN AND
YOUNG PERSONS vol 5(2) (Reissue) para 661 et seq.

3   See para 667 post; and CHILDREN AND YOUNG PERSONS vol 5(2) (Reissue) para 661 et seq.

4   See the Settled Land Act 1925 s 1(1)(ii)(d); the Trusts of Land and Appointment of Trustees Act 1996
ss 1(1), 2; the Trusts of Land and Appointment of Trustees Act 1996 (Commencement) Order 1996,
SI 1996/2974; and paras 676–677 post. See further REAL PROPERTY vol 39(2) (Reissue) paras 64–66.

5   See the Trusts of Land and Appointment of Trustees Act 1996 ss 1(1), 2; and para 676 post.

6   See paras 665–666 post; and CHILDREN AND YOUNG PERSONS vol 5(2) (Reissue) paras 657–660.

7   See para 603 note 1 ante.

8   See CHILDREN AND YOUNG PERSONS vol 5(2) (Reissue) para 655.

606. Strict settlements and resettlements of land.

Since 1 January 1997, it has not
been possible to create new strict settlements of land within the meaning of the Settled
Land Act 1925[1], and over time old strict settlements will die out[2]. Historically, the object
of strict settlements was to secure that the land should descend from father to son so that
the land as a whole could not be alienated unless and until a father and son concurred in
so doing. Alienation normally happened on the coming of age of an eldest son or other
first tenant in tail in remainder[3] expectant on the death of the tenant for life in possession,
when a family arrangement[4] was entered into and a resettlement of the land[5] was executed
for the purpose of giving effect to it[6]. However, for many years it has been impossible to
settle land in such a way that it cannot be alienated, since by statute the estate owner in
whom the legal estate is vested has an overriding power of disposition[7]. For this reason,

and also in consequence of changed economic conditions, the creation of strict settlements had already become uncommon before 1 January 1997.

A settlement created by the exercise of a power of appointment in an existing strict settlement will usually be a strict settlement and not a trust of land, unless the deed of appointment provides otherwise[8].

1 Ie within the meaning of the Settled Land Act 1925 s 1: see para 678 post.
2 See the Trusts of Land and Appointment of Trustees Act 1996 s 2(1) (see para 676 post); and the Trusts of Land and Appointment of Trustees Act 1996 (Commencement) Order 1996, SI 1996/2974. Charitable, ecclesiastical or public settlements of land and settlements with no relevant property are now trusts of land rather than strict settlements, whenever created: see the Trusts of Land and Appointment of Trustees Act 1996 s 2(4), (5), Sch 1; and paras 676–677 post.
3 As to entailed interests see para 715 et seq post; and REAL PROPERTY vol 39(2) (Reissue) para 117 et seq.
4 As to family arrangements see para 1002 et seq post.
5 As to the traditional provisions of resettlements see para 720 post; and as to resettlements restoring former life interests see para 764 post. As to the effect of resettlements on entitlement to portions see para 729 post.
6 The essential requirements of a resettlement do not differ from those of other family arrangements: see para 1007 et seq post.
7 See para 775 et seq post.
8 See the Trusts of Land and Appointment of Trustees Act 1996 s 2(2), (3); and para 676 post. As to powers of appointment see TRUSTS vol 48 (Reissue) para 708 et seq.

607. Protective settlements. Protective settlements normally contain a more or less common form set of provisions designed so as to enable the principal beneficiary to enjoy the beneficial interest intended for him without allowing him any power of alienation[1]. Such a settlement, if made by a third person, is valid against a beneficiary's trustee in bankruptcy[2], but not if made by the beneficiary himself[3].

1 The usual provision employed for this purpose is that contained in the Trustee Act 1925 s 33 (as amended): see para 917 post.
2 *Re Ashby, ex p Wreford* [1892] 1 QB 872; *Re Throckmorton, ex p Eyston* (1877) 7 ChD 145, CA. See also BANKRUPTCY AND INSOLVENCY vol 3(2) (Reissue) para 204.
3 See *Re Burroughs-Fowler, Burroughs-Fowler's Trustee v Burroughs-Fowler* [1916] 2 Ch 251; and para 916 post.

608. Settlements made to avoid or mitigate the incidence of tax. Settlements are often made with a view to avoid or mitigate the incidence of income tax, capital gains tax or inheritance tax[1]. Such settlements may be divided into two distinct categories. First, the tax legislation provides special status for a number of specific types of trust or settlement upon which tax privileges are expressly conferred[2]. Secondly, settlements are capable of being used as part of schemes designed to secure a tax advantage which may not have been specifically contemplated by Parliament. This second category of settlements is coming under increased scrutiny by the Inland Revenue Commissioners and by the courts and, in recent years the powers of the courts to strike down such schemes as artificial have evolved significantly[3]. Further, Parliament frequently enacts specific anti-avoidance provisions to override the efficacy of such schemes[4].

1 As to the fiscal consequences of settlements see further para 619 et seq post.
2 Eg accumulation and maintenance trusts (see the Inheritance Tax Act 1984 s 71; and INHERITANCE TAXATION vol 24 (Reissue) para 507); maintenance fund trusts (see s 77, Sch 4 (as amended); and INHERITANCE TAXATION vol 24 (Reissue) para 548–555); retirement benefit schemes (see the Income and Corporation Taxes Act 1988 Pt XIV Ch I (ss 590–612) (as amended); and SOCIAL SECURITY AND PENSIONS vol 44(2) (Reissue) para 747 et seq).
3 See *Ramsay v IRC* [1982] AC 300, [1981] 1 All ER 865, HL; *IRC v Burmah Oil Co Ltd* [1982] STC 30, (1981) 54 TC 200, HL; *Furniss v Dawson* [1984] AC 474, [1984] 1 All ER 530, HL; *Craven v White* [1989] AC 398, [1988] 3 All ER 495, HL; *Ensign Tankers (Leasing) Ltd v Stokes* [1992] 1 AC 655, [1992] 2 All

ER 275; *IRC v McGuckian* [1997] 3 All ER 817, [1997] 1 WLR 991, HL; *IRC v Willoughby* [1997] 4 All ER 65, [1997] 1 WLR 1071, HL.

4   See eg the changes made to the Capital Gains Tax Act 1979 (repealed) by the Finance Act 1991 ss 83–92, Sch 16, which substantially reduced the scope for avoiding or deferring a liability to capital gains tax by the use of non-resident settlements. See now the Taxation of Chargeable Gains Act 1992 s 86, Sch 5 (both as amended). As to income tax anti-avoidance provisions generally see INCOME TAXATION vol 23 (Reissue) para 1533 et seq.

(ii) Nature of the Settled Property

609. Settlements of realty and chattels real. The only estates in land which are capable of subsisting or of being conveyed or created at law are an estate in fee simple absolute in possession and a term of years absolute[1]. All other estates in land take effect as equitable interests only[2].

Important changes were made by the Trusts of Land and Appointment of Trustees Act 1996 to settlements of land[3]. Prior to 1 January 1997[4], a settlement of land took effect either as a strict settlement or as a trust for sale[5]. With limited exceptions the Act prevents the creation after that date of new strict settlements of land, although it preserves the status of most existing strict settlements[6].

The Trusts of Land and Appointment of Trustees Act 1996 created a new regime for settlements of land other than strict settlements and land to which the Universities and College Estates Act 1925 applies[7], and any such settlement is a 'trust of land' for the purpose of the Trusts of Land and Appointment of Trustees Act 1996[8]. Under that Act, existing express trusts for sale do not lose their status, nor is there any prohibition upon the creation of trusts for sale in the future[9]. Indeed, the definition of 'trust of land' expressly includes a trust for sale[10]. However, the Act makes great inroads upon the relevance of the description of a trust as a trust for sale[11]. Trusts for sale implied by statute are reclassified as trusts of land with retrospective effect[12].

It is no longer possible to create entailed interests in land[13], and any attempt to do so operates as a declaration that the land is held in trust absolutely for the person to whom the entailed interest was purportedly granted[14].

If it is desired to settle leaseholds containing onerous covenants, they are usually brought into the settlement by subdemise to the trustees[15].

An advowson or right of patronage of a benefice may be the subject of a settlement, but the statutory requirements relating to the transfer of patronage must be observed[16].

1   See the Law of Property Act 1925 s 1(1); and REAL PROPERTY vol 39(2) (Reissue) para 45.
2   See ibid s 1(3); and REAL PROPERTY vol 39(2) (Reissue) para 46. As to the transitional provisions affecting settlements of land subsisting on 1 January 1926 see the Law of Property Act 1925 s 39, Sch 1 Pt II paras 3, 5, 6(c); and REAL PROPERTY vol 39(2) (Reissue) para 49 et seq.
3   See REAL PROPERTY vol 39(2) (Reissue) paras 64–69.
4   Ie the date on which the Trusts of Land and Appointment of Trustees Act 1996 came into force: see the Trusts of Land and Appointment of Trustees Act 1996 (Commencement) Order 1996, SI 1996/2974; and para 676 post.
5   See the Settled Land Act 1925 s 1 (as amended) (see para 675 post); and the Law of Property Act 1925 ss 34–36 (as originally enacted).
6   See the Trusts of Land and Appointment of Trustees Act 1996 ss 1(2), (3), 2(1); and paras 676–677 post. As to strict settlements see para 606 ante.
7   See EDUCATION vol 15 (Reissue) para 263 et seq.
8   See the Trusts of Land and Appointment of Trustees Act 1996 s 1; and REAL PROPERTY vol 39(2) (Reissue) para 66. For the meaning of 'trust of land' see para 676 note 5 post.
9   See ibid ss 1, 4; and REAL PROPERTY vol 39(2) (Reissue) para 66.
10   See ibid s 1(2); and REAL PROPERTY vol 39(2) (Reissue) para 66.
11   See in particular the abolition of the doctrine of conversion by ibid s 3 (see REAL PROPERTY vol 39(2) (Reissue) para 77); the implication into all trusts for sale of an unexcludable power in the trustees to postpone sale by s 4 (see REAL PROPERTY vol 39(2) (Reissue) para 66); and the repeal by s 25(2), Sch 4

of the statutory powers of trustees of a trust for sale contained in the Law of Property Act 1925 ss 28–29 (repealed) (see REAL PROPERTY vol 39(2) (Reissue) para 67).

12   See the Trusts of Land and Appointment of Trustees Act 1996 s 5(1), Sch 2; and REAL PROPERTY vol 39(2) (Reissue) para 66.

13   See para 677 post. As to entailed interests see para 715 et seq post; and REAL PROPERTY vol 39(2) (Reissue) para 117 et seq.

14   See the Trusts of Land and Appointment of Trustees Act 1996 s 2, Sch 1 para 5; and para 677 post.

15   As to the settlement of leases see LANDLORD AND TENANT vol 27(1) (Reissue) paras 26–27; TRUSTS vol 48 (Reissue) para 821.

16   As to the mode and effect of transferring an advowson see *Sherrard v Lord Harborough* (1753) Amb 165 at 166; and ECCLESIASTICAL LAW. As to rights of patronage of a benefice see ECCLESIASTICAL LAW.

610. Settlements of equitable interests. Equitable interests in land, such as beneficial interests under a strict settlement[1] or trust of land[2], an equitable mortgage and an equitable easement[3], may be settled by assignment to trustees, who should give notice of the assignment to the trustees of the head settlement or the estate owner of the land affected (as the case may be) in order to perfect their interest[4].

1   As to strict settlements see para 606 ante.
2   As to trusts of land see paras 609 ante, 676–677 post.
3   As to equitable mortgages see EQUITY vol 16 (Reissue) para 779; and as to equitable easements see EASEMENTS AND PROFITS À PRENDRE.
4   See the Law of Property Act 1925 s 137(1), (2) (as amended); and CHOSES IN ACTION vol 6 (Reissue) para 41 et seq.

611. Settlements of personalty. A trust is the usual method of creating successive interests in personalty[1], and is essential for the creation of a settlement inter vivos, since at law a grant of chattels for life vests the whole legal interest in the grantee; moreover things which are exhausted by personal use, other than stock in trade of a business or farming stock, cannot be given for less than an absolute interest[2].

Although it was possible to create entailed interests in personalty between 1925[3] and 1 January 1997, it is no longer possible to do so, and any attempt to create an entailed interest in personalty will operate as a declaration that the property is held in trust absolutely for the person to whom an entailed interest in the property was purportedly granted[4].

1   See para 907 et seq post.
2   See EQUITY vol 16 (Reissue) para 782; GIFTS vol 20 (Reissue) para 23; PERSONAL PROPERTY vol 35 (Reissue) para 1230.
3   See the Law of Property Act 1925 s 130 (as originally enacted); and PERSONAL PROPERTY vol 35 (Reissue) para 1230. It was not possible to create entailed interests in personalty before the commencement of that Act (except where, by virtue of the doctrine of conversion, the property was regarded as land, eg in the case of money settled upon trust for the purchase of freehold property): see *Leventhorpe v Ashbie* (1635) 1 Roll Abr 831.
4   See the Trusts of Land and Appointment of Trustees Act 1996 s 2, Sch 1 para 5; and para 677 post.

(iii)   Manner of Creation of Settlements

612. Settlements created by deed or will. Settlements by individuals may be made either by deed or by will[1]. A settlement may be created by a deed poll, but more commonly it is created by a deed to which the intending settlor, the intended trustees of the settlement, and sometimes, and generally in the case of a marriage settlement, some of the beneficiaries, are parties. The settlement may, and in the case of a settlement for the purposes of the Settled Land Act 1925 must, be created by more than one deed, the assurance being effected by one deed and the trusts of the assured property declared by another[2]. The general rules as to interpretation of deeds apply to settlements created by deed[3].

Settlements which do not relate to land or to any interest in it[4] may be created by parol so, for example, it is possible to create a settlement of personalty orally[5].

1   The doctrine of election applies to settlements created by deed as well as to those created by will: see EQUITY vol 16 (Reissue) para 845. As to the form of settlements by deed see paras 688 et seq, 898 post. As to the form of settlements created by will see para 697 post.
2   See para 688 et seq post.
3   As to the general rules of interpretation see DEEDS AND OTHER INSTRUMENTS.
4   Ie settlements which are therefore not within the scope of the Law of Property Act 1925 s 53(1)(b): see TRUSTS vol 48 (Reissue) para 543.
5   As to settlements of personalty see para 907 et seq post.

613. Settlements created by statute. Settlements are sometimes created by either public or private Act of Parliament. A public Act creating a settlement is for the purpose of rewarding eminent public services by grants of land[1], and the Acts creating them are passed through Parliament in the same manner and with the same formalities as other public bills[2].

A private Act creating a settlement is known as an 'estate bill', being one of the class of personal bills which are introduced in the first instance in the House of Lords[3]. Formerly, recourse was often had to private Acts in order to relieve the owner of an estate from various kinds of interests by which it was encumbered, or to confer on him some administrative power, or to free the estate from the claims of persons under disability. However, by reason of the wider powers now conferred on the courts, it will seldom be necessary in future to resort to those private Acts[4].

1   Eg in the cases of the Duke of Marlborough, the Duke of Wellington and Lord Nelson. It may be observed that the entails made by such Acts are indestructible: see 6 Anne c 6 (1706) s 5; 54 Geo 3 c 161 (1814) s 28; 53 Geo 3 c 134 (1813) s 1. As to alienation see GIFTS vol 20 (Reissue) para 21. The provision can, of course, subsequently be modified by statute: see eg the Trafalgar Estates Act 1947; the Wellington Museum Act 1947; and REAL PROPERTY vol 39(2) (Reissue) para 133. A more recent example of a statutory settlement is the Chevening Estate Act 1959 (see REAL PROPERTY vol 39(2) (Reissue) para 65).
2   See PARLIAMENT vol 34 (Reissue) para 736 et seq.
3   See PARLIAMENT vol 34 (Reissue) para 872 et seq.
4   See the Settled Land Act 1925 s 64 (as amended) (see para 671 post); the Trustee Act 1925 s 57 (see para 672 post; and TRUSTS vol 48 (Reissue) para 922); and the Variation of Trusts Act 1958 s 1 (as amended) (see para 674 post; and TRUSTS vol 48 (Reissue) para 923 et seq).

(iv) Validity and Avoidance of Settlements

614. Execution of settlements. A settlement must be executed by the settlor[1], and it is generally expedient that it should be executed by the trustees. As a rule, execution by a beneficiary is only important if the beneficiary is contracting to do something[2], but, in the case of a marriage settlement, it is customary and expedient for the deed to be executed by both intending spouses, even if the property settled belongs to one of them only[3].

1   Non-execution by some of the contracting parties does not necessarily prevent a settlement from binding those parties who execute the deed: *M'Neill v Cahill* (1820) 2 Bli 228, HL; *Lady Naas v Westminster Bank Ltd* [1940] AC 366, [1940] 1 All ER 485, HL. As to the formalities of execution see DEEDS AND OTHER INSTRUMENTS.
2   *Lady Naas v Westminster Bank Ltd* [1940] AC 366, [1940] 1 All ER 485, HL.
3   See further para 628 et seq post.

615. Enforceability of settlements. A settlement is fully constituted when the settlor has done everything to be done by him to transfer the property to trustees upon trusts declared by him, or when he has declared himself to be a trustee of the property[1]. Once the settlement is fully constituted, then, unless a power of revocation has been reserved, the settlement is irrevocable[2]. For this purpose it is immaterial whether the settlement is made for valuable consideration or is voluntary, since, if a voluntary settlement is unaffected by any statutory enactment and is complete, bona fide and valid, there is no distinction between such a settlement and one executed for valuable consideration[3]. Further, a settlement which has been fully constituted binds the settlor, if he should afterwards obtain possession of the settled property, to hold it upon the trusts of the settlement[4]. However, until it is fully constituted, a settlement can be enforced, if at all, only as a contract to settle[5], or if the property vests in the trustees of the settlement[6].

1   The test is whether any act remains to be done by the settlor, and not by the beneficiaries or trustees: see GIFTS vol 20 (Reissue) para 63. As to completed and incomplete gifts see GIFTS vol 20 (Reissue) para 63 et seq. A settlement of property which is not transferred to the trustees may contain a provision which can be construed as a declaration of trust of the property pending its transfer, in which case the settlement will be enforceable: *Re Ralli's Will Trusts, Re Ralli's Marriage Settlement, Calvocoressi v Rodocanachi* [1964] Ch 288, [1963] 3 All ER 940. As to the requisites for a valid declaration of trust see *Paul v Constance* [1977] 1 All ER 195, [1977] 1 WLR 527, CA.
2   *Paul v Paul* (1882) 20 ChD 742, CA. Cf *Re Bowden, Hulbert v Bowden* [1936] Ch 71; *Re Adlard, Taylor v Adlard* [1954] Ch 29, [1953] 2 All ER 1437. See also GIFTS vol 20 (Reissue) para 56.
3   *Dickinson v Burrell, Stourton v Burrell* (1866) LR 1 Eq 337 at 343; *Paul v Paul* (1882) 20 ChD 742, CA.
4   *Re Patrick, Bills v Tatham* [1891] 1 Ch 82, CA.
5   As to contracts for settlements see para 627 et seq post. An incomplete voluntary settlement may be annulled by the settlor: *Beatson v Beatson* (1841) 12 Sim 281. If there is a covenant by the settlor with trustees to settle property for the benefit of volunteers, the court will not compel the trustees to sue for damages, and may direct them not to sue: *Re Pryce, Neville v Pryce* [1917] 1 Ch 234; *Re Kay's Settlement, Broadbent v Macnab* [1939] Ch 329, [1939] 1 All ER 245; *Re Cook's Settlement Trusts, Royal Exchange Assurance v Cook* [1965] Ch 902, [1964] 3 All ER 898. But cf *Beswick v Beswick* [1968] AC 58, [1967] 2 All ER 1197, HL. As to the enforcement of marriage settlements see para 661 post.
6   *Re Ralli's Will Trusts, Re Ralli's Marriage Settlement, Calvocoressi v Rodocanachi* [1964] Ch 288, [1963] 3 All ER 940.

616. Avoidance of settlements. Where a settlement is made by an individual at a time when he is insolvent, either at an undervalue (for example for no consideration or in consideration of marriage) or as a preference to any of the settlor's creditors during a specified period[1] ending with the presentation of a bankruptcy petition, the court will make an order restoring the position upon the application of the settlor's trustee in bankruptcy[2]. Further, where a settlement is entered into at any time at an undervalue for the purpose of defrauding creditors, the court has a wide discretion, upon the application of the settlor's trustee in bankruptcy or in certain circumstances of the victim of the transaction, to make an order (such as an order setting aside the settlement) for the purpose of restoring the position and protecting the creditors[3]. Apart from the bankruptcy laws, any voluntary settlement of land made with intent to defraud a subsequent purchaser is voidable at the instance of that purchaser[4].

A settlement, whether voluntary or not, may be set aside at the suit of the settlor himself if it is made in consequence of fraud, duress, misrepresentation or undue influence[5]. A settlement, whether voluntary or not, may also be rectified if it does not give effect to the intention of the parties[6].

1   Ie either five years, two years or six months, as appropriate: see the Insolvency Act 1986 s 341; and BANKRUPTCY AND INSOLVENCY vol 3(2) (Reissue) para 649.
2   See ibid ss 339–340; and BANKRUPTCY AND INSOLVENCY vol 3(2) (Reissue) para 642 et seq.
3   See ibid s 423; and BANKRUPTCY AND INSOLVENCY vol 3(2) (Reissue) para 653 et seq.

4　See the Law of Property Act 1925 s 173; and MISREPRESENTATION AND FRAUD vol 31 (Reissue) para 868 et seq.

5　See EQUITY vol 16 (Reissue) para 662 et seq; and MISREPRESENTATION AND FRAUD vol 31 (Reissue) para 838 et seq. As to misrepresentation see MISREPRESENTATION AND FRAUD vol 31 (Reissue) para 701 et seq; and as to undue influence see para 618 post.

6　See MISTAKE.

617. Void trusts. Trusts or limitations contained in a settlement may be void on the ground of uncertainty or public policy or because they infringe the rule against perpetuities[1]. Such trusts or limitations will be void for uncertainty if the objects are not defined with sufficient particularity[2], or are left wholly to the discretion of the trustees[3], unless the trusts are exclusively for charitable purposes[4].

A disposition in favour of illegitimate children not in being when the disposition takes effect was void at common law as being contrary to public policy[5]. However, this rule has been abolished as respects dispositions made on or after 1 January 1970[6].

In addition, the interests created by a settlement made before 16 July 1964 are void as infringing the rule against perpetuities unless they must vest indefeasibly in interest, if they vest at all, within the period of a life in being and 21 years after the determination of that life; the interests created by a settlement made on or after that date are void to the extent that they do not vest in interest within that period, or within an alternative period not exceeding 80 years specified in the settlement[7].

1　As to the rule against perpetuities see PERPETUITIES AND ACCUMULATIONS vol 35 (Reissue) para 1008 et seq.

2　*James v Allen* (1817) 3 Mer 17; *McPhail v Doulton* [1971] AC 424, [1970] 2 All ER 228, HL; *Re Baden's Deed Trusts (No 2)* [1973] Ch 9, [1972] 2 All ER 1304, CA. See also POWERS; and TRUSTS vol 48 (Reissue) para 548 et seq.

3　See *Chichester Diocesan Fund and Board of Finance Inc v Simpson* [1944] AC 341, [1944] 2 All ER 60, HL; and TRUSTS vol 48 (Reissue) para 507. Trustees can, however, be given power to appoint for such persons or purposes as they determine: *Re Hay's Settlement Trusts* [1981] 3 All ER 786, [1982] 1 WLR 202. As to powers of appointment see TRUSTS vol 48 (Reissue) para 627.

4　See CHARITIES vol 5(2) (Reissue) para 95.

5　See *Blodwell v Edwards* (1596) Cro Eliz 509; *Lomas v Wright* (1833) 2 My & K 769; *Wilkinson v Wilkinson* (1842) 1 Y & C Ch Cas 657; *Thompson v Thomas* (1891) 27 LR Ir 457. This rule did not invalidate a disposition in favour of illegitimate children in existence at the date of the settlement, including a child en ventre sa mère at the date of the settlement: *Ebbern v Fowler* [1909] 1 Ch 578, CA. As to illegitimate children see CHILDREN AND YOUNG PERSONS vol 5(2) (Reissue) para 723 et seq. As to when a reference to children in a disposition includes illegitimate children see para 731 post.

6　See the Family Law Reform Act 1969 s 15(7) (repealed); and WILLS vol 50 (Reissue) para 591.

7　See the Perpetuities and Accumulations Act 1964 ss 1, 3–5 (s 4 as amended); and PERPETUITIES AND ACCUMULATIONS vol 35 (Reissue) para 1001 et seq. The enjoyment of a person who has a vested interest under a settlement cannot be postponed by the insertion of a trust for accumulation which is exclusively for his benefit: see *Saunders v Vautier* (1841) 10 LJ Ch 354; *Wharton v Masterman* [1895] AC 186, HL; and PERPETUITIES AND ACCUMULATIONS vol 35 (Reissue) para 1120. For settlements which came into operation before 1 January 1926 there was the further restriction that, if land was limited to an unborn person during his life, a remainder could not be limited to the children or other issue of such unborn person, either at law or in equity: see *Whitby v Mitchell* (1890) 44 ChD 85, CA; *Re Nash, Cook v Frederick* [1910] 1 Ch 1, CA; and PERPETUITIES AND ACCUMULATIONS vol 35 (Reissue) para 1003. This rule was abolished as regards limitations or trusts created by an instrument coming into operation after 31 December 1925 by the Law of Property Act 1925 s 161: see PERPETUITIES AND ACCUMULATIONS vol 35 (Reissue) para 1003.

618. Settlements for the protection of the settlor. Settlements are sometimes made for the protection of the settlor himself. Such a settlement is liable to be impeached on any of the grounds on which any voluntary settlement may be impeached[1]. In particular, such a settlement may be set aside by the settlor on the ground of undue influence[2], the doctrine of undue influence not being confined to a case where the influence is exerted to secure a benefit to the person exerting it, but extending also to cases in which a person of imperfect judgment is placed or places himself under the direction of one possessing greater experience or such force as is inherent in such a relation as, for example, a father and his child[3]. Where a settlement is executed shortly after the coming of age of the settlor, it may be difficult to support it[4]. If the settlor is competent to understand and does understand the deed[5], it will not be set aside merely because it contains provisions which are unusual, or which the court may think ought not to have been inserted[6], but those who support the deed are bound to show either that the deed is in all respects proper, or, if it contains anything special or unusual, that the settlor understood and approved of it[7], and, if it should appear that the settlor did not understand, the settlement will be set aside[8]. If the settlor has understood the settlement, but his attention has not been called to the omission of any power of disposition in default of issue, the settlement may be rectified by the insertion of such a power[9]. It is desirable, but not necessary, that a settlement of this nature should contain a power of revocation[10]. The absence of a power of revocation is a circumstance to be taken into account, and is of more or less weight according to the facts of the particular case[11].

1   See para 616 ante.
2   As to undue influence see EQUITY vol 16 (Reissue) para 667 et seq; MISREPRESENTATION AND FRAUD vol 31 (Reissue) para 839 et seq.
3   *Bullock v Lloyds Bank Ltd* [1955] Ch 317, [1954] 3 All ER 726.
4   *Everitt v Everitt* (1870) LR 10 Eq 405. See also *Re Pauling's Settlement Trusts, Younghusband v Coutts & Co* [1964] Ch 303, [1964] 3 All ER 1, CA.
5   As to the degree of understanding necessary to make a gift see *Re Beaney* [1978] 2 All ER 595, [1978] 1 WLR 770. As to capacity to make a settlement see para 625 post.
6   *Dutton v Thompson* (1883) 23 ChD 278, CA. See also *James v Couchman* (1885) 29 ChD 212; *Re Brocklehurst, Hall v Roberts* [1978] Ch 14, [1978] 1 All ER 767, CA.
7   *Phillips v Mullings* (1871) 7 Ch App 244.
8   *Moore v Prance* (1851) 9 Hare 299; *Prideaux v Lonsdale* (1863) 1 De GJ & Sm 433; *Dutton v Thompson* (1883) 23 ChD 278, CA. However, this principle may not apply if it is shown that the settlor was content to rely on his advisers: *Lovell v Wallis (No 2)* (1844) 50 LT 681.
9   *James v Couchman* (1885) 29 ChD 212.
10 *Everitt v Everitt* (1870) LR 10 Eq 405. As to the binding effect of a settlement which contains no power of revocation see para 615 ante. However, a power of revocation may have adverse tax consequences: see eg the Income and Corporation Taxes Act 1988 s 660A (as added) (income arising under settlement where settlor retains an interest deemed to be that of settlor for income tax purposes) (see INCOME TAXATION vol 23 (Reissue) paras 1517–1521); the Taxation of Chargeable Gains Act 1992 s 77 (as substituted and amended) (charge to capital gains tax on settlor with interest in settlement) (see CAPITAL GAINS TAXATION vol 5(1) (Reissue) para 114–115); and the Finance Act 1986 s 102 (as amended) (gifts with reservation included in donor's estate for inheritance tax purposes) (see INHERITANCE TAXATION vol 24 (Reissue) para 446 et seq).
11 *Forshaw v Welsby* (1860) 30 Beav 243; *Toker v Toker* (1863) 3 De GJ & Sm 487; *Mountford v Keene* (1871) 24 LT 925; *Hall v Hall* (1873) 8 Ch App 430; *Henshall v Fereday* (1873) 29 LT 46; *Henry v Armstong* (1881) 18 ChD 668.

(v) Fiscal Consequences of Settlements

619. Income tax. One of the legal consequences of settling income-producing property upon the trusts of an English settlement[1], under which persons other than the settlor become beneficially entitled to the income, is that the income ceases to be the income of the settlor as a matter of property law[2]. However, by virtue of anti-avoidance provisions in the income tax legislation, this is not necessarily the consequence as between the parties to the settlement and the Inland Revenue Commissioners[3]. First, the legislation taxes income arising during the lifetime of the settlor as his income[4], if it arises under a settlement[5] under which the settlor, and in certain circumstances his spouse, has an interest[6]. Secondly, there are provisions in the legislation for taxing income which arises under a settlement, and which is paid during the lifetime of the settlor to or for the benefit of his unmarried children under the age of majority, as the settlor's income[7]. Thirdly, capital sums paid to a settlor, or to his spouse, under a settlement or by a body connected with a settlement may in certain circumstances be taxed as income[8].

1   This paragraph is not concerned with the transfer of effects abroad; as to the special provisions of the income tax legislation directed to the prevention of tax avoidance by the transfer of income-producing assets to persons abroad see INCOME TAXATION vol 23 (Reissue) para 1565 et seq.
2   See INCOME TAXATION vol 23 (Reissue) para 1497.
3   See the text and notes 4–8 infra.
4   There are provisions enabling a settlor to recover tax paid by him either from the trustees of the settlement or from the beneficiaries: see the Income and Corporation Taxes Act 1988 s 660D (as added); and INCOME TAXATION vol 23 (Reissue) para 1521.
5   For this purpose, 'settlement' includes any disposition, trust, covenant, agreement, arrangement or transfer of assets: see ibid s 660G(1) (as added); and INCOME TAXATION vol 23 (Reissue) para 1514.
6   See ibid s 660A (as added); and INCOME TAXATION vol 23 (Reissue) paras 1517–1521.
7   See ibid s 660B (as added); and INCOME TAXATION vol 23 (Reissue) paras 1517–1521. As to the age of majority see para 605 note 1 ante.
8   See ibid ss 677, 678 (as amended); and INCOME TAXATION vol 23 (Reissue) paras 1524–1525.

620. Income tax allowances and reliefs. The allowances and reliefs appropriate to the personal circumstances of a beneficiary to whom income is paid under a settlement are relevant in calculating the amount of income tax which this income should bear[1]. However, the administrative mechanism by which these allowances and reliefs are taken into account varies according to the type of settlement and nature of the income, and can give rise to considerable complexities[2]. For example, in the case of an annuity payable 'free of tax'[3] to a beneficiary, it is important to ensure that he does not, by virtue of his allowances and reliefs, receive more than his entitlement[4].

A tenant for life[5] of settled land is entitled, in the absence of any provision in the settlement to the contrary, to the benefit of income tax allowances in respect of money spent on improvements to the trust property, even if the cost of these improvements has been borne at his direction out of capital money arising under the Settled Land Act 1925[6].

1   See INCOME TAXATION vol 23 (Reissue) para 1497.
2   See INCOME TAXATION vol 23 (Reissue) para 1496 et seq.
3   As to the effect of gifts 'free of tax' see INCOME TAXATION vol 23 (Reissue) para 550.
4   *Re Batley (No 2), Public Trustee v Hert* [1952] Ch 781, [1952] 2 All ER 562, CA. Cf *Re Pettit, Le Fevre v Pettit* [1922] 2 Ch 765; *Re Lyons, Barclays Bank Ltd v Lyons* [1952] Ch 129, [1952] 1 All ER 34, CA, which are examples of the 'free of tax' cases. See also RENTCHARGES AND ANNUITIES vol 39(2) (Reissue) para 861.
5   As to tenants for life see para 761 et seq post.
6   *Re Pelly's Will Trusts, Ransome v Pelly* [1957] Ch 1, [1956] 2 All ER 326, CA. See also para 944 note 4 post. For the meaning of 'capital money arising under the Act' see para 795 post.

621. Chargeable gains. For the purposes of tax due on chargeable gains[1], a transfer into a settlement, whether revocable or irrevocable[2], is a disposal of the entire property which then becomes settled property, notwithstanding that the donor has some interest as a beneficiary under the settlement, and notwithstanding that he is a trustee, or the sole trustee, of the settlement[3].

Generally, tax due on chargeable gains accruing upon disposals of settled property by the trustees is the liability of the trustees[4]. However, if the settlor and in certain circumstances his spouse has an interest in the settlement, those gains are treated as accruing to the settlor and not to the trustees[5].

There is a deemed disposal when a person becomes absolutely entitled to any settled property as against the trustee[6], but there is an exemption from liability where the deemed disposal occurs on the death of a person entitled to a life interest in possession[7]. There is also a deemed disposal, on the termination, on the death of a person entitled to it, of a life interest in possession in settled property, in relation to assets not then ceasing to be settled property; but there is exemption from liability on that disposal[8]. Generally, in the case of a settlement where the trustees are resident and ordinarily resident in the United Kingdom, no chargeable gain accrues on the disposal of an interest created by or arising under a settlement[9].

1 Formerly known as capital gains tax: see generally the Taxation of Chargeable Gains Act 1992; and CAPITAL GAINS TAXATION. As to the liability of trustees see CAPITAL GAINS TAXATION vol 5(1) (Reissue) para 96 et seq.

2 As to revocable and irrevocable settlements see para 615 ante.

3 See the Taxation of Chargeable Gains Act 1992 s 70; and CAPITAL GAINS TAXATION vol 5(1) (Reissue) para 104. As to the position in relation to the creation of or transfer into a settlement by trustees in the exercise of powers conferred upon them in the transferor settlement see *Roome v Edwards* [1982] AC 279, [1981] 1 All ER 736, HL; *Bond v Pickford* [1983] STC 517, 57 TC 301, CA; *Swires v Renton* [1991] STC 490, 64 TC 315. Unless the context otherwise requires, and subject to the Taxation of Chargeable Gains Act 1992 s 66(4) (see CAPITAL GAINS TAXATION vol 5(1) (Reissue) para 89), 'settled property' means any property held in trust other than nominee property: see s 68; and CAPITAL GAINS TAXATION vol 5(1) (Reissue) para 101. In certain circumstances, the transferor can elect that any gain on the disposal to the trustees of the settlement is to be held over, in which case the trustees' acquisition cost is treated as reduced by the amount of the gain which would otherwise have accrued to the transferor on the disposal: see ss 165, 260 (both as amended); and CAPITAL GAINS TAXATION vol 5(1) (Reissue) paras 108, 328. If the gains are not held over, the settlor is primarily liable for tax upon the disposal into the settlement, although the trustees are liable in certain circumstances: see s 282; and CAPITAL GAINS TAXATION vol 5(1) (Reissue) para 88.

4 See CAPITAL GAINS TAXATION vol 5(1) (Reissue) para 109.

5 See the Taxation of Chargeable Gains Act 1992 s 77 (as substituted and amended); and CAPITAL GAINS TAXATION vol 5(1) (Reissue) para 114. See also, in the case of offshore settlements, s 86 (as amended) (charge to tax on settlor with an interest), s 87 (as amended) (charge to tax on beneficiaries receiving capital payments from trustees); and CAPITAL GAINS TAXATION vol 5(1) (Reissue) para 130 et seq.

6 See ibid s 71(1); and CAPITAL GAINS TAXATION vol 5(1) (Reissue) para 106. As to when a person becomes absolutely entitled as against the trustee see s 60(2); and CAPITAL GAINS TAXATION vol 5(1) (Reissue) para 97. See also *Crowe v Appleby* [1976] 2 All ER 914, [1976] 1 WLR 885, CA.

7 See the Taxation of Chargeable Gains Act 1992 s 73(1) (as amended); and CAPITAL GAINS TAXATION vol 5(1) (Reissue) para 106. If the life interest is an interest in part only of the settled property, the exemption from liability does not apply, but any chargeable gain is proportionately reduced: see s 73(2) (as amended); and CAPITAL GAINS TAXATION vol 5(1) (Reissue) para 106. Neither does the exemption from liability apply if the gain on the disposal to the trustees was held over (see note 3 supra), but the chargeable gain on the death of the person entitled to the life interest is restricted to the amount of the held-over gain or a corresponding part of it: see s 74(2); and CAPITAL GAINS TAXATION vol 5(1) (Reissue) para 106.

8 See ibid s 72; and CAPITAL GAINS TAXATION vol 5(1) (Reissue) para 105. If the life interest is in part only of the settled property, the deemed disposal is only in respect of a corresponding part of the assets: see s 72(1); and CAPITAL GAINS TAXATION vol 5(1) (Reissue) para 105. Also the exemption from liability does not apply if the gain on the disposal to the trustees was held over (see note 3 supra), but the chargeable gain on the death of the person entitled to the life interest is restricted as mentioned in note 7 supra.

9 See ibid ss 76(1) (as amended), 85(1); and CAPITAL GAINS TAXATION vol 5(1) (Reissue) para 143. This includes in particular an annuity or life interest, and the reversion to an annuity or life interest, but there is an exception where the interest disposed of has previously been acquired for a consideration in money or money's worth, other than consideration consisting of another interest under the settlement: see s 76(1) (as amended); and CAPITAL GAINS TAXATION vol 5(1) (Reissue) para 143. As to the liability where a person who has acquired an interest for consideration subsequently becomes absolutely entitled to the settled property see s 76(2); and CAPITAL GAINS TAXATION vol 5(1) (Reissue) para 143. Further, anti-avoidance provisions operate in the context of repatriated foreign settlements and transfers of beneficial interests to non-residents: see CAPITAL GAINS TAXATION vol 5(1) (Reissue) para 140 et seq.

622. Inheritance tax. For the purposes of inheritance tax[1], the creation of a settlement[2] may constitute a transfer of value[3], and, if so, it may constitute a chargeable transfer[4].

The legislation draws a distinction between settlements with an interest in possession and settlements without an interest in possession[5]. An interest in possession may subsist in whole or in part only of settled property[6]. In respect of property comprised in a settlement where there is an interest in possession, liability to inheritance tax may arise[7] on the termination of an interest in possession[8], and on the disposal of an interest in possession[9]. In the case of settled property in which no interest in possession subsists, a periodic charge arises at ten-yearly intervals[10], and there is also a charge where property ceases to be settled property in which no interest in possession subsists (whether it ceases to be comprised in the settlement or otherwise)[11], or on the trustees making a disposition reducing the value of the settled property in which no such interest subsists[12]. There will usually be no transfer of value upon the termination of an interest under a settlement without an interest in possession, although there may be a chargeable transfer upon the death of a settlor with an interest in the settlement[13]. Certain accumulation and maintenance trusts[14] where no interest in possession subsists are in a special position[15].

A person having a limited interest in any property who pays the inheritance tax attributable to the value of that property is entitled to a like charge as if the tax so attributable had been raised by means of a mortgage to him[16]. Any money held on the trusts of a settlement may be expended in paying the tax attributable to the value of any property comprised in the settlement and held on the same trusts[17].

1   As to inheritance tax generally see the Inheritance Tax Act 1984; and INHERITANCE TAXATION; and as to inheritance tax in relation to settled property see INHERITANCE TAXATION vol 24 (Reissue) para 476 et seq.
2   For the meaning of 'settlement' see ibid s 43(2); and INHERITANCE TAXATION vol 24 (Reissue) para 477.
3   For the meaning of 'transfer of value' see ibid s 3; and INHERITANCE TAXATION vol 24 (Reissue) para 409. One situation where the creation of a settlement does not constitute a transfer of value is where the settlor remains beneficially entitled to an interest in possession in the settled property, as he will be deemed to be beneficially entitled to the settled property: see s 49(1); and INHERITANCE TAXATION vol 24 (Reissue) para 480.
4   For the meaning of 'chargeable transfer' see ibid s 2; and INHERITANCE TAXATION vol 24 (Reissue) para 408. As to exempt transfers see INHERITANCE TAXATION vol 24 (Reissue) para 515 et seq. The creation of a settlement with a qualifying interest in possession will usually be potentially exempt: see s 3A (as added and amended); and INHERITANCE TAXATION vol 24 (Reissue) para 442 et seq.
5   As to settlements with an interest in possession see INHERITANCE TAXATION vol 24 (Reissue) para 479 et seq; and as to settlements without an interest in possession see INHERITANCE TAXATION vol 24 (Reissue) para 491 et seq.
6   See the Inheritance Tax Act 1984 s 50; and INHERITANCE TAXATION vol 24 (Reissue) para 482.
7   As to the rate of tax see INHERITANCE TAXATION vol 24 (Reissue) para 407 et seq; and as to the persons liable for the payment of tax see INHERITANCE TAXATION vol 24 (Reissue) para 634 et seq.
8   See the Inheritance Tax Act 1984 s 52; and INHERITANCE TAXATION vol 24 (Reissue) para 486. As to the termination of an interest in possession in particular circumstances see INHERITANCE TAXATION vol 24 (Reissue) para 488–490.
9   See ibid s 51; and INHERITANCE TAXATION vol 24 (Reissue) para 487.
10 See ibid s 64; and INHERITANCE TAXATION vol 24 (Reissue) para 496.
11 See ibid s 65(1)(a); and INHERITANCE TAXATION vol 24 (Reissue) para 499.
12 See ibid s 65(1)(b); and INHERITANCE TAXATION vol 24 (Reissue) para 499.
13 See the Finance Act 1986 s 102 (see INHERITANCE TAXATION vol 24 (Reissue) para 448); and the Inheritance Tax (Double Charges Relief) Regulations 1987, SI 1987/1130 (see INHERITANCE TAXATION vol 24 (Reissue) para 596).
14 See the Inheritance Tax Act 1984 s 71; and INHERITANCE TAXATION vol 24 (Reissue) para 507.
15 The creation of such a settlement is usually a potentially exempt transfer: see ibid s 3A (as added and amended); and INHERITANCE TAXATION vol 24 (Reissue) para 442 et seq. Such settlements are (among other things) not subject to the ten-yearly periodic charge (see ss 58(1)(b), 64; and INHERITANCE TAXATION vol 24 (Reissue) para 491), and in some cases there is no charge where the property ceases to be subject to the accumulation and maintenance trust (see s 71(3), (4); and INHERITANCE TAXATION vol 24 (Reissue) para 507).

16 See ibid s 212(2); and INHERITANCE TAXATION vol 24 (Reissue) para 652. As to the creation of a legal mortgage see para 767 post.

17 See ibid s 212(3); and INHERITANCE TAXATION vol 24 (Reissue) para 652.

(vi) Stamp Duty and Costs

623. Stamp duties. The liability to stamp duty of instruments effecting settlements or executed in relation to settlements is the subject of special statutory provisions discussed elsewhere in this work[1]. A voluntary disposition bearing the appropriate certificate is exempt from duty and from adjudication[2]. A conveyance on sale inter vivos is liable to ad valorem duty and may, without penalty, be stamped within 30 days after execution or 14 days after assessment[3]. A declaration of trust is liable to fixed duty[4].

Nothing in the Settled Land Act 1925 operates to impose any stamp duty on a vesting or other assent[5], and no stamp duty is payable in respect of a vesting order made in place of a vesting or other assent[6].

1 See STAMP DUTIES AND STAMP DUTY RESERVE TAX vol 44(1) (Reissue) para 1001 et seq.
2 See STAMP DUTIES AND STAMP DUTY RESERVE TAX vol 44(1) (Reissue) para 1002.
3 See STAMP DUTIES AND STAMP DUTY RESERVE TAX vol 44(1) (Reissue) para 1027. As to the time for stamping instruments see STAMP DUTIES AND STAMP DUTY RESERVE TAX vol 44(1) (Reissue) para 1020.
4 See STAMP DUTIES AND STAMP DUTY RESERVE TAX vol 44(1) (Reissue) para 1078.
5 For the meaning of 'vesting assent' see para 690 note 8 post.
6 See the Settled Land Act 1925 ss 12(2), 14(2), 37, Sch 2 para 2(2). No ad valorem stamp duty is payable in respect of a vesting deed or order made for giving effect to a settlement existing on 1 January 1926: Sch 2 para 1(8).

624. Costs of preparing settlement. There is a usage that an intending husband pays the costs of the solicitors of his intended wife in respect of the preparation and execution of a marriage settlement[1], and this usage requires the husband to allow the wife's solicitors to prepare the settlement[2]. 'Marriage settlement' in this respect includes any document necessary for the completion of a marriage settlement, any muniments of title or documents of that kind without which the marriage settlement is not complete; and so for instance where real estate is conveyed to trustees upon the trusts of an indenture of even date, the two documents comprise one marriage settlement[3].

1 *Helps v Clayton* (1864) 17 CBNS 553; *Re Lawrance, Bowker v Austin* [1894] 1 Ch 556 at 558–559 per Kekewich J. As to marriage settlements see para 628 et seq post.
2 *Helps v Clayton* (1864) 17 CBNS 553. A similar practice applies in the case of marriage articles, but a strict settlement of land, even if it contains provisions in favour of a husband or wife not otherwise interested in the land, is usually prepared by the solicitor of and at the expense of the settlor: see the Opinion of the Council of the Law Society dated 3 March 1927. Note that it is no longer possible to create strict settlements of land: see para 676 post.
3 *Re Lawrance, Bowker v Austin* [1894] 1 Ch 556 at 558 per Kekewich J.

(2) CAPACITY TO MAKE A SETTLEMENT

625. Capacity in general. In general, any person who can hold and dispose of property can make a settlement of property[1], but there are certain classes of person who are in law either incapable of making a settlement or whose capacity is limited to some extent.

An alien can make a settlement of any real and personal property which he is not by statute prohibited from owning[2].

The property of any person who has been adjudicated bankrupt passes from him and vests in his trustee in bankruptcy[3]. It follows that he cannot make any disposition of his property by way of settlement and this disability lasts until an order is made for his discharge[4].

A child cannot make a binding settlement, whether on marriage or otherwise[5].

A contract to settle property in consideration of marriage by a person suffering from such mental disorder as renders him incapable of understanding the transaction is good if the other party is not aware of the settlor's mental disorder[6].

A deed of settlement by a person suffering from such mental disorder as to be incapable of understanding[7] its nature and contents is void at law, but a disposition during a lucid interval is valid; a settlement by a person suffering from mental disorder might be set aside in equity, even if it is not void at law[8].

1　　See CONTRACT vol 9(1) (Reissue) para 630; PERSONAL PROPERTY vol 35 (Reissue) para 1231; REAL PROPERTY vol 39(2) (Reissue) para 229 et seq; SALE OF LAND para 64 et seq ante. As to the former rules relating to married women see HUSBAND AND WIFE.

2　　See BRITISH NATIONALITY, IMMIGRATION AND RACE RELATIONS vol 4(2) (Reissue) para 66.

3　　See the Insolvency Act 1986 s 306; and BANKRUPTCY AND INSOLVENCY vol 3(2) (Reissue) para 381.

4　　As to property devolving on a bankrupt before discharge see BANKRUPTCY AND INSOLVENCY vol 3(2) (Reissue) para 433.

5　　See CHILDREN AND YOUNG PERSONS vol 5(2) (Reissue) para 685. As to settlements made before 1970 by children with the sanction of the court see CHILDREN AND YOUNG PERSONS vol 5(2) (Reissue) para 688. As to the age of majority see para 605 note 1 ante.

6　　See MENTAL HEALTH vol 30 (Reissue) para 1391 et seq. Cf *Imperial Loan Co v Stone* [1892] 1 QB 599, CA.

7　　As to the degree of understanding required to make a gift see *Re Beaney* [1978] 2 All ER 595, [1978] 1 WLR 770; *Simpson v Simpson* [1992] 1 FLR 601, [1989] Fam Law 20.

8　　See MENTAL HEALTH vol 30 (Reissue) para 1386 et seq; EQUITY vol 16 (Reissue) para 675.

626. Settlements by trustees. Trustees of a settlement may properly settle funds advanced either under an express power of advancement contained in the settlement[1] or under the statutory power of advancement where that applies[2]. Such settlements may be made whenever the particular circumstances of the case warrant that course as being for the benefit of the object of the power[3].

Since the effect of an exercise of a power of advancement is to take the money advanced out of the original settlement, a settlement created in exercise of such a power may contain trusts not only for the beneficiary in whose favour the power is exercised but also for other persons such as his wife and issue[4]. There is a view that, unless the original power permits a delegation of powers and discretions, a settlement made in exercise of a special power of appointment cannot contain any discretionary trusts or powers, other than the ordinary power of advancement[5], since such trusts or powers would infringe the principle *delegatus non potest delegare*[6]. However, the modern view is that the relevant question is simply one of construction of the power[7]. If the power is wide enough to permit resettlement, then the trustees clearly do have the necessary authority to let the money pass out of the settlement and no question of unlawful delegation arises. If the power is not wide enough to permit resettlement, then that is the end of the matter.

1　　*Roper-Curzon v Roper-Curzon* (1871) LR 11 Eq 452; *Re Halsted's Will Trusts, Halsted v Halsted* [1937] 2 All ER 570; *Re Ropner's Settlement Trusts, Ropner v Ropner* [1956] 3 All ER 332n, [1956] 1 WLR 902; *Re Wills' Will Trusts, Wills v Wills* [1959] Ch 1, [1958] 2 All ER 472. As to express powers of advancement see para 667 post.

2　　*Re Ropner's Settlement Trusts, Ropner v Ropner* [1956] 3 All ER 332n, [1956] 1 WLR 902. As to the statutory power of advancement see the Trustee Act 1925 s 32 (as amended) (see CHILDREN AND YOUNG PERSONS vol 5(2) (Reissue) para 679); and para 667 post. The perpetuity period applicable to the resettlement is reckoned from the date of the original settlement: see PERPETUITIES AND ACCUMULATIONS vol 35 (Reissue) para 1062.

3   *Re Wills' Will Trusts, Wills v Wills* [1959] Ch 1, [1958] 2 All ER 472.

4   *Pilkington v IRC* [1964] AC 612, [1962] 3 All ER 622, HL.

5   *Re May's Settlement, Public Trustee v Meredith* [1926] Ch 136; *Re Mewburn's Settlement, Perks v Wood* [1934] Ch 112; *Re Morris' Settlement Trusts, Adams v Napier* [1951] 2 All ER 528, CA.

6   Ie the principle that delegated powers cannot be further delegated. See *Re Boulton's Settlement Trusts, Stewart v Boulton* [1928] Ch 703; *Re Morris' Settlement Trusts, Adams v Napier* [1951] 2 All ER 528, CA; *Re Hunter's Will Trusts, Gilks v Harris* [1963] Ch 372, [1962] 3 All ER 1050. See also *Re Hay's Settlement Trusts* [1981] 3 All ER 786, [1982] 1 WLR 202; cf *Re Wills' Will Trusts, Wills v Wills* [1959] Ch 1, [1958] 2 All ER 472. See further POWERS.

7   See *Pilkington v IRC* [1964] AC 612 at 639, [1962] 3 All ER 622 at 630, HL, per Viscount Radcliffe.

(3) CONTRACTS FOR SETTLEMENTS

(i) Contracts in general

627. Contracts in general. The great majority of contracts for settlements are made in contemplation of marriage[1], but such contracts may be made on other occasions[2]. Such contracts are now required to be in writing or evidenced by writing[3].

1   Such contracts are usually called 'marriage articles': see para 628 et seq post.

2   The most relevant modern example is that of an interim trust deed in an occupational pension scheme which is executed pending the execution of the definitive trust deed and rules: see eg *In re Imperial Foods Ltd Pension Scheme* [1986] 2 All ER 802, [1986] 1 WLR 717. Another example is a contract to make a gift by will: see WILLS vol 50 (Reissue) para 268 et seq.

3   See the Statute of Frauds (1677) s 4 (as amended); and CONTRACT vol 9(1) (Reissue) para 623. Contracts to settle land are within the provisions of the Law of Property (Miscellaneous Provisions) Act 1989 s 2: see CONTRACT vol 9(1) (Reissue) para 624; SALE OF LAND para 29 ante. As to contracts to settle land see paras 642–643 post.

(ii) Contracts to settle Property on Marriage

A. MARRIAGE ARTICLES

628. Definitions. Articles are clauses of a document, and hence the word 'articles' sometimes means the document itself. 'Marriage articles' commonly means a contract in consideration of marriage to settle property on terms intended to be embodied subsequently in a formal marriage settlement[1].

1   See para 629 et seq post.

629. Mode of carrying marriage articles into effect. The trusts created by marriage articles are, in most instances, in the nature of executory trusts[1]. A court of equity, therefore, directs a settlement in accordance with the intention of the parties rather than the technical meaning attached to the words used[2], and, if necessary, inserts words in order to give effect to such intention[3]. However, the legal construction of an executed settlement is not affected by proof that the settlement is not such as the court would have directed in accordance with the articles[4], but the court may rectify a settlement to give effect to marriage articles[5].

1   As to executory interests see REAL PROPERTY vol 39(2) (Reissue) para 173 et seq. Articles may so finally declare the intention of the parties that no future instrument is required to carry it out, the trusts being perfect on the articles as they stand (*De Havilland v De Saumarez, De Havilland v Bingham* (1865) 14 WR 118; cf *Johnstone v Mappin* (1891) 60 LJ Ch 241), but as a rule they are treated by the court as short notes

to be developed afterwards at length according to the usual course of settlements (*Marchioness of Blandford v Dowager Duchess of Marlborough* (1743) 2 Atk 542 at 545; *Taggart v Taggart* (1803) 1 Sch & Lef 84; *Bushell v Bushell* (1803) 1 Sch & Lef 90; and see *Randall v Willis* (1800) 5 Ves 262 at 275; *Fegan v Meegan* [1900] 2 IR 441).

2   *Webb v Kelly* (1825) 3 LJOS Ch 172; *Sackville-West v Viscount Holmesdale* (1870) LR 4 HL 543. This latter case was one of a will, but there is no distinction between an executory trust in marriage articles and in a will except that the object and purpose of the former furnish an indication of intention which in the latter must appear in some manner on the face of the instrument: *Sackville-West v Viscount Holmesdale* supra at 554; *Blackburn v Stables* (1814) 2 Ves & B 367. As to executory trusts see TRUSTS vol 48 (Reissue) paras 568–570.

3   *Kentish v Newman* (1713) 1 P Wms 234; *Targus v Puget* (1750) 2 Ves Sen 194.

4   *Doe d Daniell v Woodroffe* (1842) 10 M & W 608; affd (1849) 2 HL Cas 811. As to the construction of written instruments see DEEDS AND OTHER INSTRUMENTS.

5   *Cogan v Duffield* (1876) 2 ChD 44, CA. The proper remedy in such a case is the rectification of the settlement: see *Roberts v Kingsly* (1749) 1 Ves Sen 238; and MISTAKE. The court does not alter an agreement: *Earl of Warrington v Langham* (1699) Prec Ch 89.

630. Covenants to settle by deed or will.

A covenant to make a settlement either by deed or will is satisfied if the provisions are carried out by will[1]. If the covenant is to make provision for children or grandchildren by deed or will, the covenantor is not bound to make provision for children who die in his lifetime[2].

If a covenantor who has covenanted to settle property fails to fulfil his covenant, the remedies of the covenantee at the covenantor's death are either against any property specifically made subject to the covenant and of which the covenantor has not disposed in his lifetime[3], or are in damages against his estate[4]. A covenant to leave a specific sum by will constitutes a debt against the covenantor's estate[5]. Contracts to make wills are discussed elsewhere[6].

The wife's claim under a covenant by her husband in marriage articles to leave her, by deed or will, a sum of money at his death if she should survive him is satisfied either in whole or part, on his death intestate, out of her interest in his estate under his intestacy[7]. However, if he is bound to carry out the covenant in his lifetime, then on his death intestate, without making the agreed provision, there is a clear breach of the covenant and she is entitled to the agreed sum in addition to her interest under his intestacy[8]. The same applies if the covenant is to leave the wife an annuity; her rights under his intestacy are not a performance of the covenant either wholly or partly[9].

1   See *Jones v How* (1850) 7 Hare 267; *Re Brookman's Trust* (1869) 5 Ch App 182. As to the doctrine of satisfaction see EQUITY vol 16 (Reissue) para 857 et seq. For a case invoking a question of this doctrine in relation to marriage articles see *Lady Thynne v Earl of Glengall* (1848) 2 HL Cas 131. As to the satisfaction of debts by legacies see EQUITY vol 16 (Reissue) para 869.

2   See WILLS vol 50 (Reissue) para 270. See also *Needham v Smith* (1828) 4 Russ 318.

3   See LIEN vol 28 (Reissue) paras 777–778. Where the covenant was to leave specified property of the covenantor by will, then, in the absence of notice (now to be given, in the case of unregistered land, by registration under the Land Charges Act 1972 (see para 643 post)), the remedy against the property lies only against volunteers (see *Synge v Synge* [1894] 1 QB 466, CA) and, it seems, only if the covenant was for good consideration (see LIEN vol 28 (Reissue) para 777). As to the protection of rights affecting registered land see LAND REGISTRATION vol 26 (Reissue) para 1098 et seq.

4   See *Synge v Synge* [1894] 1 QB 466, CA; and WILLS vol 50 (Reissue) para 269. If, where the covenant was to leave specific property by will, the covenantor disposed of it in his lifetime in a manner contrary to the covenant, an action for breach of contract would arise on the disposition: *Synge v Synge* supra at 471.

5   See *Eyre v Monro* (1857) 3 K & J 305; and WILLS vol 50 (Reissue) para 269. As to the payment of debts in the administration of estates see EXECUTORS AND ADMINISTRATORS.

6   See WILLS vol 50 (Reissue) paras 268–269.

7   As to the doctrine of performance see EQUITY vol 16 (Reissue) para 872 et seq. See also *Blandy v Widmore* (1715) 1 P Wms 324; *Lee v D'Aranda* (1747) 1 Ves Sen 1; *Garthshore v Chalie* (1804) 10 Ves 1; *Goldsmid v Goldsmid* (1818) 1 Swan 211. Cf *Thacker v Key* (1869) LR 8 Eq 408. As to a widow's share on her husband's intestacy see EXECUTORS AND ADMINISTRATORS.

8   *Oliver v Brickland* (1732) cited in 3 Atk at 420, 422; *Wright v Fearris* (1791) 3 Swan 681; *Lang v Lang* (1837) 8 Sim 451.

9   *Couch v Stratton* (1799) 4 Ves 391; *Salisbury v Salisbury* (1848) 6 Hare 526; *James v Castle* (1875) 33 LT 665. See also *Creagh v Creagh* (1845) 8 I Eq R 68, where the covenant was to provide a jointure; and *Young v Young* (1871) IR 5 Eq 615. As to jointure see para 725 post.

631. Articles for settlement of land. Before the commencement of the Trusts of Land and Appointment of Trustees Act 1996, marriage articles relating to land were directed to be carried out as strict settlements[1]. By virtue of that Act, it is no longer possible to create new strict settlements of land[2]. A marriage settlement of land, other than one created before that Act came into force[3], must therefore take effect behind a trust of land within the meaning of the Act[4].

Before the commencement of the Trusts of Land and Appointment of Trustees Act 1996, limitations in marriage articles in favour of the issue of the bodies of the husband and wife or of the issue of the marriage were carried out by directing a strict settlement giving fees tail to the sons, with remainders in tail to the daughters[5]. However, the Act has abolished entailed interests so that where a person purports by an instrument coming into operation after the commencement of the Act to grant to another person an entailed interest, the instrument is not effective to grant an entailed interest, but operates instead as a declaration that the property is held on trust absolutely for the person to whom an entailed interest in the property was purportedly granted[6].

If the issue are directed by the articles to take absolute interests, the children of the marriage take as tenants in common and not as joint tenants[7], and the usual directions for vesting at majority or on marriage and survivorship and accruer clauses are inserted in the settlement[8].

No portion of any provision made by executory articles for a class merges in the residue by reason of the death of members of the class while any one member of the class remains, and that one member takes the whole provision made for the class[9].

1   Before 1926, the courts would direct marriage articles to be carried out by the creation of strict settlements rather than by fee simple or fee tail, notwithstanding the terms of the marriage articles, on the basis that it was contrary to the fundamental nature of marriage articles that the settlement could be immediately destroyed by the settlor: see eg *Rossiter v Rossiter* (1863) 14 I Ch R 247. It was otherwise in the case of fee tails, where the fee tail could not be barred by the first taker alone, in which case the settlement followed the words of the articles: see *Howel v Howel* (1751) 2 Ves Sen 358; *Highway v Banner* (1785) 1 Bro CC 584.

2   See the Trusts of Land and Appointment of Trustees Act 1996 s 2; and para 676 post.

3   Ie 1 January 1997: see the Trusts of Land and Appointment of Trustees Act 1996 (Commencement) Order 1996, SI 1996/2974; and para 676 post.

4   See the Trusts of Land and Appointment of Trustees Act 1996 ss 1, 2; and paras 609 ante, 676 post.

5   *West v Errissey* (1726) P Wms 349, HL; *Villiers v Villiers* (1740) Atk 71; *Hart v Middlehurst* (1746) 3 Atk 371; *Bash v Dalway* (1747) 3 Atk 530; *Dod v Dod* (1755) Amb 274; *Hamilton v Cathcart* (1777) Wallis by Lyne 282; *Phillips v James* (1865) 3 De GJ & Sm 72; *Grier v Grier* (1872) LR 5 HL 688. Cf *Lord Glenorchy v Bosville* (1733) Cas temp Talb 3; and see *Randall v Daniel* (1857) 24 Beav 193. For cases where the daughters have been excluded see *Powell v Price* (1729) 2 P Wms 535; *M'guire v Scully* (1829) Beat 370. 'Issue male' of a marriage has been held not to include the son of a daughter: *Lambert v Peyton* (1860) 8 HL Cas 1. 'Male issue' has been similarly construed, but not 'male descendants': *Re du Cros' Settlement, du Cros Family Trustee Co Ltd v du Cros* [1961] 3 All ER 193; [1961] 1 WLR 1252. As to entailed interests see para 715 et seq post; and REAL PROPERTY vol 39(2) (Reissue) para 117 et seq.

6   See the Trusts of Land and Appointment of Trustees Act 1996 s 2, Sch 1 para 5; and para 677 post.

7   As to tenancies in common and joint tenancies see REAL PROPERTY vol 39(2) (Reissue) para 189 et seq.

8   *Roche v Roche* (1845) 2 Jo & Lat 561; *Re Martin's Trusts* (1857) 6 I Ch R 211; *Cronin v Roche* (1858) 8 I Ch R 103; *Herring-Cooper v Herring-Cooper* [1905] 1 IR 465. Cf *Re Parrott, Walter v Parrott* (1886) 33 ChD 274, CA; *Wright v Wright* [1904] 1 IR 360 (both cases on wills); but see *Hynes v Redington* (1844) 1 Jo & Lat 589. As to the age of majority see para 605 note 1 ante. As to the directions for vesting see para 634 post.

9   *Hynes v Redington* (1834) L & G temp Plunk 33. See further WILLS vol 50 (Reissue) para 418 et seq.

632. Articles for settlement of personalty. Principles similar to those relating to the settlement of land prevail where the articles are for the settlement of personalty[1]. So far as the articles expressly provide for the destination of the capital or income the court must follow them, but in construing them it has regard to what is recognised as the usual form of settlement[2]. In accordance with this principle, a life interest has been given to the wife in personalty where articles stipulated that it should be settled on her, even though there was a subsequent provision that the income should in all cases belong to the husband[3]. A direction in a deed that a fund should be settled upon a woman and her issue has been carried out by settling the property on her for life, and after her death for her issue as she should by deed or will appoint, with trusts for her issue *per stirpes* in default of appointment, and in default of issue as she should by will appoint, and in default of such appointment to her personal representatives[4].

1   As to the principles relating to the settlement of land see para 631 ante.
2   As to the usual trusts in a settlement of personalty see para 915 et seq post. As to the manner in which directions in a will to settle personalty by reference to the limitations of realty have been carried out see *Shelley v Shelley* (1868) LR 6 Eq 540; *Sackville-West v Viscount Holmesdale* (1870) LR 4 HL 543; *Re Beresford-Hope, Aldenham v Beresford-Hope* [1917] 1 Ch 287; *Re Steele's Will Trusts, National Provincial Bank Ltd v Steele* [1948] Ch 603, [1948] 2 All ER 193. As to the manner of settling personalty to devolve with realty see paras 937–943 post.
3   *Byam v Byam* (1854) 19 Beav 58.
4   *Stanley v Jackman* (1857) 23 Beav 450. Cf *Stonor v Curwen* (1832) 5 Sim 264; *Combe v Hughes* (1872) LR 14 Eq 415 (both cases on wills). In *Samuel v Samuel* (1845) 14 LJ Ch 222, which was also a case on a will, the mother took the property absolutely. Where articles provided that the wife, in the event (which happened) of her surviving her husband, should settle and hand over two-thirds of any property remaining at the time to her children, she was held in her own right entitled to one-third of the property of which her husband died possessed: *M'Donnell v M'Donnell* (1843) 2 Con & Law 481. If the husband had survived, his obligation to settle two-thirds of his property would have been satisfied by a disposition by will: *M'Donnell v M'Donnell* supra. See also *Hankes v Jones* (1756) 5 Bro Parl Cas 136, HL. As to trusts for issue *per stirpes* in default of appointment see WILLS vol 50 (Reissue) para 628 et seq.

633. Provision for husband or wife. A direction in a will that, on the marriage of the testator's daughter, certain property should be settled for her and her issue may authorise the insertion in a settlement made on the daughter's marriage of a power to appoint a life interest to her husband[1]. Provision for an annuity by way of jointure to a widow may be authorised by a direction contained in a will that, in the event of a son marrying, his property should be put into strict settlement[2]. A husband has been entirely excluded from the trusts in default of appointment contained in a settlement made under a direction in a will that the shares of the testator's daughters should be settled on them strictly[3].

1   *Charlton v Rendall* (1853) 11 Hare 296. As to life interests see para 716 post.
2   *Wright v Wright* [1904] 1 IR 360. As to annuities see para 726 post.
3   *Loch v Bagley* (1867) LR 4 Eq 122. Note that it is no longer possible to create strict settlements of land: see para 676 post.

634. Usual powers and provisions authorised. A clause in marriage articles that the settlement is to contain all usual powers and provisions has been held to authorise the insertion of powers for the management and better enjoyment of the settled estates which are beneficial to all parties[1], such as powers of sale and exchange and reinvestment[2], leasing[3], cutting timber in due course of management[4], changing securities[5] and appointing new trustees[6]. Powers of maintenance, education and advancement have also been ordered to be inserted[7]. On the other hand, powers of jointuring and charging portions in favour of younger children are not inserted[8], unless expressly provided for by the articles[9], and a covenant to settle after-acquired property is not a usual clause[10].

A reference to specific powers has been held to exclude others[11]. A power of appointment among the children of the intended marriage should be inserted[12] unless the executory articles contain directions for equal division among children[13].

1   *Hill v Hill* (1834) 6 Sim 136 at 145. As to what are 'usual' powers see POWERS. Having regard to the wide range of the powers conferred by the Settled Land Act 1925 (see para 795 et seq post) and by the Trusts of Land and Appointment of Trustees Act 1996 (see para 902 et seq post), it will be unnecessary in future in a normal case to insert any specific powers of that nature. It may in some cases be desired to vary the statutory powers, but it is submitted that powers more extensive than the statutory powers would not be 'usual'. As to restrictions on the statutory powers see para 782 post; and as to the conferment of additional or larger powers see para 880 post.

2   *Peake v Penlington* (1813) 2 Ves & B 311; *Hill v Hill* (1834) 6 Sim 136. Cf *Wise v Piper* (1880) 13 ChD 848, distinguishing *Wheate v Hall* (1809) 17 Ves 80. A power of sale may be authorised by implication: see *Elton v Elton (No 2)* (1860) 27 Beav 634; and POWERS.

3   This includes powers of granting building or mining leases: *Hill v Hill* (1834) 6 Sim 136; *Scott v Steward* (1859) 27 Beav 367. See also *Duke of Bedford v Marquess of Abercorn* (1836) 1 My & Cr 312; and POWERS. Cf *Turner v Sargent* (1853) 17 Beav 515. However, the provisions of the articles must be followed strictly: *Pearse v Baron* (1821) Jac 158; cf *Brasier v Hudson* (1837) 9 Sim 1 at 11.

4   *Davenport v Davenport* (1863) 1 Hem & M 775.

5   *Sampayo v Gould* (1842) 12 Sim 426.

6   *Sampayo v Gould* (1842) 12 Sim 426. See also *Brasier v Hudson* (1837) 9 Sim 1; *Lindow v Fleetwood* (1835) 6 Sim 152.

7   *Turner v Sargent* (1853) 17 Beav 515; *Re Parrott, Walter v Parrott* (1886) 33 ChD 274, CA. See also *Spirett v Willows* (1869) 4 Ch App 407. The statutory powers of maintenance and advancement (see para 667 post) will in most cases be sufficient.

8   Neither power is a usual power within the meaning of an agreement to make a settlement with all the usual powers: see POWERS. As to jointure see para 725 post.

9   *Duke of Bedford v Marquess of Abercorn* (1836) 1 My & Cr 312; *Grier v Grier* (1872) LR 5 HL 688. See also *Higginson v Barneby* (1826) 2 Sim & St 516; *Wright v Wright* [1904] 1 IR 360; and note 8 supra. Where the articles were for a strict settlement, to contain a power to the father to charge £1,000 for younger children, it was said that it might well be contended that the court would insert a clause to charge the estate with £1,000 with power only to the father to apportion the shares: *Savage v Carroll* (1810) 1 Ball & B 265 at 276. However, this dictum was doubted in *Re Whitcroft's Estate* [1934] IR 649. In *Re Gowan, Gowan v Gowan* (1880) 17 ChD 778 (a case on a will) a hotchpot clause was ordered to be inserted, but in *Lees v Lees* (1871) IR 5 Eq 549 the court declined to insert such a clause. As to hotchpot clauses see para 924 post.

10   *Re Maddy's Estate, Maddy v Maddy* [1901] 2 Ch 820. As to after-acquired property see para 644 et seq post.

11   *Brewster v Angell* (1820) 1 Jac & W 625; *Pearse v Baron* (1821) Jac 158.

12   *Thompson v Simpson* (1841) 1 Dr & War 459. See also *Young v Macintosh* (1843) 13 Sim 445; *Oliver v Oliver* (1878) 10 ChD 765; *Re Gowan, Gowan v Gowan* (1880) 17 ChD 778.

13   *Re Parrott, Walter v Parrott* (1886) 33 ChD 274, CA. A power of appointment given by articles to a husband has been held not to be indefinite, but confined to the issue of the marriage, the intention being to secure a provision for the intended wife and such issue: *Bristow v Warde* (1794) 2 Ves 336. However, this case cannot be taken to establish a general rule: see *Mackinley v Sison* (1837) 8 Sim 561 at 567; *Peover v Hassel* (1861) 1 John & H 341 at 346; *Minton v Kirwood* (1868) 3 Ch App 614 at 618.

635. Satisfaction of covenant to pay money. If a covenant is to pay to the wife a certain sum after the husband's death, and the husband by his will leaves her an equal or greater sum, the court, with some reluctance, has adhered to the rule[1] that, where there is a debt due from the testator to a person, and the legacy given to that person is as much as or more than the debt, then the legacy is a satisfaction of the debt[2]. However, each case turns largely on the construction of the particular covenant and will, and the court has allowed the wife to take both the provision made for her by the articles and that made by the will on grounds of difference of value between the two provisions[3], or where the will has contained a direction to pay the testator's debts[4].

1   As to the doctrine of satisfaction generally see EQUITY vol 16 (Reissue) para 857 et seq.

2   See *Atkinson v Littlewood* (1874) LR 18 Eq 595; and EQUITY vol 16 (Reissue) para 869. See also *Lady Herne v Herne* (1706) 2 Vern 555 (where a wife was put to election to waive the marriage articles or the

will); *Corus v Farmer* (1707) 2 Eq Cas Abr 34; *Bridges v Bere* (1708) 2 Eq Cas Abr 34; *Lord Mountague v Maxwell* (1716) 4 Bro Parl Cas 598. When a husband covenanted that his executors would in each year during her life make up the wife's income to a stated sum, the covenant was held to have been performed by a direction to pay the income of his residuary estate to her for life: *Re Hall, Hope v Hall* [1918] 1 Ch 562.

3   *Jobson v Pelly* (1744) 9 Mod Rep 437; *Haynes v Mico* (1781) 1 Bro CC 129 (where the covenant was to pay a sum within one month after the husband's death, and the legacy was payable six months afterwards); *Devese v Pontet* (1785) 1 Cox Eq Cas 188 (where a share of residue was held not to be a satisfaction); *Kirkman v Kirkman* (1786) 2 Bro CC 95; *Rhodes v Rhodes* (1790) 1 Ves 96.

4   *Cole v Willard* (1858) 25 Beav 568, dissenting from *Wathen v Smith* (1819) 4 Madd 325, where Leach V-C considered that a testator must not be understood to include under the word 'debt' his liability on bond or covenant made before his marriage, even though it would be discharged after his death. As to the effect of a direction in the covenantor's will to pay his debts see *Re Hall, Hope v Hall* [1918] 1 Ch 562 (see note 2 supra); *Re Manners, Public Trustee v Manners* [1949] Ch 613, [1949] 2 All ER 201.

636. Variation of articles or settlement. The contracting parties to a marriage may, if they please, vary marriage articles by other articles before marriage[1]. Also, although a court of equity does not allow the parties to revoke before the marriage an executed settlement simply because they wish to insert provisions different from those which they desired at the time the settlement was executed[2], if the marriage contract is put an end to so that, even if a marriage subsequently took place between the parties it would, strictly speaking, be not the same marriage but another marriage than the one intended, the court has declared an executed settlement not to be binding[3].

1   *Legg v Goldwire* (1736) Cas *temp* Talb 20; *Cook v Fryer* (1842) 1 Hare 498; *Re Gundry, Mills v Mills* [1898] 2 Ch 504 at 509. It was, however, doubted whether the principle applies to a covenant to settle after-acquired property: *Re Gundry, Mills v Mills* supra at 509. As to rectification where a settlement, whether ante-nuptial or post-nuptial, differs from articles entered into before marriage see MISTAKE. As to after-acquired property see para 644 et seq post.

2   *Page v Horne* (1848) 11 Beav 227; *Bond v Walford* (1886) 32 ChD 238 at 242. See also *Re Gundry, Mills v Mills* [1898] 2 Ch 504; and cf *Goodwin v Goodwin* (1658) 1 Rep Ch 173; *Chadwick v Doleman* (1705) 2 Vern 528 at 529.

3   *Robinson v Dickenson* (1828) 3 Russ 399; *Thomas v Brennan* (1846) 15 LJ Ch 420; *Bond v Walford* (1886) 32 ChD 238. However, where, in contemplation of a marriage that did not take place, a spinster vested property in trustees upon trust for herself until her marriage, if any, the settlement was held to be irrevocable: *M'Donnell v Hesilrige* (1852) 16 Beav 346. As to the variation of settlements after a decree of divorce, nullity or judicial separation see para 603 note 1 ante; and DIVORCE.

B.   INFORMAL CONTRACTS TO SETTLE PROPERTY ON MARRIAGE

637. Requisites for enforceable contracts. An offer to make a settlement in the event of a marriage taking place may, by a marriage following on the offer, become a contract binding on all parties concerned[1]. No formal document is required to enable such a contract to be enforced[2], but it must comply with the following conditions:

(1)   any agreement to settle land must satisfy the requirements of the Law of Property (Miscellaneous Provisions) Act 1989[3];

(2)   there must be a definite offer which is turned into a contract by the celebration of the marriage[4]; a mere representation of intention to do something in the future does not suffice[5];

(3)   there must be at least reasonable certainty as to the amount and nature of the property to which the contract applies[6], although parol evidence may be admissible to explain ambiguities[7]; and

(4)   it must be proved that the marriage took place on the faith of the offer[8]; so it necessarily follows that the offer must be communicated to the person seeking to enforce it[9].

A contract so created may be enforced, if a marriage takes place on the faith of the offer, whether the offer has been made by one of the parties to the marriage to the other[10] or made by a third person to either of them[11].

1   *Hammersley v Baron De Biel* (1845) 12 Cl & Fin 45, HL; *Maunsell v White* (1854) 4 HL Cas 1039.
2   *Baron De Biel v Thomson* (1841) 3 Beav 469. A contract for a settlement could be made out by a correspondence: *Moore v Hart* (1683) 1 Vern 110; *Douglas v Vincent* (1690) 2 Vern 202; *Wankford v Fotherley* (1694) 2 Vern 322 (affd (1695) 15 Lords Journals 531, HL); *Herbert v Earl of Winchelsea* (1714) 1 Bro Parl Cas 145; *Seagood v Meale and Leonard* (1721) Prec Ch 560; *Saunders v Cramer* (1842) 3 Dr & War 87; *Luders v Anstey* (1799) 4 Ves 501; *Montgomery v Reilly* (1827) 1 Bli NS 364, HL; *Laver v Fielder* (1862) 32 Beav 1; *Coverdale v Eastwood* (1872) LR 15 Eq 121; *Keays v Gilmore* (1874) IR 8 Eq 290; *Viret v Viret* (1880) 50 LJ Ch 69.
3   See the Law of Property (Miscellaneous Provisions) Act 1989 s 2; and paras 642–643 post. See also SALE OF LAND para 29 et seq ante.
4   Expressions such as 'her share' (*Laver v Fielder* (1862) 32 Beav 1) and 'a child's share' (*Keays v Gilmore* (1874) IR 8 Eq 290) have been held to be sufficiently precise to amount to definite offers. See also *Luders v Anstey* (1799) 4 Ves 501; *Saunders v Cramer* (1842) 3 Dr & War 87; *Hammersley v Baron De Biel* (1845) 12 Cl & Fin 45, HL; *Shadwell v Shadwell* (1860) 9 CBNS 159; *Alt v Alt* (1862) 4 Giff 84; *Walford v Gray* (1865) 11 Jur NS 106 at 473; *Coverdale v Eastwood* (1872) LR 15 Eq 121; *Synge v Synge* [1894] 1 QB 466, CA; *Skeete v Silberberg* (1895) 11 TLR 491; *Re Broadwood, Edwards v Broadwood (No 2)* (1912) 56 Sol Jo 703, CA; *Re Lindrea, Lindrea v Fletcher* (1913) 109 LT 623.
5   *Moorhouse v Colvin* (1851) 15 Beav 341; *Maunsell v White* (1854) 4 HL Cas 1039; *Re Fickus, Farina v Fickus* [1900] 1 Ch 331. See also *Randall v Morgan* (1805) 12 Ves 67; *Madox v Nowlan* (1824) Beat 632; *Quinlan v Quinlan* (1834) Hayes & Jo 785; *Jorden v Money* (1854) 5 HL Cas 185; *Beaumont v Carter, Carter v Beaumont* (1863) 32 Beav 586; *M'Askie v M'Cay* (1868) IR 2 Eq 447; *Re Allen, Hincks v Allen* (1880) 49 LJ Ch 553; *Vincent v Vincent* (1887) 56 LT 243, CA.
6   *Prole v Soady* (1859) 2 Giff 1 at 22; *Kay v Crook* (1857) 3 Sm & G 407. See also *Moorhouse v Colvin* (1852) 21 LJ Ch 782; *M'Askie v M'Cay* (1868) IR 2 Eq 447; *Re Allen, Hincks v Allen* (1880) 49 LJ Ch 553.
7   *Laver v Fielder* (1862) 32 Beav 1. See further DEEDS AND OTHER INSTRUMENTS.
8   *Jameson v Stein* (1855) 21 Beav 5; *Goldicutt v Townsend* (1860) 28 Beav 445; *Dashwood v Jermyn* (1879) 12 ChD 776. See also *De Manneville v Crompton* (1813) 1 Ves & B 354. The court may infer that the marriage took place on the faith of the offer from the fact of its taking place immediately after the offer: *Luders v Anstey* (1799) 4 Ves 501; *Alt v Alt* (1862) 4 Giff 84; *Viret v Viret* (1880) 50 LJ Ch 69.
9   *Ayliffe v Tracy* (1722) 2 P Wms 65.
10   *Alt v Alt* (1862) 4 Giff 84; *Viret v Viret* (1880) 50 LJ Ch 69.
11   *Wankford v Fotherley* (1694) 2 Vern 322; *Ramsden v Oldfield and Appleyard* (1720) 4 Vin Abr 453, pl 5; *Hammersley v Baron De Biel* (1845) 12 Cl & Fin 45, HL; *Shadwell v Shadwell* (1860) 9 CBNS 159; *Laver v Fielder* (1862) 32 Beav 1; *Coverdale v Eastwood* (1872) LR 15 Eq 121. As to the parties between whom a contract may be enforced see para 640 post.

638. Effect of completed settlement. There is a presumption, which may, however, be rebutted by sufficient evidence[1], that a completed settlement contains the entire marriage contract, and, unless it is rebutted, representations or promises made by correspondence prior to the settlement which are not carried out by it are not enforced[2].

1   *Hammersley v Baron De Biel* (1845) 12 Cl & Fin 45, HL; *Loxley v Heath* (1860) 1 De GF & J 489 at 493.
2   *Loxley v Heath* (1860) 1 De GF & J 489; *Sands v Soden* (1862) 31 LJ Ch 870; *Re Badcock, Kingdon v Tagert* (1880) 17 ChD 361. Cf *White v Anderson* (1850) 1 I Ch R 419. As to the rectification of marriage settlements see MISTAKE.

C. ENFORCEMENT OF CONTRACTS TO SETTLE PROPERTY ON MARRIAGE

639. Where specific performance decreed. The court will decree specific performance of a contract for which marriage was the consideration after the marriage has taken place[1]. It is no answer to an action to enforce articles that a third person has failed to perform his portion of the contract[2], or even that the person seeking to enforce them has himself failed to perform his part under them[3]; but, if there is anything for him to do in which third persons are interested, the court takes care that he obtains no benefit until he has performed his part of the agreement[4].

Specific performance of marriage articles, as of other contracts, may be refused on the ground of ambiguity and uncertainty[5] or by reason of the agreement being dependent on a contingency which has not happened[6], or the right to it may be lost by conduct amounting to laches[7].

The courts of equity have always supported marriage articles, and have ordered specific performance of them in preference to leaving the parties interested to sue for the recovery of damages[8]. Where the only instrument was a bond given to secure an agreement to settle property on marriage, the bond was considered as articles of agreement for a settlement, and it was held that the obligor could not elect to pay the penalty, but must specifically perform his contract[9].

1   *Haymer v Haymer* (1678) 2 Vent 343. As to the enforcement of contracts to settle land see paras 642–643 post. As to specific performance generally see SPECIFIC PERFORMANCE.
2   *Perkins v Thornton* (1741) Amb 502; *Lloyd v Lloyd* (1837) 2 My & Cr 192. Cf *North v Ansell* (1731) 2 P Wms 618. *Meredeth v Jones* (1687) 1 Vern 463 cannot be considered law.
3   *Wallace v Wallace* (1842) 2 Dr & War 452; *Jeston v Key* (1871) 6 Ch App 610. Cf *Woodcock v Monckton* (1844) 1 Coll 273, where a covenantor was held discharged from his covenant in a marriage settlement executed by him by reason of the failure of another to execute the settlement. See also *Baskerville v Gore* (1701) Prec Ch 186; affd (1703) 2 Vern 448.
4   *Jeston v Key* (1871) 6 Ch App 610; *Re Smith's Trusts* (1890) 25 LR Ir 439. See also *Corsbie v Free* (1840) Cr & Ph 64; and cf *Crofton v Ormsby* (1806) 2 Sch & Lef 583 at 602.
5   *Franks v Martin* (1760) 1 Eden 309; affd 5 Bro Parl Cas 151, HL. See also *Bromley v Jefferies* (1700) 2 Vern 415; and SPECIFIC PERFORMANCE vol 44(1) (Reissue) para 844 et seq.
6   *Whitmel v Farrel* (1749) 1 Ves Sen 256.
7   *Howorth v Deem* (1758) 1 Eden 351. See, however, *Slaney v Slaney* (1714) 5 Bro Parl Cas 113. As to laches generally see EQUITY vol 16 (Reissue) para 925 et seq.
8   *Cannel v Buckle* (1724) 2 P Wms 243; *Vernon v Vernon* (1731) 2 P Wms 594 (affd 1 Bro Parl Cas 267); *Vereker v Lord Gort* (1838) 1 I Eq R 1. See also *Roper v Bartholomew, Butler v Bartholomew* (1823) 12 Price 797.
9   *Hopson v Trevor* (1723) 1 Stra 533; *Chilliner v Chilliner* (1754) 2 Ves Sen 528; *Logan v Wienholt* (1833) 7 Bli NS I 49, HL.

640. Parties between whom a contract is enforceable. Specific performance may be ordered against a contracting party either in his lifetime[1], or after his death against his estate[2]. It may be ordered at the suit of a party to the contract or his personal representative[3], at the suit of the issue of the marriage[4] or even at that of the personal representative of a party intended to be benefited[5].

1   *Sidney v Sidney* (1734) 3 P Wms 269.
2   *Haymer v Haymer* (1678) 2 Vent 343; *Laver v Fielder* (1862) 32 Beav 1; *Jeston v Key* (1871) 6 Ch App 610; *Coverdale v Eastwood* (1872) LR 15 Eq 121. See also *Williams v Williams* (1868) 37 LJ Ch 854; *Keays v Gilmore* (1874) IR 8 Eq 290.
3   *Beswick v Beswick* [1968] AC 58, [1967] 2 All ER 1197, HL.
4   *Trevor v Trevor* (1719) 1 P Wms 622, HL. However see also *Cann v Cann* (1687) 1 Vern 480, where specific performance was refused in a suit by a grandson whose father would have been tenant in tail and could have disentailed. As to entailed interests see para 715 et seq post; and REAL PROPERTY vol 39(2) (Reissue) para 117 et seq. As to the persons coming within the marriage consideration see paras 661–662 post.
5   *Wankford v Fotherley* (1694) 2 Vern 322 (affd (1695) 15 Lords Journals 531, HL); *Lovett v Lovett* (1859) John 118. Cf *Loxley v Heath* (1860) 27 Beav 523 (affd 1 De GF & J 489); *Dennehy v Delaney* (1876) IR 10 Eq 377. A wife's elopement has been held to be no bar to her claim to specific performance: *Sidney v Sidney* (1734) 3 P Wms 269. See also *Blount v Winter, Winter v Blount* (1781) 3 P Wms 276n. As to the court's power to vary a marriage settlement see para 603 note 1 ante.

641. Effect of covenant to settle or charge specified property. A covenant to settle or charge specified land or other specified property of the covenantor creates in favour of the covenantee a lien on that land or property binding on all persons to whom it might come except purchasers for value without notice[1]. A covenant to purchase and settle land of a certain value has been enforced against the representatives of the covenantor who died without purchasing the land, by directing the investment in land of a sum equivalent to what would have been the then actual value of the land if a purchase pursuant to the covenant had been made[2]. If the settlement contains something equivalent to a warranty by the settlor that the settled property is of a certain value, he is liable to make good any deficiency[3], but in each case it is a question of the construction of the particular instrument[4].

1 See LIEN vol 28 (Reissue) para 777. As to the enforcement of contracts to settle land see also paras 642–643 post.

2 *Dowager Lady Suffield v Lord Suffield* (1812) 3 Mer App 699. For a case where in very special circumstances specific performance had become impossible see *Barker v Ivers* (1724) 5 Bro Parl Cas 127, HL.

3 *Taylor v Hossack* (1838) 5 Cl & Fin 380, HL.

4 *Weldon v Bradshaw* (1873) IR 7 Eq 168. See also *Sheffield v Earl of Coventry* (1833) 2 Russ & M 317; *Milward v Milward* (1834) 3 My & K 311; *Napier v Staples* (1859) 10 I Ch R 344.

(iii) Contracts to settle Land

642. Statutory requirements. In order to be binding in law, a contract to settle land[1], must be made in writing incorporating all the terms[2] which the parties have expressly agreed and must be signed[3] by or on behalf of each party to the contract[4].

A person who makes a misrepresentation of fact, and thereby induces a marriage[5], is, in accordance with the principle of estoppel by representation[6], not allowed to deny its truth[7].

1 As to articles for the settlement of land see para 631 ante.

2 The terms may be incorporated in a document either by being set out in it or by reference to some other document: see the Law of Property (Miscellaneous Provisions) Act 1989 s 2(2); and SALE OF LAND para 29 ante. As to contracts made out by correspondence see para 637 note 2 ante.

3 The signature must be so placed to show that it was intended to relate and refer to, and that it does in fact relate and refer to, every part of the instrument: see *Caton v Caton* (1867) LR 2 HL 127. As to the general requirements regarding signature see SALE OF LAND para 39 ante.

4 See the Law of Property (Miscellaneous Provisions) Act 1989 s 2; and SALE OF LAND para 29 ante.

5 As to representations of intention amounting to offers see para 637 ante.

6 See *Jorden v Money* (1854) 5 HL Cas 185 at 207; *Warden v Jones* (1857) 23 Beav 487 at 493 (on appeal 2 De G & J 76); and ESTOPPEL vol 16 (Reissue) para 1038 et seq.

7 *Graves v White* (1680) Freem Ch 57; *Gale v Lindo* (1687) 1 Vern 475; *Hunsden v Cheyney* (1690) 2 Vern 150; *Montefiori v Montefiori* (1762) 1 Wm Bl 363; *Neville v Wilkinson* (1782) 1 Bro CC 543; *Stone v Godfrey* (1854) 5 De GM & G 76; *Maunsell v White* (1854) 4 HL Cas 1039 at 1055; *Jorden v Money* (1854) 5 HL Cas 185; *Bold v Hutchinson* (1855) 3 Eq Rep 743 (affd 5 De GM & G 558); *M'Keogh v M'Keogh* (1870) IR 4 Eq 338. The doctrine does not apply where a solemn deed has been executed from which alone the intention of the parties can be gathered: *Monypenny v Monypenny* (1858) 4 K & J 174 (revsd as to the legal construction of the deed (1859) 3 De G & J 572; affd (1861) 9 HL Cas 114); and see *Kirwan v Burchell* (1859) 10 I Ch R 63. While it is not necessary that the party making the representation should know that it was false (see *Jorden v Money* supra at 212), there must be something in the nature of a warranty of the truth of the representation, and an innocent mistake common to all parties does not give rise to an estoppel by representation (*Merewether v Shaw* (1789) 2 Cox Eq Cas 124; *Ainslie v Medlycott* (1803) 9 Ves 13; *Evans v Wyatt* (1862) 31 Beav 217), although it may give rise to an estoppel by convention. Cf *Amalgamated Investment and Property Co Ltd v Texas Commerce International Bank Ltd* [1982] QB 84, [1981] 3 All ER 577, CA.

643. Covenants to settle land. A covenant to settle land, the covenantor possessing no land, or to purchase and settle land, is satisfied wholly or pro tanto by the purchase of land suitable for settlement, even if no settlement is actually made, and, where the covenantor dies having acquired that land, it is treated as against the persons entitled to his estate as being bound by the trusts of the settlement[1].

A contract or other liability to make a settlement of land entered into after 1925 and prior to 1 January 1997[2], was required to be carried into effect by means of a vesting deed and trust instrument[3]. A settlement of land created after 1 January 1997 (even if created pursuant to a contract entered into before that date) is a trust of land rather than a settlement under the Settled Land Act 1925[4], and therefore the relevant formal requirements are to be found in the Law of Property Act 1925[5].

If the contract relates to unregistered land it should generally be registered as an estate contract[6].

1 See EQUITY vol 16 (Reissue) para 872.
2 Ie the date on which the Trusts of Land and Appointment of Trustees Act 1996 came into force: see the Trusts of Land and Appointment of Trustees Act 1996 (Commencement) Order 1996, SI 1996/2974; and para 676 post.
3 See the Settled Land Act 1925 ss 4, 11; and para 688 et seq post.
4 See the Trusts of Land and Appointment of Trustees Act 1996 s 2; and para 676 post. For the meaning of 'trust of land' see para 676 note 5 post.
5 See the Law of Property Act 1925 ss 52, 53(1)(b); and SALE OF LAND para 40 ante.
6 See the Land Charges Act 1972 s 2(4)(iv); and LAND CHARGES vol 26 (Reissue) para 532. As to the effect of such registration see LAND CHARGES vol 26 (Reissue) para 516. As to the protection of rights affecting registered land see LAND REGISTRATION vol 26 (Reissue) para 1098 et seq.

(4) COVENANTS FOR SETTLEMENT OF AFTER-ACQUIRED PROPERTY

(i) In general

644. Property not specifically settled. A provision sometimes inserted in marriage settlements is a covenant to settle property other than that which is the specific subject of the settlement[1]. Such covenants may be so framed as to sweep in all property, both present and future, even if not specifically referred to[2], of one or both of the contracting parties[3]. Such a covenant is not a 'usual covenant', and ought not to be inserted without express instructions[4]. As it is executory it is enforceable only in favour of parties within the marriage consideration[5], unless the property subsequently becomes vested in the trustees of the settlement[6].

1 *Re Wyatt, Gowan v Wyatt* (1889) 60 LT 920; *Re Rogers' Settlement, Arnott v Rogers* [1951] Ch 450, [1951] 1 All ER 236. See also *Re Benett-Stanford Settlement Trusts, Atwood v Benett-Stanford* [1947] 1 All ER 888.
2 *Caldwell v Fellowes* (1870) LR 9 Eq 410 at 417 per James V-C.
3 Such a covenant may reach property of any kind (*Lewis v Madocks* (1810) 17 Ves 48), either personalty (*Lewis v Madocks* supra) or realty (*Prebble v Boghurst* (1818) 1 Swan 309; *Gubbins v Gubbins* (1825) 1 Dr & Wal 160n), or a leasehold interest (*Lord Churston v Buller* (1897) 77 LT 45). A covenant to settle all the covenantor's after-acquired property is not too vague or general to be enforced: *Re Turcan* (1888) 40 ChD 5, CA; *Re Reis, ex p Clough* [1904] 2 KB 769, CA (affd on other grounds [1905] AC 442, HL). See also *Syrett v Egerton* [1957] 3 All ER 331, [1957] 1 WLR 1130, DC; and DEEDS AND OTHER INSTRUMENTS. As to the effect on such a covenant of the settlor's bankruptcy see BANKRUPTCY AND INSOLVENCY vol 3(2) (Reissue) para 389 et seq.
4 *Re Maddy's Estate, Maddy v Maddy* [1901] 2 Ch 820. As to the usual powers and provisions see para 634 ante.
5 As to persons within the marriage consideration see paras 661–662 post.
6 See para 615 ante.

645. Construction. The question whether property falls within the covenant or not depends in every case upon the construction of the particular covenant[1]. The instrument which contains the covenant is read as a whole, and the generality of the covenant may be cut down by reference to other parts of the instrument[2], or an ambiguity in the covenant may be explained by the recitals[3]. However, a covenant in clear terms is not restricted by a recital[4]. If possible, a covenant must be construed in such a way as not to extend to an interest which, if the covenant applied to it, would be destroyed at the moment of its creation[5].

Covenants to settle are contracts which must be performed in strict accordance with their terms[6]. Therefore general words are rejected, and a covenant to settle property derived from a particular source does not attach to property coming from another source or under another title[7]. If land is purchased out of the proceeds of personal property bound by a covenant of this kind, the land is charged with the money improperly invested[8].

1   *Scholfield v Spooner* (1884) 26 ChD 94, CA; *Re Ellis's Settlement, Ellis v Ellis* [1909] 1 Ch 618. As to covenants to settle property other than that which is the specific subject of the settlement see para 644 ante.
2   *Re Stephenson's Trusts, ex p Stephenson* (1853) 3 De GM & G 969; *Hammond v Hammond* (1854) 19 Beav 29; *Re Neal's Trusts* (1857) 4 Jur NS 6; *Childers v Eardley* (1860) 28 Beav 648; *Young v Smith* (1865) 35 Beav 87; *Re Michell's Trusts* (1878) 9 ChD 5, CA; *Re Garnett, Robinson v Gandy* (1886) 33 ChD 300, CA.
3   *Maclurcan v Lane, Melhuish v Maclurcan* (1858) 5 Jur NS 56; *Re Michell's Trusts* (1878) 9 ChD 5, CA; *Re De Ros' Trust, Hardwicke v Wilmot* (1885) 31 ChD 81, CA; *Re Coghlan, Broughton v Broughton* [1894] 3 Ch 76. See also DEEDS AND OTHER INSTRUMENTS.
4   *Re Owen's Trust* (1855) 1 Jur NS 1069; *Burn-Murdoch v Charlesworth* (1875) 23 WR 743; *Dawes v Tredwell* (1881) 18 ChD 354, CA. See also DEEDS AND OTHER INSTRUMENTS.
5   *Re Crawshay, Walker v Crawshay* [1891] 3 Ch 176; *Re Smith, Franklin v Smith* [1928] Ch 10. In both those cases the covenant preceded the acquisition under another instrument of a protected life interest. However, an attempted assignment by a person already entitled to a protected life interest may cause a forfeiture: see paras 917–918 post.
6   *Re Van Straubenzee, Boustead v Cooper* [1901] 2 Ch 779, where it was held that there is no ground for applying the rule in *Howe v Earl Dartmouth, Howe v Countess of Aylesbury* (1802) 7 Ves 137 (see EXECUTORS AND ADMINISTRATORS), to property settled by such a covenant. See also *Hope v Hope* (1855) 1 Jur NS 770; *Brooke v Hicks* (1864) 10 LT 404.
7   *Williams v Williams* (1782) 1 Bro CC 152; *Tayleur v Dickenson* (1826) 1 Russ 521; *Ibbetson v Grote* (1858) 25 Beav 17; *Childers v Eardley* (1860) 28 Beav 648; *Parkinson v Dashwood* (1861) 30 Beav 49; *Evans v Jennings* (1862) 1 New Rep 178; *Edwards v Broughton* (1863) 32 Beav 667. Cf *Re Stephenson's Trusts, ex p Stephenson* (1853) 3 De GM & G 969; *Re Neal's Trusts* (1857) 4 Jur NS 6; but see *Re Frowd's Settlement* (1864) 4 New Rep 54; *Re Crawshay, Walker v Crawshay* [1891] 3 Ch 176. An assignment of an interest in property for the time being subject to the trusts of a settlement is not a contract to assign any interest that may subsequently be acquired (*Re Walpole's Marriage Settlement, Thomson v Walpole* [1903] 1 Ch 928), and an agreement to settle property to which the covenantor 'may be' entitled does not bind future property (*Re Ridley's Agreement, Ridley v Ridley* (1911) 55 Sol Jo 838).
8   *Lewis v Madocks* (1810) 17 Ves 48.

(ii) Effect of the Covenant on Particular Interests in Property

646. Property incapable of assurance. The proper construction of a covenant to settle after-acquired property is that the property is to be conveyed for such estate and interest as is actually taken in it by the covenantor[1]. Therefore, property which is incapable of assurance[2], or in which the covenantor acquires an interest which cannot be effectively assured, such as an entailed interest[3] or a protected life interest[4], or a mere spes successionis or a contingent claim for damages which could not arise until after the husband's death[5], is not caught by the covenant.

1   See also paras 644–645 ante.

2   See *Re Pearse's Settlement, Pearse v Pearse* [1909] 1 Ch 304.

3   *Hilbers v Parkinson* (1883) 25 ChD 200; *Re Dunsany's Settlement, Nott v Dunsany* [1906] 1 Ch 578, CA. As to entailed interests see para 715 et seq post; and REAL PROPERTY vol 39(2) (Reissue) para 117 et seq. Entailed interests can no longer be created: see paras 609, 611 ante, 677 post.

4   *Brooks v Keith* (1861) 1 Drew & Sm 462; *Re Allnutt, Pott v Brassey* (1882) 22 ChD 275; *Re Currey, Gibson v Way* (1886) 32 ChD 361; *Re Crawshay, Walker v Crawshay* [1891] 3 Ch 176; *Re Smith, Franklin v Smith* [1928] Ch 10. See, however, *Re Haynes' Will Trusts, Pitt v Haynes* [1949] Ch 5, [1948] 2 All ER 243, where the acquisition of the protected life interest preceded the covenant.

5   *Re Simpson, Simpson v Simpson* [1904] 1 Ch 1, CA. See also *Re Mudge* [1914] 1 Ch 115, CA.

647. Property which does not fit the trusts. If the property does not fit the trusts of the settlement, it may be assumed that it was not intended to come within the covenant to settle after-acquired property[1]. In accordance with this principle the covenant has been held, in the absence of express words, not to attach to a life interest[2] or to an annuity[3], or to investments which represent savings of income which is not subject to the covenant[4].

1   *Re Mainwaring's Settlement* (1866) LR 2 Eq 487; *Scholfield v Spooner* (1884) 26 ChD 94, CA.

2   *White v Briggs* (1848) 22 Beav 176n; *St Aubyn v Humphreys* (1856) 22 Beav 175; *Townshend v Harrowby* (1858) 27 LJ Ch 553.

3   *Re Dowding's Settlement Trusts, Gregory v Dowding* [1904] 1 Ch 441. However, a share of residue directed to be applied in the purchase of an annuity is caught by the covenant: *Re Butler, Beatty v Vance* [1916] 1 IR 66.

4   *Finlay v Darling* [1897] 1 Ch 719; *Re Clutterbuck's Settlement, Bloxam v Clutterbuck* [1905] 1 Ch 200 (approved in *Mackenzie v Allardes* [1905] AC 285, HL), dissenting from *Re Bendy, Wallis v Bendy* [1895] 1 Ch 109, which must be taken to be overruled. Cf *Hughes v Jones* (1863) 1 Hem & M 765; *Churchill v Denny* (1875) LR 20 Eq 534; *Re Biscoe, Biscoe v Biscoe* (1914) 111 LT 902.

648. Interests existing at the date of the covenant. Interests existing at the date of the covenant are not caught by a covenant to settle property to which the covenantor is to become entitled during the marriage[1], although such interests will be caught by a covenant which on its true construction extends to present interests[2]. Whether a covenant extends to property to which the covenantor is entitled at the date of the covenant depends upon the language of the particular instrument[3], but such property is not subsequently brought within its operation by reason of an increase in value[4], or by a change of investment[5] or character, as for instance by the sale for a lump sum of an annuity which was not caught by the covenant[6].

1   *Prebble v Boghurst* (1818) 1 Swan 309 at 321; *Hoare v Hornsby* (1843) 2 Y & C Ch Cas 121; *Otter v Melvill* (1848) 2 De G & Sm 257; *Wilton v Colvin* (1856) 3 Drew 617; *Archer v Kelly* (1860) 1 Drew & Sm 300; *Churchill v Shepherd* (1863) 33 Beav 107; *Re Clinton's Trust, Hollway's Fund, Re Clinton's Trust, Weare's Fund* (1871) LR 13 Eq 295; *Re Jones' Will* (1876) 2 ChD 362; *Re Garnett, Robinson v Gandy* (1886) 33 ChD 300, CA; *Re Atkinson's Trusts, ex p Fitzroy* [1895] 1 IR 230. See also *Re Bland's Settlement, Bland v Perkin* [1905] 1 Ch 4; and para 650 note 1 post. Cf *Re Blockley, Blockley v Blockley* (1884) 49 LT 805.

2   See the text and notes 3–6 infra.

3   *Grafftey v Humpage* (1839) 3 Jur 622; *James v Durant* (1839) 2 Beav 177; *Blythe v Granville* (1842) 13 Sim 190; *Maclurcan v Lane, Melhuish v Maclurcan* (1858) 5 Jur NS 56; *Re Hughes's Trusts* (1863) 4 Giff 432; *Rose v Cornish* (1867) 16 LT 786; *Re Viant's Settlement Trusts* (1874) LR 18 Eq 436; *Williams v Mercier* (1884) 10 App Cas 1, HL; *Re Cazenove, Perkin v Bland* (1919) 122 LT 181. Cf *Re Wass, ex p Evans* (1852) 2 De GM & G 948. In some of these cases covenants or agreements binding the husband to settle property to which the wife, or the husband in her right, should become entitled during the marriage were held to cover property to which she was entitled at the date of the covenant, the words of futurity being satisfied by the interest acquired by him immediately on marriage. In some cases the decision was also founded on the language of other parts of the instrument (*Williams v Mercier* (1884) 10 App Cas 1, HL) or on expressions found in instruments other than the settlement (*Hamilton v James* (1877) IR 11 Eq 223; and see *Re Wyndham's Trusts* (1865) LR 1 Eq 290). However, it seems impossible to reconcile all the cases.

4   *Re Browne's Will* (1869) LR 7 Eq 231. Cf *Re Garnett, Robinson v Gandy* (1886) 33 ChD 300, CA.
5   *Mackenzie v Allardes* [1905] AC 285 at 293, HL, per Lord Macnaghten.
6   *Churchill v Denny* (1875) LR 20 Eq 534; *Re Biscoe, Biscoe v Biscoe* (1914) 111 LT 902.

649. Property acquired after the termination of the marriage. As the primary object of a covenant to settle the future property of a wife is to prevent it falling under the control or influence of the husband, in the absence of expressions showing a contrary intention, only property accruing to her during the intended marriage comes within its operation[1]. This is so even though the covenant relates only to property coming from a specified source[2]. On the same principle, a covenant to settle property to be acquired during the intended marriage does not attach to property the title to which has accrued after the making of a decree absolute for divorce[3]. Similarly, property acquired by a wife under her husband's will, unlike property acquired by her from her husband by way of gift inter vivos[4], is prima facie not caught by the covenant[5], nor is a joint interest given to the husband and wife[6].

1   *Howell v Howell, Howell v James* (1835) 4 LJ Ch 242; *Godsal v Webb* (1838) 2 Keen 99; *Reid v Kenrick* (1855) 1 Jur NS 897; *Dickinson v Dillwyn* (1869) LR 8 Eq 546; *Carter v Carter* (1869) LR 8 Eq 551; *Alleyne v Hussey* (1873) 22 WR 203; *Re Edwards* (1873) 9 Ch App 97 (overruling on this point *Stevens v Van Voorst* (1853) 17 Beav 305); *Holloway v Holloway* (1877) 25 WR 575; *Re Coghlan, Broughton v Broughton* [1894] 3 Ch 76. See also *Re Peel's Settlement, Millard v Peel* [1964] 3 All ER 567, [1964] 1 WLR 1232. The fictitious survivorship created by the Wills Act 1837 s 33 (as originally enacted) (which applies in relation to wills of testators who died before 1 January 1983: see WILLS vol 50 (Reissue) paras 405–406), did not prolong the marriage so as to bring within the terms of the covenant property actually acquired after the termination of the marriage: *Pearce v Graham* (1863) 9 Jur NS 568. See now the Wills Act 1837 s 33 (as substituted); and WILLS vol 50 (Reissue) para 407. See also *Re Blundell, Blundell v Blundell* [1906] 2 Ch 222 at 229.
2   *Re Campbell's Policies* (1877) 6 ChD 686.
3   Since a marriage continues until a decree absolute is made (see *Sinclair v Fell* [1913] 1 Ch 155; *Fender v St John-Mildmay* [1938] AC 1, [1937] 3 All ER 402; and DIVORCE), property the title to which accrues between decree nisi and absolute will be caught (see *Sinclair v Fell* supra). *Re Pearson's Trusts* (1872) 26 LT 393, where the contrary was held, must be considered as overruled: *Sinclair v Fell* supra at 166. A covenant to settle property to be acquired during the intended marriage did not attach to property the title to which accrued after the making of a decree of judicial separation: see *Dawes v Creyke* (1885) 30 ChD 500; *Davenport v Marshall* [1902] 1 Ch 82. However, these decisions were based on the Matrimonial Causes Act 1857 s 25 (repealed), which had the effect of putting the wife in the position of a feme sole as regards property, and, in consequence of the repeal of that provision, these decisions can no longer be regarded as applicable. Cf *Re Bankes, Reynolds v Ellis* [1902] 2 Ch 333. See also HUSBAND AND WIFE.
4   See para 653 note 2 post.
5   *Dickinson v Dillwyn* (1869) LR 8 Eq 546; *Carter v Carter* (1869) LR 8 Eq 551.
6   *Edye v Addison* (1863) 1 Hem & M 781.

650. Reversionary interests. A covenant to settle property to which the covenantor may or will at any time during the marriage become entitled does not extend to a reversionary interest which is already vested at the date of the covenant, whether it falls into possession during[1] or after[2] the marriage; but a covenant which binds a wife to settle her present and future property extends to reversionary interests to which she is entitled at the date of the covenant or acquires during the marriage, and a covenant which binds her to settle all her future acquired property extends to reversionary interests to which she becomes entitled during the marriage, notwithstanding in either case that the reversion does not fall in during the marriage[3]. Even if there are technical difficulties in the way of getting a conveyance, such property is bound in the hands of everyone, including the covenantor's personal representatives[4].

1   *Re Bland's Settlement, Bland v Perkin* [1905] 1 Ch 4, followed in *Re Yardley's Settlement, Milward v Yardley* (1908) 124 LT Jo 315; *Re Capel's Trusts, Arbuthnot v Galloway* [1914] WN 378; *Re Thompson's Settlements, Allen v Pack* (1915) 139 LT Jo 211; *Re Maltby Marriage Settlement, Aylen v Gaud* [1953] 2 All ER 220, [1953] 1 WLR 765; *Re Peel's Settlement, Millard v Peel* [1964] 3 All ER 567, [1964] 1 WLR 1232. However, the cases are not easy to reconcile: see *Blythe v Granville* (1842) 13 Sim 190; *Re London Dock Co, ex p Blake* (1853) 16 Beav 463; *Spring v Pride* (1864) 4 De GJ & Sm 395; *Re Clinton's Trust, Hollway's Fund, Re Clinton's Trust, Weare's Fund* (1871) LR 13 Eq 295; *Re Brook, Brook v Hirst* (1914) 111 LT 36; *Re Crook's Settlement, Re Glasier's Settlement, Crook v Preston* [1923] 2 Ch 339.

2   *Re Pedder's Settlement Trusts* (1870) LR 10 Eq 585; *Re Clinton's Trusts, Hollway's Fund, Re Clinton's Trust, Weare's Fund* (1871) LR 13 Eq 295. See also *Cannon v Hartley* [1949] Ch 213, [1949] 1 All ER 50.

3   *Grafftey v Humpage* (1839) 3 Jur 622; *Butcher v Butcher* (1851) 14 Beav 222; *Spring v Pride* (1864) 4 De GJ & Sm 395; *Re Mackenzie's Settlement* (1867) 2 Ch App 345; *Caldwell v Fellowes* (1870) LR 9 Eq 410; *Agar v George* (1876) 2 ChD 706; *Re D'Estampes' Settlement, D'Estampes v Crowe* (1884) 53 LJ Ch 1117; *Re Roy's Settlement, Jebb v Roy* (1906) 50 Sol Jo 256. See also *Giles v Homes* (1846) 15 Sim 359; *Re Hewett, Hewett v Hallett* [1894] 1 Ch 362 at 365; *Lloyd v Prichard* [1908] 1 Ch 265. Cf *Re Brook, Brook v Hirst* (1914) 111 LT 36; *Cannon v Hartley* [1949] Ch 213, [1949] 1 All ER 50.

4   *Lloyd v Prichard* [1908] 1 Ch 265.

651. Contingent and defeasible interests. A covenant which binds a wife to settle all her present and future property extends to contingent or defeasible interests, whether in possession or remainder[1], and whether the contingency happens or the interest becomes indefeasible during or after the marriage[2]. However, a covenant to settle future property only does not extend to a contingent or defeasible interest existing at the date of the covenant merely because it vests in interest or becomes indefeasible during the marriage[3], although it will extend to any such interest which falls into possession during the marriage[4].

1   *Agar v George* (1876) 2 ChD 706; *Cornmell v Keith* (1876) 3 ChD 767; *Re Jackson's Will* (1879) 13 ChD 189; *Re Ware, Cumberlege v Cumberlege-Ware* (1890) 45 ChD 269; *Re Hewett, Hewett v Hallett* [1894] 1 Ch 362 at 365; *Lloyd v Prichard* [1908] 1 Ch 265. *Atcherley v Du Moulin* (1855) 2 K & J 186 and *Dering v Kynaston* (1868) LR 6 Eq 210, where it was held that contingent interests are not within such a covenant, must be treated as overruled: *Agar v George* supra. As to conditions of defeasance see para 740 et seq post.

2   *Brooks v Keith* (1861) 1 Drew & Sm 462; *Agar v George* (1876) 2 ChD 706; *Lloyd v Prichard* [1908] 1 Ch 265.

3   *Re Michell's Trusts* (1878) 9 ChD 5, CA. Cf *Re Cazenove, Perkin v Bland* (1919) 122 LT 181.

4   *Archer v Kelly* (1860) 1 Drew & Sm 300; *Brooks v Keith* (1861) 1 Drew & Sm 462; *Re Worsley's Trusts* (1867) 16 LT 826; *Re Williams' Settlement, Williams v Williams* [1911] 1 Ch 441; *Re Crook's Settlement, Re Glasier's Settlement, Crook v Preston* [1923] 2 Ch 339; *Re Peel's Settlement, Millard v Peel* [1964] 3 All ER 567, [1964] 1 WLR 1232.

652. Interests under appointments and in default of appointment. An interest in default of appointment is a vested or contingent interest (as appropriate) subject to defeasance[1] and is capable of being bound by a covenant to settle present or future acquired property[2], but property acquired under an exercise of a power is derived under a new title, even where there is a gift over to the covenantor in default of appointment, and such property is not caught by a covenant which does not extend to future property[3]. Property over which the covenantor possesses a general power of appointment will not be caught unless the power is so exercised as to bring the property within the covenant[4], even if the covenantor is entitled in default of appointment[5].

1   As to conditions of defeasance see para 740 et seq post. As to powers of appointment see para 922 et seq post.

2   *Re Jackson's Will* (1879) 13 ChD 189.

3   *Sweetapple v Horlock* (1879) 11 ChD 745; *Re De la Bere's Marriage Settlement Trusts, De la Bere v Public Trustee* [1941] Ch 443, [1941] 2 All ER 533. See also *Muir (or Williams) v Muir* [1943] AC 468, HL; *Re Dowie's Will Trusts, Re Marriage Settlement of 24 September 1936, Barlas v Pennefather* [1949] Ch 547, [1949] 1 All ER 968; *Re Maltby Marriage Settlement, Aylen v Gaud* [1953] 2 All ER 220, [1953] 1 WLR 765.

4   *Ewart v Ewart* (1853) 1 Eq Rep 536; *Townshend v Harrowby* (1858) 27 LJ Ch 553; *Bower v Smith* (1871) LR 11 Eq 279.

5   The authorities are conflicting, but it is submitted that the statement in the text represents the better view: see *Townshend v Harrowby* (1858) 27 LJ Ch 553; *Re Lord Gerard, Oliphant v Gerard* (1888) 58 LT 800; *Tremayne v Rashleigh* [1908] 1 Ch 681; *Vetch v Elder* [1908] WN 137. See to the contrary *Steward v Poppleton* [1877] WN 29; *Re O'Connell, Mawle v Jagoe* [1903] 2 Ch 574.

(iii) Express Exceptions from the Covenant

653. Property and interests commonly excepted. It is usual to except from the operation of the covenant to settle after-acquired property: (1) property of less than a specified value acquired from a single source[1]; (2) gifts by the husband to the wife inter vivos[2]; (3) property purchased by the wife with savings from her income[3]; (4) life and other limited interests[4]; (5) jewels and other personal chattels[5]; (6) property which, if bound, would be liable to forfeiture[6]; and (7) property as to which the donor has expressed an intention that it should be exempt from the covenant or any similar provision[7]. Other kinds of property may also be excepted. It is desirable that any property which it is intended to exclude should be expressly mentioned[8].

1   See para 654 post.

2   Prima facie such gifts will be caught by the covenant: *Re Ellis's Settlement, Ellis v Ellis* [1909] 1 Ch 618; *Re Plumptre's Marriage Settlement, Underhill v Plumptre* [1910] 1 Ch 609; *Re Pryce, Neville v Pryce* [1917] 1 Ch 234. However, see to the contrary *Coles v Coles* [1901] 1 Ch 711; *Kingan v Matier* [1905] 1 IR 272. In *Leigh-White v Ruttledge* [1914] 1 IR 135, Barton J followed *Re Ellis's Settlement, Ellis v Ellis* supra, and *Re Plumptre's Marriage Settlement, Underhill v Plumptre* supra, in preference to his own decision in *Kingan v Matier* supra.

3   Such property will probably not be caught: *Finlay v Darling* [1897] 1 Ch 719; *Re Clutterbuck's Settlement, Bloxham v Clutterbuck* [1905] 1 Ch 200; *Mackenzie v Allardes* [1905] AC 285, HL. *Re Bendy, Wallis v Bendy* [1895] 1 Ch 109, where the contrary was decided, must be taken to have been overruled.

4   See *Scholfield v Spooner* (1884) 26 ChD 94. However see to the contrary *Re Dowding's Settlement Trusts, Gregory v Dowding* [1904] 1 Ch 441.

5   See para 656 post.

6   See para 646 ante.

7   See para 657 post.

8   As to the construction of covenants see para 645 ante.

654. Limitation as to amount, time and source. If it is intended to except from the operation of the covenant after-acquired property not exceeding a specified amount, it is usual to provide expressly that this exception is to apply to property acquired at any one time from any one source. Even if the words 'from any one source' are not inserted they are implied, and any particular fund to which the covenantor becomes entitled does not fall within the covenant unless by itself it amounts to the specified sum[1].

A legacy and a share of residue given by the same will are derived under different titles and must not be added together and treated as one sum for the purpose of seeing whether the specified amount is reached[2]; nor in making the computation may there be taken into consideration the value of property which cannot be affected by the covenant at all[3], or to which the covenantor becomes entitled under the same instrument, but not at one and the same time[4]. If property in excess of the specified amount is bequeathed upon such trusts as the covenantor may appoint, with a gift over to a stranger in default of appointment, it is open to the covenantor to defeat the covenant by a series of appointments in his own favour, each of less than the specified amount[5]; but a fund which would otherwise be bound is not withdrawn from the operation of the covenant by reason of a part of it having been paid to the covenantor under a power of advancement[6].

1 *Re Hooper's Trust* (1865) 11 Jur NS 479; *Hood v Franklin* (1873) LR 16 Eq 496; *Re Hughes' Settlement, Hughes v Schooling, Re Smith, Hughes v Schooling* [1924] 2 Ch 356. *St Leger v Magniac* [1880] WN 183, where the covenant was to settle property to which the wife should become entitled 'at one time', and was held to cover sums of money coming from different sources but falling into possession at the same time, would probably not now be followed.

2 *Re Middleton's Will* (1868) 16 WR 1107. Cf *Re Davies, Harrison v Davis* [1897] 2 Ch 204. A legacy out of general estate and another out of real estate should, however, be aggregated for the purposes of the covenant: *Re Pares, Re Scott Chad, Scott Chad v Pares* [1901] 1 Ch 708, which did not purport to differ from *Re Middleton's Will* supra, although it is difficult to see how the two cases can be reconciled. See also *Re Mackenzie's Settlement* (1867) 2 Ch App 345. As to legacies and shares of residue see WILLS vol 50 (Reissue) paras 265, 537.

3 *Forster v Davies* (1861) 4 De GF & J 133.

4 *Buller v Hornby* (1871) 25 LT 901.

5 *Bower v Smith* (1871) LR 11 Eq 279. If the gift over is to the donee of the power, there is a conflict of judicial opinion as to whether the covenant can be evaded by a series of appointments: see *Re O'Connell, Mawle v Jagoe* [1903] 2 Ch 574; *Steward v Poppleton* [1877] WN 29, for authority that it cannot be evaded. For the opposite view see *Townshend v Harrowby* (1858) 27 LJ Ch 553; *Re Lord Gerard, Oliphant v Gerard* (1888) 58 LT 800; *Tremayne v Rashleigh* [1908] 1 Ch 681.

6 *Hood v Franklin* (1873) LR 16 Eq 496. As to powers of advancement see para 667 post.

655. Estimate of value. In estimating whether the specified amount is reached, the beneficial receipt of the covenantor and not the amount of the gift must be considered[1]. Where the interest is reversionary, the value must be ascertained, not by estimating its value as a reversion[2], but according to the actual amount received when it falls into possession[3]. If, as is often the case, the true intention is only to settle interests the value of which as such exceeds a specified amount at the time at which the covenant attaches, it is in the present state of the authorities necessary to frame the clause very carefully[4].

1 *Re Pares, Re Scott Chad, Scott Chad v Pares* [1901] 1 Ch 708.

2 *Re Mackenzie's Settlement* (1867) 2 Ch App 345; *Cornmell v Keith* (1876) 3 ChD 767; *Re Clinton's Trust, Hollway's Fund, Re Clinton's Trust, Weare's Fund* (1871) LR 13 Eq 295 at 306.

3 *Re Hughes' Settlement, Hughes v Schooling, Re Smith, Hughes v Schooling* [1924] 2 Ch 356, where it was pointed out that, although there are passages in the judgments in each of the cases cited in note 2 supra, which suggest that the value should be the value of the property (not the value of the reversionary interest) at the date when the covenant attaches, the question of the date of valuation does not appear to have been before the court in any of those cases. See also *Re Welstead, Welstead v Leeds* (1882) 47 LT 331, where it was held that a reversionary interest which fell in after the termination of the marriage was not brought within the operation of the covenant because the value never exceeded the specified amount during the marriage, although the actual amount received did. The value of an endowment policy effected by a husband in favour of his wife must be ascertained at the time when the policy was effected: *Re Harcourt, White v Harcourt* (1911) 105 LT 747.

4 See note 3 supra.

656. Jewels and personal chattels. If it is desired to except from the operation of the covenant jewels and personal chattels, this must be done by express words, as no such exception is implied[1].

1 *Willoughby v Middleton* (1862) 2 John & H 344. Consumable goods are not included: *Willoughby v Middleton* supra at 355. Such an exception was held not to cover pictures and furniture forming part of an intestate's estate to a share of which the covenantor had become entitled as one of the next of kin: *Vanneck v Benham* [1917] 1 Ch 60. See also *Re Cunliffe-Owen, Mountain v IRC* [1953] Ch 545, [1953] 2 All ER 196, CA.

657. Donor's intention to exempt from the covenant. If the terms of the covenant exempt property as to which, in the instrument under which it is acquired[1], an intention is expressed that it is to be exempt from the covenant or any provision of a like nature, a gift for a declared purpose wholly inconsistent with its application under the covenant is within the exception, whether or not the donor is aware of the covenant[2]. However, if the covenant, on its true construction, does attach to property subsequently acquired, the donor's intention that it should not be bound cannot operate to exclude it[3].

1   Where property is acquired under a power of appointment, the instrument exercising the power is the instrument under which it is acquired: *Sweetapple v Horlock* (1879) 11 ChD 745; *Re De la Bere's Marriage Settlement Trusts, De la Bere v Public Trustee* [1941] Ch 443, [1941] 2 All ER 533; *Muir (or Williams) v Muir* [1943] AC 468 at 485–486, HL, per Lord Romer.
2   *Re Thorne, Thorne v Campbell-Preston* [1917] 1 Ch 360.
3   *Scholfield v Spooner* (1884) 26 ChD 94, CA, overruling on this point *Re Mainwaring's Settlement* (1866) LR 2 Eq 487, which had been followed in the Irish case of *Re Portadown, Dungannon and Omagh Junction Rly Co, ex p Young* (1867) 15 WR 979. See also *Re Wharton, Wharton v Barmby* (1910) 102 LT 531; *Re Thorne, Thorne v Campbell-Preston* [1917] 1 Ch 360; *Re Smith, Franklin v Smith* [1928] Ch 10. However, a settlement can be rectified in appropriate circumstances: see MISTAKE.

(iv) Express Covenants by Husband and Wife

658. What parties are bound. Whether a covenant is binding on the husband alone or on both husband and wife is a question of the construction of the particular instrument. In some cases a covenant in terms made by the husband alone will be binding on him alone notwithstanding that it has been prefaced by the words 'it is hereby agreed and declared'[1]. In general, the party who is to do the thing which is covenanted to be done is alone bound to perform the covenant[2]. On the other hand, where words of general agreement have prefaced a covenant by the husband alone that property coming to the wife, or under the former law to him in her right, is to be settled, the agreement has been treated as an agreement by both parties[3]. In the absence of words of general agreement, a covenant by the husband alone is his contract only[4], but joint and several covenants to settle by the husband and wife bind both parties[5]. However, it has been held that there is a covenant by the husband and wife which binds her property where the wife has been party to and has assented to the deed, and there is a covenant by the husband alone, even if it was not prefaced by words of general agreement, that he would settle the wife's property[6], or that the husband and wife should settle the wife's property[7], or even that the wife's property should be settled[8].

1   *Ramsden v Smith* (1854) 2 Drew 298; *Reid v Kenrick* (1855) 1 Jur NS 897; *Dawes v Tredwell* (1881) 18 ChD 354, CA; *Re Macpherson, Macpherson v Macpherson* (1886) 55 LJ Ch 922.
2   *Ramsden v Smith* (1854) 2 Drew 298.
3   *Butcher v Butcher* (1851) 14 Beav 222; *Stevens v Van Voorst* (1853) 17 Beav 305; *Townshend v Harrowby* (1858) 27 LJ Ch 553; *Willoughby v Middleton* (1862) 2 John & H 344; *Campbell v Bainbridge* (1868) LR 6 Eq 269; *Re D'Estampes' Settlement, D'Estampes v Crowe* (1884) 53 LJ Ch 1117. See also *Master v De Croismar* (1848) 11 Beav 184.
4   *Douglas v Congreve* (1836) 1 Keen 410; *Thornton v Bright* (1836) 2 My & Cr 230; *Hammond v Hammond* (1854) 19 Beav 29; *Young v Smith* (1865) LR 1 Eq 180; *Re Smith, Robson v Tidy* [1900] WN 75.
5   *Tawney v Ward* (1839) 1 Beav 563; *Milford v Peile* (1854) 17 Beav 602.
6   *Lee v Lee* (1876) 4 ChD 175.
7   *Re De Ros' Trust, Hardwicke v Wilmot* (1885) 31 ChD 81.
8   *Re Haden, Coling v Haden* [1898] 2 Ch 220.

(5) CONSIDERATION

659. Consideration in general. Settlements may either be for valuable consideration or voluntary[1]. If there is consideration then, unless it is plainly illusory[2], the court does not inquire into its adequacy[3], and treats the settlement as made for value[4]. A valid marriage by itself, irrespective of any pecuniary benefit or consideration, constitutes a valuable consideration for a settlement[5]; and a marriage that takes place on the faith of a voluntary settlement may supply consideration ex post facto[6]. An ordinary resettlement, even if it does not contain provisions which would amount to a valuable consideration, is supported by the court as a family arrangement[7].

1   For a definition of valuable consideration see *Currie v Misa* (1875) LR 10 Exch 153 at 162 per Lush J; and CONTRACT vol 9(1) (Reissue) para 735 et seq. As to the enforceability of settlements see para 615 ante; and as to the avoidance of settlements see para 616 ante.

2   *Kelson v Lord Kelson* (1853) 10 Hare 385; *Cornish v Clark* (1872) LR 14 Eq 184.

3   *Townend v Toker* (1866) 1 Ch App 446.

4   *Myddleton v Lord Kenyon* (1794) 2 Ves 391 at 410; *Harman v Richards* (1852) 10 Hare 81. Except in the case of persons within the marriage consideration (see paras 660–661 post) or to whom the marriage consideration extends (see para 662 post), a settlement for consideration not moving from the beneficiaries or trustees is not treated as being for value: *Re Cook's Settlement Trusts, Royal Exchange Assurance v Cook* [1965] Ch 902, [1964] 3 All ER 898.

5   *Ex p Marsh* (1744) 1 Atk 158; *Churchman v Harvey* (1757) Amb 335 at 340; *Prebble v Boghurst* (1818) 1 Swan 309 at 319; *Fraser v Thompson* (1859) 4 De G & J 659. See also *R v Lopen Inhabitants* (1788) 2 Term Rep 577. As to transactions defrauding creditors see, however, the Insolvency Act 1986 s 423; and BANKRUPTCY AND INSOLVENCY vol 3(2) (Reissue) para 652 et seq. As to when a gift is treated as being in consideration of marriage for tax purposes see para 661 note 3 post.

6   *Prodger v Langham* (1663) 1 Sid 133; *Brown v Carter* (1801) 5 Ves 862; *Guardian Assurance Co v Viscount of Avonmore* (1872) IR 6 Eq 391; *Greenwood v Lutman* [1915] 1 IR 266. See also MISREPRESENTATION AND FRAUD vol 31 (Reissue) para 876.

7   As to the nature and purpose of resettlements see para 606 ante; and as to family arrangements generally see para 1002 et seq post.

660. Marriage as consideration. To constitute valuable consideration the marriage contemplated must be one which the parties are legally capable of contracting[1]. If the contemplated marriage is one which cannot be legally contracted, the settlement is at best a voluntary settlement[2]. In such a settlement trusts to take effect from and after the solemnisation of the marriage will fail totally, marriage being construed to mean a legal and effectual marriage[3], and evidence of the knowledge and intention of the parties not being admissible to show that the words used mean something else[4]. Moreover, if the domicile of the parties remains unchanged, it makes no difference that the marriage is legal in the country in which it is celebrated[5].

1   *Ford v De Pontès, De Pontès v Kendall* (1861) 30 Beav 572; *Coulson v Allison* (1860) 2 De GF & J 521. As to what marriages are legal see HUSBAND AND WIFE.

2   *Seale v Lowndes* (1868) 17 LT 555.

3   A decree of nullity granted after 31 July 1971 in respect of a voidable marriage operates to annul the marriage only as respects any time after the decree has been made absolute, and notwithstanding the decree, the marriage is treated as if it existed up to that time: see DIVORCE.

4   *Chapman v Bradley* (1863) 4 De GJ & Sm 71; *Pawson v Brown* (1879) 13 ChD 202; *Neale v Neale* (1898) 79 LT 629, CA; *Phillips v Probyn* [1899] 1 Ch 811.

5   *Chapman v Bradley* (1863) 4 De GJ & Sm 71. As to what marriages are recognised by English law see CONFLICT OF LAWS vol 8(1) (Reissue) para 706 et seq.

661. Persons within the marriage consideration. The husband and wife and children or remoter issue[1] of the marriage[2] are within the consideration of marriage[3].

All other persons for whom provision is made by a settlement, such as children of a former marriage[4], an illegitimate child[5], children of a future marriage[6], next of kin[7], collateral relations[8] and a stranger[9], are volunteers whose interests, if the subject is land, are liable to be defeated in favour of a subsequent purchaser for valuable consideration[10], or, whether land or personalty, of the creditors of the settlor[11]. They cannot enforce a contract for settlement against the settlor[12], although an executory settlement in favour of volunteers is enforceable if the trustees of the settlement subsequently become the legal owners of the property[13], and a completed trust in favour of volunteers cannot be set aside by a settlor[14].

1   *Macdonald v Scott* [1893] AC 642 at 650, HL. Trustees of a marriage settlement are entitled to enforce on behalf of persons within the marriage consideration a contract contained in it: *Pullan v Koe* [1913] 1 Ch 9.
2   In *Smith v Cherrill* (1867) LR 4 Eq 390, an adopted child was held not to be within the consideration of marriage. However, under the Adoption Act 1976 s 39(1), the adopted child of a married couple is treated in law as if he had been born as a child of the marriage, whether or not he was in fact born after the marriage was solemnized: see CHILDREN AND YOUNG PERSONS vol 5(2) (Reissue) para 1090. As to adopted children see further para 733 post; and as to adoption generally see CHILDREN AND YOUNG PERSONS vol 5(2) (Reissue) para 1021 et seq. The question whether a legitimated child is within the consideration of marriage has not been decided, although statutory rules cover the question whether, as a matter of construction, a legitimated child is entitled to take under a settlement: see para 732 post. In relation to dispositions made before 1976, for some purposes but not others a legitimate child is treated as a child of the marriage: see the cases cited in para 732 note 2 post.
3   *Nairn v Prowse* (1802) 6 Ves 752; *Parkes v White* (1805) 11 Ves 209 at 228; *A-G v Jacobs Smith* [1895] 2 QB 341, CA. See also *Harvey v Ashley* (1748) 3 Atk 607 at 610. The question who is within the consideration of marriage is different from the question whether a gift is made in consideration of marriage: *IRC v Rennell* [1964] AC 173, [1963] 1 All ER 803, HL (estate duty, now inheritance tax). As to gifts in consideration of marriage with regard to inheritance tax see INHERITANCE TAXATION vol 24 (Reissue) para 519.
4   *Price v Jenkins* (1876) 4 ChD 483 (revsd on other grounds (1877) 5 ChD 619, CA); *Re Greer* (1877) IR 11 Eq 502; *Re Cameron and Wells* (1887) 37 ChD 32; *A-G v Jacobs Smith* [1895] 2 QB 341, CA; *Carruthers v Peake* (1911) 55 Sol Jo 291. *Newstead v Searles* (1737) 1 Atk 265; *Ithell v Beane* (1749) 1 Ves Sen 215; and *Gale v Gale* (1877) 6 ChD 144, cannot, having regard to *De Mestre v West* [1891] AC 264, PC, and *A-G v Jacobs Smith* supra, be relied on for the proposition that the case of children by a former marriage is an exception to the general rule.
5   *De Mestre v West* [1891] AC 264, PC, dissenting from *Clarke v Wright* (1861) 6 H & N 849, Ex Ch. As to illegitimate children generally see para 731 post. As to adopted and legitimated children see note 2 supra.
6   *Re Cullin's Estate* (1864) 14 I Ch R 506; *Wollaston v Tribe* (1869) LR 9 Eq 44; *De Mestre v West* [1891] AC 264, PC, explaining *Clayton v Earl of Wilton* (1813) 6 M & S 67n; *Re Kay's Settlement, Broadbent v Macnab* [1939] Ch 329, [1939] 1 All ER 245.
7   *Re D'Angibau, Andrews v Andrews* (1880) 15 ChD 228, CA; *Re Plumptre's Marriage Settlement, Underhill v Plumptre* [1910] 1 Ch 609; *Re Pryce, Nevill v Pryce* [1917] 1 Ch 234. Cf *Godsal v Webb* (1838) 2 Keen 99; *Gibbs v Grady* (1871) 41 LJ Ch 163.
8   *Staplehill v Bully* (1703) Prec Ch 224; *Reeves v Reeves* (1724) 9 Mod Rep 128 at 132; *Johnson v Legard* (1818) 3 Madd 283 (subsequent proceedings (1822) Turn & R 281); *Cormick v Trapaud* (1818) 6 Dow 60; *Cotterell v Homer* (1843) 13 Sim 506; *Stackpoole v Stackpoole* (1843) 4 Dr & War 320; *Wollaston v Tribe* (1869) LR 9 Eq 44. *Hale v Lamb* (1764) 2 Eden 292, cannot now be considered correct on this point.
9   *Sutton v Viscount Chetwynd* (1817) 3 Mer 249.
10   Ie under the Law of Property Act 1925 s 173: see MISREPRESENTATION AND FRAUD vol 31 (Reissue) para 868.
11   *Smith v Cherrill* (1867) LR 4 Eq 390.
12   *Sutton v Viscount Chetwynd* (1817) 3 Mer 249; *Godsal v Webb* (1838) 2 Keen 99; *Re D'Angibau, Andrews v Andrews* (1880) 15 ChD 228, CA; *Re Plumptre's Marriage Settlement, Underhill v Plumptre* [1910] 1 Ch 609; *Re Pryce, Nevill v Pryce* [1917] 1 Ch 234; *Re Kay's Settlement, Broadbent v Macnab* [1939] Ch 329, [1939] 1 All ER 245; *Re Cook's Settlement Trusts, Royal Exchange Assurance v Cook* [1965] Ch 902, [1964] 3 All ER 898. However, a volunteer is entitled to recover damages for breach of a covenant made with him in a deed to which he is a party: *Cannon v Hartley* [1949] Ch 213, [1949] 1 All ER 50. See also para 615 note 5 ante.

13   *Re Ralli's Will Trusts, Re Ralli's Marriage Settlement, Calvocoressi v Rodocanachi* [1964] Ch 288, [1963] 3 All ER 940.

14   *Kekewich v Manning* (1851) 1 De GM & G 176; *Paul v Paul* (1882) 20 ChD 742, CA; *Re Flavell, Murray v Flavell* (1883) 25 ChD 89, CA; *Osborn v Bellman* (1860) 6 Jur NS 1325. Cf *Ayerst v Jenkins* (1873) LR 16 Eq 275. See also EQUITY vol 16 (Reissue) para 783; GIFTS vol 20 (Reissue) para 63; TRUSTS vol 48 (Reissue) para 566; and para 615 ante.

662. Extension to parties not within the consideration. If the order of the limitations[1] in a settlement is such that the limitations which are not within the marriage consideration are covered by those that are, so that those which are within the marriage consideration cannot take effect in the form and manner provided by the instrument without also giving effect to the others, then the marriage consideration extends to all the limitations[2].

Further, where in a marriage settlement one of the parties to the marriage settles property and the settlement contains limitations in favour of the other party, or his or her issue, or even his or her collateral relations, it may be presumed that the last-mentioned party stipulated, as part of the marriage bargain, for their insertion in the settlement, and so may properly be regarded as having by the marriage purchased them on behalf of those who are intended to be benefited by them. However, an intended wife cannot be inferred to have stipulated on behalf of the relations of the intended husband, nor the intended husband on behalf of the relations of the intended wife[3]; and a party settling property will not be considered as having purchased any interest in that property limited to that party[4].

1   As to limitations in settlements see para 715 et seq post.

2   *Newstead v Searles* (1737) 1 Atk 265; *Clayton v Earl of Wilton* (1813) 6 M & S 67n, as explained by *Mackie v Herbertson* (1884) 9 App Cas 303 at 336, HL, and *De Mestre v West* [1891] AC 264, PC. See also *Re Cullin's Estate* (1864) 14 I Ch R 506; *Re Sheridan's Estate* (1878) 1 LR Ir 54. These cases all arose under 27 Eliz 1 c 4 (Fraudulent Conveyances) (1584–5), replaced by the Law of Property Act 1925 ss 172 (repealed) and 173 (see MISREPRESENTATION AND FRAUD vol 31 (Reissue) para 868 et seq). However, the principle would appear to be of general application.

3   *Heap v Tonge* (1851) 9 Hare 90 at 104; *Ford v Stuart* (1852) 15 Beav 493 at 500; *Clarke v Wright* (1861) 6 H & N 849, Ex Ch.

4   *Barham v Earl of Clarendon* (1852) 10 Hare 126; *Clarke v Wright* (1861) 6 H & N 849, Ex Ch; *Re Brown's Estate* (1862) 13 I Ch R 283. Cf *Dilkes v Broadmead* (1860) 2 De GF & J 566, where a limitation to the wife of her own property for her life to her separate use without power of anticipation was held not to be a voluntary settlement for her benefit, inasmuch as the husband derived a benefit from the manner in which the property was settled.

663. Effect of concurrence of third persons. If persons other than the intended husband and wife, being persons whose concurrence is necessary to give effect to the settlement, join as parties to it, their concurrence is sufficient to constitute a consideration for trusts in favour of other branches of the family or of strangers[1].

If a person agrees with another to make a provision for a volunteer in consideration of the other doing the like, the contract is not voluntary[2], and, if it is enforced by either party, the volunteer gets the benefit of it[3], although the volunteer could not enforce it against either of the contracting parties, since they are at liberty either to vary or to abandon their contract[4].

1   *Jenkins v Keymis* (1664) 1 Lev 150; *Jenkins v Keymes* (1668) 1 Lev 237; *Osgood v Strode* (1724) 2 P Wms 245 at 256; *Goring v Nash* (1774) 3 Atk 186; *Stephens v Trueman* (1748) 1 Ves Sen 73; *Roe d Hamerton v Mitton* (1767) 2 Wils 356; *Pulvertoft v Pulvertoft* (1811) 18 Ves 84 at 92. These decisions are not affected by *Mackie v Herbertson* (1884) 9 App Cas 303, HL, and *De Mestre v West* [1891] AC 264, PC (see para 661 notes 4–5 ante): *A-G v Baron Rathdonnell* [1896] WN 141 at 143.

2   *Bentley v Mackay* (1862) 31 Beav 143; on appeal 4 De GF & J 279.

3   *Davenport v Bishopp* (1843) 2 Y & C Ch Cas 451; affd (1846) 1 Ph 698. See also *Beswick v Beswick* [1968] AC 58, [1967] 2 All ER 1197, HL.

4   *Hill v Gomme* (1839) 5 My & Cr 250; *Re Anstis, Chetwynd v Morgan, Morgan v Chetwynd* (1886) 31 ChD 596, CA.

(6) TRUSTEES' DUTIES OF ADMINISTRATION

664. Duties of trustees in general. It is the duty of the trustees of a settlement to make themselves acquainted with the terms of the trust, to obtain possession of all trust property which should be under their control, to comply strictly with the provisions of the settlement, to keep proper accounts, to exercise in good faith any discretion conferred on them either by the settlement or by statute, to act impartially between the beneficiaries and, in the case of a settlement by deed, to inform the beneficiaries of their interest under the settlement[1].

1   See *Hawkesley v May* [1956] 1 QB 304, [1955] 3 All ER 353. As to the duties of trustees generally see TRUSTS vol 48 (Reissue) para 825 et seq. As to delegation by trustees see the Trustee Act 1925 s 25 (as amended); the Powers of Attorney Act 1971 s 9; the Trusts of Land and Appointment of Trustees Act 1996 s 9; and TRUSTS vol 48 (Reissue) para 854 et seq.

665. Trustees' powers of management in relation to land. The ambit of trustees' powers of management in relation to land depends upon whether the trust is a settlement within the Settled Land Act 1925[1] or whether it is a trust of land[2].

Trustees of land have in general the powers of an absolute owner[3]. Additionally, the trustees have the following express powers:

(1)   a power to convey the land to the beneficiaries in certain circumstances[4];
(2)   a power to purchase land[5];
(3)   an express power of partition[6]; and
(4)   a power to delegate their duties by power of attorney to any beneficiary of full age and beneficially entitled to an interest in possession in the land[7].

All these powers, except the power to delegate, are subject to any provision in the disposition[8] by which the trust was created to the contrary[9]. Further, and unless provision to the contrary is made in the disposition, the trustees must, in the exercise of their powers so far as practicable, consult with the beneficiaries of full age and beneficially entitled to an interest in possession in the land and, generally, give effect to their wishes[10]. The disposition may also provide for the consent of certain persons to the exercise of these powers[11].

The trustees of a strict settlement have the powers set out in the Settled Land Act 1925[12]. As long as any child[13] is entitled to a beneficial interest in possession affecting land, the trustees[14] may[15] enter into and continue in possession of the land on the child's behalf[16]. In such a case the trustees must manage or superintend the management of the land[17], with full power:

(a)   to fell timber or cut underwood from time to time in the usual course for sale, or for repairs or otherwise[18];
(b)   to erect, pull down, rebuild and repair houses and other buildings and erections[19];
(c)   to continue the workings of mines, minerals and quarries which have usually been worked[20];
(d)   to drain or otherwise improve the land or any part of it[21];
(e)   to insure against loss by fire[22];
(f)   to make allowances to and arrangements with tenants and others[23];

(g)   to determine tenancies and to accept surrenders of leases and tenancies[24]; and

(h)   generally to deal with the land in a proper and due course of management[25].

However, where the child is impeachable for waste, the trustees may not commit waste, and may cut the timber on the same terms only, and subject to the same restrictions on and subject to which the child could, if of full age, cut the same[26].

These powers are also available where any person is contingently entitled to land under an instrument coming into operation on or after 1 January 1926 and before 1 January 1997[27], subject to any prior interests or charges affecting the land, until his interest vests or, if his interest vests during minority, until he attains the age of 18 years[28].

1   See para 675 post.
2   See paras 609 ante, 676–677 post.
3   See the Trusts of Land and Appointment of Trustees Act 1996 s 6(1); and TRUSTS vol 48 (Reissue) para 894. The more complex powers of trustees for sale set out in the Law of Property Act 1925 ss 28, 29 (repealed) have been abolished: see the Trusts of Land and Appointment of Trustees Act 1996 s 25(2), Sch 4.
4   See ibid s 6(2); and TRUSTS vol 48 (Reissue) para 894.
5   See ibid s 6(3); and TRUSTS vol 48 (Reissue) para 894.
6   See ibid s 7; and TRUSTS vol 48 (Reissue) para 908.
7   See ibid s 9; and TRUSTS vol 48 (Reissue) para 895.
8   'Disposition' includes a conveyance and also a devise, bequest, or an appointment of property contained in a will: Law of Property Act 1925 s 205(1)(ii); definition applied by the Trusts of Land and Appointment of Trustees Act 1996 s 23(2). The relevant document will usually be the transfer by the settlor to the trustees, but the better view is that the definition extends to a declaration of trust by a beneficial owner.
9   See ibid s 8; and TRUSTS vol 48 (Reissue) para 894.
10 See ibid s 11; and TRUSTS vol 48 (Reissue) para 895. Additionally, the trustees are directed to have regard to the rights of the beneficiaries when exercising the powers conferred by s 6 (see the text and notes 3–5 supra): see s 6(5); and TRUSTS vol 48 (Reissue) para 894.
11 See ibid s 10; and TRUSTS vol 48 (Reissue) para 895.
12 See further para 750 et seq post.
13 The Settled Land Act 1925 refers to infants but 'child' has been substituted throughout this title: see CHILDREN AND YOUNG PERSONS vol 5(2) (Reissue) para 603.
14 Ie the trustees appointed for this purpose by the settlement, or if there are none so appointed, then the trustees of the settlement, unless the settlement or the order of the court by which they or their predecessors in the office were appointed to be such trustees expressly provides to the contrary, or if there are none, then any persons appointed as trustees for this purpose by the court on the application of the child's guardian or next friend: see the Settled Land Act 1925 s 102(1). For the meaning of 'trustees of the settlement' see para 750 note 1 post. As to the age of majority see para 605 note 1 ante.
15 The trustees have a discretion whether to enter: *Re Lethbridge, Couldwell v Lethbridge* [1917] WN 243.
16 See the Settled Land Act 1925 s 102(1), which has effect subject to an express appointment by the settlement, or the court, of trustees for the purposes of s 102 (as amended): s 102(4). Section 102 (as amended) applies only if and as far as a contrary intention is not expressed in the instrument, if any, under which the child's interest arises, and has effect subject to the terms of that instrument and the provisions contained in it: see s 102(6); and CHILDREN AND YOUNG PERSONS vol 5(2) (Reissue) para 658.
17 Ibid s 102(2).
18 Ibid s 102(2)(a).
19 Ibid s 102(2)(b).
20 Ibid s 102(2)(c).
21 Ibid s 102(2)(d).
22 Ibid s 102(2)(e). Money received on insurances effected by trustees is capital money: see the Trustee Act 1925 s 20 (as amended); and TRUSTS vol 48 (Reissue) para 892. Money received under insurances effected under the Conveyancing Act 1881 s 42 (repealed by the Law of Property Act 1925, except so far as it relates to instruments in operation before 1926, subject to the right to have the money applied in rebuilding under the Fires Prevention (Metropolis) Act 1774), belongs to the child: *Re Quicke's Trusts, Poltimore v Quicke* [1908] 1 Ch 887.
23 Settled Land Act 1925 s 102(2)(f).
24 Ibid s 102(2)(g).
25 Ibid s 102(2)(h).
26 See ibid s 102(2). As to waste see para 986 et seq post.

27 Ie after the coming into force of the Settled Land Act 1925 and before the coming into force of the Trusts of Land and Appointment of Trustees Act 1996: see para 676 post.
28 See the Settled Land Act 1925 s 102(5) (amended by the Family Law Reform Act 1969 s 1(3), Sch 1); and the Trusts of Land and Appointment of Trustees Act 1996 s 2(1) (see paras 676–677 post).

666. Expenses of management and keeping down charges. Where the trustees of a settlement[1] under the Settled Land Act 1925 enter into possession[2], they may pay from time to time, out of the income of the land, including the produce of the sale of timber and underwood, the expenses incurred in the management, or in the exercise of any power conferred on them in relation to the land[3], and all outgoings not payable by any tenant or other person, and must keep down any annual sum, and the interest of any principal sum, charged on the land[4].

1 For the meaning of 'trustees of the settlement' see para 750 note 1 post.
2 As to the power for the trustees to enter see para 665 ante.
3 Ie any power conferred on them by the Settled Land Act 1925 s 102 (as amended) (see para 665 ante) or otherwise: see s 102(3).
4 Ibid s 102(3). As to payment for repairs as between capital and income see para 963 post.

667. Powers of maintenance and advancement. Statutory powers enable trustees of a settlement at their sole discretion to apply income arising from it for the maintenance, education or benefit of a child, subject to any contrary intention expressed in the trust instrument[1]. It is usual in settlements to rely on these statutory powers, although it is also usual to supplement them with express powers of accumulation and maintenance[2]. Express powers should be inserted in any event if the interests provided are of such a nature that the statutory powers do not apply[3], or if it is desired to vary the statutory powers[4]. For certain types of trust it is important to exclude the statutory powers[5].

It has, moreover, long been recognised that trustees of a settlement may be expressly authorised by the trust instrument to raise sums out of the capital of the personal estate in which a beneficiary has an interest, for placing him out in life or otherwise for a special benefit to him as distinct from ordinary maintenance and education[6]. In addition, in the case of trusts constituted or created after 1925, a statutory power of advancement[7] is conferred on trustees which, subject to certain limitations[8], enables them at any time to apply capital money in such manner as they may in their absolute discretion think fit for the advancement or benefit of any person entitled absolutely or contingently to the capital or any share of it[9].

1 See the Trustee Act 1925 s 31 (as amended); and CHILDREN AND YOUNG PERSONS vol 5(2) (Reissue) para 666 et seq. As to the age of majority see para 605 note 1 ante.
2 As to powers of accumulation and maintenance see CHILDREN AND YOUNG PERSONS vol 5(2) (Reissue) para 661 et seq.
3 For example, an express power should be included if the settlor wishes the trustees to have powers of accumulation in relation to the income of beneficiaries of full age: see further TRUSTS vol 48 (Reissue) para 845 et seq.
4 As to express powers of maintenance see CHILDREN AND YOUNG PERSONS vol 5(2) (Reissue) para 661.
5 The exclusion of the Trustee Act 1931 s 31 (as amended) (see CHILDREN AND YOUNG PERSONS vol 5(2) (Reissue) para 666 et seq) is important if it is desired to give an interest in possession to a beneficiary under the age of majority for the purposes of the Inheritance Tax Act 1984: see INHERITANCE TAXATION vol 24 (Reissue) para 507.
6 This is usually called a power of advancement. As to express powers of advancement see CHILDREN AND YOUNG PERSONS vol 5(2) (Reissue) para 676 et seq.
7 The power arises under the Trustee Act 1925 s 32 (as amended) (see CHILDREN AND YOUNG PERSONS vol 5(2) (Reissue) para 679). It is excluded if a contrary intention is expressed in the trust instrument: see s 69(2); and CHILDREN AND YOUNG PERSONS vol 5(2) (Reissue) para 679. See also *IRC v Bernstein* [1961] Ch 399, [1961] 1 All ER 320, CA.
8 As to these limitations see CHILDREN AND YOUNG PERSONS vol 5(2) (Reissue) para 680.

9   See the Trustee Act 1925 s 32 (as amended) (see CHILDREN AND YOUNG PERSONS vol 5(2) (Reissue) para 679); and para 626 ante. The statutory power of advancement under s 32 (as amended) does not apply to capital money arising under the Settled Land Act 1925 (as to which see para 795 post): see the Trustee Act 1925 s 32(2) (amended by the Trusts of Land and Appointment of Trustees Act 1996 s 25(1), Sch 3 para 3(8)). See, however, *Re Collard's Will Trusts, Lloyds Bank Ltd v Rees* [1961] Ch 293, [1961] 1 All ER 821, where settled land was nevertheless validly advanced. An express power of advancement should be inserted in instruments if it is desired to vary the statutory power, or if the statutory power does not apply, or if the settlement is not to be governed by English law. It is usual to vary the statutory power in a settlement, so that it extends over the whole rather than one half of a beneficiary's presumptive or vested entitlement in the trust fund: see CHILDREN AND YOUNG PERSONS vol 5(2) (Reissue) para 682.

668. Duty to invest. A settlement, whether created by deed or will, usually contains a clause specifying what investments of the trust funds may lawfully be made by the trustees[1]. This clause primarily determines the powers of the trustees of the settlement in making investments, but, unless expressly forbidden by the settlement[2], they have the extensive powers of investment which are now conferred on them by statute[3]. If the investment clause purports still further to enlarge these powers, it should be construed strictly for the protection of the trustees and remaindermen[4].

1   See generally TRUSTS vol 48 (Reissue) para 862 et seq.
2   A direction that the trustees are to invest in a particular way is not an express prohibition: *Re Maire, Maire v De La Batut* (1905) 49 Sol Jo 383; *Re Burke, Burke v Burke* [1908] 2 Ch 248; *Re Warren, Public Trustee v Fletcher* [1939] Ch 684, [1939] 2 All ER 599.
3   Ie by the Trustee Act 1925 ss 2, 5–11 (as amended); the Trustee Investments Act 1961; and the Trusts of Land and Appointment of Trustees Act 1996 s 6 (in relation to trusts of land). As to these powers and the powers and duties of trustees to invest see TRUSTS vol 48 (Reissue) para 869 et seq.
4   *Re Maryon-Wilson's Estate* [1912] 1 Ch 55, CA. As regards trustee investments and the construction of investment clauses see TRUSTS vol 48 (Reissue) para 862 et seq.

669. Duty in respect of policies and choses in action. If a settlement contains a covenant by any person to pay the premiums on an insurance policy which forms part of the subject matter of the settlement, it is the duty of the trustees of the settlement to take all necessary steps to enforce payment of the premiums by the covenantor, although it is usual to restrict their responsibility by the instrument creating the trust[1]. However, the trustees incur no liability if their efforts are unsuccessful, nor are they bound to take any steps to enforce payment if by reason of the covenantor's poverty there is ground for believing that such steps would be ineffectual[2]. If there are no funds properly applicable to the keeping up of the policy, it is the trustees' duty to do what they can to protect the policy and advance or obtain money for the purpose of paying the premiums[3]. In such case the trustees, or any person advancing money for the purpose at their request, will be entitled to a lien on the policy for the amount so advanced, together with interest[4]. Where no funds are available to keep up a policy, it may be ordered to be surrendered[5] or sold, and the trustees may be reimbursed out of the proceeds the amount of premiums paid by them[6]. If, however, the beneficiary supplies funds, or if, by duly performing their trust, the trustees ought to be in possession of funds applicable for the purpose, then the trustees acquire no lien on the policy, and cannot confer one on another person who provides the necessary funds[7]. Trustees should insist on having the policy and assignment handed over to them for custody even though the possession may not confer on them any legal estate or advantage[8].

Where the subject of the settlement is an insurance policy or any other chose in action, the trustees should see that their title is perfected by giving the necessary notices[9].

If a chose in action which is the subject of the settlement is capable of reduction into possession, it is the trustees' duty to reduce it into possession without unnecessary delay, and if they fail to do so they will be guilty of a breach of trust unless they can prove that even if speedy steps had been taken the money could not have been recovered[10].

1 As to a life policy taken out by a husband for the benefit of his wife and children see HUSBAND AND WIFE; INSURANCE vol 25 (Reissue) para 558. As to life insurance generally see INSURANCE vol 25 (Reissue) para 525 et seq.
2 *Ball v Ball* (1847) 11 I Eq R 370; *Clack v Holland* (1854) 19 Beav 262; *Hobday v Peters (No 3)* (1860) 28 Beav 603.
3 *Clack v Holland* (1854) 19 Beav 262 at 276.
4 *Clack v Holland* (1854) 19 Beav 262. Cf *Shearman v British Empire Mutual Life Assurance Co* (1872) LR 14 Eq 4; *Gill v Downing* (1874) LR 17 Eq 316. As to liens on policies see INSURANCE vol 25 (Reissue) para 560. The traditional rate of interest is 4% per annum, but cf para 945 note 5 post.
5 *Beresford v Beresford* (1857) 23 Beav 292. It is desirable in settlements of policies to insert express powers enabling the trustees to surrender the policy.
6 *Hill v Trenery* (1856) 23 Beav 16.
7 *Clack v Holland* (1854) 19 Beav 262.
8 See *Meux v Bell* (1841) 1 Hare 73 at 89.
9 As to these notices see CHOSES IN ACTION vol 6 (Reissue) para 20 et seq.
10 *Styles v Guy* (1849) 1 Mac & G 422; *Wiles v Gresham* (1854) 5 De GM & G 770; *Grove v Price* (1858) 26 Beav 103; *Re Brogden, Billing v Brogden* (1888) 38 ChD 546, CA. As to the duty of trustees to get in outstanding property see TRUSTS vol 48 (Reissue) para 827–828.

(7) UNAUTHORISED TRANSACTIONS EFFECTED UNDER COURT ORDERS

670. Jurisdiction of the court. It is not the function of the court in exercise of its inherent jurisdiction[1] to alter a trust because alteration is thought to be advantageous[2], and, in general, the court has no jurisdiction to sanction acts being done by trustees which are not, on the face of the trust instrument, authorised by its terms[3]. Within specified limits, however, the court has inherent jurisdiction to authorise transactions that are not authorised, or may not be authorised, by the trust[4]. Such transactions may:

(1) change the nature of property to which a child is absolutely entitled[5];
(2) provide maintenance out of trust income for a child and, but rarely, for an adult beneficiary, even if the income is directed to be accumulated or applied in reduction of incumbrances[6];
(3) sanction the compromise of disputed rights[7] notwithstanding that some of the beneficiaries are children or are unborn[8]; and
(4) authorise by way of salvage some unauthorised transaction to be carried out[9].

In addition to the inherent jurisdiction of the court, certain special powers of authorising transactions to be carried out by tenants for life[10] or trustees[11], or of approving arrangements varying trusts[12], have been conferred on the court by statute. Moreover there is statutory power, for the purpose of enabling a child's property to be applied for his maintenance, education or benefit, to make vesting orders or appoint persons to convey the property[13].

1 As to this inherent jurisdiction see generally TRUSTS vol 48 (Reissue) para 921. Special statutory jurisdiction, overriding to some extent the principle stated in the text, has been conferred by the Variation of Trusts Act 1958. As to this jurisdiction see TRUSTS vol 48 (Reissue) para 923 et seq; and para 674 post.
2 See *Chapman v Chapman* [1954] AC 429 at 446, [1954] 1 All ER 798 at 802, HL, per Viscount Simonds LC, after citing with approval a proposition stated by Farwell J in *Re Walker, Walker v Duncombe* [1901] 1 Ch 879 at 885.
3 See *Re New, Re Leavers, Re Morley* [1901] 2 Ch 534 at 544, CA, per Romer LJ, cited with approval by Lord Morton of Henryton in *Chapman v Chapman* [1954] AC 429 at 452, [1954] 1 All ER 798 at 808, HL.
4 See *Chapman v Chapman* [1954] AC 429 at 445, [1954] 1 All ER 798 at 802, HL, per Lord Simonds LC, at 451 and 807–808 per Lord Morton of Henryton, and at 469 and 818 per Lord Asquith of Bishopstone.

5　　See *Chapman v Chapman* [1954] AC 429 at 452, [1954] 1 All ER 798 at 808, HL, per Lord Morton of
　　　Henryton; and TRUSTS vol 48 (Reissue) para 921; CHILDREN AND YOUNG PERSONS vol 5(2) (Reissue)
　　　para 1389. A like jurisdiction was exercised in the case of persons suffering from mental disorders: see
　　　Chapman v Chapman supra at 452 and 808 per Lord Morton of Henryton. In the case of children's
　　　property there was a distinction between realty and personalty: see eg *Re Heyworth's Settlements* [1956] Ch
　　　364 at 371, [1956] 2 All ER 21 at 24 per Upjohn J. As to the age of majority see para 605 note 1 ante.
6　　See *Chapman v Chapman* [1954] AC 429 at 455, [1954] 1 All ER 798 at 810, HL, per Lord Morton of
　　　Henryton; and CHILDREN AND YOUNG PERSONS vol 5(2) (Reissue) para 1389. For a further statutory
　　　power in relation to property of a child see para 673 post.
7　　*Chapman v Chapman* [1954] AC 429 at 461, [1954] 1 All ER 798 at 814, HL, per Lord Morton of
　　　Henryton; *Re Lord Hylton's Settlement, Barclays Bank Ltd v Jolliffe* [1954] 2 All ER 647n, [1954] 1 WLR
　　　1055, CA; *Re Powell-Cotton's Resettlement, Henniker-Major v Powell-Cotton* [1956] 1 All ER 60, [1956] 1
　　　WLR 23, CA.
8　　See *Re Trenchard, Trenchard v Trenchard* [1902] 1 Ch 378; and CHILDREN AND YOUNG PERSONS vol 5(2)
　　　(Reissue) para 1389. However, as to this decision see *Chapman v Chapman* [1954] AC 429 at 446, [1954]
　　　1 All ER 798 at 803, HL, per Lord Simonds LC, and at 464 and 815 per Lord Morton of Henryton.
9　　*Conway v Fenton* (1888) 40 ChD 512; *Re Waldegrave, Earl Waldegrave v Earl Selborne* (1899) 81 LT 632.
　　　The inherent jurisdiction to authorise a transaction by way of salvage was exercised with great caution and
　　　only in a case which amounted to actual salvage: *Re De Teissier's Settled Estates, Re De Teissier's Trusts, De
　　　Teissier v De Teissier* [1893] 1 Ch 153; *Re New, Re Leavers, Re Morley* [1901] 2 Ch 534, CA; *Chapman v
　　　Chapman* [1954] AC 429 at 452, [1954] 1 All ER 798 at 808, HL, per Lord Morton of Henryton. This
　　　jurisdiction has been largely superseded by the wider statutory powers conferred on the court: see the text
　　　and notes 10–13 infra. In exercising this jurisdiction in a case concerning settled land, these statutory
　　　powers, whether or not they exclude the inherent jurisdiction, afford a guide to the court in arriving at a
　　　proper conclusion concerning the exercise of this jurisdiction: see *Re De Teissier's Settled Estates* supra at
　　　165; *Re Willis, Willis v Willis* [1902] 1 Ch 15 at 21–22, CA. See further TRUSTS vol 48 (Reissue) para 921.
10　See the Settled Land Act 1925 s 64 (as amended); and para 671 post.
11　See the Trustee Act 1925 s 57; and para 672 post. See also TRUSTS vol 48 (Reissue) para 922.
12　See the Variation of Trusts Act 1958 s 1 (as amended) (see TRUSTS vol 48 (Reissue) paras 923–924); and
　　　para 674 post.
13　See para 673 post.

671. Court's power to order transactions affecting settled land. If there is any
transaction[1] affecting or concerning settled land, or any part of settled land, or any other
land[2], which is not a transaction authorised by the Settled Land Act 1925 or by the
settlement, and which, in the opinion of the court[3], would be for the benefit of the settled
land or any part of it, or the persons interested under the settlement, and if it is one which
could have been validly effected[4] by an absolute owner, the court has jurisdiction to
authorise the tenant for life[5] to effect the transaction[6].

This jurisdiction includes power to make an order authorising any expense of action
taken or proposed in or for the management[7] of settled land to be treated as a capital
outgoing, notwithstanding that in other circumstances that expense could not properly
have been so treated[8]. Before making such an order the court must be satisfied that the
action taken or proposed was or would be for the benefit of the persons entitled under
the settlement generally[9], and either (1) that the available income from all sources of a
person who, as being beneficially entitled to possession or receipt of the rents and profits
of the land or to reside in a house comprised in it might otherwise have been expected
to bear the expense of the action taken or proposed, has been so reduced as to render him
unable to bear its expense or unable to bear it without undue hardship[10]; or (2) in a case
in which there is no such person, that the income available for meeting that expense has
become insufficient[11].

In determining whether to make an order the court must have regard to all the
circumstances of the case, including (a) the extent of the obligations, whether legally
enforceable or not and whether or not relating to the land, of the person referred to[12];
(b) the extent to which other persons entitled under the settlement are likely to benefit
from the action taken or proposed or from the relief which would accrue to that person

from the making of the order; and (c) the extent to which the making of the order would be likely to involve a loss to any other person so entitled without his receiving any corresponding benefit[13].

1   'Transaction' includes any sale, exchange, assurance, grant, lease, surrender, reconveyance, release, reservation, or other disposition, and any purchase or other acquisition, and any covenant, contract or option, and any application of capital money, and any compromise or other dealing or arrangement: see the Settled Land Act 1925 s 64(2) (amended by the Settled Land and Trustee Acts (Court's General Powers) Act 1943 s 2; and the Statute Law (Repeals) Act 1969). 'Transaction' is not limited to acts of an administrative character: *Re Downshire Settled Estates, Marquess of Downshire v Royal Bank of Scotland, Re Chapman's Settlement Trusts, Chapman v Chapman, Re Blackwell's Settlement Trusts, Blackwell v Blackwell* [1953] Ch 218, [1953] 1 All ER 103, CA; affd in part on another point sub nom *Chapman v Chapman* [1954] AC 429, [1954] 1 All ER 798, HL. The following matters have been held to be transactions within the definition: (1) raising money to pay debts incurred by the tenant for life (*Re White-Popham Settled Estates* [1936] Ch 725, [1936] 2 All ER 1486, CA); (2) raising money to enable the tenant for life to continue to live in the mansion house (*Re Scarisbrick Re-settlement Estates* [1944] Ch 229, [1944] 1 All ER 404); (3) raising money for the purchase of furniture and chattels to equip the mansion house (*Re Earl of Mount Edgcumbe* [1950] Ch 615, [1950] 2 All ER 242); or (4) payment of capital to the tenant for life in return for a provision for compensating remaindermen (*Re Simmons, Simmons v Public Trustee* [1956] Ch 125, [1955] 3 All ER 818). The court's power in the Settled Land Act 1925 s 64 (as amended) extends to authorising a maintenance fund trust within the Inheritance Tax Act 1984 s 27, Sch 4 (as amended) (see INHERITANCE TAXATION vol 24 (Reissue) para 548 et seq): see *Raikes v Lygon* [1988] 1 All ER 884, [1988] 1 WLR 281.

2   References to land include references to restrictions and burdens affecting land: see the Settled Land Act 1925 s 64(2) (as amended: see note 1 supra).

3   See para 792 post.

4   'Effected' has the meaning appropriate to the particular transaction: Settled Land Act 1925 s 64(2) (as amended: see note 1 supra).

5   'Tenant for life' includes a person (not being a statutory owner) (see para 766 post) who has the powers of a tenant for life under the Settled Land Act 1925, and also (where the context requires) one of two or more persons who together constitute the tenant for life: s 117(1)(xviii). The court's powers under s 64 (as amended) are in certain circumstances exercisable in the case of a trust of land: see the Settled Land and Trustee Acts (Court's General Powers) Act 1943 s 1 (as amended); and the text and notes 7–13 infra).

6   Settled Land Act 1925 s 64(1). The court's powers under s 64 (as amended) are not limited by the Variation of Trusts Act 1958 s 1: see s 1(6) (as amended) (see TRUSTS vol 48 (Reissue) para 922); and para 674 post. The court's jurisdiction under the Settled Land Act 1925 s 64 (as amended), is more ample than its jurisdiction under the Trustee Act 1925 s 57 (see para 672 post; and TRUSTS vol 48 (Reissue) para 922): *Re Downshire Settled Estates, Marquess of Downshire v Royal Bank of Scotland, Re Chapman's Settlement Trusts, Chapman v Chapman, Re Blackwell's Settlement Trusts, Blackwell v Blackwell* [1953] Ch 218, [1953] 1 All ER 103, CA; affd in part on another point sub nom *Chapman v Chapman* [1954] AC 429, [1954] 1 All ER 798, HL.

7   'Management' includes all the acts referred to in the Settled Land Act 1925 s 102(2) (see para 665 ante); and references to expense of management include references to the expense of the employment of a solicitor, accountant, surveyor or other person in an advisory or supervisory capacity: see the Settled Land and Trustee Acts (Court's General Powers) Act 1943 s 1(5) (amended by the Emergency Laws (Miscellaneous Provisions) Act 1953 ss 9, 14, Sch 3). Although the Act authorises the expenditure of capital money only in or for the management of settled land, it does not restrict the court's jurisdiction under the Settled Land Act 1925 s 64 (as amended): *Re Scarisbrick Re-settlement Estates* [1944] Ch 229, [1944] 1 All ER 404.

8   See the Settled Land and Trustee Acts (Court's General Powers) Act 1943 s 1(1) (amended by the Trusts of Land and Appointment of Trustees Act 1996 s 25(1), Sch 3 para 8). As to payments out of capital money see para 808 post.

9   Settled Land and Trustee Acts (Court's General Powers) Act 1943 s 1(2)(a).

10 Ibid s 1(2)(b) (amended by the Emergency Laws (Miscellaneous Provisions) Act 1953 Sch 3).

11 Settled Land and Trustee Acts (Court's General Powers) Act 1943 s 1(2)(c) (amended by the Emergency Laws (Miscellaneous Provisions) Act 1953 Sch 3).

12 Ie referred to in head (1) in the text: see the Settled Land and Trustee Acts (Court's General Powers) Act 1943 s 1(3).

13   Ibid s 1(3). Such an order may be made notwithstanding that the action in question was taken, or the expense of it was discharged, before the application for the order, and the court may direct such adjustments of accounts and such repayments to be made as may appear to the court to be requisite for giving full effect to the purposes of any such order: see s 1(4).

672. Court's power to authorise dealings with any trust property. If in the management or administration of any property vested in trustees, any sale, lease, mortgage, surrender, release or other disposition, or any purchase, investment, acquisition, expenditure or other transaction is, in the court's opinion, expedient, but cannot be effected by reason of the absence of any power for that purpose vested in the trustees by the trust instrument, if any, or by law, the court may by order confer upon the trustees, either generally or in any particular instance, the necessary power for the purpose[1].

1   See the Trustee Act 1925 s 57(1); and TRUSTS vol 48 (Reissue) para 922. These powers of the court have been extended by the Settled Land and Trustee Acts (Court's General Powers) Act 1943 s 1 (as amended) (see para 671 ante), to the same extent as have its powers under the Settled Land Act 1925 s 64 (as amended): see para 671 ante. The court's powers under the Trustee Act 1925 s 57 are not limited by the Variation of Trusts Act 1958 (see para 674 post; and TRUSTS vol 48 (Reissue) para 923 et seq): see s 1(6) (as amended); and TRUSTS vol 48 (Reissue) para 922. For an example of the application of the enactment to a settlement see *Re Beale's Settlement Trusts, Huggins v Beale* [1932] 2 Ch 15 (authorisation of sale notwithstanding individual's consent refused).

673. Orders affecting child's property. Where a child is beneficially entitled to any property, then, with a view to the application of its capital or income for the maintenance, education or benefit of the child, the court may make an order appointing a person to convey such property, or, in the case of stock or a thing in action, make a vesting order[1].

1   See the Trustee Act 1925 s 53; and CHILDREN AND YOUNG PERSONS vol 5(2) (Reissue) para 674. As to the age of majority see para 605 note 1 ante.

674. Approval of arrangements varying trusts. Where real or personal property is held on trusts arising under a settlement, then, if it thinks fit, the court may approve on behalf of certain specified persons any arrangement varying or revoking all or any of the trusts or enlarging the trustees' powers of managing or administering any of the property subject to the trusts[1]. These persons are:

(1)   any person having an interest, directly or indirectly, whether vested or contingent, under the trusts who by reason of being a child or other incapacity is incapable of assenting[2];

(2)   any person, whether ascertained or not, who may become entitled, directly or indirectly, to such an interest as being at a future date or on the happening of a future event a person of any specified description or a member of any specified class of persons[3];

(3)   any person unborn[4]; or

(4)   any person in respect of any discretionary interest[5] of his under protective trusts[6] where the interest of the principal beneficiary[7] has not failed or determined[8].

The power does not extend to trusts affecting property settled by Act of Parliament[9].

1   See the Variation of Trusts Act 1958 s 1(1); and TRUSTS vol 48 (Reissue) para 923. The Act applies whether the trusts arose before or after the passing of the Act: see s 1(1); and TRUSTS vol 48 (Reissue) para 923.

2   See ibid s 1(1)(a); and TRUSTS vol 48 (Reissue) para 924.

3   See ibid s 1(1)(b); and TRUSTS vol 48 (Reissue) para 924. This does not include any person who would be of that description, or a member of that class, if that date had fallen or that event had happened at the date of the application to the court: see s 1(1)(b); and TRUSTS vol 48 (Reissue) para 924.
4   See ibid s 1(1)(c); and TRUSTS vol 48 (Reissue) para 924.
5   'Discretionary interest' means an interest arising under the trust specified in the Trustee Act 1925 s 33(1)(ii) (see para 917 post), or any like trust: see the Variation of Trusts Act 1958 s 1(2).
6   'Protective trusts' means the trusts specified in the Trustee Act 1925 s 33(1)(i), (ii) (see para 917 post), or any like trusts: see the Variation of Trusts Act 1958 s 1(2).
7   'The principal beneficiary' has the same meaning as in the Trustee Act 1925 s 33(1) (see para 917 post): see the Variation of Trusts Act 1958 s 1(2).
8   See ibid s 1(1)(d); and TRUSTS vol 48 (Reissue) para 924. Except under s 1(1)(d), the court must not approve an arrangement on behalf of any person unless its being carried out would be for the benefit of that person: see s 1(1) proviso.
9   See ibid s 1(5).

2.   SETTLEMENTS OF LAND UNDER THE SETTLED LAND ACT 1925

(1) SETTLEMENTS WITHIN THE ACT

675. Settlements of land within the Settled Land Act 1925. Since 1 January 1997, when the Trusts of Land and Appointment of Trustees Act 1996 came into force, it has been impossible to create settlements for the purposes of the Settled Land Act 1925, save in a very limited class of cases[1]. Settlements governed by the Settled Land Act 1925 on 1 January 1997, however, generally retain their status and are not trusts of land within the meaning of the Trust of Land and Appointment of Trustees Act 1996[2]. The paragraphs set out below deal with that decreasing number of settlements which are governed by the Settled Land Act 1925[3].

1   See para 676 post.
2   See para 676 post.
3   See paras 678–896 post.

676. Trusts in place of settlements. No settlement created after 1 January 1997[1] is a settlement for the purposes of the Settled Land Act 1925[2]; and no settlement is to be deemed to be made under that Act[3] after that date[4]. Any trust of property relating to land created after 1 January 1997 is a trust of land[5].

This provision does not apply to a settlement created on the occasion of an alteration in any interest in, or of a person becoming entitled under, a settlement which is in existence at that date, or derives from such a settlement[6]. However, such a settlement is not a settlement for the purposes of the Settled Land Act 1925 if provision to the effect that it is not is made in the instrument, or any of the instruments, by which it is created[7].

Where at any time after 1 January 1997 there is in the case of any settlement which is a settlement for the purposes of the Settled Land Act 1925 no relevant property[8] which is, or is deemed to be, subject to the settlement, the settlement permanently ceases at that time to be a settlement for the purposes of that Act[9].

No land held on charitable, ecclesiastical or public trusts is or is deemed to be settled land after 1 January 1997, even if it was or was deemed to be settled land before that date[10].

Provision is made for the imposition of a trust in circumstances in which, apart from the above provisions, there would be a settlement for the purposes of the Settled Land Act 1925 and there would not otherwise be a trust[11].

1   Ie the commencement of the Trusts of Land and Appointment of Trustees Act 1996: see s 27(2); and the
     Trusts of Land and Appointment of Trustees Act 1996 (Commencement) Order 1996, SI 1996/2974.
2   As to settlements within the Settled Land Act 1925 see paras 675 ante, 678 et seq post.
3   As to settlements deemed to be made under the Settled Land Act 1925 see para 679 post.
4   Trusts of Land and Appointment of Trustees Act 1996 s 2(1).
5   See ibid s 1; and REAL PROPERTY vol 39(2) (Reissue) para 66. 'Trust of land' means any trust of property
     which consists of or includes land; and 'trustees of land' means trustees of a trust of land: see s 1(1); and
     REAL PROPERTY vol 39(2) (Reissue) para 66. The reference to land does not include land which is settled
     land: see s 1(3); and REAL PROPERTY vol 39(2) (Reissue) para 66. As to the creation of trusts of land see
     paras 897–899 post; and as to trustees of land see para 900 et seq post.
6   Ibid s 2(2).
7   Ibid s 2(3).
8   'Relevant property' means land and personal chattels to which the Settled Land Act 1925 67(1)
     (heirlooms) (see para 941 post) applies: Trusts of Land and Appointment of Trustees Act 1996 s 2(4).
9   Ibid s 2(4). See also para 677 post.
10   Ibid s 2(5). See also para 677 post.
11   See ibid s 2(6); and para 677 post.

677. Imposition of trusts. Where after 1 January 1997[1] a person purports to convey
a legal estate[2] in land to a child[3], or two or more children, alone, the conveyance[4] is not
effective to pass the legal estate, but operates as a declaration that the land is held in trust
for the child or children (or if he purports to convey it to the child or children in trust
for any persons, for those persons)[5]. Where after that date a person purports to convey a
legal estate in land to a child, or two or more children, and another person who is, or
other persons who are, of full age, the conveyance operates to vest the land in the other
person or persons in trust for the child or children and the other person or persons (or if
he purports to convey it to them in trust for any persons, for those persons)[6]. Where
immediately before 1 January 1997, a conveyance was operating[7] as an agreement to
execute a settlement[8] in favour of a child or children the agreement ceased to have effect
on that date, and the conveyance subsequently operated instead as a declaration that the
land was held in trust for the child or children[9]. Where after that date, a legal estate in
land would, by reason of intestacy or in any other circumstances not dealt with above,
vest in a person who is a child if he were a person of full age, the land is held in trust for
the child[10].

Where, by virtue of an instrument[11] coming into operation after 1 January 1997, land
becomes charged voluntarily (or in consideration of marriage[12]) or by way of family
arrangement[13], whether immediately or after an interval, with the payment of a
rentcharge for the life of a person or a shorter period, or capital, annual or periodical sums
for the benefit of a person[14], the instrument operates as a declaration that the land is held
in trust for giving effect to the charge[15].

Where there is a conveyance of land held on charitable, ecclesiastical or public trusts
(other than land to which the Universities and College Estates Act 1925 applies[16]) if the
statutory provisions relating to dispositions and mortgages[17] do not apply to the
conveyance, it must state that the land is held on such trusts, and if the specified
provisions[18] have not been complied with in relation to the conveyance and a purchaser
has notice that the land is held on such trusts, he must see that any consents or orders
necessary to authorise the transaction have been obtained[19]. Where any trustees or the
majority of any set of trustees have power to transfer or create any legal estate in the land,
the estate must be transferred or created by them in the names and on behalf of the
persons in whom it is vested[20].

Where a person purports by an instrument coming into operation after 1 January 1997
to grant to another person an entailed interest[21] in real or personal property, the
instrument is not effective to grant an entailed interest, but operates instead as a
declaration that the property is held in trust absolutely for the person to whom an entailed

interest in the property was purportedly granted[22]. Where a person purports by an instrument coming into operation after that date to declare himself a tenant in tail of real or personal property, the instrument is not effective to create an entailed interest[23].

Where a settlement ceases to be a settlement for the purposes of the Settled Land Act 1925 because no relevant property[24] is, or is deemed to be, subject to the settlement, any property which is or later becomes subject to the settlement is held in trust for the persons interested under the settlement[25].

1 Ie the commencement of the Trusts of Land and Appointment of Trustees Act 1996: see para 676 note 1 ante.
2 'Legal estates' means the estates, interest and charges, in or over land (subsisting or created at law) which are by the Law of Property Act 1925 authorised to subsist or be created as legal estates (see REAL PROPERTY vol 39(2) (Reissue) para 47 et seq): s 205(1)(x); definition applied by the Trusts of Land and Appointment of Trustees Act 1996 s 23(2).
3 The Trusts of Land and Appointment of Trustees Act 1996 refers to minors but 'child' has been substituted throughout this title: see CHILDREN AND YOUNG PERSONS vol 5(2) (Reissue) para 603.
4 For the meaning of 'conveyance' see REAL PROPERTY vol 39(2) (Reissue) para 232; definition applied by ibid s 23(2).
5 Ibid s 2(6), Sch 1 para 1(1).
6 Ibid Sch 1 para 1(2).
7 Ie by virtue of the Settled Land Act 1925 s 27 (repealed): see the Trusts of Land and Appointment of Trustees Act 1996 Sch 1 para 1(3).
8 For the meaning of 'settlement' see para 678 note 1 post; definition applied by ibid s 23(2).
9 Ibid Sch 1 para 1(3).
10 Ibid Sch 1 para 2.
11 'Instrument' does not include a statute, unless the statute creates a settlement: Law of Property Act 1925 s 205(1)(viii); definition applied by the Trusts of Land and Appointment of Trustees Act 1996 s 23(2).
12 As to marriage as consideration see para 660 et seq ante.
13 As to family arrangements see para 1002 et seq post.
14 As to rentcharges and annual payments see generally RENTCHARGES AND ANNUITIES.
15 Trusts of Land and Appointment of Trustees Act 1996 Sch 1 para 3.
16 See EDUCATION vol 15 (Reissue) paras 263–264.
17 Ie the Charities Act 1993 ss 37(1), 39(1) (see CHARITIES vol 5(2) (Reissue) paras 330, 332): see the Trusts of Land and Appointment of Trustees Act 1996 Sch 1 para 4(2).
18 Ie the Charities Act 1993 ss 37(2), 39(2) (see CHARITIES vol 5(2) (Reissue) paras 330, 332): see the Trusts of Land and Appointment of Trustees Act 1996 Sch 1 para 4(2).
19 Ibid Sch 1 para 4(1), (2).
20 Ibid Sch 1 para 4(3).
21 As to entailed interests see para 715 et seq post; and REAL PROPERTY vol 39(2) (Reissue) para 117 et seq.
22 Trusts of Land and Appointment of Trustees Act 1996 Sch 1 para 5(1).
23 Ibid Sch 1 para 5(2).
24 For the meaning of 'relevant property' see para 676 note 8 ante.
25 Trusts of Land and Appointment of Trustees Act 1996 Sch 1 para 6.

678. What constitutes a settlement. If a settlement[1] is capable of being governed by the Settled Land Act 1925, having regard to the provisions of the Trusts of Land and Appointment of Trustees Act 1996[2], it will be a settlement for the purposes of the Settled Land Act 1925 if it is created by or is any deed, will, agreement for a settlement or other agreement[3], Act of Parliament (public or private[4]), or other instrument, or any number of instruments[5], whenever made or passed, under or by virtue of which instrument or instruments any land[6] (not held upon trust for sale[7]), after 31 December 1925 stands for the time being[8]:

(1) limited in trust[9] for any persons by way of succession[10];
(2) limited in trust for any person in possession (a) for an entailed interest[11] whether or not capable of being barred or defeated[12]; (b) for an estate in fee simple or for a term of years absolute[13] subject to an executory limitation, gift or disposition

over on failure of his issue or in any other event[14]; (c) for a base or determinable fee[15] or any corresponding interest in leasehold land[16]; or (d) being a child[17], for an estate in fee simple or for a term of years absolute[18];

(3)   limited in trust for any person for an estate in fee simple or for a term of years absolute contingently on the happening of any event[19]; or

(4)   charged, whether voluntarily or in consideration of marriage[20] or by way of family arrangement[21], and whether immediately or after an interval, with the payment of any rentcharge for the life of any person[22], or any less period, or of any capital, annual, or periodical[23] sums for the portions, advancement, maintenance or otherwise for the benefit[24] of any persons, with or without any term of years for securing or raising the rentcharge or other sums[25].

If land is held on an immediate binding[26] trust for sale[27], whether or not exercisable at the request or with the consent of any person, and with or without a power at discretion to postpone sale[28], a settlement is not created in respect of it by any of the limitations or charges or in any of the circumstances mentioned above[29].

1   'Settlement' includes an instrument or instruments which, under the Settled Land Act 1925, or the Acts which it replaces (ie the Settled Land Acts 1882 to 1890, namely the Settled Land Act 1882, the Settled Land Act 1884, the Settled Land Acts (Amendment) Act 1887, the Settled Land Act 1889, and the Settled Land Act 1890: Short Titles Act 1896 s 2, Sch 2), is or are deemed (see para 679 post) to be or which together constitute (see paras 681–683 post) a settlement, and a settlement which is deemed to have been made by any person or to be subsisting for the purposes of the Settled Land Act 1925: s 117(1)(xxiv). 'Settlement' includes compound settlement if one subsists: see s 1(1) proviso; and para 681 post. See also *Re Cradocks Settled Estates* [1926] Ch 944; *Re Cayley and Evans' Contract* [1930] 2 Ch 143; *Re Curwen, Curwen v Graham* [1931] 2 Ch 341. As to retrospective amendments of the Settled Land Acts 1882 to 1890 see the Settled Land Act 1925 s 118, Sch 4. For the purposes of the Settled Land Act 1925, a settlement may either mean the document or documents creating the settlement or may be a particular state of affairs brought or deemed to have been brought about by one or more documents; and documents may create more than one settlement: *Re Ogle's Settled Estates* [1927] 1 Ch 229. See also *Roome v Edwards* [1982] AC 279 at 292–293, [1981] 1 All ER 736 at 739–740, HL, per Lord Wilberforce.

2   It is no longer possible to create settlements under the Settled Land Act 1925: see para 676 ante.

3   See *Bacon v Bacon* [1947] P 151, [1947] 2 All ER 327, where it was held that a consent order, made on divorce, for securing to a wife for life occupation of a house constitutes an agreement creating a settlement within the Settled Land Act 1925 s 1(1) (as amended). As to consent orders see DIVORCE.

4   *Vine v Raleigh* [1896] 1 Ch 37. An Act which neither incorporates nor affects the limitations of a settlement, but merely confers powers of management upon its trustees, is not part of the settlement: *Talbot v Scarisbrick* [1908] 1 Ch 812. See also *Re Buttle's Will Trusts, Buttle v IRC* [1977] 3 All ER 1039, [1977] 1 WLR 1200, CA, where no settlement arose on a partial intestacy by virtue of the will and the Administration of Estates Act 1925 (see EXECUTORS AND ADMINISTRATORS).

5   As to compound settlements see para 681 et seq post.

6   For the meaning of 'land' see para 680 note 1 post.

7   See the text and notes 26–29 infra. See also para 609 ante; and REAL PROPERTY vol 39(2) (Reissue) para 64 et seq. The Settled Land Act 1925 s 1 (as amended) does not apply to land held on any trust arising by virtue of the Trusts of Land and Appointment of Trustees Act 1996 s 5(1), Sch 2 (see REAL PROPERTY vol 39(2) (Reissue) para 66): see s 5(2).

8   See the Settled Land Act 1925 s 1(1).

9   'Trust' includes an implied or constructive trust: ibid s 117(1)(xii). As to implied and constructive trusts see TRUSTS vol 48 (Reissue) para 585 et seq.

10   Ibid s 1(1)(i). The words 'stands ... limited ... by way of succession' have no technical force, and must be construed broadly (see *Re Mundy and Roper's Contract* [1899] 1 Ch 275, CA; *Re Phillimore's Estate, Phillimore v Milnes* [1904] 2 Ch 460; *Re Marshall's Settlement, Marshall v Marshall* [1905] 2 Ch 325; *Re Trafford's Settled Estates* [1915] 1 Ch 9; *Re Monckton's Settlement, Monckton v Calder* [1917] 1 Ch 224); and they may include land subject to a right of residence (*Re Hanson, Hanson v Eastwood* [1928] Ch 96; *Binions v Evans* [1972] Ch 359, [1972] 2 All ER 70, CA). See further para 762 note 18 post. However, the words were held not to include an instrument by which land stood limited to, or in trust for, one and the same person for various estates and interests by way of succession (see *Re Pocock and Prankerd's Contract* [1896] 1 Ch 302), or by which land was limited to A B and his successors, vicars of X (see *Ex p Vicar of Castle Bytham, ex p Midland Rly Co* [1895] 1 Ch 348; *Re Bishop of Bath and Wells* [1899] 2 Ch 138), or by which a house was given upon trust to permit the minister for the time being officiating at a particular church

to reside in it (*Re Higgs, Symonds v Rhodes* [1927] WN 316). As to land held upon ecclesiastical trusts see para 680 post. Where a trust deed created under the Settled Land Act 1925 s 1 (as amended) provides a person with a life interest in a property, the sale proceeds of that property may be used by the trustees to purchase another property in which the person has a life interest, even if the deed makes no such provision: *Costello v Costello* [1996] 3 FCR 40, [1996] 1 FLR 805, CA.

11 'Entailed interest' means an interest in tail or in tail male or in tail female or in tail special: see the Law of Property Act 1925 s 130(1); definition applied by the Settled Land Act 1925 s 117(1)(xxviii). The Law of Property Act 1925 s 130(1) has been repealed by the Trusts of Land and Appointment of Trustees Act 1996 s 25(2), Sch 4 except in relation to any entailed interest created before 1 January 1997: see REAL PROPERTY vol 39(2) (Reissue) para 119. As to the application of this provision to personalty settled after 1925 see para 939 post. As to entailed interests generally see para 715 et seq post; and REAL PROPERTY vol 39(2) (Reissue) para 117 et seq.

12 Settled Land Act 1925 s 1(1)(ii)(a). As to disentail see REAL PROPERTY vol 39(2) (Reissue) para 121.

13 'Term of years absolute' means a term of years, taking effect either in possession or in reversion, with or without impeachment for waste, whether at a rent or not and whether subject or not to another legal estate, and whether certain or liable to determination by notice, re-entry, operation of law, or by a provision for cesser on redemption, or in any other event (other than the dropping of a life, or the determination of a determinable life interest), but does not include any term of years determinable with life or lives or with the cesser of a determinable life interest, nor, if created after 1925, a term of years which is not expressed to take effect in possession within 21 years after its creation where required by statute to take effect within that period; and 'term of years' includes a term for less than a year, or for a year or years and a fraction of a year or from year to year: ibid s 117(1)(xxix). 'Legal estate' means an estate interest or charge in or over land (subsisting or created at law) which is by statute authorised to subsist or to be created at law: s 117(1)(xi). As to legal estates and terms of years generally see REAL PROPERTY vol 39(2) (Reissue) para 45.

14 Ibid s 1(1)(ii)(b).

15 Ie other than a fee which is a fee simple absolute by virtue of the Law of Property Act 1925 s 7 (as amended) (see REAL PROPERTY vol 39(2) (Reissue) para 91): see the Settled Land Act 1925 s 1(1)(ii)(c) (as amended: see note 16 infra). 'Determinable fee' means a fee determinable whether by limitation or condition: s 117(1)(iv). See also REAL PROPERTY vol 39(2) (Reissue) paras 114–116.

16 Ibid s 1(1)(ii)(c) (amended by the Trusts of Land and Appointment of Trustees Act 1996 s 25(1), Sch 3).

17 See para 665 note 13 ante.

18 Settled Land Act 1925 s 1(1)(ii)(d). A child is deemed to be entitled in possession notwithstanding any subsisting right of dower (not assigned by metes and bounds) affecting the land: see s 1(3); and para 679 post. Where a child is beneficially entitled to land for an estate in fee simple or for a term of years absolute and by reason of an intestacy or otherwise there is no instrument under which his interest arises or is acquired, a settlement is deemed to have been made by the intestate or by the person whose interest the child has acquired: s 1(2). See also *Re Taylor, Pullan v Taylor* [1931] 2 Ch 242; and CHILDREN AND YOUNG PERSONS vol 5(2) (Reissue) para 632. As to the age of majority see para 605 note 1 ante.

19 Settled Land Act 1925 s 1(1)(iii). See also *Re Bird, Watson v Nunes* [1927] 1 Ch 210. See further REAL PROPERTY vol 39(2) (Reissue) para 115.

20 As to marriage as consideration see paras 660–663 ante.

21 As to family arrangements see para 1002 et seq post.

22 As to rentcharges for the life of a person see RENTCHARGES AND ANNUITIES vol 39(2) (Reissue) para 74 et seq.

23 A perpetual annuity is an annual or periodical sum for the 'benefit' of the person receiving it: *Re Austen, Collins v Margetts* [1929] 2 Ch 155.

24 'Benefit' is not to be construed ejusdem generis with portions, advancement and maintenance: *Re Bird, Watson v Nunes* [1927] 1 Ch 210; *Re Austen, Collins v Margetts* [1929] 2 Ch 155. See also *Pilkington v IRC* [1964] AC 612 at 634–635, [1962] 3 All ER 622 at 627, HL.

25 See the Settled Land Act 1925 s 1(1)(v). The statutory prohibition on creating rentcharges does not apply to the creation of a rentcharge which has the effect of making the land settled land, or which would have that effect but for the fact that the land is already settled land or is held on a trust of land: see the Rentcharges Act 1977 s 2(3)(a), (b) (as substituted); and RENTCHARGES AND ANNUITIES vol 39(2) (Reissue) para 774. Such a rentcharge is not subject to the provisions of the Rentcharges Act 1977 relating to the extinguishment of rentcharges (see s 3(3); and RENTCHARGES AND ANNUITIES vol 39(2) (Reissue) para 894), or to the redemption of rentcharges (see s 8(4); and RENTCHARGES AND ANNUITIES vol 39(2) (Reissue) para 900). Settled land which on 1 January 1926 became subject to a settlement by reason only of the existence of a charge was not settled land immediately prior to that date: *Re Earl of Carnarvon's Chesterfield Settled Estates, Re Earl of Carnarvon's Highclere Settled Estates* [1927] 1 Ch 138; *Re Ogle's Settled Estates* [1927] 1 Ch 229; *Re Lord Alington and London County Council's Contract* [1927] 2 Ch 253; *Re Blake's Settled Estates* [1932] IR 637. The 'settlement' is the instrument creating the charge: *Re Earl of*

Carnarvon's Chesterfield Settled Estates, Re Earl of Carnarvon's Highclere Settled Estates supra; *Re Ogle's Settled Estates* supra. This provision has been held to include land subject to a charge given to two or more persons as joint tenants (*Re Gaul and Houlston's Contract* [1928] Ch 689, CA), or as tenants in common (*Re Bird, Watson v Nunes* [1927] 1 Ch 210). When different portions of an estate had, prior to 1 January 1926, been sold to different purchasers subject to a family charge, each portion became on that date the subject matter of a separate settlement and accordingly separate sets of trustees could be appointed in respect of each settlement: *Re Ogle's Settled Estates* supra. As to the power to convey settled land subject to a charge see para 703 post.

26   This concept is relevant in determining the status of a settlement as at 1 January 1997, although the word 'binding' is excluded from the definition of 'trust for sale' in the Law of Property Act 1925 s 205(1)(xxix) by the Trusts of Land and Appointment of Trustees Act 1996 s 25(2), Sch 4: see note 27 infra. In any event the word 'binding' does not exclude a trust for sale as usually understood (*Re Parker's Settled Estates, Parker v Parker* [1928] Ch 247; not following *Re Leigh's Settled Estates* [1926] Ch 852, and *Re Leigh's Settled Estates (No 2)* [1927] 2 Ch 13), but there will not be an immediate binding trust for sale unless the trust for sale comprises the whole estate which is the subject matter of the settlement (*Re Parker's Settled Estates, Parker v Parker* supra; *Re Norton, Pinney v Beauchamp* [1929] 1 Ch 84; *Re Beaumont Settled Estates* [1937] 2 All ER 353; *Re Sharpe's Deed of Release, Sharpe and Fox v Gullick* [1939] Ch 51, [1938] 3 All ER 449; *Bacon v Bacon* [1947] P 151, [1947] 2 All ER 327).

27   'Trust for sale', in relation to land, means an immediate trust for sale, whether or not exercisable at the request or with the consent of any person: Law of Property Act 1925 s 205(1)(xxix) (amended by the Trusts of Land and Appointment of Trustees Act 1996 Sch 4); definition applied by the Settled Land Act 1925 s 117(1)(xxx). 'Trustees for sale' means the persons (including a personal representative (see para 697 note 6 post) holding land on trust for sale: Law of Property Act 1925 s 205(1)(xxix); definition applied by the Settled Land Act 1925 s 117(1)(xxx).

28   A power to postpone sale is now implied into express trusts for sale, whenever created, and the reference to a power to postpone sale has now been deleted from the definition of 'trust for sale' in the Law of Property Act 1925: see note 27 supra.

29   See the Settled Land Act 1925 s 1(7) (added by the Law of Property (Amendment) Act 1926 s 7, Schedule). If a settlement is expressed to direct trustees for sale to permit a person who is not entitled to the rents and profits until sale to reside free of rent in the property, that person is tenant for life under the Settled Land Act 1925, and the land is not held on an immediate binding trust for sale: *Dodsworth v Dodsworth* (1973) 228 Estates Gazette 1115, CA, distinguishing *Re Herklots' Will Trusts, Temple v Scorer* [1964] 2 All ER 66, [1964] 1 WLR 583, where the person to whom the right of occupation was given was entitled to the rents and profits until sale, and overruling *Ayer v Benton* (1967) 204 Estates Gazette 359. As to when land subject to a right of residence is settled land see also note 10 supra.

679. Where land is deemed to be the subject of a settlement. In certain cases land which is not the subject of a settlement[1] is deemed for the purposes of the Settled Land Act 1925, to be the subject of a settlement. These are:

(1)   where there is a subsisting right of dower[2] (not assigned by metes and bounds) affecting land to which a child[3] is entitled in possession, in which case the right of dower is deemed to be an interest comprised in the subject of the settlement and coming to the dowress under or by virtue of the settlement[4];

(2)   where dower has been assigned by metes and bounds, in which case the letters of administration or probate granted in respect of the estate of the husband of the dowress is deemed a settlement made by the husband[5];

(3)   an estate or interest not disposed of by a settlement and remaining in or reverting to the settlor, or any person deriving title under him, is for the purposes of the Settled Land Act 1925 an estate or interest comprised in the subject of the settlement and coming to the settlor or such person under or by virtue of the settlement[6];

(4)   where a settlement creates an entailed interest which is incapable of being barred or defeated[7], or a base or determinable fee[8], whether or not the reversion or right of reverter is in the Crown, or any corresponding interest in leasehold land[9];

(5)   where the subject of a settlement is an entailed interest, or base or determinable fee, whether or not the reversion or right of reverter is in the Crown, or any corresponding interest in leasehold land[10]; and

(6)   the estate or interest of a tenant by the curtesy, which is deemed to be an estate or interest arising under a settlement made by his wife[11].

1   For the meaning of 'settlement' see para 678 note 1 ante.
2   'Dower' includes freebench: Settled Land Act 1925 s 117(1)(vi). Dower and freebench have been abolished with certain savings: see the Administration of Estates Act 1925 ss 45(1)(c), 51(2) (as amended); and EXECUTORS AND ADMINISTRATORS; REAL PROPERTY vol 39(2) (Reissue) para 161. As to estates in dower see REAL PROPERTY vol 39(2) (Reissue) para 161.
3   See para 665 note 13 ante.
4   See the Settled Land Act 1925 s 1(3). See also *Re Taylor, Pullan v Taylor* [1931] 2 Ch 242.
5   See the Settled Land Act 1925 s 1(3). This provision applies whether the person entitled subject to the right of dower is a child or of full age. As to letters of administration or probate see EXECUTORS AND ADMINISTRATORS.
6   Ibid s 1(4). See also *Re Hunter and Hewlett's Contract* [1907] 1 Ch 46; and cf *Re Bond, Panes v A-G* [1901] 1 Ch 15. This provision binds the Crown: Settled Land Act 1925 s 1(6).
7   For the meaning of 'entailed interest' see para 678 note 11 ante. See also para 677 text and note 22 ante.
8   For the meaning of 'determinable fee' see para 678 note 15 ante.
9   Settled Land Act 1925 s 1(5)(a). See also note 10 infra.
10   Ibid s 1(5)(b). Under s 1(5)(a) or (b) (see heads (4) and (5) in the text) the reversion or right of reverter upon the cesser of the interest so created or settled is deemed to be an interest comprised in the subject of the settlement, and limited by the settlement: s 1(5). This provision binds the Crown: s 1(6).
11   Ibid s 20(3). Tenancy by the curtesy has been abolished with certain savings: see the Administration of Estates Act 1925 ss 45(1)(b), 51(2); Law of Property Act 1925 s 130(4). See further EXECUTORS AND ADMINISTRATORS; REAL PROPERTY vol 39(2) (Reissue) paras 157–160; and para 939 post.

680. Meaning of 'settled land'. 'Settled land' means land[1] which is or is deemed to be the subject of a settlement[2]. The fact that part of an estate is settled land does not make the whole estate settled land[3]. Land held upon trust for sale is not settled land within the Settled Land Act 1925[4].

Land held on charitable, ecclesiastical or public trusts is no longer settled land, whenever the trust was created[5].

1   'Land' includes land of any tenure, and mines and minerals whether or not held apart from the surface, buildings or parts of buildings (whether the division is horizontal, vertical or made in any other way) and other corporeal hereditaments; also a manor, an advowson, and a rent and other incorporeal hereditaments, and an easement, right, privilege or benefit in, over or derived from land, and any estate or interest in land, but does not (except in the phrase 'trust of land') include an undivided share in land: Settled Land Act 1925 s 117(1)(ix) (amended by the Trusts of Land and Appointment of Trustees Act 1996 s 25(1), Sch 3 para 2). This includes the benefit of a restrictive covenant: *Earl of Leicester v Wells-next-the-Sea UDC* [1973] Ch 110, [1972] 3 All ER 77. As to settlements of advowsons see para 609 ante. 'Hereditaments' means real property which on an intestacy might before 1926 have devolved on an heir (Settled Land Act 1925 s 117(1)(vii)) (see further EXECUTORS AND ADMINISTRATORS); 'manor' includes lordship, and reputed manor or lordship (s 117(1)(xiv)) (see further CUSTOM AND USAGE vol 12(1) (Reissue) para 695 et seq); and 'mines and minerals' means mines and minerals whether already opened or in work or not, and includes all minerals and substances in, on or under the land, obtainable by underground or by surface working (s 117(1)(xv)) (see generally MINES, MINERALS AND QUARRIES). The settled land may consist entirely of ground rents (see *Re Wilkinson, Lloyd v Steel* (1901) 85 LT 43); and where prior to 1926 two moieties of land were settled by separate instruments upon the same limitations, it was held that they became merged and that the entirety of the land was settled land (*Re Egton Settled Estate, Foster v Foster* [1931] 2 Ch 180).
2   See the Settled Land Act 1925 ss 2, 117(1)(xxiv). For the meaning of 'settlement' see para 678 note 1 ante; and as to land deemed to be the subject of a settlement see para 679 ante.
3   See *Re Bective Estate* (1891) 27 LR Ir 364.
4   See para 678 ante.
5   See the Trusts of Land and Appointment of Trustees Act 1996 s 2(5); and para 676 ante.

681. Meaning of 'compound settlement'. A settlement[1] for the purposes of the Settled Land Act 1925, may be created by or consist of any number of instruments[2]. Where a series of settlements extending over several generations has been effected by means of powers of appointment and disentailing assurances, the whole series forms one settlement, called a 'compound settlement'[3].

1   For the meaning of 'settlement' see para 678 note 1 ante.
2   See the Settled Land Act 1925 s 1(1) (as amended); and para 678 ante. As to the position before the Settled Land Act 1925 came into force see para 682 post.
3   Where land is the subject of a compound settlement, references in the Settled Land Act 1925 to the settlement must be construed as meaning such compound settlements, unless the context otherwise requires: ibid s 1(1) proviso. For the meaning of 'land' see para 680 note 1 ante. A settlement by reference to the trusts of another settlement does not constitute a compound settlement: *Re Adair, Adair v Treherne* [1927] WN 229; *Re Shelton's Settled Estates* [1928] WN 27. As to powers of appointment see para 922 et seq post. As to disentailing deeds see REAL PROPERTY vol 39(2) (Reissue) para 121 et seq.

682. Co-existing settlements before 1926. Under the law in force prior to 1926[1] there might be at the same time a more comprehensive settlement consisting of several deeds, and a less comprehensive settlement constituted by one of the deeds only[2], or even a number of settlements each constituted by one or a number of deeds. When a tenant for life wished to exercise his statutory powers, it was necessary to determine what settlements were subsisting and under which one or more of them the tenant for life could exercise his powers[3].

1   Ie before the Settled Land Act 1925 came into force. As to the position after 1925 see para 683 post.
2   *Re Du Cane and Nettlefold's Contract* [1898] 2 Ch 96 at 105; *Re Mundy and Roper's Contract* [1899] 1 Ch 275 at 295, CA; *Re Lord Wimborne and Browne's Contract* [1904] 1 Ch 537.
3   *Re Cornwallis-West and Munro's Contract* [1903] 2 Ch 150; *Parr v A-G* [1926] AC 239, HL. See also the cases cited in note 2 supra. A tenant for life could sell settled land free from jointures created under powers prior to the deed by which his life estate was created: *Re Marquis of Ailesbury and Lord Iveagh* [1893] 2 Ch 345; *Re Mundy and Roper's Contract* [1899] 1 Ch 275, CA; *Re Phillimore's Estate, Phillimore v Milnes* [1904] 2 Ch 460.

683. Since 1925 a compound settlement is the only settlement. Since 31 December 1925, where a settlement consists of more than one instrument, there can be one settlement only for the purposes of the Settled Land Act 1925, namely the compound settlement[1]; and, except in one case[2], the settled land can only be dealt with by the tenant for life in exercise of his powers under the compound settlement[3]. However, it is of no importance to a purchaser dealing with the tenant for life under which instrument the life estate of the tenant for life arises, because the tenant for life will in every case be able to exercise all the powers conferred by any of the instruments constituting the settlement[4].

1   See para 681 text and note 3 ante. See also *Re Cradock's Settled Estates* [1926] Ch 944; *Re Cayley and Evans' Contract* [1930] 2 Ch 143; *Re Curwen, Curwen v Graham* [1931] 2 Ch 341.
2   Ie where a person is beneficially entitled to land subject to a prior interest, in which case he may convey the legal estate subject to that interest as if the land had not been settled land: see the Law of Property (Amendment) Act 1926 s 1(1), (3); and para 703 post.
3   See para 761 et seq post.
4   *Re Cowley Settled Estates* [1926] Ch 725. Cf *Re Beaumont Settled Estates* [1937] 2 All ER 353.

684. Effect of dealings with beneficial interests. Any instrument by which either a tenant for life[1] or a remainderman deals with his beneficial interest and by which new beneficial interests[2] in the settled land[3] are created is one of the documents declaring trusts concerning the settled land, and, as such, is one of the instruments constituting a compound settlement[4]. However, an instrument by which a tenant for life merely makes an absolute assignment of his beneficial interest does not form part of a compound settlement[5], and the same principle applies in the case of an instrument by which a tenant for life creates a charge upon his beneficial interest by way of security, as well as in the case of any similar dealings by a remainderman[6]. An assignment by a tenant for life of his beneficial interest, whether or not his interest was in possession at the time when the assignment was made, does not operate to pass the statutory powers to the assignee[7]. While, therefore, a tenant for life must give effect to all equitable interests affecting the settled land of which he has notice[8], including the rights of an assignee or chargee of his own beneficial interest, any disposition by him of that interest must be ignored in ascertaining the person who is entitled to have a vesting instrument executed in his favour[9].

An apparent exception to this principle is created by the provision that an instrument by which a tenant for life, in consideration of marriage or as part or by way of any family arrangement, not being a security for payment of money advanced, makes an assignment of or creates a charge upon his estate or interest under the settlement is to be deemed one of the instruments creating the settlement[10]. However, such an instrument is not one of the instruments creating the settlement for all the purposes of the Settled Land Act 1925, but is only to be deemed such for the purpose of avoiding the necessity of obtaining the assignee's consent to the exercise of the statutory powers where such consent would otherwise be required[11]. Such an instrument does not, therefore, form any exception to the general rule.

1 For the meaning of 'tenant for life' see para 671 note 5 ante. See also para 761 et seq post.
2 As to beneficial interests see para 761 et seq post.
3 For the meaning of 'settled land' see para 680 text to note 2 ante.
4 As to the meaning of 'compound settlement' see para 681 text and note 3 ante.
5 *Re Earl of Carnarvon's Chesterfield Settled Estates, Re Earl of Carnarvon's Highclere Settled Estates* [1927] 1 Ch 138.
6 *Re Earl of Carnarvon's Chesterfield Settled Estates, Re Earl of Carnarvon's Highclere Settled Estates* [1927] 1 Ch 138. See also MORTGAGE.
7 See the Settled Land Act 1925 s 104(1); and para 777 post. The only exception to this rule is where the tenant for life surrenders his life estate to the next remainderman: see para 778 post.
8 See ibid s 16(1)(i); and para 767 post.
9 See para 688 et seq post.
10 Settled Land Act 1925 s 104(11). Any such instrument is not an assignment for value for the purposes of s 104 (see para 777 et seq post): s 104(11). This provision does not have effect with respect to any disposition made before 18 August 1890, if inconsistent with the nature or terms of the disposition: s 104(11) proviso.
11 *Re Du Cane and Nettlefold's Contract* [1898] 2 Ch 96.

685. Settlements by different instruments on the same limitations. Where estates[1] are settled by different settlements[2] upon the same limitations[3], whether by reference or otherwise, the following provisions apply[4]:

(1) the estates or any two or more of them, as the case may require, may be treated as one aggregate estate, in which case the aggregate estate will be, for all the purposes of the Settled Land Act 1925, the settled land[5];

(2) where the trustees for the purposes of the Settled Land Act 1925[6] of the two or several settlements are the same persons, they will be the trustees of the settlement of the aggregate estate for all the purposes of that Act, and all or any part of the capital money arising from one of the estates may be applied by the direction of the tenant for life[7] or statutory owner[8] as if the money had arisen from any other of the estates[9];

(3) where the trustees for the purposes of the Settled Land Act 1925 of the settlements or of any two or more of them are not the same persons[10], then (a) any notice

required to be given by the Act[11] to the trustees of the settlement and to the solicitor of such trustees must be given to the trustees of every settlement which comprises any part of the land to which such notice relates and to the solicitor of those trustees[12]; (b) any capital money arising on any sale, exchange, lease[13], mortgage, charge or other disposition[14] of land comprised in more than one settlement must be apportioned between the trustees of the different settlements in such manner as the tenant for life or statutory owner may think fit[15]; and (c) all or any part of the capital money arising from the land comprised in one of the settlements may be paid by the trustees of that settlement, by such direction, to the trustees of any of the other settlements, to be applied by such last-mentioned trustees as if the money had arisen from land comprised in that other settlement[16]; and

(4)   for the purposes of these provisions, money liable to be laid out in the purchase of land to be settled upon the same limitations as other land may be applied and dealt with in like manner in all respects as if land had been purchased and settled, and the money were capital money arising from it[17].

1   'Estate' means the land, capital money and securities representing capital money for the time being subject to a particular settlement: Settled Land Act 1925 s 91(4). For the meaning of 'capital money arising under the Act' see para 795 post.
2   For the meaning of 'settlement' see para 678 note 1 ante.
3   Estates are to be deemed to be settled upon the same limitations, notwithstanding that any of them may be subject to incumbrances, charges or powers of charging to which the other or others of them may not be subject: Settled Land Act 1925 s 91(2). Cf *Re Lord Stamford's Settled Estates* (1889) 43 ChD 84; *Re Byng's Settled Estates* [1892] 2 Ch 219. As to limitations see para 715 et seq post.
4   See the Settled Land Act 1925 s 91(1).
5   Ibid s 91(1)(i). As many vesting instruments may be executed as may be convenient: *Re Clayton's Settled Estates* [1926] Ch 279. As to the application of money settled by one deed in the improvement of land settled by another see para 809 text and note 12 post. For the meaning of 'settled land' see para 680 text to note 2 ante.
6   See para 750 et seq post.
7   For the meaning of 'tenant for life' see para 671 note 5 ante. See also para 761 et seq post.
8   As to the statutory owner see para 766 post.
9   Settled Land Act 1925 s 91(1)(ii). Capital money arising under one settlement may be applied in discharging incumbrances which are charged on land comprised in that as well as in another settlement, even though the incumbrances are not charged on the capital money: *Re Symons, Symons-Jeune v Bunbury* [1927] 1 Ch 344. For the meaning of 'trustees of the settlement' see para 750 note 1 post. As to trustees of settlements by reference see para 755 post. As to life interests see para 716 post.
10 Settled Land Act 1925 s 91(1)(iii).
11 See paras 783–784 post.
12 Settled Land Act 1925 s 91(1)(iii)(a).
13 'Lease' includes an agreement for a lease: ibid s 117(1)(x).
14 'Disposition' includes a mortgage, charge by way of legal mortgage, lease, assent, vesting declaration, vesting instrument, disclaimer, release and every other assurance of property or of an interest in it by any instrument except a will, and 'dispose of' has a corresponding meaning: ibid s 117(1)(v). Where any provision in the Settled Land Act 1925 refers to sale, purchase, exchange, mortgaging, charging, leasing, or other disposition or dealing, or to any power, consent, payment, receipt, deed, assurance, contract, expenses, act, or transaction, it is to be construed (unless the contrary appears) as extending only to sales, purchases, exchanges, mortgages, charges, leases, dispositions, dealings, powers, consents, payments, receipts, deeds, assurances, contracts, expenses, acts, and transactions under that Act: s 112(2).
15 Ibid s 91(1)(iii)(b).
16 Ibid s 91(1)(iii)(c).
17 Ibid s 91(1)(iv). As to what is covered by the expression 'money liable to be laid out in the purchase of land' see para 796 post.

686. Position where all estates are not subject to the same incumbrances. If any of the estates are subject to incumbrances, charges or powers of charging to which the other or others of them is or are not subject[1], the powers relating to the payment or application of capital money[2] may not be exercised without a court order unless the settlement[3] under which the capital money is held otherwise provides[4]. However, a court order is not necessary if part, at any rate, of the land comprised in each settlement is subject to the same incumbrance[5].

1 See para 685 note 3 ante.
2 Ie the powers contained in the Settled Land Act 1925 s 91 (see para 685 ante): see s 91(2) proviso.
3 For the meaning of 'settlement' see para 678 note 1 ante.
4 Ibid s 91(2) proviso. As to the court see para 792 post.
5 *Re Symons, Symons-Jeune v Bunbury* [1927] 1 Ch 344.

687. Appointment by the court of trustees of the settlement of an aggregate estate. The foregoing provisions as to different estates settled upon the same limitations[1] have effect without prejudice to any appointment made by the court before 1926 of trustees of the settlement of an aggregate estate, and to the court's power in any case after 1925 to make any such appointment, and, in any case where such appointment has been or is made, those provisions have effect as if the trustees so appointed and their successors in office were the trustees for the purposes of the Settled Land Act 1925 of each of the settlements constituting the settlement[2] of the aggregate estate, and there were no other trustees of it for the purposes of that Act[3].

1 Ie the Settled Land Act 1925 s 91: see paras 685–686 ante.
2 For the meaning of 'settlement' see para 678 note 1 ante.
3 See the Settled Land Act 1925 s 91(3). As to the appointment of trustees by the court see paras 756–758 post.

(2) VESTING DEEDS AND TRUST INSTRUMENTS

688. Method of creating a settlement inter vivos. It has not been possible to create a new settlement under the Settled Land Act 1925 since 1 January 1997[1]. However, this does not affect existing settlements and the law relating to the method of creating a settlement is still of relevance in relation to those existing settlements.

Every settlement[2] of a legal estate[3] in land[4] inter vivos[5], save as otherwise provided in the Settled Land Act 1925, must have been effected by two deeds, namely, a vesting deed[6] and a trust instrument[7], and if effected in any other way did not operate to transfer or create a legal estate[8].

1 See the Trusts of Land and Appointment of Trustees Act 1996 s 2; and para 676 ante.
2 For the meaning of 'settlement' see para 678 note 1 ante.
3 For the meaning of 'legal estate' see para 678 note 13 ante.
4 For the meaning of 'land' see para 680 note 1 ante.
5 As to settlements created by will see para 697 post.
6 In relation to settled land, 'vesting deed' or 'vesting order' means the instrument by which settled land is conveyed to or vested or declared to be vested in a tenant for life (see para 671 note 5 ante) or statutory owner (see para 766 post): Settled Land Act 1925 s 117(1)(xxxi).
7 'Trust instrument' means the instrument by which the trusts of the settled land are declared, and includes any two or more such instruments and a settlement or instrument which is deemed to be a trust instrument: ibid s 117(1)(xxxi). 'Instrument' does not include a statute unless the statute creates a settlement: s 117(1)(viii). See also para 695 post.
8 Ibid s 4(1).

689. Function of a principal vesting deed. By the vesting deed[1] the land is conveyed[2] to the tenant for life[3] or statutory owner[4], and if more than one as joint tenants, for the legal estate[5] the subject of the intended settlement[6], except that, if the legal estate is already vested in the tenant for life or statutory owner, it is sufficient, without any other conveyance, if the vesting deed declares that the land is vested in him for that estate[7]. A vesting deed for giving effect to a settlement[8], or for conveying settled land to a tenant for life or statutory owner during the subsistence of the settlement, is referred to in the Settled Land Act 1925 as a 'principal vesting deed'[9]. There can, if desired, be more than one principal vesting deed, and different parcels of the settled land can be comprised in separate principal vesting deeds[10].

1   For the meaning of 'vesting deed' see para 688 note 6 ante.
2   As to the procedure where the land is registered land see LAND REGISTRATION vol 26 (Reissue) paras 763 et seq, 1032 et seq.
3   For the meaning of 'tenant for life' see para 671 note 5 ante. See also para 761 et seq post.
4   As to the statutory owner see para 766 post.
5   For the meaning of 'legal estate' see para 678 note 13 ante.
6   See the Settled Land Act 1925 s 4(2). When a person settles an estate, prima facie, he intends to include in the conveyance every interest which he can part with and does not except: *Johnson v Webster* (1854) 4 De GM & G 474 at 488. See also the Law of Property Act 1925 s 63; and REAL PROPERTY vol 39(2) (Reissue) para 199.
7   See the Settled Land Act 1925 s 4(2) proviso. However, a person can convey land to himself: see the Law of Property Act 1925 s 72(3); and REAL PROPERTY vol 39(2) (Reissue) para 244.
8   For the meaning of 'settlement' see para 678 note 1 ante.
9   See the Settled Land Act 1925 s 5(1). As to the form of the deed see para 690 post. New settlements can no longer be created: see para 688 ante.
10   *Re Clayton's Settled Estates* [1926] Ch 279.

690. Form of principal vesting deed. A principal vesting deed[1] must contain:
  (1)   a description, either specific or general, of the settled land[2];
  (2)   a statement that the settled land is vested in the person or persons to whom it is conveyed or in whom it is declared to be vested upon the trusts from time to time affecting the settled land[3];
  (3)   the names of the persons who are appointed the trustees of the settlement[4];
  (4)   any additional or larger powers conferred by the trust instrument[5] relating to the settled land which by virtue of the Settled Land Act 1925 operate and are exercisable as if conferred by the Act on a tenant for life[6]; and
  (5)   the name of any person for the time being entitled under the trust instrument to appoint new trustees of the settlement[7].

These statements or particulars may be incorporated by reference to an existing vesting instrument[8], but not by reference to a trust instrument or a disentailing deed, except in the case of a settlement subsisting at the commencement of the Settled Land Act 1925[9], in which case they may be incorporated by reference to that settlement and to any instrument by which land has been conveyed to the uses or upon the trusts of that settlement[10].

As a rule the conveyance or declaration by a settlor in a vesting deed is expressed to be made by him 'as settlor'. This expression implies a covenant for further assurance by the person so conveying in favour of the person or persons to whom the property is conveyed[11].

1   For the meaning of 'principal vesting deed' see para 689 text to note 9 ante. New settlements can no longer be created: see para 688 ante.
2   Settled Land Act 1925 s 5(1)(a). For the meaning of 'settled land' see para 680 text to note 2 ante.
3   Ibid s 5(1)(b).
4   See ibid s 5(1)(c). For the meaning of 'trustees of the settlement' see para 750 note 1 post.
5   For the meaning of 'trust instrument' see para 688 note 7 ante.
6   Settled Land Act 1925 s 5(1)(d). As to the extension of statutory powers see paras 880–881 post. For the meaning of 'tenant for life' see para 671 note 5 ante. See also para 761 et seq post.
7   Ibid s 5(1)(e).

8   'Vesting instrument' means a vesting deed, a vesting assent or, where the land affected remains settled land, a vesting order: ibid s 117(1)(xxxi). 'Vesting assent' means the instrument by which a personal representative, after the death of a tenant for life or statutory owner, or the survivor of two or more tenants for life or statutory owners, vests settled land in a person entitled as tenant for life or statutory owner: s 117(1)(xxxi). For the meaning of 'vesting deed' or 'vesting order' see para 688 note 6 ante.

9   Ie 1 January 1926. 'A settlement subsisting at the commencement of the Settled Land Act 1925' includes a settlement created by virtue of the Act immediately on its commencement: s 117(1)(xxiv).

10   Ibid s 5(2). For forms of principal vesting deeds see s 15, Sch 1 Form 2; and the Law of Property (Miscellaneous Provisions) Act 1994 s 9(1), (2).

11   In respect of dispositions on or before 1 July 1995, the relevant covenant is to be found in the Law of Property Act 1925 s 76(1)(E), Sch 2, Pt V (repealed as regards dispositions of property made after that date by the Law of Property (Miscellaneous Provisions) Act 1994 ss 10(1), 21(2), Sch 2) in terms that the person so conveying, and every person deriving title under him by deed or act or operation of law in his lifetime subsequent to that conveyance, or by testamentary disposition or devolution in law, on his death, will, from time to time, and at all times, after the date of that conveyance, at the request and cost of any person deriving title under it, execute and do all such lawful assurances and things for further or more perfectly assuring the subject matter of the conveyance to the persons to whom the conveyance is made and those deriving title under them, as by them or any of them are reasonably required, subject as, if so expressed, and in the manner in which the conveyance is expressed to be made: see the Law of Property Act 1925 Sch 2 Pt V (repealed). For the purposes of this covenant, 'conveyance' includes, among other things, a vesting instrument: see s 205(1)(ii). In respect of dispositions after 1 July 1995, the relevant covenant is to be found in the Law of Property (Miscellaneous Provisions) Act 1994 s 2 in terms that the person making the disposition will at his own cost do all that he reasonably can to give the person to whom he disposes of the property the title he purports to give, including (1) in relation to a disposition of an interest in land the title to which is registered, doing all that he reasonably can to ensure that the person to whom the disposition is made is entitled to be registered as proprietor with at least the class of title registered immediately before the disposition; and (2) in relation to a disposition of an interest in land the title to which is required to be registered by virtue of the disposition, giving all reasonable assistance fully to establish to the satisfaction of the Chief Land Registrar the right of the person to whom the disposition is made to registration as proprietor: see s 2; and SALE OF LAND para 338 ante.

691. Form of subsidiary vesting deed. If, after the creation of a settlement[1] by means of a vesting deed[2], land[3] is acquired with capital money arising under the Settled Land Act 1925[4], or in exchange for settled land[5], such land must be conveyed to the tenant for life[6] or statutory owner[7] by means of a deed, which is referred to in that Act as a 'subsidiary vesting deed'[8]. It must contain:

(1)   particulars of the last or only principal vesting instrument[9] affecting land subject to the settlement[10];

(2)   a statement that the land conveyed is to be held upon and subject to the same trusts and powers as the land comprised in such last or only principal vesting instrument[11];

(3)   the names of the persons who are the trustees of the settlement[12]; and

(4)   the name of any person for the time being entitled to appoint new trustees of the settlement[13].

The acquisition of the land will not operate to increase or multiply charges or powers of charging[14].

Similarly, where on a grant of settled land a rentcharge can be[15] and is reserved, the deed by which the rentcharge is reserved is a 'subsidiary vesting deed'[16], and must contain:

(a)   a statement that the rentcharge is vested in the grantor and is subject to the settlement which, immediately before the grant, was subsisting with respect to the land out of which it was reserved[17]; and

(b)   particulars of the last or only principal vesting instrument affecting such land[18].

An extended lease granted under the Leasehold Reform Act 1967 to a tenant for life or statutory owner is treated as a subsidiary vesting deed[19].

1   For the meaning of 'settlement' see para 678 note 1 ante. It is no longer possible to create settlements under the Settled Land Act 1925: see paras 676, 688 ante.

2   For the meaning of 'vesting deed' see para 688 note 6 ante. The same principle applies where the original vesting instrument is a vesting assent: see para 698 post. For the meaning of 'vesting assent' see para 690 note 8 ante.

3   For the meaning of 'land' see para 680 note 1 ante.

4   As to capital money see para 795 et seq post.

5   For the meaning of 'settled land' see para 680 text to note 2 ante.

6   For the meaning of 'tenant for life' see para 671 note 5 ante. See also para 761 et seq post.

7   As to the statutory owner see para 766 post.

8   See the Settled Land Act 1925 s 10(1).

9   For the meaning of 'vesting instrument' see para 690 note 8 ante.

10 Settled Land Act 1925 s 10(2)(a). As to the principal vesting deed see paras 689–690 ante.

11 Ibid s 10(2)(b).

12 Ibid s 10(2)(c). For the meaning of 'trustees of the settlement' see para 750 note 1 post.

13 Ibid s 10(2)(d). For forms of subsidiary vesting deeds on the acquisition of land see s 15, Sch 1 Form 4; and the Law of Property (Miscellaneous Provisions) Act 1994 s 9(1), (2). A subsidiary vesting deed is also required where a long term is enlarged by a tenant for life or a statutory owner under the Law of Property Act 1925 s 153 (as amended): see para 858 post. As to the procedure where the land is registered land see LAND REGISTRATION vol 26 (Reissue) paras 1032 et seq.

14 Settled Land Act 1925 s 10(5). See also para 704 note 8 post.

15 The Rentcharges Act 1977 prohibits, subject to exceptions, the creation of new rentcharges: see RENTCHARGES AND ANNUITIES vol 39(2) (Reissue) para 751.

16 See the Settled Land Act 1925 s 10(1).

17 Ibid s 10(3)(a).

18 Ibid s 10(3)(b).

19 See the Leasehold Reform Act 1967 s 6(2); and LANDLORD AND TENANT vol 27(2) (Reissue) para 1277. As to leasehold enfranchisement see para 877 post; and LANDLORD AND TENANT vol 27(2) (Reissue) para 1253 et seq.

692. Effect of errors in vesting deed. Neither a principal vesting deed[1] nor a subsidiary vesting deed[2] will be invalidated by reason only of any error in any of the statements or particulars which the Settled Land Act 1925 requires to be contained in it[3]. However, a vesting deed will be invalid if it does not comply with the requirements of that Act; for example, if a compound settlement[4] exists, the vesting deed will be invalid if it does not give effect to the compound settlement or if it is not executed by the trustees of the compound settlement[5].

1   For the meaning of 'principal vesting deed' see para 689 text to note 9 ante.

2   For the meaning of 'subsidiary vesting deed' see para 691 text to notes 8, 16 ante.

3   Settled Land Act 1925 ss 5(3), 10(4).

4   As to the meaning of 'compound settlement' see para 681 text and note 3 ante.

5   *Re Cayley and Evans' Contract* [1930] 2 Ch 143. See, however, *Re Curwen, Curwen v Graham* [1931] 2 Ch 341, where a vesting deed to give effect to a compound settlement was held to be valid although the trustees of the compound settlement were described in it merely as being the trustees of the earliest of the documents which constituted the compound settlement. As to trustees of compound settlements see para 754 post.

693. Settlements of personal estates to be invested in land. In the case of an instrument subsisting on 1 January 1926, or made or coming into operation after that date, by virtue of which any money or securities[1] were or are liable, by statute or under a trust or direction contained in the instrument, to be invested in the purchase of land[2] to be conveyed so as to become settled land[3], but on that date or when that instrument was made or came into operation, as the case may be, there was no land in respect of which a principal vesting deed could be executed, the first deed thereafter by which any land was acquired is regarded as a principal vesting deed[4] and must be framed accordingly[5]. A vesting deed need not be executed in respect of money or securities[6].

1   'Securities' include stocks, funds and shares: Settled Land Act 1925 s 117(1)(xxiii).
2   For the meaning of 'land' see para 680 note 1 ante.
3   For the meaning of 'settled land' see para 680 text to note 2 ante.
4   For the meaning of 'principal vesting deed' see para 689 text to note 9 ante.
5   See the Settled Land Act 1925 s 10(1) proviso. See also *Re Draycott Settled Estate* [1928] Ch 371. As to the
    form of a principal vesting deed see para 690 ante.
6   *Re Clayton's Settled Estates* [1926] Ch 279.

694. Form of trust instrument. The trust instrument[1] must:

(1)   declare the trusts affecting the settled land[2];

(2)   appoint or constitute trustees of the settlement[3];

(3)   contain the power, if any, to appoint new trustees of the settlement[4];

(4)   set out, either expressly or by reference, any powers intended to be conferred by
      the settlement in extension of those conferred by the Settled Land Act 1925[5]; and

(5)   bear any ad valorem stamp duty which was payable (whether by virtue of the
      vesting deed or otherwise) in respect of the settlement[6].

1   For the meaning of 'trust instrument' see para 688 note 7 ante. New settlements can no longer be created:
    see para 688 ante.
2   Settled Land Act 1925 s 4(3)(a). As to the usual limitations see para 715 et seq post. For the meaning of
    'settled land' see para 680 text to note 2 ante.
3   Ibid s 4(3)(b). For the meaning of 'trustees of the settlement' see para 750 note 1 post.
4   Ibid s 4(3)(c). As to the appointment of trustees see para 756 post.
5   Ibid s 4(3)(d). As to the statutory powers see para 775 et seq post.
6   Ibid s 4(3)(e). For forms of trust instruments see s 15, Sch 1 Form 3; and the Law of Property
    (Miscellaneous Provisions) Act 1994 s 9(1), (2). As to the stamp duty on settlements see para 623 ante;
    and see generally STAMP DUTIES AND STAMP DUTY RESERVE TAX.

695. Instruments deemed to be trust instruments. The following settlements and
instruments are for the purposes of the Settled Land Act 1925 deemed to be trust
instruments[1]:

(1)   an instrument[2] executed or, in the case of a will[3], coming into operation after
      1925 which by virtue of that Act is deemed to be a settlement[4];

(2)   a settlement which by virtue of that Act is deemed to have been made by any
      person after 1925[5];

(3)   an instrument inter vivos intended to create a settlement of a legal estate[6] in land
      which is executed after 1925 and does not comply with the requirements of that
      Act with respect to the method of effecting such a settlement[7]; and

(4)   a settlement made after 1925 (including a settlement by the will of a person who
      dies after 1925) of (a) an equitable interest in land which is capable, when in
      possession, of subsisting at law[8]; or (b) an entailed interest[9]; or (c) a base or
      determinable fee[10] or any corresponding interest in leasehold land[11], but only if
      and when the interest settled takes effect free from all equitable interests and
      powers under every prior settlement, if any[12].

1   Settled Land Act 1925 s 9(1). Any reference to a trust instrument in the Settled Land Act 1925 applies to
    the settlements and instruments set out in heads (1) to (4) in the text: see s 9(1). For the meaning of 'trust
    instrument' see para 688 note 7 ante.
2   For the meaning of 'instrument' see para 688 note 7 ante.
3   'Will' includes codicil: Settled Land Act 1925 s 117(1)(xxxiii). See generally WILLS.
4   See ibid s 9(1)(i). As to land deemed to be the subject of a settlement see para 679 ante. For the meaning
    of 'settlement' see para 678 note 1 ante.
5   See ibid s 9(1)(ii). This provision covers the following cases: (1) if a child (see para 665 note 13 ante) is
    beneficially entitled to land for an estate in fee simple or for a term of years absolute, and by reason of an
    intestacy or otherwise there is no instrument under which the interest of the child arises or is acquired, a
    settlement is deemed to have been made by the intestate, or by the person whose interest the child has

acquired (see s 1(2); and para 678 ante); (2) if dower has been assigned by metes and bounds, the letters of administration or probate granted in respect of the estate of the husband of the dowress is deemed a settlement made by the husband (see s 1(3); and para 679 ante); and (3) if the estate or interest of a tenant by the curtesy is deemed to be an estate or interest arising under a settlement by his wife (see s 20(3); and para 679 ante).

6   For the meaning of 'legal estate' see para 678 note 13 ante.
7   See the Settled Land Act 1925 s 9(1)(iii). As to such requirements see para 688 ante.
8   See ibid s 9(1)(iv)(a). 'Equitable interests' mean all other interests and charges in or over land or in the proceeds of sale of it other than an estate, interest or charge in or over land (subsisting or created at law) which is by statute authorised to subsist or be created at law; and an equitable interest 'capable of subsisting at law' means such an equitable interest as could validly subsist at law, if clothed with the legal estate: s 117(1)(xi). As to what estates, interests and charges are capable of subsisting or being created at law see the Law of Property Act 1925 s 1 (as amended); and REAL PROPERTY vol 39(2) (Reissue) para 45 et seq.
9   Settled Land Act 1925 s 9(1)(iv)(b). For the meaning of 'entailed interest' see para 678 note 11 ante.
10   For the meaning of 'determinable fee' see para 678 note 15 ante. As to what is a 'base fee' see REAL PROPERTY vol 39(2) (Reissue) paras 134–139.
11   Settled Land Act 1925 s 9(1)(iv)(c).
12   Ibid s 9(1)(iv).

696. Vesting deed to be executed to give effect to a trust instrument. As soon as practicable after a settlement[1], or an instrument[2] which for the purposes of the Settled Land Act 1925 is deemed to be a trust instrument[3], took effect as such[4], the trustees of the settlement[5] could, and on the request of the tenant for life[6] or statutory owner[7] had to, execute a principal vesting deed[8] containing the proper statements and particulars, declaring that the legal estate[9] in the settled land was to vest or was vested in the person or persons named in it, being the tenant for life or statutory owner, including the trustees themselves if they were the statutory owners, and, unless the legal estate was already so vested, this deed operated to convey or vest the legal estate in the settled land to or in such person or persons, and, if more than one, as joint tenants[10].

1   For the meaning of 'settlement' see para 678 note 1 ante.
2   For the meaning of 'instrument' see para 688 note 7 ante.
3   For the meaning of 'trust instrument' see para 688 note 7 ante. As to instruments deemed to be trust instruments see para 695 ante.
4   New settlements can no longer be created: see para 688 ante.
5   For the meaning of 'trustees of the settlement' see para 750 note 1 post. As to the position where there are no trustees see para 699 post.
6   For the meaning of 'tenant for life' see para 671 note 5 ante. See also para 761 et seq post.
7   As to the statutory owner see para 766 post.
8   For the meaning of 'principal vesting deed' see para 689 text to note 9 ante. See further paras 689–690 ante.
9   For the meaning of 'legal estate' see para 678 note 13 ante.
10   See the Settled Land Act 1925 s 9(2); and the Law of Property Act 1925 s 9(1) (see REAL PROPERTY vol 39(2) (Reissue) para 246).

697. Settlements created by will. Where a settlement[1] was created by the will[2] of an estate owner[3] who died after 1925, the will is a trust instrument[4] for the purposes of the Settled Land Act 1925[5], and the personal representatives[6] of the testator hold the settled land[7] upon trust, if and when required so to do, to convey it to the person who, under the will or by virtue of the Settled Land Act 1925, is the tenant for life[8] or statutory owner[9], and, if more than one, as joint tenants[10].

1   For the meaning of 'settlement' see para 678 note 1 ante.
2   For the meaning of 'will' see para 695 note 3 ante. New settlements can no longer be created: see para 688 ante.
3   'Estate owner' means the owner of a legal estate: Settled Land Act 1925 s 117(1)(xi). For the meaning of 'legal estate' see para 678 note 13 ante.
4   For the meaning of 'trust instrument' see para 688 note 7 ante.

5   See the Settled Land Act 1925 s 6(a).
6   'Personal representative' means the executor, original or by representation, or administrator, for the time
    being of a deceased person, and where there are special personal representatives for the purposes of settled
    land means those personal representatives: ibid s 117(1)(xviii). As to special personal representatives see
    EXECUTORS AND ADMINISTRATORS.
7   For the meaning of 'settled land' see para 680 text to note 2 ante.
8   For the meaning of 'tenant for life' see para 671 note 5 ante. See also para 761 et seq post.
9   As to the statutory owner see para 766 post.
10 Settled Land Act 1925 s 6(b). This may be done by a vesting assent: see para 698 post. As to joint tenancies
    see REAL PROPERTY vol 39(2) (Reissue) para 190 et seq.

698. Vesting instruments on change of ownership. A principal vesting instrument[1]
is also necessary on a change of ownership, which will occur in any of the following cases:

  (1)   if on the death of a tenant for life[2] or statutory owner[3], or of the survivor of two
        or more tenants for life or statutory owners, in whom the settled land was vested,
        the land remains settled land[4];

  (2)   if a person by reason of attaining full age becomes a tenant for life for the purposes
        of the Settled Land Act 1925 of settled land, either alone[5] or jointly with any
        other person or persons[6]; and

  (3)   if by reason of forfeiture, surrender or otherwise the estate owner[7] of the settled
        land ceases to have the statutory powers of a tenant for life and the land remains
        settled land[8].

In any such case the person or persons in whom the settled land is vested, including
the personal representatives[9] of a deceased tenant for life or statutory owner, is or are
bound to convey the settled land, if and when required so to do, to the person who under
the trust instrument or by virtue of the Settled Land Act 1925 becomes the tenant for life
or statutory owner, and, if more than one, as joint tenants[10].

If in any case in which settled land ought to be conveyed to a tenant for life or
statutory owner the land is vested in personal representatives, they may execute either a
principal vesting deed or a vesting assent[11]. Such vesting assent, which operates as a
conveyance[12], must be in writing signed by them and must contain the like statements
and particulars as are required by the Settled Land Act 1925 in the case of a principal
vesting deed[13].

Every vesting instrument executed for the purpose of giving effect to a settlement or
instrument which is deemed to be a trust instrument[14], or to a settlement created by a
will[15], or on a change of ownership, must be made at the cost of the trust estate[16].

The obligation to execute any such vesting instrument is subject and without
prejudice (a) where the settlement is created by a will, to the rights and powers of the
personal representatives for the purposes of administration[17]; and (b) in any case, to the
person on whom the obligation is imposed being satisfied that provision has been or will
be made for the payment of any unpaid death duties[18] in respect of the land or any interest
in it for which he is accountable, and any interest and costs in respect of such duties, or
that he is otherwise effectually indemnified against such duties, interest and costs[19]. A
conveyance, if made by deed (but not a vesting assent) may contain a reservation to the
person by whom it is made of a term of years absolute[20] in the settled land, upon trusts
for indemnifying him against any unpaid death duties in respect of the settled land or any
interest in it, and any interest and costs in respect of such duties[21]. Furthermore, the
obligation does not affect the right of personal representatives to transfer or create such
legal estates to take effect in priority to the vesting deed or assent as may be required for
giving effect to the obligations imposed on them by statute[22], or any right which a person
entitled to an equitable charge for securing money actually raised, and affecting the whole
estate the subject of the settlement, may have to require effect to be given to it by a legal
mortgage[23] before the execution of a vesting deed or assent[24].

1   'Principal vesting instrument' includes any vesting instrument other than a subsidiary vesting deed: Settled Land Act 1925 s 117(1)(xxxi). For the meaning of 'vesting instrument' see para 690 note 8 ante. For the meaning of 'subsidiary vesting deed' see para 691 text to notes 8, 16 ante.

2   For the meaning of 'tenant for life' see para 671 note 5 ante. See also para 761 et seq post.

3   As to the statutory owner see para 766 post.

4   See the Settled Land Act 1925 s 7(1). As to the duration of settlements for the purposes of that Act see para 708 post. For the meaning of 'settled land' see para 680 text to note 2 ante; and for the meaning of 'land' see para 680 note 1 ante.

5   See ibid s 7(2).

6   See ibid s 7(3). As to the age of majority see para 605 note 1 ante.

7   For the meaning of 'estate owner' see para 697 note 2 ante.

8   See the Settled Land Act 1925 s 7(4). See also *Re Shawdon Estates Settlement* [1930] 2 Ch 1, CA. For the purposes of determining, where the estate owner of any settled land is bankrupt, whether the legal estate in the settled land is comprised in or is capable of being claimed for, the bankrupt's estate, the legal estate in the settled land is deemed not to vest in the estate owner unless and until the estate owner becomes absolutely and beneficially entitled to the settled land free from all limitations, powers, and charges taking effect under the settlement: Settled Land Act 1925 s 103 (amended by the Insolvency Act 1985 s 235(1), Sch 8 para 3). See also BANKRUPTCY AND INSOLVENCY vol 3(2) (Reissue) para 418. As to when the powers of the tenant for life cease see paras 684 ante, 778 post.

9   For the meaning of 'personal representative' see para 697 note 6 ante.

10 See the Settled Land Act 1925 s 7(1)–(4). As to the procedure where the land is registered land see LAND REGISTRATION vol 26 (Reissue) paras 1039 et seq.

11 See ibid ss 8(4), 9(4). For the meaning of 'vesting assent' see para 690 note 8 ante. That definition is not exhaustive, as a personal representative under a will which creates a settlement can execute a vesting assent: see para 697 ante.

12 See ibid s 8(1). 'Conveyance' includes a mortgage, charge by way of legal mortgage, lease, assent, vesting declaration, vesting instrument, disclaimer, release and every other assurance of property or of an interest in it by any instrument, except a will, and 'convey' has a corresponding meaning: s 117(1)(v).

13 See ibid ss 8(1), 9(4); Law of Property Act 1925 s 9(1); and para 695 ante. For a form of vesting assent see the Settled Land Act 1925 s 15, Sch 1 Form 5; and the Law of Property (Miscellaneous Provisions) Act 1994 s 9(1), (2).

14 See para 695 ante. For the meaning of 'settlement' see para 678 note 1 ante; for the meaning of 'instrument' see para 695 note 2 ante; and for the meaning of 'trust instrument' see para 688 note 7 ante.

15 See para 697 ante. For the meaning of 'will' see para 695 note 3 ante.

16 See the Settled Land Act 1925 ss 8(2), 9(4).

17 Ibid ss 8(3)(a), 9(4). As to the rights and powers of personal representatives see EXECUTORS AND ADMINISTRATORS.

18 'Death duty' means estate duty and every other duty leviable or payable on death: ibid s 117(1)(iii) (amended by the Finance Act 1949 s 52(10), Sch 11 Pt IV). This includes inheritance tax: see INHERITANCE TAXATION vol 24 (Reissue) para 401 et seq.

19 Settled Land Act 1925 ss 8(3)(b), 9(4). As to the liability of personal representatives or other estate owners see INHERITANCE TAXATION vol 24 (Reissue) para 636.

20 For the meaning of 'term of years absolute' see para 678 note 13 ante.

21 See the Settled Land Act 1925 ss 8(6), 9(4).

22 See ibid ss 8(5), 9(4). See also para 712 post. As to the obligations imposed on personal representatives by statute see EXECUTORS AND ADMINISTRATORS.

23 'Legal mortgage' means a mortgage by demise or sub-demise or a charge by way of legal mortgage, and 'legal mortgagee' has a corresponding meaning: ibid s 117(1)(xi).

24 See ibid ss 8(7), 9(4). As to equitable mortgages and charges see MORTGAGE. As to creating a legal mortgage to give effect to an equitable charge see para 767 post.

699. Power of the court to make vesting orders. If, when a vesting deed[1] or vesting assent[2] ought to be executed, any person who ought to execute it, or in whom the settled land[3] is wrongly vested, refuses or neglects to execute the requisite vesting deed or vesting assent within one month after demand in writing[4], or any such person is outside the United Kingdom[5], or cannot be found, or it is not known whether he is alive or dead[6], or for any reason the court[7] is satisfied that the vesting deed or vesting assent cannot be executed, or cannot be executed without undue delay or expense[8], the court, on the application of any person interested, may make an order vesting the settled land in the tenant for life[9] or statutory owner[10] or person, if any, of full age absolutely entitled (whether beneficially or as personal representative or trustee of land or otherwise) and, if the land remains settled land, the provisions of the Settled Land Act 1925 relating to a principal vesting deed or a subsidiary vesting deed[11], as the case may be, apply to any order so made and every such order must contain the like statements and particulars[12].

If a vesting deed or assent ought to be executed by the trustees of the settlement[13], but there are no such trustees, then (in default of a person able and willing to appoint such trustees) an application must be made to the court for the appointment of the trustees[14].

1   For the meaning of 'vesting deed' see para 688 note 6 ante.
2   For the meaning of 'vesting assent' see para 690 note 8 ante.
3   For the meaning of 'settled land' see para 680 text to note 2 ante.
4   See the Settled Land Act 1925 s 12(1)(a). See also *Re Shawdon Estates Settlement* [1930] 2 Ch 1, CA.
5   'United Kingdom' means Great Britain and Northern Ireland: Settled Land Act 1925 s 117(1)(xxxii). 'Great Britain' means England, Scotland and Wales: Union with Scotland Act 1706 preamble art I; Interpretation Act 1978 s 22(1), Sch 2 para 5(a). See further CONSTITUTIONAL LAW AND HUMAN RIGHTS vol 8(2) (Reissue) para 3.
6   Settled Land Act 1925 s 12(1)(b).
7   As to the court see para 792 post.
8   Settled Land Act 1925 s 12(1)(c).
9   For the meaning of 'tenant for life' see para 671 note 5 ante. See also para 761 et seq post.
10 As to the statutory owner see para 766 post.
11 See paras 690–691 ante.
12 See the Settled Land Act 1925 s 12(1) (amended by the Trusts of Land and Appointment of Trustees Act 1996 s 25(1), Sch 3 para 2). As to the statutory owner see para 766 post. The provisions of the Trustee Act 1925 relating to vesting orders and orders appointing a person to convey (see ss 44–56 (as amended); and TRUSTS vol 48 (Reissue) para 754 et seq) apply to all vesting orders authorised to be made by the Settled Land Act 1925: s 113(9).
13 For the meaning of 'trustees of the settlement' see para 750 note 1 post.
14 See the Settled Land Act 1925 s 9(3). As to applications to the court see para 792 post.

700. Vesting instruments where a settlement was subsisting on 1 January 1926. Where a settlement of a legal estate[1] in land (not held at law or in equity in undivided shares vested in possession[2]) was subsisting on 1 January 1926[3], the legal estate in the land became vested on that day in the tenant for life[4] or statutory owner[5] and the settlement became a trust instrument for the purposes of the Settled Land Act 1925[6]. That Act contains provisions similar to those[7] under which the tenant for life or statutory owner became entitled to have a principal vesting deed or vesting assent (containing the proper statements and particulars[8]) executed in his favour at the cost of the trust estate[9]. A like power was conferred on the tenant for life or statutory owner or any other person interested to apply to the court for the appointment of trustees of the settlement, if none existed[10], and for a vesting order if default was made in executing a principal vesting deed[11]. There were also similar savings in favour of personal representatives and any person entitled to an equitable charge for securing money actually raised[12].

All the estates, interests and powers limited by the settlement, other than any legal estate or interest vested in a mortgagee or other purchaser for money or money's worth, which were not by statute otherwise converted into equitable interests or powers[13], took effect, as from the date of the principal vesting deed or order, only in equity[14].

1   For the meaning of 'legal estate' see para 678 note 13 ante.
2   Settled Land Act 1925 s 37, Sch 2 para 1(5). As to land held in undivided shares see REAL PROPERTY vol 39(2) (Reissue) para 189 et seq.
3   See para 690 note 8 ante.
4   For the meaning of 'tenant for life' see para 671 note 5 ante. See also para 761 et seq post.
5   As to the statutory owner see para 766 post.

6   See the Settled Land Act 1925 Sch 2 para 1(1); and the Law of Property Act 1925 s 39, Sch 1 Pt II
     paras 2, 5, 6(c) (see REAL PROPERTY vol 39(2) (Reissue) para 52). For the meaning of 'trust instrument'
     see para 688 note 7 ante.
7   Ie the Settled Land Act 1925 ss 6, 8(1), (2), (4), 9(2): see paras 696, 698 ante.
8   See paras 690, 698 ante. For the meaning of 'principal vesting deed' see para 689 text to note 9 ante; and
     for the meaning of 'vesting assent' see para 690 note 8 ante.
9   See the Settled Land Act 1925 Sch 2 paras 1(2), 2(1), (2), (4). For forms see s 15, Sch 1 Forms 1, 5; and
     the Law of Property (Miscellaneous Provisions) Act 1994 s 9(1), (2).
10   See the Settled Land Act 1925 Sch 2 para 1(3); and para 699 ante. For the meaning of 'trustees of the
     settlement' see para 750 note 1 post.
11   See ibid Sch 2 para 1(4); and para 699 ante.
12   See ibid Sch 2 para 2(3), (5)–(7); and para 698 ante. For the meaning of 'personal representative' see
     para 697 note 6 ante.
13   See the Law of Property Act 1925 s 1(1)–(3); and REAL PROPERTY vol 39(2) (Reissue) para 43 et seq.
14   Settled Land Act 1925 Sch 2 para 1(6) (amended by the Law of Property (Amendment) Act 1926 s 7,
     Schedule).

701. Vesting not to operate as breach of covenant or forfeiture. Any vesting
effected under the powers conferred by the Settled Land Act 1925 in relation to settled
land[1] does not operate as a breach of a covenant or condition against alienation or give
rise to a forfeiture[2].

1   For the meaning of 'settled land' see para 680 text to note 2 ante.
2   Settled Land Act 1925 s 14(1). This provision applies to any settlement subsisting on 1 January 1926 (see
     para 700 ante) and also where a vesting instrument is executed for the purposes of giving effect to any
     instrument which is deemed to be a trust instrument (see para 695 ante). However, it will not avoid the
     necessity of obtaining a licence where there is a covenant or condition against alienation, when a
     settlement is made, at any rate if the vesting deed is executed before the trust instrument. It is, however,
     arguable that it enables a settlor to make a settlement after 1925 without obtaining a licence, by executing
     an instrument which is deemed to be a trust instrument (eg a declaration of trust) to which effect can then
     be given by a vesting instrument. The effect of this provision is far from clear and in practice it would
     always be wise to apply for a licence. It is thought that a licence is unnecessary when a vesting instrument
     is executed on a change of ownership (see para 698 ante), but this also is open to doubt. As to covenants
     and conditions against alienation see LANDLORD AND TENANT vol 27(1) (Reissue) para 390 et seq.

702. Dispositions not effective until a vesting instrument is executed. Where
a tenant for life[1] or statutory owner[2] has become entitled to have a principal vesting deed[3]
or a vesting assent[4] executed in his favour then, except in specific cases[5], until a vesting
instrument[6] is executed or made pursuant to the Settled Land Act 1925 in respect of the
settled land[7], any purported disposition[8] of it inter vivos by any person, other than a
personal representative[9] (not being a disposition which he has power to make in right of
his equitable interests[10] or powers under a trust instrument[11]), will not take effect except
in favour of a purchaser[12] of a legal estate[13] without notice of such tenant for life or
statutory owner having become so entitled, but, except as already stated, will operate only
as a contract for valuable consideration to carry out the transaction after the requisite
vesting instrument has been executed or made, and a purchaser of a legal estate will not
be concerned with such disposition unless the contract is registered as a land charge[14].
This provision does not affect the creation or transfer of a legal estate by virtue of a court
order or an order of the Minister of Agriculture, Fisheries and Food[15] or other competent
authority[16]. However, if before a vesting instrument is executed the settlement comes to
an end, no vesting instrument need, or can, be executed, and the restrictions on
dispositions imposed by these provisions cease to apply to the land which had been subject
to the settlement[17].

1   For the meaning of 'tenant for life' see para 671 note 5 ante. See also para 761 et seq post.
2   As to the statutory owner see para 766 post.
3   For the meaning of 'principal vesting deed' see para 689 text to note 9 ante.

4   For the meaning of 'vesting assent' see para 690 note 8 ante.
5   See para 703 post.
6   For the meaning of 'vesting instrument' see para 690 note 8 ante.
7   This means a vesting instrument which complies with the provisions of the Settled Land Act 1925: *Re Cayley and Evans' Contract* [1930] 2 Ch 143. For the meaning of 'settled land' see para 680 text to note 2 ante.
8   For the meaning of 'disposition' see para 685 note 14 ante. The expression here means a disposition under the Settled Land Act 1925: see s 112(2); and para 685 note 14 ante. See also *Re Alefounder's Will Trusts, Adnams v Alefounder* [1927] 1 Ch 360. 'Lease' includes the lease of an easement over the park or grounds: see *Dowager Duchess of Sutherland v Duke of Sutherland* [1893] 3 Ch 169 at 194; *Pease v Courtney* [1904] 2 Ch 503 at 510.
9   For the meaning of 'personal representative' see para 697 note 6 ante.
10   For the meaning of 'equitable interests' see para 695 note 8 ante.
11   For the meaning of 'trust instrument' see para 688 note 7 ante.
12   'Purchaser' means a purchaser in good faith for value, and includes a lessee, mortgagee or other person who in good faith acquires an interest in settled land for value; and in reference to a legal estate includes a chargee by way of legal mortgage: Settled Land Act 1925 s 117(1)(xxi).
13   For the meaning of 'legal estate' see para 678 note 13 ante. As to legal estates in land see the Law of Property Act 1925 s 1; and REAL PROPERTY vol 39(2) (Reissue) para 91 et seq.
14   Settled Land Act 1925 s 13 (amended by the Law of Property (Amendment) Act 1926 ss 6, 7, Schedule). As to the registration of land charges see LAND CHARGES vol 26 (Reissue) para 501 et seq. As to the protection of rights affecting registered land see LAND REGISTRATION vol 26 (Reissue) para 1098 et seq.
15   As to the Minister of Agriculture, Fisheries and Food see CONSTITUTIONAL LAW AND HUMAN RIGHTS vol 8(2) (Reissue) paras 435–437.
16   Settled Land Act 1925 s 13 (as amended: see note 14 supra); s 117(1)(xvi) (amended by the Transfer of Functions (Ministry of Food) Order 1955, SI 1955/554).
17   *Re Alefounder's Will Trusts, Adnams v Alefounder* [1927] 1 Ch 360. As to the duration of settlements see para 708 post.

703. When a vesting instrument is unnecessary. In the following cases settled land[1] can be dealt with by an estate owner even if no vesting deed has been executed[2]:
(1)   a person beneficially entitled to land[3] for an estate in fee simple or for a term of years absolute[4] subject to any estates, interests, charges or powers of charging subsisting or capable of being exercised under a settlement[5] may convey or create a legal estate[6] subject to a prior interest[7] as if the land had not been settled land[8]; and
(2)   where (a) a legal estate has been conveyed or created under the power set out in head (1) above, or under the statutory procedure for the enforcement of equitable interests and powers against estate owners[9], subject to any prior interest[10]; or (b) before 1 January 1926, land was conveyed to a purchaser[11] for money or money's worth subject to any prior interest, whether or not on the purchase the land was expressed to be exonerated from, or the grantor agreed to indemnify the purchaser against, such prior interest[12], the estate owner[13] for the time being of the land subject to that prior interest may, notwithstanding anything in the Settled Land Act 1925, but without prejudice to any power by which that prior interest is capable of being overreached, convey or create a legal estate subject to that prior interest as if the instrument[14] creating the prior interest was not an instrument or one of the instruments constituting a settlement of the land[15].

1   For the meaning of 'settled land' see para 680 text to note 2 ante; definition applied by the Law of Property (Amendment) Act 1926 s 8(1).
2   See ibid s 1.
3   For the meaning of 'land' see para 680 note 1 ante.
4   For the meaning of 'term of years absolute' see para 678 note 13 ante.
5   For the meaning of 'settlement' see para 678 note 1 ante.
6   For the meaning of 'legal estate' see para 678 note 13 ante; definition applied by the Law of Property (Amendment) Act 1926 s 8(1).
7   'Interest' means an estate, interest, charge or power of charging subsisting, or capable of arising or of being exercised under a settlement: ibid s 1(3).

8   Ibid s 1(1). Such a person has the powers of a tenant for life under the Settled Land Act 1925 s 20(1)(ix): see para 762 post.

9   Ie under ibid s 16 (see paras 767–769 post): see the Law of Property (Amendment) Act 1926 s 1(2)(a).

10   Ibid s 1(2)(a).

11   For the meaning of 'purchaser' see para 702 note 12 ante; definition applied by ibid s 8(1).

12   Ibid s 1(2)(b).

13   This power can be exercised by an absolute owner, tenant for life or statutory owner, trustee for sale or personal representative: see *Re Gaul and Houlston's Contract* [1928] Ch 689 at 691, CA, per Clauson J.

14   Where a prior interest arises under the exercise of a power, 'instrument' includes both the instrument conferring the power and the instrument exercising it: Law of Property (Amendment) Act 1926 s 1(3).

15   Ibid s 1(2).

704. Vesting deed on acquisition of land.

Where land[1] is acquired with capital money arising under the Settled Land Act 1925[2], the land must be conveyed to the tenant for life[3] or statutory owner[4], and the conveyance must be framed as a subsidiary vesting deed[5], unless prior to the execution of the conveyance there has not been any land in respect of which a principal vesting deed[6] was capable of being executed, in which case the conveyance must be framed as a principal vesting deed[7]. The acquisition of the land does not operate to increase or multiply charges or powers of charging[8].

Where (1) mortgage money[9] is capital money for the purposes of the Settled Land Act 1925; (2) land (other than any forming the whole or part of any property vested in trustees by way of security which is discharged from the right of redemption)[10] is, or is deemed to be, subject to the settlement[11]; and (3) the tenant for life or statutory owner requires the trustees to execute with respect to land forming the whole or part of that property a vesting deed such as would have been required in relation to the land if it had been acquired on a purchase with capital money, the trustees must execute such a vesting deed[12].

1   For the meaning of 'land' see para 680 note 1 ante.

2   For the meaning of 'capital money arising under the Act' see para 795 post.

3   For the meaning of 'tenant for life' see para 671 note 5 ante. See also para 761 et seq post.

4   As to the statutory owner see para 766 post.

5   For the meaning of 'conveyance' see para 698 note 12 ante. As to the form of a subsidiary vesting deed see para 691 ante.

6   For the meaning of 'principal vesting deed' see para 689 text to note 9 ante. As to the form of a principal vesting deed see para 690 ante.

7   See the Settled Land Act 1925 s 10(1); and paras 691, 693 ante. See also *Re Draycott Settled Estate* [1928] Ch 371. As to the procedure where the land is registered land see LAND REGISTRATION vol 26 (Reissue) para 1032 et seq. As to when there is no relevant property in a settlement see para 676 text to notes 8–9 ante.

8   Settled Land Act 1925 s 10(5). It is a general rule of construction that the court does not impute an intention to multiply charges, or trusts in the nature of charges, upon a trust estate in the absence of anything in the particular document to be construed to show such an intention: see *Trew v Perpetual Trustee Co* [1895] AC 264, PC; and para 723 post.

9   'Mortgage money' means money or money's worth secured by a mortgage; and 'mortgage' includes any charge or lien on any property for securing money or money's worth: Law of Property Act 1925 s 205(1)(xvi). See further MORTGAGE.

10   Ie land which forms the whole or part of the property mentioned in ibid s 31(1) (as amended) (see TRUSTS VOL 48 (Reissue) para 879): see s 31(4) (as substituted: see note 12 infra).

11   For the meaning of 'settlement' see para 678 note 1 ante; definition applied by ibid s 205(1)(xxvi).

12   See ibid s 31(4) (substituted by the Trusts of Land and Appointment of Trustees Act 1996 s 5(1), Sch 2 para 1(5)). If a subsidiary vesting deed is not so required, the property must be held on trust: see the Settled Land Act 1925 s 31(1) (as amended); and TRUSTS VOL 48 (Reissue) para 879.

705. Vesting deed by owner entitled subject to equitable interests.
Notwithstanding any stipulation to the contrary, a person of full age who is beneficially
entitled in possession to a legal estate[1] subject to any equitable interests[2] or powers, for
the purpose of overreaching such interests or powers, may by deed, which has effect as a
principal vesting deed[3], declare that the legal estate is vested in him on trust to give effect
to all equitable interests and powers affecting the legal estate[4]. The deed must be executed
by two or more individuals approved or appointed by the court[5] or a trust corporation[6],
who must be stated to be trustees of the settlement for the purposes of the Settled Land
Act 1925[7].

Then, so long as any of the equitable interests and powers are subsisting:

(1) the person so entitled and each of his successors in title being an estate owner[8]
     will have the powers of a tenant for life[9] and the land[10] will be deemed to be
     settled land[11];

(2) the instrument[12], if any, under which his estate arises or is acquired, and the
     instrument, if any, under which the equitable interests or powers are subsisting
     or capable of taking effect, will be deemed to be the trust instrument[13];

(3) the persons stated in the principal vesting deed to be the trustees of the
     settlement[14] for the purposes of the Settled Land Act 1925 will also be the trustees
     of the trust instrument for those purposes[15]; and

(4) capital money arising on any disposition[16] of the land must be paid to or by the
     direction of the trustees of the settlement or into court[17], and will be applicable
     towards discharging or providing for payment in due order of any principal
     money payable in respect of such interests or charges as are overreached by such
     disposition, and until so applied must be invested or applied as capital money
     under the trust instrument[18], and its income must be applied as the income of that
     capital money, and is liable for keeping down in due order any annual or
     periodical sum which may be overreached by the disposition[19].

1 For the meaning of 'legal estate' see para 678 note 13 ante. This provision applies to land which is not
   the subject of a settlement within the Settled Land Act 1925: see para 675 et seq ante. As to the age of
   majority see para 605 note 1 ante.
2 For the meaning of 'equitable interests' see para 695 note 8 ante. As to the equitable interests which are
   excepted from the operation of this provision see para 706 post.
3 Ie within the meaning of the Settled Land Act 1925 (see paras 688–690 ante): see s 21(1).
4 Ibid s 21(1), which has effect notwithstanding any stipulation to the contrary.
5 As to the court see para 792 post. The approval of trustees need not be an ad hoc approval for the purposes
   of sale: *Re Leigh's Settled Estates (No 2)* [1927] 2 Ch 13.
6 'Trust corporation' means the Public Trustee or a corporation either appointed by the court in any
   particular case to be a trustee or entitled by rules made under the Public Trustee Act 1906 s 4(3) (see
   TRUSTS vol 48 (Reissue) para 682 et seq), to act as custodian trustee, and includes the Church of
   England Pensions Board (see ECCLESIASTICAL LAW) and certain other officials and persons: see the
   Settled Land Act 1925 s 117(1)(xxx); the Trustee Act 1925 s 68(1) para (18); the Law of Property Act
   1925 s 205(1)(xxviii); the Law of Property (Amendment) Act 1926 s 3 (as amended); the Clergy
   Pensions Measure 1961 s 31; and TRUSTS vol 48 (Reissue) para 688.
7 Settled Land Act 1925 s 21(1). Examples of equitable interests which can be overreached under these
   provisions are: (1) any rentcharge for the life of any person, or any less period, or any capital, annual
   or periodical sums for the portions, advancement, maintenance or otherwise for the benefit of any
   person charged otherwise than voluntarily or in consideration of marriage or by way of family
   arrangement (cf s 1(1)(v); see para 678 ante); (2) an annuity within the Land Charges Act 1972 (see
   s 17(1); and LAND CHARGES vol 26 (Reissue) para 567 et seq); (3) a limited owner's charge within
   that Act (see s 2(4)(ii); and LAND CHARGES vol 26 (Reissue) para 530); and (4) a general equitable
   charge within the Land Charges Act 1972 (see s 2(4)(iii); and LAND CHARGES vol 26 (Reissue) para
   531). These include land charges registered under corresponding repealed provisions of the Land
   Charges Act 1925: see the Land Charges Act 1972 s 18(5), (6); and LAND CHARGES vol 26 (Reissue)
   para 532. As to overreaching powers see REAL PROPERTY vol 39(2) (Reissue) para 247 et seq.
8 For the meaning of 'estate owner' see para 697 note 2 ante.

9   For the meaning of 'tenant for life' see para 671 note 5 ante. See also para 761 et seq post. By virtue of the Settled Land Act 1925 s 72, the estate owner will be able to overreach the equitable interests: see para 874 post.

10   For the meaning of 'land' see para 680 note 1 ante.

11   Settled Land Act 1925 s 21(1)(a). For the meaning of 'settled land' see para 680 text to note 2 ante.

12   For the meaning of 'instrument' see para 688 note 7 ante.

13   Settled Land Act 1925 s 21(1)(b). For the meaning of 'trust instrument' see para 688 note 7 ante. Where there is no such instrument, then a deed, which will take effect as a trust instrument, must be executed contemporaneously with the vesting deed, and must declare the trusts affecting the land: s 21(1)(b) proviso.

14   For the meaning of 'trustees of the settlement' see para 750 note 1 post. For the meaning of 'settlement' see para 678 note 1 ante.

15   Settled Land Act 1925 s 21(1)(c). In the case of an ordinary settlement the trust instrument appoints or constitutes trustees of the settlement (see s 4(3)(b); and para 694 ante), and the principal vesting deed states who are the trustees of the settlement (see s 5(1)(c); and para 690 ante).

16   For the meaning of 'disposition' see para 685 note 14 ante.

17   As to applications to the court see para 792 post.

18   As to the application of capital money see para 808 post.

19   Settled Land Act 1925 s 21(1)(d).

706. Equitable interests and powers not overreached. The following equitable interests and powers cannot be overreached[1]:

(1)   an equitable interest protected by a deposit of documents relating to the legal estate[2] affected[3];

(2)   the benefit of a covenant or agreement restrictive of the user of land[4];

(3)   an easement, liberty or privilege over or affecting land and being merely an equitable interest[5];

(4)   the benefit of a contract to convey or create a legal estate, including a contract conferring either expressly or by statutory implication a valid option of purchase, a right of pre-emption or any other like right[6]; and

(5)   any equitable interest protected by registration under the Land Charges Act 1972[7] other than an annuity within the meaning of that Act[8], or a limited owner's charge or a general equitable charge within the meaning of that Act[9].

1   Ie under the Settled Land Act 1925 s 21(1) (see para 705 ante): see s 21(2). For the meaning of 'equitable interests' see para 695 note 8 ante.

2   For the meaning of 'legal estate' see para 678 note 13 ante.

3   Settled Land Act 1925 s 21(2)(i). See also MORTGAGE.

4   Ibid s 21(2)(ii). For the meaning of 'land' see para 680 note 1 ante. See also EQUITY vol 16 (Reissue) para 787 et seq; LANDLORD AND TENANT vol 27(1) (Reissue) para 466 et seq; SALE OF LAND para 331 et seq ante.

5   Ibid s 21(2)(iii). This includes any easement, right or privilege for an interest less than an estate in fee simple absolute in possession or a term of years absolute: see the Law of Property Act 1925 s 1(2)(a), (3); and EASEMENTS AND PROFITS À PRENDRE.

6   Settled Land Act 1925 s 21(2)(iv). As to options to purchase and rights of pre-emption see SALE OF LAND paras 27–28 ante.

7   As to rights capable of being registered under the Land Charges Act 1972 see LAND CHARGES vol 26 (Reissue) para 522 et seq. This covers also any registration made under any statute which has effect as if the registration had been made under that Act: see the Settled Land Act 1925 s 117(3); the Land Charges Act 1972 s 18(5), (6); and LAND CHARGES vol 26 (Reissue) para 501.

8   Settled Land Act 1925 s 21(2)(v)(a); Land Charges Act 1972 s 18(6). As to annuities within the meaning of the Land Charges Act 1972 see LAND CHARGES vol 26 (Reissue) paras 518, 567, 570.

9   Settled Land Act 1925 s 21(2)(v)(b); Land Charges Act 1972 s 18(6). As to the charge of a limited owner and a general equitable charge see LAND CHARGES vol 26 (Reissue) paras 518, 530–531. As to overreaching such interests see para 705 note 7 ante.

707. Protection of equitable chargees. Subject to the powers conferred by the Settled Land Act 1925 on a tenant for life[1], nothing contained in the foregoing powers of an owner entitled subject to equitable interests[2], deprives an equitable chargee of any of his rights or of his remedies for enforcing those rights[3].

1 For the meaning of 'tenant for life' see para 671 note 5 ante. See also para 761 et seq post. As to the statutory powers of a tenant for life see para 775 et seq post.
2 Ie the powers contained in the Settled Land Act 1925 s 21(1), (2) (see para 705 ante): see s 21(3).
3 Ibid s 21(3). As to the rights and remedies of mortgagees see MORTGAGE.

(3) DURATION AND DETERMINATION OF SETTLEMENTS

708. Duration of settlements. Land[1] which has been subject to a settlement[2] which is a settlement for the purposes of the Settled Land Act 1925, is deemed for the purposes of that Act to remain and be settled land[3], and the settlement is deemed to be a subsisting settlement for those purposes, so long as: (1) any limitation[4], charge or power of charging under the settlement[5] subsists, or is capable of being exercised[6]; or (2) the person who, if of full age, would be entitled as beneficial owner to have that land vested in him for a legal estate is a child[7]. A settlement within the Settled Land Act 1925 ceases to be a settlement within that Act if at any time there is no relevant trust property[8].

1 For the meaning of 'land' see para 680 note 1 ante.
2 For the meaning of 'settlement' see para 678 note 1 ante.
3 Settled Land Act 1925 s 3 (amended by the Trusts of Land and Appointment of Trustees Act 1996 s 25(1), Sch 3 para 2). For the meaning of 'settled land' see para 680 text to note 2 ante.
4 'Limitation' includes a trust: Settled Land Act 1925 s 117(1)(xii). For the meaning of 'trust' see para 678 note 9 ante.
5 'Under the settlement' means under the settlement deemed to be subsisting, and a limitation, charge or power of charging can only be said to subsist under a settlement if it is necessary to resort to the settlement for the purpose of overriding it: *Re Draycott Settled Estate* [1928] Ch 371.
6 Settled Land Act 1925 s 3(a). This provision covers cases where a settlement came into existence on 1 January 1926 by virtue of the Settled Land Act 1925, even if there was no settlement immediately prior to that date: *Re Earl of Carnarvon's Chesterfield Settled Estates, Re Earl of Carnarvon's Highclere Settled Estates* [1927] 1 Ch 138; *Re Ogle's Settled Estates* [1927] 1 Ch 229; *Re Lord Alington and London County Council's Contract* [1927] 2 Ch 253.
7 Settled Land Act 1925 s 3(b). See also para 665 note 13 ante. As to land limited on trust for a child in possession see para 678 ante. As to the age of majority see para 605 note 1 ante.
8 See the Trusts of Land and Appointment of Trustees Act 1996 s 2(4); and para 676 ante. See also REAL PROPERTY vol 39(2) (Reissue) para 65.

709. Conveyance on termination of settlement. If any person of full age[1] becomes absolutely entitled to the settled land[2] (whether beneficially, or as personal representative[3], or as trustee of land[4] or otherwise) free from all limitations[5], powers and charges taking effect under the settlement, he is entitled to require the trustees of the settlement[6], personal representatives[7] or other persons in whom the settled land is vested to convey the land to him, and if more persons than one being of full age become so entitled to the settled land they are entitled to require such persons to convey the land to them as joint tenants[8]. The court has power to make an order vesting the land in such person or persons in the same cases as those in which it can make an order in favour of a tenant for life[9] or statutory owner[10] where the land remains settled land[11].

1 As to the age of majority see para 605 note 1 ante.
2 For the meaning of 'settled land' see para 680 text to note 2 ante.
3 For the meaning of 'personal representative' see para 697 note 6 ante.

4   For the meaning of 'trustees of land' see para 676 note 5 ante; definition applied by the Interpretation Act 1978 s 5, Sch 1.

5   For the meaning of 'limitation' see para 708 note 4 ante.

6   For the meaning of 'trustees of the settlement' see para 750 note 1 post.

7   If on the death of a tenant for life or statutory owner the land ceases to be settled land, his general personal representatives are entitled to probate without any exception of settled land, which will vest in them accordingly: *Re Bridgett and Hayes' Contract* [1928] Ch 163. See further EXECUTORS AND ADMINISTRATORS.

8   Settled Land Act 1925 s 7(5). If the land is vested in personal representatives the conveyance may be made by means of an assent: see s 8(1); and para 698 ante. As to the procedure where the land is registered land see LAND REGISTRATION vol 26 (Reissue) para 1032 et seq. If the conveyance or assent does not state who are the trustees of the settlement for the purposes of the Settled Land Act 1925, a purchaser of a legal estate is bound and entitled to act on the assumption that the person in whose favour it has been made is absolutely entitled to the land free from all limitations, powers and charges taking effect under the settlement: see s 110(5) (as amended); and para 889 post. If when the settlement comes to an end the land is already vested in the person who has become absolutely entitled, a deed of discharge must be executed: see para 710 post.

    The obligation to convey the settled land is subject and without prejudice: (1) where the settlement is created by will, to the rights and powers of the personal representatives for the purposes of administration (s 8(3)(a)); and (2) in any case to the person on whom the obligation is imposed being satisfied that provision has been or will be made for the payment of any unpaid death duties in respect of the land or any interest in it for which he is accountable, and any interest and costs in respect of such duties, or that he is otherwise effectually indemnified against such duties, interest and costs (see s 8(3)(b)). Death duties include inheritance tax payable on the death of a life tenant by virtue of the Inheritance Tax Act 1984 s 49 (as amended): see INHERITANCE TAXATION vol 24 (Reissue) para 480. As to security for inheritance tax, debts or liabilities see EXECUTORS AND ADMINISTRATORS.

9   For the meaning of 'tenant for life' see para 671 note 5 ante. See also para 761 et seq post.

10   As to the statutory owner see para 766 post.

11   See the Settled Land Act 1925 s 12(1) (amended by the Trusts of Land and Appointment of Trustees Act 1996 s 25(1), Sch 3 para 2); and para 699 ante.

710. Deed of discharge on the termination of a settlement. Where the estate owner[1] of any settled land[2] holds the land free from all equitable interests[3] and powers under a trust instrument[4], the persons who, in the last or only principal vesting instrument[5] or the last or only indorsement on or annex to it, are declared to be trustees of the settlement[6] or the survivors of them are, unless they have notice of any derivative settlement, trust of land[7] or equitable charge affecting the land, bound to execute, at the cost of the trust estate, a deed declaring that they are discharged from the trust so far as regards that land[8].

If the trustees have notice of any derivative settlement or trust of land affecting the land, they must not execute a deed of discharge until a vesting instrument or a conveyance has been executed or made for giving effect to it[9]. In such a case the deed of discharge must contain a statement that the land is settled land by virtue of the vesting instrument and the trust instrument referred to in it, or is subject to a trust of land by virtue of the conveyance, as the case may require[10].

If the trustees have notice of an equitable charge affecting the land, they must not execute a deed of discharge until they are satisfied that the charge is or will be secured by a legal mortgage[11], or is protected by registration as a land charge[12] or by deposit of the documents of title, or that its owner consents to the execution of the deed of discharge[13].

If, in these circumstances and when these conditions have been complied with, the trustees of a settlement, on being requested to execute a deed of discharge by the estate owner[14], or by a person interested under, or by the trustees of, a derivative settlement[15], or by the trustees of land[16], refuse to do so, or if for any reason the discharge cannot be effected without undue delay or expense, the estate owner, person interested or trustees may apply to the court[17] for an order discharging the first-mentioned trustees as respects the whole or any part of the settled land, and the court may make such order as it thinks fit[18].

Where a deed or order of discharge contains no statement to the contrary, a purchaser[19] of a legal estate in the land to which the deed or order relates is entitled to assume that the land has ceased to be settled land, and is not subject to any trust of land[20].

1   For the meaning of 'estate owner' see para 697 note 2 ante.
2   For the meaning of 'settled land' see para 680 text to note 2 ante.
3   For the meaning of 'equitable interests' see para 695 note 8 ante.
4   For the meaning of 'trust instrument' see para 688 note 7 ante. It includes all the instruments, constituting a compound settlement: see para 681 ante.
5   For the meaning of 'principal vesting instrument' see para 698 note 1 ante.
6   For the meaning of 'trustees of the settlement' see para 750 note 1 post.
7   For the meaning of 'trust of land' see para 676 note 5 ante; definition applied by the Interpretation Act 1978 s 5, Sch 1.
8   See the Settled Land Act 1925 s 17(1) (amended by the Trust of Land and Appointment of Trustees Act 1996 s 25(1), Sch 3 para 2). As to the procedure where the land is registered land see LAND REGISTRATION vol 26 (Reissue) para 1038. As to distribution where the settlement has been lost see *Hansell v Spink* [1943] Ch 396; and as to distribution where death is presumed see para 711 post.
9   Settled Land Act 1925 s 17(1) proviso (a) (amended by the Trusts of Land and Appointment of Trustees Act 1996 Sch 3 para 2). For the meaning of 'conveyance' see para 698 note 12 ante.
10 See the Settled Land Act 1925 s 17(1).
11 For the meaning of 'legal mortgage' see para 698 note 23 ante. See also MORTGAGE.
12 See LAND CHARGES vol 26 (Reissue) paras 522, 528, 531.
13 Settled Land Act 1925 s 17(1) proviso (b).
14 Ibid s 17(2)(a).
15 Ibid s 17(2)(b).
16 Ibid s 17(2)(c) (amended by the Trusts of Land and Appointment of Trustees Act 1996 Sch 3 para 2).
17 As to applications to the court see para 792 post.
18 Settled Land Act 1925 s 17(2).
19 For the meaning of 'purchaser' see para 702 note 12 ante.
20 Settled Land Act 1925 s 17(3) (amended by the Trusts of Land and Appointment of Trustees Act 1996 Sch 3 para 2). As to the deed or order of discharge containing a statement to the contrary see the text and note 10 supra.

711.   Order for distribution where death is presumed. Where a person interested in trust property has disappeared and has not been heard of for a considerable time, then, if satisfied of the probability of death[1], the court[2] may authorise distribution on the footing that he has died[3].

1   As to the presumption of death see EVIDENCE.
2   As to applications to the court see para 792 post.
3   *Re Benjamin, Neville v Benjamin* [1902] 1 Ch 723; *Re Newson-Smith's Settlement, Grice v Newson-Smith* [1962] 3 All ER 963n, [1962] 1 WLR 1478. Cf *Re Wilson* [1964] 1 All ER 196, [1964] 1 WLR 214.

712.   Restrictions on dispositions of settled land. Where land[1] is the subject of a vesting instrument[2] and the trustees of the settlement have not been discharged under the Settled Land Act 1925[3], then: (1) any disposition[4] by the tenant for life[5] or statutory owner[6] of the land, other than a disposition authorised by that Act or any other statute, or made in pursuance of any additional or larger powers mentioned in the vesting instrument, is void, except for the purpose of conveying or creating such equitable interests[7] as he has power, in right of his equitable interests and powers under the trust instrument, to convey or create[8]; (2) if any capital money[9] is payable in respect of a transaction, a conveyance[10] to a purchaser[11] of the land only takes effect under the Settled Land Act 1925 if the capital money is paid to or by the direction of the trustees of the settlement or into court[12]; and (3) notwithstanding anything to the contrary in the vesting instrument or the trust instrument, capital money must not, except where the trustee is a trust corporation[13], be paid to or by the direction of fewer persons than two as trustees of the settlement[14].

However, these restrictions do not affect: (a) the right of a personal representative[15] in whom the settled land is vested to convey or deal with the land for the purposes of administration[16]; (b) the right of a person of full age who has become absolutely entitled (whether beneficially or as trustee of land[17] or personal representative or otherwise) to the settled land, free from all limitations[18], powers and charges taking effect under the trust instrument, to require the land to be conveyed to him[19]; or (c) the power of the tenant for life, statutory owner or personal representative in whom the settled land is vested to transfer or create such legal estates, to take effect in priority to the settlement, as may be required for giving effect to any obligations imposed on him by statute[20], but, where any capital money is raised or received in respect of the transaction, the money must be paid to or by the direction of the trustees of the settlement or in accordance with an order of the court[21].

1   For the meaning of 'land' see para 680 note 1 ante.
2   For the meaning of 'vesting instrument' see para 690 note 8 ante.
3   For the meaning of 'trustees of the settlement' see para 750 note 1 post. As to the discharge of trustees see para 759 post.
4   For the meaning of 'disposition' see para 685 note 14 ante.
5   For the meaning of 'tenant for life' see para 671 note 5 ante. See also note 8 infra; and para 761 et seq post.
6   As to the statutory owner see para 766 post.
7   For the meaning of 'equitable interests' see para 695 note 8 ante.
8   Settled Land Act 1925 s 18(1)(a). This provision is not limited to transactions by, or purporting to be by, a tenant for life as such: *Weston v Henshaw* [1950] Ch 510.
9   As to capital money arising under the Act see para 795 post.
10 For the meaning of 'conveyance' see para 698 note 12 ante.
11 For the meaning of 'purchaser' see para 702 note 12 ante.
12 Settled Land Act 1925 s 18(1)(b).
13 For the meaning of 'trust corporation' see para 705 note 6 ante.
14 Settled Land Act 1925 s 18(1)(c). As to the court's powers where on a sale the consideration attributable to timber on, or fixtures attached to, settled land which has been sold is paid by mistake to anyone other than the trustees see para 832 post.
15 For the meaning of 'personal representative' see para 697 note 6 ante.
16 Settled Land Act 1925 s 18(2)(a). See also para 698 ante. For the meaning of 'settled land' see para 680 text to note 2 ante.
17 For the meaning of 'trustees of land' see para 676 note 5 ante; definition applied by the Interpretation Act 1978 s 5, Sch 1.
18 For the meaning of 'limitation' see para 708 note 4 ante.
19 Settled Land Act 1925 s 18(2)(b) (amended by the Trusts of Land and Appointment of Trustees Act 1996 s 25(1), Sch 3 para 2). See also para 709 ante.
20 Eg to give effect to equitable interests: see para 767 post.
21 Settled Land Act 1925 s 18(2)(c). As to the court see para 792 post.

713. Settled land held upon trust for persons entitled in undivided shares. If settled land[1] is held in trust for persons entitled in possession under a trust instrument[2] in undivided shares[3], the trustees of the settlement[4] (if the settled land is not already vested in them) may require the estate owner[5] in whom the settled land is vested (but, in the case of a personal representative, subject to his rights and powers for purposes of administration[6]), at the cost of the trust estate, to convey the land to them or to assent to the land vesting in them as joint tenants[7]. If and when the settled land so held in trust in undivided shares is or becomes vested in the trustees of the settlement, the land is held by them (subject to any incumbrances affecting the settled land which are secured by a legal mortgage[8], but freed from any incumbrances affecting the undivided shares or not so secured, and from any interests, powers and charges subsisting under the trust instrument which have priority to the trust for the persons entitled to the undivided shares) in trust for the persons interested in the land[9]. If the settled land is not vested in the trustees, it is held, until it is so vested, by the estate owner in whom it is vested in trust for the persons interested in the land[10]. An undivided share in land is not capable of being created except under a trust instrument or under the Law of Property Act 1925[11], and then takes effect behind a trust of land[12]. The priority among themselves of any incumbrances, whether affecting the entirety of the land or an undivided share, is not affected[13].

1   For the meaning of 'settled land' see para 680 text to note 2 ante.

2   For the meaning of 'trust instrument' see para 688 note 7 ante.

3   This provision applies immediately the persons entitled in undivided shares have interests in possession. This may occur either during the subsistence of the interest of the tenant for life (*Re Hind, Bernstone v Montgomery* [1933] Ch 208) or on its termination (*Re Cugny's Will Trusts, Smith v Freeman* [1931] 1 Ch 305; *Re Thomas* [1939] Ch 513, [1939] 1 All ER 379). It also applies although the division into undivided shares is brought about, not by the trust instrument, but by a subsequent deed or event, and a conveyance of an undivided moiety of a base fee has been held to be a trust instrument within this provision: *Re Hind, Bernstone v Montgomery* supra. As to base fees see REAL PROPERTY vol 39(2) (Reissue) paras 134–139.

4   For the meaning of 'trustees of the settlement' see para 750 note 1 post.

5   For the meaning of 'estate owner' see para 697 note 2 ante.

6   See para 698 ante. For the meaning of 'personal representative' see para 697 note 6 ante.

7   See the Settled Land Act 1925 s 36(1).

8   For the meaning of 'legal mortgage' see para 698 note 23 ante.

9   Settled Land Act 1925 s 36(2) (amended by the Trusts of Land and Appointment of Trustees Act 1996 s 25(1), Sch 3 para 2). The Settled Land Act 1925 s 36 (as amended) binds the Crown: s 36(7). References to the persons interested in the land include persons interested as trustees or personal representatives (as well as persons beneficially interested): s 36(6) (substituted by the Trusts of Land and Appointment of Trustees Act 1996 Sch 3 para 2).

10   See the Settled Land Act 1925 s 36(1).

11   See the Law of Property Act 1925 s 34 (as amended); and REAL PROPERTY vol 39(2) (Reissue) para 211.

12   Settled Land Act 1925 s 36(4) (amended by the Trusts of Land and Appointment of Trustees Act 1996 Sch 3 para 2). For the meaning of 'trust of land' see para 676 note 5; definition applied by the Interpretation Act 1978 s 5, Sch 1.

13   Settled Land Act 1925 s 36(5).

714. Vesting order. If an estate owner[1] refuses or neglects for one month after a written demand to convey to the trustees the settled land[2] which is held in trust in undivided shares[3], or if by reason of his being outside the United Kingdom[4], or being unable to be found, or by reason of the dissolution of a corporation, or for any other reason, the court[5] is satisfied that the conveyance cannot otherwise be made, or cannot be made without undue delay or expense, then, on the application of the trustees of the settlement[6], the court may make an order vesting the settled land in them in trust for the persons interested in the land[7].

1   For the meaning of 'estate owner' see para 697 note 2 ante.

2   For the meaning of 'settled land' see para 680 text to note 2 ante.

3   See para 713 ante.

4   For the meaning of 'United Kingdom' see para 699 note 5 ante.

5   As to the court see para 792 post.

6   For the meaning of 'trustees of the settlement' see para 750 note 1 post.

7   Settled Land Act 1925 s 36(3) (amended by the Trusts of Land and Appointment of Trustees Act 1996 s 25(1), Sch 3 para 2). As to the statutory provisions applying to such vesting orders see the Settled Land Act 1925 s 113(9); and para 699 ante.

(4) BENEFICIAL INTERESTS

(i) Traditional Limitations

715. In general. The traditional limitations to be found in a strict settlement of land not made on marriage[1] are a life interest to the settlor[2], with remainder to his first and other sons in tail male, with remainder to his first and other sons in tail general, with remainder to his daughters as tenants in common in tail with cross remainders between them[3]. The settlement might contain powers of charging for pin money[4] and a jointure[5] for the wife of the tenant for life, and powers for raising portions for younger children[6]. Where a settlement is made on marriage, the sons and daughters to be provided for would usually be confined to the children of the marriage, and the settlement would traditionally contain trusts for the purpose of providing pin money and a jointure for the wife and portions for the younger children of the marriage[7]. However, it is now more common for a settlement to benefit the settlor's children equally[8].

1 It is no longer possible to create settlements under the Settled Land Act 1925: see para 676 ante. As to settlements made on marriage see para 628 et seq ante.
2 As to life interests see para 716 post.
3 As to interests in remainder see para 717 post. It is no longer possible to create entailed interests: see para 677 ante; and REAL PROPERTY VOL 39(2) (Reissue) para 119.
4 As to pin money see para 724 post.
5 As to jointure see para 725 post.
6 As to portions see paras 727–739 post.
7 See para 628 et seq ante.
8 As to the rights of illegitimate, legitimated and adopted children see paras 731–733 post.

716. Life interests. In settlements of realty[1], whether made on marriage or not, the first life interest is usually given to the settlor[2]. In the case of a settlement made in favour of the living children of the settlor or of another named person, a life interest was traditionally given to the sons and daughters successively upon failure of the prior limitations, and the same practice was usually followed in the case of a settlement by will[3].

Life interests are generally expressed to be without impeachment of waste, so as to enable the tenant for life for the time being to cut timber, open mines and commit other wasteful acts for his own profit[4].

1 It is no longer possible to create settlements under the Settled Land Act 1925: see para 676 ante.
2 As to the limitation of life interests see REAL PROPERTY vol 39(2) (Reissue) para 144 et seq. As to settlements made on marriage see para 628 et seq ante.
3 As to settlements by will see para 630 ante.
4 As to liability for waste see para 986 et seq post.

717. Interests in remainder. Subject to any prior life interests and to the trusts, if any, for pin money, jointures and portions[1], realty was traditionally settled by a marriage settlement upon trust for the first and all other sons of the intended marriage successively according to seniority in tail male[2], with remainder upon trust for the daughters of the marriage in tail with cross remainders[3] between them, but provision might be made for sons of a subsequent marriage in priority to daughters of the intended marriage. However, it is now more common for a settlement to benefit the settlor's children equally[4].

1 See paras 724–739 post.
2 As to the nature, incidents and mode of creation of entailed interests see REAL PROPERTY vol 39(2) (Reissue) para 117 et seq; and as to the descent of entailed interests see EXECUTORS AND ADMINISTRATORS. It is no longer possible to create entailed interests: see para 677 ante; and REAL

PROPERTY vol 39(2) (Reissue) para 119. Under a settlement, not made on marriage, under which the sons of the settlor or of any other person are given life interests, it was usual to follow each life interest with a trust for the sons of the life tenant successively in tail male. This was also the practice in the case of strict settlements by will. A trust in favour of the first and other sons of a person in tail will take effect in their favour successively according to seniority, even if the word 'successively' is omitted: *Re Close's Estate* [1910] 1 IR 357; *Re Gosset's Settlement, Gribble v Lloyds Bank* [1943] Ch 351, [1943] 2 All ER 515.

3   As to cross remainders see para 718 post.

4   As to the rights of illegitimate, legitimated and adopted children see paras 731–733 post. It is no longer possible to create settlements under the Settled Land Act 1925: see para 676 ante.

718. Cross remainders. In the case of a deed, unlike a will, cross remainders in tail cannot be raised by implication, however plainly the intention of the settlor may have been expressed, as technical words of limitation are essential for the creation of an entailed interest[1]. However, if a deed contains express limitations by way of cross remainder, so that the court is not asked to supply words of limitation, the same rule of construction applies to both deeds and wills, and the court gives effect to the plain intention of the settlor[2].

1   *Cole v Levingston* (1672) 1 Vent 224; *Doe d Tanner v Dorvell* (1794) 5 Term Rep 518; *Doe d Foquett v Worsley* (1801) 1 East 416; *Doe d Clift v Birkhead* (1849) 4 Exch 110 at 125; *Bainton v Bainton* (1865) 34 Beav 563; *Gaussen and French v Ellis* [1930] IR 116, Ir CA. See also the Law of Property Act 1925 s 130(1) (repealed except in relation to any entailed interest created before 1 January 1997); and para 939 post. Where technical words are unnecessary, as in the case of an interest pur autre vie, cross remainders in tail may be implied even in a deed: *Re Battersby's Estate* [1911] 1 IR 453. It is no longer possible to create new entailed interests: see para 677 ante; and REAL PROPERTY vol 39(2) (Reissue) para 119.

2   *Doe d Watts v Wainewright* (1793) 5 Term Rep 427; *Cole v Sewell* (1848) 2 HL Cas 186. Accordingly, 'survivors' may be construed as 'others' (*Doe d Watts v Wainewright* supra; *Cole v Sewell* supra; *Re Palmer's Settlement Trusts* (1875) LR 19 Eq 320), and 'shares' as including accrued shares (*Doe d Clift v Birkhead* (1849) 4 Exch 110, overruling *Edwards v Alliston* (1827) 4 Russ 78).

719. Ultimate limitations. The ultimate limitation in a settlement of realty, as in a settlement of personalty, is sometimes designed to bring the settled property back to its original ownership, and is expressed to be upon trust for the settlor in fee simple[1]. The settlor under such a limitation takes the ultimate estate as a purchaser by virtue of the settlement, and is not entitled to it as his former estate or part of it[2]. However, there may be an ultimate trust in favour of other persons.

Where a deed is executed after 1925 words of limitation are not necessary to pass a fee simple[3].

1   See REAL PROPERTY vol 39(2) (Reissue) para 117. It is no longer possible to create settlements under the Settled Land Act 1925: see para 676 ante. As to the ultimate trusts of settlements of personalty see para 932 post.

2   See the Inheritance Act 1833 s 3 (as amended); and REAL PROPERTY vol 39(2) (Reissue) para 164. See also EXECUTORS AND ADMINISTRATORS.

3   See the Law of Property Act 1925 s 60(1); and REAL PROPERTY vol 39(2) (Reissue) para 93.

720. Traditional provisions in a resettlement. Where an estate was settled upon the traditional trusts in strict settlement[1] and the first-born son, being tenant in tail in remainder, had attained full age, he would generally execute a disentailing deed and this would then be followed by a resettlement[2]. By the disentailing deed[3], in which the father would join both as protector of the settlement[4] and for the purpose of conveying his life estate, the estate would usually be conveyed to a grantee upon such trusts as the father and son would jointly appoint, and in default of such appointment upon the trusts subsisting under the existing settlement. The resettlement proper would then be effected by the father and son in exercise of the joint power conferred on them by the disentailing deed[5]. The new trusts were generally expressed to be subject to the trusts and charges preceding the son's former estate tail, except the father's life estate. If the resettlement was made on the marriage of the son, the first of the new trusts was generally to provide by rentcharges pin money[6] for the son's wife, and then an annuity for the son during the joint lives of himself and his father, and a jointure for the son's wife if she survived him[7]. If the son was neither married nor about to marry, power was generally reserved to him to charge the estate with pin money and jointure rentcharges. Subject to these charges, the father's old life estate was restored by the resettlement, and this restoration had the effect of also giving back to him the powers annexed to the life estate by the original settlement, in addition to which he was capable of exercising all the powers conferred by the resettlement[8]. That estate was followed by the limitation of an estate to the son for his life. After the determination of this latter estate, the property was given to the son's first and other unborn sons successively in tail, or in tail male, with remainder to such sons successively in tail general. These were followed by limitations of life estates to the son's younger brothers and estates tail or tail male in favour of the issue of the son's younger brothers, and sometimes by limitations in favour of collateral branches of the family. If limitations in favour of daughters of the son or of the son's younger brothers were introduced, they were generally made to the daughters successively in tail male. The ultimate limitation was generally to the son in fee simple[9].

1   See para 715 ante. The traditional trusts of a strict settlement and of a resettlement are now less common. It is no longer possible to create settlements under the Settled Land Act 1925: see para 676 ante.

2   A resettlement cannot be made while the tenant in tail is a child, except by a court order under the Variation of Trusts Act 1958: see para 674 ante; and TRUSTS vol 48 (Reissue) paras 923–927. In order to avoid full ad valorem stamp duty, the resettlement is sometimes postponed until the son's marriage, when it may be effected as a marriage settlement: see the Stamp Duty (Exempt Instruments) Regulations 1987, SI 1987/516; and STAMP DUTIES AND STAMP DUTY RESERVE TAX vol 44(1) (Reissue) para 1083. See also para 623 ante. As to marriage settlements see para 628 et seq ante. As to the age of majority see para 605 note 1 ante.

3   As to disentail see REAL PROPERTY vol 39(2) (Reissue) para 122 et seq. As to entailed interests see REAL PROPERTY vol 39(2) (Reissue) para 117 et seq. It is no longer possible to create new entailed interests: see para 677 ante; and REAL PROPERTY vol 39(2) (Reissue) para 119.

4   See REAL PROPERTY vol 39(2) (Reissue) paras 124, 128.

5   See REAL PROPERTY vol 39(2) (Reissue) paras 123–124.

6   As to pin money see para 724 post; and HUSBAND AND WIFE. As to rentcharges see para 724 et seq post; and generally RENTCHARGES AND ANNUITIES.

7   As to jointure see para 725 post; and POWERS. As to annuities see para 724 et seq post; an RENTCHARGES AND ANNUITIES vol 39(2) (Reissue) para 790 et seq.

8   See the Settled Land Act 1925 s 22(2); and para 773 post. The statutory powers conferred by the Settled Land Act 1925 are not affected by the resettlement: see para 777 post. Concurrence in a resettlement, which revoked the uses, trusts, limitations, intents and purposes of the original settlement, did not put an end to a power to charge conferred by it: *Evans v Evans* (1853) 1 WR 215.

9   See further REAL PROPERTY vol 39(2) (Reissue) paras 118–120.

721. Referential trusts. Property is frequently settled by reference to the trusts of other property settled by the same or a different instrument[1]. The effect of a referential trust depends in every case upon the particular words employed to refer to the principal trusts[2]. A reference to the trusts of a subsisting settlement so far as they are capable of taking effect means the trusts of that settlement as then subsisting without regard to intermediate appointments[3], and a reference to the trusts of a subsisting settlement in favour of particular beneficiaries incorporates the provisions relating to those beneficiaries, but not the directions as to the time when the benefits are to arise[4]. Where property was settled by reference to trusts declared in a deed of even date which was never executed[5], or was devised and bequeathed to be assigned on the trusts of a settlement which was no longer subsisting and of which there were no longer trustees to receive the property on the trusts[6], there was in one case a resulting trust to the settlor and in another case an intestacy[7].

Where property is directed to be held upon the same trusts as property already settled, it is not by that direction made an accretion to the original property, and it may not devolve with the original property in all respects[8], unless there is some context from which such an intention can be inferred[9].

1   As to vesting deeds and trust instruments see para 688 et seq ante. It is no longer possible to create settlements under the Settled Land Act 1925: see para 676 ante.

2   As to the effect of various phrases incorporating other trusts see *Wortham v Mackinnon* (1831) 4 Sim 485 ('uses ... existing, undetermined or capable of taking effect'); *Ford v Ruxton* (1844) 1 Coll 403 ('the same trusts'); *Marshall v Baker* (1862) 31 Beav 608 ('the same or the like trusts'); *Re Shirley's Trusts* (1863) 32 Beav 394 ('in like manner ... as if such trusts and provisions were here fully repeated'); *Re Smith, Bashford v Chaplin* (1881) 45 LT 246 ('the like trusts'); *Brigg v Brigg* (1885) 33 WR 454; *Re Shelton's Settled Estates, Shelton v Shelton* [1945] Ch 158, [1945] 1 All ER 283 ('or as nearly corresponding thereto as the circumstances of the case ... will admit'); *Re Benett-Stanford Settlement Trusts, Attwood v Benett-Stanford* [1947] 1 All ER 888 ('or as near thereto as circumstances will permit'). If the meaning of the original trusts is clear, a subsequent inaccurate recital of their effect will be rejected: *Grade v Grade* (1843) 3 Dr & War 435. The proviso for redemption in a mortgage may be so worded as to revive the original trusts of a settlement: see *Re Oxendon's Settled Estates, Oxendon v Chapman* (1904) 74 LJ Ch 234; and MORTGAGE. As to the circumstances in which the limitations of a settlement might be varied by the proviso see *Hipkin v Wilson* (1850) 3 De G & Sm 738; *Meadows v Meadows* (1853) 16 Beav 401; *Whitbread v Smith* (1854) 3 De GM & G 727.

3   *Smyth-Pigott v Smyth-Pigott* [1884] WN 149, CA.

4   *Hare v Hare* (1876) 24 WR 575. See further POWERS.

5   *Re Wilcock, Wilcock v Johnson* (1890) 62 LT 317.

6   *Re Slade, Witham v Watson* (1919) 89 LJ Ch 412, HL. It should be noted that in this case there was no gift to the persons interested under the settlement.

7   As to resulting trusts see EQUITY vol 16 (Reissue) para 904; TRUSTS vol 48 (Reissue) para 599 et seq. Revocation of a will does not, however, invalidate a settlement containing trusts for payment of legacies bequeathed by that will: *Re Hall's Settlement Trusts, Samuell v Lamont* [1937] Ch 227, [1937] 1 All ER 571. Cf *Darley v Langworthy* (1774) 3 Bro Parl Cas 359; *Re Whitburn, Whitburn v Christie* [1923] 1 Ch 332.

8   *Montague v Montague* (1852) 15 Beav 565; *Re North, Meates v Bishop* (1887) 76 LT 186; *Re Marquis of Bristol, Earl Grey v Grey* [1897] 1 Ch 946; *Re Wood, Wodehouse v Wood* [1913] 2 Ch 574, CA; *Re Campbell's Trusts, Public Trustee v Campbell* [1922] 1 Ch 551; *Re Gooch, Gooch v Gooch* [1929] 1 Ch 740.

9   *Baskett v Lodge* (1856) 23 Beav 138; *Baker v Richards* (1859) 27 Beav 320; *Re Perkins, Perkins v Bagot* [1893] 1 Ch 283; *Re Fraser, Ind v Fraser* [1913] 2 Ch 224; *Re Paul's Settlement Trusts, Paul v Nelson* [1920] 1 Ch 99; *Re Playfair, Palmer v Playfair* [1951] Ch 4, [1950] 2 All ER 285. There is no rule of law preventing the coalescence of two funds subject to a charge peculiar to one of them: *Re Rydon's Settlement, Barclays Bank v Everitt Ltd* [1955] Ch 1, [1954] 3 All ER 1, CA. Cf *Re Cavendish, Grosvenor v Butler* [1912] 1 Ch 794.

722. Referential powers. Powers created by reference to other powers are naturally construed as being of the same nature and extent as such other powers[1], but divested of any conditions or restrictions personal to the donee of the original power[2]. However, if the original power is inconsistent with the limitations in the instrument creating the referential power, the referential power is, as a matter of construction, limited so as to conform with those limitations[3].

Where estates are devised to the same uses and subject to like powers as those to which settled estates have been limited, they are subject to all the trusts, powers and provisos contained in the settlement, so that powers of sale, leasing and exchange will have to be exercised by the same persons as those who have to exercise the similar powers contained in the original settlement[4]. A power of appointment may nevertheless be incorporated in a settlement by reference, even though the power is to be given to a person other than the appointor under the original settlement[5].

A power of appointment over an original share operates on an accruing share which becomes subject to the same trusts, powers and provisos as the original share[6].

1   See *Cox v Cox* (1855) 1 K & J 251, where a power to give receipts was not implied in a referential power of sale; and POWERS. A power to make loans of a limited amount is not increased by the accruer of property by way of referential trust: *Eustace v Robinson* (1880) 7 LR Ir 83, Ir CA.
2   *Earl of Harrington v Countess Dowager of Harrington* (1868) LR 3 HL 295.
3   *Crossman v Bevan* (1859) 27 Beav 502.
4   *Taylor v Miles* (1860) 28 Beav 411; cf *Morgan v Rutson* (1848) 16 Sim 234; *Earl of Shrewsbury v Keightley* (1866) LR 2 CP 130, Ex Ch. It is no longer possible to create settlements under the Settled Land Act 1925: see para 676 ante.
5   *Countess of Berchtoldt v Marquis of Hertford* (1844) 7 Beav 172.
6   *Re Hutchinson's Settlement, ex p Dunn* (1852) 5 De G & Sm 681. As to powers of appointment see para 922 et seq post.

723. Multiplication of charges. Where trusts are created by reference[1], a proviso is commonly inserted that charges on the estate are not to be increased or multiplied. In the absence of such a proviso, as a general rule a trust created by reference is not read so as to make a duplication of charges[2], although an intention to do so may be inferred from the language of any particular instrument[3].

1   As to referential trusts see para 721 ante. It is no longer possible to create settlements under the Settled Land Act 1925: see para 676 ante.
2   *Hindle v Taylor* (1855) 5 De GM & G 577; *Boyd v Boyd* (1863) 9 LT 166; *Trew v Perpetual Trustee Co* [1895] AC 264, PC. Cf *Re Campbell's Trusts, Public Trustee v Campbell* [1922] 1 Ch 551.
3   *Cooper v Macdonald* (1873) LR 16 Eq 258; *Re Arnell, Re Edwards, Prickett v Prickett* [1924] 1 Ch 473. See also *Re Beaumont, Bradshaw v Packer* [1913] 1 Ch 325.

(ii) Rentcharges and Annuities

724. Pin money. Pin money is an allowance made by a husband to his wife for her separate personal expenses[1]. This allowance can be secured either by the limitation to the trustees during the joint lives of the husband and wife of a yearly rentcharge secured on the husband's real estate, or by a trust to pay the rentcharge to the trustees out of the rents and profits of the estate in trust for the wife[2]. Such a rentcharge accrues from day to day, and no provision for its apportionment is required[3]. As a rule, the statutory means of compelling payment are relied on, and no express provisions for that purpose are inserted in the settlement[4].

1   *Howard v Earl of Digby* (1834) 2 Cl & Fin 634 at 654, HL. As to pin money generally see HUSBAND AND WIFE. It is no longer possible to create settlements under the Settled Land Act 1925: see para 676 ante.
2   It is not now necessary to create a rentcharge to secure pin money since a trust for this purpose can be enforced against the tenant for life: see paras 767–768 post. As to the power to create rentcharges in the case of settlements see para 678 note 25 ante. As to rentcharges generally see RENTCHARGES AND ANNUITIES vol 39(2) (Reissue) para 753 et seq.
3   See the Apportionment Act 1870 ss 2 (as amended), 5; and para 957 post.
4   As to the statutory means of compelling payment see the Law of Property Act 1925 s 121 (as amended); and RENTCHARGES AND ANNUITIES vol 39(2) (Reissue) para 865.

725. Jointure. A jointure is prima facie a provision for a wife after the death of her husband[1]. Such provision is made out of the husband's land and can be created either by limiting a yearly rentcharge upon trust for the wife or by a trust to pay the rentcharge to her out of the rents and profits of the land, if she survives her husband[2]. The rentcharge need not be made apportionable[3], and the statutory means of recovering it are usually relied on as in the case of pin money[4].

It is not unusual to insert a power for the husband, if he survives the wife, to appoint a jointure for a subsequent wife. In the case of a deficiency, unless the settlement otherwise provides, jointures and portions[5] abate proportionately[6].

1   *Re De Hoghton, De Hoghton v De Hoghton* [1896] 2 Ch 385; *Greenwood v Lutman* [1915] 1 IR 266. See also *Jamieson v Trevelyan* (1854) 10 Exch 269, which turned on the peculiar language of the will then in question; and POWERS.
2   As in the case of pin money (see para 724 ante) a jointure can be created by means of a trust: see para 724 note 2 ante. As to the power to create rentcharges in the case of settlements see para 678 note 25 ante. It is no longer possible to create settlements under the Settled Land Act 1925: see para 676 ante.
3   See the Apportionment Act 1870 ss 2 (as amended), 5; and para 957 post.
4   See the Law of Property Act 1925 s 121 (as amended); and RENTCHARGES AND ANNUITIES vol 39(2) (Reissue) para 865.
5   As to portions see para 727 et seq post.
6   *Re Keele Estates, Aveling v Sneyd* [1952] Ch 306, [1952] 1 All ER 44; revsd on another point [1952] Ch 603, [1952] 2 All ER 164, CA.

726. Annuities. If it is desired that a certain income be secured to a person out of the rents and profits of land for life or some other period, it is usual to limit the land to trustees upon trust that the proposed annuitant is to receive a yearly rentcharge of the proposed amount[1]. The limitation should state the period during which the rentcharge is payable, but no technical words of limitation are necessary[2].

It is no longer usual to insert express provisions as to the recovery of rentcharges, reliance being placed on the remedies afforded by statute[3], and they need not be made apportionable[4].

1   It is not necessary to create a rentcharge: see para 724 note 2 ante. As to the power to create rentcharges in the case of settlements see para 678 note 25 ante. It is no longer possible to create settlements under the Settled Land Act 1925: see para 676 ante.
2   See the Law of Property Act 1925 s 60(1); and REAL PROPERTY vol 39(2) (Reissue) para 93. As to the commencement and duration of rentcharges and annuities see RENTCHARGES AND ANNUITIES vol 39(2) (Reissue) para 751 et seq.
3   See ibid s 121 (as amended); and RENTCHARGES AND ANNUITIES vol 39(2) (Reissue) para 865.
4   See the Apportionment Act 1870 ss 2 (as amended), 5; and para 957 post.

(iii) Portions

727. Nature of portions. Since the principal trusts of a strict settlement were traditionally framed so as to carry the settled land in its entirety to one son of the settlor and his descendants, further provisions were commonly inserted for the purpose of providing sums of money for the benefit of the other, and generally younger, children of the settlor who did not succeed to the land. Such sums are known as portions[1]. Formerly, such sums were secured by limiting the settled land to trustees for a long term[2] upon trust by mortgage or sale of the land or otherwise to raise such sums. However, after 1925 it became usual to declare trusts for raising portions without limiting a term of years[3]. The portions were generally directed to be held in trust for such children on their attaining the age of 21, or, if female, marrying under that age, in such shares and proportions as the husband and wife might jointly appoint by deed, and subject to any such appointment as the survivor might by deed or will appoint, and in default of any such appointment for the qualified children in equal shares[4]. It was not unusual to insert a power for the settlor, if he or she was the surviving spouse, to charge portions for the children of a subsequent marriage[5].

1   *Jones v Maggs* (1852) 9 Hare 605. This use of the word 'portions' should not be confused with its use in
     connection with the doctrine of satisfaction or the rule against double portions, as to which see EQUITY
     vol 16 (Reissue) para 857 et seq. Portions charged by a father under a power contained in a settlement
     made by himself and a son take priority over any estate given to the son, unless a contrary intention is
     expressed or implied in the settlement: *Mills v Mills* (1846) 3 Jo & Lat 242. As to powers of charging
     portions generally see POWERS. The traditional trusts of a strict settlement, while still permissible, are less
     common. It is no longer possible to create settlements under the Settled Land Act 1925: see para 676 ante.
2   Such a term can be limited to commence more than 21 years from the date of the settlement: see the Law
     of Property Act 1925 s 149(3); and LANDLORD AND TENANT vol 27(1) (Reissue) para 83. The statutory
     restrictions on the number of the trustees of a settlement (see para 756 note 3 post) do not apply in the
     case of the trustees of a portions term: see the Trustee Act 1925 s 34(3)(c); and TRUSTS vol 48 (Reissue)
     para 694.
3   Such a trust can be enforced against the tenant for life: see para 767 post.
4   Where the ultimate trust of the sum raised was that it should go as part of the personal estate of the settlor,
     the sum, having been raised, was held to devolve as personalty, notwithstanding that when it was raised
     the settlor could not be compelled to pay it and that the estate charged with it might not have been well
     discharged: *Tucker v Loveridge* (1858) 2 De G & J 650. As to the abatement of jointures and portions in
     case of a deficiency see para 725 text and note 6 ante.
5   See POWERS.

728. Meaning of 'eldest son'. The object of raising portions being to make provision
for the children other than the one who takes the settled estate, the court leans against a
strict construction of the clause when the position of the children has been changed, as
for instance by the death of the first-born son. Where the trusts have been for the younger
children, or the children other than an eldest son[1], or the children other than a son or
sons who should by means of the settlement become entitled to the first estate of freehold
or inheritance, the questions who is an eldest son and who are younger children ought
prima facie to be decided at the time of the distribution of the portions fund[2], and in
construing the words 'eldest son' the court is not bound to say that 'eldest son' is the
person who originally answered that description, as being the first-born son, but that it
really means the person who may have become, in the events that have happened, an
eldest son, and who as such eldest son comes into actual enjoyment of the bulk of the
estate[3]. A daughter taking the estate has been treated as an eldest son[4].

     The vesting of a portion by appointment or otherwise does not exclude this rule[5].
However, a payment when made in accordance with the terms of the settlement, or,
where the period of distribution has been accelerated by the release of the prior life estate,
upon the eldest son actually succeeding, is final and irrevocable[6], and the application of
the rule may be excluded by the terms of the settlement[7].

1   If the portions are provided for children 'other than an eldest or only son', daughters take portions as
     being others than an eldest or only son, but a provision for children 'besides an eldest or only son' requires
     the existence of a son to bring it into operation: *Walcott v Bloomfield* (1843) 4 Dr & War 211; *Re Flemyngs's
     Trusts* (1885) 15 LR Ir 363; *L'Estrange v Winniett* [1911] 1 IR 62. See, however, *Simpson v Frew* (1856) 5
     I Ch R 517. As to illegitimate, legitimated and adopted children see paras 731–733 post.
2   *Ellison v Thomas* (1862) 1 De GJ & Sm 18; *Collingwood v Stanhope* (1869) LR 4 HL 43; *Morton's Trusts*
     [1902] 1 IR 310n; *Re Stawell's Trusts, Poole v Riversdale* [1909] 1 Ch 534 (revsd on the construction of
     the documents [1909] 2 Ch 239, CA).
3   *Chadwick v Doleman* (1705) 2 Vern 528; *Lord Teynham v Webb* (1751) 2 Ves Sen 198; *Loder v Loder* (1754)
     2 Ves Sen 530; *Earl of Northumberland v Earl of Egremont* (1759) 1 Eden 435; *Broadmead v Wood* (1780) 1
     Bro CC 77; *Matthews v Paul* (1819) 3 Swan 328; *Gray v Earl of Limerick* (1848) 2 De G & Sm 370; *Richards
     v Richards* (1860) John 754; *Ellison v Thomas* (1862) 1 De GJ & Sm 18; *Davies v Huguenin* (1863) 1 Hem
     & M 730; *Re Flemyngs's Trusts* (1885) 15 LR Ir 363. Cf *Re Bayley's Settlement* (1871) 6 Ch App 590. On
     the other hand, a child who was originally a younger child does not become an eldest son because at the
     time of distribution he is in fact the eldest child, if he does not take the bulk of the estate: *Re Wrottesley's
     Settlement, Wrottesley v Fowler* [1911] 1 Ch 708 at 713.
4   *Earl of Northumberland v Earl of Egremont* (1759) 1 Eden 435; *Stirum v Richards* (1861) 12 I Ch R 323. As
     a rule, however, an elder daughter, where there is a son, is accounted a younger child: *Heneage v Hunloke*
     (1742) 2 Atk 456.

5   *Chadwick v Doleman* (1705) 2 Vern 528; *Re Stawell's Trusts, Poole v Riversdale* [1909] 1 Ch 534 (revsd on
     another point [1909] 2 Ch 239, CA). As to powers of appointment see para 922 et seq post.
6   *Re Stawell's Trusts, Poole v Riversdale* [1909] 1 Ch 534; revsd on another point [1909] 2 Ch 239, CA.
7   *Windham v Graham* (1826) 1 Russ 331; *Re Bankes, Alison v Bankes* (1909) 101 LT 778; *Re Wise's
     Settlement, Smith v Waller* [1913] 1 Ch 41; *Re Beresford's Settlement, Irvine v Beresford* [1914] 1 IR 222.

729. Meaning of 'younger sons'. As the principle is generally that no child who
takes the bulk of the estate is to share in the portions fund[1], if under the settlement the
estate goes to a younger son, and not to the first-born son, then in relation to the portions
the first-born is regarded as a younger son and the younger is regarded as the eldest son[2].
However, a son who takes the estate cannot claim a portion on the ground that his
inheritance is valueless[3]. A son who, while interested in remainder, joins in a resettlement
will be treated as an eldest son and excluded from sharing in the portions provision
whatever the value of his interest under the resettlement may be[4]. If the first-born son
joins with his father in resettling the estate, a younger son who actually comes into
possession of the estate by virtue, not of the limitations of the original settlement, but of
the subsequent resettlement, is entitled to his portion as a younger son[5]. Similarly, where
a settlement contained a power of revocation and reappointment to new uses, a younger
son to whom the estate was appointed did not take any estate under the settlement in such
a sense that he should be deemed an eldest son[6].

1   See paras 727–728 ante.
2   *Beale v Beale* (1713) 1 P Wms 244; *Duke v Doidge* (1746) 2 Ves Sen 203n; *Ellison v Thomas* (1862) 1 De
     GJ & Sm 18; *Davies v Huguenin* (1863) 1 Hem & M 730; *Swinburne v Swinburne* (1868) 17 WR 47;
     Collingwood v Stanhope (1869) LR 4 HL 43 at 52; *L'Estrange v Winniett* [1911] 1 IR 62; *Re Cavendish's
     Settlement, Grosvenor v Lady Butler* (1912) 106 LT 510. Where, however, the trusts were for children other
     than an eldest son for the time being entitled to a life interest, the personal representatives of a deceased
     eldest son who had in the past enjoyed a life interest were excluded: *Re Gunter's Settlements, Owen v
     Pritchard-Barrett* [1949] Ch 502, [1949] 1 All ER 680, not following *Ellison v Thomas* supra.
3   *Collingwood v Stanhope* (1869) LR 4 HL 43; *Reid v Hoare* (1884) 26 ChD 363; *Re Fitzgerald's Settled Estates,
     Saunders v Boyd* [1891] 3 Ch 394; *Rooke v Plunkett* [1902] 1 IR 299.
4   *Re Leeke's Settlement Trusts, Borough v Leeke* [1937] Ch 600, [1937] 2 All ER 563. As to resettlements see
     para 720 ante.
5   *Spencer v Spencer* (1836) 8 Sim 87; *Tennison v Moore* (1850) 13 I Eq R 424; *Wyndham v Fane* (1853) 11 Hare
     287; *Macoubrey v Jones* (1856) 2 K & J 684; *Adams v Beck* (1858) 25 Beav 648; *Re Smyth's Trusts, ex p Smyth*
     (1861) 12 I Ch R 487; *Sing v Leslie* (1864) 2 Hem & M 68; *Domvile v Winnington* (1884) 26 ChD 382; *Re
     Fitzgerald's Settled Estates, Saunders v Boyd* [1891] 3 Ch 394; *Re Wrottesley's Settlement, Wrottesley v Fowler*
     [1911] 1 Ch 708.
6   *Wandesforde v Carrick* (1871) IR 5 Eq 486.

730. Designation by name. The fact that the persons to take or be excluded from
portions are designated by name may or may not make a difference, according as the view
is taken, on the construction of the particular instrument, that the named individual is
intended, or that the named person is included or excluded as fulfilling a certain
qualification[1].

1   *Jermyn v Fellows* (1735) Cas temp Talb 93; *Savage v Carroll* (1810) 1 Ball & B 265; *Sandeman v Mackenzie*
     (1861) 1 John & H 613. See also *Wood v Wood* (1867) LR 4 Eq 48; *Re Prytherch, Prytherch v Williams*
     (1889) 42 ChD 590. As to the nature of portions see para 727 ante.

731. Illegitimate children. In a disposition made before 1970, a gift in favour of
future illegitimate children is void as being contrary to public policy[1]. Further, in such a
disposition, a gift to 'the children' of a person prima facie does not include his illegitimate
children[2], and other expressions which are a term of art denoting a person's relations
prima facie do not include persons who are illegitimate, or who deduce the relationship
through an illegitimate person[3].

In a disposition made after 1969 and before 4 April 1988, a gift in favour of future illegitimate children is not void as being contrary to public policy[4].

In dispositions made inter vivos on or after 4 April 1988 or by will or codicil executed on or after that date, references (however expressed) to any relationship between two persons, unless the contrary intention appears, are to be construed without regard to whether or not the father and mother of either of them, or the father and mother of any person through whom the relationship is deduced, have or had been married to each other at any time[5]. The use, without more, of the word 'heir' or 'heirs' or any expression purporting to create an entailed interest in real or personal property does not show a contrary intention for these purposes[6]. A disposition of real or personal property devolving with a dignity or title of honour is unaffected by these reforms[7].

1   See para 617 ante.
2   *Hill v Crook* (1873) LR 6 HL 265. This prima facie rule does not apply if, to the settlor's knowledge, there is an impossibility or strong improbability of the person having legitimate children, or if the context indicates that the term 'children' is not confined to legitimate children: *Hill v Crook* supra; *Re Fletcher, Barclays Bank Ltd v Ewing* [1949] Ch 473, [1949] 1 All ER 732; *Re Jones Will Trusts, Jones v Hawtin Squire* [1965] Ch 1124, [1965] 2 All ER 828; *Re Jebb, Ward-Smith v Jebb* [1966] Ch 666, [1965] 3 All ER 358, CA. Cf *Re Brinkley's Will Trusts, Westminster Bank Ltd v Brinkley* [1968] Ch 407, [1967] 3 All ER 805. See also WILLS vol 50 (Reissue) para 590.
3   *Sydall v Castings Ltd* [1967] 1 QB 302, [1966] 3 All ER 770, CA. See also note 2 supra.
4   See para 617 ante.
5   See the Family Law Reform Act 1987 ss 1, 19(1); and CHILDREN AND YOUNG PERSONS vol 5(2) (Reissue) para 723; WILLS vol 50 (Reissue) para 592. As to dispositions in cases of adoption see para 733 post.
6   See ibid s 19(2) (as amended); and WILLS vol 50 (Reissue) para 592.
7   See ibid s 19(4); and WILLS vol 50 (Reissue) para 592.

732. Legitimated children. In a disposition made before 1976[1], subject to any contrary indication, a legitimated person and his spouse, children and more remote issue are entitled to take any interest under any disposition coming into operation after the date of the legitimation in like manner as if he had been born legitimate[2].

In a disposition made after 1975, subject to any contrary indication, a legitimated person and any other person, is entitled to take any interest as if the legitimated person had been born legitimate[3].

1   The Legitimacy Act 1926 s 3 (see note 2) was repealed by the Children Act 1975 s 108(1)(b), Sch 4, Pt II (now itself repealed), but not in relation to instruments made before 1 January 1976: see s 8(9), Sch 1 paras 1(5), 12(9) (repealed); and the Legitimacy Act 1976 s 11(1), Sch 1 para 2. The regime introduced by the Family Law Reform Act 1969 s 15 in relation to dispositions made between 1969 and 1976 was repealed (with savings in relation to the operation of the Trustee Act 1925 s 33): see the Family Law Reform Act 1987 s 33(2), (4), Sch 3 para 9, Sch 4.
2   See the Legitimacy Act 1926 s 3 (repealed: see note 1 supra); and WILLS vol 50 (Reissue) para 586. This does not apply to property settled to devolve (as nearly as the law permits) along with a dignity or title of honour: see s 3(3) (repealed: see note 1 supra). As to whether a legitimated child is entitled to take as a child 'of the marriage' of his parents see *Re Askew, Marjoribanks v Askew* [1930] 2 Ch 259; *Re Wicks Marriage Settlement, Public Trustee v Wicks* [1940] Ch 475; *Colquitt v Colquitt* [1948] P 19, [1947] 2 All ER 50, DC. As to the meaning of 'disposition' see *Re Billson's Settlement Trusts* [1984] Ch 409 at 415, [1984] 2 All ER 401 at 404, CA, per Browne-Wilkinson LJ ('disposition' means the instrument creating the interest, not the interest itself). As to whether a legitimated child is within the marriage consideration see para 661 note 2 ante.
3   See the Legitimacy Act 1976 s 5(3). This does not apply to property settled to devolve (as nearly as the law permits) along with a dignity or title of honour: see s 11, Sch 1 para 4(3); and CHILDREN AND YOUNG PERSONS vol 5(2) (Reissue) para 728.

733. Adopted children. In a disposition made before 1950, an adoption order does not deprive the adopted child of any right to or in property to which, but for the order, the child would have been entitled under the disposition, whether occurring or made before or after the making of the adoption order, or confer on the adopted child any right to or interest in property as a child of the adopter[1]. Further, in a disposition made before 1950, whether made before or after the making of the adoption order, the expressions 'child', 'children' and 'issue' do not, unless the contrary intention appears, include an adopted child or children or the issue of an adopted child[2].

In a disposition made after 1949 and before 1976, being one made after the date of an adoption order: (1) any reference, whether express or implied, to the child or children of the adopter is, unless a contrary intention appears, to be construed as, or including a reference to, the adopted person; (2) any reference, whether express or implied, to the child or children of the adopted person's natural parents or either of them is, unless a contrary intention appears, to be construed as not being, or as not including, a reference to the adopted person; and (3) any reference, whether express or implied, to a person related to the adopted person in any degree refers to the person who would be related to him in that degree if he were the child of the adopter born in lawful wedlock and were not the child of any other person[3].

The rights of an adopted child in respect of a disposition made after 1975 are set out elsewhere[4].

1   See note 2 infra.
2   See the Adoption of Children Act 1926 s 5(2) (repealed by the Adoption of Children Act 1949 s 10(5), but continuing to apply to dispositions made before 1 January 1950, the date on which the latter Act came into operation: see the Interpretation Act 1978 s 16(1)). See also *Re Gilpin, Hutchinson v Gilpin* [1954] Ch 1, [1953] 2 All ER 1218. As to adoption see generally CHILDREN AND YOUNG PERSONS vol 5(2) (Reissue) para 1021 et seq. As to whether a contrary intention appears for the purposes of the Adoption of Children Act 1926 s 5(2) (repealed) see the principle stated and the cases cited in para 731 note 2 ante.
3   See the Adoption Act 1958 s 16(2), replacing provisions formerly contained in the Adoption of Children Act 1949 s 3 (repealed), and the Adoption Act 1950 s 13(2) (repealed), and itself repealed by the Children Act 1975 s 108(1)(b), Sch 4 Pt I (repealed), but not so as to affect its application in relation to a disposition of property effected by an instrument made before 1 January 1976: see s 8(9), Sch 1 paras 1(5), 5(2) (repealed). The Adoption Act 1958 s 16(2) (repealed), does not affect the devolution of property limited (whether subject to any preceding limitation or charge or not) to devolve (as nearly as the law permits) with a dignity or title of honour: s 16(4) (repealed). The Adoption Act 1976 s 73(1), Sch 2 para 6(2), likewise provides that the Adoption Act 1958 s 16 (repealed), continues to apply to dispositions of property effected by instruments made before 1 January 1976.
4   See CHILDREN AND YOUNG PERSONS vol 5(2) (Reissue) para 1089 et seq; WILLS vol 50 (Reissue) para 593. As to whether an adopted child is within the consideration of marriage see para 661 note 2 ante. As to the succession rights of a child adopted under a foreign order see CONFLICT OF LAWS vol 8(1) (Reissue) para 794.

734. Amount of portions. The amount to be raised for portions may vary with the number of children to be provided for, and it is a matter of the construction of the particular settlement whether this amount depends upon the original number of children, where this has been reduced before the period of distribution, or the number who actually take[1]. Where the paramount intention of the settlement is that, subject to the provision of portions, the settled property is to go to the eldest child, the trusts for portions will not come into operation at all if their only effect would be to benefit the personal representatives of a deceased younger child[2]. However, when the trusts are certain, and the amount to be raised is certain, and the events have happened on the occurrence of which the trusts are expressed to come into operation, then the whole amount is raised for the benefit of the surviving portioner[3]. In the case of a marriage settlement, it is presumed that the intention of the parties is to make provision for every child of the marriage who requires it, and accordingly the court may construe the trust for portions according to the number of children attaining vested interests, and not according to the number of children born, even if this involves a departure from the strict grammatical construction[4].

1   As to the nature of portions see para 727 ante.
2   *Hubert v Parsons* (1751) 2 Ves Sen 261. Cf *Clarke v Jessop* (1844) Drury *temp* Sug 301. See also *Hemming v Griffith, Griffith v Hemming* (1860) 2 Giff 403.
3   *Hemming v Griffith, Griffith v Hemming* (1860) 2 Giff 403; *Knapp v Knapp* (1871) LR 12 Eq 238. A portion which has once become vested is not divested by the death of the portioner before the period of distribution: *Willis v Willis* (1796) 3 Ves 51; *Vane v Lord Dungannon* (1804) 2 Sch & Lef 118. As to the vesting of portions see para 738 post.
4   *Rye v Rye* (1878) 1 LR Ir 413. As to marriage settlements see para 628 et seq ante.

735. Time for raising portions. The time for raising portions depends in each case upon the construction of the particular settlement[1], but, as a general rule, if the portions are vested or the contingencies on which they are to be paid have happened, and they are required[2], they must be raised, even if to do so involves a considerable sacrifice and waste of property, as where the only means of raising them is by the sale or mortgage of a reversionary term[3].

The following general rules have been deduced from the cases[4]:

(1)   where a term is limited in remainder to commence in possession after the death of a parent, yet if the trust is to raise a portion payable at a fixed period, the child need not wait for the death of the parent before the portion is raised, but at the fixed period may compel a sale of the term[5];

(2)   where the period is not fixed by the original settlement, but depends on a contingency, that rule applies as soon as the contingency happens[6];

(3)   where not only the period, but the class of children in favour of whom the portions are to be raised, depends on a contingency, as where the term is limited to take effect in case the father dies without issue male by his wife, on the contingency happening on the death of either parent without issue male, the portions are to be raised immediately, and the term is saleable in the lifetime of the surviving parent[7]; and

(4)   portions are not raised in the lifetime of the parents if there is a clear indication in the settlement to the contrary[8].

1   *Codrington v Lord Foley* (1801) 6 Ves 364; *Smyth v Foley* (1838) 3 Y & C Ex 142; *Keily v Keily* (1843) 4 Dr & War 38; *Massy v Lloyd* (1863) 10 HL Cas 248. Where the trustees were to raise portions by sale or mortgage or any other reasonable means, with power at their discretion to postpone the raising of the portions, they were bound, when exercising their discretion, to consider the interests of the persons entitled to the estate as well as those of the portioners: *Re Sandys, Union of London and Smith's Bank v Litchfield* [1916] 1 Ch 511. As to the nature of portions see para 727 ante. As to the method of raising portions see para 737 post.
2   *Edgeworth v Edgeworth* (1829) Beat 328. As to the vesting of portions see para 738 post.
3   *Ravenhill v Dansey* (1723) 2 P Wms 179; *Codrington v Lord Foley* (1801) 6 Ves 364; *Whaley v Morgan* (1839) 2 Dr & Wal 330; *Massy v Lloyd* (1863) 10 HL Cas 248; *Re Lord Gisborough's Settled Estates* [1921] 2 Ch 39. See also *Reresby v Newland* (1723) 6 Bro Parl Cas 75; and *Re Sandys, Union of London and Smith's Bank v Litchfield* [1916] 1 Ch 511.
4   *Smyth v Foley* (1838) 3 Y & C Ex 142 at 157 per Alderson B.
5   *Hellier v Jones* (1689) 1 Eq Cas Abr 337; *Stanley v Stanley* (1737) 1 Atk 549; *Cotton v Cotton* (1738) 3 Y & C Ex 149n; *Smith v Evans* (1766) Amb 633; *Whaley v Morgan* (1839) 2 Dr & Wal 330; *Michell v Michell* (1842) 4 Beav 549. A portion to be raised by means of a term ceases to be raisable when the term comes to an end: *Re Marshall's Estate* [1899] 1 IR 96.
6   *Staniforth and Clerkson v Staniforth* (1703) 2 Vern 460; *Hebblethwaite v Cartwright* (1734) Cas temp Talb 31.
7   *Gerrard v Gerrard* (1703) 2 Vern 458; *Lyon v Duke of Chandos* (1746) 3 Atk 416; *Smyth v Foley* (1838) 3 Y & C Ex 142.

8   The court has found indications that portions are not to be raised in the lifetime of the parents in the following cases: *Corbett v Maydwell* (1710) 2 Vern 640 (portion for daughter unmarried or not provided for at father's death); *Brome v Berkley* (1728) 2 P Wms 484 (direction for maintenance, which precedes portion, after trust estate chargeable with portion comes into possession); *Churchman v Harvey* (1757) Amb 335 (precedent estate of a jointress). Cf *Hall v Carter* (1742) 2 Atk 354.

736. Anticipation in favour of portioners. Whether the whole sum for portions is raisable as soon as part becomes payable depends upon the construction of the particular settlement, but in general the whole sum probably is so raisable[1]. Although the time for raising portions may therefore be anticipated in favour of portioners whose interests have vested[2], it will not be anticipated in favour of the persons entitled to the inheritance[3], in the absence of contrary indication in the settlement[4].

1   *Gillibrand v Goold* (1833) 5 Sim 149; *Leech v Leech* (1842) 2 Dr & War 568; *Peareth v Greenwood* (1880) 28 WR 417. See, however, *Hays v Bailey* (1813) cited in 2 Dr & War 576; *Wynter v Bold* (1823) 1 Sim & St 507; *Sheppard v Wilson* (1845) 4 Hare 392. As to the nature of portions see para 727 ante; and as to the method of raising portions see para 737 post.
2   As to the vesting of portions see para 738 post.
3   *Oldfield v Oldfield* (1685) 1 Vern 336; *Sheppard v Wilson* (1845) 4 Hare 392 at 394. Contingent legacies may not be anticipated in favour of a devisee of land charged with them: *Dickenson v Dickenson* (1789) 3 Bro CC 19.
4   *Marsh v Keith* (1861) 29 Beav 625.

737. Method of raising portions. Where a settlement directs a particular method of raising portions, they cannot be raised in any other way[1]. If no method is directed, they may be raised by a sale or mortgage[2]. In deciding between a sale or mortgage, the court has regard to the wishes of the persons immediately interested[3]. An express prohibition against raising portions by sale excludes the possibility of raising them by mortgage[4].

If portions are directed to be raised out of land they cannot be raised out of personalty[5]. A power to charge portions on land authorises a charge on any part of land[6], and a direction to raise portions out of rents and profits will enable them to be raised out of corpus[7], unless they are directed to be raised only out of annual rents and profits[8] or there are other indications that they are to be raised out of the rents and profits as they accrue[9].

If the trustees have power to raise portions either by sale or mortgage or out of the rents and profits, then, in the absence of an indication to the contrary in the settlement, they should charge the principal on the inheritance and secure the application of the annual profits to keep down the interest on the portions[10]. Where the ordinary profits of a term are insufficient to raise the portions, timber may be felled or a mine may be worked[11].

The costs of raising portions are payable out of the estate and not out of the portions[12], but the costs of dealing with the portions must be borne by the portioners themselves[13].

1   *Ivy v Gilbert* (1722) 2 P Wms 13 (affd (1723) 6 Bro Parl Cas 68, HL); *Mills v Banks* (1724) 3 P Wms 1; *Bennett v Wyndham* (1857) 23 Beav 521 (on appeal (1862) 4 De GF & J 259). A portion to be raised by means of a term ceases to be raisable when the term comes to an end: *Re Marshall's Estate* [1899] 1 IR 96. As to the nature of portions see para 727 ante.
2   *Meynell v Massey* (1686) 2 Vern 1; *Kelly v Lord Bellew* (1707) 4 Bro Parl Cas 495, HL; *Ashton v—* (1718) 10 Mod Rep 401.
3   *Metcalfe v Hutchinson* (1875) 1 ChD 591. A sale may be ordered at the instance of the person entitled to the estate against the wishes of the portioners: *Warburton v Warburton* (1701) 2 Vern 420; on appeal (1702) 4 Bro Parl Cas 1, HL. As to the duty of the trustees to consider the interests both of the persons entitled to the estate and of the portioners see *Re Sandys, Union of London and Smith's Bank v Litchfield* [1916] 1 Ch 511. As to the sale or mortgage of a reversionary term see para 735 text and note 3 ante.
4   *Bennett v Wyndham* (1857) 23 Beav 521; on appeal (1862) 4 De GF & J 259.

5   *Edwards v Freeman* (1727) 2 P Wms 435; *Burgoigne v Fox* (1738) 1 Atk 575; *Lechmere v Charlton* (1808) 15
     Ves 193.
6   *Mosley v Mosley* (1800) 5 Ves 248. As to the apportionment of a charge see *Otway-Cave v Otway* (1866)
     LR 2 Eq 725.
7   *Backhouse v Middleton* (1670) 1 Cas in Ch 173; *Sheldon v Dormer* (1693) 2 Vern 309; *Blagrave v Clunn*
     (1706) 2 Vern 576; *Trafford v Ashton* (1718) 1 P Wms 415; *Green v Belchier* (1737) 1 Atk 505; *Okeden v
     Okeden* (1738) 1 Atk 550; *Allan v Backhouse* (1813) 2 Ves & B 65 (affd (1821) Jac 631). Cf *Phillips v
     Gutteridge* (1862) 3 De GJ & Sm 332; *Pearson v Helliwell* (1874) LR 18 Eq 411; *Re Buchanan, Stephens v
     Draper* [1915] 1 IR 95, Ir CA. See also *Countess of Shrewsbury v Earl of Shrewsbury* (1790) 1 Ves 227 at 234;
     Bootle v Blundell (1815) 1 Mer 193 at 233; *Metcalfe v Hutchinson* (1875) 1 ChD 591.
8   *Stanhope v Thacker* (1716) Prec Ch 435; *Trafford v Ashton* (1718) 1 P Wms 415. Cf *Re Green, Baldock v
     Green* (1888) 40 ChD 610.
9   *Ivy v Gilbert* (1722) 2 P Wms 13 (affd (1723) 6 Bro Parl Cas 68, HL); *Mills v Banks* (1724) 3 P Wms 1;
     Green v Belchier (1737) 1 Atk 505. Cf *Ridout v Earl of Plymouth* (1740) 2 Atk 104; *Stone v Theed* (1787) 2
     Bro CC 243; *Wilson v Halliley* (1830) 1 Russ & M 590; *Foster v Smith* (1846) 1 Ph 629; *Earle v Bellingham
     (No 1)* (1857) 24 Beav 445. See also *Evelyn v Evelyn* (1731) 2 P Wms 659; *Warter v Hutchinson* (1823) 1
     Sim & St 276; *Balfour v Cooper* (1883) 23 ChD 472, CA.
10   *Marker v Kekewich* (1850) 8 Hare 291; *Kekewich v Marker* (1851) 3 Mac & G 311; *Re Marquess of Bute,
     Marquess of Bute v Ryder* (1884) 27 ChD 196.
11   *Offley v Offley* (1691) Prec Ch 26; *Marker v Kekewich* (1850) 8 Hare 291; *Marker v Marker* (1851) 9 Hare
     1; *Kekewich v Marker* (1851) 3 Mac & G 311; *Bennett v Wyndham* (1857) 23 Beav 521 (on appeal (1862)
     4 De GF & J 259).
12   *Michell v Michell* (1842) 4 Beav 549; *Armstrong v Armstrong* (1874) LR 18 Eq 541.
13   *Stewart v Marquis of Donegal* (1845) 2 Jo & Lat 636.

738. Vesting of portions. Portions charged on land and payable at a future time do
not in general vest until the time appointed for payment[1]. If no time for payment is
specified, they vest traditionally on the attainment of the age of 21[2] or on marriage on the
principle that a portion does not vest until it is wanted[3]. Upon the death of the portioner
before the time appointed for payment the portion sinks into the inheritance[4]. On the
other hand, if portions are directed to be raised out of the rents and profits of land, but
no time is mentioned for payment, they are payable presently and become an immediate
vested interest, and the representatives of a child who dies during his minority are entitled
to that child's portion[5].

However, if the payment of portions is postponed, not from any consideration
personal to the portioner, but for the convenience of the estate, as where it is postponed
until after the death of the tenant for life, the portions will nevertheless vest before the
time appointed for payment, even if the term out of which they are to be raised may not
then have arisen[6]. However, this rule will yield to a contrary intention in the settlement,
so that the personal representatives of a deceased portioner who had attained 21 or
married will be excluded if the settlement provides either that the right to a portion
depends upon the portioner surviving both or either of his parents[7], or that the issue of a
deceased portioner should take by substitution their parent's share in the portion fund[8].

1   As to the nature of portions see para 727 ante.
2   There have been no reported cases on the point since the age of majority was reduced to 18, as to which
     see para 605 note 1 ante.
3   *Warr v Warr* (1702) Prec Ch 213; *Bruen v Bruen* (1702) 2 Vern 439; *Remnant v Hood* (1860) 2 De GF &
     J 396; *Davies v Huguenin* (1863) 1 Hem & M 730; *Haverty v Curtis* [1895] 1 IR 23. In the case of a marriage
     settlement (see para 628 et seq ante), there is a strong presumption that the shares of the children are to
     become vested in the case of sons at 21 (see note 2 supra), and in the case of daughters at 21 or marriage:
     Re Willmott's Trusts (1869) LR 7 Eq 532 at 537 per James V-C. The same rule applies where the portion
     is payable out of personalty: *Jeffreys v Reynous* (1767) 6 Bro Parl Cas 398; *Schenck v Legh* (1803) 9 Ves 300;
     Perfect v Lord Curzon (1820) 5 Madd 442; *Swallow v Binns* (1855) 1 K & J 417. Cf *Bayard v Smith* (1808)
     14 Ves 470.
4   *Lady Poulet v Lord Poulet* (1685) 1 Vern 204 at 321; *Carter v Bletsoe* (1708) 2 Vern 617; *Prowse v Abingdon*
     (1738) 1 Atk 482 (commenting on *Jackson v Farrand* (1701) 2 Vern 424); *Boycot v Cotton* (1738) 1 Atk 552;
     Ruby v Foot and Beamish (1817) Beat 581; *Edgeworth v Edgeworth* (1829) Beat 328; *Evans v Scott* (1847) 1

HL Cas 43; *Remnant v Hood* (1860) 2 De GF & J 396; *Bagge v Bagge* [1921] 1 IR 213. Cf *Henty v Wrey* (1882) 21 ChD 332 at 359, CA. A power to charge portions may be validly exercised and the portions may be raisable, notwithstanding that no portioner attains a vested interest: *Fosberry v Smith* (1856) 5 I Ch R 321. See also *Simmons v Pitt* (1873) 8 Ch App 978. Cf the vesting of legacies: see WILLS vol 50 (Reissue) para 644 et seq.

5   *Earl Rivers v Earl of Derby* (1688) 2 Vern 72 (affd (1689) 14 Lords Journals 195, HL); *Evelyn v Evelyn* (1731) 2 P Wms 659; *Cowper v Scott* (1731) 3 P Wms 119. The same rule applies in the case of portions payable out of personalty (*Lady Poulet v Lord Poulet* (1685) 1 Vern 204 (affd 14 Lords Journals 87, HL); *Gordon v Raynes* (1732) 3 P Wms 134; *Prowse v Abingdon* (1738) 1 Atk 482; *Mount v Mount* (1851) 13 Beav 333; *Currie v Larkins* (1864) 4 De GJ & Sm 245; *Jopp v Wood* (1865) 2 De GJ & Sm 323), unless a contrary intention appears in the settlement (*Mostyn v Mostyn* (1844) 1 Coll 161 at 167; *Re Colley's Trusts* (1866) LR 1 Eq 496. See also *Re Dennis's Trusts* (1857) 6 I Ch R 422).

6   *Emperor v Rolfe* (1748–9) 1 Ves Sen 208; *Cholmondeley v Meyrick* (1758) 1 Eden 77; *Rooke v Rooke* (1761) 2 Eden 8; *Woodcock v Duke of Dorset* (1792) 3 Bro CC 569; *Willis v Willis* (1796) 3 Ves 51; *Hope v Lord Clifden* (1801) 6 Ves 499; *Powis v Burdett* (1804) 9 Ves 428; *King v Hake* (1804) 9 Ves 438; *Howgrave v Cartier* (1814) 3 Ves & B 79; *Fry v Lord Sherborne* (1829) 3 Sim 243; *Evans v Scott* (1847) 1 HL Cas 43; *Remnant v Hood* (1860) 2 De GF & J 396; *Wakefield v Maffet* (1885) 10 App Cas 422, HL; *Waller v Stevenson* (1912) 56 Sol Jo 666, HL.

7   *Wingrave v Palgrave* (1717) 1 P Wms 401; *Howgrave v Cartier* (1814) 3 Ves & B 79 at 85; *Hotchkin v Humfrey* (1817) 2 Madd 65; *Fitzgerald v Field* (1826) 1 Russ 416; *Whatford v Moore* (1837) 3 My & Cr 270; *Skipper v King* (1848) 12 Beav 29; *Jeffrey v Jeffrey* (1849) 17 Sim 26. Cf *Gordon v Raynes* (1732) 3 P Wms 134; *Worsley v Earl of Granville* (1751) 2 Ves Sen 331.

8   *Re Wilmott's Trusts* (1869) LR 7 Eq 532 (commenting on *Mocatta v Lindo* (1837) 9 Sim 56; and *Mendham v Williams* (1866) LR 2 Eq 396); *Jeyes v Savage* (1875) 10 Ch App 555; *Day v Radcliffe* (1876) 3 ChD 654; *Selby v Whittaker* (1877) 6 ChD 239, CA.

739. Interest on portions. If there is no direction in the settlement as to interest, portions carry interest[1] from the time when they ought to be raised[2], but not from the time when the title to the portion vests[3]. The interest should be paid annually and not allowed to accumulate[4]. Where there is a power of charging interest on a portion it is considered as maintenance[5], and no interest is given on arrears[6].

The donee of a power to charge has a right to fix the rate of interest[7], but this rule does not apply where the trustees have a trust vested in them to raise a specific sum of money, and the only power given to anybody in connection with the money so raised is to state in what proportion the money is to be divided between the parties and at what time it is to be payable[8].

In the absence of any express direction a portion carries interest at the rate current in the country where the land charged is situated, which rate in England is traditionally 4 per cent[9].

1   *Clayton v Earl of Glengall* (1841) 1 Dr & War 1. A contrary intention may be implied from the terms of the instrument creating the trust: *Selby v Gillum* (1836) 2 Y & C Ex 379; *Bredin v Bredin* (1841) 1 Dr & War 494. As to interest by way of maintenance on portions arising under a settlement by a parent or person in loco parentis see CHILDREN AND YOUNG PERSONS vol 5(2) (Reissue) para 661 et seq. As to the nature of portions see para 727 ante.

2   *Lord Roseberry v Taylor* (1702) 6 Bro Parl Cas 43, HL; *Bagenal v Bagenal* (1725) 6 Bro Parl Cas 81, HL; *Evelyn v Evelyn* (1731) 2 P Wms 659 at 669, HL; *Conway v Conway* (1791) 3 Bro CC 267. See also *Lyddon v Lyddon* (1808) 14 Ves 558; and POWERS.

3   *Churchman v Harvey* (1757) Amb 335; *Massy v Lloyd* (1863) 10 HL Cas 248. See also *Reynolds v Meyrick* (1758) 1 Eden 48; *Gardner v Perry* (1851) 20 LJ Ch 429, where, however, the decision seems to have turned on the language of the particular instrument. As to the vesting of portions see para 738 ante.

4   *Boycot v Cotton* (1738) 1 Atk 552.

5   *Boycot v Cotton* (1738) 1 Atk 552.

6   *Mellish v Mellish* (1808) 14 Ves 516.

7   *Boycot v Cotton* (1738) 1 Atk 552; *Lewis v Freke* (1794) 2 Ves 507. See also *Balfour v Cooper* (1883) 23 ChD 472, CA.

8   *Balfour v Cooper* (1883) 23 ChD 472, CA.

9   *Sitwell v Bernard* (1801) 6 Ves 520; *Young v Lord Waterpark* (1842) 13 Sim 199 (on appeal (1845) 15 LJ Ch 63); *Balfour v Cooper* (1883) 23 ChD 472, CA; *Re Drax, Savile v Drax* [1903] 1 Ch 781, CA. See also POWERS. As to rates of interest generally see MONEY; and para 945 note 5 post.

(iv) Conditions of Defeasance

740. Conditions of defeasance generally. Conditions of defeasance, also known as shifting clauses, forfeiture clauses or defeasance clauses[1], are provisions inserted in settlements for the purpose of shifting the estates from the persons taking under the settlement on the happening of a contingency specified in the clause[2]. Such clauses must be so framed as to take effect within the period laid down by the rule against perpetuities[3], and if so expressed as to be divisible they may be good in one event and bad in another[4].

1   See eg *Clayton v Ramsden* [1943] AC 320 at 326, [1943] 1 All ER 16 at 17, HL, per Lord Russell of Killowen, and at 329 and 19 per Lord Wright; *Bromley v Tryon* [1952] AC 265 at 267, 271, [1951] 2 All ER 1058 at 1060, 1063, HL, per Lord Simonds LC.
2   For examples of such contingencies see para 741 et seq post.
3   As to the rule against perpetuities and its applicability to conditions see PERPETUITIES AND ACCUMULATIONS vol 35 (Reissue) para 1008 et seq. If the condition is not limited to the perpetuity period, but the Perpetuities and Accumulations Act 1964 applies, the 'wait and see' rule applies to the condition: see PERPETUITIES AND ACCUMULATIONS vol 35 (Reissue) para 1009.
4   *Miles v Harford* (1879) 12 ChD 691.

741. Events bringing the clause into operation. Conditions of defeasance are commonly employed to carry over the settled estate in the event of accession to another estate[1], but they may also be employed to impose a penalty for a failure to comply with a condition contained in the settlement. Examples of the matters commonly required by such conditions are the profession of a specified religion[2], compliance with a name and arms clause[3] or residence at a specified place[4].

1   See para 743 post. As to conditions of defeasance generally see para 740 ante.
2   See eg the cases referred to in para 742 note 4 post.
3   See para 745 et seq post.
4   Residence implies not domicile but personal presence in the locality at some time or other, not necessarily involving the spending of a night there: *Walcot v Botfield* (1854) Kay 534. A condition requiring residence for a fixed period in every year in a house comprised in the settlement is valid, and requires personal residence: *Walcot v Botfield* supra; *Wynne v Fletcher* (1857) 24 Beav 430; *Dunne v Dunne* (1885) 7 De GM & G 207; *Re Wright, Mott v Issott* [1907] 1 Ch 231; *Re Vivian v Swansea* (1920) 36 TLR 222 (affd 36 TLR 657, CA); but cf *Re Moir, Warner v Moir* (1884) 25 ChD 605. If no period is fixed, the condition may be void for uncertainty: see para 742 post. Absence on official duty is not a breach of such a condition: *Re Adair and Settled Land Act* [1909] 1 IR 311. The condition as to residence is now less important, in as much as it may be defeated by the exercise of the powers of sale and leasing conferred by the Settled Land Act 1925 ss 38–43 (as amended): see para 827 et seq post. However, the condition is effectual so far as it does not hinder the tenant for life from disposing of the property: *Re Haynes, Kemp v Haynes* (1887) 37 ChD 306; *Re Trenchard, Trenchard v Trenchard* [1902] 1 Ch 378; *Re Adair and Settled Land Act* supra; *Re Acklom, Oakeshott v Hawkins* [1929] 1 Ch 195; *Re Orlebar, Orlebar v Orlebar* [1936] Ch 147.

742. Requirement of certainty. In order to be valid, conditions of defeasance[1] must be so framed that the persons affected, or the court, if they seek its guidance, can from the outset know with certainty the exact event on the happening of which their interests are to be divested[2]. If the court cannot say with reasonable certainty, from the moment of the creation of the estate, in what event the defeasance will occur, the condition will be void[3], but if the condition is clearly expressed, it is not necessary that the words of the condition should be of such a character that the question whether forfeiture has or has not occurred can be ascertained, not only with certainty, but with perfect ease[4].

1   As to conditions of defeasance generally see para 740 ante.

2   *Fillingham v Bromley* (1823) Turn & R 530; *Clavering v Ellison* (1859) 7 HL Cas 707 at 725; *Clayton v Ramsden* [1943] AC 320, [1943] 1 All ER 16, HL. See also *Re Viscount Exmouth, Viscount Exmouth v Praed* (1883) 23 ChD 158 at 164; *Re Sandbrook, Noel v Sandbrook* [1912] 2 Ch 471 at 477; *Re Hanlon, Heads v Hanlon* [1933] Ch 254; *Sifton v Sifton* [1938] AC 656, [1938] 3 All ER 435, PC. However, if the condition is clearly expressed, it is not necessary that the donee be in a position at all times to know whether he is committing a breach of it: *Re Lanyon, Lanyon v Lanyon* [1927] 2 Ch 264. For discussion of the rule see *Sifton v Sifton* supra; *Bromley v Tryon* [1952] AC 265, [1951] 2 All ER 1058, HL. Although a gift over will normally only take effect if the event expressly mentioned occurs, it will also take effect by implication if it must, a fortiori, have been intended to operate in some other event: *Jones v Westcomb* (1711) Prec Ch 316; *Re Fox's Estate, Dawes v Druitt* [1937] 4 All ER 664, CA; *Re Bowen, Treasury Solicitor v Bowen* [1949] Ch 67, [1948] 2 All ER 979. As to certainty in connection with trusts and powers see *Whishaw v Stephens* [1970] AC 508, [1968] 3 All ER 785, HL; *McPhail v Doulton* [1971] AC 424, [1970] 2 All ER 228, HL; *Re Baden's Deed Trusts (No 2)* [1973] Ch 9, [1972] 2 All ER 1304, CA; and TRUSTS vol 48 (Reissue) para 554.

3   As to the distinction between conditions subsequent and conditions precedent (which are valid unless their terms are such that it is impossible to give them any meaning at all) see *Re Allen, Faith v Allen* [1953] Ch 810, [1953] 2 All ER 898, CA; *Re Wolffe's Will Trusts, Shapley v Wolffe* [1953] 2 All ER 697, [1953] 1 WLR 1211; *Re Selby's Will Trusts, Donn v Selby* [1965] 3 All ER 386, [1966] 1 WLR 43; *Re Barlow's Will Trusts* [1979] 1 All ER 296, [1979] 1 WLR 278. See, however, *Re Perry Almshouses* [1898] 1 Ch 391 (affd [1899] 1 Ch 21, CA); *Re Tampolsk, Barclays Bank Ltd v Hyer* [1958] 3 All ER 479, [1958] 1 WLR 1157. As to the distinction between conditions subsequent and determinable limitations see *Re Viscount Exmouth, Viscount Exmouth v Praed* (1883) 23 ChD 158; *Re Wilkinson, Page v Public Trustee* [1926] Ch 842. A condition relating to religion is not void as being contrary to public policy on the ground of impermissible discrimination or on the ground that it might influence parents as to how to bring up their child: *Blathwayt v Baron Cawley* [1976] AC 397, [1975] 3 All ER 625, HL.

4   *Re Lanyon, Lanyon v Lanyon* [1927] 2 Ch 264; *Sifton v Sifton* [1938] AC 656 at 671, [1938] 3 All ER 435 at 442, HL; *Re Gape, Verey v Gape* [1952] Ch 743, [1952] 2 All ER 579, CA. Even if the condition is valid, the court will construe it strictly, and lean against defeasance: see *Clavering v Ellison* (1859) 7 HL Cas 707; *Walmesley v Gerard* (1861) 29 Beav 321; *Re Hinckes, Dashwood v Hinckes* [1921] 1 Ch 475, CA.

   The following cases are examples of conditions held to be void for uncertainty:

   (1)   conditions relating to religion: see *Re Blaiberg, Blaiberg and Public Trustee v De Andia Yrarrzaval and Blaiberg* [1940] Ch 385, [1940] 1 All ER 632; *Re Donn, Donn v Moses* [1944] Ch 8, [1943] 2 All ER 564, HL; *Re Moss's Trusts, Moss v Allen* [1945] 1 All ER 207; *Re Wolffe's Will Trusts, Shapley v Wolffe* [1953] 2 All ER 697, [1953] 1 WLR 1211 (marriage to a person of the Jewish faith and the child of Jewish parents); *Re Tampolsk, Barclays Bank Ltd v Hyer* [1958] 3 All ER 479, [1958] 1 WLR 1157 (of the Jewish race and religion); *Clayton v Ramsden* [1943] AC 320, [1943] 1 All ER 16, HL (of Jewish faith and parentage); *Re Krawitz's Will Trusts, Krawitz v Crawford* [1959] 3 All ER 793, [1959] 1 WLR 1192 (practise the Jewish religion); *Re Tegg, Public Trustee v Bryant* [1936] 2 All ER 878 (conform to and be members of the Church of England). See, however, the cases relating to religion cited infra;

   (2)   conditions relating to residence: *Fillingham v Bromley* (1823) Turn & R 530 (live and reside); *Re M'Cleary, Moffat v M'Cleary* [1923] 1 IR 16 (come to live); *Sifton v Sifton* [1938] AC 656, [1938] 3 All ER 435, PC (continue to reside in Canada). Such conditions are valid, however, where the requirement of residence relates to a house comprised in a settlement: see para 741 note 4 ante; and

   (3)   other conditions: see *Clavering v Ellison* (1859) 7 HL Cas 707 (being educated abroad); *Duddy v Gresham* (1878) 2 LR Ir 442, Ir CA (retire to a convent etc); *Jeffreys v Jeffreys* (1901) 84 LT 417 (not to associate, correspond with or visit certain persons); *Re Gassiot, Brougham v Rose-Gassiot* (1907) 51 Sol Jo 570 (as to taking name); *Re Sandbrook, Noel v Sandbrook* [1912] 2 Ch 471 (child to be under control of father); *Re Reich, Public Trustee v Guthrie* (1924) 40 TLR 398 (to adopt and carry on a profession); *Re Murray, Martins Bank Ltd v Dill* [1955] Ch 69, [1954] 3 All ER 129, CA (to assume surname). Cf *Re Neeld, Carpenter v Inigo-Jones* [1962] Ch 643, [1962] 2 All ER 335, CA.

   As to examples of conditions, some being conditions precedent, held to be not uncertain, but such as the court enforces see *Tattersall v Howell* (1816) 2 Mer 26 (donee to give up low company etc); *Maud v Maud* (1860) 27 Beav 615 ('should she follow the paths of virtue' etc); *Evanturel v Evanturel* (1874) LR 6 PC 1 (not to dispute will); *Re Moore's Trusts, Lewis v Moore* (1906) 96 LT 44 (donee to marry person of ample fortune to maintain her in comfort and affluence); *Patton v Toronto General Trusts Corpn* [1930] AC 629, PC (to be of the Lutheran religion); *Re Hanlon, Heads v Hanlon* [1933] Ch 254 (not to marry or live or misconduct himself with a named person); *Re Talbot-Ponsonby's Estate, Talbot-Ponsonby v Talbot-Ponsonby* [1937] 4 All ER 309 (to make an estate the devisee's home and not to let a named person set foot on the property); *Re Evans, Hewitt v Edwards* [1940] Ch 629 (become a convert to the Roman Catholic religion); *Bromley v Tryon* [1952] AC 265, [1951] 2 All ER 1058, HL (to succeed to the bulk of the estate); *Re Gape, Verey v Gape* [1952] Ch 743, [1952] 2 All ER 579, CA (permanent residence); *Re Allen, Faith v Allen* [1953] Ch 810, [1953] 2 All ER 898, CA (member of the Church of England and adherent of its doctrine); *Re Neeld, Carpenter v Inigo-Jones* supra (to use surname on all occasions and bear arms); *Re Selby's Will Trusts, Donn v Selby* [1965] 3 All ER 386, [1966] 1 WLR 43 (marrying out of the Jewish faith); *Blathwayt v Baron Cawley* [1976] AC 397, [1975] 3 All ER 625, HL; *Re Tuck's Settlement Trusts, Public Trustee v Tuck* [1978] Ch 49, [1978] 1 All ER 1047, CA (condition referring to the Jewish faith and of Jewish blood). A gift to trustees upon trust for a person if he behaves well, and to their satisfaction, may sometimes be construed as giving them only a discretion to deprive him of the gift as a condition subsequent: see *Kingsman v Kingsman* (1706) 2 Vern 559; *Re Coe's Trust* (1858) 4 K & J 199; *Re Drax, Baroness Dunsany v Sawbridge* (1906) 75 LJ Ch 317.

743. Conditions of defeasance on succession to the principal family estate.
Conditions providing for defeasance in the event of succession to the principal family estate used to be commonly found in settlements of realty. There are five points which deserve special attention[1]

(1)   The event in which the defeasance is to occur must be accurately described[2]. The condition, like all conditions of defeasance[3], is strictly construed[4], so that a direction that it is to take effect on a person's accession to the principal family estate is not satisfied by his succeeding to a part of it, however large[5]; or by his succeeding to the whole, if it is charged with an incumbrance to which it was not, in fact or in contingency, liable when the settlement was framed[6]; or by accession to the principal family estate under a subsequent and independent instrument or by act of law[7].

(2)   The clause should describe accurately what estates or interests the younger brother solely, or both the younger brother and his issue male, are to take in the principal family estate, so as to give the clause the effect of making the second estate shift from them[8].

(3)   Equal attention must be observed in describing the person to whom the settlor wishes the second estate to devolve when the party accedes to the principal family estate[9].

(4)   It is also necessary to provide for the case where the next taker is not in existence at the time of defeasance, but may afterwards come into being, and to direct the destination of the intermediate rents and profits[10].

(5)   In many cases it is necessary to provide for the return of the principal family estate to the person from whom it has been divested by the condition of defeasance, in order to prevent it from devolving upon collateral relations of the settlor under the ultimate limitations in the settlement while there should still be issue of his own body[11].

1   See Co Litt 327a, Butler's note. As to conditions of defeasance generally see para 740 ante.
2   If the estate is stated to be divested because other provision has been made for the person from whom it is taken, the gift over fails if the provision turns out not to have been made: *Carter v Earl of Ducie* (1871) 41 LJ Ch 153. As to when a gift over will take effect by implication see para 742 note 2 ante.
3   See paras 740–742 ante.
4   *Walmesley v Gerard* (1861) 29 Beav 321; *Re Hinckes, Dashwood v Hinckes* [1921] 1 Ch 475, CA. Cf *Bromley v Tryon* [1952] AC 265, [1951] 2 All ER 1058, HL. In construing such conditions, the words 'eldest' or 'younger' son are always read and construed in their primary significance (see *Scarisbrick v Eccleston* (1838) 5 Cl & Fin 398, HL; *Wilbraham v Scarisbrick* (1847) 1 HL Cas 167; cf *Meredith v Treffry* (1879) 12 ChD 170; and para 728 ante), unless it is impossible to interpret the shifting clause according to the literal meaning of the words (*Bathurst v Errington* (1877) 2 App Cas 698, HL).
5   *Meyrick v Laws, Meyrick v Mathias* (1874) 9 Ch App 237; *Gardiner v Jellicoe* (1862) 12 CBNS 568 (affd (1865) 11 HL Cas 323); *Re Hinckes, Dashwood v Hinckes* [1921] 1 Ch 475, CA. Cf *Bromley v Tryon* [1952] AC 265, [1952] 2 All ER 1058, HL. See also *Stackpoole v Stackpoole* (1843) 2 Con & Law 489; *Micklethwait v Micklethwait* (1859) 4 CBNS 790.

6   See *Fazakerley v Ford* (1831) 4 Sim 390; *Harrison v Round* (1852) 2 De GM & G 190; *Meyrick v Laws, Meyrick v Mathias* (1874) 9 Ch App 237.

7   *Taylor v Earl of Harewood* (1844) 3 Hare 372; *Meyrick v Laws, Meyrick v Mathias* (1874) 9 Ch App 237. Whether a resettlement confers an independent title depends upon whether the estate descends in the mode in which it was limited to descend under the principal settlement: *Harrison v Round* (1852) 2 De GM & G 190. Cf *Fazakerley v Ford* (1831) 4 Sim 390; *Monypenny v Dering* (1852) 2 De GM & G 145; *Re Meeking, Meeking v Meeking* [1922] 2 Ch 523.

8   *Bagot v Legge* (1864) 10 Jur NS 994. 'Entitled' in such a clause means beneficially entitled in possession: see *Chorley v Loveband* (1863) 33 Beav 189; *Umbers v Jaggard* (1870) LR 9 Eq 200; and para 744 note 2 post. A person does not come into possession of a estate for the purposes of a shifting clause by becoming entitled to an estate in remainder either for life (see *Monypenny v Dering* (1852) 2 De GM & G 145; *Curzon v Curzon* (1859) 1 Giff 248), or in tail (*Bagot v Legge* (1864) 10 Jur NS 994), or by actual possession obtained as a purchaser for value, a mortgagee from the owner, a tenant from year to year, or a lessee for years rendering rent, a judgment creditor, or (formerly) tenant by elegit (*Taylor v Earl of Harewood* (1844) 3 Hare 372 at 386). See also *Leslie v Earl of Rothes* [1894] 2 Ch 499, CA; *Re Hinckes, Dashwood v Hinckes* [1921] 1 Ch 475, CA. A person may be entitled in possession notwithstanding that the whole income of the property is eaten up by charges and that there are no surplus rents and profits: *Re Varley, Thornton v Varley* (1893) 62 LJ Ch 652.

9   A direction that, on defeasance, the estate divested from a tenant for life should devolve upon the person next entitled in remainder, or should devolve as though the tenant for life were dead, may cause it to devolve upon the son of the tenant for life (*Bagot v Legge* (1864) 10 Jur NS 994) or, formerly, upon the trustees to preserve contingent remainders to unborn sons of the tenant for life whose estate had determined (see *Doe d Heneage v Heneage* (1790) 4 Term Rep 13; *Stanley v Stanley* (1809) 16 Ves 491; *Morrice v Langham* (1840) 11 Sim 260; *Lambarde v Peach* (1859) 4 Drew 553; *Turton v Lambarde, Lambarde v Turton* (1860) 1 De GF & J 495). A limitation that the estate should devolve as though the tenant for life had died without issue causes it to devolve upon the next vested remainderman: *Carr v Earl of Erroll* (1805) 6 East 59; *Doe d Lumley v Earl of Scarborough* (1835) 3 Ad & El 2 (revsd without affecting this point, sub nom *Earl of Scarborough v Doe d Savile* (1836) 3 Ad & El 897, Ex Ch); *Re Harcourt, Fitzwilliam v Portman* [1920] 1 Ch 492. See also *Morrice v Langham* (1841) 8 M & W 194; *Sanford v Morrice* (1844) 11 Cl & Fin 667, HL. For a case where 'die without issue' was held to mean die without issue of a particular class see *Jellicoe v Gardiner* (1865) 11 HL Cas 323; but see *Doe d Lumley v Earl of Scarborough* supra.

10   If an intention to dispose of the beneficial interest is either expressed in the instrument on which the question arises, or can be gathered from its provisions, the rents and profits cannot result to the settlor, and the next remainderman takes them (*Turton v Lambarde, Lambarde v Turton* (1860) 1 De GF & J 495; *D'Eyncourt v Gregory* (1864) 34 Beav 36; cf *Re Conyngham, Conyngham v Conyngham* [1921] 1 Ch 491, CA); but, if no such intention is expressed in or can be gathered from the instrument, the intermediate rents and profits revert to the settlor (*Stanley v Stanley* (1809) 16 Ves 491; *Lambarde v Peach* (1859) 4 Drew 553).

11   See *Trevor v Trevor* (1842) 13 Sim 108; on appeal (1847) 1 HL Cas 239.

744. Time when condition takes effect. A condition of defeasance[1] takes effect immediately on the happening of the specified event, and there is no difference for this purpose whether the clause is expressed to take effect 'then' or 'then and immediately thereupon'[2]. If it is to operate as often as the event referred to should recur, this should appear from its terms, but an intention may be gathered from the meaning of the clause as a whole in the absence of express words[3]. A condition will normally be treated as not requiring compliance by the beneficiary before he attains his majority[4].

1   As to conditions of defeasance generally see para 740 ante.

2   *Cope v Earl De La Warr* (1873) 8 Ch App 982. A life tenant of property specifically devised does not become entitled to the actual receipt of the rents and profits of the property until either a vesting assent has been executed or he is entitled to call for a vesting assent: *Re Neeld, Carpenter v Inigo-Jones* [1962] Ch 643, [1962] 2 All ER 335, CA. See also *Re Gape, Verey v Gape* [1952] Ch 743, [1952] 2 All ER 579, CA; *Blathwayt v Baron Cawley* [1976] AC 397, [1975] 3 All ER 625, HL; and para 743 note 8 ante.

3   *Doe d Lumley v Earl of Scarborough* (1835) 3 Ad & El 2 at 38. See, however, *Earl of Scarborough v Doe d Savile* (1836) 3 Ad & El 897 at 964, Ex Ch; *Monypenny v Dering* (1852) 2 De GM & G 145 at 188.

4   *Partridge v Partridge* [1894] 1 Ch 351; *Re May, Eggar v May* [1917] 2 Ch 126; *Patton v Toronto General Trusts Corpn* [1930] AC 629, PC; *Blathwayt v Baron Cawley* [1976] AC 397, [1975] 3 All ER 625, HL. See also para 745 note 8 post.

745. Name and arms clauses. A common use of a condition of defeasance formerly was to compel compliance with a name and arms clause by which a settlor imposed upon all persons succeeding to the estate under the settlement an obligation to take his name[1] and bear his arms[2]. Such a clause first indicates the persons on whom the obligation is imposed, that is, every person becoming entitled[3] under the settlement as tenant for life or tenant in tail male, or in tail, to the possession or receipt of the rents and profits of the settled property, and who must not then use or bear the specified surname and arms[4]. It then directs that any such person[5] within a specified period after becoming so entitled[6], unless he is a child, in which case the obligation is to be performed within the specified period after attaining his majority[7], is to apply for and endeavour to obtain a licence from the Crown[8] expressly authorising him to take and use[9] the specified surname[10] and the specified arms[11].

1   As to the changing of a name and the invalidity of a clause requiring a first name to be changed see para 748 post. As to conditions of defeasance generally see para 740 ante.

2   See eg *Re Neeld, Carpenter v Inigo-Jones* [1962] Ch 643, [1962] 2 All ER 335, CA.

3   As to the meaning of 'entitled' see paras 743 note 8, 744 note 2 ante.

4   A direction to use a particular surname on all occasions is not void for uncertainty: *Re Neeld, Carpenter v Inigo-Jones* [1962] Ch 643, [1962] 2 All ER 335, CA. See also *Re Howard's Will Trusts, Levin v Bradley* [1961] Ch 507, [1961] 2 All ER 413; *Blathwayt v Baron Cawley* [1976] AC 397, [1975] 3 All ER 625, HL. Cf *Re Murray, Martins Bank Ltd v Dill* [1955] Ch 69, [1954] 3 All ER 129, CA. As to entailed interests see para 715 et seq ante; and REAL PROPERTY vol 39(2) (Reissue) para 117 et seq.

5   If the person entitled is a woman, the obligation is sometimes imposed on her husband (*Re Williams* (1860) 6 Jur NS 1064), but an exception is sometimes made in favour of husbands who are peers or sons of peers (see *Egerton v Earl Brownlow* (1853) 4 HL Cas 1 at 7). A condition requiring a woman, whether married or not, to change her name, is not void as being contrary to public policy: *Re Neeld, Carpenter v Inigo-Jones* [1962] Ch 643, [1962] 2 All ER 335, CA.

6   If no period is specified it is a sufficient compliance with the clause if the change of name is effected within a reasonable time, considering the circumstances of the case (*Davies v Lowndes* (1835) 1 Bing NC 597 at 618), but in the absence of a time limit the clause may be void as transgressing the rule against perpetuities (see *Bennett v Bennett* (1864) 2 Drew & Sm 266; *Re Fry, Reynolds v Denne* [1945] Ch 348, [1945] 2 All ER 205). As to this rule see para 740 note 3 ante.

7   As to compliance with conditions by children see para 744 ante and note 8 infra.

8   If no method of assuming the name is specified, the voluntary assumption of it even by a child is sufficient (*Doe d Luscombe v Yates* (1822) 5 B & Ald 544; *Davies v Lowndes* (1835) 1 Bing NC 597; *Bevan v Mahon-Hagan* (1893) 31 LR Ir 342, CA; *Barlow v Bateman* (1730) 3 P Wms 64; on appeal (1735) 2 Bro Parl Cas 272, HL); but in *Re Talbot* [1932] IR 714, doubt was expressed whether it was possible for a child to accomplish the act of taking or assuming a surname by any voluntary act on his part. However, a beneficiary is not normally required to comply with a condition before he attains his majority: see para 744 ante. Where the condition was to 'take the name for themselves and their heirs', it was said that many acts are to be done to oblige the heirs to take it, such as a grant from the Sovereign or an Act of Parliament: *Gulliver d Corrie v Ashby* (1766) 4 Burr 1929 at 1940. As to the methods by which a new name can be assumed see para 748 post.

9   'Take and use' means 'take and thereafter use', so that discontinuance of the name involves forfeiture: *Re Drax, Baroness Dunsany v Sawbridge* (1906) 75 LJ Ch 317. See also *Blagrove v Bradshaw* (1858) 4 Drew 230. However, the mere inadvertent use of the former surname does not involve forfeiture: *Re Neeld, Carpenter v Inigo-Jones* [1962] Ch 643, [1962] 2 All ER 335, CA.

10   If the clause does not enjoin the assumption of the name as surname it is sufficient that the devisee has the name as a first name: *Bennett v Bennett* (1864) 2 Drew & Sm 266. If the devisee is required to assume the prescribed surname, the use of it before his own family name is not a compliance with the condition (*D'Eyncourt v Gregory* (1876) 1 ChD 441 at 445; *Re Llangattock, Shelley v Harding* (1917) 33 TLR 250; *Re Berens, Re Dowdeswell, Berens-Dowdeswell v Holland-Martin* [1926] Ch 596); but, if the prescribed surname is to be assumed 'along or together with' the devisee's family name, it may be used before the family name (*Re Eversley, Mildmay v Mildmay* [1900] 1 Ch 96).

11   As to the assumption of arms see para 749 post. A condition requiring a person to quarter the arms of another with his own requires him, if he has none, to obtain his own: *Re Neeld, Inigo-Jones v Inigo-Jones* [1969] 2 All ER 1025, [1969] 1 WLR 988.

746. Condition of defeasance for breach of name and arms clause. A name and arms clause is generally followed by a condition of defeasance[1] of the interest of any person who fails to comply with its provisions[2] in favour of the next remainderman[3]. In the case of a defaulting tenant for life, the estate may be made to devolve on the remainderman, who may be his child[4], but in the case of a defaulting tenant in tail the estate cannot be made to devolve upon the next remainderman in tail as though the person in default were dead, since to do so would be to allow an estate tail to be partially good and partially bad[5].

A forfeiture clause, with no gift over, is effective to determine an estate tail[6], but is repugnant to an absolute gift[7]. Accordingly the condition is defeated by the execution of a disentailing assurance[8].

1   Where the words are capable of construction either as a condition subsequent or a condition precedent, the former will be preferred: *Bennett v Bennett* (1864) 2 Drew & Sm 266 at 275; *Re Greenwood, Goodhart v Woodhead* [1903] 1 Ch 749 at 755, CA; *Re Talbot* [1932] IR 714. As to conditions of defeasance generally see para 740 ante. As to name and arms clauses see para 745 ante.
2   As to what amounts to a breach see para 747 post. If there is any discrepancy between the requirements of the name and arms clause and the defeasance clause the resulting confusion may cause both clauses to be void for uncertainty: *Re Murray, Martins Bank Ltd v Dill* [1955] Ch 69, [1954] 3 All ER 129, CA. Cf *Re Neeld, Carpenter v Inigo-Jones* [1962] Ch 643, [1962] 2 All ER 335, CA, where missing words were able to be supplied.
3   In the absence of a gift over, the condition may be void for perpetuity (see *Re Fry, Reynolds v Denne* [1945] Ch 348, [1945] 2 All ER 205; *Re Engels, National Provincial Bank Ltd v Mayer* [1943] 1 All ER 506; and para 740 note 3 ante), and failure to invest a gift over may cause the name and arms clause to be construed as precatory only (*Gulliver d Corrie v Ashby* (1766) 4 Burr 1929 at 1940; *Vandeleur v Sloane* [1919] 1 IR 116; *Re Evans's Contract* [1920] 2 Ch 469; *Re Talbot* [1932] IR 714).
4   *Doe d Lumley v Earl of Scarborough* (1835) 3 Ad & El 2 at 39.
5   *Corbet's Case* (1600) 1 Co Rep 83b at 85b; *Mildmay's Case* (1605) 6 Co Rep 40a; *Seymour v Vernon* (1864) 10 Jur NS 487. As to entailed interests see para 715 et seq ante; and REAL PROPERTY vol 39(2) (Reissue) para 117 et seq.
6   *Astley v Earl of Essex* (1874) LR 18 Eq 290.
7   *Re Catt's Trusts* (1864) 2 Hem & M 46; *Musgrave v Brooke* (1884) 26 ChD 792; *Re Fry, Reynolds v Denne* [1945] Ch 348, [1945] 2 All ER 205. The absence of a gift over may cause the condition to be void for perpetuity, there being no vested remaindermen in such a case: *Re Fry, Reynolds v Denne* supra. Cf *Re Hanlon, Heads v Hanlon* [1933] Ch 254.
8   *Doe d Lumley v Earl of Scarborough* (1835) 3 Ad & El 2 (revsd sub nom *Earl of Scarborough v Doe d Savile* (1836) 3 Ad & El 897, Ex Ch); *Milbank v Vane* [1893] 3 Ch 79, CA; *Re Hind, Bernstone v Montgomery* [1933] Ch 208. See also *Blathwayt v Baron Cawley* [1976] AC 397, [1975] 3 All ER 625, HL. As to the effect of a name and arms clause in referential trusts in tail of personalty see *Re Cornwallis, Cornwallis v Wykeham-Martin* (1886) 32 ChD 388. As to referential trusts see para 721 ante. As to disentailing deeds see REAL PROPERTY vol 39(2) (Reissue) para 121 et seq.

747. What amounts to a breach. Ignorance of a condition of defeasance is no excuse for failure to comply with it[1]. What will amount to a breach of a condition will depend on the wording of the condition in the particular case. If a condition is expressed to take effect if the donee 'omits' or 'fails' to take the name and arms, this will cover every case of non-compliance[2]. However, the word 'refuse' implies a conscious act of volition, so that a person who was ignorant of the condition or was under a disability cannot be said to have refused to comply with it[3], but if a person knows of the existence of the condition, a refusal need not be express[4]. 'Neglect', when used alone, prima facie covers only omissions that are negligent[5], but when used in certain contexts it may mean no more than 'fail'[6]. The expression 'neglect or refuse' also implies a conscious act of volition[7].

1   *Lady Anne Fry's Case* (1674) 1 Vent 199; *Re Hodges' Legacy* (1873) LR 16 Eq 92; *Astley v Earl of Essex* (1874) LR 18 Eq 290. The case would be different if the party could make a good title apart from the instrument containing the condition and he was ignorant of the condition: *Doe d Kenrick v Lord Beauclerk*

(1809) 11 East 657. As to conditions of defeasance generally see para 740 ante.

2   *Astley v Earl of Essex* (1874) LR 18 Eq 290; *Partridge v Partridge* [1894] 1 Ch 351; *Re Quintin Dick, Lord Cloncurry v Fenton* [1926] Ch 992. However, the mere inadvertent use of the former surname does not involve forfeiture: *Re Neeld, Carpenter Inigo-Jones* [1962] Ch 643, [1962] 2 All ER 335, CA. As to name and arms clauses see paras 745–746 ante.

3   *Doe d Kenrick v Lord Beauclerk* (1809) 11 East 657 at 667; *Re Quintin Dick, Lord Cloncurry v Fenton* [1926] Ch 992.

4   *Doe d Duke of Norfolk v Hawke* (1802) 2 East 481 at 487.

5   *Re Conington's Will* (1860) 6 Jur NS 992; *Re Quintin Dick, Lord Cloncurry v Fenton* [1926] Ch 992.

6   *Hawkes v Baldwin* (1838) 9 Sim 355; *Re Hodges' Legacy* (1873) LR 16 Eq 92; *O'Higgins v Walsh* [1918] 1 IR 126; *Re Quintin Dick, Lord Cloncurry v Fenton* [1926] Ch 992.

7   *Partridge v Partridge* [1894] 1 Ch 351; *Re Edwards, Lloyd v Boyes* [1910] 1 Ch 541 at 550; *Re Quintin Dick, Lord Cloncurry v Fenton* [1926] Ch 992.

748. Change of name. A surname may be changed by mere user, without formality, or by deed poll, but a first name may be changed only by private Act[1] or at confirmation[2]. Recourse to Parliament for authority to adopt a new name is unusual, but it may be necessary to obtain a private Act, as for instance where the clause requires the adoption of that course, or requires a change of the first name[3]. Such an Act is not imperative in its terms, but merely permits the assumption of the new name[4].

1   See eg the Baines Name Act 1907, a private Act under which the name of Henry Rodd was assumed in place of the original name Raymond Hill.

2   *Re Parrott, Cox v Parrott* [1946] Ch 183, [1946] 1 All ER 321. See also ECCLESIASTICAL LAW; PERSONAL PROPERTY vol 35 (Reissue) para 1273. A clause requiring the beneficiary to change his first name by deed poll is impossible to fulfil and so void: *Re Parrott, Cox v Parrott* supra. As to change of name see PERSONAL PROPERTY vol 35 (Reissue) para 1272 et seq.

3   As to the procedure on personal bills see PARLIAMENT vol 34 (Reissue) para 850 et seq. As to the voluntary assumption of a name where no method is specified see para 745 note 8 ante.

4   See PERSONAL PROPERTY vol 35 (Reissue) para 1277. As to changing the surname of a child when a residence order is in force see the Children Act 1989 s 13(1)(a); and CHILDREN AND YOUNG PERSONS vol 5(2) (Reissue) para 775.

749. Assumption of arms. An obligation to assume arms is not satisfied by mere user unless the person assuming them is entitled by descent to bear them[1]. Arms can lawfully be assumed[2] only by applying for a royal licence[3].

1   *Re Berens, Re Dowdeswell, Berens-Dowdeswell v Holland-Martin* [1926] Ch 596, 605. See also *Austen v Collins* (1886) 54 LT 903; *Bevan v Mahon-Hagan* (1891) 27 LR Ir 399 (on appeal (1893) 31 LR Ir 342 at 366, Ir CA); *Re Croxon, Croxon v Ferrers* [1904] 1 Ch 252. The right to bear arms is a dignity conferred by the Crown, and not an incorporeal hereditament. It is not cognisable by the common law; jurisdiction in these matters is in the High Court of Chivalry of the Earl Marshal of England, which although still extant, will intervene only in cases of substance: *Manchester Corpn v Manchester Palace of Varieties Ltd* [1955] P 133, [1955] 1 All ER 387. See further PEERAGES AND DIGNITIES vol 35 (Reissue) paras 974–976.

2   A clause which requires the assumption of arms which the College of Arms will not grant, as being the arms of some other family, is void for impossibility: *Re Croxon, Croxon v Ferrers* [1904] 1 Ch 252; *Re Berens, Re Dowdeswell, Berens-Dowdeswell v Holland-Martin* [1926] Ch 596. See also *Austen v Collins* (1886) 54 LT 903. As to the College of Arms see PEERAGES AND DIGNITIES vol 35 (Reissue) para 913.

3   As to applications for a royal licence see PEERAGES AND DIGNITIES vol 35 (Reissue) para 974.

(5) SETTLED LAND ACT TRUSTEES

750. Trustees for the purposes of the Settled Land Act 1925. The following persons are trustees of a settlement[1] for the purposes of the Settled Land Act 1925[2]:

   (1)   the persons, if any, who are for the time being under the settlement[3] trustees with power of sale of the settled land[4] (subject or not to the consent of any person), or

with power of consent to or approval of the exercise of such a power of sale, or, if there are no such persons[5]; then

(2) the persons, if any, for the time being, who are by the settlement declared to be trustees of it for the purposes of the Settled Land Acts 1882 to 1890[6], or any of them, or the Settled Land Act 1925, or, if there are no such persons[7]; then

(3) the persons, if any, who are for the time being under the settlement trustees with a power or duty to sell any other land comprised[8] in the settlement and subject to the same limitations as the land to be sold or otherwise dealt with, or with power of consent to or approval of the exercise of such a power of sale, or, if there are no such persons[9]; then

(4) the persons, if any, who are for the time being under the settlement trustees with a future power or duty to sell the settled land[10], or with power of consent to or approval of the exercise of such a future power of sale, and whether the power or duty takes effect in all events or not, or, if there are no such persons[11]; then

(5) the persons, if any, appointed by deed to be trustees of the settlement by all the persons who at the date of the deed were together able, by virtue of their beneficial interests or by the exercise of an equitable power, to dispose of the settled land in equity for the whole estate the subject of the settlement[12].

If, on 1 January 1926, any persons who had been appointed under the Settled Land Act 1882[13] had power to act generally or for any specific purpose on behalf of a child[14], those persons became trustees of the settlement[15].

1   'Trustees of the settlement' means the trustees of the settlement for the purposes of the Settled Land Act 1925, however appointed or constituted: ss 30(1), 117(1)(xxiv).

2   See the Settled Land Act 1925 s 30(1).

3   For the meaning of 'settlement' see para 678 note 1 ante.

4   For the meaning of 'settled land' see para 680 text to note 2 ante. The power of sale must be general and not limited; that is it must be a power exercisable at any time and for any purpose: *Re Coull's Settled Estates* [1905] 1 Ch 712. See also *Re Morgan* (1883) 24 ChD 114. Where a power of sale given to trustees was exercisable only during the lifetime of the tenant for life, on her death they ceased to be trustees for the purposes of the former Acts: *Re Collis's Estate* [1911] 1 IR 267. If realty is settled by reference to the trusts of personalty (see para 907 et seq post), a power to vary investments makes the trustees of the personalty trustees with a power of sale of the settled realty (*Re Garnett Orme and Hargreaves' Contract* (1883) 25 ChD 595), and a power to vary or transfer securities has been held to imply a power to sell ground rents which were an investment authorised by the settlement (*Re Tapp and London and India Docks Co's Contract* (1905) 74 LJ Ch 523). Trustees of a term with power to raise money by mortgage or any other means do not have a power of sale of the settled land: *Re Carne's Settled Estates* [1899] 1 Ch 324. The Settled Land Act 1925 s 30(1)(i), (iii), (iv) (s 30(1)(iii), (iv) as amended) takes effect as if the powers referred to there had not by that Act been made exercisable by the tenant for life or statutory owner: s 30(2). For the meaning of 'tenant for life' see para 671 note 5 ante. See also para 761 et seq post. As to the statutory owner see para 766 post. By virtue of s 108, the trustees are not entitled to exercise the power of sale (see para 827 post) unless they are statutory owners and entitled to sell in that capacity (see para 766 post), but the effect of conferring the power of sale is to make the persons on whom it is conferred trustees.

5   Ibid s 30(1)(i).

6   As to these Acts see para 678 note 1 ante.

7   Settled Land Act 1925 s 30(1)(ii).

8   For the meaning of 'land' see para 680 note 1 ante. 'Comprised in' means 'at any time comprised in', and includes land not originally subject to the trusts of the settlement, but subsequently purchased by the trustees out of personalty: see *Re Moore, Moore v Bigg* [1906] 1 Ch 789.

9   Settled Land Act 1925 s 30(1)(iii) (amended by the Trusts of Land and Appointment of Trustees Act 1996 s 25(1), Sch 3 para 2).

10   It is immaterial that the power or trust is to take effect only after the death of one of the trustees (*Re Jackson's Settled Estate* [1902] 1 Ch 258), or that one or both of the trustees are themselves tenants for life (*Re Jackson's Settled Estate* supra; *Re Davies and Kent's Contract* [1910] 2 Ch 35, CA).

11   Settled Land Act 1925 s 30(1)(iv) (amended by the Trusts of Land and Appointment of Trustees Act 1996 Sch 3 para 2).

12 Settled Land Act 1925 s 30(1)(v).
13 See the Settled Land Act 1882 s 60 (repealed), now replaced by the Settled Land Act 1925 s 26 (see CHILDREN AND YOUNG PERSONS vol 5(2) (Reissue) para 633).
14 See para 665 note 13 ante.
15 Settled Land Act 1925 s 37, Sch 2 para 3(3).

751. Personal representatives as trustees. If a settlement[1] has been created by will[2], or a settlement has arisen by the effect of an intestacy, and apart from this provision there would be no trustees of that settlement for the purposes of the Settled Land Act 1925, then, until other trustees are appointed, the personal representatives[3] of the deceased are by virtue of that Act the trustees of the settlement, but if there is a sole personal representative, not being a trust corporation[4], it is obligatory on him to appoint an additional trustee to act with him for the purposes of the Settled Land Act 1925, and the provisions of the Trustee Act 1925[5] relating to the appointment of new trustees and the vesting of trust property apply accordingly[6].

1 For the meaning of 'settlement' see para 678 note 1 ante.
2 For the meaning of 'will' see para 695 note 3 ante.
3 For the meaning of 'personal representative' see para 697 note 6 ante.
4 For the meaning of 'trust corporation' see para 705 note 6 ante.
5 See generally TRUSTS.
6 Settled Land Act 1925 s 30(3). This provision applies even if the estate is fully administered (per Russell J in chambers (1926) 62 L Jo 436), but the words 'and the provisions accordingly' apply only to the case of a sole personal representative, and if two or more personal representatives wish to retire and appoint new trustees in their place they must do so under the powers conferred by the Trustee Act 1925 s 64(1) (see para 756 post; and TRUSTS vol 48 (Reissue) para 724 et seq): *Re Dark, Glover v Dark* [1954] Ch 291, [1954] 1 All ER 681. Where a testator devised land to trustees of a settlement to be held on the trusts of that settlement and at his death there were no trustees of a settlement, the testator's personal representatives were trustees of the settlement created by his will: *Re Shelton's Settled Estates* [1928] WN 27. As to the powers of personal representatives of a sole or last surviving trustee see para 753 post.

752. Continuance of trustees in office. If any persons have been appointed or constituted trustees of a settlement[1], whether by court order[2] or otherwise, or have by reason of a power or duty to sell, or by reason of a power of consent to or approval of the exercise of a power of sale, or by virtue of the Settled Land Act 1925 or otherwise at any time become trustees of a settlement for the purposes of the Settled Land Acts 1882 to 1890[3], or the Settled Land Act 1925, then those persons or their successors in office[4] remain and are trustees of the settlement as long as that settlement is subsisting or deemed to be subsisting for the purposes of the Settled Land Act 1925[5].

1 For the meaning of 'trustees of the settlement' see para 750 note 1 ante.
2 See para 792 post.
3 As to these Acts see para 678 note 1 ante.
4 'Successors in office' means the persons who, by appointment or otherwise, have become trustees for such purposes: Settled Land Act 1925 s 33(1). As to the powers of the personal representatives of a last surviving or continuing trustee see para 753 post.
5 Ibid s 33(1) (amended by the Trusts of Land and Appointment of Trustees Act 1996 s 25(1), Sch 3 para 2). As to the duration of settlements see para 708 ante. Trustees for the purposes of the Settled Land Act 1925 are trustees of the settlement, not of the land subject to it, so that trustees appointed by the court in Ireland of a settlement which then comprised only land in Ireland did not cease to be trustees of the settlement by reason of the sale of all the land in Ireland: *Re Earl of Arran and Knowlesden and Creer's Contract* [1912] 2 Ch 141. As to a case where, before 1 January 1926, a settlement had ceased to subsist but was again brought into existence by the Settled Land Act 1925 on that date see para 754 note 4 post. As to the position when no relevant property remains subject to a settlement see para 676 ante.

753. Powers of surviving or continuing trustees. The provisions of the Settled Land Act 1925 referring to the trustees of a settlement[1] apply to the surviving or continuing trustees or trustee of the settlement[2] for the time being[3], except that capital money arising under the Settled Land Act 1925[4] must not be paid to a sole trustee unless the trustee is a trust corporation[5]. Subject to that exception, until the appointment of new trustees, the personal representatives or representative for the time being of a sole trustee, or, where there were two or more trustees, of the last surviving or continuing trustee, are or is capable of exercising or performing any power or trust which was given to, or capable of being exercised by, the sole or last surviving or continuing trustee, or the other trustees or trustee for the time being of the trust[6].

1 See the Settled Land Act 1925 s 94(2). For the meaning of 'trustees of the settlement' see para 750 note 1 ante.
2 For the meaning of 'settlement' see para 678 note 1 ante.
3 Settled Land Act 1925 s 94(2).
4 For the meaning of 'capital money arising under the Act' see para 795 post.
5 See the Settled Land Act 1925 s 94(1); and para 786 post. For the meaning of 'trust corporation' see para 705 note 6 ante.
6 See the Trustee Act 1925 s 18(2); and TRUSTS vol 48 (Reissue) para 707. As to the power of the personal representatives of a last surviving or continuing trustee to give receipts see para 785 post.

754. Trustees of compound settlements. Persons who are for the time being trustees for the purposes of the Settled Land Act 1925[1] of an instrument[2] which is a settlement[3], or is deemed to be a subsisting settlement for those purposes[4], are the trustees for the purposes of that Act of any settlement constituted by that instrument and any instruments subsequent in date or operation[5]. Further, if there are trustees for the purposes of that Act of the instrument under which there is a tenant for life[6] or statutory owner[7] but there are no trustees for those purposes of a prior instrument, being one of the instruments by which a compound settlement[8] is constituted, those trustees, unless and until trustees are appointed[9] of the prior instrument or of the compound settlement, are the trustees for those purposes of that Act of the compound settlement[10].

These provisions apply whenever any of the instruments came into operation, but have effect without prejudice to any appointment made by the court before 1926 of trustees of a settlement constituted by more than one instrument, and to the power of the court in any case after 1925 to make any such appointment, and if any such appointment has been or is made, these provisions do not apply or will cease to apply to the settlement consisting of the instruments to which the appointment relates[11].

1 See paras 750–752 ante.
2 For the meaning of 'instrument' see para 688 note 7 ante.
3 For the meaning of 'settlement' see para 678 note 1 ante.
4 See para 679 ante. As to the duration of settlements see para 708 ante. Where, before 1 January 1926, a compound settlement had ceased to subsist but was again brought into existence by the Settled Land Act 1925 on that date, the trustees of the compound settlement who had been appointed before it ceased to subsist were held to be the trustees of that settlement for the purposes of that Act: *Re Lord Alington and London County Council's Contract* [1927] 2 Ch 253.
5 Settled Land Act 1925 s 31(1); *Re Cayley and Evans' Contract* [1930] 2 Ch 143.
6 For the meaning of 'tenant for life' see para 671 note 5 ante. See also para 761 et seq post.
7 As to statutory owners see para 766 post.
8 As to compound settlements see para 681 et seq ante.
9 Such an appointment can be made either by the court or out of court under the statutory or an express power: see para 756 et seq post.
10 Settled Land Act 1925 s 31(1) (amended by the Law of Property (Amendment) Act 1926 s 7, Schedule).
11 Settled Land Act 1925 s 31(2). As to the appointment of trustees by the court see paras 756–757 post.

755. Trustees of settlements by reference. If a settlement[1], whenever made[2], takes effect by reference to another settlement[3], the trustees for the time being of the settlement to which reference is made are the trustees of the settlement[4] by reference, unless the settlement by reference contains an appointment of trustees of the settlement for the purposes of the Settled Land Acts 1882 to 1890[5], or any of them, or the Settled Land Act 1925[6]. However, this provision has effect without prejudice to any appointment made by the court before 1926 of trustees of a settlement by reference, or of the compound settlement consisting of a settlement and any other settlement or settlements made by reference to them[7], and to the power of the court, in any case after 1925, to make any such appointment, and, if any such appointment has been or is made, this provision does not apply or will cease to apply[8].

1   For the meaning of 'settlement' see para 678 note 1 ante.
2   See the Settled Land Act 1925 s 32(2).
3   'A settlement by reference to another settlement' means a settlement of property upon the limitations and subject to the powers and provisions of an existing settlement, with or without variation: ibid s 32(3).
4   For the meaning of 'trustees of the settlement' see para 750 note 1 ante.
5   As to these Acts see para 678 note 1 ante.
6   Settled Land Act 1925 s 32(1). As to the trustees of an aggregate estate see para 687 ante.
7   As to compound settlements see para 681 et seq ante. As to the difference between a compound settlement and a settlement by reference to the trusts of another settlement see para 681 note 3 ante.
8   Settled Land Act 1925 s 32(2).

756. Appointment of trustees. It is unusual to insert in a settlement express powers of appointing new trustees, and, as a rule, the only clause inserted in a settlement is the nomination of the persons or person, commonly the settlor or, in the case of a marriage settlement, the husband and wife and the survivor of them, who may exercise the statutory power of appointment[1].

There should be inserted in the trust instrument a declaration that the trustees of the settlement are trustees of the settlement for the purposes of the Settled Land Act 1925[2]. The statutory powers and provisions with reference to the appointment of new trustees for such purposes and the discharge and retirement of such trustees are applicable[3]. If at any time there are no trustees of a settlement[4], or if in any other case it is expedient for the purposes of the Settled Land Act 1925, that new trustees of a settlement should be appointed, the court[5] may[6], if it thinks fit, on the application of the tenant for life, statutory owner[7] or of any other person having under the settlement[8] an estate or interest in the settled land[9] in possession, remainder or otherwise, or, in the case of a child[10], of his testamentary or other guardian or next friend, appoint fit persons to be trustees of the settlement[11]. The persons so appointed, and the survivors and survivor of them, while continuing to be trustees or trustee, and, until the appointment of new trustees, the personal representatives or representative[12] for the time being of the last surviving or continuing trustee, become and are the trustees or trustee of the settlement[13].

If at any time trustees of a settlement have been appointed by the court for the purposes of the Settled Land Acts 1882 to 1890, or of the Settled Land Act 1925, then after 1925 the person or persons nominated for the purpose of appointing new trustees by the instrument, if any, creating the settlement, even though no trustees for the purposes of those Acts were thereby appointed, or, if there is no such person, or no such person able and willing to act, the surviving or continuing trustees or trustee for the time being for the purposes of those Acts, or the personal representatives of the last surviving or continuing trustee for those purposes, has or have the statutory powers to appoint new or additional trustees of the settlement for those purposes[14].

1   See the Trustee Act 1925 s 36 (as amended); and TRUSTS vol 48 (Reissue) para 724 et seq. As to marriage
     settlements see para 628 et seq ante.
2   As to trust instruments see para 694 ante. The vesting deed states the names of the trustees: see para 690
     ante. It is no longer possible to create settlements under the Settled Land Act 1925: see para 676 ante.
3   See the Trustee Act 1925 s 64(1); and TRUSTS vol 48 (Reissue) para 724 et seq. Two or more personal
     representatives who are trustees of the settlement by virtue of the Settled Land Act 1925 s 30(3) (see
     para 751 ante), can retire and appoint new trustees in their places: *Re Dark, Glover v Dark* [1954] Ch
     291, [1954] 1 All ER 681. In the case of settlements for the purposes of the Settled Land Act 1925, or
     of dispositions on trust for sale subsisting on 1 January 1926, no new trustees may be appointed if the
     effect of the appointment would be to cause the number of the trustees to exceed four: see the Trustee
     Act 1925 s 34(1); and para 900 post. Where such settlements or dispositions are made or come into
     operation after 1925, the number of the trustees must not exceed four: see s 34(2) (as amended); and
     TRUSTS vol 48 (Reissue) para 694 et seq.
4   For the meaning of 'trustees of the settlement' see para 750 note 1 ante.
5   As to the court see para 792 post.
6   The power is discretionary: see *Williams v Jenkins* [1894] WN 176. In *Burke v Gore* (1884) 13 LR Ir 367
     it was stated that the court should not only require to be satisfied of the fitness of the proposed trustees,
     but also that the purpose for which their appointment is applied for is such as to render their appointment
     safe and beneficial to all parties interested, but this has not been followed in practice, at any rate in
     England.
7   For the meaning of 'tenant for life' see para 671 note 5 ante. See also para 761 et seq post. As to statutory
     owners see para 766 post.
8   For the meaning of 'settlement' see para 678 note 1 ante.
9   For the meaning of 'settled land' see para 680 text to note 2 ante.
10   See para 665 note 13 ante.
11   Settled Land Act 1925 s 34(1). As to the procedure see para 792 post. The court has power under the
     Judicial Trustees Act 1896 s 1 (as amended) (see TRUSTS vol 48 (Reissue) para 646 et seq) to appoint a
     judicial trustee sole trustee for the purposes of the Settled Land Act 1925: *Re Marshall's Will Trusts* [1945]
     Ch 217, [1945] 1 All ER 550. An order appointing two persons trustees for the purposes of the Settled
     Land Acts 1882 to 1890 (see para 678 note 1 ante) of a settlement created by a will was held to have the
     effect of appointing the persons named separate trustees of three several settlements created by the will:
     Re Skerritt's Estate [1899] WN 240. However, if an instrument creates more than one settlement, persons
     appointed to be trustees of one of those settlements will not thereby become trustees of any of the other
     settlements: *Re Ogle's Settled Estates* [1927] 1 Ch 229. As to the persons whom the court will appoint see
     para 757 post.
12   For the meaning of 'personal representative' see para 697 note 6 ante.
13   Settled Land Act 1925 s 34(2). Until the appointment of new trustees the personal representatives of a
     sole or a last surviving or continuing trustee can exercise and perform all powers and trusts: see the Trustee
     Act 1925 s 18(2); and TRUSTS vol 48 (Reissue) para 707.
14   Ibid s 64(2).

757. Qualification of persons appointed by the court.

Since the appointment of trustees is required to impose a check upon the extensive powers given by the Settled Land Act 1925 to a tenant for life[1], the court has declined to appoint the tenant for life[2] or his solicitor[3], and has even refused to appoint two persons who were near relatives to one another[4]; but these cases are not now treated as laying down a general principle. There is no rule of practice that the subsisting trustees of a settlement ought to be appointed trustees for the purposes of the Settled Land Act 1925, and the tenant for life may propose other persons if he sees fit[5], but the existing trustees, if willing and fit to act, are, as a general rule, appointed[6]. In a proper case persons resident abroad have been appointed, but this will only be done in exceptional circumstances[7].

1   For the meaning of 'tenant for life' see para 671 note 5 ante. See also para 761 et seq post. As to the
     statutory powers see para 775 et seq post.
2   *Re Harrop's Trusts* (1883) 24 ChD 717. However, if a tenant for life has been appointed as a trustee the
     appointment is not invalid: *Re Davies and Kent's Contract* [1910] 2 Ch 35, CA.
3   *Re Kemp's Settled Estates* (1883) 24 ChD 485, CA; *Re Earl of Stamford, Payne v Stamford* [1896] 1 Ch 288;
     Re Spencer's Settled Estates [1903] 1 Ch 75. The appointment by the donee of a power of appointment of
     his own solicitor as a trustee is not, however, invalid: *Re Earl of Stamford, Payne v Stamford* supra; *Re Cotter,
     Jennings v Nye* [1915] 1 Ch 307.

4   *Re Knowles' Settled Estates* (1884) 27 ChD 707. Cf *Re Norris, Allen v Norris* (1884) 27 ChD 333. See also
     TRUSTS vol 48 (Reissue) paras 745–749.
5   *Re Nicholas* [1894] WN 165.
6   *Re Stoneley's Will* (1883) 27 Sol Jo 554.
7   *Re Simpson, Re Whitchurch* [1897] 1 Ch 256, CA. See also *Re Maberley's Settled Estate* (1887) 19 LR Ir
     341; *Re Whitehead's Will Trusts, Burke v Burke* [1971] 2 All ER 1334, [1971] 1 WLR 833.

758.   Trustees for management of child's estate. Trustees may be appointed for
the management of an estate during the minority of a beneficiary, or where a beneficiary
is contingently entitled to land[1].

1   As to the persons who are such trustees, and as to their powers see paras 665–666 ante. As to the age of
     majority see para 605 note 1 ante.

759.   Deed of declaration on appointment or discharge of trustees. Whenever
a new trustee for the purposes of the Settled Land Act 1925 is appointed of a trust
instrument[1], or a trustee of a trust instrument for those purposes is discharged from the
trust without a new trustee being appointed, a deed must be executed, supplemental to
the last or only principal vesting instrument[2], containing a declaration that the persons
named in it, being the persons who after such appointment or discharge, as the case may
be, are the trustees of the trust instrument for those purposes, are the trustees of the
settlement for those purposes[3]. A memorandum of the names and addresses of the persons
who are for the time being such trustees must be indorsed on or annexed to the last or
only principal vesting instrument by or on behalf of the trustees of the settlement, and
that vesting instrument must, for that purpose, be produced by the person having
possession of it to the trustees of the settlement when so required[4].

If the trustee is appointed or discharged by the court, the deed must be executed by
such person as the court may direct, and in any other case it must be executed by[5]: (1) the
person, if any, named in the principal vesting instrument as the person for the time being
entitled to appoint new trustees of the settlement, or, if no person is so named or the
person is dead or unable or unwilling to act, the persons who if the principal vesting
instrument had been the only instrument constituting the settlement would have had
power to appoint new trustees[6]; (2) the persons named in the deed of declaration as the
trustees of the settlement[7]; and (3) any trustee who is so discharged or retires[8].

A statement contained in any such deed of declaration to the effect that the person
named in the principal vesting instrument as the person for the time being entitled to
appoint new trustees of the settlement is unable or unwilling to act, or that a trustee has
remained outside the United Kingdom[9] for more than 12 months, or refuses or is unfit
to act, or is incapable of acting, is, in favour of a purchaser[10] of a legal estate[11], conclusive
evidence of the matter stated[12].

1   For the meaning of 'trust instrument' see para 688 note 7 ante.
2   For the meaning of 'principal vesting instrument' see para 698 note 1 ante.
3   Settled Land Act 1925 s 35(1). As to the trustees of the settlement see para 750 et seq ante.
4   Ibid s 35(1); Trustee Act 1925 s 35(2).
5   Settled Land Act 1925 s 35(2).
6   Ibid s 35(2)(i). For the meaning of 'settlement' see para 678 note 1 ante.
7   Ibid s 35(2)(ii).
8   Ibid s 35(2)(iii).
9   For the meaning of 'United Kingdom' see para 699 note 5 ante.
10   For the meaning of 'purchaser' see para 702 note 12 ante.
11   For the meaning of 'legal estate' see para 678 note 13 ante.
12   Settled Land Act 1925 s 35(3).

760. Nomination of trust corporation to receive notices. A settlement may nominate a trust corporation[1] to which notices of dealings affecting real or personal property[2] may be given, and in default of such nomination the trustees, if any, of the settlement, or the court[3], on the application of any person interested, may make the nomination[4].

1 For the meaning of 'trust corporation' see para 705 note 6 ante.
2 'Property' includes any thing in action, and any interest in real or personal property: Law of Property Act 1925 s 205(1)(xx).
3 As to applications to the court see para 905 post.
4 See the Law of Property Act 1925 s 138(1); and TRUSTS vol 48 (Reissue) para 693.

(6) THE ESTATE OWNER

(i) Tenant for Life or Statutory Owner

761. Nature of tenant for life. The person of full age[1] who is for the time being beneficially entitled under a settlement[2] to possession[3] of settled land[4] for his life is, for the purposes of the Settled Land Act 1925, the tenant for life[5] of that land and the tenant for life under that settlement[6]. There is only one tenant for life for the purposes of that Act, but that tenant for life may be constituted by two or more persons of full age so entitled as joint tenants[7]. If in any case there are two or more persons so entitled as joint tenants and they are not all of full age, such one or more of them as is or are for the time being of full age is or, if more than one, together constitute the tenant for life, but the beneficial interests of such of them as are not for the time being of full age are not affected[8]. However, a tenant for life under the Settled Land Act 1925 must be both beneficially entitled to possession and entitled for his life, so that such a tenant for life is not constituted by the several objects of a discretionary trust for distribution of the rents and profits during the life of one of them[9].

If there is a tenant for life within the above meaning, he is deemed to be such notwithstanding that, under the settlement or otherwise, the settled land, or his estate or interest in it, is incumbered or charged in any manner or to any extent, and notwithstanding any assignment by operation of law or otherwise of his estate or interest under the settlement, whether before or after it came into possession, other than an assurance which extinguishes that estate or interest[10].

1 The words 'of full age' mean not being a minor and so a corporation may be a tenant for life: *Re Earl of Carnarvon's Chesterfield Settled Estates, Re Earl of Carnarvon's Highclere Settled Estates* [1927] 1 Ch 138. As to the age of majority see para 605 note 1 ante. As to the application of the powers conferred by the Settled Land Act 1925 to children see s 26; and CHILDREN AND YOUNG PERSONS vol 5(2) (Reissue) para 659. As to the application of the provisions of the Settled Land Act 1925 to married women see s 25 (amended by the Married Women (Restraint upon Anticipation) Act 1949 s 1(4), Sch 2).
2 For the meaning of 'settlement' see para 678 note 1 ante.
3 'Possession' includes receipt of rents and profits, or the right to receive them, if any: Settled Land Act 1925 s 117(1)(xix).
4 For the meaning of 'settled land' see para 680 text to note 2 ante.
5 For the meaning of 'tenant for life' see para 671 note 5 ante.
6 Settled Land Act 1925 s 19(1). A person who is entitled to reside in a house for life is a tenant for life within this provision, even if extensive powers of management are given to trustees (see *Re Baroness Llanover's Will, Herbert v Freshfield* [1902] 2 Ch 679; affd [1903] 2 Ch 16, CA), or even if an option must first be exercised (see *Re Anderson, Halligey v Kirkley* [1920] 1 Ch 175; *Re Gibbons, Gibbons v Gibbons* [1920] 1 Ch 372, CA). See also *Re Hanson, Hanson v Eastwood* [1928] Ch 96; *Binions v Evans* [1972] Ch 359, [1972] 2 All ER 70, CA. As to whether a person entitled to reside in a house is tenant for life where the settlement is expressed to create a trust for sale see para 678 note 29 ante. When dower has been

assigned by metes and bounds, the dowress is a tenant for life under a settlement deemed to have been made by her husband: see para 679 ante. The words 'for life' mean for life and not for a greater interest: *Re Earl of Carnarvon's Chesterfield Settled Estates, Re Earl of Carnarvon's Highclere Settled Estates* [1927] 1 Ch 138. An annuitant is not a tenant for life: *Re Bird, Watson v Nunes* [1927] 1 Ch 210. An exclusive right to occupy property for life does not necessarily constitute a life interest in that property under the Settled Land Act 1925: *Dent v Dent* [1996] 1 All ER 659, [1996] 1 WLR 683.

7   Settled Land Act 1925 s 19(2). Persons entitled to land in undivided shares do not constitute the tenant for life: *Re Stamford and Earl of Warrington, Payne v Grey* [1927] 2 Ch 217; but see *Re Stevens and Dunsby's Contract* [1928] WN 187. Where, immediately before 1926, there were two or more tenants for life of full age entitled under the same settlement in undivided shares, and after the cesser of all their interests in the income of the settled land, the entirety of the land was limited so as to devolve together (not in undivided shares), their interests were, but without prejudice to any beneficial interest, converted into a joint tenancy, and the joint tenants and the survivor of them, until such cesser occurs, constitute the tenant for life for the purposes of the Settled Land Act 1925 and the Law of Property Act 1925: s 39, Sch 1 Pt IV para 4 (added by the Law of Property (Amendment) Act 1926 s 7, Schedule). In ascertaining whether this last-mentioned provision applies, regard must be had to the limitations of the settlement subsisting immediately before 1926, but not to any dealing with or devolution of the interest of any person taking under the limitations of the settlement; it only applies where the interests of the tenants for life are followed by a vested indefeasible limitation not in undivided shares: *Re Colyer's Farningham Estate* [1927] 1 Ch 677. It does not apply where after the cesser of the interests of the life tenants the limitation is to trustees on trust for sale (*Re Higgs' and May's Contract* [1927] 2 Ch 249; *Re Robins, Holland v Gillam* [1928] Ch 721), or to one of the tenants for life (*Re Barrat, Body v Barrat* [1929] 1 Ch 336). As to where two persons constituting the tenant for life cannot agree whether the settled land should be sold see para 793 text and note 12 post. As to joint tenancy generally see REAL PROPERTY vol 39(2) (Reissue) para 190 et seq.

8   Settled Land Act 1925 s 19(3). As to the position when the sole tenant for life is a child see CHILDREN AND YOUNG PERSONS vol 5(2) (Reissue) para 659.

9   See *Re Atkinson, Atkinson v Bruce* (1886) 31 ChD 577, CA.

10   Settled Land Act 1925 s 19(4). As to the effect on the exercise of the statutory powers of an assignment or surrender by a tenant for life of his estate or interest see paras 777–782 post.

762. Persons having the powers of tenant for life.

Certain persons who are not tenants for life within the statutory meaning[1] but have the specified beneficial[2] estates or interests in possession, as distinguished from reversion or remainder[3], can exercise the statutory powers, and the statutory provisions referring to a tenant for life[4], either as conferring powers on him or otherwise, extend to each of them, any reference to the death of a tenant for life being deemed to refer to the determination by death or otherwise of the estate or interest of such person[5]. If the reversion, right of reverter or other reversionary right is in the Crown, the exercise by such a person of his powers under the Settled Land Act 1925 binds the Crown[6].

Each of the following persons being of full age, when his estate or interest is in possession has the powers of a tenant for life[7]:

(1)   a tenant in tail[8], including a tenant in tail after possibility of issue extinct[9], and a tenant in tail restrained by Act of Parliament[10] from barring or defeating his estate tail, and even though the reversion is in the Crown, unless the land in respect of which such restraint is imposed was purchased with money provided by Parliament in consideration of public services[11];

(2)   a person entitled to land for an estate in fee simple or for a term of years absolute[12] with or subject to, in any of such cases, an executory limitation[13], gift or disposition over on failure of his issue or in any other event[14];

(3)   a person entitled to a base or determinable fee, even though the reversion or right of reverter is in the Crown, or to any corresponding interest in leasehold land[15];

(4)   a tenant for years determinable on life, not holding merely under a lease at a rent[16];

(5)   a tenant for the life of another, not holding merely under a lease at a rent[17];

(6) a tenant for his own or any other life[18], or for years determinable on life[19], whose estate is liable to cease in any event during that life, whether by expiration of the estate or by conditional limitation or otherwise, or to be defeated by an executory limitation, gift or disposition over, or is subject to a trust for accumulation of income[20] for any purpose[21];

(7) a tenant by the curtesy[22];

(8) a person entitled to the income of land under a trust[23] or direction for payment of the income to him during his own or any other life[24], whether or not subject to expenses of management[25] or to a trust for accumulation of income for any purpose, or until sale of the land, or until forfeiture, cesser or determination by any means of his interest in it[26], unless the land is subject to a trust of land[27]; and

(9) a person beneficially entitled to land for an estate in fee simple or for a term of years absolute subject to any estates, interests, charges or powers of charging subsisting or capable of being exercised under a settlement[28].

1 For the meaning of 'tenant for life' see para 671 note 5 ante.
2 See *Re Jemmett and Guest's Contract* [1907] 1 Ch 629 (trustees holding on discretionary trusts cannot exercise the statutory powers). Personal representatives may be entitled to exercise the powers of a tenant for life: *Re Johnson, Johnson v Johnson* [1914] 2 Ch 134. It is apprehended that these powers only last so long as the specified estate lasts, eg those vested in a tenant in tail or in a tenant in fee with an executory limitation over are extinguished if such person becomes absolute owner in fee. As to entailed interests see para 715 et seq ante; and REAL PROPERTY vol 39(2) (Reissue) para 117 et seq.
3 *Re Morgan* (1883) 24 ChD 114; *Re Strangways, Hickley v Strangways* (1886) 34 ChD 423, CA; *Re Baroness Llanover, Herbert v Ram* [1907] 1 Ch 635; *Re Bird, Watson v Nunes* [1927] 1 Ch 210. However, a term of years whatever its length, if it is merely a security for charges, does not prevent the person entitled to the income subject to the term from being in possession within the meaning of this provision: see *Re Jones* (1884) 26 ChD 736, CA; *Re Clitheroe Estate* (1885) 31 ChD 135, CA. Cf *Re Richardson, Richardson v Richardson* [1900] 2 Ch 778; *Re Money Kyrle's Settlement, Money Kyrle v Money Kyrle* [1900] 2 Ch 839.
4 See para 761 ante.
5 Settled Land Act 1925 s 20(2).
6 Ibid s 20(4).
7 Ibid s 20(1). As to the meaning of 'of full age' see para 761 note 1 ante; and as to the age of majority see para 605 note 1 ante.
8 'Tenant in tail' includes a person entitled to an entailed interest in property: ibid s 117(xxviii). For the meaning of 'entailed interest' see para 678 note 11 ante.
9 See REAL PROPERTY vol 39(2) (Reissue) para 148.
10 See REAL PROPERTY vol 39(2) (Reissue) para 133.
11 Settled Land Act 1925 s 20(1)(i). See also REAL PROPERTY vol 39(2) (Reissue) para 133. As to property owned by the Crown see generally CROWN PROPERTY.
12 For the meaning of 'term of years absolute' see para 678 note 13 ante.
13 For the meaning of 'limitation' see para 708 note 4 ante.
14 Settled Land Act 1925 s 20(1)(ii). See also REAL PROPERTY vol 39(2) (Reissue) para 45. This includes the case of a person to whom land is devised on condition of residence in a house and maintenance of a home there for a named person suffering from mental disorder: see *Re Richardson, Richardson v Richardson* [1904] 2 Ch 777.
15 Settled Land Act 1925 s 20(1)(iii). As to base fees see REAL PROPERTY vol 39(2) (Reissue) paras 134–139. For the meaning of 'determinable fee' see para 678 note 15 ante.
16 Ibid s 20(1)(iv). A person entitled to receive, if he so long lives, the rents payable by a tenant for years under an ordinary lease at a rent during the continuance of that tenant's term is not a tenant for years determinable on life within s 20(1)(iv), or under s 20(1)(vi) (see head (6) in the text): see *Re Hazle's Settled Estates* (1885) 29 ChD 78, CA. See also notes 17–19 infra. It is a necessary implication from this provision that a tenant of settled land under a lease at a rent is excluded from the class of persons who have the powers of a tenant for life: *Re Catling, Public Trustee v Catling* [1931] 2 Ch 359.
17 Settled Land Act 1925 s 20(1)(v). See also REAL PROPERTY vol 39(2) (Reissue) para 151 et seq. A person entitled for the life of another to receive the rents and profits of real estate whose interest has arisen in consequence of a direction for accumulation having become void under the Accumulations Act 1800 (repealed), or the replacing Law of Property Act 1925 s 164, and the Perpetuities and Accumulations Act 1964 s 13 (see PERPETUITIES AND ACCUMULATIONS vol 35 (Reissue) para 1121), is within this provision: see *Vine v Raleigh* [1896] 1 Ch 37, which, however, in so far as it decided that persons entitled in

undivided shares had collectively the powers of a tenant for life, is no longer law. The assignee of the interest of a tenant for life under a settlement does not come within this provision: *Re Earl of Carnarvon's Chesterfield Settled Estates, Re Earl of Carnarvon's Highclere Settled Estates* [1927] 1 Ch 138.

18   A person entitled during his own or another's life to receive surplus rents from trustees who are in possession of the estates is not within this provision (see *Re Jones* (1884) 26 ChD 736, CA; *Re Baroness Llanover, Herbert v Ram* [1907] 1 Ch 635), but a residuary legatee entitled to put an end to accumulation of rents directed to be made during the life of another person comes within it (see *Re Drinkwater's Settled Estates* (1905) 49 Sol Jo 237). A person entitled to occupy a house during pleasure has during such occupation the powers of a tenant for life under this provision (see *Re Paget's Settled Estates* (1885) 30 ChD 161; *Re Eastman's Settled Estates* [1898] WN 170; *Re Carne's Settled Estates* [1899] 1 Ch 324; *Re Baroness Llanover's Will, Herbert v Freshfield* [1902] 2 Ch 679 (affd [1903] 2 Ch 16, CA); *Re Boyer's Settled Estates* [1916] 2 Ch 404; *Re Acklom, Oakeshott v Hawkins* [1929] 1 Ch 195; *Re Patten, Westminster Bank Ltd v Carlyon* [1929] 2 Ch 276; and see *Binions v Evans* [1972] Ch 359, [1972] 2 All ER 70, CA), unless he has precluded himself for the time being from occupying personally, eg by concurring in a lease of the house (see *Re Edwards' Settlement* [1897] 2 Ch 412). However, there must be a direction to permit a specified person to reside in a specified house: see *Re Bond's Estate, Burrell v Bond* (1904) 48 Sol Jo 192. As to the position where the settlement confers a right of occupation but is expressed to create a trust for sale see para 678 note 29 ante. This provision also includes the case of a widow to whom land was devised during widowhood for the maintenance of herself and her children (see *Re Pollock, Pollock v Pollock* [1906] 1 Ch 146; *Re Martin* [1919] 1 IR 71), and of a person whose estate was suspended in the event, which happened, of a claim being enforced against the testator's estate (see *Williams v Jenkins* [1893] 1 Ch 700).

19   It should be noted that the words 'not holding merely under a lease at a rent' are not inserted here, but a tenant under a lease at a rent does not come within this provision: *Re Catling, Public Trustee v Catling* [1931] 2 Ch 359.

20   'Income' includes rents and profits: Settled Land Act 1925 s 117(1)(xix).

21   Ibid s 20(1)(vi). This includes a widow entitled to reside in the property until remarriage or until her son attains a stated age: *Re Hanson, Hanson v Eastwood* [1928] Ch 96. See also para 678 note 29 ante. Where property is given to a person for life subject to a trust for accumulation, this provision applies: see *Re Woodhouse, Annesley v Woodhouse* [1898] 1 IR 69; *Re Martyn, Coode v Martyn* (1900) 69 LJ Ch 733; *Re Llewellyn, Llewellyn v Llewellyn* [1911] 1 Ch 451; *Re Musgrave, Machell v Parry* [1916] 2 Ch 417. However, if the interest of the tenant for life does not arise until after the trust for accumulation has ceased, he does not come within this provision: see *Re Strangways, Hickley v Strangways* (1886) 34 ChD 423, CA. See, however, *Re Beauchamp's Will Trusts, Cadge v Barker-Hahlo* [1914] 1 Ch 676. As to trusts for accumulation see TRUSTS vol 48 (Reissue) para 583.

22   Settled Land Act 1925 s 20(1)(vii). As to tenancy by the curtesy see para 679 note 11 ante; and REAL PROPERTY vol 39(2) (Reissue) para 157–160. The estate or interest of a tenant by the curtesy is deemed to be an estate or interest arising under a settlement made by his wife: see s 20(3).

23   For the meaning of 'trust' see para 678 note 9 ante.

24   To come within this provision a person must be entitled for his own or some other life: see *Re Astor, Astor v Astor* [1922] 1 Ch 364 at 391, CA. A person entitled to a terminable life interest comes within the provision: see *Re Sumner's Settled Estates* [1911] 1 Ch 315. So also does a person entitled to rents for a term of years if he should so long live: *Re Waleran Settled Estates* [1927] 1 Ch 522. A person does not come within this provision if he is entitled only to a share of the income, the remainder being held as capital money (*Re Frewen* [1926] Ch 580), neither do the objects of a discretionary trust (see *Re Atkinson, Atkinson v Bruce* (1886) 31 ChD 577, CA; *Re Horne's Settled Estate* (1888) 39 ChD 84, CA), nor does a person who is entitled to a mere expectancy such as a right to surplus income, if any, subject to a discretionary trust in favour of another person (*Re Alston-Roberts-West's Settled Estate* [1928] WN 41; cf *Re Gallenga Will Trusts, Wood v Gallenga* [1938] 1 All ER 106), nor does a person absolutely entitled subject to annuities (*Re Sharpe's Deed of Release, Sharpe and Fox v Gullick* [1939] Ch 51, [1938] 3 All ER 449). In *Re Stevens and Dunsby's Contract* [1928] WN 187, it was held that persons entitled under the same will to rents in undivided shares were within this provision, distinguishing *Re Earl of Stamford and Warrington, Payne v Grey* [1927] 2 Ch 217, where persons entitled in undivided shares under separate settlements were held not to come within it.

25   The fact that the trustees are directed to manage the property does not prevent the person entitled to the rents from coming within this provision: see *Clarke v Thornton* (1887) 35 ChD 307.

26   See *Re Sumner's Settled Estates* [1911] 1 Ch 315. See also note 27 infra.

27   Settled Land Act 1925 s 20(1)(viii) (amended by the Trusts of Land and Appointment of Trustees Act 1996 s 25(1), Sch 3 para 2). For the meaning of 'trust of land' see para 676 note 5 ante; definition applied by the Interpretation Act 1978 s 5, Sch 1. The fact that the whole income is exhausted by charges does not prevent the person who would be entitled to it, if there were any, from having the powers of a tenant for life under this provision: see *Re Jones* (1884) 26 ChD 736, CA; *Re Cookes' Settled Estates, Cookes v Cookes* [1885] WN 177. A person entitled in remainder after a valid trust for accumulation has not the

powers of a tenant for life, his estate not being in possession: see *Re Strangways, Hickley v Strangways* (1886) 34 ChD 423, CA. It is otherwise if the term is in the nature of an incumbrance which may be redeemed at any moment: see *Re Clitheroe Estate* (1885) 31 ChD 135, CA.

28	Settled Land Act 1925 s 20(1)(ix). A purchaser of a fee simple subject to a family charge comes within this provision (*Re Earl of Carnarvon's Chesterfield Settled Estates, Re Earl of Carnarvon's Highclere Settled Estates* [1927] 1 Ch 138), and, if part of the land subject to a charge is sold, the rest being retained by the vendor, the purchaser and the vendor both come within this provision in respect of the land held by them (*Re Ogle's Settled Estates* [1927] 1 Ch 229).

763. Tenant for life suffering from mental disorder. Where the nominated judge or master of the Court of Protection[1] is satisfied that a tenant for life is incapable, by reason of mental disorder[2], of managing and administering his property and affairs, the judge or master may: (1) make such orders or give such directions or authorities as he thinks fit for the exercise of any power vested in the tenant for life[3]; and (2) appoint a receiver for the tenant for life in relation to his property and affairs[4].

1	As to the exercise of powers by the nominated judge or master see the Mental Health Act 1983 ss 93, 94 (as amended); and MENTAL HEALTH vol 30 (Reissue) para 1433 et seq.
2	For the meaning of 'mental disorder' see ibid s 1(2); and MENTAL HEALTH vol 30 (Reissue) para 1202.
3	See ibid s 96(1)(k); and MENTAL HEALTH vol 30 (Reissue) para 1442.
4	See ibid s 99(1); and MENTAL HEALTH vol 30 para 1463.

764. Effect of restoring original life estate. Where by a disentailing assurance[1] settled land[2] is expressed to be limited (whether subject or not to any estates, interests, charges or powers expressly created or conferred by it) upon the trusts subsisting with respect to it immediately before the execution of that disentailing assurance, or any of such trusts, then, for the purposes of the Settled Land Act 1925 and otherwise, a person entitled to any estate or interest in the settled land under any such previously subsisting trust is entitled to it after the execution of the disentailing assurance as of his former estate or interest[3].

Where by a resettlement[4] of settled land any estate or interest in it is expressed to be limited to any person (whether subject or not to any estate, interest, charge or power expressly created or conferred by the resettlement) in restoration or confirmation of his estate or interest under a prior settlement, then, for the purposes of the Settled Land Act 1925 and otherwise, that person is entitled to the estate or interest so restored or confirmed as of his former estate or interest, and, in addition to the powers exercisable by him in respect of his former estate or interest, he is capable of exercising all such further powers as he could have exercised by virtue of the resettlement if his estate or interest under the prior settlement had not been so restored or confirmed, but he had been entitled under the resettlement only[5].

1	As to disentailing deeds see REAL PROPERTY vol 39(2) (Reissue) para 121 et seq.
2	For the meaning of 'settled land' see para 680 text to note 2 ante.
3	Settled Land Act 1925 s 22(1). See also *Re Cradock's Settled Estates* [1926] Ch 944.
4	As to resettlements see para 720 ante.
5	Settled Land Act 1925 s 22(2).

765. Position where tenant for life has parted with interest. If it is shown to the satisfaction of the court[1] that a tenant for life[2] who has by reason of bankruptcy, assignment, incumbrance or otherwise ceased in the court's opinion to have a substantial interest in his estate or interest in the settled land[3], or any part of it, has unreasonably refused to exercise any of the powers conferred on him by the Settled Land Act 1925[4], or consents[5] to an order[6], then, on the application of any person interested in the settled land or the part of it affected, the court may make an order authorising the trustees of the settlement[7] to exercise in the name and on behalf of the tenant for life, any of the powers of a tenant for life under that Act in relation to the settled land or the part of it affected, either generally and in such manner and for such period as the court may think fit, or in a particular instance, and the court may by the order direct that any documents of title in the possession of the tenant for life relating to the settled land be delivered to the trustees of the settlement[8]. Such an order may be made at any time after the estate or interest of the tenant for life under the settlement[9] has taken effect in possession[10], and notwithstanding that he disposed of it when it was an estate or interest in remainder or reversion[11].

While any such order is in force the tenant for life may not, in relation to the settled land or the part of it affected, exercise any of the powers authorised by the order to be exercised in his name and on his behalf, but no person dealing with the tenant for life is affected by any such order, unless the order is for the time being registered as an order affecting land[12].

1   As to the court see para 792 post.
2   For the meaning of 'tenant for life' see para 671 note 5 ante. See also *Re Craven Settled Estates* [1926] Ch 985.
3   For the meaning of 'settled land' see para 680 text to note 2 ante.
4   As to the statutory powers see para 775 et seq post. It is necessary to prove a definite refusal on the part of the tenant for life and mere neglect or failure is not sufficient: *Re Thornhill's Settlement* [1941] Ch 24, [1940] 4 All ER 249, CA.
5   The tenant for life must either be a party to the proceedings or his consent in writing must be proved strictly: *Re Cecil's Settled Estates* [1926] WN 262.
6   Ie an order under the Settled Land Act 1925 s 24: see s 24(1).
7   For the meaning of 'trustees of the settlement' see para 750 note 1 ante. As to the trustees see para 750 et seq ante.
8   Settled Land Act 1925 s 24(1). As to the procedure see para 792 post.
9   For the meaning of 'settlement' see para 678 note 1 ante.
10 For the meaning of 'possession' see para 761 note 3 ante.
11 Settled Land Act 1925 s 24(3).
12 Ibid s 24(2). As to the registration of orders affecting land see LAND CHARGES vol 26 (Reissue) para 554 et seq; LAND REGISTRATION vol 26 (Reissue) para 1158.

766. Statutory owners. If under a settlement[1] there is no tenant for life[2] nor, independently of this provision, a person having by virtue of the Settled Land Act 1925 the powers of a tenant for life[3], then: (1) any person of full age on whom such powers are by the settlement expressed to be conferred[4]; and (2) in any other case the trustees of the settlement[5], have the powers of a tenant for life under that Act[6]. This provision applies to trustees of settlements of land[7] purchased with money provided by Parliament in consideration of public services where the tenant in tail is restrained from barring or defeating his estate tail[8], except that, if the tenant in tail is of full age and capacity[9], the powers may not be exercised without his consent, but a purchaser[10] is not concerned to see or inquire whether such consent has been given[11].

1   For the meaning of 'settlement' see para 678 note 1 ante.
2   For the meaning of 'tenant for life' see para 671 note 5 ante.
3   As to the statutory powers see para 775 et seq post.
4   Settled Land Act 1925 s 23(1)(a). In the case of a compound settlement (see paras 681–683 ante) the powers can be conferred by any of the instruments constituting the compound settlement: *Re Cowley Settled Estates* [1926] Ch 725; *Re Beaumont Settled Estates* [1937] 2 All ER 353. As to the meaning of 'of full age' see para 761 note 1 ante; and as to the age of majority see para 605 note 1 ante.
5   Settled Land Act 1925 s 23(1)(b). For the meaning of 'trustees of the settlement' see para 750 note 1 ante. As to the trustees see para 750 et seq ante.
6   Ibid s 23(1). The persons on whom the powers of a tenant for life are conferred by this provision are generally called 'statutory owners', but they are not so called in the provision itself. 'Statutory owner' means the trustees of the settlement or other persons who, during a minority, or at any other time when there is

no tenant for life, have the powers of a tenant for life under the Settled Land Act 1925, but does not include the trustees of the settlement, where by virtue of a court order or otherwise the trustees have power to convey the settled land in the name of the tenant for life (ie under ss 24 (see para 765 ante), 68 (as amended) (see para 879 post)): s 117(1)(xxvi). Cases in which this provision has been held to apply are *Re Frewen* [1926] Ch 580; *Re Bird, Watson v Nunes* [1927] 1 Ch 210; *Re Stamford and Earl of Warrington, Payne v Grey* [1927] 2 Ch 217; *Re Alston-Roberts-West's Settled Estates* [1928] WN 41; *Re Norton, Pinney v Beauchamp* [1929] 1 Ch 84. The powers conferred on statutory owners under this provision, unlike those of a tenant for life, may be released or assigned: *Re Craven Settled Estates* [1926] Ch 985. As to powers of management during a minority or when a person is contingently entitled see paras 665–666 ante.

7   For the meaning of 'land' see para 680 note 1 ante.

8   See para 762 ante; and REAL PROPERTY vol 39(2) (Reissue) para 133. As to entailed interests see para 715 et seq ante; and REAL PROPERTY vol 39(2) (Reissue) para 117 et seq.

9   For the meaning of 'tenant in tail' see para 762 note 8 ante.

10 For the meaning of 'purchaser' see para 702 note 12 ante.

11 Settled Land Act 1925 s 23(2).

(ii) Enforcement of Equitable Interests

767. Method of enforcing equitable interests. All equitable interests[1] and powers in or over settled land[2], whether created[3] before or after the date of any vesting instrument[4] affecting the legal estate[5], are enforceable against the estate owner[6], but in the case of personal representatives[7] without prejudice to their rights and powers for purposes of administration[8], in the following manner[9]:

(1)   the estate owner must stand possessed of the settled land and its income upon such trusts and subject to such powers and provisions as may be requisite for giving effect to the equitable interests and powers affecting the settled land or its income of which he has notice[10] according to their respective priorities[11];

(2)   where any person of full age[12] becomes entitled to require a legal estate in the settled land to be vested in him in priority to the settlement[13], by reason of a right of reverter, statutory or otherwise, or an equitable right of entry[14] taking effect, or on the ground that his interest ought no longer to be capable of being overreached under the powers of the Settled Land Act 1925, the estate owner is bound, if so requested in writing, to transfer or create such legal estate as may be required for giving legal effect to the rights of the person so entitled[15]; and

(3)   where (a) any principal sum is required to be raised on the security of the settled land, by virtue of any trust or by reason of the exercise of an equitable power affecting the settled land, or by any person or persons who under the settlement is or are entitled or together entitled to or has or have a general power of appointment over the settled land[16], whether subject to any equitable charges or powers of charging subsisting under the settlement or not[17]; or (b) the settled land is subject to any equitable charge for securing money actually raised and affecting the whole estate the subject of the settlement[18], the estate owner is bound, if so requested[19] in writing, to create such legal estate or charge by way of legal mortgage[20] as may be required for raising the money or giving legal effect to the equitable charge[21]. So long, however, as the settlement remains subsisting[22], any legal estate or charge by way of legal mortgage so created takes effect, and must be expressed to take effect, subject to any equitable charges or powers of charging subsisting under the settlement which have priority to the interests or powers of the person or persons by or on behalf of whom the money is required to be raised or legal effect is required to be given to the equitable charge, unless the persons entitled to the prior charges or entitled to exercise the powers consent in writing to the same being postponed, but such consent need not be expressed in the instrument creating such legal estate or charge by way of legal mortgage[23].

Except as expressly provided[24], no legal estate may, so long as the settlement is subsisting, be transferred or created by the estate owner for giving effect to any equitable interest or power under the settlement[25].

A purchaser[26] of a legal estate taking free from any equitable interest or power is not affected by these provisions[27].

1   For the meaning of 'equitable interests' see para 695 note 8 ante.
2   For the meaning of 'settled land' see para 680 text to note 2 ante.
3   Where an equitable interest in or power over property arises by statute or operation of law, references to the 'creation' of an interest or power include any interest or power so arising: Settled Land Act 1925 s 117(2).
4   For the meaning of 'vesting instrument' see para 690 note 8 ante.
5   For the meaning of 'legal estate' see para 678 note 13 ante.
6   For the meaning of 'estate owner' see para 697 note 2 ante.
7   For the meaning of 'personal representative' see para 697 note 6 ante. As to personal representatives in the case of settled land see EXECUTORS AND ADMINISTRATORS.
8   As to the rights and powers of personal representatives see the Administration of Estates Act 1925 ss 2(1), 24, 39 (as amended); and EXECUTORS AND ADMINISTRATORS.
9   Settled Land Act 1925 s 16(1).
10 'Notice' includes constructive notice: ibid s 117(1)(xvii).
11 Ibid s 16(1)(i).
12 See para 761 note ante.
13 For the meaning of 'settlement' see para 678 note 1 ante.
14 As to the right of reverter or right of entry see REAL PROPERTY vol 39(2) (Reissue) para 187.
15 Settled Land Act 1925 s 16(1)(ii).
16 An estate owner having a general power of appointment over the settled land is entitled under this provision to mortgage the settled land for the purpose of raising money for his own use and benefit: *Re Egerton Settled Estates* [1926] Ch 574.
17 Settled Land Act 1925 s 16(1)(iii)(a).
18 Ibid s 16(1)(iii)(b).
19 Where the estate owner is borrowing for his own purposes the request must come from the lender; in other cases, such as one of money being required to be raised by virtue of any trust, the request may be made by the trustees, the beneficiaries or the lender: *Re Egerton Settled Estates* [1926] Ch 574 at 579.
20 For the meaning of 'legal mortgage' see para 698 note 23 ante.
21 Settled Land Act 1925 s 16(1)(iii). This provision does not affect the power conferred by the Settled Land Act 1925 on a tenant for life of raising money by mortgage (see paras 849–850 post), or of directing capital money to be applied in discharge of incumbrances (see para 808 post): s 16(3). For the meaning of 'tenant for life' see para 671 note 5 ante. See also para 761 et seq ante.
22 As to the duration of settlements see para 708 ante.
23 Settled Land Act 1925 s 16(1) proviso. It will usually be preferable for the estate owner, where possible, to raise the money required by mortgage under s 71 (as amended) (see para 849 post), in order to avoid bringing equitable charges on to the title.
24 Ie under ibid s 16(1): see s 16(5).
25 Ibid s 16(5).
26 For the meaning of 'purchaser' see para 702 note 12 ante.
27 Settled Land Act 1925 s 16(8). A purchaser from a tenant for life or statutory owner under the statutory powers will take free from all equitable interests and powers: see para 874 post.

768. Effect of mortgage or charge by estate owner. If a mortgage or charge is expressed to be made by an estate owner[1] pursuant to the statutory provisions[2], then, in favour of the mortgagee or chargee and persons deriving title under him[3], it takes effect in priority to all the trusts of the settlement[4] and all equitable interests[5] and powers subsisting or to arise under the settlement except those to which it is expressly made subject, and so takes effect whether or not the mortgagee or chargee has notice of any such trusts, interests or powers, and the mortgagee or chargee is not concerned to see that a case has arisen to authorise the mortgage or charge, or that no more money than was wanted was raised[6].

Under these provisions effect may be given by means of a legal mortgage[7] to an agreement for a mortgage, or a charge or lien, whether or not arising by operation of law, if the agreement, charge or lien ought to have priority over the settlement[8].

1   For the meaning of 'estate owner' see para 697 note 2 ante.
2   Ie pursuant to the Settled Land Act 1925 s 16 (see para 767 ante): see s 16(2).
3   See further MORTGAGE.
4   For the meaning of 'settlement' see para 678 note 1 ante.
5   For the meaning of 'equitable interests' see para 695 note 8 ante.
6   Settled Land Act 1925 s 16(2).
7   For the meaning of 'legal mortgage' see para 698 note 23 ante. As to legal mortgages see MORTGAGE.
8   Settled Land Act 1925 s 16(4). As to legal lien and equitable lien see LIEN vol 28 (Reissue) para 716 et seq.

769. Applications to the court. An application may be made to the court[1] for directions if a question arises or a doubt is entertained whether any and what legal estate ought to be transferred or created pursuant to the statutory provisions[2] for the enforcement of equitable interests and powers against an estate owner[3]. If an estate owner refuses or neglects for one month after written demand to transfer or create any such legal estate, or if, by reason of his being outside the United Kingdom[4], or being unable to be found, or by reason of the dissolution of a corporation[5], or for any other reason, the court is satisfied that the transaction cannot otherwise be effected, or cannot be effected without undue delay or expense, then, on the application of any person interested, the court may make a vesting order[6] transferring or creating the requisite legal estate[7].

1   As to applications to the court see paras 792–793 post.
2   Ie pursuant to the Settled Land Act 1925 s 16 (see paras 767–768 ante): see s 16(6).
3   Ibid s 16(6). For the meaning of 'estate owner' see para 697 note 2 ante.
4   For the meaning of 'United Kingdom' see para 699 note 5 ante.
5   As to the dissolution of corporations see CORPORATIONS vol 9(2) (Reissue) para 1196 et seq.
6   For the meaning of 'vesting order' see para 688 note 6 ante.
7   Settled Land Act 1925 s 16(7). As to the provisions applying to such vesting orders see s 113(9); and para 699 ante.

(iii) Right to Possession

770. Nature of the right. A tenant for life or statutory owner[1] is ordinarily entitled to possession[2], by virtue of his position as the estate owner[3], but, as he is a trustee for all persons interested in the settled land[4], it is conceived that his right to possession, being subject to his obligation to give effect to any legal or equitable interest having priority to or equality with his own beneficial interest, would be controlled by the court accordingly[5].

1   As to the tenant for life or statutory owner see para 761 et seq ante.
2   The right of the tenant for life or statutory owner is not barred by reason of any other person entitled to a beneficial interest in the settled land being in possession: see LIMITATION OF ACTIONS vol 28 (Reissue) para 993.
3   Prior to 1926, a legal tenant for life was entitled as of course to possession and receipt of the rent and profits, notwithstanding the existence of a prior term to secure the payment of annuities: *Ferrand v Wilson* (1845) 4 Hare 344 at 368. An equitable tenant for life was not so entitled as of course (*Taylor v Taylor, ex p Taylor* (1875) LR 20 Eq 297), but he could usually obtain possession by applying to the court. As to the principles on which the court exercised its discretion in such cases see *Re Earl of Stamford and Warrington, Payne v Grey* [1925] Ch 162 (revsd on another ground [1925] Ch 589, CA), and the cases there considered. See also REAL PROPERTY vol 39(2) (Reissue) para 2 et seq.
4   See para 767 ante.

5   For example, an assignee of the beneficial interest of a tenant for life would clearly be entitled to
     possession as against the tenant for life: see REAL PROPERTY vol 39(2) (Reissue) para 184; EQUITY vol 16
     (Reissue) para 775. As to the method of enforcing equitable interests see para 767 ante. As to outgoings
     see para 961 et seq post.

771. Custody of title deeds. A tenant for life[1], being the person in whom the legal
estate is vested, is normally, but not necessarily[2], entitled to the custody of the title deeds[3].
The court does not interfere with this right, except in cases where the tenant for life has
been guilty of misconduct so that the safety of the deeds has been endangered[4], or where
the rights of others intervene and it becomes necessary for the court to take charge of the
title deeds in order to carry out the administration of the property[5]. However, where it
is shown to the satisfaction of the court[6] that a tenant for life who has, by reason of
bankruptcy, assignment, incumbrance or otherwise, ceased in the court's opinion to have
a substantial interest in his estate or interest in the settled land or any part of it, has
unreasonably refused to exercise any of the powers conferred on him by the Settled Land
Act 1925 or consents to an order, then, on the application of any person interested in the
settled land or the part of it affected, the court may make an order directing that any
documents of title in the possession of the tenant for life relating to the settled land be
delivered to the trustees of the settlement[7].

1   As to the tenant for life see para 761 et seq ante.
2   See the Settled Land Act 1925 s 98(3) (see para 892 post); and SALE OF LAND para 131 ante. See also
     Allwood v Heywood (1863) 1 H & C 745; *Re Beddoe, Downes v Cottam* [1893] 1 Ch 547 at 557, CA, per
     Lindley LJ; *Clayton v Clayton* [1930] 2 Ch 12.
3   *Strode v Blackburne* (1796) 3 Ves 222; *Garner v Hannyngton* (1856) 22 Beav 627. This does not include deeds
     of appointment of trustees (*Clayton v Clayton* [1930] 2 Ch 12) or securities for capital money (see the
     Settled Land Act 1925 s 98(3); and para 892 post).
4   The fact that the tenant for life has taken the deeds out of the jurisdiction may be a ground for thinking
     that there is danger to them if they remain in his custody (*Jenner v Morris* (1866) 1 Ch App 603), but the
     mere fact that he has for many years been resident abroad is no objection (*Leathes v Leathes* (1877) 5 ChD
     221). If the dicta in *Reeves v Reeves* (1724) 9 Mod Rep 128; *Ivie v Ivie* (1738) 1 Atk 429; and *Smith v Cooke*
     (1746) 3 Atk 378 at 382, assert an unqualified right in the remainderman to have the title deeds brought
     into court, they will not now be followed: see *Ford v Peering* (1789) 1 Ves 72.
5   *Stanford v Roberts* (1871) 6 Ch App 307; *Leathes v Leathes* (1877) 5 ChD 221 (dissenting from *Pyncent v
     Pyncent* (1747) 3 Atk 571, and *Warren v Rudall, ex p Godfrey* (1860) I John & H 1). Where a sale has been
     ordered to raise portions, but the tenant for life refused to produce the title deeds of the estate, a receiver
     of the rents and profits was appointed: *Brigstocke v Mansel* (1818) 3 Madd 47. Where deeds have been
     brought into court by the tenant for life for the purposes of an action, the court on the conclusion of the
     proceedings has ordered them to be redelivered to him: *Webb v Lord Lymington, Webb v Webb* (1757) 1
     Eden 8; *Duncombe v Mayer* (1803) 8 Ves 320; but see *Hicks v Hicks* (1785) 2 Dick 650; *Lady Langdale v
     Briggs* (1856) 8 De GM & G 391; *Jenner v Morris* (1866) 1 Ch App 603. However, the court only delivers
     deeds out to the party who has deposited them: *Plunkett v Lewis* (1847) 6 Hare 65.
6   As to the court see para 792 post.
7   See the Settled Land Act 1925 s 24(1); and para 765 ante. Such a direction will only be given in an order
     under this provision authorising the trustees to execute the statutory powers: see para 765 ante.

772. Indorsement of notice of vesting instrument. Where, if the settlement[1] were
not disclosed, it would appear that the tenant for life[2] had a general power of appointment
over, or was absolutely and beneficially entitled to, the settled land[3], the trustees of the
settlement[4] must, before they deliver the documents of title to him, require that notice
of the last or only principal vesting instrument[5] be written on one of the documents under
which the tenant for life acquired his title, and may, if the documents are not in their
possession, require such notice to be written, but in the latter case they will not be liable
in any way for not requiring the notice to be written[6].

1   For the meaning of 'settlement' see para 678 note 1 ante.
2   For the meaning of 'tenant for life' see para 671 note 5 ante. See also para 761 et seq ante.
3   For the meaning of 'settled land' see para 680 text to note 2 ante.
4   For the meaning of 'trustees of the settlement' see para 750 note 1 ante. As to the trustees see para 750 et
    seq ante.
5   For the meaning of 'principal vesting instrument' see para 698 note 1 ante.
6   Settled Land Act 1925 s 98(3) proviso.

773. Effect of purchase of life interest. The tenant for life[1] is expressly prohibited from delivering the documents of title relating to the settled land[2] to a purchaser[3] of his beneficial interest who is not also a purchaser of the whole of the settled land to which those documents relate[4]. In the case of a conveyance of or dealing with his beneficial interest by a tenant for life after 1925 in favour of a purchaser, the purchaser is not entitled to the possession of the documents of title relating to the settled land but has the same rights with respect to the title deeds as if the tenant for life had given to him a statutory acknowledgment of his right to production and delivery of copies of them, and a statutory undertaking for their safe custody[5].

1   For the meaning of 'tenant for life' see para 671 note 5 ante. See also para 761 et seq ante.
2   For the meaning of 'settled land' see para 680 text to note 2 ante.
3   For the meaning of 'purchaser' see para 702 note 12 ante.
4   Settled Land Act 1925 s 111.
5   Ibid s 111 proviso. As to acknowledgments of the right to production of title deeds see SALE OF LAND para 132 ante. The statutory powers remain exercisable by the tenant for life notwithstanding any assignment by him of his beneficial interest: see para 777 post.

774. Insurance by the tenant for life. In the absence of special contract or obligation[1], a tenant for life is not bound to insure the settled premises[2]. Accordingly, where policies have been effected and kept up by or on behalf of a tenant in tail[3], who is under no obligation to insure and, being a child, cannot be credited with any intention of making the policy money a present to the settled estate, the policy money belongs absolutely to the tenant in tail[4]. In the case of a tenant for life without impeachment of waste, the absence of liability to insure carries with it a right to receive money forthcoming by reason of the insurance which he is under no liability to effect[5], and this is so in the case both of an insurance of buildings and of chattels settled to devolve with land[6]. However, the remaindermen have a statutory right to require insurance money on buildings to be applied in replacing the buildings insured[7], and if they exercise this right the tenant for life is not entitled to a charge for the amount so applied[8].

Any money received since 1925[9], either by trustees or any beneficiary, under a policy of insurance against the loss or damage, whether by fire or otherwise, of any property subject to a trust or to a settlement within the Settled Land Act 1925[10], is, however, capital money for the purposes of the trust or settlement, as the case may be, whenever the policy was effected, if the policy has been kept up under any trust in that behalf, or under any power statutory or otherwise, or in performance of any covenant or of any obligation statutory or otherwise, or by a tenant for life impeachable for waste[11].

1   As to the obligation on the tenant for life to insure buildings comprised in an improvement executed under the statutory provisions see the Settled Land Act 1925 s 88; and para 964 post. As to the obligation on a tenant for life of settled leaseholds to bear the cost of insurance if there is a covenant to insure see para 961 post. A tenant for life is not bound to keep furniture insured: *Re Betty, Betty v A-G* [1899] 1 Ch 821. As to the tenant for life see para 761 et seq ante.
2   *Re Bennett, Jones v Bennett* [1896] 1 Ch 778 at 787, CA; *Re McEacharn, Gambles v McEacharn* (1911) 103 LT 900. As to the power of trustees to insure personal property see the Trustee Act 1925 s 19 (as amended); and TRUSTS vol 48 (Reissue) para 891.
3   As to entailed interests see para 715 et seq ante; and REAL PROPERTY vol 39(2) (Reissue) para 117 et seq.

4   *Seymour v Vernon* (1852) 16 Jur 189; *Warwicker v Bretnall* (1882) 23 ChD 188 (distinguishing *Rook v Worth*
    (1750) 1 Ves Sen 460; *Norris v Harrison* (1817) 2 Madd 268; *Parry v Ashley* (1829) 3 Sim 97).
5   *Gaussen v Whatman* (1905) 93 LT 101. As to the right of the tenant for life and remaindermen to insure
    in respect of their respective beneficial interests see INSURANCE vol 25 (Reissue) para 614. If the tenant
    for life insures for the full value of the property and the insurance company pays the entire sum over to
    him without raising any question as to the extent of his interest, he does not become a trustee of the sum
    for all persons interested in the property: *Gaussen v Whatman* supra. A condition in a settlement that a
    tenant for life is to keep the settled property in good and tenantable repair creates an obligation upon him
    to rebuild premises destroyed by fire: *Re Skingley* (1851) 3 Mac & G 221; *Gregg v Coates, Hodgson v Coates*
    (1856) 23 Beav 33. As to waste see para 986 et seq post.
6   *Re Quicke's Trusts, Poltimore v Quicke* [1908] 1 Ch 887; *Re Bladon, Dando v Porter* [1911] 2 Ch 350 at 354
    per Neville J. As to chattels settled to devolve with land see paras 799, 937 et seq post.
7   See the Fires Prevention (Metropolis) Act 1774 s 83; and INSURANCE vol 25 (Reissue) paras 637–639.
    This provision applies to the whole of England: *Re Barker, ex p Gorely* (1864) 4 De GJ & Sm 477; *Re
    Quicke's Trusts, Poltimore v Quicke* [1908] 1 Ch 887; *Sinnott v Bowden* [1912] 2 Ch 414. See, however,
    Westminster Fire Office v Glasgow Provident Investment Society (1888) 13 App Cas 699 at 716, HL.
8   *Re Quicke's Trusts, Poltimore v Quicke* [1908] 1 Ch 887.
9   See the Trustee Act 1925 s 20(6); and TRUSTS vol 48 (Reissue) para 892.
10 As to the meaning of 'settlement within the Settled Land Act 1925' see para 675 et seq ante.
11 See the Trustee Act 1925 s 20(1); and TRUSTS vol 48 (Reissue) para 892. See also *Mumford Hotels Ltd v
    Wheler* [1964] Ch 117, [1963] 3 All ER 250. As to the effect of, and qualifications on, this provision see
    TRUSTS vol 48 (Reissue) para 892. The same principle applied prior to 1926, if a tenant for life was under
    an obligation to insure or trustees had power to insure: *Re Bladon, Dando v Porter* [1911] 2 Ch 350 at 354
    per Neville J. As to capital money generally see para 795 et seq post.

(7) STATUTORY POWERS

(i) Characteristics

775. Fiduciary position of tenant for life. In exercising[1] the statutory powers[2], or
any additional or larger powers conferred by the settlement[3], a tenant for life[4] or statutory
owner[5] must have regard to the interests of all parties entitled under the settlement[6], and
is deemed in relation to the exercise to be in the position and to have the duties and
liabilities of a trustee for those parties[7], but only according to their rights as created by the
settlement[8]. It follows that a purchaser who knows that the tenant for life is exercising a
statutory power improperly, and is aware that what the tenant for life is doing would
amount to a breach of trust, has a right to decline to complete[9].

It is no objection to a proposed transaction that it will benefit the tenant for life
personally, and may be to the detriment of the remaindermen[10], especially where the
evidence adduced on behalf of the remaindermen is speculative evidence of a future
increase of the value of the settled property, for it is the right of the tenant for life to derive
any benefit he can from his estate[11], but he must not act unjustly towards those whose
interests he is bound to protect[12], including the tenants on the estate[13] and existing
incumbrancers[14]. Moreover, the exercise by the tenant for life of his powers must be in
good faith for the benefit of the estate as a whole, and not for the sole purpose of
obtaining a benefit for himself or some person connected with him, such as his wife, at
the expense of the remaindermen[15], and he is not justified in forwarding his private views
to their detriment[16]. It necessarily follows that, if a bribe is given to induce the tenant for
life to exercise his powers, the transaction can be set aside by the remaindermen, whether
they are injured or not[17].

Although the corresponding statutory provisions which were in force prior to 1926
imposed on the tenant for life the duties of a trustee, they did not confer on him the rights
of a trustee as to, for instance, his costs[18]. However, a tenant for life is not necessarily a
trustee of every adventitious profit which may accrue to him as a consequence of an
exercise in good faith of his statutory powers[19].

1   Whether a statutory power is exercised or not depends on statute and intention, and accordingly, a deed expressed to operate under the Settled Land Act 1925 to effect a sale, exchange, lease, mortgage, charge or other disposition is effective, so far as it can be (see para 874 post), and a purchaser of a legal estate from personal representatives is entitled to assume that they act under their statutory powers (see para 887 post). A lease granted by a tenant for life who believed that he was absolute owner was valid to the extent of the statutory power of leasing, even though not expressed to be made in exercise of that power, since it was the obvious intention that the lease should be good: *Mogridge v Clapp* [1892] 3 Ch 382 at 395, CA. As to the effect of leases not authorised by statutory or express powers see para 883 post.

2   Ie all powers conferred by the Settled Land Act 1925 on a tenant for life or person having the powers of a tenant for life: see para 762 ante. As to the particular powers see para 794 et seq post.

3   *Re Duke of Westminster's Settled Estates, Duke of Westminster v Earl of Shaftesbury* [1921] 1 Ch 585; *Re Cowley Settled Estates* [1926] Ch 725. As to the exercise of such additional or larger powers see para 880–881 post.

4   For the meaning of 'tenant for life' see para 671 note 5 ante. See also para 761 et seq ante.

5   For the meaning of 'statutory owner' see para 766 note 6 ante.

6   For the meaning of 'settlement' see para 678 note 1 ante.

7   Settled Land Act 1925 s 107(1). See also *Owen v Williams* (1773) Amb 734; *Pole v Pole* (1865) 2 Drew & Sm 420; *Lloyd-Jones v Clark-Lloyd* [1919] 1 Ch 424, CA; *Re Lord Boston's Will Trusts, Inglis v Boston* [1956] Ch 395, [1956] 1 All ER 593.

8   *Re Lacon's Settlement, Lacon v Lacon* [1911] 2 Ch 17, CA. The provision by a tenant for life or statutory owner, at his own expense, of dwellings available for the working classes on any settled land is not to be deemed to be an injury to any interest in reversion or remainder in that land, but such provision may not be made by a tenant for life or statutory owner without the previous approval in writing of the trustees of the settlement: Settled Land Act 1925 s 107(2). For the meaning of 'settled land' see para 680 text to note 2 ante; and for the meaning of 'trustees of the settlement' see para 750 note 1 ante. The meaning of the expression 'working classes' as used in the Housing Act 1936 (repealed) was discussed by Denning J in *H E Green & Sons v Minister of Health* [1948] 1 KB 34 at 38, [1947] 2 All ER 469 at 470–471. See also *Belcher v Reading Corpn* [1950] Ch 380 at 392, [1949] 2 All ER 969 at 984 per Romer J.

9   *Hatten v Russell* (1888) 38 ChD 334 at 345. See also para 784 post. Cf *Re Handman and Wilcox's Contract* [1902] 1 Ch 599, CA; and SALE OF LAND para 239 ante. As to the fiduciary position of trustees see TRUSTS vol 48 (Reissue) para 829.

10   *Re Lord Stamford's Estate* (1887) 56 LT 484; *Re Hare, Leycester-Penrhyn v Leycester-Penrhyn* (1908) 43 L Jo 659. See also *Re Wix, Hardy v Lemon* [1916] 1 Ch 279.

11   *Thomas v Williams* (1883) 24 ChD 558.

12   *Re Richardson, Richardson v Richardson* [1900] 2 Ch 778; *Re Earl of Stamford and Warrington, Payne v Grey* [1916] 1 Ch 404.

13   *Re Duke of Marlborough's Settlement, Duke of Marlborough v Marjoribanks* (1885) 30 ChD 127 (affd (1886) 32 ChD 1, CA); *Lord Bruce v Marquess of Ailesbury* [1892] AC 356, HL; *Re Lord Stafford's Settlement and Will, Gerard v Stafford* [1904] 2 Ch 72.

14   *Hampden v Earl of Buckinghamshire* [1893] 2 Ch 531, CA.

15   *Dowager Duchess of Sutherland v Duke of Sutherland* [1893] 3 Ch 169; *Middlemas v Stevens* [1901] 1 Ch 574; *Re Hunt's Settled Estates, Bulteel v Lawdeshayne* [1905] 2 Ch 418 (on appeal [1906] 2 Ch 11, CA); *Re Wharncliffe's Trusts, Wharncliffe v Stuart Wortley* (1904) 48 Sol Jo 176, CA; *Re Gladwin's Trust* [1919] 1 Ch 232; *Re Cornwallis-West, ex p Trustee* (1919) 88 LJKB 1237; *Re Sutherland Settlement Trusts* [1953] Ch 792, [1953] 2 All ER 27.

16   *Re Earl of Somers, Cocks v Lady Somerset* (1895) 11 TLR 567. See, however, *Re Earl of Egmont's Settled Estates, Lefroy v Earl of Egmont* [1906] 2 Ch 151.

17   *Chandler v Bradley* [1897] 1 Ch 315.

18   *Sebright v Thornton* [1885] WN 176; *Re Llewellin, Llewellin v Williams* (1887) 37 ChD 317. After 1925, however, in any case in which the tenant for life can be said to be acting as trustee of the legal estate under the Settled Land Act 1925 s 16(1)(i) (see para 767 ante), it would seem that he would be entitled to the same rights as to costs as an ordinary trustee. As to costs incurred by trustees see TRUSTS vol 48 (Reissue) para 787 et seq.

19   See *Re Pelly's Will Trusts, Ransome v Pelly* [1957] Ch 1 at 13, [1956] 2 All ER 326 at 329, CA, per Lord Evershed MR (a tenant for life was entitled to retain the benefit of income tax relief for improvements the cost of which was paid out of capital money, there being no right of recoupment in respect of the capital money expended). See also para 944 post.

776.   Delegation of powers. For a period not exceeding 12 months, a tenant for life[1] or statutory owner[2] may delegate to any person, including a trust corporation[3], the execution or exercise of all or any of the trusts, powers and discretions vested in him[4]. Before or within seven days after giving a power of attorney, the donor of the power must give written notice[5]:

(1)   in the case of a tenant for life, to the trustees of the settlement[6] and to each person, if any, who together with the person giving the notice constitutes the tenant for life[7]; and

(2)   in the case of a statutory owner, to each of the persons, if any, who together with the person giving the notice constitute the statutory owner, and in the case of a statutory owner, being a person of full age on whom the powers of a tenant for life are by the settlement expressed to be conferred[8] to the trustees of the settlement[9].

1   For the meaning of 'tenant for life' see para 671 note 5 ante; definition applied by the Trustee Act 1925 s 68(1) para (15).
2   For the meaning of 'statutory owner' see para 766 note 6 ante; definition applied by ibid s 68(1) para (15).
3   See ibid s 25(2) (as substituted); and TRUSTS vol 48 (Reissue) para 854. For the meaning of 'trust corporation' see para 705 note 6 ante.
4   See ibid s 25(1), (8) (as substituted); and TRUSTS vol 48 (Reissue) para 854. If the person delegating such trusts, powers or discretions is one of two persons constituting the tenant for life or statutory owner and the other of such persons is not a trust corporation, that other person may not be appointed to be an attorney under this provision: see s 25(2) (as substituted); and TRUSTS vol 48 (Reissue) para 854. Delegation cannot be effected by a tenant for life or statutory owner by a general power of attorney under the Powers of Attorney Act 1971: see s 10; and AGENCY vol 1(2) (Reissue) para 45.
5   The notice must specify the date on which the power comes into operation and its duration, the donee of the power, the reason why the power is given and, where some only are delegated, the trusts, powers and discretions delegated: see the Trustee Act 1925 s 25(4) (as substituted); and TRUSTS vol 48 (Reissue) para 854.
6   As to the trustees of the settlement see para 750 et seq ante.
7   See the Trustee Act 1925 s 25(4), (8)(b) (as substituted); and TRUSTS vol 48 (Reissue) para 854.
8   As to such person being a statutory owner see the Settled Land Act 1925 s 23(1)(a); and para 766 ante.
9   Trustee Act 1925 s 25(4), (8)(c) (as substituted: see TRUSTS vol 48 (Reissue) para 854). The instrument creating the power of attorney must be attested by at least one witness: see s 25(3) (as substituted); and TRUSTS vol 48 (Reissue) para 854.

777.   Statutory powers inalienable. A tenant for life may make any arrangement that he pleases for disposing of his beneficial interest[1], but a contract by him not to exercise his statutory powers or any of them is void[2]. The statutory powers[3] are not capable of assignment[4] or release and do not pass to an assignee, by operation of law or otherwise, of the tenant for life, but remain exercisable by the tenant for life after and notwithstanding any assignment, by operation of law or otherwise, of his estate or interest under the settlement[5] and notwithstanding that the estate or interest of the tenant for life under the settlement was not in possession when the assignment was made or took effect by operation of law[6]. This prohibition against alienation does not apply to statutory owners[7].

1   *Re Trenchard, Trenchard v Trenchard* [1902] 1 Ch 378.
2   Settled Land Act 1925 s 104(2). For the meaning of 'tenant for life' see para 671 note 5 ante. See also para 761 et seq ante.
3   Any additional or larger powers conferred by the settlement are also incapable of assignment or release: see ibid s 109(2); and paras 880–881 post.
4   Ibid s 104 extends to assignments made or coming into operation before or after 1925, and for these purposes, 'assignment' includes assignment by way of mortgage, and any partial or qualified assignment and any charge or incumbrance, 'assignee' has a corresponding meaning, and 'assignee for value' includes persons deriving title under the original assignee: s 104(12). As to the power to delegate the statutory powers see para 776 ante.

5 For the meaning of 'settlement' see para 678 note 1 ante.
6 Settled Land Act 1925 s 104(1). As to the effect of an assurance to the next remainderman, however, see para 778 post. In the case of bankruptcy of the tenant for life, the legal estate in the settled land does not vest in the trustee in bankruptcy unless and until the tenant for life becomes absolutely and beneficially entitled to the settled land free from all limitations, powers and charges taking effect under the settlement: see para 698 ante. As to the powers of the court where a tenant for life has parted with his interest see para 765 ante.
7 *Re Craven Settled Estates* [1926] Ch 985. As to statutory owners see para 766 ante.

778. Effect of assurance of life estate to next remainderman. If the estate or interest of a tenant for life[1] under a settlement[2] has been or is absolutely assured either by the tenant for life himself or by any one in whom the life estate is vested[3] with intent[4] to extinguish the same, whenever the assurance[5] was effected, to the person next entitled in remainder or reversion under the settlement[6], then the statutory powers of the tenant for life under the Settled Land Act 1925, in reference to the property[7] affected by the assurance, and notwithstanding the provisions rendering his statutory powers inalienable[8], cease to be exercisable by him and from that time become exercisable as if he were dead, but without prejudice to any incumbrance affecting the estate or interest assured, and to the rights to which any incumbrancer would have been entitled if those powers had remained exercisable by the tenant for life[9]. This provision applies whether or not any term of years or charge intervenes, or the estate of the remainderman or reversioner is liable to be defeated, and whether or not the estate or interest of the tenant for life under the settlement was in possession at the date of the assurance, but unless the assurance provides to the contrary, it does not operate to accelerate any such intervening term of years or charge[10].

These provisions apply so long as the settlement subsists, but an assignment by a tenant for life of his life estate may bring the settlement to an end[11].

1 For the meaning of 'tenant for life' see para 671 note 5 ante. See also para 761 et seq ante.
2 For the meaning of 'settlement' see para 678 note 1 ante.
3 *Re Shawdon Estates Settlement* [1930] 2 Ch 1, CA.
4 The intent must be that of the assignor: *Re Shawdon Estates Settlement* [1930] 2 Ch 1, CA.
5 In this provision, 'assurance' means any surrender, conveyance, assignment or appointment under a power (whether vested in any person solely, or jointly in two or more persons) which operates in equity to extinguish the estate or interest of the tenant for life, and 'assured' has a corresponding meaning: Settled Land Act 1925 s 105(2). For the meaning of 'conveyance' see para 698 note 12 ante. As to assurances generally see REAL PROPERTY vol 39(2) (Reissue) para 232 et seq.
6 A person is not next entitled for this purpose if there is an intervening limitation which may still take effect: *Re Maryon-Wilson's Instruments, Blofeld v Maryon-Wilson* [1971] Ch 789, [1969] 3 All ER 558.
7 'Property' includes any thing in action, and any interest in real or personal property: Settled Land Act 1925 s 117(1)(xx).
8 See para 777 ante.
9 Settled Land Act 1925 s 105(1) (amended by the Law of Property (Amendment) Act 1926 s 7, Schedule). On such an assurance being executed the assignee will, if the land remains settled land, become entitled to have a vesting deed executed in his favour (see para 698 ante), but until a new vesting deed is executed a purchaser will be entitled to deal with the person named in the existing vesting deed as the tenant for life: see para 886 post.
10 Settled Land Act 1925 s 105(1). This provision does not prejudice anything done by the tenant for life before 1926 in exercise of any power operating under the Settled Land Acts 1882 to 1890 (see para 678 note 1 ante): Settled Land Act 1925 s 105(1).
11 Cf *Re Hind, Bernstone v Montgomery* [1933] Ch 208.

779. Effect of assignment for value. In the case of an assignment for value[1] made or coming into operation after 1925, the consent of the assignee is not requisite for the exercise by the tenant for life[2] of any of the statutory powers[3]. However,

(1) the assignee is entitled to the same or the like estate or interest in or charge on the land, money or securities[4] for the time being representing the land, money or

securities comprised in the assignment as he had by virtue of the assignment in the last-mentioned land, money or securities[5];

(2)   if the assignment so provides, or if it takes effect by operation of the law of bankruptcy, and after notice of it to the trustees of the settlement[6], no investment or application of capital money for the time being affected by the assignment may be made without the consent of the assignee, except an investment in securities authorised by statute for the investment of trust money[7]; and

(3)   unless the assignment otherwise provides, notice of the intended transaction must be given to the assignee, but a purchaser is not concerned to see or inquire whether such notice has been given[8].

1   For the meaning of 'assignment' see para 777 note 4 ante. An assignment, by operation of the law of bankruptcy, which comes into operation after 1925 is deemed to be an assignment for value for the purpose of the Settled Land Act 1925 s 104: s 104(10). As to assignment taking effect by operation of the law of bankruptcy see BANKRUPTCY AND INSOLVENCY vol 3(2) (Reissue) para 204 et seq.

2   For the meaning of 'tenant for life' see para 671 note 5 ante. See also para 761 et seq ante.

3   Settled Land Act 1925 s 104(4).

4   For the meaning of 'land' see para 680 note 1 ante; and for the meaning of 'securities' see para 693 note 1 ante.

5   Settled Land Act 1925 s 104(4) proviso (a).

6   For the meaning of 'trustees of the settlement' see para 750 note 1 ante. As to the trustees see para 750 et seq ante.

7   Settled Land Act 1925 s 104(4) proviso (b). As to such consent see para 780 post. As to what securities are authorised for the investment of trust money see para 668 ante; and TRUSTS vol 48 (Reissue) para 871 et seq.

8   Ibid s 104(4) proviso (c). For the meaning of 'purchaser' see para 702 note 12 ante. As to the position where the assignment was made before 1926 see s 104(3), (5).

780. Consent to investment after assignment. Where there has been an assignment for value[1], consent to any such investment or application of capital money may be given by specified persons[2].

The consent may be given by a trustee or personal representative[3] who is an assignee for value[4], and the trustee or personal representative may by the consent bind all persons interested in the trust estate, or the estate of the testator or intestate[5].

If, by the original assignment or by any subsequent disposition, the estate or interest assigned or created by the original assignment, or any part of it or any derivative interest, is settled on persons in succession, whether subject to any prior charge or not, and there is no trustee or personal representative in whom the entirety of the estate or interest so settled is vested, the consent may be given by the person for the time being entitled in possession under the limitations of that settlement, whether as trustee or beneficiary, or who would, if of full age[6], be so entitled, and notwithstanding any charge or incumbrance subsisting or to arise under that settlement, and that person may by the consent bind all persons interested or to become interested under the settlement[7].

If an assignee for value or any person who has power to give such consent is a child[8], the consent may be given on his behalf by his parents or parent or testamentary or other guardian named in the order[9].

The court[10] has power to authorise any person interested under any assignment to consent to any such investment or application of capital money, on behalf of himself and all other persons interested, or who may become interested under the assignment[11].

1   For the meaning of 'assignment' see para 777 note 4 ante. See also para 779 note 1 ante.

2   See the Settled Land Act 1925 s 104(6)–(9) (see the text and notes 5–11 infra). As to the consent to the exercise by the tenant for life of his statutory powers where the assignment was made before 1926 see s 104(3), (6)–(9). For the meaning of 'tenant for life' see para 671 note 5 ante.

3   For the meaning of 'personal representative' see para 697 note 6 ante.

4   As to the meaning of 'assignee for value' see para 777 note 4 ante.
5   See the Settled Land Act 1925 s 104(6).
6   As to consents on behalf of a child see the text to note 8 infra. As to the age of majority see para 605 note 1 ante.
7   Settled Land Act 1925 s 104(7).
8   See para 665 note 13 ante.
9   See the Settled Land Act 1925 s 104(8). As to guardians see CHILDREN AND YOUNG PERSONS vol 5(2) (Reissue) para 739 et seq.
10 As to the court see para 792 post.
11 See the Settled Land Act 1925 s 104(9). As to capital money see para 795 post.

781. Rights of purchaser of life interest. Where (1) on 1 January 1926 the legal beneficial interest of a tenant for life[1] under a settlement[2] was vested in a purchaser[3]; or (2) after 31 December 1925 a tenant for life conveys or deals with his beneficial interest in possession in favour of a purchaser, and the interest so conveyed or created would, but for the restrictions imposed by statute on the creation of legal estates[4], have been a legal interest[5], the purchaser (without prejudice to the powers conferred by the Settled Land Act 1925 on the tenant for life) has and is entitled to exercise all the same rights and remedies[6] as he would have had or have been entitled to exercise if the interest had remained or been a legal interest and the reversion, if any, on any leases or tenancies derived out of the settled land[7] had been vested in him[8].

1   For the meaning of 'tenant for life' see para 671 note 5 ante. See also para 761 et seq ante.
2   For the meaning of 'settlement' see para 678 note 1 ante.
3   Settled Land Act 1925 s 111(a). For the meaning of 'purchaser' see para 702 note 12 ante.
4   As to what legal estates can be created see REAL PROPERTY vol 39(2) (Reissue) para 91 et seq.
5   Settled Land Act 1925 s 111(b).
6   Eg to distrain or recover possession on forfeiture: see REAL PROPERTY vol 39(2) (Reissue) para 253.
7   For the meaning of 'settled land' see para 680 text to note 2 ante.
8   Settled Land Act 1925 s 111. The purchaser is not entitled to the possession of the documents of title: see para 773 ante.

782. Prohibitions against exercise of powers void. Notwithstanding anything in a settlement[1], the exercise by a tenant for life[2] or statutory owner[3] of his statutory powers cannot occasion a forfeiture[4]. If in a settlement, will, assurance or other instrument[5], whenever made[6], a provision is inserted: (1) purporting or attempting, by way of direction, declaration or otherwise, to forbid a tenant for life or statutory owner to exercise any statutory power, or his right to require the settled land to be vested in him[7]; or (2) attempting or tending or intended, by a limitation[8], gift or disposition over of settled land, or of other real or any personal property[9], or by the imposition of any condition[10], or by forfeiture, or in any other manner whatever, to prohibit or prevent him from exercising, or to induce him to abstain from exercising, or to put him into a position inconsistent with his exercising any power under the Settled Land Act 1925, or his right to require the settled land to be vested in him[11], that provision, so far as it purports, or attempts or tends or is intended to have, or would or might have, such operation, is deemed to be void[12]. For these purposes, an estate or interest limited to continue so long only as a person abstains from exercising any such power or right is and takes effect as an estate or interest to continue for the period for which it would continue if that person were to abstain from exercising the power or right, discharged from liability to determination or cesser by or on his exercising the same[13].

It follows that a gift over on failure to comply with a condition as to residence in a particular house may be defeated by the exercise of the statutory powers[14], and it is immaterial that the gift over is of property settled by a person other than the original settlor by an instrument other than the original settlement[15]. Such a condition, however, is void only so far as it is a fetter on the exercise of the statutory powers[16], and a testator can oblige a tenant for life to reside in a mansion until it is disposed of by exercise of the statutory powers, and his failure to comply with this condition causes him to forfeit his interest[17]. However, a provision that the tenant for life of a house while in occupation is to be free from all outgoings does not tend to induce him to refrain from exercising the statutory power of sale[18], nor does a direction terminating a provision which is neither for the benefit of the tenant for life nor ancillary to the enjoyment by him of the trust property[19].

1   For the meaning of 'settlement' see para 678 note 1 ante.
2   For the meaning of 'tenant for life' see para 671 note 5 ante. See also para 761 et seq ante.
3   For the meaning of 'statutory owner' see para 766 note 6 ante.
4   Settled Land Act 1925 s 106(3).
5   For the meaning of 'will' see para 695 note 3 ante; and for the meaning of 'instrument' see para 688 note 7 ante.
6   See *Re Smith, Grose-Smith v Bridger* [1899] 1 Ch 331.
7   Settled Land Act 1925 s 106(1)(a). For the meaning of 'settled land' see para 680 text to note 2 ante.
8   For the meaning of 'limitation' see para 708 note 4 ante.
9   See *Re Ames, Ames v Ames* [1893] 2 Ch 479; *Re Smith, Grose-Smith v Bridger* [1899] 1 Ch 331; *Re Fitzgerald, Brereton v Day* [1902] 1 IR 162; *Re Patten, Westminster Bank Ltd v Carlyon* [1929] 2 Ch 276; *Re Herbert, Herbert v Lord Bicester* [1946] 1 All ER 421.
10   See *Re Richardson, Richardson v Richardson* [1904] 2 Ch 777, where a direction that a beneficiary should provide a home for a named person was held to be a condition. See also para 762 note 14 ante.
11   Settled Land Act 1925 s 106(1)(b).
12   Ibid s 106(1). See also *Re Patten, Westminster Bank Ltd v Carlyon* [1929] 2 Ch 276. This provision does not apply unless the settlement contains a provision which, but for an attempted prohibition, would constitute a tenant for life capable of exercising the statutory powers: *Re Hazle's Settled Estates* (1885) 29 ChD 78, CA; *Re Atkinson, Atkinson v Bruce* (1886) 31 ChD 577, CA. It is no longer possible to create settlements under the Settled Land Act 1925: see para 676 ante.
13   Ibid s 106(2).
14   *Re Paget's Settled Estates* (1885) 30 ChD 161; *Re Dalrymple, Bircham v Springfield* (1901) 49 WR 627; *Re Adair and Settled Land Act* [1909] 1 IR 311; *Re Acklom, Oakeshott v Hawkins* [1929] 1 Ch 195; *Re Orlebar, Orlebar v Orlebar* [1936] Ch 147. As to conditions as to residence generally see para 741 note 4 ante.
15   *Re Smith, Grose-Smith v Bridger* [1899] 1 Ch 331; *Re Orlebar, Orlebar v Orlebar* [1936] Ch 147.
16   *Re Trenchard, Trenchard v Trenchard* [1902] 1 Ch 378; *Re Bellew, O'Reilly v Bellew* [1924] 1 IR 1, Ir CA; *Re Patten, Westminster Bank Ltd v Carlyon* [1929] 2 Ch 276.
17   *Re Haynes, Kemp v Haynes* (1887) 37 ChD 306; *Re Edwards' Settlement* [1897] 2 Ch 412; *Re Trenchard, Trenchard v Trenchard* [1902] 1 Ch 378.
18   *Re Simpson, Clarke v Simpson* [1913] 1 Ch 277; *Re Burden, Mitchell v Trustees of St Luke's Hostel* [1948] 1 All ER 31.
19   *Re Aberconway's Settlement Trusts, McLaren v Aberconway* [1953] Ch 647, [1953] 2 All ER 350, CA.

(ii) Preliminaries to exercise of Statutory Powers

A. NOTICE TO, AND RECEIPT OF, TRUSTEES

783. Requirement, form and effect of notice. A tenant for life[1] or statutory owner[2], when intending to make a sale, exchange, lease[3], mortgage or charge, or to grant an option, must give notice[4], which (except in the case of a mortgage or charge[5]) may be notice of a general intention, of his intention in that behalf to each of the trustees of the settlement[6], unless the intention is to grant a lease for a term not exceeding 21 years at the best rent that can be reasonably obtained without fine and by which the lessee is not exempted from punishment for waste[7]. Such a lease may be made without notice[8], and notwithstanding that there are no such trustees of the settlement[9].

The notice must be given by posting registered letters or the recorded delivery service addressed to the trustees severally, and to the solicitor for the trustees, if any such solicitor is known to the tenant for life or statutory owner, and posted not less than one month before the making or granting of the sale, exchange, lease, mortgage, charge or option, or of a contract for the same[10].

The notice is not a mere formality, as, if the tenant for life attempted to commit a fraud, for example by proposing to sell the property for something very much below its real value, the trustees can apply for an injunction[11]. A notice will not be valid unless at its date the trustee is a trust corporation or the number of the trustees is not less than two[12]. Consequently, unless one or other of those conditions is fulfilled, a tenant for life may be restrained from exercising any of the powers mentioned until trustees have been appointed[13], and, if the sanction of the court is required to such exercise, an application for leave will be ordered to stand over until trustees have been appointed[14]. Any trustee, by writing under his hand, may waive notice, either in any particular case or generally, and may accept less than one month's notice[15].

On request by a trustee of the settlement, a tenant for life or statutory owner must also furnish to him such particulars and information as may reasonably be required by him from time to time with reference to sales, exchanges or leases effected, or in progress, or immediately intended[16].

1 For the meaning of 'tenant for life' see para 671 note 5 ante. See also para 761 et seq ante.
2 For the meaning of 'statutory owner' see para 766 note 6 ante.
3 For the meaning of 'lease' see para 685 note 13 ante.
4 A distinction is drawn between the making of the sale, exchange, lease, mortgage or charge, and the making of the contract; if the notice is given before either one of these two things it is good, and it is no objection that the notice given did not expire until after the contract became binding between the parties: see *Duke of Marlborough v Sartoris* (1886) 32 ChD 616. As to the giving of notice by the receiver for a tenant for life who is suffering from mental disorder see MENTAL HEALTH vol 30 (Reissue) para 1459.
5 In the case of a mortgage or charge the notice should specify the particular transaction intended: see *Re Ray's Settled Estates* (1884) 25 ChD 464.
6 For the meaning of 'trustees of the settlement' see para 750 note 1 ante. As to the trustees see para 750 et seq ante.
7 See the Settled Land Act 1925 ss 42(5)(i)(a), 101(1)(a), (2). As to waste see para 986 et seq post.
8 Ibid s 42(5)(i)(a).
9 Ibid s 42(5)(i)(b).
10 See ibid s 101(1); and the Recorded Delivery Service Act 1962 s 1(1) (see POST OFFICE).
11 See *Wheelwright v Walker* (1883) 23 ChD 752 at 762 (where it was stated that the trustees would be under a duty to apply for an injunction); *Re Lord Monson's Settled Estates* [1898] 1 Ch 427 at 432. However, the Settled Land Act 1925 s 97 (see para 891 post), relieves them from liability for not taking proceedings: see *England v Public Trustee* (1967) 205 Estates Gazette 651, CA, where the trustee was under no liability for not taking proceedings to prevent a bona fide, but improvident, sale.
12 Settled Land Act 1925 s 101(1) proviso. For the meaning of 'trust corporation' see para 705 note 6 ante.
13 See *Wheelwright v Walker* (1883) 23 ChD 752; *Re Bentley, Wade v Wilson* (1885) 54 LJ Ch 782. See also INJUNCTIONS vol 24 (Reissue) para 930.
14 *Re Taylor* (1883) 52 LJ Ch 728, CA.
15 Settled Land Act 1925 s 101(4).
16 Ibid s 101(3).

784. Persons dealing with tenant for life. A person dealing in good faith with the tenant for life[1] is not concerned to inquire respecting the giving to the trustees of notice of intention to exercise statutory powers[2]. Default in giving notice to the trustees is not a defect in the title of the tenant for life[3], nor is the non-existence of trustees[4], unless the transaction involves the payment of capital money, which must be paid either to the trustees or into court at the option of the tenant for life[5], and, since he can only exercise his option if there are trustees, the person paying the capital money is thus bound to ascertain that there are trustees to whom it could be paid[6]. However, a person dealing with the tenant for life, if he knows that there are no trustees, is probably justified in refusing to complete, even if no capital money has to be received by them[7]; and a purchaser who knows that there are no trustees cannot be compelled to pay his purchase money into court, but he would get a good title if he did so in ignorance of the non-existence of the trustees[8]. An agreement for a lease when the intending lessee knows that there are no trustees in existence is not binding on the remaindermen[9].

1   For the meaning of 'tenant for life' see para 671 note 5 ante. See also para 761 et seq ante.
2   Settled Land Act 1925 s 101(5). The notice referred to in the text is that required under s 101 (see para 783 ante): see s 101(5). See further *Duke of Marlborough v Sartoris* (1886) 32 ChD 616 at 623; *Hatten v Russell* (1888) 38 ChD 334. As to the protection of purchasers see para 885 et seq post.
3   *Hatten v Russell* (1888) 38 ChD 334.
4   *Mogridge v Clapp* [1892] 3 Ch 382, CA.
5   See the Settled Land Act 1925 s 75(1); and para 804 post. As to capital money see para 795 post.
6   *Mogridge v Clapp* [1892] 3 Ch 382, CA.
7   *Mogridge v Clapp* [1892] 3 Ch 382 at 400, CA. Under the Settled Land Act 1925 s 110(4), where no capital money arises under a transaction, a disposition by a tenant for life or statutory owner, in favour of a purchaser of a legal estate, has effect under the Act notwithstanding that at the date of the transaction there are no trustees of the settlement (see para 888 post); but 'purchaser' means a purchaser in good faith for value, and includes a lessee, mortgagee, or other person who in good faith acquires an interest in settled land for value (see para 702 note 12 ante), so it would seem that a purchaser who knows that there are no trustees would not be able to claim that protection.
8   *Re Fisher and Grazebrook's Contract* [1898] 2 Ch 660.
9   *Hughes v Fanagan* (1891) 30 LR Ir 111, Ir CA.

785. Effect of receipt or direction of trustees. The receipt or direction in writing of or by the trustees of the settlement[1], or, where a sole trustee is a trust corporation[2], of or by that trustee, or of or by the personal representatives[3] of the last surviving or continuing trustee, for or relating to any money[4] or securities[5] paid or transferred to or by the direction of the trustees, trustee or representatives, as the case may be, effectually discharges the payer or transferor from payment, and from being bound to see to the application or being answerable for any loss or misapplication of it, and, in the case of a mortgagee or other person advancing money, from being concerned to see that any money advanced by him is wanted for any purpose of the Settled Land Act 1925, or that no more than is wanted is raised[6].

1   For the meaning of 'trustees of the settlement' see para 750 note 1 ante. As to the trustees see para 750 et seq ante.
2   For the meaning of 'trust corporation' see para 705 note 6 ante.
3   For the meaning of 'personal representative' see para 697 note 6 ante.
4   As to the restriction on payment of capital money to a sole trustee see para 786 post.
5   For the meaning of 'securities' see para 693 note 1 ante.
6   Settled Land Act 1925 s 95.

786. Restriction on payment of capital money to a sole trustee. Notwithstanding anything in the Settled Land Act 1925, capital money arising under that Act[1] must not be paid[2] to fewer than two persons[3] as trustees of a settlement[4], unless the trustee is a trust corporation[5]. Trustees of a settlement must concur in a conveyance to receive or direct payment of capital money, since no one else can give a purchaser a good discharge[6]. Where the settlement comes to an end, however, a sole personal representative of a deceased tenant for life can give a good receipt[7].

1   For the meaning of 'capital money arising under the Act' and as to powers in respect of capital money see para 795 et seq post.
2   Capital money must be paid to trustees or into court: see para 797 post.
3   As to the powers of surviving or continuing trustees see para 753 ante.
4   For the meaning of 'trustees of the settlement' see para 750 note 1 ante. As to the trustees see para 750 et seq ante.

5   Settled Land Act 1925 s 94(1). For the meaning of 'trust corporation' see para 705 note 6 ante.
6   *Re Norton and Las Casas' Contract* [1909] 2 Ch 59 (payment must be made to or by the direction of the trustees or into court). As to the payment of capital money in accordance with an order of, or into, court see the Settled Land Act 1925 ss 18(2)(c), 75(1); and paras 712 ante, 804 post.
7   *Re Bridgett and Hayes' Contract* [1928] Ch 163.

B. LEAVE OF THE COURT OR CONSENT OF TRUSTEES

787. Where leave of the court is required. The leave of the court[1] is required to the exercise of the statutory powers in the following cases:

(1)   if it is desired to vary the statutory terms or conditions of a building or mining lease[2];

(2)   on a sale or purchase of personal chattels settled to devolve with land[3];

(3)   on a grant or lease for the purpose of the erection of dwellings for the working classes[4], or the provision of gardens to be held with them, or for the purpose of the Small Holdings and Allotments Acts 1908 to 1931[5], of any part of the settled land exceeding two acres in the case of land situate in a district, or ten acres in the case of land situate in a parish, in any one parish if the full consideration is not paid or reserved in respect of the excess[6];

(4)   on the investment or application of capital money in the purchase of any leasehold interest where the immediate reversion is settled land[7];

(5)   on the execution of a deed confirming past transactions[8]; and

(6)   if it is desired to effect a transaction affecting or concerning the settled land or any other land which is not authorised[9].

1   As to the court see para 792 post.
2   See the Settled Land Act 1925 s 46; and para 844 post.
3   See ibid s 67(3); and para 941 post.
4   As to the phrase 'working classes' see para 775 note 8 ante.
5   As to these Acts and the Acts amending them see ALLOTMENTS AND SMALLHOLDINGS vol 2 (Reissue) para 1 et seq.
6   See the Settled Land Act 1925 s 57(2); the Local Government Act 1972 ss 1(9), 179(3); and paras 831, 841 post.
7   See the Settled Land Act 1925 s 73(1)(xiv); and para 808 head (12) post.
8   See the Law of Property Act 1925 s 66 (as amended); and para 876 post.
9   See the Settled Land Act 1925 s 64 (as amended); and para 671 ante.

788. When consent of the trustees is required. The written consent of the trustees of the settlement[1] is required:

(1)   if the tenant for life[2] desires to compromise, compound, abandon, submit to arbitration or otherwise settle any claim, dispute or question relating to the settled land[3] or any part of it, including in particular claims, disputes or questions as to boundaries, the ownership of mines and minerals[4], rights and powers of working mines and minerals, local laws and customs relative to the working of mines and minerals and other matters, easements and restrictive covenants, and whether or not any consideration in money or otherwise is given or taken[5]; and

(2)   if the tenant for life desires or agrees to release, waive or modify any covenant, agreement or restriction imposed on any other land for the benefit of the settled land, or any part of it, or release or agree to release any other land from any easement, right or privilege, including a right of pre-emption, affecting that land for the benefit of the settled land or any part of it, and whether with or without consideration in money or otherwise[6].

1   For the meaning of 'trustees of the settlement' see para 750 note 1 ante. As to the trustees see para 750 et seq ante.
2   For the meaning of 'tenant for life' see para 671 note 5 ante. See also para 761 et seq ante.
3   For the meaning of 'settled land' see para 680 text to note 2 ante.
4   For the meaning of 'mines and minerals' see para 680 note 1 ante. As to mines and minerals generally see MINES, MINERALS AND QUARRIES.
5   See the Settled Land Act 1925 s 58(1) (as amended); and para 872 post. As to easements and restrictive covenants see EASEMENTS AND PROFITS À PRENDRE; EQUITY vol 16 (Reissue) para 789 et seq.
6   See ibid s 58(2); and para 873 post. A tenant for life may contract that a transaction which is affected by the Railway Clauses Consolidation Act 1845 s 78 (whether subject or not to any variation by the Mines (Working Facilities and Support) Act 1923) or the Waterworks Clauses Act 1847 s 22 takes effect as if some other distance than 40 yards or the prescribed distance had been mentioned: see the Settled Land Act 1925 s 58(3); and MINES, MINERALS AND QUARRIES vol 31 (Reissue) para 151. As to rights of pre-emption see SALE OF LAND para 28 ante.

789. When consent of trustees or court order is required. The consent of the trustees of the settlement[1] or a court order[2], is required:

(1)   to the cutting and sale of timber by a tenant for life[3] impeachable for waste[4]; and

(2)   to the exercise of the statutory powers of disposing of settled land[5] as respects the principal mansion house[6], if any, on any settled land, and the pleasure grounds and park[7] and lands, if any, usually occupied with it[8], where the settlement is made or comes into operation before 1926, if the settlement did not expressly provide to the contrary[9], and where the settlement is made or comes into operation after 1925, if the settlement expressly provides that those powers or any of them are not to be exercised without such consent or order[10]. For this purpose, the court may at any time say whether or not a particular house is the principal mansion house, and, having regard to the state of facts existing at the date of the application to it, may come to the conclusion that a house which was formerly a principal mansion house has ceased to be such[11]. If two estates are settled by the same settlement, with a mansion house on each, there may be two principal mansion houses on the settled land[12].

1   For the meaning of 'trustees of the settlement' see para 750 note 1 ante. As to the trustees see para 750 et seq ante.
2   As to the court see paras 792–793 post.
3   For the meaning of 'tenant for life' see para 671 note 5 ante. See also para 761 et seq ante.
4   See the Settled Land Act 1925 s 66; and para 848 post. As to waste see para 986 et seq post.
5   For the meaning of 'dispose of' see para 685 note 14 ante. For the meaning of 'settled land' see para 680 text to note 2 ante.
6   Where a house is usually occupied as a farmhouse, or where the site of any house and the pleasure grounds and park and land, if any, usually occupied with it do not together exceed 25 acres in extent, the house is not to be deemed a principal mansion house for this purpose and may accordingly be disposed of in like manner as any other part of the settled land: Settled Land Act 1925 s 65(2).
7   The word 'park' is not used in the sense of an ancient legal park, but according to its ordinary meaning in common parlance: see *Pease v Courtney* [1904] 2 Ch 503.
8   Settled Land Act 1925 s 65(1). The words 'usually occupied therewith' apply merely to the words 'lands, if any', immediately preceding them, so that a park not usually occupied with the principal mansion house may be within this restriction: see *Pease v Courtney* [1904] 2 Ch 503. See, however, *Lord Bruce v Marquess of Ailesbury* [1892] AC 356 at 360, HL.
9   See the Settled Land Act 1925 s 65(1) proviso (a).
10   Ibid s 65(1) proviso (b). As to consents to dispositions to the National Trust see OPEN SPACES AND ANCIENT MONUMENTS vol 34 (Reissue) para 113. It is no longer possible to create settlements under the Settled Land Act 1925: see para 676 ante.
11   See *Re Wythes' Settled Estates* [1908] 1 Ch 593; *Re Feversham Settled Estates* [1938] 2 All ER 210.
12   See *Gilbey v Rush* [1906] 1 Ch 11.

790. How consent of the trustees is given. The consent of the trustees[1] must be the consent of all the trustees, given at the time and with reference to the particular transaction proposed, but it need not be in writing, and it is immaterial whether it is expressed orally or otherwise to the parties. Provided that it is given to the actual transaction proposed, it makes no difference that it was given in the belief that the house affected was not the principal mansion house[2].

1 Ie the consent of the trustees to disposal of the mansion house: see para 789 ante.
2 *Gilbey v Rush* [1906] 1 Ch 11.

791. Principles on which the court acts. In sanctioning a sale of the principal mansion house[1], the court is bound to consider the interests of the persons entitled under the settlement, but in the Settled Land Act 1925 the paramount object of the legislature is the well-being of the settled land, and the public interests, in the sense of the interests of those who live upon the soil, ought to outweigh all considerations of sentimental interest in the family[2]. The facts that the estate is not an old family estate and that the settlor has directed a sale on the death of the tenant for life may make the court readier to consent to a sale[3], but, on the other hand, the consent is not refused merely because the settlor in creating the settlement has annexed a qualification that the mansion house is not to be sold[4], or a condition as to residence[5]. However, if the tenant for life has mortgaged his life interest to its full value, the court declines to make an order to sanction a sale without the consent of the mortgagee being obtained to it, and without full information as to the proposed sale[6].

The same principles apply to the exercise of the statutory power of leasing the principal mansion house, and the pleasure grounds and park and land usually occupied with it, the consent of the trustees or of the court being required to any exercise of such power, and a condition as to residence is inoperative to prevent such exercise[7].

1 See para 789 ante.
2 See *Re Marquis of Ailesbury's Settled Estates* [1892] 1 Ch 506, CA; affd sub nom *Lord Bruce v Marquess of Ailesbury* [1892] AC 356, HL.
3 See *Re Wortham's Settled Estates* (1896) 75 LT 293.
4 See *Re Brown's Will* (1884) 27 ChD 179 (where the court declined to grant leave without a direction as to what was to be done with chattels settled to devolve with the house). As to sanctioning a sale of settled chattels see para 942 post.
5 See *Re Paget's Settled Estates* (1885) 30 ChD 161; and para 782 ante.
6 See *Re Sebright's Settled Estates* (1886) 33 ChD 429 at 442, CA. See also MORTGAGE.
7 See *Re Thompson's Will* (1888) 21 LR Ir 109.

C. APPLICATIONS TO THE COURT

792. Jurisdiction and procedure. All matters within the jurisdiction of the court under the Settled Land Act 1925 are, subject to the enactments for the time being in force with respect to the procedure of the Supreme Court of Judicature, assigned to the Chancery Division of the High Court[1].

The powers of the court may, as regards land[2] not exceeding in capital value the county court limit[3], or in net annual value for rating the county court limit[4], and, as regards capital money arising under the Settled Land Act 1925[5], and securities[6] in which the same is invested, not exceeding in amount or value the county court limit, and as regards personal chattels settled or to be settled in accordance with that Act[7], not exceeding the county court limit, be exercised by any county court[8]. The jurisdiction of the county court can, however, be extended by the consent of the parties[9], and the High Court has power to transfer proceedings to the county court even if the limits set out above are exceeded[10].

1 Settled Land Act 1925 s 113(1). As to the Supreme Court of Judicature see COURTS. Payment of money into court effectually exonerates from payment the person making the payment: s 113(4). As to applications to the court see s 113(5); RSC Ord 5 r 3; CCR Ord 3 r 4; and, as from 26 April 1999, CPR Pts 7, 8. See further PRACTICE AND PROCEDURE. On any application notice must be served on such persons, if any, as the court thinks fit, and on an application by the trustees of a settlement notice must be served in the first instance on the tenant for life: see the Settled Land Act 1925 s 113(6), (7). For the meaning of 'trustees of the settlement' see para 750 note 1 ante; and for the meaning of 'tenant for life' see para 671 note 5 ante.

   The court has full power and discretion to make such order as it thinks fit respecting the costs, charges, or expenses of all or any of the parties to any application, and may, if it thinks fit, order that all or any of those costs, charges, or expenses be paid out of property subject to the settlement: s 113(8). For the meaning of 'property' see para 778 note 7 ante; and for the meaning of 'settlement' see para 678 note 1 ante. Costs have been allowed where the application was unsuccessful (*Re Horne's Settled Estate* (1888) 39 ChD 84, CA), and, on the other hand, the costs of a successful application have been ordered to be paid by the tenant for life (*Re Bagot's Settlement, Bagot v Kittoe* [1894] 1 Ch 177). Where trustees are the applicants the ordinary rule as to their costs is followed: see TRUSTS vol 48 (Reissue) para 787 et seq. Where trustees concurred in an application as to improvements without appearing separately, the court declined to allow their costs out of the estate: see *Re Broadwater Estate* (1885) 54 LJ Ch 1104, CA. Where trustees acted reasonably in taking different views, they were allowed separate costs: see *Re Marquis of Ailesbury's Settled Estates* [1892] 1 Ch 506 at 548, CA. As to costs see generally RSC Ord 62; as from 26 April 1999, CPR Pts 43–48; and PRACTICE AND PROCEDURE.
2 For the meaning of 'land' see para 680 note 1 ante.
3 For these purposes, 'the county court limit' means the county court limit for the time being specified by an Order in Council under the County Courts Act 1984 s 145 (see COUNTY COURTS) as the county court limit for the purposes of the Settled Land Act 1925 s 113(3) (as substituted): s 113(3A) (added by the Administration of Justice Act 1982 s 37, Sch 3 Pt II para 4; and amended by the County Courts Act 1984 s 148(1), Sch 2 Pt V para 20). As to the county court limit see COUNTY COURTS.
4 Rates and rateable values were abolished by the Local Government Finance Act 1988: see RATING AND COUNCIL TAX vol 39(1) (Reissue) para 602. However, references in the Settled Land Act 1925 s 113 (as amended) to net annual value for rating or rateable value are to be construed as references to a sum equivalent to the last such value of the property concerned immediately before 1 April 1990, or, if it did not have one, to the rateable value of the hereditament of which it is, or was, part or failing that, the value by the year which the land has at the commencement of proceedings: see the Local Government Finance (Repeals, Savings and Consequential Amendments) Order 1990, SI 1990/776, art 4.
5 As to such capital money see para 795 et seq post.
6 For the meaning of 'securities' see para 693 note 1 ante.
7 It is no longer possible to create settlements under the Settled Land Act 1925: see para 676 ante.
8 Ibid s 113(3) (substituted by the County Courts Act 1984 Sch 2 Pt V para 20). As to payment or transfer of money, securities or proceeds of sale being paid or transferred into the court see para 798 note 8 post.
9 See the County Courts Act 1984 s 24 (as amended); and COUNTY COURTS.
10 See ibid s 40 (as substituted); and PRACTICE AND PROCEDURE. As to the power of the Lord Chancellor to make orders allocating business between the High Court and county courts see the Courts and Legal Services Act 1990 s 1; and PRACTICE AND PROCEDURE; COUNTY COURTS.

793. Reference of questions to the court. If a question arises or a doubt is entertained:

(1) respecting the exercise or intended exercise of any of the powers conferred by the Settled Land Act 1925, or any enactment replaced by that Act[1], or the settlement[2], or any matter relating to it[3];

(2) as to the person in whose favour a vesting deed or assent[4] ought to be executed, or as to its contents[5]; or

(3) otherwise in relation to property[6] subject to a settlement[7],

the tenant for life[8] or statutory owner[9], or the trustees of the settlement[10], or any other person interested under the settlement, may apply to the court for its decision or directions on it, or for the court's sanction to any conditional contract, and the court may make such order or give such directions respecting the matter as it thinks fit[11]. In the absence of bad faith, the court will not order a sale under this power where two persons who jointly constitute the tenant for life disagree as to whether the property should be sold[12].

1 Ie the Settled Land Acts 1882 to 1890: see para 678 note 1 ante.
2 For the meaning of 'settlement' see para 678 note 1 ante.
3 Settled Land Act 1925 s 93(a).
4 For the meaning of 'vesting deed' see para 688 note 6 ante; and for the meaning of 'vesting assent' see para 690 note 8 ante.
5 Settled Land Act 1925 s 93(b).
6 For the meaning of 'property' see para 778 note 7 ante.
7 Settled Land Act 1925 s 93(c).
8 For the meaning of 'tenant for life' see para 671 note 5 ante. See also para 761 et seq ante.
9 For the meaning of 'statutory owner' see para 766 note 6 ante.
10 For the meaning of 'trustees of the settlement' see para 750 note 1 ante. As to the trustees see para 750 et seq ante.
11 Settled Land Act 1925 s 93. In addition to this provision which gives the court a general jurisdiction, the Settled Land Act 1925 also confers on the court jurisdiction to determine a considerable number of specific matters. The various provisions of the Act conferring such jurisdiction are set out in the text in conjunction with the matters to which they relate.
12 *Re 90, Thornhill Road, Tolworth, Surrey, Barker v Addiscott* [1970] Ch 261, [1969] 3 All ER 685.

(iii) Power to effect Improvements

794. Powers as regards improvements. The tenant for life[1] and each of his successors in title having under the trust instrument[2] a limited estate or interest in the settled land[3], and all persons employed by or under contract with him or them, may from time to time enter on the settled land and, without impeachment of waste by any remainderman or reversioner, execute on it any improvement authorised by the Settled Land Act 1925[4], or inspect, maintain and repair it[5]. For these purposes such persons may do, make and use on the settled land all proper acts, works and conveniences, and may get and work freestone, limestone, clay, sand and other substances, make tramways and other ways, burn and make bricks, tiles and other things, and cut down and use timber and other trees not planted or left standing for shelter or ornament[6].

A tenant for life may enter into a contract for or relating to the execution of any improvement authorised by the Settled Land Act 1925, and may vary or rescind it[7]. He may also join or concur with any other person interested in executing, or contributing to the costs of, any improvement authorised by the Settled Land Act 1925[8].

1 For the meaning of 'tenant for life' see para 671 note 5 ante. See also para 761 et seq ante. As to the exercise of the powers of a tenant for life by statutory owners see para 766 ante.
2 For the meaning of 'trust instrument' see para 688 note 7 ante.
3 For the meaning of 'settled land' see para 680 text to note 2 ante.
4 As to these improvements see para 815 et seq post. As to impeachment for waste see para 986 et seq post.
5 Settled Land Act 1925 s 89.
6 Ibid s 89. As to cutting timber see further para 848 et seq post.
7 Ibid s 90(1)(v). As to such contracts see further paras 869–870 post.
8 Ibid s 86. This includes the investment of capital money in a water company formed to supply water to a building estate: see *Re Orwell Park Estate* (1894) 8 R 521.

(iv) Powers in respect of Capital Money

795. Meaning of 'capital money arising under the Act'. 'Capital money arising under the Settled Land Act 1925' means capital money arising under the powers and provisions of that Act, or the Acts replaced by it[1], and receivable for the trusts and purposes of the settlement[2], and includes securities[3] representing capital money[4]. Capital money may arise either by reason of the exercise of the statutory powers[5] or by virtue of other statutory provisions[6].

1 Ie the Settled Land Acts 1882 to 1890: see para 678 note 1 ante.
2 For the meaning of 'settlement' see para 678 note 1 ante.
3 For the meaning of 'securities' see para 693 note 1 ante.
4 Settled Land Act 1925 s 117(1)(ii).
5 See eg para 920 post (sale of investments); para 921 et seq post (sale of land); para 778 note 7 ante (grant of lease subject to fine); para 843 post (lease of mines); para 848 post (sale of timber); para 941 post (sale of heirlooms); and para 849 post (sums raised by mortgage). As to money arising on the exercise of a number of the powers grouped in the Settled Land Act 1925 under the heading 'Miscellaneous Powers' see para 856 et seq post.
6 Compensation payable under the Land Compensation Act 1973 Pt I (ss 1–19) (as amended), for injury to the value of settled land (see COMPULSORY ACQUISITION OF LAND vol 8(1) (Reissue) para 360 et seq) is treated as capital money arising under the Settled Land Act 1925: see the Land Compensation Act 1973 s 10(3); and COMPULSORY ACQUISITION OF LAND vol 8(1) (Reissue) para 374. An advance payment on account of compensation payable for a compulsory purchase of settled land is also treated as such capital money: see s 52(7); and COMPULSORY ACQUISITION OF LAND vol 8(1) (Reissue) para 136. See also paras 796–797 post.

796. Money liable under settlement to be laid out in purchase of land. Where (1) under any instrument[1], whenever it came into operation, money is in the hands of trustees, including money in court[2], and is liable[3] to be laid out in the purchase of land[4] to be made subject to the trusts declared by that instrument[5]; or (2) under any instrument which came into operation after 1925, money or securities[6] or the proceeds of sale of any property[7] is or are held by trustees on trusts creating entailed interests in it[8], then, in addition to such powers of dealing with them as the trustees have independently of the Settled Land Act 1925, they may, at the option of the tenant for life[9], invest or apply the money, securities or proceeds as if they were capital money arising under that Act[10].

On the principle that the erection of a building is substantially the same thing as the purchase of land[11], money liable to be laid out in the purchase of land, independently of the above power to invest or apply the money as if it were capital money arising under that Act, may be applied in the erection of new buildings on settled land or in rebuilding houses which are in a ruinous state (if the rebuilding would be beneficial to the estate) either on the land settled or on the land to be purchased[12], although not under this principle in improvements[13] or repairs of existing buildings or in reinstating a mansion house destroyed by fire[14].

Money liable to be laid out in the purchase of land to be made subject to the settlement includes money bequeathed to trustees on trust to be laid out in land in strict settlement[15], the proceeds of sale of settled land directed by a court order to be invested in consols pending the purchase of other hereditaments to be settled in the same manner as the land that was sold[16], money the investment of which in land is deferred[17], a sinking fund to replace a sum raised by mortgage for the purposes of improvements on settled estates[18], and money subject to a disposition under which it may be, although it is not bound to be, laid out in the purchase of land[19], or of some particular parcel of land[20], or of freehold ground rents[21].

1 For the meaning of 'instrument' see para 688 note 7 ante.
2 See *Clarke v Thornton* (1887) 35 ChD 307 at 314. The Settled Land Act 1925 s 77 does not expressly refer to money in court.
3 This includes a mere power: see *Re Hill, Hill v Pilcher* [1896] 1 Ch 962.
4 For the meaning of 'land' see para 680 note 1 ante.
5 Settled Land Act 1925 s 77(a). As to the proceeds of investments sold see para 826 post.
6 For the meaning of 'securities' see para 693 note 1 ante.

7   For the meaning of 'property' see para 778 note 7 ante.

8   Settled Land Act 1925 s 77(b). For the meaning of 'entailed interest' see para 678 note 11 ante. As to entailed interests see para 715 et seq ante; and REAL PROPERTY vol 39(2) (Reissue) para 117 et seq.

9   See *Re Gee, Pearson Gee v Pearson* (1895) 64 LJ Ch 606. For the meaning of 'tenant for life' see para 671 note 5 ante. See also para 761 et seq ante.

10   Settled Land Act 1925 s 77. For the meaning of 'capital money arising under the Act' see para 795 ante. As to modes of application of capital money see para 808 post.

11   *Re Newman's Settled Estates* (1874) 9 Ch App 681 at 683 per James LJ; *Vine v Raleigh* [1891] 2 Ch 13, CA.

12   *Re Lord Hotham's Trusts* (1871) LR 12 Eq 76; *Lord Cowley v Wellesley* (1877) 46 LJ Ch 869; *Re Blake's Settled Estates* [1923] 2 Ch 128.

13   Capital money may be applied on improvements independently of this principle if the improvements are authorised under the Settled Land Act 1925: see the text to notes 1–10 supra; and para 808 et seq post.

14   See *Re Leigh's Estate* (1871) 6 Ch App 887; *Brunskill v Caird* (1873) LR 16 Eq 493; *Re Newman's Settled Estates* (1874) 9 Ch App 681; *Drake v Trefusis* (1875) 10 Ch App 364. This last-mentioned case has been consistently followed: see *Re Venour's Settled Estates, Venour v Sellon* (1876) 2 ChD 522; *Re Speer's Trusts* (1876) 3 ChD 262; *Donaldson v Donaldson* (1876) 3 ChD 743; *Jesse v Lloyd* (1883) 48 LT 656; *Conway v Fenton* (1888) 40 ChD 512 at 515 per Kekewich J; *Vine v Raleigh* [1891] 2 Ch 13, CA. If any cases (eg *Re Johnson's Settlements* (1869) LR 8 Eq 348; *Earl Poulett v Somerset* (1871) 25 LT 56; *Re Leadbitter* (1882) 30 WR 378) are inconsistent with the principles laid down in *Re Newman's Settled Estates* supra they cannot now be treated as having authority.

15   *Re Mackenzie's Trusts* (1883) 23 ChD 750. See further note 16 infra.

16   *Re Tennant* (1889) 40 ChD 594. This case and *Re Mackenzie's Trusts* (1883) 23 ChD 750 (see note 15 supra) proceeded on the ground that, if the investment had been made, the land purchased could have been sold and the proceeds invested under the Settled Land Acts. Both these decisions were approved in *Re Mundy's Settled Estates* [1891] 1 Ch 399, CA.

17   *Re Maberly, Maberly v Maberly* (1886) 33 ChD 455. See, however, *Burke v Gore* (1884) 13 LR Ir 367.

18   *Re Sudbury and Poynton Estates, Vernon v Vernon* [1893] 3 Ch 74. As to improvements see para 809 et seq post.

19   *Re Soltau's Trust* [1898] 2 Ch 629.

20   *Re Hill, Hill v Pilcher* [1896] 1 Ch 962.

21   *Re Thomas, Weatherall v Thomas* [1900] 1 Ch 319 at 323.

797. Money in court liable under statute to be laid out in purchase of land.

Where under an Act, or an order or scheme confirmed by or having the force of an Act of Parliament, incorporating or applying, wholly or in part, the Lands Clauses Acts[1], or under any Act, public general, or local or private, money is in court and is liable to be laid out in the purchase of land[2] to be made subject to a settlement[3], then, in addition to any mode of dealing with it authorised by the statute under which the money is in court, that money may be invested or applied as capital money arising under the Settled Land Act 1925[4] on the like terms, if any, respecting costs[5] and other things, as nearly as circumstances admit, and notwithstanding anything in that Act, according to the same procedure, as if the modes of investment or application authorised by the Act were authorised by the statute under which the money is in court[6]. Such money may be paid out to the trustees of the settlement at the request of the tenant for life[7]. Reason must be shown for supposing that the payment will be to the advantage of the settlement. There is no jurisdiction to impose as a condition of such payment out that the trustees are to give notice to the remainderman of all proposed investments or other applications of the money, although it may be right that they should give such notice[8].

1   As to these Acts see COMPULSORY ACQUISITION OF LAND vol 8(1) (Reissue) para 11 et seq.

2   For the meaning of 'land' see para 680 note 1 ante.

3   This includes the purchase money on a compulsory purchase of land belonging to a charity absolutely (see *Re Byron's Charity* (1883) 23 ChD 171; *Re Bethlehem and Bridewell Hospitals* (1885) 30 ChD 541), of glebe land (see *Ex p Vicar of Castle Bytham, ex p Midland Rly Co* [1895] 1 Ch 348), and of land belonging to a local authority (see *Ex p City of London Corpn, ex p West Ham Corpn* (1901) 17 TLR 232). For the meaning of 'settlement' see para 678 note 1 ante.

4   For the meaning of 'capital money arising under the Act' see para 795 ante.

5   As to costs where land is compulsorily acquired see COMPULSORY ACQUISITION OF LAND vol 8(1) (Reissue) paras 140–141.

6   Settled Land Act 1925 s 76. See also COMPULSORY ACQUISITION OF LAND vol 8(1) (Reissue) para 156.

7   *Re Wright's Trusts* (1883) 24 ChD 662; *Re Harrop's Trusts* (1883) 24 ChD 717; *Re Duke of Rutland's Settlement* (1883) 49 LT 196; *Re Rathmines etc Drainage Act, ex p Verschoyle* (1885) 15 LR Ir 576; *Re Wootton's Estate* [1890] WN 158; *Re Belfast Improvement Acts, ex p Reid* [1898] 1 IR 1.

8   *Re Bolton Estates Act 1863* (1885) 52 LT 728.

798. Personalty settled on trusts of capital money. Where money or securities[1] or the proceeds of sale of any property[2] is or are by any instrument[3], whenever it came into operation, directed to be held on trusts declared by reference to capital money arising under the Settled Land Act 1925[4] from land[5] settled by that instrument or any other instrument, the money, securities or proceeds are to be held on the like trusts as if they had been or represented money which had actually arisen under that Act from the settled land[6].

The money, securities or proceeds of sale must be paid or transferred to the trustees of the settlement[7] of the settled land, or paid or transferred into court[8], and invested or applied accordingly[9]. Where the settled land includes freehold land, the money, securities or proceeds of sale must be held on the like trusts as if they had been or represented capital money arising from the freehold land[10]. This provision has effect notwithstanding any direction in the instrument creating the trust that the trust property is not to vest absolutely in any tenant in tail[11] or in tail male or in tail female under the limitations[12] of the settled land who dies under a specified age, or before the happening of a specified event, but otherwise has effect with any variations and subject to any contrary intention expressed in the instrument creating the trust[13].

1   For the meaning of 'securities' see para 693 note 1 ante.

2   For the meaning of 'property' see para 778 note 7 ante.

3   For the meaning of 'instrument' see para 688 note 7 ante.

4   For the meaning of 'capital money arising under the Act' see para 795 ante.

5   For the meaning of 'land' see para 680 note 1 ante.

6   Settled Land Act 1925 s 78(1). This is without prejudice to the rights of any person claiming under a disposition for valuable consideration of any such money, securities or proceeds made before 1926: s 78(1) (amended by the Law of Property (Amendment) Act 1926 s 7, Schedule). For the meaning of 'disposition' see para 685 note 14 ante. Before 1926 personalty could be converted into realty only by imposing an imperative trust to invest in land: *Re Walker, Macintosh-Walker v Walker* [1908] 2 Ch 705; *Re Twopeny's Settlement, Monro v Twopeny* [1924] 1 Ch 522, CA. For the meaning of 'settled land' see para 680 text to note 2 ante.

7   For the meaning of 'trustees of the settlement' see para 750 note 1 ante. As to the trustees see para 750 et seq ante.

8   As to the court see para 792 ante. Any reference in the Settled Land Act 1925 to money, securities or proceeds of sale being paid or transferred into court is to be construed as referring to the money, securities or proceeds being paid or transferred into the Supreme Court or any other court that has jurisdiction, and any reference in that Act to the court, in a context referring to the investment or application of money, securities or proceeds of sale paid or transferred into court, is to be construed, in the case of money, securities or proceeds paid or transferred into the Supreme Court, as referring to the High Court, and, in the case of money, securities or proceeds paid or transferred into another court, as referring to that other court: s 117(1A) (added by the Administration of Justice Act 1965 s 17(1), Sch 1).

9   See the Settled Land Act 1925 s 78(3).

10 Ibid s 78(4).

11 For the meaning of 'tenant in tail' see para 762 note 8 ante.

12 For the meaning of 'limitation' see para 708 note 4 ante. As to entailed interests see para 715 et seq ante; and REAL PROPERTY vol 39(2) (Reissue) para 117 et seq.

13 Settled Land Act 1925 s 78(5). As to the effect of such a direction see para 938 note 8 post.

799. Personalty settled together with land. Where money or securities[1] or the proceeds of sale of any property[2] is or are by any instrument[3] coming into operation after 1925 directed to be held on the same trusts as, or on trusts corresponding as nearly as may be with the limitations[4] of land[5] settled by that instrument or any other instrument, the money, securities or proceeds are to be held on the like trusts as if they had been or represented capital money arising under the Act from the settled land[6]. The money, securities or proceeds of sale must be paid or transferred and held on trust, and the trust instrument has the same effect, as in the foregoing case of personalty settled on trusts of capital money[7].

1   For the meaning of 'securities' see para 693 note 1 ante.
2   For the meaning of 'property' see para 778 note 7 ante.
3   For the meaning of 'instrument' see para 688 note 7 ante.
4   For the meaning of 'limitation' see para 708 note 4 ante.
5   For the meaning of 'land' see para 680 note 1 ante.
6   Settled Land Act 1925 s 78(2). For the meaning of 'capital money arising under the Act' see para 795 ante. For the meaning of 'settled land' see para 680 text to note 2 ante.
7   See ibid s 78(3)–(5); and para 798 ante.

800. Capital money arising otherwise than under the Act. Any money arising after 1925 from settled land[1] otherwise than under the Settled Land Act 1925[2], as well as any money or securities[3] in the names or under the control of the tenant for life[4] or the trustees of the settlement[5], being or representing money which had arisen before 1926 from the settled land otherwise than under the Settled Land Acts 1882 to 1890[6], and which, as between the persons interested in the settled land, ought to be or to have been treated as capital[7], is (without prejudice to any other statutory provisions affecting the same) deemed to be or to represent capital money arising under the Settled Land Act 1925[8], and must be paid or transferred to or retained by the trustees of the settlement, or paid or transferred into court[9], and invested or applied accordingly[10].

1   For the meaning of 'settled land' see para 680 text to note 2 ante.
2   The purposes authorised for the application of capital money by the Settled Land Act 1925 s 73 include the payment of any sum recoverable as compensation where planning permission is revoked or modified under the Town and Country Planning Act 1990 (see ss 111, 112) (both as amended) (see TOWN AND COUNTRY PLANNING vol 46 (Reissue) paras 701–702): see s 328 (as amended); and TOWN AND COUNTRY PLANNING vol 46 (Reissue) para 701.
3   For the meaning of 'securities' see para 693 note 1 ante.
4   For the meaning of 'tenant for life' see para 671 note 5 ante. See also para 761 et seq ante.
5   For the meaning of 'trustees of the settlement' see para 750 note 1 ante. As to the trustees see para 750 et seq ante.
6   As to these Acts see para 678 note 1 ante.
7   As to cases in which money arising otherwise than under the Settled Land Act 1925 has been held to be capital see para 944 note 5 post.
8   For the meaning of 'capital money arising under the Act' see para 795 ante.
9   As to the court see para 792 ante. As to money paid or transferred into court see para 798 note 8 ante.
10 Settled Land Act 1925 s 81. Section 81 does not give the court a discretion unfettered by previous authority to decide what in fact is capital money: *Re Pomfret's Settlement, Guest v Pomfret* [1952] Ch 48, [1951] 2 All ER 951.

801. Damages for breach of lessee's covenants. Money, not being rent[1], received after 1925 by way of damages or compensation for breach of any covenant by a lessee or grantee contained in any lease[2] or grant of settled land[3] (whenever the lease or grant was made and whether under the statutory powers or not), unless in any case the court[4] on the application of the tenant for life or the trustees of the settlement[5] otherwise directs, is deemed to be capital money arising under the Act[6], and must be paid to or retained by the trustees of the settlement, or paid into court, and invested or applied accordingly[7].

This provision: (1) does not apply to money received by way of damages or compensation for the breach of a covenant to repay to the lessor or grantor money laid out or expended by him, or to any case in which, if the money received were applied in making good the breach of covenant or its consequences, such application would not enure for the benefit of the settled land, or any buildings on it[8]; and (2) applies only if and as far as a contrary intention is not expressed in the settlement[9], and has effect subject to the terms of the settlement, and to any provisions contained in it, but a contrary intention is not to be deemed to be expressed merely by words negativing impeachment for waste[10].

1   'Rent' includes yearly or other rent, and toll, duty, royalty, or other reservation, by the acre, or the ton, or otherwise; and, in relation to rent, 'payment' includes delivery; and 'fine' includes premium or fore-gift, and any payment, consideration, or benefit in the nature of a fine, premium or fore-gift: Settled Land Act 1925 s 117(1)(xxii).
2   For the meaning of 'lease' see para 685 note 13 ante.
3   For the meaning of 'settled land' see para 680 text to note 2 ante.
4   As to the court see para 792 ante.
5   For the meaning of 'tenant for life' see para 671 note 5 ante. See also para 761 et seq ante. For the meaning of 'trustees of the settlement' see para 750 note 1 ante. As to the trustees see para 750 et seq ante.
6   For the meaning of 'capital money arising under the Act' see para 795 ante.
7   Settled Land Act 1925 s 80(1), (5). As to the application of such money see also para 808 note 23 post. As to the payment of money into court see para 798 note 8 ante.
8   Ibid s 80(4).
9   For the meaning of 'settlement' see para 678 note 1 ante.
10   Settled Land Act 1925 s 80(6). As to impeachment for waste see para 986 et seq post.

802. Money received under insurance policy. Money receivable by trustees or any beneficiary under a policy of insurance against the loss or damage of any property subject to a settlement within the Settled Land Act 1925[1], whether by fire or otherwise, where the policy has been kept up under any trust in that behalf or under any power statutory or otherwise, or in performance of any covenant or of any obligation statutory or otherwise, or by a tenant for life impeachable for waste[2], is: (1) if the money was receivable in respect of settled land within that Act[3], or any building or works on it, deemed to be capital money arising under that Act[4] from the settled land, and must be invested or applied by the trustees, or, if in court, under the direction of the court, accordingly[5]; or (2) if it was receivable in respect of personal chattels settled as heirlooms within that Act[6], deemed to be capital money arising under that Act, and is applicable by the trustees, or, if in court, under the direction of the court, in like manner as provided by that Act with respect to money arising by a sale of chattels settled as heirlooms[7].

1   For the meaning of 'settlement' see para 678 note 1 ante.
2   See the Trustee Act 1925 s 20(1); and para 774 ante. As to liability for waste see para 986 et seq post.
3   For the meaning of 'settled land within the Settled Land Act 1925' see para 680 ante.
4   For the meaning of 'capital money arising under the Act' see para 795 ante.
5   See the Trustee Act s 20(3)(a); and TRUSTS vol 48 (Reissue) para 892.
6   See para 937 et seq post.
7   See the Trustee Act 1925 s 20(3)(b); and TRUSTS vol 48 (Reissue) para 892. This provision extends to chattels within the Settled Land Act 1925 s 67(4): see para 943 post. As to the sale of settled chattels see paras 940–943 post. As to insurance money being capital see *Mumford Hotels Ltd v Wheler* [1964] Ch 117, [1963] 3 All ER 250.

803. Commutation money for additional rent on conversion of perpetually renewable leaseholds. Money received for the commutation of any additional rent payable in respect of a perpetually renewable lease converted by the Law of Property Act 1922[1] into a long term, where the reversion is settled land, is treated as capital money[2].

1   See LANDLORD AND TENANT vol 27(1) (Reissue) para 453. See also para 978 post.
2   See the Law of Property Act 1922 s 145, Sch 15 para 17(3).

804. Capital money to be paid to trustees or into court. In order that it may be invested or applied in an authorised manner[1], capital money arising under the Settled Land Act 1925[2] must be paid either to the trustees of the settlement[3] or into court[4], at the option of the tenant for life[5], and must be invested or applied by the trustees, or under the direction of the court, as the case may be, accordingly[6]. This option may only be exercised if there are trustees for the purposes of that Act in existence at the time of payment[7]. Consequently a purchaser cannot be compelled to pay into court if there are no trustees in existence at the time of completion of the contract, although he might get a good title if he paid into court in ignorance of the fact that there were no trustees[8].

1   As to the making of investments see paras 805–808 post.
2   For the meaning of 'capital money arising under the Act' see para 795 ante.
3   For the meaning of 'trustees of the settlement' see para 750 note 1 ante. As to the trustees see para 750 et seq ante. As to the restriction on the payment of capital money to a sole trustee see para 786 ante. See also SALE OF LAND para 312 ante.
4   As to the court see para 792 ante. As to the payment of money into court see para 798 note 8 ante.
5   For the meaning of 'tenant for life' see para 671 note 5 ante. See also para 761 et seq ante.
6   Settled Land Act 1925 s 75(1). A purchaser should not pay purchase money to an incumbrancer by the direction of the tenant for life in order to pay off an incumbrance which is prior to the settlement, even where the purchase money is insufficient to discharge the incumbrance; he should pay it to or by the direction of the trustees: see *Re Norton and Las Casas' Contract* [1909] 2 Ch 59.
7   *Hatten v Russell* (1888) 38 ChD 334; *Mogridge v Clapp* [1892] 3 Ch 382, CA; *Re Fisher and Grazebrook's Contract* [1898] 2 Ch 660.
8   *Re Fisher and Grazebrook's Contract* [1898] 2 Ch 660. Cf *Hughes v Fanagan* (1891) 30 LR Ir 111, Ir CA. See further para 784 ante.

805. Investment or application by trustees. If the investment or other application is to be made by the trustees, it must be made according to the direction of the tenant for life[1]. The trustees are bound to see that the proposed application is for an authorised object, and they are entitled to be satisfied that the direction is given on proper professional advice[2], but, so long as the tenant for life really and honestly exercises his discretion, he cannot be controlled by the trustees or by the court[3]. However, the court may interfere to prevent a tenant for life, who in these matters is in the same position as a trustee, from investing in a security which is not suitable, even if it is within the words of the power[4].

In default of any direction by the tenant for life, the investment or other application must be made according to the discretion of the trustees, subject to any consent required or direction given by the settlement with respect to the investment or other application by the trustees of trust money of the settlement[5]. All investments must be in the names or under the control of the trustees[6].

During the subsistence of the beneficial interest of the tenant for life, an investment, or other application, of capital money may not be altered without his consent[7].

1   Settled Land Act 1925 s 75(2). For the meaning of 'tenant for life' see para 671 note 5 ante. See also para 761 et seq ante. In giving such a direction, as in exercising any of the statutory powers, the tenant for life is acting as a trustee: see *Re Hunt's Settled Estates, Buh*eel *v Lawdeshayne* [1905] 2 Ch 418 (on appeal [1906] 2 Ch 11, CA); *Re Peel's Settled Estates* [1910] 1 Ch 389; *Re Gladwin's Trust* [1919] 1 Ch 232; *Re Cowley Settled Estates* [1926] Ch 725; *Re Boston's Will Trusts, Inglis v Boston* [1956] Ch 395, [1956] 1 All ER 593. See also para 775 ante.
2   See *Re Lord Coleridge's Settlement* [1895] 2 Ch 704; *Re Hotham, Hotham v Doughty* [1902] 2 Ch 575, CA. If the order of the Court of Appeal in the latter case is to be taken as laying down a principle of law, it seems to follow that the tenant for life can consult his own brokers as to proposed investments, and that the trustees, on being satisfied that he has been properly advised, can safely pay the money to his brokers

for investment, and are not entitled to employ their own brokers, contrary to *Re Duke of Cleveland's Settled Estates* [1902] 2 Ch 350, which followed *Re Hotham, Hotham v Doughty* [1901] 2 Ch 790 (subsequently varied: [1902] 2 Ch 575, CA). As to the trustees' duty to seek professional advice see *Re Duke of Northumberland, Halifax v Northumberland* [1951] Ch 202, [1950] 2 All ER 1181. See also the Trustee Investments Act 1961 s 6; and TRUSTS vol 48 (Reissue) para 878.

3   *Re Lord Coleridge's Settlement* [1895] 2 Ch 704. The trustees will be protected for acting on the direction of the tenant for life: see the Settled Land Act 1925 ss 97, 98; and paras 891–892 post.

4   *Re Hunt's Settled Estates, Bulteel v Lawdeshayne* [1905] 2 Ch 418 (on appeal [1906] 2 Ch 11, CA); *Re Cowley Settled Estates* [1926] Ch 725.

5   See the Settled Land Act 1925 s 75(2). For the meaning of 'settlement' see para 678 note 1 ante.

6   Ibid s 75(2).

7   Ibid s 75(4).

806. Investment or application under direction of the court. If the investment or other application[1] is to be made under the direction of the court, it must be made on the application of the tenant for life or of the trustees[2]. All or any part of any capital money paid into court may, if the court thinks fit, be at any time paid out to the trustees of the settlement[3], although the tenant for life has in the first instance exercised his option to have it paid into court[4]. Capital money may be paid to trustees of the settlement residing abroad[5]. On such an application the court will act on the same principle as it would if the money had been in the hands of the trustees and they had referred the matter to the court[6].

1   See para 804 ante.

2   Settled Land Act 1925 s 75(3). As to applications to the court see paras 792–793 ante. For the meaning of 'tenant for life' see para 671 note 5 ante. See also para 761 et seq ante.

3   Ibid s 75(8). For the meaning of 'trustees of the settlement' see para 750 note 1 ante. As to the trustees see para 750 et seq ante. As to the payment of money into court see para 798 note 8 ante.

4   As to such option see para 804 ante.

5   *Re Lloyd, Edwards v Lloyd* (1886) 54 LT 643; *Re Simpson, Re Whitchurch* [1897] 1 Ch 256, CA.

6   *Clarke v Thornton* (1887) 35 ChD 307.

807. Application of purchase money for interest less than fee simple. If capital money arising under the Settled Land Act 1925[1] is purchase money paid in respect of (1) a lease for years[2]; (2) any other estate or interest in land less than the fee simple[3]; or (3) a reversion dependent on any such lease, estate or interest[4], the trustees of the settlement[5], or the court[6], as the case may be, and, in the case of the court, on the application of any party interested in that money, may require and cause it to be laid out, invested, accumulated and paid in such manner as, in the judgment of the trustees or of the court, as the case may be, will give to the parties interested in that money the like benefit from it as they might lawfully have had from the lease, estate, interest or reversion in respect of which the money was paid or as near to it as may be[7].

1   For the meaning of 'capital money arising under the Act' see para 795 ante.

2   Settled Land Act 1925 s 79(a). For the meaning of 'lease' see para 685 note 13 ante.

3   Ibid s 79(b). As to interests in land see REAL PROPERTY vol 39(2) (Reissue) para 74 et seq.

4   Ibid s 79(c).

5   For the meaning of 'trustees of the settlement' see para 750 note 1 ante. As to the trustees see para 750 et seq ante.

6   As to the court see para 792 ante.

7   Settled Land Act 1925 s 79. The words in this provision which direct apportionment follow those of the Settled Estates Act 1877 s 37 (repealed), which are similar to the words of the Lands Clauses Consolidation Act 1845 s 74 (as amended), the cases on which form a precedent for the interpretation of the present enactment: see *Cottrell v Cottrell* (1885) 28 ChD 628. See also COMPULSORY ACQUISITION OF LAND vol 8(1) (Reissue) para 164. On a sale of settled leaseholds by the court where there is no trust or power of sale, the same method of distribution is adopted as in a case of compulsory purchase: *Re Lingard, Lingard v Squirrell* [1908] WN 107. As to the principles on which apportionment should be

applied see *Cottrell v Cottrell* supra; *Re Robinson's Settlement Trusts* [1891] 3 Ch 129; *Re Fullerton's Will* [1906] 2 Ch 138; *Re Duke of Westminster's Settled Estates, Duke of Westminster v Earl of Shaftesbury* [1921] 1 Ch 585.

808. Modes of application. Capital money arising under the Settled Land Act 1925[1], when received, must be invested or otherwise applied wholly in one, or partly in one and partly in another or others, of certain specified modes, subject to payment of claims properly payable out of it and to the application of it for any special authorised object for which it was raised[2]. The modes are as follows.

(1) Investment in government securities[3], or other securities in which the trustees of the settlement[4] are by the settlement or by law authorised to invest trust money of the settlement, with power to vary the investment into or for any other such securities[5].

(2) Discharge, purchase or redemption of incumbrances affecting the whole estate the subject of the settlement[6], or of Crown rent, chief rent or quit rent[7] charged on or payable out of the settled land[8], or of any charge in respect of an improvement created on a holding under the Agricultural Holdings Act 1986, or any similar previous enactment[9].

A mortgage of a long term is a mortgage affecting the inheritance, whether it is in possession[10] or reversion[11]. A mortgage of part of the land may be discharged out of capital money arising from another part[12], even when the two parts are settled by different instruments[13], or in the actual event devolve on different persons[14]; and capital money arising from the proceeds of sale of chattels settled to devolve with land may be applied in the discharge of incumbrances affecting the inheritance of the land, by reference to the limitations of which, although by another instrument, the chattels are settled, notwithstanding that different persons may become entitled to the proceeds of the chattels and to the land[15]. Capital money arising from land may be applied in discharging inheritance tax on heirlooms settled on corresponding trusts[16]. So much of a charge on land for expenses incurred by a local authority in sewering, paving and flagging new streets[17] as represents capital, although payable by instalments, may be paid out of capital money[18], but not a terminable rentcharge of which the tenant for life is bound to pay the instalments[19], unless it comes within the definition of an improvement rentcharge[20]. The tenant for life may direct the application of capital money arising under the Settled Land Act 1925 in discharge of incumbrances, notwithstanding that his interest is subject to a term created by the settlement for that purpose, provided that his direction is in good faith and in the interest of all parties[21]. However, a purchaser is not justified in paying his purchase money, at the request of the tenant for life, to an incumbrancer who has priority over the settlement[22].

(3) Payment for any improvement authorised by the Settled Land Act 1925[23].

(4) Payment as for an improvement authorised by that Act of any money expended and costs incurred by a landlord in or about the execution of certain specified improvements to agricultural holdings[24].

(5) Payment for equality of exchange of settled land[25].

(6) Redemption of any compensation rentcharge created in respect of the extinguishment of manorial incidents, and affecting the settled land[26].

(7) Commuting any additional rent made payable on the conversion of a perpetually renewable leasehold interest into a long term, and satisfying any claim for compensation on such conversion by any officer, solicitor or other agent of the lessor in respect of fees or remuneration which would have been payable by the lessee or underlessee on any renewal[27].

(8) Purchase of the freehold reversion in fee of any part of the settled land, being leasehold land held for years[28].

(9) Purchase of land[29] in fee simple, or of leasehold land held for 60 years or more unexpired at the time of purchase, subject or not to any exception or reservation of or in respect of mines or minerals in it[30], or of or in respect of rights or powers relative to the working of mines or minerals in it or in other land[31].

Land may be acquired on a purchase or exchange to be made subject to a settlement, notwithstanding that the land is subject to any Crown rent, quit rent, chief rent or other incident of tenure, or to any easement, right or privilege, or to any restrictive covenant, or to any liability to maintain or repair walls, fences, sea walls, river banks, dykes, roads, streets, sewers or drains, or to any improvement rentcharge which is capable under the Settled Land Act 1925 of being redeemed out of capital money[32]. Ground rents may be purchased[33], but not an equity of redemption[34]. Capital money arising from settled land in England or Wales cannot be applied in the purchase of land out of England or Wales, unless the purchase is expressly authorised by the settlement[35].

(10) Purchase, either in fee simple or for a term of 60 years or more, of mines and minerals convenient to be held or worked with the settled land, or of any easement, right or privilege convenient to be held with the settled land for mining or other purposes[36].

(11) Redemption of an improvement rentcharge[37].

(12) Purchase, with the leave of the court[38], of any leasehold interest where the immediate reversion is settled land, so as to merge the leasehold interest (unless the court otherwise directs) in the reversion, and notwithstanding that the leasehold interest may have less than 60 years to run[39].

(13) Payment of the costs and expenses of all plans, surveys and schemes[40] made with a view to, or in connection with the improvement or development of, the settled land or any part of it, or the exercise of any statutory powers, and of all negotiations entered into by the tenant for life with a view to the exercise of any of such powers, notwithstanding that the negotiations may prove abortive, and payment of the costs and expenses of opposing any such proposed scheme affecting the settled land, whether or not the scheme is made[41].

(14) Payment to a local or other authority of such sum as may be agreed in consideration of the authority taking over and becoming liable to repair a private road on the settled land or a road for the maintenance of which a tenant for life is liable *ratione tenurae*[42].

(15) Financing any person who may have agreed to take a lease[43] or grant for building purposes[44] of the settled land, or any part of it, by making advances to him in the usual manner on the security of an equitable mortgage of his building agreement[45].

(16) Payment to any person becoming absolutely entitled or empowered to give an absolute discharge[46].

(17) Payment of costs, charges and expenses of or incidental to the exercise of any of the powers or the execution of any of the provisions of the Settled Land Act 1925, including the costs and expenses incidental to any of the authorised modes of investing or applying capital money[47].

(18) Any other mode authorised by the settlement with respect to money produced by the sale of the settled land[48].

Capital money may also be applied:

(a) in payment of inheritance tax in respect of property comprised in the settlement[49];

(b) where the settled land is leased, in payment of money expended and costs incurred by a landlord under the Landlord and Tenant Act 1927 in or about the execution of any improvement or of any sum due to a tenant under that Act in respect of compensation for an improvement, and any costs, charges and expenses incidental to it, or in payment of the costs, charges and expenses of opposing any proposal by a tenant to execute an improvement[50];

(c)　in payment of a coast protection charge or expenses incurred in carrying out work under a works scheme under the Coast Protection Act 1949[51];

(d)　in payment of certain expenses and making certain payments under the Landlord and Tenant Act 1954[52];

(e)　in payment of expenses incurred in, or in connection with, proceedings taken relating to the acquisition of the freehold or an extended lease under the Leasehold Reform Act 1967[53];

(f)　in payment of compensation to a tenant where rights under the Leasehold Reform Act 1967 are excluded[54];

(g)　in payment of expenses incurred by a landlord under a farm business tenancy in, or in connection with, the making of any physical improvement on the holding, in payment of compensation for tenant's improvements, and in payment of the costs, charges and expenses incurred on a reference to arbitration under the Agricultural Tenancies Act 1995[55].

1　For the meaning of 'capital money arising under the Act' see para 795 ante.

2　Settled Land Act 1925 s 73(1). As to the raising of capital money for special authorised purposes see s 71 (as amended); and paras 849–850 post.

3　For the meaning of 'securities' see para 693 note 1 ante. As to government securities see MONEY.

4　For the meaning of 'trustees of the settlement' see para 750 note 1 ante. As to the trustees see para 750 et seq ante. For the meaning of 'settlement' see para 678 note 1 ante.

5　Settled Land Act 1925 s 73(1)(i). As to what investments are permitted by law to trustees see the Trustee Act 1925 Pt I (ss 2–11) (as amended); the Trustee Investments Act 1961; and TRUSTS vol 48 (Reissue) para 867 et seq.

6　Arrears of a jointure rentcharge are an incumbrance affecting the inheritance: see *Re Duke of Manchester's Settlement* [1910] 1 Ch 106. It seems that future payments of a jointure or pin money cannot be redeemed out of capital money: see *Re Knatchbull's Settled Estate* (1884) 27 ChD 349 at 353 (affd (1885) 29 ChD 588, CA); *Re Frewen, Frewen v James* (1888) 38 ChD 383 at 384; *Re Duke of Manchester's Settlement* supra at 115. As to pin money and jointure see paras 724–725 ante.

7　As to Crown rent, chief rent and quit rent see REAL PROPERTY vol 39(2) (Reissue) para 84.

8 ·　For the meaning of 'settled land' see para 680 text to note 2 ante.

9　Settled Land Act 1925 s 73(1)(ii) (amended by the Finance Act 1963 s 73(8)(b), Sch 11 Pt VI; and the Agricultural Holdings Act 1986 s 100, Sch 14 para 11). As to the redemption of rentcharges generally see the Rentcharges Act 1977 ss 8–10 (as amended); and RENTCHARGES AND ANNUITIES vol 39(2) (Reissue) para 900 et seq. The Settled Land Act 1925 s 73(1)(ii) (as amended) also authorises capital money to be applied in the discharge, purchase or redemption of rentcharge in lieu of tithe. However, tithe rentcharge was extinguished on 2 October 1936: see ECCLESIASTICAL LAW. As to the redemption of a charge in respect of compensation for improvements paid to an agricultural tenant see *Re Duke of Wellington's Parliamentary Estates, King v Wellesley* [1972] Ch 374, [1971] 2 All ER 1140. See also note 24 infra. As to agricultural holdings generally see AGRICULTURE vol 1(2) (Reissue) para 301 et seq.

10　See *Re Frewen, Frewen v James* (1888) 38 ChD 383.

11　See *Re Lord Gisborough's Settled Estates* [1921] 2 Ch 39, where the court authorised the application of capital money in payment of portions, although the similar provisions in the Settled Land Act 1882 s 21(ii) (repealed), did not expressly sanction this. See also MORTGAGE.

12　*Re Chaytor's Settled Estate Act* (1884) 25 ChD 651; *Re Navan and Kingscourt Rly Co, ex p Dyas* (1888) 21 LR Ir 369.

13　*Re Lord Stafford's Settlement and Will, Gerard v Stafford* [1904] 2 Ch 72.

14　*Re Freme, Freme v Logan* [1894] 1 Ch 1, CA. See para 685 ante.

15　*Re Duke of Marlborough's Settlement, Duke of Marlborough v Marjoribanks* (1886) 32 ChD 1, CA; *Re Lord Stafford's Settlement and Will, Gerard v Stafford* [1904] 2 Ch 72. See para 937 et seq post.

16　*Re Earl of Egmont's Settled Estate, Lefroy v Egmont* [1912] 1 Ch 251, a decision relating to estate duty (now inheritance tax). See INHERITANCE TAXATION vol 24 (Reissue) para 401 et seq.

17　See HIGHWAYS, STREETS AND BRIDGES vol 21 (Reissue) para 731.

18　See *Re Legh's Settled Estate* [1902] 2 Ch 274; and HIGHWAYS, STREETS AND BRIDGES vol 21 (Reissue) para 736. A liability to repair *ratione tenurae* is not an incumbrance affecting the inheritance of the settled land (*Re Hodgson's Settled Estate, Altamont v Forsyth* [1912] 1 Ch 784), but capital money can now be applied for the purpose of discharging such a liability (see the Settled Land Act 1925 s 73(1)(xvii): see head (14) in the text). As to liability *ratione tenurae* see HIGHWAYS, STREETS AND BRIDGES vol 21 (Reissue) paras 196–199.

19   See ibid s 85(3) (see para 814 post); and *Re Knatchbull's Settled Estate* (1885) 29 ChD 588, CA.

20   As to the redemption of improvement rentcharges see para 822 post.

21   *Re Richardson, Richardson v Richardson* [1900] 2 Ch 778. See also *Re Earl of Stamford and Warrington, Payne v Grey* [1925] Ch 162 at 175; revsd on another point [1925] Ch 589, CA.

22   *Re Norton and Las Casas' Contract* [1909] 2 Ch 59. See also para 804 note 6 ante.

23   Settled Land Act 1925 s 73(1)(iii). As to applying capital money on improvements see paras 809 et seq post; and for a list of authorised improvements see para 815 et seq post. As to the payment of the cost of repairs out of capital see paras 671 ante, 963 post. Money, not being rent, received since 1925 by way of damages or compensation for breach of any covenant by a lessee or grantee contained in any lease or grant of settled land (except in the cases mentioned in para 801 ante) may be applied, at any time within 12 months after its receipt or such extended period as the court may allow, in or towards payment of the costs of making good in whole or in part the breach of covenant in respect of which it was received, or its consequences, and the trustees of the settlement, if they think fit, may require any money so received, or any part of it, to be so applied, the work required to be done for the purpose being deemed to be an improvement authorised by s 83, Sch 3 Pt I: see s 80(1)–(3), (5); and para 801 ante. Improvements may be paid for out of capital money notwithstanding that the settlement contains a power to pay for them out of income: see *Clarke v Thornton* (1887) 35 ChD 307; *Re Lord Stamford's Settled Estates* (1889) 43 ChD 84; *Re Thomas, Weatherall v Thomas* [1900] 1 Ch 319; *Re Tubbs, Dykes v Tubbs* [1915] 2 Ch 137, CA. Cf *Re Partington, Reigh v Kane* [1902] 1 Ch 711, where the decision turned on the special facts of the case. As to the retention by the tenant for life of sums recovered by way of relief from income tax in respect of expenditure on improvements which have been paid for out of capital money see *Re Pelly's Will Trusts, Ransome v Pelly* [1957] Ch 1, [1956] 2 All ER 326, CA; *Menzies' Trustees v Lindsay* 1957 SC 44. See also para 820 post; and AGRICULTURE vol 1(2) (Reissue) para 492. As to the power to charge the settled land with the cost of erecting a new mansion house see AGRICULTURE vol 1(2) (Reissue) para 509 et seq.

24   Settled Land Act 1925 s 73(1)(iv) (amended by the Agricultural Holdings Act 1986 Sch 14 para 11). The improvements are those specified in the Agricultural Holdings Act 1986 s 64(1), Sch 7 (see AGRICULTURE vol 1(2) (Reissue) paras 412, 492): see the Settled Land Act 1925 s 73(1)(iv) (as so amended). This includes repairs to fixed equipment: *Re Duke of Northumberland, Halifax v Northumberland* [1951] Ch 202, [1950] 2 All ER 1181; *Re Lord Brougham and Vaux's Settled Estates* [1954] Ch 24, [1953] 2 All ER 655; *Re Wynn, Public Trustee v Newborough* [1955] 2 All ER 865, [1955] 1 WLR 940; cf *Re Boston's Will Trusts, Inglis v Boston* [1956] Ch 395, [1956] 1 All ER 593, all of which cases were decisions on the effect of the Agricultural Holdings Act 1948 s 96 (repealed), but repairs done before that Act came into force cannot, it seems, be paid for out of capital money (*Re Sutherland Settlement Trusts* [1953] Ch 792, [1953] 2 All ER 27). See further paras 809, 817 post; and AGRICULTURE vol 1(2) (Reissue) para 405 et seq. Capital money cannot be applied under the Settled Land Act 1925 s 73(1)(iv) (as amended) in reimbursing a tenant for life with compensation for improvements paid to an agricultural tenant but if the landlord obtains an order from the minister charging the holding with the repayment of the compensation, the trustees can redeem that charge out of capital money under the Settled Land Act 1925 s 73(1)(ii) (see head (2) in the text): see *Re Duke of Wellington's Parliamentary Estates, King v Wellesley* [1972] Ch 374, [1971] 2 All ER 1140 (decided under the Agricultural Holdings Act 1948 (repealed): see now the Agricultural Holdings Act 1986; and AGRICULTURE vol 1(2) (Reissue) para 383 et seq).

25   Settled Land Act 1925 s 73(1)(v). As to equality of exchange see paras 834–835 post.

26   Ibid s 73(1)(viii). As to the extinguishment of manorial incidents see CUSTOM AND USAGE vol 12(1) (Reissue) para 643.

27   Ibid s 73(1)(ix). As to commuting additional rent see the Law of Property Act 1922 s 145, Sch 15 paras 14 (as amended), 15, 17(1), (4) (as amended); and LANDLORD AND TENANT vol 27(1) (Reissue) paras 453–454. See also para 978 post.

28   Settled Land Act 1925 s 73(1)(x). There is no statutory power to adjust the rights as between the tenant for life and the remaindermen on the purchase of a reversion.

29   For the meaning of 'land' see para 680 note 1 ante.

30   For the meaning of 'mines and minerals' see para 680 note 1 ante.

31   Settled Land Act 1925 s 73(1)(xi). This provision may cover an expenditure on repairs up to the amount by which the value of the property acquired would have been increased if such repairs had been executed by the vendor before the sale: see *Re Blake's Settled Estate* [1923] 2 Ch 128. The conveyance of the land must be framed either as a principal or subsidiary vesting deed: see the Settled Land Act 1925 s 10(1); and paras 691, 693 ante.

32 Ibid s 74(1). The acquisition on a purchase or exchange before 1926 of any land subject to any such burden is confirmed: see s 74(2). As to what improvement rentcharges are capable of being redeemed out of capital money see para 822 post.

33 *Re Peyton's Settlement Trust* (1869) LR 7 Eq 463. See, however, *Ex p Gartside* (1837) 6 LJ Ch 266.

34 *Re Earl Radnor's Settled Estates* [1898] WN 174.

35 Settled Land Act 1925 s 73(2). Capital money may be expended on improvements on land out of England but settled by an English settlement: see *Re Gurney's Marriage Settlement, Sullivan v Gurney* [1907] 2 Ch 496, following an unreported decision, *Re Strousberg* (1886) (see 32 Sol Jo 625). See also *Re Earl of Dunraven's Settled Estates* [1907] 2 Ch 417.

36 Settled Land Act 1925 s 73(1)(xii). 'Mining purposes' includes the sinking and searching for, winning, working, getting, making merchantable, smelting or otherwise converting or working for the purposes of any manufacture, carrying away and disposing of mines and minerals in or under the settled land, or any other land, and the erection of buildings, and the execution of engineering and other works suitable for those purposes: s 117(1)(xv). 'Privilege' includes sporting rights: see *Re Earl of Portarlington's Settled Estates* [1918] 1 IR 362. As to sporting rights see ANIMALS vol 2 (Reissue) para 248 et seq; FISHERIES. As to mines see generally MINES, MINERALS AND QUARRIES.

37 Settled Land Act 1925 s 73(1)(xiii). This provision applies to a rentcharge (temporary or permanent) whenever created, in pursuance of any Act of Parliament, with the object of paying off any money advanced for defraying the expenses of an improvement of any kind authorised by s 83, Sch 3 Pt I (see para 816 post): see s 73(1)(xiii). As to the redemption of improvement rentcharges see para 822 post.

38 As to the court see para 792 ante.

39 Settled Land Act 1925 s 73(1)(xiv).

40 This includes schemes under the Town Planning Act 1925 (repealed), or any similar previous enactments: see the Settled Land Act 1925 s 73(1)(xv). The development plans made under the Town and Country Planning Act 1990 Pt II (ss 10–28A) (as amended) (see TOWN AND COUNTRY PLANNING vol 46 (Reissue) para 39 et seq) cannot be considered as schemes for this purpose as only enactments previous to the Settled Land Act 1925 are referred to in s 73(1)(xv).

41 Settled Land Act 1925 s 73(1)(xv). As to the court's power to approve proceedings for the protection of the settled land see para 825 post.

42 Ibid s 73(1)(xvii). As to liability *ratione tenurae* see HIGHWAYS, STREETS AND BRIDGES vol 21 (Reissue) paras 196–199.

43 For the meaning of 'lease' see para 685 note 13 ante.

44 'Building purposes' includes the erecting and the improving of, and the adding to, and the repairing of buildings: Settled Land Act 1925 s 117(1)(i).

45 Ibid s 73(1)(xviii). As to sales for less than the best price or rent see para 831 post; and as to building leases see para 842 post. As to equitable mortgages see MORTGAGE.

46 Ibid s 73(1)(xix). This allows payment out to trustees (see *Re Smith, ex p London and North Western Rly Co and Midland Rly Co* (1888) 40 ChD 386, CA) who, if necessary, are appointed for the purpose of receiving the money (see *Re Wright's Trusts* (1883) 24 ChD 662; *Re Harrop's Trusts* (1883) 24 ChD 717; *Re Wootton's Estate* [1890] WN 158). The power to order payment out to trustees is, however, discretionary on the part of the court: *Re Smith, ex p London and North Western Rly Co and Midland Rly Co* supra. See also the Settled Land Act 1925 s 75(8); and para 806 ante.

47 Ibid s 73(1)(xx). As to what costs, charges and expenses may be paid under this provision see para 823 et seq post. Under the law in force prior to 1926, where the tenant for life was constituted by several persons entitled as tenants in common, each was entitled to employ his own solicitor in completing a sale, and to have his separate costs out of the purchase money: *Smith v Lancaster* [1894] 3 Ch 439, CA. Under the present law the persons constituting the tenant for life are joint tenants and the land is vested in them as express trustees (see para 767 ante), and it would seem that the ordinary rule that trustees should not sever would apply to them. As to the severance of joint tenancies see REAL PROPERTY vol 39(2) (Reissue) para 198 et seq.

48 Settled Land Act 1925 s 73(1)(xxi). A testator may add to the methods of applying capital, but he cannot limit the discretion given to the tenant for life by the Settled Land Act 1925, though it may be controlled by the court if its exercise, although in good faith, would work injustice to any parties concerned: see *Re Richardson, Richardson v Richardson* [1900] 2 Ch 778. See also para 775 ante.

49 See the Inheritance Tax Act 1984 s 212(1), (3); and INHERITANCE TAXATION vol 24 (Reissue) para 652.

50 See the Landlord and Tenant Act 1927 s 13(1) (as amended); and LANDLORD AND TENANT vol 27(1) (Reissue) para 652. See further para 821 post,

51 See the Coast Protection Act 1949 s 11(2)(a) (as amended); and WATER vol 49(2) (Reissue) para 73.

52 See the Landlord and Tenant Act 1954 s 8, Sch 2 para 6 (as amended); and LANDLORD AND TENANT vol 27(2) (Reissue) para 1070.

53   See the Leasehold Reform Act 1967 s 6(2), (3), (5) (as amended); and para 877 post. As to leasehold enfranchisement see also the Leasehold Reform, Housing and Urban Development Act 1993; and LANDLORD AND TENANT vol 27(1) (Reissue) para 1253 et seq.

54   Ie under ibid ss 17, 18 (as amended): see Sch 2 para 9 (as amended); and LANDLORD AND TENANT vol 27(2) (Reissue) para 1343.

55   See the Agricultural Tenancies Act 1995 s 33(1) (as amended); and AGRICULTURE vol 1(2) (Reissue) para 500.

809. Payment for improvements generally. Capital money arising under the Settled Land Act 1925[1] may be applied in or towards payment for any improvement authorised[2] by the Act or by the settlement[3] without any scheme[4] for the execution of the improvement being first submitted for approval to, or approved by, the trustees of the settlement[5] or the court[6]. In any case where it appears proper, the court may by order direct or authorise capital money to be applied in or towards payment for any improvement authorised by the Settled Land Acts 1882 to 1890[7], or the Settled Land Act 1925, notwithstanding that a scheme was not submitted for approval as required by the Settled Land Act 1882 to the trustees of the settlement or to the court, or even that the tenant for life was not competent to submit a scheme, and notwithstanding that no capital money is immediately available for the purpose[8]. The fact that there is no capital money immediately available does not prevent the determination of the legal question whether the proposed works are improvements within the meaning of the Settled Land Act 1925[9].

If the trustees of a settlement do not oppose an application by a tenant for life for the application of capital money in payment for an improvement, when his interest is opposed to the remaindermen, it is their duty to remain neutral, and the court will not hear counsel on their behalf in support of the application[10].

In some circumstances capital money so expended may be required to be repaid to capital[11].

When lands are settled by different instruments on the same trusts, capital money arising under one deed may be applied in the improvement of land settled by another[12].

Apart from statute, and in the absence of some express provision in the instrument under which his estate or interest arises, a tenant for life of, or any other owner having a limited interest in, land has no claim against the inheritance for the cost of buildings erected or improvements made by him[13].

The court has jurisdiction to order capital money to be applied towards payment for an improvement authorised by the Settled Land Act 1925 notwithstanding that it was executed prior to the Act[14]. The court's jurisdiction continues even though the property improved has been sold[15].

In the exercise of this retrospective jurisdiction, the court will scrutinise a claim closely[16], and in general will refuse to allow recoupment where the applicant has deliberately carried out improvements knowing that the expenditure could not then be recovered from capital, but would be borne by himself[17]. Delay in asking for recoupment is a ground for refusal[18]. A power in or direction to trustees to effect improvements out of income[19] does not deprive a tenant for life of his right to require capital money to be applied in payment for them; nevertheless a provision by the settlor that the expense of executing improvements is to fall on income is a ground for refusing the application of a tenant for life[20]. A claim was allowed for recoupment by the executors of a life tenant who, having been erroneously advised that improvements could not be paid out of capital, paid for them himself[21].

It seems that the court has no jurisdiction to authorise capital money to be applied in paying for the cost of repairs and maintenance authorised by the Agricultural Holdings Act 1948 where they were incurred before that Act came into operation[22].

1   For the meaning of 'capital money arising under the Act' see para 795 ante.

2   As to what improvements are authorised see the Settled Land Act 1925 s 83, Sch 3; and para 815 et seq post.

3   For the meaning of 'settlement' see para 678 note 1 ante.

4   Before the coming into operation of the Settled Land Act 1925, a scheme had to be submitted by the tenant for life for the approval of the trustees of the settlement or of the court under the Settled Land Act 1882 s 26(1) (repealed): see *Re Wormald's Settled Estate, Wormald v Ollivant* [1908] WN 214.

5   For the meaning of 'trustees of the settlement' see para 750 note 1 ante. As to the trustees see para 750 et seq ante.

6   Settled Land Act 1925 s 84(1). As to the court see para 792 ante.

7   As to these Acts see para 678 note 1 ante.

8   See the Settled Land Act 1925 s 87. The principles upon which the court acts were considered in *Re Tucker's Settled Estates* [1895] 2 Ch 468, CA; *Re St Germans Settled Estates* [1924] 2 Ch 236. See also *Re Keck's Settlement* [1904] 2 Ch 22.

9   *Re Calverley's Settled Estates* [1904] 1 Ch 150.

10   *Re Hotchkin's Settled Estates* (1887) 35 ChD 41 at 43, CA, per North J. See, however, *Re Marquis of Ailesbury's Settled Estates* [1892] 1 Ch 506 at 548, CA, where trustees taking different sides were allowed separate costs.

11   As to the repayment of capital money see para 812 post.

12   *Re Mundy's Settled Estates* [1891] 1 Ch 399, CA; *Re Byng's Settled Estates* [1892] 2 Ch 219; *Re Lord Stamford's Settled Estates* (1889) 43 ChD 84. Cf *Re Clitheroe's Settled Estates* (1869) 20 LT 6; *Donaldson v Donaldson* (1876) 3 ChD 743. So, too, capital money arising from the sale of settled land in Ireland is applicable for the improvement of English property settled by the same settlement (*Re Eyre Coote, Coote v Cadogan* (1899) 81 LT 535), and money liable to be laid out in the purchase of settled land in England is available for improvements on land in Scotland comprised in the same settlement (*Re Gurney's Marriage Settlement, Sullivan v Gurney* [1907] 2 Ch 496).

13   *Bostock v Blakeney* (1789) 2 Bro CC 653; *Caldecott v Brown* (1842) 2 Hare 144; *Mathias v Mathias* (1858) 3 Sm & G 552; *Rowley v Ginnever* [1897] 2 Ch 503.

14   *Re Lord Sherborne's Settled Estate* [1929] 1 Ch 345; *Re Borough Court Estate* [1932] 2 Ch 39. Where the value of the improvements has diminished, a rebate will be made: *Re Jacques Settled Estates* [1930] 2 Ch 418; *Re Lord Sherborne's Settled Estate* supra.

15   *Re Borough Court Estate* [1932] 2 Ch 39.

16   *Re Tucker's Settled Estates* [1895] 2 Ch 468, CA.

17   *Re Ormrod's Settled Estate* [1892] 2 Ch 318; *Re Borough Court Estate* [1932] 2 Ch 39. Recoupment of the cost of electric light installation made before 1926 has been allowed because, although it was not then an authorised improvement, it was an improvement that would have to be made sooner or later, and became authorised by the Settled Land Act 1925 s 83, Sch 3 Pt III para (ii) (see para 818 post): *Re Jacques Settled Estates* [1930] 2 Ch 418. See also *Re Sutherland Settlement Trusts* [1953] Ch 792, [1953] 2 All ER 27.

18   *Re Allen's Settled Estate* (1909) 126 LT Jo 282.

19   *Clarke v Thornton* (1887) 35 ChD 307; *Re Lord Stamford's Estate* (1887) 56 LT 484. It is otherwise if there is a trust coming before the trust for the tenant for life and providing for payment of improvements out of income: *Re Partington, Reigh v Kane* [1902] 1 Ch 711. If a tenant for life resorts to a fund created by the settlement for the purposes of improvement, he is bound to comply with any condition imposed by the settlement for the repayment of that fund: *Re Sudbury and Poynton Estates, Vernon v Vernon* [1893] 3 Ch 74.

20   *Countess of Cardigan v Curzon-Howe* (1893) 9 TLR 244; *Re Partington, Reigh v Kane* [1902] 1 Ch 711.

21   *Re St Germans Settled Estates* [1924] 2 Ch 236.

22   See *Re Sutherland Settlement Trusts* [1953] Ch 792, [1953] 2 All ER 27, where Harman J did not follow on this point the decision of Vaisey J in *Re Duke of Northumberland, Halifax v Northumberland* [1951] Ch 202, [1950] 2 All ER 1181. See also *Re Lord Boston's Will Trusts, Inglis v Lord Boston* [1956] Ch 395, [1956] 1 All ER 593. See further para 808 head (4) and note 24 ante.

810. Payment out of capital money in the hands of the trustees. Capital money[1] in the hands of trustees of the settlement[2] may be applied by them in or towards payment for the whole or any part of any work or operation comprised in an authorised improvement[3] on: (1) a certificate of a competent engineer or able practical surveyor employed independently of the tenant for life, certifying that the work or operation comprised in the improvement or some specific part of it, has been properly executed and what amount is properly payable in respect of it[4]; or (2) a court order directing or authorising the trustees so to apply a specified portion of the capital money[5].

Capital money so applied may be required in certain cases to be replaced[6].

Settlements of Land under the Settled Land Act 1925

1   For the meaning of 'capital money arising under the Act' see para 795 ante.
2   For the meaning of 'trustees of the settlement' see para 750 note 1 ante. As to the trustees see para 750 et seq ante.
3   Ie an improvement authorised by the Settled Land Act 1925 (see para 815 et seq post) or by the settlement: see the Settled Land Act 1925 s 84(1).
4   Ibid s 84(2)(i). The certificate does not vouch for the propriety of the improvements or that it is authorised by the Act or by the settlement, but is conclusive as an authority and discharge to the trustees for any payment made by them in pursuance of it: see s 84(2)(i).
5   Settled Land Act 1925 s 84(2)(ii). On an application under this provision it is apprehended that the court will have to be satisfied not merely of the fact of the expenditure, but of the propriety of it; the court has a discretion, and its duties are not merely ministerial: see *Re Keck's Settlement* [1904] 2 Ch 22, where, however, there was an approved scheme which, since 1925, is no longer necessary (see para 809 note 4 ante).
6   As to the repayment of capital money see para 812 et seq post.

811. Payment out of funds in court. If the capital money to be expended is in court, then, if it thinks fit, on a report or certificate of the Minister of Agriculture, Fisheries and Food or of a competent engineer or able practical surveyor approved by the court, or on such other evidence as the court may think sufficient, the court may direct the application of the money, or any part of it, in or towards payment for the whole or part of any work or operation comprised in the improvement[1].

1   Settled Land Act 1925 ss 84(3), 117(1)(xvi) (amended by the Transfer of Functions (Ministry of Food) Order 1955, SI 1955/554). As to the minister's powers see para 965 post. As to the Minister of Agriculture, Fisheries and Food generally see CONSTITUTIONAL LAW AND HUMAN RIGHTS vol 8(2) (Reissue) para 435 et seq. As to applications to the court see para 792 et seq ante.

(v) Repayment of Capital Money

812. Repayment by instalments. If capital money is applied in or towards payment for an improvement authorised by Part I of the Third Schedule to the Settled Land Act 1925[1], or by the settlement, the money is not repayable, but in relation to other improvements there may, and in some circumstances must, be a requirement for repayment[2].

If the improvement is authorised by Part II of that Schedule[3], the trustees may, if they think fit, and must, if so directed by the court, before they make any such application of capital money require that the money, or any part of it, be repaid to them out of the income of the settled land[4] by not more than 50 half-yearly instalments, the first of such instalments to be paid or to be deemed to have become payable at the expiration of six months from the date when the work or operation in payment for which the money is to be applied was completed[5]. If the court authorises capital money to be applied in payment for the improvement, as a condition of making the order it may require that the capital money, or any part of it, be repaid to the trustees of the settlement out of the income of the settled land by a fixed number of periodical instalments to be paid at the times appointed by the court[6].

If the improvement is authorised by Part III of that Schedule[7], then, before they make any such application of capital money, the trustees must require the money to be repaid to them out of the income of the settled land by not more than 50 half-yearly instalments, commencing as mentioned above[8]. If the court authorises capital money to be applied in payment for the improvement, as a condition of making the order it must[9] require that the whole of the capital money be repaid to the trustees of the settlement out of the income of the settled land by a fixed number of periodical instalments to be paid at the times appointed by the court[10].

The court may require that any incumbrancer of the estate or interest of the tenant for life be served with notice of the proceedings[11].

All money received by the trustees of the settlement in respect of these instalments is to be held by them as capital money arising from freehold land under the settlement unless the court otherwise directs[12].

1   Ie authorised by the Settled Land Act 1925 s 83, Sch 3 Pt I: see para 816 post. As to the expenditure of capital money on improvements see para 809 ante. Improvements specified in the Agricultural Holdings Act 1986 s 64, Sch 7 are deemed to be authorised by the Settled Land Act 1925 Sch 3 Pt I (see the Agricultural Holdings Act 1986 s 89(1) (as amended), and their cost is not repayable: see AGRICULTURE vol 1(2) (Reissue) para 492.

2   See the Settled Land Act 1925 s 84(2) proviso.

3   Ie authorised by ibid Sch 3 Pt II, and not by Sch 3 Pt I, or by the settlement. As to the improvements authorised by Sch 3 Pt II see para 817 post.

4   For the meaning of 'settled land' see para 680 text to note 2 ante.

5   Settled Land Act 1925 s 84(2) proviso (a).

6   See ibid s 84(4).

7   Ie authorised by ibid Sch 3 Pt III, and not by the settlement. As to the improvements authorised by Sch 3 Pt III see para 818 post.

8   See ibid s 84(2) proviso (b). As to the commencement of the instalments see the text to note 5 supra.

9   However, as to the court's powers under the Settled Land and Trustee Act (Court's General Powers) Act 1943 see para 671 ante.

10   See the Settled Land Act 1925 s 84(4).

11   See ibid s 84(4). For the meaning of 'tenant for life' see para 671 note 5 ante. See also para 761 et seq ante.

12   Ibid s 84(5). For the meaning of 'trustees of the settlement' see para 750 note 1 ante. As to the trustees see para 750 et seq ante.

813. Creation of rentcharges to discharge instalments.

When a tenant for life[1] is required by the trustees of the settlement[2] to repay the capital money expended or any part of it by instalments[3], he may create out of the settled land[4] or any part of it a yearly rentcharge in favour of the trustees sufficient for that purpose[5].

Where a court order is made requiring repayment by instalments, the settled land stands charged with the payment to the trustees of the settlement of a yearly rentcharge sufficient in amount to discharge the periodical instalments and such a rentcharge takes effect as if limited by the settlement prior to the estate of the tenant for life and the trustees have all statutory and other powers for its recovery[6].

1   For the meaning of 'tenant for life' see para 671 note 5 ante. See also para 761 et seq ante.

2   For the meaning of 'trustees of the settlement' see para 750 note 1 ante. As to the trustees see para 750 et seq ante.

3   As to repayment of capital money by instalments see para 812 ante.

4   For the meaning of 'settled land' see para 680 text to note 2 ante.

5   Settled Land Act 1925 s 85(1). The rentcharge does not charge the equitable interest of the tenant for life, and a life interest determinable on alienation does not cease upon the execution of the charge: see *Re Liberty's Will Trusts, Blackmore v Stewart Liberty* [1937] Ch 176, [1937] 1 All ER 399; and para 918 post. The Rentcharges Act 1977 s 2 does not prevent the creation of such a rentcharge: see s 2(3)(d); and RENTCHARGES AND ANNUITIES vol 39(2) (Reissue) para 774.

6   Settled Land Act 1925 s 85(2). The rentcharge accrues from day to day and is payable at the times appointed for payment of the periodical instalments: s 85(2). As to the recovery of rentcharges see the Law of Property Act 1925 ss 121 (as amended), 122; and RENTCHARGES AND ANNUITIES vol 39(2) (Reissue) para 865 et seq. The instalments of the rentcharge are capital money unless the court otherwise directs: see para 812 ante.

814. Overreaching of rentcharges.

Rentcharges created to discharge instalments of capital money[1] are not redeemable out of capital money[2], but they may be overreached[3] in like manner as if they were limited by the settlement[4] and cease when the land affected by the improvement ceases to be settled land[5], or is sold or exchanged[6]. They may be shifted on to other land with the consent of the incumbrancer so as to exonerate the land originally charged[7].

1   As to the creation of rentcharges for this purpose see para 813 ante.
2   As to the redemption out of capital money of an improvement rentcharge, created to pay for an improvement where the tenant for life is not obliged to replace the cost see para 822 post.
3   As to overreaching see para 874 post.
4   For the meaning of 'settlement' see para 678 note 1 ante.
5   For the meaning of 'settled land' see para 680 text to note 2 ante.
6   See the Settled Land Act 1925 s 85(3); and para 808 ante. If part of the land affected by the improvement remains subject to the settlement the rentcharge remains in force in regard to the settled land: see s 85(3).
7   As to the power to shift incumbrances see para 851 post.

815. Improvements payable out of capital money. The improvements authorised by the Settled Land Act 1925 are the making or execution on or in connection with, and for the benefit of, settled land[1] of any of the specified works[2] and any operation[3] incident to or necessary or proper in the execution of any of those works, or necessary or proper for carrying into effect any of those purposes, or for securing the full benefit of any of those works or purposes[4].

In order that improvements are to be paid for out of capital money[5], they must fall within the improvements enumerated in Schedule 3 to the Settled Land Act 1925[6], or be authorised by other legislation[7], or by the settlement[8], or by the court[9]. The code provided by the Settled Land Act 1925 supersedes and enlarges the lists contained in the Settled Land Acts 1882 to 1890[10], but decisions interpreting any part of those lists will in general be in point as regards the corresponding part of the Settled Land Act 1925 and are cited accordingly.

1   For the meaning of 'settled land' see para 680 text to note 2 ante.
2   Ie works mentioned in the Settled Land Act 1925 s 83, Sch 3: see s 83.
3   In *Re De Crespigny's Settled Estates* [1914] 1 Ch 227, CA, an estate office, to be constructed in connection with the development of the land as a building estate, was treated as such an operation. See further paras 816 note 18, 817 note 4 post.
4   Settled Land Act 1925 s 83.
5   As to payment for improvements out of capital money see para 809 et seq ante.
6   See *Re Lord Gerard's Settled Estates* [1893] 3 Ch 252, CA; *Re Willis, Willis v Willis* [1902] 1 Ch 15 at 23, CA, per Romer LJ; *Re Blagrave's Settled Estates* [1903] 1 Ch 560 at 564, CA, per Cozens-Hardy LJ. As to the improvements see paras 816–818 post.
7   See the Landlord and Tenant (War Damage) Act 1939 s 3 (amended by the Trusts of Land and Appointment of Trustees Act 1996 s 25(2), Sch 4); the Hill Farming Act 1946 s 11 (as amended: see AGRICULTURE vol 1(2) (Reissue) para 509); and the Agricultural Holdings Act 1986 s 89(1), Sch 7 (see para 808 head (4) ante; and AGRICULTURE vol 1(2) (Reissue) para 412). As to charging the inheritance with the cost of improvements in consequence of the Improvement of Land Act 1864 see AGRICULTURE vol 1(2) (Reissue) para 501 et seq.
8   *Re Earl Egmont's Settled Estates, Egmont v Lefroy* (1900) 16 TLR 360.
9   As to the court's power to sanction an unauthorised transaction see paras 670–672 ante. As to payment for repairs (not being authorised improvements) out of capital see para 963 post.
10 As to these Acts see para 678 note 1 ante.

816. Improvements the costs of which are not liable to be replaced by instalments. The costs of the following improvements authorised by Part I of the Third Schedule to the Settled Land Act 1925[1] are not liable to be replaced by instalments[2]:

(1)   drainage[3], including the straightening, widening or deepening[4] of drains, streams and watercourses[5];
(2)   bridges[6];
(3)   irrigation[7] and warping[8];
(4)   drains, pipes and machinery for supply and distribution of sewage as manure[9];
(5)   embanking or weiring from a river or lake, or from the sea or a tidal water[10];
(6)   groynes, sea walls[11] and defences against water[12];
(7)   enclosing, straightening of fences and redivision of fields[13];

(8) reclamation and dry warping[14];

(9) farm roads, private roads[15] and roads or streets in villages or towns[16];

(10) clearing, trenching and planting[17];

(11) cottages[18] for labourers, farm servants and artisans, employed on the settled land or not[19];

(12) farmhouses, offices and outbuildings, and other buildings for farm purposes[20];

(13) sawmills, scutchmills and other mills, water wheels, enginehouses, and kilns which will increase the value of the settled land for agricultural purposes or as woodland or otherwise[21];

(14) reservoirs, tanks, conduits, watercourses, pipes, wells, ponds, shafts, dams, weirs, sluices and other works and machinery for supply and distribution of water for agricultural, manufacturing or other purposes, or for domestic or other consumption[22];

(15) tramways, railways, canals and docks[23];

(16) jetties, piers and landing places on rivers, lakes, the sea or tidal waters for facilitating transport of persons and of agricultural stock and produce, and of manure and other things required for agricultural purposes, and of minerals, and of things required for mining purposes[24];

(17) markets and market places[25];

(18) streets, roads, paths, squares, gardens or other open spaces for the use, gratuitously or on payment, of the public or of individuals, or for dedication to the public, being necessary or proper in connection with the conversion of land into building land[26];

(19) sewers, drains, watercourses, pipe-making, fencing, paving, brick-making, tile-making and other works necessary or proper in connection with any of the objects previously mentioned[27];

(20) trial pits for mines and other preliminary works necessary or proper in connection with development of mines[28];

(21) reconstruction, enlargement or improvement of any of those works[29];

(22) the provision of small dwellings[30], either by means of building new buildings or by means of the reconstruction, enlargement or improvement of existing buildings, if that provision of small dwellings is, in the court's opinion, not injurious[31] to the settled land or is agreed to by the tenant for life and the trustees of the settlement[32];

(23) additions to or alterations in buildings reasonably necessary or proper to enable them to be let[33];

(24) erection of buildings in substitution for buildings within its area taken by a local or other public authority, or for buildings taken under compulsory powers[34], but so that no more money be expended than the amount received for the buildings taken and their sites[35];

(25) the rebuilding[36] of the principal mansion house[37] on the settled land, provided that the sum to be applied under this head may not exceed one-half of the annual rental[38] of the settled land[39].

1 See the Settled Land Act 1925 s 83; and paras 812, 815 ante.

2 The improvements listed are those contained in ibid s 83, Sch 3 Pt I paras (i)–(xxv), which correspond with heads (1)–(25) in the text. By subsequent enactments many other improvements are deemed to be authorised under Sch 3 Pt I: see paras 815 note 7 ante, 817 note 1 post.

3 See *Re Lord Leconfield's Settled Estates* [1907] 2 Ch 340, where a complete system of drainage in a mansion house was allowed.

4 As to the drainage of land see WATER vol 49(2) (Reissue) para 311 et seq. As to the landowner's power to execute drainage works see WATER vol 49(2) (Reissue) para 327 et seq.

5 Settled Land Act 1925 Sch 3 Pt I para (i).

6   Ibid Sch 3 Pt I para (ii).
7   The rights of riparian owners must be respected: *Embrey v Owen* (1851) 6 Exch 353. See also WATER vol 49(2) (Reissue) para 113.
8   Settled Land Act 1925 Sch 3 Pt I para (iii). Warping is a method of improving, and sometimes of reclaiming, land by causing mud to be deposited on it from tidal or flooded rivers. As to dry warping see note 14 infra.
9   Ibid Sch 3 Pt I para (iv). See also the Public Health Act 1936 s 33 by which works for the supply of sewage to land for agricultural purposes are brought within the improvements authorised by the Improvement of Land Act 1864: see AGRICULTURE vol 1(2) (Reissue) para 509. See further PUBLIC HEALTH.
10   Settled Land Act 1925 Sch 3 Pt I para (v).
11   This includes the erection of a sea wall for improving land for building purposes: see *Re Bethlehem and Bridewell Hospitals* (1885) 30 ChD 541.
12   Settled Land Act 1925 Sch 3 Pt I para (vi).
13   Ibid Sch 3 Pt I para (vii). This includes the erection of new fences partly in substitution for old ones and partly to divide a park (see *Re Verney's Settled Estates* [1898] 1 Ch 508), and the rebuilding of a garden wall so as to enclose more ground (see *Re Earl Dunraven's Settled Estates* [1907] 2 Ch 417), but not the reconstruction of unmortared stone walls to divide fields (see *Re Duke of Marlborough's Settlement* (1892) 8 TLR 201).
14   Settled Land Act 1925 Sch 3 Pt I para (viii). Dry warping is a method of improving poor soil by spreading upon it a layer of better soil, and is distinguishable from warping (see note 8 supra) in which the coating of soil is deposited by water.
15   This includes a new carriage drive to the mansion house, but not garden paths: see *Re Windham's Settled Estate* [1912] 2 Ch 75.
16   Settled Land Act 1925 Sch 3 Pt I para (ix).
17   Ibid Sch 3 Pt I para (x).
18   A gardener's cottage comes within this heading (*Re Earl Lisburne's Settled Estates* [1901] WN 91), but a residence for an estate agent does not (*Re Lord Gerard's Settled Estate* [1893] 3 Ch 252). See also the Settled Land Act 1925 Sch 3 Pt I para (xxii) (see the text head (22)); cf Sch 3 Pt II para (i) (see para 817 head (1) post).
19   Ibid Sch 3 Pt I para (xi). For the meaning of 'settled land' see para 680 text to note 2 ante.
20   Ibid Sch 3 Pt I para (xii). In *Re Broadwater Estate* (1885) 54 LJ Ch 1104, CA, silos were considered to be buildings, but the cost was disallowed on the ground that ensilage was in an experimental stage. This decision would probably not now be followed. In any case, silos are covered by the Agricultural Holdings Act 1986: see s 64, Sch 7 Pt II para 12; and AGRICULTURE vol 1(2) (Reissue) para 412. Reconstruction of unmortared stone walls was not allowed either under this head or under head (21): see *Re Duke of Marlborough's Settlement* (1892) 8 TLR 201.
21   Settled Land Act 1925 Sch 3 Pt I para (xiii). 'Other mills' does not include mills for commercial purposes: see *Re Earl Harrington's Settled Estates* (1906) 75 LJ Ch 460, CA. The expression 'or otherwise' must be construed ejusdem generis: *Re Lord Leconfield's Settled Estates* [1907] 2 Ch 340.
22   Settled Land Act 1925 Sch 3 Pt I para (xiv). This includes fire extinguishing equipment: *Re Earl Dunraven's Settled Estates* [1907] 2 Ch 417. Boring for water and preliminary works are authorised by the Settled Land Act 1925 Sch 3 Pt II para (vi) (see para 817 head (6) post), and the cost may therefore be required to be replaced by instalments.
23   Ibid Sch 3 Pt I para (xv).
24   Ibid Sch 3 Pt I para (xvi). For the meaning of 'mining purposes' see para 808 note 36 ante.
25   Ibid Sch 3 Pt I para (xvii). As to the meaning of 'market' see MARKETS AND FAIRS. The erection of market places and market houses is authorised by Sch 3 Pt II para (iii): see para 817 head (3) post.
26   Ibid Sch 3 Pt I para (xviii). For the meaning of 'land' see para 680 note 1 ante. A cricket ground has been allowed, but not a pavilion (*Re Orwell Park Estate* (1904) 48 Sol Jo 193); a golf course and golf club-house have been allowed (*Re Lord De La Warr's Settled Estates* (1911) 27 TLR 534), but not the amount paid to an agricultural tenant by way of compensation on determining his tenancy in order to obtain possession of the land for the golf course (*Re Earl De La Warr's Cooden Beach Settled Estate* [1913] 1 Ch 142, CA). An estate office has been allowed (*Re De Crespigny's Settled Estates* [1914] 1 Ch 227, CA), as being an operation as now mentioned in the Settled Land Act 1925 s 83 (see para 815 ante); see now, however, Sch 3 Pt II para (ii) (see para 817 head (2) post). As to the dedication of land for open spaces under s 56 (as amended) see para 865 post.
27   Ibid Sch 3 Pt I para (xix). It is submitted that this means those previously mentioned in Sch 3 Pt I paras (i)–(xix) (see heads (1)–(19) in the text): see *Re Earl Dunraven's Settled Estates* [1907] 2 Ch 417; and note 29 infra.
28   Settled Land Act 1925 Sch 3 Pt I para (xx). So long as any part of the area remains to be opened up development is going on, and at every stage in the operation of extracting all the workable minerals from the area there may be works to be executed which are accurately described as works preliminary to

development: *Re Hanbury's Settled Estates* [1913] 1 Ch 50 at 55 per Eve J. As to the privatisation of the coal industry see MINES, MINERALS AND QUARRIES vol 31 (Reissue) para 3.

29   Settled Land Act 1925 Sch 3 Pt I para (xxi). The works referred to in the text are any of the works mentioned in Sch 3 Pt I paras (i)–(xx) (see note 27 supra), however or whenever those works were made, whether under the powers of a Settled Land Act or otherwise: see *Re Earl Dunraven's Settled Estates* [1907] 2 Ch 417. The item includes the reconstruction, enlargement or improvement of preliminary works constructed under the Settled Land Act 1925 Sch 3 Pt I para (xx), even though such works have ceased to be merely preliminary and have become permanent (see *Re Mundy's Settled Estates* [1891] 1 Ch 399, CA), but it is apprehended that it does not apply to new works constructed under any of the subsequent provisions of the Settled Land Act 1925 Sch 3 Pt I or of Sch 3 Pt II or Pt III. Where repairs are necessary in order to carry out an improvement, the work may be treated as a whole and the cost of the repairs as part of the improvement: *Re Lindsay's Settlement (No 2)* [1941] Ch 119, [1941] 1 All ER 143.

30   'Small dwellings' means dwelling houses of a rateable value not exceeding £100 per annum: Settled Land Act 1925 s 117(1)(xxv). As to the rateable value see RATING AND COUNCIL TAX vol 39(1) (Reissue) para 683. Each flat intended to be separately occupied by a workman and his family is a small dwelling: *Re Paddington's Estate* [1940] Ch 43. A limited acreage of settled land may be granted gratuitously or at a nominal rent for the erection of houses for the working classes or the provision of allotments and smallholdings: see para 831 post.

31   The provision of dwellings available for the working classes is not to be deemed injurious, but the tenant for life may not make such provision without the trustees' written consent: see the Settled Land Act 1925 s 107(2); and para 775 note 8 ante.

32   Ibid Sch 3 Pt I para (xxii). For the meaning of 'tenant for life' see para 671 note 5 ante. See also para 761 et seq ante. For the meaning of 'trustees of the settlement' see para 750 note 1 ante. As to the trustees see para 750 et seq ante.

33   Ibid Sch 3 Pt I para (xxiii). These additions or alterations need not be structural additions or alterations: *Re Lindsay's Settlement (No 2)* [1941] Ch 119, [1941] 1 All ER 143. 'Reasonably necessary or proper' was considered in *Stanford v Roberts* [1901] 1 Ch 440. There must be a present intention to let as distinguished from an intention to occupy: see *Re De Teissier's Settled Estates* [1893] 1 Ch 153; *Stanford v Roberts* supra. This condition is satisfied if the tenant gives notice that he will quit unless the work is done: see *Re Calverley's Settled Estates* [1904] 1 Ch 150. Under this item, or the corresponding one in the Settled Land Act 1890 s 13 (repealed), the following works have been allowed: a new billiard room (*Re De Teissier's Settled Estates* supra at 156); rearrangement of the main entrance to a house, and reroofing of a house (*Re Gaskell's Settled Estates* [1894] 1 Ch 485); reconstructing drainage to houses (*Re Thomas, Weatherall v Thomas* [1900] 1 Ch 319; *Re Lord Leconfield's Settled Estates* [1907] 2 Ch 340; *Standing v Gray* [1903] 1 IR 49); substitution of solid concrete floors for floorboards (*Stanford v Roberts* supra); erection of washhouse and privy (*Re Calverley's Settled Estates* supra); structural alterations in public house required as condition of renewal of licence (*Re Gurney's Marriage Settlement, Sullivan v Gurney* [1907] 2 Ch 496); structural alterations in buildings of historic interest open to sightseers (*Re Battle Abbey Settled Estate, Webster v Troubridge* [1933] WN 215); and the conversion of a dwelling house, cottage and shop into residential flats and shops to increase the rental value of the settled land (*Re Swanwick House, Prestbury* [1939] 3 All ER 531). As to when repairs amount to additions or alterations see *Re Conquest, Royal Exchange Assurance v Conquest* [1929] 2 Ch 353. The following works have been disallowed: erection of new building in place of old (*Re Leveson-Gower's Settled Estate* [1905] 2 Ch 95); heating apparatus (*Re Gaskell's Settled Estates* supra); electric light installation (*Re Clarke's Settlement* [1902] 2 Ch 327; *Re Blagrave's Settled Estates* [1903] 1 Ch 560, CA); engine house for electric light (*Re Blagrave's Settled Estates* supra); lengthening shaft in silk mill (*Re Earl Harrington's Settled Estates* (1906) 75 LJ Ch 460, CA); repairs to a mansion house, the cost of which the tenant for life desired to be repaid out of a forfeited deposit upon an abortive sale (*Re Foster's Settled Estates* [1922] 1 Ch 348).

     Cf the Settled Land Act 1925 Sch 3 Pt II para (v), and Sch 3 Pt III paras (i), (ii): see paras 817 head (5), 818 heads (1), (2) post.

34   As to compulsory acquisition of land generally see COMPULSORY ACQUISITION OF LAND.

35   See the Settled Land Act 1925 Sch 3 Pt I para (xxiv). This item refers to buildings 'within an urban sanitary district'. As to such districts see PUBLIC HEALTH.

36   Rebuilding involves a question of fact in each case: see *Re Wright's Settled Estate* (1900) 83 LT 159; *Re Kensington Settled Estates* (1905) 21 TLR 351. It does not include structural repairs (see *Re De Teissier's Settled Estates* [1893] 1 Ch 153), or merely architectural improvements (see *Re Lord Gerard's Settled Estate* [1893] 3 Ch 252, CA), or the erection of a laundry 250 yards away from the house (see *Re Earl Dunraven's Settled Estates* [1907] 2 Ch 417). On the other hand, it has been held to include partial reconstruction of a mansion house (see *Re Walker's Settled Estate* [1894] 1 Ch 189), heating and electric light apparatus (see *Re Kensington Settled Estates* supra; *Re Dunham Massey Settled Estates* (1906) 22 TLR 595), and stables connected with the house physically and by use (see *Re Lord Gerard's Settled Estate* supra).

37   As to the meaning of 'principal mansion house' see para 789 note 5 ante.

38 In calculating the annual rental, no deduction should be made for mortgage interest, tithes, drainage rates or rentcharges (see *Re Windham's Settled Estate* [1912] 2 Ch 75), or income tax or capital transfer tax (see *Re Fife's Settlement Trusts* [1922] 2 Ch 348), or costs of repairs (see *Re Kensington Settled Estates* (1905) 21 TLR 351). There should be included the income of invested capital money (see *Re De Teissier's Settled Estates* [1893] 1 Ch 153), the whole rental of the settled property (see *Re Lord Gerard's Settled Estate* [1893] 3 Ch 252, CA), and the rental value of settled property usually let but temporarily unlet, but not of land in the occupation of the tenant for life (see *Re Walker's Settled Estate* [1894] 1 Ch 189). The point of time to be taken in ascertaining the annual rental was the date when the scheme was approved by the trustees or the court (see *Re Fife's Settlement Trusts* supra), but now that no scheme has to be prepared and approved (see para 809 ante), it is submitted that the point of time will be the date of a binding contract for the execution of the work.

39 Settled Land Act 1925 Sch 3 Pt I para (xxv). As to the use of this power by a landowner under the Improvement of Land Act 1864, and as to the provisions of the Limited Owners Residences Act 1870, and the Limited Owners Residences Act (1870) Amendment Act 1871 see AGRICULTURE vol 1(2) (Reissue) para 508 et seq.

817. Improvements the costs of which may be replaced by instalments. The following are the improvements under Part II of the Third Schedule to the Settled Land Act 1925, the cost of which may be required by the trustees of the settlement or the court to be replaced by instalments[1]:

(1)   residential houses for land or mineral agents, managers, clerks, bailiffs, woodmen, gamekeepers and other persons employed on the settled land[2] or in connection with its management or development[3];

(2)   any offices[4], workshops and other buildings of a permanent nature required in connection with the management or development of the settled land or any part of it[5];

(3)   the erection and building of dwelling houses, shops, buildings for religious, educational, literary, scientific or public purposes, market places, market houses, places of amusement and entertainment, gasworks, electric light or power works or any other works necessary or proper in connection with the development of the settled land or any part of it as a building estate[6];

(4)   restoration or reconstruction of buildings damaged or destroyed by dry rot[7];

(5)   structural additions[8] to or alterations in buildings reasonably required, whether the buildings are intended to be let or not, or are already let[9];

(6)   boring for water and other preliminary works in connection with it[10]; and

(7)   works specified as being required for properly maintaining a listed building of special architectural or historic interest[11].

1   The improvements listed are those contained in the Settled Land Act 1925 s 83, Sch 3 Pt II, which correspond with heads (1)–(6) in the text. As to repayment by instalments see para 812 ante. Improvements specified in the Agricultural Holdings Act 1986 s 64, Sch 7, are deemed to be authorised by the Settled Land Act 1925 s 83, Sch 3 Pt I (see the Agricultural Holdings Act 1986 s 89(1) (as amended), and their cost is not repayable: see AGRICULTURE vol 1(2) (Reissue) para 492.

2   For the meaning of 'settled land' see para 680 text to note 2 ante.

3   Settled Land Act 1925 Sch 3 Pt II para (i).

4   The erection of an estate office had already been allowed on other grounds (see *Re De Crespigny's Settled Estates* [1914] 1 Ch 227, CA): see paras 815 note 3, 816 text and note 26 ante.

5   Settled Land Act 1925 Sch 3 Pt II para (ii).

6   Ibid Sch 3 Pt II para (iii).

7   Ibid Sch 3 Pt II para (iv). This removes difficulties which were considered in *Re Legh's Settled Estate* [1902] 2 Ch 274.

8   The test whether a building is a structural addition is whether it forms with the principal house a whole or unit, not whether the new building is physically attached to the principal house: *Re Insole's Settled Estate* [1938] Ch 812, [1938] 3 All ER 406, CA.

9   Settled Land Act 1925 Sch 3 Pt II para (v). Cf Sch 3 Pt I para (xxiii) (see para 816 head (23) ante).

10 Ibid Sch 3 Pt II para (vi). As to the supply and distribution of water see Sch 3 Pt I paras (xiv), (xix); and para 816 heads (14), (19) ante.

11   This class of works is added by the Planning (Listed Buildings and Conservation Areas) Act 1990 s 87: see TOWN AND COUNTRY PLANNING vol 46 (Reissue) para 897. As to listed buildings generally see TOWN AND COUNTRY PLANNING vol 46 (Reissue) para 888 et seq.

818. Improvements the costs of which must be replaced by instalments. The following are the improvements under Part III of the Third Schedule to the Settled Land Act 1925, the costs of which the trustees and the court must require to be replaced by instalments[1]:

(1)   heating, hydraulic or electric power apparatus for buildings, and engines, pumps, lifts, rams, boilers, flues and other works required for use in connection with them[2];

(2)   engine houses, engines, gasometers, dynamos, accumulators, cables, pipes, wiring, switchboards, plant and other works required for the installation of electric, gas or other artificial light, in connection with any principal mansion house[3], or other house or buildings, but not electric lamps, gas fittings or decorative fittings required in any such house or building[4]; and

(3)   steam rollers, traction engines, motor lorries and movable machinery for farming or other purposes[5].

1   See the Settled Land Act 1925 s 83, Sch 3 Pt III paras (i)–(iii). Improvements specified in the Agricultural Holdings Act 1986 s 64, Sch 7, are deemed to be authorised by the Settled Land Act 1925 s 83, Sch 3 Pt I (see the Agricultural Holdings Act 1986 s 89(1) (as amended), and their cost is not repayable: see AGRICULTURE vol 1(2) (Reissue) para 492. As to repayment by instalments see para 812 ante. As to the court's power to treat an income expense as a capital liability see para 671 ante.
2   Settled Land Act 1925 Sch 3 Pt III para (i).
3   As to the meaning of 'principal mansion house' see para 789 note 6 ante.
4   Settled Land Act 1925 Sch 3 Pt III para (ii).
5   Ibid Sch 3 Pt III para (iii).

819. Interpretation of statutory improvements. The Settled Land Act 1925 includes, with considerable additions, all the agricultural improvements enumerated in the Improvement of Land Act 1864[1], and the fact that an improvement has been sanctioned under the latter Act, as coming within a provision substantially identical with a provision of the Settled Land Act 1925, is good evidence that it is an improvement within the Settled Land Act 1925[2]. The list has been interpreted by the courts with some liberality[3], but those items which by the language employed are limited to works incidental to the use of the land itself as agricultural land will not be construed in a wider sense[4].

1   See *Re Newton's Settled Estates* [1890] WN 24, CA. As to the improvements specified in the Improvement of Land Act 1864 s 9 see AGRICULTURE vol 1(2) (Reissue) para 509.
2   *Re Verney's Settled Estates* [1898] 1 Ch 508.
3   This appears evident from the cases in the footnotes to para 816 et seq ante; but where the Settled Land Act 1925 s 83, Sch 3 makes provision for the execution of work of a certain class, the court will regard itself as bound by it: see *Re Lord Gerard's Settled Estate* [1893] 3 Ch 252, CA.
4   See *Re Earl Harrington's Settled Estates* (1906) 75 LJ Ch 460, CA. Thus an engine house to supply electric light (*Re Lord Leconfield's Settled Estates* [1907] 2 Ch 340), or mills for commercial purposes (*Re Earl Harrington's Settled Estates* supra), were not allowed as improvements under an enactment which corresponded to the Settled Land Act 1925 Sch 3 Pt I para (xiii) (see para 816 head (13) ante). Provision is now made under Sch 3 Pt III para (ii) for works required for the installation of electric or other artificial light: see para 818 head (2) ante.

820. Payment of expenses of improvements. The expenses of making any authorised improvement may be paid out of capital money under the Settled Land Act 1925[1], or they may be raised by legal mortgage on the security of the settled land or any part of it[2]. A tenant for life who is entitled under the settlement to the whole income and enjoyment of the settled property during his life is under no obligation to account to the trustees for sums recovered by him by way of income tax allowances or reliefs referable to his expenditure on improvements[3] to the settled land, notwithstanding that the expenditure has been recouped to him by the trustees of the settlement at his direction[4]. Where the costs of works of public improvement have been assessed on land, the landowner may apply to have these costs charged on the land as if the works had been improvements under the Improvement of Land Act 1864[5]. It would appear, moreover, that where such expenses have been charged by the local authority upon the settled land under statutory powers, the tenant for life is entitled to have them repaid out of capital[6].

1   For the meaning of 'capital money arising under the Act' see para 795 ante.
2   See the Settled Land Act 1925 ss 71(1) (as amended), 84; and paras 809–812 ante, 849–850 post. As to repayment of the costs of certain improvements out of income see para 812 ante.
3   The improvements were within ibid s 83, Sch 3 Pt I, and accordingly no part of their cost had to be recouped to capital by instalments: see para 812 ante.
4   *Re Pelly's Will Trusts, Ransome v Pelly* [1957] Ch 1, [1956] 2 All ER 326, CA. The decision in that case left open the question of what the position would be as regards income tax reliefs if the cost of the improvements had been paid for by the trustees direct to the contractors who did the work. See further para 808 note 23 ante.
5   See the Improvement of Land Act 1864 ss 57, 58; and AGRICULTURE vol 1(2) (Reissue) para 520. In effect this provision extends the scope of authorised improvements, although by an indirect method.
6   *Re Legh's Settled Estate* [1902] 2 Ch 274.

821. Improvements and initial repairs to tenanted premises. Capital money arising under the Settled Land Act 1925[1] may be applied:

(1)   in payment as for an improvement authorised by that Act of any money expended or costs incurred by a landlord under or in pursuance of Part I of the Landlord and Tenant Act 1927[2] in or about the execution of any improvement[3];

(2)   in payment of any sum due to a tenant in respect of compensation[4] for an improvement and any costs, charges and expenses incidental to it[5]; and

(3)   in payment of the costs, charges and expenses of opposing any proposal by a tenant to execute an improvement[6]. Similarly, capital money so arising may be applied in the payment of expenses incurred in carrying out certain initial repairs[7].

1   For the meaning of 'capital money arising under the Act' see para 795 ante. Where the landlord liable to pay compensation for an improvement is a tenant for life or in a fiduciary position, he may require the sum payable as compensation, and any costs, charges and expenses incidental to it, to be paid out of any capital money held on the same trusts as the settled land; and in this provision, 'capital money' includes any personal estate held on the same trusts as the land: Landlord and Tenant Act 1927 s 13(3) (amended by the Landlord and Tenant Act 1954 s 45, Sch 7 Pt I; and by the Trusts of Land and Appointment of Trustees Act 1996 s 25(2), Sch 4). For the meaning of 'tenant for life' under the Settled Land Act 1925 see para 671 note 5 ante.
2   Ie under the Landlord and Tenant Act 1927 Pt I (ss 1–17) (as amended) (see LANDLORD AND TENANT vol 27(1) (Reissue) para 637 et seq): see s 13(1)(a).
3   Ibid s 13(1)(a).
4   Ie due under ibid Pt I: see s 13(1)(b) (as amended: see note 5 infra). As to the compensation payable under Pt I see ss 1–3 (s 1 as amended); and LANDLORD AND TENANT vol 27(1) (Reissue) para 642 et seq. The satisfaction of a claim for compensation is included among the purposes for which a tenant for life or statutory owner may raise money under the Settled Land Act 1925 s 71 (as amended), ie by a legal mortgage: see the Landlord and Tenant Act 1927 s 13(2) (amended by the Trusts of Land and Appointment of Trustees Act 1996 Sch 4); and LANDLORD AND TENANT vol 27(1) (Reissue) para 652. As to the power to mortgage settled land see paras 849–850 post.
5   Landlord and Tenant Act 1927 s 13(1)(b) (amended by the Landlord and Tenant Act 1954 Sch 7 Pt I).
6   Landlord and Tenant Act 1927 s 13(1)(c).
7   See the Landlord and Tenant Act 1954 s 8, Sch 2 para 6 (as amended); and LANDLORD AND TENANT vol 27(2) (Reissue) para 1070. The repairs referred to in the text are the repairs relating to premises let under

long tenancies at low rents specified in s 8: see LANDLORD AND TENANT vol 27(2) (Reissue) para 1073. Capital money applied in respect of repairs is subject to the like provisions as if it were applied in respect of improvements under the Settled Land Act 1925 s 83, Sch 3 Pt II (see para 817 ante), and is therefore money which the trustees of the settlement or the court may require to be replaced by instalments: see the Landlord and Tenant Act 1954 Sch 2 para 6 proviso (see LANDLORD AND TENANT vol 27(1) (Reissue) para 1070); and para 812 ante. As to the maintenance, repair and insurance of improvements see para 964 post.

822. Redemption of improvement rentcharges. Capital money may be applied in the redemption of certain improvement rentcharges[1]. Redemption here means the discharge of all instalments due or to become due, principal as well as interest, by the payment of a lump sum, as distinct from the mere payment of instalments as and when they become due[2]. An improvement rentcharge for this purpose is a rentcharge, whether temporary or permanent, created at any time pursuant to an Act of Parliament, with the object of paying off any money advanced for defraying the expenses of an authorised[3] improvement[4], but a rentcharge created to repay capital money which a tenant for life is required to replace is not itself redeemable out of capital[5]. Recoupment of expenditure on improvements borne by a tenant for life but properly chargeable to capital may, it seems, be allowed in the absence of circumstances showing that recoupment was waived or that it would be inequitable[6]. The fact that the improved portion of the estate has been sold and that the rentcharge has been transferred to other portions is no objection to such an application of capital money[7].

A payment made by a tenant for life to induce the original holders of charges to consent to a transfer of the charges by which the interest is reduced may not be repaid to him out of capital money[8]. When an improvement rentcharge has been redeemed out of capital money, the obligations of the tenant for life to maintain and insure[9] apply to the improvement in respect of which the rentcharge was created[10].

1   See the Settled Land Act 1925 s 73(1)(xiii); and para 808 ante.
2   *Re Sandbach* [1951] Ch 791 at 803, [1951] 1 All ER 971 at 977, CA, explaining *Re Lord Egmont's Settled Estates* (1890) 45 ChD 395, CA. Past payments by a tenant for life in respect of instalments, representing capital and interest, of loans for improvements, the payments being made as and when the instalments became due, may not be recouped out of capital money under the Settled Land Act 1925 s 73(1)(xiii): see *Re Sandbach* supra. The words 'or otherwise providing for the payment' of an improvement rentcharge, which were in the former enactment (see the Settled Land Acts (Amendment) Act 1887 s 1 (repealed)) and were the basis of the decision in *Re Lord Sudeley's Settled Estates* (1887) 37 ChD 123 that periodical payments of instalments in so far as consisting of capital, could be recouped, are not in the Settled Land Act 1925 s 73(1)(xiii).
3   Ie authorised by ibid s 83, Sch 3 Pt I (see para 816 ante): see s 73(1)(xiii). It is essential that the improvement should be of such a kind: see *Re Newton's Settled Estates* (1889) 61 LT 787; *Re Verney's Settled Estates* [1898] 1 Ch 508 at 511.
4   Settled Land Act 1925 s 73(1)(xiii).
5   See ibid s 85(1), (3); and paras 808, 813 ante. As to charging the inheritance with the cost of improvements authorised by the Settled Land Act 1925 Sch 3, pursuant to the Improvement of Land Act 1864 see AGRICULTURE vol 1(2) (Reissue) para 511.
6   See *Re Sandbach* [1951] Ch 791 at 806–807, [1951] 1 All ER 971 at 979, CA, where Jenkins LJ distinguished *Re Howard's Settled Estates* [1892] 2 Ch 233, *Re Dalison's Settled Estate* [1892] 3 Ch 522, and *Re Verney's Settled Estates* [1898] 1 Ch 508 as being related to the wording of the Settled Land Acts (Amendment) Act 1887 ss 1, 2 (repealed), which was different from that of the corresponding provisions of the Settled Land Act 1925: see note 2 supra. Similar considerations apply to *Re Marquis of Bristol's Settled Estates* [1893] 3 Ch 161 at 165.
7   *Re Howard's Settled Estates* [1892] 2 Ch 233.
8   *Re Verney's Settled Estates* [1898] 1 Ch 508.
9   As to the maintenance and insurance of improvements see para 964 post.
10 See the Settled Land Act 1925 s 88(6).

823. Costs incurred by tenant for life. The tenant for life is entitled to be paid out of capital money arising under the Settled Land Act 1925[1] the costs incurred but not recovered by him of an unsuccessful action by the remaindermen to prevent his exercising his statutory power of sale[2], and also the costs of a wholly or partially unsuccessful attempt to sell[3]. An estate agent's commission for procuring a building lease for a long term is payable out of capital money[4], but commission on a short letting is an income charge which cannot be thrown on capital[5]. An architect's fees and solicitor's remuneration incurred in connection with a letting have been allowed out of capital[6], but an intention to deal with portions of an estate does not enable a tenant for life to obtain out of capital money payment of the costs of making an elaborate survey of the whole estate[7]. The costs of obtaining the consent of a mortgagee of the life estate to a sale, although costs incidental to the exercise of the statutory power, ought not as a rule to be directed by the court to be paid out of capital money[8], and the tenant for life must bear the cost of obtaining vacant possession of settled land, including the payment of compensation, for the purpose of executing an authorised improvement[9].

1   As to the tenant for life see para 761 et seq ante. For the meaning of 'capital money arising under the Act' see para 795 ante.
2   *Re Llewellin, Llewellin v Williams* (1887) 37 ChD 317.
3   *Re Smith's Settled Estates* [1891] 3 Ch 65. As to the form of order for payment of costs of sale see *Re Rudd* [1887] WN 251. The trustees need not tax the costs of the tenant for life, but are entitled to an opportunity of considering the bills and deciding whether they will require them to be taxed: *Re Peel's Settled Estates* [1910] 1 Ch 389. As to costs see generally RSC Ord 62; as from 26 April 1999, CPR Pts 43–48; and PRACTICE AND PROCEDURE.
4   *Re Maryon-Wilson's Settled Estates* [1901] 1 Ch 934.
5   *Re Leveson-Gower's Settled Estate* [1905] 2 Ch 95. See, however, *Re Watson, Brand v Culme-Seymour* [1928] WN 309.
6   *Re Watson, Brand v Culme-Seymour* [1928] WN 309.
7   *Re Eyton's Settled Estate* [1888] WN 254. Cf *Re Tubbs, Dykes v Tubbs* [1915] 2 Ch 137, CA.
8   *Sebright v Thornton* [1885] WN 176; *Countess Cardigan v Curzon-Howe* (1889) 41 ChD 375, CA. This is so whether the money is in court or held by the trustees: *Re Peel's Settled Estates* [1910] 1 Ch 389.
9   *Re Earl of De La Warr's Cooden Beach Settled Estate* [1913] 1 Ch 142, CA.

824. Costs directed by the court to be paid out of capital money. The court[1], in its discretion, may order the costs, charges or expenses of all or any of the parties to any application to it under the Settled Land Act 1925[2] to be paid out of the settled property[3]. When the court directs that any costs, charges or expenses be paid out of property subject to a settlement[4], then, subject to the court's direction, they are to be raised and paid (1) out of capital money arising under that Act[5] or other money liable to be laid out in the purchase of land[6] to be made subject to the settlement[7]; (2) out of securities[8] representing such money, or out of income of any such money or securities[9]; (3) out of any accumulations of income of land, money or securities[10]; (4) by means of a sale of part of the settled land[11] in respect of which the costs, charges or expenses are incurred, or of other settled land comprised in the same settlement and subject to the same limitations[12]; or (5) by means of a legal mortgage[13] of the settled land or any part of it to be made by such person as the court directs[14], or partly in one of those modes and partly in another or others, or in any such other mode as the court thinks fit[15].

1   As to the court see para 792 ante.
2   As to applications to the court see para 792 ante.
3   See the Settled Land Act 1925 s 113(8); and para 792 ante.
4   For the meaning of 'property' see para 778 note 7 ante; and for the meaning of 'settlement' see para 678 note 1 ante.
5   For the meaning of 'capital money arising under the Act' see para 795 ante.
6   For the meaning of 'land' see para 680 note 1 ante.

7 Settled Land Act 1925 s 114(a).
8 For the meaning of 'securities' see para 693 note 1 ante.
9 Settled Land Act 1925 s 114(b).
10 Ibid s 114(c).
11 For the meaning of 'settled land' see para 680 text to note 2 ante.
12 Settled Land Act 1925 s 114(d). For the meaning of 'limitation' see para 708 note 4 ante.
13 For the meaning of 'legal mortgage' see para 698 note 23 ante.
14 Settled Land Act 1925 s 114(e).
15 Ibid s 114.

825. Costs of protecting the settled land. If it thinks fit, the court[1] may approve of any action, defence, petition to Parliament, parliamentary opposition or other proceeding taken or proposed to be taken for the protection of settled land[2], or of any action or proceeding taken or proposed to be taken for the recovery of land being or alleged to be subject to a settlement[3], and may direct that any costs, charges or expenses incurred or to be incurred in relation to it, or any part of it, be paid out of property subject to the settlement[4]. The tenant for life is not bound to obtain the court's sanction before commencing proceedings, but, if he does so without first obtaining the court's sanction, it is at the risk of having payment of his costs out of capital refused[5].

The court has power under its general jurisdiction to order that money forming part of the settled estate and subject to a trust to be laid out in the purchase of land may be applied in repaying to the tenant for life the expenditure incurred in opposing a bill before Parliament[6], or in an action to establish rights[7].

1 As to the court see para 792 ante.
2 For the meaning of 'settled land' see para 680 text to note 2 ante.
3 In special circumstances this has been held to cover proceedings successfully prosecuted before the House of Lords to establish a claim to an earldom (see *Re Earl of Aylesford's Settled Estates* (1886) 32 ChD 162), a petition by the lord of a manor to the ecclesiastical courts for a new faculty (see *Re Mosley's Settled Estates* (1912) 56 Sol Jo 325), and surveying properties let and serving notices on the tenants (see *Re Tubbs, Dykes v Tubbs* [1915] 2 Ch 137, CA). For the meaning of 'land' see para 680 note 1 ante; and for the meaning of 'settlement' see para 678 ante.
4 Settled Land Act 1925 s 92.
5 *Re Yorke, Barlow v Yorke* [1911] 1 Ch 370. In *Re Wilkie's Settlement, Wade v Wilkie* [1914] 1 Ch 77, costs were allowed even though the proceedings had been abandoned.
6 *Re Ormrod's Settled Estate* [1892] 2 Ch 318. See, however, *Stanford v Roberts* (1882) 52 LJ Ch 50.
7 *Hamilton v Tighe* [1898] 1 IR 123.

826. Devolution of capital money. Capital money arising under the Settled Land Act 1925[1], while remaining uninvested or unapplied, and securities[2] on which an investment of any such capital money is made, are, for all purposes of disposition, transmission and devolution, treated as land[3], and must be held for and go to the same persons successively, in the same manner and for and on the same estates, interests and trusts as the land from which the money arises would, if not disposed of, have been held and have gone under the settlement[4], and the income of the securities must be paid or applied as the income of the land, if not disposed of, would have been payable or applicable under the settlement[5]. However, an appointee under a will of land does not become entitled to fines or premiums paid to the appointor in consideration of the granting of building leases by him[6].

Securities on which an investment of capital money is made may be converted into money, which in turn is capital money arising under the Settled Land Act 1925[7].

1 For the meaning of 'capital money arising under the Act' see para 795 ante.
2 For the meaning of 'securities' see para 693 note 1 ante.
3 For the meaning of 'land' see para 680 note 1 ante.

4   Settled Land Act 1925 s 75(5). For the meaning of 'settlement' see para 678 note 1 ante. See also *Re Cartwright, Cartwright v Smith* [1939] Ch 90, [1938] 4 All ER 209, CA; *Re Cutcliffe's Will Trusts, Brewer v Cutcliffe* [1940] Ch 565, [1940] 2 All ER 297; *Re Armstrong's Will Trusts, Graham v Armstrong* [1943] Ch 400, [1943] 2 All ER 537. This provision does not effect a conversion of capital money into land for all purposes: *Re Midleton's Settlement, Lord Cottesloe and Loyd v A-G and Earl of Midleton* [1947] Ch 583 at 591–592, [1947] 2 All ER 134 at 137, CA (affd sub nom *Earl of Midleton v Baron Cottesloe* [1949] AC 418, [1949] 1 All ER 841, HL); *Bank of Ireland v Domvile* [1956] IR 37 at 57.
5   Settled Land Act 1925 s 75(6).
6   *Re Moses, Beddington v Beddington* [1902] 1 Ch 100, CA; affd sub nom *Beddington v Baumann* [1903] AC 13, HL.
7   See the Settled Land Act 1925 s 75(7).

(vi)   Powers of Sale and Exchange

827.   Power of sale. The tenant for life[1] may sell the settled land[2], or any part of it[3], or any easement, right or privilege of any kind over or in relation to it[4]. This power is absolute, and may be exercised free from any restrictions on a power of sale given to the trustees by the settlement, or by a private Act of Parliament[5]. However, the purchase money must be paid to the trustees of the settlement or into court[6].

1   For the meaning of 'tenant for life' see para 671 note 5 ante.
2   For the meaning of 'settled land' see para 680 text to note 2 ante. As to the power to sell the principal mansion house see paras 789–790 ante. As to the notice to be given before a sale is made see para 783 ante.
3   The tenant for life is empowered to sell the subsoil without the surface: *Re Pearson's Will* (1900) 83 LT 626. As to the power to deal with the surface and minerals separately see para 856 post.
4   Settled Land Act 1925 s 38(i). As to the exercise of this power where persons together constituting the tenant for life disagree see para 793 ante. As to equitable interests in land see EQUITY vol 16 (Reissue) para 775 et seq.
5   *Wheelwright v Walker* (1883) 23 ChD 752; *Re Chaytor's Settled Estate Act* (1884) 25 ChD 651. As to the exercise by the tenant for life of powers given to the trustees see para 880 post.
6   See para 804 ante.

828.   Consideration for sale. Except in certain circumstances[1], every sale must be made either for the best consideration in money that can reasonably be obtained[2], or, where a rentcharge can still validly be created, in consideration wholly or partially of a perpetual rent, or a terminable rent[3] consisting of principal and interest combined, payable yearly or half-yearly to be secured upon the land[4] sold, or the land to which the easement, right or privilege sold is to be annexed in enjoyment or an adequate part of it[5]. It is a breach of duty for the tenant for life[6] to enter into an agreement to sell for a price to be fixed by someone else, for example by an arbitrator[7], except that timber on or fixtures attached to the land sold may be sold at a valuation[8].

1   As to sale for less than the best price see para 831 post.
2   Settled Land Act 1925 s 39(1). See also *Wheelwright v Walker* (1883) 48 LT 867. A sale in consideration of consols has been held to be a sale for 'money': *Re Sutton's Contract* (1920) 65 Sol Jo 259. In granting authority to sell Scottish estates belonging to an English trust, the court in Scotland has held that it is inappropriate to include in its order the words 'provided every sale shall be made for the best consideration in money that can reasonably be obtained' as being a provision from a system of land tenure alien to Scotland: *Campbell's Petition* 1958 SC 275. As to options to purchase see para 871 post.
3   For the meaning of 'rent' see para 801 note 1 ante. As to perpetual or terminable rents see also RENTCHARGES AND ANNUITIES vol 39(2) (Reissue) para 787.
4   For the meaning of 'land' see para 680 note 1 ante.
5   Settled Land Act 1925 s 39(2). Subject to certain exceptions, a rentcharge can no longer be created: see the Rentcharges Act 1977 s 2 (as amended); and RENTCHARGES AND ANNUITIES vol 39(2) (Reissue) para 751.
6   As to the tenant for life see para 761 et seq ante.
7   *Re Earl of Wilton's Settled Estates* [1907] 1 Ch 50 at 55. However, the tenant for life may in certain circumstances delegate his powers: see para 776 ante.
8   See the Settled Land Act 1925 s 49(2); and para 832 post.

829. Sale in consideration of rent. If a sale is made in consideration of a rent[1] certain conditions must be observed.

(1) The rent[2] reserved on any such sale must be the best rent that can reasonably be obtained, regard being had to any money paid as part of the consideration, or laid out, or to be laid out, for the benefit of the settled land[3], and generally to the circumstances of the case, but a peppercorn rent, or a nominal or other rent less than the rent ultimately payable, may be made payable during any period not exceeding five years from the date of the conveyance[4].

(2) Where there is a terminable rent, the conveyance must distinguish the part attributable to principal (which is capital money arising under the Settled Land Act 1925[5]) and that attributable to interest[6]. Unless the part of the terminable rent attributable to interest varies according to the amount of the principal repaid, the trustees of the settlement[7] must during the subsistence of the rent, accumulate the income of the capital money in the way of compound interest by investing it and the resulting income in securities[8] authorised for the investment of capital money and must add the accumulations to capital[9].

(3) The conveyance must contain a covenant by the purchaser[10] for the payment of the rent, and the statutory powers and remedies for the recovery of the rent will apply[11], and the conveyance must be framed as a subsidiary vesting deed[12].

(4) A duplicate of the conveyance must be executed by the purchaser and delivered to the tenant for life or statutory owner[13], of which execution and delivery the execution of the conveyance by the tenant for life or statutory owner is sufficient evidence[14].

(5) A statement, contained in the conveyance or in an indorsement on it, signed by the tenant for life or statutory owner, respecting any matter of fact or of calculation under the Settled Land Act 1925 in relation to the sale is, in favour of the purchaser and those claiming under him, sufficient evidence of the matter stated[15].

1 As to the prohibition on creating a rentcharge see para 828 note 5 ante.
2 For the meaning of 'rent' see para 801 note 1 ante.
3 For the meaning of 'settled land' see para 680 text to note 2 ante.
4 Settled Land Act 1925 s 39(3). For the meaning of 'conveyance' see para 698 note 12 ante.
5 For the meaning of 'capital money arising under the Act' see para 795 ante.
6 Settled Land Act 1925 s 39(2). See also para 828 ante.
7 For the meaning of 'trustees of the settlement' see para 750 note 1 ante. As to the trustees see para 750 et seq ante.
8 For the meaning of 'securities' see para 693 note 1 ante.
9 Settled Land Act 1925 s 39(2) proviso.
10 For the meaning of 'purchaser' see para 702 note 12 ante.
11 Settled Land Act 1925 s 39(4)(i) (amended by the Law of Property (Amendment) Act 1926 s 7, Schedule). As to the statutory powers and remedies for recovery of the rent see the Law of Property Act 1925 s 121 (as amended); and RENTCHARGES AND ANNUITIES vol 39(2) (Reissue) para 865 et seq.
12 See the Settled Land Act 1925 s 10(1), (3); and para 691 ante.
13 For the meaning of 'tenant for life' see para 671 note 5 ante; and for the meaning of 'statutory owner' see para 766 note 6 ante. See also para 761 et seq ante.
14 Settled Land Act 1925 s 39(4)(ii).
15 Ibid s 39(4)(iii).

830. Sale to statutory company. The consideration on a sale to any company incorporated by special Act of Parliament[1], or by provisional order confirmed by Parliament or by any other order, scheme or certificate having the force of an Act of Parliament, may, with the consent of the tenant for life[2], consist, wholly or in part, of fully-paid securities[3] of any description of the company; such securities must be vested in the trustees of the settlement[4] and will be subject to the provisions of the Settled Land Act 1925 relating to securities representing capital money arising under that Act[5], and may be retained and held by the trustees in like manner as if they had been authorised by that Act for the investment of capital money[6].

1   This provision does not apply to companies registered under the Companies Act 1985, or any of the Acts which it replaced (see COMPANIES vol 7(1) (1996 Reissue) para 7 et seq), or to companies incorporated by royal charter (see CORPORATIONS vol 9(2) (Reissue) para 1034 et seq). As to companies incorporated by authority of Parliament see CORPORATIONS vol 9(2) (Reissue) para 1048 et seq.

2   For the meaning of 'tenant for life' see para 671 note 5 ante. See also para 761 et seq ante.

3   For the meaning of 'securities' see para 693 note 1 ante.

4   For the meaning of 'trustees of the settlement' see para 750 note 1 ante. As to the trustees see para 750 et seq ante.

5   For the meaning of 'capital money arising under the Act' see para 795 ante. As to the modes of application of capital money see para 808 ante.

6   Settled Land Act 1925 s 39(5).

831. Sale for less than best price or rent. A sale for less than the best price or rent[1] may be made only in the following cases.

(1)   A tenant for life[2] has a restricted power to make a grant in fee simple or absolutely for a nominal price or rent[3], or for less than the best price or rent that can reasonably be obtained, of any part of the settled land[4], for certain public and charitable purposes[5].

(2)   If land[6] is sold for the purpose of the erection on such land of small dwellings[7], or to a county council for the purposes of smallholdings[8], the sale may be made for such consideration in money or land, or in land and money, or may reserve such rent, as having regard to such purposes and to all the circumstances of the case, is the best that can reasonably be obtained, notwithstanding that a better consideration or rent might have been obtained if the land were sold, exchanged or leased for another purpose[9].

(3)   For the purpose of the erection of dwellings for the working classes[10], or the provision of gardens to be held with them[11] or for the purpose of the Small Holdings and Allotments Acts 1908 to 1931[12], a tenant for life may make a grant in fee simple or absolutely of any part of the settled land, with or without any easement, right or privilege of any kind over or in relation to the settled land or any part of it, for a nominal price or rent, or for less than the best price or rent that can reasonably be obtained or gratuitously[13], but, except under a court order[14], not more than two acres in the case of land situate in a district, or ten acres in the case of land situate in a parish, in any one parish may be granted under this power, unless the full consideration be paid or reserved in respect of the excess[15].

(4)   A tenant for life has a restricted power to make a grant in fee simple or absolutely of certain water rights to any statutory authority for a nominal price or rent, or for less than the best price or rent that can reasonably be obtained[16].

All money, not being rent, received on the exercise of any of these powers is capital money arising under the Settled Land Act 1925[17].

1   As to the consideration for sale or rent generally see para 828 ante. As to the prohibition on creating a rentcharge see para 828 note 5 ante.

2   For the meaning of 'tenant for life' see para 671 note 5 ante. See also para 761 et seq ante.

3   For the meaning of 'rent' see para 801 note 1 ante.

4   For the meaning of 'settled land' see para 680 text to note 2 ante.

5   See the Settled Land Act 1925 s 55(1); and para 864 post. As to grants to the National Trust see OPEN SPACES AND ANCIENT MONUMENTS vol 34 (Reissue) para 113.

6   For the meaning of 'land' see para 680 note 1 ante.

7   Settled Land Act 1925 s 57(1)(a). For the meaning of 'small dwellings' see para 816 note 30 ante.

8   See ibid s 57(1)(b).

9   Ibid s 57(1). See also ALLOTMENTS AND SMALLHOLDINGS vol 2 (Reissue) paras 14, 16. As to county councils see the Local Government Act 1972 s 1; and LOCAL GOVERNMENT.

10   As to the phrase 'working classes' see para 775 note 8 ante.

11   Settled Land Act 1925 s 57(2)(a).

12   Ibid s 57(2)(b). As to the Small Holdings and Allotments Acts 1908 to 1931 and the Acts amending them see ALLOTMENTS AND SMALLHOLDINGS vol 2 (Reissue) para 1 et seq.

13   See the Settled Land Act 1925 s 57(2).

14   As to the court see para 792 ante.

15   See the Settled Land Act 1925 s 57(2) proviso; and the Local Government Act 1972 ss 1(10), 179 (see LOCAL GOVERNMENT). See also ALLOTMENTS AND SMALLHOLDINGS vol 2 (Reissue) paras 14, 16.

16   See the Settled Land Act 1925 s 54(1); and para 868 post.

17   See ibid ss 54(4), 55(2), 57(3). For the meaning of 'capital money arising under the Act' see para 795 ante.

832. Mode of sale. A sale may be made in one lot or in several lots[1], and either by auction or by private contract, and may be made subject to any stipulations respecting title, or evidence of title, or other things[2]. The tenant for life may fix reserve biddings, and buy in at an auction[3].

A sale may also be made subject to a stipulation that all or any of the timber[4] on the land sold, or any fixtures[5], are to be taken by the purchaser[6] at a valuation, and the amount of the valuation forms part of the price of the land and is capital money accordingly[7]. If on a sale the consideration attributable to any timber or fixtures is by mistake paid to a tenant for life or other person not entitled to receive it, then, if that person or the purchaser or the persons deriving title under either of them subsequently pay the consideration, with such interest, if any, on it as the court[8] may direct, to the trustees of the settlement[9] or other persons entitled to it, or into court[10], the court may, on the application[11] of the purchaser or the persons deriving title under him, declare that the disposition is to take effect as if the whole of the consideration had at its date been duly paid to the trustees of the settlement or other persons entitled to receive it[12]. The person not entitled to receive it to whom the consideration is paid, and his estate and effects, remain liable to make good any loss attributable to the mistake[13].

1   A tenant for life selling lands held under a fee farm grant was held entitled to sell in lots, carrying out the sales by making sub-fee farm grants or long leases to the respective purchasers: *Re Braithwaite's Settled Estate* [1922] 1 IR 71. As to fee farm see REAL PROPERTY vol 39(2) (Reissue) para 5.

2   Settled Land Act 1925 s 39(6). If the sale is by lots, the tenant for life is vendor in relation to each of the contracts into which he eventually enters, and there is no objection in principle to his solicitors giving him notice before the sale that on all sales under a certain amount they will not make scale charges, but will make detailed charges: *Re Peel's Settled Estates* [1910] 1 Ch 389. As to sale of land generally see SALE OF LAND. As to sales by persons in a fiduciary position see TRUSTS vol 48 (Reissue) para 902 et seq; POWERS.

3   Settled Land Act 1925 s 39(7). For the meaning of 'tenant for life' see para 671 note 5 ante. See also para 761 et seq ante. As to reserve biddings see AUCTION vol 2 (Reissue) para 940.

4   Ie any of the timber and other trees, pollards, tellers, underwood, saplings and plantations on the land sold: see ibid s 49(2). For the meaning of 'land' see para 680 note 1 ante.

5   Ie any articles attached to the land: see ibid s 49(2).

6   For the meaning of 'purchaser' see para 702 note 12 ante.

7   Settled Land Act 1925 s 49(2). See also para 848 post. As to capital money arising under the Act see para 795 ante.

8   As to the court see para 792 ante.

9   For the meaning of 'trustees of the settlement' see para 750 note 1 ante. As to the trustees see para 750 et seq ante.

10   As to the payment of money into court see para 798 note 8 ante.

11   As to applications to the court see para 792 ante.

12 Settled Land Act 1925 s 49(3). As to the effect of receipts of trustees see para 785 ante. As to the confirmation of past transactions see also para 876 post.
13 Ibid s 49(3).

833. Power to leave part of purchase money on mortgage. On a sale of land for an estate in fee simple or for a term having at least 500 years to run by a tenant for life or statutory owner[1], the tenant for life or statutory owner on behalf of the trustees of the settlement[2], where the proceeds are liable to be invested, may contract that the payment of any part, not exceeding two-thirds, of the purchase money is to be secured by a charge by way of legal mortgage or a mortgage by demise or sub-demise for a term of at least 500 years (less a nominal reversion when by sub-demise), of the land sold, with or without the security of any other property, such charge or mortgage, if any buildings are comprised in the mortgage, to contain a covenant by the mortgagor to keep them insured against loss or damage by fire to their full value[3]. The trustees are bound to give effect to such contract made by the tenant for life or statutory owner[4].

1 For the meaning of 'tenant for life' see para 671 note 5 ante; and for the meaning of 'statutory owner' see para 766 note 6 ante; definitions applied by the Trustee Act 1925 s 68(1) para (15).
2 For the meaning of 'trustees of the settlement' see para 750 note 1 ante; definition applied by ibid s 68(1) para (15).
3 Trustee Act 1925 s 10(2) (amended by the Trusts of Land and Appointment of Trustees Act 1996 s 25(2), Sch 4).
4 Trustee Act 1925 s 10(2) (as amended: see note 3 supra).

834. Power of exchange. A tenant for life[1] may make an exchange of the settled land[2], or any part of it, or of any easement right or privilege of any kind, whether or not newly created over or in relation to the settled land, or any part of it, for other land[3], or for any easement, right or privilege of any kind, whether or not newly created, over or in relation to other land, including an exchange in consideration of money paid for equality of exchange[4]. Land may be acquired on an exchange to be made subject to a settlement, notwithstanding that the land is subject to any Crown rent, quit rent, chief rent or other incident of tenure, or to any easement, right or privilege, or to any restrictive covenant, or to any liability to maintain or repair walls, fences, sea walls, river banks, dykes, roads, streets, sewers or drains, or to any improvement rentcharge which is capable under the Settled Land Act 1925 of being redeemed out of capital money[5]. Settled land in England or Wales may not be given in exchange for land out of England or Wales[6]. An exchange may be made subject to any stipulations respecting title, or evidence of title, or other things[7].

1 For the meaning of 'tenant for life' see para 671 note 5 ante. See also para 761 et seq ante.
2 For the meaning of 'settled land' see para 680 text to note 2 ante. As to the power to exchange the principal mansion house see paras 789–791 ante. As to the notice to be given before an exchange is made see para 783 ante.
3 In *Duke of Westminster's Settled Estates, Duke of Westminster v Earl of Shaftesbury* [1921] 1 Ch 585 at 596 Sargant J suggested that the words 'other land' would preclude an exchange for a further interest in land already comprised in the settlement. In view of the meaning of 'land' in the Settled Land Act 1925 (see para 680 note 1 ante) it is submitted that this view is no longer correct.
4 Ibid s 38(iii). As to exchange generally see REAL PROPERTY vol 39(2) (Reissue) para 240 et seq.
5 See ibid s 74(1); and para 808 head (11) ante. As to what improvement rentcharges are capable of being redeemed out of capital money see para 822 ante. As to Crown rent, quit rent and chief rent see REAL PROPERTY vol 39(2) (Reissue) para 84.
6 Ibid s 40(3).
7 Ibid s 40(2).

835. Consideration for exchange. Every exchange must be made for the best consideration in land[1], or in land and money, that can reasonably be obtained[2], unless land is given in exchange for the purpose of the erection on the land so given of small dwellings[3], or to a county council for the purposes of smallholdings, in which case the exchange may be made for such consideration in money or land, or in land and money, as having regard to those purposes and to all the circumstances of the case is the best that can reasonably be obtained, notwithstanding that a better consideration might have been obtained if the land were sold, exchanged or leased for another purpose[4].

1   For the meaning of 'land' see para 680 note 1 ante. Leaseholds having less than 60 years to run may not be taken in exchange: *Re Duke of Westminster's Settled Estates, Duke of Westminster v Earl of Shaftesbury* [1921] 1 Ch 585.
2   Settled Land Act 1925 s 40(1). As to the prohibition on creating a rentcharge see para 828 note 5 ante.
3   For the meaning of 'small dwellings' see para 816 note 30 ante.
4   See the Settled Land Act 1925 s 57(1); the Local Government Act 1972 s 1; and para 831 ante.

836. Conveyance of land acquired on exchange. Where land is acquired in exchange for settled land, the land must be conveyed to the tenant for life or statutory owner[1], the conveyance being framed as a subsidiary vesting deed[2].

1   As to the tenant for life or statutory owner see para 761 et seq ante.
2   See the Settled Land Act 1925 s 10(1); and para 691 ante.

(vii) Power to grant and accept Leases

837. Power to lease. A tenant for life[1] has statutory power to lease the settled land[2], or any part of it[3], or any easement, right or privilege of any kind over or in relation to it[4], for any purpose whatever, whether involving waste or not[5], for a term not exceeding[6]: (1) in the case of a building lease 999 years[7]; (2) in the case of a mining lease 100 years[8]; (3) in the case of a forestry lease 999 years[9]; and (4) in the case of any other lease 50 years[10]. Failure to comply with the statutory requirements may render void a lease granted in purported exercise of the statutory power, but a tenant for life may be bound by it to the extent of his beneficial interest[11].

1   For the meaning of 'tenant for life' see para 671 note 5 ante. See also para 761 et seq ante.
2   For the meaning of 'settled land' see para 680 text to note 2 ante. As to the power to lease the principal mansion house see paras 789–791 ante.
3   As to the power to lease the surface of the settled land reserving the mines and minerals see para 856 post.
4   A right to lessees of mines during the continuance of their lease so to work the mines as to let down or damage the surface of the land is the lease of an easement, right or privilege over the settled land: *Sitwell v Earl of Londesborough* [1905] 1 Ch 460; *IRC v New Sharlston Collieries Co Ltd* [1937] 1 KB 583, [1937] 1 All ER 86, CA.
5   As to waste see para 986 et seq post.
6   Settled Land Act 1925 s 41.
7   Ibid s 41(i). As to building leases see para 842 post.
8   Ibid s 41(ii). As to mining leases see para 843 post.
9   Ibid s 41(iii). As to forestry leases see para 845 post.
10 Ibid s 41(iv). For the meaning of 'lease' see para 685 note 13 ante.
11 See para 883 post; and POWERS.

838. Extent of statutory power of leasing. The leasing power of a tenant for life[1] extends to the making of: (1) a lease[2] for giving effect to a contract entered into by a predecessor in title for making a lease, and which, if made by that predecessor, would have been valid against his successors in title[3]; (2) a lease for giving effect (in such manner and so far as the law permits) to a covenant of renewal, performance of which could be enforced against the owner for the time being of the settled land[4]; and (3) a lease for confirming, as far as may be, a previous lease being void or voidable, but so that every lease, as and when confirmed, is such a lease as might at the date of the original lease have been lawfully granted under the Settled Land Act 1925 or otherwise, as the case may require[5].

1   For the meaning of 'tenant for life' see para 671 note 5 ante. See also para 761 et seq ante.
2   For the meaning of 'lease' see para 685 note 13 ante.
3   See the Settled Land Act 1925 ss 63, 117(1)(v). Under this provision a tenant for life can grant a lease with such terms and having exactly the same effect as if it had been granted by the settlor, a valid contract having been made by the settlor (owner in fee): see *Re Kemeys-Tynte, Kemeys-Tynte v Kemeys-Tynte* [1892] 2 Ch 211.
4   Settled Land Act 1925 s 43(i). For the meaning of 'settled land' see para 680 text to note 2 ante. As to covenants for renewal see LANDLORD AND TENANT vol 27(1) (Reissue) para 450–454.
5   Ibid s 43(ii). As to the effect of leases not authorised by statutory or express powers see para 883 post.

839. Statutory requirements for leases. Every lease[1] must be by deed, and must be made to take effect in possession[2] not later than 12 months after its date[3], or in reversion after an existing lease having not more than seven years to run at the date of the new lease[4], unless the new lease is for a term that does not extend beyond three years at the best rent that can be reasonably obtained without fine and does not exempt the lessee from punishment for waste[5], in which case it may be made by writing under hand only containing an agreement instead of a covenant by the lessee for payment of rent[6].

Except in certain circumstances[7], every lease must reserve the best rent that can reasonably be obtained[8], regard being had to any fine taken[9], and to any money laid out, or to be laid out, for the benefit of the settled land[10], and generally to the circumstances of the case[11]. A lease may be made partly in consideration of the lessee having executed or agreeing to execute, on the land leased, an improvement authorised by the Settled Land Act 1925[12] for or in connection with mining purposes[13]. Every lease must contain a covenant by the lessee for payment[14] of the rent, and a condition of re-entry on the rent not being paid within a time specified in it, not exceeding 30 days[15].

A counterpart of every lease must be executed by the lessee and delivered to the tenant for life or statutory owner[16], of which execution and delivery the execution of the lease by the tenant for life or statutory owner is sufficient evidence[17].

Failure to observe these conditions may render the lease void at law, although it may have a limited effect in equity[18].

A tenant for life may not grant a lease of the settled property together with other property of which he is absolute owner without providing for apportionment of the rent[19].

A tenant for life cannot grant a lease to himself, either alone or jointly with others[20].

1   For the meaning of 'lease' see para 685 note 13 ante.
2   For the meaning of 'possession' see para 761 note 3 ante.
3   As to the validity in equity of a lease granted to take effect more than 12 months after its date see *Kisch v Hawes Bros Ltd* [1935] Ch 102 (overruled on another point in *Warner v Sampson* [1959] 1 QB 297, [1959] 1 All ER 120, CA); and LANDLORD AND TENANT vol 27(1) (Reissue) paras 119–120.
4   Settled Land Act 1925 s 42(1)(i). If a lease is surrendered and a new lease granted without an underlease being surrendered, the new lease takes effect in possession: *Re Grosvenor Settled Estates, Duke of Westminster v McKenna* [1932] 1 Ch 232.
5   As to the extent of a tenant's liability for waste see LANDLORD AND TENANT vol 27(1) (Reissue) para 348.
6   Settled Land Act 1925 s 42(5)(ii). For the meaning of 'rent' see para 801 note 1 ante.
7   As to the exceptions see para 841 post.
8   Rent includes a reservation in kind: Co Litt 142a; *Campbell v Leach* (1775) Amb 740 at 748; *R v Earl of Pomfret* (1816) 5 M & S 139 at 143; *Re Moody and Yates' Contract* (1885) 30 ChD 344 at 346–347, CA. If money is paid to the tenant for life to induce him to grant a lease, the rent reserved by the lease so granted

cannot be considered as the best rent, even if there is no evidence that a better rent could have been obtained: *Chandler v Bradley* [1897] 1 Ch 315; *Re Handman and Wilcox's Contract* [1902] 1 Ch 599, CA. The rent must be one which is legally recoverable: *Pumford v W Butler & Co Ltd* [1914] 2 Ch 353.

9 For the meaning of 'fine' see para 801 note 1 ante. A fine received on any grant of a lease under the statutory powers is capital money arising under the Settled Land Act 1925 (s 42(4)), and must be paid to the trustees of the settlement or into court (see para 804 ante). As to fines arising on the renewal of a lease see para 859 post. As to capital money see para 795 ante.

10 These words refer to money to be laid out under an obligation imposed by the transaction of lease on the tenant, and do not include voluntary past expenditure by him: see *Re Chawner's Settled Estates* [1892] 2 Ch 192.

11 Settled Land Act 1925 s 42(1)(ii). See also *Dowager Duchess of Sutherland v Duke of Sutherland* [1893] 3 Ch 169 at 195; *Re Aldam's Settled Estates* [1902] 2 Ch 46 at 59. The onus is on anyone alleging that the best rent has not been given to prove that fact: *Davies v Hall* [1954] 2 All ER 330, [1954] 1 WLR 855, CA. As to the protection of the lessee see paras 840, 885–886 post.

12 As to the improvements authorised by the Settled Land Act 1925 see para 815 et seq ante.

13 Ibid s 45(2). As to mining leases see para 843 post.

14 For the meaning of 'payment' in relation to rent see para 801 note 1 ante.

15 Settled Land Act 1925 s 42(1)(iii). A condition of re-entry need not be inserted in a lease where it is not appropriate (see *Sitwell v Earl of Londesborough* [1905] 1 Ch 460), and this provision may not apply to leases for less than three years (*Davies v Hall* [1954] 2 All ER 330 at 334, [1954] 1 WLR 855 at 860, CA). An outrageous omission of covenants might be evidence of fraud: see *Davies v Davies* (1888) 38 ChD 499. As to re-entry for non-payment of rent see LANDLORD AND TENANT vol 27(1) (Reissue) para 502 et seq.

16 For the meaning of 'tenant for life' see para 671 note 5 ante; and for the meaning of 'statutory owner' see para 766 note 6 ante.

17 Settled Land Act 1925 s 42(2). As to the lease and counterpart see LANDLORD AND TENANT vol 27(1) (Reissue) para 91.

18 See para 883 post; and POWERS.

19 *Re Rycroft's Settlement, Rycroft v Rycroft* [1962] Ch 263, [1961] 3 All ER 581.

20 *Boyce v Edbrooke* [1903] 1 Ch 836. The same result continues to apply, notwithstanding the Law of Property Act 1925 s 82 (see DEEDS AND OTHER INSTRUMENTS), as the tenant for life is a trustee of the settled land (see para 767 ante). See also *Rye v Rye* [1962] AC 496, [1962] 1 All ER 146, HL. However, the trustees of the settlement can now grant a lease to the tenant for life: see para 879 post.

840. Statements in leases or indorsements. A statement, whether contained in a lease[1] or in an indorsement on a lease, signed by the tenant for life or statutory owner[2] respecting any matter of fact or of calculation under the Settled Land Act 1925 in relation to the lease is, in favour of the lessee and those claiming under him, sufficient evidence of the matter stated[3].

1 For the meaning of 'lease' see para 685 note 13 ante.

2 For the meaning of 'tenant for life' see para 671 note 5 ante; and for the meaning of 'statutory owner' see para 766 note 6 ante.

3 Settled Land Act 1925 s 42(3). This refers to any statement that the rent reserved is the best rent (see s 42(1)(ii); and para 839 ante), or as to apportionment of rents on a contract for lease in lots (see s 44(3) (as amended); and para 842 post), or as to the value of the lessee's interest in a surrendered lease (see s 52(5); and para 859 post). A lessee cannot rely on such a statement if he has reason to believe that it is incorrect: cf *Re Duce and Boots Cash Chemists (Southern) Ltd's Contract* [1937] Ch 642, [1937] 3 All ER 788.

841. Leases at less than the best rent. The following are the only cases in which a lease may be made at less than the best rent.

(1) A tenant for life[1] has a restricted power to lease any part of the settled land[2] for any term of years absolute[3] for a nominal rent[4], or for less than the best rent that can reasonably be obtained, for certain public and charitable purposes[5].

(2) If land is leased for the purpose of the erection on such land of small dwellings[6], or to a county council for the purposes of smallholdings, the lease may reserve such rent as, having regard to such purposes and to all the circumstances of the

case, is the best that can reasonably be obtained, notwithstanding that a better consideration or rent might have been obtained if the land were sold, exchanged or leased for another purpose[7].

(3) For the purpose of the erection of dwellings for the working classes[8], or the provision of gardens to be held with them, or for the purpose of the Small Holdings and Allotments Acts 1908 to 1931[9], a tenant for life may grant a lease for any term of years absolute of any part of the settled land, with or without any easement, right or privilege of any kind over or in relation to the settled land or any part of it, for a nominal rent, or for less than the best rent that can reasonably be obtained or gratuitously, but, except under a court order[10], not more than two acres in the case of land situate in a district, or 10 acres in the case of land situate in a parish, in any one parish may be leased under this power unless the full consideration is paid or reserved in respect of the excess[11].

(4) A tenant for life has a restricted power to grant a lease for any term of years absolute of certain water rights to any statutory authority for a nominal rent, or for less than the best rent that can reasonably be obtained or gratuitously[12].

All money, not being rent, received on the exercise of any of the above powers is capital money arising under the Settled Land Act 1925[13].

1 For the meaning of 'tenant for life' see para 671 note 5 ante. See also para 761 et seq ante.
2 For the meaning of 'settled land' see para 680 text to note 2 ante.
3 For the meaning of 'term of years absolute' see para 678 note 13 ante.
4 For the meaning of 'rent' see para 801 note 1 ante.
5 See the Settled Land Act 1925 s 55(1); and para 864 post.
6 For the meaning of 'small dwellings' see para 816 note 30 ante.
7 See the Settled Land Act 1925 s 57(1); the Local Government Act 1972 s 1; and para 831 ante.
8 As to the phrase 'working classes' see para 775 note 8 ante.
9 As to the Small Holdings and Allotments Acts 1908 to 1931 and the Acts amending them see ALLOTMENTS AND SMALLHOLDINGS vol 2 (Reissue) para 1 et seq.
10 As to the court see para 792 ante.
11 See the Settled Land Act 1925 s 57(2); and the Local Government Act 1972 ss 1(10), 179 (see LOCAL GOVERNMENT). See also ALLOTMENTS AND SMALLHOLDINGS vol 2 (Reissue) paras 14, 16.
12 See the Settled Land Act 1925 s 54(1); and para 868 post.
13 See ibid ss 54(4), 55(2), 57(3); and para 831 ante. For the meaning of 'capital money arising under the Act' see para 795 ante.

842. Building leases. Every building lease[1] must be made partly in consideration of the lessee, or some person by whose direction the lease is granted, or some other person, having erected[2] or agreeing to erect buildings, new or additional, or having improved or repaired or agreeing to improve or repair[3] buildings, or having executed, or agreeing to execute, on the land[4] leased an authorised improvement for or in connection with building purposes[5]. A peppercorn or a nominal or other rent[6] less than the rent ultimately payable may be made payable for the first five years, or any less part of the term[7].

Where the land is contracted to be leased in lots, the entire amount of rent to be ultimately payable may be apportioned among the lots in any manner[8]. However, the annual rent reserved by any lease must not be less than 50p[9]. The total amount of the rents reserved on all leases for the time being granted must not be less than the total amount of the rents which, in order that the leases may conform with the statutory requirements, ought to be reserved in respect of the whole land for the time being leased[10], and the rent reserved by any lease must not exceed one-fifth of the full annual value of the land comprised in that lease with the buildings on it when completed[11].

1 'Building lease' means a lease for any building purposes or purposes connected with building purposes: Settled Land Act 1925 s 117(1)(i). For the meaning of 'building purposes' see para 808 note 44 ante; and

for the meaning of 'lease' see para 685 note 13 ante. See also *Re Earl of Ellesmere* [1898] WN 18. A lease may be a building lease if it contains a covenant by the lessee to rebuild existing buildings when it becomes necessary, but without prescribing any definite time within which the rebuilding is to be carried out or begun: *Re Grosvenor Settled Estates, Duke of Westminster v McKenna* [1933] Ch 97.

2   These words do not include the case of a past voluntary expenditure by the lessee: see *Re Chawner's Settled Estates* [1892] 2 Ch 192. See also para 839 note 10 ante.

3   These words include an agreement to lay out a fixed sum in improvements and repairs (see *Re Daniell's Settled Estates* [1894] 3 Ch 503, CA), and appear to include a lease by which the tenant covenants to do all necessary repairs (see *Truscott v Diamond Rock Boring Co* (1882) 20 ChD 251, CA).

4   For the meaning of 'land' see para 680 note 1 ante.

5   Settled Land Act 1925 s 44(1). As to authorised improvements see para 815 et seq ante.

6   For the meaning of 'rent' see para 801 note 1 ante.

7   Settled Land Act 1925 s 44(2).

8   Ibid s 44(3). However, it seems that a lease may be an improper exercise of the power, although it conforms to these provisions: see *Re Sabin's Estates* [1885] WN 197. Without leave of the court (see paras 671 ante, 844 post) a tenant for life cannot enter into an agreement for leasing the land in lots if the rent cannot be apportioned under these provisions: *Re Rycroft's Settlement, Rycroft v Rycroft* [1962] Ch 263, [1961] 3 All ER 685.

9   See the Settled Land Act 1925 s 44(3) proviso (i) (amended by the Decimal Currency Act 1969 s 10(1)).

10   Settled Land Act 1925 s 44(3) proviso (ii).

11   Ibid s 44(3) proviso (iii).

843. Mining leases. In a mining lease[1] the rent[2] may be made to be ascertainable by or to vary according to the acreage worked[3], or by or according to the quantities of any mineral or substance gotten[4], made merchantable, converted, carried away[5] or disposed of, in or from the settled land[6], or any other land[7], or by or according to any facilities[8] given in that behalf[9]. The rent may also be made to vary according to the price of the minerals or substances gotten, or any of them, and such price may be the saleable value, or the price or value appearing in any trade or market or other price list or return from time to time, or may be the marketable value as ascertained in any manner prescribed by the lease, including a reference to arbitration, or may be an average of any such prices or values taken during a specified period[10]. A fixed[11] or minimum rent[12] may be made payable, with or without power for the lessee, in case the rent, according to acreage or quantity or otherwise, in any specified period does not produce an amount equal to the fixed or minimum rent, to make up the deficiency in any subsequent specified period, free of rent other than the fixed or minimum rent[13]. The execution by the lessee of an improvement may be part of the consideration[14].

Unless a contrary intention[15] is expressed in the settlement[16], part of the rent[17] under a mining lease, whether the mines or minerals leased are already opened or in work or not[18], must be set aside as capital money arising under the Settled Land Act 1925[19], that is, if the tenant for life or statutory owner is impeachable for waste[20] in respect of minerals, three-quarters of the rent and otherwise one-quarter, and the residue of the rent is applicable as rents and profits[21].

1   'Mining lease' means a lease for any mining purposes or purposes connected with them, and includes a grant or licence for any mining purposes: Settled Land Act 1925 s 117(1)(xv). For the meaning of 'mining purposes' see para 808 note 36 ante; and for the meaning of 'lease' see para 685 note 13 ante. It may include surface land necessary for the effective working of minerals: see *Re Reveley's Settled Estates* (1863) 32 LJ Ch 812. For the meaning of 'mines and minerals' see para 680 note 1 ante.

2   For the meaning of 'rent' see para 801 note 1 ante.

3   If the lease reserves a royalty or rent per acre worked, that rent is then called 'acreage royalty' or 'acreage rent', and the acreage may be measured horizontally or along the inclination of the seam. The acre may be a statute acre, or a customary acre, eg Cheshire acre. As to mining royalties see MINES, MINERALS AND QUARRIES vol 31 (Reissue) para 324 et seq.

4   Eg per ton, in which case the rent or royalty is known as a 'tonnage rent' or 'tonnage royalty'. The number of pounds per ton is usually specified.

5   Where a right of wayleave or shaft-leave is granted, the rent may be based on the acreage of mineral carried over the way or brought up the shaft, or may be based on the quantity in tons so carried or brought. As to wayleave royalties see MINES, MINERALS AND QUARRIES vol 31 (Reissue) para 337.

6   For the meaning of 'settled land' see para 680 text to note 2 ante.

7   The words 'other land' refer to minerals worked by outstroke from the settled land. As to the meaning of 'outstroke' see MINES, MINERALS AND QUARRIES vol 31 (Reissue) para 333.

8   Eg by means of wayleaves: see MINES, MINERALS AND QUARRIES vol 31 (Reissue) para 259–260.

9   Settled Land Act 1925 s 45(1)(i).

10   Ibid s 45(1)(ii). Rents are sometimes reserved according to the selling price of the minerals, and the proportion of the selling price often varies with the selling price and is not a fixed proportion. Such rents are sometimes known as 'sliding-scale royalties'.

11   The words 'fixed rent' are sometimes used as synonymous with 'minimum' or 'dead' rent. Sometimes a fixed rent only is reserved, irrespective of the quantity of mineral gotten, but the more usual practice is to reserve a fixed or minimum or dead rent coupled with and merging into royalties, the fixed or minimum or dead rent being either a rent according to acreage of surface over the minerals (eg £1 per acre), or a rent proportionate to the expected annual royalties, so as to produce to the lessor a certain fixed annual sum whether mineral is worked or not, and so as also to operate to compel the lessee to work in order to avoid payment of rent for nothing but the right to work. As to such rents see further MINES, MINERALS AND QUARRIES vol 31 (Reissue) para 335.

12   See note 11 supra. The minimum rent need not commence immediately, and may increase year by year during the earlier years of the term, and the lease may contain a proviso, where the circumstances warrant it, for cesser of the minimum rent when all the minerals demised or so much of them as are workable have been paid for at the royalty rate, and may also reserve a wayleave rent for minerals brought through the demised mines from other land after such cesser, at a nominal rent: *Re Aldam's Settled Estate* [1902] 2 Ch 46, CA.

13   Settled Land Act 1925 ss 45(1)(iii). It is usual to insert in mining leases a power to the lessee, in case the minimum rent paid in any year or half-year exceeds the royalty value of the minerals actually worked, to recoup such excess out of royalties otherwise payable in excess of minimum rent in any subsequent year or half-year of the term. As to covenants to pay rent and royalties in mining leases generally see MINES, MINERALS AND QUARRIES vol 31 (Reissue) paras 338–340.

14   See ibid s 45(2); and para 839 ante.

15   As to what will amount to the expression of a contrary intention see *Re Duke of Newcastle's Estates* (1883) 24 ChD 129; *Re Bagot's Settlement, Bagot v Kittoe* [1894] 1 Ch 177 at 184; *Re Daniels, Weeks v Daniels* [1912] 2 Ch 90; *Re Rayer, Rayer v Rayer* [1913] 2 Ch 210; *Re Hanbury's Settled Estates* [1913] 2 Ch 357. Cf *Re Royal Victoria Pavilion, Ramsgate, Whelan v FTS (Great Britain) Ltd* [1961] Ch 581, [1961] 3 All ER 83. An express power to grant a mining lease, coupled with a provision that the tenant for life is to take the rents and profits, constitutes sufficient expression of contrary intention: see *Re Arkwright's Settlement, Phoenix Assurance Co Ltd v Arkwright* [1945] Ch 195 at 211, [1945] 1 All ER 404 at 414 per Romer J.

16   For the meaning of 'settlement' see para 678 note 1 ante.

17   As to the application, as between capital and income, of compensation paid in respect of mines acquired under the Coal Act 1938 see para 944 post.

18   As to the distinction between open and unopened mines see MINES, MINERALS AND QUARRIES vol 31 (Reissue) paras 7–11.

19   For the meaning of 'capital money arising under the Act' see para 795 ante.

20   A tenant for life, even if not expressly made unimpeachable for waste, may work open mines, and if he grants a lease of such mines only one-quarter of the rents need be set aside (*Re Chaytor* [1900] 2 Ch 804), and the position is the same even if the lease was granted by a predecessor and the mines are not opened until after he becomes tenant for life in possession (*Re Fitzwalter, Wright v Plumtre* [1943] Ch 285, [1943] 2 All ER 328, CA). A person entitled until sale to the income of land held upon trust for sale is in the position of tenant for life impeachable for waste: *Re Ridge, Hellard v Moody* (1885) 31 ChD 504, CA. As to the liability of a tenant for life for waste see para 986 et seq post. As to the working of mines and the doctrine of waste in relation to limited owners see MINES, MINERALS AND QUARRIES vol 31 (Reissue) paras 373–380.

21   See the Settled Land Act 1925 s 47. This provision does not apply to a lease for giving effect to the contract of a predecessor in title who was absolutely entitled (see *Re Kemeys-Tynte, Kemeys-Tynte v Kemeys-Tynte* [1892] 2 Ch 211; and para 947 post), or to a lease granted by a tenant for life under an express power in the settlement (see *Earl Lonsdale v Lowther* [1900] 2 Ch 687). Where land is settled subject to a mining lease already granted, the rights of the tenant for life are governed either by the terms of the settlement or by the law as to open mines: see *Re Hall, Hall v Hall* [1916] 2 Ch 488; and MINES, MINERALS AND QUARRIES vol 31 (Reissue) para 373 et seq. Where the term of a lease is extended under the Settled Land Act 1925 s 59(1) (see para 860 post), the tenant for life is not deprived of his right, if any, to the entire rent during the period of the original term: *Re Bruce, Brudenell v Brudenell* [1932] 1 Ch 316;

Re Arkwright's Settlement, Phoenix Assurance Co Ltd v Arkwright [1945] Ch 195, [1945] 1 All ER 404. Apart from the provisions of the Settled Land Act 1925, the produce of mines, whether royalties or otherwise, belongs to the tenant for life: see *Daly v Beckett* (1857) 24 Beav 114 at 123. See further para 947 post; and MINES, MINERALS AND QUARRIES vol 31 (Reissue) para 374.

844. Variation of statutory terms or conditions for building or mining leases. If it is shown to the court[1] with respect to the district in which any settled land[2] is situated either that it is the custom for land[3] in the district to be leased for building or mining purposes[4] for a longer term, or on other conditions than the statutory term or conditions specified in that behalf[5], or that it is difficult to make leases for building or mining purposes of land in it, except for a longer term or on other conditions than the statutory term or conditions specified in that behalf[6], the court may, if it thinks fit, authorise generally the tenant for life or statutory owner[7] to make from time to time leases of or affecting the settled land in that district or parts of it for any term[8] or on any conditions as expressed in the order of the court, or may, if it thinks fit, authorise the tenant for life or statutory owner to make any such lease in any particular case[9]. The tenant for life or statutory owner and, subject to any direction in the order to the contrary, each of his successors in title, being a tenant for life or statutory owner, may then make in any case, or in the particular case, a lease of the settled land, or part of it, in conformity with the order[10].

1 As to the court see para 792 ante.
2 For the meaning of 'settled land' see para 680 text to note 2 ante.
3 For the meaning of 'land' see para 680 note 1 ante.
4 For the meaning of 'building purposes' see para 808 note 44 ante; and for the meaning of 'mining purposes' see para 808 note 36 ante. For the meaning of 'lease' see para 685 note 13 ante.
5 Settled Land Act 1925 s 46(1)(i). As to the statutory terms and conditions see paras 837, 842–843 ante.
6 Ibid s 46(1)(ii).
7 For the meaning of 'tenant for life' see para 671 note 5 ante; and for the meaning of statutory owner see para 766 note 6 ante.
8 See *Re O'Connell's Estate* [1903] 1 IR 154, where a building lease of 500 years was sanctioned under a previous similar provision at a time when the normal maximum term for such leases of settled land was only 99 years. As to the present normal maximum terms for buildings or mining leases see para 837 ante.
9 Settled Land Act 1925 s 46(1). As to a more general power for the court to sanction transactions affecting settled land see para 671 ante.
10 Ibid s 46(2).

845. Forestry leases. Where there is a forestry lease[1] a peppercorn rent, or a nominal or other rent[2] less than the rent ultimately payable, may be made payable for the first ten years or any less part of the term[3]. The rent may be made to be ascertainable by or to vary according to the value of the timber[4] on the land comprised in the lease, or the produce of it, which may during any year be cut, converted, carried away or otherwise disposed of[5]. A fixed or minimum rent may be made payable, with or without power for the lessee, in case the rent according to value in any specified period does not produce an amount equal to the fixed or minimum rent, to make up the deficiency in any subsequent specified period, free of rent other than the fixed or minimum rent[6]. Any other provisions may be made for the sharing of the proceeds or profits of the user of the land between the reversioner and the Minister of Agriculture, Fisheries and Food[7].

1 As respects England, 'forestry lease' means a lease to the Minister of Agriculture, Fisheries and Food for any purpose for which he is authorised to acquire land by the Forestry Act 1967: see the Settled Land Act 1925 s 117(1)(x); the Forestry Act 1967 ss 49(1), 50, Sch 6 para 5; and FORESTRY vol 19(1) (Reissue) para 22. For the meaning of 'lease' see para 685 note 13 ante. As to the position with respect to Wales see FORESTRY vol 19(1) (Reissue) para 10. As to the Minister of Agriculture, Fisheries and Food see CONSTITUTIONAL LAW AND HUMAN RIGHTS vol 8(2) (Reissue) paras 435–437.
2 For the meaning of 'rent' see para 801 note 1 ante.

3   Settled Land Act 1925 s 48(1)(i).
4   'Timber' includes all forest products: ibid s 48(2).
5   Ibid s 48(1)(ii).
6   Ibid s 48(1)(iii).
7   Ibid s 48(1)(iv); Forestry Act 1967 Sch 6 para 5. See also note 1 supra.

846. Power to accept leases. A tenant for life[1] may accept a lease[2] of any land, or of any mines and minerals[3], or of any easement, right or privilege, convenient to be held or worked with or annexed in enjoyment to the settled land[4], or any part of the settled land, for such period, and upon such terms and conditions, as the tenant for life thinks fit[5], but no fine may be paid out of capital money[6] in respect of the lease[7]. The lease may contain an option to purchase the reversion expectant on the term granted by it[8]. The lease must be granted to the tenant for life or statutory owner, and will be deemed a subsidiary vesting deed[9], and the statements and particulars required in the case of subsidiary vesting deeds must either be inserted in it or indorsed on it[10].

1   For the meaning of 'tenant for life' see para 671 note 5 ante. See also para 761 et seq ante.
2   For the meaning of 'lease' see para 685 note 13 ante. The tenant for life may accept an extended lease under the Leasehold Reform Act 1967: see s 6(2) (see LANDLORD AND TENANT vol 27(2) (Reissue) para 1277); and para 877 post.
3   For the meaning of 'land' and 'mines and minerals' see para 680 note 1 ante.
4   For the meaning of 'settled land' see para 680 text to note 2 ante.
5   Settled Land Act 1925 s 53(1).
6   As to capital money arising under the Settled Land Act 1925 see para 795 ante. For the meaning of 'fine' see para 801 note 1 ante.
7   Settled Land Act 1925 s 53(1) proviso. It would seem that, unlike the case of a lease which is to be acquired with capital money (see para 808 head (12) ante), a lease may be acquired under this provision even if it has less than 60 years unexpired and that the consent of the court need not be obtained.
8   Ibid s 53(3). As to options to purchase in a lease see LANDLORD AND TENANT vol 27(1) (Reissue) paras 110–113.
9   For the meaning of 'statutory owner' see para 766 note 6 ante. For the meaning of 'subsidiary vesting deed' see para 691 text to notes 8, 16 ante.
10 Settled Land Act 1925 s 53(2). As to the statements and particulars required in the case of subsidiary vesting deeds see para 691 ante.

847. Power to procure variation of leases, grants and covenants. If the settled land[1] or any part of it is held or derived under a lease[2], or under a grant reserving rent[3], or subject to covenants, agreements or conditions, whether that lease or grant comprises other land[4] or not, and whenever such lease or grant was made[5], the tenant for life[6] may at any time by deed, with or without giving or taking any consideration in money or otherwise[7], procure the variation, release, waiver or modification, either absolutely or otherwise, of the terms, covenants, agreements or conditions contained in the lease or grant, in respect of the whole or any part of the settled land comprised in it, including the apportionment of any rent, covenants, agreements, conditions and provisions reserved, created by or contained in the lease or grant[8].

1   For the meaning of 'settled land' see para 680 text to note 2 ante.
2   For the meaning of 'lease' see para 685 note 13 ante.
3   For the meaning of 'rent' see para 801 note 1 ante.
4   For the meaning of 'land' see para 680 note 1 ante.
5   See the Settled Land Act 1925 s 60(3).
6   For the meaning of 'tenant for life' see para 671 note 5 ante. See also para 761 et seq ante.
7   'Consideration in money or otherwise' means: (1) a capital sum of money or a rent; (2) land being freehold or leasehold for any term of years of which not less than 60 years are unexpired; (3) any easement, right or privilege over or in relation to the settled land, or any part of it, or any other land; (4) the benefit of any restrictive covenant or condition; and (5) the release of the settled land, or any part of it, or any other land, from any easement, right or privilege, including a right of pre-emption, or from the burden

of any restrictive covenant or condition affecting the same: Settled Land Act 1925 s 61(2). As to the payment of consideration other than rent in respect of transactions effected under this power see s 61(1); and para 863 post.

8   Ibid s 60(2).

(viii) Powers as regards Timber

848. Power to cut timber. Where a tenant for life[1] is impeachable for waste in respect of timber[2], and there is on the settled land[3] timber ripe and fit for cutting, then, on obtaining the consent of the trustees of the settlement[4] or a court order[5], the tenant for life may cut and sell that timber or any part of it[6].

Three-quarters of the net proceeds of the sale must be set aside as and be capital money arising under the Settled Land Act 1925[7], and the other quarter goes as rents and profits[8].

1   For the meaning of 'tenant for life' see para 671 note 5 ante. See also para 761 et seq ante.
2   As to the rights of a tenant for life generally to cut down timber see paras 964, 988 et seq post. As to the meaning of 'timber' see FORESTRY vol 19(1) (Reissue) para 32; as to felling licences see FORESTRY vol 19(1) (Reissue) para 46 et seq; and as to compensation payable to the trustees see FORESTRY vol 19(1) (Reissue) para 65.
3   For the meaning of 'settled land' see para 680 text to note 2 ante.
4   For the meaning of 'trustees of the settlement' see para 750 note 1 ante. As to the trustees see para 750 et seq ante.
5   As to the court see para 792 ante.
6   Settled Land Act 1925 s 66(1). As to the cutting of timber planted as an improvement see s 88(2); and paras 964, 994 post. As to the cutting of timber for executing authorised improvements see s 89; and para 794 ante. As to the cutting of timber during minority see s 102(2)(a); and para 665 ante.
7   For the meaning of 'capital money arising under the Act' see para 795 ante.
8   Settled Land Act 1925 s 66(2). See also paras 990–992 post. On a sale of the estate with the timber where the price of the timber is to be ascertained at a valuation, the amount of the valuation must be considered as capital money: *Re Llewellin, Llewellin v Williams* (1887) 37 ChD 317. Cf *Re Earl of Londesborough, Spicer v Earl of Londesborough* [1923] 1 Ch 500. See also para 832 ante.

(ix) Power to Mortgage

849. Purposes for which mortgage may be made. By a legal mortgage[1] on the security of the settled land[2] or of any part of it, the tenant for life[3] may raise money required for[4]:

(1)   discharging an incumbrance[5] on the settled land or part of it[6];
(2)   paying for any improvement authorised by the Settled Land Act 1925[7] or by the settlement[8];
(3)   equality of exchange[9];
(4)   redeeming a compensation rentcharge in respect of the extinguishment of manorial incidents and affecting the settled land[10];
(5)   commuting any additional rent[11] made payable on the conversion of a perpetually renewable leasehold interest into a long term[12];
(6)   satisfying any claims for compensation on the conversion of a perpetually renewable leasehold interest into a long term by any officer, solicitor or other agent of the lessor in respect of fees or remuneration which would have been payable by the lessee or underlessee on any renewal[13];
(7)   paying the costs of any of the foregoing transactions[14] or of shifting any incumbrance[15], or of varying the provisions of an incumbrance or charging by way of additional security or consolidation[16];
(8)   satisfying any claim under the Landlord and Tenant Act 1927 for compensation for an improvement[17];

(9) paying a coast protection charge or expenses incurred in carrying out work under a works scheme under the Coast Protection Act 1949[18];

(10) paying certain expenses and making certain payments under the Landlord and Tenant Act 1954 in respect of repairs to a dwelling house[19];

(11) paying expenses incurred in, or in connection with, proceedings relating to the acquisition of the freehold or an extended lease under the Leasehold Reform Act 1967[20]; or

(12) paying compensation to a tenant where rights under the Leasehold Reform Act 1967 are excluded[21].

The money so raised is capital money for the purpose, and may be paid or applied accordingly[22].

1   For the meaning of 'legal mortgage' see para 698 note 23 ante. See also MORTGAGE. As to charging registered land see LAND REGISTRATION vol 26 (Reissue) para 967 et seq.

2   For the meaning of 'settled land' see para 680 text to note 2 ante. As to the power to mortgage the principal mansion house see paras 789–791 ante.

3   For the meaning of 'tenant for life' see para 671 note 5 ante. See also para 761 et seq ante.

4   See the Settled Land Act 1925 s 71(1). 'Required' does not mean absolutely necessary, but reasonably required having regard to the circumstances of the settled land: see *Re Clifford, Scott v Clifford* [1902] 1 Ch 87; *Re Bruce, Halsey v Bruce* [1905] 2 Ch 372 at 376.

5   For these purposes, 'incumbrance' does not include any annual sum payable only during a life or lives, or during a term of years absolute or determinable: Settled Land Act 1925 s 71(2). For the meaning of 'term of years absolute' see para 678 note 13. 'Incumbrance' does include the expenses of making up a street or of other works which have become a charge on the settled land under the Highways Act 1980 ss 212, 305 (see HIGHWAYS, STREETS AND BRIDGES vol 21 (Reissue) paras 731, 872): see *Re Smith's Settled Estates* [1901] 1 Ch 689; *Re Pizzi, Scrivener v Aldridge* [1907] 1 Ch 67. As to whether a trust for accumulation is an incumbrance see *Re Strangways, Hickley v Strangways* (1886) 34 ChD 423, CA; *Re Woodhouse, Annesley v Woodhouse* [1898] 1 IR 69.

6   Settled Land Act 1925 s 71(1)(i).

7   As to improvements authorised by the Settled Land Act 1925 see para 815 et seq ante. The purposes authorised by s 71 (as amended) as purposes for which money may be raised by mortgage include the payment of compensation under the Agricultural Tenancies Act 1995 s 16: see s 33(2) (as amended); and AGRICULTURE vol 1(2) (Reissue) para 500. A mortgage to the Agriculture Mortgage Corporation Ltd, which was incorporated in pursuance of the Agricultural Credits Act 1928, may provide that the loan secured by it is to be repayable by equal yearly or half-yearly instalments of capital and interest spread over a period not exceeding 60 years, or repayable on such other terms as may be authorised by the memorandum or articles of that company: see the Agricultural Credits Act 1932 s 3(1) (repealed with a saving in relation to mortgages subsisting on 25 September 1991: see the Agriculture and Forestry (Financial Provisions) Act 1991 s 1(3)); and AGRICULTURE vol 1(2) (Reissue) para 526.

8   Settled Land Act 1925 s 71(1)(ii). For the meaning of 'settlement' see para 678 note 1 ante.

9   Ibid s 71(1)(iii). As to exchange see REAL PROPERTY vol 39(2) (Reissue) para 240 et seq.

10   Ibid s 71(1)(vi). As to the extinguishment of manorial incidents see CUSTOM AND USAGE vol 12(1) (Reissue) para 643.

11   For the meaning of 'rent' see para 801 note 1 ante.

12   Settled Land Act 1925 s 71(1)(vii). As to commuting additional rent see the Law of Property Act 1922 s 145, Sch 15 paras 14 (as amended), 15, 17(1), (4) (as amended); and LANDLORD AND TENANT vol 27(1) (Reissue) paras 453–454. See also para 978 post.

13   Settled Land Act 1925 s 71(1)(viii). See the Law of Property Act 1922 Sch 15 paras 15, 17(2) and note 12 supra.

14   Ie under the Settled Land Act 1925 s 71(1)(i)–(viii): see s 71(1)(ix).

15   Ie under ibid s 69 (see para 851 post): see s 71(1)(ix).

16   Ie under ibid s 70 (see para 855 post): see s 71(1)(ix). As to raising costs on mortgage by court order see para 824 ante. As to the power to make any disposition (which includes a mortgage) to give effect to a contract entered into by a predecessor in title see para 876 post.

17   See the Landlord and Tenant Act 1927 s 13(2) (as amended); and LANDLORD AND TENANT vol 27(1) (Reissue) para 652. As to claims for compensation for improvements see LANDLORD AND TENANT vol 27(1) (Reissue) para 637 et seq.

18   See the Coast Protection Act 1949 s 11(2)(a) (as amended); and WATER vol 49(2) (Reissue) para 73.

19   See the Landlord and Tenant Act 1954 s 8, Sch 2 para 6 (as amended); and LANDLORD AND TENANT vol 27(2) (Reissue) para 1070.

20 See the Leasehold Reform Act 1967 s 6(2), (3), (5) (as amended); and para 877 post.
21 Ie under ibid ss 17, 18 (as amended): see Sch 2 para 9 (as amended); and LANDLORD AND TENANT vol 27(2) (Reissue) para 1343.
22 See the Settled Land Act 1925 s 71(1); and notes 17–21 supra. As to the payment of capital money see para 804 ante; and as to its application see para 808 ante.

850. How the power may be exercised. The mortgage may be of the settled land or any part of it, and may be given over the entire property, even if the incumbrance to be discharged affects only a part[1], but a tenant for life is not justified in trying to preserve a heavily incumbered estate by mortgaging it if by doing that he sacrifices the interest of existing incumbrancers upon it[2]. The statutory restrictions on the leasing powers of a tenant for life[3] do not apply in relation to a mortgage term created under the Settled Land Act 1925[4].

1 *Hampden v Earl of Buckinghamshire* [1893] 2 Ch 531, CA; *Re Lord Monson's Settled Estates* [1898] 1 Ch 427; *Re Coull's Settled Estates* [1905] 1 Ch 712.
2 *Hampden v Earl of Buckinghamshire* [1893] 2 Ch 531, CA.
3 As to the power of leasing see para 837 et seq ante. For the meaning of 'tenant for life' see para 671 note 5 ante.
4 Settled Land Act 1925 s 71(3). As to the purposes for which mortgage may be raised see para 849 ante.

(x) Power to Shift and Vary Incumbrances

851. Power to shift incumbrances. Where there is an incumbrance[1] affecting any part of the settled land[2] (whether capable of being overreached on the exercise by the tenant for life[3] of his statutory powers or not[4]) then, with the consent of the incumbrancer, the tenant for life may charge that incumbrance on any other part of the settled land, or on all or any part of the capital money or securities[5] representing capital money subject or to become subject to the settlement[6], whether already charged with it or not, in exoneration of the first-mentioned part, and, by a legal mortgage[7] or otherwise, make provision accordingly[8].

1 This includes an improvement rentcharge, as to which see para 852 post.
2 For the meaning of 'settled land' see para 680 text to note 2 ante.
3 For the meaning of 'tenant for life' see para 671 note 5 ante. See also para 761 et seq ante.
4 These words within parentheses accord with the earlier decision in *Re Knight's Settled Estates* [1918] 1 Ch 211. As to overreaching equitable interests see paras 705–706 ante, 874 post.
5 For the meaning of 'securities' see para 693 note 1 ante.
6 For the meaning of 'settlement' see para 678 note 1 ante.
7 For the meaning of 'legal mortgage' see para 698 note 23 ante.
8 Settled Land Act 1925 s 69. Incumbrances, at any rate such as might lawfully be discharged out of capital money, might on a sale be discharged by the method provided by the Law of Property Act 1925 s 50: see SALE OF LAND para 268 ante.

852. Exoneration by agreement of land improvement rentcharges. The incumbrances which may be shifted under the statutory power[1] include an improvement rentcharge under the Improvement of Land Act 1864, or the Acts amending or extending it[2]. The consent of the Minister of Agriculture, Fisheries and Food[3] is not required for this purpose, but the new charge does not take priority over existing incumbrances in the way that a charge created by an absolute order of the minister does[4].

1 As to the statutory power see para 851 ante.
2 *Re Earl of Strafford and Maples* [1896] 1 Ch 235, CA. As to improvement rentcharges see AGRICULTURE vol 1(2) (Reissue) para 501 et seq. The Rentcharges Act 1977 s 2 (as amended), does not prohibit the creation of a rentcharge under any Act of Parliament providing for the creation of rentcharges in connection with the execution of works on land, whether by way of improvements or otherwise, or the

commutation of any obligation to do any such work: see s 2(3)(d); and RENTCHARGES AND ANNUITIES vol 39(2) (Reissue) para 774.

3   As to the Minister of Agriculture, Fisheries and Food see CONSTITUTIONAL LAW AND HUMAN RIGHTS vol 8(2) (Reissue) paras 435–437.

4   *Re Earl of Strafford and Maples* [1896] 1 Ch 235, CA. As to the effect of a charge created by absolute order see AGRICULTURE vol 1(2) (Reissue) para 513 et seq.

853. Land acquired as substituted security. Land[1] acquired by purchase or in exchange or otherwise under the powers of the Settled Land Act 1925 may be made a substituted security for any charge from which the settled land[2] or any part of it has already been released on the occasion and in order to complete a sale, exchange or other disposition[3]. However, where a charge[4] does not affect the whole of the settled land, the land acquired may not be subjected to it unless that land is acquired either by purchase with money arising from the sale of land which was before the sale subject to the charge, or by an exchange of land which was before the exchange subject to the charge[5].

1   For the meaning of 'land' see para 680 note 1 ante.
2   For the meaning of 'settled land' see para 680 text to note 2 ante.
3   Settled Land Act 1925 s 82(1). For the meaning of 'disposition' see para 685 note 14 ante. As to exchange see REAL PROPERTY vol 39(2) (Reissue) paras 240–242.
4   'Charge' is not limited to charges existing in priority to the settlement: see *Re Lord Stamford's Settled Estates* (1889) 43 ChD 84 at 94.
5   Settled Land Act 1925 s 82(1) proviso. Land purchased with money arising from the sale of heirlooms settled to devolve with land subject to a charge does not become subject to the charge affecting the settled land: *Re Duke of Marlborough and Governors of Queen Anne's Bounty* [1897] 1 Ch 712. As to the protection of the person conveying by direction of the tenant for life see para 890 post. As to settlements of personalty to devolve with realty see para 937 et seq post. As to exchange see REAL PROPERTY vol 39(2) (Reissue) paras 240–242.

854. Power to exonerate from capital and annual sums. On a sale or other disposition[1] or dealing under the powers of the Settled Land Act 1925, the whole or any part of any capital or annual sum (and in the case of an annual sum whether temporary or perpetual) charged on or payable out of the land[2] disposed of, or any part of it, and other land subject to the settlement[3], may, as between the tenant for life or statutory owner[4] and his successors in title and the other party and persons deriving title under or in succession to him (but without prejudice to the rights of the person entitled to that capital or annual sum), be charged exclusively on the land disposed of, or any part of it, or such other land, or any part of it, in exoneration of the rest of the land on or out of which the capital or annual sum is charged or payable[5].

1   For the meaning of 'disposition' see para 685 note 14 ante.
2   For the meaning of 'land' see para 680 note 1 ante.
3   For the meaning of 'settlement' see para 678 note 1 ante.
4   For the meaning of 'tenant for life' see para 671 note 5 ante; and for the meaning of 'statutory owner' see para 766 note 6 ante. See also para 761 et seq ante.
5   Settled Land Act 1925 s 49(1)(c).

855. Power to vary incumbrances. If an incumbrance[1] affects any part of the settled land[2], the tenant for life[3] may, with the incumbrancer's consent, vary the rate of interest charged and any of the other provisions of the instrument, if any, creating the incumbrance, and with the like consent charge that incumbrance on any part of the settled land, whether already charged with it or not, or on all or any part of the capital money or securities[4] representing capital money subject or to become subject to the settlement, by way of additional security, or of consolidation of securities, and, by a legal mortgage[5] or otherwise, make provision accordingly[6].

1   For these purposes, 'incumbrance' includes any annual sum payable during a life or lives or during a term of years absolute or determinable, but in any such case an additional security may be effected only so as to create a charge or security similar to the original charge or security: Settled Land Act 1925 s 70(2). For the meaning of 'term of years absolute' see para 678 note 13 ante.

2   For the meaning of 'settled land' see para 680 text to note 2 ante.

3   For the meaning of 'tenant for life' see para 671 note 5 ante. See also para 761 et seq ante.

4   For the meaning of 'securities' see para 693 note 1 ante.

5   For the meaning of 'legal mortgage' see para 698 note 23 ante.

6   Settled Land Act 1925 s 70(1).

(xi) Miscellaneous Powers

856. Power to deal with surface and minerals separately. A sale, exchange, lease or other authorised disposition[1] may be made either of land[2], with or without an exception or reservation of all or any of the mines and minerals[3] in it, or of any mines and minerals, and in any such case with or without a grant or reservation of powers of working, wayleaves[4] or rights of way, rights of water and drainage and other powers, easements, rights or privileges for or incident to, or connected with mining purposes[5], in relation to the settled land[6], or any part of it, or any other land[7].

1   For the meaning of 'lease' see para 685 note 13 ante; and for the meaning of 'disposition' see para 685 note 14 ante. As to exchange see REAL PROPERTY vol 39(2) (Reissue) paras 240–242.

2   For the meaning of 'land' see para 680 note 1 ante.

3   For the meaning of 'mines and minerals' see para 680 note 1 ante.

4   This enables the grant of a wayleave for foreign coal. In respect of such a wayleave no separate rent need be reserved and, if the circumstances of the particular case justify it, it may be granted for only a nominal rent after the cesser of the minimum rent required by a mining lease: see *Re Aldam's Settled Estate* [1902] 2 Ch 46, CA. See also *Re Lord Wallace's Settled Estates* [1869] WN 66. As to wayleaves generally see MINES, MINERALS AND QUARRIES vol 31 (Reissue) paras 259–260, 337.

5   For the meaning of 'mining purposes' see para 808 note 36 ante.

6   For the meaning of 'settled land' see para 680 text to note 2 ante.

7   Settled Land Act 1925 s 50.

857. Power to create easements and impose restrictions. On a sale or other disposition[1] or dealing under the statutory powers:

(1)   any easement, right or privilege of any kind may be reserved or granted over or in relation to the settled land[2], or any part of it, or other land[3], including the land disposed of, and, in the case of an exchange, the land taken in exchange[4]; and

(2)   any restriction with respect to building on or other user of land, or with respect to mines and minerals[5], or with respect to or for the purpose of the more beneficial working of it, or with respect to any other thing, may be imposed and made binding, as far as the law permits, by covenant, condition or otherwise, on the tenant for life or statutory owner[6] and the settled land or any part of it, or on the other party and any land disposed of to him[7].

1   For the meaning of 'disposition' see para 685 note 14 ante.

2   For the meaning of 'settled land' see para 680 text to note 2 ante.

3   For the meaning of 'land' see para 680 note 1 ante.

4   Settled Land Act 1925 s 49(1)(a). As to exchange see REAL PROPERTY vol 39(2) (Reissue) paras 240–242.

5   For the meaning of 'mines and minerals' see para 680 note 1 ante.

6   For the meaning of 'tenant for life' see para 671 note 5 ante; and for the meaning of 'statutory owner' see para 766 note 6 ante. See also para 761 et seq ante.

7   Settled Land Act 1925 s 49(1)(b).

858. Power to enlarge residue of long terms. A tenant for life or statutory owner[1] has power to enlarge the residue of a long term into a fee simple in the same manner and subject to the same restrictions as an absolute owner[2].

1   See para 761 et seq ante.
2   See the Law of Property Act 1925 s 153(1), (6) (as amended); and REAL PROPERTY vol 39(2) (Reissue) paras 108–111.

859. Power to accept surrenders of leases and regrants. A tenant for life[1] may accept, with or without consideration, a surrender of any lease[2] of settled land[3], whether made under the statutory power[4] or not, or a regrant of any land granted in fee simple[5], whether under the statutory power[6] or not, in respect of the whole land leased or granted, or any part of it, with or without an exception of all or any of the mines and minerals[7] in it, or in respect of mines and minerals, or any of them, and with or without an exception of any easement, right or privilege of any kind over or in relation to the land surrendered or regranted[8].

On a surrender of a lease or a regrant of land granted in fee simple, in respect of part only of the land or mines or minerals leased or granted, the rent or rentcharge may be apportioned[9]. On a surrender or regrant, the tenant for life may in relation to the land or mines and minerals surrendered or regranted, or of any part of it, make a new or other lease, or grant in fee simple, or new or other leases, or grants in fee simple, in lots[10]. The new or other lease or grant in fee simple may comprise additional land or mines and minerals, and may reserve any apportioned or other rent or rentcharge[11], but it must conform with the statutory requirements[12]. A regrant must be made to the tenant for life or statutory owner[13], and will be deemed a subsidiary vesting deed[14], and the statements and particulars required in the case of subsidiary vesting deeds must be inserted in it[15]. On a surrender or regrant, and the making of a new or other lease, whether for the same or for any extended or other term, or of a new or other grant in fee simple, and whether or not subject to the same or to any other covenants, provisions or conditions, the value of the lessee's or grantee's interest in the lease surrendered or the land regranted may be taken into account in the determination of the amount of the rent or rentcharge to be reserved, and of any fine[16] or consideration in money to be taken, and of the nature of the covenants, provisions and conditions to be inserted in the new or other lease or grant in fee simple[17].

All money, not being rent or a rentcharge, received on the exercise by the tenant for life of the above power is capital money arising under the Settled Land Act 1925[18] unless the court[19], on an application made within six months after its receipt or within such further time as the court may in special circumstances allow, otherwise directs[20].

1   For the meaning of 'tenant for life' see para 671 note 5 ante. See also para 761 et seq ante.
2   For the meaning of 'lease' see para 685 note 13 ante.
3   For the meaning of 'settled land' see para 680 text to note 2 ante.
4   As to the power of leasing see para 837 et seq ante.
5   For these purposes, 'land granted in fee simple' means land so granted with or subject to a reservation out of it of a perpetual or terminable rentcharge which is or forms part of the settled land, and 'grant in fee simple' has a corresponding meaning: Settled Land Act 1925 s 52(9). For the meaning of 'land' see para 680 note 1 ante. As to rentcharges see generally RENTCHARGES AND ANNUITIES.
6   As to the various statutory powers see para 827 et seq ante.
7   For the meaning of 'mines and minerals' see para 680 note 1 ante.
8   Settled Land Act 1925 s 52(1).
9   Ibid s 52(2). For the meaning of 'rent' see para 801 note 1 ante.
10   Ibid s 52(3).
11   Ibid s 52(4). As to the prohibition on creating a rentcharge see para 828 note 5 ante.
12   See ibid s 52(6). As to the statutory requirements see para 839 et seq ante.

13   For the meaning of 'statutory owner' see para 766 note 6 ante. See also para 761 et seq ante.

14   For the meaning of 'subsidiary vesting deed' see para 691 text to notes 8, 16 ante.

15   Settled Land Act 1925 s 52(8). As to the statements and particulars required to be inserted in a subsidiary vesting deed see para 691 ante.

16   For the meaning of 'fine' see para 801 note 1 ante.

17   Settled Land Act 1925 s 52(5). A tenant for life who in good faith accepts a surrender and grants a new lease at an increased rent is entitled to the whole of the increased rent: *Re Wix, Hardy v Lemon* [1916] 1 Ch 279.

18   For the meaning of 'capital money arising under the Act' see para 795 ante. As to the payment of capital money see para 804 ante.

19   As to the court see para 792 ante.

20   Settled Land Act 1925 s 52(7). As to applications to the court see paras 792–793 ante. As to the law in force prior to 1926 see para 949 note 1 post. In the case of a surrender of a term having 60 years or more to run or of a regrant in fee simple, any consideration payable by the tenant for life may be paid out of capital money arising under the Act: see s 73(1)(xi); and para 808 head (9) ante. However, compensation payable to the tenant cannot be paid out of capital money: *Re Earl De La Warr's Cooden Beach Settled Estate* [1913] 1 Ch 142, CA. As to payment out of capital money of compensation for improvements to an agricultural tenant see para 808 note 24 ante.

860. Power to vary leases and grants. At any time, by deed, either with or without consideration in money or otherwise[1], a tenant for life[2] may vary, release, waive or modify, either absolutely or otherwise, the terms of any lease[3], whenever made, of the settled land[4] or any part of it, or any covenants or conditions contained in any grant in fee simple, whenever made, of land with or subject to a reservation out of it of a rent[5] which is or forms part of the settled land, and in either case in respect of the whole or any part of the land comprised in such lease or grant; but, after such variation, release, waiver or modification, every such lease or grant must be such a lease or grant as might then have been lawfully made under the Settled Land Act 1925[6] if the lease had been surrendered, or the land comprised in the grant had never been so comprised, or had been regranted[7].

1   For the meaning of 'consideration in money or otherwise' see para 847 note 7 ante. As to the payment of consideration other than rent in respect of transactions effected under this power see the Settled Land Act 1925 s 61(1); and para 863 post.

2   For the meaning of 'tenant for life' see para 671 note 5 ante. See also para 761 et seq ante.

3   For the meaning of 'lease' see para 685 note 13 ante.

4   For the meaning of 'settled land' see para 680 text to note 2 ante.

5   For the meaning of 'rent' see para 801 note 1 ante.

6   As to what grants of leases can be made see paras 827 et seq, 837 et seq ante.

7   Settled Land Act 1925 s 59(1). The same result could be effected by means of a surrender and a new grant (see para 859 ante), but this provision is not limited to cases where at common law there would be a surrender and a new grant: *Re Savile Settled Estates, Savile v Savile* [1931] 2 Ch 210. A variation of the terms of a lease may operate by way of estoppel as between lessor and lessee as a surrender and new demise, but the remaindermen are not entitled to rely on the estoppel against the tenant for life, so that as between them the original lease is not destroyed: *Re Bruce, Brudenell v Brudenell* [1932] 1 Ch 316; *Re Arkwright's Settlement, Phoenix Assurance Co Ltd v Arkwright* [1945] Ch 195, [1945] 1 All ER 404. See also para 883 post. As to estoppel see ESTOPPEL vol 16 (Reissue) para 951 et seq.

861. Power to give licences, consents and approval. If land[1] is or has been disposed of subject to any covenant requiring the licence, consent or approval of the covenantee or his successors in title as to:

(1)   the user of the land in any manner[2];

(2)   the erection, construction or alteration of or addition to buildings or works of any description on the land[3];

(3)   the plans or elevations of any proposed buildings or other works on the land[4];

(4)   any other act, matter or thing relating to the land, or any buildings or works on it[5]; or

(5)   any assignment, underletting or parting with the possession of all or any part of the property comprised in any lease[6] affecting the settled land[7],

and the covenant enures for the benefit of settled land (including, where the disposition is a lease, the reversion expectant on its determination) the licence, consent or approval may be given by the tenant for life[8] of the settled land affected[9].

1   For the meaning of 'land' see para 680 note 1 ante.
2   Settled Land Act 1925 s 59(2)(a).
3   Ibid s 59(2)(b).
4   Ibid s 59(2)(c).
5   Ibid s 59(2)(d).
6   For the meaning of 'lease' see para 685 note 13 ante.
7   Settled Land Act 1925 s 59(2)(e). For the meaning of 'settled land' see para 680 text to note 2 ante.
8   For the meaning of 'tenant for life' see para 671 note 5 ante. See also para 761 et seq ante.
9   Settled Land Act 1925 s 59(2).

862. Power to apportion rents. At any time, by deed, either with or without consideration in money or otherwise[1], a tenant for life[2] may agree for the apportionment of any rent[3] reserved or created by any lease or grant[4], whenever made[5], or any rent being or forming part of the settled land[6], so that the apportioned parts of the rent are from that time to be payable exclusively out of or in respect of such respective portions of the land[7] subject to it as may be thought proper, and may also agree that any covenants, agreements, powers or remedies for securing the rent and any other covenants or agreements by the lessee or grantee and any conditions are also to be apportioned and made applicable exclusively to the respective portions of the land out of or in respect of which the apportioned parts of the rent are from that time to be payable[8].

1   For the meaning of 'consideration in money or otherwise' see para 847 note 7 ante. As to the payment of consideration other than rent in respect of transactions effected under this power see the Settled Land Act 1925 s 61(1), and para 863 post.
2   For the meaning of 'tenant for life' see para 671 note 5 ante. See also para 761 et seq ante.
3   For the meaning of 'rent' see para 801 note 1 ante.
4   Ie any lease or grant as mentioned in the Settled Land Act 1925 s 59 (see paras 860–861 ante): see s 60(1). For the meaning of 'lease' see para 685 note 13 ante.
5   See ibid s 60(3).
6   For the meaning of 'settled land' see para 680 text to note 2 ante.
7   For the meaning of 'land' see para 680 note 1 ante.
8   Settled Land Act 1925 s 60(1).

863. Payment of consideration other than rent in respect of certain transactions. All money, not being rent[1], payable by the tenant for life[2] in respect of any transaction effected under the statutory powers to compromise claims[3], or to release, waive or modify restrictions[4], or to procure variation of leases, grants and covenants[5], or to vary leases and grants[6], or to give licences, consents and approval[7], or to apportion rents[8], must be paid out of capital money arising under the Settled Land Act 1925[9], and all money, not being rent, received[10] on the exercise by the tenant for life of any of those powers is capital money arising under that Act, unless the court[11], on an application made within six months after the receipt of the money or within such further time as the court may in special circumstances allow, otherwise directs[12].

1   For the meaning of 'rent' see para 801 note 1 ante.
2   For the meaning of 'tenant for life' see para 671 note 5 ante. See also para 761 et seq ante.
3   See para 872 post.
4   See para 873 post.
5   See para 847 ante.
6   See para 860 ante.

7   See para 861 ante.
8   See para 862 ante.
9   For the meaning of 'capital money arising under the Act' see para 795 ante.
10 As to the payment of capital money see para 804 ante.
11 As to the court see para 792 et seq ante.
12 Settled Land Act 1925 s 61(1).

864. Power to make grants for public and charitable purposes. For the development, improvement or general benefit of the settled land[1], or any part of it, a tenant for life[2] may make a grant in fee simple, or absolutely, or a lease for any term of years absolute[3], for a nominal price or rent[4] or for less than the best price or rent that can reasonably be obtained, or gratuitously, of any part of the settled land, with or without any easement, right or privilege over or in relation to the settled land or any part of it, for all or any one or more of certain specified purposes[5]. The purposes are:

(1)   for the site, or the extension of any existing site, of a place of religious worship, residence for a minister of religion, school house, town hall, market house, public library, public baths, museum, hospital, infirmary or other public building, literary or scientific institution, drill hall, working men's club, parish room, reading room or village institute, with or without in any case any yard, garden or other ground to be held with any such building[6];

(2)   for the construction, enlargement or improvement of any railway, canal, road (public or private), dock, sea wall, embankment, drain, watercourse or reservoir[7]; or

(3)   for any other public or charitable purpose in connection with the settled land, or any part of it, or tending to the benefit of the persons residing, or for whom dwellings may be erected, on the settled land or any part of it[8].

Not more than one acre may in any particular case be conveyed for any purpose mentioned under head (1) or head (3), nor more than five acres for any purpose mentioned in head (2), unless the full consideration is paid or reserved in respect of the excess[9]. All money, not being rent, received on the exercise of any of the above powers is capital money arising under the Settled Land Act 1925[10].

1   For the meaning of 'settled land' see para 680 text to note 2 ante.
2   For the meaning of 'tenant for life' see para 671 note 5 ante. See also para 761 et seq ante.
3   For the meaning of 'lease' see para 685 note 13 ante; and for the meaning of 'term of years absolute' see para 678 note 13 ante.
4   For the meaning of 'rent' see para 801 note 1 ante.
5   See the Settled Land Act 1925 s 55(1).
6   Ibid s 55(1)(i).
7   Ibid s 55(1)(ii).
8   Ibid s 55(1)(iii). As to charitable purposes see CHARITIES vol 5(2) (Reissue) para 1 et seq.
9   Ibid s 55(1). As to grants and leases to the National Trust see OPEN SPACES AND ANCIENT MONUMENTS vol 34 (Reissue) para 113.
10 Ibid s 55(2). See also para 831 ante. For the meaning of 'capital money arising under the Act' see para 795 ante. As to the payment of capital money see para 804 ante.

865. Power to dedicate land for streets and open spaces. On or after or in connection with a sale or grant for building purposes[1], or a building lease[2], or the development as a building estate of the settled land[3], or any part of the settled land, or at any other reasonable time, the tenant for life[4], for the general benefit of the residents on the settled land, or on any part of it[5], may:

(1)   cause or require any parts of the settled land to be appropriated and laid out for streets, roads, paths, squares, gardens or other open spaces for the use, gratuitously

or on payment, of the public or of individuals, with sewers, drains, watercourses, fencing, paving or other works necessary or proper in connection with it[6];

(2)   secure the continuance of that appropriation and the continued repair or maintenance of streets or those other places and works by providing that the lands are to be conveyed to or vested in the trustees of the settlement[7], or other trustees, or any company or public body, with or without provision for appointment of new trustees when required[8]; and

(3)   may execute any general or other deed[9] necessary or proper for giving effect to these provisions declaring the mode, terms and conditions of the appropriation and the manner in which and the persons by whom the benefit of it is to be enjoyed, and the nature and extent of the privileges and conveniences granted[10].

In regard to the dedication of land for such public purposes, a tenant for life is in the same position as if he were an absolute owner[11]. A tenant for life has power (a) to enter into any agreement for recompense to be made for any part of the settled land which is required for the widening of a highway under the Highways Act 1980[12] or otherwise[13]; and (b) to consent to the diversion of any highway over the settled land under that Act[14] or otherwise[15]. Any agreement or consent so made or given is as valid and effectual, for all purposes, as if made or given by an absolute owner of the settled land[16]. All money, not being rent[17], received on the exercise of any of the above powers is capital money arising under the Settled Land Act 1925[18].

A tenant for life may also enter into an agreement, binding upon any person deriving title or otherwise claiming title under him, in respect of an experimental project or scheme designed to facilitate the enjoyment of the countryside or to conserve its natural beauty[19] or with a local authority in connection with the provision of a country park[20]. Such an agreement may be entered into either for consideration or gratuitously[21].

1   For the meaning of 'building purposes' see para 808 note 44 ante.
2   For the meaning of 'building lease' see para 842 note 1 ante.
3   For the meaning of 'settled land' see para 680 text to note 2 ante.
4   For the meaning of 'tenant for life' see para 671 note 5 ante. See also para 761 et seq ante.
5   Settled Land Act 1925 s 56(1).
6   Ibid s 56(1)(i). The expenses of making streets and other works under this provision may be raised out of capital money: see para 816 head (18) ante. As to open spaces generally see OPEN SPACES AND ANCIENT MONUMENTS vol 34 (Reissue) para 101 et seq.
7   For the meaning of 'trustees of the settlement' see para 750 note 1 ante. As to the trustees see para 750 et seq ante.
8   See the Settled Land Act 1925 s 56(1)(ii).
9   The deed may be enrolled in the Central Office of the Supreme Court: see ibid s 56(1)(iii). As to such enrolment see PRACTICE AND PROCEDURE.
10   Ibid s 56(1)(iii).
11   Ibid s 56(2).
12   See the Highways Act 1980 s 72 (as amended); and HIGHWAYS, STREETS AND BRIDGES vol 21 (Reissue) para 348.
13   Settled Land Act 1925 s 56(3)(a) (amended by the Highways Act 1980 s 343(2), Sch 24 para 2).
14   See ibid ss 116–122 (as amended); and HIGHWAYS, STREETS AND BRIDGES vol 21 (Reissue) paras 151–155, 297 et seq.
15   Settled Land Act 1925 s 56(3)(b) (amended by the Highways Act 1980 Sch 24 para 2).
16   Settled Land Act 1925 s 56(3). As to the dedication of settled land as a highway otherwise than under s 56 (as amended) see HIGHWAYS, STREETS AND BRIDGES vol 21 (Reissue) para 72.
17   For the meaning of 'rent' see para 801 note 1 ante.
18   See the Settled Land Act 1925 s 56(4). For the meaning of 'capital money arising under the Act' see para 795 ante. As to the payment of capital money see para 804 ante.
19   See the Countryside Act 1968 ss 4, 45 (both as amended); and OPEN SPACES AND ANCIENT MONUMENTS vol 34 (Reissue) paras 156, 319.
20   See ibid ss 7, 8 (as amended), 45 (as amended); and OPEN SPACES AND ANCIENT MONUMENTS vol 34 (Reissue) para 319 et seq.

21 See ibid s 45(1), (2) (as amended); and OPEN SPACES AND ANCIENT MONUMENTS vol 34 (Reissue) para 319. For the purposes of the Settled Land Act 1925 s 72 (see para 874 post), such an agreement is treated as a disposition: see the Countryside Act 1968 s 45(1), (2) (as amended); and OPEN SPACES AND ANCIENT MONUMENTS vol 34 (Reissue) para 319.

866. Powers as regards land in the Green Belt area. A tenant for life[1] of land in the Green Belt area around London may by deed expressly declare that the land is part of that Green Belt, may enter into covenants restrictive of the user of that land and may by agreement confer a right of pre-emption, binding his successors, on a local authority[2].

1 As to the tenant for life see para 761 et seq ante.
2 See the Green Belt (London and Home Counties) Act 1938 ss 3(a), 18, 19 (as amended); and OPEN SPACES AND ANCIENT MONUMENTS vol 34 (Reissue) paras 331, 337–338.

867. Powers to enter into forestry dedication covenants and agreements as to cattle-grids or by-passes. A tenant for life[1] may enter into a forestry dedication covenant relating to the settled land or any part of it either for consideration or gratuitously[2]. He may also enter into an agreement with the appropriate authority for the use of part of the settled land for the purpose of providing, altering or improving a cattle-grid or by-pass[3].

1 As to the tenant for life see para 761 et seq ante.
2 See the Forestry Act 1967 s 5(4), Sch 2 para 1 (as amended); and FORESTRY vol 19(1) (Reissue) para 45.
3 See the Highways Act 1980 s 87(1), (4) (as amended); and HIGHWAYS, STREETS AND BRIDGES vol 21 (Reissue) para 380.

868. Power to grant water rights. For the development, improvement or general benefit of the settled land[1], or any part of it, a tenant for life[2] may make a grant in fee simple or absolutely, or a lease[3] for any term of years absolute[4], for a nominal price or rent[5], or for less than the best price or rent that can reasonably be obtained, or gratuitously, to any statutory authority[6] of any water or streams or springs of water in, upon or under the settled land, and of any rights of taking, using, enjoying and conveying water, and of laying, constructing, maintaining and repairing mains, pipes, reservoirs, dams, weirs and other works of any kind proper for the supply and distribution of water, and of any part of the settled land required as a site for any of such works, and of any easement, right or privilege over or in relation to the settled land or any part of it in connection with any such works[7]. However, no greater rights can be created than could have been created by a person absolutely entitled for his own benefit to the settled land affected[8]. All money, not being rent, received on the exercise of any of the above powers is capital money arising under the Settled Land Act 1925[9].

1 For the meaning of 'settled land' see para 680 text to note 2 ante.
2 For the meaning of 'tenant for life' see para 671 note 5 ante. See also para 761 et seq ante.
3 For the meaning of 'lease' see para 685 note 13 ante.
4 For the meaning of 'term of years absolute' see para 678 note 13 ante.
5 For the meaning of 'rent' see para 801 note 1 ante.
6 For these purposes, 'statutory authority' means an authority or company for the time being empowered by any Act of Parliament, public general, local or private, or by any order or certificate having the force of an Act of Parliament, to provide with a supply of water any town, parish or place in which the settled land or any part of it is situated: Settled Land Act 1925 s 54(3).
7 Ibid s 54(1). As to water authorities see WATER vol 49(2) (Reissue) para 148 et seq.
8 Ibid s 54(2). See also WATER vol 49(2) (Reissue) para 97.
9 See ibid s 54(4); and para 831 ante. For the meaning of 'capital money arising under the Act' see para 795 ante. As to the payment of capital money see para 804 ante.

869. Power to contract. A tenant for life[1] may contract to exercise the statutory powers conferred on him, that is, he may contract to make any sale, exchange, mortgage, charge or other disposition authorised by the Settled Land Act 1925[2], and may, with or without consideration, vary or rescind the contract as if he were absolute owner of the settled land[3], provided that the varied contract is within the statutory powers[4]. He may contract to make any lease[5], and in making the lease may vary the terms, with or without consideration, but so that the lease is within the statutory powers[6], and may accept the surrender of a contract for a lease or a grant in fee simple at a rent[7], in like manner and on the like terms in and on which he might accept a surrender of a lease or a regrant[8], and may then make a new or other contract for or relative to a lease or leases, or a grant or grants in fee simple at a rent, in like manner and on the like terms in and on which he might make a new or other lease or grant, or new or other leases or grants, where a lease or a grant in fee simple at a rent had been executed[9]. However, a preliminary contract under the Settled Land Act 1925 for or relating to a lease, and a contract conferring an option does not form part of the title or evidence of the title of any person to the lease, or to its benefit, or to the land the subject of the option[10]. The tenant for life may also enter into a contract for or relating to the execution of any statutory improvement, or to do any act for carrying any statutory purpose into effect, and may vary or rescind any such contract[11].

All money, not being rent, received on the exercise by the tenant for life or statutory owner[12] of any of the above powers is capital money arising under the Settled Land Act 1925[13] unless the court[14], on an application made within six months after the receipt of the money or within such further time as the court may in special circumstances allow, otherwise directs[15].

1   For the meaning of 'tenant for life' see para 671 note 5 ante. See also para 761 et seq ante.
2   Settled Land Act 1925 s 90(1)(i). For the meaning of 'disposition' see para 685 note 14 ante.
3   For the meaning of 'settled land' see para 680 text to note 2 ante.
4   See the Settled Land Act 1925 s 90(1)(ii). As to the various statutory powers see para 827 et seq ante.
5   For the meaning of 'lease' see para 685 note 13 ante.
6   See the Settled Land Act 1925 s 90(1)(iii). This empowers the tenant for life to contract to grant a lease which, when granted, complies with the statutory requirements: *Re Rycroft's Settlement, Rycroft v Rycroft* [1962] Ch 263, [1961] 3 All ER 581. As to the power of leasing see para 837 et seq ante.
7   For the meaning of 'rent' see para 801 note 1 ante.
8   As to the acceptance of surrenders of leases and regrants see para 859 ante.
9   Settled Land Act 1925 s 90(1)(iv). See also para 860 ante. As to the power to make grants in fee simple at a rent see paras 828–829 ante.
10   Ibid s 90(4). See also *Hughes v Fanagan* (1891) 30 LR Ir 111 at 117, Ir CA. As to evidence of title see SALE OF LAND para 137 et seq ante.
11   See the Settled Land Act 1925 s 90(1)(v), (vi); and para 794 ante. As to statutory improvements see para 809 et seq ante.
12   For the meaning of 'statutory owner' see para 766 note 6 ante. See also para 761 et seq ante.
13   For the meaning of 'capital money arising under the Act' see para 795 ante. As to the payment of capital money see para 804 ante.
14   As to applications to the court see paras 792–793 ante.
15   Settled Land Act 1925 s 90(5).

870. Effect of contract. A contract, including a contract arising by reason of the exercise of an option[1], made under the statutory power binds and enures for the benefit of the settled land[2], and is enforceable against and by every successor in title for the time being of the tenant for life or statutory owner[3], and may be carried into effect by any such successor, who may vary or rescind it as if it had been made by himself[4]. On the application of the tenant for life or statutory owner, or of any such successor, or of any person interested in any contract, the court[5] may give directions respecting the enforcing, carrying into effect, varying or rescinding of the contract[6], but it cannot adjudicate on the claims of persons not parties to it[7].

1   As to the power to grant options see para 871 post.
2   For the meaning of 'settled land' see para 680 text to note 2 ante.
3   For the meaning of 'tenant for life' see para 671 note 5 ante; and for the meaning of 'statutory owner' see para 766 note 6 ante. See also para 761 et seq ante.
4   Settled Land Act 1925 s 90(2). As the contract enures for the benefit of the settled land, a forfeited deposit is capital money: see the cases cited in para 944 note 5 post. As to the completion of contracts made by a predecessor see para 876 post.
5   As to applications to the court see paras 792–793 ante.
6   Settled Land Act 1925 s 90(3). See also *Re Marquis of Ailesbury and Lord Iveagh* [1893] 2 Ch 345 at 358.
7   *Re Ailesbury Settled Estates* (1893) 62 LJ Ch 1012.

871. Power to grant options. A tenant for life[1] may at any time, either with or without consideration, grant by writing an option to purchase or take a lease[2] of the settled land[3], or any part of it, or any easement, right or privilege over or in relation to it at a price or rent[4] fixed at the time of the granting of the option[5]. Every such option must be made exercisable within an agreed number of years not exceeding ten[6]. The price or rent must be the best which, having regard to all the circumstances, can reasonably be obtained, and either:

(1)   may be a specified sum of money or rent, or at a specified rate according to the superficial area of the land[7] with respect to which the option is exercised, or its frontage or otherwise[8];

(2)   in the case of an option to purchase contained in a lease or agreement for a lease, may be a stated number of years' purchase of the highest rent reserved by the lease or agreement[9]; or

(3)   if the option is exercisable as regards part of the land comprised in the lease or agreement, may be a proportionate part of such highest rent[10],

and any aggregate price or rent may be made to be apportionable in any manner, or according to any system, or by reference to arbitration[11]. An option to take a mining lease[12] may be coupled with the grant of a licence to search for and prove any mines or minerals[13] under the settled land, or any part of it, pending the exercise of the option[14]. The consideration for the grant of the option is capital money arising under the Settled Land Act 1925[15].

1   For the meaning of 'tenant for life' see para 671 note 5 ante. See also para 761 et seq ante.
2   For the meaning of 'lease' see para 685 note 13 ante. As to options to purchase contained in leases and options to renew leases see LANDLORD AND TENANT vol 27(1) (Reissue) para 110 et seq. As to options to purchase land generally see SALE OF LAND para 27 ante.
3   For the meaning of 'settled land' see para 680 text to note 2 ante.
4   For the meaning of 'rent' see para 801 note 1 ante.
5   Settled Land Act 1925 s 51(1).
6   Ibid s 51(2).
7   For the meaning of 'land' see para 680 note 1 ante.
8   Settled Land Act 1925 s 51(3)(a).
9   Ibid s 51(3)(b).
10   Ibid s 51(3)(c).
11   Ibid s 51(3). As to arbitration see ARBITRATION vol 2 (Reissue) para 601 et seq.
12   For the meaning of 'mining lease' see para 843 note 1 ante.
13   For the meaning of 'mines and minerals' see para 680 note 1 ante.
14   Settled Land Act 1925 s 51(4).
15   See ibid s 51(5). For the meaning of 'capital money arising under the Act' see para 795 ante. As to the payment of capital money see para 804 ante.

872. Power to compromise claims. With the written consent of the trustees of the settlement[1], either with or without giving or taking any consideration in money or otherwise[2], a tenant for life[3] may compromise, compound, abandon, submit to arbitration or otherwise settle any claim, dispute or question whatsoever relating to the settled land[4] or any part of it, including in particular claims, disputes or questions as to boundaries, the ownership of mines and minerals[5], rights and powers of working mines and minerals, local laws and customs relative to the working of mines and minerals and other matters, easements and restrictive covenants, and for any of those purposes may enter into, give, execute and do such agreements, assurances, releases and other things as the tenant for life may, with such consent, think proper[6].

1   For the meaning of 'trustees of the settlement' see para 750 note 1 ante. As to the trustees see para 750 et seq ante.
2   For the meaning of 'consideration in money or otherwise' see para 847 note 7 ante. As to the payment of consideration other than rent in respect of transactions effected under this power see para 863 ante.
3   For the meaning of 'tenant for life' see para 671 note 5 ante. See also para 761 et seq ante.
4   For the meaning of 'settled land' see para 680 text to note 2 ante.
5   For the meaning of 'mines and minerals' see para 680 note 1 ante.
6   See the Settled Land Act 1925 s 58(1) (amended by the Statute Law (Repeals) Act 1969); and para 788 ante.

873. Power to release, waive or modify restrictions. With the written consent of the trustees of the settlement[1], a tenant for life[2] may at any time, by deed or writing, either with or without consideration in money or otherwise[3], release, waive or modify, or agree to release, waive or modify any covenant, agreement or restriction imposed on any other land[4] for the benefit of the settled land[5] or any part of it, or release, or agree to release, any other land from any easement, right or privilege, including a right of pre-emption, affecting that land for the benefit of the settled land or any part of it[6].

1   For the meaning of 'trustees of the settlement' see para 750 note 1 ante. As to the trustees see para 750 et seq ante.
2   For the meaning of 'tenant for life' see para 671 note 5 ante. See also para 761 et seq ante.
3   For the meaning of 'consideration in money or otherwise' see para 847 note 7 ante. As to the payment of consideration other than rent in respect of transactions effected under this power see para 863 ante.
4   For the meaning of 'land' see para 680 note 1 ante.
5   For the meaning of 'settled land' see para 680 text to note 2 ante.
6   Settled Land Act 1925 s 58(2). A tenant for life has a right of pre-emption in respect of any part of the settled land acquired under the Defence of the Realm (Acquisition of Land) Act 1916, and has power to release that right: see s 5(3) (as amended), (4); the Defence of the Realm (Acquisition of Land) Act 1920 s 2; and WAR AND ARMED CONFLICT vol 49(1) (Reissue) para 612.

874. Power to complete transactions by conveyance. On a sale, exchange, lease, mortgage, charge or other disposition[1], as regards land[2] sold, given in exchange, leased, mortgaged, charged or otherwise disposed of, or intended so to be, or as regards easements or other rights or privileges sold, given in exchange, leased, mortgaged or otherwise disposed of, or intended so to be, the tenant for life[3] may effect the transaction by deed to the extent of the estate or interest vested or declared to be vested in him by the last or only vesting instrument affecting the settled land[4] or any less estate or interest, in the manner requisite for giving effect to the sale, exchange, lease, mortgage, charge or other disposition, but a mortgage must be effected by the creation of a term of years absolute[5] in the settled land, or by charge by way of legal mortgage[6], and not otherwise[7].

     To the extent and in the manner to and in which it is expressed or intended to operate and can operate under the Settled Land Act 1925, such a deed[8] is effectual to pass the land conveyed, or the easements, rights, privileges or other interests created, discharged from all the limitations[9], powers and provisions of the settlement[10], and from all estates, interests and charges subsisting or to arise under it[11], but subject to and with the exception of (1) all legal estates[12] and charges by way of legal mortgage having priority to the settlement[13]; (2) all legal estates and charges by way of legal mortgage which have been conveyed or created for securing money actually raised at the date of the deed[14]; and (3) all leases and grants at fee farm rents[15] or otherwise, and all grants of easements, rights of common or other rights or privileges which were before the date of the deed granted or made for value in money or money's worth, or agreed so to be, by the tenant for life or statutory owner[16], or by any of his predecessors in title or any trustees for them, under the settlement, or under any statutory power, or are at that date otherwise binding on the successors in title of the tenant for life or statutory owner[17], and which are at the date of the deed protected by registration under the relevant Act if capable of registration under it[18]. Notwithstanding registration under the relevant Act of an annuity[19], or of a limited owner's charge[20] or a general equitable charge within the meaning of the relevant Act[21], a disposition under the Settled Land Act 1925 operates to overreach such annuity or charge which, according to its priority, takes effect as if limited by the settlement[22].

This provision does not validate a deed which under the Settled Land Act 1925 the tenant for life has no power to execute[23], but a lease made by a tenant for life who believes himself to be an absolute owner is valid, provided that it is one within the statutory powers[24].

1   For the meaning of 'lease' see para 685 note 13 ante; and for the meaning of 'disposition' see para 685 note 14 ante. For the purposes of the Settled Land Act 1925 s 72, entering into a forestry dedication covenant is treated as a disposition: see para 867 ante. An agreement under the Countryside Act 1968 is also treated as a disposition: see para 865 ante.

2   For the meaning of 'land' see para 680 note 1 ante.

3   For the meaning of 'tenant for life' see para 671 note 5 ante. See also para 761 et seq ante.

4   For the meaning of 'vesting instrument' see para 690 note 8 ante. For the meaning of 'settled land' see para 680 text to note 2 ante. A tenant for life or statutory owner cannot make an effective disposition of the settled land under the statutory powers until after a vesting instrument has been executed in his favour: see the Settled Land Act 1925 s 13 (as amended); and para 702 ante.

5   For the meaning of 'term of years absolute' see para 678 note 13 ante.

6   For the meaning of 'legal mortgage' see para 698 note 23 ante.

7   Settled Land Act 1925 s 72(1).

8   A lease in writing under hand has the same operation as if it had been a deed in any case where a lease is authorised by the Settled Land Act 1925 to be made in that manner: see s 72(4); and para 839 ante.

9   For the meaning of 'limitation' see para 708 note 4 ante.

10   For the meaning of 'settlement' see para 678 note 1 ante.

11   Settled Land Act 1925 s 72(2). The land may be conveyed free from charges arising under the settlement, so long as they have not been actually raised (*Re Keck and Hart's Contract* [1898] 1 Ch 617; *Re Du Cane and Nettlefold's Contract* [1898] 2 Ch 96), and where there is a compound settlement (see para 681 ante), even if the charges in question have been created by a deed prior to that by which the estate of the tenant for life is limited (*Re Marquis of Ailesbury and Lord Iveagh* [1893] 2 Ch 345, approved in *Re Mundy and Roper's Contract* [1899] 1 Ch 275, CA; *Re Phillimore's Estate, Phillimore v Milnes* [1904] 2 Ch 460). A terminable rentcharge created by a tenant for life under the Settled Land Act 1925 s 85(1) (see para 813 ante) will be overreached: see s 85(3); and para 808 ante.

12   For the meaning of 'legal estate' see para 678 note 13 ante.

13   Settled Land Act 1925 s 72(2)(i). 'Priority' means priority in interest, so that eg a legal estate created by the tenant for life under s 16(1)(ii) (see para 767 ante) will not be overreached. Examples of other legal estates having priority to the settlement are a legal mortgage created prior to the settlement, or the freehold in the case of a settlement of leaseholds.

14   Ibid s 72(2)(ii). These include legal mortgages or charges by way of legal mortgage created under the statutory powers (see paras 849–850 ante) or under any powers for that purpose contained in the settlement (*Re Dickin and Kelsall's Contract* [1908] 1 Ch 213 at 221; *Re Davies and Kent's Contract* [1910] 2 Ch 35 at 57, CA), and mortgages and charges for securing sums of money actually raised for portions (*Re Keck and Hart's Contract* [1898] 1 Ch 617 at 624). As the estates or interests of the beneficiaries under the settlement are equitable only (see REAL PROPERTY vol 39(2) (Reissue) para 46 et seq), these words will not cover mortgages or charges on the estate or interest of any beneficiary: see *Re Dickin and Kelsall's Contract* supra; *Re Davies and Kent's Contract* supra. In an Irish case (*Connolly v Keating* [1903] 1 IR 353)

the deed was taken to mean the deed creating the charge, not the deed for effecting the conveyance. It seems doubtful whether this interpretation is consistent with what has been said in *Re Keck and Hart's Contract* supra; *Re Du Cane and Nettlefold's Contract* [1898] 2 Ch 96; *Re Mundy and Roper's Contract* [1899] 1 Ch 275, CA; and *Re Dickin and Kelsall's Contract* supra.

15   As to fee farm rents see REAL PROPERTY vol 39(2) (Reissue) para 5.

16   For the meaning of 'statutory owner' see para 766 note 6 ante. See also para 761 et seq ante.

17   Settled Land Act 1925 s 72(2)(iii)(a).

18   Ibid s 72(2)(iii)(b). The relevant Act is the Land Charges Act 1925 (repealed) or the Land Charges Act 1972: see s 18(5), (6). This includes registration under any statute which is to have effect as if registered under those Acts: see the Settled Land Act 1925 s 117(3); the Land Charges Act 1972 s 3(7), (8) (as amended); and LAND CHARGES vol 26 (Reissue) para 506. Registration in the Yorkshire deeds registries, now closed (see the Law of Property Act 1969 ss 16, 17 (as amended); and LAND CHARGES vol 26 (Reissue) para 529), previously also had such effect: see the Land Charges Act 1925 s 10(6) (repealed). See also *Re Dickin and Kelsall's Contract* [1908] 1 Ch 213. As to the registration of estate contracts and equitable easements see LAND CHARGES vol 26 (Reissue) paras 522, 532, 536. As to the inapplicability of the Land Charges Act 1972 to registered land see LAND CHARGES vol 26 (Reissue) para 505.

19   See the Settled Land Act 1925 s 72(3)(a). As to the registration of annuities see LAND CHARGES vol 26 (Reissue) paras 522, 567–570.

20   See ibid s 72(3)(b). As to the registration of a limited owner's charge see LAND CHARGES vol 26 (Reissue) paras 522, 530.

21   See ibid s 72(3)(b). As to the registration of a general equitable charge see LAND CHARGES vol 26 (Reissue) paras 522, 531.

22   See ibid s 72(3). As to the effect of a conveyance by a tenant for life see the Law of Property Act 1925 s 2(1)(i), (4), (5); and REAL PROPERTY vol 39(2) (Reissue) para 247 et seq. As to overreaching of equitable interests protected by registration see LAND CHARGES vol 26 (Reissue) para 518.

23   *Re Newell and Nevill's Contract* [1900] 1 Ch 90, overruled on another point by *Re Gladstone, Gladstone v Gladstone* [1900] 2 Ch 101, CA.

24   *Mogridge v Clapp* [1892] 3 Ch 382, CA. See also *Re Pennant's Will Trusts, Pennant v Ryland* [1970] Ch 75, [1969] 2 All ER 862. As to the effect of leases not authorised by statutory or express powers see para 883 post. The case of a sale is different since the purchaser must ascertain that there are trustees to whom his purchase money can be paid: *Mogridge v Clapp* supra at 400. As to statutory powers of leasing see para 837 et seq ante.

875. Exercise of powers. Where any statutory or express[1] power of sale, exchange, leasing, mortgaging or charging or other power is exercised by a tenant for life or statutory owner[2], or by the trustees of a settlement[3], he and they may respectively execute, make and do all deeds, instruments and things necessary or proper in that behalf[4].

1   As to express powers see paras 880–881 post.

2   For the meaning of 'tenant for life' see para 671 note 5 ante; and for the meaning of 'statutory owner' see para 766 note 6 ante. See also para 761 et seq ante.

3   For the meaning of 'trustees of the settlement' see para 750 note 1 ante. As to the trustees see para 750 et seq ante.

4   See the Settled Land Act 1925 s 112(1).

876. Power to complete predecessor's contracts and confirm past transactions. A tenant for life[1] may make any disposition[2] necessary or proper for giving effect to a contract entered into by a predecessor in title which, if made by such predecessor, would have been valid as against his successors in title[3]. With the leave of the court[4], he may also execute a deed for the purpose of confirming any interests intended to affect the settled land (provided that they are capable of subsisting as legal estates[5]) which, at some prior date, were expressed to have been transferred or created, and of confirming also any dealings with it which would have been legal if those interests had been legally and validly transferred or created[6].

1   For the meaning of 'tenant for life' see para 671 note 5 ante. See also para 761 et seq ante.
2   For the meaning of 'disposition' see para 685 note 14 ante.
3   Settled Land Act 1925 s 63. See also para 838 ante. As to the validation of defective leases see para 883 post.
4   As to the court see paras 792 ante, 905 post.
5   As to what estates are capable of subsisting as legal estates see the Law of Property Act 1925 s 1 (as amended); and REAL PROPERTY vol 39(2) (Reissue) para 45.
6   See ibid s 66(1), (2) (as amended); and REAL PROPERTY vol 39(2) (Reissue) para 246.

877. Leasehold enfranchisement. The statutory provisions relating to leasehold enfranchisement[1] apply in certain circumstances to a tenant for life[2] and to the trustees of a settlement[3]. Capital money may be applied[4] or raised by mortgage of the settled land[5] for the payment of expenses incurred[6] in or in connection with proceedings taken to acquire the freehold or an extended lease[7]. The statutory provisions relating to the rights of members of the family to succeed to a tenancy on the death of a tenant of a house[8] also apply on the death of a tenant for life in specified circumstances[9].

1   See the Leasehold Reform Act 1967; and LANDLORD AND TENANT vol 27(2) (Reissue) para 1253 et seq.
2   As to the tenant for life see para 761 et seq ante.
3   See the Leasehold Reform Act 1967 s 6 (as amended); and LANDLORD AND TENANT vol 27(2) (Reissue) para 1277.
4   As to modes of application of capital money see para 808 et seq ante.
5   As to the power to mortgage the settled land see paras 849–850 ante.
6   Ie by a tenant for life or statutory owner: see the Leasehold Reform Act 1967 s 6(5) (as amended); and LANDLORD AND TENANT vol 27(2) (Reissue) para 1277.
7   See ibid s 6(5) (as amended); and LANDLORD AND TENANT vol 27(2) (Reissue) para 1277.
8   See ibid s 7 (as amended); and LANDLORD AND TENANT vol 27(2) (Reissue) para 1278.
9   See ibid s 7(3), (5); and LANDLORD AND TENANT vol 27(2) (Reissue) para 1278.

(xii) Dealings between Tenant for Life and Estate

878. Authorised dealings. The Settled Land Act 1925 authorises certain specified dealings between the tenant for life and the settled estate[1]. The dealings so authorised are:

(1)   a sale, grant, lease[2], mortgage, charge or other disposition[3] to him of settled land[4], or of any easement, right or privilege over it[5];

(2)   an advance to him of capital money on mortgage[6];

(3)   a purchase from him of land[7] to be made subject to the limitations[8] of the settlement[9]; and

(4)   an exchange with him of settled land for other land[10].

Any such disposition, advance, purchase or exchange may be made to, from or with any persons of whom the tenant for life is one[11].

1   See the Settled Land Act 1925 s 68(1). As to the procedure see para 879 post. For the meaning of 'tenant for life' see para 671 note 5 ante. See also para 761 et seq ante.
2   For the meaning of 'lease' see para 685 note 13 ante.
3   For the meaning of 'disposition' see para 685 note 14 ante.
4   For the meaning of 'settled land' see para 680 text to note 2 ante.
5   See the Settled Land Act 1925 s 68(1)(a).
6   For the meaning of 'capital money arising under the Act' see para 795 ante.
7   For the meaning of 'land' see para 680 note 1 ante.
8   For the meaning of 'limitation' see para 708 note 4 ante.
9   Settled Land Act 1925 s 68(1)(c). For the meaning of 'settlement' see para 678 note 1 ante.
10   Ibid s 68(1)(d).
11   Ibid s 68(1)(e). A transaction may be a valid exercise of this power even if the parties purport to act in a different capacity: *Re Pennant's Will Trusts, Pennant v Ryland* [1970] Ch 75, [1969] 2 All ER 862.

879. Powers exercisable by trustees. In dealings between the tenant for life and the settled estate[1], the trustees of the settlement[2], in addition to their powers as trustees, have all the powers of a tenant for life in reference to negotiating and completing the transaction, and have power to enforce any covenants by the tenant for life, or where the tenant for life is himself one of the trustees, then the others or other of them have such power, and the powers of the tenant for life may be exercised by the trustees of the settlement in the name and on behalf of the tenant for life[3].

These provisions[4] apply notwithstanding that the tenant for life is one of the trustees of the settlement, or that an order has been made authorising the trustees to act on his behalf[5], or that he is a person suffering from mental disorder, but they do not apply to dealings with any body of persons which includes a trustee of the settlement, not being the tenant for life, unless the transaction is either previously or subsequently approved by the court[6].

1   As to such authorised dealings see para 878 ante. For the meaning of 'tenant for life' see para 671 note 5 ante. See also para 761 et seq ante.
2   For the meaning of 'trustees of the settlement' see para 750 note 1 ante. As to the trustees see para 750 et seq ante.
3   Settled Land Act 1925 s 68(2). A single trustee could act under this provision, provided that no capital money arises in respect of that transaction: see para 786 ante. Where settled land is purchased by the tenant for life who is also one of the trustees, he should be expressed to be one of the conveying parties as well as the purchaser: *Re Pennant's Will Trust, Pennant v Ryland* [1970] Ch 75, [1969] 2 All ER 862.
4   Ie the Settled Land Act 1925 s 68 (as amended): see s 68(3) (as amended: see note 6 infra).
5   As to the position where the tenant for life has parted with the interest see para 765 ante.
6   Settled Land Act 1925 s 68(3) (amended by the Mental Health Act 1959 s 149(1), Sch 7 Pt I). As to the court see para 792 ante. If the body of persons with whom a dealing is proposed includes both the tenant for life and one or more of the trustees of the settlement, the transaction must be approved by the court: see para 792 ante.

(xiii)   Extension of Statutory Powers

880. Conferment of additional or larger powers. A settlor may confer on the tenant for life[1], or (subject to a specified restriction[2]) the trustees of the settlement[3], any powers additional to or larger than the statutory powers[4], and such additional or larger powers, as far as may be, operate and are exercisable in the like manner, and with all the like incidents, effects and consequences as if they were conferred by the Settled Land Act 1925, and, if relating to the settled land[5], as if they were conferred by that Act on a tenant for life[6]. The statutory powers are cumulative, and nothing in the Settled Land Act 1925 takes away, abridges or prejudicially affects any power for the time being subsisting under a settlement, or by statute[7] or otherwise, exercisable by a tenant for life, or (subject to the specified restriction) by trustees with his consent, on his request or by his direction, or otherwise[8].

If a tenant for life purports to exercise 'every power and authority enabling him' he is presumed to have exercised the power which is most beneficial to him[9]. If a tenant for life has no express power to mortgage, but has an express power to lease, not confined to leasing at a rackrent, he can mortgage by demise for a term of years[10].

1   For the meaning of 'tenant for life' see para 671 note 5 ante. See also para 761 et seq ante.
2   Ie in case of conflict between the settlement and the statutory provisions: see para 881 post.
3   For the meaning of 'trustees of the settlement' see para 750 note 1 ante. As to the trustees see para 750 et seq ante.
4   See the Settled Land Act 1925 s 109(1).
5   For the meaning of 'settled land' see para 680 text to note 2 ante.
6   See the Settled Land Act 1925 s 109(2). Where there is a compound settlement (see para 681 et seq ante) the tenant for life is entitled to exercise any larger or additional powers conferred by any deed forming

part of it: *Re Cowley Settled Estates* [1926] Ch 725. As to the fiduciary position of the tenant for life in exercising any larger or additional powers see para 775 ante.

7   Eg the Lands Clauses Consolidation Act 1845 (see COMPULSORY ACQUISITION OF LAND vol 8(1) (Reissue) para 11 et seq). See also *Re Lady Bentinck and London and North Western Rly Co* (1895) 12 TLR 100; and COMPULSORY ACQUISITION OF LAND vol 8(1) (Reissue) paras 96, 164–165.

8   See the Settled Land Act 1925 s 108(1). The words 'or otherwise' refer not to the consent, request or direction of some person other than the tenant for life, but to something which the tenant for life is to do or abstain from doing: *Re Jefferys, Finch v Martin* [1939] Ch 205, [1938] 4 All ER 120.

9   *Earl Lonsdale v Lowther* [1900] 2 Ch 687; *Re Lady Bentinck and London and North Western Rly Co* (1895) 12 TLR 100.

10   *Mostyn v Lancaster, Taylor v Mostyn* (1883) 23 ChD 583, CA.

881. Conflict between settlement and statutory provisions. In case of conflict between the provisions of a settlement[1] and the statutory provisions[2] relative to any matter in respect of which the tenant for life or statutory owner[3] exercises or contracts or intends to exercise any statutory power, the statutory provisions prevail; and, notwithstanding anything in the settlement, any power (not being merely a power of revocation or appointment) relating to the settled land[4] conferred by the settlement on the trustees of the settlement[5] or other persons exercisable for any purpose, whether or not provided for in the Settled Land Act 1925, is exercisable by the tenant for life or statutory owner as if it were an additional power conferred on the tenant for life and not otherwise[6]. The result is that if the tenant for life has one power by statute and the trustees have another power under the settlement, and there is a conflict between the provisions of the settlement and the statutory provisions, the power of the tenant for life is paramount[7], and can be exercised free from any restraint imposed by the settlement[8] or by a private Act of Parliament[9].

1   For the meaning of 'settlement' see para 678 note 1 ante.

2   The provisions here referred to are provisions connected with the execution of the power, eg consent of a third person, not with the results of such execution; they deal with the act of execution, not with its proceeds: see *Earl Lonsdale v Lowther* [1900] 2 Ch 687.

3   For the meaning of 'tenant for life' see para 671 note 5 ante; and for the meaning of 'statutory owner' see para 766 note 6 ante. See also para 761 et seq ante.

4   For the meaning of 'settled land' see para 680 text to note 2 ante. A power to appoint new trustees of the settlement is not one relating to the settled land for this purpose: *Re Maryon-Wilson's Instruments, Blofeld v Maryon-Wilson* [1971] Ch 789, [1969] 3 All ER 558.

5   For the meaning of 'trustees of the settlement' see para 750 note 1 ante. As to the trustees see para 750 et seq ante.

6   See the Settled Land Act 1925 s 108(2); and para 880 ante.

7   *Clarke v Thornton* (1887) 35 ChD 307; *Re Lord Stamford's Settled Estates* (1889) 43 ChD 84; *Re Thomas, Weatherall v Thomas* [1900] 1 Ch 319. The effect of these decisions is that if there is a power under the settlement to pay for improvements out of income and a power under the Act to pay for them out of capital, effect will be given to the statutory power, but the statutory provisions do not override an absolute trust to pay for improvements out of income, the tenant for life in such a case being entitled only to the net balance: see *Re Partington, Reigh v Kane* [1902] 1 Ch 711.

8   *Re Jefferys, Finch v Martin* [1939] Ch 205, [1938] 4 All ER 120.

9   See *Re Chaytor's Settled Estate Act* (1884) 25 ChD 651. As to private Acts of Parliament see PARLIAMENT vol 34 (Reissue) para 845 et seq.

882. Court decision on matters of doubt. If a question arises or a doubt is entertained respecting any of the foregoing matters[1], the tenant for life or statutory owner[2], the trustees of the settlement[3] or any other person interested under the settlement may apply to the court[4] for its decision, and the court may make such order respecting the matter as it thinks fit[5].

1   Ie any matter within the Settled Land Act 1925 s 108: see paras 880–881 ante.
2   For the meaning of 'tenant for life' see para 671 note 5 ante; and for the meaning of 'statutory owner' see
     para 766 note 6 ante. See also para 761 et seq ante.
3   For the meaning of 'trustees of the settlement' see para 750 note 1 ante. As to the trustees see para 750 et
     seq ante.
4   As to the court see para 792 ante.
5   Settled Land Act 1925 s 108(3).

883. Effect of leases not authorised by statutory or express powers. A lease by
a tenant for life which is not authorised by his statutory powers[1] may be valid in equity.
It will be valid so long as his beneficial interest subsists[2], but on the determination of his
interest it is void[3]. However, if the remainderman allows the tenant to continue in
possession and stands by while he expends money on the property, he may be bound to
grant him a new lease[4]. Merely allowing a yearly tenant to continue in possession for a
substantial time is a recognition of his tenancy and entitles him to notice to quit[5].

   As between the parties to the lease, it is in any case good by way of estoppel[6]. Further,
a lessee dealing in good faith with a tenant for life is, as against all parties entitled under
the settlement, conclusively taken to have given the best rent reasonably obtainable and
to have complied with all the statutory requirements[7]; and leases invalidated by reason of
non-compliance with the terms of the powers under which they are granted may in
certain circumstances take effect in equity as a contract for the grant of a valid lease[8].

1   This will include any additional express powers: see the Settled Land Act 1925 s 109; and para 880 ante.
     As to the tenant for life see para 761 et seq ante.
2   *Bragg v Wiseman* (1614) 1 Brownl 22. See also *Re Smyth, ex p Smyth* (1818) 1 Swan 337; *Symons v Symons
     and Powell* (1821) 6 Madd 207. However, the lease subsists for his life, notwithstanding the determination
     of his estate by surrender, or even, it has been said, by forfeiture: *Sutton's Case* (1701) 12 Mod Rep 557.
     The position regarding forfeiture is less certain, but it is thought that the statement in the text is accurate.
     As to covenants for renewal entered into by a limited owner see *Macartney v Blundell* (1789) 2 Ridg Parl
     Rep 113; *Higgins v Rosse* (1821) 3 Bli 112, HL; *Brereton v Tuohey* (1858) 8 ICLR 190.
3   *Doe d Simpson v Butcher* (1778) 1 Doug KB 50; *Roe d Jordan v Ward* (1789) 1 Hy Bl 97; *Doe d Pulteney v
     Lady Cavan* (1794) 5 Term Rep 567 at 570–571; *Doe d Potter v Archer* (1796) 1 Bos & P 531; *Mogridge v
     Clapp* [1892] 3 Ch 382 at 392, CA; *Chandler v Bradley* [1897] 1 Ch 315. Therefore, the remainderman
     cannot confirm the lease (*Jones d Cowper v Verney* (1739) Willes 169; *James d Aubrey v Jenkins* (1758) Bull
     NP 96; *Jenkins d Yate v Church* (1776) 2 Cowp 482; *Doe d Simpson v Butcher* supra; *Ludford v Barber* (1786)
     1 Term Rep 90), although the receipt of rent will constitute a yearly tenancy under the remainderman
     (see *Doe d Martin v Watts* (1797) 7 Term Rep 83), and the tenancy will commence from the day and be
     on the terms of the original demise, so far as applicable to a yearly tenancy (*Roe d Jordan v Ward* supra).
     However, to have this effect the rent must be suitable to a tenancy from year to year (see *Reynolds v
     Reynolds* (1848) 12 I Eq R 172), and the receipt of a nominal sum as 'chief rent' will not suffice (*Smith v
     Widlake* (1877) 3 CPD 10, CA; cf *Jegon v Vivian* (1865) LR 1 CP 9 (affd (1868) LR 3 HL 285)).
     Nevertheless, in *Handman and Wilcox's Contract* [1902] 1 Ch 599, CA, the point whether the lease was
     void or voidable was left open. See also *Smith v Hobbs* (1980) Times, 13 November, CA (see note 4 infra).
4   See *Stiles v Cowper* (1748) 3 Atk 692; *Hardcastle v Shafto* (1794) 1 Anst 184 at 186; *Dann v Spurrier* (1802)
     7 Ves 231 at 236; *Pilling v Armitage* (1805) 12 Ves 78 at 85. Cf *Bowes v East London Waterworks* (1818) 3
     Madd 375 at 384; *O'Fay v Burke* (1858) 8 I Ch R 511. If there has been an unauthorised purchase and
     letting of land, ratification of the purchase involves ratification also of the letting: *Smith v Hobbs* (1980)
     Times, 13 November, CA.
5   *Doe d Cates v Somerville* (1826) 6 B & C 126 at 132; *O'Keeffe v Walsh* (1880) 8 LR Ir 184, Ir CA. The
     acceptance of a lessee by the remainderman will import into the new tenancy a covenant in the original
     lease by the lessee to repair: *Morrogh v Alleyne* (1873) 7 IR Eq 487.
6   *Yellowly v Gower* (1855) 11 Exch 274. A tenant for life who agrees to grant a lease for a term in excess of
     the power is bound to carry out his agreement to the extent of his own interest (cf *Byrne v Acton* (1721)
     1 Bro Parl Cas 186, HL; *Dyas v Cruise* (1845) 2 Jo & Lat 460) with compensation (*Leslie v Crommelin*
     (1867) IR 2 Eq 134). However, the remaindermen cannot have specific performance of the agreement:
     see *Ricketts v Bell* (1847) 1 De G & Sm 335. See also ESTOPPEL vol 16 (Reissue) paras 1074–1082.
7   See the Settled Land Act 1925 ss 109(2), 110(1); and paras 880 ante, 885 post.
8   See the Law of Property Act 1925 ss 152, 154; and LANDLORD AND TENANT vol 27(1) (Reissue) para 120.

884. Leases by tenants in tail. A tenant in tail[1] has all the powers of leasing of a tenant for life under the Settled Land Act 1925[2]. In addition, however, a lease not authorised under those powers, if made by deed, will take effect under the Fines and Recoveries Act 1833[3], but only in equity[4]. If not made by deed, it will be void as against the persons entitled subject to the entailed interest[5], but will be voidable only as against the issue in tail[6], and may be confirmed either expressly or impliedly by a subsequent tenant in tail[7].

1   As to entailed interests see para 715 et seq ante; and REAL PROPERTY vol 39(2) (Reissue) para 117 et seq.
2   See the Settled Land Act 1925 s 20(1)(i); and para 762 ante. For the meaning of 'tenant for life' see para 671 note 5 ante. See also para 761 et seq ante. As to the powers of leasing of a tenant for life see para 837 et seq ante.
3   See the Fines and Recoveries Act 1833 ss 15, 40 (both as amended); and REAL PROPERTY vol 39(2) (Reissue) para 121 et seq.
4   See the Law of Property (Amendment) Act 1924 s 9, Sch 9; and REAL PROPERTY vol 39(2) (Reissue) para 121.
5   Co Litt 45b; *Andrew v Pearce* (1805) 1 Bos & PNR 158 at 162. As to the effect of leases not authorised by statutory or express powers see para 883 ante.
6   Co Litt 45b; *Earl of Bedford's Case* (1586) 7 Co Rep 7b. See also LANDLORD AND TENANT vol 27(1) (Reissue) para 27.
7   *Stiles v Cowper* (1748) 3 Atk 692; *Doe d Southhouse v Jenkins* (1829) 5 Bing 469 at 476; cf *Doe d Phillips v Rollings* (1847) 4 CB 188. See, however, *Osborn v Duke of Marlborough* (1866) 14 LT 789.

(xiv) Protection of Trustees and Third Persons

885. Protection of purchasers from tenant for life. On a sale, exchange, lease[1], mortgage, charge or other disposition[2], a purchaser[3] dealing in good faith with a tenant for life or statutory owner[4] is, as against all parties entitled under the settlement[5], conclusively taken to have given the best price, consideration or rent[6], as the case may require, that could reasonably be obtained by the tenant for life or statutory owner, and to have complied with all the statutory requirements[7]. The fact that the transaction is at an undervalue, without anything more, is insufficient to invalidate it if the person dealing with the tenant for life acted in good faith[8], but, if he is not acting in good faith, the transaction may be set aside at the instance of the beneficiaries, not only against such person himself, but possibly also against his transferees who have acquired the property without notice of the defect[9].

1   For the meaning of 'lease' see para 685 note 13 ante.
2   For the meaning of 'disposition' see para 685 note 14 ante.
3   For the meaning of 'purchaser' see para 702 note 12 ante.
4   For the meaning of 'tenant for life' see para 671 note 5 ante; and for the meaning of 'statutory owner' see para 766 note 6 ante. See also para 761 et seq ante.
5   For the meaning of 'settlement' see para 678 note 1 ante.
6   For the meaning of 'rent' see para 801 note 1 ante.
7   Settled Land Act 1925 s 110(1). This provision is not limited to cases where the only defect is insufficiency of the consideration, and, subject to the requirement of good faith, it applies to an executory transaction: *Re Morgan's Lease, Jones v Norsesowicz* [1972] Ch 1, [1971] 2 All ER 235. Subject to that requirement, it applies whether the purchaser knew or did not know that he was dealing with a tenant for life or statutory owner: *Re Morgan's Lease, Jones v Norsesowicz* supra, not following *Weston v Henshaw* [1950] Ch 510. As to notice to and receipt by the trustees of the settlement see para 783 et seq ante.
8   *Hurrell v Littlejohn* [1904] 1 Ch 689.
9   *Re Handman and Wilcox's Contract* [1902] 1 Ch 599, CA, where the court left open the questions whether the transaction was void or voidable and, if only voidable, whether it could be set aside against a subsequent purchaser for value without notice.

886. Assumptions to be made by purchaser of legal estate. Except in certain specified cases[1], a purchaser[2] of a legal estate[3] in settled land[4] is not bound or entitled to call for the production of the trust instrument[5] or any information concerning it or any ad valorem stamp duty on it[6], and, whether or not he has notice of its contents, he is, except in the specified cases, bound and entitled if the last or only principal vesting instrument[7] contains the requisite statements and particulars[8] to assume that[9]:

(1)   the person in whom the land is by the instrument vested or declared to be vested is the tenant for life or statutory owner[10] and has all the statutory powers of a tenant for life, including such additional or larger powers, if any, as are mentioned in it[11];

(2)   the persons by the instrument stated to be the trustees of the settlement[12], or their successors appearing to be duly appointed, are the properly constituted trustees of the settlement[13];

(3)   the statements and particulars required by the Settled Land Act 1925 and contained (expressly or by reference) in the instrument were correct at its date[14];

(4)   the statements contained in any deed executed in accordance with that Act declaring who are the trustees of the settlement for the purposes of that Act are correct[15]; and

(5)   the statements contained in any deed of discharge executed in accordance with that Act are correct[16].

In the case of the first vesting instrument executed for the purpose of giving effect to (a) a settlement subsisting on 1 January 1926[17]; (b) an instrument which by virtue of the Settled Land Act 1925 is deemed to be a settlement[18]; (c) a settlement which by virtue of that Act is deemed to have been made by any person after 1925[19]; or (d) an instrument inter vivos intended to create a settlement of a legal estate in land which is executed after 1925 and which does not comply with the statutory requirements with respect to the method of effecting such a settlement[20], a purchaser is concerned to see that the land disposed of to him is comprised in the settlement or instrument[21], that the person in whom the settled land is by the vesting instrument vested or declared to be vested is the person in whom it ought to be vested as tenant for life or statutory owner[22], and that the persons stated to be the trustees of the settlement are the properly constituted trustees of the settlement[23].

1   As to these cases see the text to notes 17–23 infra.
2   For the meaning of 'purchaser' see para 702 note 12 ante.
3   For the meaning of 'legal estate' see para 678 note 13 ante.
4   For the meaning of 'settled land' see para 680 text to note 2 ante.
5   For the meaning of 'trust instrument' see para 688 note 7 ante. See also paras 694–695 ante.
6   As to stamp duty see para 623 ante.
7   For the meaning of 'principal vesting instrument' see para 698 note 1 ante.
8   As to what statements and particulars are required see para 690 ante.
9   Settled Land Act 1925 s 110(2).
10   For the meaning of 'tenant for life' see para 671 note 5 ante; and for the meaning of 'statutory owner' see para 766 note 6 ante. See also para 761 et seq ante.
11   Settled Land Act 1925 s 110(2)(a). As to the powers of a tenant for life see para 775 et seq ante.
12   For the meaning of 'trustees of the settlement' see para 750 note 1 ante. As to the trustees see para 750 et seq ante.
13   Settled Land Act 1925 s 110(2)(b).
14   Ibid s 110(2)(c).
15   Ibid s 110(2)(d). As to such deeds see para 759 ante.
16   Ibid s 110(2)(e). As to deeds of discharge see para 710 ante.
17   Ibid s 110(2) proviso (a). The date of commencement of the Act was 1 January 1926: see para 690 note 8 ante.
18   Ibid s 110(2) proviso (b). See further para 695 note 1 ante.
19   Ibid s 110(2) proviso (c). See further para 695 note 5 ante.

20   Ibid s 110(2) proviso (d). As to the effect of not complying with the statutory requirements as to vesting instruments see para 702 ante.

21   Ibid s 110(2) proviso (i).

22   Ibid s 110(2) proviso (ii).

23   Ibid s 110(2) proviso (iii). In the case of a compound settlement, the purchaser must see that the trustees are trustees of the compound settlement: *Re Cayley and Evans' Contract* [1930] 2 Ch 143. As to who are trustees of a compound settlement see para 754 ante.

887. Assumptions to be made by purchasers from personal representatives.

A purchaser[1] of a legal estate[2] in settled land[3] from a personal representative[4] is entitled to act on the following assumptions[5]:

(1)   if the capital money, if any, payable in respect of the transaction is paid to the personal representative, that the representative is acting under his statutory or other powers[6] and requires the money for purposes of administration[7];

(2)   if such capital money is, by the direction of the personal representative, paid to persons who are stated to be the trustees of a settlement, that such persons are the duly constituted trustees of the settlement for the purposes of the Settled Land Act 1925[8], and that the personal representative is acting under his statutory powers during a minority[9]; and

(3)   in any other case, that the personal representative is acting under his statutory or other powers[10].

1   For the meaning of 'purchaser' see para 702 note 12 ante.

2   For the meaning of 'legal estate' see para 678 note 13 ante.

3   For the meaning of 'settled land' see para 680 text to note 2 ante.

4   For the meaning of 'personal representative' see para 697 note 6 ante.

5   Settled Land Act 1925 s 110(3).

6   As to the powers of a personal representative see EXECUTORS AND ADMINISTRATORS.

7   Settled Land Act 1925 s 110(3)(i). The general personal representative of a deceased tenant for life on whose death the settlement comes to an end can give a good title to a purchaser: *Re Bridgett and Hayes' Contract* [1928] Ch 163. See also para 786 ante.

8   For the meaning of 'trustees of the settlement' see para 750 note 1 ante. As to the trustees see para 750 et seq ante.

9   Settled Land Act 1925 s 110(3)(ii). As to the statutory powers of a personal representative during a minority see CHILDREN AND YOUNG PERSONS vol 5(2) (Reissue) para 633 et seq.

10   Ibid s 110(3)(iii).

888. Effect of dispositions where no capital money arises.

If no capital money arises under a transaction, a disposition[1] by a tenant for life or statutory owner[2] in favour of a purchaser[3] of a legal estate[4] has effect under the Settled Land Act 1925[5] notwithstanding that at the date of the transaction there are no trustees of the settlement[6].

1   For the meaning of 'disposition' see para 685 note 14 ante.

2   For the meaning of 'tenant for life' see para 671 note 5 ante; and for the meaning of 'statutory owner' see para 766 note 6 ante. See also para 761 et seq ante.

3   For the meaning of 'purchaser' see para 702 note 12 ante.

4   For the meaning of 'legal estate' see para 678 note 13 ante.

5   As to the effect of a disposition under the Settled Land Act 1925 see para 874 ante.

6   Ibid s 110(4). However, as to the position where the purchaser knows that there are no trustees see para 784 note 7 ante. For the meaning of 'trustees of the settlement' see para 750 note 1 ante. As to the trustees see para 750 et seq ante.

889. Effect where no trustees named in conveyance or assent.

If a conveyance[1] of, or an assent relating to, land which was formerly subject to a vesting instrument[2] does not state who are the trustees of the settlement[3] for the purposes of the Settled Land Act 1925, a purchaser of a legal estate[4] is bound and entitled to act on the assumption that the person in whom the land was vested by the instrument was entitled to the land free from all limitations[5], powers and charges taking effect under that settlement[6], absolutely and beneficially, or, if so expressed in the conveyance or assent, as personal representative, or trustee of land or otherwise, and that every statement of fact in such conveyance or assent is correct[7].

1   For the meaning of 'conveyance' see para 698 note 12 ante.
2   For the meaning of 'land' see para 680 note 1 ante. For the meaning of 'vesting instrument' see para 690 note 8 ante.
3   For the meaning of 'trustees of the settlement' see para 750 note 1 ante. As to the trustees see para 750 et seq ante.
4   For the meaning of 'purchaser' see para 702 note 12 ante; and for the meaning of 'legal estate' see para 678 note 13 ante.
5   For the meaning of 'limitation' see para 708 note 4 ante.
6   For the meaning of 'settlement' see para 678 note 1 ante.
7   Settled Land Act 1925 s 110(5) (amended by the Trusts of Land and Appointment of Trustees Act 1996 s 25(1), Sch 3 para 2). This provides a method of putting an end to a settlement on the death of the last tenant for life without executing a deed of discharge: see paras 709–710 ante.

890. Person conveying by way of substituted security by direction of tenant for life. On land being acquired by purchase or in exchange or otherwise under the statutory powers[1], any person who, by the direction of the tenant for life[2], so conveys it as to subject it to a legal estate[3] or charge by way of legal mortgage[4] by way of substituted security[5] is not concerned to inquire whether or not it is proper that the land should be subjected to that legal estate or charge[6].

1   As to the statutory powers of sale and exchange see para 827 et seq ante.
2   For the meaning of 'tenant for life' see para 671 note 5 ante. See also para 761 et seq ante.
3   For the meaning of 'legal estate' see para 678 note 13 ante.
4   For the meaning of 'legal mortgage' see para 698 note 23 ante.
5   As to the land being acquired as substituted security see para 853 ante.
6   See the Settled Land Act 1925 s 82(2).

891. Protection of trustees in general. The trustees of the settlement[1], or any of them, are not liable:

(1)   for giving any consent[2], or for not making, bringing, taking or doing any such application, action, proceeding or thing as they might make, bring, take or do[3];

(2)   in case of a purchase of land with capital money arising under the Settled Land Act 1925[4] or of an exchange, lease or other disposition[5], for adopting any contract made by the tenant for life or statutory owner[6], nor are they bound to inquire as to the propriety of the purchase, exchange, lease or other disposition, or answerable as regards any price, consideration or fine[7];

(3)   to see to, or answerable for, the investigation of the title[8], or answerable for a conveyance[9] of land, if the conveyance purports to convey the land in the proper mode[10]; and

(4)   in respect of purchase money paid by them by the direction of the tenant for life or statutory owner to any person joining in the conveyance as a conveying party, or as giving a receipt for the purchase money, or in any other character, or in respect of any other money paid by them by the direction of the tenant for life or statutory owner on the purchase, exchange, lease or other disposition[11].

1   For the meaning of 'trustees of the settlement' see para 750 note 1 ante. As to the trustees see para 750 et seq ante.
2   As to cases where the consent of the trustees is required see paras 788–789 ante.

3 Settled Land Act 1925 s 97(a). As to whether trustees are under a duty to prevent an improper disposition of which they have notice see further para 783 ante.

4 For the meaning of 'land' see para 680 note 1 ante. For the meaning of 'capital money arising under the Act' see para 795 ante.

5 For the meaning of 'lease' see para 685 note 13 ante; and for the meaning of 'disposition' see para 685 note 14 ante.

6 For the meaning of 'tenant for life' see para 671 note 5 ante; and for the meaning of 'statutory owner' see para 766 note 6 ante. See also para 761 et seq ante.

7 Settled Land Act 1925 s 97(b). For the meaning of 'fine' see para 801 note 1 ante.

8 However, the trustees are entitled to see that the tenant for life has had proper professional advice as to the investigation of title (*Re Hotham, Hotham v Doughty* [1902] 2 Ch 575, CA), and they are entitled to inquire into both the title and value of land which it is proposed to purchase (*Re Theobald* (1903) 19 TLR 536), and they are not bound to apply capital money at the direction of the tenant for life for an investment which is undesirable (*Re Gladwin's Trust* [1919] 1 Ch 232). As to the investigation of title generally see SALE OF LAND para 137 et seq ante.

9 For the meaning of 'conveyance' see para 698 note 12 ante.

10 Settled Land Act 1925 s 97(c).

11 Ibid s 97(d).

892. Protection of trustees in respect of authorised investments or application of capital money.

If the tenant for life or statutory owner[1] directs capital money to be invested on any authorised security or investment[2], the trustees of the settlement[3] are not liable for the acts of any agent employed by the tenant for life or statutory owner in connection with the transaction, or for not employing a separate agent in or about the valuation of the subject of the security or the investigation of its title, or for the form of the security or of any deed conveying the subject of it to the trustees[4], or for paying or applying any capital money by the direction of the tenant for life or statutory owner for any authorised purpose[5].

Further, the trustees of the settlement are not liable in any way on account of any vesting instrument[6] or other documents of title relating to the settled land[7], other than securities[8] for capital money, being placed in the possession of the tenant for life or statutory owner[9], but where, if the settlement[10] were not disclosed, it would appear that the tenant for life had a general power of appointment over, or was absolutely and beneficially entitled to, the settled land, they must, before they deliver the documents to him, require that notice of the last or only principal vesting instrument[11] be written on one of the documents under which the tenant for life acquired his title, and, if the documents are not in their possession, may require such notice to be written, but, in the latter case, they will not be liable in any way for not requiring the notice to be written[12].

1 For the meaning of 'tenant for life' see para 671 note 5 ante; and for the meaning of 'statutory owner' see para 766 note 6 ante. See also para 761 et seq ante.

2 As to the modes of application of capital money see para 808 ante.

3 For the meaning of 'trustees of the settlement' see para 750 note 1 ante. As to the trustees see para 750 et seq ante.

4 Settled Land Act 1925 s 98(1).

5 Ibid s 98(2). As to the purposes for which capital money may be applied see paras 795 et seq ante, 891 note 8 ante.

6 For the meaning of 'vesting instrument' see para 690 note 8 ante.

7 For the meaning of 'settled land' see para 680 text to note 2 ante.

8 For the meaning of 'securities' see para 693 note 1 ante.

9 As to custody of the title deeds see paras 771–773 ante.

10 For the meaning of 'settlement' see para 678 note 1 ante.

11 For the meaning of 'principal vesting instrument' see para 698 note 1 ante.

12 Settled Land Act 1925 s 98(3). As to the notice see para 772 ante.

893. Trustees' liability for personal acts only. Each person who is for the time being a trustee of a settlement[1] is answerable for what he actually receives only, notwithstanding his signing any receipt for conformity, and in respect of his own acts, receipts and defaults only, and is not answerable in respect of those of any other trustee, or of any banker, broker or other person, or for the insufficiency or deficiency of any securities[2], or for any loss not happening through his own wilful default[3]. He is also entitled to the ordinary protection afforded to trustees[4].

1	For the meaning of 'trustees of the settlement' see para 750 note 1 ante. As to the trustees see para 750 et seq ante.
2	For the meaning of 'securities' see para 693 note 1 ante.
3	Settled Land Act 1925 s 96.
4	As to the liability of trustees for the acts of their agents and co-trustees generally see TRUSTS vol 48 (Reissue) paras 861, 981. As to the protection of trustees generally see TRUSTS vol 48 (Reissue) para 795 et seq.

894. Indemnity to personal representatives and others. Personal representatives[1], trustees or other persons who have in good faith, pursuant to the Settled Land Act 1925, executed a vesting deed, assent or other conveyance[2] of the settled land[3], or a deed of discharge of trustees, are absolutely discharged from all liability in respect of the equitable interests[4] and powers taking effect under the settlement[5], and are entitled to be kept indemnified at the cost of the trust estate from all liabilities affecting the settled land, but the person to whom the settled land is conveyed (not being a purchaser[6] taking free from them) holds the settled land upon the trusts, if any, affecting it[7].

1	For the meaning of 'personal representative' see para 697 note 6 ante.
2	For the meaning of 'vesting deed' see para 688 note 6 ante; for the meaning of 'vesting assent' see para 690 note 8 ante; and for the meaning of 'conveyance' see para 698 note 12 ante.
3	For the meaning of 'settled land' see para 680 text to note 2 ante.
4	For the meaning of 'equitable interests' see para 695 note 8 ante.
5	For the meaning of 'settlement' see para 678 note 1 ante.
6	For the meaning of 'purchaser' see para 702 note 12 ante. As to a purchaser taking free from equitable interests and powers see para 874 ante.
7	Settled Land Act 1925 s 99.

895. Reimbursement of trustees' expenses. Trustees of a settlement[1] may reimburse themselves or pay and discharge out of the trust property all expenses properly incurred by them[2].

1	For the meaning of 'trustees of the settlement' see para 750 note 1 ante. As to the trustees see para 750 et seq ante.
2	Settled Land Act 1925 s 100. As to the rights of trustees to reimbursement generally see TRUSTS vol 48 (Reissue) para 785 et seq.

896. Protection of purchasers under compound settlements. If settled land[1] is or has been expressed to be disposed of under a compound settlement[2] of which trustees were appointed by the court[3], and the capital money, if any, arising on the disposition[4] is or was paid to the persons who by virtue of the order or any subsequent appointment appear to be or to have been the trustees of that settlement[5], and if the person by or on whose behalf the disposition is or was made is or was the tenant for life or statutory owner[6] of the land[7] disposed of under a principal instrument mentioned in the order as constituting part of the compound settlement, then the title of the person to whom the disposition is made is not impeachable on the ground[8]:

(1) that the instruments mentioned in the order did not constitute a compound settlement[9];

(2) that those instruments were not all the instruments at the date of the order or of the disposition constituting the compound settlement of the land disposed of[10]; or

(3) that any of the instruments mentioned in the order did not form part of the settlement of the land disposed of, or had ceased to form part of the settlement at the date of the disposition[11].

This provision does not, however, prejudice the rights of any person in respect of any estate, interest or charge under any instrument existing at the date of the order and not mentioned in it which would not have been overreached if the disposition had been made by or on behalf of the tenant for life or statutory owner under the principal instrument as such, and there had been trustees of that instrument for the purposes of the Settled Land Acts 1882 to 1890[12] or of the Settled Land Act 1925, and the capital money, if any, arising on the disposition had been paid to the trustees[13].

These provisions operate to confirm all dispositions made before 1926, but not so as to render invalid or prejudice any court order or any title or right acquired before 1926, and operate without prejudice to any appointment already made by the court of trustees of a settlement and to the court's power in any case after 1925 to make any such appointment[14].

1 For the meaning of 'settled land' see para 680 text to note 2 ante.
2 As to compound settlements see para 681 et seq post. For the meaning of 'settlement' see para 678 note 1 ante.
3 This provision applies whenever the appointment was made. As to the appointment of trustees by the court see paras 756–757 ante.
4 For the meaning of 'disposition' see para 685 note 14 ante.
5 For the meaning of 'trustees of the settlement' see para 750 note 1 ante. As to the trustees see para 750 et seq ante.
6 For the meaning of 'tenant for life' see para 671 note 5 ante; and for the meaning of 'statutory owner' see para 766 note 6 ante. See also para 761 et seq ante.
7 For the meaning of 'land' see para 680 note 1 ante.
8 See the Settled Land Act 1925 s 33(2).
9 Ibid s 33(2)(a).
10 Ibid s 33(2)(b).
11 Ibid s 33(2)(c).
12 As to these Acts see para 678 note 1 ante.
13 Settled Land Act 1925 s 33(2). For the meaning of 'capital money arising under the Act' see para 795 ante.
14 Ibid s 33(3).

3. TRUSTS OF LAND

(1) CREATION OF TRUSTS OF LAND

897. Creation generally. Land may be settled either by deed or by will upon a trust of land[1]. By the Trusts of Land and Appointment of Trustees Act 1996, a trust of land is any trust of property (whether created before or after the commencement of the Act) which consists of or is land[2]. References in the Act to a trust of land are to any description of trust (whether express, implied, resulting or constructive), including a trust for sale and a bare trust, but excludes settled land[3]. Settlements of land upon trust of land may also arise by statute[4]. Wherever land is held upon trust of land the legal estate in the land settled is, or should be, vested in the trustees[5].

Since the enactment of the Trusts of Land and Appointment of Trustees Act 1996, the interest of a beneficiary under a trust of land is usually in the land itself, the doctrine of conversion having been abolished[6].

1   For the meaning of 'trust of land' see para 676 note 5 ante. Before the Trusts of Land and Appointment of Trustees Act 1996 came into force (ie 1 January 1997: see para 676 note 1 ante) an alternative to creating a settlement of land under the Settled Land Act 1925 was to settle land upon trust for sale. Since that date, it is no longer possible to create settlements under the Settled Land Act 1925: see para 676 ante. In addition, from that date every trust for sale of property which consists of or includes land is a trust of land: see the Trusts of Land and Appointment of Trustees Act 1996 s 1; and REAL PROPERTY vol 39(2) (Reissue) paras 64–66. See further paras 676–677 ante.
2   See ibid s 1(1), (2); and para 676 ante.
3   See ibid s 1(3); and REAL PROPERTY vol 39(2) (Reissue) para 66. As to the position when there is no relevant property subject to the settlement see para 676 text to notes 8–9 ante.
4   As to trusts of land arising by statute see para 899 post.
5   As to the method of settling land upon trust of land see para 898 post.
6   See the Trusts of Land and Appointment of Trustees Act 1996 s 3; and REAL PROPERTY vol 39(2) (Reissue) para 77. The doctrine of conversion, whereby the beneficiary's interest is notionally in the proceeds of sale rather than in the land, continues to apply to trusts created by will if the testator died before the commencement of the Act: see s 3(2); and REAL PROPERTY vol 39(2) (Reissue) para 77.

898.   Method of settling land upon trust of land. If a legal estate in land is settled inter vivos upon a trust of land[1], the legal estate is still frequently conveyed or transferred to the trustees upon trust to sell and to hold the net proceeds of sale, and the net rents and profits of the land until sale, upon the trusts declared by a deed of even date[2]. This practice is likely to change over time, and there is clearly scope since the introduction of trusts of land to economise with the words used.

There is no statutory provision requiring the transaction to be carried out by means of two deeds, but it is clearly convenient to carry out the transaction by two separate deeds, whether or not the land in question is registered land, so that the trustees can ensure they are able to retain the document containing the settlement. If a legal estate in land is settled by a will upon a trust of land, the personal representatives, if they are not themselves the trustees, must as soon as the estate has been fully administered assent to the land vesting in the trustees upon trust[3]. Even if they are themselves the trustees, they should execute an assent in their own favour[4].

1   See para 897 ante. For the meaning of 'trust of land' see para 676 note 5 ante.
2   This is despite the provisions of the Trusts of Land and Appointment of Trustees Act 1996 which imply in every trust for sale of land a power to retain the land: see s 4; and REAL PROPERTY vol 39(2) (Reissue) para 66.
3   See *Re Yerburgh, Yerburgh v Yerburgh* [1928] WN 208 (a case of intestacy); and EXECUTORS AND ADMINISTRATORS.
4   See *Re King's Will Trusts, Assheton v Boyne* [1964] Ch 542, [1964] 1 All ER 833; *Re Edward's Will Trusts, Edwards v Edwards* [1982] Ch 30, [1981] 2 All ER 941, CA; and EXECUTORS AND ADMINISTRATORS.

899.   Trust of land arising by statute. Trusts of land[1] are imposed by statute in the following cases:
(1)   if property vested in trustees by way of security becomes discharged from the right of redemption[2];
(2)   if by a conveyance executed, or by a will coming into operation, after 1925 land is conveyed, devised, bequeathed or appointed to persons in undivided shares[3];

(3)   if a legal estate (not being settled land[4]) is beneficially limited to or held in trust for any persons as joint tenants[5];

(4)   if immediately before 1926 land was held at law or in equity in undivided shares vested in possession[6];

(5)   if there was a tenancy by entireties existing immediately before 1926[7]; and

(6)   on the death after 1925 of a person intestate[8].

1   For the meaning of 'trust of land' see para 676 note 5 ante; definition applied by the Interpretation Act 1978 s 5, Sch 1. As to when land is held on trust of land see para 676 ante. For the meaning of 'land' see REAL PROPERTY vol 39(2) (Reissue) para 77. For the definition of 'land' in the Settled Land Act 1925 see para 680 note 1 ante.
2   See the Law of Property Act 1925 s 31(1) (as amended); and TRUSTS vol 48 (Reissue) para 879.
3   See ibid s 34(2), (3) (as amended); and REAL PROPERTY vol 39(2) (Reissue) para 207 et seq.
4   For the meaning of 'settled land' see para 680 text to note 2 ante; definition applied by ibid s 205(1)(xxvi).
5   See ibid s 36(1) (as amended); and REAL PROPERTY vol 39(2) (Reissue) para 190.
6   See ibid s 39(4), Sch 1 Pt IV (as amended); and REAL PROPERTY vol 39(2) (Reissue) para 55 et seq.
7   See ibid ss 36(1), 39(6), Sch 1 Pt VI (as amended); and REAL PROPERTY vol 39(2) (Reissue) para 55 et seq.
8   See the Administration of Estates Act 1925 s 33(1) (as amended); and EXECUTORS AND ADMINISTRATORS.

(2) TRUSTEES OF LAND

(i) Appointment of Trustees of Land

900. Appointment of trustees of a trust of land where there is a separate trust of the proceeds of sale. The persons having power to appoint new trustees of land[1] are bound to appoint the same persons (if any) who are for the time being trustees of any trust of the proceeds of sale of the land, whenever the trust of land and the trust of proceeds of sale are created[2].

It is not necessary to have more than one trustee of a trust of land except where capital money arises on the transaction, in which case either there must be at least two trustees or the trustee must be a trust corporation[3]. Where a settlement or disposition on trust of land is made or comes into operation after 1925, the number of the trustees must not exceed four[4]. If more than four persons are named as trustees, the first four named who are able and willing to act will alone be the trustees and the other persons named are not to be trustees unless appointed on the occurrence of a vacancy[5].

1   For the meaning of 'trustees of land' and 'trust of land' see para 676 note 5 ante; definitions applied by the Interpretation Act 1978 s 5, Sch 1.
2   See the Law of Property Act 1925 s 24(1), (3) (substituted by the Trusts of Land and Appointment of Trustees Act 1996 s 25(1), Sch 3 para 4). A purchaser is not concerned to see that this provision has been complied with: see the Law of Property Act 1925 s 24(2) (as so substituted). As to the manner of appointment of the trustees see para 901 post.
3   See the Law of Property Act 1925 s 27(2) (as substituted and amended); and TRUSTS vol 48 (Reissue) para 689. This provision does not affect the right of a sole personal representative as such to give valid receipts for, or direct the application of, proceeds of sale or other capital money: see s 27(2) (as substituted and amended); and TRUSTS vol 48 (Reissue) para 689. For the meaning of 'trust corporation' see para 705 note 6 ante.
4   See the Trustee Act 1925 s 34(2) (as amended); and TRUSTS vol 48 (Reissue) paras 694, 712.
5   See ibid s 34(2)(a); and TRUSTS vol 48 (Reissue) para 694. The number of trustees may not be increased beyond four: see s 34(2)(b); and TRUSTS vol 48 (Reissue) para 712. This restriction does not apply in the case of land vested in trustees for charitable, ecclesiastical or public purposes, or where the net proceeds of sale are held for like purposes: see s 34(3); and TRUSTS vol 48 (Reissue) para 694. If on 1 January 1926 there were more than four trustees holding land on trust for sale, then, except where as the result of the appointment the number was reduced to four or less, no new trustees could be appointed until the number was reduced to less than four and thereafter the number cannot be increased beyond four: see s 34(1).

901. Appointment of new trustees of land. Appointments of new trustees of land[1] and of new trustees of any trust of the proceeds of sale of the land must, subject to any order of the court, be effected by separate instruments, but in such manner as to secure that the same persons become trustees of land and trustees of the trust of the proceeds of sale[2].

Where new trustees of land are appointed, a memorandum of the persons who are for the time being the trustees of the land must be indorsed on or annexed to the conveyance by which the land was vested in the trustees of land; and that conveyance must be produced to the persons who are for the time being the trustees of the land by the person in possession of it in order for that to be done when the trustees require its production[3].

1   For the meaning of 'trustees of land' see para 676 note 5 ante; definition applied by the Interpretation Act 1978 s 5, Sch 1. 'New trustee' includes an additional trustee: Trustee Act 1925 s 68(17).
2   Ibid s 35(1) (substituted by the Trusts of Land and Appointment of Trustees Act 1996 s 25(1), Sch 3).
3   Trustee Act 1925 s 35(3) (substituted by the Trusts of Land and Appointment of Trustees Act 1996 s 25(1), Sch 3). There is no statutory provision requiring a memorandum to be indorsed on or annexed to the conveyance on the discharge of a trustee under the Trustee Act 1925 s 39(1) (as amended) (see TRUSTS vol 48 (Reissue) para 776) but the same course should be followed in that case.

(ii)   Powers of Trustees of Land

902. Necessary consents. When executing a trust of land[1] or exercising any statutory or other powers, trustees must comply strictly with any provisions of the instrument creating the trust with regard to obtaining the consent of any person or persons to the execution of that trust or the exercise of those powers[2].

If a disposition[3] creating a trust of land requires the consent of more than two persons to the exercise by the trustees of any function relating to the land, the consent of any two of them to the exercise of the function is sufficient in favour of a purchaser[4].

Where the person whose consent is required is suffering from mental disorder, the trustees must obtain the consent of his or her receiver[5].

Trustees of land in carrying out any function relating to land must, so far as practicable, consult the beneficiaries of full age and beneficially entitled to an interest in possession in the land and, so far as consistent with the general interests of the trust, give effect to the wishes of those beneficiaries, or (in case of dispute) of the majority (according to the value of their combined interests)[6].

1   For the meaning of 'trust of land' see para 676 note 5 ante. See also para 897 et seq ante.
2   See *Bateman v Davis* (1818) 3 Madd 98; and TRUSTS vol 48 (Reissue) para 895. As to applications to the court where consent cannot be obtained see para 905 post. As to the protection of a purchaser if consents are not obtained see para 906 post.
3   For the meaning of 'disposition' see para 665 note 8 ante.
4   See the Trusts of Land and Appointment of Trustees Act 1996 s 10; and TRUSTS vol 48 (Reissue) para 895. As to the application of this rule to trustees of land held on charitable, ecclesiastical or public trusts, personal representatives and children see TRUSTS vol 48 (Reissue) para 895.
5   A receiver of the property of a person with a mental disorder appointed under the Mental Health Act 1983 s 99 may be authorised to consent to the exercise by trustees of their powers: see ss 99(2), 96(1)(k); and MENTAL HEALTH vol 30 (Reissue) para 1442 et seq.
6   See the Trusts of Land and Appointment of Trustees Act 1996 s 11(1); and TRUSTS vol 48 (Reissue) para 895. This rule does not apply in certain circumstances: see s 11(2); and TRUSTS vol 48 (Reissue) para 895. The rule also does not apply to annuitants or to personal representatives holding land on trust for sale: see ss 18(1), 22(3); and TRUSTS vol 48 (Reissue) paras 894, 624.

903. General powers of trustees. In the case of every trust for sale of land[1] created by a disposition[2] there is to be implied, despite any provision to the contrary made by the disposition, a power for the trustees to postpone sale of the land[3]. In cases where a trust of land is implied by statute, the trustees do not have a duty to sell the property[4].

For the purpose of exercising their functions as trustees, the trustees of land have in relation to the land subject to the trust all the powers of an absolute owner[5].

Where in the case of any land subject to a trust of land each of the beneficiaries interested in the land is a person of full age and capacity who is absolutely entitled to the land, the trustees may convey the land to the beneficiaries even though they have not required the trustees to do so[6].

The trustees of land have the power to purchase a legal estate in any land in England or Wales and may exercise this power to purchase land by way of investment, for occupation by any beneficiary, or for any other reason[7].

Trustees of land may, where beneficiaries of full age are absolutely entitled in undivided shares to land subject to the trust, partition the land, or any part of it, and provide (by way of mortgage or otherwise) for the payment of any equality money[8]. The trustees must, prior to the exercise of this power, obtain the consent of each such beneficiary[9].

The trustees of land may by power of attorney, delegate to any beneficiary of full age and beneficially entitled to an interest in possession in land subject to the trust any of their functions as trustees which relate to the land[10]. Such a delegation may be for any period, definite or indefinite[11]. Where any function has been delegated to a beneficiary under the statutory power, the trustees are jointly and severally liable for any act or default of the beneficiary in the exercise of the function if, but only if, the trustees did not exercise reasonable care in deciding to delegate the function to the beneficiary[12].

1   As to trusts for sale see REAL PROPERTY vol 39(2) (Reissue) para 55. For the meaning of 'land' see REAL PROPERTY vol 39(2) (Reissue) para 77.
2   For the meaning of 'disposition' see para 665 note 8 ante.
3   See the Trusts of Land and Appointment of Trustees Act 1996 s 4(1); and REAL PROPERTY vol 39(2) (Reissue) para 66. The trustees are not liable in any way for postponing sale of the land, in the exercise of their discretion, for an indefinite period: see s 4(1); and REAL PROPERTY vol 39(2) (Reissue) para 66. This provision does not affect any liability incurred by trustees before 1 January 1997: see s 4(3); and REAL PROPERTY vol 39(2) (Reissue) para 66.
4   See ibid s 5(1), Sch 2; and REAL PROPERTY vol 39(2) (Reissue) para 66. For the meaning of 'trust of land' see para 676 note 5 ante.
5   See ibid s 6(1); and TRUSTS vol 48 (Reissue) para 894. For the meaning of 'trustees of land' see para 676 note 5 ante.
6   See ibid s 6(2); and TRUSTS vol 48 (Reissue) para 894. Where land is so conveyed, the beneficiaries must do whatever is necessary to secure that it vests in them, and if they fail to do so, the court may make an order requiring them to do so: see s 6(2); and TRUSTS vol 48 (Reissue) para 894. There is no requirement for consultation with beneficiaries in relation to the exercise of this power: see s 11(2)(c); and TRUSTS vol 48 (Reissue) para 895.
7   See ibid s 6(3), (4); and TRUSTS vol 48 (Reissue) para 894. In exercising these powers, the trustees must have regard to the rights of the beneficiaries, and must not act in contravention of, or of any order made in pursuance of, any other enactment or any rule of law or equity: see s 6(5), (6); and TRUSTS vol 48 (Reissue) para 894. As to the effect of restrictions, limitations or conditions in other enactments see s 6(8); and TRUSTS vol 48 (Reissue) para 894.
8   See ibid s 7(1); and TRUSTS vol 48 (Reissue) para 908. As to the method of giving effect to any such partition see s 7(2); and TRUSTS vol 48 (Reissue) para 908. As to where a share of land is affected by an incumbrance or is vested in a child see s 7(4), (5); and TRUSTS vol 48 (Reissue) para 908.
9   See ibid s 7(3); and TRUSTS vol 48 (Reissue) para 908.
10   See ibid s 9(1); and TRUSTS vol 48 (Reissue) para 855. As to the position when a beneficiary ceases to be beneficially entitled to an interest in possession in land see s 9(4); and TRUSTS vol 48 (Reissue) para 855. Beneficiaries to whom functions have been delegated under the statutory power are, in relation to the exercise of the functions, in the same position as trustees, with the same duties and liabilities, but such

beneficiaries are not regarded as trustees for any other purposes (including, in particular, the purposes of any enactment permitting the delegation of functions by trustees or imposing requirements relating to the payment of capital money): see s 9(7); and TRUSTS vol 48 (Reissue) para 855.

11　See ibid s 9(4); and TRUSTS vol 48 (Reissue) para 855.

12　See ibid s 9(8); and TRUSTS vol 48 (Reissue) para 855.

904. Miscellaneous powers. In addition to the foregoing powers, trustees of land have all the powers conferred on ordinary trustees[1], including the following, the operation of which may, except as specifically stated, be excluded by the expression of a contrary intention in the settlement[2]:

(1)　power to sell or concur with any other person in selling all or any part of the property, either subject to prior charges or not, and either together or in lots, by public auction or by private contract, subject to any conditions respecting title or evidence of title or other matters as the trustees think fit, with power to vary any contract for sale, and to buy in at any auction, or to rescind any contract for sale and to resell, without being answerable for any loss[3];

(2)　power to sell or dispose of part of the land, whether the division is horizontal, vertical or made in any other way[4];

(3)　if they are authorised by the instrument creating the trust or by law to pay or apply capital money subject to the trust for any purpose or in any manner, power to raise the money required by sale, conversion, calling in or mortgage of all or any part of the trust property for the time being in possession[5];

(4)　power to insure any personal property against loss and damage, and to pay the premiums for such insurance out of its income or out of the income of any other property subject to the same trusts without obtaining the consent of any person entitled to the income[6]; and

(5)　power to deposit any documents held by them relating to the trust or the trust property with any banker or banking company or any other company whose business includes the undertaking of the safe custody of documents, any sum payable in respect of such deposit being payable only out of the income of the trust property[7].

1　As to the powers of trustees see the Trustee Act 1925 Pt II (ss 12–33) (as amended); and TRUSTS vol 48 (Reissue) para 845 et seq.

2　See ibid s 69(2).

3　See ibid s 12(1) (as amended); and TRUSTS vol 48 (Reissue) para 904. Trustees for sale have the same power as a tenant for life to leave part of the purchase money on mortgage: see s 10(2) (as amended); and para 833 ante. The power of the trustees to sell is subject to depreciatory conditions: see s 13; and TRUSTS vol 48 (Reissue) para 906.

4　See ibid s 12(2) (as amended); and TRUSTS vol 48 (Reissue) para 904. See also note 3 supra.

5　See ibid s 16(1); and TRUSTS vol 48 (Reissue) para 915. This provision applies notwithstanding anything to the contrary in the instrument creating the trust: see s 16(2); and TRUSTS vol 48 (Reissue) para 915.

6　See ibid s 19(1) (as amended); and TRUSTS vol 48 (Reissue) para 891. As to the application of the insurance money see TRUSTS vol 48 (Reissue) para 892.

7　See ibid s 21; and TRUSTS vol 48 (Reissue) para 916. In special circumstances trustees may be justified in depositing title deeds with their solicitors: see *Field v Field* [1894] 1 Ch 425; and TRUSTS vol 48 (Reissue) para 827.

905. Applications to the court. Any person who is a trustee of land[1] or has an interest in property subject to a trust of land[2] may make an application to the court for an order relating to the exercise by the trustees of any of their functions (including an order relieving them of any obligation to obtain the consent of, or to consult, any person in connection with the exercise of their functions), or declaring the nature or extent of a person's interest in the property subject to the trust[3].

1   For the meaning of 'trustees of land' see para 676 note 5 ante.
2   For the meaning of 'trust of land' see para 676 note 5 ante.
3   See the Trusts of Land and Appointment of Trustees Act 1996 s 14(1), (2). The court may not make an
    order under this provision as to the appointment or removal of trustees: see s 14(3). As to the matters to
    which the court is to have regard in determining an application for an order see s 15. See generally
    TRUSTS vol 48 (Reissue) (Supp) para 893A. As to applications to the court by a trustee of a bankrupt's
    estate see the Insolvency Act 1986 s 335A (as added); and BANKRUPTCY AND INSOLVENCY vol 3(2)
    (Reissue) paras 635, 637.

(iii) Purchaser protection

906. Purchaser protection. A purchaser of land which is or has been subject to a trust
need not be concerned to see that the trustees have obtained the necessary consents, or
that they have consulted with the beneficiaries or had regard to their rights as they are
required to do by the Trusts of Land and Appointment of Trustees Act 1996[1].

Where there is a trust of the proceeds of sale of land, and the persons having power
to appoint new trustees have failed to ensure that they have appointed as trustees of land
the same persons as are the trustees of the proceeds of sale, this does not affect a
purchaser[2].

Notwithstanding anything to the contrary in the trust instrument (either relating to
the land or to the proceeds of sale), the proceeds of sale or other capital money must not
be paid to or applied by the direction of fewer than two persons as trustees, except where
the trustee is a trust corporation[3]. A purchaser of a legal estate from trustees of land is not
concerned with the trusts affecting the land, the net income of the land or the proceeds
of sale of the land whether or not those trusts are declared by the same instrument as that
by which the trust of land is created[4].

Certain provisions of the Trusts of Land and Appointment of Trustees Act 1996
expressly apply to the trusts of the proceeds of sale[5].

Where trustees purport to delegate functions relating to any land to a person by power
of attorney under the Trusts of Land and Appointment of Trustees Act 1996[6], and
another person in good faith deals with him in relation to the land, he is presumed in
favour of that other person to have been a person to whom the functions could be
delegated unless that other person has knowledge at the time of the transaction that he
was not such a person[7].

1   See the Trusts of Land and Appointment of Trustees Act 1996 s 16(1); and TRUSTS vol 48 (Reissue)
    para 895. As to the necessary consents and consultation see para 902 ante. As to the consequences of
    contravention by the trustees see s 16(2). As to the duty of trustees to bring any limitation of their
    powers to the notice of a purchaser see s 16(3). As to the position of a purchaser buying from a
    beneficiary to whom the trustees have conveyed the property see s 16(4), (5). As to the application of
    this provision to land held on charitable, ecclesiastical or public trusts, and to registered land see s 16(6),
    (7). See further TRUSTS vol 48 (Reissue) paras 894–895.
2   See the Law of Property Act 1925 s 24 (as substituted); and para 900 ante.
3   Ibid s 27(2) (amended by the Trusts of Land and Appointment of Trustees Act 1996 s 25(1), Sch 3 para 4(1),
    (8)). For the meaning of 'trust corporation' see para 705 note 6 ante. This provision does not affect the right
    of a sole personal representative as such to give valid receipts for, or direct the application of, the proceeds
    of sale or other capital money, nor, except where capital money arises on the transaction, render it necessary
    to have more than one trustee: see the Law of Property Act 1925 s 27(2) (as so amended).
4   See ibid s 27(1) (substituted by the Trusts of Land and Appointment of Trustees Act 1996 Sch 3 para 4(1), (8)).
5   See ibid s 17(1); and TRUSTS vol 48 (Reissue) para 894. The provisions are s 6(3) (trustees' power to
    purchase land in England and Wales), s 14 (applications to court): see s 17(1); and paras 903, 905 ante.
    For the meaning of 'trust of proceeds of sale of land' see TRUSTS vol 48 (Reissue) para 894. A settlement
    still governed by the Settled Land Act 1925 cannot be a trust of proceeds of sale of land: see the Trusts of
    Land and Appointment of Trustees Act 1996 s 17(5); and TRUSTS vol 48 (Reissue) para 894.
6   See para 903 text and notes 10–12 ante.

7   See the Trusts of Land and Appointment of Trustees Act 1996 s 9(2); and TRUSTS vol 48 (Reissue) para 855. It is conclusively presumed in favour of any purchaser whose interest depends on the validity of that transaction that that other person dealt in good faith and did not have such knowledge if that other person makes a statutory declaration to that effect before or within three months after the completion of the purchase: see s 9(2); and TRUSTS vol 48 (Reissue) para 855.

4. SETTLEMENTS OF PERSONALTY

(1) CONSTITUTION OF THE SETTLEMENT

907. Constitution generally. A voluntary settlement is fully constituted when the settlor has done everything necessary to be done by him to transfer the property to trustees upon trusts declared by him, or when he has declared himself to be a trustee of the property[1].

Where money and other property passes by delivery, only one instrument is necessary, but in other cases deeds of transfer or assignment may be required[2].

1   As to completed and incomplete gifts see para 615 ante; and GIFTS vol 20 (Reissue) para 63 et seq. As to when writing is required in respect of a declaration of trust or a disposition of an equitable interest or trust see the Law of Property Act 1925 s 53(1)(b), (c); CHOSES IN ACTION vol 6 (Reissue) para 31; GIFTS vol 20 (Reissue) para 39. If the property is held on a bare trust for the settlor, and is transferred at his direction, no separate assignment of his beneficial interest is necessary: *Vandervell v IRC* [1967] 2 AC 291, [1967] 1 All ER 1, HL.
2   See para 908 et seq post. As to delivery see GIFTS vol 20 (Reissue) para 36 et seq; and as to the transfer of things in action generally see CHOSES IN ACTION vol 6 (Reissue) para 9 et seq. A settlement may itself operate as an effective disposition of the settlor's equitable interest where the legal title was outstanding at the date of the settlement: *Re Wale, Wale v Harris* [1956] 3 All ER 280, [1956] 1 WLR 1346.

908. Debts. A debt is settled by assigning it to the trustees of the settlement. Such an assignment, coupled with notice of it to the debtor in writing, vests in the trustees the legal right to the debt and the remedies for it, with power to give a good discharge[1].

1   See the Law of Property Act 1925 s 136(1); and CHOSES IN ACTION vol 6 (Reissue) para 12.

909. Mortgage debts. Money secured by a mortgage is settled by transferring it to the trustees by one deed (without disclosing that the mortgage debt is trust money), and declaring the trusts by another. This avoids the inconvenience that would otherwise arise on the sale or redemption of the mortgaged property of having to produce and acknowledge the right to production of the deed containing the trusts[1]. For similar reasons a portion charged on land is settled by assigning it to the trustees of the settlement by a separate deed[2].

1   *Capper v Terrington* (1844) 1 Coll 103; *Dobson v Land* (1851) 4 De G & Sm 575. See also MORTGAGE.
2   As to portions see para 727 et seq ante.

910. Stocks and shares. Stocks and shares in public or private companies are settled by transferring them to the trustees in accordance with the regulations of the particular company[1]. The transfer of government stocks and funds is effected in the books of the Bank of England[2], while certain bonds and securities may be transferred by delivering them to the trustees[3]. The transfer of local government stock is regulated by special provisions[4]. In each case the settlement normally recites that the transfer has been or is intended to be made, as the case may be[5].

1   See GIFTS vol 20 (Reissue) para 31; STOCK EXCHANGE.
2   See BANKING vol 3(1) (Reissue) para 16; MONEY; STOCK EXCHANGE.
3   See GIFTS vol 20 (Reissue) paras 38, 69. Premium savings bonds are not transferable: see MONEY.
4   See LOCAL GOVERNMENT.
5   An erroneous recital that investments have been transferred does not invalidate the settlement if, on its
     true construction, it operates as an equitable assignment of the settlor's interest in them: *Re Wale, Wale v
     Harris* [1956] 3 All ER 280, [1956] 1 WLR 1346.

911. Reversionary interests. A reversionary interest is settled by being assigned to the
trustees of the settlement, who should perfect their title, as in the case of other choses in
action, by giving notice in writing of the assignment to the trustees of the instrument
under which the reversionary interest is derived[1]. The principle on which the court acts
in discouraging dealing by expectant heirs with their reversionary interests has no
application to the case of a settlement by an expectant heir[2].

1   See CHOSES IN ACTION vol 6 (Reissue) para 41 et seq.
2   *Shafto v Adams* (1864) 4 Giff 492. Cf MISREPRESENTATION AND FRAUD vol 31 (Reissue) para 855–858.

912. Share of personalty under or in default of appointment. A fund or share of
a fund of personalty to which the settlor is entitled, either under or in default of
appointment, in the estate of a testator or intestate is settled by assigning to the trustees
the settlor's interest. This should be described with precision, since settlements of an
interest in a fund derived under a will by survivorship or otherwise do not include a share
in the fund coming to the settlor as next of kin of another beneficiary under the will, and
shares taken under appointments do not pass under settlements which deal with shares in
the same property taken in default of appointment[1].

1   *Re Newbolt's Trust* (1856) 4 WR 735; *Parkinson v Dashwood* (1861) 30 Beav 49; *Edwards v Broughton* (1863)
     32 Beav 667; cf *Smith v Osborne* (1857) 6 HL Cas 375; *Re Walpole's Marriage Settlement, Thomson v Walpole*
     [1903] 1 Ch 928; *Re Dowie's Will Trusts, Re Marriage Settlement of September 24 1936, Barlas v Pennefather*
     [1949] Ch 547, [1949] 1 All ER 968. In the case of a settlement for valuable consideration a purported
     assignment of an interest in a fund to which the settlor has no title will catch any interest in the fund
     subsequently acquired by him: *Re Harper's Settlement, Williams v Harper* [1919] 1 Ch 270. See ESTOPPEL
     vol 16 (Reissue) para 1034.

913. Insurance policies. Policies of insurance are frequently made the subject of
settlements[1]. The settlement may either declare the trusts of money to arise from a policy
which is taken out by the trustees in their own names[2], or the settlor may take out the
policy in his own name and assign it to the trustees to be held upon the trusts declared by
the settlement[3]. The trustees should give to the insurance company written notice of the
assignment[4]. An assignment of a policy generally carries with it any bonuses that may
accrue[5], although the settlor may be entitled to exercise any option that is given to him
by the rules of the company to apply the bonuses in reduction of premiums or receive
them in cash[6]. Where bonuses are excluded from the settlement, the trustees who receive
them are not allowed to retain them, as against the personal representatives of the settlor,
to make good a misappropriation of trust funds by him[7].

The settlement usually contains covenants with the trustees by the person whose life
is assured not to avoid the policy, to pay premiums, to effect a substituted policy if
necessary, and not to prejudice the trustees' rights to the policy money. If the covenant
is merely to keep up the policy, there is no right of action against the covenantor's estate
on the forfeiture of the policy by reason of a breach of the stipulations contained in it[8].

Failure to effect a substituted policy will render the covenantor liable in damages to
the trustees, even if his life has in fact become uninsurable[9]. If, in breach of his covenant,
a settlor allows a policy to become void, neither he nor his assigns can claim any interest

in other property comprised in the settlement until the loss has been made good[10]. Failure to pay premiums gives the trustees a right to substantial damages[11], and, should the covenantor become bankrupt, his contingent future liability to pay premiums is a debt that may be proved in his bankruptcy[12]. It is desirable always to give the trustees power to surrender the policy for a fully paid up one of a smaller amount.

1   As to life policies see INSURANCE vol 25 (Reissue) para 525 et seq. A covenant by an intending husband to effect a policy with an insurance company is not satisfied by effecting a less beneficial policy with a friendly society: *Courtenay v Courtenay* (1846) 3 Jo & Lat 519.
2   *Tidswell v Ankerstein* (1792) Peake 151; *Collett v Morrison* (1851) 9 Hare 162. See also INSURANCE vol 25 (Reissue) para 543.
3   See INSURANCE vol 25 (Reissue) para 545 et seq.
4   See the Policies of Assurance Act 1867 s 3; and INSURANCE vol 25 (Reissue) para 549. As to assignments of policies generally see INSURANCE vol 25 (Reissue) para 545 et seq. A policy of insurance of his life subsequently effected by the settlor may be caught by a covenant by him to settle after-acquired property: *Re Turcan* (1888) 40 ChD 5, CA.
5   *Courtney v Ferrers* (1827) 1 Sim 137; *Parkes v Bott* (1838) 9 Sim 388; *Gilly v Burley* (1856) 22 Beav 619; *Warren v Wybault* (1866) 12 Jur NS 639. Bonuses do not pass if the policies are only securities for a specified sum which is settled: *Domville v Lamb* (1853) 1 WR 246. Cf *Re Armstrong's Trusts* (1857) 3 K & J 486, not following *Plunkett v Mansfield* (1845) 2 Jo & Lat 344.
6   *Hughes v Searle* [1885] WN 79. Cf *Gilly v Burley* (1856) 22 Beav 619.
7   *Hallett v Hallett* (1879) 13 ChD 232. The case is different where the claim is made under the trusts of the settlement: *Re Weston, Davies v Tagart* [1900] 2 Ch 164.
8   *Dormay v Borrodaile* (1847) 10 Beav 335.
9   *Re Arthur, Arthur v Wynne* (1880) 14 ChD 603.
10   *Re Jewell's Settlement, Watts v Public Trustee* [1919] 2 Ch 161.
11   *Schlesinger and Joseph v Mostyn* [1932] 1 KB 349.
12   See the Insolvency Act 1986 s 382(1), (3) (as amended); and BANKRUPTCY AND INSOLVENCY vol 3(2) (Reissue) para 479.

914. Personal chattels. Personal chattels are sometimes made the subject of a settlement[1]. Such a settlement should provide that the beneficiaries should have the enjoyment of the settled chattels, and that the trustees should not interfere with their custody, management or legal ownership, or be responsible for their custody, preservation or insurance against fire or other damage or loss. It is expedient to provide for the substitution of new articles of equal value for those originally settled[2].

The settled chattels need not be specifically described, but they must be described in such a way as to be clearly identifiable[3]. It is often convenient to enumerate them in a schedule.

A settlement, on marriage, of chattels does not require registration as a bill of sale[4].

The transfer of the chattels may usually be effected simply by delivery[5].

1   See also PERSONAL PROPERTY vol 35 (Reissue) para 1230. As to the position on bankruptcy where the chattels are in the reputed ownership of the bankrupt see BANKRUPTCY AND INSOLVENCY vol 3(2) (Reissue) para 389 et seq. A settlement of a house together with the fixtures and fittings does not include household furniture (*Simmons v Simmons* (1847) 6 Hare 352), and articles for the settlement of household goods or utensils of household stuff did not attach to household goods in a building employed by the settlor as a hospital (*Pratt v Jackson* (1726) 1 Bro Parl Cas 222), but 'furniture' may include silver plate (*Re Torrington's Settled Estates* (1924) 157 LT Jo 408). As to the powers and duties of trustees under such a settlement see para 940 post. As to the settlement of chattels to devolve with realty see para 937 et seq post.
2   For a case where fresh furniture was substituted see *Lane v Grylls* (1862) 6 LT 533. As to the sale of personal chattels settled without reference to settled land see para 941 post.
3   *Dean v Brown* (1826) 5 B & C 336.
4   See the Bills of Sale Act 1878 s 4; and BILLS OF SALE vol 4(1) (Reissue) para 637. As to marriage settlements see para 628 et seq ante.
5   See GIFTS vol 20 (Reissue) paras 36–38.

(2) BENEFICIAL INTERESTS

(i) Life Interests

915. Life interests generally. In a marriage settlement of personalty the first life interest in the settled property is usually taken by whichever party to the marriage brings the property into settlement[1]. If both parties bring property into settlement, usually each takes the first life interest in the property settled by or on behalf of him or her and, after the death of either spouse, the survivor is given a life interest in the entire fund[2].

1 As to marriage settlements see para 628 et seq ante.
2 A divorced woman survives her coverture (*Re Crawford's Settlement, Cooke v Gibson* [1905] 1 Ch 11), but a marriage settlement, in so far as it is not varied by the proper tribunal, remains unaffected by the dissolution of the marriage (*Fitzgerald v Chapman* (1875) 1 ChD 563; *Burton v Sturgeon* (1876) 2 ChD 318, CA). As to variation of marriage settlements on divorce see para 603 note 1 ante. As to coverture see HUSBAND AND WIFE. Sometimes the interest of the survivor is made to determine on remarriage. A trust to pay the income of the husband's fund, after his death, to the wife during her life or until she marries again is not determined, after the marriage has been dissolved, by her remarriage during the lifetime of the first husband: *Re Monro's Settlement, Monro v Hill* [1933] Ch 82. See, however, to the contrary *Re Mathew's Trusts* (1876) 24 WR 960. See also *Re Pilkington's Settlement, Pilkington v Wright* (1923) 129 LT 629; and para 936 post.

916. Protected life interests. A provision in a settlement which reserves to the settlor a life interest in property settled by him determinable on his bankruptcy is void as against his trustee in bankruptcy[1], but a provision reserving to the settlor a life interest in such property determinable if he assigns, charges or incumbers it is valid[2]. A person bringing property into settlement may settle it so as to give to any other person taking an interest under the settlement a life interest determinable on bankruptcy[3], or on any attempted alienation or other disposition[4], and it is by no means unusual to give the husband such a protected life interest in the property brought into the settlement by his wife[5].

1 See BANKRUPTCY AND INSOLVENCY vol 3(2) (Reissue) para 418.
2 *Re Walsh's Estate* [1905] 1 IR 261; *Re Perkins' Settlement Trusts, Leicester-Warren v Perkins* [1912] WN 99. See BANKRUPTCY AND INSOLVENCY vol 3(2) (Reissue) para 398. Once it has taken effect, the limitation over is not avoided by the subsequent bankruptcy of the settlor: *Re Detmold, Detmold v Detmold* (1889) 40 ChD 585.
3 *Mackintosh v Pogose* [1895] 1 Ch 505. As to conditions for forfeiture on bankruptcy see generally BANKRUPTCY AND INSOLVENCY vol 3(2) (Reissue) para 398.
4 *Re Throckmorton, ex p Eyston* (1877) 7 ChD 145, CA.
5 Where the husband took a life interest determinable on bankruptcy followed by a gift after his death, on failure of issue of the marriage, to the wife's next of kin, the husband's trustee in bankruptcy was entitled to the income during the interval between the husband's bankruptcy and death: *Frank v Mackay* (1873) IR 7 Eq 287; *Upton v Brown* (1879) 12 ChD 872. Where the gift over is expressed to take effect upon the happening of some, but not all, of the events on which the prior life interest is determinable, it may be possible to fill the gap by construction (*Re Muggeridge's Trusts* (1860) John 625; *Re Akeroyd's Settlement, Roberts v Akeroyd* [1893] 3 Ch 363, CA; *O'Donoghue v O'Donoghue* [1906] 1 IR 482); but this cannot be done if, from the form of the trusts, it is impossible to say what trust should be inserted to fill the gap (*Re Cochrane, Shaw v Cochrane* [1955] Ch 309, [1955] 1 All ER 222). As to supplying words see *Re Whitrick, Sutcliffe v Sutcliffe* [1957] 2 All ER 467, [1957] 1 WLR 884, CA.

917. Statutory protective trusts. A determinable life interest is now generally given[1] by directing that the trustees are to hold the income on protective trusts for the benefit of the principal beneficiary during his life or for some lesser period[2]. In such a case the income, without prejudice to any prior interest, must be held on the statutory protective trusts[3], namely upon trust for the principal beneficiary during the specified period or until he, whether before or after the termination of any prior interest, does or attempts[4] to do or suffers[5] any act or thing, or until any event happens, other than an advance under any statutory or express power[6], by which, if the income were payable to him absolutely during the specified period, he would be deprived of the right to receive the income or any part of it[7]; and, if such trust should fail or determine during the specified period, then, during the residue of that period, the income is applicable, at the discretion of the trustees, for the maintenance or support, or otherwise for the benefit, of any one or more of the following persons, namely the principal beneficiary and his or her wife or husband, if any, and his or her children or more remote issue[8], if any, or, if there is no wife or husband or issue[9] of the principal beneficiary in existence, the principal beneficiary and the persons who would if he were actually dead, be entitled to the trust property or its income[10].

1   As to the construction of express forfeiture clauses and provisions for determination of life interests in wills see eg *Re Mair, Williamson v French* [1909] 2 Ch 280; *Re Walker, Public Trustee v Walker* [1939] Ch 974, [1939] 3 All ER 902. See further WILLS vol 50 (Reissue) para 696 et seq. As to conditions of defeasance in settlements generally see para 740 et seq ante.

2   If no period is specified, the gift may be construed as an indefinite gift of income, entitling the beneficiary to call for the capital: cf *Re Wittke, Reynolds and Gorst v King Edward's Hospital Fund for London and Custodian of Enemy Property* [1944] Ch 166, [1944] 1 All ER 383.

3   Ie the trusts set out in the Trustee Act 1925 s 33 (as amended) (see the text and notes 7–10 infra), which does not apply to trusts which came into operation before 1926 (see s 33(2)) and does not operate to validate any trust which would, if contained in the instrument creating the trust, be liable to be set aside (see s 33(3)).

4   See *Re Porter, Coulson v Capper* [1892] 3 Ch 481, where a post-nuptial settlement, although partially inoperative, was held to be an attempt to assign a reversionary interest.

5   'Suffer' applies to an involuntary proceeding: see *Roffey v Bent* (1867) LR 3 Eq 759; *Re Throckmorton, ex p Eyston* (1877) 7 ChD 145, CA; *Re Sartoris Estate, Sartoris v Sartoris* [1892] 1 Ch 11, CA. Cf *Re Hall, Public Trustee v Montgomery* [1944] Ch 46, [1943] 2 All ER 753.

6   Even in the absence of an express provision, a consent to an exercise of a power of advancement does not cause a forfeiture: *Re Hodgson, Weston v Hodgson* [1913] 1 Ch 34; *Re Shaw's Settlement Trusts, Shaw v Shaw* [1951] Ch 833, [1951] 1 All ER 656; *Re Rees, Lloyds Bank Ltd v Rees* [1954] Ch 202, [1954] 1 All ER 7. *Re Stimpson's Trusts, Stimpson v Stimpson* [1931] 2 Ch 77, where the contrary was held, can no longer be regarded as good law.

7   See the Trustee Act 1925 s 33(1)(i). The words 'or any part of it', if not inserted, will be implied: *Re Dennis's Settlement Trusts, Dennis v Dennis* [1942] Ch 283, [1942] 1 All ER 520; *Re Haynes Will Trusts, Pitt v Haynes* [1949] Ch 5, [1948] 2 All ER 423.

8   In a disposition made on or after 1 January 1970, the reference to the children or more remote issue of the principal beneficiary includes a reference to any illegitimate child of the principal beneficiary, and anyone who would rank as such issue if he, or some other person through whom he is descended from the principal beneficiary, had been born legitimate: see the Family Law Reform Act 1969 s 15(3)(a) (repealed); and WILLS vol 50 (Reissue) para 591. In relation to dispositions inter vivos made on or after 4 April 1988 and dispositions by will or codicil where the will or codicil is made after that date the Trustee Act 1925 s 33 (as amended) has effect as if any reference, however expressed, to any relationship between two persons were construed in accordance with the Family Law Reform Act 1987 s 1: see s 19(3) (see WILLS vol 50 (Reissue) para 592; Trustee Act 1925 s 33(4) (added by the Family Law Reform Act 1987 s 33(1), Sch 2 para 2). See also CHILDREN AND YOUNG PERSONS vol 5(2) (Reissue) para 723.

9   In a disposition made on or after 1 January 1970, the reference to the issue of the principal beneficiary includes a reference to anyone who would rank as such issue if he, or some other person through whom he is descended from the principal beneficiary, had been born legitimate: see the Family Law Reform Act 1969 s 15(3)(b) (repealed); and WILLS vol 50 (Reissue) para 591. In relation to dispositions inter vivos made on or after 4 April 1988 and dispositions by will or codicil where the will or codicil is made after that date see note 8 supra.

10   See the Trustee Act 1925 s 33(1)(ii).

918. Events causing forfeiture. Whether or not an act or event has caused a forfeiture depends in every case upon the true construction of the particular clause, which will not be construed so as to extend its limits beyond the fair meaning of the words used[1]. Where the clause adopts or follows the language of the statutory protective trusts[2], no forfeiture is caused by a settlement by the principal beneficiary of his protected life interest if, under the terms of the settlement, the income remains payable to him[3], but a covenant to pay the income, if and when received, to a third person is an equitable assignment of the income and causes a forfeiture[4]. A forfeiture also occurs where the income is impounded by the trustees to make good a breach of trust[5], or where a creditor obtains a charging order against the trust fund[6], or where a writ of sequestration is issued against the property of the principal beneficiary[7], or where under a statute the income becomes payable to the Custodian of Enemy Property[8], but not where his interest is reduced after divorce by a court order[9], nor where he elects against the instrument conferring the protected life interest[10].

A forfeiture is not caused by the fact that fees, expenses or other sums are payable in priority out of the income, as where a receiver is appointed by an order of the Court of Protection[11], or where the trustees are entitled to their management expenses out of the income of the protected interest[12] or where a rentcharge is created to secure the repayment of capital money expended in payment for improvements under the Settled Land Act 1925[13].

Further, no forfeiture is caused by the exercise by the court of an overriding power either to vary the trusts[14] or to authorise a transaction affecting the trust property[15].

1   *Re Greenwood, Sutcliffe v Gledhill* [1901] 1 Ch 887 at 891. In general, the court cannot supply words in such a clause: *Re Brewer's Settlement, Morton v Blackmore* [1896] 2 Ch 503; *Re Dennis's Settlement Trusts, Dennis v Dennis* [1942] Ch 283, [1942] 1 All ER 520. As to implying when a gift over takes effect see para 742 ante.

2   Ie the Trustee Act 1925 s 33 (as amended): see para 917 ante.

3   *Lockwood v Sikes* (1884) 51 LT 562; *Re Tancred's Settlement, Somerville v Tancred, Re Selby, Church v Tancred* [1903] 1 Ch 715. It is otherwise if the effect is to make the beneficiary's interest contingent: *Re Dennis's Settlement Trusts, Dennis v Dennis* [1942] Ch 283, [1942] 1 All ER 520. Receipt of income by trustees is not necessarily payment to a beneficiary: *Johnstone v Lumb* (1846) 15 Sim 308.

4   *Re Spearman, Spearman v Lowndes* (1900) 82 LT 302, CA; *Re Gillott's Settlement, Chattock v Reid* [1934] Ch 97; *Re Haynes Will Trusts, Pitt v Haynes* [1949] Ch 5, [1948] 2 All ER 423. An authority to the trustees to pay the income to a third person which is not communicated to the third person is, however, revocable and does not cause a forfeiture (*Re Hamilton, FitzGeorge v FitzGeorge* (1921) 124 LT 737, CA), nor does a like authority which is not acted on (*Re Salting, Baillie-Hamilton v Morgan* [1932] 2 Ch 57). See also CHOSES IN ACTION vol 6 (Reissue) para 34.

5   *Re Balfour's Settlement, Public Trustee v Official Receiver* [1938] Ch 928, [1938] 3 All ER 259.

6   *Roffey v Bend* (1867) LR 3 Eq 759. In *Re Richardson's Will Trusts, Public Trustee v Llewellyn Evans' Trustees* [1958] Ch 504, [1958] 1 All ER 538 it was held that forfeiture occurred where in divorce proceedings the principal beneficiary was ordered to charge his interest to secure maintenance, even if no deed was executed to give effect to the charge. However, this cannot be considered correct: see *General Accident Fire and Life Assurance Corpn Ltd v IRC* [1963] 3 All ER 259, [1963] 1 WLR 1207, CA (see the text and note 9 infra). In *Edmonds v Edmonds* [1965] 1 All ER 379n, [1965] 1 WLR 58 it was held that an attachment of earnings order in respect of maintenance payments caused forfeiture of a pension held on protective trusts.

7   *Re Baring's Settlement Trusts, Baring Bros & Co Ltd v Liddell* [1940] Ch 737, [1940] 3 All ER 20. As to writs of sequestration see EXECUTION.

8   *Re Gourju's Will Trusts, Starling v Custodian of Enemy Property* [1943] Ch 24, [1942] 2 All ER 605; cf *Re Munster* [1920] 1 Ch 268. See also *Re Hall, Public Trustee v Montgomery* [1944] Ch 46, [1943] 2 All ER 753; *Re Harris, Cope v Evans* [1945] Ch 316, [1945] 1 All ER 702; *Re Pozot's Settlement Trusts, Westminster Bank Ltd v Guerbois* [1952] Ch 427, [1952] 1 All ER 1107, CA, where on the construction of the particular clauses no forfeiture was incurred. As to the Custodian of Enemy Property see WAR AND ARMED CONFLICT vol 49(1) (Reissue) para 643.

9   *General Accident Fire and Life Assurance Corpn Ltd v IRC* [1963] 3 All ER 259, [1963] 1 WLR 1207, CA. Where the order extinguishes the interest of the beneficiary as if he were dead, the discretionary trusts engrafted onto the determinable life interest are, however, extinguished with it: *Re Allsopp's Marriage Settlement Trusts, Public Trustee v Cherry* [1959] Ch 81, [1958] 2 All ER 393.

10   *Re Gordon's Will Trusts, National Westminster Bank Ltd v Gordon* [1978] Ch 145, [1978] 2 All ER 969, CA. As to election generally see EQUITY vol 16 (Reissue) para 842 et seq.

11   *Re Westby's Settlement, Westby v Ashley* [1950] Ch 296, [1950] 1 All ER 479, CA. As to receivers for patients see generally MENTAL HEALTH vol 30 (Reissue) para 1463 et seq. Income payable to an agent of

the beneficiary is not payable to another person within the meaning of a forfeiture clause: *Re Marshall, Marshall v Whateley* [1920] 1 Ch 284; *Re Oppenheim's Will Trusts, Westminster Bank Ltd v Oppenheim* [1950] Ch 633, [1950] 2 All ER 86.

12 *Re Tancred's Settlement, Somerville v Tancred, Re Selby, Church v Tancred* [1903] 1 Ch 715.

13 See *Re Liberty's Will Trusts, Blackmore v Stewart Liberty* [1937] Ch 176, [1937] 1 All ER 399; and para 813 ante.

14 See the Variation of Trusts Act 1958 s 1 (as amended); and para 674 ante.

15 *Re Mair, Richards v Doxat* [1935] Ch 562; cf *Re Salting, Baillie-Hamilton v Morgan* [1932] 2 Ch 57.

919. Express protective trusts. The statutory protective trusts[1] may be varied both as regards the events which will cause a forfeiture and the objects of the discretionary trusts by the instrument creating the trust[2].

A clause conferring a protected life interest, even if future in terms, applies to a bankruptcy existing at the date of the settlement or at the time when the interest would, but for the bankruptcy, have fallen into possession[3]. If the forfeiture is expressed to take effect on alienation only, an involuntary act, such as the filing by a creditor of a bankruptcy petition, does not operate as a forfeiture[4]. The filing by a debtor of a petition which is not followed by adjudication does not work a forfeiture of his life interest under a limitation 'until he should do or suffer something whereby the income, if payable absolutely to him, would become vested in any other person'[5]. The word 'forfeited' in a gift over in case the settled property should be 'forfeited to or become vested in any other person' means liable to be taken away, not merely actually taken away[6]. A trust until insolvency means until the beneficiary is unable to pay his debts[7].

Forfeiture is now restricted in the case of interests in occupational pension schemes[8].

1 See the Trustee Act 1925 s 33 (as amended); and para 917 ante.

2 See ibid s 33(2).

3 See BANKRUPTCY AND INSOLVENCY vol 3(2) (Reissue) para 397. The position is different if the bankruptcy is annulled in the interval between the time when the title to the fund accrues to the bankrupt and the time when it would have become payable to him but for the bankruptcy: see BANKRUPTCY AND INSOLVENCY vol 3(2) (Reissue) para 397. A clause which is future in its terms will not be construed so as to include past charges where the settlement contains a recital that charges have been created: *West v Williams* [1899] 1 Ch 132, CA.

4 *Lear v Leggett* (1830) 1 Russ & M 690; *Pym v Lockyer* (1841) 12 Sim 394. The result may be different if the petition is presented by the beneficiary and is followed by an adjudication: *Re Cotgrave, Mynors v Cotgrave* [1903] 2 Ch 705. See, however, *Re Griffiths, Jones v Jenkins* [1926] Ch 1007; and BANKRUPTCY AND INSOLVENCY vol 3(2) (Reissue) para 395. The fact that in such a clause the income is expressed to be given to the husband and his assigns during his life does not make the life interest absolute: *Re Kelly's Settlement, West v Turner* (1888) 59 LT 494. A charging order obtained by a creditor terminates an interest limited until the execution of some assignment or act by which the interest might be incumbered: *Montefiore v Behrens* (1865) LR 1 Eq 171. On the other hand, a gift over, if the beneficiary should be precluded from personal enjoyment by any legal disability, takes effect only on a personal disability being imposed involuntarily by the law, such as bankruptcy, not on a disability voluntarily created, such as an alienation or charge (*Re Carew, Carew v Carew* [1896] 2 Ch 311, CA), and a clause which provided for forfeiture only in case of acts or events which were done or happened without the beneficiary's consent was not brought into operation by an act of the legislature, to which no effective consent was possible (*Re Viscount Furness, Wilson v Kenmare* [1943] Ch 415, [1944] 1 All ER 66).

5 *Re Moon, ex p Dawes* (1886) 17 QBD 275, CA; *Re Griffiths, Jones v Jenkins* [1926] Ch 1007. Cf *Re Weibking, ex p Ward* [1902] 1 KB 713 (where the words 'become bankrupt' meant 'be adjudicated a bankrupt'); *Re Hamilton, FitzGeorge v FitzGeorge* (1921) 124 LT 737, CA (where neither a receiving order nor a scheme for composition worked a forfeiture). See, however, *Re Amherst's Trusts* (1872) LR 13 Eq 464.

6 *Re Levy's Trusts* (1885) 30 ChD 119. However, where land was settled until the tenant for life should commit, or knowingly permit or suffer to be committed, any act by which his interest in the land might become the property of a third person, or until the land should be taken in execution, the interest was held not to be forfeited by a judgment being obtained and a writ of fieri facias issued against the tenant for life: *Re Ryan* (1887) 19 LR Ir 24. As to writs of fieri facias see EXECUTION.

7 *De Tastet v Le Tavernier, De Tastet v Smith, Smith v De Tastet* (1836) 1 Keen 161; *Freeman v Bowen* (1865) 35 Beav 17; *Billson v Crofts* (1873) LR 15 Eq 314; *Nixon v Verry* (1885) 29 ChD 196. Cf *Montefiore v*

Enthoven (1867) LR 5 Eq 35, where the limitation was until the beneficiary should become bankrupt or take the benefit of any Act for the relief of insolvent debtors.

8   See the Pensions Act 1995 ss 91–94; and SOCIAL SECURITY AND PENSIONS vol 44(2) (Reissue) para 865 et seq. See also, in relation to the effect of forfeiture provisions in occupational pension clauses, *In re Landau (a bankrupt)* [1998] Ch 223, [1997] 3 All ER 322.

920. Life interests by implication. A settlement on a husband and wife during their joint and natural lives means during their joint lives and the natural life of each of them[1]. Where there was a trust of income for the separate use of the wife during marriage, with a gift over in the event of her dying in her husband's lifetime, the wife took a life interest by implication[2].

In some cases, on the construction of the particular instrument, trusts for the benefit of a parent and children have conferred only a life interest on the parent[3].

Where there is a determinable life interest and the ultimate gift is expressed to take effect only on the death of the life tenant, it may be possible to fill the gap in the trusts by necessary implication[4], but this cannot be done if it is impossible to see what trust must be implied[5]. Cross-remainders for life between children have been implied where the intention apparent from the deed was that the property should be kept together as a whole until the death of the survivor of the children and that the income should go among the children who survived[6].

1   *Smith v Oakes* (1844) 14 Sim 122.
2   *Tunstall v Trappes* (1830) 3 Sim 286 at 308, 312; *Allin v Crawshay* (1851) 9 Hare 382; *Sweetman v Butler* [1908] 1 IR 517. Cf *Re Stanley's Settlement, Maddocks v Andrews* [1916] 2 Ch 50. For cases where the wife has been held, on the construction of the settlement, to take a greater interest see *Clarke v Hackwell* (1788) 2 Bro CC 304; *Smith v King* (1826) 1 Russ 363.
3   *Chambers v Atkins* (1823) 1 Sim & St 382; *Fowler v Hunter* (1829) 3 Y & J 506.
4   *Re Akeroyd's Settlement, Roberts v Akeroyd* [1893] 3 Ch 363, CA.
5   *Re Cochrane, Shaw v Cochrane* [1955] Ch 309, [1955] 1 All ER 222. As to supplying words generally see *Re Whitrick, Sutcliffe v Sutcliffe* [1957] 2 All ER 467, [1957] 1 WLR 884, CA.
6   *Re Hey's Settlement Trusts, Hey v Nickell-Lean* [1945] Ch 294, [1945] 1 All ER 618 (implication of trust of share and income of child dying before period of distribution in favour of surviving children), applying *Re Tate, Williamson v Gilpin* [1914] 2 Ch 182 at 185. See further WILLS vol 50 (Reissue) para 700 et seq. As to the use and effect of an accruer clause in trusts for issue see para 928 note 4 post.

921. Acceleration of subsequent interests. The doctrine of acceleration usually arises in relation to gifts by will[1], but it may also apply to settlements[2]. Where there is a gift to a person for life, and a vested gift in remainder expressed to take effect on the death of the first taker, the gift in remainder is construed as a gift taking effect on the death of the first taker or on any earlier failure or determination of his interest; the result is that if the gift to the first taker fails in his lifetime or is disclaimed or surrendered then the person entitled in remainder will take immediately on the failure or determination of the prior interest, and will not be kept waiting until the death of the first taker[3]. The principle applies to personalty as well as to realty[4]. It applies if the remainder is vested, but subject to defeasance[5], but not if it is contingent[6], unless the contingency is not related to the determination of the prior interest or to the words of futurity[7].

1   See eg *Jull v Jacobs* (1876) 3 ChD 703. See also WILLS vol 50 (Reissue) para 419.
2   See *Re Flower's Settlement Trusts, Flower v IRC* [1957] 1 All ER 462 at 465, [1957] 1 WLR 401 at 405, CA, per Jenkins LJ; *Re Young's Settlement Trusts, Royal Exchange Assurance v Taylor-Young* [1959] 2 All ER 74 at 78, [1959] 1 WLR 457 at 462 per Harman J; *Re Dawson's Settlement, Lloyds Bank Ltd v Dawson* [1966] 3 All ER 68, [1966] 1 WLR 1456. However, it may be more difficult in the case of a settlement to collect the necessary intention: see *Re Flower's Settlement Trusts, Flower v IRC* supra at 465 and 405 per Jenkins LJ; *Re Young's Settlement Trusts, Royal Exchange Assurance v Taylor-Young* supra.
3   *Re Flower's Settlement Trusts, Flower v IRC* [1957] 1 All ER 462 at 465, [1957] 1 WLR 401 at 405, CA, per Jenkins LJ. Cf para 936 post.

4   *Re Flower's Settlement Trusts, Flower v IRC* [1957] 1 All ER 462 at 465, [1957] 1 WLR 401 at 405, CA, per Jenkins LJ; *Re Hodge, Midland Bank Executor and Trustee Co Ltd v Morrison* [1943] Ch 300 at 301, [1943] 2 All ER 304 at 305 per Simonds J.

5   *Re Conyngham, Conyngham v Conyngham* [1921] 1 Ch 491, CA; *Re Taylor, Lloyds Bank Ltd v Jones* [1957] 3 All ER 56, [1957] 1 WLR 1043. As to conditions of defeasance generally see para 740 et seq ante.

6   *Re Townsend's Estate, Townsend v Townsend* (1886) 34 ChD 357.

7   *Re Bellville's Settlement Trusts, Westminster Bank Ltd v Bellville* [1964] Ch 163, [1963] 3 All ER 270; *Re Dawson's Settlement, Lloyds Bank Ltd v Dawson* [1966] 3 All ER 68, [1966] 1 WLR 1456. See also *Re Harker's Will Trusts, Kean v Harker* [1969] 3 All ER 1, [1969] 1 WLR 1124; cf *Re Kebty-Fletcher's Will Trusts, Public Trustee v Swan and Snowden* [1969] 1 Ch 339, [1967] 3 All ER 1076. As to contingent interests see further WILLS vol 50 (Reissue) para 420.

(ii) Trusts for Issue

922. Nature of powers of appointment among issue. As a rule, in marriage settlements of personalty the settled fund is held by the trustees after the death of the survivor of the husband and wife upon trust for the children or more remote issue of the marriage in such shares and for such interests as the husband and wife by deed, revocable or irrevocable, jointly appoint[1], and in default of such appointment as the survivor by deed, revocable or irrevocable, or by will or codicil, appoints[2].

The extension of this power to the more remote issue of the marriage was rendered necessary by the inconvenience of a limitation to children of the marriage only, which prevented parents from providing for their grandchildren[3], so that the issue of a child predeceasing the parent might be left unprovided for, it being impossible to appoint either to the issue or to the personal representatives of the deceased child[4]. The donee of the power must be careful in exercising it to select only such objects of the power as are within the limits prescribed by the rule against perpetuities[5].

If the appointment under such a power is made by will and the appointee dies in the lifetime of the donee of the power, the appointment fails and the share goes as unappointed among the persons entitled in default of appointment[6].

1   For the purposes of the rule against perpetuities a joint power has been held not to be a general power: *Re Churston's Settled Estates* [1954] Ch 334, [1954] 1 All ER 725. See also PERPETUITIES AND ACCUMULATIONS vol 35 (Reissue) para 1091; POWERS. As to illegitimate, legitimated and adopted children see paras 731–733 ante.

2   As to powers of appointment among a class, powers of revocation and the invalid exercise of powers see POWERS.

3   See *Alexander v Alexander* (1755) 2 Ves Sen 640; *Smith v Lord Camelford* (1795) 2 Ves 698; *Kennerley v Kennerley* (1852) 10 Hare 160.

4   See *Maddison v Andrew* (1747) 1 Ves Sen 57; *Re Susanni's Trusts* (1877) 47 LJ Ch 65.

5   As to who are lawful appointees see PERPETUITIES AND ACCUMULATIONS vol 35 (Reissue) para 1090 et seq.

6   *Griffiths v Gale* (1844) 12 Sim 354; *Holyland v Lewin* (1884) 26 ChD 266, CA. See also WILLS vol 50 (Reissue) para 408.

923. Form of power of appointment. A power of appointment among issue is usually expressed to be to appoint to one or more exclusively of the others or other of the children or issue, although every power is now prima facie exclusive[1].

A trust for children at such ages as the donee of the power may appoint authorises an appointment to a child en ventre sa mere at the date of the appointment[2], and such a child can take by virtue of an appointment made under a power to appoint to issue born before the date of appointment[3].

The donee is generally authorised to make provision for the maintenance, education and advancement of the objects of the power[4]. The statutory powers as to maintenance, and, in the case of trusts created after 1925, as to advancement, are available, in relation to interests taken by minors under a power of appointment[5].

A special power of appointment by will given to the survivor of a husband and wife is not well exercised by an appointment made during the joint lives by the will of the actual survivor[6].

1   See the Law of Property Act 1925 s 158(1); and POWERS. As to illegitimate, legitimated and adopted children see paras 731–733 ante.
2   *Fearon v Desbrisay* (1851) 14 Beav 635.
3   *Re Farncombe's Trusts* (1878) 9 ChD 652.
4   As to settlements made in exercise of special powers of appointment see also para 626 ante.
5   See CHILDREN AND YOUNG PERSONS vol 5(2) (Reissue) para 661 et seq; TRUSTS vol 48 (Reissue) paras 909–910.
6   See *Re Moir's Settlement Trusts* (1882) 46 LT 723; and POWERS. As to the exercise of powers generally see POWERS. A general power exercisable by the survivor is, however, well exercised by them jointly: *Macarmick v Buller* (1787) 1 Cox Eq Cas 357.

924. Hotchpot clauses. A clause, called a 'hotchpot clause'[1], is often inserted in order to preclude appointees[2] of a share of the fund from participating in the unappointed fund without treating the appointed shares as received in or towards satisfaction of the shares to which they would be entitled if the whole fund were to go in default of appointment[3].

The clause applies to appointments of life or reversionary interests[4]. A life interest must be brought into hotchpot on the basis of an actuarial calculation of its value on the date when it fell into possession, irrespective of subsequent events[5].

The ordinary hotchpot clause in settlements does not apply to advancements[6].

1   As to hotchpot clauses in wills see WILLS vol 50 (Reissue) paras 636–638.
2   If the power of appointment extends to issue more remote than children, the hotchpot clause should be made expressly to apply to such issue: *Langslow v Langslow* (1856) 21 Beav 552; *Hewitt v Jardine* (1872) LR 14 Eq 58.
3   In the absence of a hotchpot clause the appointee of a share in a fund is entitled to share in the unappointed residue: *Wilson v Piggott* (1794) 2 Ves 351; *Alloway v Alloway* (1843) 4 Dr & War 380; *Wombwell v Hanrott* (1851) 14 Beav 143; *Foster v Cautley* (1855) 6 De GM & G 55; *Walmsley v Vaughan* (1857) 1 De G & J 114; *Close v Coote* (1880) 7 LR Ir 564; *Re Alfretons Trust Estates* (1883) 52 LJ Ch 745. However, the rule may be excluded by clear expression of intention on the part of the appointor (*Fortescue v Gregor* (1800) 5 Ves 553; *Foster v Cautley* supra), or by the appointee agreeing to take under the appointment in lieu of his share in the unappointed property (*Clune v Apjohn* (1865) 17 I Ch R 25; *Armstrong v Lynn* (1875) IR 9 Eq 186). As to the time for valuing appointed shares cf *Re Gollin's Declaration of Trust, Turner v Williams* [1969] 3 All ER 1591, [1969] 1 WLR 1858; *Re Marquess of Abergavenny's Estate Act Trusts, Marquess of Abergavenny v Ram* [1981] 2 All ER 643, [1981] 1 WLR 843 (concerning the valuation of advanced property).
4   *Rucker v Scholefield* (1862) 1 Hem & M 36; *Eales v Drake* (1875) 1 ChD 217; *Wheeler v Humphreys* [1898] AC 506, HL. See, however, *Williamson v Jeffreys* (1854) 18 Jur 1071. Where the interest appointed is a life interest with a general power of appointment by will in default of issue, only the life interest need be brought into hotchpot: *Re Gordon, Public Trustee v Bland* [1942] Ch 131, [1942] 1 All ER 59.
5   *Re Heathcote, Trench v Heathcote* [1891] WN 10; *Re Westropp* (1903) 37 ILT 183; *Re Thomson Settlement Trusts, Robertson v Makepeace* [1953] Ch 414, [1953] 1 All ER 1139. See also *Re North Settled Estates, Public Trustee v Graham* [1946] Ch 13; and cf *Re West, Denton v West* [1921] 1 Ch 533, where the life interests never fell into possession and a retrospective actuarial calculation was rejected.
6   *Re Fox, Wodehouse v Fox* [1904] 1 Ch 480. As to advancement see para 667 ante; and CHILDREN AND YOUNG PERSONS vol 5(2) (Reissue) para 676 et seq.

925. Application of hotchpot clause where two settled funds. If two distinct funds are settled for the same purposes by two distinct deeds, each containing a hotchpot clause, each hotchpot clause applies only to the fund settled by the deed containing it[1]. Where a settlement declared express trusts of one fund, with a hotchpot clause referring to that fund, the hotchpot clause was not incorporated with reference to a second and distinct fund by a general reference to the trusts, powers, provisos and agreements expressed in reference to the former fund[2]. However, where it appeared on the true construction of the settlement that the second fund was to be amalgamated with or treated as an accretion to the first fund, the hotchpot clause was applicable to both funds[3], and in the absence of express words a settlement may contain a plain indication of intention that the hotchpot clause is to apply to all funds settled by it[4].

1   *Montague v Montague* (1852) 15 Beav 565; *Lady Wellesley v Earl of Mornington* (1855) 1 Jur NS 1202. See also para 722 ante. As to hotchpot clauses see para 924 ante.
2   *Re Marquis of Bristol, Earl Grey v Grey* [1897] 1 Ch 946; *Re Cavendish, Grosvenor v Butler* [1912] 1 Ch 794; *Re Wood, Wodehouse v Wood* [1913] 2 Ch 574, CA. Cf *Re Campbell's Trusts, Public Trustee v Campbell* [1922] 1 Ch 551; *Re Rydon's Settlement, Barclays Bank Ltd v Everitt* [1955] Ch 1, [1954] 3 All ER 1, CA.
3   *Re Fraser, Ind v Fraser* [1913] 2 Ch 224.
4   *Hutchinson v Tottenham* [1898] 1 IR 403; *Re Perkins, Perkins v Bagot* (1892) as reported in 67 LT 743; cf *Stares v Penton* (1867) LR 4 Eq 40; *Middleton v Windross* (1873) LR 16 Eq 212.

926. Trusts in default of appointment. In default of and subject to any appointment, in settlements made on marriage, the settled property is traditionally directed to go to all the children or any child of the marriage[1] who, being sons or a son, attain the age of 21 years[2], or, being daughters or a daughter, attain that age or marry under that age, and if more than one in equal shares[3]. A rule of convenience has been established in the case of wills[4] that, where there is an immediate gift to a class to be paid on their attaining a specified age, the time for distribution is the death of the testator, if any member of the class has then attained that age and, if not, the first occasion when a member attains that age, and so that persons born after the time for distribution are excluded; this rule applies also to settlements, at any rate if made by voluntary deed[5], but by reason of the previous life estate in the parent it is not normally called into play in relation to a marriage settlement[6].

1   An ultimate trust for children of the intended husband includes children by a subsequent marriage, notwithstanding a limitation to him in default of children of the then intended marriage (*Isaac v Hughes* (1870) LR 9 Eq 191); and a trust in a post-nuptial settlement for children to be born of the marriage includes children in existence at the date of the settlement (*Slingsby v—* (1718) 10 Mod Rep 397; *Hewet v Ireland* (1718) 1 P Wms 426; and see *Cook v Cook* (1706) 2 Vern 545). As to illegitimate, legitimated and adopted children see paras 731–733 ante.
2   As to the age of majority see para 605 note 1 ante. A trust in a marriage settlement executed before 1926 in favour of children at any later age than 21 is void for remoteness, but on a settlement executed after 1925, if a trust is made to take effect at an age exceeding 21 and the settlement would as a result be rendered void for remoteness, the settlement takes effect with the substitution of a lower age (see the Law of Property Act 1925 s 163 (repealed in relation to instruments taking effect on or after 16 July 1964; Perpetuities and Accumulations Act 1964 s 4(1), applying in relation to instruments taking effect on or after that date): see PERPETUITIES AND ACCUMULATIONS vol 35 (Reissue) para 1070.
3   Where there was a trust for such a class of persons 'as being male shall have attained the age of 21 years or being female shall have married under that age' the trust was, on the construction of the settlement as a whole, given effect to as if it read 'or being female shall have attained the age of 21 years or shall have married under that age': *Re Hargraves' Trusts, Leach v Leach* [1937] 2 All ER 545. A reference to marriage without more means marriage during infancy: *Lang v Pugh* (1842) 1 Y & C Ch Cas 718.
4   See eg *Andrews v Partington* (1791) 3 Bro CC 401; *Re Edmondson's Will Trusts, Baron Sandford of Banbury v Edmondson* [1972] 1 All ER 444, [1972] 1 WLR 183, CA. See also WILLS vol 50 (Reissue) para 546 et seq.
5   *Re Knapp's Settlement, Knapp v Vassall* [1895] 1 Ch 91. It seems that it also applies to settlements for value: see *Re Knapp's Settlement, Knapp v Vassall* supra at 99. See also *Re Wernher's Settlement Trusts, Lloyds Bank Ltd v Earl Mountbatten* [1961] 1 All ER 184, [1961] 1 WLR 136; *Re Chapman's Settlement Trusts, Jones v Chapman* [1978] 1 All ER 1122, [1977] 1 WLR 1163, CA.
6   As to marriage settlements see para 628 et seq ante.

927. Marriage with consent. The provision for daughters is sometimes made dependent on their marrying with the consent of their parents, or of the trustees of the settlement[1]. In such a case, if the consent required is that of a class of persons who, without the beneficiary's fault or default, have ceased to exist and cannot be brought into existence, as in the case of the consent of the parents being required and one or both being dead at the time of the marriage, the consent may be dispensed with[2]. However, the consent is not dispensed with on the ground that the class of persons whose consent is required is not actually in existence at the time of marriage, if such a class could have been brought into existence, as where the consent required is that of trustees or guardians[3].

A direction that the shares of daughters are to be settled is inserted only to provide for the daughters' children, if any, so that if a daughter never has any children the object in cutting down her interest is gone, and she takes absolutely[4].

1   Such a condition is enforceable if it is accompanied by a gift over on marriage without the required consent: *Re Whiting's Settlement, Whiting v De Rutzen* [1905] 1 Ch 96, CA. See also GIFTS vol 20 (Reissue) para 54; WILLS vol 50 (Reissue) para 370 et seq.

2   *Green v Green* (1845) 2 Jo & Lat 529; *Dawson v Oliver-Massey* (1876) 2 ChD 753, CA.

3   *Re Brown's Will, Re Brown's Settlement* (1881) 18 ChD 61, CA. As to gifts of legacies conditional on marriage with consent see further WILLS vol 50 (Reissue) paras 374–375.

4   *Re Sidway Hall Estate* (1877) 37 LT 457. See also WILLS vol 50 (Reissue) para 566.

928. Time of vesting. As in the case of portions[1], so in the case of provision for issue, the rule is that if the settlement clearly and unequivocally throughout all its provisions makes the right of a child depend upon its surviving both its parents, the court has no authority to control that disposition[2]. However, if the settlement is in any of its provisions ambiguously expressed, so as to leave it in any degree uncertain whether it was intended that the right of a child should depend upon the event of its surviving both its parents, then the court is bound by authority to declare, upon what may be called the presumed intention in instruments of this nature, that the interest of a child, although not to take effect in possession until after the death of both parents, did, upon the limitations in the settlement, vest in the case of sons at 21 and of daughters at 21 or on marriage[3].

If limitations or trusts giving a vested interest at birth are employed, they are generally accompanied by an accruer clause, so that on the death of a child under 21 or if a daughter, without having been married, his or her share devolves on the other children or child[4].

1   As to the vesting of portions see para 738 ante.

2   *Bright v Rowe* (1834) 3 My & K 316; *Jeffery v Jeffery* (1849) 17 Sim 26; *Lloyd v Cocker* (1854) 19 Beav 140; *Barnett v Blake* (1862) 2 Drew & Sm 117; *Beale v Connolly* (1874) IR 8 Eq 412. Cf *Re Edgington's Trusts* (1855) 3 Drew 202, where a gift over to children 'then living' was held to refer to the period at which the prior life interest determined.

3   *Perfect v Lord Curzon* (1820) 5 Madd 442; *Torres v Franco* (1830) 1 Russ & M 649; *Re Orlebar's Settlement Trusts* (1875) LR 20 Eq 711; *Martin v Dale* (1884) 15 LR Ir 345. Cf *Bree v Perfect* (1844) 1 Coll 128. The court's policy is to accelerate, if possible, the period of vesting unless there is something in the document to show an intention to postpone enjoyment until the happening of some event personal to the parties interested themselves: *Darley v Perceval* [1900] 1 IR 129. See also para 926 ante; and WILLS vol 50 (Reissue) para 645.

4   Cross-remainders may sometimes be implied as a matter of construction: *Re Bickerton's Settlement, Shaw v Bickerton* [1942] Ch 84, [1942] 1 All ER 217; *Adamson v A-G* [1933] AC 257 at 279, HL. As to the implication of cross-remainders in wills see WILLS vol 50 (Reissue) para 709. As to the implication of cross-remainders for life between children see para 920 ante. In construing an accruer clause there is no distinction between a deed and a will: *Re Friend's Settlement, Cole v Allcot* [1906] 1 Ch 47; *Cole v Sewell* (1848) 2 HL Cas 186 at 236. The court construes 'survivors' as 'others' if there is a sufficient context to enable this to be done (*Re Palmer's Settlement Trusts* (1875) LR 19 Eq 320; *Re Friend's Settlement, Cole v Allcot* supra), but otherwise the words must bear their grammatical meaning (*Cole v Sewell* supra). See also *Re Allsop, Cardinal v Warr* [1968] Ch 39, [1967] 2 All ER 1056, CA; and WILLS vol 50 (Reissue) para 554 et seq. Survivorship has also been referred to the period of vesting (*Re Acott's Settlement* (1859) 28 LJ Ch 383), and of distribution (*Reid v Reid* (1862) 30 Beav 388). As to conditions of defeasance generally see para 740 et seq ante.

929. Meaning of 'issue'. Where trusts are declared in favour of issue the question frequently arises whether 'issue' is confined to children, or whether and to what extent it includes grandchildren. The word 'issue' occurring in a deed or in a will[1] prima facie includes descendants in all degrees, unless there is some context to displace that construction[2]. However, if issue are pointed out as persons to take with reference to the share of the parent a gift which, so far as regards the parent, fails, they take on the principle which may be called the quasi-representative principle; that is to say, the children of each parent whose share fails take that parent's share, but grandchildren are not admitted to take in competition with children[3]. There may also be such a context in a deed as to cause 'issue' to be construed as children[4].

A substitutional gift in favour of the issue of a named parent, in the event of that parent dying in the settlor's lifetime, does not fail by reason of the parent being dead at the date of the settlement[5].

A gift in favour of male issue prima facie includes only issue in the exclusively male line[6], but a gift to male descendants is not so confined[7].

1   With regard to wills the court always looks at the intention of the testator, and adopts in practice, if not in theory, a more benignant rule of construction than in the case of an executed settlement, which it always takes as it finds it: *Re Warren's Trusts* (1884) 26 ChD 208 at 217. For cases under wills where 'issue' has been restricted to children see *Re Hopkins' Trusts* (1878) 9 ChD 131; *Ralph v Carrick* (1879) 11 ChD 873 at 882, CA. As to whether a reference to issue taking their deceased parent's share raises a presumption that only children can take see *Re Manly's Will Trusts, Burton v Williams* [1969] 3 All ER 1011, [1969] 1 WLR 1818; *Re Manly's Will Trusts (No 2), Tickle v Manly* [1976] 1 All ER 673. See also WILLS vol 50 (Reissue) para 572 et seq. 'Issue' has also been restricted to children in marriage articles, which are treated only as a memorandum of instruction: *Swift v Swift* (1836) 8 Sim 168; *Thompson v Simpson* (1841) 1 Dr & War 459; *Campbell v Sandys* (1803) 1 Sch & Lef 281.

2   *South v Searle* (1856) 2 Jur NS 390; *Harrison v Symons* (1866) 14 WR 959; *Donoghue v Brooke* (1875) IR 9 Eq 489; *Re Warren's Trusts* (1884) 26 ChD 208; *Hobbs v Tuthill* [1895] 1 IR 115 (commenting on *Re Dixon's Trusts* (1869) IR 4 Eq 1, and *Re Denis' Trusts* (1875) IR 10 Eq 81). Cf *Haydon v Wilshire* (1789) 3 Term Rep 372.

3   *Robinson v Sykes* (1856) 23 Beav 40 (following *Ross v Ross* (1855) 20 Beav 645 (will)); *Anderson v Viscount St Vincent* (1856) 2 Jur NS 607; *Marshall v Baker* (1862) 31 Beav 608; *Barraclough v Shillito* (1884) 53 LJ Ch 841; *Re Manly's Will Trusts, Burton v Williams* [1969] 3 All ER 1011, [1969] 1 WLR 1818; *Re Manly's Will Trusts (No 2), Tickle v Manly* [1976] 1 All ER 673.

4   As where a gift to issue was followed by a gift to one child if there should be but one (*Re Biron's Contract* (1878) 1 LR Ir 258, Ir CA), or where a power of appointment given in the event of death without leaving lawful issue was followed by a gift over in default of appointment, in case there should be no children (*Re Heath's Settlement* (1856) 23 Beav 193; *Gordon v Hope* (1849) 3 De G & Sm 351). 'Issue of our marriage' includes only children: *Reed v Braithwaite* (1871) LR 11 Eq 514; *Re Noad, Noad v Noad* [1951] Ch 553, [1951] 1 All ER 467, not following *Walsh v Johnston* [1899] 1 IR 501. See also WILLS vol 50 (Reissue) para 572. As to illegitimate, legitimated and adopted children see paras 731–733 ante.

5   *Barnes v Jennings* (1866) LR 2 Eq 448. See also WILLS vol 50 (Reissue) para 486.

6   *Re Du Cros' Settlement, Du Cros Family Trustee Co Ltd v Du Cros* [1961] 3 All ER 193, [1961] 1 WLR 1252.

7   *Re Du Cros' Settlement, Du Cros Family Trustee Co Ltd v Du Cros* [1961] 3 All ER 193, [1961] 1 WLR 1252; *Re Drake, Drake v Drake* [1971] Ch 179, [1970] 3 All ER 32, CA.

930. Effect of no trust in default of appointment. If a settlement contains a power to appoint among certain objects but no gift to those objects and no gift over in default of appointment, or a gift to a class and a power to appoint in what shares and what manner the members may take, the court may imply a trust for, or a gift to, those objects equally if the power is not exercised[1].

1   See *Cruwys v Colman* (1804) 9 Ves 319; *Parsons v Baker* (1812) 18 Ves 476; *Re Llewellyn's Settlement, Official Solicitor v Evans* [1921] 2 Ch 281. See also POWERS.

931. Provision for issue of subsequent marriage. Provision for issue of a subsequent marriage is usually made by the insertion of a power to appoint in favour of a subsequent spouse and the children of the subsequent marriage a portion of the trust fund, the amount being commonly made to depend on the number of children of the first marriage who become adult[1]. Such a power is sometimes made conditional on the making of a settlement on a subsequent marriage[2].

1 As to the age of majority see para 605 note 1 ante. As to gifts to children see also WILLS vol 50 (Reissue) para 569.
2 As to marriage settlements see para 628 et seq ante.

(iii) Trusts in default of Issue

932. Usual trusts in default of issue. As a rule the aim of the trusts in default of issue contained in a marriage settlement is to return the settled property to the destination to which it would have gone if no settlement had been made[1].

The ordinary ultimate limitation of personal property settled by the husband is for the husband absolutely in default of issue[2].

The wife's fund may be settled if the wife survives the husband, in trust for the wife absolutely[3], but, if he survives her, on such trusts as she by will or codicil appoints and, in default of and subject to any such appointment, in trust for the person or persons who would have been entitled to it if she had died domiciled in England a widow and intestate and in the same shares and proportions[4].

1 Trusts in default of issue may arise on the dissolution of a marriage, there being no issue of the marriage: *Bond v Taylor* (1861) 2 John & H 473. A gift over on the death of issue under age was held to take effect on there being no issue of the marriage: *Osborn v Bellman* (1860) 2 Giff 593.
2 If and so long as the settled property or its income cannot become payable to the settlor except on the death under the age of 25 or some lower age of some person who would be beneficially entitled to the property or its income on attaining that age, an ultimate trust for the settlor will not be an interest retained by him within the Income and Corporation Taxes Act 1988 s 660A (as added): see para 619 ante; and INCOME TAXATION vol 23 (Reissue) para 1517.
3 A trust for such children of a future marriage as the wife, if she survives her husband, by will appoints does not interfere with her right to the trust funds under an absolute trust for her if she survives her husband and there is no issue of the intended marriage: *Hanson v Cooke and Hanson* (1825) 4 LJOS Ch 45. Failure to give an absolute interest to a married woman in the event of her surviving her husband, so that the next of kin acquire an indefeasible interest, has been held to be a ground for rectification upon the unsupported testimony of the wife that her intention was only to protect the settled property during marriage: *Wolterbeek v Barrow* (1857) 23 Beav 423; *Smith v Iliffe* (1875) LR 20 Eq 666; *Cook v Fearn* (1878) 48 LJ Ch 63; *Edwards v Bingham* (1879) 28 WR 89; *Hanley v Pearson* (1879) 13 ChD 545.
4 Ie in accordance with the Administration of Estates Act 1925 Pt IV (ss 45–52) (as amended); and the Family Law Reform Act 1987 ss 1, 18(1): see EXECUTORS AND ADMINISTRATORS. As to the construction of references in settlements, whenever made, to the Statutes of Distribution or to statutory next of kin see paras 934–935 post; and EXECUTORS AND ADMINISTRATORS.

933. Trusts for personal representatives. A trust for executors and administrators gives them the property in their representative capacity, notwithstanding the addition of the words 'for their own use and benefit'[1]. Trusts for the representatives, or personal representatives, or legal personal representatives of a person have the same meaning and effect as trusts for the executors and administrators[2], unless sufficiently strong grounds can be found in the particular instrument to justify a different construction, as for example treating them as equivalent to 'next of kin'[3].

When such a trust follows a life interest to the person whose representatives are to take, that person takes an absolute interest[4], notwithstanding the interposition between the life interest and the ultimate trust of a power of appointment by deed or will[5] or by will only[6]. In this respect a trust for personal representatives differs from a trust for next of kin, since a limitation to a person for life, and then as he should appoint by will, and in default of appointment for his next of kin, takes effect according to its tenor[7].

1   *Collier v Squire* (1827) 3 Russ 467; *Wellman v Bowring* (1830) 3 Sim 328; *Marshall v Collett* (1835) 1 Y & C Ex 232; *Hames v Hames* (1838) 2 Keen 646; *Meryon v Collett* (1845) 8 Beav 386; *Johnson v Routh* (1857) 27 LJ Ch 305; *O'Brien v Hearn* (1870) 18 WR 514.
2   *Re Crawford's Trusts* (1854) 2 Drew 230; *Re Best's Settlement Trusts* (1874) LR 18 Eq 686. See also *Topping v Howard* (1851) 4 De G & Sm 268.
3   *Smith v Dudley* (1738) 9 Sim 125('executors or administrators of her own family'); *Bailey v Wright* (1811) 18 Ves 49 ('next of kin or personal representative') (affd (1818) 1 Swan 39); *Bulmer v Jay* (1830) 4 Sim 48 (affd (1834) 3 My & K 197); *Daniel v Dudley* (1841) 1 Ph 1; *A-G v Malkin* (1846) 2 Ph 64; *Briggs v Upton* (1872) 7 Ch App 376 ('legal representatives in due course of administration'); *Robinson v Evans* (1873) 43 LJ Ch 82 ('person or persons who should happen to be legal personal representatives at time of death'); and see *Howell v Gayler* (1842) 5 Beav 157; *Morris v Howes* (1845) 4 Hare 599; on appeal (1846) 16 LJ Ch 121; *Walker v Marquis of Camden* (1848) 16 Sim 329; *Mackenzie v Mackenzie* (1851) 3 Mac & G 559; *Lindsay v Ellicott* (1876) 46 LJ Ch 878.
4   *Anderson v Dawson* (1808) 15 Ves 532; *Page v Soper* (1853) 11 Hare 321. Cf *Malcolm v O'Callaghan* (1835) 5 LJ Ch 137. A trust for the executors and administrators of a living person does not, however, entitle that person to demand the fund: *Horseman v Abbey* (1819) 1 Jac & W 381.
5   *Holloway v Clarkson* (1843) 2 Hare 521.
6   *Devall v Dickens* (1845) 9 Jur 550; *St John v Gibson* (1847) 12 Jur 373; *Page v Soper* (1853) 11 Hare 321.
7   *Anderson v Dawson* (1808) 15 Ves 532. See also *Wolterbeek v Barrow* (1857) 23 Beav 423; *Paul v Paul* (1882) 20 ChD 742, CA. As to trusts for next of kin see paras 934–935 post.

934. Trusts for heirs or next of kin. A trust of personalty for the heirs of a person, contained in a settlement which came into operation before 1 January 1926, was not affected by the Administration of Estates Act 1925[1]. Under such a trust contained in a settlement whenever made, the heir-at-law (who will be ascertained according to the law in force prior to that date) takes and not the next of kin[2], although a substitutional gift to persons or their heirs may be treated as referring to the next of kin[3].

A trust for the next of kin of a person, without more, is not a trust for the next of kin according to the statute which would have regulated the distribution of his property if he had died intestate[4], but a trust for his nearest blood relations, so that brothers and sisters take to the exclusion of the children of deceased brothers and sisters[5]; and, in the absence of some indication to the contrary, such persons will take as joint tenants[6]. A husband is not next of kin to his wife[7], nor is a wife next of kin to her husband[8]. Prima facie, the next of kin of a person are to be ascertained at his death[9].

1   See the Administration of Estates Act 1925 s 51(1); and EXECUTORS AND ADMINISTRATORS.
2   See the Law of Property Act 1925 ss 131 (as amended), 132 (see WILLS vol 50 (Reissue) para 576; EXECUTORS AND ADMINISTRATORS); *Hamilton v Mills* (1861) 29 Beav 193; *Re Bourke's Will Trusts, Barclays Bank Trust Co Ltd v Canada Permanent Trust Co* [1980] 1 All ER 219, [1980] 1 WLR 539. The husband cannot take under a limitation of personalty to the right heirs of the wife: *Newenham v Pittar* (1838) 7 LJ CP 300. As to who was the heir-at-law under the law in force prior to 1926 see EXECUTORS AND ADMINISTRATORS.
3   *Re Whitehead, Whitehead v Hemsley* [1920] 1 Ch 298; *Re Kilvert, Midland Bank Executor and Trustee Co Ltd v Kilvert* [1957] Ch 388, [1957] 2 All ER 196. See, however, *Re Bourke's Will Trusts, Barclays Bank Trust Co Ltd v Canada Permanent Trust Co* [1980] 1 All ER 219, [1980] 1 WLR 539.
4   Ie in the case of deaths before 1926, the Statute of Distribution (1670), in the case of deaths after 1925 and before 1953, the Administration of Estates Act 1925, and in the case of deaths after 1952, the Administration of Estates Act 1925 (construed as including references to the Intestates' Estates Act 1952 and the Family Law Reform Act 1987 (as the case may require)): see EXECUTORS AND ADMINISTRATORS.
5   *Elmsley v Young* (1835) 2 My & K 780; *Withy v Mangles* (1843) 10 Cl & Fin 215, HL; *Rook v A-G* (1862) 31 Beav 313; *Re Gray's Settlement, Akers v Sears* [1896] 2 Ch 802. See also *—v—* (1815) 1 Madd 36; *Re Clanchy's Will Trusts, Lynch v Edwards* [1970] 2 All ER 489, CA.
6   *Withy v Mangles* (1843) 10 Cl & Fin 215, HL; *Lucas v Brandreth (No 2)* (1860) 28 Beav 274.

7   *Watt v Watt* (1796) 3 Ves 244; *Bailey v Wright* (1811) 18 Ves 49 (affd (1818) 1 Swan 39); *Grafftey v Humpage* (1838) 1 Beav 46 (affd (1839) 3 Jur 622). However, where the wife was illegitimate it was held that the fund resulted to her and went to her husband as her personal representative: *Hawkins v Hawkins* (1834) 7 Sim 173.

8   *Worseley v Johnson* (1753) 3 Atk 758; *Garrick v Lord Camden* (1807) 14 Ves 372; *Cholmondeley v Lord Ashburton* (1843) 6 Beav 86; *Kilner v Leech* (1847) 10 Beav 362; *Re Fitzgerald* (1889) 58 LJ Ch 662.

9   *Re Winn, Brook v Whitton* [1910] 1 Ch 278; cf *Re Clanchy's Will Trusts, Lynch v Edwards* [1970] 2 All ER 489, CA. As to the time for ascertaining next of kin see also para 935 post.

935. Trusts for statutory next of kin. If the trust for the next of kin of a person contains any reference, express or implied[1], to any statute regulating the distribution of the estates of intestates[2], those persons take who would have taken if he had died intestate and, in the absence of any provision to the contrary, they take as tenants in common in the shares and manner in which they would have taken on an intestacy[3]. On a death intestate before 1926, a husband was not[4], but a wife was[5], a person entitled under the description of statutory next of kin, but they are both entitled as such on a death intestate since 1925[6].

In a marriage settlement, the ultimate trust of the wife's fund, in the event of the husband surviving her, may be for the persons who would be her statutory next of kin if she had survived the husband and died intestate[7]. As a general rule, when a trust is created in favour of persons who take under any statute, and the only hypothesis stated is the death of some person intestate possessed of the personal property settled by the instrument creating the trust, the persons who take are the persons determined by the statute and ascertained at the time, that is to say at the death of the person in question[8]. However, the trust may be so worded as to show that the class of persons to be ascertained is not to be ascertained when the death did happen, but at some other time, as if the death had happened at that other time[9]. The question in each case is a question of grammatical construction. In the case of the foregoing ultimate trust of a wife's fund, the next of kin would have to be ascertained at the date of the husband's death[10].

1   A reference to intestacy implies a reference to the Statute of Distribution (1670), or the Administration of Estates Act 1925, or the latter Act as amended by the Intestates' Estates Act 1952 and the Family Law Reform Act 1987 (as the case may require): see *Kidd v Frasier* (1851) 1 I Ch R 518; *Re Gray's Settlement, Akers v Sears* [1896] 2 Ch 802; following *Garrick v Lord Camden* (1807) 14 Ves 372; *Maclean v Smith* [1927] NI 109, NI CA, where the next of kin were held entitled to settled realty; *Re Jackson* (1943) 113 LJ Ch 78. See also *Cotton v Scarancke* (1815) 1 Madd 45. A reference to death unmarried contains no such implication: see *Halton v Foster* (1868) 3 Ch App 505; *Re Webber's Settlement* (1850) 19 LJ Ch 445. A trust for 'relations' or 'relatives' is construed as a trust for the statutory next of kin, but no reference to the relevant statute is implied in such a trust for the purpose of determining the shares and manner in which the next of kin are to take: *Eagles v Le Breton* (1873) LR 15 Eq 148; *Re Gansloser's Will Trusts, Chartered Bank of India, Australia and China v Chillingworth* [1952] Ch 30, [1951] 2 All ER 936, CA. See also *Re Kilvert, Midland Bank Executor and Trustee Co Ltd v Kilvert* [1957] Ch 388, [1957] 2 All ER 196, distinguished in *Re Bourke's Will Trusts, Barclays Bank Trust Co Ltd v Canada Permanent Trust Co* [1980] 1 All ER 219, [1980] 1 WLR 539. In *Re Hughes, Loddiges v Jones* [1916] 1 Ch 493, a gift in a will of both real and personal estate to the persons entitled 'under the statute for the distribution of the estates of intestate persons' meant no more than 'by law', so that the heir-at-law was entitled to the real estate.
     As to the construction of references in settlements to the Statutes of Distribution and to statutory next of kin see EXECUTORS AND ADMINISTRATORS.

2   As to the relevant statutes see para 934 note 4 ante.

3   *Downes v Bullock* (1858) 25 Beav 54 (affd (1860) 9 HL Cas 1 (will)); *Re Ranking's Settlement Trusts* (1868) LR 6 Eq 601; *Re Nightingale* [1909] 1 Ch 385. See, however, *Re Krawitz's Will Trusts, Krawitz v Crawford* [1959] 3 All ER 793, [1959] 1 WLR 1192.

4   *Garrick v Lord Camden* (1807) 14 Ves 372; *Milne v Gilbart* (1854) 5 De GM & G 510; *Noon v Lyon* (1875) 33 LT 199. Before 1926 a husband took the whole of his wife's personal estate on an intestacy by husband's right, and not under the Statute of Distribution (1670): see EXECUTORS AND ADMINISTRATORS.

5   See the Statute of Distribution (1670) s 3 (repealed); and EXECUTORS AND ADMINISTRATORS.

6 See the Administration of Estates Act 1925 Pt IV (ss 45–52) (as amended); the Family Law Reform Act 1987 ss 1, 18(1); and EXECUTORS AND ADMINISTRATORS. See also *Re Gilligan* [1950] P 32, [1949] 2 All ER 401.

7 See para 932 ante.

8 *Wheeler v Addams* (1853) 17 Beav 417; cf *Smith v Smith* (1841) 12 Sim 317; *Day v Day* (1870) 18 WR 417. See also *Wharton v Barker* (1858) 4 K & J 483; *Bullock v Downes* (1860) 9 HL Cas 1 (where the rule is stated with reference to wills).

9 *Re King's Settlement, Gibson v Wright* (1889) 60 LT 745 per Chitty J. As to the time for ascertaining next of kin see also para 934 ante.

10 *Pinder v Pinder* (1860) 28 Beav 44; *Chalmers v North* (1860) 28 Beav 175; *Re King's Settlement, Gibson v Wright* (1889) 60 LT 745; *Clarke v Hayne* (1889) 42 ChD 529; *Re Peirson's Settlement, Cayley v De Wend* (1903) 88 LT 794. There has, however, been a considerable conflict of authority on the point. For the contrary view see *Druitt v Seaward, Re Ainsworth, Ainsworth v Seaward* (1885) 31 ChD 234; *Re Bradley, Brown v Cottrell* (1888) 58 LT 631. The balance of judicial authority supports the view stated in the text.

936. Effect of the phrase 'without having been married'. A trust for the statutory next of kin of the wife as if she had died intestate and 'without having been married', or 'without ever having been married', used to exclude the wife's issue, whether issue of the intended marriage who fail to attain a vested interest[1], or issue of a former[2] or subsequent marriage[3]. There might, however, be a context[4] or special circumstances in connection with the particular settlement that might lead to the conclusion that it could not have been the intention to exclude the wife's children[5]. If the words used were as if she had died intestate and 'unmarried', the word 'unmarried', in the absence of any context, was taken to bear its primary meaning of 'never having been married'[6]. However, 'unmarried' is a word of flexible meaning, and might be construed according to the obvious intention of the persons using the word[7]. Accordingly, where the effect of giving the word its primary meaning would be to favour collaterals at the expense of lineals, the court interpreted it as meaning 'not having a husband living at her death', thus admitting issue[8] and excluding a subsequent husband[9].

A trust for the wife's next of kin on the death or remarriage of the husband, who took an interest for life or until remarriage if he survived his wife, has been held to take effect on the cesser of the prior interests and, the marriage having been terminated by divorce and the husband having remarried, the next of kin took on the death of the wife in the lifetime of her husband[10].

1 *Re Deane's Trusts, Dudley v Deane* [1900] 1 IR 332; *Re Brydone's Settlement, Cobb v Blackburne* [1903] 2 Ch 84, CA; *Re Smith's Settlement, Wilkins v Smith* [1903] 1 Ch 373. The two last-mentioned cases, following the decision of Jessel MR in *Emmins v Bradford, Johnson v Emmins* (1880) 13 ChD 493, negative the view which was taken in several cases (*Re Ball's Trust* (1879) 11 ChD 270; *Upton v Brown* (1879) 12 ChD 872; *Re Arden's Settlement* [1890] WN 204; *Stoddart v Saville* [1894] 1 Ch 480; *Re Mare, Mare v Howey* [1902] 2 Ch 112) that a general rule was laid down in *Wilson v Atkinson* (1864) 4 De GJ & Sm 455 that such words of limitation were introduced merely to exclude the husband of the wife, and not to exclude any persons who might be her descendants. The view taken in *Re Brydone's Settlement, Cobb v Blackburne* supra was approved by the House of Lords in *Boyce v Wasbrough* [1922] 1 AC 425, HL.

2 *Emmins v Bradford, Johnson v Emmins* (1880) 13 ChD 493; *Boyce v Wasbrough* [1922] 1 AC 425, HL.

3 *Hardman v Maffett* (1884) 13 LR Ir 499.

4 There was such a context in *Wilson v Atkinson* (1864) 4 De GJ & Sm 455, where the trust was followed by a declaration that an illegitimate daughter should for the purposes of the trust be deemed to be a lawful child of the wife, the settlement containing no express provision for children or issue.

5 Eg the absence of any provision for the children or issue of the marriage: see *Re Deane's Trusts, Dudley v Deane* [1900] 1 IR 332.

6 *Blundell v De Falbe* (1888) 57 LJ Ch 576. See also *Heywood v Heywood* (1860) 29 Beav 9; *Clarke v Colls* (1861) 9 HL Cas 601 at 612, 615. Cf *Dalrymple v Hall* (1881) 16 ChD 715; *Re Sergeant, Mertens v Walley* (1884) 26 ChD 575 (cases on wills).

7 *Maugham v Vincent* (1840) 9 LJ Ch 329. See, however, *Boyce v Wasbrough* [1922] 1 AC 425 at 445–446, HL, per Lord Sumner.

8 *Maugham v Vincent* (1840) 9 LJ Ch 329; *Re Norman's Trust* (1853) 3 De GM & G 965 (where the expression 'without being married' was said to mean without having a husband at the time of death); *Pratt*

v Mathew (1856) 8 De GM & G 522; *Re Saunders' Trust* (1857) 3 K & J 152; *Clarke v Colls* (1861) 9 HL Cas 601; *Re Woodhouse's Trusts* [1903] 1 IR 126. Cf *Day v Barnard* (1860) 1 Drew & Sm 351; *Re Jones, Last v Dobson* [1915] 1 Ch 246 (cases on wills).

It appears that a trust for the statutory next of kin of a wife as if she had died intestate and 'without having been married' or 'without ever having been married' includes her legitimate or illegitimate children or, if they predecease her, their issue. See also the Family Law Reform Act 1987 s 1 (see para 917 note 8 ante); and CHILDREN AND YOUNG PERSONS vol 5(2) (Reissue) para 723. As to the position prior to 4 April 1988 see EXECUTORS AND ADMINISTRATORS.

9   *Re Saunders' Trust* (1857) 3 K & J 152.

10   *Re Mathew's Trusts* (1876) 24 WR 960. However, the decision in that case, in so far as it was held that the husband's interest was destroyed by his second marriage during the wife's lifetime seems to be in conflict with *Re Pilkington's Settlement, Pilkington v Wright* (1923) 129 LT 629 and *Re Monro's Settlement, Monro v Hill* [1933] Ch 82. See also para 915 note 2 ante. As to the acceleration of subsequent interests generally see para 921 ante.

(3) SETTLEMENTS OF PERSONALTY TO DEVOLVE WITH REALTY

937. In general. It is often desired that the enjoyment and devolution of personal property and personal chattels, without conversion, is to accompany the limitations of some freehold estate settled by the same or another settlement[1]. This is usually effected by assigning such personal property or personal chattels to trustees to be enjoyed or held with, or upon trusts corresponding as nearly as may be with the trusts affecting, the settled estate[2].

A settlement of chattels to devolve with land is commonly called making them heirlooms[3].

1   As to the settlement of land see para 675 et seq ante. It is no longer possible to create settlements of land: see para 676 ante.

2   Jewels settled as heirlooms along with a settled estate which is subject to a power of appointment may themselves be subject to a corresponding but independent power of appointment: *Re Penton's Settlement Trusts, Penton v Langley* [1924] 2 Ch 192.

3   'Heirlooms' means something which although not by its own nature heritable, is to have a heritable character impressed upon it: *Byng v Byng* (1862) 10 HL Cas 171 at 183. This character may be imposed by a voluntary donor: *Seale v Hayne* (1863) 9 LT 570. As to heirlooms at common law see REAL PROPERTY vol 39(2) (Reissue) paras 89–90; EXECUTORS AND ADMINISTRATORS. Articles which can only be enjoyed by consumption or are perishable in a short time are not included in a direction that furniture and household goods, chattels and effects in or about a house are to be annexed to the house as heirlooms: *Hare v Pryce* (1864) 11 LT 101.

938. Devolution of personalty settled before 1926. Where instruments came into operation before 1926, it was impossible to create an estate tail in personalty[1], and an assignment or bequest of personalty, either by way of immediate gift or executed trust[2], to devolve with realty or, in the case of chattels, a direction that they should be treated as heirlooms so far as the rules of law and equity permitted[3], gave life interests in the personalty or chattels to those who took life interests in the realty[4], but such personalty or chattels vested absolutely at birth in the first person who became entitled to the real estate for a vested estate of inheritance, whether in possession or remainder[5], subject of course, if the estate was in remainder, to all prior limited interests, such as estates for life[6].

Accordingly, a gift of chattels as heirlooms, or so far as the rules of law and equity permitted, to such persons as should from time to time be holders of a title, conferred an absolute interest on the first person who became beneficially entitled to the chattels as holder of the title[7]. This rule could be modified by an appropriate provision in the settlement[8], provided that the words used were reasonably clear and certain[9].

1   *Earl of Stafford v Buckley* (1750) 2 Ves Sen 170. See also *Ex p Sterne* (1801) 6 Ves 156. As to entailed interests see para 715 et seq ante; and REAL PROPERTY vol 39(2) (Reissue) para 117 et seq.

2   As to executory trusts to settle personalty as realty see PERSONAL PROPERTY vol 35 (Reissue) paras 1229–1230; WILLS vol 50 (Reissue) para 279.

3   These words did not make the trust executory or alter the trusts affecting the personalty (*Lord Scarsdale v Curzon* (1860) 1 John & H 40), or prevent the settlement from transgressing the rule against perpetuities (*Portman v Viscount Portman* [1922] 2 AC 473, HL; *Re Hind, Bernstone v Montgomery* [1933] Ch 208 at 225). See also PERPETUITIES AND ACCUMULATIONS vol 35 (Reissue) para 1081.

4   *Gower v Grosvenor* (1740) 5 Madd 337; *Savile v Earl of Scarborough* (1818) 1 Swan 537; *Harrington v Harrington* (1868) 3 Ch App 564 at 573; *Robinson v Robinson* (1875) 33 LT 663. Cf *Montague v Lord Inchiquin* (1875) 32 LT 427; *Re Fowler, Fowler v Fowler* [1917] 2 Ch 307, CA.

5   *Trafford v Trafford* (1746) 3 Atk 347; *Duke of Bridgwater v Egerton* (1751) 2 Ves Sen 121; *Foley v Burnell* (1783) 1 Bro CC 274 (affd (1785) 4 Bro Parl Cas 319, HL); *Vaughan v Burslem* (1790) 3 Bro CC 101; *Fordyce v Ford* (1795) 2 Ves 536; *Ware v Polhill* (1805) 11 Ves 257; *Carr v Lord Erroll* (1808) 14 Ves 478; *Lord Southampton v Marquis of Hertford* (1813) 2 Ves & B 54 at 63; *Doncaster v Doncaster* (1856) 3 K & J 26; *Lord Scarsdale v Curzon* (1860) 1 John & H 40; *Re Johnson's Trusts* (1866) LR 2 Eq 716; *Re Fothergill's Estate, Price-Fothergill v Price* [1903] 1 Ch 149; *Re Parker, Parker v Parkin* [1910] 1 Ch 581; *Re Beresford-Hope, Aldenham v Beresford-Hope* [1917] 1 Ch 287; *Re Fowler, Fowler v Fowler* [1917] 2 Ch 307, CA; *Portman v Viscount Portman* [1922] 2 AC 473, HL; *Pole v Pole, Mundy Pole v Pole, Martin v Pole* [1924] 1 Ch 156, CA; *Barton v Moorhouse* [1935] AC 300, PC. Cf *Schank v Scott* (1874) 22 WR 513, where a life interest in a sum of money was given to a tenant in tail with remainder upon the trusts of the settled land, and an absolute interest was acquired in the personalty on the execution of a disentailing deed. As to disentailing deeds see REAL PROPERTY vol 39(2) (Reissue) para 121 et seq.

6   Such an interest might be defeated by any event which would defeat the estate of the person becoming entitled to it in the realty (*Lady Pelham v Gregory* (1760) 3 Bro Parl Cas 204, HL; *Re Parker, Parker v Parkin* [1910] 1 Ch 581); but once vested it was not divested by death under 21 (*Foley v Burnell* (1783) 1 Bro CC 274 (affd (1785) 4 Bro Parl Cas 319, HL); *Vaughan v Burslem* (1790) 3 Bro CC 101; *Carr v Lord Erroll* (1808) 14 Ves 478; *Re Parker, Parker v Parkin* supra), or by death before the interest became indefeasibly vested, if ultimately in fact it did so vest (*Re Cresswell, Parkin v Cresswell* (1883) 24 ChD 102). Consequently such a phrase did not make the trust executory (*Vaughan v Burslem* (1790) 3 Bro CC 101 (overruling on this point *Gower v Grosvenor* (1740) 5 Madd 337; *Trafford v Trafford* (1746) 3 Atk 347; *Lord Scarsdale v Curzon* (1860) 1 John & H 40 at 50; *Countess Harrington v Earl of Harrington* (1871) LR 5 HL 87; *Portman v Viscount Portman* [1922] 2 AC 473 at 484, 495, HL), or extend or alter the disposition made of the personal estate (*Christie v Gosling* (1866) LR 1 HL 279 at 299), or imply a provision that the interest of a tenant in tail by purchase who died under the age of 21 would be defeated (*Re Parker, Parker v Parkin* supra).

7   *Lady Laura Tollemache v Earl and Countess of Coventry* (1834) 2 Cl & Fin 611, HL; *Mackworth v Hinxman* (1836) 2 Keen 658; *Re Viscount Exmouth, Viscount Exmouth v Praed* (1883) 23 ChD 158; *Re Hill, Hill v Hill* [1902] 1 Ch 537 (affd [1902] 1 Ch 807, CA). Cf *Rowland v Morgan* (1848) 2 Ph 764; *Campbell v Ingilby* (1856) 25 LJ Ch 761; *Re Johnston, Cockerell v Earl of Essex* (1884) 26 ChD 538; *Re Marquess of Bute, Marquess of Bute v Ryder* (1884) 27 ChD 196. The Legitimacy Act 1976, so far as it affects the succession to the dignity or title of honour, or the devolution of property settled with it, applies only to children born after 28 October 1959: see s 11, Sch 1 para 4(1), (3); and CHILDREN AND YOUNG PERSONS vol 5(2) (Reissue) para 728. As to legitimation generally see CHILDREN AND YOUNG PERSONS vol 5(2) (Reissue) para 723 et seq. As to the rights of legitimated children see para 732 ante.

8   In this way it was possible to defeat the interest of a tenant in tail by purchase who died under the age of 21 (*Christie v Gosling* (1866) LR 1 HL 279; *Countess Harrington v Earl of Harrington* (1871) LR 5 HL 87; *Martelli v Holloway* (1872) LR 5 HL 532; *Viscount Hill v Dowager Viscountess Hill* [1897] 1 QB 483 at 495, CA; *Re Dayrell, Hastie v Dayrell* [1904] 2 Ch 496; *Re Lewis, Busk v Lewes* [1918] 2 Ch 308), or who did not come into actual possession of the land (*Potts v Potts* (1848) 1 HL Cas 671; *Lord Scarsdale v Curzon* (1860) 1 John & H 40; *Re Angerstein, Angerstein v Angerstein* [1895] 2 Ch 883; *Re Fothergill's Estate, Price-Fothergill v Price* [1903] 1 Ch 149; cf *Barton v Moorhouse* [1935] AC 300, PC). See also *Cox v Sutton* (1856) 25 LJ Ch 845. See also, as to 'actual possession', *Re Petre's Settlement Trusts, Legh v Petre* [1910] 1 Ch 290; *Re Duckett, Phillpotts v Fitzmaurice* [1918] 1 IR 110, Ir CA; *Re Duncombe, Wrixon-Becher v Faversham* [1932] 1 Ch 622, CA. As to the meaning of 'actually entitled to possession' see *Re Morrison's Settlement, Gatty v Dent-Brocklehurst* [1974] Ch 326, [1973] 3 All ER 1094.

9   *Foley v Burnell* (1783) 1 Bro CC 274 (affd (1785) 4 Bro Parl Cas 319, HL); *Lord Scarsdale v Curzon* (1860) 1 John & H 40; *Re Parker, Parker v Parkin* [1910] 1 Ch 581; *Re Lewis, Busk v Lewes* [1918] 2 Ch 308; *Portman v Viscount Portman* [1922] 2 AC 473, HL; *Re Coote, Cavers and Evans v Kaye* [1940] Ch 549, [1940] 2 All ER 363; *Re Morrison's Settlement, Gatty v Dent-Brocklehurst* [1974] Ch 326, [1973] 3 All ER 1094.

939. Devolution of personalty settled after 1925. Where an instrument came into operation after 1925, but before 1 January 1997[1], an interest in tail, or in tail male, or in tail female, or in tail special, which interests are usually included in the expression 'entailed interests', could be created by way of trust in personal, as well as in real, property. An entailed interest could only be created by a settlement of real or personal property or its proceeds of sale (including the will of a person dying after 1925), or by an agreement for a settlement in which the trusts to affect the property were sufficiently declared[2].

If an entailed interest has been created in personalty, it will have the like results as the creation of a similar estate in realty, including the right to bar the entail either absolutely or so as to create an interest equivalent to a base fee, and all statutory provisions relating to estates tail in real property apply to entailed interests in personal property[3]. In default of and subject to the execution of a disentailing assurance or the exercise of the testamentary power conferred by statute[4], an entailed interest (to the extent of the property affected) devolves as an equitable interest, from time to time, upon the persons who would have been successively entitled to it as the heirs of the body (either generally or of a particular class) of the tenant in tail or other person, or as tenant by the curtesy[5], if the entailed interest had, before 1 January 1926, been limited in respect of freehold land governed by the general law in force immediately before that date and such law had remained unaffected[6].

1   As from 1 January 1997, it has no longer been possible to create entailed interests: see the Trusts of Land and Appointment of Trustees Act 1996 s 2, Sch 1 para 5; and REAL PROPERTY vol 39(2) (Reissue) para 119. See also paras 611, 677 ante.
2   Such an interest in personalty could be created either by means of the like expressions as those by which, before 1926, a similar estate tail could have been created by deed (not being an executory instrument) in freehold land (see the Law of Property Act 1925 s 130(1)) (repealed except in relation to any entailed interest created before 1 January 1997: see REAL PROPERTY vol 39(2) (Reissue) para 119; and para 678 note 11 ante) or by directing personal estate (including the proceeds of sale of land directed to be sold and chattels directed to be held as heirlooms (which expression extends to chattels to which the Settled Land Act 1925 s 67 applies: see s 67(4); and paras 802 ante, 941 post)) to be enjoyed or held with or upon trusts corresponding to trusts affecting land in which an entailed interest has at any time been created and is subsisting: see the Law of Property Act 1925 s 130(3) (repealed). In the latter case, the trusts must follow the exact words of s 130(3) (repealed): *Re Jones, Public Trustee v Jones* [1934] Ch 315. As to the method of creating an entailed interest since 1925 see REAL PROPERTY vol 39(2) (Reissue) para 119.
3   Intermediate income pending the birth of a person who, on being born, would be entitled in possession as tenant in tail should not be accumulated, but is payable to the person next entitled in remainder: *Re Crossley's Settlement Trusts, Chivers v Crossley* [1955] Ch 627, [1955] 2 All ER 801.
4   See the Law of Property Act 1925 s 176; and REAL PROPERTY vol 39(2) (Reissue) para 141; WILLS vol 50 (Reissue) para 619.
5   As to the abolition of tenancy by the curtesy see para 679 ante.
6   Law of Property Act 1925 s 130(4).

940. Powers and duties of trustees in respect of settled chattels. If furniture, jewels or other personal chattels are the subject of a settlement, the trustees, if and while the chattels are in their possession, are bound to keep them as if they were their own, as in the case of any other trust property[1]. However, since such articles by their nature can only be enjoyed by the beneficiaries by delivery to them, it is usual to provide in the settlement that the trustees are not to be liable for such articles or to see to their condition or insurance. However, if the beneficiary in whose possession such articles are fails to insure them, the trustees have power to insure them and pay the premiums out of the income of capital money in their hands[2].

The trustees should keep an inventory of the articles, and should take any steps necessary to safeguard them in the event of its being apprehended that the beneficiary will dispose of them. The beneficiary may be required to sign an inventory of, but not to give security for, the chattels, unless there is reason to suppose that they will be in danger in his custody[3]. If the articles are assigned to the trustees by the settlement, the possession of them is that of the trustees, who may maintain an action against a wrongdoer for their conversion[4].

1   As to the duties of trustees in respect of safe custody of trust property see TRUSTS vol 48 (Reissue) para 827.
2   See the Trustee Act 1925 s 19 (as amended) (see TRUSTS vol 48 (Reissue) para 891); *Re Earl of Egmont's Trusts, Lefroy v Earl of Egmont* [1908] 1 Ch 821. The statutory power to insure is only in respect of loss or fire damage to an amount (including the amount of any insurance already on foot) not exceeding three quarters of the full value of the property (see the Trustee Act 1925 s 19(1)), but a wider power is often included in the settlement.
3   *Foley v Burnell* (1783) 1 Bro CC 274 at 279; *Conduitt v Soane* (1844) 1 Coll 285; *Temple v Thring* (1887) 56 LJ Ch 767.
4   *Barker v Furlong* [1891] 2 Ch 172. As to the rights of the trustees against the beneficiary's creditors see BANKRUPTCY AND INSOLVENCY vol 3(2) (Reissue) para 417.

941. Power to sell settled chattels. If personal chattels have been settled without reference to settled land[1] on trusts creating entailed interests[2] in them, the trustees have power to sell the chattels or any of them provided that they obtain the consent of the usufructuary for the time being if of full age[3].

If personal chattels have been settled so as to devolve with settled land[4], or to devolve with it as nearly as may be in accordance with the law or practice in force at the date of the settlement[5], or are settled together with land[6], or upon trusts declared by reference to the trusts affecting land, a tenant for life of the land[7] may sell the chattels or any of them[8]. However, no such sale may be made without a court order[9].

Trustees having a power of sale of settled land, but having no power of sale of chattels settled to devolve with the land, are trustees for the purposes of the Settled Land Act 1925[10] for the sale of such chattels, and can give a good discharge for the purchase money[11].

1   For the meaning of 'settled land' see para 680 text to note 2 ante; definition applied by the Law of Property Act 1925 s 205(1)(xxvi).
2   As to entailed interests see paras 715 et seq, 939 ante; and REAL PROPERTY vol 39(2) (Reissue) para 117 et seq.
3   See the Law of Property Act 1925 s 130(5). As to the proceeds of sale see para 943 post.
4   Chattels settled to devolve with a dignity, eg a baronetcy, are chattels settled to devolve with settled land according to this provision, and can be sold under it by the holder for the time being of the dignity: see *Re Sir J Rivett-Carnac's Will* (1885) 30 ChD 136.
5   For the meaning of 'settlement' see para 678 note 1 ante.
6   For the meaning of 'land' see para 680 note 1 ante.
7   For the meaning of 'tenant for life' see para 671 note 5 ante. See also para 761 et seq ante. 'The land' means the land with which the chattels are to devolve, and it makes no difference that the land and chattels are settled by different instruments: see *Re Lord Stafford's Settlement and Will, Gerard v Stafford* [1904] 2 Ch 72. As to the settlement of chattels to devolve with land see para 937 et seq ante.
8   Settled Land Act 1925 s 67(1). As to the proceeds of sale see para 943 post. The Settled Land Act 1925 does not confer any power to lease chattels, and a tenant for life who lets a house with the chattels in it under the statutory powers is not entitled to any part of the compensation recovered from the tenant in respect of chattels damaged or missing: see *Re Lacon's Settlement, Lacon v Lacon* [1911] 1 Ch 351; revsd on another point [1911] 2 Ch 17, CA.
9   See the Settled Land Act 1925 s 67(3). As to applications to the court see para 792 et seq ante. Service on the children of the tenant for life is not required when their interests are sufficiently represented by the trustees: *Re Brown's Will* (1884) 27 ChD 179. On the other hand, service on a remainderman has been directed, to relieve the trustees from the sole burden of arguing the case: *Re Earl of Radnor's Will Trusts* (1890) 45 ChD 402 at 404, CA.
10   As to trustees for the purposes of the Settled Land Act 1925 see para 750 et seq ante.
11   See *Constable v Constable* (1886) 32 ChD 233.

942. Exercise of court's power to approve sale or purchase. The court's power to authorise a sale or purchase is discretionary, and must be exercised having regard to the circumstances of each particular case[1].

As a general rule, the circumstances that the tenant for life, who is in the position of a trustee having a discretionary power of sale which must be honestly exercised in the interest of all parties concerned[2], has incumbered his life estate under the settlement, ought to be excluded from consideration by the court[3], and the court does not sanction a sale merely to relieve a tenant for life from the consequences of his own extravagance[4], or to enable him to pay inheritance tax and live in the mansion house[5], or merely to increase his income[6]. Moreover, as public considerations do not intervene, the court may be less ready to consent to the sale of heirlooms than to the sale of a mansion house[7]. However, a sale has been sanctioned to enable the tenant for life to keep up his position where he was in straitened circumstances through no fault of his own[8].

On the purchase of a new mansion house, chattels settled to devolve with the old one may be sold if not suitable to be removed[9], and, where chattels were directed to be annexed to and at all times kept in the mansion house, the court declined to make an order for sale of the house without a direction as to what should be done with the chattels[10]. No statutory provision is made for the court's authority being given retrospectively, but where an advantageous sale had been made a direction was given that the trustees should take no steps to recover the sold chattels[11].

1 Re Earl of Radnor's Will Trusts (1890) 45 ChD 402 at 407, 418, 424, CA; Re Hope's Settled Estates (1910) 26 TLR 413.
2 Re Earl of Radnor's Will Trusts (1890) 45 ChD 402, CA; Re Hope's Settled Estates (1910) 26 TLR 413.
3 Re Duke of Marlborough's Settlement, Duke of Marlborough v Marjoribanks (1885) 30 ChD 127 (affd (1886) 32 ChD 1, CA); Re Beaumont's Settled Estates (1888) 58 LT 916; Re Earl of Radnor's Will Trusts (1890) 45 ChD 402 at 410, CA.
4 Re Hope's Settlement (1893) [1899] 2 Ch 691n; Re Hope, De Cetto v Hope [1899] 2 Ch 679, CA.
5 Re Fetherstonhaugh's Estate (1898) 14 TLR 167 (a case concerning death duties which are now inheritance tax: see INHERITANCE TAXATION vol 24 (Reissue) para 401 et seq).
6 Re Sebright, Sebright v Brownlow (1912) 28 TLR 191.
7 Lord Bruce v Marquess of Ailesbury [1892] AC 356 at 363, HL. As to sanctioning a sale of the principal mansion house see para 791 ante.
8 Re Lord John Thynne (1884) 77 LT Jo 195 (where the income had been reduced by agricultural depression); Re Townshend's Settlement (1903) 89 LT 691. Cf Re Sebright, Sebright v Earl Brownlow (1914) 31 TLR 25; but see Re Beaumont's Settled Estates (1888) 58 LT 916.
9 Browne v Collins (1890) 62 LT 566.
10 Re Brown's Will (1884) 27 ChD 179.
11 Re Ames, Ames v Ames [1893] 2 Ch 479. The power to confirm past transactions (see para 876 ante) does not apply to chattels.

943. Application of proceeds of sale of settled chattels and entailed personalty. The net proceeds of sale of personal chattels settled without reference to settled land on trusts creating entailed interests[1] in them must be held in trust for and go to the same persons successively, in the same manner and for the same interests, as the chattels sold would have been held and gone if they had not been sold, and the income of investments representing such proceeds of sale must be applied accordingly[2].

The net proceeds of sale of personal chattels settled so as to devolve with settled land[3] are capital money arising under the Settled Land Act 1925, and must be paid, invested or applied and otherwise dealt with in like manner in all respects as directed by that Act with respect to other capital money arising under the Act[4], or may be invested in the purchase of other chattels of the same or any other nature which, when purchased, must be settled and held on the same trusts and devolve in the same manner as the chattels sold[5]. However, no such purchase may be made without a court order[6].

Personal estate entailed (not being chattels settled as heirlooms[7]) may be invested, applied and otherwise dealt with as if it was capital money or securities representing capital money arising under the Settled Land Act 1925 from land settled on the like trusts[8].

1   For the meaning of 'entailed interest' see para 678 note 11 ante. As to entailed interests see para 715 et seq ante; and REAL PROPERTY vol 39(2) (Reissue) para 117 et seq.

2   See the Law of Property Act 1925 s 130(5).

3   As to the sale of personal chattels see para 941 ante. For the meaning of 'settled land' see para 680 text to note 2 ante.

4   For the meaning of 'capital money arising under the Act' see para 795 ante. As to its application see para 808 ante. Money arising from the sale of chattels settled to devolve with land has been allowed to be applied in the discharge of incumbrances notwithstanding that the position of a minor tenant in tail in remainder was thereby prejudiced: see *Re Duke of Marlborough's Settlement, Duke of Marlborough v Marjoribanks* (1885) 30 ChD 127 (affd (1886) 32 ChD 1, CA); *Re Lord Stafford's Settlement and Will, Gerard v Stafford* [1904] 2 Ch 72. It has also been applied in payment for authorised improvements: see *Re Houghton Estate* (1885) 30 ChD 102. As to authorised improvements see para 809 et seq ante.

5   See the Settled Land Act 1925 s 67(2). The repair and renovation of other heirlooms settled by the same settlement, but remaining unsold, is within this provision: see *Re Waldegrave, Earl Waldegrave v Earl of Selborne* (1899) 81 LT 632.

6   See the Settled Land Act 1925 s 67(3). Cf para 941 note 9 ante.

7   Any reference to personal chattels settled as heirlooms extends to chattels to which ibid s 67 applies: s 67(4). See also para 941 ante.

8   Law of Property Act 1925 s 130(1) (repealed except in relation to any entailed interest created before 1 January 1997 by the Trusts of Land and Appointment of Trustees Act 1996 s 25(2), Sch 4). As to the investment and application of capital money arising under the Settled Land Act 1925 see para 805 et seq ante.

5. CAPITAL AND INCOME AND WASTE

(1) INCOME AND CAPITAL RECEIPTS

(i) In general

944. Rights of tenant for life and remainderman. A tenant for life of settled property is entitled ordinarily to the net income of the property[1]. He will be entitled also to casual profits which accrue during the subsistence of the life interest, but not to capital receipts[2], unless, in either instance, the settlement provides otherwise[3]. Receipts that accrue to settled property may be either casual profits[4], which accordingly belong to the tenant for life, or capital accretions[5] or substitutions[6]. The answer to the question whether a particular receipt is capital or income may depend, not merely on its nature, but on the intention of the person from whom it comes[7] or on statutory provision[8].

The rule that a tenant for life is entitled to the income of property applies in general to wasting assets settled by deed or specifically by will, so, apart from statute[9] and apart from the equitable principles applicable to a residuary bequest of property on trust for persons entitled in succession[10], a tenant for life is entitled to the income of wasting property such as leaseholds[11] or to the income of mines lawfully worked[12]. Whether a tenant for life may cut timber or open new mines depends, apart from statutory powers[13], on whether he is unimpeachable for waste. If he is unimpeachable for waste, he will be entitled to the rents and profits[14]. If he is impeachable for waste but exercises the statutory power, he will be entitled beneficially to the proportion allowed him by statute[15].

If property settled by will includes a reversionary interest in personalty, which interest is subject to a trust or duty that it should be sold but is retained unsold in the exercise by the trustees of a power for the benefit of the estate, the tenant for life will be entitled, in the absence of a contrary intention shown by the settlement, to a proportion of the capital in lieu of the income that has not been earned[16].

1   See eg *Verner v General and Commercial Investment Trust* [1894] 2 Ch 239 at 258 (on appeal [1894] 2 Ch 239, CA); *Re Forster's Settlement, Forster v Custodian of Enemy Property for England* as reported in [1942] 1 All ER 180 at 184 (discretionary trust). The right of the tenant for life to income extends to the income of a fund set aside to provide portions payable on his death, subject, of course, to a contrary provision in the settlement: see *Wellesley v Earl of Mornington* (1857) 27 LJ Ch 150. As to the outgoings to be borne out of income see para 961 et seq post. As to the tenant for life see para 761 et seq ante.

2   See eg *Re Wilson's Estate* (1863) 3 De GJ & Sm 410 (compulsory enfranchisement of copyholds on acquisition compulsorily by a railway company, no fines being payable to the lord of the manor who was tenant for life).

3   See *Simpson v Bathhurst, Shepherd v Bathhurst* (1869) 5 Ch App 193 (fines on renewal of leases given to the tenant for life).

4   Examples of such casual profits are fines payable where leases are renewed under an obligation or custom (*Brigstocke v Brigstocke* (1878) 8 ChD 357, CA; *Re Medows, Norie v Bennett* [1898] 1 Ch 300); a bonus paid under the Irish Land Act 1903 on a sale by a tenant for life (*Re Goodall's Settlement, Fane v Goodall* [1909] 1 Ch 440, where the decision was the consequence of an express provision in the Irish Land Act 1904 s 3 (repealed); but in *Re Thorngate's Settlement, Churcher v A-G* (1915) 84 LJ Ch 561, such a bonus was held to be capital where the sale was by trustees and the provision previously mentioned did not apply); compensation for damage done during military occupation of land in wartime (*Re Williams' Settlement, Williams Wynn v Williams* [1922] 2 Ch 750; *Re Pomfret's Settlement, Guest v Pomfret* [1952] Ch 48, [1951] 2 All ER 951, in which cases the tenant for life was unimpeachable for waste; cf *Gage and Roper v Pigott and de Jenner* [1919] 1 IR 23, Ir CA; *Re Thompson, Westminster Bank Ltd v Thompson* [1949] Ch 1, [1948] 2 All ER 223 (see note 5 infra)); damages for injury to a ferry caused in the exercise of statutory powers (*Re Lindsay's Settlement (No 1)* [1941] Ch 170, [1941] 1 All ER 104); a bonus payable under the Finance (No 2) Act 1931 (*Re Schopperle's Trusts* [1932] IR 457; see also *Re Fulford, Fulford v Hyslop* [1930] 1 Ch 71, where a tenant for life was held entitled to a sum in respect of money paid or deducted on account of income tax in respect of income accumulated during her minority). See also *Re Pelly's Will Trusts, Ransome v Pelly* [1957] Ch 1, [1956] 2 All ER 326, CA; *Menzies Trustees v Lindsay* 1957 SC 44, where a life tenant was entitled to allowances by way of discharge and repayment of tax in respect of capital expenditure on agricultural land. As to such allowances see para 820 ante.

5   The following receipts have been held to be capital: a bonus payable on repayment of the value of securities deposited with the government during war (see *Re Oppenheim, Oppenheim v Oppenheim* [1917] 1 Ch 274); compensation paid for ornamental timber felled by the Crown for military purposes (see *Gage and Roper v Pigott and de Jenner* [1919] 1 IR 23, Ir CA); compensation for damage done during requisition in wartime (*Re Thompson, Westminster Bank Ltd v Thompson* [1949] Ch 1, [1948] 2 All ER 223; but cf *Re Pomfret's Settlement, Guest v Pomfret* [1952] Ch 48, [1951] 2 All ER 951 (see note 4 supra)); a forfeited deposit on an abortive sale by the tenant for life of part of the settled property (*Re Foster's Settled Estates* [1922] 1 Ch 348; see also *Earl of Shrewsbury v Countess of Shrewsbury* (1854) 18 Jur 397; *Re Ward's Settled Estate* [1919] WN 51); compensation paid under the Welsh Church Act 1914 for the extinction of the right of patronage of a benefice (*Re Lord Penrhyn's Settlement Trusts, Penrhyn v Robarts* [1923] 1 Ch 143); compensation in the nature of a gratuity awarded by the Compensation (Ireland) Commission for damage to the settled property (*Re Macnamara, Macnamara v Macnamara* [1936] 1 All ER 602); such part of the sum received on the encashment of national savings certificates after the death of the holder as represents interest earned during his life and capitalised at the end of each completed month (*Re Holder, National Provincial Bank Ltd v Holder* [1953] Ch 468, [1953] 2 All ER 1); the additional amount added to compensation under what is now the Town and Country Planning Act 1990 Pt IV (ss 107–118) (as amended), at all events where the parties have not expressly agreed to treat it as income (see *Re Hasluck, Sully v Duffin* [1957] 3 All ER 371, [1957] 1 WLR 1135); compensation paid for depreciation of land values, and compensation receivable for refusal, revocation or modification of planning permission (*Re Meux, Gilmour v Gilmour* [1958] Ch 154, [1957] 2 All ER 630). As to compensation payable under the Town and Country Planning Act 1990 see para 800 note 2 ante; and TOWN AND COUNTRY PLANNING vol 46 (Reissue) para 697 et seq.

6   The fact that, through fortuitous circumstances, money has been substituted for an interest in property affords no ground for effecting a substitution of beneficial interests. Accordingly war damage value payments received in respect of settled leaseholds were applied in buying annuities for periodscorresponding to the period of the leases, the annuities being themselves applied as the rents of the properties would have been applied: see *Re Scholfield's Will Trusts, Scholfield v Scholfield* [1949] Ch 341, [1949] 1 All ER 490.

7   Eg where a company makes a distribution, its intention may control whether the payment is capital or income: see eg *Re Whitehead's Will Trusts, Public Trustee v White* [1959] Ch 579 at 588, [1959] 2 All ER 497 at 501 per Harman LJ. See also paras 951–952 post.

8   See eg the Coal Act 1938 s 6, Sch 3 para 21(2) (repealed), under which the compensation was applicable as a substitution, so as to give the beneficiaries the like benefits that they would have had from the property (cf the principle stated in note 6 supra). See also *Re Duke of Leeds, Duke of Leeds v Davenport* [1947] Ch 525, [1947] 2 All ER 200; *Re Lucas, Bethune v Lucas* [1947] Ch 558, [1947] 2 All ER 213n; *Re Blandy-Jenkins, Blandy-Jenkins v Public Trustee* [1948] Ch 322, [1948] 1 All ER 582; *Williams v Sharpe* [1949] Ch 595, [1949] 2 All ER 102, CA.

9   See the Settled Land Act 1925 s 47 (capitalisation of part of mining rent: see para 843 ante), s 66 (capitalisation of part of proceeds of sale of timber: see paras 848 ante, 989–992 post).

10   As to such entitlement see para 945 post.

11   See *Milford v Peile* (1854) 17 Beav 602; *Hope v Hope* (1855) 1 Jur NS 770.

12   See *Daly v Beckett* (1857) 24 Beav 114. As to mines see further para 947 post.

13   As to the statutory power to cut timber see para 989 post; and as to the statutory power to grant mining leases see para 843 ante.

14   A provision that a tenant for life is unimpeachable for waste expresses an intention excluding the general rule that the price of land carried away and sold in the shape of minerals, stones or bricks is treated as capital: see *Re Ridge, Hellard v Moody* (1885) 31 ChD 504 at 508, CA; *Re Chaytor* [1900] 2 Ch 804 at 809. As to the position of a tenant for life in relation to waste see para 986 et seq post.

15   See para 843 ante (capitalisation of part of mining rent), para 947 post (mining royalties), and para 990 post (as regards timber).

16   As to the rights of the tenant for life in such a case see para 946 post.

945. Income of unauthorised investments pending sale. If, under a disposition by will of residuary personal estate, personal property[1], not being an authorised investment[2], is held on trust to be converted[3] and the proceeds are given in trust for persons entitled in succession, the general rule, which is always subject to a contrary intention found on the true construction of the will[4], is that, if the property is retained unconverted without impropriety for the benefit of the trust, the person entitled to the life interest in the proceeds of sale is not entitled to the income of the property pending conversion but only to interest, conventionally at 4 per cent[5], on the value of the property[6]. It seems that this principle[7] does not apply to a settlement of personalty by deed in the absence of any express trust for conversion[8]. The principle never applied to a residuary gift of real estate by will[9], and does not now apply to leaseholds with an unexpired term of more than 60 years[10], but it continues to apply to a residuary gift of pure personalty[11]. Where in the will there is a trust for sale with power to postpone sale or to retain investments unconverted, the tenant for life is ordinarily only entitled to interest on the capital value[12], but the will may well show an intention that the tenant for life should have the income[13]. The principle does not apply where the trust for sale does not arise until the death of the life tenant[14], and the position is the same where the consent of the life tenant is necessary for a sale in his lifetime[15]. If there is no trust for sale and unauthorised investments are retained under a power, the tenant for life is entitled to the income[16].

Where unauthorised investments which are to be sold are retained without impropriety for realisation, there should be an apportionment, subject to any contrary provision in the will, between income and capital[17].

If the unauthorised investments have been made by trustees in breach of trust, and the trustees make good the breach, the remainderman is not entitled to an adjustment limiting any interest received by the life tenant to 4 per cent, since no loss has been sustained[18]. However, if in such circumstances there has been depreciation, the life tenant, although not a party to the breach of trust, is not entitled to any adjustment to make good any arrears of income unless he brings into account such income from the unauthorised investments as he has received[19].

1   Although there is no difference for the purposes of the rule in *Howe v Earl of Dartmouth* (1802) 7 Ves 137 (as to which see EXECUTORS AND ADMINISTRATORS) between unauthorised investments of a permanent nature and of a wasting nature (*Re Nicholson, Eade v Nicholson* [1909] 2 Ch 111), yet, where trust property is of a wasting nature, realisation of it is necessary if it is to be enjoyed by persons beneficially entitled in succession. For this reason the first part of the rule in *Howe v Earl of Dartmouth* supra imposed an obligation to realise wasting property, and accordingly the tenant for life was entitled only to interest on the sum realised: see *Meyer v Simonsen* (1852) 5 De G & Sm 723; *Stroud v Gwyer* (1860) 28 Beav 130; *Brown v Gellatly* (1867) 2 Ch App 751.

2   See *Brown v Gellatly* (1867) 2 Ch App 751.

3   This applies even if the will contains a power to postpone conversion: see the text and notes 12–13 infra. The position is the same whether the will contains an express trust for conversion (*Dimes v Scott* (1828) 4 Russ 195) or the obligation for conversion arises by reason of the first part of the rule in *Howe v Earl of Dartmouth* (1802) 7 Ves 137 (see note 1 supra). Both *Howe v Earl of Dartmouth* supra and *Meyer v Simonsen* (1852) 5 De G & Sm 723 were cases where there was no express trust for conversion.

4   See eg *Scholefield v Redfern* (1863) 2 Drew & Sm 173; *Thursby v Thursby* (1875) LR 19 Eq 395. Commonly, the principle stated here is excluded by express provision that income of property until conversion is to be applied as income arising from the proceeds of sale: see eg *Morley v Mendham* (1856) 2 Jur NS 998; *Re Norrington, Brindley v Partridge* (1879) 13 ChD 654, CA; *Re Sherry, Sherry v Sherry* [1913] 2 Ch 508. For an example where the contrary intention was not made out see *Re Evans' Will Trusts, Pickering v Evans* [1921] 2 Ch 309.

5   The general practice has been to allow interest at 4% per annum, but this is not a universal rule: see *Gibson v Bott* (1802) 7 Ves 89; *Meyer v Simonsen* (1852) 5 De G & Sm 723; *Brown v Gellatly* (1867) 2 Ch App 751; *Wentworth v Wentworth* [1900] AC 163, PC; *Re Woods, Gabellini v Woods* [1904] 2 Ch 4; *Re Beech, Saint v Beech* [1920] 1 Ch 40; *Re Baker, Baker v Public Trustee* [1924] 2 Ch 271; *Re Ellis, Nettleton v Crimmins* [1935] Ch 193; *Re Fawcett, Public Trustee v Dugdale* [1940] Ch 402 at 407; *Re Parry, Brown v Parry* [1947] Ch 23, [1946] 2 All ER 412. See also *Bartlett v Barclays Bank Trust Co Ltd (No 2)* [1980] Ch 515, [1980] 2 All ER 92. As to rates of interest generally see MONEY.

6   *Meyer v Simonsen* (1852) 5 De G & Sm 723; *Brown v Gellatly* (1867) 2 Ch App 751. See also *Wentworth v Wentworth* [1900] AC 163 at 171, HL, per Lord Macnaghten; *Re Oliver, Wilson v Oliver* [1908] 2 Ch 74 at 78. For general consideration of the rule see *Re Fawcett, Public Trustee v Dugdale* [1940] Ch 402; and EXECUTORS AND ADMINISTRATORS.

7   The principle is referred to as the second part of the rule in *Howe v Earl of Dartmouth* (1802) 7 Ves 137 or, where there is a trust for conversion, as the rule in *Dimes v Scott* (1828) 4 Russ 195: see EXECUTORS AND ADMINISTRATORS.

8   *Re Van Straubenzee, Boustead v Cooper* [1901] 2 Ch 779. See also *Milford v Peile* (1854) as reported in 2 WR 181; *Hope v Hope* (1855) 1 Jur NS 770; *Slade v Chaine* [1908] 1 Ch 522 at 533, CA.

9   See *Re Woodhouse* [1941] Ch 332, [1941] 2 All ER 265. See also EXECUTORS AND ADMINISTRATORS.

10   See *Re Gough, Phillips v Simpson* [1957] Ch 323, [1957] 2 All ER 193.

11   *Re Trollope's Will Trusts, Public Trustee v Trollope* [1927] 1 Ch 596.

12   *Re Chaytor, Chaytor v Horn* [1905] 1 Ch 233; *Re Beech, Saint v Beech* [1920] 1 Ch 40; *Re Berry, Lloyds Bank Ltd v Berry* [1962] Ch 97, [1961] 1 All ER 529. As to the rate of interest see note 5 supra.

13   See *Re Sheldon, Nixon v Sheldon* (1888) 39 ChD 50 (power to continue investments); *Re Thomas, Wood v Thomas* [1891] 3 Ch 482; *Re Inman, Inman v Inman* [1915] 1 Ch 187. As regards bequests of businesses see *Re Chancellor, Chancellor v Brown* (1884) 26 ChD 42, CA; *Re Elford, Elford v Elford* [1910] 1 Ch 814. See also TRUSTS vol 48 (Reissue) para 634.

14   *Alcock v Sloper* (1833) 2 My & K 699. See also *Green v Britten* (1863) 1 De GJ & Sm 649, as explained in *Brown v Gellatly* (1867) 2 Ch App 751 at 757.

15   *Re Rogers, Public Trustee v Rogers* [1915] 2 Ch 437.

16 *Re Wilson, Moore v Wilson* [1907] 1 Ch 394; *Re Nicholson, Eade v Nicholson* [1909] 2 Ch 111.

17 See eg *Re Owen, Slater v Owen* [1912] 1 Ch 519; and EXECUTORS AND ADMINISTRATORS. Income tax at the basic rate is deductible in the computation of what sum put out at 4% interest will amount to the actual annual product: see *Re Hengler, Frowde v Hengler* [1893] 1 Ch 586. As to the rate of interest see note 5 supra.

18 *Stroud v Gwyer* (1860) 28 Beav 130; *Re Appleby, Walker v Lever, Walker v Nisbet* [1903] 1 Ch 565 at 566, CA; *Slade v Chaine* [1908] 1 Ch 522, CA, distinguishing *Re Hill, Hill v Hill* (1881) 50 LJ Ch 551. The rule stated here applies even where the same person is both the trustee and the tenant for life: *Re Hoyles, Row v Jagg (No 2)* [1912] 1 Ch 67. As to the rate of interest see note 5 supra.

19 *Re Bird, Re Evan Dodd v Evans* [1901] 1 Ch 916, cited in *Re Alston, Alston v Houston* [1901] 2 Ch 584.

946. Apportionment of amount realised on sale. Where under a residuary gift contained in a will personal property that has not been bearing income is held on trust for sale but, without impropriety, has not been sold, the tenant for life is entitled to a proportion of the capital when it is received[1]. This principle is the corollary of the rule previously discussed[2], and, like it, does not apply to realty[3] and yields to the expression of a contrary intention in the will[4]. The principle does not apply to a settlement which does not contain a trust for conversion[5].

If an authorised security proves insufficient on realisation to meet both arrears of income and capital, the amount realised should be apportioned[6], unless the settlement otherwise provides, between income and capital, so that the loss falls fairly on both[7]. Until realisation of the security the tenant for life is generally entitled to the income[8] and, in the case of dividends from shares, is normally entitled to dividends declared during his lifetime[9].

However, where interest, as and when it is credited, is capitalised under agreement, in effect, between the person acquiring a security and the borrower, and is payable ultimately with the capital, the accretions arising before but paid after the testator's death are capital as between the remainderman and the tenant for life[10].

1 *Re Earl of Chesterfield's Trusts* (1883) 24 ChD 643. See further EXECUTORS AND ADMINISTRATORS.

2 Ie the rule in *Howe v Earl of Dartmouth* (1802) 7 Ves 137 at 148: see para 945 ante. It is, indeed, a branch of that rule: see *Re Hey's Settlement Trusts, Hey v Nickell-Lean* [1945] Ch 294 at 315, [1945] 1 All ER 618 at 627 per Cohen J.

3 *Re Woodhouse, Public Trustee v Woodhouse* [1941] Ch 332, [1941] 2 All ER 265.

4 See eg *Re Lewis, Davies v Harrison* [1907] 2 Ch 296 where the will contained a clause that property not actually producing income was not to be treated as producing income, but the clause did not apply to the property in question as the income was produced and only its payment had been postponed.

5 *Re Van Straubenzee, Boustead v Cooper* [1901] 2 Ch 779.

6 Where a receiver was in possession of a mortgaged colliery, the proceeds of working the colliery, as and when received, were apportioned between capital and income, the apportionment being made by computing what sum put out at 4% interest at the testator's death would amount to the proceeds received: *Re Godden, Teague v Fox* [1893] 1 Ch 292. As to the rate of interest see para 945 note 5 ante.

7 *Re Moore, Moore v Johnson* (1885) 54 LJ Ch 432; *Re Alston, Alston v Houston* [1901] 2 Ch 584; *Re Atkinson, Barbers' Co v Grose-Smith* [1904] 2 Ch 160, CA; *Re Walker's Settlement Trusts, Watson v Walker* [1936] Ch 280; *Re Morris's Will Trusts, Public Trustee v Morris* [1960] 3 All ER 548, [1960] 1 WLR 1210. A provision that property not actually producing income should not be treated as producing any income does not exclude this apportionment: *Re Hubbuck, Hart v Stone* [1896] 1 Ch 754, CA.

8 *Re Broadwood's Settlements, Broadwood v Broadwood* [1908] 1 Ch 115; *Re Coaks, Coaks v Bayley* [1911] 1 Ch 171.

9 See *Re Sale, Nisbet v Philp* [1913] 2 Ch 697 at 703; and para 950 post.

10 See *Re Holder, National Provincial Bank Ltd v Holder* [1953] Ch 468, [1953] 2 All ER 1 (national savings certificates), in which such accretions were capital, despite a direction that no part of any interest received after the testator's death should be treated as capital.

(ii) Particular Receipts

947. Mines and minerals. Apart from statute, the general principle is that, as between tenant for life and remainderman, the price of minerals[1] gotten that is paid by a mining lessee is capital, as it is paid in respect of a part of the land that is carried away and sold; however, this rule yields to an expression of contrary intention in the settlement and, if the mines were open mines when they were settled, such a contrary intention is inferred unless the inference is excluded by the settlement[2]. Accordingly the tenant for life of a settled estate, where mines were opened[3], or contracted to be leased[4], by the settlor, is entitled to royalties payable in respect of minerals gotten; and the same applies where the mines were demised by trustees of the settlement in exercise of a power of leasing given by the settlor[5]. Subject to statute, the principle extends to stone[6], brickfields[7] and gravel[8].

A tenant for life impeachable for waste was not entitled to open new mines although he had the right to work open mines[9].

However, where the statutory power of granting mining leases[10] is exercised[11], a fraction of the rent[12] must be set aside as capital, whether the mines were or were not already worked, unless a contrary intention is expressed in the settlement[13].

1   The principle extends equally to stone and brick earth: *Re Ridge, Hellard v Moody* (1885) 31 ChD 504, CA.
2   *Re Ridge, Hellard v Moody* (1885) 31 ChD 504 at 508, CA; *Re Chaytor* [1900] 2 Ch 804 at 809 (the exception with regard to open mines rests on inference of the settlor's intention). The tenant for life is entitled to whatever the settlor, as owner in fee, would have taken as income, including the dead rent and royalties: *Re Kemeys-Tynte, Kemeys-Tynte v Kemeys-Tynte* [1892] 2 Ch 211 at 215. As to the meaning of 'open mines' see MINES, MINERALS AND QUARRIES vol 31 (Reissue) paras 7–11.
3   See *Brigstocke v Brigstocke* (1878) 8 ChD 357 at 363, CA; *Re Canner, Bury v Canner* (1923) 155 LT Jo 211.
4   *Re Kemeys-Tynte, Kemeys-Tynte v Kemeys-Tynte* [1892] 2 Ch 211.
5   *Daly v Beckett* (1857) 24 Beav 114 at 123.
6   See *Re Ridge, Hellard v Moody* (1885) 31 ChD 504 at 508, CA, per Lindley LJ; *Leppington v Freeman* (1891) 40 WR 348, CA.
7   *Miller v Miller* (1872) LR 13 Eq 263; *Leppington v Freeman* (1891) 40 WR 348, CA; *Re North, Garton v Cumberland* [1909] 1 Ch 625.
8   *Earl of Cowley v Wellesley* (1866) LR 1 Eq 656.
9   As to this aspect of the doctrine of waste see para 987 post.
10   Ie the power conferred by the Settled Land Act 1925 s 41(ii): see paras 837–839, 843 ante.
11   As to the position where the tenant for life has an express power of leasing see *Earl Lonsdale v Lowther* [1900] 2 Ch 687.
12   For the meaning of 'rent' see para 801 note 1 ante.
13   See the Settled Land Act 1925 s 47; and para 843 ante.

948. Damages for breach of lessee's covenants. Money, not being rent, received since 1925[1] by way of damages or compensation for breach of any covenant[2] by a lessee or grantee contained in any lease[3] or grant of settled land[4], whenever the lease or grant was made and whether it was made under the statutory powers or not, unless in any case the court[5] on the application of the tenant for life[6] or the trustees of the settlement[7] otherwise directs, is deemed to be capital money arising under the Settled Land Act 1925[8] and must be paid to or retained by the trustees of the settlement, or paid into court[9], and invested or applied, accordingly[10].

1   Before 1926 damages paid by a lessee to a tenant for life, unimpeachable for waste, for breach of repairing covenants in a lease of settled land belonged to the tenant for life and were not capital money: see *Re Lacon's Settlement, Lacon v Lacon* [1911] 2 Ch 17, CA, where the lease had been granted in 1888 by a predecessor in title. As to the liability of the tenant for life for waste see para 986 et seq post.
2   As to damages recoverable from a lessee for breach of covenants see LANDLORD AND TENANT vol 27(1) (Reissue) para 368 et seq.
3   For the meaning of 'lease' see para 685 note 13 ante.
4   For the meaning of 'settled land' see para 680 text to note 2 ante.

5   As to applications to the court see paras 792–793 ante.
6   For the meaning of 'tenant for life' see para 671 note 5 ante. See also para 761 et seq ante.
7   For the meaning of 'trustees of the settlement' see para 750 note 1 ante. As to the trustees see para 750 et seq ante.
8   As to capital money arising under the Settled Land Act 1925 see para 795 ante.
9   As to the payment of money into court see para 798 note 8 ante.
10   See the Settled Land Act 1925 s 80(1), (5). See also s 80(4), (6); and para 801 ante. As to the application of fire insurance money where the settled land was leased see *Mumford Hotels Ltd v Wheler* [1964] Ch 117, [1963] 3 All ER 250.

949. Consideration for accepting surrender of leases. Since 1925[1] all money, not being rent[2] or a rentcharge, received on the exercise by a tenant for life[3] of the statutory power to accept a surrender[4], unless the court[5], on an application made within six months after its receipt or within such further time as the court may in special circumstances allow, otherwise directs[6], is capital money arising under the Settled Land Act 1925[7].

1   Before 1926 money paid to a legal tenant for life as the consideration for accepting the surrender of a lease by virtue of his common law powers belonged to him even if the lease surrendered had been granted under statutory power (*Re Hunloke's Settled Estates, Fitzroy v Hunloke* [1902] 1 Ch 941; *Re Penrhyn's Settlement, Lord Penrhyn v Pennant* [1922] 1 Ch 500); although, where a surrender was accepted by an equitable tenant for life, any consideration for it did not belong to him but had to be paid by instalments to him and the other persons entitled to the rent (*Re Rodes, Sanders v Hobson* [1909] 1 Ch 815). Under the law in force since 1925 the tenant for life is the legal reversioner in every case, but it seems that the effect of the Settled Land Act 1925 s 16(1)(i), which makes him an express trustee of the settled land (see para 767 ante), is to prevent him from exercising his common law powers so as to obtain any such consideration for himself.
2   For the meaning of 'rent' see para 801 note 1 ante. A tenant for life who in good faith accepts a surrender and grants a new lease at an increased rent is entitled to the increased rent during the unexpired part of the original term: see *Re Wix, Hardy v Lemon* [1916] 1 Ch 279.
3   For the meaning of 'tenant for life' see para 671 note 5 ante. See also para 761 et seq ante.
4   As to the power to accept such surrenders see para 859 ante.
5   As to applications to the court see paras 792–793 ante.
6   There appears to be no reported case in which the court has given such a direction, but as to the principles which it might be expected to apply in directing apportionment between capital and income see *Cottrell v Cottrell* (1885) 28 ChD 628; *Re Robinson's Settlement Trusts* [1891] 3 Ch 129; *Re Fullerton's Will* [1906] 2 Ch 138; *Re Duke of Westminster's Settled Estates, Duke of Westminster v Earl of Shaftesbury* [1921] 1 Ch 585 (transaction regarded as cross-sales and purchase of the surrendered leases).
7   See the Settled Land Act 1925 s 52(7); and para 859 ante. For the meaning of 'capital money arising under the Act' see para 795 ante.

950. Income of stocks and shares. If stocks or shares of a public company[1] are settled, the tenant for life is entitled to all dividends declared out of current profits in respect of any period commencing and ending[2] during the continuance of his interest at whatever rate[3], and whether described as extraordinary or special dividends[4] or bonuses[5]. His rights to the entire dividend declared are not affected by the fact that the profits out of which the dividend is declared include money received by the company in respect of an old debt[6], or profits made in past years which have been put by under the name of a reserve fund[7], or that the amount declared covers arrears of a cumulative dividend[8]. Moreover, where during the continuance of a life interest arrears of dividend are satisfied by, for example, an issue of funding certificates or shares or other property, the tenant for life is entitled to the property so issued[9].

Conversely, a tenant for life is not entitled to any part of dividends declared in a financial year of the company that falls wholly after his death, as there is no right to a dividend until it is declared[10]. Therefore, where preference shares carried a right to a cumulative preferential dividend as and when the directors decided that one should be declared and the tenant for life of the shares died while the preference dividends were in arrear, all future dividends (including any that might cover the arrears) in respect of periods after the death of the tenant for life belonged to the remainderman[11]. The position is the same where preference shares carry a right to a fixed cumulative preferential dividend and, no dividends having been paid for some years before the death of the tenant for life, dividends are paid in financial years after his death to meet the arrears[12].

In general, a limited company that is not in liquidation cannot, except by reduction of capital, return capital to shareholders, and accordingly other distributions are by way of dividing profits, so that, when these are paid to the trustees of settled shares, they are received as income[13], but other considerations apply where there is an increase of capital by way of capitalisation of profits[14]. In accordance with these principles, proper distributions of surplus assets to shareholders prior to the liquidation of a company are usually income[15], and, where trustees sell stock inflated in value by a contingent right to receive an income payment, the existence of such right makes the price in the hands of the trustees partially an income receipt[16]. However, a distribution out of money standing to the credit of a company's share premium account is to be regarded as a payment made in reduction of capital[17].

Distributions to shareholders made in the liquidation of a limited company are capital[18].

Where units in a fixed investment trust are settled, the trustees must inquire into the source of all distributions distributed by the investment trust as capital distributions, and must treat them as capital or income as if the trustees were the holders of the shares from which the sums distributed are derived[19].

Where shares have been purchased in breach of trust there is jurisdiction to apportion whatever may have been received by way of dividend distribution, or to allocate it to capital, so that beneficial rights are not altered[20].

1   See *Re White, Theobald v White* [1913] 1 Ch 231. As to stocks and shares of public companies see COMPANIES vol 7(1) (1996 Reissue) para 173 et seq.
2   See generally *Re Armitage, Armitage v Garnett* [1893] 3 Ch 337 at 346, CA, applied in *Re Sale, Nisbet v Philip* [1913] 2 Ch 697. As to the apportionment of dividends under the Apportionment Act 1870 see paras 957–960 post.
3   *Barclay v Wainewright* (1807) 14 Ves 66; *Price v Anderson* (1847) 15 Sim 473.
4   *Re Hopkins' Trusts* (1874) LR 18 Eq 696.
5   *Preston v Melville* (1848) 16 Sim 163; *Johnson v Johnson* (1850) 15 Jur 714; *Hebert v Bateman* (1853) 1 WR 191; *Murray v Glasse* (1853) 23 LJ Ch 126; *Plumbe v Neild* (1860) 29 LJ Ch 618; *Dale v Hayes* (1871) 40 LJ Ch 244. Cf *Re Tedlie, Holt v Croker* (1922) 91 LJ Ch 346.
6   *Maclaren v Stainton* (1861) 3 De GF & J 202; *Edmondson v Crosthwaite* (1864) 34 Beav 30.
7   *Re Alsbury, Sugden v Alsbury* (1890) 45 ChD 237; *Re Northage, Ellis v Barfield* (1891) 60 LJ Ch 488. As to reserve funds see COMPANIES vol 7(1) (1996 Reissue) para 728.
8   *Re Wakley, Wakley v Vachell* [1920] 2 Ch 205, CA; *Re Marjoribanks, Marjoribanks v Dansey* [1923] 2 Ch 307; *Re Joel, Johnson v Joel* [1936] 2 All ER 962. Cf *First Garden City Ltd v Bonham-Carter* [1928] Ch 53. As to cumulative dividends see COMPANIES vol 7(1) (1996 Reissue) para 717.
9   *Re Pennington, Stevens v Pennington* [1915] WN 333; *Re Sandbach, Royds v Douglas* [1933] Ch 505; *Re MacIver's Settlement, MacIver v Rae* [1936] Ch 198; *Re Smith's Will Trusts* [1936] 2 All ER 1210. However, a cash bonus paid in consideration of a release of preferential rights in respect of capital has been held to be capital: *Bates v Mackinley* (1862) 31 Beav 280; *Re Tedlie, Holt v Croker* (1922) 91 LJ Ch 346.
10   However, it may be that, on the true construction of the testator's will and having regard to special circumstances of the distribution, a distribution of compensation stock by way of capital profits dividend declared after the testator's death in respect of a date during his lifetime will be capital of his estate: see *Re Winder's Will Trusts, Westminster Bank Ltd v Fausset* [1951] Ch 916 at 921, [1951] 2 All ER 362 at 365 per Romer J. Cf *Manclark v Thomson's Trustees* 1958 SC 147. So, too, when a tenant for life has consented to a capital investment of trust funds by purchasing shares in a company which proposes to distribute stock that it has received by way of compensation, the tenant for life will fail, by reason of his prior consent, to make good a claim based on the principle that the distribution of the stock by the company is a distribution of income: see *Re Maclaren's Settlement Trusts, Royal Exchange Assurance v Maclaren* [1951] 2 All ER 414.

11   *Re Sale, Nisbet v Philp* [1913] 2 Ch 697, applying *Re Taylor's Trusts, Matheson v Taylor* [1905] 1 Ch 734. See also *Re Marjoribanks, Marjoribanks v Dansey* [1923] 2 Ch 307, where arrears of cumulated preference dividend (some of which had accrued before the testatrix's death) paid after her death were held to pass as income of her residuary estate.

12   *Re Grundy, Grundy v Holme* (1917) 117 LT 470; *Re Wakley, Wakley v Vachell* [1920] 2 Ch 205, CA.

13   See *Re Bates, Mountain v Bates* [1928] Ch 682; *Hill v Permanent Trustee Co of New South Wales Ltd* [1930] AC 720 at 731, PC; *Re Doughty, Burridge v Doughty* [1947] Ch 263 at 270, [1947] 1 All ER 207 at 211, CA, per Cohen LJ; *Re Harrison's Will Trusts, Re Harrison's Settlement, Harrison v Milborne-Swinnerton-Pilkington* [1949] Ch 678. The fact that a company describes an income distribution as being capital does not alter its nature: see *Re Doughty, Burridge v Doughty* supra at 272 and 212 per Morton LJ; *Re Morris's Will Trusts, Public Trustee v Morris* [1960] 3 All ER 548, [1960] 1 WLR 1210.

14   *Hill v Permanent Trustee Co of New South Wales Ltd* [1930] AC 720 at 731, PC. As to the effect of capitalisation of profits see para 951 post.

15   See *Re Palmer, Palmer v Cassel* (1912) 28 TLR 301; *Re Tedlie, Holt v Croker* (1922) 91 LJ Ch 346. The following group of cases arose out of the distribution, as 'capital profits dividend', of a sum of British Transport Stock issued to a company as compensation on nationalisation: *Re Sechiari, Argenti v Sechiari* [1950] 1 All ER 417 (distribution treated as income); *Re Kleinwort's Settlements, Westminster Bank Ltd v Bennett* [1951] Ch 860, [1951] 2 All ER 328; *Re Rudd's Will Trusts, Wort v Rudd* [1952] 1 All ER 254.

16   See *Thomson's Trustees v Thomson* 1955 SC 476 (where trustees sold stock with the right attached to it, by resolution of the company, to receive a sum of government stock to be distributed by way of capital profits dividend to which the tenant for life would have been entitled (see note 10 supra) if the stock had not been sold). *Thomson's Trustees v Thomson* supra was distinguished in *Manclark v Thomson's Trustees* 1958 SC 147, where the settlement was by will and the resolution had been passed before the testator's death.

17   See the Companies Act 1985 s 130; and COMPANIES vol 7(1) (1996 Reissue) para 188. See also *Re Duff's Settlements, National Provincial Bank Ltd v Gregson* [1951] 1 Ch 923, [1951] 2 All ER 534, CA.

18   *Nicholson v Nicholson* (1861) 30 LJ Ch 617; *Re Armitage, Armitage v Garnett* [1893] 3 Ch 337, CA; *Re Palmer, Palmer v Cassel* (1912) 28 TLR 301; *IRC v Burrell* [1924] 2 KB 52, CA; *Hill v Permanent Trustee Co of New South Wales Ltd* [1930] AC 720 at 729, PC. Cf *Re Pennington, Pennington v Pennington* [1914] 1 Ch 203, CA, where payments made in respect of debenture interest in a winding up were income. As to the apportionment of mortgage interest see para 982 post.

19   *Re Whitehead's Will Trusts, Public Trustee v White* [1959] Ch 579, [1959] 2 All ER 497. As to fixed investment trusts see STOCK EXCHANGE.

20   See *Re Maclaren's Settlement Trusts, Royal Exchange Assurance v Maclaren* [1951] 2 All ER 414 at 420 per Harman J; *Re Kleinwort's Settlements, Westminster Bank Ltd v Bennett* [1951] Ch 860 at 963, [1951] 2 All ER 328 at 330 per Vaisey J; *Re Rudd's Will Trusts, Wort v Rudd* [1952] 1 All ER 254 at 258–259 per Upjohn J.

951. Effect of capitalisation of profits. A company which has the power of increasing its capital[1] can either distribute its profits as dividend or convert them into capital, and, if the company validly exercises this power, that exercise is binding on all persons interested under the testator or settlor in the shares, and consequently what is paid by the company as dividend goes to the tenant for life, and what is paid by the company to the shareholder as capital, or appropriated as an increase of the capital stock in the concern, enures to the benefit of all interested in the capital[2]. Accordingly, where a company having these powers issued new shares which represented a portion of its current earnings that had been applied to necessary works, those new shares were held to be capital[3]. Where a company declared a bonus dividend out of accumulated profits, and at the same time made an issue of new shares for a corresponding amount among its shareholders in proportion to the existing interests, and applied the bonus dividend in paying the calls on such new shares, undivided profits had been effectively appropriated and dealt with so as to become capital stock[4]. Also, where a trust held shares in a company, which underwent a demerger into two companies (the original company and the new company), the trust being issued with shares in the new company, the new shares were held to form part of the capital of the trust fund[5].

1   This power is possessed by all companies limited by shares or limited by guarantee and having a share
     capital, if authorised by their articles: see the Companies Act 1985 s 121(1), (2); and COMPANIES vol 7(1)
     (1996 Reissue) para 201 et seq. Formerly, where a bonus was distributed by a company as an
     extraordinary distribution out of profits and the company had no power to increase capital, the bonus
     (not being by way of increased dividend) was treated as a capital receipt: see eg *Paris v Paris* (1804) 10 Ves
     185; *Witts v Steere* (1807) 13 Ves 363; *Ward v Combe* (1836) 7 Sim 634.
2   *Bouch v Sproule* (1887) 12 App Cas 385, HL. If the company's intention to capitalise is clear, the fact that
     the shareholders have an option to take cash or new shares does not affect the position as between the
     tenant for life and the remainderman: *Re Evans, Jones v Evans* [1913] 1 Ch 23. If the option in such a case
     is vested in trustees, there is no right to elect between them and their beneficiaries and they must take the
     dividend in the capitalised form: *Re Evans, Jones v Evans* supra.
3   *Re Barton's Trust* (1868) LR 5 Eq 238.
4   *Baring v Lady Ashburton* (1868) 16 WR 452; *Bouch v Sproule* (1887) 12 App Cas 385, HL.
5   *Re Lee, Sinclair v Lee* [1993] Ch 497, [1993] 3 All ER 926.

952. Determination of question whether profits capitalised. A company has the
power to determine conclusively against the world whether or not it will capitalise its
profits[1], and it is a question of fact in each case whether a company has or has not done
so. Regard must be had to both the form and the substance of the transaction[2], and a
statement by a company that the distribution is one of capital will be ineffective if the
company has not taken the necessary steps to effect a capitalisation[3]. Where a company
has power to increase its capital and appropriate its profits to such increase, it cannot be
considered as having converted any part of its profits into capital when it has made no
such increase[4]. It follows that the mere carrying over of profits by such a company to a
reserve fund[5] or suspense account[6], or the temporary devotion of them to capital
purposes[7], does not suffice to convert them into capital. Distributions out of profits by
way of redemption of subscribed capital of a company are capital[8], unless such payments
are invalid by reason of failure on the part of the company to observe the necessary
formalities, in which case they belong as income to the tenant for life[9].

If an option is given to the shareholder to take either a cash dividend or shares, the
court determines from the scheme as a whole whether the profits dealt with are or are
not capitalised[10]. However, in the latter case the tenant for life is not entitled to the entire
value of the shares allotted in respect of dividend, but only to so much of the proceeds of
realisation of such shares as represent the dividend, and the balance ought to be applied
as capital[11].

If the settlement contains an express declaration that bonuses are to be treated as
income or as capital, the rights of the tenant for life are governed by the declaration[12].

1   *IRC v Blott, IRC v Greenwood* [1921] 2 AC 171, HL; *IRC v Fisher's Executors* [1926] AC 395, HL; *Re
     Taylor, Waters v Taylor* [1926] Ch 923; *IRC v Wright* [1927] 1 KB 333, CA. Cf *Re Schopperle's Trusts*
     [1932] IR 457, where it was held that a similar determination by a foreign government was binding as
     between the tenant for life and remaindermen. See also COMPANIES vol 7(1) (1996 Reissue) para 732.
2   *Bouch v Sproule* (1887) 12 App Cas 385, HL; *Re Malam, Malam v Hitchens* [1894] 3 Ch 578 at 585. In
     determining the question the surrounding circumstances must be considered: *Re Joel, Johnson v Joel* [1936]
     2 All ER 962.
3   See para 950 note 13 ante.
4   *Bouch v Sproule* (1887) 12 App Cas 385 at 398, HL.
5   *Re Alsbury, Sugden v Alsbury* (1890) 45 ChD 237; *Re Thomas, Andrew v Thomas* [1916] 2 Ch 331, CA. As
     to reserve funds see COMPANIES vol 7(1) (1996 Reissue) para 728.
6   *Re Bates, Mountain v Bates* [1928] Ch 682.
7   *Bouch v Sproule* (1887) 12 App Cas 385 at 401, HL; *Re Lord Alfred Paget, Listowel v Paget* (1892) 9 TLR
     88. Cf para 951 note 1 ante.
8   *Re Lord Alfred Paget, Listowel v Paget* (1892) 9 TLR 88. Cf *Re Duff's Settlements, National Provincial Bank
     Ltd v Gregson* [1951] Ch 923, [1951] 2 All ER 534, CA (distribution of sums from share premium
     account). See also para 950 ante.
9   *Re Piercy, Whitwham v Piercy* [1907] 1 Ch 289.

10 *Bouch v Sproule* (1887) 12 App Cas 385, HL; *Re Despard, Hancock v Despard* (1901) 17 TLR 478; *Blyth's Trustees v Milne* 1905 7 F (Ct of Sess) 799; *Re Evans, Jones v Evans* [1913] 1 Ch 23; *Re Hatton, Hockin v Hatton* [1917] 1 Ch 357; *Re Taylor, Waters v Taylor* [1926] Ch 923; *IRC v Wright* [1927] 1 KB 333, CA. See also para 951 note 2 ante. See further COMPANIES vol 7(1) (1996 Reissue) para 717 et seq.

11 *Re Northage, Ellis v Barfield* (1891) 60 LJ Ch 488; *Re Tindal* (1892) 9 TLR 24; *Re Hume Nisbet's Settlement* (1911) 27 TLR 461. See also *Rowley v Unwin* (1855) 2 K & J 138.

12 *Re Mittam's Settlement Trusts* (1858) 4 Jur NS 1077. Cf *Plunkett v Mansfield* (1845) 2 Jo & Lat 344. The court may decide as a question of construction that bonuses paid out of current profits are not within a proviso in the settlement for the capitalisation of bonuses: *Hollis v Allan* (1866) 14 WR 980; *Re Baker, Ruddock v Baker* (1891) 8 TLR 7. In *Re Speir, Holt v Speir* [1924] 1 Ch 359, CA, it was held that a trust to pay the 'dividends, bonuses and income' of settled shares to a tenant for life did not cover a capital bonus. Cf *Re Wright's Settlement Trusts, Wright v Wright* [1945] Ch 211, [1945] 1 All ER 587.

953. Options to take shares. Unless a settlement contains an express clause authorising the trustees to relinquish in favour of the tenant for life any preferential right to take new shares in a company that may accrue to them in respect of settled shares, they must exercise their option to take new shares on behalf of all their beneficiaries, and such new shares or any money received by sale of the option or the shares are capital[1]. If the calls on the new shares are paid out of income, the tenant for life has a lien on them for the amount so paid[2].

1 *Rowley v Unwin* (1855) 2 K & J 138; *Re Bromley, Sanders v Bromley* (1886) 55 LT 145; *Re Curtis, Hawes v Curtis* (1885) 1 TLR 332; *Re Malam, Malam v Hitchens* [1894] 3 Ch 578 at 586–587. See also the Trustee Act 1925 s 10(3)(bb) (as added), (4); and TRUSTS vol 48 (Reissue) para 885. As to options to take shares see COMPANIES vol 7(1) (1996 Reissue) para 377.

2 *Rowley v Unwin* (1855) 2 K & J 138. If money is advanced by the tenant for life, at the request of the trustees, for payment of calls or shares, he has a lien on the shares for the repayment of the amount advanced with interest: *Todd v Moorhouse* (1874) LR 19 Eq 69. See further LIEN vol 28 (Reissue) para 771.

954. Directors' fees accounted for by trustees. Where trustees are accountable to the trust for remuneration as directors of a company in which they hold shares subject to the trust, as they are where their appointment as directors was procured by virtue of the settled shares[1], and they are not exempted from liability to account by the terms of the settlement[2], the sums accounted for are capital and not income[3].

1 *Re Francis, Barrett v Fisher* (1905) 74 LJ Ch 198; *Re Macadam, Dallow v Codd* [1946] Ch 73, [1945] 2 All ER 664. It is otherwise where the remuneration is received by the trustee independently of any use made by him of the trust holding: *Re Dover Coalfield Extension Ltd* [1908] 1 Ch 65, CA, as explained in *Re Gee, Wood v Staples* [1948] Ch 284, [1948] 1 All ER 498. See further TRUSTS vol 48 (Reissue) para 810.

2 Cf *Re Llewellin's Will Trusts, Griffiths v Wilcox* [1949] Ch 225, [1949] 1 All ER 487.

3 *Re Francis, Barrett v Fisher* (1905) 74 LJ Ch 198.

955. Partnerships. If a share in a partnership business is settled, or if settled funds are properly employed in a partnership business, the question what is income and what is capital must be determined by the articles of partnership, and all that is divided between the partners as profit goes to the tenant for life[1]. What is properly retained as capital in the business is treated as capital, and belongs to the remainderman, only the interest on it being payable to the tenant for life[2]. Where a tenant for life is entitled to the profits arising from a business carried on by the trustees, they may be justified in deducting a reasonable and proper annual sum for depreciation[3].

1 *Stroud v Gwyer* (1860) 28 Beav 130; *Browne v Collins* (1871) LR 12 Eq 586; *Gow v Forster* (1884) 26 ChD 672; *Re Robbins, Midland Bank Executor and Trustee Co Ltd v Melville* [1941] Ch 434, [1941] 2 All ER 601. As to shares in partnerships see PARTNERSHIP vol 35 (Reissue) para 109 et seq.

2 *Stroud v Gwyer* (1860) 28 Beav 130; *Straker v Wilson* (1871) 6 Ch App 503; *Re Robbins, Midland Bank Executor and Trustee Co Ltd v Melville* [1941] Ch 434, [1941] 2 All ER 601.

3 *Re Crabtree, Thomas v Crabtree* (1911) 106 LT 49, CA.

956. Right to emblements. Where a tenant for life has sown the land for crops which usually repay the sowing within the year, and dies before he has obtained the advantage of his expense and labour, his personal representatives are entitled to take the crops as emblements[1]. However, he is not entitled to emblements if his estate determines in his lifetime by his own act[2].

1   Co Litt 55b. The sowing must be by or at the expense of the tenant for life himself: *Grantham v Hawley* (1615) Hob 132; 9 Vin Abr 369, Emblements (17). As to emblements generally see AGRICULTURE vol 1(2) (Reissue) para 382; EXECUTORS AND ADMINISTRATORS.

2   Eg where a widow, who holds during widowhood, remarries: *Oland's Case* (1602) 5 Co Rep 116a, Co Litt 55b.

(2) APPORTIONMENT IN RESPECT OF TIME

957. In general. Unless the settlement expressly stipulates[1] that no apportionment is to take place[2], all rents, annuities, dividends and other periodical payments in the nature of income are considered as accruing from day to day, and on the cesser of the interest of the tenant for life by death or otherwise[3] are apportionable accordingly[4] between him or his personal representatives and the remainderman[5].

Accordingly, whenever there are periodical payments accruing when the event calling for apportionment occurs, the Apportionment Act 1870[6] must be applied, and when subsequently the accruing payments become due they must be distributed accordingly, the portion attributable to the period before the death of a tenant for life being payable to his estate[7]. Moreover, if an investment on which a dividend is so accruing is transferred by trustees to a person absolutely entitled before the dividend is paid, the estate of the deceased tenant for life still remains entitled to the portion accruing prior to his death, and some arrangement should be made to secure payment to the estate of that amount[8].

1   It seems that the express stipulation must be found in the will or other instrument of gift: *Re Oppenheimer, Oppenheimer v Boatman* [1907] 1 Ch 399.

2   See the Apportionment Act 1870 s 7; and RENTCHARGES AND ANNUITIES vol 39(2) (Reissue) para 840. There must either be an express direction against apportionment or terms of gifts so clear as necessarily to exclude apportionment; an inference to be collected from the general terms of the will is not sufficient (*Tyrrell v Clark* (1854) 2 Drew 86, decided on similar language in the Apportionment Act 1834 s 3 (repealed)); and neither is a clause drafted with reference to the rule in *Howe v Earl of Dartmouth, Howe v Countess of Aylesbury* (1802) 7 Ves 137 (see para 945 note 1 ante), and plainly directed only to the exclusion of that rule (see *Re Edwards, Newbery v Edwards* [1918] 1 Ch 142). For examples of 'express stipulations' see *Re Duke of Cleveland's Estate, Viscount Wolmer v Forester* [1894] 1 Ch 164, CA; *Re Lysaght, Lysaght v Lysaght* [1898] 1 Ch 115, CA; *Re Meredith, Stone v Meredith* (1898) 67 LJ Ch 409; *Macpherson's Trustees v Macpherson* 1907 SC 1067; *Re Jenkins, Williams v Jenkins* [1915] 1 Ch 46.

3   *Re Jenkins, Williams v Jenkins* [1915] 1 Ch 46. Income applicable under the Trustee Act 1925 s 31 (see para 667 ante; and CHILDREN AND YOUNG PERSONS vol 5(2) (Reissue) para 666 et seq) for the benefit of a class is apportionable on an increase in that class, unless the settlement excludes such apportionment: *Re Joel's Will Trusts, Rogerson v Brudenell-Bruce* [1967] Ch 14, [1966] 2 All ER 482.

4   See the Apportionment Act 1870 s 2; and RENTCHARGES AND ANNUITIES vol 39(2) (Reissue) para 839. As to the sums liable to apportionment see para 958 post. Interest payable under what is now the Town and Country Planning Act 1990 on compensation for depreciation of land values (see TOWN AND COUNTRY PLANNING vol 46 (Reissue) para 697 et seq) is not apportionable: *Re Sneyd, Robertson-MacDonald v Sneyd* [1961] 1 All ER 744, [1961] 1 WLR 575. The apportionment of income involves an apportionment of outgoings in regard to that income: *Re Joel's Will Trusts, Rogerson v Brudenell-Bruce* [1967] Ch 14, [1966] 2 All ER 482.

5   *Re Clines' Estate* (1874) LR 18 Eq 213; *Pollock v Pollock* (1874) LR 18 Eq 329.

6   See para 958 post.

7   *Re Muirhead, Muirhead v Hill* [1916] 2 Ch 181 at 186; *Re Henderson, Public Trustee v Reddie* [1940] Ch 368 at 375, [1940] 1 All ER 623 at 626–627 per Morton J; *Re Winder's Will Trust, Westminster Bank Ltd v*

Fausset [1951] Ch 916 at 921, [1951] 2 All ER 362 at 366 per Romer J. See also *Pollock v Pollock* (1874) LR 18 Eq 329.

8   *Re Henderson, Public Trustee v Reddie* [1940] Ch 368 at 378, [1940] 1 All ER 623 at 628 per Morton J.

958. Sums liable to apportionment. Apportionment by virtue of the Apportionment Act 1870[1] takes place in respect of all rents[2], which includes rent service, rentcharge and rent seck, and all periodical payments or renderings in lieu of or in the nature of rent[3]. Apportionment also takes place in respect of annuities, which includes salaries or pensions[4], dividends on stock[5] and all payments made by the name of dividend, bonus or otherwise out of the revenue of trading or other public companies[6], whether such payments are usually made or declared at any fixed times or otherwise[7]. However, a payment will not be apportionable unless it is declared or expressed to be made for or in respect of some definite period[8].

Profits arising from a private trading partnership[9] or a newspaper carried on by trustees[10] are not apportionable. There is no apportionment in respect of any sum duly or properly paid or accruing due before the happening of the event which is said to require the apportionment[11]. Annual sums made payable on policies of assurance of any description are not apportionable[12].

1   See REAL PROPERTY vol 39(2) (Reissue) para 839 et seq. As to the apportionment of rent as between landlord and tenant see LANDLORD AND TENANT vol 27(1) (Reissue) para 245. As to the apportionment of inheritance tax and interest on it as between life tenant and remainderman see INHERITANCE TAXATION vol 24 (Reissue) para 634 et seq.
2   *Roseingrave v Burke* (1873) IR 7 Eq 186; *Capron v Capron* (1874) LR 17 Eq 288.
3   See the Apportionment Act 1870 s 5; and EXECUTORS AND ADMINISTRATORS. As to rents see REAL PROPERTY vol 39(2) (Reissue) para 755. In the Apportionment Act 1870, 'rents' includes tithes and all periodical payments or renderings in lieu of or in the nature of a tithe (see s 5), but 'tithe rentcharge', as defined in the Tithe Act 1936 s 47(1) was extinguished by s 1: see ECCLESIASTICAL LAW.
4   See the Apportionment Act 1870 s 5; and EXECUTORS AND ADMINISTRATORS.
5   *Pollock v Pollock* (1874) LR 18 Eq 329.
6   See *Re White, Theobald v White* [1913] 1 Ch 231.
7   See the Apportionment Act 1870 s 5. 'Dividends' includes (besides dividends strictly so called) all payments made by the name of dividend, bonus or otherwise out of the revenue of trading or other public companies, divisible between all or any of the members of such respective companies, whether such payments are usually made or declared, at any fixed times or otherwise, and all such divisible revenue is deemed to have accrued by equal daily increment during and within the period for or in respect of which the payment of the same revenue is declared or expressed to be made, but 'dividend' does not include payments in the nature of a return or reimbursement of capital: Apportionment Act 1870 s 5. See also *Re Griffith, Carr v Griffith* (1879) 12 ChD 655; *Re Lysaght, Lysaght v Lysaght* [1898] 1 Ch 115, CA.
8   *Re Jowitt, Jowitt v Keeling* [1922] 2 Ch 442.
9   *Jones v Ogle* (1872) 8 Ch App 192. Cf *Andrew's Trustees v Hallett* 1926 SC 1087. Partnership profits are deemed to have accrued at the end of the relevant accounting period. Accordingly, where executors continue a partnership at the direction of the testator, the tenant for life is entitled to the whole of the profits for an accounting period partly before and partly after the testator's death, but any withdrawn profits for a period wholly before the death are capital unless the will otherwise provides: *Re Robbins, Midland Bank Executor and Trustee Co Ltd v Melville* [1941] Ch 434, [1941] 2 All ER 601. See also PARTNERSHIP vol 35 (Reissue) para 120.
10   *Re Cox's Trusts* (1878) 9 ChD 159.
11   *Trevalion v Anderton* (1897) 66 LJQB 489, CA; *Ellis v Rowbotham* [1900] 1 QB 740 at 744, CA. On this principle, income payable to a testator before his death forms capital of his estate without apportionment as between tenant for life and remainderman, although income payable on the date of his death is apportionable: *Re Aspinall, Aspinall v Aspinall* [1961] Ch 526, [1961] 2 All ER 751.
12   Apportionment Act 1870 s 6.

959. Sale and purchase of investments. As a general rule, on a sale of investments, whether for purposes of reinvestment or distribution, the court declines to make any apportionment between the tenant for life and the remainderman of the proceeds of sale on account of income accrued but not payable at the time of sale, in as much as to do otherwise would be to impose a heavy burden on trustees[1]. This rule is not affected by the Apportionment Act 1870, and is applied in cases where the tenant for life has died between the last payment of income and the sale[2]. However, apportionment has been allowed in special circumstances, for instance where the sale has been by order of the court for the benefit of the estate, or to facilitate distribution among the beneficiaries[3]. If a purchase of stock carries with it the right to receive dividends which have been earned and declared but not paid, there is no question of apportionment, and the tenant for life is not entitled to be paid by the trustees the amount of such dividends[4].

1 *Scholefield v Redfern* (1863) 2 Drew & Sm 173; *Freman v Whitbread* (1865) LR 1 Eq 266. See also *Re Maclaren's Settlement Trusts, Royal Exchange Assurance v Maclaren* [1951] 2 All ER 414.
2 *Bulkeley v Stephens* [1896] 2 Ch 241; *Re Firth, Sykes v Ball* [1938] Ch 517, [1938] 2 All ER 217. As to the provisions of the Apportionment Act 1870 see paras 957–958 ante.
3 *Bulkeley v Stephens* (1863) 3 New Rep 105; *Bulkeley v Stephens* [1896] 2 Ch 241; *Re Winterstoke's Will Trusts, Gunn v Richardson* [1938] Ch 158, [1937] 4 All ER 63. See also *Lord Londesborough v Somerville* (1854) 19 Beav 295; *Re Henderson, Public Trustee v Reddie* [1940] Ch 368 at 382, [1940] 1 All ER 623 at 631 per Morton J. The fact that the amount of the income is known or is easily ascertainable is not sufficient to entitle the court to depart from the rule: *Re Walker, Walker v Patterson* [1934] WN 104; *Re Firth, Sykes v Ball* [1938] Ch 517, [1938] 2 All ER 217; *Re Henderson, Public Trustee v Reddie* supra at 382 and 631 per Morton J.
4 *Re Peel's Settled Estates* [1910] 1 Ch 389. As to the right to receive dividends see COMPANIES vol 7(1) (1996 Reissue) para 718.

960. Payment or recovery of apportioned parts. An apportioned part of any continuing rent, annuity, dividend[1] or other payment is payable or recoverable when the entire portion of which such apportioned part forms part becomes due or payable, and not before, and in the case of a rent, annuity or other payment determined by re-entry, death or otherwise, when the next entire portion of the same would have been payable, if it had not so determined, and not before[2].

The personal representatives of the tenant for life have the same remedies for recovering apportioned parts as they would have had for recovering the entire portions if entitled to them, except that entire or continuing rents, including the apportioned parts, must be recovered by the person who, if the rent had not been apportionable, would have been entitled to the entire or continuing rent, and the apportioned part is recoverable from that person by the executors or other person entitled to it[3].

1 For the meaning of 'rent' see para 958 text and note 3 ante; for the meaning of 'annuities' see para 958 text and note 4 ante; and for the meaning of 'dividends' see para 958 note 7 ante.
2 Apportionment Act 1870 s 3. As to the recovery of apportioned parts of rents and annuities see LANDLORD AND TENANT vol 27(1) (Reissue) para 245 et seq; RENTCHARGES AND ANNUITIES vol 39(2) (Reissue) para 839 et seq. As to the time of day when an instalment of rent becomes payable see *Re Aspinall, Aspinall v Aspinall* [1961] Ch 526, [1961] 2 All ER 751; and LANDLORD AND TENANT vol 27(1) (Reissue) para 229.
3 See the Apportionment Act 1870 s 4; and LANDLORD AND TENANT vol 27(1) (Reissue) para 246.

(3) ADJUSTMENT OF BURDENS BETWEEN CAPITAL AND INCOME

(i) Outgoings

961. Outgoings payable out of income. In the absence of an express direction by a settlor to the contrary, it is presumed that the settled property is intended to descend intact. Income must, therefore, bear all ordinary outgoings of a recurrent nature in respect of the property[1], such as rates and taxes[2], the interest on charges and incumbrances on the property[3], any fee farm rents and quit rents to which the property is subject[4], rents reserved by the leases under which settled leaseholds are held[5], and the expense of performing and observing all continuing obligations, covenants and conditions on the part of the lessee[6], the cost of insurance effected by trustees[7], and the costs of ordinary repairs[8]. The tenant for life must also bear the costs of legal proceedings for his sole benefit in respect of his life interest, such as the costs of an application by the tenant for life of a fund which has been paid into court[9], including the costs of the trustees if it is necessary for them to appear[10], the costs of an application in an administration action for payment of income[11], the costs of an application to change investments in order to increase income[12], the costs of rendering an income account unnecessarily demanded by a tenant for life in an administration action[13], the costs of a reference to inquire whether a tenant for life is capable of managing his own affairs where his income would be reduced if he were found incapable[14] and the expenses of a receiver of the rents[15], and the costs of an application to be let into possession of land settled on trust for sale[16].

1 *Fountaine v Pellet* (1791) 1 Ves 337 at 342; *Shore v Shore* (1859) 4 Drew 501; *Re Copland's Settlement, Johns v Carden* [1900] 1 Ch 326. Compensation to an outgoing tenant under a covenant in his lease has been held to be a current expense: *Mansel v Norton* (1883) 22 ChD 769, CA. However, as to such compensation in the case of an agricultural tenant see para 808 ante; and AGRICULTURE vol 1(2) (Reissue) para 405 et seq.

2 *Fountaine v Pellet* (1791) 1 Ves 337 at 342; *Kingham v Kingham* [1897] 1 IR 170; *Re Redding, Thompson v Redding* [1897] 1 Ch 876. Where the real value of property could only be ascertained and its real benefit enjoyed by means of a sale, the tenant for life was held entitled to the income of the proceeds of sale without contributing to the charges accrued since the life interest came into possession: see *Earl of Lonsdale v Countess Berchtoldt* (1857) 3 K & J 185. The deductions from rent which the tenants of licensed houses were entitled to make under the Licensing Act 1964 s 17(4) (repealed) in respect of charges imposed by that Act were annual outgoings, and not charges to be paid out of capital (see *Re Smith, Smith v Dodsworth* [1906] 1 Ch 799), but it would seem that payments of monopoly value under the Licensing Act 1953 s 6(1) (repealed), even if made by annual instalments, had to be borne by capital (*Appenrodt v Central Middlesex Assessment Committee* [1937] 2 KB 48, CA). The tenant for life must bear tithe redemption annuities: see *Re Leicester's Settled Estates, Coke v Earl of Leicester* [1939] Ch 77, [1938] 3 All ER 553; and ECCLESIASTICAL LAW.

3 *Revel v Watkinson* (1748) 1 Ves Sen 93; *Whitbread v Smith* (1854) 3 De GM & G 727 at 741; *Marshall v Crowther* (1874) 2 ChD 199; *Re Harrison, Townson v Harrison* (1889) 43 ChD 55; *Honywood v Honywood* [1902] 1 Ch 347.

4 As to fee farm rents and quit rents see REAL PROPERTY vol 39(2) (Reissue) para 84.

5 *Kingham v Kingham* [1897] 1 IR 170; *Redding, Thompson v Redding* [1897] 1 Ch 876; *Re Betty, Betty v A-G* [1899] 1 Ch 821; *Re Gjers, Cooper v Gjers* [1899] 2 Ch 54. The same rule applies in the case of unsaleable leaseholds included in a residuary estate, and any loss must be borne by the tenant for life (*Allen v Embleton* (1858) 4 Drew 226; *Re Owen, Slater v Owen* [1912] 1 Ch 519) but, in the case of leaseholds settled by will, the liability of the tenant for life does not commence until he has been put by the executors into possession of the income, and any outgoings incurred before then must be apportioned between capital and income on the principle of *Allhusen v Whittell* (1867) LR 4 Eq 295: see *Re Shee, Taylor v Stoger* [1934] Ch 345. See also *Earl Lonsdale v Countess Berchtoldt* (1857) 3 K & J 185, where a tenant for life had refused to take possession of specifically bequeathed leaseholds, and the ground rent and outgoings were ordered to be paid out of capital.

6 See para 774 ante.

7 As to the power of trustees to insure see the Trustee Act 1925 s 19 (as amended); and TRUSTS vol 48 (Reissue) para 891. See also para 904 ante. As to insurance see further para 774 ante.

8 As to the cost of repairs see para 963 post; and as to the apportionment of outgoings in regard to income which is apportioned see para 957 note 4 ante.

9 *Ingram's Trust* (1854) 2 WR 679; *Re — (a lunatic)* (1860) 8 WR 333; *Re Marner's Trusts* (1866) LR 3 Eq 432; *Re Whitton's Trusts* (1869) LR 8 Eq 352; *Re Smith's Trusts* (1870) LR 9 Eq 374; *Re Evans' Trusts* (1872) 7 Ch App 609; *Re T—* (1880) 15 ChD 78. As to payment into court under the Trustee Act 1925 s 63 (as amended) see TRUSTS vol 48 (Reissue) para 798.

10 *Re Evans' Trusts* (1872) 7 Ch App 609.

11 *Eady v Watson* (1864) 12 WR 682. See, however, *Scrivener v Smith* (1869) LR 8 Eq 310; *Longuet v Hockley* (1870) 22 LT 198.

12 *Equitable Reversionary Interest Society v Fuller* (1861) 1 John & H 379 (on appeal 30 LJ Ch 848); *Re Tennant* (1889) 40 ChD 594.

13 *Croggan v Allen* (1882) 22 ChD 101.
14 *Winthrop v Winthrop* (1846) 15 LJ Ch 403.
15 *Bainbridge v Blair* (1835) 4 LJ Ch 207; *Shore v Shore* (1859) 4 Drew 501.
16 *Re Bagot's Settlement, Bagot v Kittoe* [1894] 1 Ch 177; *Re Newen, Newen v Barnes* [1894] 2 Ch 297. As to the costs of remaindermen see *Re Hunt, Pollard v Geake* [1900] WN 65 (on appeal [1901] WN 144, CA). Cf *Re Newen, Newen v Barnes* supra at 309.

962. Capital outgoings. The corpus of a trust estate must be resorted to for all costs, charges and expenses properly incurred for the benefit of the whole estate, such as the costs of carrying into execution the trusts of a will[1]; the premiums on insurance policies forming part of the settled property[2]; the costs of legal proceedings for the administration and protection of the whole estate[3], such as the costs of paying the trust fund into court[4] and of actions by the trustees for the protection of the estate[5]; the costs of a yearly audit and stocktaking where capital is left in a business[6]; and the costs of appointing new trustees[7]. The costs of proceedings for the administration and protection of the settled property are payable out of capital even where they are incurred by the tenant for life primarily for his own benefit, as where he applies to the court to decide questions as to the proper investment of trust funds[8], brings a redemption action[9], incurs costs in settling a foreclosure action brought by the mortgagees[10], or defends an action by a purchaser to recover a deposit[11]. Where the sole question is one of apportionment between the tenant for life and the remainderman, however, the costs may also be apportioned[12].

Costs which ought to be borne by capital may be retained out of income by the trustees until they can be raised out of capital[13], but the tenant for life is entitled to have such costs defrayed by an immediate sale[14].

1 *Bainbridge v Blair* (1835) 4 LJ Ch 207.
2 *Macdonald v Irvine* (1878) 8 ChD 101, CA; *Re Sherry, Sherry v Sherry* [1913] 2 Ch 508. Cf *Re Jones' Settlement, Stunt v Jones* [1915] 1 Ch 373, where a tenant for life was held not entitled to be repaid premiums paid voluntarily and without any request by the trustees.
3 *Re Earl De La Warr's Estates* (1881) 16 ChD 587.
4 *Re Staples' Settlement* (1849) 13 Jur 273; *Ingram's Trust* (1854) 2 WR 679; *Re Whitton's Trusts* (1869) LR 8 Eq 352.
5 *Stott v Milne* (1884) 25 ChD 710, CA; *Re Ormrod's Settled Estate* [1892] 2 Ch 318; *Re Blake (a lunatic)* (1895) 72 LT 280. Expenses incurred by trustees in compelling lessees of settled land to perform their covenants to repair have, however, been directed to be raised by mortgage of the settled land, so that the tenant for life and the remainderman should bear them in fair proportion: *Re McClure's Trusts, Carr v Commercial Union Insurance Co* (1906) 76 LJ Ch 52. As to the costs of legal proceedings for the protection of the settled land see para 825 ante.
6 *Re Bennett, Jones v Bennett* [1896] 1 Ch 778, CA.
7 *Re Fulham (a lunatic)* (1850) 15 Jur 69; *Ex p Davies* (1852) 16 Jur 882; *Lord Brougham v Lord Poulett* (1855) 19 Beav 119 at 135; *Re Fellows' Settlement* (1856) 2 Jur NS 62; *Carter v Sebright* (1859) 26 Beav 374 at 377; *Harvey v Olliver* [1887] WN 149. Where the settlor has appointed a single trustee, the costs of appointing an additional trustee are payable out of corpus (*Re Ratcliff* [1898] 2 Ch 352; but see *Finlay v Howard* (1842) 2 Dr & War 490; *Re Brackenbury's Trusts* (1870) LR 10 Eq 45); and where trustees rightly retired in consequence of the acts of the tenant for life, the costs were directed to be paid out of income (*Coventry v Coventry* (1837) 1 Keen 758). See also TRUSTS vol 48 (Reissue) para 775.
8 *Beauclerk v Ashburnham* (1845) 8 Beav 322; *Hume v Richardson* (1862) 31 LJ Ch 713.
9 *Colyer v Colyer, Pawley v Colyer* (1863) 3 De GJ & Sm 676.
10 *More v More* (1889) 37 WR 414. See also *Selby v Selby* (1838) 2 Jur 106.
11 *Re Foster's Settled Estates* [1922] 1 Ch 348. See also para 823 ante.
12 *Reeves v Creswick* (1839) 3 Y & C Ex 715; *Re Earl of Chesterfield's Trusts* (1883) 24 ChD 643 at 654.
13 *Stott v Milne* (1884) 25 ChD 710, CA. See also TRUSTS vol 48 (Reissue) para 637.
14 *Burkett v Spray* (1829) 1 Russ & M 113. As to the recovery by the tenant for life of costs incurred on a compulsory purchase under the Lands Clauses Consolidation Act 1845 see COMPULSORY ACQUISITION OF LAND vol 8(1) (Reissue) para 165.

963. Cost of repairs. Casual repairs effected by trustees should usually be paid out of income[1]. The trustees may pay for any repairs out of income, and if they do so the court will not interfere with their discretion[2]. However, if they think the repairs are such that they should not be paid for out of income, the trustees may apply to the court for a direction for payment out of capital[3]. Repairs amounting to structural reconstruction[4] and permanent improvements[5] should generally be borne by capital[6].

1   *Re Smith, Vincent v Smith* [1930] 1 Ch 88; *Re Earl of Berkeley, Inglis v Countess of Berkeley* [1968] Ch 744, [1968] 3 All ER 364, CA. As to repairs of improvements see para 964 post. As to the court's power to sanction payment out of capital in special circumstances see para 671 ante. As to the management powers of trustees see paras 665–666 ante. As to whether a tenant for life is bound to repair see paras 995–996 post.
2   *Re Gray, Public Trustee v Woodhouse* [1927] 1 Ch 242.
3   *Re Jackson, Jackson v Talbot* (1882) 21 ChD 786; *Re Robins, Holland v Gillam* [1928] Ch 721.
4   *Re Whitaker, Rooke v Whitaker* [1929] 1 Ch 662.
5   *Re Conquest, Royal Exchange Assurance v Conquest* [1929] 2 Ch 353; *Re Smith, Vincent v Smith* [1930] 1 Ch 88.
6   *Re Hotchkys, Freke v Calmady* (1886) 32 ChD 408, CA; *Re Robins, Holland v Gillam* [1928] Ch 721 at 737; *Re Conquest, Royal Exchange Assurance v Conquest* [1929] 2 Ch 353; *Re Howlett, Howlett v Howlett* [1949] Ch 767, [1949] 2 All ER 490. See further TRUSTS vol 48 (Reissue) para 901. As to expenditure of capital money on authorised improvements under the Settled Land Act 1925 see para 809 et seq ante. Where trustees of a settlement exercise their powers of management under s 102 (as amended) (see paras 665–666 ante), or trustees of land exercise such powers (see para 903 ante), repairs in the nature of permanent improvements may be directed to be borne out of capital, even if not authorised improvements under the Settled Land Act 1925: *Re Robins, Holland v Gillam* supra; *Re Smith, Vincent v Smith* [1930] 1 Ch 88.

964. Maintenance, repair and insurance of improvements. Improvements[1] must be maintained and repaired and, if they include a building or work in its nature insurable against damage by fire, insured, at the expense of the tenant for life[2] and each of his successors in title having under the trust instrument[3] a limited interest only in the settled land[4], for such period, if any, and in such amount, if any, as the Minister of Agriculture, Fisheries and Food prescribes by certificate in any case[5]. The tenant for life and each of his successors in title is also bound from time to time, if required by the Minister on or without the application of any person having under the settlement any estate or interest in the settled land in possession, remainder or otherwise, to report to the Minister the state of every improvement and the fact and particulars of any fire insurance[6]. Failure to comply with these requirements gives any person having any estate or interest in the settled land, in possession, remainder or reversion, under the trust instrument, a right to an action for damages against the tenant for life or his estate after his death[7]. The tenant for life and each of his successors in title having under the trust instrument a limited interest only in the settled land is protected, in executing, repairing or maintaining authorised improvements, against liability for waste in respect of any acts, works or user of the land for such purposes[8]. However, the tenant for life or his successors in title are not authorised to cut down and use timber and other trees planted or left standing for shelter or ornament[9], and he and they are prohibited from cutting down, except in proper thinning, any trees planted as an authorised improvement[10].

1   Ie improvements authorised under the Settled Land Act 1925 or the enactments replaced by it: see para 815 et seq ante.
2   For the meaning of 'tenant for life' see para 671 note 5 ante. See also para 761 et seq ante.
3   For the meaning of 'trust instrument' see para 688 note 7 ante.
4   For the meaning of 'settled land' see para 680 text to note 2 ante.
5   Settled Land Act 1925 ss 88(1), 117(1)(xvi) (amended by the Transfer of Functions (Ministry of Food) Order 1955, SI 1955/554). As to the minister's powers see para 965 post. As to the Minister of Agriculture, Fisheries and Food generally see CONSTITUTIONAL LAW AND HUMAN RIGHTS vol 8(2)

(Reissue) para 435 et seq. As to the insurance money see paras 774, 802 ante. The certificate may be varied from time to time, but not so as to increase the liability of the tenant for life or any of his successors in title: see the Settled Land Act 1925 s 88(4).

Every certificate and report approved and made by the Minister under the Settled Land Act 1925 must be filed in the office of the Minister of Agriculture, Fisheries and Food, and an office copy of any certificate or report so filed must be delivered out of such office to any person requiring the same, on payment of the proper fee, and is sufficient evidence of the certificate or report of which it purports to be a copy: s 116 (amended by the Transfer of Functions (Ministry of Food) Order 1955, SI 1955/554).

6   Settled Land Act 1925 s 88(3).
7   See ibid s 88(5).
8   See ibid s 89; and para 794 ante. As to liability for waste see para 986 et seq post.
9   See ibid s 89. As to cutting timber see paras 848 ante, 988 et seq post. It is for the court to determine whether timber has been planted or left for shelter or ornament, but the question is not determined by saying whether in the opinion of the court the timber is ornamental or not; if the timber has been planted or left by the owners of the estate for the time being for shelter or for ornament, it is protected even though the opinion may be that it is not in fact ornamental: *Weld-Blundell v Wolseley* [1903] 2 Ch 664.
10 See the Settled Land Act 1925 s 88(2). Planting is an authorised improvement: see s 83, Sch 3 Pt I para (x); and para 816 head (10) ante. The prohibition is not limited to timber trees. It is unclear whether, if timber has been planted as an authorised improvement, this prohibition would prevent the exercise by a tenant for life of his right to cut ripe timber under s 66: see para 848 ante. As to the powers of limited owners to enter into a forestry dedication covenant see para 867 ante; and FORESTRY vol 19(1) (Reissue) para 45.

965. Extension of the minister's powers. For the purposes of any Act, public general, local or private, making provision for the execution of improvements on settled land[1], the Minister of Agriculture, Fisheries and Food has all such powers and authorities as he has for the purposes of the Improvement of Land Act 1864[2]. The provisions of that Act relating to proceedings and inquiries, and to authentication of instruments and to declarations, statements, notices, applications, forms, security for expenses, inspections and examinations extend and apply, as far as the nature and circumstances of the case admit, to acts and proceedings done or taken by or in relation to the Minister under any Act making provision for the execution of improvements on settled land[3]. The provisions of any Act relating to security for costs in respect of business transacted under the Acts administered by the Minister as successor of the Land Commissioners for England extend and apply to the business transacted by or under the direction of the Minister under any Act, public general, or local or private, by which any power or duty is conferred or imposed on him as such successor[4].

1   For the meaning of 'settled land' see para 680 text to note 2 ante.
2   Settled Land Act 1925 ss 115(1), 117(1)(xvi) (amended by the Transfer of Functions (Ministry of Food) Order 1955, SI 1955/554). As to the Minister of Agriculture, Fisheries and Food see CONSTITUTIONAL LAW AND HUMAN RIGHTS vol 8(2) (Reissue) paras 435–437. As to the powers of the Minister under the Improvement of Land Act 1864 see AGRICULTURE vol 1(2) (Reissue) para 509 et seq.
3   Settled Land Act 1925 ss 115(2), 117(1)(xvi) (as amended: see note 2 supra).
4   Ibid ss 115(3) (amended by the Agriculture (Miscellaneous Provisions) Act 1963 s 28, Schedule Pt II), 117(1)(xvi) (as amended: see note 2 supra). As to the Land Commissioners for England see AGRICULTURE vol 1(2) (Reissue) para 509.

(ii) Duty of Tenant for Life to keep down Interest and Annuities

966. Liability for incumbrances and interest on them. Apart from any question arising on the special terms of the instrument creating the settlement, a tenant for life is under no obligation to discharge any portion of the principal of paramount incumbrances[1], but he is bound as between himself and the remainderman[2] to keep down the interest accruing during his lifetime to the extent of, and out of, the rents and profits received by him[3]. If the rents are at any time insufficient to keep down the interest, subsequent rents arising during his lifetime are applicable to liquidate arrears accruing during his own life tenancy[4] and, if part of the property is sold, principal, interest and costs due on the mortgage being then paid off out of the proceeds, the rents of the unsold portion subsequently received by the tenant for life remain liable as between himself and the remainderman to recoup amounts paid out of capital in satisfaction of arrears of interest[5].

1   *Lord Penrhyn v Hughes* (1799) 5 Ves 99 at 107; *Kekewich v Marker* (1851) 3 Mac & G 311 at 328.
2   The obligation does not exist as between the tenant for life and the incumbrancers: *Re Morley, Morley v Saunders* (1869) LR 8 Eq 594. See also MORTGAGE.
3   *Revel v Watkinson* (1748) 1 Ves Sen 93; *Amesbury v Brown* (1750) 1 Ves Sen 477 at 480; *Earl of Peterborough v Mordaunt* (1760) 1 Eden 474; *Faulkner v Daniel* (1843) 3 Hare 199 at 207. See also *Syer v Gladstone* (1885) 30 ChD 614, as explained in *Frewen v Law Life Assurance Society* [1896] 2 Ch 511 at 517. See also MORTGAGE.
4   *Revel v Watkinson* (1748) 1 Ves Sen 93; *Tracy v Viscountess Dowager Hereford* (1786) 2 Bro CC 128. This applies to interest on unpaid instalments of estate duty (now replaced by inheritance tax): *Re Earl Howe's Settled Estates, Earl Howe v Kingscote* [1903] 2 Ch 69, CA; *Re Earl of Egmont's Settled Estates, Lefroy v Egmont* [1912] 1 Ch 251. See also para 971 post.
5   *Honywood v Honywood* [1902] 1 Ch 347.

967. Extent of obligation of tenant for life. The obligation of the tenant for life to keep down interest applies even if there is an ultimate limitation to the tenant for life in fee[1], or if he has an absolute power of appointment, by reason of which he might make the estate his own[2]. A purchaser of his estate, although himself the mortgagee, is bound to discharge the obligations[3].

If real estate is charged by will with payment of debts, and subject to that is settled, every tenant for life must keep down all the interest upon all the debts bearing interest which are ascertained to be a charge upon the estate[4] from the day of the testator's death[5], and also pay all interest payable on any legacies charged on the estate[6].

The liability of the tenant for life is not personal[7], but is a charge on his life estate, and if he fails to keep down interest, future rents and profits payable during his tenancy for life are liable to recoup to the remainderman the full amount of his default[8], and he is not entitled to have any portion of the settled estates sold for the purposes of paying off interest and arrears[9]. However, he may have an incumbrance paid off by sale if the rents are insufficient to keep down the interest[10].

1   *Burges v Mawbey* (1823) Turn & R 167. As to the obligation of the tenant for life to keep down interest see para 966 ante. As to the tenant for life generally see para 761 et seq ante. As to limitations see para 715 et seq ante.
2   *Whitbread v Smith* (1854) 3 De GM & G 727 at 741. The rule applies to the case of an owner in fee with an executory devise over (*Butcher v Simmonds* (1876) 35 LT 304), or of a tenant in tail who is a child (*Sergeson v Sealey* (1742) 2 Atk 412; *Burges v Mawbey* (1823) Turn & R 167), but not to the case of an adult tenant in tail because he is in fact the owner of the estate, and has the remainderman at his mercy (*Amesbury v Brown* (1750) 1 Ves Sen 477; *Burges v Mawbey* supra at 175). However, if the tenant in tail, having kept down interest during his life, dies without barring the entail, his personal representative has no charge on the reversion for the interest: *Amesbury v Brown* supra. As to entailed interests see para 715 et seq ante; and REAL PROPERTY vol 39(2) (Reissue) para 117 et seq.
3   *Lord Penrhyn v Hughes* (1799) 5 Ves 99; *Raffety v King* (1836) 1 Keen 601.
4   *Faulkner v Daniel* (1843) 3 Hare 199; *Wastell v Leslie, Carter v Leslie* (1844) 13 LJ Ch 205; *Marshall v Crowther* (1874) 2 ChD 199. See also EXECUTORS AND ADMINISTRATORS.
5   *Barnes v Bond* (1863) 32 Beav 653; *Marshall v Crowther* (1874) 2 ChD 199, following *Allhusen v Whittell* (1867) LR 4 Eq 295, and not following *Greisley v Earl of Chesterfield* (1851) 13 Beav 288.
6   *Earl of Milltown v Trench* (1837) 4 Cl & Fin 276, HL; *Faulkner v Daniel* (1843) 3 Hare 199; *Coote v Lord Milltown* (1844) 1 Jo & Lat 501. See also EXECUTORS AND ADMINISTRATORS.
7   *Honywood v Honywood* [1902] 1 Ch 347 at 351.
8   *Waring v Coventry* (1834) 2 My & K 406; *Fitzmaurice v Murphy* (1859) 8 I Ch R 363; *Makings v Makings* (1860) 1 De GF & J 355; *Lord Kilworth v Earl of Mountcashell* (1864) 15 I Ch R 565. The remainderman's remedy is to apply to the court for the appointment of a receiver, whose costs must be borne by the tenant

for life (*Shore v Shore* (1859) 4 Drew 501), and have the rents appropriated for the purpose of paying the accruing interest (*Hill v Browne* (1844) Drury *temp* Sug 426 at 434; *Coote v O'Reilly* (1844) 1 Jo & Lat 455 at 461; *Lord Kensington v Bouverie* (1859) 7 HL Cas 557 at 575; *Kirwan v Kennedy* (1869) IR 3 Eq 472 at 481). See also RECEIVERS vol 39(2) (Reissue) para 335 et seq.

9   *Hawkins v Hawkins* (1836) 6 LJ Ch 69; *Shore v Shore* (1859) 4 Drew 501.
10   *Lord Penrhyn v Hughes* (1799) 5 Ves 99; *Cooke v Cholmondeley* (1857) 4 Drew 244.

968. Remainderman's rights. The remainderman is entitled to be repaid arrears of interest out of the assets of a deceased tenant for life to the extent of the rents received during the life tenancy[1], subject to any set-off there may be in respect of capital charges paid by the tenant for life[2]. However, he is not entitled to have arrears of interest which have accrued during a previous life tenancy discharged by a subsequent tenant for life out of the rents and profits as such arrears are primarily a charge on the inheritance[3], and if the subsequent tenant for life is forced to pay them they are repayable to him out of capital[4].

1   *Baldwin v Baldwin* (1856) 6 I Ch R 156; *Re Fitzgerald's Estate* (1867) IR 1 Eq 453; *Kirwan v Kennedy* (1869) IR 3 Eq 472 at 481; *Re Gore* (1874) IR 9 Eq 83. The remainderman has not, however, a specific lien on rents collected or to be collected by a personal representative after the death of the tenant for life: *Dillon v Dillon* (1853) 4 I Ch R 102.
2   *Re Whyte* (1857) 7 I Ch R 61n; *Howlin v Sheppard* (1872) IR 6 Eq 497. As to set-off generally see SET-OFF AND COUNTERCLAIM.
3   *Caulfield v Maguire* (1845) 2 Jo & Lat 141; *Sharshaw v Gibbs* (1854) Kay 333; *Kennedy v Daley* (1858) 7 I Ch R 445.
4   *Kirwan v Kennedy* (1870) IR 4 Eq 499. However, where the tenant for life has overpaid interest by mistake, this is not recoverable out of capital: see *Kirwan v Kennedy* supra.

969. Several estates in one settlement. If several estates are included in the same settlement, the tenant for life is bound out of the whole rents and profits to keep down the interest on charges on all the estates[1]. If a charge in respect of which arrears of interest have arisen is paid off by means of a sale of one of the estates, he remains liable to make good the arrears out of subsequent rents received by him from any of the estates[2].

1   *Tracy v Viscountess Dowager Hereford* (1786) 2 Bro CC 128; *Scholefield v Lockwood* (1863) 4 De GJ & Sm 22; *Frewen v Law Life Assurance Society* [1896] 2 Ch 511; *Honywood v Honywood* [1902] 1 Ch 347. See also *Re Hotchkys, Freke v Calmady* (1886) 32 ChD 408 at 418–419, CA. As to the tenant for life generally see para 761 et seq ante.
2   *Honywood v Honywood* [1902] 1 Ch 347.

970. Annuities. On a gift of real estate charged with annuities, the tenant for life is bound to keep down the annuities[1], and if he fails to do so and the estate is sold to pay the arrears, the remainderman is entitled to have the arrears recouped out of interest on the surplus of the purchase money accruing during the life tenancy[2]. However, if the income is insufficient to pay the annuities in full and the deficiency is raised out of capital, the remainderman is not entitled to have the deficiency recouped out of future income accruing during the life tenancy[3]. Arrears unpaid at the death of a tenant for life become a charge upon and must be raised out of corpus, and the succeeding tenant for life is only bound to keep down the interest on them[4].

If the annuity charged on the settled estate is a debt of the settlor, the tenant for life and the remainderman must contribute to the annuity proportionately[5].

1   *Re Grant, Walker v Martineau* (1883) 52 LJ Ch 552; *Re Popham, Butler v Popham* (1914) 111 LT 524. As to annuities generally see RENTCHARGES AND ANNUITIES vol 39(2) (Reissue) para 762 et seq.
2   *Coote v O'Reilly* (1844) 1 Jo & Lat 455.
3   *Re Croxon, Ferrers v Croxton* [1915] 2 Ch 290.
4   *Playfair v Cooper, Prince v Cooper* (1853) 17 Beav 187.

5   As to the rules for ascertaining the respective liabilities of the tenant for life and the remainderman see
     EXECUTORS AND ADMINISTRATORS. As to whether an annuity is payable out of the corpus or income
     of property charged see RENTCHARGES AND ANNUITIES vol 39(2) (Reissue) para 826 et seq.

(iii)   Discharge of Incumbrances by Tenant for Life

971.   Discharge of interest. A tenant for life in possession of an estate subject to a
charge bearing interest who pays the interest, although the rents and profits are
insufficient to enable him to do so, may make himself an incumbrancer[1] for the excess of
his payments beyond the amount of the rents and profits, but if he pays the interest during
his life without any intimation that the rents and profits are insufficient, or that he has any
intention of charging the corpus of the estate with any deficiency, his personal
representatives cannot after his death set up any such charge[2]. If the charge is a continuing
charge on income as well as a charge on the corpus, it is doubtful whether a tenant for
life is entitled, until after the termination of his life interest, to recoupment out of the
corpus in respect of a deficiency which he has made good out of his own money[3].

1   See MORTGAGE. Cf *Fetherstone v Mitchell* (1847) 9 I Eq R 480.
2   *Dixon v Peacock* (1855) 3 Drew 288; *Lord Kensington v Bouverie* (1859) 7 HL Cas 557. See also MORTGAGE;
     and paras 966–967 ante.
3   In *Re Warwick's Settlement Trusts, Greville Trust Co v Grey* [1937] Ch 561, [1937] 2 All ER 828, Farwell
     J held that a tenant for life was not entitled to recoupment until after the tenancy for life had come to an
     end, or at any rate until the estate had been sold. The Court of Appeal affirmed his decision on other
     grounds ([1938] Ch 530, [1938] 1 All ER 639, CA), but Sir Wilfrid Greene MR expressed a strong view
     that a tenant for life was entitled at any time to an immediate recoupment out of corpus, provided that
     he had shown a sufficient intention to claim a charge on corpus. However, Clauson LJ, without
     expressing a concluded view, appeared to agree with Farwell J.

972.   Payment off of capital charge by tenant for life. A tenant for life who pays
off a capital charge on the inheritance is prima facie entitled to that charge for his own
benefit[1]. The presumption applies equally in favour of a tenant for life in remainder[2], or
in any case where the charge is paid off by the trustees out of rents and profits[3]. If
successive tenants for life pay off a mortgage by instalments, the money must be repaid to
them rateably in proportion to the payments made by them, and not divided among them
in order of priority[4].

1   *Countess of Shrewsbury v Earl of Shrewsbury* (1790) 1 Ves 227; *Faulkner v Daniel* (1843) 3 Hare 199 at 217;
     Burrell v Earl of Egremont (1844) 7 Beav 205 at 226; *Morley v Morley, Harland v Morley* (1855) 5 De GM &
     G 610; *Howlin v Sheppard* (1872) IR 6 Eq 497; *Re Godley's Estate* [1896] 1 IR 45. See also *Re Pride, Shackell
     v Colnett* [1891] 2 Ch 135. The rule applies where the tenant for life in exercise of a power of charging
     has himself created the charge which he pays off: *Re Duchess Dowager of Norfolk, ex p Earl of Digby* (1821)
     Jac 235; *Jenkinson v Harcourt* (1854) Kay 688. See also EQUITY vol 16 (Reissue) para 885 et seq;
     MORTGAGE.
2   *Re Chesters, Whittingham v Chesters* [1935] Ch 77.
3   *Re Harvey, Harvey v Hobday* [1896] 1 Ch 137, CA.
4   *Re Nepean's Settled Estate* [1900] 1 IR 298.

973.   Evidence of intention. A tenant for life is under no obligation to prove his
intention to pay off the charge for his own benefit[1]. The simple payment of the charge
by him is sufficient to establish his prima facie right to have the charge raised out of the
estate and he is under no obligation or duty to make any declaration, or to do any act
demonstrating his intention[2]. However, in every case, what the court has to ascertain is
the intention of the party paying off the charge. In the absence of direct evidence the
intention must be gathered from what it was his interest to do, but any evidence to the
contrary must be regarded[3], and the smallest demonstration that he meant to discharge

the estate is sufficient[4]. Such a demonstration may be made by his acts as well as by his words which, being against interest, are legitimate evidence even after the event[5]. The burden of proving an intention to exonerate the estate, however, lies on the remainderman[6], and evidence drawn from recitals in a deed, or the form of reconveyance, may in its turn be rebutted by a long series of acts consistent only with an intention to keep the charge alive[7], or by the personal evidence of the tenant for life[8].

The fact that the tenant for life who pays off the charge and the remainderman stand in the relationship of parent and child is material if there is anything else to rebut the presumption that the tenant for life paid the charge off for his own benefit, but is not by itself sufficient to rebut it[9].

1   *Lindsay v Earl of Wicklow* (1873) IR 7 Eq 192. As to the payment off of capital charges by the tenant for life see para 972 ante.
2   *Redington v Redington* (1809) 1 Ball & B 131; *Burrell v Earl of Egremont* (1844) 7 Beav 205; *Lord Kensington v Bouverie* (1859) 7 HL Cas 557 at 595; *Lindsay v Earl of Wicklow* (1873) IR 7 Eq 192; *Re Harvey, Harvey v Hobday* [1896] 1 Ch 137, CA.
3   *Pitt v Pitt* (1856) 22 Beav 294; *Williams v Williams-Wynn* (1915) 84 LJ Ch 801. For a case where there was a covenant to assign to the trustees of the settlement the benefit of charges paid off see *Cochrane v St Clair* (1855) 1 Jur NS 302.
4   *Jones v Morgan* (1783) 1 Bro CC 206 at 218; *Lord Kensington v Bouverie* (1859) 7 HL Cas 557; *Re Warwick's Settlement Trusts, Greville Trust Co v Grey* [1938] Ch 530, [1938] 1 All ER 639, CA. In the present state of the authorities, a tenant for life who wishes to keep a charge alive would be well advised to give express notice to the trustees whenever he makes a payment out of his own money.
5   *Lord Kensington v Bouverie* (1859) 7 HL Cas 557 at 574; *Conolly v Barter* [1904] 1 IR 130 at 138, Ir CA.
6   *Re Harvey, Harvey v Hobday* [1896] 1 Ch 137, CA.
7   *Lindsay v Earl of Wicklow* (1873) IR 7 Eq 192.
8   *Lord Gifford v Lord Fitzhardinge* [1899] 2 Ch 32; *Williams v Williams-Wynn* (1915) 84 LJ Ch 801. On the other hand, an assignment of a charge to a trustee for the benefit of the tenant for life has been held not to keep the charge alive in the face of evidence contained in his will that he regarded it as extinguished: *Re Lloyd's Estate* [1903] 1 IR 144. For a case where an intention to keep a charge alive was evidenced by the will see *Lysaght v Lysaght* (1851) 4 Ir Jur 110. As to proof of intention generally and hearsay evidence see EVIDENCE.
9   *Re Harvey, Harvey v Hobday* [1896] 1 Ch 137, CA. As to the presumption of advancement generally see GIFTS vol 20 (Reissue) para 45 et seq.

974. Extinction of charge by mistake. A tenant for life who extinguishes a charge on the estate in a mistaken belief as to his own rights is entitled on discovering his error to keep the charge alive against the inheritance[1]. A vague intention of not requiring repayment, if he should find that he could conveniently do without it, does not convert the payment into a gift for the benefit of the inheritance[2].

1   *Burrell v Earl of Egremont* (1844) 7 Beav 205; *Conolly v Barter* [1904] 1 IR 130, Ir CA. Apart from mistake, an intention to discharge the incumbrance cannot afterwards be changed: see MORTGAGE. See also *Lindsay v Earl of Wicklow* (1873) IR 7 Eq 192 at 209; but see *Lysaght v Lysaght* (1851) 4 Ir Jur 110. On the question of merger generally see EQUITY vol 16 (Reissue) para 882 et seq; MORTGAGE; REAL PROPERTY vol 39(2) (Reissue) para 255 et seq. As to mistake generally see MISTAKE.
2   *Cuddon v Cuddon* (1876) 4 ChD 583.

(iv) Expenses of Renewing Leases

975. Renewable leaseholds. After 1925, perpetually renewable leases which formerly were frequently the subject of settlements no longer exist as such but take effect as a demise for a term of 2,000 years, and perpetually renewable underleases take effect as a demise for a term less in duration by one day than the term out of which they are derived[1]. Leases and underleases may, however, still contain a provision for renewal for a term not exceeding 60 years from the termination of the lease or underlease[2] and, if such renewable leaseholds are included in the subject matter of a settlement, the settlement should make it plain whether an imperative trust for renewal is intended to be created. A direction to renew may be couched in discretionary terms in order to avoid placing the estate and the persons interested at the mercy of the lessor, and yet impose on the trustees a trust which the court will execute if they do not[3]. If there is a direction to renew, whether express or implied[4], it must be obeyed, and the persons whose duty it is to renew, whether the trustees or the tenant for life, are liable to compensate the remainderman for the loss occasioned by their default[5], or, if he himself renews, to repay him the amount of the fine, provided that it is reasonable[6]. In the absence of a direction to renew, the mere circumstance of there being limitations over imposes no necessity on the tenant for life, and he may renew or allow the term to expire[7]. However, if a tenant for life in such circumstances chooses to renew, he is a trustee of the lease for all persons interested under the subsequent limitations, in accordance with the principle of equity that parties interested jointly with others in a lease cannot take to themselves the benefit of a renewal to the exclusion of the other parties interested with them[8].

1   See the Law of Property Act 1922 s 145, Sch 15 paras 1(1), 2(1), 5, 6(1), 7(1); and LANDLORD AND TENANT vol 27(1) (Reissue) paras 453–454.
2   See ibid Sch 15 para 7(2); and LANDLORD AND TENANT vol 27(1) (Reissue) para 450. As to renewable leaseholds see LANDLORD AND TENANT vol 27(1) (Reissue) para 450 et seq.
3   *Viscount Milsington v Earl Mulgrave* (1818) 3 Madd 491 (subsequent proceedings *Viscount Milsintown v Earl Portmore, Earl Mulgrave* (1821) 5 Madd 471); *Mortimer v Watts* (1852) 14 Beav 616.
4   *Lock v Lock* (1710) 2 Vern 666. However, the court is slow on mere inference to impose an obligation on the tenant for life to renew: *Capel v Wood* (1828) 4 Russ 500.
5   *Lord Montfort v Lord Cadogan* (1810) 17 Ves 485 (varied (1816) 19 Ves 635); *Bennett v Colley* (1833) 2 My & K 225. See also *Hulkes v Barrow* (1829) Taml 264. The trustees have a right to be recouped by the tenant for life who has received the rents and profits that ought to have made good the fine (*Lord Montfort v Lord Cadogan* supra), but where the estate of a tenant for life who neglected to renew was insolvent the loss was borne by capital and not by the tenant for life in remainder (*Wadley v Wadley* (1845) 2 Coll 11).
6   *Colegrave v Manby* (1826) 2 Russ 238.
7   *Stone v Theed* (1787) 2 Bro CC 243; *White v White* (1804) 9 Ves 554 at 561; *O'Ferrall v O'Ferrall* (1834) L & G temp Plunk 79. A tenant for life ought not, however, by surrendering a lease, to deprive himself of the option of renewing for the benefit of the parties in remainder: *Harvey v Harvey* (1842) 5 Beav 134.
8   *Taster v Marriott* (1768) Amb 668; *Rawe v Chichester* (1773) Amb 715; *Pickering v Vowles* (1783) 1 Bro CC 197; *Parker v Brooke* (1804) 9 Ves 583; *Eyre v Dolphin* (1813) 2 Ball & B 290; *Giddings v Giddings* (1827) 3 Russ 241; *Cridland v Luxton* (1834) 4 LJ Ch 65; *Waters v Bailey* (1843) 2 Y & C Ch Cas 219; *Trumper v Trumper* (1873) 8 Ch App 870; *Re Biss, Biss v Biss* [1903] 2 Ch 40 at 61, CA; *Hahesy v Guiry* [1918] 1 IR 135, Ir CA. See also *Griffith v Owen* [1907] 1 Ch 195; and EQUITY vol 16 (Reissue) para 903.

976. Liability for expenses of renewal. The settlement should provide how and by whom the expenses of renewal are to be raised and borne. If provision is made for raising the expenses of renewal by sale or mortgage of the estate itself, or of another estate, the tenant for life loses the rents of the part sold in the case of sale and keeps down the interest in the case of a mortgage[1]. However, if there is a direction to renew leases out of rents and profits, the whole expense has to be borne by the tenant for life[2].

If there is no special direction in the settlement as to the raising of expenses of renewal[3], or the special direction is limited in amount[4], the expenses of renewal, or the excess of them over the limited sum, must be borne by the tenant for life and remainderman in proportion to their actual enjoyment of the renewed lease[5]. Therefore, if the tenant for life derives no benefit from the renewal, as where he dies before the expiration of the original lease, the whole expense must fall on the remainderman[6]. On the other hand, if the remainderman derives no benefit from the renewal, the estate of the tenant for life cannot make any claim in respect of the fines[7].

1 *Plumtre v Oxenden* (1855) 25 LJ Ch 19; *Ainslie v Harcourt* (1860) 28 Beav 313; *Bradford v Brownjohn* (1868) 3 Ch App 711 at 715.

2 *Earl of Shaftesbury v Duke of Marlborough* (1833) 2 My & K 111; *Solley v Wood* (1861) 29 Beav 482. Where the custom was to renew annually and underlet, it was held that the fines upon renewal were payable out of rents and profits, and the tenant for life, undertaking to pay those fines, was entitled to the fines on renewal of the underleases: *Milles v Milles* (1802) 6 Ves 761. A direction to raise fines out of rents and profits has been held to authorise the raising of a gross sum by sale or mortgage: *Allan v Backhouse* (1813) 2 Ves & B 65.

3 If there is a power in the trustees to raise expenses of renewal either by sale or mortgage or out of rents and profits, and the trustees do not exercise their discretion, the court treats the case as one in which there is no direction binding the court: *Jones v Jones* (1846) 5 Hare 440 at 462; *Ainslie v Harcourt* (1860) 28 Beav 313. See, however, *Viscount Milsintown v Earl Portmore, Earl Mulgrave* (1821) 5 Madd 471.

4 *Plumtre v Oxenden* (1855) 25 LJ Ch 19.

5 *Nightingale v Lawson* (1785) 1 Bro CC 440; *White v White* (1804) 9 Ves 554; *Giddings v Giddings* (1827) 3 Russ 241; *Cridland v Luxton* (1834) 4 LJ Ch 65; *Jones v Jones* (1846) 5 Hare 440; *Hudleston v Whelpdale* (1852) 9 Hare 775; *Bradford v Brownjohn* (1868) 3 Ch App 711. In *Re Baring, Jeune v Baring* [1893] 1 Ch 61, Kekewich J thought that the enjoyment might properly be ascertained by actuarial valuation, but the point was not argued.

6 *Nightingale v Lawson* (1785) 1 Bro CC 440; *Adderley v Clavering* (1789) 2 Cox Eq Cas 192; *Harris v Harris (No 3)* (1863) 32 Beav 333.

7 *Lawrence v Maggs* (1759) 1 Eden 453.

977. Reimbursement of tenant for life and remainderman. If the expenses of renewal are paid by the tenant for life, his estate has a lien upon the residue of the term for whatever ought to be paid by the remainderman in respect of the period of which the tenant for life has not had the enjoyment[1], but the tenant for life cannot require repayment of the sum advanced in his lifetime[2]. The remainderman pays compound interest on the amount found due from him for the period down to the death of the tenant for life and simple interest from that date until payment[3]. If the renewal is made by or at the expense of the remainderman, or the money is raised by a mortgage of the corpus, the difficulty arises that, unless some course is taken to protect the remainderman's interest, the tenant for life may enjoy the estate during his whole life without bearing any greater charge than the interest on the debt created by the renewal, and he may have no assets to pay his proportion of the principal money. This inconvenience has been avoided by requiring the tenant for life to give security for an amount calculated upon the assumption that his life will last during a portion of the renewed lease[4]. If he dies within the time during which it is assumed his life will last, the security is void for the excess. If he outlives that time, he may be called on to give a further security to cover the additional proportion then to be attributed to him[5], but his income cannot be impounded on account of a security that he may have to give in the future[6].

1 *Adderley v Clavering* (1789) 2 Cox Eq Cas 192; *Jones v Jones* (1846) 5 Hare 440 at 465. See also LIEN vol 28 (Reissue) para 769 et seq.

2 *Harris v Harris (No 3)* (1863) 32 Beav 333.

3 *Nightingale v Lawson* (1785) 1 Bro CC 440; *Giddings v Giddings* (1827) 3 Russ 241; *Cridland v Luxton* (1834) 4 LJ Ch 65; *Bradford v Brownjohn* (1868) 3 Ch App 711. The rate of interest which has been allowed is 4% (*Bradford v Brownjohn* supra), but see para 945 note 5 ante.

4 See notes 5–6 infra.

5 *White v White* (1804) 9 Ves 554; *Reeves v Creswick* (1839) 3 Y & C Ex 715; *Greenwood v Evans* (1841) 4 Beav 44; but see *Jones v Jones* (1846) 5 Hare 440; *Hudleston v Whelpdale* (1852) 9 Hare 775 at 788.

6 *Hudleston v Whelpdale* (1852) 9 Hare 775 at 789.

978. Commutation of additional rent where leaseholds formerly perpetually renewable. The additional rent into which any fine or other money (including a heriot) payable on the renewal of a perpetually renewable lease or underlease[1] was converted on 1 January 1926[2] may be commuted in whole or in part[3]. A power contained in a settlement authorising or directing the application or raising of any money for or in the discharge of the costs, fines and other sums payable on the renewal of any perpetually renewable lease or underlease is deemed to authorise the payment, application or raising of money for such commutation[4]. If the land comprised in the lease or underlease is settled land or subject to a trust of land[5], the commutation money may be paid out of capital money[6] or personal estate (not being chattels real) held on the same trusts as the land[7].

1   As to renewable leases see para 975 ante.
2   See LANDLORD AND TENANT vol 27(1) (Reissue) para 453.
3   See the Law of Property Act 1922 s 145, Sch 15 para 14(1)(a) (amended by the Law of Property (Amendment) Act 1924 s 2, Sch 2). A tenant for life of settled land may enter into such agreements and do such acts and things in relation to the conversion of perpetually renewable leases or underleases into long terms as the lessor or lessee or underlessee, as the case may require, is by any enactment authorised to enter into or do: see the Settled Land Act 1925 s 62(4). For the meaning of 'tenant for life' see para 671 note 5 ante. See also para 761 et seq ante. For the meaning of 'settled land' see para 680 text to note 2 ante.
4   See the Law of Property Act 1922 Sch 15 para 17(1).
5   For the meaning of 'trust of land' see para 676 note 5; definition applied by the Interpretation Act 1978 s 5, Sch 1.
6   See para 795 ante. If the reversion is settled land, or subject to a trust of land, any commutation money must be treated as capital money or proceeds of sale of the land as the case may be: see the Law of Property Act 1922 Sch 15 para 17(3) (amended by the Trusts of Land and Appointment of Trustees Act 1996 s 25(1), Sch 3 para 1).
7   Law of Property Act 1922 Sch 15 para 17(4).

979.   Trust to renew becoming impossible to perform. Where there is a paramount trust to renew a lease for the benefit of all persons entitled in succession, the lease must be sold if from any cause renewal becomes impossible, and the proceeds of sale and of any sum set apart to provide for renewals invested as capital[1], or, if possible, the reversion in fee simple should be purchased by the trustees for the benefit of the estate[2]. If, however, the court on the construction of the settlement comes to the conclusion that the tenant for life is entitled in specie to the whole rents and profits, charged only with the payment of such a sum as may be required for the renewal, then, on the renewal becoming impracticable, there is nothing by which the charge can be ascertained, and no means by which any substituted benefit to be given to the remainderman can be ascertained by the court; the tenant for life is, therefore, entitled to all rents and profits accruing during the co-existence of the existing term and his life, including any sums directed to be accumulated for purpose of renewal and, if the term is sold, to a corresponding proportion of the price obtained for it[3]. The court does not sanction the purchase of the reversion to the prejudice of the tenant for life by trustees who have a mere power of renewal[4].

1   *Maddy v Hale* (1876) 3 ChD 327, CA; *Re Barber's Settled Estates* (1881) 18 ChD 624.
2   *Re Lord Ranelagh's Will* (1884) 26 ChD 590.
3   *Richardson v Moore* (1817) Madd & G 83n; *Tardiff v Robinson* (1819) 27 Beav 630n; *Morres v Hodges* (1859) 27 Beav 625; *Re Money's Trusts* (1862) 2 Drew & Sm 94.
4   *Hayward v Pile* (1870) 5 Ch App 214.

980.   Purchase of reversion on renewable lease. If the tenant for life or his assignee purchases the reversion on a renewable lease, he can only hold it as trustee for the remainderman[1], but he is entitled to a charge on the property for the purchase money, which carries interest at 4 per cent from his death[2].

1   *Re Lord Ranelagh's Will* (1884) 26 ChD 590; *Phillips v Phillips* (1885) 29 ChD 673, CA.
2   *Mason v Hulke* (1874) 22 WR 622; *Isaac v Wall* (1877) 6 ChD 706. As to the purchase of reversions on settled leaseholds with capital money arising under the Settled Land Act 1925 see para 808 ante. As to the rate of interest see, however, para 945 note 5 ante.

(4) ADJUSTMENT OF LOSSES BETWEEN TENANT FOR LIFE AND REMAINDERMAN

981. Losses on authorised investments generally. A tenant for life under an ordinary settlement of personal property[1] is entitled to the whole income arising from authorised investments, notwithstanding any shrinkage or decrease of the capital value, but he is not entitled to share in any augmentation of the capital value[2]. Therefore, in the case of the settled property producing a diminished or no income, the loss must be borne by the tenant for life, and he has no claim to have the loss, or any portion of it, made good out of capital[3]. Accordingly, a tenant for life has no claim against capital in respect of loss of income by the reduction of dividends on government stock[4], or by the non-payment of interest on railway bonds where the covenant is to pay out of net earnings available, and no earnings are available, even though the bonds are cumulative[5], or by the non-payment of cumulative dividends until after the cesser of his interest[6]. Any loss arising from the misappropriation by a trustee of the rents of settled property must be borne by the tenant for life[7].

1   As to settlements of personalty see para 907 et seq ante.
2   *Verner v General and Commercial Investment Trust* [1894] 2 Ch 239 at 258, 270, CA.
3   *Shore v Shore* (1859) 4 Drew 501 at 509; *Yates v Yates* (1860) 28 Beav 637. See, however, *Re Carr's Settlement, Riddell v Carr* [1933] Ch 928, where settled annuities were redeemed under what is now the Rentcharges Act 1977 ss 8–10 (s 10 as amended) (see RENTCHARGES AND ANNUITIES vol 39(2) (Reissue) paras 900–902), and the income from the investments of the redemption money being insufficient to pay the annuities in full, the tenants for life were held entitled to have the deficiency made good out of the capital.
4   *Bague v Dumergue* (1853) 10 Hare 462.
5   *Re Taylor's Trusts, Matheson v Taylor* [1905] 1 Ch 734.
6   *Re Sale, Nisbet v Philp* [1913] 2 Ch 697; *Re Grundy, Grundy v Holme* (1917) 117 LT 470; *Re Wakley, Wakley v Vachell* [1920] 2 Ch 205, CA.
7   *Solley v Wood* (1861) 29 Beav 482.

982. Losses on authorised mortgage investments. If the authorised investment is a security, such as a mortgage, not only for principal but also for interest, then, notwithstanding any payment of interest to the tenant for life, he has a right as against the remainderman to have arrears of interest charged upon the security, and the proceeds of the insufficient security must be apportioned in the proportions which the amount due for capital and the amount due to the tenant for life for arrears of interest bear to one another[1]. This right to apportionment is not defeated by a provision that no property not actually producing income is to be treated as producing income[2]. Where the mortgagees enter into possession of the mortgaged property, the rents of the property, pending realisation, ought to be applied in the first place in payment to the tenant for life of sums not exceeding the interest on the mortgages, and any excess should be applied as capital[3]. Interest on arrears of interest is not allowed[4], but where a mortgage contained a proviso for reduction of interest on punctual payment the arrears were calculated on the full rate of interest[5].

If the equity of redemption becomes barred, by virtue either of the Limitation Act 1980[6], or of an order for foreclosure or otherwise, the tenant for life is then entitled to the actual net rents, even if they exceed the amount of the interest which was previously payable under the mortgage, but he is not entitled to have any subsequent deficiency recouped out of capital[7]. However, this will not affect any right to apportionment which had accrued prior to the equity of redemption becoming barred[8].

1   *Re Moore, Moore v Johnson* (1885) 54 LJ Ch 432; *Re Barker, Barker v Barker* [1897] WN 154; *Lyon v Mitchell* [1899] WN 27; *Re Alston, Alston v Houston* [1901] 2 Ch 584; *Stewart v Kingsale* [1902] 1 IR 496; *Re Atkinson, Barbers' Co v Grose-Smith* [1904] 2 Ch 160, CA (overruling *Re Foster, Lloyd v Carr* (1890) 45 ChD 629, and *Re Phillimore, Phillimore v Herbert* [1903] 1 Ch 942); *Re Southwell, Carter v Hungerford* (1915) 85 LJ Ch 70; *Re Walker's Settlement Trusts, Watson v Walker* [1936] Ch 280; *Re Morris's Will Trusts, Public Trustee v Morris* [1960] 3 All ER 548, [1960] 1 WLR 1210. Cf *Re Pennington, Pennington v Pennington* [1914] 1 Ch 203, CA.
2   *Re Hubbuck, Hart v Stone* [1896] 1 Ch 754, CA; *Re Lewis, Davies v Harrison* [1907] 2 Ch 296.
3   *Re Coaks, Coaks v Bayley* [1911] 1 Ch 171. In *Re Broadwood's Settlements, Broadwood v Broadwood* [1908] 1 Ch 115, where there were successive tenants for life, sums received as income were ordered to be distributed between the personal representatives of the deceased tenants for life and the remainderman in proportion to the amounts owing to them for arrears of interest when the particular sum was received. In *Re Southwell, Carter v Hungerford* (1915) 85 LJ Ch 70, rents distributed under a similar order had to be brought into hotchpot (as to which see para 924 ante) when the security was realised, the ultimate distribution being made on the principle laid down in *Re Atkinson, Barbers' Co v Grose-Smith* [1904] 2 Ch 160, CA. See, however, *Re Ancketill's Estate, ex p Scottish Provident Institution* (1891) 27 LR Ir 331, where a receiver had been appointed; and *Re Godden, Teague v Fox* [1893] 1 Ch 292. See also MORTGAGE.
4   *Re Moore, Moore v Johnson* (1885) 54 LJ Ch 432.
5   *Re Atkinson, Barbers' Co v Grose-Smith* [1904] 2 Ch 160, CA.
6   See the Limitation Act 1980 ss 16, 17; and LIMITATION OF ACTIONS vol 28 (Reissue) para 994 et seq.
7   See the Law of Property Act 1925 s 31 (as amended). See also *Re Horn's Estate, Public Trustee v Garnett* [1924] 2 Ch 222. This principle does not apply if, before 1912, the land was accepted and settled as land: see the Law of Property Act 1925 s 31(5). See also *Re Bogg, Allison v Paice* [1917] 2 Ch 239.
8   *Re Horn's Estate, Public Trustee v Garnett* [1924] 2 Ch 222.

983.   Losses on investments not immediately realisable.   A loss arising on the ultimate realisation of a security covering both principal and interest, which for some time after entitlement to its possession could not be realised, must be shared between the tenant for life and the remainderman in the same way as they would have shared it if the loss had occurred when they first became entitled in possession to the fund, the principle being that neither may gain an advantage over the other[1]. In such cases a calculation is made of what principal sum, if invested at the date when the conversion should have taken place, would amount with interest to the sum actually recovered. Interest on this principal sum, or, in other words, the difference between such principal sum and the amount actually recovered, goes to the tenant for life and the rest is treated as principal[2].

1   *Cox v Cox* (1869) LR 8 Eq 343.
2   *Turner v Newport* (1846) 2 Ph 14; *Cox v Cox* (1869) LR 8 Eq 343. In both these cases the rate of interest was calculated at 4%, but as to the rate of interest see para 945 note 5 ante. The same principle was applied in *Re Duke of Cleveland's Estate, Hay v Wolmer* [1895] 2 Ch 542, where money was paid away under an erroneous court order and subsequently recovered, but without interest.

984.   Loss on conversion of authorised investment into unauthorised security.   The same principle as in the case of investments not immediately realisable[1] has been applied to a trustee wrongfully selling out an authorised investment and investing the proceeds in an unauthorised equitable mortgage[2]. If the tenant for life in such a case was responsible for the breach of trust, the remainderman would have the right to have the income received refunded to capital[3].

1   As to such investments see para 983 ante.
2   See *Re Bird, Re Evans, Dodd v Evans* [1901] 1 Ch 916 (a case on consols, where the executor of the tenant for life gave credit for interest actually received, but was not liable to refund any overpayment, as the tenant for life was in no way responsible for, or cognisant of, the breach of trust). This case is difficult to

reconcile with *Re Grabowski's Settlement* (1868) LR 6 Eq 12, except that in the latter case the dividends actually received by the tenant for life were in excess of anything that could have been recovered on an apportionment.

3   *Raby v Ridehalgh* (1855) 7 De GM & G 104.

985. Losses on trust business. Where a business is vested in trustees in trust for successive tenants for life, losses incurred in carrying on the business must normally be made good out of subsequent profits[1], but a direction to defray losses out of the estate throws them on capital[2], and, where a share in a partnership was settled, the practice of the partnership was followed, and accordingly, losses were written off against capital[3]. Where a business is only carried on temporarily until it can be sold profitably, and not pursuant to a direction in the settlement, it seems that any loss ought to be apportioned between capital and interest[4].

1   *Upton v Brown* (1884) 26 ChD 588.
2   *Re Millichamp, Goodale and Bullock* (1885) 52 LT 758; *Re Clapham, Rutter v Clapham* (1886) 2 TLR 424, where it was held that the losses and profits on the working of several steamboats, part of the estate, should be set off against each other, and that the tenant for life should take the net income.
3   *Gow v Forster* (1884) 26 ChD 672.
4   See *Re Hengler, Frowde v Hengler* [1893] 1 Ch 586, where the sale of a leasehold circus forming part of a testator's residuary estate was postponed for the benefit of the estate, and the annual profit, if any, or loss on it was apportioned between income and capital by calculating what sum, accumulating at compound interest at 4%, with yearly rests from the day appointed for conversion would, together with such interest and accumulations, after deducting income tax, have been equivalent to the amount of such profit or loss, and crediting to or charging against capital the sum so calculated, and crediting to or charging against income the rest of such profit or loss.

(5) WASTE

986. Liability for waste. A tenant for life has the right to the full enjoyment of the land during the continuance of his estate[1] subject to the duty of leaving it unimpaired for the remainderman. This duty is defined by the doctrine of waste[2]. Waste may be legal or equitable[3], and legal waste may be either voluntary[4] or permissive[5].

The liability of a tenant for life[6] for voluntary waste depends on the terms of the settlement, for he is so liable unless, as is frequently the case, he is expressly made unimpeachable for waste[7]. A tenant for life, even though impeachable for waste, is not liable for permissive waste unless his estate is expressly made subject to the condition of maintaining the premises[8]. On the other hand every tenant for life, whether impeachable for waste or not, is liable for equitable waste[9].

1   As to the right to emblements after the estate determines see para 956 ante.
2   Co Litt 53a. As to the nature of waste see generally LANDLORD AND TENANT vol 27(1) (Reissue) para 345.
3   As to equitable waste see para 997 post.
4   As to voluntary waste see para 987 post.
5   As to permissive waste see para 995 post.
6   An action for waste will lie against a tenant by the curtesy, a tenant in dower, or a tenant for life, for years, or half a year: Co Litt 53a et seq. A tenant in tail cannot be impeached for waste, either legal or equitable. A tenant in tail after possibility of issue extinct, however, or a tenant in fee simple subject to an executory devise over, may be restrained from committing equitable, but not legal, waste: *Turner v Wright* (1860) 2 De GF & J 234; *Re Hanbury's Settled Estates* [1913] 2 Ch 357; cf *A-G v Duke of Marlborough* (1818) 3 Madd 498; *Lowndes v Norton* (1864) 33 LJ Ch 583; *Re Ridge, Hellard v Moody* (1885) 31 ChD 504 at 507, CA; *Pardoe v Pardoe* (1900) 82 LT 547; *Re Fitzwalter, Wright v Plumptre* [1943] Ch 285, [1943] 2 All ER 328, CA. As to entailed interests see para 715 et seq ante; and REAL PROPERTY vol 39(2) (Reissue) para 117 et seq.
7   *Woodhouse v Walker* (1880) 5 QBD 404. See also para 994 post.
8   As to such a condition see para 995 post.
9   See para 997 post.

987. Voluntary waste. Voluntary waste is an act which is injurious to the inheritance either: (1) by diminishing the value of the estate; (2) by increasing the burden upon it; or (3) by impairing the evidence of title[1]. Unless unimpeachable for waste[2], a tenant for life may not, therefore, plough up ancient pasture[3], pull down buildings, even though ruinous, without rebuilding, or erect new buildings, or suffer such new buildings, if erected, to be wasted[4]. He may not open new mines, quarries or claypits, or work old abandoned pits or mines[5], but he may work mines or pits which have been previously opened[6] in the sense that they have been worked, not necessarily for profit, so long as such previous working or use was not limited to any special or restricted purpose, such as the purpose of fuel or repair to some particular tenements[7].

1   *Doe d Grubb v Earl of Burlington* (1833) 5 B & Ad 507. Waste by impairing evidence of title is, however, a very peculiar head of the law which has not been extended in modern times (*Jones v Chappell* (1875) LR 20 Eq 539 at 541) and may be regarded as obsolete.
2   As to tenants for life unimpeachable for waste see para 994 post.
3   *Cole v Peyson* (1637) 1 Rep Ch 106; *Tregonwell v Lawrence* (1674) 2 Rep Ch 94; *Simmons v Norton* (1831) 7 Bing 640 at 648; *Bobbett v Kennedy* (1916) 50 ILT 171. See, however, *Duke of St Albans v Skipwith* (1845) 8 Beav 354. In fee simple estates a continuance in pasture for 20 years during the life of the donor or testator impresses on land the character of ancient pasture: *Morris v Morris* (1825) 1 Hog 238 at 241. See also *Murphy v Daly* (1860) 13 ICLR 239, Ir CA. See further AGRICULTURE vol 1(2) (Reissue) para 329; LANDLORD AND TENANT vol 27(1) (Reissue) para 345.
4   Co Litt 53a. However, the erection of new buildings which constitute improvements is permitted (see paras 794 ante, 993 post). See also LANDLORD AND TENANT vol 27(1) (Reissue) para 348.
5   *Viner v Vaughan* (1840) 2 Beav 466. As to the statutory power to grant mining leases see para 843 ante; and MINES, MINERALS AND QUARRIES vol 31 (Reissue) para 373 et seq.
6   As to what is an open mine see MINES, MINERALS AND QUARRIES vol 31 (Reissue) paras 7–11.
7   See MINES, MINERALS AND QUARRIES vol 31 (Reissue) para 9.

988. Common law exception for timber. Apart from statute, a tenant for life, even if impeachable for waste, can cut timber necessary for repairs[1] in the exercise of his right to estovers or botes[2]. He can also cut trees, with certain exceptions[3], other than timber trees[4] or trees which would be timber if they were over 20 years old, but timber trees under 20 years old may be cut down in the course of the proper management of the estate for the purpose of allowing the growth of other timber[5]. If there is a local usage to fell timber trees periodically when grown in woods with a view to ensuring a succession of timber and to preserving the woods, the tenant for life is entitled to cut them, and if it is a necessary implication from the terms of the settlement that the settlor intended the woods to be enjoyed as an annual source of revenue, the tenant for life takes the proceeds of the sale[6]. If timber is decaying or injurious to the growth of other trees, so that to cut it is beneficial to the inheritance, the court can authorise a tenant for life to cut it[7].

1   Timber for repairs may not be cut in advance (*Gorges v Stanfield* (1597) Cro Eliz 593), or sold to pay the wages of men employed to do the repairs (Bro Abr, Waste, pl 112) or in order to purchase other timber with the proceeds (Co Litt 53b; *Simmons v Norton* (1831) 7 Bing 640). As to the statutory right to cut timber see para 989 post.
2   Co Litt 53a. These rights must be distinguished from common of estovers: see COMMONS vol 6 (Reissue) para 509. The estovers taken must be reasonable: Co Litt 41b, 53b. The right to take them may be restricted by special covenant (Co Litt 41b), but this does not make the taking of estovers waste (see *Anon* (1561) 2 Dyer 198b).
3   Ornamental trees or germins, that is, stools of underwood, trees planted for the protection of the house, and quickset fences of whitethorn, or fruit trees growing in a garden or an orchard, may not be cut by a tenant for life impeachable for waste: Co Litt 53a.
4   As to what trees are timber see FORESTRY vol 19(1) (Reissue) para 32.
5   *Pidgeley v Rawling* (1845) 2 Coll 275; *Bagot v Bagot, Legge v Legge* (1863) 32 Beav 509 at 517; *Earl of Cowley v Wellesley* (1866) LR 1 Eq 656; *Honywood v Honywood* (1874) LR 18 Eq 306. Cf *Dunn v Bryan* (1872) IR 7 Eq 143.

6   *Dashwood v Magniac* [1891] 3 Ch 306, CA (considering the law laid down by Jessel MR in *Honywood v Honywood* (1874) LR 18 Eq 306, that the tenant for life is entitled to cut timber on timber estates, ie estates which are cultivated merely for the produce of saleable timber, and where the timber is cut periodically); *Re Trevor-Batye's Settlement, Bull v Trevor-Batye* [1912] 2 Ch 339.
7   *Bewick v Whitfield* (1734) 3 P Wms 267; *Hussey v Hussey* (1820) 5 Madd 44; *Seagram v Knight* (1867) 2 Ch App 628, CA.

989. Statutory exception for timber. Under the Settled Land Act 1925, a tenant for life[1] who is impeachable for waste in respect of timber may, on obtaining the consent of the trustees of the settlement[2] or a court order[3], cut and sell timber which is ripe and fit for cutting[4]. He may also cut down and use timber and other trees, provided that they have not been planted or left standing for shelter or ornament[5], for the purpose of executing, maintaining or repairing any improvement authorised by that Act[6].

1   As to the tenant for life see para 761 et seq ante.
2   As to the trustees of the settlement see para 750 et seq ante.
3   As to applications to the court see paras 792–793 ante.
4   See the Settled Land Act 1925 s 66(1); and para 848 ante. As to what trees are timber see FORESTRY vol 19(1) (Reissue) para 32.
5   As to ornamental timber see paras 998–1000 post.
6   See the Settled Land Act 1925 s 89; and para 794 ante. As to authorised improvements see para 815 et seq ante.

990. Proceeds of timber and other trees properly cut. Where the cutting of timber is authorised at common law either under a court order or otherwise[1], the proceeds follow the interests of the estate and are accordingly invested and the income given to the tenant for life impeachable for waste in the first place[2]. After his death the proceeds become the property of the first tenant for life unimpeachable for waste[3], or the owner of the first estate of inheritance, whichever estate first comes into possession[4].

On any exercise by a tenant for life impeachable for waste of the statutory power to cut and sell timber[5] three quarters of the net proceeds of sale must be set aside as capital money arising under the Settled Land Act 1925[6], and the other quarter goes as rents and profits[7].

A tenant for life impeachable for waste is entitled to the proceeds of sale of trees (not being timber) cut in the ordinary course of management[8].

1   *Waldo v Waldo* (1841) 12 Sim 107; *Gent v Harrison* (1859) John 517.
2   *Wickham v Wickham* (1815) 19 Ves 419 at 423; *Tooker v Annesley* (1832) 5 Sim 235; *Waldo v Waldo* (1841) 12 Sim 107; *Phillips v Barlow* (1844) 14 Sim 263; *Gent v Harrison* (1859) John 517; *Bagot v Bagot, Legge v Legge* (1863) 32 Beav 509; *Honywood v Honywood* (1874) LR 18 Eq 306; *Lowndes v Norton* (1877) 6 ChD 139; *Hartley v Pendarves* [1901] 2 Ch 498.
3   *Waldo v Waldo* (1841) 12 Sim 107; *Phillips v Barlow* (1844) 14 Sim 263; *Gent v Harrison* (1859) John 517; *Lowndes v Norton* (1877) 6 ChD 139. As to tenants unimpeachable for waste see para 994 post.
4   *Honywood v Honywood* (1874) LR 18 Eq 306. The statement in *Honywood v Honywood* supra that the income is given to the successive owners of the estate until the owner of the first absolute estate of inheritance is reached who can take away the money must be taken to refer to the case of successive tenants for life impeachable for waste.
5   See the Settled Land Act 1925 s 66(1); and paras 848, 989 ante.
6   For the meaning of 'capital money arising under the Act' see para 795 ante.
7   See the Settled Land Act 1925 s 66(2); and para 848 ante. Any compensation for refusal of a felling licence under the Forestry Act 1967 s 11, or sum paid by the Forestry Commissioners under s 26 for trees felled and removed by them, where the tenant for life is impeachable for waste in respect of the trees, must be paid to the trustees and applied by them as if it were proceeds of sale of timber cut in exercise of the statutory power: see s 29(3); and FORESTRY vol 19(1) (Reissue) para 65.
8   *Honywood v Honywood* (1874) LR 18 Eq 306; *Re Harker's Will Trusts, Harker v Bayliss* [1938] Ch 323, [1938] 1 All ER 145.

991. Proceeds of timber wrongfully cut. A tenant for life impeachable for waste who takes upon himself to cut and sell timber without authority does so at his peril, and can never be permitted to derive any advantage from his wrongful act[1]. In such a case the timber cut or its produce belongs to the owner of the first vested estate of inheritance[2], notwithstanding that other persons may come into existence who would be entitled to a first estate tail, and notwithstanding the existence of an intervening estate in a tenant for life without impeachment of waste[3]. However, if in such a case there is fraudulent collusion between the tenant for life and the owner of the inheritance in remainder, the court interferes and orders the value of the timber which was wrongfully cut to be impounded and held for the benefit of the estate and all persons interested in it[4], and the same course will be adopted where the tenant for life is himself the owner of the first vested estate of inheritance[5].

1   *Williams v Duke of Bolton* (1784) 1 Cox Eq Cas 72; *Seagram v Knight* (1867) 2 Ch App 628, CA. As to the devolution of timber on the death of the tenant for life see EXECUTORS AND ADMINISTRATORS.

2   *Bowles Case* (1615) 11 Co Rep 79b; *Whitfield v Bewit* (1724) 2 P Wms 240; *Bewick v Whitfield* (1734) 3 P Wms 267; *Honywood v Honywood* (1874) LR 18 Eq 306 at 311.

3   *Dashwood v Magniac* [1891] 3 Ch 306 at 387, CA. See also *Pigot v Bullock* (1792) 1 Ves 479 at 484; *Gent v Harrison* (1859) John 517 at 524; *Re Cavendish, Cavendish v Mundy* [1877] WN 198, dissenting from the dictum of Romilly MR in *Bagot v Bagot, Legge v Legge* (1863) 32 Beav 509 at 523, that the produce does not belong to the first tenant in tail in being while there is a possibility of prior tenants in tail coming into existence. As to entailed interests see para 715 et seq ante; and REAL PROPERTY vol 39(2) (Reissue) para 117 et seq. As to the tenant for life unimpeachable for waste see para 994 post.

4   *Garth v Cotton* (1753) 3 Atk 751; *Birch-Wolfe v Birch* (1870) LR 9 Eq 683; *Re Cavendish, Cavendish v Mundy* [1877] WN 198.

5   *Williams v Duke of Bolton* (1784) 1 Cox Eq Cas 72; *Powlett v Duchess of Bolton* (1797) 3 Ves 374; *Birch-Wolfe v Birch* (1870) LR 9 Eq 683.

992. Windfalls. Timber blown down in a storm belongs, at law, to the owner of the first vested estate of inheritance[1], but, in the absence of improper conduct on the part of the tenant for life, the rule is to treat the produce of such timber trees as capital and allow the income to the tenant for life[2]. If trees on a settled estate, other than timber, are blown down, courts of equity, so far as may be, struggle to prevent accident interfering with the rights of the parties, and endeavour to place the tenant for life and the remainderman in the same position as if the windfall had not occurred. Accordingly, where larch plantations were so damaged by a gale that it became necessary to clear and replant the ground, the court directed the proceeds of sale of the larch trees to be invested, but fixed an annual sum, determined by the average income which would have been derived from the plantation if the gales had not occurred, to be paid to the tenant for life out of the income, and, if necessary, the capital of the invested fund[3]. Generally, a tenant for life is entitled to have the benefit of the sale of all such trees blown down by the wind as he would himself be entitled to cut[4].

1   *Whitfield v Bewit* (1724) 2 P Wms 240; *Aston v Aston* (1750) 1 Ves Sen 264, 396; *Garth v Cotton* (1753) 3 Atk 751; *Honywood v Honywood* (1874) LR 18 Eq 306.

2   *Bateman v Hotchkin* (1862) 31 Beav 486; *Bagot v Bagot, Legge v Legge* (1863) 32 Beav 509; *Re Harrison's Trusts, Harrison v Harrison* (1884) 28 ChD 220 at 228, CA. See also *Gage and Roper v Pigott and De Jenner* [1919] 1 IR 23, Ir CA.

3   *Re Harrison's Trusts, Harrison v Harrison* (1884) 28 ChD 220, CA. Cf *Re Terry, Terry v Terry* (1918) 87 LJ Ch 577, CA, where larch trees were sold in exceptional circumstances, and the court ordered half the proceeds of sale to be capitalised and the other half to be paid to the tenants for life. See also *Gage and Roper v Pigott and De Jenner* [1919] 1 IR 23, Ir CA.

4   *Bateman v Hotchkin* (1862) 31 Beav 486. It is a question of fact as regards each particular tree whether it has been blown down so as to be detached from the soil: *Re Ainslie, Swinburn v Ainslie* (1885) 30 ChD 485, CA.

993. Meliorating waste. A tenant for life impeachable for waste is not liable in respect of acts which, although technically voluntary waste[1], in fact improve the inheritance[2] and are commonly known as meliorating waste[3]. Nevertheless, the opinion has been expressed that such acts are not waste at all[4]. If the acts done in fact constitute an injury to the land, it is no defence to show that there are compensating advantages[5].

1   As to voluntary waste see para 987 ante.
2   *Birch-Wolfe v Birch* (1870) LR 9 Eq 683; *Harris v Ekins* (1872) 26 LT 827.
3   See LANDLORD AND TENANT vol 27(1) (Reissue) para 346.
4   *Jones v Chappell* (1875) LR 20 Eq 539.
5   *West Ham Central Charity Board v East London Waterworks Co* [1900] 1 Ch 624. See also LANDLORD AND TENANT vol 27(1) (Reissue) paras 345–346.

994. Privilege of tenant for life unimpeachable for waste. If, as is usual, the tenant for life is made tenant for life without impeachment of waste, he has as great power to commit legal waste as a tenant in tail has[1] and so is not liable for voluntary waste[2]. He is entitled, therefore, to open new mines or pits, and to fell timber (but not, except in proper thinning, trees planted as an improvement under the Settled Land Acts 1882 to 1890[3], or the Settled Land Act 1925[4]), and the produce of minerals or timber belongs to him, whether severed from the estate by his act or not, but not until severance[5]. This remains the law even if the sale was made not under a power contained in the settlement, but under the statutory powers conferred by the Settled Land Act 1882 or the Settled Land Act 1925[6]. It follows that on a sale of the estate with timber he is not entitled to the produce of the timber[7].

The exemption from liability for waste of a tenant for life without impeachment for waste is a special power given to him to appropriate part of the inheritance, and may be controlled or qualified, either impliedly or expressly, by special powers given to the trustees[8], or it may be restricted by exceptions, for example for pulling down houses[9], for voluntary waste[10], for wilful waste[11], for spoil or destruction or voluntary or permissive waste or suffering buildings or houses to go to decay and not repairing them[12]. If the words used are 'without impeachment of any action of waste', no action can be brought, but it would seem that the tenant for life is not entitled to the thing severed[13]. The privilege 'without impeachment of waste' is annexed to the privity of the estate[14], and it is consequently lost by change of the estate, as where a lessee for years accepts a confirmation to him for his life[15], but it devolves on the assignee of the estate[16].

1   *Bowles Case* (1615) 11 Co Rep 79b; Littleton's Tenures s 352; Co Litt 220a. See also *Re Hanbury's Settled Estates* [1913] 2 Ch 357; and para 986 note 6 ante. As to entailed interests see para 715 et seq ante; and REAL PROPERTY vol 39(2) (Reissue) para 117 et seq.
2   *Lowndes v Norton* (1864) 33 LJ Ch 583; *Re Ridge, Hellard v Moody* (1885) 31 ChD 504 at 507, CA; *Pardoe v Pardoe* (1900) 82 LT 547. As to voluntary waste see para 987 ante.
3   As to these Acts see para 678 note 1 ante.
4   See the Settled Land Act 1925 s 88(2); and para 964 ante.
5   *Anon* (1729) Mos 237; *Pyne v Dor* (1785) 1 Term Rep 55; *Wolf v Hill* (1806) 2 Swan 149n; *Williams v Williams* (1808) 15 Ves 419 at 425; *Bridges v Stephens* (1817) 2 Swan 150n; *Re Hall, Hall v Hall* [1916] 2 Ch 488; *Re Earl of Londesborough, Spicer v Earl of Londesborough* [1923] 1 Ch 500.
6   See *Re Llewellin, Llewellin v Williams* (1887) 37 ChD 317.
7   *Doran v Wiltshire* (1792) 3 Swan 699; *Wolf v Hill* (1806) 2 Swan 149n.
8   *Kekewich v Marker* (1851) 3 Mac & G 311; *Briggs v Earl of Oxford* (1851) 5 De G & Sm 156. See also *Lord Lovat v Duchess of Leeds (No 1)* (1862) 2 Drew & Sm 62, where an overriding trust to discharge mortgages out of the rents and profits of the settled estates was held not to interfere with the rights of a tenant for life to cut timber.
9   *Aston v Aston* (1750) 1 Ves Sen 264.
10 *Garth v Cotton* (1753) 3 Atk 751.
11 *Wickham v Wickham* (1815) 19 Ves 419.

12 See *Vincent v Spicer* (1856) 22 Beav 380, where it was declared that the tenant for life was entitled to cut
    such timber (except ornamental) as the owner of an estate in fee simple having not only a due regard to
    his own interest, but to the permanent advantage of the estate, might properly cut in due course of
    management.
13 Co Litt 220a; *Bowles Case* (1615) 11 Co Rep 79b.
14 *Bowles Case* (1615) 11 Co Rep 79b.
15 See *Bowles Case* (1615) 11 Co Rep 79b.
16 *Anon* (1729) Mos 237; *Watlington v Waldron* (1853) 4 De GM & G 259; *Beaumont v Marquis of Salisbury*
    (1854) 19 Beav 198. See also *Davis v Duke of Marlborough* (1819) 2 Swan 108 at 144. As to the rights of
    assignees of the timber who claim under the tenant for life see *Gordon v Woodford* (1859) 27 Beav 603.

995. Permissive waste. Permissive waste is an omission by which damage results to
premises, such as allowing houses to fall into decay[1]. A tenant for life, whether or not
made impeachable for waste, is not liable for permissive waste[2]. If, however, the settlor
has imposed a condition that the tenant for life is to keep the premises in repair, there is
a personal liability which can be enforced by the court[3], even in respect of dilapidations
existing at the time when the settlement came into force[4]. Damages may be recovered in
respect of such a liability from the estate of the tenant for life after his death, the proper
measure of such damages being such sum as is reasonably necessary to put the premises in
the state of repair in which he ought to have left them[5].

1 2 Co Inst 145.
2 *Lord Castlemaine v Lord Craven* (1733) 22 Vin Abr 523, pl 11; *Wood v Gaynon* (1761) Amb 395; *Powys v
   Blagrave* (1854) 4 De GM & G 448; *Barnes v Dowling* (1881) 44 LT 809, DC; *Re Hotchkys, Freke v Calmady*
   (1886) 32 ChD 408, CA; *Re Cartwright, Avis v Newman* (1889) 41 ChD 532; *Re Parry and Hopkin* [1900]
   1 Ch 160; *Re Owen, Slater v Owen* [1912] 1 Ch 519. The principle applies equally to land settled by the
   instrument creating the settlement and to land purchased under a direction contained in such an
   instrument: *Re Freman, Dimond v Newburn* [1898] 1 Ch 28. In the face of these cases, *Parteriche v Powlet*
   (1742) 2 Atk 383 cannot be relied on. See also *Gibson v Wells* (1805) 1 Bos & PNR 290 (tenancy at will);
   Herne v Bembow (1813) 4 Taunt 764 (lessee under a lease which contained no covenant to repair). As to
   the liability of tenants for years for permissive waste generally see LANDLORD AND TENANT vol 27(1)
   (Reissue) para 348. As to tenants unimpeachable for waste see para 994 ante.
3 *Caldwall v Baylis* (1817) 2 Mer 408; *Gregg v Coates, Hodgson v Coates* (1856) 23 Beav 33; *Woodhouse v
   Walker* (1880) 5 QBD 404; *Re Williames, Andrew v Williames* (1885) 54 LT 105, CA; *Batthyany v Walford*
   (1886) 33 ChD 624 (affd (1887) 36 ChD 269, CA); *Re Bradbrook, Lock v Willis* (1887) 56 LT 106;
   Dashwood v Magniac [1891] 3 Ch 306 at 335, CA; *Dingle v Coppen, Coppen v Dingle* [1899] 1 Ch 726; *Jay
   v Jay* [1924] 1 KB 826, DC; *Haskell v Marlow* [1928] 2 KB 45 (where the tenant for life was bound to
   keep the property in good repair and condition 'reasonable wear and tear excepted'); *Brown v Davies*
   [1958] 1 QB 117, [1957] 3 All ER 401, CA. Cf *Re Field, Sanderson v Young* [1925] Ch 636. As to the
   meaning of 'fair wear and tear excepted' see *Regis Property Co Ltd v Dudley* [1959] AC 370, [1958] 3 All
   ER 491, HL. If on renewal of leaseholds the tenant for life covenants with the lessor to do repairs he is
   under the same personal liability if he neglects to perform the covenant: *Marsh v Wells* (1824) 2 Sim & St
   87. A direction that trustees are to pay for repairs out of rents throws the cost of ordinary repairs on
   income (*Crowe v Crisford* (1853) 17 Beav 507; *Clarke v Thornton* (1887) 35 ChD 307; *Re Baring, Jeune v
   Baring* [1893] 1 Ch 61; *Debney v Eckett* (1894) 43 WR 54; *Re Thomas, Weatherall v Thomas* [1900] 1 Ch
   319 at 323), but not the cost of extraordinary repairs which would be equivalent to rebuilding (*Crowe v
   Crisford* supra; *Cooke v Cholmondeley* (1858) 4 Drew 326). However, where the tenant for life has power
   to direct the repairs, and the trustees' expenses in carrying out the repairs are charged on the estate, they
   are borne by capital: *Skinner v Todd* (1881) 46 LT 131.
4 *Cooke v Cholmondeley* (1858) 4 Drew 326; *Re Bradbrook, Lock v Willis* (1887) 56 LT 106.
5 *Woodhouse v Walker* (1880) 5 QBD 404; *Re Williames, Andrew v Williames* (1885) 54 LT 105, CA;
   Batthyany v Walford (1886) 33 ChD 624; *Re Bradbrook, Lock v Willis* (1887) 56 LT 106. Cf *Batthyany v
   Walford* (1887) 36 ChD 269, CA.

996. Liability in respect of leaseholds. A tenant for life of settled leaseholds is not
liable to the remainderman for permissive waste in the absence of an express condition
that he is to keep the settled leaseholds in repair[1]. Nevertheless he, and every successive
owner of the lease, is bound as between himself and the estate of the settlor to perform
the covenants in the lease, including the covenant to repair, and indemnify the estate

against any breach[2]. This liability of the tenant for life is unaffected by the fact that he is entitled not to the clear rack rent of the property but only to a small improved ground rent[3]. However, he is not bound to make good the settlor's deficiencies and put premises into repair which were out of repair at the time when the settlement came into force[4].

1 This was the law before 1926 whether the estate of the tenant for life was legal or equitable: *Re Parry and Hopkin* [1900] 1 Ch 160; *Re Field, Sanderson v Young* [1925] Ch 636 at 640.

2 *Re Redding, Thompson v Redding* [1897] 1 Ch 876; *Kingham v Kingham* [1897] 1 IR 170; *Re Betty, Betty v A-G* [1899] 1 Ch 821; *Re Gjers, Cooper v Gjers* [1899] 2 Ch 54; *Re Waldron and Bogue's Contract* [1904] 1 IR 240. On this point *Re Baring, Jeune v Baring* [1893] 1 Ch 61, and *Re Tomlinson, Tomlinson v Andrew* [1898] 1 Ch 232, are overruled. The court has power to sanction payment out of capital in special circumstances: see para 671 ante. As to covenants to repair see LANDLORD AND TENANT vol 27(1) (Reissue) para 350 et seq.

3 *Re Copland's Settlement, Johns v Carden* [1900] 1 Ch 326 (expenses of complying with sanitary notice and dangerous structure notice). As to the nature of rent see LANDLORD AND TENANT vol 27(1) (Reissue) para 212.

4 *Harris v Poyner* (1852) 1 Drew 174; *Re Courtier, Coles v Courtier, Courtier v Coles* (1886) 34 ChD 136, CA, distinguishing *Re Fowler, Fowler v Odell* (1881) 16 ChD 723; *Brereton v Day* [1895] 1 IR 518; *Re Smith, Bull v Smith* (1901) 84 LT 835. See also *Pinfold v Shillingford* (1877) 46 LJ Ch 491; *Re Sutton, Sutton v Sutton* (1912) 56 Sol Jo 650.

997. Equitable waste. Equitable waste is such an unconscionable or unreasonable use of legal powers as goes to the destruction of the subject matter[1]. Unless expressly authorised by the settlement, a tenant for life, although made unimpeachable for waste, is not entitled to commit equitable waste[2]. Accordingly, the courts have restrained a tenant for life unimpeachable for waste from pulling down the mansion house[3], or other houses[4], from grubbing up a wood so as to destroy it absolutely[5], from cutting underwood or saplings of insufficient growth, or at unreasonable times[6], and from cutting down timber planted or left standing for shelter or ornament[7] of the settled property[8].

Fixtures which have become part of the inheritance cannot be removed by a limited owner without the commission of waste except in the case of trade fixtures and certain ornamental fixtures[9].

A tenant in tail after possibility of issue extinct, although from the nature of his estate unimpeachable for voluntary waste[10], has been restrained by the courts from committing equitable waste[11].

1 *Aston v Aston* (1750) 1 Ves Sen 264.

2 See the Law of Property Act 1925 s 135; and EQUITY vol 16 (Reissue) para 777.

3 *Vane v Lord Barnard* (1716) 2 Vern 738.

4 *Abrahal v Bubb* (1679) Freem Ch 53; *Williams v Day* (1680) 2 Cas in Ch 32; *Cook v Winford* (1701) 1 Eq Cas Abr 221; *Cooke v Whaley* (1701) 1 Eq Cas Abr 400. See also *Aston v Aston* (1750) 1 Ves Sen 264, where it was said that the court would restrain the pulling down of farmhouses unless two were pulled down to make into one.

5 *Aston v Aston* (1750) 1 Ves Sen 264.

6 *O'Brien v O'Brien* (1751) Amb 107; *Chamberlayne v Dummer* (1782) 1 Bro CC 166; *Chamberlayne v Dummer* (1792) 3 Bro CC 549; *Brydges v Stephens* (1821) 6 Madd 279. See also *Hole v Thomas* (1802) 7 Ves 589; *Dunn v Bryan* (1872) IR 7 Eq 143 at 154.

7 As to ornamental timber see paras 998–1000 post.

8 *Abrahal v Bubb* (1679) Freem Ch 53; *Packington's Case* (1744) 3 Atk 215; *O'Brien v O'Brien* (1751) Amb 107; *Chamberlayne v Dummer* (1782) 1 Bro CC 166; *Marquis of Downshire v Lady Sandys* (1801) 6 Ves 107; *Lord Tamworth v Lord Ferrers* (1801) 6 Ves 419; *A-G v Duke of Marlborough* (1818) 3 Madd 498; *Wombwell v Belasyse* (1825) 6 Ves (2 Edn) 116n; *Wellesley v Wellesley* (1834) 6 Sim 497; *Morris v Morris* (1847) 15 Sim 505 (affd 11 Jur 196); *Turner v Wright* (1860) 2 De GF & J 234; *Ford v Tynte* (1864) 2 De GJ & Sm 127; *Weld-Blundell v Wolseley* [1903] 2 Ch 664; *Gage and Roper v Pigott and De Jenner* [1919] 1 IR 23 at 42, Ir CA. See also *Baker v Sebright* (1879) 13 ChD 179. It is stated in *Coffin v Coffin* (1821) Jac 70 that in one case the court went so far as to restrain a man from cutting down trees that he had planted himself.

9 *Bain v Brand* (1876) 1 App Cas 762 at 767, HL. See also *Re Lord Chesterfield's Settled Estates* [1911] 1 Ch 237. As to what are fixtures see LANDLORD AND TENANT vol 27(1) (Reissue) para 143 et seq. As to

questions between the representatives of a tenant for life who has annexed a chattel to the freehold and the remainderman see EXECUTORS AND ADMINISTRATORS.

10　See para 986 note 6 ante. As to entailed interests see para 715 et seq ante; and REAL PROPERTY vol 39(2) (Reissue) para 117 et seq.

11　*Abrahal v Bubb* (1679) Freem Ch 53; *Cooke v Whaley* (1701) 1 Eq Cas Abr 400; *Anon* (1704) Freem Ch 278; *A-G v Duke of Marlborough* (1818) 3 Madd 498 at 538. Tenants in tail after possibility of issue extinct are not referred to in the Law of Property Act 1925 s 135: see EQUITY vol 16 (Reissue) para 777.

998. Test whether timber is ornamental. In determining whether timber is or is not ornamental, the question for the court is not whether it is or is not ornamental in the court's opinion, but whether on the evidence it was planted or left by the owner of the estate for the time being for the purposes of ornament or shelter[1]. The taste of a testator binds the parties and, if the object in planting timber or leaving it standing is ornamental, the timber is protected whether the object is achieved or not[2].

The test to be applied in each case is whether the settlor has by his disposition or acts indicated that there is to be a continuous enjoyment in succession of that which he has himself enjoyed, in which case it is against conscience that a tenant for life, claiming under his disposition, should by the exercise of a legal power defeat that intention[3]. If, therefore, a testator or settlor occupies a mansion house with trees planted or left standing for ornament around or about it, or keeps such a house in a state for occupation, and devises or settles it so as to go in a course of succession, he may reasonably be presumed to anticipate that those who are to succeed him will occupy the mansion house, and it cannot be presumed that he meant it to be denuded of that ornament which he has himself enjoyed. Therefore, in such circumstances the court will protect the trees against the acts of the tenant for life[4].

1　*Weld-Blundell v Wolseley* [1903] 2 Ch 664. See also *Annesley v Annesley* (1918) 52 ILT 189. As to the cutting of timber see para 988 et seq ante.

2　*Marquis of Downshire v Lady Sandys* (1801) 6 Ves 107; *Wombwell v Belasyse* (1825) 6 Ves (2 Edn) 116; *Ashby v Hincks* (1888) 58 LT 557.

3　See note 4 infra.

4　*Micklethwait v Micklethwait* (1857) 1 De G & J 504 at 524–525; *Turner v Wright* (1860) 2 De GF & J 234 at 245; *Weld-Blundell v Wolseley* [1903] 2 Ch 664 at 669.

999. Protection of ornamental timber. The protection given to ornamental timber about a mansion house by making it equitable waste to fell it[1] has been extended to groups of firs planted two miles away from a mansion house[2], and to rides and avenues cut through a wood at a considerable distance from a mansion house, but not to the whole wood[3]. However, a whole wood may be considered ornamental[4], but in such a case the court directs an inquiry as to what trees can be felled without impairing the beauty of the place as it stood at the time of the settlement[5]. The protection has been extended to trees planted for the purpose of excluding unsightly objects[6], and even to trees in a park and pleasure grounds which surrounded a mansion house that had been pulled down under a power in the settlement[7].

A tenant for life who wrongfully pulls down a mansion house does not by doing that acquire a right to cut down ornamental timber[8], but trees originally planted for the ornament of a mansion house that has been pulled down by the settlor, without any intention of rebuilding, are not protected as ornamental timber between parties claiming under him[9].

Trees planted for profit are not ornamental timber[10], but in one case the protection was extended to fruit trees in a garden as being ornamental to the house[11].

1 As to this protection see paras 997–998 ante.
2 *Marquis of Downshire v Lady Sandys* (1801) 6 Ves 107.
3 *Wombwell v Belasyse* (1825) 6 Ves (2 Edn) 116.
4 *Marker v Marker* (1851) 9 Hare 1 at 21. See also *Ford v Tynte* (1864) 2 De GJ & Sm 127 at 131.
5 *Marker v Marker* (1851) 9 Hare 1; *Ashby v Hincks* (1888) 58 LT 557.
6 *Day v Merry* (1810) 16 Ves 375.
7 *Wellesley v Wellesley* (1834) 6 Sim 497. However, no judgment was delivered in this case, and it is not clear whether the decision went on the ground that the mansion house might be rebuilt, or that the trees in question were ornamental to villas that had been erected on the property.
8 *Morris v Morris* (1847) 15 Sim 505. See also *Duke of Leeds v Lord Amherst* (1846) 14 Sim 357.
9 *Micklethwait v Micklethwait* (1857) 1 De G & J 504.
10 *Halliwell v Phillips* (1858) 4 Jur NS 607.
11 *Anon* (1704) Freem Ch 278.

1000. Decaying ornamental timber. What would be done by a prudent owner in the ordinary and proper course of management is no measure of the obligation upon a tenant for life with reference to timber planted or left standing for ornament[1], and decaying timber, even if injurious to other trees, may not be cut down if it is ornamental[2]. However, the cutting of decayed wood which is beneficial to the ornamental timber that remains may be directed by the court[3] or even done by the tenant for life[4]. If a storm has produced gaps in a piece of ornamental planting, the cutting of a few trees to produce a uniform and consistent appearance instead of an unpleasant and disjointed one would not be construed to be waste[5].

1 *Ford v Tynte* (1864) 2 De GJ & Sm 127, differing on this point from *Halliwell v Phillips* (1858) 4 Jur NS 607.
2 *Bewick v Whitfield* (1734) 3 P Wms 267; *Lushington v Boldero* (1819) 6 Madd 149.
3 *Lushington v Boldero* (1819) 6 Madd 149; *Ford v Tynte* (1864) 2 De GJ & Sm 127.
4 *Baker v Sebright* (1879) 13 ChD 179. In such a case, however, the court, at the instance of the remainderman, may restrain the tenant for life from cutting and direct the cutting to be done under its supervision: *Baker v Sebright* supra.
5 *Lord Mahon v Lord Stanhope* (1808) 3 Madd 523n.

1001. Remedies for waste. Where a tenant for life has committed waste for which he is liable[1] the remainderman entitled to have the waste made good is entitled to a remedy by way of equitable lien against the profits receivable by him during the remainder of his life[2].

An injunction to restrain the commission of waste may be granted where either voluntary or equitable waste is threatened or apprehended[3].

The obligation not to commit voluntary or permissive waste is an obligation in tort[4]. Equitable waste is treated as a breach of trust[5].

1 As to the liability for voluntary waste, permissive waste and equitable waste see para 986 et seq ante.
2 See LIEN vol 28 (Reissue) para 757.
3 See EQUITY vol 16 (Reissue) para 777; INJUNCTIONS vol 24 (Reissue) paras 890–892.
4 See LANDLORD AND TENANT vol 27(1) (Reissue) para 345; LIMITATION OF ACTIONS vol 28 (Reissue) para 1057.
5 See EQUITY vol 16 (Reissue) para 777.

6. FAMILY ARRANGEMENTS

(1) DEFINITION

1002. Meaning of family arrangements. A family arrangement is an agreement between members of the same family, intended to be generally and reasonably for the benefit of the family[1] either by compromising doubtful or disputed rights or by preserving the family property[2] or the peace and security of the family by avoiding litigation[3] or by saving its honour[4].

The agreement may be implied from a long course of dealing[5], but it is more usual to embody or to effectuate the agreement in a deed to which the term 'family arrangement' is applied[6].

1   The meaning of 'family' is a wide one and includes illegitimate members *(Stapilton v Stapilton* (1739) 1 Atk 2 at 5; *Westby v Westby* (1842) 2 Dr & War 502 at 525–526; *Smith v Mogford* (1873) 21 WR 472), and persons yet to be born *(Re New, Re Leavers, Re Morley* [1901] 2 Ch 534, CA).
2   *Hoblyn v Hoblyn* (1889) 41 ChD 200 at 204.
3   *Hoghton v Hoghton* (1852) 15 Beav 278.
4   *Stapilton v Stapilton* (1739) 1 Atk 2; and the notes on that case in 1 White & Tud LC (9 Edn) 178 et seq.
5   *Clifton v Cockburn* (1834) 3 My & K 76; *Williams v Williams* (1867) 2 Ch App 294. However, any right to set aside a family arrangement which is invalid may be lost by a long period of acquiescence. As to acquiescence generally see EQUITY vol 16 (Reissue) para 924.
6   As to examples of family arrangements see para 1003 post.

1003. Examples generally. The following different types of settlements, resettlements and agreements have been supported as family arrangements:

(1)   a resettlement by a tenant in tail on attaining full age[1] reducing his interest to a life estate, with remainder to his issue in tail[2], even though the resettlement provides a jointure for the mother of the tenant in tail, and limits the estate to his younger brothers and their issue in tail, in priority to his own daughters[3];

(2)   an agreement to provide for the sisters of the tenant in tail as part of a transaction resettling the family estates[4];

(3)   a settlement made by parents on the occasion of their child's marriage making provision for the mother, though outside the marriage consideration, on her giving up her right to dower in her husband's estate[5];

(4)   an agreement between father and son altering the limitations of a family settlement[6];

(5)   an agreement between father and son that property to which the former would become entitled as heir at law of a person of unsound mind, and which formerly had been in the family, should be settled to the same uses as the family estates[7];

(6)   an agreement providing for payment of the son's debts in consideration of his giving up his interest in the family business[8];

(7)   a conveyance of the father's life estate to the son, a tenant in tail, in consideration of payment of the father's debts, provision being made for the father, mother, brothers and sisters[9];

(8)   a covenant to settle property on a nephew alienated from his father by a marriage without his father's consent, in order to reconcile father and son[10]; and

(9)   a resettlement of the family property making provision for an illegitimate son[11], or a division of the family property for the same purpose[12].

1   As to the age of majority see para 605 note 1 ante. As to resettlements see para 720 ante. As to entailed interests see para 715 et seq ante; and REAL PROPERTY vol 39(2) (Reissue) para 117 et seq.
2   *Winnington v Foley* (1719) 1 P Wms 536. See also the case referred to by Lord Hardwicke as having occurred in Lord Cowper's time, in *Tendril v Smith* (1740) 2 Atk 85 at 86. See further *Jenner v Jenner* (1860) 2 De GF & J 359; *Wakefield v Gibbon* (1857) 1 Giff 401; *Dimsdale v Dimsdale* (1856) 3 Drew 556.
3   See *Hartopp v Hartopp* (1856) 21 Beav 259, where a sum was provided for payment of the tenant in tail's debts, and for the purchase of a commission in the army.
4   *Wycherley v Wycherley* (1763) 2 Eden 175.
5   *Jones v Boulter* (1786) 1 Cox Eq Cas 288. As to dower and its abolition see REAL PROPERTY vol 39(2) (Reissue) para 161.
6   *Tendril v Smith* (1740) 2 Atk 85; *Davis v Uphill* (1818) 1 Swan 129. As to limitations see para 715 et seq ante.

7   *Persse v Persse* (1840) 7 Cl & Fin 279, HL. As to dealings with expectancies see CHOSES IN ACTION vol 6 (Reissue) para 32; MISREPRESENTATION AND FRAUD vol 31 (Reissue) para 855 et seq.
8   *Tennent v Tennents* (1870) LR 2 Sc & Div 6, HL.
9   *Bellamy v Sabine* (1847) 2 Ph 425; *Wakefield v Gibbon* (1857) 1 Giff 401.
10 *Wiseman v Roper* (1645) 1 Rep Ch 158.
11 *Stapilton v Stapilton* (1739) 1 Atk 2; *Westby v Westby* (1842) 2 Dr & War 502. As to illegitimate children see para 731 ante.
12 See *Gordon v Gordon* (1821) 3 Swan 400, where the arrangement was set aside on the ground that one party to it suppressed from the other material facts.

1004. Examples relating to the division of property. The following arrangements for division of property have been supported as family arrangements:

(1)   an agreement for the division of family property by way of compromise of a family quarrel or litigation about a disputed or lost will[1], or even to prevent family friction, where there is no question as to the devolution of the property nor any disputed right, there being some consideration for the arrangement other than love and affection[2], or any arrangement as to division of property where the construction of a will or other instrument under which the parties claim is doubtful[3];

(2)   an agreement dividing up family property, though entered into under a misapprehension of the legal rights of the parties, provided the misapprehension is not induced by any party to the agreement[4], even where the fact that misapprehension existed has been established by subsequent legal decision[5];

(3)   an agreement between members of a family to divide equally whatever they obtain under the will of an ancestor[6];

(4)   an agreement between co-heiresses dividing the property between them[7];

(5)   an agreement between the heir at law and a person supposed to be entitled under a lost will dividing the property between themselves and other members of the family[8]; and

(6)   an agreement dividing the family property between members of the family where some of the members had a title independently of the will of their father, who purported to dispose of the whole among his sons and daughters[9].

1   *Cann v Cann* (1721) 1 P Wms 723; *Pullen v Ready* (1743) 2 Atk 587; *Gascoyne v Chandler* (1755) 3 Swan 418n; *Neale v Neale* (1837) 1 Keen 672; *Wilcocks v Carter* (1875) LR 19 Eq 327 (overruled on the construction of the agreement of compromise 10 Ch App 440). As to disputed and lost wills see EXECUTORS AND ADMINISTRATORS.
2   *Williams v Williams* (1867) 2 Ch App 294.
3   *Gibbons v Caunt* (1799) 4 Ves 840; *Stockley v Stockley* (1812) 1 Ves & B 23; *Hotchkis v Dickson* (1820) 2 Bli 303, HL; *Fowler v Fowler* (1859) 4 De G & J 250; *Partridge v Smith* (1863) 11 WR 714. If the parties had not present to their minds the doubts alleged to be compromised, the transaction cannot be supported as a family arrangement: *Harvey v Cooke* (1827) 4 Russ 34; *Ashhurst v Mill* (1848) 7 Hare 502; *Cloutte v Storey* [1911] 1 Ch 18 at 33–34, CA, per Farwell LJ.
4   *Frank v Frank* (1667) 1 Cas in Ch 84; *Stephens v Bateman* (1778) 1 Bro CC 22; *Stewart v Stewart* (1839) 6 Cl & Fin 911, HL; *Bentley v Mackay* (1862) 8 Jur NS 857 (affd 8 Jur NS 1001). As to misrepresentation see MISREPRESENTATION AND FRAUD vol 31 (Reissue) para 701 et seq.
5   *Lawton v Campion* (1854) 18 Beav 87.
6   *Beckley v Newland* (1723) 2 P Wms 182 (this case is treated as an example of a family arrangement in *Hoghton v Hoghton* (1852) 15 Beav 278 at 301, although this is not the ground upon which the judgment proceeded); *Harwood v Tooke* (1812) 2 Sim 192; *Wethered v Wethered* (1828) 2 Sim 183; *Higgins v Hill* (1887) 56 LT 426.
7   *Head v Godlee* (1859) John 536.
8   *Heap v Tonge* (1851) 9 Hare 90.
9   *Houghton v Lees* (1854) 1 Jur NS 862.

(2) GENERAL PRINCIPLES

1005. Principles governing family arrangements. Family arrangements are governed by principles which are not applicable to dealings between strangers[1]. When deciding the rights of parties under a family arrangement or a claim to upset such an arrangement, the court considers what in the broadest view of the matter is most in the interest of the family, and has regard to considerations which, in dealing with transactions between persons not members of the same family, would not be taken into account[2]. Matters which would be fatal to the validity of similar transactions between strangers are not objections to the binding effect of family arrangements[3]. Conversely, an intention to create a legally enforceable contract may be negatived more readily where the parties to an arrangement are members of the same family than where they are not[4].

Although usually and necessarily present where a family arrangement is made, parental influence will not by itself render the transaction voidable[5], but where, at a time when he is not fully emancipated from his parent's influence[6], a child enters into a family arrangement under which the parent benefits to the total exclusion of the child[7] or benefits to an extent out of all proportion to the benefit accruing to the child[8], there is a presumption of undue influence[9]. The presumption will be rebutted if it appears that, when the arrangement was entered into, the child was able to form a free and unfettered judgment independent of any sort of control[10].

1 *Persse v Persse* (1840) 7 Cl & Fin 279 at 318, HL, per Lord Cottenham LC.
2 *Jodrell v Jodrell* (1851) 14 Beav 397 at 412–413 per Sir John Romilly MR. See also *Hardwicke v Johnson* [1978] 2 All ER 935, [1978] 1 WLR 683, CA.
3 *Jodrell v Jodrell* (1851) 14 Beav 397 at 412 per Sir John Romilly MR; *Hoblyn v Hoblyn* (1889) 41 ChD 200 at 204; *Westby v Westby* (1842) 2 Dr & War 502 (where the doctrine as to family arrangements is elaborately examined and explained). See also *Persse v Persse* (1840) 7 Cl & Fin 279, HL; *Williams v Williams* (1867) 2 Ch App 294.
4 *Balfour v Balfour* [1919] 2 KB 571, CA. See also CONTRACT vol 9(1) (Reissue) paras 723–726.
5 *Hoghton v Hoghton* (1852) 15 Beav 278 at 305; *Hartopp v Hartopp* (1856) 21 Beav 259 at 266. As to voidable contracts see CONTRACT vol 9(1) (Reissue) para 607 et seq.
6 As to the time at which a child can be said to be fully emancipated from his parent's influence see MISREPRESENTATION AND FRAUD vol 31 (Reissue) para 844.
7 See eg *Savery v King* (1856) 5 HL Cas 627, where the arrangement between father and son was effected for the purpose of borrowing money on the family property exclusively for the father's benefit.
8 See eg *Hoghton v Hoghton* (1852) 15 Beav 278. *Kinchant v Kinchant* (1784) 1 Bro CC 369 is to the contrary, but has been questioned: see *Brown v Carter* (1801) 5 Ves 862 at 877. See also *Talbot v Staniforth* (1861) 1 John & H 484 (where a purchase by a father, the tenant for life, from his son, the reversioner, was set aside although the object was the laudable one of keeping the estate in the family); *Playford v Playford* (1845) 4 Hare 546 (similar purchase by father again set aside, although purchase money used to pay off son's debts and other consideration given to him). In *Willoughby v Brideoake* (1865) 11 Jur NS 524 (which appears at variance with *Playford v Playford* supra) the court refused to set aside such a purchase as against a purchaser from the father after a delay of 17 years, but on appeal (11 Jur NS 706) the decision of the court below was affirmed without prejudice to any question between the son and his father's estate.
9 *Archer v Hudson* (1844) 7 Beav 551 at 560. As to the effect of parental and other influence on the validity of family arrangements see para 1021 post. As to the presumption of undue influence between parent and child see MISREPRESENTATION AND FRAUD vol 31 (Reissue) para 843 et seq.
10 *Archer v Hudson* (1844) 7 Beav 551 at 560; *Hoghton v Hoghton* (1852) 15 Beav 278 at 306; *Dimsdale v Dimsdale* (1856) 3 Drew 556 at 571; *Turner v Collins* (1871) 7 Ch App 329 at 338. As to the need for separate advice see para 1022 post.

1006. Considerations favouring family arrangements. Considerations which will lead a court to support a family arrangement are that as a result of the family arrangement disputes are avoided in the family[1]; the honour of the family is safeguarded[2], or various obligations, morally binding on a family, are provided for[3]; or family property is continued in the family[4].

1 *Hoghton v Hoghton* (1852) 15 Beav 278; *Neale v Neale* (1837) 1 Keen 672.

2 See eg *Stapilton v Stapilton* (1739) 1 Atk 2 (where provision was made for an illegitimate child); *Westby v Westby* (1842) 2 Dr & War 502 (compromise of dispute arising out of invalid marriage).

3 Eg in *Hartopp v Hartopp* (1856) 21 Beav 259, by a resettlement made shortly after the tenant in tail attained 21, a jointure was secured to his mother, and the interest of his daughters was postponed to that of his younger brothers. In *Wycherley v Wycherley* (1763) 2 Eden 175 provision was made in the settlement for the tenant in tail's sisters, in as much as these provisions were not for the benefit of the persons through whose influence the settlements were procured, they were not considered objections to the arrangement. In *Hoblyn v Hoblyn* (1889) 41 ChD 200 at 204, Kekewich J stated that the duty to provide for those members of the family who are not intended to succeed to the family property is one recognised by the court.

4 *Hoghton v Hoghton* (1852) 15 Beav 278 at 300, 307 per Sir John Romilly MR; *Dimsdale v Dimsdale* (1856) 3 Drew 556 at 569 per Kindersley V-C; *Hoblyn v Hoblyn* (1889) 41 ChD 200 at 204 per Kekewich J. An arrangement by which an extravagant son was excluded from his interest in the family business, so preserving it for the rest of the family, was supported in *Tennent v Tennents* (1870) LR 2 Sc & Div 6, HL. As to examples of particular arrangements which have been upheld see paras 1003–1004 ante.

(3) FORMALITIES

1007. Formalities in general. The necessary and sufficient formalities of a family arrangement are the same generally as those of any contract relating to the same subject matter[1]. Accordingly, where land is concerned, writing is necessary[2]. Where land is not concerned writing is not necessary[3].

For effectuating the division of the estate of a deceased person under a family arrangement in respect of the legal estate in land, a written assent by the personal representatives is, it appears, sufficient[4].

1 See CONTRACT vol 9(1) (Reissue) para 620 et seq; DEEDS AND OTHER INSTRUMENTS.

2 See the Law of Property (Miscellaneous Provisions) Act 1989 s 2 (as amended), which requires contracts for the sale or other disposition of an interest in land to be in writing and incorporate all the terms expressly agreed by the parties. See further SALE OF LAND paras 29–40 ante.

3 *Gibbons v Caunt* (1799) 4 Ves 840.

4 See the Administration of Estates Act 1925 s 36(1), under which an assent to the vesting in any person who (whether by devise, bequest, devolution, appropriation or otherwise) may be entitled to the property operates to vest the legal estate in such person even if he turns out to be the wrong person (see s 36(2), (4)), subject, however, to the rights of recovery afforded by ss 36(7), (9), 38(1). See further EXECUTORS AND ADMINISTRATORS.

1008. Need for concluded agreement. There must be a concluded agreement between the parties on the point in dispute[1]. An agreement will not necessarily be implied from a mere course of dealing[2], although third parties acquiring rights under such a course of dealing will in some cases be protected[3].

1 *Heald v Walls* (1870) 39 LJ Ch 217.

2 *Bullock v Downes* (1860) 9 HL Cas 1; *Re Moulton, Grahame v Moulton* (1906) 94 LT 454, CA. A course of dealing is strong evidence, however, of an agreement in existence: *Miller v Harrison* (1871) IR 5 Eq 324.

3 *Clifton v Cockburn* (1834) 3 My & K 76, where family arrangements had taken place under a mistaken construction of a settlement.

1009. All parties must adopt the arrangement. Subject to any express or implied provision to the contrary[1], a family arrangement come to by persons who have executed the instrument embodying the arrangement without the knowledge, or in the absence, of one member of the family intended to be affected by it is regarded as having been entered into on the assumption that the absentee will in due time join in the transaction. His concurrence, therefore, either by execution of the document[2] or by adoptive acts[3], is an implied condition of the validity of the arrangement, and if such concurrence is not obtained the arrangement is not binding even on those parties who executed the document[4]. The execution of the arrangement or acts adopting it will be ineffective if the person concerned does not have the capacity to contract[5].

1   *Peto v Peto* (1849) 16 Sim 590; *Bolitho v Hillyar* (1865) 34 Beav 180.
2   *Peto v Peto* (1849) 16 Sim 590; *Re Morton, Morton v Morton* [1932] 1 Ch 505.
3   *Dimsdale v Dimsdale* (1856) 3 Drew 556; *Westby v Westby* (1842) 2 Dr & War 502.
4   The effect of non-execution of a deed by one or more parties to it is discussed in DEEDS AND OTHER INSTRUMENTS. See also CONTRACT vol 9(1) (Reissue) para 686.
5   *Bolitho v Hillyar* (1865) 34 Beav 180. As to the capacity to contract see CONTRACT vol 9(1) (Reissue) para 630.

(4) PARTIES

1010. Parties in general. Any members of a family may be parties to a family arrangement. Agreements between husband and wife[1], parent and child[2], legitimate or illegitimate[3], uncle and nephews and nieces[4], co-heiresses[5], and brothers[6], have all been supported as family arrangements[7].

In arrangements between husband and wife by which the wife charges her property to pay the husband's debts, an inference that she is lending to her husband, and therefore is entitled to be indemnified by him, will only arise if there are facts justifying the inference, and there is no presumption for the husband to rebut[8].

1   *Jodrell v Jodrell* (1845) 9 Beav 45; *Jodrell v Jodrell* (1851) 14 Beav 397; *Harrison v Harrison* [1910] 1 KB 35.
2   *Hartropp v Hartropp* (1856) 21 Beav 259. However, as to the limits within which such arrangements must be made see para 1021 post.
3   *Stapilton v Stapilton* (1739) 1 Atk 2; *Heap v Tonge* (1851) 9 Hare 90. As to illegitimate and legitimated children see paras 731–732 ante.
4   *Lawton v Campion* (1854) 18 Beav 87; *Wiseman v Roper* (1645) 1 Rep Ch 158.
5   *Head v Godlee* (1859) John 536.
6   *Cann v Cann* (1721) 1 P Wms 723.
7   As to examples of family arrangements see paras 1003–1004 ante.
8   *Paget v Paget* [1898] 1 Ch 470, CA. See also HUSBAND AND WIFE.

1011. Parties under disability. Unless an arrangement is made with the sanction of the court[1], if a party is under a disability at the time of execution, and it is in his or her interest to repudiate the arrangement, repudiation may be inferred or not according to the rules applicable to other contracts of such persons[2]. It is no objection that one of the parties is a reversioner or an expectant heir[3].

1   See para 1012 post.
2   See CHILDREN AND YOUNG PERSONS vol 5(2) (Reissue) para 625; MENTAL HEALTH vol 30 (Reissue) para 1389 et seq. As to capacity to contract see para 1010 ante; and CONTRACT vol 9(1) (Reissue) para 630.
3   *Tweddell v Tweddell* (1822) Turn & R 1; *Bellamy v Sabine* (1847) 2 Ph 425 at 439; *Willoughby v Brideoake* (1865) 11 Jur NS 524, on appeal 11 Jur NS 706. See, however, *Talbot v Staniforth* (1861) 1 John & H 484; *Playford v Playford* (1845) 4 Hare 546. As to the rule in ordinary cases with regard to dealings with reversioners and expectant heirs see MISREPRESENTATION AND FRAUD vol 31 (Reissue) paras 855–858; EQUITY vol 16 (Reissue) para 674.

1012. Court's jurisdiction to sanction arrangements on behalf of persons under disability. Apart from its statutory powers in respect of the variation of trusts[1], the court has a limited inherent jurisdiction to sanction on behalf of all parties acts that are desirable and necessary for the benefit of the trust estate and the interests of the beneficiaries, but which, without such sanction, the trustees would have no power to do[2].

This jurisdiction is confined to those cases in which the variation is justified either by reasons of salvage arising from practical necessity[3]; or to allow maintenance out of income which the settlor has directed to be accumulated, where it may be assumed that he did not intend the children to be left unprovided for during the accumulation period[4]; or to compromise doubtful or disputed rights or settle questions of construction[5]. It does not extend to the re-arrangement of beneficial interests merely because that seems expedient or beneficial[6], nor does it enable, for example, the court to alter a man's will because it thinks it beneficial[7]. In those cases where it is exercised by way of salvage, it is a jurisdiction to confer on trustees administrative powers[8]. The jurisdiction to sanction a compromise of disputed rights is not, in a true sense, a jurisdiction to alter beneficial interests[9].

The court has a wide statutory jurisdiction, on behalf of persons under disability and others, to approve arrangements varying or revoking the trusts of any property or enlarging the trustees' powers of management or administration[10]. The court also has a more limited statutory jurisdiction, in relation to trust property other than settled land, to confer on the trustees powers of management or administration beyond those authorised by the trust instrument or by law[11]. The court has a further statutory jurisdiction to sanction certain transactions by the tenant for life of settled land or by trustees of land[12].

1   As to such powers see the text and notes 10–12 infra.
2   *Re New, Re Leavers, Re Morley* [1901] 2 Ch 534 at 544–545, CA, per Romer LJ; *Re Wells, Boyer v Maclean* [1903] 1 Ch 848; *Re Downshire Settled Estates, Marquess of Downshire v Royal Bank of Scotland* [1953] Ch 218, [1953] 1 All ER 103, CA; *Chapman v Chapman* [1954] AC 429, [1954] 1 All ER 798, HL. As to the powers of trustees in relation to settlements see para 750 et seq ante; and as to the powers of trustees generally see TRUSTS vol 48 (Reissue) para 845 et seq.
3   *Re New, Re Leavers, Re Morley* [1901] 2 Ch 534, CA; *Re Tollemache* [1903] 1 Ch 955, CA; *Re Heyworth's Contingent Reversionary Interest* [1956] Ch 364, [1956] 2 All ER 21 (beneficiary a child; variation of trusts). See further TRUSTS vol 48 (Reissue) para 921.
4   *Re Walker, Walker v Duncombe* [1901] 1 Ch 879. As to powers of maintenance see CHILDREN AND YOUNG PERSONS vol 5(2) (Reissue) para 661 et seq.
5   *Re Lord Hylton's Settlement, Barclays Bank Ltd v Jolliffe* [1954] 2 All ER 647n, [1954] 1 WLR 1055, CA; *Chapman v Chapman* [1954] AC 429 at 445, [1954] 1 All ER 798 at 802, HL, per Viscount Simonds. See also *Brooke v Lord Mostyn* (1864) 2 De GJ & Sm 373.
6   *Chapman v Chapman* [1954] AC 429, [1954] 1 All ER 798, HL.
7   *Re Walker, Walker v Duncombe* [1901] 1 Ch 879 at 885; *Re New, Re Leavers, Re Morley* [1901] 2 Ch 534, CA; *Re Wells, Boyer v Maclean* [1903] 1 Ch 848; *Chapman v Chapman* [1954] AC 429 at 445, [1954] 1 All ER 798 at 802, HL, per Viscount Simonds; *Re Cockerell's Settlement Trusts, Cockerell v National Provincial Bank Ltd* [1956] Ch 372, [1956] 2 All ER 172.
8   *Re Downshire Settled Estates, Marquess of Downshire v Royal Bank of Scotland* [1953] Ch 218, [1953] 1 All ER 103; *Chapman v Chapman* [1954] AC 429, [1954] 1 All ER 798, HL. See also TRUSTS vol 48 (Reissue) para 921.
9   *Chapman v Chapman* [1954] AC 429 at 461, [1954] 1 All ER 798 at 814, HL, per Lord Morton of Henryton.
10 See the Variation of Trusts Act 1958; and TRUSTS vol 48 (Reissue) para 923 et seq.
11 See the Trustee Act 1925 s 57; and TRUSTS vol 48 (Reissue) para 922.
12 See the Settled Land Act 1925 s 64(1) (see para 671 ante); and the Trusts of Land and Appointment of Trustees Act 1996 s 14 (see TRUSTS vol 48 (Reissue) (Supp) para 893A). See also *Re Simmons, Simmons v Public Trustee* [1956] Ch 125, [1955] 3 All ER 818. In view of the wide jurisdiction conferred by the Variation of Trusts Act 1958, the powers conferred by the Trustee Act 1925 s 57, and the Settled Land Act 1925 s 64 (as amended), are now usually invoked only where the court's sanction is sought in respect of a particular transaction. As to the court's jurisdiction to order provision to be made for dependants out of the estate of a deceased person under the Inheritance (Provision for Family and Dependents) Act 1975 see EXECUTORS AND ADMINISTRATORS.

(5) CONSIDERATION

1013. How far consideration is required. Since the consideration for a family arrangement is partly value and partly love and affection, the pecuniary worth of the consideration is not regarded too closely[1]. The court will not, as a general rule, inquire into the adequacy of the consideration[2], but there is an equity to set aside a family arrangement where the inadequacy of the consideration is so gross as to lead to the conclusion that the party either did not understand what he was about, or was the victim of some imposition[3].

1   See *Persse v Persse* (1840) 7 Cl & Fin 279, HL; *Bellamy v Sabine* (1847) 2 Ph 425. As to the treatment of family arrangements, in which a consideration for money or money's worth is involved, in the context of certain statutory provisions see para 1026 et seq post. As to consideration generally see CONTRACT vol 9(1) (Reissue) para 727 et seq.

2   *Houghton v Lees* (1854) 1 Jur NS 862; *Wycherley v Wycherley* (1763) 2 Eden 175; *Stephens v Bateman* (1778) 1 Bro CC 22; *Williams v Williams* (1867) 2 Ch App 294 at 304.

3   *Tennent v Tennent* (1870) LR 2 Sc & Div 6 at 9, HL, per Lord Westbury. See also EQUITY vol 16 (Reissue) para 673.

1014. Compromise of doubtful rights. The intention formed after due deliberation to compromise doubtful rights is sufficient consideration for a family arrangement, and the agreement will be enforceable even if the rights turn out to be different from what they were thought to be[1]. There must, however, be an intention to compromise such rights, and not a mere agreement fixing the amount to which a party is entitled on a particular interpretation of those rights, adopted by the parties as unquestionable[2]. In such a case the collateral point of the extent of the right will be left open, and the agreement will not preclude a subsequent action to determine the right[3]. A deed of arrangement involving the compromise of specific questions will not be construed so as to deprive parties of rights not in dispute at the time of the deed[4].

1   *Stapilton v Stapilton* (1739) 1 Atk 2; *Naylor v Winch* (1824) 1 Sim & St 555; *Lawton v Campion* (1854) 18 Beav 87; *Houghton v Lees* (1854) 1 Jur NS 862. As to compromises as constituting consideration generally see CONTRACT vol 9(1) (Reissue) para 740.

2   *Lawton v Campion* (1854) 18 Beav 87; *Bennett v Merriman* (1843) 6 Beav 360.

3   See note 4 infra.

4   *Cloutte v Storey* [1911] 1 Ch 18 at 34, CA, per Farwell LJ. Cf *Cocking v Pratt* (1750) 1 Ves Sen 400 (agreement as to distribution of personal estate; value found to be much greater than was known); *Bennett v Merriman* (1843) 6 Beav 360 (compromise under the court; subsequent point of construction); *Lindo v Lindo* (1839) 1 Beav 496.

1015. Concurrence of members of family. As between two parties the concurrence of another member of the family is sufficient consideration for a family arrangement if that member brings property into the arrangement or if, without that member's concurrence, the arrangement could not be effectuated[1].

1   *Williams v Williams* (1867) 2 Ch App 294 (widow concurring in an agreement between two sons to relinquish her rights); *Heap v Tonge* (1851) 9 Hare 90.

(6) VALIDITY

1016. Duty of disclosure. In any family arrangement there must be honest disclosure by each party to the other of all such material facts known to him, relative to the rights and title of either, as are calculated to influence the other's judgment in the adoption of the arrangement, and any advantage taken by either of the parties of the other's known ignorance of such facts will render the agreement liable to be set aside[1].

If one party to the arrangement has material information in his possession which, without any dishonest intention, he does not communicate to the others, proceedings by them to set aside the transaction may succeed even though they made inquiries on the subject[2].

1 *Groves v Perkins* (1834) 6 Sim 576; *Pickering v Pickering* (1839) 2 Beav 31 at 56; *Reynell v Sprye, Sprye v Reynell* (1849) 8 Hare 222 at 257; *Cashin v Cashin* [1938] 1 All ER 536, PC. See also *Scott v Scott* (1847) 11 I Eq R 74 at 96. Mere silence as regards a material fact which one party is not bound to disclose to the other is not a ground for rescission nor a defence to specific performance: *Turner v Green* [1895] 2 Ch 205. A compromise sanctioned by the court on behalf of a minor cannot be set aside by him on any ground which would be insufficient to set aside a compromise between persons sui juris. It is not clear whether it can always be set aside on grounds which, as between parties sui juris, would be sufficient. In no case can a compromise be set aside unless there has been, on the part of the person claiming to uphold it, conduct which in the view of a court of equity amounts to fraud: *Brooke v Lord Mostyn* (1864) 2 De GJ & Sm 373 at 416. See also EQUITY vol 16 (Reissue) para 662 et seq; CHILDREN AND YOUNG PERSONS vol 5(2) (Reissue) para 1392.

2 *Greenwood v Greenwood* (1863) 2 De GJ & Sm 28; *Leonard v Leonard* (1812) 2 Ball & B 171 at 188. In *Pusey v Desbouvrie* (1734) 3 P Wms 315 the executor kept to himself the value of the personal estate. In *Cocking v Pratt* (1750) 1 Ves Sen 400; *Groves v Perkins* (1834) 6 Sim 576 and *Greenwood v Greenwood* supra, some of the parties had more information as to the value of the property in question than the others. In *Bowles v Stewart* (1803) 1 Sch & Lef 209 deeds were kept back. In *Gordon v Gordon* (1821) 3 Swan 400 the fact of a secret marriage was known to one party and not to the other. In *Harvey v Cooke* (1827) 4 Russ 34 the party complaining was not informed as to certain legal opinions that had been taken. In *Pickering v Pickering* (1839) 2 Beav 31 counsel's opinion on the construction of a will had been obtained by the executor upon an imperfect statement of the terms of the will and the facts of the case; and in *Smith v Pincombe* (1852) 3 Mac & G 653 a will was not disclosed. In *Re Roberts, Roberts v Roberts* [1905] 1 Ch 704, CA, a legal opinion was incorrectly explained to the parties. See also *Dougan v Macpherson* [1902] AC 197, HL, a case of a trustee purchasing from a beneficiary. See further MISTAKE. As to the duties of the solicitor in advising see para 1023 post.

1017. Mistake in general.

If a family arrangement has been fairly entered into without concealment or imposition upon either side, and with no suppression of what is true or suggestion of what is false, then, even though the parties may have greatly misunderstood the situation and mistaken their rights, the court will not disturb the arrangement[1], even if it rests upon grounds which would not have been considered satisfactory had the transaction occurred between mere strangers[2]. Where, on the other hand, the transaction has been unfair and founded upon falsehood and misrepresentation, the court will have very great difficulty in permitting the contract to bind the parties[3].

1 *Gordon v Gordon* (1821) 3 Swan 400 at 463 per Lord Eldon LC, cited with approval in *Cashin v Cashin* [1938] 1 All ER 536 at 543, PC.

2 *Westby v Westby* (1842) 2 Dr & War 502 at 525 per Lord Sugden LC. As to mistake generally see MISTAKE.

3 *Gordon v Gordon* (1821) 3 Swan 400 at 463 per Lord Eldon LC, cited with approval in *Cashin v Cashin* [1938] 1 All ER 536 at 543, PC. As to misrepresentation generally see MISREPRESENTATION AND FRAUD vol 31 (Reissue) para 701 et seq.

1018. Mistake in cases of compromise.

While in general it would defeat the object of a family arrangement based upon the compromise of doubtful rights if the agreement could be set aside on the grounds of mistake, equity will nevertheless relieve a party who, in ignorance of a plain and settled principle of law, is induced to give up a portion of his indisputable property to another under the name of a compromise[1]. Relief will also be granted where parties, being ignorant of facts on which their rights depend or erroneously assuming that they know their rights, deal with the property accordingly and not upon the principle of compromising doubts[2].

1 *Naylor v Winch* (1824) 1 Sim & St 555 at 564, cited with approval in *Lawton v Campion* (1854) 18 Beav 87 at 93. See also EQUITY vol 16 (Reissue) para 684. As to compromise see CONTRACT vol 9(1) (Reissue) para 740.

2 *Stockley v Stockley* (1812) 1 Ves & B 23 at 31; *Harvey v Cooke* (1827) 4 Russ 34 at 57–58; *Reynell v Sprye, Sprye v Reynell* (1849) 8 Hare 222 at 255; *Lawton v Campion* (1854) 18 Beav 87 at 97–98. The plaintiff's right to relief is not forfeited by the mere fact that throughout he had the means, equally with the defendant, of knowing what his rights were and obtaining competent advice, or by the fact that the defendant was in ignorance and under mistake also: *Reynell v Sprye, Sprye v Reynell* supra.

1019. Ignorance. Ignorance of one party as to the true state of his rights is not a fatal defect in a family arrangement, nor is ignorance of its true nature, so long as the transaction is in good faith and the ignorant party is not misled by any party to it, and the ignorant party has an intention not widely different from that actually expressed by the arrangement[1]. In such cases the knowledge of the solicitor or agent is the knowledge of the client or principal[2].

1 *Frank v Frank* (1667) 1 Cas in Ch 84; *Stewart v Stewart* (1839) 6 Cl & Fin 911, HL; *Lawton v Campion* (1854) 18 Beav 87; *Dimsdale v Dimsdale* (1856) 3 Drew 556 at 571. The decision in *Turner v Turner* (1679) 2 Rep Ch 154 was to the opposite effect, but the case is very imperfectly reported, and the grounds of the decision are not given. The headnote to *Gee v Spencer* (1681) 1 Vern 32 is inaccurate, and the decision appears to have gone on the fact that the releasor had been led to believe something contrary to the fact, the case cited in support being one of fraud. The intention of the ignorant party may be shown by evidence, for example, of his desire to unite two estates which the arrangement settles in strict settlement: *Persse v Persse* (1840) 7 Cl & Fin 279, HL. As to the duties of the solicitor in advising see para 1023 post.

2 *Stewart v Stewart* (1839) 6 Cl & Fin 911 at 970, HL, per Lord Cottenham LC.

1020. Misrepresentation. A compromise of a claim of estates founded on a mistake as to title induced by the misrepresentation or suppression of facts within the knowledge of one of the parties to the compromise may be set aside[1]. A family arrangement may be rendered voidable by misrepresentation even though innocent[2], and for this purpose an insufficient or erroneous explanation may be sufficient misrepresentation[3]. An innocent misrepresentation will also give rise to a claim for damages where the misrepresentor is unable to prove that he had reasonable ground to believe and did believe up to the time the arrangement was entered into that the facts represented were true[4]. In the absence of fraud the court also has a discretion to award damages in lieu of rescission if it would be equitable to do so[5].

1 *Leonard v Leonard* (1812) 2 Ball & B 171. See also EQUITY vol 16 (Reissue) para 684.

2 *Fane v Fane* (1875) LR 20 Eq 698; *Lansdown v Lansdown* (1730) Mos 364, which was adversely criticised in *Stewart v Stewart* (1839) 6 Cl & Fin 911 at 964, HL, per Lord Cottenham LC, but no doubt was thrown on the correctness of the decision so far as it decided that a positive misrepresentation, even as to legal rights, made by one of the parties to a family arrangement, is a ground for upsetting the arrangement at the suit of the party misled. See also *Gordon v Gordon* (1821) 3 Swan 400. See further MISREPRESENTATION AND FRAUD vol 31 (Reissue) para 783.

3 *Harvey v Cooke* (1827) 4 Russ 34; *Re Roberts, Roberts v Roberts* [1905] 1 Ch 704, CA. As to innocent misrepresentation see MISREPRESENTATION AND FRAUD vol 31 (Reissue) para 762 et seq.

4 See the Misrepresentation Act 1967 s 2(1); and MISREPRESENTATION AND FRAUD vol 31 (Reissue) para 801.

5 See ibid s 2(2); and MISREPRESENTATION AND FRAUD vol 31 (Reissue) para 834.

1021. Influence of parents and other persons. Parental influence is inseparable from most cases of family arrangement[1]. Where such influence is exercised by a father to obtain some undue benefit[2] for himself, it is prima facie fatal to the validity of the arrangement so far as that benefit to the father is concerned[3]. The exercise of parental influence, however, does not invalidate an arrangement where the benefits obtained are for third persons[4], even though the influence amounts to strong pressure[5]. If the parent, as well as the third party, derives some benefit, the question whether that is fatal to the validity of the whole arrangement must be determined by the principles applicable to ordinary cases where transactions between parent and child for the benefit of the former are impeached[6]. An undue benefit so obtained by a parent may be given up or set aside and the rest of the arrangement may still be upheld[7].

Influence other than parental is generally subject to the usual rules applicable to ordinary contracts[8].

1   See para 1005 ante.

2   The benefit need not be of a direct nature: *McCausland v Young* [1949] NI 49.

3   Provisions in a resettlement reserving to the father (1) a general power of appointment upon the failure of the earlier trusts in favour of issue (*Hoghton v Hoghton* (1852) 15 Beav 278 at 307; *Fane v Fane* (1875) LR 20 Eq 698 at 710); and (2) a power to appoint an annual sum out of the settled property (*Hoghton v Hoghton* supra), have been considered unreasonable. It would be otherwise if the power, though reserved to the father, is exercisable only in favour of persons other than the father: *Hoblyn v Hoblyn* (1889) 41 ChD 200; *Tennent v Tennent* (1870) LR 2 Sc & Div 6, HL.

4   Ie persons other than the parent through whose influence the arrangement was brought about, for example mother, brothers, sisters, or other collateral relatives: *Tendril v Smith* (1740) 2 Atk 85; *Hoghton v Hoghton* (1852) 15 Beav 278; *Hartopp v Hartopp* (1856) 21 Beav 259; *Jenner v Jenner* (1860) 2 Giff 232 (affd 2 De GF & J 359); *Fane v Fane* (1875) LR 20 Eq 698 at 706 per Hall V-C; *Hoblyn v Hoblyn* (1889) 41 ChD 200 at 206.

5   *Wycherley v Wycherley* (1763) 2 Eden 175 (warmth of temper without improper exercise of influence). The influence may be equally effectual though silent: *Hartopp v Hartopp* (1856) 21 Beav 259.

6   *Hoghton v Hoghton* (1852) 15 Beav 278 at 306 per Sir John Romilly MR; *Dimsdale v Dimsdale* (1856) 3 Drew 556 at 571; *Hoblyn v Hoblyn* (1889) 41 ChD 200. As to undue influence generally see MISREPRESENTATION AND FRAUD vol 31 (Reissue) para 839 et seq. As to transactions between parent and child see also EQUITY vol 16 (Reissue) para 669; GIFTS vol 20 (Reissue) para 10; CHILDREN AND YOUNG PERSONS vol 5(2) (Reissue) para 612 et seq. As to frauds on powers see POWERS.

7   *Dimsdale v Dimsdale* (1856) 3 Drew 556. In *Jenner v Jenner* (1860) 2 Giff 232 (affd 2 De GF & J 359) the provision for the father's benefit was not complained of, and the court refused to set aside the settlement. Had the provision been impeached, the decision might have been different. In *Hoblyn v Hoblyn* (1889) 41 ChD 200 the father gave up the provision for his benefit, and the mother her jointure, and accordingly the action to set aside the settlement was dismissed.

8   *Bentley v Mackay* (1862) 31 Beav 143; affd 4 De GF & J 279 (although in this case the agreement was not set aside); *Ellis v Barker* (1871) 7 Ch App 104. As to the general law on this subject see CONTRACT vol 9(1) (Reissue) para 712 et seq. As to the presumption of undue influence where a solicitor takes a benefit under the arrangement see MISREPRESENTATION AND FRAUD vol 31 (Reissue) para 846.

1022. Separate advice. It is not essential to the validity of a family arrangement that the various parties should have separate advice[1]. Any party may be properly advised by the family solicitor[2], or even by another party having opposing interests[3].

It is, however, advisable to have separate advice, particularly if some of the parties are at a disadvantage as regards knowledge, experience, education, means or social position[4], and generally where there is a risk of the doctrine of undue influence being invoked[5]. To omit it is to incur the risk of the arrangement being set aside[6].

The advice may be obtained either by employing a separate solicitor, or by the family solicitor instructing separate counsel to advise the party[7].

1   *Jenner v Jenner* (1860) 2 Giff 232 (affd 2 De GF & J 359); *Bentley v Mackay* (1862) 31 Beav 143 (affd 4 De GF & J 279); *Cashin v Cashin* [1938] 1 All ER 536 at 543, PC.

2   *Hartopp v Hartopp* (1856) 21 Beav 259; *Hoblyn v Hoblyn* (1889) 41 ChD 200.

3   *Hotchkis v Dickson* (1820) 2 Bli 303, HL.

4   *Hoblyn v Hoblyn* (1889) 41 ChD 200 at 205 per Kekewich J; *Cashin v Cashin* [1938] 1 All ER 536. See also *Bruty v Edmundson* (1915) 113 LT 1197 at 1201–1202.

5   See para 1021 ante. Cf *Bullock v Lloyds Bank Ltd* [1955] Ch 317, [1954] 3 All ER 726. See further MISREPRESENTATION AND FRAUD vol 31 (Reissue) para 853.

6   *Sturge v Sturge* (1849) 12 Beav 229 at 239. In such a case it will not be sufficient that the documents contain a full recital of the circumstances; the parties should also have time given them to consider their position and take the advice of their friends: *Evans v Llewellin* (1787) 1 Cox Eq Cas 333.
7   *Hoblyn v Hoblyn* (1889) 41 ChD 200.

1023.   Duties of solicitor in advising. A solicitor who advises parties to a family arrangement must take care that any representations he makes on the title to and rights in the property, and the effect of the arrangement, are accurate[1]. If the solicitor's view is inaccurate as to facts or law, or if he considers it advisable to keep the parties in ignorance of the facts in order to effect the compromise, the arrangement may be voidable on the ground of non-disclosure or misrepresentation[2]. It is not sufficient merely to read over the documents, the party must be made to understand their effect[3].

1   *Fane v Fane* (1875) LR 20 Eq 698 at 707; *Hoblyn v Hoblyn* (1889) 41 ChD 200; *Willis v Barron* [1902] AC 271, HL. As to the duties of a solicitor advising a party where there is a risk of undue influence see MISREPRESENTATION AND FRAUD vol 31 (Reissue) para 853.
2   *Re Roberts, Roberts v Roberts* [1905] 1 Ch 704, CA. As to solicitors' obligations towards their clients see SOLICITORS vol 44(1) (Reissue) para 148 et seq. See also *Powell v Powell* [1900] 1 Ch 243 as modified in *Inche Noriah v Shaik Allie Bin Omar* [1929] AC 127, PC.
3   *Sturge v Sturge* (1849) 12 Beav 229.

1024.   Drunkenness. Dissolute habits, though not constituting absolute incapacity, will lead the court to examine a transaction strictly, particularly where the instrument contains in itself evidence that unfair advantage has been taken[1]. Additional care is therefore necessary on the part of other parties in case a party is drunk or addicted to drink, for the state of such a person's mind and the circumstances are considered even if he is sober at the time[2]. If the party is made drunk for the purpose, the arrangement is voidable[3], but it is not voidable if no unfair advantage is taken, and the arrangement is reasonable[4]. The court refused to give effect to an agreement as to division of property where the heir gave up property to which he had undoubted rights without consideration, and where he was ignorant, a drunkard, and without professional assistance, though there was no evidence of fraud or undue influence[5].

1   See CONTRACT vol 9(1) (Reissue) para 717.
2   *Dunnage v White* (1818) 1 Swan 137.
3   *Johnson v Medlicott* (1734) 3 P Wms 131 note [A]; *Cooke v Clayworth* (1811) 18 Ves 12. See also CONTRACT vol 9(1) (Reissue) para 717.
4   *Cory v Cory* (1747) 1 Ves Sen 19.
5   *Dunnage v White* (1818) 1 Swan 137. As to undue influence see MISREPRESENTATION AND FRAUD vol 31 (Reissue) para 839 et seq.

(7)   EFFECT

1025.   Benefits to persons not parties. Whether a family arrangement is enforceable by a person who is not a party to it depends on the same principles as apply to other contracts[1]. An arrangement is not enforceable by a person not a party to it merely because it confers a benefit on him[2], but if, in a deed of family arrangement, A covenants to confer a benefit on B, and B is not named as a party to the deed, B may nevertheless sue upon the covenant[3], at all events if the covenant relates to real property[4]. A family arrangement, whether or not made by deed, in which A confers an interest on T, who takes as trustee for B, is enforceable by B even though he is not a party[5]. The peculiar considerations applicable to the validity of family arrangements do not arise in favour of persons who are not parties[6].

1 See CONTRACT vol 9(1) (Reissue) para 748 et seq.
2 See CONTRACT vol 9(1) (Reissue) para 749.
3 See the Law of Property Act 1925 s 56(1) (see CONTRACT vol 9(1) (Reissue) para 617; DEEDS AND OTHER INSTRUMENTS); *Beswick v Beswick* [1968] AC 58 at 105–107, [1967] 2 All ER 1197 at 1223–1224, HL, per Lord Upjohn.
4 *Beswick v Beswick* [1968] AC 58 at 77, [1967] 2 All ER 1197 at 1204–1205, HL, per Lord Reid, at 81 and 1207 per Lord Hodson, and at 87 and 1211 per Lord Guest. See also DEEDS AND OTHER INSTRUMENTS.
5 *Priestley v Ellis* [1897] 1 Ch 489.
6 *Willis v Barron* [1902] AC 271, HL.

1026. Creditor's rights to avoid an arrangement. A deed genuinely made by way of family arrangement and which is made for good or valuable consideration will not be liable to be set aside[1] as a transaction defrauding creditors[2]. Likewise so long as it is made for valuable consideration, such a deed will not be voidable at the instance of the trustee in bankruptcy[3] as a transaction at an undervalue or a preference[4]. If, however, the deed is made in such circumstances as to show that it was meant to defraud creditors, it will be set aside at their request[5].

A provision for the benefit of creditors in a family arrangement is subject to the rules usually applicable to such a provision[6].

1 Ie under the Insolvency Act 1986 s 423: see BANKRUPTCY AND INSOLVENCY vol 3(2) (Reissue) para 653. See also the Law of Property Act 1925 s 173 (voluntary dispositions made with intent to defraud purchasers); and MISREPRESENTATION AND FRAUD vol 31 (Reissue) para 867 et seq.
2 See *Jones v Boulter* (1786) 1 Cox Eq Cas 288; *Hotchkis v Dickson* (1820) 2 Bli 303, HL; *Wakefield v Gibbon* (1857) 1 Giff 401; *Re Johnson, Golden v Gillam* (1881) 20 ChD 389; affd (1882) 51 LJ Ch 503, CA. See also *Denny's Trustee v Denny and Warr* [1919] 1 KB 583. See generally MISREPRESENTATION AND FRAUD vol 31 (Reissue) para 867 et seq.
3 Ie under the Insolvency Act 1986 ss 339 or 340: see BANKRUPTCY AND INSOLVENCY vol 3(2) (Reissue) para 642 et seq.
4 See *Hance v Harding* (1888) 20 QBD 732, CA (a settlement of property by a parent there forming a valuable consideration); *Re Eyre, ex p Eyre* (1881) 44 LT 922. See also BANKRUPTCY AND INSOLVENCY vol 3(2) (Reissue) para 642 et seq.
5 *Penhall v Elwin* (1853) 1 Sm & G 258; *Re Maddever, Three Towns Banking Co v Maddever* (1884) 27 ChD 523, CA.
6 *Priestley v Ellis* [1897] 1 Ch 489. See TRUSTS vol 48 (Reissue) para 567.

1027. Effect of presence or absence of valuable consideration. The courts have from time to time had to consider whether a particular family arrangement was or was not a 'voluntary disposition', 'purchase', 'sale' or 'disposition for valuable consideration' in a particular statutory context[1].

Accordingly, a deed of family arrangement disposing of land has been held not to be a voluntary disposition for the purposes of the statutory provisions[2] rendering voidable voluntary dispositions which are made with intent to defraud a subsequent purchaser for value[3]. For the purposes of stamp duty[4], while some deeds of family arrangements for which valuable consideration is given may not be and have not been regarded as conveyances on sale[5], other such deeds may and have been so regarded[6]. Conversely, for the purposes of the Rent Acts[7], a person who acquired a dwelling house by way of family arrangement, albeit giving valuable consideration for the acquisition, was held not to have become landlord by purchasing[8].

It presumably depends on the nature and terms of the family arrangement in question, and the circumstances in which it was made, whether the arrangement is regarded as a disposition for valuable consideration if it is sought to be impeached in the course of a claim for financial relief in divorce proceedings[9], or as a disposition for full valuable consideration if it is sought to be impeached in the course of a claim for financial provision from a deceased's estate[10].

1   See the text and notes 2–10 infra.

2   Ie the Law of Property Act 1925 s 173, re-enacting 27 Eliz 1 c 4 (Fraudulent Conveyances) (1584–5) (repealed), and the Voluntary Conveyances Act 1893 (repealed): see MISREPRESENTATION AND FRAUD vol 31 (Reissue) para 868.

3   See *Heap v Tonge* (1851) 9 Hare 90; *Bennett v Bernard* (1848) 10 I Eq R 584. See generally MISREPRESENTATION AND FRAUD vol 31 (Reissue) para 867 et seq.

4   See the Stamp Act 1891 s 54; and STAMP DUTIES AND STAMP DUTY RESERVE TAX vol 44(1) (Reissue) para 1030.

5   *Marquess of Bristol v IRC* [1901] 2 KB 336 at 340, DC; *Denn d Manifold v Diamond* (1825) 4 B & C 243; *Cormack's Trustees v IRC* 1924 SC 819.

6   *Marquess of Bristol v IRC* [1901] 2 KB 336, DC; *Oughtred v IRC* [1960] AC 206, [1959] 3 All ER 623, HL. See also *Lethbridge v A-G* [1907] AC 19, HL.

7   See the Rent Act 1977 s 98 (as amended), Sch 15 Pt I Case 9; and LANDLORD AND TENANT vol 27(1) (Reissue) para 812 et seq.

8   See *Thomas v Fryer* [1970] 2 All ER 1, [1970] 1 WLR 845, CA. See further *IRC v Gribble* [1913] 3 KB 212 at 218, CA, per Buckley LJ; *HL Bolton (Engineering) Co Ltd v TJ Graham & Sons Ltd* [1957] 1 QB 159 at 170, [1956] 3 All ER 624 at 628, CA, per Denning LJ; *Frederick Lawrence Ltd v Freeman, Hardy and Willis Ltd* [1959] Ch 731, [1959] 3 All ER 77, CA. See also LANDLORD AND TENANT vol 27(1) (Reissue) para 812 et seq.

9   See the Matrimonial Causes Act 1973 s 37(4); and DIVORCE. See also note 10 infra.

10   See the Inheritance (Provision for Family and Dependants) Act 1975 s 10(2); and EXECUTORS AND ADMINISTRATORS. A genuine deed of family arrangement would probably not be liable to be impeached under this provision or under the provision referred to in note 9 supra.

1028. Tax considerations. Except in certain special cases[1], a disposition by way of family arrangement stands on the same footing for the purposes of capital gains tax and inheritance tax as any other inter vivos disposition[2].

Where within the period of two years after a person's death any of the dispositions (whether effected by will, under the law relating to intestacy or otherwise) of the property of which he was competent to dispose are varied, or the benefit conferred by any of those dispositions is disclaimed, by an instrument in writing made by the persons who benefit or would benefit under the dispositions (which includes, but is clearly not confined to, a deed of family arrangement or similar instrument)[3], provided the requisite notices of election are given to the Commissioners of Inland Revenue: (1) the variation or disclaimer is not a disposal for the purposes of capital gains tax, the variation is treated as if it had been effected by the deceased, or as the case may be, as if the disclaimed benefit had never been conferred[4]; and (2) the Inheritance Tax Act 1984 applies as if the variation had been effected by the deceased or, as the case may be, the disclaimed benefit had never been conferred[5].

1   See the text and notes 3–5 infra.

2   See CAPITAL GAINS TAXATION vol 5(1) (Reissue) para 40 et seq; INHERITANCE TAXATION vol 24 (Reissue) para 407 et seq.

3   The position is to be contrasted, therefore, with the original capital gains tax and inheritance tax provisions governing post-death variations (see the Finance Act 1965 s 24(11) (repealed) and the Finance Act 1975 s 47(1) respectively (repealed)), which were limited to deeds of family arrangement or similar instruments. Difficulties were sometimes caused when it was desired to benefit a stranger to the family under the variation.

4   See the Taxation of Chargeable Gains Act 1992 s 62(6), (7); and CAPITAL GAINS TAXATION vol 5(1) (Reissue) para 95. The variation is only treated as having been effected by the deceased (or the disclaimed benefit treated as never having been conferred) for the purposes of s 62 (as amended) (and in particular, s 62(4), applying where a person acquires an asset as legatee from personal representatives), and not for the purposes of capital gains tax generally: see *Marshall (Inspector of Taxes) v Kerr* [1995] 1 AC 148, [1994] 2 All ER 106, HL; and CAPITAL GAINS TAXATION vol 5(1) (Reissue) para 95.

5   See the Inheritance Tax Act 1984 s 142(1), (2); and INHERITANCE TAXATION vol 24 (Reissue) para 471. As to other circumstances where alteration is allowed of dispositions taking effect on death for inheritance tax purposes see ss 143–146; and INHERITANCE TAXATION vol 24 (Reissue) para 472 et seq.

1029–1100. Effect of arrangement assigning interest in settled land. A deed of family arrangement, otherwise than as a security for payment of money advanced, by which the estate or interest of a tenant for life[1] under the Settled Land Act 1925 is assigned or charged is deemed to be one of the instruments creating the settlement, and not an assignment for value[2]. The deed of family arrangement does not affect the powers of the tenant for life[3] but, in relation to the exercise of those powers, he is a trustee for the assignee[4]. The trustees of the original settlement are the trustees of the compound settlement constituted by the original settlement and the deed of family arrangement[5].

1 For the meaning of 'tenant for life' see para 671 note 5 ante. See also para 761 et seq ante.
2 See the Settled Land Act 1925 s 104(11); and para 684 ante.
3 See ibid s 104(1); and para 777 ante. As to the powers of a tenant for life see para 775 et seq ante.
4 See ibid s 107(1); and para 775 ante.
5 See ibid s 31(1) (as amended); and para 754 ante. This provision removed the conveyancing difficulty occasioned by the Settled Land Act 1890 s 4 (repealed) (see now the Settled Land Act 1925 s 104(11); and the text to note 2 supra): see *Re Du Cane and Nettlefold's Contract* [1898] 2 Ch 96; *Re Lord Wimborne and Browne's Contract* [1904] 1 Ch 537. As to compound settlements see para 681 et seq ante.

SHERIFFS

1. THE OFFICE

(1) SHERIFFS

(i) High Sheriffs of Counties

1101. Introduction. A high sheriff[1] must be appointed annually for every county[2]. The authority of a sheriff does not extend beyond his own county[3]. The power of the Crown at common law to grant to a town or city the franchise or liberty of choosing its own officer to exercise the powers and duties of a sheriff[4] was abolished in 1974[5]. Most of these franchises or liberties, as regards the powers and duties of the sheriff, have been merged by statute in the counties in which they are situated[6].

The office of sheriff is of great antiquity[7], but its importance has declined as many of the sheriff's powers and duties have been transferred to the courts and to departments under the authority of the Lord Chancellor[8].

A person duly qualified[9] to serve in the office can claim exemption only by virtue of an Act of Parliament or letters patent[10], and if a person duly appointed refuses to serve he is liable to a criminal information or to be indicted[11].

1 Sheriffs appointed for a county or Greater London are known as 'high sheriffs', and any reference in any enactment or instrument to a sheriff must be construed accordingly in relation to sheriffs for a county or Greater London: Local Government Act 1972 s 219(1). 'Greater London' in s 219 (as amended) does not include the City or the Temples: s 219(8). 'County' in s 219 (as amended) has the same meaning as in the Sheriffs Act 1887 (see note 2 infra): Local Government Act 1972 s 219(8) (amended by the Local Government Changes for England (Miscellaneous Provision) Regulations 1995, SI 1995/1748, reg 8(2) (amended by SI 1996/330)).

2 Sheriffs Act 1887 s 3(1). 'County' in relation to Wales, means a preserved county (as defined by the Local Government (Wales) Act 1994 s 64): Sheriffs Act 1887 s 3(4) (added by the Local Government (Wales) Act 1994 s 62(1)). For lists of the counties of England and Wales see the Local Government Act 1972 ss 1(2), 20(2), Sch 1 Pts I, II, Sch 4 Pt I (substituted by the Local Government (Wales) Act 1994 s 1(2), Sch 1); and LOCAL GOVERNMENT. 'County', in relation to England, means, subject to the provisions of the Sheriffs Act 1887 s 38, Sch 2A (added by the Local Government Changes for England (Miscellaneous Provision) Regulations 1995, SI 1995/1748, reg 8(1)(b)), a county for the purposes of the Local Government Act 1972: Sheriffs Act 1887 s 38 (amended by Local Government Changes for England (Miscellaneous Provision) Regulations 1995, SI 1995/1748, reg 8(1)(a)). Subject to certain necessary modifications, Greater London other than the City of London, which includes the Inner Temple and the Middle Temple, is treated as a county for the purposes of the Sheriffs Act 1887: see the Administration of Justice Act 1964 ss 19, 26, 38(1) (all as amended); and LONDON GOVERNMENT. As to the appointment of sheriffs for counties see para 1103 et seq post; and as to the election of sheriffs for the City of London see paras 1109–1110 post. For a directory showing the sheriffs' shrievalties see Atkin's Court Forms (2nd Edn) Directory of High Court, District Registries and County Courts.

3 *Platt v Sheriffs of London* (1550) 1 Plowd 35 at 37a. As to the functions of sheriffs see para 1128 et seq post.

4 As to the application of the Sheriffs Act 1887 to franchises see s 34 (repealed).

5 See the Local Government Act 1972 ss 219(7), 272(1), Sch 30.

6 Most of them were so merged under the Liberties Act 1850 (repealed). However, the Cinque Ports and ancient towns of Winchelsea and Rye were merged under the Cinque Ports Act 1855 (see s 2 (repealed in part)), and by the County of Hertford and Liberty of St Alban Act 1874 (repealed) the liberty of St Alban was made part of the county of Hertford for all purposes (see s 7 (repealed)), although provision was made for saving the rights and privileges of the hundred or hereditary sheriff of the hundred of Cashio (see s 38 (repealed)). In the Isle of Ely the chief bailiff, who was appointed by the Crown, acted as sheriff except with regard to summoning juries, that duty being performed by the sheriff of the counties of Cambridge and Huntingdon: Liberties Act 1836 ss 12, 15 (both repealed). In the liberty of the Honor of Pontefract it was the duty of the sheriff of the county of York, and not the bailiff of the liberty, to execute all writs of execution: 8 & 9 Vict c 72 (Liberty of Pontefract) (1845) s 4 (repealed). The former franchise of Swansea is now preserved as a bailiwick: see para 1111 note 6 post. As to bailiwicks see para 1111 post.

7   For a general description of the office of sheriff, both past and present see the Guide to the Office of High
    Sheriff (1992), published by the Shrievalty Association.
8   As to the decline of the sheriff's jurisdiction see para 1128 post.
9   As to the qualifications to serve as sheriff see para 1106 post.
10 *R v Larwood* (1694) 1 Ld Raym 29 at 32–33. As to the exemptions from liability to serve see para 1107
    post. As to letters patent see CONSTITUTIONAL LAW AND HUMAN RIGHTS vol 8(2) (Reissue) para 920.
11 *A-G v Read* (1678) 2 Mod Rep 299; *R v Larwood* (1694) 1 Ld Raym 29; *R v Woodrow* (1788) 2 Term
    Rep 731; *R v Hutchinson* (1893) 32 LR Ir 142. In practice, the Privy Council requires the written consent
    of the nominee before his name is added to the roll.

1102. Tenure of office of sheriff. The office of high sheriff, which is held during the
pleasure of the Crown, is an annual one, the grant of the office for more than a year being
void[1]. The office is not avoided by the demise of the Crown[2] or the Duchy of Cornwall[3],
nor by the succession of the sheriff to a peerage[4].

Every sheriff of a county must continue to act as such until his successor has made the
requisite declaration and entered upon office[5]. The sheriff of a county may not transfer
his office[6], nor, while holding that office, may he act as a justice of the peace of his
county[7].

1   Sheriffs Act 1887 s 3(1), (2). Although the high sheriff of a county may be dismissed at the pleasure of the
    Crown, the Monarch cannot legally deprive him of part only of his office or grant any portion of the
    office to another: *Mitton's Case* (1584) 4 Co Rep 32b. As to the procedure for the appointment of sheriffs
    see paras 1103–1105, 1108 post.
2   See the Demise of the Crown Act 1901 s 1(1); and CROWN AND ROYAL FAMILY VOL 12(1) (Reissue)
    paras 15, 17.
3   Sheriffs Act 1887 s 3(3) (amended by the Statute Law (Repeals) Act 1973). As to the appointment of
    sheriffs of Cornwall see para 1105 post. The person holding office continues in office for the remainder
    of his term, unless sooner removed or superseded, as if the demise had not taken place: Sheriffs Act 1887
    s 3(3) (as so amended).
4   *Mordant's Case* (1583) Cro Eliz 12. As to the effect of the death of a high sheriff see para 1115 post.
5   Sheriffs Act 1887 s 7(2). As to the declaration of office see para 1108 post.
6   As to the duty of the coroner to act in place of the sheriff where the sheriff is personally interested see
    CORONERS vol 9(2) (Reissue) para 839.
7   As to the offices which a high sheriff is disqualified from holding see para 1106 post.

1103. Nomination of high sheriffs. On 12 November in every year or, if that day
falls on a Sunday, then on the ensuing Monday, persons fit to serve as high sheriffs[1] must
be nominated at the Royal Courts of Justice in the customary manner[2] for every county
other than the counties of Cornwall, Lancashire, Greater Manchester and Merseyside[3].
Nominations are made by the Lord Chancellor, the Chancellor of the Exchequer, the
Lord President and others of the Privy Council, and the Lord Chief Justice of England,
or any two or more of them, with the judges of the High Court, or any two or more of
them[4].

1   As to the qualifications for office see para 1106 post.
2   The method of nomination is as follows: after the great officials and judges have taken their places on the
    bench, the Queen's Remembrancer reads the names of nominees for service as sheriffs in the various
    counties in the preceding year. The names of the sheriffs actually in office are then struck out, and one
    of the judges present gives in another name from the Roll of the county, which has previously been sent
    to the Queen's Remembrancer. As a rule, the name is adopted and placed on the nomination list. If deaths
    have occurred or excuses are made and allowed, other names are supplied, so as to make up a list of three
    names for each county, the names so settled being read out by the Queen's Remembrancer and taken to
    be nominated as placed on the roll. Excuses, such as lack of sufficient means or illness, or requests to alter
    the order of names on the roll, may be made in open court. There will have been prior correspondence
    with the Privy Council, and the clerk to the Privy Council hands up the letters to the Lord Chief Justice
    who confers as to their contents with those on the bench. As to the procedure generally see 13 L Jo 718.

The Roll of a county, which is a private document, is the list of high sheriffs maintained in each Shrievalty by the sheriffs. As to the Queen's Remembrancer see COURTS; and as to the Privy Council see CONSTITUTIONAL LAW AND HUMAN RIGHTS vol 8(2) (Reissue) paras 521–526.

3 Sheriffs Act 1887 s 6(1), (4) (amended by the Statute Law Revision Act 1908); Local Government Act 1972 s 219(3) (amended by the Statute Law (Repeals) Act 1993). As to the appointment of sheriffs for Cornwall, Lancashire, Greater Manchester and Merseyside see para 1105 post.

4 Sheriffs Act 1887 s 6(1) (amended by the Statute Law Revision Act 1908; and the Statute Law (Repeals) Act 1998). In ancient times sheriffs were elected by the inhabitants of counties, and in some cases the office was hereditary: 1 Bl Com (14th Edn) 339, 340. The elections by the inhabitants were put an end to by 9 Edw 2 Stat 2 (Sheriffs) (1315) (repealed), and the last of the hereditary shrievalties, that of Westmorland, was abolished by 13 & 14 Vict c 30 (Sheriff of Westmorland) (1850) (repealed).

1104. Pricking the sheriffs; warrant of appointment. The names of the persons nominated as high sheriffs are afterwards engrossed on the Roll[1] and presented to the Queen in Council. The Queen appoints the person to serve by pricking with a bodkin[2] opposite the names in the list of persons nominated, a ceremony known as 'pricking the sheriffs'. One name, usually the first, is pricked for each county, except for the counties of Lancashire, Greater Manchester, Merseyside and Cornwall[3]. The names of the persons so appointed must then be notified in the London Gazette, and warrants must be made out[4], signed by the Clerk of the Privy Council and transmitted by him to the persons pricked[5]. The appointments so made are of the same effect as if made by patent under the Great Seal[6]. Within ten days of the date of each warrant of appointment the Clerk of the Privy Council must send a duplicate to the proper officer[7] of each of the respective county councils, who must enroll and keep it without fee[8].

1 As to the nomination of sheriffs see para 1103 ante; and as to the Roll see para 1104 note 2 ante.
2 The bodkin has been variously described as being of silver (see the earlier editions of this work) or golden (Account of the Nomination of Sheriffs at Westminster 1878; 13 L Jo 719). It is understood that the bodkin in present use has a brass handle and a steel shaft.
3 As to the appointment of sheriffs for these counties see para 1105 post.
4 For the form of warrant see the Sheriffs Act 1887 s 6(2), Sch 1.
5 Ibid s 6(2).
6 Ibid s 6(2). Prior to 1833, the appointment was made by patent under the Great Seal: see the Fines Act 1833 s 3 (repealed). As to grants under the Great Seal see CONSTITUTIONAL LAW AND HUMAN RIGHTS vol 8(2) (Reissue) para 849 et seq.
7 As to proper officers see LOCAL GOVERNMENT.
8 Sheriffs Act 1887 s 6(3); Courts Act 1971 s 56(1), Sch 8 para 1(1), (2), (4); Local Government Act 1972 s 251(1), Sch 29 paras 1(1), 4(1). In relation to Wales the Sheriffs Act 1887 s 6(3) (as amended) applies as if it required the duplicate warrant to be transferred to, and enrolled and kept by, the proper officer of the appropriate county or county borough council: Sheriffs Act 1887 s 6(3A)(a) (s 6(3A), (3B) added by the Local Government (Wales) Act 1994 s 62(4)). In that case the Sheriffs Act 1887 s 3(4) (as added) does not apply: s 6(3A)(b) (as so added). In the case of the high sheriff of Greater London (see para 1101 note 2 ante), the duplicate must be sent to the proper officer of each London commission area: Administration of Justice Act 1964 s 19(4)(c); Local Government Act 1972 Sch 29 paras 1(1), 4(1). As to the London commission areas see MAGISTRATES. Any question as to which is the appropriate county or county borough council in relation to a particular warrant must be determined by the Secretary of State: Sheriffs Act 1887 s 6(3B) (as so added).

1105. Sheriffs of Lancashire, Greater Manchester, Merseyside and Cornwall. The high sheriffs of the counties of Lancashire, Greater Manchester and Merseyside are appointed by the Monarch in right of the Duchy of Lancaster, the list of persons liable to serve being submitted by the Chancellor of the Duchy of Lancaster[1].

The shrievalty of the county of Cornwall is annexed to the Duchy of Cornwall and the appointment of the high sheriff is made by the Prince of Wales as Duke of Cornwall or by the Monarch in the duke's name during his minority and is determinable on his attaining the age of 18[2].

1   The Sheriffs Act 1887 s 6 (as amended) (see paras 1103–1104 ante) does not apply to the appointment of sheriffs of the counties of Lancashire, Greater Manchester or Merseyside: s 6(4) (amended by the Statute Law Revision Act 1908); Local Government Act 1972 s 219(3) (amended by the Statute Law (Repeals) Act 1993). Appointment to the office of sheriff of these counties is notified through the office of the Duchy of Lancaster and not the office of the Lord Chancellor. The Monarch annually receives the Chancellor of the Duchy of Lancaster in private audience for 'pricking' the names on the list of sheriffs for each of the three counties. As to 'pricking' the sheriffs see para 1104 ante.

     The grant of the office of Sheriff of Lancaster was held by the family of William of Lancaster from the early 13th century. Since 1399, when John of Gaunt's son, Henry of Bolingbroke, came to the throne as Henry IV, the sheriffs of the County Palatine of Lancaster have been appointed by the Monarch in right of the Duchy of Lancaster. The three counties of Lancashire, Greater Manchester and Merseyside were created from within the general area of the original county palatine: see the Local Government Act 1972 s 1(2), Sch 1 Pts I, II; and LOCAL GOVERNMENT. As to the Duchy and County Palatine of Lancaster generally see CROWN LANDS AND PRIVILEGES vol 12(1) (Reissue) para 300 et seq.

2   Sheriffs Act 1887 s 6(4) (as amended: see note 1 supra), s 37; Duchy of Cornwall Management Act 1863 s 38 (amended by the Family Law Reform Act 1969 s 10(3)); Local Government Act 1972 s 219(3) (as amended: see note 1 supra). See also *Rowe v Brenton* (1828) 3 Man & Ry KB 133. At the request of the office of the Duchy of Cornwall a list of names is put forward for consideration, one name is chosen and the appointment is then duly made and notified in the London Gazette. As to the Duchy of Cornwall generally see CROWN LANDS AND PRIVILEGES vol 12(1) (Reissue) para 318 et seq.

1106. Qualification and disqualification.

Although there are no age limits on persons eligible for nomination as high sheriffs[1], a person may not be appointed high sheriff of a county unless he has sufficient land within his county to answer the Queen and her people[2]. While holding office, the high sheriff of a county is disqualified both from acting as a justice of the peace for the county[3] and from membership of the House of Commons for any constituency comprising the whole or part of the area for which he is appointed[4].

1   *Young v Fowler* (1640) Cro Car 555 at 556; *Claridge v Evelyn* (1821) 5 B & Ald 81 at 86. However, the nomination of a person who was either very young or over 70 would be discouraged by the Privy Council. As to the nomination of sheriffs see para 1103 ante.

2   Sheriffs Act 1887 s 4 (amended by the Local Government Act 1972 s 272(1), Sch 30). What constitutes sufficient land for this purpose has never been laid down. As to persons exempt from liability to serve as sheriff see para 1107 post. The requirement to have sufficient land within his or her bailiwick does not apply in relation to any appointment to the office of high sheriff of the county of Rutland of the person who is for the time being high sheriff of the county of Leicestershire: Local Government Changes for England (Sheriffs) Order 1996, SI 1996/2009, art 2(2). As to bailiwicks see para 1111 et seq post.

3   Sheriffs Act 1887 s 17. See also *Ex p Colville* (1875) 1 QBD 133. Any acts done by a sheriff contrary to this provision are void: Sheriffs Act 1887 s 17. In its application to Greater London (as to which see para 1101 note 2 ante) s 17 is to be construed as referring to a justice of the peace for any of the London commission areas: Administration of Justice Act 1964 s 19(4)(a). As to the London commission areas see MAGISTRATES.

4   See the House of Commons Disqualification Act 1975 s 1(2), Sch 1 Pt IV; and PARLIAMENT vol 34 (Reissue) para 610. See also para 1107 post. As the Queen's representative, it is not appropriate for a high sheriff to take part in party politics.

1107. Exemptions from liability to serve.

Members of the House of Commons are exempt from liability to assume the office of or serve as high sheriff[1]. Officers of the regular military or air forces on the active list are incapable of being nominated for or elected to the office of high sheriff[2].

    A person who has been high sheriff of a county for a whole year may not be appointed high sheriff of that county within the following three years unless there is no other person in the county qualified to fill the office[3].

1   As to the qualifications to serve as high sheriff see para 1106 ante. A resolution of the House of Commons of 7 January 1689 declares it to be a breach of privilege to nominate any member for the office of high sheriff of a county: 9 Commons Journals 378; 10 Commons Journals 325, 335. See also para 1106 ante.
2   See the Army Act 1955 s 182; the Air Force Act 1955 s 182; and ROYAL FORCES.
3   Sheriffs Act 1887 s 5.

1108. Declaration of office. Before entering on the execution of his office, every high sheriff must make and sign a declaration[1] either before a judge of the High Court or before a justice of the peace of the county for which he is sheriff[2]. On making the declaration the sheriff is entitled, without payment of any fee, to exercise all the powers, privileges and authorities incident to his office[3].

The declaration of office must be transmitted to the proper officer[4] of the appropriate county council and be filed by him among the records of his office[5].

1   For the form of declaration see the Sheriffs Act 1887 s 7(1), Sch 2 (amended by the Statute Law (Repeals) Act 1978). For the Welsh version of the declaration see the Sheriffs Act 1887 (Welsh Forms) Order 1969, SI 1969/1276 (made under the Welsh Language Act 1967 s 2(1) (repealed); and now continued under the Welsh Language Act 1993 s 26).
2   Sheriffs Act 1887 s 7(1) (amended by the Statute Law Revision Act 1908). In the case of the high sheriff of Greater London (see para 1101 note 2 ante), the declaration may be made and signed before a justice of the peace for the appropriate London commission area: Administration of Justice Act 1964 s 19(4)(a). As to the London commission areas see MAGISTRATES.
3   Sheriffs Act 1887 s 6(2). This provision does not apply to the counties of Cornwall, Lancashire, Greater Manchester and Merseyside: s 6(4) (amended by the Statute Law Revision Act 1908); Local Government Act 1972 s 219(3) (amended by the Statute Law (Repeals) Act 1993). As to sheriffs for these counties see para 1105 ante. As to a sheriff's tenure of office see para 1102 ante; and as to his statutory functions see para 1128 et seq post.
4   As to proper officers see LOCAL GOVERNMENT.
5   Sheriffs Act 1887 s 30(1) (amended by the Statute Law (Repeals) Act 1981); Courts Act 1971 s 56(1), Sch 8 para 1(1), (2), (4); Local Government Act 1972 s 251(1), Sch 29 paras 1(1), 4(1). In the case of the high sheriff of Greater London the proper officer is the proper officer of each of the London commission areas: Administration of Justice Act 1964 s 19(4)(c); Courts Act 1971 Sch 8 para 1(1), (2), (4); Local Government Act 1972 Sch 29 paras 1(1), 4(1). In practice all the records for the shrievalty within England and Wales are maintained in the office of the Queen's Remembrancer (Central Office, Royal Courts of Justice, Strand, London WC2A 2LL).

(ii) Sheriffs of the City of London

1109. Election of sheriffs. It is an ancient privilege of the Corporation of the City of London to elect sheriffs for the City[1]. Two sheriffs, elected annually, jointly exercise the office of sheriff within the City[2]. The office is held of the corporation, which is answerable to the Crown for its due execution on the part of the sheriffs and their officers[3].

The election of the sheriffs of the City takes place on 24 June, unless that date happens to be either a Saturday or Sunday, in which case the election must be held on the Monday next immediately following either of those days[4], in the Common Hall of Guildhall[5] from among candidates nominated from: (1) all aldermen who have not yet held the office of sheriff[6]; (2) freemen, not exceeding three in number, nominated by the Lord Mayor between 14 February and 14 April[7]; and (3) freemen nominated in writing by any two liverymen before 1 May[8]. No person may be nominated who has served as sheriff before[9]. Any candidate nominated may withdraw his name by written notice delivered to the Town Clerk[10] before 8 May[11]. The precepts for the election are issued by the Lord Mayor and the election is decided by a show of hands unless a poll is demanded by any candidate or any two electors[12]. A bond of £1,000 is required to be given by the sheriffs–elect for due attendance at Guildhall to be sworn in[13].

1   See the Sheriffs Act 1887 s 33(1) (amended by the Statute Law Revision Act 1908); and LONDON
    GOVERNMENT. As to the approval of elections by the Monarch see para 1110 post.
        From at least the 12th century, under charters granted by the Crown, the sheriffs of the City of London
    were elected jointly as sheriffs of London and Middlesex: see the 3rd Charter of King John, 5 July 1199,
    and the Report of the Royal Commission on the Amalgamation of the City and County of London
    (1894) (C 2nd series 7493) paras 6102–6107. However, the right of the Corporation of the City of
    London to elect the sheriff of Middlesex was abolished by the Local Government Act 1888 s 46(6)
    (repealed), and the authority of the sheriffs of the City of London now does not extend beyond the City:
    s 41(8) (repealed). As to the high sheriff of Greater London see para 1101 note 2 ante. As to the
    administration of London generally see LONDON GOVERNMENT.
2   See the Sheriffs Act 1887 s 33(4) (amended by the Statute Law Revision Act 1908; and the Statute Law
    (Repeals) Act 1998), which applies the Act to the duly elected sheriffs of the City in the same way as
    it applies to high sheriffs of counties (as to whom see para 1101 ante). See also the Report of the Royal
    Commission on the Amalgamation of the City and County of London (1894) (C 2nd series 7493), App
    iii, 20, App v, 4, and the Corporation of London, Origin, Constitution, Powers and Duties (1953),
    paras 24–26. See also note 1 supra.
        The duties of the sheriffs of the City of London are almost entirely ceremonial, their legal duties being
    performed by the Secondary (as to whom see para 1116 post). They attend the Lord Mayor on state
    occasions and present petitions on behalf of the corporation to the House of Commons. It is also their
    privilege to wait on the Monarch, by the direction of the corporation, with the City Remembrancer, to
    ascertain the royal will and pleasure as to the reception of addresses from the corporation: see the Report
    of the Royal Commission on the Amalgamation of the City and County of London (1894) (C 2nd series
    7493), App iii, 21. See also evidence on sheriffs submitted to the Royal Commission on London
    Government (1921) (Cmd 1830) by the City of London.
3   See the Report of the Royal Commission on the Amalgamation of the City and County of London
    (1894) (C 2nd series 7493), App iii, 53, 54. See also the evidence submitted to the Royal Commission
    on London Government (1921) (Cmd 1830) by the City of London on Sheriffs.
4   Act of Common Council of 21 January 1932 cl 3 (amended by Act of Common Council of 22 March
    1973 cl 1). However, the Court of Common Council, by solemn resolution, may appoint some other
    day for the election: Act of Common Council of 21 January 1932 cl 3. As to the Court of Common
    Council see LONDON GOVERNMENT.
5   Ibid cll 2, 14.
6   Ibid cl 7. Aldermen in their first year in that office are not liable to serve against their will: cl 7 proviso.
7   Ibid cl 8; Act of Common Council of 25 June 1998 cl 1.
8   Act of Common Council of 21 January 1932 cl 10; Act of Common Council of 4 November 1937 cl 2;
    Act of Common Council of 25 June 1998 cl 2.
9   Act of Common Council of 21 January 1932 cl 24.
10 As to the Town Clerk see LONDON GOVERNMENT.
11 Act of Common Council of 21 January 1932 cl 12; Act of Common Council of 25 June 1998 cl 3.
12 As to the legislation governing and the procedure for such polls see LONDON GOVERNMENT.
13 Act of Common Council of 21 January 1932 cl 17.

1110. Approval of election. The election of the sheriffs of the City of London[1] must
be approved by the Monarch[2]. Approval is signified by royal warrants under the seal of
the Chancellor of the Exchequer which are prepared at the Central Office of the Supreme
Court[3] and delivered to the sheriffs, or their duly authorised agents, without fee, between
30 September and 12 November in every year[4]. Unless the warrants are stayed by order
of Her Majesty in Council on or before 30 September the election is deemed to be
approved[5]. The sheriffs are sworn in at Guildhall on 28 September unless that date
happens to be either a Saturday or a Sunday, in which case then upon the Friday next
immediately preceding either of those days[6].

    A person who, having been duly elected, fails to appear to be sworn in is liable to a
fine[7].

1   As to the election of sheriffs in the City of London see para 1109 ante.
2   See the evidence submitted to the Royal Commission on London Government (1921) (Cmd 1830) by
    the City of London on Sheriffs.
3   The documents are prepared in the office of the Queen's Remembrancer (as to which see COURTS), who
    attests to the seal.

4   Sheriffs Act 1887 s 33(2) (amended by the Statute Law Revision Act 1908). The warrants are filed and recorded in the Central Office of the Supreme Court: Sheriffs Act 1887 s 33(3) (amended by the Statute Laws Revision Act 1908).

5   Sheriffs Act 1887 s 33(2) (as amended: see note 4 supra).

6   Act of Common Council of 21 January 1932 cl 17 (amended by the Act of Common Council of 22 March 1973 cl 3).

7   The fine is £600 for aldermen and £400 for other persons: Act of Common Council of 21 January 1932 cll 18–21. The fine, which is recoverable in the Mayor's and City of London Court (as to which see COURTS), is paid to the City of London's Freemen's School (formerly the Freeman's Orphan School): cl 23.

(2) UNDER-SHERIFFS, DEPUTIES, BAILIFFS AND OTHER OFFICERS

(i) Under-Sheriffs

1111. Appointment and jurisdiction. Every high sheriff[1] is required, within one month of the notification of his appointment in the London Gazette, to appoint by writing under his hand a fit person[2] to be his under-sheriff[3]. The high sheriff must send a duplicate of the written appointment to the proper officer of the county council, who must file it in his records[4].

The area for which an under-sheriff acts is known as a bailiwick[5], each bailiwick being the same area as that for which an under-sheriff acted prior to the reorganisation of local government in 1974[6]. One of the effects of the reorganisation was that some of the old counties, together with a number of cities and towns which had been counties in themselves, for which high sheriffs and therefore under-sheriffs had been appointed, disappeared. Thus, many of the bailiwicks do not have the same boundaries as the new counties for which high sheriffs are appointed[7], with the result that in many cases there are two or more bailiwicks within a county and a bailiwick may be situated in more than one county[8]. Where a bailiwick is situated in two or more counties[9], the duty of appointing the under-sheriff for that area must be discharged by the high sheriff of the county containing the greater part of that area[10], after consulting any other high sheriff concerned[11].

1   As to the meaning of 'high sheriff' see para 1101 note 1 ante.

2   Although there are no particular qualifications for the office of under-sheriff, a solicitor of standing is usually appointed.

3   Sheriffs Act 1887 s 23(1). In the case of Greater London (as to which see para 1101 note 2 ante) the high sheriff is required to appoint an under-sheriff for each of the London commission areas (see the Administration of Justice Act 1964 s 19(1)), although in recent practice the same person has been appointed for each area. As to the London commission areas see MAGISTRATES. As to the under-sheriff of the City of London see para 1116 post.

4   Sheriffs Act 1887 s 23(1); Courts Act 1971 s 56(1), Sch 8 para 1(1), (2), (4); Local Government Act 1972 s 251(1), Sch 29 paras 1(1), 4(1). As to proper officers see LOCAL GOVERNMENT. As to the office of under-sheriff see para 1112 et seq post.

5   Under-Sheriffs' Bailiwicks Order 1974, SI 1974/222, art 2(1) (made under the Local Government Act 1972 s 219(4)). See also note 8 infra.

6   Under-Sheriffs' Bailiwicks Order 1974, SI 1974/222, art 2(2). However, in the area for which the under-sheriff of Glamorgan acted before the reorganisation there are two bailiwicks, Glamorgan and Swansea: see art 3, Schedule. As to the reorganisation of local government effected by the Local Government Act 1972 see LOCAL GOVERNMENT.

7   As to the appointment of high sheriffs of counties see para 1101 ante.

8   Although a writ of execution (as to which see para 1132 post) must be directed to the high sheriff of the county in which the writ is to be executed, it must be sent to the same under-sheriff as it would have been sent to prior to the reorganisation of 1974, notwithstanding that his bailiwick is situated in a different county. Thus, a writ for execution at an address near Gatwick Airport will be addressed to the high sheriff of West Sussex, in which county the airport is now situated, but will be sent for execution

to the under-sheriff of Surrey, whose bailiwick extends to the whole of the old county of Surrey in which the airport was previously situated. By arrangement with the Queen's Remembrancer and the Under-Sheriffs' Association the list of High Sheriffs and Under-Sheriffs' Bailiwicks, which is maintained in the High Court and in each district registry, has an asterisk against the name of one under-sheriff for each county in which there is more than one bailiwick, indicating that that under-sheriff will answer inquiries to ascertain the high sheriff to whom the writ should be directed and the under-sheriff to whom it should be sent for execution.

The following list shows, as regards England, each shrievalty of a high sheriff to whom a writ is to be directed and, in parentheses, the bailiwick or bailiwicks of the under-sheriff with whom the writ is to be lodged: Greater London (Greater London); City of London (City of London); *Metropolitan counties*: Greater Manchester (Lancashire*; Cheshire; Yorkshire); Merseyside (Lancashire*; Cheshire); South Yorkshire (Yorkshire*; Hallamshire; Nottinghamshire); Tyne and Wear (City of Newcastle upon Tyne; Northumberland*; Durham); West Midlands (Staffordshire; Worcestershire; Warwickshire*); West Yorkshire (Yorkshire); *Non-metropolitan counties*: Avon (Somerset*; City of Bristol; Gloucestershire); Bedfordshire (Bedfordshire); Berkshire (Berkshire*; Buckinghamshire); Buckinghamshire (Buckinghamshire); Cambridgeshire (Cambridgeshire and Isle of Ely; Huntingdonshire and Peterborough); Cheshire (City of Chester; Lancashire; Cheshire*); Cleveland (Durham*; Yorkshire); Cornwall (Cornwall); Cumbria (Lancashire; Cumberland*; Westmorland; Yorkshire); Derbyshire (Derbyshire*; Cheshire); Devon (City of Exeter; Devonshire*; Dorset (Hampshire; Dorset*; Borough of Poole); Durham (Durham*; Yorkshire); East Sussex (Sussex); Essex (Essex); Gloucestershire (City of Gloucester; Gloucestershire*); Hampshire (Hampshire*; Southampton Town); Hereford and Worcester (City of Worcester; Herefordshire; Worcestershire*); Hertfordshire (Hertfordshire); Humberside (Lincolnshire; City of Kingston-upon-Hull; Yorkshire*); Isle of Wight (Hampshire); Kent (City of Canterbury; Kent); Lancashire (Lancashire*; Yorkshire); Leicestershire (Leicestershire*; Rutlandshire); Lincolnshire (City of Lincoln; Lincolnshire); Norfolk (City of Norwich; Norfolk*; Suffolk); North Yorkshire (City of York; Yorkshire*); Northamptonshire (Northamptonshire); Northumberland (Northumberland; Berwick upon Tweed); Nottinghamshire (City of Nottingham; Nottinghamshire*); Oxfordshire (Oxfordshire*; Berkshire); Rutlandshire (Leicestershire*) Salop (Shropshire); Somerset (Somersetshire); Staffordshire (Staffordshire*; City of Lichfield); Suffolk (Suffolk); Surrey (Surrey); Warwickshire (Warwickshire); West Sussex (Sussex*; Surrey); Wiltshire (Wiltshire).

The following list shows, in the same way, the shrievalties and bailiwicks for Wales: Clwyd (Flintshire*; Denbighshire; Merionethshire); Dyfed (Cardiganshire; Carmarthenshire; Town of Carmarthen; Pembrokeshire*; Town of Haverfordwest); Gwent (Monmouthshire*; Breconshire); Gwynedd (Anglesey; Caernarvonshire*; Merionethshire; Denbighshire); Mid-Glamorgan (Glamorganshire*; Breconshire; Monmouthshire); Powys (Montgomeryshire*; Radnorshire; Breconshire); South Glamorgan (Glamorganshire*; Monmouthshire); West Glamorgan (Glamorganshire districts of Afan and Neath; Glamorganshire districts of Swansea and Lliw Valley).

9 'County', in the Local Government Act 1972 s 219(5), includes Greater London and the City of London (including the Temples): see ss 219(5), 270(1) (as amended); and LOCAL GOVERNMENT.

10 Any question as to which county contains the greater part of a bailiwick is decided by the Lord Chancellor: ibid s 219(5).

11 Ibid s 219(5).

1112. Declaration and tenure of office; security. Before entering on the execution of his office[1] every under-sheriff must make a declaration in similar form to that made by the high sheriff[2] either before a judge of the High Court or before a justice of the peace for the county for which he is appointed[3]. On his appointment an under-sheriff may execute an indemnity, with sureties, in favour of each high sheriff whose bailiwick[4] covers the area administered by the under-sheriff for the due and faithful discharge of his duties, and either may indemnify the high sheriff against any liability for breach of duty on his part or on the part of his servants in the execution of the office or may arrange for appropriate insurance cover.

An under-sheriff may be removed at the pleasure of the high sheriff even though his appointment is purported to be irrevocable[5]. Otherwise, the office of under-sheriff comes to an end on the expiration of that of the high sheriff who appointed him[6], although he may be reappointed by the sheriff's successor.

1   As to the appointment of under-sheriffs see para 1111 ante.

2   For the form of declaration see the Sheriffs Act 1887 s 23(3) (as amended: see note 3 infra), Sch 2 (amended by the Statute Law (Repeals) Act 1978). As to the meaning of 'high sheriff' see para 1101 note 1 ante.

3   Sheriffs Act 1887 s 23(3) (amended by the Statute Law Revision Act 1908). The under-sheriff of any London commission area (see para 1111 note 3 ante) may make his declaration before a justice of the peace for any of the London commission areas: Administration of Justice Act 1964 s 19(4)(a).

4   As to bailiwicks see para 1111 ante.

5   Com Dig, Viscount (B1); *Norton v Simmes* (1614) Hob 12.

6   Com Dig, Viscount (B1). As to the effect of the death of the high sheriff see para 1115 post.

1113. Prohibition of sale or letting of office. The office of under-sheriff may not, directly or indirectly, be bought or sold, nor may any valuable consideration be given or received for the office[1]. However, this prohibition does not prevent the high sheriff[2] or under-sheriff from demanding and taking the lawful fees and perquisites relating to the office or from accounting or giving security to account, and does not prevent the high sheriff from giving or the under-sheriff from receiving a salary or remuneration for the execution of the office[3].

1   See the Sheriffs Act 1887 s 27(1) (amended by the Statute Law (Revision) Act 1998). This provision also applies to deputy-sheriffs (see paras 1117–1118 post), and to bailiffs and other sheriffs' officers (see para 1121 post). Any person other than an under-sheriff, deputy-sheriff, bailiff or other officer who acts in contravention of the Sheriffs Act 1887 s 27 (as amended) is liable to the same punishment as if he were an under-sheriff, deputy-sheriff, bailiff or officer: s 27(2). As to penalties for misconduct see para 1155 post.

2   As to the meaning of 'high sheriff' see para 1101 note 1 ante.

3   Sheriffs Act 1887 s 27(3). As to fees and accounts see para 1123 et seq post.

1114. Duties and powers. The under-sheriff usually performs all the duties of the office of high sheriff[1], subject to certain exceptions where the personal presence of the high sheriff is necessary[2]. In respect of the area for which he acts[3] the under-sheriff is treated as the deputy of the high sheriff for the purpose of all the functions of the high sheriff except those as returning officer at parliamentary elections[4].

An under-sheriff has all the powers incident to the sheriff's office which are not personal to the high sheriff, and a covenant or condition in restraint of such powers is void[5]. By virtue of his office an under-sheriff has authority, in the course of the execution of the office, to execute a deed in the name and under the seal of the high sheriff[6]. However, in all cases it is the duty of the under-sheriff to act in the name of the high sheriff[7] and any action in respect of the non-performance of the duties of the office must be brought against the high sheriff, who alone is liable[8].

1   As to the meaning of 'high sheriff' see para 1101 note 1 ante. As to the duties and functions of the high sheriff see para 1128 et seq post; and as to the circumstances in which an under-sheriff is required to act as high sheriff see para 1115 post.

2   1 Bl Com (14 Edn) 345; Com Dig, Viscount (B1).

3   See para 1111 ante.

4   Local Government Act 1972 s 219(6). As to the functions of a high sheriff in connection with parliamentary elections see para 1129 post.

5   Eg a covenant or condition by an under-sheriff that he will not execute process for a sum in excess of a certain amount without a warrant from the high sheriff will be void: *Boucher v Wiseman* (1595) Cro Eliz 440; *Chamberlaine v Goldsmith* (1609) 2 Brownl 280; *Norton v Simmes* (1614) Hob 12; *Parker v Kett* (1701) 1 Salk 95. See also Com Dig, Viscount (B1).

6   *Doe d James v Brawn* (1821) 5 B & Ald 243 (assignment by deed of a term of years in execution); *Wood v Rowcliffe* (1846) 6 Hare 183 at 186 (bill of sale by under-sheriff).

7   *Parker v Kett* (1701) 1 Salk 95.

8   *Cameron v Reynolds* (1776) 1 Cowp 403; *Scarfe v Hallifax* (1840) 7 M & W 288. As to the liability of a high sheriff for the acts of his officers see para 1146 et seq post.

1115.   Duty to act as high sheriff in certain cases. Where a high sheriff[1] dies before the expiration of his year of office or before his successor has entered on the office, his under-sheriff nevertheless continues in office, and it is his duty to exercise the office of high sheriff in the name of the deceased sheriff until another high sheriff for the county has been appointed and made the declaration of office[2]. The under-sheriff is answerable for the execution of the office as the deceased sheriff would have been if living and the security given to the deceased sheriff[3] operates as security to the Crown and all other persons for the due execution by the under-sheriff of the offices of high sheriff and under-sheriff[4].

1   As to the meaning of 'high sheriff' see para 1101 note 1 ante.
2   Sheriffs Act 1887 s 25(1). However, this provision does not authorise the under-sheriff to discharge the duties of returning officer, and upon a sheriff's death the acting returning officer must discharge all the sheriff's duties as returning officer until another sheriff is appointed and has made the declaration of office: Representation of the People Act 1983 s 28(6). As to the appointment of high sheriffs see para 1101 et seq ante; and as to their duties as returning officers see para 1129 post. As to the office of acting returning officer see ELECTIONS vol 15 (Reissue) paras 459–460.
3   See para 1112 ante.
4   Sheriffs Act 1887 s 25(1). See also *Gloucestershire Banking Co v Edwards* (1887) 20 QBD 107, CA, where the executors of a deceased under-sheriff, who had acted in the place of a deceased high sheriff, were held liable to execution creditors for a sum improperly deducted by the under-sheriff for charges to which he was not entitled. As to the power of an under-sheriff to appoint a deputy on the death of the high sheriff see para 1118 post.

1116.   Secondary and under-sheriff of the City of London. In the City of London[1] the Secondary[2], who is appointed by the Court of Aldermen[3], occupies a similar position to that of an under-sheriff[4] and performs, in the names of the sheriffs, all the duties ordinarily incident to the office of an under-sheriff[5]. The office of Secondary is held of the Corporation of the City of London, which is liable to the Crown for any breach of duty on his part[6].

1   As to the appointment of sheriffs for the City of London see paras 1109–1110 ante.
2   The Secondary's full title is 'Secondary of the City of London and Under-Sheriff, High Bailiff of Southwark'. See also note 5 infra.
3   As to the Court of Aldermen see LONDON GOVERNMENT.
4   As to under-sheriffs see para 1111 et seq ante.
5   The appointment and duties of the Secondary and Under-Sheriff together with a list of the establishment of the department are contained in the Report of the Establishment Committee 'Central Criminal Court Administration' which was presented to and approved by the Court of Common Council on 27 June 1968, as amended by the Report of the City Secretary relative to the Management Review at the Central Criminal Court which was approved by the Establishment Committee on 19 November 1998. The functions of the Secondary relating to the preparation of registers of electors and jury lists were transferred to the Town Clerk by the City of London (Various Powers) Act 1968 s 3 (as amended): see LONDON GOVERNMENT.
6   Report of the Royal Commission on the Amalgamation of the City and County of London (1894) (C 2nd series 7493) App iii, 53–55.

(ii) Deputies

1117.   London deputy. Every high-sheriff[1] is required to appoint a sufficient deputy, who must reside or have an office within a mile from the Inner Temple Hall, for the receipt of writs, the granting of warrants, the making of returns, and the acceptance of all rules and orders to be made on or touching the execution of any process or writ directed to the sheriff[2]. The delivery of a writ to the London deputy operates as a delivery to the sheriff[3], and the writ obtains priority as from the time of delivery[4].

1   As to the meaning of 'high sheriff' see para 1101 note 1 ante.
2   Sheriffs Act 1887 s 24. As to the execution of writs see para 1132 post.
3   *Woodland v Fuller* (1840) 11 Ad & El 859 at 867.
4   Under the Supreme Court Act 1981 s 138(1), a writ of fieri facias or other writ of execution against goods issued from the High Court binds the property in the goods of the execution debtor as from the time it is delivered to the sheriff to be executed. It is, therefore, the duty of a sheriff to indorse on the back of the writ the hour, day, month and year when he received the writ: see s 138(3). See also EXECUTION.

1118. Deputy of under-sheriff. Where an under-sheriff is under the duty to act as high-sheriff[1] he may by writing appoint a deputy[2]. Before the deputy sheriff takes upon himself the execution of any writ issued by a court of record[3] he must make a declaration[4] as to the manner in which he will exercise his office[5].

An under-sheriff has no power to appoint a deputy in any other circumstances, although he may authorise another to do a particular act[6].

1   Ie due to the death of the high sheriff: see para 1115 ante. As to the meaning of 'high sheriff' see para 1101 note 1 ante.
2   Sheriffs Act 1887 s 25(2). A deputy sheriff may not sell or let his office: see s 27(1), (2) (s 27(1) as amended); and para 1113 ante.
3   As to courts of record see COURTS.
4   For the form of declaration see the Sheriffs Act 1887 s 26 (as amended: see note 5 infra), Sch 2 (amended by the Courts Act 1971 s 56(4), Sch 11 Pt I).
5   Sheriffs Act 1887 s 26 (amended by the Statute Law Revision Act 1908; the Courts Act 1971 Sch 11 Pt I; the Local Government Act 1972 s 272(1), Sch 30; and the Statute Law (Repeals) Act 1981). The declaration, which is exempt from stamp duty, must be made before a judge of the High Court or before a justice of the peace for the county in which the deputy exercises authority or, in the case of a deputy in Greater London (see para 1101 note 2 ante), before a justice of the peace for any of the London commission areas: Sheriffs Act 1887 s 26 (as so amended); Administration of Justice Act 1964 s 19(4)(a). As to the London commission areas see MAGISTRATES.
6   *Parker v Kett* (1701) 1 Salk 95.

(iii)   Sheriff's Officers

1119. Appointment and nature of office. Sheriff's officers, are appointed by high sheriffs[1] for the purpose of executing writs and processes[2]. Before a sheriff's officer takes upon himself the execution of any writ issued by a court of record[3] he must make a declaration[4] as to the manner in which he will exercise his office[5].

A sheriff's officer may be required to give to the sheriff a bond, with sureties, for the due execution of the office and the accounting to the sheriff for the fees[6] received, and indemnifying him against liability for any breach of duty on the officer's part[7]. Officers who have given such a bond are sometimes called 'bound bailiffs'[8]. Alternatively, the sheriff's officer will arrange for appropriate insurance cover.

The office of sheriff's officer being one of responsibility and trust, a minor cannot be appointed[9]. The office is a personal one, and cannot be executed by a deputy[10], nor is any partnership possible between two officers so as to render the acts of one binding on the other[11]. All sheriff's officers are disqualified from holding licences to retail intoxicating liquor[12].

It is an offence for any sheriff's officer to take or demand money other than the statutory fees allowed[13].

The Bailiffs of Jersey and Guernsey have special powers and are appointed by the Crown[14].

1   As to the meaning of 'high sheriff' see para 1101 note 1 ante. The larger counties have full time sheriff's officers paid either by salary or by retaining certain of the sheriff's fees. Smaller counties have part-time officers. As to bailiffs of the City of London see para 1120 post; and as to special bailiffs see para 1122 post.

2   1 Bl Com (14 Edn) 345. See also EXECUTION. As to county court bailiffs see COUNTY COURTS. References to a high bailiff (the office of which has been abolished: see COUNTY COURTS) in any enactment, Order in Council, order, rule, regulation or other document must be construed as a reference to a district judge of a county court: County Courts Act 1984 s 148(2), Sch 3 para 7. As to district judges see COUNTY COURTS.

3   As to the meaning of 'court of record' see COURTS.

4   For the form of declaration, which is the same as that required from a deputy sheriff see the Sheriff's Act 1887 s 26, Sch 2 (both as amended); and para 1118 ante.

5   Ibid s 26 (amended by the Statute Law Revision Act 1908; the Courts Act 1971 s 56(4), Sch 11 Pt I; the Local Government Act 1972 s 272(1), Sch 30; and the Statute Law (Repeals) Act 1981). The declaration must be made in the same way as that of a deputy sheriff: see the Sheriffs Act 1887 s 26 (as so amended); and para 1118 note 5 ante.

6   As to the fees of sheriffs and sheriffs' officers see para 1123 et seq post.

7   As to sheriffs' liability for the acts of their officers see para 1146 et seq post.

8   1 Bl Com (14 Edn) 346. In *Farebrother v Worsley* (1831) 5 C & P 102, it was held that a sheriff who defended an action for a false return as well as he could was entitled to recover his costs from the sureties of the bailiff who executed the writ, although the verdict was given against the sheriff on the ground of the non-production of certain evidence which ought to have been produced. See also *Cook v Palmer* (1827) 6 B & C 739; *Farebrother v Worsley* (1831) 1 Tyr 424.

9   *Cuckson v Winter* (1828) 2 Man & Ry KB 313 at 317.

10   *Jackson v Hill* (1839) 10 Ad & El 477 at 484 per Patteson J.

11   *Jons v Perchard* (1794) 2 Esp 507.

12   See the Licensing Act 1964 s 9(1)(a); and INTOXICATING LIQUOR VOL 26 (Reissue) para 143.

13   See the Sheriffs Act 1887 ss 20(3), 29(2) (both as amended); and paras 1123, 1151 post.

14   See COMMONWEALTH AND DEPENDENCIES vol 6 (Reissue) paras 841–847.

1120. City of London. In the City of London[1] the bound bailiffs[2] are called 'serjeants-at-mace' and their assistants 'yeomen'. It is the duty of the Secondary[3] to take securities on behalf of the sheriffs from the serjeants-at-mace.

1   As to the sheriffs of the City of London see para 1109 ante.

2   As to bound bailiffs see para 1119 ante.

3   As to the Secondary of the City of London see para 1116 ante.

1121. Prohibition on sale or letting of office. The statutory prohibition on the sale or letting of the office of under-sheriff[1] also applies to the office of bailiff or any other office or place appertaining to the high sheriff[2]. However, this does not prevent a sheriff's officer from accounting to the sheriff for fees received in respect of his office[3] or from giving security so to account, nor does it prevent a sheriff from giving nor an officer from receiving a salary or remuneration for the execution of his office[4].

1   Ie the Sheriffs Act 1887 s 27(1) (as amended): see para 1113 ante.

2   See ibid s 27(1), (2) (s 27(1) as amended); and para 1113 ante. As to the meaning of 'high sheriff' see para 1101 note 1 ante.

3   As to fees see para 1123 et seq post.

4   Sheriffs Act 1887 s 27(3).

1122. Special bailiffs. The term 'special bailiff' refers to a particular officer appointed by a high sheriff[1] to execute a writ at the request of the person issuing the writ[2]. Such an officer is regarded, as between the person issuing the writ and the sheriff, as the agent of that person rather than of the sheriff, thus exonerating the sheriff, as a general rule, from liability to the person issuing the writ for any misconduct or breach of duty on the part of the officer in the execution of the writ[3].

A mere request by an execution creditor or his solicitor that a particular officer may be employed to execute the writ does not necessarily constitute the officer a special bailiff[4], even if it is coupled with information given direct to the officer to assist him in the execution of the writ[5]. However, if the execution creditor or his solicitor requests that the warrant be directed to a particular officer, and instructs him as to the manner in which the writ is to be executed, the officer is thereby constituted a special bailiff of the execution creditor[6].

1   As to the appointment of bailiffs see para 1119 ante; and as to the meaning of 'high sheriff' see para 1101 note 1 ante.
2   Such an appointment is rare but might be made where the plaintiff sought special expertise in the bailiff, eg on an execution involving the seizure and sale of specialised goods. The sheriff may require the special bailiff to make a declaration under the Sheriffs Act 1887 s 26 (as amended) (see para 1119 ante) before issuing his warrant to him. A special bailiff must account to the sheriff for the sheriff's fees levied under the warrant against the defendant but the bailiff may make an arrangement with the plaintiff for the terms of his employment by the plaintiff. As to fees see para 1123 et seq post.
3   As to sheriffs' liability for the acts of their officers see para 1146 et seq post.
4   *Balson v Meggat* (1836) 4 Dowl 557; *Corbet v Brown* (1838) 6 Dowl 794; *Seal v Hudson* (1847) 4 Dow & L 760.
5   *Alderson v Davenport* (1844) 13 M & W 42 at 46.
6   *Doe v Trye* (1839) 7 Dowl 636; *Alderson v Davenport* (1844) 13 M & W 42.

(3) FEES, POUNDAGE AND ACCOUNTS

1123. Statutory right to fees and poundage. A high sheriff[1] or his officer[2] concerned in the execution of process directed to the sheriff[3] may only demand, take and receive such fees and poundage as are prescribed[4], and may not take, directly or indirectly, any reward for doing, or abstaining from doing, his duty or in respect of the mode in which he executes his office or duty, other than such fees or poundage[5].

Before any prescribed fees become payable a formal seizure must have been made under the warrant of execution[6].

1   As to the meaning of 'high sheriff' see para 1101 note 1 ante.
2   As to sheriffs' officers see para 1111 et seq ante.
3   As to the execution of process see para 1132 et seq post.
4   The Lord Chancellor is empowered to fix, with the advice and consent of the judges of the Court of Appeal and the High Court, or any three of them, and with Treasury concurrence, the fees and rate of poundage which are allowed: Sheriffs Act 1887 s 20(2) (amended by the Statute Law Revision Act 1908). For the amounts of fees and the rate of poundage see the Order dated 8 July 1920, SR & O 1920/1250 (as amended); the Order dated 2 May 1921, SR & O 1921/827 (as amended); and para 1139 et seq post. Special bailiffs (as to whom see para 1122 ante) are not bound by the statutory scale of fees and charges: see EXECUTION. As to expenses in relation to the levying of distress see DISTRESS.
     For cases where sheriffs' expenses in excess of the prescribed fees and rate of poundage were disallowed see *Slater v Hames* (1841) 7 M & W 413; *Davies v Edmonds* (1843) 12 M & W 31, where it was held that on the execution of a writ of fieri facias the sheriff was not entitled to the extra expense incurred by keeping two men in possession for the protection of the property against an adverse claim as such expense was not included in the statutory table of fees; *Phillips v Viscount Canterbury* (1843) 11 M & W 619, where the sheriff was not allowed to deduct the expenses of disposing of goods seized under a writ of fieri facias by appraisement and sale because the prescribed fees only covered sales by auction; *Gill v Jose* (1856) 6 E & B 718, where, although it was proved to be customary in the particular county to take more than the prescribed mileage, the excess was disallowed; *Halliwell v Heywood* (1862) 10 WR 780, where it was held to be extortion to charge for a second man in possession under a writ of fieri facias; *Braithwaite v Marriott* (1862) 1 H & C 591; *Re Ludmore* (1884) 13 QBD 415, where it was held that when a debtor's bankruptcy supervenes after seizure, but before sale, by a sheriff acting under a writ of fieri facias, the 'costs of execution' under what is now the Insolvency Act 1986 s 346, do not include poundage; *Re Thomas, ex p Sheriff of Middlesex* [1899] 1 QB 460, CA (similar case). See also *Re Woodham, ex p Conder* (1887) 20 QBD 40, where the expenses of reaping growing crops were disallowed; *Lee v Dangar, Grant & Co* [1892] 2 QB 337, CA, where it was held that a sheriff's officer was not entitled to rely on a writ of fieri facias in the County of London under a writ paid out under fieri facias in the City of London. As to the effect of taking excess fees and poundage see para 1124 post.
5   See the Sheriffs Act 1887 s 20(2) (amended by the Statute Law Revision Act 1908); the Sheriffs Act 1887 s 20(3) (amended by the Statute Law (Repeals) Act 1998). For an analysis of the right to poundage see

Mortimore v Cragg, ex p Sheriff of Surrey (1878) 3 CPD 216 at 219, CA, per Brett LJ. See also *Montague v Davies, Benachi & Co* [1911] 2 KB 595 at 605, DC, where the development of the sheriff's right to fees and the earlier cases are considered. As to the levy of fees and poundage see para 1125 post.

The fees and emoluments of the sheriffs of the City of London (as to whom see para 1109 ante) are retained by the Corporation of the City of London and it is the duty of the Secondary (as to whom see para 1116 ante) to account to the Chamberlain for all fees in respect of the execution of process at the end of every three months: Report of the Royal Commission on the Amalgamation of the City and County of London (1894) (C 2 series 7493) App iii 21, 54, 55.

6   *Nash v Dickenson* (1867) LR 2 CP 252. Whether or not a seizure has been made is a question of fact: *Lloyds and Scottish Finance Ltd v Modern Cars and Caravans (Kingston) Ltd* [1966] 1 QB 764, [1964] 2 All ER 732. As to seizure see para 1140 post; and EXECUTION.

1124. Taking excess fees. If a sheriff's bailiff or officer[1] takes too large a sum in respect of fees or poundage[2], an action based on an implied contract will lie against the sheriff for the excess, without any proof that the money has come to his hands[3]. Such an action survives against the sheriff's executors or administrators[4].

A sheriff may not take a bond for his fees[5] because under colour of it he might recover more than the fees allowed[6], and a sheriff or under-sheriff is not entitled to refuse to execute process until his fees have been paid[7]. An express promise to pay extra remuneration for the execution of process is void[8].

1   As to bailiffs and officers see para 1119 et seq ante.
2   As to the right to fees and poundage see para 1123 ante.
3   *Jons v Perchard* (1794) 2 Esp 507; *Dew v Parsons* (1819) 2 B & Ald 562; *Blake v Newburn* (1848) 5 Dow & L 601. See also CONTRACT vol 9(1) (Reissue) para 1099; EXECUTION; GUARANTEE AND INDEMNITY vol 20 (Reissue) paras 347–349. As to the liability of a sheriff or his officers to punishment for extortion see para 1155 post.
4   *Gloucestershire Banking Co v Edwards* (1887) 20 QBD 107, CA.
5   As to bonds by under-sheriffs and bailiffs see paras 1112, 1119 ante.
6   *Lyster v Bromley* (1632) Cro Car 286.
7   *Hescott's Case* (1694) 1 Salk 330. If a sheriff or under-sheriff does so refuse he is liable to an action for not doing his duty or, if the fees are paid, to punishment for extortion: *Hescott's Case* supra.
8   *Bridge v Cage* (1605) Cro Jac 103.

1125. Levy of fees, poundage and expenses. Subject to one exception[1], the amount of the fees, poundage and expenses of the execution[2] may be levied over and above the sum recovered[3], even though the judgment creditor may not be entitled to the costs of the action in which the judgment was obtained[4]. The amount of the fees allowed may be levied even though they are not indorsed on the writ of execution, and it is not necessary for the sheriff to particularise the respective items in his return to the writ[5]. If, after seizure, the judgment creditor becomes disentitled to recover the amount of the debt, the sheriff is not entitled to sell any portion of the goods seized for the purpose of paying his fees and expenses[6].

The exception to the right so to levy fees, poundage and expenses is where the judgment or order to be executed is for less than £600 and does not entitle the plaintiff to costs against the person against whom the writ of fieri facias to enforce the judgment or order is issued[7].

1   See the text to note 7 infra.
2   As to costs and expenses of execution generally see EXECUTION.
3   The right to levy fees, poundage and expenses is expressly incorporated in the prescribed forms of writs of execution. As to the statutory right to fees and poundage see para 1123 ante; and as to the amounts allowed see para 1139 et seq post.
4   *Armitage v Jessop* (1866) LR 2 CP 12, where it was held that costs of execution are not costs of the action.
5   *Curtis v Mayne* (1842) 2 Dowl NS 37. As to the recovery of sheriff's charges under a writ of possession see para 1144 post; and as to the return to the writ see para 1136 post.

6 *Sneary v Abdy* (1876) 1 Ex D 299, DC, where the sheriff was held liable to the execution debtor as for an unlawful sale. See also *Goode v Langley* (1827) 7 B & C 26.

7 RSC Ord 47 r 4; CPR Sch 1 RSC Ord 47 r 4. In such a case the writ may not authorise the sheriff to whom it is directed to levy any fees, poundage or other costs of execution.

1126. Right to sue creditor for fees. If a high sheriff[1] is unable, without any default on his part, to levy his fees against the execution debtor[2], he has a right of action for them against the execution creditor by whom or on whose behalf he was requested to execute the writ of execution[3]. Where the execution is withdrawn, satisfied or stopped the sheriff's statutory fees[4] must be paid either by the person issuing the execution or by the person at whose instance the sale is stopped, as the case may be[5]. The sheriff who has done nothing of any benefit in pursuance of the writ is not entitled to recover fees from the execution creditor[6].

1 As to the meaning of 'high sheriff' see para 1101 note 1 ante.

2 As to the right to levy fees see paras 1123, 1125 ante.

3 *Stanton v Suliard* (1599) Cro Eliz 654; *Tyson v Paske* (1705) 2 Ld Raym 1212; *Rawstorne v Wilkinson* (1815) 4 M & S 256; *Bunbury v Matthews* (1844) 1 Car & Kir 380; *Maybery v Mansfield* (1846) 9 QB 754; *Marshall v Hicks* (1847) 10 QB 15; *Montague v Davies, Benachi & Co* [1911] 2 KB 595 at 605, 606, DC; *The Ile de Ceylan* [1922] P 256. In an action by a sheriff for poundage (as to which see generally para 1123 ante), proof that he has acted as sheriff is sufficient evidence of his being so without any further proof of his appointment: *Bunbury v Matthews* supra. It may be convenient for a sheriff first to tax his fees (see para 1127 post) and then to sue on the taxing master's certificate.

4 For the statutory fees see para 1139 et seq post.

5 Order dated 8 July 1920, SR & O 1920/1250, preamble, Schedule Fee 10 (Fee 10 substituted by SI 1971/808).

6 *Bilke v Havelock* (1813) 3 Camp 374; *Lane v Sewell* (1819) 1 Chit 175; *Cole v Terry* (1861) 5 LT 347, where it was held that the sheriff's levy was ineffectual by reason of the claim of an assignee; *Newman v Merriman* (1872) 26 LT 397 (goods of stranger seized). See also *Thomas v Peek* (1888) 20 QBD 727 at 728 per A L Smith J. As to the recovery of fees by a sheriff or a bailiff and the liability of a creditor's solicitor for fees see generally EXECUTION.

1127. Detailed assessment and sheriff's fees. In relation to proceedings begun on or after 26 April 1999[1], where a sheriff and the party liable to pay his fees and charges[2] differ as to the amount payable, the amount must be assessed by an authorised court officer[3] or where a party objects to the detailed assessment of costs being made by an authorised court officer, the court may order it to be made by a costs judge or a district judge[4].

The jurisdiction of the authorised court officer is confined to fixing the amount the sheriff is entitled to[5], and no appeal lies from his decision[6]. The costs of detailed assessment are within the discretion of the authorised court officer[7]. The receiving party is entitled to his costs except where it is otherwise provided[8], or where the court, having regard to all the circumstances[9] makes some other order[10].

1 Ie the date on which the CPR come into force. For the position with regard to proceedings commenced before that date see RSC Ord 62.

2 As to the recovery of fees and charges see para 1125 ante.

3 See the Order dated 8 July 1920, SR & O 1920/1250, preamble, Schedule Fee 10 (Fee 10 substituted by SI 1971/808). To begin detailed assessment proceedings (formally taxation), the party requiring the detailed assessment must produce a notice of commencement in the relevant practice form and a copy of the bill of costs: see CPR 47.6(1). As to the procedure on detailed assessment generally see CPR Pt 47; and PRACTICE AND PROCEDURE.

4 CPR 47.3(2).

5 Where the difference between the parties depends on a matter of principle it must be settled by action: *Union Bank of Manchester Ltd v Grundy* [1924] 1 KB 833, CA.

6 *Townend v Sheriff of Yorkshire* (1890) 24 QBD 621. However, where the authorised court officer (formerly known as the taxing officer) refuses to consider a particular head of fees the Divisional Court on motion

may direct him to subject them to detailed assessment: *Madeley v Greenwood* (1897) 42 Sol Jo 34, DC. See also *Tramp Leasing Ltd v Turnbull* (1991) 135 Sol Jo LB 54, Times, 12 June, CA.

7   *Butler v Smith* (1895) 39 Sol Jo 406.

8   Ie provided by the provisions of any Act, any of the Civil Procedure Rules or any relevant Practice Direction: see CPR 47.18(1).

9   See CPR 47.18(2).

10   See CPR 47.18(1).

2. POWERS, DUTIES AND LIABILITIES

(1) FUNCTIONS OF SHERIFFS GENERALLY

1128. Decline of sheriff's jurisdiction. The sheriff's original civil and criminal jurisdictions, which were exercised by him in the sheriff's court[1] and sheriff's tourn[2] respectively, are now merged in the jurisdictions of the county court, the High Court[3] and the Crown Court[4]. Further, the sheriff has ceased to have responsibility in the collection of fines[5], the summoning of jurors[6], and for the execution of judgment of death[7].

The sheriff's functions are now concerned solely with the execution of writs of execution[8] and warrants[9], limited functions in connection with parliamentary elections[10] and various ceremonial and administrative duties which often vary according to the traditions of the different counties[11].

1   The sheriff was required to hold a court for the due execution of certain writs, for instance writs of elegit (abolished by the Administration of Justice Act 1956 s 34(1) (repealed): see EXECUTION), writs of extent (abolished by the Crown Proceedings Act 1947 s 33), and writs of inquiry (abolished in 1957 by RSC Ord 36B r 1 (revoked): see also note 3 infra): Sheriffs Act 1887 s 18(1), (2) (repealed by the Administration of Justice Act 1977 s 32(4), Sch 5 Pt V).

2   The sheriff's tourn was abolished by the Sheriffs Act 1887 s 18(4) (repealed).

3   As to the procedure for the assessment of damages in the High Court (which replaced the procedure on a writ of inquiry) see RSC Ord 37 r 1; and PRACTICE AND PROCEDURE. See now Practice Direction— Case Management—Preliminary Stage: Allocation and Re-allocation (1999) PD26 para 12.10.

4   The sheriff's power under any commission or writ to take an inquest by which any person is indicted was abolished by the Sheriffs Act 1887 s 18(3) (repealed).

5   The Criminal Justice Act 1967 s 47 (repealed) provided for the enforcement of fines imposed and recognisances forfeited in criminal proceedings by magistrates' courts instead of sheriffs. As to fines and recognisances see CRIMINAL LAW, EVIDENCE AND PROCEDURE vol 11(2) (Reissue) paras 1232–1237; MAGISTRATES. See also the Supreme Court Act 1981 s 140; CONFLICT OF LAWS vol 8(1) (Reissue) para 1060.

6   See the Sheriffs Act 1887 s 12 (repealed); and the Juries Acts 1825–1949 (all repealed), which empowered the sheriff to summon juries. As to the present method of summoning jurors see JURIES vol 26 (Reissue) para 411 et seq.

7   See the Sheriffs Act 1887 s 13 (repealed), which charged the sheriff with the execution of a judgment of death. As to the sentence of death see CRIMINAL LAW, EVIDENCE AND PROCEDURE vol 11(2) (Reissue) para 1199.

8   See RSC Ords 45–47; CPR Sch 1 RSC Ords 45–47. See also the Family Proceedings Rules 1991, SI 1991/1247, r 7.3, under which an order of a county court in matrimonial jurisdiction may be transferred to the High Court for enforcement; and para 1132 et seq post. As the financial limit on the county court jurisdiction increases (cf COUNTY COURTS), the number of writs of execution issued out of the High Court decreases and the number of county court judgments transferred to the sheriffs increases.

9   See para 1137 post.

10   See para 1129 post.

11   Until 1904 the sheriff, by virtue of his office as the keeper of the Queen's peace, both by common law
     and by commission, was the first man in the county, and superior in rank to any nobleman of the county:
     Ex p Fernandez (1861) 10 CBNS 3 at 52. However, by Royal Warrant issued on 18 February 1904, prior
     place is given to the Lord Lieutenant.
        The Crown Court may order the sheriff to pay rewards to persons who have been active in or towards
     the apprehension of any person charged with an arrestable offence: see the Criminal Law Act 1826 s 28
     (as amended); and CRIMINAL LAW, EVIDENCE AND PROCEDURE vol 11(2) (Reissue) para 1525. The
     sheriff may apply for repayment from the Lord Chancellor on producing the order and receipt: see s 29
     (as amended); and CRIMINAL LAW, EVIDENCE AND PROCEDURE VOL 11(2) (Reissue) para 1525. The
     exercise of this power gives sheriffs the opportunity of holding formal presentation ceremonies. Although
     it is sufficient for royal proclamations to be published in the Gazettes (see CONSTITUTIONAL LAW AND
     HUMAN RIGHTS vol 8(2) (Reissue) para 916), the Lord President of the Council, if he thinks it expedient,
     may send copies of all royal proclamations to such sheriffs as he thinks fit who are then required to make
     them known locally: see the Crown Office (Forms and Proclamations Rules) Order 1992, SI 1992/1730
     (amended by SI 1996/276) (made under the Crown Office Act 1877 s 3).

1129. Functions in connection with parliamentary elections. The high sheriff[1]
of a county is the returning officer[2] for parliamentary elections (1) in a county
constituency which is coterminous with or wholly contained in the county of which he
is sheriff[3]; (2) in a constituency, wholly outside Greater London, for which he has been
designated returning officer by the Secretary of State by order made by statutory
instrument[4].

The high sheriff as returning officer must give to the acting returning officer[5] written
notice of any duties which he reserves to himself; and in the case of any election, only
those duties are reserved in relation to which such a notice is given not later than the day
following that on which the writ is received[6].

1   As to the meaning of 'high sheriff' see para 1101 note 1 ante.
2   As to returning officers generally see ELECTIONS vol 15 (Reissue) paras 456–467.
3   Representation of the People Act 1983 s 24(1)(a) (amended by the Local Government (Wales) Act 1994
    s 66(6), Sch 16; and the Local Government Changes for England (Miscellaneous Provision) Regulations
    1995, SI 1995/1748, reg 8(3)); and the Representation of the People Act 1983 s 24(1)(aa) (added by the
    Local Government (Wales) Act 1994 Sch 16).
4   Representation of the People Act 1983 s 24(1)(c) (amended by the Local Government (Wales) Act 1994
    Sch 16); and the Representation of the People Act 1983 s 24(1)(cc) (added by the Local Government
    (Wales) Act 1994 Sch 16). For a list of the constituencies of which the high sheriff is the returning officer
    see the Returning Officers (Parliamentary Constituencies) (England) Order 1995, SI 1995/2061 (as
    amended); the Returning Officers (Parliamentary Constituencies) (Wales) Order 1996, SI 1996/897; and
    ELECTIONS VOL 15 (Reissue) para 456.
5   As to the office of acting returning officer see ELECTIONS vol 15 (Reissue) paras 459–460.
6   See the Representation of the People Act 1983 s 28(1), (3) (s 28(1) as amended); and ELECTIONS VOL 15
    (Reissue) para 459. In the event of the death of a high sheriff the acting returning officer and not the
    under-sheriff discharges all the duties as returning officer until another high sheriff is appointed and has
    made his declaration of office: see s 28(6); and ELECTIONS VOL 15 (Reissue) para 458. As to the office of
    under-sheriff see paras 1111–1116 ante.

1130. Sheriffs' functions as conservators of the peace. As conservator of the
Queen's peace it was the sheriff's duty to suppress unlawful assemblies and riots, to
apprehend offenders and to defend his county against invasion[1]. Although these ancient
powers and rights have been preserved[2], in modern times all duties for the enforcement
of law and order are the responsibility of the police forces[3]. However, the sheriff is
entitled to arrest and commit to prison any person who resists the execution of a writ,
and for that purpose may call upon the police for assistance[4].

1   1 Bl Com (14 Edn) 343; Com Dig Viscount (C2); 17 Ric 2 c 8 (Suppression of Riots) (1393); the Riot
    Act 1411 (repealed); and the Riot Act 1414 (repealed). By the Sheriffs Act 1887 s 8(1) (repealed), every
    person in a county was bound to be ready at the sheriff's command and at the cry of the county to arrest
    a felon and in default was liable to a fine. As to the duty of private persons to assist constables see POLICE.

As to the duty of private persons to assist magistrates see *R v Pinney* (1832) 5 C & P 254. In 1939 the Privy Council warned the sheriffs that in the event of invasion they might have to exercise their powers to call upon the civilian population to assist them in the defence of their counties.

2 The Sheriffs Act 1887 s 39(1)(d) expressly preserves such of the powers, rights, privileges, obligations, liabilities and duties of any sheriff or sheriff's officer as existed at common law. In *R v Lydford* [1914] 2 KB 378, CCA, it was held that if the court has power to make an order, there must be someone whose duty it is to carry it out and that therefore the duty of carrying out a sentence of whipping fell on the sheriff as the person entrusted, at common law, with the duty of carrying out the court's order.

3 As to the functions and powers of the police in relation to the preservation of the Queen's peace see POLICE.

4 See the Sheriffs Act 1887 s 8(2), under which any person who resists the execution is guilty of an offence. By letter of 15 September 1969 it was acknowledged that the Metropolitan Police Commissioner would give assistance to the sheriff of Greater London in executing writs of possession where premises were occupied by squatters. See also para 1131 post.

1131. Obstruction of court officers in execution of process for possession. A person who resists or intentionally obstructs any person who is in fact an officer of a court[1] engaged in executing any process issued by the High Court or any county court for the purpose of enforcing any judgment or order for the recovery or delivery of possession of any premises is guilty of an offence[2]. However, this provision does not apply unless the judgment or order in question was given or made in proceedings brought under any provisions of rules of court applicable only in circumstances where the person claiming possession of any premises alleges that the premises in question are occupied solely by a person or persons, not being a tenant or tenants holding over after the termination of the tenancy, who entered into or remained in occupation of the premises without the licence or consent of the person claiming possession or any predecessor in title of his[3].

In any proceedings for an offence under these provisions it is a defence for the accused to prove that he believed that the person he was resisting or obstructing was not an officer of the court[4].

A constable in uniform or any officer of a court may arrest without warrant anyone who is or whom he, with reasonable cause, suspects to be, guilty of an offence under these provisions[5].

1 'Officer of the court' means any sheriff, under-sheriff, deputy sheriff, bailiff or sheriff's officer (Criminal Law Act 1977 s 10(6)(a)), and any bailiff or other person who is an officer of a county court within the meaning of the County Courts Act 1984 (see s 147(1); and COUNTY COURTS) (Criminal Law Act 1977 s 10(6)(b); Interpretation Act 1978 s 17(2)(a)).

2 Criminal Law Act 1977 s 10(1). This provision is without prejudice to the Sheriffs Act 1887 s 8(2) (see para 1130 ante): Criminal Law Act 1977 s 10(1). 'Premises' means any building, any part of a building under separate occupation, any land ancillary to a building, the site comprising any building or buildings together with any ancillary land, and any other place (s 12(1)(a)); and 'building' includes any structure other than a movable one, and any movable structure, vehicle or vessel designed or adapted for use for residential purposes (s 12(2)). For the purposes of s 12(1), part of a building is under separate occupation if anyone is in occupation or is entitled to occupation of that part as distinct from the whole (s 12(2)(a)), and land is ancillary to a building if it is adjacent to it and used or intended for use in connection with the occupation of that building or any part of it (s 12(2)(b)).

3 Ibid s 10(1), (2). For the rules of court applicable see RSC Ord 113; CPR Sch 1 RSC Ord 113; and REAL PROPERTY vol 39(2) (Reissue) para 270; and CCR Ord 24; CPR Sch 2 CCR Ord 24; and COUNTY COURTS.

4 Criminal Law Act 1977 s 10(3). A person guilty of an offence under s 10 is liable on summary conviction to imprisonment for a term not exceeding six months, or to a maximum fine of level 5 on the standard scale or both: s 10(4) (amended by the Criminal Justice Act 1982 ss 38, 46). 'Standard scale' means the standard scale of maximum fines for summary offences as set out in the Criminal Justice Act 1982 s 37(2) (as substituted): Interpretation Act 1978 s 5, Sch 1 (amended by the Criminal Justice Act 1988 s 170(1), Sch 15 para 58(a). See CRIMINAL LAW, EVIDENCE AND PROCEDURE vol 11(2) (Reissue) para 808; and MAGISTRATES. At the date at which this volume states the law, the standard scale is as follows: level 1, £200; level 2, £500; level 3, £1,000; level 4, £2, 500; level 5, £5000: Criminal Justice Act 1982 s 37(2)

(substituted by the Criminal Justice Act 1991 s 17(1)). As to the determination of the amount of the fine actually imposed, as distinct from the level on the standard scale which it may not exceed, see the Criminal Justice Act 1991 s 18 (substituted by the Criminal Justice Act 1993 s 65); and MAGISTRATES.

5   Criminal Law Act 1977 s 10(5). The power of arrest without a warrant is specifically preserved by the Police and Criminal Evidence Act 1984 s 26(2), Sch 2. As to the constable's power of entry for the purpose of arrest see the Police and Criminal Evidence Act 1984 s 17 (as amended); and CRIMINAL LAW, EVIDENCE AND PROCEDURE vol 11(1) (Reissue) para 683.

(2) EXECUTION OF PROCESS

(i) Receipt and Execution of Writs

1132. Writs of execution. Subject to certain exceptions[1], all writs of execution on judgments and orders of the Supreme Court[2] are directed to the high sheriff[3], who is under a duty to execute them[4]. In exercising his functions in executing writs the sheriff acts as an officer of the court[5].

1   The exceptions are writs of sequestration and writs of fieri facias de bonis ecclesiasticis: see EXECUTION.
2   The Supreme Court consists of the Court of Appeal, the High Court of Justice and the Crown Court: Supreme Court Act 1981 s 1(1).
3   As to the issue and form of writs of execution and the manner in which they are executed see EXECUTION. As to the meaning of 'high sheriff' see para 1101 note 1 ante.
4   As to the execution of writs by sheriffs' officers see para 1119 ante. Although it is primarily the sheriff's duty to know the extent of his bailiwick (as to which see para 1111 ante), the execution creditor must define reasonably exactly the property on which he requires the sheriff to levy, and should correctly state the address of the execution debtor in the county. If, on receipt of the writ of fieri facias in the under-sheriff's office, the address is seen to be in another county the writ should be returned unexecuted without fee, but, if there is doubt as to the situation of the premises, the sheriff's officer must make inquiries on the spot and is entitled to his fee for so doing: see the propositions agreed with the Under Sheriffs Association, set out in (1953) 50 Law Society's Gazette 122. As to execution of process in the county court see COUNTY COURTS; as to execution against a tenant see DISTRESS; and as to the duty of the sheriff in case of supervening bankruptcy see BANKRUPTCY AND INSOLVENCY vol 3(2) (Reissue) para 664–665; COMPANIES VOL 7(3) (1996 Reissue) paras 2643–2645.
5   Although for some purposes the sheriff is the agent of the party who puts the writ into his hands, he is not a mere agent but is a public functionary with duties towards those to whom the writ in his hands is directed: *Hooper v Lane* (1857) 6 HL Cas 443 at 549 per Lord Cranworth. See also *Re a Debtor (No 2 of 1977), ex p the Debtor v Goacher* [1979] 1 All ER 870, [1979] 1 WLR 956, DC, where it was held that the sheriff is not simply an agent of the judgment creditor but has wider responsibilities which include duties towards the Official Receiver or the trustee in bankruptcy. In *Fredericks and Pelhams Timber Buildings v Wilkins (Read, claimant)* [1971] 3 All ER 545, [1971] 1 WLR 1197, CA, it was held that the sheriff is the officer charged with the carrying out of the orders of the court and as such is in the same position as an officer of the court and should maintain a neutral position in interpleader proceedings.

1133. Sheriff's liability in executing writs. The writ of execution is an absolute justification to the sheriff for what is done in pursuance of it[1], even though the judgment on which it is founded may be afterwards set aside[2], and the fact that advice is given to the sheriff's officers[3] by the solicitors for the execution creditor does not of itself make the officers agents of the execution creditor[4]. However, the sheriff is liable if any act is done in excess of the authority given by the writ[5], and in an action against him for trespass it is not necessary to prove actual damage[6]. The sheriff may also be sued by the execution creditor for not duly enforcing the writ, and by either the creditor or the debtor for any unreasonable delay or negligence in the execution, provided actual damage is shown[7].

A sheriff is entitled to the benefit of the interpleader process[8].

1   *Hunt v Hooper* (1844) 12 M & W 664; and cf *Withers v Parker* (1860) 5 H & N 725, Ex Ch. As to wrongful and irregular execution see EXECUTION.

2   *Countess of Rutland's Case* (1605) 5 Co Rep 25b; *Parsons v Loyd* (1772) 3 Wils 341; *Ives v Lucas* (1823) 1 C & P 7; *Williams v Williams and Nathan* [1937] 2 All ER 559, CA; *Barclays Bank Ltd v Roberts* [1954] 3 All ER 107, [1954] 1 WLR 1212, CA. A sheriff selling, under an execution, goods in the possession of the execution debtor at the time of the seizure, without any claim being made to them, is protected from liability in regard to the sale unless he had notice or, by making reasonable inquiry, might have ascertained that the goods were not the debtor's: see the Supreme Court Act 1981 s 138B (as added). See also *Curtis v Maloney* [1951] 1 KB 736 at 745, [1950] 2 All ER 982 at 986, CA. A similar provision applies to the registrar of a county court selling under an execution: see the County Courts Act 1984 s 98 (as amended); and COUNTY COURTS.

3   As to the execution of writs by sheriffs' officers see para 1119 ante.

4   *Barclays Bank Ltd v Roberts* [1954] 3 All ER 107, [1954] 1 WLR 1212, CA, where it was held that a sheriff's officer who executed a writ of possession against a sub-tenant on the advice of the landlord's solicitors had acted in accordance with the writ and that therefore, as the solicitors were not the landlord's agents, the landlord was not liable for wrongful ejectment.

5   *Saunderson v Baker and Martin* (1772) 3 Wils 309 (trespass for seizing goods of the wrong person); *Ash v Dawnay* (1852) 8 Exch 237 (trespass for remaining in possession an unreasonable time); *Playfair v Musgrove* (1845) 14 M & W 239 (remaining on premises after property sold); *Lee v Dangar, Grant & Co* [1892] 2 QB 337, CA (refusing to withdraw until fees improperly demanded paid). Trespass will lie if premises are wrongfully entered and a substantial grievance is suffered: *De Coppett v Barnett* (1901) 17 TLR 273, CA. See also *Watson v Murray & Co* [1955] 2 QB 1, [1955] 1 All ER 350. An officer of a county court is not liable as a trespasser by reason of a mere irregularity or informality in the execution of a warrant although the person aggrieved may bring an action against him for special damage suffered: see the County Courts Act 1984 s 126 (as amended); and COUNTY COURTS. As to trespass generally see TORT. There was an action for trover if more goods than sufficient to satisfy the levy were sold (*Batchelor v Vyse* (1834) 4 Moo & S 552; *Stead v Gascoigne* (1818) 8 Taunt 527; *Aldred v Constable* (1844) 6 QB 370), and if the sheriff seized and sold the goods of a third person (*Jelks v Hayward* [1905] 2 KB 460). As to actions for trover (also called conversion of goods and which is now actionable as wrongful interference with goods) see the Torts (Interference with Goods) Act 1977 s 1(a); PRACTICE AND PROCEDURE; and TORT. As to the liability of the execution creditor for wrongful seizure and the sheriff's right to indemnity against him when misled by the indorsement on the writ see EXECUTION. As to the liability of the sheriff for the wrongful acts of his officers see para 1146 et seq post.

6   *Saunderson v Baker and Martin* (1772) 3 Wils 309; *Lee v Dangar, Grant & Co* [1892] 2 QB 337, CA.

7   *Mullet v Challis* (1851) 16 QB 239 (sale at an undervalue in consequence of negligence); *Aireton v Davis* (1833) 9 Bing 740; *Clifton v Hooper* (1844) 6 QB 468; *Carlile v Parkins* (1822) 3 Stark 163 (unreasonable delay). In an action by a judgment creditor for the sheriff's breach of duty, the measure of damages is the amount which could have been recovered if the sheriff had performed his duty: see EXECUTION.

8   See INTERPLEADER vol 25 (Reissue) para 1003 et seq. The court has to look at all the relevant facts surrounding the execution, including the conduct of the claimant; it is the quality of the sheriff's admitted wrong which is relevant: *Neumann v Bakeaway Ltd* [1983] 2 All ER 935, [1983] 1 WLR 1016n, CA.

1134. Right of entry in civil process.

In the execution of process, the overriding rule is that the sheriff may not gain entry into the debtor's dwelling house or the premises of any stranger to which the debtor's goods have been removed by breaking down the outer door or using force, although he may enter by any of the usual means[1]. However, the sheriff will be a trespasser if he enters a stranger's premises and the goods are not there[2]. Once an entry has been effected, the sheriff may break open inner doors and cupboards but he must not remain on the premises for an unreasonable length of time[3]. A sheriff executing a writ of fieri facias is not entitled to re-enter a dwelling house by force except where, having gained entry peaceably, he is expelled by force or has been deliberately excluded by the tenant. What would amount to deliberate exclusion is to be considered in the light of the individual circumstances[4].

1   As to seizure and right of entry see EXECUTION.
2   See EXECUTION.
3   As to rights after entry see EXECUTION. See also para 1141 post.
4   *Khazanchi v Faircharm Investments Ltd; McLeod v Butterwick* [1998] 2 All ER 901, [1998] 1 WLR 1603, CA.

1135. Property in goods seized. After goods have been seized by the sheriff[1] the goods are placed in the custody of the law and are held on behalf of the legal owners[2]. The general property in the goods until sale remains in the execution debtor, if they belong to him[3], but the sheriff has a special property in them and may maintain trespass or conversion against a person taking them out of his custody[4]. No property passes to the execution creditor by virtue of the seizure[5].

1 As to the seizure of goods see EXECUTION. As to excessive seizure of goods see also *Watson v Murray & Co* [1955] 2 QB 1, [1955] 1 All ER 350, where damages were awarded against the sheriff's officers for trespass in taking exclusive possession of premises for the purpose of holding a sale there even though no damage had resulted from excessive execution.
2 *Richards v Jenkins* (1887) 18 QBD 451 at 455, CA, per Lord Esher MR. As to the right of the sheriff to interplead where the goods are claimed by a third person see INTERPLEADER vol 25 (Reissue) para 1005 et seq.
3 *Giles v Grover* (1832) 9 Bing 128, HL; *Playfair v Musgrove* (1845) 14 M & W 239; *Re Clarke* [1898] 1 Ch 336, CA.
4 *Wilbraham v Snow* (1670) 2 Wms Saund 47; *Giles v Grover* (1832) 9 Bing 128, HL. See also EXECUTION.
5 *Giles v Grover* (1832) 9 Bing 128, HL.

1136. Return to the writ. Any party at whose instance a writ of execution has been issued or the person against whom the writ was issued may serve a notice on the sheriff to whom it was directed requiring him to indorse on the writ, within a specified time, a statement of the manner in which it has been executed and to send a copy of the statement to that party[1].

1 CPR Sch 1 RSC Ord 46 r 9(1). The return is in effect the sheriff's report as to the result of the execution and may be necessary where an official record is required. If the sheriff fails to comply with the notice the court may order the sheriff to supply the statement: see CPR Sch 1 RSC Ord 46 r 9(2). See further EXECUTION. As to the position in relation to proceedings commenced before 26 April 1999 see RSC Ord 46 r 9.

1137. Warrant for possession of land after compulsory acquisition. Where undertakers or an acquiring authority are authorised to enter upon and take possession of land required for the purposes of the undertaking and the owner or occupier of the land or any other person refuses to give up possession, or hinders the taking of possession, the undertakers or the authority may issue their warrant to the sheriff to deliver possession[1].

1 See the Lands Clauses Consolidation Act 1845 s 91; the Compulsory Purchase Act 1965 s 13(1); and COMPULSORY ACQUISITION OF LAND vol 8(1) (Reissue) para 130. This power is often used by acquiring authorities. The sheriff executes the warrant in the same way as any other writ of possession. As to the costs of a warrant of possession issued and executed under this provision see COMPULSORY ACQUISITION OF LAND vol 8(1) (Reissue) para 131.

(ii) Fees for Execution of Process

1138. Types of fees. The fees to which a sheriff is entitled in connection with the execution of process[1] fall into the following categories: (1) an allowance for particular action taken[2]; or (2) a sum in respect of actual expenses incurred[3]; or (3) a percentage based on the amount of money received or recovered[4]; or (4) the value of the goods seized and sold[5].

1 As to the statutory right to fees see para 1123 ante.
2 Eg fees allowed in respect of mileage: see para 1139 post.
3 Eg incidental expenses: see para 1142 post.
4 Eg a percentage of money received on a sale by auction: see para 1143 post. See also para 1144 post.
5 Eg poundage: see para 1144 post.

1139. Mileage. A sheriff's officer[1] concerned in the execution of a writ of fieri facias may demand, take and receive a fixed sum per mile in respect of journeys from his residence to the place of levy and return[2]. One journey may be made to seize the goods and, where appropriate, one journey to remove them[3]. In the case of a writ of possession or delivery, mileage is allowed for one journey from the residence of the sheriff's officer to the place where the land or goods are situated and return[4].

1   As to sheriffs' officers see para 1119 ante.
2   Order dated 8 July 1920, SR & O 1920/1250, preamble, Schedule Fee 1 (amended by SI 1971/808; and SI 1988/1384). The rate is 29.2p per mile: Order dated 8 July 1920, SR & O 1920/1250, Schedule Fee 1 (amended by SI 1988/1384). Where the place of levy is more than 1t expenses actually and reasonably incurred for conveyance from the station to the place of levy and back may be allowed in lieu of mileage: Order dated 8 July 1920, SR & O 1920/1250, Schedule Fee 1 (amended by SI 1971/808). In *Townend v Sheriff of Yorkshire* (1890) 24 QBD 621, a sheriff who executed a writ of fieri facias by seizing goods at different, separately rated, addresses of the debtor was allowed mileage for each seizure.
3   Order dated 8 July 1920, SR & O 1920/1250, Schedule Fee 1 (as amended: see note 2 supra).
4   Order dated 2 May 1921, SR & O 1921/827, preamble, Schedule Fee 7A (added by SI 1971/808; and amended by SI 1998/1384). The rate is 29.2p per mile: Order dated 2 May 1921, SR & O 1921/827, Schedule Fee 7A (as so added and amended).

1140. Seizure and work done. In executing a writ of fieri facias a sheriff's officer is entitled to a fee for seizure[1] for each building or place separately rated at which a seizure is made[2].

Where written claims are received by the sheriff's officer from third persons, such as from a landlord for unpaid rent or from persons claiming ownership of goods seized, a charge is allowed for making inquiries as to such claims, including giving the necessary notices to all parties, and towards out-of-pocket expenses[3].

1   As to seizure see EXECUTION.
2   Order dated 8 July 1920, SR & O 1920/1250, preamble, Schedule Fee 2 (amended by SI 1971/808). The fee is £2 for each building: Order dated 8 July 1920, SR & O 1920/1250, Schedule Fee 2 (as so amended). See also *Re Wells, ex p Sheriff of Kent* (1893) 68 LT 231, where it was held that fees for seizure or mileage (see para 1139 ante) are not payable on a second writ where the sheriff is in possession under the first unless the seizure under the second is made in a different place.
3   Order dated 8 July 1920, SR & O 1920/1250, Schedule Fee 3 (amended by SI 1956/502; and SI 1971/808). A fee not exceeding £2 is allowed for work done and a further fee, again not exceeding £2, for all out-of-pocket expenses actually and reasonably incurred in relation to such work: Order dated 8 July 1920 SR & O 1920/1250, Schedule Fee 3 (amended by SI 1971/808). If necessary, details of the work must be given by the sheriff.

1141. Possession of goods and animals. A sheriff concerned in the execution of a writ of fieri facias is entitled to a fee for keeping possession of the debtor's goods or animals[1]. Where a man is left in physical possession a daily fee is allowed per man, but he must provide his own board and accommodation[2]. However, a fee for physical possession must not be charged where an agreement for walking possession[3] is signed at the time of the levy[4], although a lesser fee for walking possession is allowed[5].

The sheriff is only allowed to charge for possession money for a reasonable period while he prepares for sale unless the debtor consents to the period being extended[6]. However, if the sheriff remains in possession of the debtor's goods without selling at the request of the execution creditor and of the debtor he will be entitled to his fees for the period[7].

Where the sheriff is in possession against the same debtor under more than one writ, possession money can only be charged in respect of the writ that has priority[8].

1   Order dated 8 July 1920, SR & O 1920/1250, preamble, Schedule Fee 4 (Fee 4 substituted by SI 1956/502; and further amended by the Decimal Currency Act 1969 s 10(1); and by SI 1971/808). As to possession money generally see further EXECUTION.

2   Order dated 8 July 1920, SR & O 1920/1250, Schedule Fee 4(a) (as substituted and amended: see note 1 supra). The fee is £3 per man per day: Schedule Fee 4(a) (as so substituted and amended).

3   The concept of walking possession, where the bailiff makes regular visits to the debtor's premises after the initial seizure, has been adapted from the county court. See also the County Courts Act 1984 s 89 (as amended); COUNTY COURTS; EXECUTION.

4   Order dated 8 July 1920, SR & O 1920/1250, Schedule Fee 4 (as substituted and amended: see note 1 supra). For the form of a walking possession agreement see the Sheriffs' Fees (Amendment) Order 1956, SI 1956/502, art 1, Schedule. The agreement may be signed either by the defendant or by a person in possession or control of the goods: see *National Commercial Bank of Scotland v Arcam Demolition and Construction Ltd and Hatherley Hall Ltd* [1966] 2 QB 593, [1966] 3 All ER 113, CA.

5   Order dated 8 July 1920, SR & O 1920/1250, Schedule Fee 4(b) (as substituted and amended: see note 1 supra). The daily fee for walking possession under an agreement is 25p: Schedule Fee 4(b) (as so substituted and amended).

6   *Re Finch, ex p Sheriff of Essex* (1891) 65 LT 466.

7   *Re Hurley* (1893) 41 WR 653, where the sheriff was allowed possession money from the date of seizure until the date of the receiving order: *Re Beeston, ex p Board of Trade* [1899] 1 QB 626, CA, where the sheriff was allowed possession money for 15 months, being the period he was in possession at the request of the execution creditor and debtor.

8   *Glasbrook v David and Vaux* [1905] 1 KB 615. However, where the sheriff appropriates different goods to answer each execution he may charge possession money on each: *Re Morgan, ex p Board of Trade* [1904] 1 KB 68.

1142. Incidental expenses and charges. A sheriff concerned in the execution of a writ of fieri facias may charge for the sums actually and reasonably paid (1) for the removal of goods or animals to a place of safe keeping[1]; (2) for their warehousing or for taking charge of them when they have been removed[2]; and (3) for the keep of animals while in the sheriff's custody[3]. However, no fees for the keeping of goods or animals may be charged after the goods or animals have been removed[4].

Where there is no prescribed fee to cover the cost or expenses of any duty which the sheriff may have to undertake, the fee is such sum as may be allowed on a special application to a Supreme Court Master or a District Judge[5].

The amount of any fees and charges payable are to be assessed in case the sheriff and the party liable to pay such fees differ as to the amount[6].

1   See Order dated 8 July 1920, SR & O 1920/1250, preamble, Schedule Fee 5.
2   See ibid Schedule Fee 6.
3   See ibid Schedule Fee 7.
4   See ibid Schedule Fees 5–7.
5   See Order dated 2 May 1921, SR & O 1921/827, preamble, Schedule Fee 9.
6   See ibid Schedule Pt I (amended by SI 1992/1379). As to detailed assessment see para 1127 ante.

1143. Sales by auction and private sales. Where goods seized under a writ of fieri facias are sold[1] by public auction[2] at the auctioneer's premises, the auctioneer is entitled to an inclusive charge for all out-of-pocket expenses except the costs of removal[3]. Where the auction is held on the debtor's premises the auctioneer is entitled, in addition to out-of-pocket expenses actually and reasonably incurred, to a commission on the sum realised[4]. Where the court orders that the goods may be sold otherwise than by public auction[5] the auctioneer is entitled to half the percentage allowed on a sale by auction[6], plus a commission in respect of work actually done in preparing for sale by auction[7] and the sums actually and reasonably paid for advertising any intended sale by auction and for necessary labour[8].

Where no sale takes place, either by public auction or as ordered by the court, the auctioneer is entitled to a commission on the value of the goods[9].

1   As to the sale of goods generally see EXECUTION.
2   Where goods are sold under an execution for a sum exceeding £20, the sale must be by public auction unless the court from which the process issued orders otherwise: see the Supreme Court Act 1981 s 138A(1) (as added); and EXECUTION.
3   Order dated 8 July 1920, SR & O 1920/1250, preamble, Schedule Fee 8(1)(a) (Fee 8 substituted by SI 1962/2417). The rates are £15 per cent on the first £100; £12.50 per cent on the next £900; and £10 per cent above £1,000: Order dated 8 July 1920, SR & O 1920/1250, Schedule Fee 8(1)(a) (as so substituted; and further amended by the Decimal Currency Act 1969 s 10(1)).
4   Order dated 8 July 1920, SR & O 1920/1250, Schedule Fee 8(1)(b) (as substituted: see note 3 supra). The rate of commission is 7o substituted).
5   Ie on an application under RSC Ord 47 r 6, or CPR Sch 1 RSC Ord 47 r 6: see EXECUTION.
6   Order dated 8 July 1920, SR & O 1920/1250, Schedule Fee 9(a).
7   Ie in preparing inventory and valuation and all other preparatory work: ibid Schedule Fee 9(b). The rate of commission is 2dule Fee 9(b).
8   See ibid Schedule Fee 9(c).
9   Where the goods have been removed to the auctioneer's premises the rate of commission is 10% to include all out-of-pocket expenses except the costs of removal: Order dated 8 July 1920, SR & O 1920/1250, Schedule Fee 8(2)(a) (as substituted: see note 3 supra). Where the goods have not been removed but work has been done by the auctioneer or sheriff's officer in preparation for sale, the rate is 5%, in addition to out-of-pocket expenses actually and reasonably incurred: Schedule Fee 8(2)(b) (as so substituted; and Fee 8(2)(b) further substituted by SI 1971/808). This fee may be charged only where the work done includes the preparation of a detailed inventory of the goods seized: Order dated 8 July 1920, SR & O 1920/1250, Schedule Fee 8(2) (as so amended).

1144. Poundage. In the case of an execution under a writ of fieri facias the sheriff is entitled to poundage[1] on the amount recovered[2] at the rate of 5 per cent up to £100 and 2.5 per cent above that sum[3]. The basis for calculating poundage on a writ of possession was changed in 1992[4]. Following the abolition of domestic rating by the Local Government Finance Act 1988[5], where the value for a domestic property[6] (either as a whole or part) is ascertainable from the valuation list in force immediately before 1 April 1990, that value forms the basis for calculating the sheriff's fee in respect of the property or the relevant part of it[7]. Otherwise, the fee is calculated by reference to the value by the year of the property or the relevant part of it[8]. The fee charged in relation to non-domestic property was reduced to reflect the revaluation of non-domestic property under the Local Government Finance Act 1988 and the fee is calculated by reference to the annual value for rating of the property[9]. In executing a writ of delivery a sheriff is entitled to charge poundage at the rate of 4 per cent on the value of the goods as stated in the writ of summons or judgment[10].

The sheriff is also entitled to poundage where, after seizure, a payment is made by the debtor or a third person under the compulsion of the writ and the plaintiff agrees to withdraw the sheriff from possession in consequence of the compromise between the parties[11].

1   As to the sheriff's statutory right to poundage see para 1123 ante.
2   To be entitled to poundage the sheriff must levy the money: *Colls v Coates* (1840) 11 Ad & El 826. See also EXECUTION.
3   Order dated 8 July 1920, SR & O 1920/1250, preamble, Schedule Fee 10 (Fee 10 substituted by SI 1971/808).
4   See Order dated 2 May 1921, SR & O 1921/827, preamble, Schedule Fee 7B (Fee 7B added by SI 1971/808; and later substituted by SI 1992/1379).
5   As to the abolition of domestic rating see RATING AND COUNCIL TAX vol 39(1) (Reissue) para 817.
6   Ie domestic property within the meaning of the Local Government Finance Act 1988 s 66 (as amended): see RATING AND COUNCIL TAX vol 39(1) (Reissue) para 713.
7   See Order dated 2 May 1921, SR & O 1921/827, Schedule Fee 7B(1) (as added and substituted: see note 4 supra).
8   See ibid Schedule Fee 7B(3) (as added and substituted: see note 4 supra).
9   See ibid Schedule Fee 7B(2), (4) (as added and substituted: see note 4 supra). As to the valuation of non-domestic property for rating see RATING AND COUNCIL TAX vol 39(1) (Reissue) para 679 et seq.

10 Ibid Schedule Fee 7C (added by SI 1971/808).
11 See *Madeley v Greenwood* (1897) 42 Sol Jo 34, DC; *Re Thomas, ex p Sheriff of Middlesex* [1899] 1 QB 460 at 462, CA, per Lindley MR; *Montague v Davies, Benachi & Co* [1911] 2 KB 595, DC.

1145. Value added tax on sheriff's fees. Where value added tax is chargeable in respect of the provision by a sheriff of any service[1] for which a fee is prescribed[2] the amount of tax must be paid in addition to that fee[3]. Accordingly, any person delivering a writ of execution to a sheriff to be executed by him, or serving a request[4] for the writ to be indorsed with the manner in which it has been executed, must pay the value added tax at the appropriate rate, in addition to the prescribed sheriff's fee, at the time of delivery or service[5].

1 Where a person, in the course or furtherance of a trade, profession or vocation, accepts any office, services supplied by him as holder of that office are treated as supplied in the course or furtherance of the trade, profession or vocation: Value Added Tax Act 1994 s 94(4); and see VALUE ADDED TAX vol 49(1) (Reissue) para 19. The effect of this provision is that the supply of sheriffs' services, not being an exempt supply are chargeable to value added tax.
2 Ie under the Order dated 8 July 1920, SR & O 1920/1250 (as amended); or the Order dated 2 May 1921, SR & O 1921/827 (as amended): see paras 1123, 1139 et seq ante.
3 Sheriffs' Fees (Amendment No 2) Order 1977, SI 1977/2111, art 2.
4 Ie under RSC Ord 46 r 9, or CPR Sch 1 RSC Ord 46 r 9: see para 1136 ante
5 *Practice Direction* [1978] 1 WLR 144.

(3) LIABILITY OF SHERIFF FOR ACTS OF OFFICERS

1146. Principles of liability. A sheriff is liable for any fraud or wrongful act or omission on the part of his under-sheriff, bailiff or officer in the course of their employment[1], even though there may be no proof of any recognition by the sheriff of the act or default complained of[2]. However, a sheriff is not liable for the acts of a bailiff or officer which are quite outside the scope of his duties and which are not done for the purpose of executing the authority entrusted to him, or under colour of such authority[3], or for money received by the bailiff or officer otherwise than in the course of exercising or purporting to exercise his authority[4].

A sheriff is not liable at the suit of an execution creditor or debtor for an act of misconduct on the part of his officer which was done at the request or with the knowledge and assent of the person complaining[5]. However, the mere fact that the debtor or creditor induces the officer to commit a breach of his duty does not absolve the sheriff from his general responsibility for the misconduct of the officer, but only exonerates him from liability for the particular act or omission assented to by the plaintiff[6].

1 *Laicock's Case* (1627) Lat 187; *Woodgate v Knatchbull* (1787) 2 Term Rep 148; *Raphael v Goodman* (1838) 8 Ad & El 565; *Brown v Copley* (1844) 8 Scott NR 350, where it was held that a sheriff is not liable for the acts of his officers done after he has countermanded the execution of the writ; *Wright v Child* (1866) LR 1 Exch 358. 'The reason that the sheriff is held liable, is, that, having a duty imposed upon him by law, instead of performing it himself, he delegates it to another; and therefore it is but just that he should be responsible for the misconduct of those to whom he so delegates the performance of his duty': *Smith v Pritchard* (1849) 8 CB 565 at 588 per Maule J. The sheriff is liable in trespass if, on the execution of a writ of fieri facias, his bailiff takes the goods of a person other than the execution debtor (*Saunderson v Baker and Martin* (1772) 3 Wils 309; *Ackworth v Kempe* (1778) 1 Doug KB 40; *Smith v Milles* (1786) 1 Term Rep 475 at 480), or wrongfully seizes goods after payment (*Gregory v Cotterell* (1855) 5 E & B 571, Ex Ch), or wrongfully breaks and enters the premises of a third person (*Smith v Pritchard* supra), or for false imprisonment by his officers (*Saunderson v Baker and Martin* supra at 317). See also *Moore v Lambeth County Court Registrar (No 2)* [1970] 1 QB 560, [1970] 1 All ER 980, CA; and *Khazanchi v Faircharm Investments Ltd; McLeod v Butterwick* [1998] 2 All ER 901, [1998] 1 WLR 1603, CA, where many of the earlier cases

were reviewed. As to wrongful and irregular execution generally see EXECUTION. The sheriff's officers are themselves liable in damages for their wrongful acts: *Watson v Murray & Co* [1955] 2 QB 1, [1955] 1 All ER 350 (trespass).

2   *Saunderson v Baker and Martin* (1772) 3 Wils 309; *Ackworth v Kempe* (1778) 1 Doug KB 40. See also para 1149 post.

3   *Brown v Gerard* (1834) 3 Dowl 217, where it was held that the sheriff was not bound by an undertaking of his officer on behalf of the defendant that, in consideration of the plaintiff accepting a certain amount, the defences in the action should be withdrawn and the plaintiff should have judgment. In *Smith v Pritchard* (1849) 8 CB 565, the high sheriff of a county court was held to be not liable for assault and false imprisonment by a bailiff, not under colour of his warrant, but in assertion of a statutory power given to the individual officer wrongfully obstructed.

4   *Cook v Palmer* (1827) 6 B & C 739, where it was held that the sheriff was not liable to the assignees of the debtor for the balance of proceeds of goods taken in execution by a bailiff since the bailiff's authority to realise more than sufficient to satisfy the levy derived from the assignees, not from the sheriff; *Woods v Finnis* (1852) 7 Exch 363, where the bailiff, on the execution of a writ of *capias ad satisfaciendum* (since abolished), received the debt and costs and failed to pay over the amount and it was held that the sheriff was not liable, it being no part of the officer's duty, in executing such a writ, to receive the amount due on behalf of the creditor.

5   See *Crowder v Long* (1828) 8 B & C 598.

6   See *Wright v Child* (1866) LR 1 Exch 358; *Barclays Bank Ltd v Roberts* [1954] 3 All ER 107, [1954] 1 WLR 1212, CA.

1147. Extent of liability. The sheriff's liability[1] extends not merely to acts done by his bailiff or officer in pursuance of his warrant[2], but also to anything done by him by colour of the warrant, the reason for the extended liability being that the sheriff is supposed to be executing his duty in person. The impossibility of so doing authorises him to delegate his duty, but he puts the delegate in his place and is therefore liable not only for acts done under the express authority of the warrant, but also for acts done in pursuance of the warrant generally[3]. Thus, if a bailiff to whom a warrant is delivered to execute a writ of fieri facias improperly authorises an assistant to execute it in his absence, the sheriff is liable for the acts and misconduct of the assistant, and for money received by him in reference to the execution, even though it may not have been paid over[4].

The sheriff is liable even though the act done may have been contrary to the express terms of the writ[5], or in disobedience to his express instructions[6], provided only that it is done in the purported exercise of the officer's authority.

1   As to the principles of liability see para 1146 ante.

2   Where there is variance between the writ and the warrant, the sheriff is not necessarily liable for an illegal execution: *Rose v Tomblinson* (1834) 3 Dowl 49. As to the sheriff's warrant see EXECUTION.

3   *Raphael v Goodman* (1838) 8 Ad & El 565; *Smith v Pritchard* (1849) 8 CB 565 at 588 per Maule J; *Gregory v Cotterell* (1855) 5 E & B 571 at 585, Ex Ch. In practice, liability insurance is usually taken out to cover the actions of the sheriff and all persons executing a warrant under his authority. As to liability insurance generally see INSURANCE vol 25 (Reissue) para 660 et seq.

4   *Gregory v Cotterell* (1855) 5 E & B 571, Ex Ch.

5   *Smart v Hutton* (1833) 8 Ad & El 568n, where a debtor was wrongfully detained under a writ of fieri facias.

6   *Scarfe v Hallifax* (1840) 7 M & W 288 at 290.

1148. Liability for acts of special bailiff. Where a special bailiff[1] is employed to execute a writ at the request of the execution creditor who gives him his instructions, the sheriff is not liable to the execution creditor for the bailiff's negligence or misconduct[2]. In such a case, the sheriff is not bound to make a return to the writ, and if he does so he is not liable for a false return[3]. However, the employment of a special bailiff does not relieve the sheriff from his own general responsibility and duty, or from his liability to the execution creditor for his own negligence or that of his under-sheriff[4]: it only absolves him from liability to the execution creditor for the acts and defaults of the special bailiff[5].

1   As to special bailiffs see para 1122 ante.

2   *De Moranda v Dunkin* (1790) 4 Term Rep 119; *Ford v Leche* (1837) 6 Ad & El 699; *Doe v Trye* (1839) 7 Dowl 636; *Futcher v Hinder* (1858) 3 H & N 757.

3   *De Moranda v Dunkin* (1790) 4 Term Rep 119; *Porter v Viner* (1815) 1 Chit 613n; *Pallister v Pallister* (1816) 1 Chit 614n; *Harding v Holden* (1841) 2 Man & G 914. As to the return to the writ see para 1136 ante.

4   As to the principles and extent of the sheriff's liability see paras 1146–1147 ante.

5   *Taylor v Richardson* (1800) 8 Term Rep 505.

1149. Evidence to connect sheriff with officer. In order to maintain an action against a sheriff for the wrongful act or default of a bailiff or officer[1] it is necessary to show that the officer whose conduct is complained of was authorised by the sheriff in the particular transaction[2]. As a general rule, either the original warrant directed by the sheriff to the bailiff should be produced and proved[3], or the non-production of the original should be accounted for in such a manner as to warrant the admission of secondary evidence[4]. The production of a warrant proved to have been issued by the under-sheriff or the sheriff's London deputy to the particular officer under the sheriff's seal of office is sufficient, without proof of the writ of execution[5]. Proof of the warrant may also be dispensed with where there is other satisfactory evidence that the officer was duly authorised by the sheriff in the particular transaction[6]. If, by his conduct, the sheriff has recognised or shown an intention to adopt the officer's acts, that is sufficient evidence of privity, and such a recognition or adoption may be indicated by the pleadings in the action[7].

1   As to the principles of liability see para 1146 ante.

2   *Drake v Sikes* (1797) 7 Term Rep 113; *George v Perring* (1801) 4 Esp 63; *Martin v Bell* (1816) 1 Stark 413; *Snowball v Goodricke* (1833) 4 B & Ad 541.

3   *Drake v Sikes* (1797) 7 Term Rep 113; *George v Perring* (1801) 4 Esp 63; *Martin v Bell* (1816) 1 Stark 413; *Snowball v Goodricke* (1833) 4 B & Ad 541.

4   To allow the admission of secondary evidence it is generally sufficient to give reasonable proof of loss of the original (*Moon v Raphael* (1835) 2 Bing NC 310; *Minshall v Lloyd* (1837) 2 M & W 450), or of service of a notice to produce on the sheriff's London agents to whom the warrant was sent (*Suter v Burrell* (1858) 2 H & N 867). As to secondary evidence generally see EVIDENCE.

5   *Grey v Smith* (1808) 1 Camp 387; *Shepherd v Wheble* (1838) 8 C & P 534; *Bessey v Windham* (1844) 6 QB 166.

6   *Jones v Wood* (1812) 3 Camp 228, where documents were produced which were shown to have been written in the sheriff's office and directed to the particular officer requiring him to give instructions for a return to the writ; *Tealby v Gascoigne* (1817) 2 Stark 202; *Francis v Neave* (1821) 6 Moore CP 120 (proof of indorsement of officer's name on the writ by a clerk in the office of the under-sheriff); *Scott v Marshall* (1832) 2 Cr & J 238, where a copy of the writ indorsed with the bailiff's name was held to be sufficient on proof that it was the custom of the sheriff's office to indorse on the writ the name of the bailiff to whom the warrant was granted. However, it has been held insufficient merely to prove the writ with the bailiff's name written in the margin (*Jones v Wood* supra), or to produce an examined copy of the writ indorsed with the bailiff's name without proof that the indorsement was made by the sheriff's authority (*Hill v Sheriff of Middlesex* (1816) 7 Taunt 8). See also *Fermor v Philips* (1817) 5 Moore CP 184n; *Morgan v Brydges* (1818) 1 B & Ald 647; *Sarjeant v Cowan* (1832) 5 C & P 492.

7   *Martin v Bell* (1816) 1 Stark 413; *Smart v Hutton* (1833) 8 Ad & El 568n; *Barsham v Bullock* (1839) 10 Ad & El 23 (defence traversing the alleged wrong, but admitting in effect that the act was that of the defendant's officer); *Reed v Thoyts* (1840) 6 M & W 410 (similar case); *Brickell v Hulse* (1837) 7 Ad & El 454, where it was held that an affidavit of the officer used by the sheriff on a motion could be used against the sheriff in subsequent proceedings.

1150. Knowledge imputed to sheriff. Except in cases where there is a statutory requirement that specific notice be given to the sheriff[1], the knowledge of a sheriff's officer of any fact or circumstance connected with his employment which it is his duty to communicate to the sheriff or under-sheriff operates as notice to the sheriff of that fact or circumstance[2].

1 See eg the Insolvency Act 1986 s 184(4); *Hellyer v Sheriff of Yorkshire* [1975] Ch 16, [1974] 2 All ER 712, CA; and COMPANIES VOL 7(3) (1996 Reissue) para 2643. See also the Insolvency Act 1986 s 346; the Insolvency Rules 1986, SI 1986/1925 (as amended); and BANKRUPTCY AND INSOLVENCY vol 3(2) (Reissue) para 664.
2 See generally AGENCY VOL 1(2) (Reissue) paras 149–150.

(4) OFFENCES

1151. Offences punishable as contempt of court and by penalty. A sheriff, under-sheriff, bailiff or officer of a sheriff who acts in breach of the provisions of the Sheriffs Act 1887 is guilty of an offence[1]. In addition, a sheriff, under-sheriff, bailiff or officer of a sheriff who (1) grants a warrant for the execution of any writ before he has actually received it[2]; or (2) is guilty of any offence against or breach of the provisions of the Act, or of any wrongful act or neglect or default in the execution of his office or of any contempt of a superior court[3], is liable to be punished as for a contempt of court[4] and to forfeit £200 and to pay all damages suffered by any person aggrieved[5]. Any proceedings under those provisions must be taken within two years after the commission of the alleged offence[6], and the court may order that the costs of proceedings for contempt of court be paid by one party to the other[7].

1 Sheriffs Act 1887 s 29(1)(d) (amended by the Local Government Act 1972 s 272(1), Sch 30). The offence is punishable on conviction with a term of imprisonment not exceeding one year and a fine or, if the defendant cannot pay a fine, a term of imprisonment not exceeding three years: Sheriffs Act 1887 s 29(1). There have been no reported cases under s 29 (as amended) this century, but see *Lee v Dangar, Grant & Co* [1892] 1 QB 231 (affd [1892] 2 QB 337, CA); *Woolford's Estate Trustee v Levy* [1892] 1 QB 772, CA (overcharging of sheriff's fees); *Bagge v Whitehead* [1892] 2 QB 355, CA.
2 Sheriffs Act 1887 s 29(2)(c).
3 Ibid s 29(2)(d).
4 See ibid s 29(2)(i), (3), (5) (s 29(3) amended by the Statute Law Revision Act 1908; and the Courts Act 1971 s 56, Sch 11 Pt IV). The Sheriffs Act 1887 s 29 (as amended) also applies to any person procuring the commission of an offence.
5 Ibid s 29(2)(ii). See also note 4 supra. The forfeiture and damages can be recovered as a debt by an action in the High Court: s 29(2) (amended by the Statute Law Revision Act 1908). The penalty of £200 is imposed for acts in the nature of a criminal offence and to support an action for its recovery there must be evidence of criminal intent on the part of the defendant, a person making an unintentional overcharge not being liable: *Lee v Dangar, Grant & Co* [1892] 1 QB 231 (affd [1892] 2 QB 337, CA); *Woolford's Estate Trustee v Levy* [1892] 1 QB 772, CA. The only persons liable are those actually committing the offence or procuring its commission: *Bagge v Whitehead* [1892] 2 QB 355, CA. A more appropriate remedy is an action for damages against the sheriff: see EXECUTION. Where malice is proved, the court may consider awarding exemplary damages: see *Moore v Lambeth County Court Registrar (No 2)* [1970] 1 QB 560 at 572, [1970] 1 All ER 980 at 986, CA, per Sachs LJ.
6 See the Sheriffs Act 1887 s 29(7). No person is liable to be punished twice for the same offence: see s 29(8).
7 See ibid s 29(4) (amended by the Statute Law Revision Act 1908). The order for costs has the same effect as a judgment of the High Court, and may be enforced accordingly: Sheriffs Act s 29(4) (as so amended).

1152. Wrongful assumption of office. Any person, not being an under-sheriff, bailiff, or officer of a sheriff, who assumes or pretends to act as such, is liable to punishment as if he were an under-sheriff guilty of a contempt of the High Court[1].

1 Sheriffs Act 1887 s 29(6) (amended by the Statute Law Revision Act 1908; and the Theft Act 1968 s 33(3), Sch 3 Pt I): see para 1151 ante.

INDEX

Sale of Land

ABSTRACT OF TITLE
  sale of land, on. *See under* TITLE TO LAND
ADVERTISEMENT
  control of display—
    pre-contract searches, 22
    preliminary inquiries on sale of land, 14
AGENT
  misrepresentation by, 53
  signature of contract for sale of land, 40
AGREEMENT
  sale of land, for. *See under* SALE OF LAND
AGRICULTURAL CHARGE
  pre-contract search of register, 22
  searches of register, 22, 168
AGRICULTURAL HOLDING
  preliminary inquiries on sale of land, 9
ALIEN
  real property, capacity as to, 64
APPEAL
  sale under court direction, as to, 135
  summary order as to sale of land, from, 229
APPROPRIATION
  purchase money on sale of land, as to, 197
ASSURANCE
  sale of land. *See under* SALE OF LAND
AUCTION
  conditions of sale, 84, 85
  offer by purchaser, 24
  oral contract, 29
  sale of land. *See under* SALE OF LAND
  sales under court direction, 134
  written contract, signature of, 40
AUCTIONEER
  stakeholder, as, 86n[1]
BANKRUPTCY
  purchaser of land, of, 210, 211
  real property, capacity as to, 65
  vendor of land, of. *See under* CONTRACT OF
    SALE (LAND)
BANKRUPTCY ORDER
  proof of, 157
  registration of, 209
BANKRUPTCY PETITION
  pending action, registration as, 209
BIRTH
  proof of, 161
BOUNDARY
  preliminary inquiries, 16
BREACH OF COVENANT (LEASE)
  conditions of sale as to, 99

BUILDING SOCIETIES
  conditions of sale as to instruments of, 96
CHARGE (COMPANY)
  searches of registers on sale of land, 168
CHARGING ORDER
  sale of land, effect on, 216
CHARITY TRUSTEES
  land transactions, capacity, 75
COMMONS REGISTRATION
  search on sale of land, 22
COMPANY
  real property, capacity as to, 66n[3]
COMPENSATION
  conditions of sale as to. *See under* CONDITIONS
    OF SALE (LAND)
  sale of land, as to. *See under* CONTRACT OF SALE
    (LAND)
COMPULSORY ACQUISITION
  capacity of persons purchasing under, 73
  conditions of sale, 80
  costs of transfer on, payment of, 325
  preliminary inquiries on sale of land, 12, 15
COMPULSORY PURCHASE ORDER
  completion of contract, pending, 80
CONDITIONS OF SALE (LAND)
  abstract of title—
    delivery, 100
    failure to deliver, 101
  acceptance of title, 174n[1,5]
  adjoining land retained by vendor, where, 81
  auction—
    bidding, 84
    reserve, 85
    vendor's right to bid, 85
  compensation, for—
    error or omission, for, 111
    misdescription, 110
    recovery of compensation, 113
    rescission where, 108
  compensation, restricting, 115, 116
  completion, as to—
    contractual date, 120
    entry into possession, 124
    expenses charged on property, 126
    interest on purchase money, 122
    notice to complete, 121
    occupation before, 119
    outgoings: meaning, 125
    payment by instalments, 128
    receipt of rents, 124

References are to paragraph numbers; superior figures refer to notes

References are to paragraph numbers; superior figures refer to notes

References are to paragraph numbers; superior figures refer to notes

SALE OF LAND—*continued*
  incumbered land—*continued*
    payment of purchase money to incum-
      brancers, 314
    recitals, 286
    registration of discharge, 267n[10]
    sale of, 267
  inquiries, preliminary. *See under* CONTRACT OF
    SALE (LAND)
  insurance—
    common law position, 117
    conditions of sale, effect, 118
    preliminary inquiries, 18
    statute, effect of, 118
  interest on purchase money. *See under* purchase
    money *below*
  investigation of title. *See* TITLE TO LAND
  land charges—
    pre-contract searches, 21
    searches, 167
  leaseholds—
    assurance. *See* assurance of leaseholds *above*
    deed, transfer by, 264
    preliminary inquiries, 8
    See also tenanted property *below*
  licence on occupation before completion, 119
  lien—
    purchaser's, 256
    vendor's. *See* VENDOR'S LIEN
  local authority, capacity to contract, 68
  local land charges—
    pre-contract searches, 20
    preliminary inquiries, 13
  loss of bargain, damages for, 258
  lots, in—
    assurance of leaseholds, 304
    expenses of abstract of title, 173
  maintenance, vendor's duty pending com-
    pletion, 180, 181
  material facts, disclosure of. *See under*
    CONTRACT OF SALE (LAND)
  misdescription—
    compensation for, 110
    quality, as to, 51, 52
    specific performance, effect on, 250
  misrepresentation—
    agent, by, 53
    answers to preliminary inquiries, in, 5
    conditions of sale as to liability, 116
    damages for, 42, 259
    quality, as to, 51
    rescission after completion, 356
  mistake—
    rectification of transfer, 354
    rescission after completion, for, 356
  National Conveyancing Protocol, 19
  non-party—
    benefit of covenants running with land, 335
    right to take interest in land, 283
  notice—
    adverse claims, of, 330
    completion notice, 121

SALE OF LAND—*continued*
  notice—*continued*
    death of intended recipient, 322
    equitable estates, as to, 320
    equity of redemption, as to, 321
    tenant's interest, of, 329
  objections, summary order as to. *See under*
    CONTRACT OF SALE (LAND)
  occupation rent payable by vendor, 191
  option to purchase—
    recitals, 288
    requirements, 27
  outgoings—
    meaning, 125
    expenses charged on property, 126
    preliminary inquiries, 18
    vendor's liability, 193
  parcels, 239, 291
  part property—
    assignment of leaseholds, 303
    transfer by separate deeds, 263
  patent defects—
    notice of, 6, 7
    quality, of, 45
  payment into court, discharge of incumbrances
    by, 268
  plan, description by, 291
  planning control—
    pre-contract searches, 22
    preliminary inquiries, 11
  possession—
    completion of contract, dates for, 185
    interest on purchase money, 195, 196
    rents and profits, and right to, 188
    time for transfer of, 186
  power of attorney, acts done under, 307
  preliminary agreement, 1
  preservation of property, vendor's duty
    pending completion, 181
  private treaty, by, pre-contractual stage, 1
  procedure—
    signing of contract, after, 2
    stages of, 1
  purchase money—
    appropriation to meet, 197
    cheque, payment by, 309n[4]
    evidence of payment, 310
    incumbrancers, payment to, 314
    interest on—
      appropriation, 197
      completion date fixed by contract, 196
      completion date not fixed, 195
      vendor's right to, 194
    licensed conveyancer, payment to, 315
    mode of payment, 309n[4]
    receipt—
      evidence of, 310
      form of, 309
      mortgagee, by, 311
      superfluous land, as to, 313
      trustees, by, 312
    return after completion, remedy of, 353

Set-off and Counterclaim

References are to paragraph numbers; superior figures refer to notes

Settlements

References are to paragraph numbers; superior figures refer to notes

References are to paragraph numbers; superior figures refer to notes

References are to paragraph numbers; superior figures refer to notes

SETTLEMENT OF PROPERTY—*continued*
Trusts of Land and Appointment of Trustees Act 1996, effect of, 609
types of, 602
unauthorised transactions—
  child's property, 673
  jurisdiction of court, 670
  settled land, court's powers, 671
  statutory powers, 670
  trust property, court's powers as to, 672
  variation of trusts, approval of, 674
undue influence—
  family arrangements, 1005, 1021
  setting aside for, 616
void, grounds, 617
voluntary—
  avoidance, 616
  enforceability, 615
  incomplete, annulment by settlor, 615n[5]
  post-nuptial settlement, 604
  protection of settlor, for, 618
  rectification, 616
will, manner of creation by, 612
written contract for, 627
SETTLOR
capacity, 625
setting aside settlement at suit of, 616
settlements for protection of, 618
SHARE IN COMPANY
settlement of, 910
tenant for life entitled to income of, 950
SOLICITOR
family arrangements, duties in giving advice as to, 1023
SPECIFIC PERFORMANCE
marriage settlement, 639
STAMP DUTY
family arrangements, 1027
settlements, 623
STATUTE
settlements created by, 613
STATUTORY OWNER
meaning, 766n[6]
alienation of powers, 777n[7]
deeds etc, power to execute, 875
delegation of powers, 776
dispositions, restrictions, 712
fiduciary position, 775
mortgage of part purchase money on sale by, 833
notice of intention to exercise powers, 783
possession, nature of right, 770
powers of tenant for life, 766
statutory powers. *See under* TENANT FOR LIFE
STOCK (INVESTMENT)
settlement of, 910
tenant for life entitled to income of, 950
STRICT SETTLEMENT. *See under* SETTLEMENT OF PROPERTY
TENANT FOR LIFE
meaning, 671n[5], 761
alienation of powers, prohibition, 777

TENANT FOR LIFE—*continued*
annuities, duty to keep down, 970
apportionment—
  amount realised on sale, 946
  rents, 862
  time, as to, 957–960
assignment for value—
  consent to investment after, 780
  effect, 779
assignment of interest, 765
bankruptcy of, 765
blown down trees and timber, 992
building lease—
  dedication of land for streets etc, 865
  statutory powers, 842, 844
breach of lessee's covenants, damages as capital money, 801
calls or shares, payment of, 953
capital charge, payment off, 972
capital money—
  meaning, 795
  arising otherwise than under 1925 Act, 800
  commutation money as to perpetually renewable leaseholds, 803
  consideration other than rent, payment of, 863
  court, in, liable under statute to be laid out in purchase of land, 797
  court direction as to investment or application, 806
  damages for breach of lessee's covenants, 801
  devolution of, 826
  direction as to investment or application by trustees, 805
  improvements, payment for, 809
  insurance money, 802
  modes of application, 808
  payment into court, 804
  payment to trustees, 804
  personalty settled on trusts of, 798
  personalty settled together with land, 799
  purchase money for interest less than fee simple, application of, 807
  purchase of land, money liable to be laid out in, 796, 797
  repayment. *See* repayment of capital money *below*
  See also under SETTLED LAND; SETTLEMENT OF PROPERTY
casual profits, right to, 944n[4]
cattle-grids and by-passes, powers, 867
charitable etc purposes, grants for, 864
compromise of claims, powers, 872
confirmation of past transactions, 876
consent of trustees to exercise of powers. *See* trustees' consent *below*
consent or approval by, powers, 861
contract—
  effect, 870
  powers, 869
  predecessor's, completion of, 876
conveyance, completion of transactions by, 874

References are to paragraph numbers; superior figures refer to notes

Sheriffs

Words and Phrases

Words in parentheses indicate the context in which the word or phrase is used

References are to paragraph numbers; superior figures refer to notes

References are to paragraph numbers; superior figures refer to notes

royalty—
  acreage, 843n[3]
  sliding-scale, 843n[10]
  tonnage, 843n[4]
sale (Law of Property Act 1925), 139n[2]
serjeants-at-mace, 1120
set-off, 406
settled land, 680
settlement—
  (property), 601
  (settled land), 678n[1]
  compound, 601, 681
  marriage, 603, 624
  protective, 607
  reference to another settlement, by, 755n[3]
  trustees of the (land), 750n[1]
  under the, 708n[5]
sheriff, high, 1101n[1]
signed (document), 33
sliding-scale royalties, 843n[10]
solicitor (Standard Conditions of Sale), 86n[1]
son—
  eldest, 728
  younger, 729
special bailiff, 1122
standard scale, 1131n[4]
statutory owner (settled land), 766n[6]
subsidiary vesting deed, 691
successors in office (trustee), 752n[4]
tenant for life (settled land), 671n[5], 761
tenant in tail, 762n[8]
term of years absolute, 678n[13]
title—
  abstract of, 141
  good holding, 137n[3]

title—*continued*
  marketable, 137n[3]
  perfect, 170
  root of, 142
tonnage rent or royalty, 843n[4]
transaction (settled land), 671n[1]
transfer (Standard Conditions of Sale), 118n[4]
trust—
  land, of, 146n[3], 676n[5], 897
  (settled land), 678n[9]
trust corporation, 705n[6]
trust instrument (settled land), 688n[7]
trustees of the settlement (settled land), 750n[1]
under the settlement (settled land), 708n[5]
United Kingdom, 699n[5]
valuable consideration, 659n[1]
vesting assent (settled land), 690n[8]
vesting deed—
  (settled land), 688n[6]
  principal, 689
  subsidiary, 691
vesting instrument (settled land), 690n[8]
vesting order (settled land), 688n[6]
voluntary waste, 987
waste—
  equitable, 997
  meliorating, 993
  permissive, 995
  voluntary, 987
will (settled land), 695n[3]
working day (Standard Conditions of Sale), 101n[3]
writing (contract), 39
yeomen (sheriff's), 1120
younger sons, 729